HUDSONS

Historic Houses & Gardens

Castles and Heritage Sites

HERITAGE HOUSE GROUP

Long Library, Blenheim Palace

2011

I am delighted to have been asked to provide a few words for this 24th edition of Hudson's Historic Houses and Gardens. And, as the first member of the Government to hold the title Minister for Tourism and Heritage, I am really happy to be able to do so.

And there really has never been a more exciting time to have this job. 2012 will soon be upon us, of course, with all the excitement that the Olympic and Paralympic Games in London bring and the chance to celebrate The Queen's Diamond Jubilee. Between them, these events provide an extraordinary opportunity for everyone in the tourism and leisure businesses. They will shine a spotlight on this country that I hope and believe will leave behind a long-term legacy for us all. Their potential impact, as a long-term boost for the travel and tourism industries, cannot be overestimated.

The Government believes that tourism is an absolutely vital element in the UK's economy in the 21st century, and will play a huge part in our country's recovery. It's worth a staggering £115 billion to the economy and employs one in ten of our work force. And we also know that the UK's heritage and historic environment are probably the single most important reason why people come here from overseas, and why so many of our own people choose to holiday here too. Tourism and heritage are inextricably linked.

This means that publications like Hudson's - rightly seen by many as the 'bible' for Britain's historic properties that are open to visitors - really is an essential starting point for people wanting to make the most of their UK holiday. This edition will be a welcome addition to a huge number of homes, whether it's to help plan a complete holiday or just a Sunday afternoon trip out.

I heartily commend this 2011 edition of Hudson's to you, and hope that it helps you enjoy the richness of our heritage, in all its forms, throughout the year.

John Penrose

JOHN PENROSE
Minister for Tourism and Heritage

Contents

Hudson's Historic Houses & Gardens

Publisher....Kate Kaegler
Publishing Manager....Sarah Phillips
Production Controller....Deborah Coulter
HHG Design....Jamieson Eley
HHG Director....Kelvin D Ladbrook
Production....PDQ Digital Media
Print Management....Bluepoint Cambridge
Printer....St Ives
UK Trade Sales....Portfolio Books
UK Distribution....NBN International
US Distribution....Globe Pequot

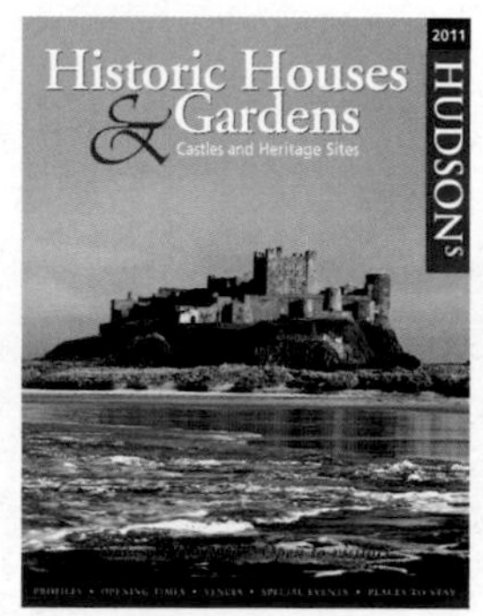

PUBLISHED BY:

Heritage House Group
Ketteringham Hall
Wymondham
Norfolk
NR18 9RS
Tel: 01603 813319
Fax: 01603 814992
Email: hudsons@hhgroup.co.uk
Web: www.hudsonsguide.co.uk

HERITAGE HOUSE GROUP

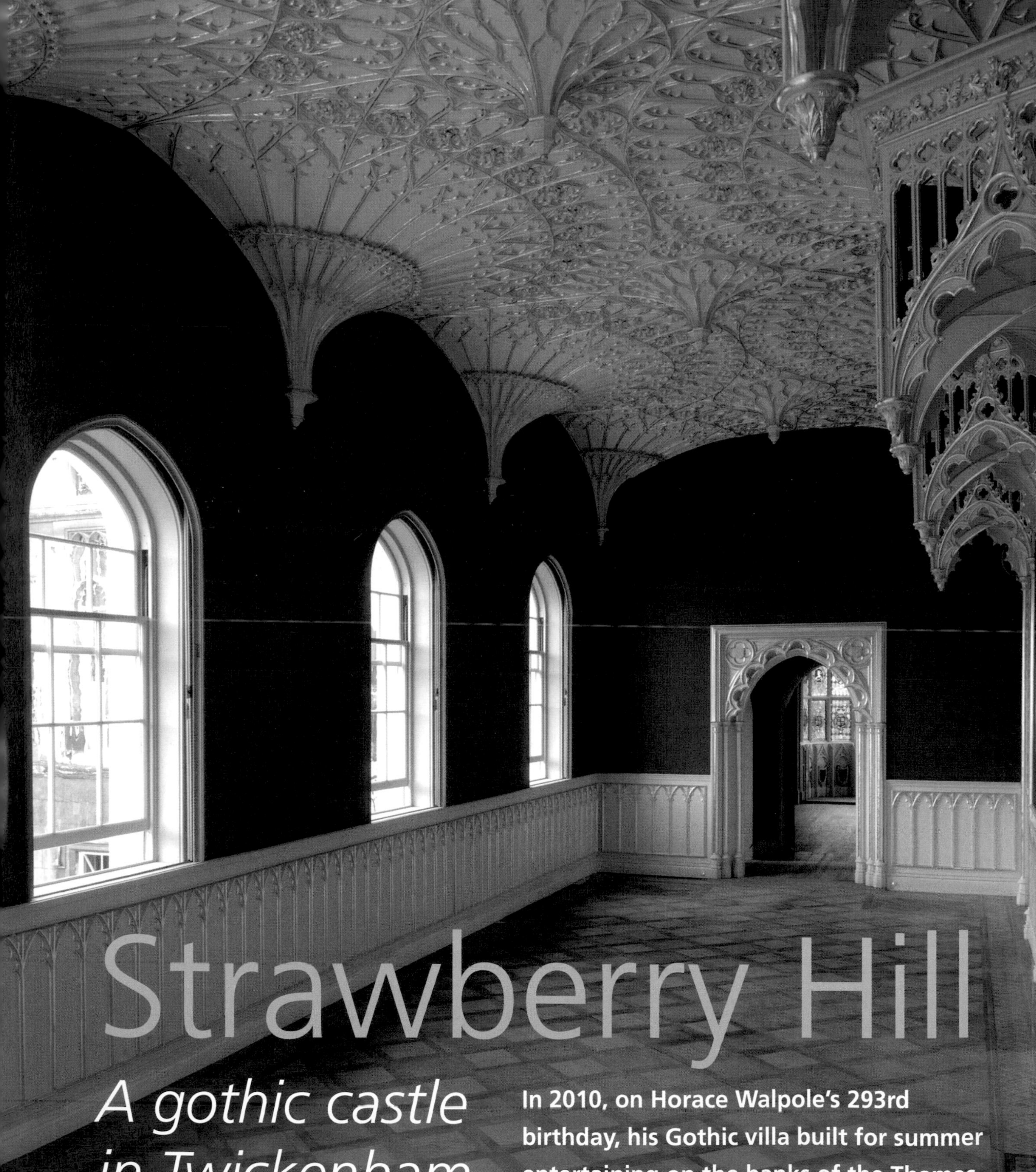

Strawberry Hill

A gothic castle in Twickenham

The restored Gallery at Strawberry Hill

In 2010, on Horace Walpole's 293rd birthday, his Gothic villa built for summer entertaining on the banks of the Thames at Twickenham, re-opened to the public after an extensive restoration programme.

18th century painting of Strawberry Hill by Müntz. Courtesy of Lewis Walpole Library.

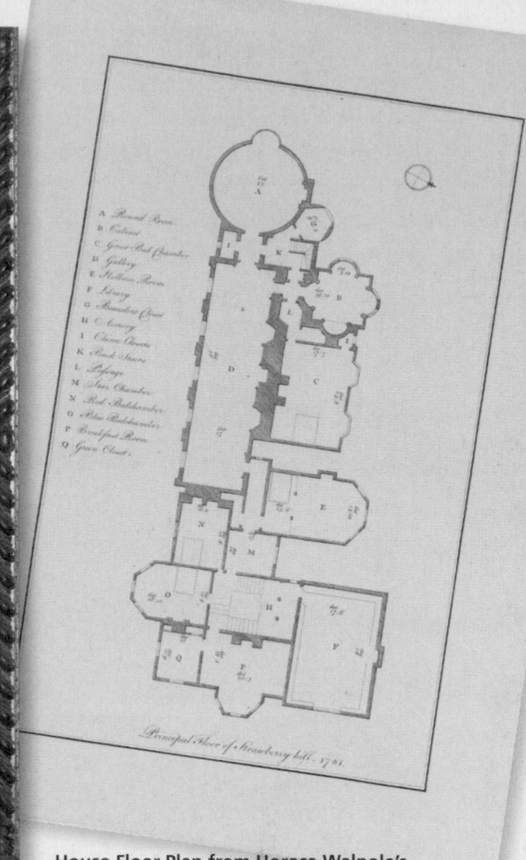

House Floor Plan from Horace Walpole's "Decription of the Villa'

Private Collection

Portrait of Horace Walpole 1754 - John Giles Eccart

Kilian O'Sullivan

Detail of the Gallery ceiling

"My house is built of paper..."

Walpole had ignored the popular Georgian choice of classically inspired architecture and turned instead to Gothic. His style swept England and inspired buildings throughout Europe and America. His vision was all embracing, and promoted an architectural style, the Gothic revival, which included furniture that reflected architectural elements and a literature of mystery, terror and imagination. Both grew out of Britain's past coupled with a strong sense of theatre. These elements were embodied in Strawberry Hill.

Strawberry Hill was listed, in 2004, by The World Monuments Fund as one of the 100 most endangered sites in the world and was also included on English Heritage's register of Buildings at Risk. It closed to the public in 2008 for an extensive restoration organised by The Strawberry Hill Trust. The Trust had been set up in 2002 to fund and mastermind a comprehensive programme of conservation and restoration. It was decided at the same time to restore the garden and to open it to the public.

The project was completed under the chairmanship of Michael Snodin with the Trust appointing Peter Inskip, of Inskip and Jenkins, as architect. Kevin Rogers, from the practice was placed in charge of the historical research on which the restoration would be based. The Heritage Lottery Fund granted £4.9 million of the £9 million needed, with other donations and support given by The World Monuments Fund, The Architectural Heritage Fund and English Heritage. Substantial contributions came also from charitable foundations, from individual donors and from numerous local or small charities and societies.

Initially, the problems facing the team were both less and, at the same time, greater than would normally be expected in restoring an historic house. Strawberry Hill is a house about which so much was already known. The problems were partly because Walpole never expected his house to last long beyond his death and had used some flimsy materials in the construction, and partly because there was almost too much information: choices had to be made. Obviously accuracy of detail was the first requisite, and as the greatest body of information covered the last Walpolian decorative period it was decided to restore the House to about 1790. In its time it was breathtakingly different to all other houses: unique. Irregularity and lack of symmetry created a mood of the unexpected, grisaille and painted glass filtered light to produce shadows and replicate the mood of medieval churches, grey paint absorbed the remaining light. By reinstating these elements the perception of the House, so carefully constructed by Walpole, would be reinstated in Strawberry Hill.

Richard Spiers

Yellow bedchamber chimneypiece showing ghosting from 18th century

Kilian O'Sullivan

Extensive renovation work in the Cloister

Kilian O'Sullivan

Wallpapers revealed during restoration

Martin Charles

"It is a little play-thing house... and is the prettiest bauble you ever saw"

HORACE WALPOLE AND THE HISTORY OF STRAWBERRY HILL

During early exploratory work Stephen Gee, the architect on site, found extensive evidence of a pre-Walpole building dating from the 17th century. Immediately before Walpole bought the house and land it had been used as a lodging house and rented to a 'toymaker', or seller of trinkets. Walpole was charmed by the thought of living in a 'play-thing house' and it became his home from 1747 until 1797.

Born in 1717, the son of Prime Minister Robert Walpole, Horace was educated at Eton where he demonstrated a lamentable inability for maths and forged friendships which lasted throughout his life. He went on the Grand Tour accompanied by Thomas Gray whom he had met at Cambridge. Journeying through France and Italy he was one of the earliest travellers to enter the newly discovered Herculaneum. On returning to England he searched for somewhere to live, outside London, to house his growing Collection and entertain his friends: he found Strawberry Hill. Over the next 50 years he built, amassed a famous Collection of extraordinary and beautiful objects, found a lack of space to display them and built again. He was advised on Gothic taste by a 'Committee' of his friends which included John Chute and Richard Bentley. This 'Committee' helped Walpole realise his vision. Strawberry Hill reflects Horace Walpole's passions from 1747 to 1797.

In character he was notably eccentric in an age of eccentricity. He displayed great loyalty and generosity to friends and family, was patriotic, popular with his servants most of whom remained with him throughout their lives, was fond of practical jokes and thought of himself as a writer of social and political history above all else. He died in 1797 leaving over 3,000 letters recording contemporary events, personalities of the day and the building of Strawberry Hill with its pitfalls and successes. He wrote a Gothic novel set in Strawberry Hill, *The Castle of Otranto*, which started the taste for Gothic horror which is alive in both literature and film today. His influential book, *The History of the Modern Taste in Gardening* recorded the arrival of the landscape garden. The best of what he or his friends wrote was published by his private press, The Strawberry Hill Press. When he died he bequeathed the House to his cousin's daughter, Anne Damer, for her life.

Anne was a sculptress. She had little money to spend on the house and there were few changes during her occupancy, or during that of early members of the Waldegrave family who inherited the house after she left it in 1811. However, Frances Braham, daughter of a fashionable singer, married two Waldegrave sons, one after the other. George, her second husband, became 7th Earl Waldegrave. In 1842, following his imprisonment for attacking a police officer, he put the contents

Richard Holttum

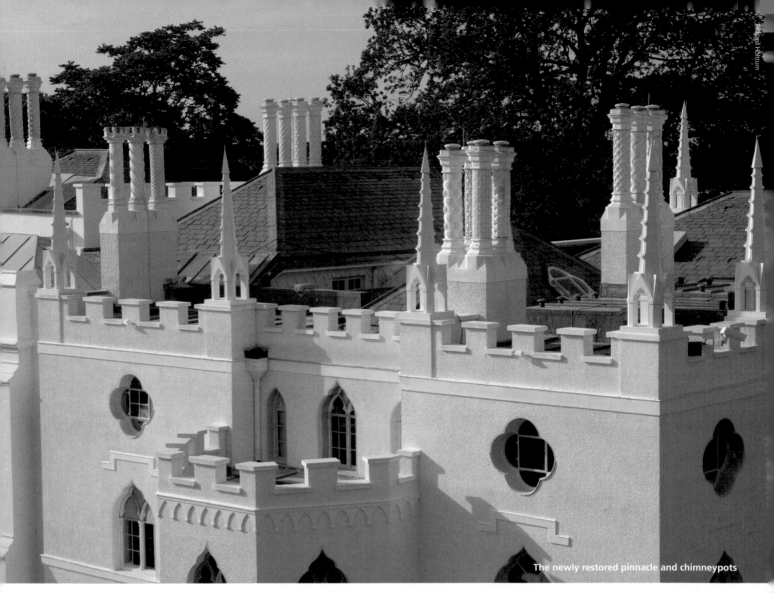

The newly restored pinnacle and chimneypots

Kilian O'Sullivan

The ceiling of The Round Room with gilding complete

Richard Holttum

Restored ceiling and stained glass of The Round Room

of Walpole's Strawberry Hill up for sale. The house was stripped of contents which took 32 days to sell, objects were dispersed around the world. Frances went on to marry twice more. She added a very grand wing to the 18th century Strawberry Hill, making it once more a place where society could gather. Following her death in 1879 it was bought by the de Stern family who owned it until 1923 when the Catholic Education Trust purchased it to house members of the Vincentian Order and to build a teacher training college in the grounds. Strawberry Hill remained in their ownership until it was leased to the Strawberry Hill Trust in 2007.

The gift conferred on Strawberry Hill by these groups and individuals is that they all decorated or built around the 18th century material without removing earlier work. Once their alterations were removed, under Peter Inskip's direction, long hidden areas of early wallpapers, repositioned windows, papier-mâché decoration, paint schemes and timber floors were revealed. This enabled the Trust to retain much of the original.

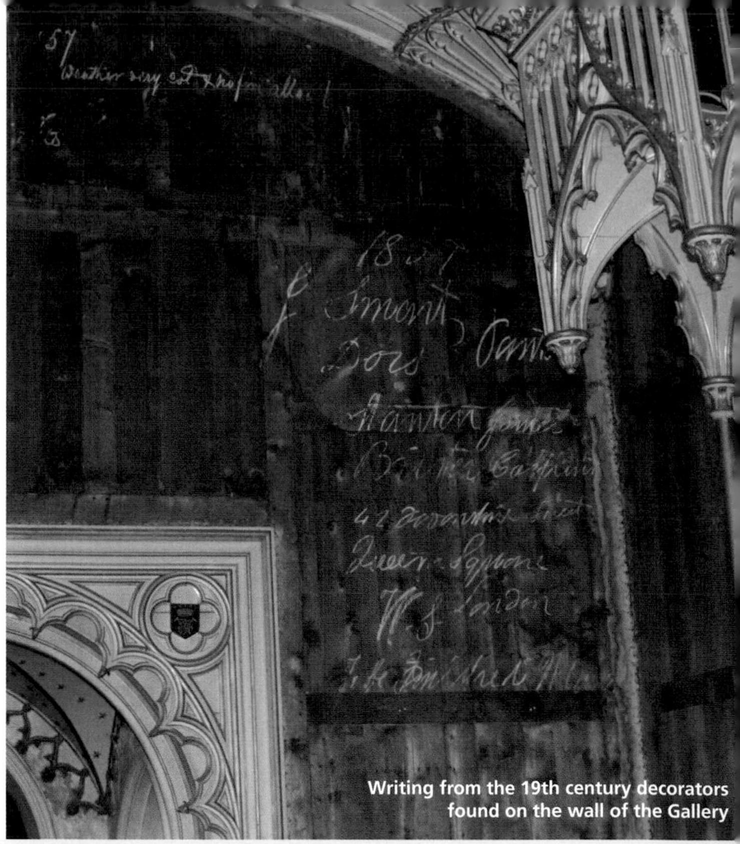

Writing from the 19th century decorators found on the wall of the Gallery

"The variety is little, and admits no charming irregularities."

BACKGROUND TO THE RESTORATION

Fanshawe LLP were appointed by the Trust to Project Manage the restoration. The decision was made to photograph each action taken and to record the process on film. All finds were listed and fragments used to date or advise on materials. Because of monetary constraints the decision was taken to restore comprehensively the Hall Staircase and state rooms together with other areas which could be used to house a museum, an education wing, a cafe and office space. However, after an in-depth investigation of the whole house was completed the findings revealed so many unexpected details that it was also decided to show at least one room un-restored, with revelations intact, and documented for visitors. Other areas would be made safe but not fully restored until later.

Initial discoveries were substantiated by printed records which included Walpole's own illustrated guidebook to the House, *The Description of the Villa*, which he compiled and published in 1774 and reprinted in 1784 in an enlarged edition. This book, together with his letters and accounts, were the first point of reference. Subsequent owners had been forced to sell objects from his Collection, or from the house, at auction and the catalogues for these sales were also consulted. Strawberry Hill was on the tourist route in the 18th century, with Walpole issuing tickets to those wishing to view it, and it continued to be visited until the 21st century. All of these facts combined to make it one of the best documented houses of the 18th century and one from which so much was expected.

Walpole's correspondence had been published in 48 volumes: the House Guides were detailed to check through each letter and list every mention of rooms, building or decoration. From their work, and other research, an historically accurate description of every room was produced, year by year, the objects within the rooms, the decorators employed and the purpose of the rooms. A set of watercolours show the most important rooms as they were around 1788. After this date Walpole, who was suffering badly from gout, spent less money on interior decoration and there were fewer changes.

Over a period of fifty years Walpole strove to build the interiors using details from known Gothic sources. He referred to engravings which had been made in the 17th and early 18th centuries and showed neither scale nor materials. The chimneypieces are among the greatest objects within Strawberry Hill, but only three are made of stone, the others are wood. The house was built using mainly inexpensive materials and modern (18th century) technology. The best and most fashionable craftsmen were employed to decorate, including Thomas Bromwich. Their work reinventing an earlier period was interspersed with genuine medieval or renaissance objects. The whole was conceived and put together by amateurs. This was, and is its charm and had to be retained.

Lisa Ferguson of Angel Interiors, gilding the the networking in the Gallery

Kilian O'Sullivan

The Chapel Studio stain glass window restoration

The ceiling of the Library and restored stained glass

Richard Holttum

Martin Charles

"I have carpenters to direct, plasterers to hurry, papermen to scold, and glaziers to help; this last has been my greatest pleasure."

THE RESTORATION

Once the restoration began a team of conservators and craftsmen were brought in. The earliest work was structural. The roof required re-leading with new pinnacles put in place and the 'battlements' repaired. Dry and wet rot were dealt with wherever they were found, the structure made safe and the crumbling Great South Tower rebuilt using Georgian principles and techniques. The restoration covered twenty rooms accessible to the public as well as accommodation and offices on the upper floor. Some rooms have been conserved, but not restored, and left to reveal the history of Strawberry Hill. With budgetary constraints some of the private rooms have been left for a future date and new campaign.

Throughout the restoration as fragments and artifacts appeared beneath floorboards, bricked into old walls, or as broken off architectural elements, they were listed and catalogued. At the start of the project some unexpected facts came to light. Among them, multiple layers of wallpaper were discovered, dating from pre-Walpole to the 20th century, showing the fashionable trends, tastes and status of those who had lived in Strawberry Hill. Throughout the period of restoration paint and fabric analysis was carried out which revealed large areas of 18th century paint and confirmed the unexpectedness of Walpole's palette. The use of dark grey paint enlivened by gilding conferred a richness and pageantry which surprised everyone involved with the project. The house emerged with an interior, except for the state rooms, painted in a dark grey which provided uniformity. It also increased the feeling of being in a stone, pre-Georgian, building. Painted glass used in the upper lights of the windows filtered the light with grey paint absorbing much of what remained, making sense of Walpole's description of the interior as having 'gloomth'.

The Renaissance glass had to be crated and removed by the restorers before the builders could start other work throughout the house. It was decided to re-assemble it according to Walpole's original plan which had been researched by glass expert, Michael Peover. Where glass was missing decisions were made whether to copy and replace or insert new grisaille glass. The famous lapis lazuli coloured glass used on the upper lights by Walpole to filter light was replaced, and the dramatic effect immediately perceived.

The Refectory or Great Parlour was restored to an overall background blue-grey imparting Gothic gloomth to the start of any visit to Strawberry Hill. The chimneypiece designed in 1754 by Richard Bentley was fully restored. In this room where the reference between architecture and furniture design is pivotal, replica settees and chairs have been made. They demonstrate how each item is part of Walpole's integral design.

In the Hall and Staircase sections of the 1791 hand-painted Gothic trompe l'oeil wallpaper was conserved demonstrating how the low-relief painting on the wall reinforced the impression of standing within a stone-walled building. Glass was commissioned to replace missing glass either side of the front door to complete this mood. A replica lantern lights the darkness.

The Yellow Bedchamber or Beauty Room, on the ground floor, has been conserved but left with the layers of three hundred years of living exposed. In this room it is possible to see the ingenious window system of horizontal sliding shutters and glass.

On the first floor in the Library, the pierced Gothic arches, book presses and chimneypiece now look magnificent. The Holbein Chamber is a vision in purple and the state rooms, Gallery, Round Room and Great North Bedchamber are all transformed by hangings of crimson Norwich damask. In the Gallery the effect is enhanced by mirrored alcoves which reflect the garden on the opposite wall. The proportion of the Gallery has been reinstated by raising the dado to its Georgian height. The papier-mâché ceiling for which the Gallery has been famed since it was built in 1762 has been cleaned and re-gilded. To complete the room the great door of St Alban has been copied and replaced. The Round Room and Great North Bedchamber have both been restored in a similar way with emphasis on their chimneypieces, one of them in scagliola by Robert Adam. The Bedchamber had been altered considerably by the Victorian owner and had lost its magnificence; it has now been restored to Walpolian grandeur and a state bed is being sought to complete it.

The Tribune or Cabinet contains what is possibly the most interesting placement of window glass in the house with a system whereby the painted glass panel is protected by both one of clear glass and by shutters, sliding into the wall between two 'skins'.

On entering the state rooms from dark passages the effect in the 18th century was spectacular; crimson damask on the walls and gilding provided the 'wow' factor. The design of the ceilings, chimneypieces and dados was Gothic but the furniture was fashionably up to date and predominately French. The effect was achieved through Walpole's sense of theatre. Painted and glazed arms were emblazoned everywhere. The use of heraldry coupled the Walpole family with monarchs and heroes. By progressing through objects from English history (for example, a copy of Magna Carta hung in Walpole's bedchamber), through the use of heraldry and through the impact of light the visitor was alerted to an approaching grand finale. The grandeur and finale have been replaced although, sadly, the French furniture is missing. The Trust is actively seeking to locate these treasures with a view to borrowing, or even buying them in order to return them to their former home.

Outside the house 20th century additions were removed and the garden front restored to its 18th century state. The house is startlingly white, a quality remarked upon in Walpole's time.

Kilian O'Sullivan

Chimneypiece with 18th century inscription

Martin Charles

17th century glass, a hunting scene

Kilian O'Sullivan

Round Roo[m] chimneypie[ce]

"For the rest of the house, I could send it to you in this letter, only that I should have nowhere to live till the return of the post."

THE FUTURE

In the service wing and cloistered area there have been major changes. The Great Cloister has been taken back to its 18th century state by the removal of interior walls; the arcade which had been infilled in the early 19th century has been reopened, and simply glazed, to enable the area to be used as a tea room. In summer this should be a magical space with a view of the garden. Close by, the Servants' Hall will be used as a museum room relating the stories of those who lived in the house and showing objects from Walpole's Collection. Elsewhere in this wing an education suite of rooms have been added and every inch of space utilised.

An archive of objects found within the house during the course of the work has been started but the greatest archival achievement is a database created by The Lewis Walpole Library, Yale University. This aims to list all the objects owned by Walpole, with images wherever possible, and follows them through later ownership. It will assist future research into Strawberry Hill by students and scholars alike.

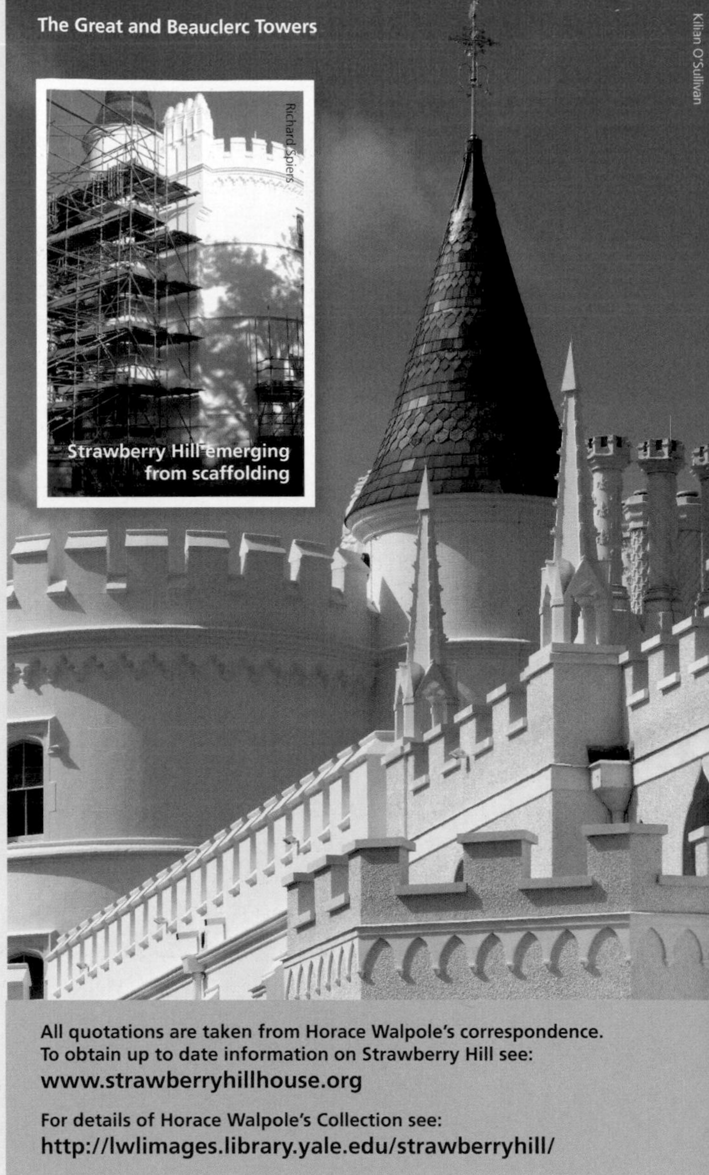
The Great and Beauclerc Towers

Kilian O'Sullivan

Strawberry Hill emerging from scaffolding

Richard Spiers

All quotations are taken from Horace Walpole's correspondence.
To obtain up to date information on Strawberry Hill see:
www.strawberryhillhouse.org

For details of Horace Walpole's Collection see:
http://lwlimages.library.yale.edu/strawberryhill/

"It is set in enamelled meadows, with filigree hedges."

THE GARDEN

Horace Walpole loved the garden. He built the house and furnished rooms to complement the views to the river Thames and the planting of the garden. Thus, the small tower overlooking the garden was hung with green wallpaper and displayed flower paintings. The garden was designed with skilful planting to carry the eye back to the house. It is integral to an enjoyment and understanding of the house. Although less garden space is available now than in the Georgian period the core survives and will be planted as accurately as possible. However, trees could not be planted until the main work of restoration finished therefore we, like Walpole, await the growth of trees to maturity. In the front of the house the Prior's Garden wafts the scent of roses and herbs to approaching visitors.

Horace Walpole's vision was to create a spectacular house which his friends and visitors could enjoy. They were encouraged to make a journey, stepping back into the past, to encounter the most beautiful and precious man-made objects which he could obtain for his Collection. At the same time they entered his own theatre in which each room of the house was presented as if it were a scene of a play, with the Gallery providing the denouement and the Great North Bedchamber seen as the climax. He succeeded so well that Strawberry Hill became one of the most famous houses of the time. The Trust aims to return it to this position, a 'must be seen' venue for every visitor to London and the United Kingdom.

As more people come to visit and more money is raised further areas will be restored and opened to the public. In 1766 Walpole wrote... ***'I almost think there is no wisdom comparable to that of exchanging what is called the realities of life for dreams. Old castles, old pictures, old histories, and the babble of old people make one live back into centuries that cannot disappoint one.'***

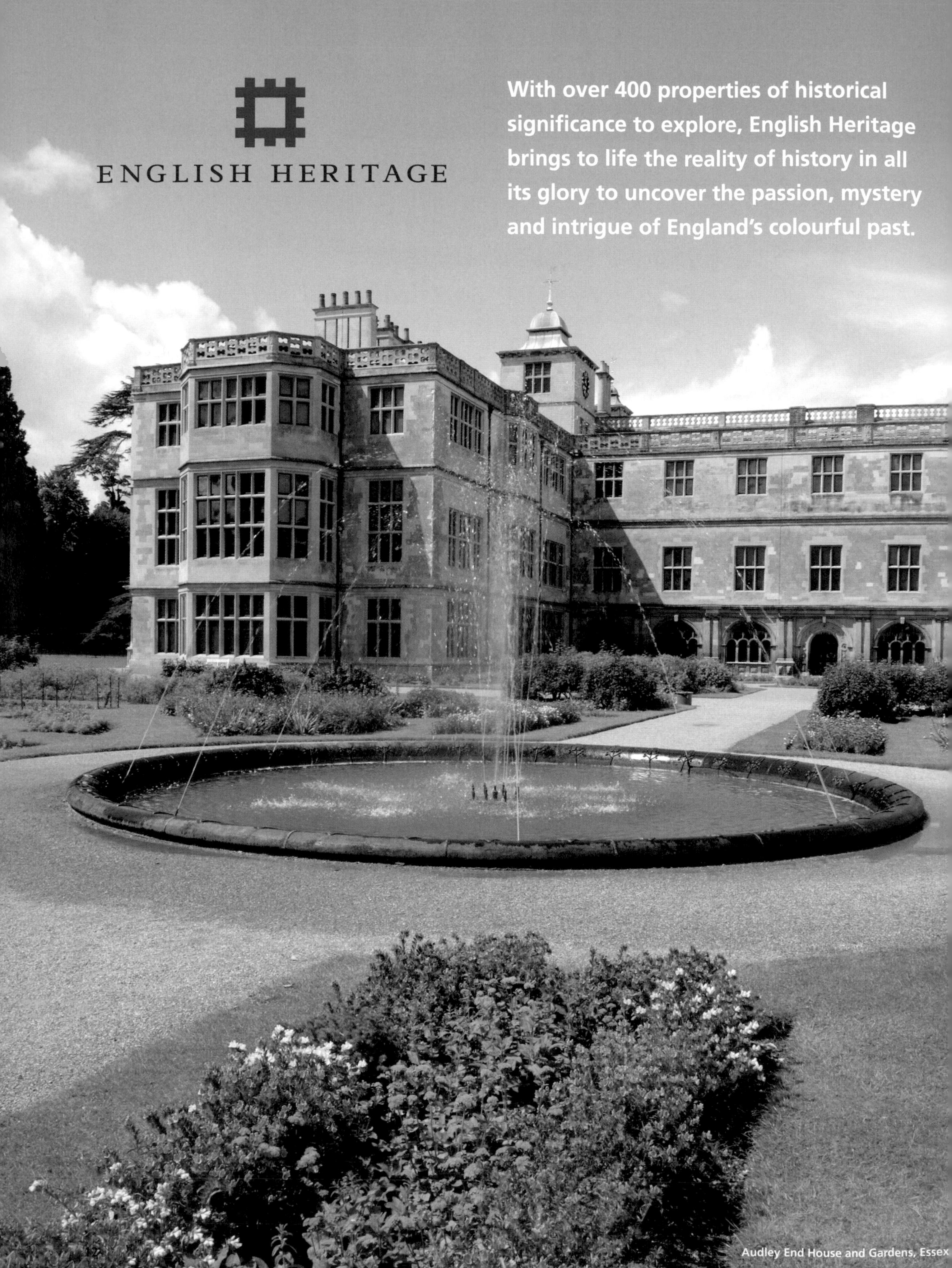

Audley End House and Gardens, Essex

English Heritage

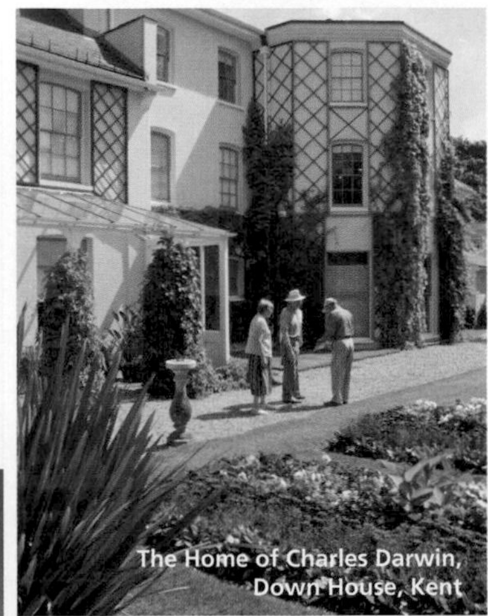
The Home of Charles Darwin, Down House, Kent

Discover days out with a difference

Come and visit some of our fantastic properties including mighty castles, beautiful houses, English gardens, magnificent roman sites, ancient monuments, ruins and much more.

Stonehenge, Wiltshire

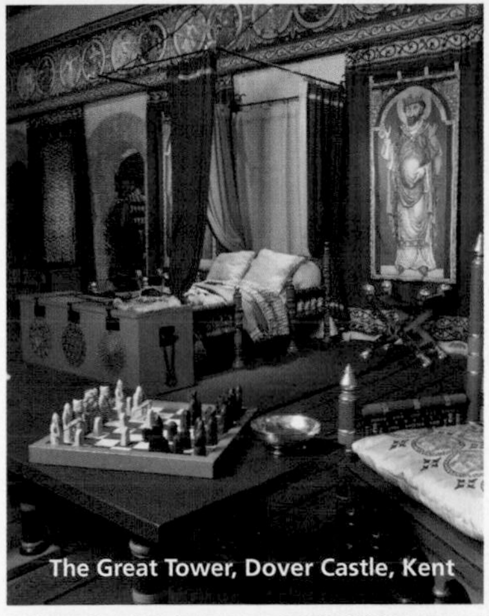
The Great Tower, Dover Castle, Kent

You can journey back to the 12th century at **Dover Castle** and visit the Great Tower which has recently been transformed to its former glory by our dedicated team at English Heritage. Originally created by King Henry II this medieval treasure is definitely worth a visit and you could meet the mighty King himself!

Explore **The Home of Charles Darwin, Down House** where the famous scientist lived with his family for over 40 years. Unravel the mystery of the ancient stone circle of **Stonehenge** which dates back to around 3,000 BC or discover the grand stables that have been beautifully restored at **Audley End House and Gardens.**

"At English Heritage membership really does offer something special."

The Sevice Wing, Audley End House and Garder

Audley End House from lake

For children, there are dressing up clothes in the stables as well as a new themed play area and don't forget to visit the new Cart Yard Café for a delicious treat to finish your day.

AUDLEY END HOUSE AND GARDENS

At Audley End House & Gardens you'll enjoy a truly unique visitor experience, there's plenty to explore. Take in the spectacular Jacobean mansion, built to entertain royalty with it's stunning art collection and luxurious interiors. Stroll through the formal gardens, organic kitchen garden and parklands designed by Capability Brown, and then discover how life would have been 'below stairs' for the servants and staff in the fascinating Service Wing.

Recently restored, these are the rooms that were never intended to be seen. Immerse yourself in the sights, sounds and smells of the 1800s kitchen, scullery, pantry and laundries. The cook, Mrs Crocombe, and her staff can regularly be seen trying out new recipes and going about their chores.

Horse and groom, Audley End House and Gardens

BRINGING NEW LIFE TO AUDLEY END STABLES

After over 60 years and following a major restoration project in 2010, Audley End House and Gardens has reopened the doors to its stables, complete with resident horses and costumed groom. The stables make a fascinating addition to Audley End as the typical daily routine of a Victorian stable yard is brought to life.

This important early 17th century building is the grandest surviving example of the period, and is one of the most significant stable buildings English Heritage has in its care. The stables would have housed up to 30 pampered horses, with the grooms, coaches, and other equipment needed to service the demands of this great country house.

The new stables experience includes an exhibition where you can find out about the workers who lived on the estate in the 1880s, the tack house and the Audley End fire engine.

Stables, Audley End House and Gardens

Rangers House, London

" By becoming a member of English Heritage, you'll also be supporting the essential work of preserving, restoring and exhibiting England's historic legacy for years to come."

English Heritage Members benefits include:

- Free entry to over 400 places of historical interest
- Free entry for up to 6 accompanied children within your family group under 19 years of age
- Free or reduced price entry to an exciting calendar of historical events
- Free full colour guide detailing each property
- Free members magazine; Heritage Today.

Find out more:
www.english-heritage.org.uk *or* call 0870 333 1184

Brodsworth Hall and Gardens, South Yorkshire

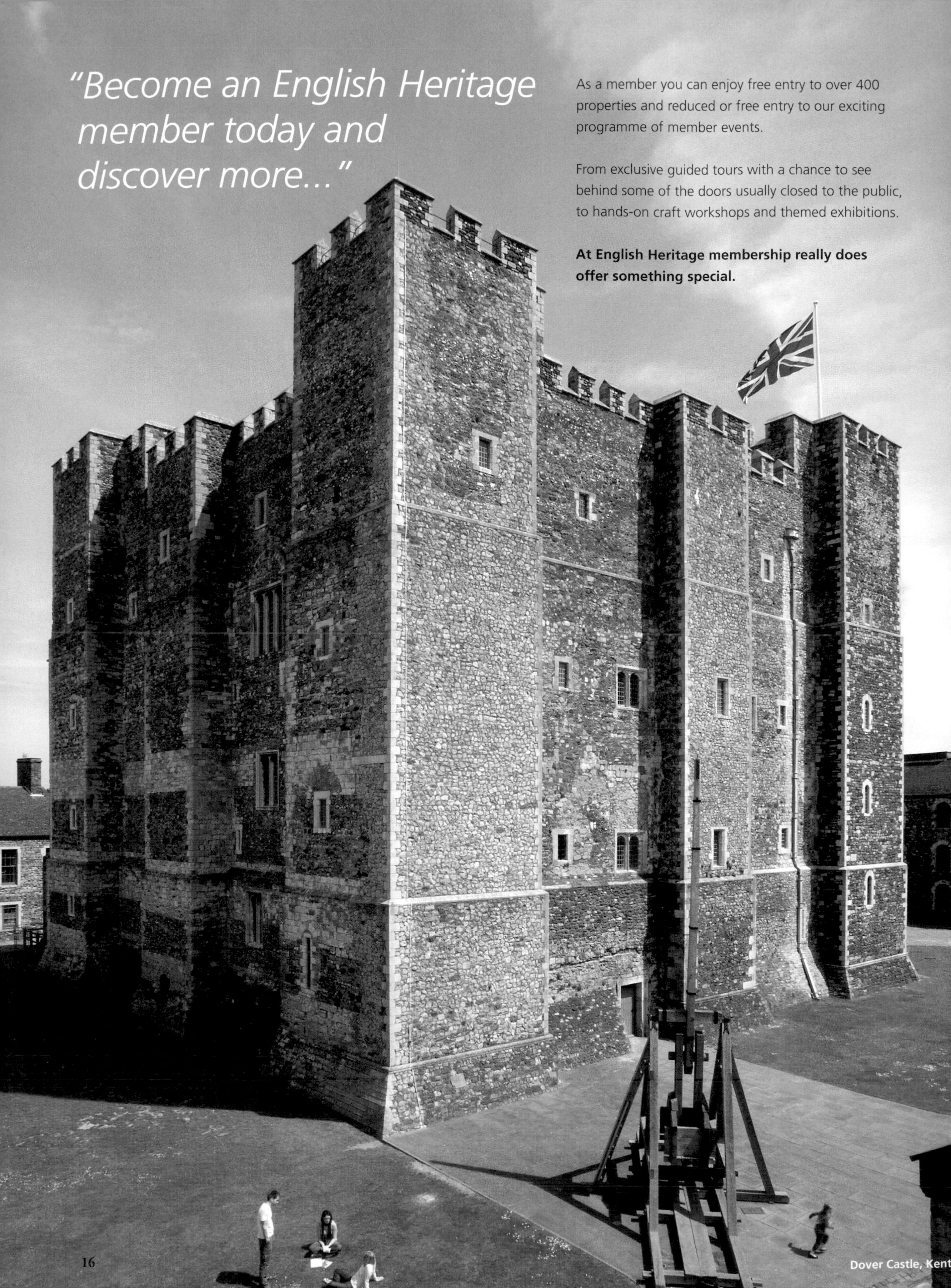

"Become an English Heritage member today and discover more..."

As a member you can enjoy free entry to over 400 properties and reduced or free entry to our exciting programme of member events.

From exclusive guided tours with a chance to see behind some of the doors usually closed to the public, to hands-on craft workshops and themed exhibitions.

At English Heritage membership really does offer something special.

Dover Castle, Kent

The Palace Project

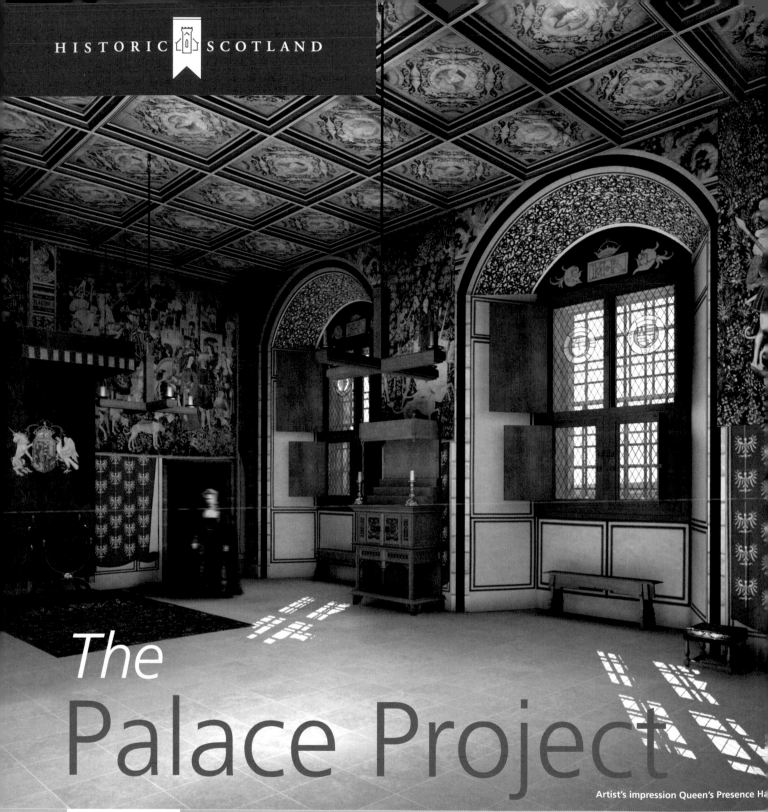

Artist's impression Queen's Presence Ha

In centuries past the likes of Daniel Defoe lamented how James V's once magnificent palace at Stirling Castle had been allowed to fade and crumble. At last it has been returned to its Renaissance majesty thanks to a £12 million refurbishment by Historic Scotland.

The result is that from Easter 2011 visitors will be able to step back into the childhood world of Mary, Queen of Scots. They can admire six refurbished royal apartments which have been redecorated and furnished by some of the best traditional craftsmen from Scotland, England and France, to look as they might have done in the mid-16th century. To complete the sense of time travel there are costumed performers who seamlessly slip in and out of character – one minute they are modern guides, the next they are lords, ladies, servants or guards letting people in on court gossip and intrigue. And the palace certainly saw its share of conspiracies and plots.

"It was here that the infant Mary was brought to live in 1543 by her mother - the beautiful, charming, rich and politically astute Mary of Guise."

The palace had been built by James V and was intended to match anything that his French queen would have known in her homeland. For the ruler of a poor northern kingdom to hope to match the accomplishments of France, a powerhouse of Renaissance culture, was ambitious indeed. But Mary's large dowry was a big help. And while the unfortunate king achieved his objective he possibly never saw his grand scheme realised, dying aged 30 in late 1542, before the palace is thought to have been finished, and leaving his throne to a baby girl less than a week old.

James is believed to have died thinking the Stewart dynasty was doomed but, in part thanks to the determination and character of his widow, it not only survived but went on to bring about the union of the Scottish and English crowns through their grandson James VI and I. And the palace at Stirling is where the two Marys spent critical years, hoping they were far enough north to avoid possible English attempts to kidnap the 'little queen' and force her to wed Henry VIII's son, Prince Edward.

But the threat from the Auld Enemy was not always the most pressing. Scotland was riven by competing factions, with rival parties insisting that their own people were at Stirling Castle to watch over the child – and each other. In the meantime Mary of Guise gradually used her political skills, backed by French cash and troops, to build her own position – indeed she ultimately became regent and ruled the kingdom on her daughter's behalf. So, in these early years of the 1540s the palace was simultaneously a gilded cage and a powerbase.

Music performance

Outer walls of palace

TODAY'S VISITORS CAN SEE JUST HOW THAT POWER WAS EXERCISED...

Three apartments were designed for the king and three for his queen, in 'his and hers' style, each with an outer hall, inner hall and bedchamber. Historic Scotland has furnished the queen's apartments as if Mary of Guise was in residence, giving a glimpse of what it must have been like for a subject turning up to petition the young widow for favours or justice.

First the Queen's Outer Hall, splendidly painted, but simply furnished with a few benches round the side for those too old or infirm to stand. And stand they did, sometimes hour upon hour, waiting to speak to officials or to Mary herself and perhaps having to return for several days. Waiting was very much part of the theatre of royalty, leaving no one in any doubt about who

John Donaldson (carver) with replica Stirling Hea

was in charge. And all the time there would be gentry, nobles, servants, soldiers and others milling about, perhaps including your own rivals, all with their own competing schemes and dreams.

Recent research by historian John Harrison has also shown that Mary of Guise probably often dined in the outer hall. And this would have been quite a sight as trestle tables were hastily assembled and preparations made for the arrival of the queen and her entourage. What's especially intriguing is that unlike in Tudor England, where royalty often dined in splendid isolation, the hall would have been packed with folk from many social backgrounds from minor landholders and junior officers up. And this was part of Mary's genius, she became liked and admired because she chatted, laughed and listened – today we call it networking.

After the meals the furniture was cleared and there would sometimes have been music, dance and jesters' tricks. This in itself would have been quite a sight, not least because of the diverse people there would have been including poets, jugglers, singers, lutenists and others. Some may have come from far away, Mr Harrison has identified records of two 'Moors' in the royal household at this time, who are among the first Arabs or Africans firmly identified in Scotland. Perhaps they were entertainers, it's not clear. What is known is that the ceilings of some of the palace apartments were decorated with great oak medallions, a metre wide, intricately carved with characters from court life. They include a jester, a poet and one carving with the earliest-known instrumental musical notation carved round the edge. Historic Scotland has worked with experts in Renaissance music to rediscover what it may have sounded like, and the interpretations have been performed several times. Whose music it was is unknown, but there is the tantalizing possibility that it was a court favourite or even a royal composition.

"More than 30 original roundels survive, collectively known as the Stirling Heads and they are so special they are sometimes known as Scotland's other crown jewels."

The 16th century heads are now on display in their own purpose-built gallery above the refurbished apartments, while a full set of hand-carved replicas have been used to decorate the ceiling of the King's Inner Hall. They are astounding, bringing visitors face to face not just with Renaissance entertainers, but with kings, queens, emperors and classical heroes. Among them are James V, Mary of Guise, Margaret Tudor and Henry VIII – cloaked and armour-clad with a lion draped across his shoulders.

King's Presence Hall

The Queen's Inner Hall is decorated with something equally remarkable, a set of huge hand-woven tapestries telling the popular tale of The Hunt of the Unicorn. Records show that Scotland's royal family had, among its collection of around 100 tapestries, a set which told this story. But they were much more than just something to admire, they expressed power and wealth, as well as performing a practical function as draft excluders. An indication of the investment involved is that the set of seven commissioned for Stirling cost around £2 million, and are a stand alone project largely funded by philanthropic donations.

The inner hall was where those granted an audience would meet Mary of Guise, and they would bow deeply in reverence. She would be seated on a chair stood on a dais, probably covered in imported carpets. Above her head would be a cloth of estate bearing her arms – one side had the red lion rampant of Scotland and the other the complex and colourful heraldry of her own great Guise family.

Visitors nowadays see a version which took some of Scotland's finest embroiderers six months to make. The shield is supported by a unicorn and eagle, above it is a crown stitched with gold and pearls. Professor Malcolm Lochhead, the Glasgow Caledonian University textiles expert leading the embroiders, likened a cloth of estate to a modern brand image that vividly flashed out your family's importance and pedigree. Even in the 21st century when we are surrounded by so much colour and imagery, this exquisite craftsmanship still has the power to dazzle.

Finally there are the bedchambers, where only a chosen few could venture, close friends, personal servants and confidants.

Embroiderers from top: Liz Boulton, Eileen Rumble and Mary McCarron

"The Palace and Royal apartments are very magnificent, but all in Decay ... we thought it would be much better to pull them down than to let such Buildings sink into their own Rubbish ..."

DANIEL DEFOE

Artist's impression Queen's Outer Hall

Palace gardens

Carvings palace exterior

The queen's is furnished with cupboards and chests, and a personal altar topped with a triptych showing pious scenes. Pride of place is reserved for the bed itself, which is sumptuously dressed in beautiful materials and surrounded by hand-made carpets from a specialist business in Lahore.

What comes as a surprise to some people is that at this time the four posters were not the objects of tradition and antiquity they are for us. Quite the opposite, they were innovative and must-have furniture. When James V ventured to France he was hugely impressed and ordered some to be sent back to Scotland flat-pack style. They were probably considered far too good to sleep on. Proud owners had their portraits painted in front of them, would receive honoured guests beside them, but mostly took their rest elsewhere.

In Stirling palace there is a tiny room, smaller than the cabin of a cross channel ferry, just off the King's Bedchamber which was probably intended as his sleeping area. And as the palace stood on top of a volcanic rock, exposed to the worst that the northern winter weather could throw at it, having a cosy cubbyhole to sleep in was very wise.

Historic Scotland has also invested in superb new displays telling the story of the palace from the Wars of Independence to the centuries after the royals departed – preferring the warmer climes of England. The vaults beneath the palace also have family-orientated interactive displays which give youngsters the chance to discover all sorts of interesting people from the castle's past.

Overall the palace project has provided Scotland with a superb new visitor attraction which, however, would not have been possible had the likes of Daniel Defoe got their way. Like other visitors of the past he commented on how the palace, transformed into an army barracks, was a shadow of its former self. In 1727 he wrote: "The Palace and Royal apartments are very magnificent, but all in Decay … we thought it would be much better to pull them down than to let such Buildings sink into their own Rubbish …" Thankfully they survived and with them the superb statues on the outside walls. One of the finest is of James V, thickly bearded with one hand resting on his dagger hilt. After 450 years he remains a striking figure, staring intently at the visitors flowing through the main entrance of the palace which he never got to enjoy for himself.

ENGLISH HERITAGE
Come and see the heritage you have helped save.

There are many fascinating places to visit which have recently been repaired with the help of grants from English Heritage financed by the taxpayer.

With over 1,200 to choose from, there's bound to be something near you and something to suit every taste. Some of them are opening their doors to the public for the first time.

We give grants for major repair projects on important heritage sites throughout England. The range is huge: houses from medieval to modern, forts and castles from the Romans to the Victorians, mills and mausoleums, follies and parks, and all sorts of places of worship. We also grant aid essential professional work such as investigation, research and surveys to help plan repairs and future management more effectively. Alongside these grants for individual sites, we contribute to the costs of some public and charitable organisations working to care for the historic environment and to get more people involved. Last year, we spent a total of £32.3 million in grants.

It has always been a principle of English Heritage grant-giving that the public should be able to see the sites and buildings they have helped repair. The extent of public access varies from one property to another. Some are open throughout the year, some on certain days only and others by prior arrangement. Some open on Heritage Open Days as well. Full details of opening arrangements at grant-aided places are published on our website, at: **www.english-heritage.org.uk –** follow the links for Days Out and then Visit Grant Aided Places. Here you can find a database of over 1,200 different buildings, monuments, parks and gardens, searchable by location and type. Most of the properties are open free, but we give details of admission charges where they apply. There is also a brief description of each property and information on parking and access for people with disabilities. A selection of current examples is shown on the page opposite.

English Heritage is grateful to all those owners and custodians with whom we work; their commitment to keeping the nation's heritage in good repair and their support for these public access arrangements is vital. The vast majority of this country's heritage is in the hands and care of private individuals and voluntary groups. We are pleased to be able to help through grant aid where we can, but we will only ever provide a fraction of the sums needed to pass on our historic environment to future generations. The private owners and voluntary groups who look after listed buildings, monuments and landscapes are today's principal custodians of tomorrow's heritage. Their contribution to the beauty and history of this country is vital.

We very much hope you enjoy the sites and properties you find, from the famous to the many lesser-known treasures - they are all worth a visit.

Birkenhead Park Grand Entrance

Windmill Hill Windmill

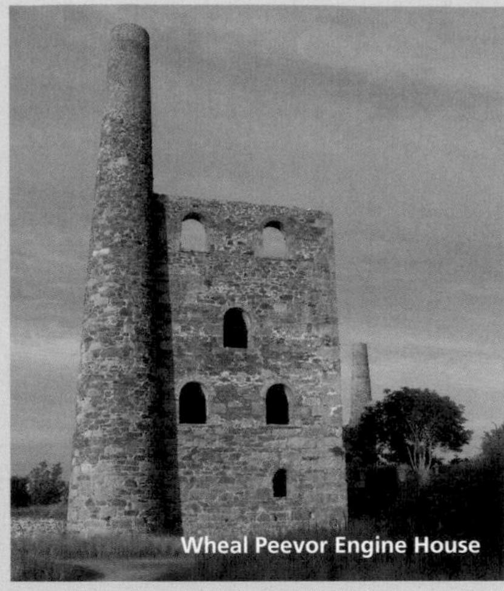

Wheal Peevor Engine House

GRAND ENTRANCE, BIRKENHEAD PARK

Park Road North, Birkenhead, Wirral, Merseyside CH41 4HD

Grand triple entrance archway to Birkenhead Park, with two-storey lodges on either side. Dated 1847, by L Hornblower and J Robertson for Sir Joseph Paxton. Full-height coupled Ionic columns which also continue across the flanking lodges. Balustraded parapet. Listed Grade II*. English Heritage grant-aided refurbishment of upper and lower roofs and front elevation repairs between 2005 and 2006.

www.wirral.gov.uk

Grant Recipient: Wirral Council

Access contact: Mr Adam King, Park Manager

T: 0151 652 5197 **F:** 0151 652 4521

E-mail: adamking@wirral.gov.uk

Open: March - September: Friday, tour 2 - 3pm. At other times by prior arrangement.

Heritage Open Days: Yes

Parking: 20 spaces. Additional parking in park.

Access for the disabled: Entrance arches wheelchair accessible but not internal buildings. WC for the disabled at Birkenhead Park Pavilion (visitor centre) and coffee shop. WC for the disabled. Assistance dogs allowed.

Admission charge: No

WINDMILL HILL WINDMILL

Herstmonceux, Hailsham, East Sussex BN27 4RT

Grade II* listed, dating from 1815, the second tallest and largest post mill in body size in the country. The mill last worked by wind in 1894 and has been authentically restored. English Heritage provided funds towards a detailed survey in 1999 and from 2002 contributed along with other funders to the restoration of the mill frame and roundhouse. It opened to the public in 2006.

www.windmillhillwindmill.co.uk

Grant Recipient: Windmill Hill Windmill Trust (reg charity 1054504)

Access contact: Mrs B Frost

T: 01323 833033 **F:** 01323 833744

E-mail: admin@windmillhillwindmill.co.uk

Open: Easter to October: first and third Sunday of the month and Bank Holidays 2.30pm - 5pm. School parties and groups by prior arrangement throughout the year.

Heritage Open Days: Yes

Parking: 4 spaces

Access for the disabled: Wheelchair access to visitor centre. Film enables full visitor experience without climbing long ladder to mill body. WC for the disabled. Assistance dogs allowed.

Admission charge: No

WHEAL PEEVOR ENGINE HOUSE AND MINE COMPLEX

Wheal Peevor, Sinns Common, Redruth, Cornwall TR16 4BH

Engine houses and mine complex of former deep tin mine, all a Scheduled Monument. The engine houses, also listed Grade II, date from the 1870s. The buildings have been consolidated and viewing platforms installed allowing visitors to enter the structures. A network of trails has been created within the site to link up to the Coast to Coast multi-use trail. English Heritage grant-aided consolidation works to mine engine houses, mine stack chimney, calciner remains and associated flue structures between 2005 and 2007.

www.cornish-mining.org.uk/sites/peevor.htm

Grant Recipient: Kerrier District Council

Access contact: Mr Adam Warden, Cornwall Council

T: 0300 1234 202 **F:** 01209 614493

E-mail: adam.warden@cornwall.gov.uk

Open: All reasonable times.

Heritage Open Days: No

Parking: 6 spaces. Access to Coast to Coast multi-use trail.

Access for the disabled: Wheelchair access to the three key engine houses and main route throughout the site. No WC for the disabled. Assistance dogs allowed.

Admission charge: No

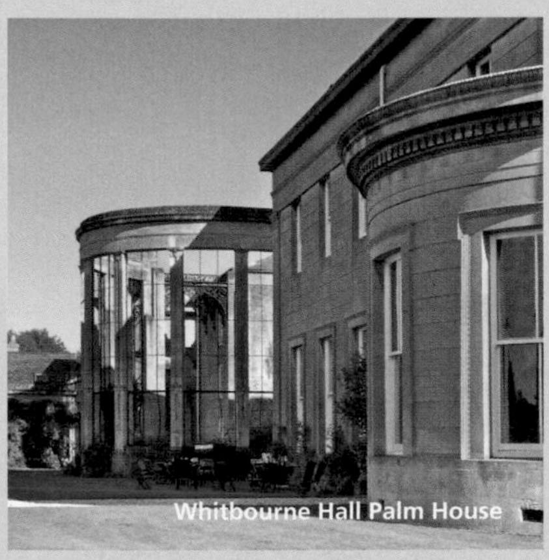

Whitbourne Hall Palm House

WHITBOURNE HALL AND PALM HOUSE

Whitbourne, Worcester, Worcestershire WR6 5SE

Victorian Greek Revival style country house, 1860-62, with large palm house built later (circa 1865-77) in the space between main block and service wing. The south front has an imposing Ionic portico. The main hall, with Maw and Co. mosaic tiled floor, is lit entirely by glazed blue-glass ceiling and surrounded by a gallery accessed by a white marble staircase with limestone balustrade. English Heritage grant aided work to stabilise and repair the palm house structure between 2001 and 2006.

www.whitbournehall.com

Grant Recipient: Whitbourne Hall Community Ltd

Access contact: Heather Colley

T: 01886 821165

E-mail: HeatherDColley@aol.com

Open: 2, 9, 16, 23 and 30 May, 6, 13, 20 and 27 June 11am - 4pm.
Also Daffodil Day (to be confirmed at time of publication - see website).
At other times for groups by prior arrangement.

Heritage Open Days: No

Parking: 100 spaces. Parking around the House for 30 cars.

Access for the disabled: Wheelchair access to part of the garden. Mobile ramp available for access to the house (three steps). Open areas of the house accessible for wheelchairs (wide doors). WC for the disabled. Assistance dogs allowed.

Admission charge: Adult: £5.00, Child: £2.50, Other: £3.50

Heritage Open Days is an annual event over four days in September which celebrates England's architecture and culture by allowing visitors free access to properties that are either not usually open, or would normally charge an entrance fee.

ENGLISH HERITAGE

ENGLISH HERITAGE 138-142 Holborn, London EC1N 2ST
Customer services: Tel: +44 (0) 870 333 1181 Fax: +44 (0) 1793 414 926
Minicom text telephone for the deaf or hard of hearing: 0800 015 0516
Email: customers@english-heritage.org.uk
www.english-heritage.org.uk

The Poison Garden

The Alnwick Garden's locked garden of killer plants

A little visitor

The Alnwick Garden, a contemporary garden created by the Duchess of Northumberland alongside Alnwick Castle in Northumberland, is home to the unusual and the unexpected. From one of the world's largest wooden treehouses to shooting jets of water and innovative programmes of tours, exhibitions and events, there's much to take visitors by surprise.

"Visitors enter a world of lethal lovelies..."

Lithospermum officinale

The Garden's most infamous feature is the Poison Garden; a locked garden of killer plants. Stepping through the dramatic gates, visitors enter a world of lethal lovelies, used for centuries in murder, execution, hunting and warfare. The Poison Garden challenges our ideas about what a garden can or should be, creating a place for drama and death in an otherwise lovely landscape.

Hyposycamus niger

Euphorbia x martini

In The Alnwick Garden's early days, the Duchess wondered why so many gardens around the world focused on the healing powers of plants rather than their ability to kill. She visited gardens in Padua, Italy, learning that they had been built to find more effective ways for the Medicis to kill their enemies.
Our ancestors were masters of the toxic arts. They could select a poison that would take days or even months to take effect, leaving no clue to the source of a lingering sickness. Of course, many people poisoned themselves by accident, using the wrong plant or the wrong dose in the quest for beauty or health.

The plant-world is steeped in myth, legend and folklore, with some plants prized for their special powers while others are avoided. These stories inspire the tours given by the Poison Garden guides once behind the locked gates. Each tour is different as the guides share their favourite stories, entertaining with gruesome details and ensuring there's no touching, tasting or even smelling of the plants.

Artemisia absinthium

Dangerous plants grow behingd bars

Flame shaped bec

Following the Duchess's vision, the Poison Garden was designed by internationally-renowned designer Jacques Wirtz, within the master plan for The Alnwick Garden. Within The Garden's footprint, it contrasts with the romance of the Rose Garden and the sensory experiences of the Bamboo Labyrinth and the water-filled Serpent Garden. The heavy and dark Poison Garden gates feature a skull and crossbones, reminding visitors of the danger within, and are interwoven with a snake and a spider. They lead to gloomy ivy-covered tunnels, and moving through the Garden, flame-shaped beds lick at visitors' feet.

The mandrake, made famous by Harry Potter, grows at Alnwick. It has long been known for its poisonous properties, and is steeped in history and intrigue. The forked root is known as the 'root of life' or the 'divine root', and resembling the human form, it was thought to be in the power of dark earth spirits. It was believed to possess magical powers that could rejuvenate lost youth, as well as induce a feeling of love, affection and happiness. Mandrakes were once more prized than gold. Roman physicians reported complicated surgical operations having been performed in Alexandria under the anesthetic effect of mandrake.

Strychnos nux-vomica or Poison nut, also found here, was familiar to the Egyptian queen Cleopatra. When deciding to end her life, she used her slaves as guinea pigs to test the effects of many different poisonous plants. Among the toxic sources she tried were belladonna, henbane and the seed of the strychnine tree. Death by strychnine poisoning is accompanied by violent spasms that distort the facial muscles into a hideous mask. To look beautiful in death, she chose a venomous snake instead.

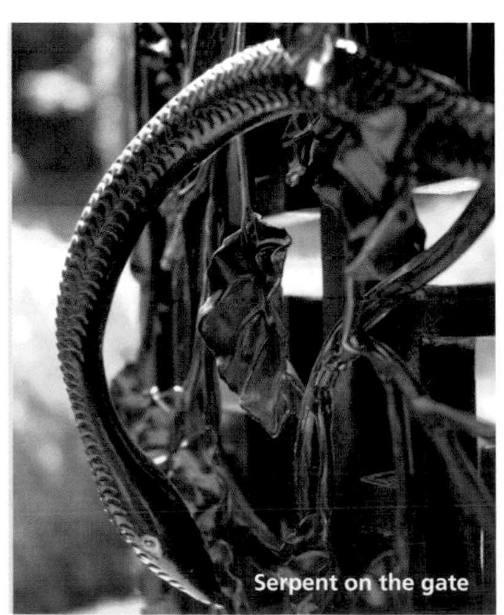
Serpent on the gate

Ricinus communis, grown by Alnwick's gardening team, is the source of castor oil, which is still widely used as a stomach medication. However, it is also the source of ricin, a deadly poison with no known antidote, and was the poison placed on the tip of the umbrella used to murder Bulgarian dissident Georgi Markov in 1978. The Anglo Saxons believed the seeds would turn away hail and rough weather and if taken on board ship would prevent tempests.

The most dangerous plants are in cages so they can't be touched, and The Garden has a licence from The Home Office to grow cannabis and coca. Plants like these become killers only in the hands of men, and so the Poison Garden is also a place where people of all ages can learn more about drugs and the effects they have on people's lives.

The Garden also features many plants grown unwittingly in back gardens, and those that grow in the British countryside.

How much do you know about the plants you grow?

Cannabis sativa

Aquilegia alpina

Helleborus odorus

"The Poison Garden gives a fascinating glimpse into the darker side of nature."

A gloomy Ivy covered tunnel

Glynde Place, Sussex

Eyam Hall, Derbyshire

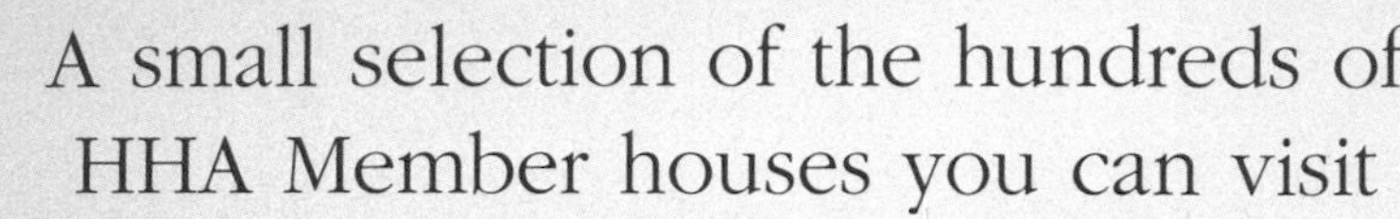
A small selection of the hundreds of HHA Member houses you can visit

Athelhampton, Dorset

Duart Castle, West Highlands & Islands

Squerryes Court, Kent

Longleat, Wiltshire

Forde Abbey, Dorset

Holkham Hall, Norfolk

Kingston Bagpuize House, Oxfordshire

Castle Howard, Yorkshire

Layer Marney Tower, Essex

Chenies Manor House, Buckinghamshire

Cadw

Medieval Magic

Cadw Style

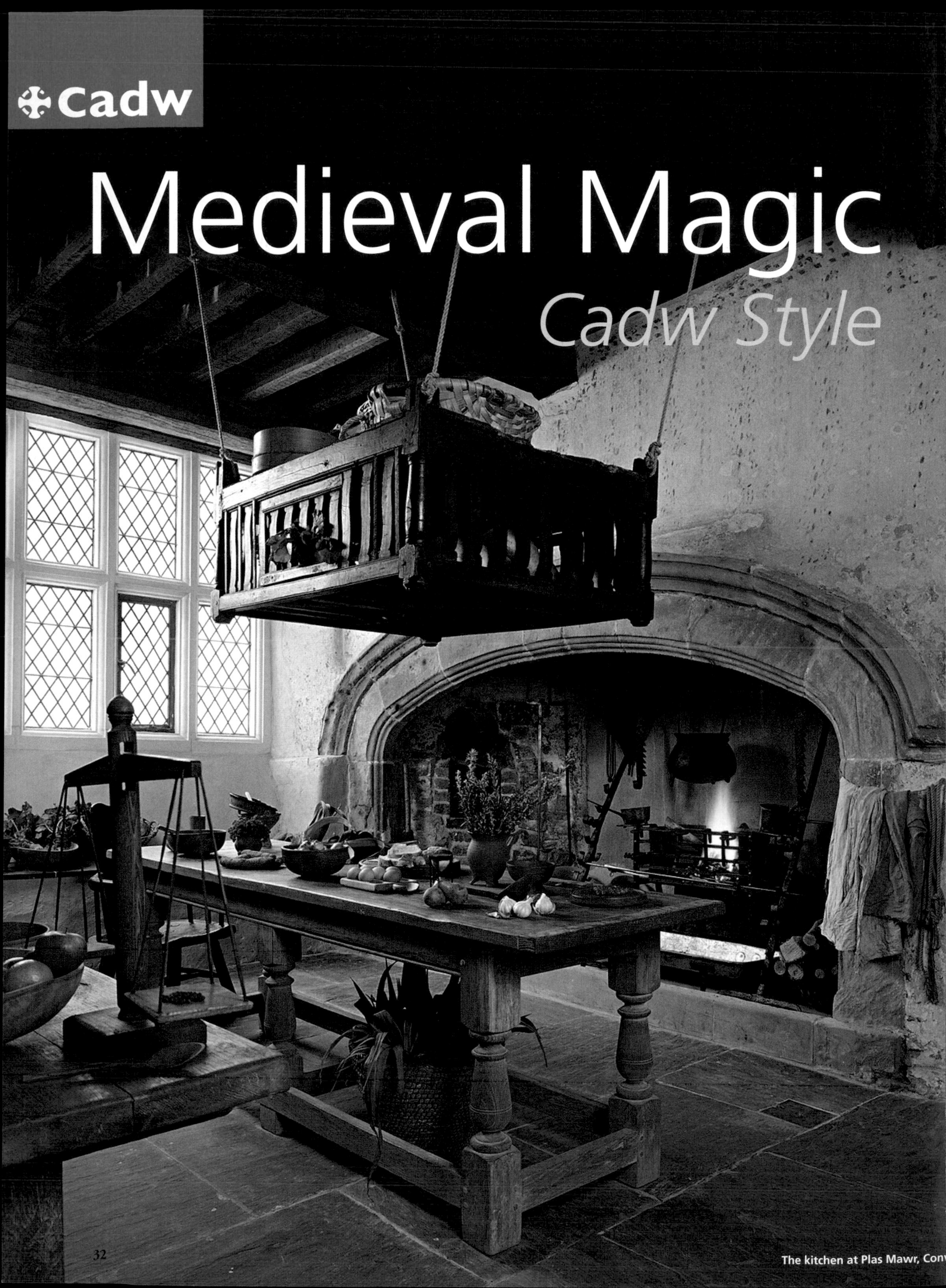

The kitchen at Plas Mawr, Conv

Plas Mawr's gatehouse

The headline-grabbing castles of Wales rightly deserve their impressive reputations, but there are also a number of somewhat smaller, yet no less important, historic houses in the care of Cadw, the Welsh Assembly Government's historic environment service. These provide the visitor with a unique insight into the development of the domestic house in Wales.

"Plas Mawr... the finest Elizabethan townhouse in Britain."

Ornate plasterwork in Plas Mawr

A furnished chamber in Plas Mawr

One such property is Plas Mawr - "The Great Hall" - described as the 'finest Elizabethan townhouse in Britain'. With its main façade hidden in a narrow lane, many visitors pass the gatehouse entrance in Conwy's High Street without realising that behind it lies an unspoilt 16th century house. Another is the majestic Tretower Court and Castle near Crickhowell in the south east of the country. Tretower, which recently opened again following a two-year major restoration and presentation project, guarantees a rare and unique insight into 15th century life.

Through such rare examples of surviving high status domestic houses, we can trace the progression from open hall to storeyed mansion, displaying how the gentry lived in the 15th century (Hafoty on Anglesey and Tretower Court) and later 16th century (Plas Mawr)

It is fair to say that any house, whatever its scale, is a mirror to the lives and ambitions of its occupiers. This can be reflected in the way space is arranged as well as in the quality of construction and decoration. What we see is the evolution of the house from the relative simplicity of the hall house with its limited number of rooms, to the later sophisticated complexity of Tretower and Plas Mawr.

The ways in which these buildings changed, through the placing of fireplaces into the open halls or the insertion of floors, also indicated changing ideas about how to live, and changing needs for space. The increasing elaboration and sophistication of these buildings also has a lot to say about the increasing wealth and status of their gentry builders.

Plas Mawr is a particularly dramatic testimony to the new wealth available to the Tudor gentry in Wales after the Act of Union and is architecturally elaborate with its lavish interior decoration, its ornate fire-places and colourful intricate plasterwork. This was the house of Robert Wynn (d. 1598), whose initials – R.W. – appear so frequently on its ornamental plasterwork. Having travelled widely in Europe, Robert Wynn married at the age of fifty and bought land for his new house in Conwy. In its design he incorporated elements that were fashionable in London and beyond, as well as reminders of his own and his wife's family connections with the gentry families of Wales. Specialist plasterers created decorative schemes in the main rooms that incorporated heraldic emblems of the families to whom Robert Wynn was related.

Tretower by contrast shows the emergence of domestic architecture from other origins, primarily defensive in nature. Tretower Court was built as a direct replacement of the castle, and in its layout and architectural detail it reveals the status of its owners and demonstrates particular patterns of use.

Heraldic emblems in Plas Mawr's hall

The north range at Tretower Court

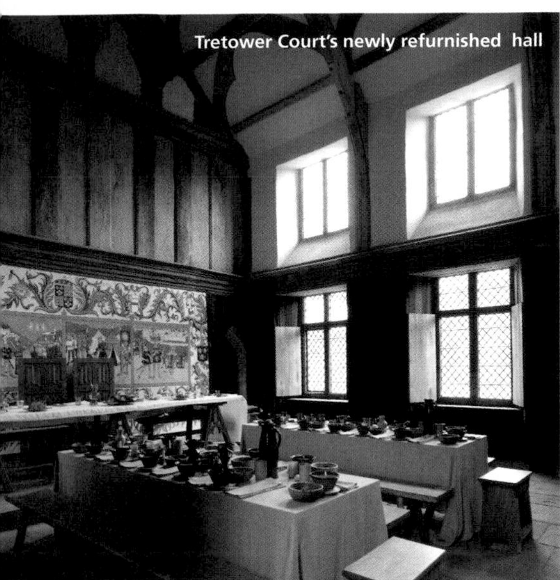
Tretower Court's newly refurnished hall

Tretower recreated medieval garde

Set against the beautiful background of the Brecon Beacons, a visit to Tretower Court and Castle is a unique journey through history that dates back to Norman times. The recent medieval makeover has taken over two years to complete and the court has been transformed, under the careful scrutiny and guidance of numerous stakeholders, building and conservation specialists, to its former splendour. The house now looks and feels as it would have done around 540 years ago, when the Vaughans of Tretower were in their pomp.

The rooms on the ground floor were once the beating heart of the court — in essence, a late medieval mansion built around a rectangular courtyard. Here, feasts and banquets were enjoyed, guests were entertained, Welsh poets proclaimed their verse and batteries of servants scurried backwards and forwards with heaving trenchers of food.

A state-of-the-art audio tour takes visitors back to a momentous event in the life of Tretower - the preparations for a feast in

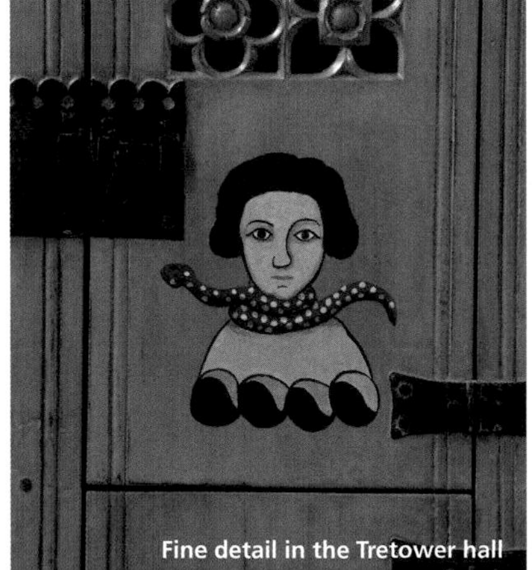
Fine detail in the Tretower hall

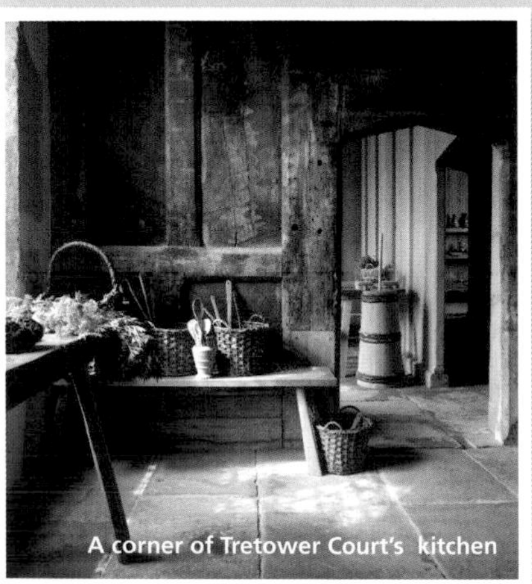
A corner of Tretower Court's kitchen

1471 which were marred when news arrived of the death of Sir Roger Vaughan at the hands of Jasper Tudor. Visitors enter the kitchen and, through the audio tour and discreet interpretation displays, see the rooms through the eyes of two young servants.

Both properties also offer replanted gardens in the style of the period for visitors to enjoy. Evidence for both gardens was revealed in illustrations and archaeological excavations which took place before the gardens were recreated. The sheer natural beauty of both sites has also proved popular with couples seeking to tie the knot in medieval splendour and anyone wishing to spend their special day at either Plas Mawr or Tretower is advised to book well in advance. Medieval feasts are also now on the menu at Tretower and proving a big hit with guests seeking a trip back through the centuries in authentic style.

For more information on Cadw and sites in its care, visit www.cadw.wales.gov.uk.

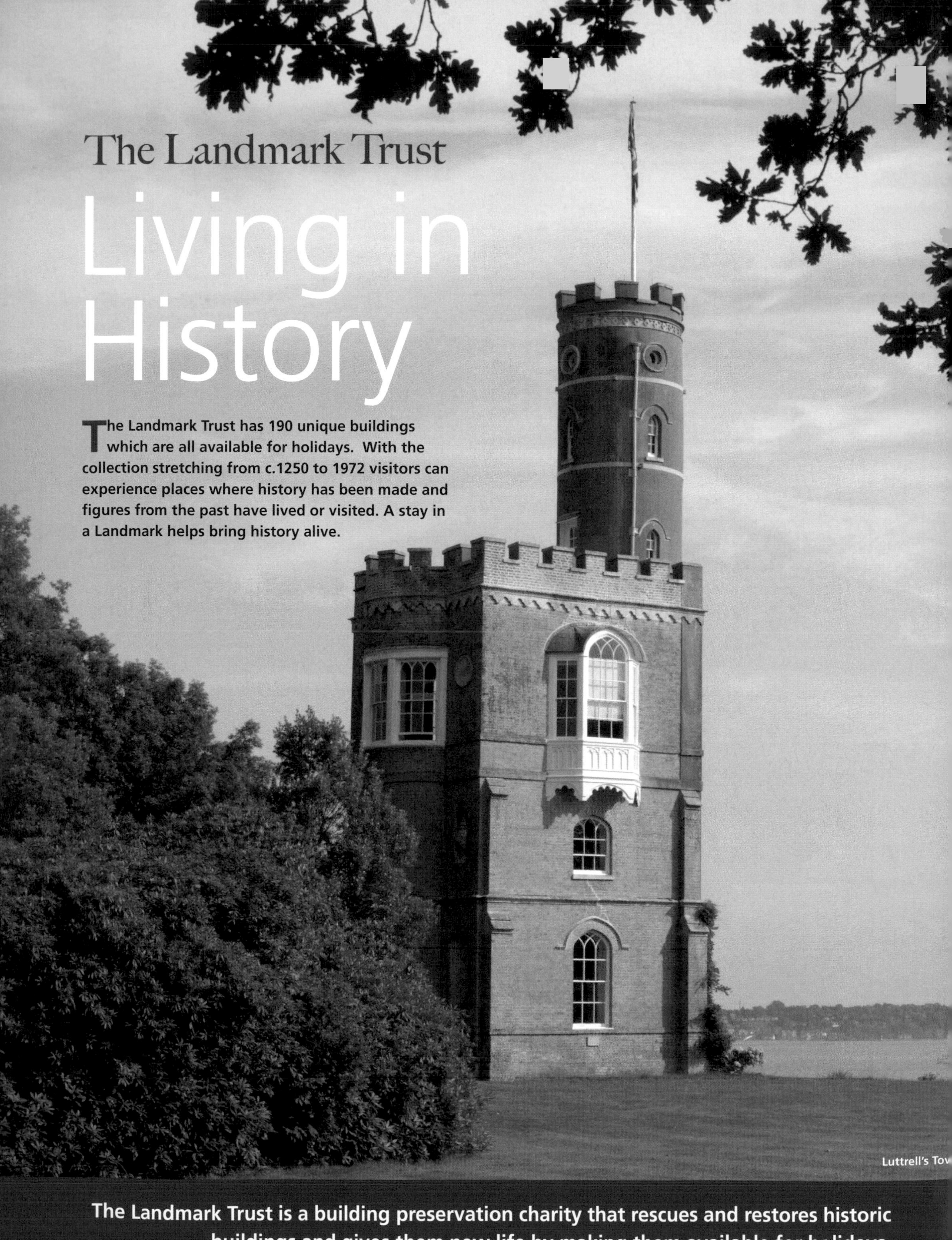

The Landmark Trust

Living in History

The Landmark Trust has 190 unique buildings which are all available for holidays. With the collection stretching from c.1250 to 1972 visitors can experience places where history has been made and figures from the past have lived or visited. A stay in a Landmark helps bring history alive.

Luttrell's Tov

The Landmark Trust is a building preservation charity that rescues and restores historic buildings and gives them new life by making them available for holidays.

Astley Castle

Astley Castle in Warwickshire is one of Landmark's current restoration projects and its most challenging one ever due to the terrible condition the structure was in. The castle has been owned by three Queens of England (Elizabeth Woodville, Elizabeth of York and Lady Jane Grey) and having been occupied for nearly 1000 years is a building of national importance. Once restored it will sleep up to 8 people in modern accommodation inserted within the ruined walls.

Auchinleck House in Ayrshire was the family home of James Boswell, renowned eighteenth-century diarist and biographer. Boswell's friend and mentor Dr. Samuel Johnson famously argued over politics with Lord Auchinleck in the library here, when they visited at the end of their tour of the Hebrides in 1773.
(Now for 13 people)

Auchinleck House

Mackintosh Building

Mackintosh Building in Perthshire was designed by Charles Rennie Mackintosh and dates from 1903–4, a time when he was doing his very best work (such as The Hill House where there is a Landmark apartment which can be rented for holidays). It was commissioned by a local draper and ironmonger, Peter Macpherson, as a shop with a flat above and workrooms in the attics. The main room runs into the projecting turret, or tourelle, which Mackintosh added to the outer angle of the building in a nod towards Scottish Baronial architecture.
(Now for 4 people)

Coombe in Cornwall is a hamlet of 8 cottages. It is partly in the parish of Morwenstow and its most famous vicar, the Reverend Stephen Hawker, lived here for a short time. He was the inventor (or perhaps reviver) of harvest festivals. He raised funds to build the bridge below Coombe and the cross-shaped window in No 1 Hawker's Cottages is said to have been his idea. Coombe was also the home of Rose Saltern, the heroine of Charles Kingsley's Westward Ho!
(Now 8 cottages for 3 – 6 people)

Luttrell's Tower in Hampshire was built for Temple Luttrell, a Member of Parliament (but reputedly a smuggler here) who died in Paris in 1803. His brother-in-law, Lord Cavan, who commanded our forces in Egypt from 1801, was the next owner. He brought with him two mysterious feet on a plinth of Nubian granite, now at the tower and thought to be the base of a XIXth dynasty statue of Rameses II. Thereafter the tower passed through various hands. Marconi used it for his wireless experiments of 1912 and Sir Clough Williams-Ellis designed the double staircase that gives access from the beach. *(Now for 4 people)*

Hawker's Cottages, Coombe

Through the Landmark Trust you can holiday in extraordinary places - places which have witnessed history in the making. A castle, a tower, a fort or a cottage can all be yours to stay in.

Tixall Gatehouse

Beckford's Tower

North Street

Sant'Antonio

Beckford's Tower in Bath was built by William Beckford who is best known for his extraordinary Gothic folly, Fonthill Abbey in Wiltshire. Born immensely rich, Beckford became a collector, patron, writer and eccentric builder. He lived in Bath as a recluse and each morning, accompanied by 'his dwarf' and pack of spaniels, would ride up to his Tower to play with his treasures in its opulent rooms.
(Now for 4 people)

North Street in Derbyshire is the earliest planned industrial housing in the world and the finest of its type ever built – vastly superior to that of the next century, and now lying at the heart of a designated World Heritage Site. It was built in 1771 by Richard Arkwright to house his mill workers, and named after the Prime Minister. The three-storey gritstone houses have one room on each floor, with a room for framework-knitting in the attic. Each had a small garden and an allotment at a distance.
(Now for 4 people)

Tixall Gatehouse in Staffordshire was built in about 1580 by Sir Walter Aston to stand in front of an older house, now disappeared. It was described in 1598 as 'one of the fairest pieces of work made of late times in all these counties'. Mary, Queen of Scots, was imprisoned at Tixall for two weeks in 1586. Her son James I came here once for two days. In 1678 the Aston of the day was sent briefly to the Tower, accused of a part in the Titus Oates conspiracy. A century later, his descendant Thomas Clifford, guided by 'the celebrated Brown' and his pupil Eames, ingeniously made use of a new canal to form a lake in his park – known to boaters as Tixall Wide.
(Now for 6 people)

Sant'Antonio at Tivoli, near Rome is one of four Landmarks in Italy. At Sant'Antoinio the walls of a Roman villa, dated to about 60 BC and believed to have belonged to the poet Horace, survive up to the middle floor of the present house, itself begun in about 850 AD. Franciscan monks have lived here and Popes. The final additions were made 'as late as the 17th century'. It was abandoned around 1870 and rescued by Fredrick Searle in 1878, who spent many years gently repairing it.
(Now for 12 people)

For further details about any of Landmark's buildings please visit **www.landmarktrust.org.uk** or telephone 01628 825925. The website also gives details of the restoration projects underway as well as those buildings in need of funds to save them.

Duchess Georgiana by Conway before cleaning

2011 is another landmark year for Chatsworth with the continuation of the major restoration and investment in the visitor route.

Duchess Georgiana by Conway after cleanin

Revealed lantern over the Oak Stairs

Chatsworth in 2011
The Story Continues

The cleaned and conserved stone of the inner court and the north front were unveiled in 2010, together with the opening of three new galleries on the second floor and the restored Oak Stairs. The opportunity to conserve some of the Devonshire Collection's most important works of art which were unveiled in 2010 continues, and this article highlights some of the transforming results of last year's conservation.

Oak Stairs

Lady Dorothy Cavendish by Romney

The South Sketch Gallery, which focuses on the life of the 5th Duke and Duchess Georgiana, is furnished and decorated with many art works which they acquired. A magical painting of Georgiana flying through the clouds as the Goddess Diana, by the artist Maria Cosway, was returned from conservation just in time for the opening of the Gallery last year. The painting was badly discoloured with dirt and old varnishes as well as previous restorations. The sky has been transformed from a sludgy brown to its original moonlit blue studded with stars. Eagle eyed visitors might notice that she is painted with six toes… a detail not evident in its pre-conserved state. New acquisitions were made with the purchase by the Chatsworth House Trust of a portrait of the 5th Duke's sister, Lady Dorothy Cavendish, by George Romney. There was previously no painting in the collection by Romney, so this acquisition complements the other paintings by the artists such as Sir Joshua Reynolds and Thomas Gainsborough.

At the end of the Gallery is an important group of furniture by the German cabinet maker David Roentgen, who worked for Catherine the Great of Russia and whose work can be seen in national museums and the Royal Collection. The ensemble contains a cylinder bureau, revolving desk chair, dressing table and small oval writing table. The fact that this group is in the same collection suggests that it was bought new from Roentgen by the 5th Duke of Devonshire. Each piece was conserved in 2009 and the group is now displayed together, as originally intended, for the first time in living memory.

In the adjoining West Sketch Gallery the display is all about the 3rd Earl of Burlington, an important figure in the architectural development of the 18th century and the introduction of Palladianism which was a key development of the English country house. The 3rd Earl's daughter, and heiress married the 4th Duke of Devonshire and through her inheritance the Devonshire Collection was enriched with many old master paintings, drawings, sculpture and other works of art, not to mention the properties of Chiswick House and Burlington House in London, as well as country estates. The Gallery now displays nearly fifty old

Chapel passa

master paintings in the manner of Chiswick House, together with 18th century portraits. In 2009 many of these paintings were given minor conservation treatments for the new display. The portrait of the 3rd Earl of Burlington by George Knapton of 1743 is displayed together with the John Michael Rysbrack's marble busts of the Earl's great architectural heroes, Andrea Palladio and Inigo Jones. The busts are displayed on a pair of richly inlaid pietra dura pedestals from Chiswick, enriched with gilt bronze mounts. The pedestals were cleaned and conserved as part of this project. It is now thought that these must be the pedestals that the sculptures were originally displayed on at Chiswick.

One of the most striking results of the conservation undertaken recently at Chatsworth is the group portrait of the 3rd Earl of Burlington with his family by J.B. Van Loo. The heavily discoloured varnish and layers of dirt were carefully cleaned, and structural problems attended to, to prepare it for its new home on the Oak Stairs, where it last hung in 1850. The portrait is displayed as part of an all embracing display of family portraits from the 1st Duke to the 11th Duke, and some royal portraits, covering three storeys of the building. The complicated hang took over three weeks to install. The view of the space from the upper landing with the top light from Sir Jeffry Wyatville's restored lantern is spectacular.

3rd Earl of Burlington with his family by Van Loo after cleaning

West Sketch Gallery
Portrait of Richard Boyle, 3rd Earl of Burlington (1694-1753) by George Knapton 1698-1778

Flanked by Portrait bust of Andrea Palladio (1508-1580) and Portrait bust of Inigo Jones c.1725 by John Michael Rysbrack (1694-1770)

North Sketch Gallery

South Sketch Gallery. A grouping of Roentgen furniture

"2011 sees the continuation of the conservation of the building, which now moves to the south and west fronts, perhaps the best known and loved of Chatsworth's façades.."

The work will take over 60 weeks and there will be a special viewing platform on the scaffolding of the south front allowing visitors to inspect the elaborate carvings at the top of the house in a way that hasn't been done since it was built over 300 years ago.

Inside there will be a new gallery for temporary exhibitions created in the North Wing which this year has a celebration of the life of the 6th Duke of Devonshire, the Bachelor Duke. The exhibition includes many items not normally on view such as archives, books from the library and familiar favourites such as Landseer's "Trial by Jury" into which the 6th Duke had one of his dogs painted. There will also be a festival of innovation exploring some of the extraordinary achievements of the 6th Duke and his gardener Joseph Paxton, from the Emperor fountain to the magical light displays he put on in the gardens for Queen's Victoria's visits.

There will also be a new purpose made display space for some of Chatsworth's treasures, the Old Master drawings. The new room will be created at the end of the State Apartment and the space will include restored cornices from the first Duke's house, removed in the 19th century and put into storage until now. Finally the important suite of Regency bedrooms, known as the Scots and Leicester Apartments, will be returned to their original appearance and furnishings. There are six grand beds, including three massive four-posters with domed canopies and their original furniture to go with them. The project will be presented to visitors in varying stages so that they can see some of the behind-the-scenes elements of the work involved in recreating these rooms. Eventually the rooms will demonstrate to visitors the tradition of the 19th century house party and highlight some of the famous people that slept in them, including Queen Victoria, the Duke of Wellington and crowned heads of Europe.

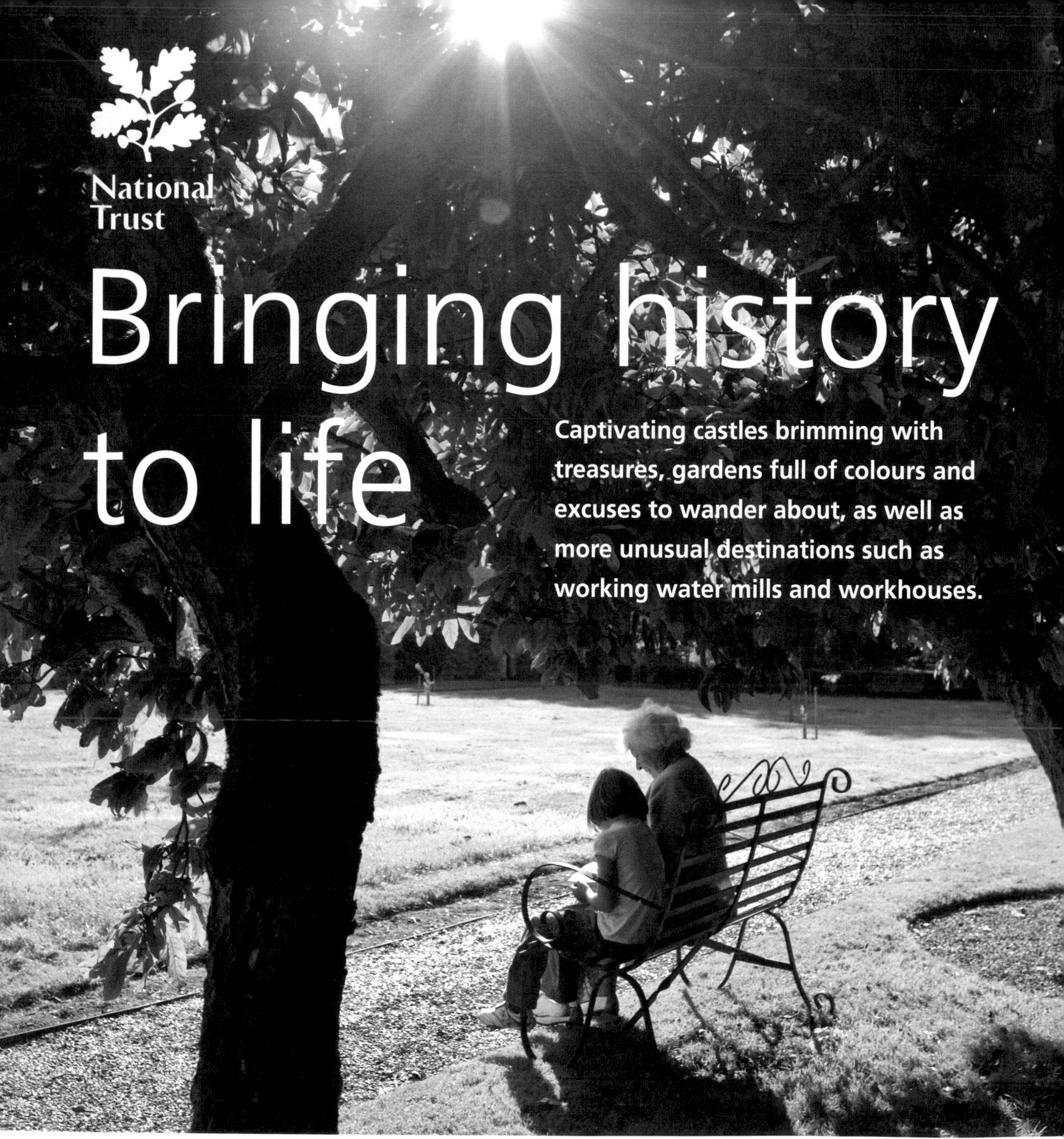

Bringing history to life

Captivating castles brimming with treasures, gardens full of colours and excuses to wander about, as well as more unusual destinations such as working water mills and workhouses.

" Discover historic houses that will fire your imagination... "

Walk into wild landscapes and let the views take your breath away. Make it a great big adventure for all the family, or just a place to stop and share the best cakes with your friends. Whatever you're looking for, wherever you are in the country, with places across England, Wales and Northern Ireland, we're never far away so come along for a visit.

The Argory Drawing Room

"Here are a few of the great experiences on offer in 2011..."

Looking for an unforgettable day out? Walk into past times and discover houses alive with the look, sounds and even smells of their history. Experience the lives of the former residents and their servants as you venture below the stairs, play the piano, sit and read books or even play a game of billiards.

Tinkle the ivories at The Argory, County Armagh
Take an upgraded guided house tour and enjoy the opportunity to step back in time and experience a little slice of 1900s life. Challenge friends and family to a game of billiards, tinkle the ivories of a Steinway in the drawing room or help with some conservation cleaning.

Look into the 19th-century luggage at Arlington Court, Devon
In 1878 Sir Bruce Chichester, his wife and 12 year-old daughter took a year long Mediterranean cruise and at the end of it sent their luggage ahead to be unpacked. Rummage through the contents and discover some fascinating souvenirs, treasures and trinkets.

See what's cooking at Basildon Park, Berkshire
Come and see what's cooking at Basildon Park. Its kitchen has been restored 1950s style, with period fixtures and fittings. Find out how it operated through hands-on activities, cookery demonstrations and the coolest gadgets, from iconic Salter scales to a Bel Cream Maker.

Peer into Lady Brownlow's boudoir at Belton House, Lincolnshire
Travel back in time as an invited guest to experience the house of Lord and Lady Brownlow. Glimpse the blue bedroom as it would have been when prepared for a visit, afternoon tea in Lady Brownlow's boudoir, an extravagant formal dinner in the dining room and re-live King Edward VIII's abdication speech in the tapestry room.

Enjoy a game or two at Beningbrough Hall and Gardens, Yorkshire
Do you know your Snip from your Snap and your Snorum? Or do you prefer a bit of Speculation on your Loo? Confused? Don't be. They are all 18th century card games, available to play in the card room, with staff in period costume on hand to cut the decks and ensure fair play prevails.

Peek into the newly-weds bedroom at Berrington Hall, Herefordshire
Life upstairs and down is put in the spotlight as special rooms in the house have been dressed to portray events in 1891. Spend time in the bedroom of the newly-wed Lady Rodney, sit at her dressing table, see her wedding dress and read the day's news, before hearing the sad tale of the butler, William Kemp, in the butler's bedroom.

Meet the guards at Chirk Castle, Wrexham
From the austere medieval towers to the elegant state rooms and dramatic dungeons there's plenty for the costumed medieval guards to protect at Chirk. Find them doing their rounds in the courtyard of this magnificent castle.

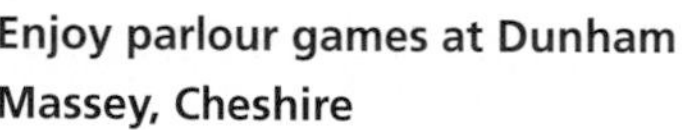

Belton House

The Billiard Room
Upton House and garden

Enjoy parlour games at Dunham Massey, Cheshire
Make yourself at home in the finest country house in Cheshire. Enjoy Victorian games in the great gallery; try your hand at Snap, Happy Families, Snakes and Ladders or the Victorian game of 'Crinkinole'. Or get cosy on the original sofas with a good read - choose from period books and magazines.

Experience a servant's life at Ickworth House, Park and Gardens, Suffolk
Walk in the (many) footsteps of those who lived and worked at Ickworth as you explore the newly opened servants' basement. Travel from Edwardian times to the end of the Second World War and discover just what life was like below stairs.

Get warm and cosy at Kingston Lacy, Dorset
This elegant country mansion houses a priceless art collection and is famous for its Spanish Room with gilded leather walls, but amidst the treasures listen out for atmospheric recordings, alive with the sounds of the past. Find peace and quiet next to crackling log fires and relax on comfy seats - perfect for soaking up the lavish 17th century interiors.

Feel like one of Mrs Grenville's party guests at Polesden Lacey, Surrey
Make yourself at home in this extraordinary Edwardian house - it must be special if King George V and Queen Elizabeth honeymooned here, rack up a few games of billiards, wind up the gramophone, plump the cushions and sit on the sofa with papers 'of the time' or play a tune on the piano.

Imagine the life of a millionaire at Upton House & Gardens, Warwickshire
Enjoy the atmosphere of a 1930s millionaire's house party as you're encouraged to listen, touch, delve and read what you can to explore what life was like in 1938, before the Second World War changed the world forever. You can also sit in the cosy Inglenook and answer the phone in the library.

Run the household at Wallington, Northumberland
Visit the kitchen and make yourself at home as you discover just how the household of this grand mansion would have been run in the 1880s. Pick up mystery gadgets and try and guess their use, and get some advice from Mrs Beeton's bestselling Book of Household Management.

The Kitchen at Wallington

past time
From stunning houses and breathtaking beauty, to relaxing strolls and dazzling views. Why not come along and relive the past, we're closer than you think.
To find a place near you just visit
nationaltrust.org.uk
Members go FREE
An independent charity looking after special places for ever, for everyone.
Oxburgh Hall, Norfolk. Registered charity number 205846
National Trust
Time well spent

A Walk on the Wild Side

Leighton Hall

Heritage House Group's Creative Director, Nick McCann, has designed guidebooks for many of this country's independent country houses, castles and heritage sites. Over the years Nick has gained a unique and broad perspective on their wildlife and birds; his abiding passion. Illustrated by his photographs and paintings, he gives a flavour of what can be seen and where, and why historic houses and gardens are starting to make more of this abundant and precious natural resource.

"I have been bird-watching or birding since I was knee-high to a heron. It started, not with a kiss, but with a pair of plastic binoculars from Woolworths in Birkenhead."

Throughout the ensuing years this perennial interest has comforted, excited, rewarded and led me to places and experiences no other interest could provide. The great thing about 'birding', as it's now properly termed, is one can 'do it' anywhere, at any time of the year and with limited equipment and resources. No surprise perhaps, that it is now one of the most popular leisure activities, with membership of its major organisation, the RSPB (the Royal Society for the Protection of Birds) well over a million and rising inexorably, year on year. The organisation now reckons that 6 million of us in the UK regularly go 'birding'.

Puffins, Oil Painting by Nick McCann

Raby Castle and Lake

Television programmes such as the BBC's *Springwatch* and *Autumnwatch* and other shows featuring wildlife such as *Coast* attract huge viewing figures and are becoming powerful political lobbying tools. The annual Bird Fair in August at Rutland Water is truly astounding in its scope and size. Birding and wildlife watching are no longer the preserve of the silent 'anoraks', but are seriously cool things to do: Vic Reeves, Sean Bean, Joanna Lumley, Mick Jagger, Jarvis Cocker and the band British Sea Power are all birders. One of our most-loved comedians, the late Eric Morecambe, gained relaxation from the stresses of performing in his passion for birds; the reserve at Leighton Moss, near **Leighton Hall** in Lancashire has a hide dedicated in his name. It's a multi-million pound 'industry' that is growing in influence, stature and importance in the leisure life of the nation. Country houses, their gardens, parks and estates are beautifully positioned to capitalise on the public's interest in birds and wildlife generally. Recently the RSPB held a roadshow at **Burghley House**, they are holding events at **Leeds Castle** in Kent, and many more houses are becoming more and more pro-active in conservation and wildlife management and activities. When the visitor has marvelled at the paintings, sculptures and furniture and drunk in the history, the coffee and eaten the cakes, how better to end the day than with a great breath of fresh air and some exercise, seeking out the natural treasures our estates

Red Kite at Deene

Shags on a rock

Inveraray from Dun na Cua

have to offer. Every house I have been to has had something special, and some are truly nature reserves, in all but name.

Forty years ago, the only place in this country that you could reliably see an osprey, arguably our most spectacular bird of prey, was through a telescope at Loch Garten in Speyside. Today, on migration from Southern Europe or Africa, or during the summer, wherever there is water that supports fish, there's a chance to see this magnificent creature… and increasingly at, and in the vicinity of, a number of Britain's historic houses. With the help and support of British Telecom and the local water authority, one enlightened house manager in the Midlands recently erected a telegraph pole with a suitably nest-friendly platform on his estate, having seen ospreys regularly surveying the house's park and lake. The birds have bred successfully this year and have been feeding their young with small fish from the lake. For the moment this location is secret, but ospreys visit and fish at a number of sites in England including **Holkham Hall**, **Burghley** (with birds from nearby Rutland Water) and **Powderham Castle** in Devon. In Scotland in summer, if there is a river or lake at hand, ospreys frequent many places such as the castles of **Ballindalloch**, **Balmoral**, **Blair** and many more. Birds of prey have a particular appeal to the public: they're generally large, and therefore highly visible, their 'glamour' as hunters enhanced by a regal and majestic appearance. Red kites – superb fliers and remarkably undaunted by the presence of man – have made a spectacular comeback since their decline to virtual extinction during the 18th and 19th centuries. In Charles Dickens' day, the skies of London would have been alive with these beautiful birds. A resident, primarily scavenging bird, the kite can be seen today soaring and diving over many

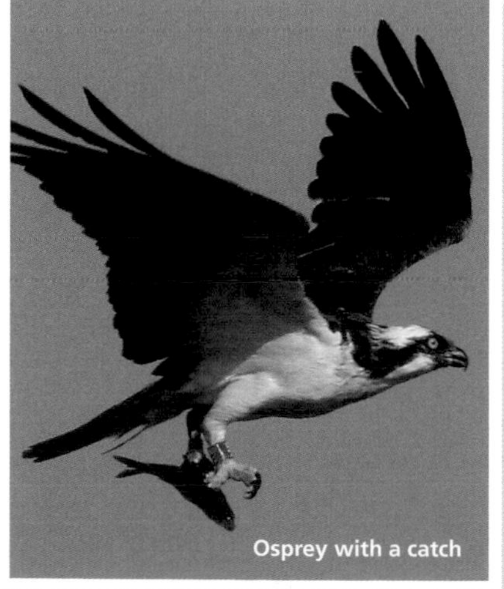

Osprey with a catch

estates in England. Anywhere in central England and locations in Yorkshire, central Wales and Inverness-shire are best, with birds regularly seen at **Blenheim Palace**, **Boughton House**, **Burghley**, **Rockingham Castle**, **Castle Howard** and **Harewood House**. Spectacular views can be obtained at **Deene Park** in Northamptonshire where many pairs breed. Deene, like many of our smaller and lesser-visited properties, is a beautiful, 'secret' spot: accompanying the kites are kingfishers, woodpeckers, a variety of water birds and animals. In the kites' own ancestral home of central Wales, places such as **Strata Florida Abbey**, quoted in Hudsons as "remotely set in the green, kite-haunted Teifi Valley", are good spots to see this remarkable bird. Throughout the country, there are many other historic houses where wild birds of prey can be seen with patience. At **Duart Castle** on the Isle of Mull (dubbed 'eagle island') I've seen spectacular golden and white-tailed eagles, as at **Dunvegan Castle** on Skye. There are peregrine falcons (now nesting on many of our tall buildings, such as **Derby Cathedral**, on the **Liverpool Historic Waterfront** and in the **City of London**) and merlins (from where the Spitfire's Rolls-Royce engine took its name), can be seen at many places such

Lapwing

Sunset Godwits

Oystercatchers

"Birding here on the most northerly mainland part of Britain, can be truly spectacular..."

Castle of Mey beach

Powderham Belvedere

Common

Little Egret in fl

The Short-eared owl on Benbecula, oil painting by Nick McCann

Common seal

as the **Castle of Mey**. Birding here on the most northerly mainland part of Britain, can be truly spectacular, with great skuas, seabirds and waders all in abundance with the opportunity to see sea mammals off-shore. Her Majesty The Queen Mother certainly enjoyed the castle's unspoilt position overlooking the wild Pentland Firth and Orkney. The gift shop at the castle has books on the birdlife of Caithness and I've noticed several house shops now featuring more titles in this vein. The dashing summer-visiting falcon, the hobby, made an appearance, in July, at **Bamburgh Castle** and this bird visits many other properties, such as **Leeds Castle** and anywhere with water and dragonflies; their main diet. **Bamburgh's** ramparts, like **Dunrobin** in Sutherland, are also home to a close relative of the

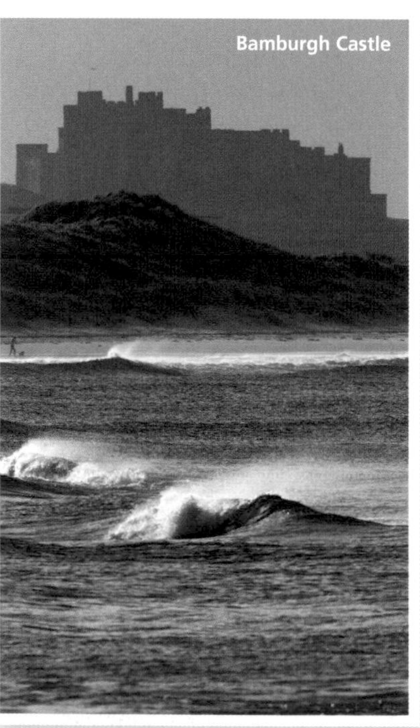
Bamburgh Castle

albatross, the fulmar. Spending most of the year far out to sea, the birds come back to these castles to breed, the steep seaward walls resembling cliffs. All of our coastal castles and houses are great places to see seabirds, estuary visitors and migrants. **Powderham Castle** in Devon has the Exe estuary at the bottom of the garden, attracting birds not usually associated with a stately home, such as avocets (the symbol of the RSPB), little egrets and in 2010, a pair of spoonbills. At many places, sea mammal watching is also growing in popularity. Bottle-nosed dolphins are a famous attraction opposite **Fort George** in the Moray Firth, and around the coasts, whales, dolphins, porpoises, basking sharks and seals can be seen at the right time all round Britain, either from castle grounds, or very nearby.

Tissington Hall

Cock Wheatear

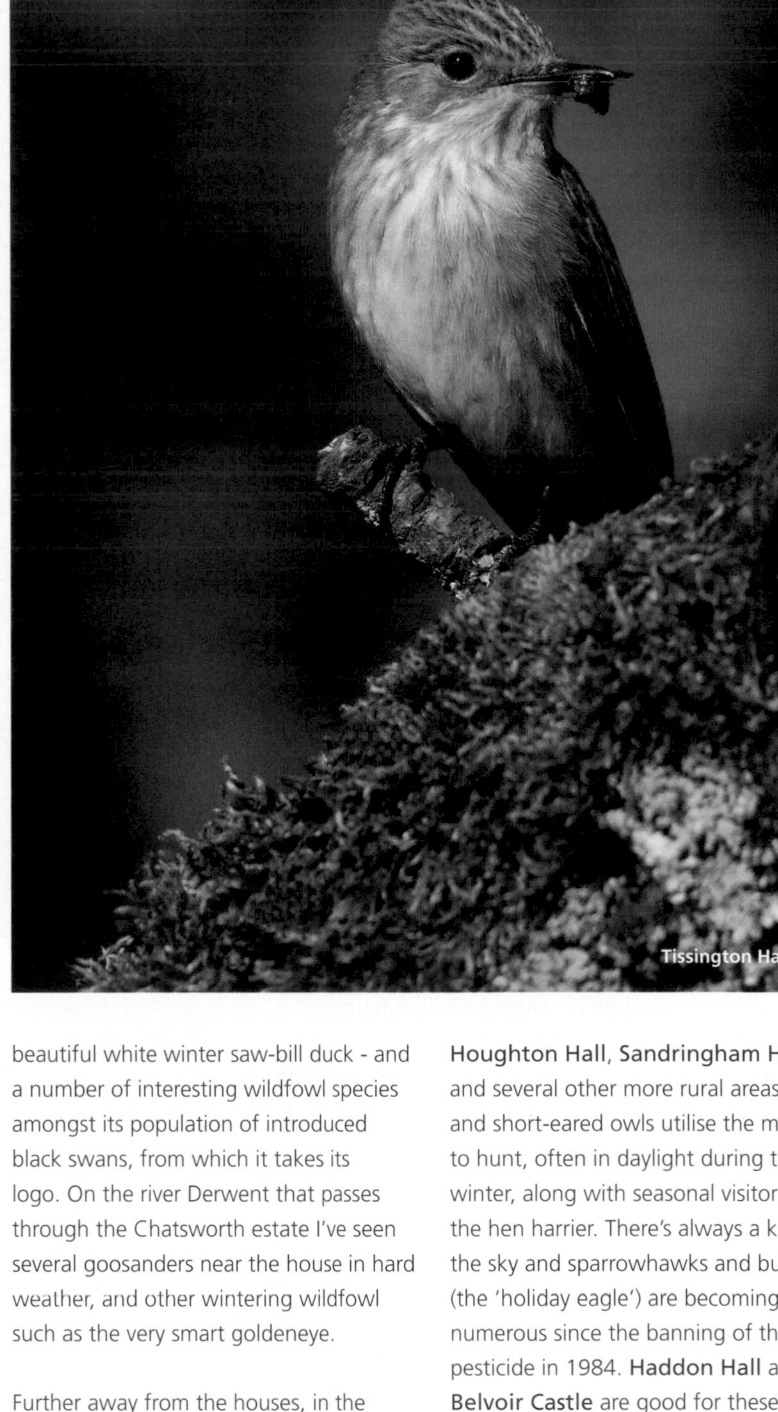
Tissington Hall's Spotted Flycatcher

Fortunately, the main visitor season at historic houses (Easter to October) coincides with the passage of migrants in spring and late summer through August and September. In the gardens and around the estates, very good birding can be enjoyed away from the 'madding crowd' with the potential for rarities. Spring sees the arrival of summer visitors and many houses have nesting flycatchers close to the buildings, such as **Tissington Hall**, and a range of other birds such as warblers, whitethroats, blackcaps and the beautiful wheatear, favouring coastal and moorland sites. Some houses such as **Chatsworth** and **Leeds Castle** are open all year round, and as such, are nature reserves to be enjoyed even in the bleakest of weather. The lake at Leeds in Kent, has attracted smew – a beautiful white winter saw-bill duck - and a number of interesting wildfowl species amongst its population of introduced black swans, from which it takes its logo. On the river Derwent that passes through the Chatsworth estate I've seen several goosanders near the house in hard weather, and other wintering wildfowl such as the very smart goldeneye.

Further away from the houses, in the fields, meadows, moorland and woods, country estates form a hugely valuable habitat. In summer, upland areas support grouse (red and in some cases, black) and other game birds such as woodcock (woodlands) and snipe in more marshy areas, with waders such as the redshank and oystercatchers. In Norfolk – at locations such as **Blickling Hall**, **Houghton Hall**, **Sandringham House** and several other more rural areas, barn and short-eared owls utilise the meadows to hunt, often in daylight during the winter, along with seasonal visitors such as the hen harrier. There's always a kestrel in the sky and sparrowhawks and buzzards (the 'holiday eagle') are becoming very numerous since the banning of the DDT pesticide in 1984. **Haddon Hall** and **Belvoir Castle** are good for these species with a range of other woodland birds to be enjoyed in great surroundings.

Some stately homes have their own aristocratic star wildlife attractions, both for the casual visitor and the more ardent enthusiast. The daily 'heron-feeding' attraction at **Muncaster Castle** in Cumbria is a big draw for visitors, as are the red

Parham Pa

squirrels at the castles of **Ballindalloch**, **Chillingham** and **Glamis**, among several other sites, where our indigenous squirrel survives over its much more aggressive introduced cousin; the grey. Wild and semi-wild deer of course, feature heavily at many places - some having particular and unique 'branding' appeal: **Houghton Hall** has a herd of stunning white fallow deer as the star attraction among many other deer species and some estates, such as **Raby Castle**, can trace the red deer herd back to the Norman Conquest. At **Scone Palace** and **Holkham**, if you are very lucky and very persistent, you may be able to see one of our shyest 'difficult' birds up in the tops of the trees: the hawfinch, which favours hornbeams.

At one of my favourite places, **Parham House** in Sussex, there are stoats and weasels in the grounds and doubtless snakes and other reptiles in the sandy downland soil. As the climate changes, the fauna and flora is adapting; some species are re-locating or diminishing, whereas others are flourishing. The once continental small white heron, the little egret, whose plumes once adorned the hats of a thousand fashionable ladies, is now a common sight around Britain, nesting in increasing numbers throughout England. **Powderham**, **Holkham** and many places on the south coast with water are good bets if you want to see them.

Wild flower meadows and carefully managed woods and pastures, such as those at **Houghton Hall** are good for butterflies, birds, mammals and the general ecology, with nest boxes and bird feeders near visitor centres all helping the cause and appeal of the environment for birds and visitors alike. It is good to see more and more nature trails, awareness and interpretation at houses of the natural heritage at hand, and it is good to see websites, such as **Hopetoun House's**, on the Firth of Forth, making such a great feature of their ecology and wildlife.

When you next visit one of our great country estates or stately homes, try and find the time to venture outside and explore what is around and about, you may be surprised at what lies beyond the castle walls. Happy birding.

Nick McCann would love to hear from visitors, houses and estates, for his forthcoming guide to the birds and wildlife of Britain's historic houses. Email: hughmcnicholas@yahoo.co.uk

Westminster Cathedral

London

England's vibrant capital city contains not just the 'must-see' attractions such as Buckingham Palace and the Tower of London, but also many smaller and no less interesting properties. London's parks are the lungs of the city. From Regent's Park in the north to Battersea Park south of the river, via Hyde Park and St James's it is possible to walk for miles, hardly touching a pavement.

Myddelton House Gardens

St Paul's Cathedral © Matt Prince

LONDON

Somerset House

Keats House

St John's Gate

The Library, St Paul's Cathedral

©English Heritage/Nigel Corrie

APSLEY HOUSE ⌗

THE HOME OF THE DUKES OF WELLINGTON

www.english-heritage.org.uk/apsleyhouse

Apsley House (also known as No. 1 London) is the former residence of the first Duke of Wellington.

The Duke made Apsley House his London home after a dazzling military career culminating in his victory over Napoleon at Waterloo in 1815. Wellington enlarged the house (originally designed and built by Robert Adam between 1771–78) adding the magnificent Waterloo Gallery by Benjamin Dean Wyatt which holds many of the masterpieces from the Duke's extensive painting collection. It has been the London home of the Dukes of Wellington ever since.

The seventh Duke gave the house and contents to the Nation in 1947, with apartments retained for the family. With its collections of outstanding paintings, porcelain, silver, sculpture, furniture, medals and memorabilia largely intact and the family still in residence, Apsley House is the last great aristocratic town house in London.

©English Heritage/Nigel Corrie

No photography in house.

By arrangement.

Free. English, French, Spanish & German.

In Park Lane.

Owner
English Heritage

Contact
House Manager
Apsley House
Hyde Park Corner
London W1J 7NT

Tel: 020 7499 5676
E-mail: customers@english-heritage.org.uk

Location
MAP 20:L8
OS Ref. TQ284 799

N. side of Hyde Park Corner.

Underground:
Hyde Park Corner exit 1 Piccadilly Line.

Bus:
9, 22, 148.

Opening Times
1 April–31 October, Wed–Sun & BHs, 11am–5pm.
1 November–31 March, Wed–Sun, 11am–4pm.
Closed 24–26 Dec & 1 Jan.

Admission

Adult	£6.00
Children	£3.00
Child (under 5yrs)	Free
Conc.	£5.10

Joint ticket with Wellington Arch:

Adult	£7.40
Children	£3.70
Child (under 5yrs)	Free
Conc.	£6.30
Family	£18.50

15% discount for groups (11+). Free for English Heritage members and for Overseas Visitor Pass holders. Opening times and prices are valid until 31st March 2011, after this date details are subject to change please visit www.english-heritage.org.uk for the most up-to-date information.

■ **Owner**
Chiswick House and Gardens Trust and English Heritage

■ **Contact**
Visits:
House Manager
Chiswick House
Burlington Lane
London W4 2RP
Tel: 020 8995 0508
E-mail: customers@english-heritage.org.uk

Venue Hire and Hospitality:
Hospitality Co-ordinator
Tel: 020 8742 2762

■ **Location**
MAP 19:C8
OS Ref: TQ210 775

Burlington Lane
London W4.

Rail: ½ mile NE of Chiswick Station.

Tube:
Turnham Green, ¾ mile

Bus: 190, E3.

■ **Opening Times**
1–30 April, Daily, 10am–5pm.
1 May–31 October, Sun–Wed & BHs, 10am–5pm.
1 November–31 March, available for group tours - please call for details.

■ **Admission**

Adult	£5.00
Child (5–15yrs)	£2.50
Conc	£4.30
Family	£12.50

Groups (11+)
15% discount.

EH Members free.

Opening times and prices are valid until 31st March 2011, after this date details are subject to change please visit www.english-heritage.org.uk or www.chgt.org.uk for the most up-to-date information.

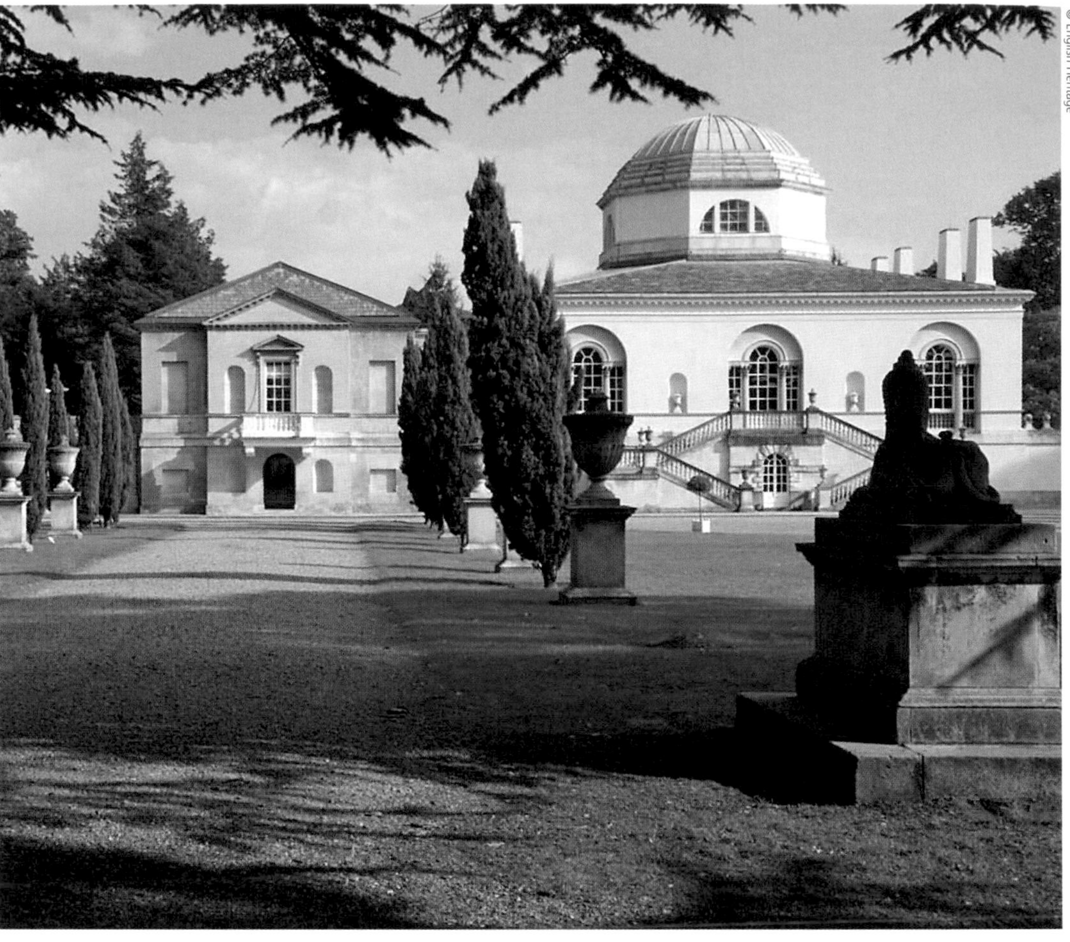
© English Heritage

CHISWICK HOUSE AND GARDENS

www.english-heritage.org.uk/chiswickhouse

Chiswick House is internationally renowned as one of the first and finest English Palladian villas. Lord Burlington, who built the villa from 1725–1729, was inspired by the architecture and gardens of ancient Rome and this house is his masterpiece. His aim was to create a fit setting to show his friends his fine collection of art and his library. The opulent interior features gilded decoration, velvet walls and painted ceilings. The important 18th century gardens surrounding Chiswick House have, at every turn, something to surprise and delight the visitor from the magnificent cedar trees to the beautiful Italianate gardens with their cascade, statues, temples, urns and obelisks.

2010 saw the culmination of a major project to restore the historic gardens to their former glory, including the Conservatory and its world famous camellia collection. Visitor facilities have also been improved and a new modern café, designed by award winning architects Caruso St John, offers a light airy space to enjoy a seasonal menu of freshly cooked dishes.

© English Heritage

WCs. Filming, plays, photographic shoots.

Private & corporate hospitality.

Personal guided tours must be booked in advance.

Free audio tours in English, French & German.

Free if booked in advance. Tel: 020 7973 3485.

ELTHAM PALACE AND GARDENS ⌗

www.english-heritage.org.uk/eltham

The epitome of 1930s chic, Eltham Palace dramatically demonstrates the glamour and allure of the period.

Bathe in the light flooding from a spectacular glazed dome in the Entrance Hall as it highlights beautiful blackbean veneer and figurative marquetry. It is a tour de force only rivalled by the adjacent Dining Room – where an Art Deco aluminium-leafed ceiling is a perfect complement to the bird's-eye maple walls. Step into Virginia Courtauld's magnificent gold-leaf and onyx bathroom and throughout the house discover lacquered, 'ocean liner' style veneered walls and built-in furniture.

A Chinese sliding screen is all that separates chic Thirties Art Deco from the medieval Great Hall. You will find concealed electric lighting, centralised vacuum cleaning and a loud-speaker system that allowed music to waft around the house. Authentic interiors have been recreated by the finest contemporary craftsmen. Their appearance was painstakingly researched from archive photographs, documents and interviews with friends and relatives of the Courtaulds.

Outside you will find a delightful mixture of formal and informal gardens including a rose garden, pergola and loggia, all nestled around the extensive remains of the medieval palace.

A display celebrating the Royal Army Education Corps' (RAEC) post World War II illustrates a further chapter in the Palace's history, including a recreation of an officer's bedroom of the 1960s.

- i WCs. Filming, plays and photographic shoots.
- Exclusive private and corporate hospitality.
- WCs.
- Guided tours on request.
- Free. English, German & French.
- P Coaches must book.

Owner
English Heritage

Contact
Eltham Palace
Court Yard
Eltham
London SE9 5QE

Visits:
Administrator
Tel: 020 8294 2548
E-mail: customers@english-heritage.org.uk

Venue Hire and Hospitality:
Hospitality Manager
Tel: 020 8294 2577

Location
MAP 19:F8
OS Ref. TQ425 740

M25/J3, then A20 towards Eltham. The Palace is signposted from A20 and from Eltham High Street.
A2 from Central London.

Rail: 30 mins from Victoria or London Bridge Stations to Eltham or Mottingham, then 15 mins walk.

Opening Times
1 April–31 October, Sun–Wed, 10am–5pm.

1 November–31 December, Sun–Wed, 11am–4pm.

Closed 1–31 January.

1 February–31 March Sun–Wed 11am–4pm.

Eltham Palace is also open on Saturdays; 7 May, 18 June and 10 September.

The property may close at short notice, please ring in advance for details

English Heritage offers exclusive use of the Palace on Thu, Fri or Sat for daytime conferences, meetings and weddings and in the evenings for dinners, concerts and receptions.

Admission
House and Gardens

Adult	£8.70
Child	£4.40
Conc.	£7.40
Family (2+3)	£21.80

Gardens only

Adult	£5.60
Child	£2.80
Conc.	£4.80

EH Members free.

Group discount available.

Opening times and prices are valid until 31 Mar 2011, after this date please visit www.english-heritage.org.uk for the most up to date information.

Conference/Function

ROOM	MAX CAPACITY
Great Hall	300 standing 200 dining
Entrance Hall	100 seated
Drawing Room	120 standing 80 theatre-style
Dining Room	10 dining

Owner
English Heritage

Contact
Kenwood House
Hampstead Lane
London NW3 7JR

Visits:
The House Manager
Tel: 020 8348 1286
E-mail: customers@english-heritage.org.uk

Location
MAP 20:K1
OS Ref. TQ271 874

M1/J2. Signed off A1, on leaving A1 turn right at junction with Bishop's Ave, turn left into Hampstead Lane. Visitor car park on left.

Bus: London Transport 210.

Rail: Hampstead Heath.

Underground: Archway or Golders Green Northern Line then bus 210.

Opening Times
1 April–31 March, daily. 11.30am–4pm.

Closed 24–26 December & 1 January.

The Park opens earlier and stays open later, please see site notices. Pre-booked group tours available.

Events are available for up to 100 guests in the Service Wing. Please ring Company of Cooks on 020 8341 5384.

Admission
House & Grounds
Free. Donations welcome.

Opening times and prices are valid until 31 Mar 2011, after this date details are subject to change please visit www.english-heritage.org.uk for the most up-to-date information.

© English Heritage

KENWOOD HOUSE ⌗

www.english-heritage.org.uk/kenwoodhouse

Kenwood, one of the treasures of London, is an idyllic country retreat close to the popular villages of Hampstead and Highgate.

The house was remodelled in the 1760s by Robert Adam, the fashionable neo-classical architect. The breathtaking library or 'Great Room' is one of his finest achievements.

Kenwood is famous for the internationally important collection of paintings bequeathed to the nation by Edward Guinness, 1st Earl of Iveagh. Some of the world's finest artists are represented by works such as a Rembrandt *Self Portrait*, Vermeer's *The Guitar Player; Mary, Countess Howe* by Gainsborough and paintings by Turner, Reynolds and many others.

As if the house and it's contents were not riches enough, Kenwood stands in 112 acres of landscaped grounds on the edge of Hampstead Heath, commanding a fine prospect towards central London. The meadow walks and ornamental lake of the park, designed by Humphry Repton, contrast with the wilder Heath below.

© English Heritage

© English Heritage

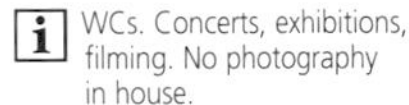
WCs. Concerts, exhibitions, filming. No photography in house.

Exclusive private and corporate hospitality.

Available on request (in English). Please call for details.

West Lodge car park (Pay & Display) on Hampstead Lane. Parking for the disabled.

Free when booked in advance on 020 7973 3485.

Guide dogs only.

NATIONAL MARITIME MUSEUM, QUEEN'S HOUSE & ROYAL OBSERVATORY, GREENWICH

www.nmm.ac.uk

The National Maritime Museum details inspirational stories of exploration, discovery and endeavour from Britain's seafaring past as well as examining the continuing effects the oceans still have on the world today. See Nelson's bullet-pierced coat from his final, fatal battle and discover the courage shown by renowned explorers including Captain Cook, all at the world's largest maritime museum.

The Queen's House, completed in around 1638 and designed by Inigo Jones, introduced England to the beauties of Palladian architecture. Once a richly furnished summer villa for Queen Henrietta Maria, wife of Charles I, it is now the principal showcase for the National Maritime Museum's world-class collection of fine art.

The Royal Observatory, Greenwich is the home of Greenwich Mean Time and the famous Prime Meridian of the World - 0° 0′ 0″. Built for the purpose of finding longitude at sea, Sir Christopher Wren's Royal Observatory is also a museum of time and astronomy, where it is still possible to see how the Astronomers Royal used to live and work. The Royal Observatory also houses London's only planetarium which provides a magnificent introduction to the mysteries and wonders of the night sky.

 WCs. 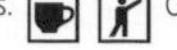 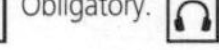 Obligatory.  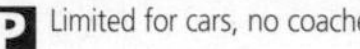 Limited for cars, no coaches.   Guide dogs only. 

Owner

National Maritime Museum

Contact

National Maritime Museum
Park Row
Greenwich
London SE10 9NF

Tel: 020 8312 6565
Fax: 020 8312 6632

Group Bookings:
Tel: 020 8312 6608
Fax: 020 8312 6522
E-mail:
bookings@nmm.ac.uk

Venue Hire:
Events
Tel: 020 8312 8517
Fax: 020 8312 6572
E-mail:
events@nmm.ac.uk

Location

MAP 19:E7
OS Ref. TQ388 773

M25 (S) via A2. From M25 (N) M11, A12 and Blackwall Tunnel.

Bus: 177, 180, 188, 199, 286, 380, 386

Rail: Greenwich rail (8 minutes from London Bridge) or DLR Cutty Sark

Boat: From Westminster, Waterloo, Embankment, Bankside or Tower Piers

Opening Times

Open daily, 10am–5pm.

Last admission 30 minutes before closing.

Late summer opening times apply.

Visit nmm.ac.uk for further details.

Closed 24–26 December.

Admission

Admission is free. Charges and age restrictions apply for planetarium shows, some special events and exhibitions. All information correct at time of print but may be subject to change.

Special Events

The Sammy Ofer Wing, due for completion by summer 2011, will include a major new gallery for special exhibitions, an open archive centre and library, new learning spaces and improved visit facilities. For further information visit nmm.ac.uk/ofer.

Conference/Function

ROOM	SIZE	MAX CAPACITY
Queen's House	40′ x 40′	Dining 120 Standing 200
Observatory, Octagon Rm	25′ x 25′	Dining 60 Standing 150
Observatory, Planetarium		Dining 110 Standing 150
NMM Upper Deck	140′ x 70′	Dining 500 Standing 750
NMM Lecture Theatre		Conference 130
Queen's House Observatory		Daytime business meetings 12–50

■ **Owner**

Dean & Chapter of St Paul's Cathedral

■ **Contact**

The Chapter House
St Paul's Churchyard
London EC4M 8AD
Tel: 020 7246 8350
020 7236 4128
Fax: 020 7248 3104
E-mail: chapter@stpaulscathedral.org.uk

■ **Location**

MAP 20:N7
OS Ref. TQ321 812

Central London.

Underground: St Paul's, Mansion House, Blackfriars, Bank.

Rail: Blackfriars, City Thameslink.

Air: London Airports.

■ **Opening Times**

Mon–Sat, 8.30am–4.30pm, last admission 4pm.

Guided tours: Mon–Sat, 10.45am, 11.15am, 1.30pm & 2pm.

Tours of the Triforium: Mon & Tues, 11.30am & 2pm. Fri, 2pm.

All tours are subject to an additional charge.

Cathedral Shop & Café: Mon–Sat, 9am–5pm, Shop Sun,10am–4.30pm, Cafe Sun,12pm–4pm.

Restaurant: Mon–Sat, Lunch 12pm–3pm, Afternoon tea 3pm–4.30pm. Sun, 12pm–3pm.

Service Times
Mon–Sat, 7.30am Mattins 8am Holy Communion (said), 12.30pm Holy Communion (said) 5pm Choral Evensong

Sun: 8am Holy Communion (said) 10.15am Choral Mattins & sermon, 11.30am Choral Eucharist & sermon, 3.15pm Choral Evensong & sermon 6pm Evening service

The Cathedral may be closed to tourists on certain days of the year. It is advisable to phone or check our website for up-to-date information.

■ **Admission**

Adult	£12.50
Child	£4.50
OAP	£11.50
Student	£9.50
Family	£29.50
Groups (10+)	
Adult	£11.50
Child	£4.00
OAP	£10.50
Student	£8.50

(Subject to change).

© Matt Prince
Beneath the Dome

ST PAUL'S CATHEDRAL

www.stpauls.co.uk

St Paul's, with its world-famous Dome, is an iconic feature of the London skyline, but there is much more to Sir Christopher Wren's masterpiece than its impressive façade.

A spiritual focus for the nation since its first service in 1697, many important events have taken place within its walls, from the State funerals of Lord Nelson, the Duke of Wellington and Sir Winston Churchill to the wedding of the Prince of Wales to Lady Diana Spencer and the Thanksgiving services for Her Majesty the Queen's Golden Jubilee and 80th Birthday.

The results of the Cathedral's programme of cleaning and repair, now in its final stages, are breathtaking.

Visitors in 2011 can enjoy a new multimedia exhibition located in the Cathedral's famous Crypt. 'Oculus: an eye into St Paul's' is a 270° HD film that brings the 1400 years of the cathedral's history to life. The films offer visitors a unique insight into the history of the site and St Paul's as a vibrant working church. Visitors can also enjoy a multimedia audio guide included in the entry price.

The pinnacle of any trip to St Paul's is making the winding journey up the spiral staircases to the Whispering Gallery, to experience the unique acoustic effects before climbing up and out to the Stone and Golden Galleries, which afford a panoramic view of London that is second to none.

© Graham Lacdao
Timeline

© St Paul's Cathedral / Peter Smith
Down the Nave

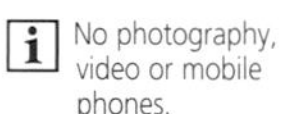
No photography, video or mobile phones.

Licensed.

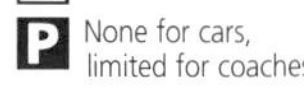
None for cars, limited for coaches.

© Spencer House / Mark Fiennes

SPENCER HOUSE

www.spencerhouse.co.uk

Spencer House, built 1756–66 for the first Earl Spencer, an ancestor of Diana, Princess of Wales (1961–97), is London's finest surviving 18th century town house. The magnificent private palace has regained the full splendour of its late 18th century appearance, after a painstaking ten-year restoration programme.

Designed by John Vardy and James 'Athenian' Stuart, the nine State rooms are amongst the first neo-classical interiors in Europe. Vardy's Palm Room, with its spectacular screen of gilded palm trees and arched fronds, is a unique Palladian set-piece, while the elegant mural decorations of Stuart's Painted Room reflect the 18th century passion for classical Greece and Rome. Stuart's superb gilded furniture has been returned to its original location in the Painted Room by courtesy of the V&A and English Heritage. Visitors can also see a fine collection of 18th century paintings and furniture, specially assembled for the house, including five major Benjamin West paintings, graciously lent by Her Majesty The Queen.

The State rooms are open to the public for viewing on Sundays. They are also available on a limited number of occasions each year for private and corporate entertaining during the rest of the week.

© Spencer House / Mark Fiennes

© Spencer House / Mark Fiennes

No photography inside House or Garden.

House only, ramps and lifts. WC.

Obligatory. Comprehensive colour guidebook.

None.

Contact

Jane Rick
Director
Spencer House
27 St James's Place
London SW1A 1NR

Tel: 020 7514 1958
Fax: 020 7409 2952
Recorded Info Line: 020 7499 8620
Email: tours@spencerhouse.co.uk

Location

MAP 20:L8
OS Ref. TQ293 803

Central London: off St James's Street, overlooking Green Park.

Underground: Green Park.

Opening Times

All Year (except January & August) Suns, 10.30am–5.45pm.

Last tour 4.45pm.

Regular tours throughout the day. Maximum number on each tour is 20.

Mon mornings for pre-booked groups only. Group size: min 15–60.

Open for private and corporate hospitality except during January & August.

Admission

Adult	£9.00
Conc.*	£7.00

*Students, Members of the V&A, Friends of the Royal Academy, Tate Members and senior citizens (only on production of valid identification), children under 16. No children under 10 admitted.

Prices include guided tour.

Garden
For updated information on opening dates for the restored 18th century garden view: www.spencerhouse.co.uk or telephone the recorded information line: 020 7499 8620.

Conference/Function

ROOM	MAX CAPACITY
Receptions	400
Lunches & Dinners	126
Board Meetings	40
Theatre-style Meetings	100

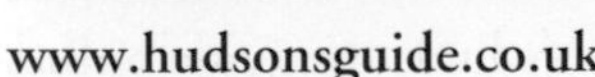

■ **Owner**

Strawberry Hill Trust

■ **Contact**

Nick Smith
268 Waldegrave Road
Twickenham
London
TW1 4ST

Tel: 020 8744 3124
E-mail: info@strawberryhillhouse.org.uk

■ **Location**

MAP 19:C8
OS Ref. TQ158 722

Off A310 between Twickenham and Teddington.

Bus: 33 Hammersmith - Fulham or R68 Kingston - Kew

Rail: Strawberry Hill (National Rail) 0.3 miles.

Underground: Richmond (District Line)

■ **Opening Times**

Apr–Oct, Sat–Wed, 12noon–4.30pm. NB.

Gardens only
April–October

Monday, Tuesday, Wednesday, Saturday, Sunday

12.00–4.30pm

■ **Admission**

Adult	£8.00 (£7.25)
Child	£5.20 (£4.45)
Family	£20.00 (£18.10)

(2 adults up to three children under 16)
Under 5 free admission

Prices include a 10% voluntary donation above the standard admission price, which goes towards the preservation of Strawberry Hill. If you are a UK taxpayer you can fill out a Gift Aid declaration enabling the Trust to claim an additional 28% from the government at no additional cost to you.

STRAWBERRY HILL

strawberryhillhouse.org.uk

Strawberry Hill is Britain's finest example of Gothic Revival architecture and interior decoration. It began life in 1698 as a modest house, later transformed by Horace Walpole, the son of England's first Prime Minister.

Between 1747 and 1792 Walpole doubled its size, creating extraordinary rooms and adding towers and battlements in fulfilment of his dream.

Strawberry Hill was a tourist site in its own day and has survived into ours, its rural surroundings gone, but its charm undiminished.

As they approach Strawberry Hill visitors will be met by the remarkable exterior, restored to its original 'wedding cake' appearance, lime washed in white. The castellated parapets and 3-metre high pinnacles create a dramatic and spiky silhouette.

There are 25 show rooms on the ground and first floors, 20 of which will have been fully restored to take the house back to the 1790s when Walpole had completed his creation.

In addition to extensive repairs to the roof, much work has been done to repair and conserve the fabric of the building employing the same structural design as the original. Of particular note is the huge collection of renaissance glass for which Strawberry Hill is famed.

Horace set up a private press, publishing historical texts and his own writings including a novel, *The Castle of Otranto*, considered to be the first piece of Gothic literature.

Following an £8.9 million restoration with the support of the Heritage Lottery Fund, the house is now open to the public as an extraordinary fairytale experience.

 WCs.

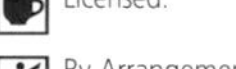 Licensed.

 By Arrangement.

 Limited for cars. No coaches.

 Guide dogs only.

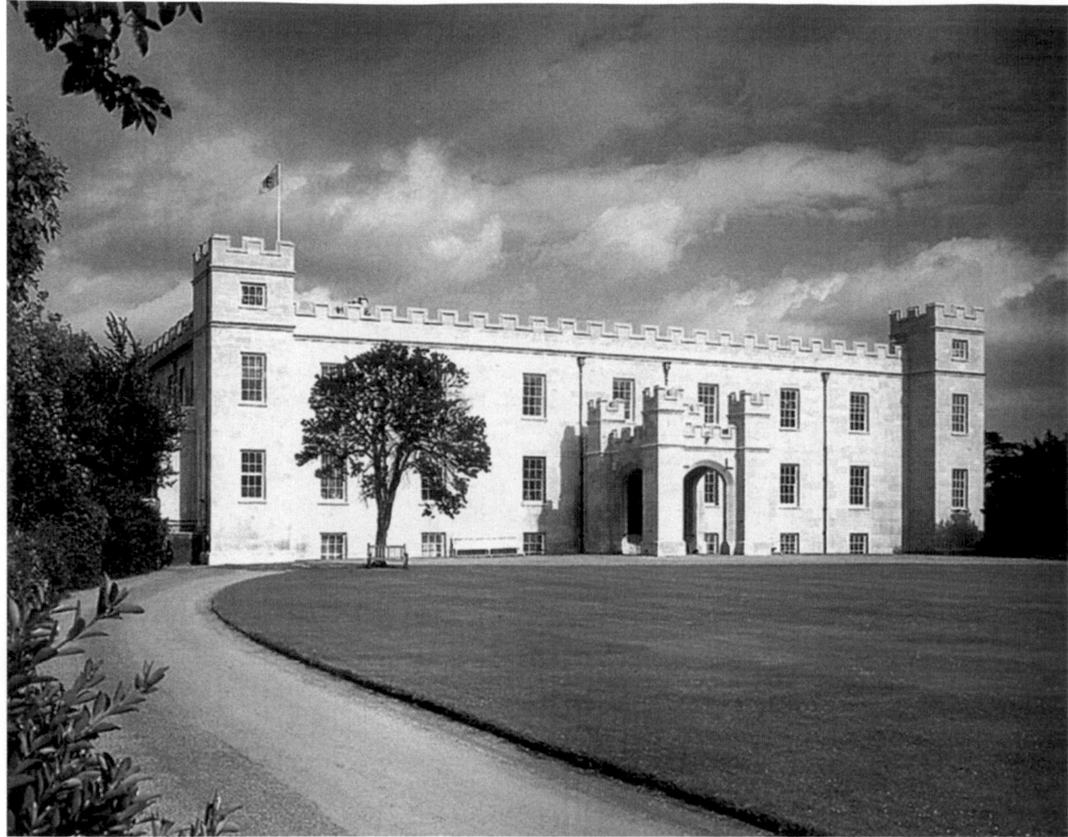

SYON PARK

www.syonpark.co.uk

Described by John Betjeman as the 'Grand Architectural Walk', Syon House and its 200-acre park is the London home of the Duke of Northumberland, whose family, the Percys, have lived here for 400 years.

Originally the site of a late medieval monastery, excavated by Channel 4's *Time Team*, Syon Park has a fascinating history. The present house has Tudor origins but contains some of Robert Adam's finest interiors, which were commissioned by the 1st Duke in the 1760s. The private apartments and State bedrooms are available to view. The house can be hired for filming and photo shoots subject to availability.

Within the 'Capability' Brown landscaped park are 40 acres of gardens which contain the spectacular Great Conservatory designed by Charles Fowler in the 1820s. The House and Great Conservatory are available for corporate and private hire.

The Northumberland Room in Syon House is an excellent venue for conferences, meetings, lunches and dinners (max 60). The State Apartments make a sumptuous setting for dinners, concerts, receptions, launches and wedding ceremonies (max 120). Marquees can be erected on the lawn adjacent to the house for balls and corporate events. The Great Conservatory is available for summer parties, launches, filming, photoshoots and wedding receptions (max 150).

© Tony Marshall

No photography in house. Indoor adventure playground.

Garden centre.

By arrangement.

■ Owner

The Duke of Northumberland

■ Contact

Estate Office
Syon House
Syon Park
Brentford
TW8 8JF

Tel: 020 8560 0882
Fax: 020 8568 0936
E-mail: info@syonpark.co.uk

■ Location

MAP 19:B8
OS Ref. TQ173 767

Between Brentford and Twickenham, off the A4, A310 in SW London.

Rail: Kew Bridge or Gunnersbury Underground then Bus 237 or 267.

Air: Heathrow 8m.

■ Opening Times

Syon House
16 March–30 October
Wed, Thur, Sun & BHs
11am–5pm
(open Good Fri & Easter Sat).

Other times by appointment for groups.

Gardens only
April–October
Daily, 10.30am–5pm
November–March
Sats & Suns, &
New Year's day,
10.30am–4pm or dusk, whichever is earlier.

Last admissions House & Gardens 1 hr before closing.

■ Admission

House and Gardens

Adult	£10.00
Child	£4.00
Conc.	£8.00
Family (2+2)	£22.00

Group bookings (15–50)

Adult	£8.50
Conc.	£7.50
School Group	£2.00

Gardens & Great Conservatory

Adult	£5.00
Child	£2.50
Conc.	£3.50
Family (2+2)	£11.00

Group bookings (15–50)
Price on application (please telephone).

Syon House Ventures & The Lovaine Trust reserve the right to alter opening times.

Conference/Function

ROOM	SIZE	MAX CAPACITY
Great Hall	50' x 30'	120
Great Conservatory	60' x 40'	150
Northumberland Room	35' x 20'	60
Marquee		1000

2 WILLOW ROAD

Hampstead, London NW3 1TH

Tel: 020 7435 6166

Owner: National Trust **Contact:** The Custodian

Former home of Ernö Goldfinger.

Location: MAP 20:J2, OS Ref. TQ270 858. Hampstead, London.

18 FOLGATE STREET

Spitalfields, East London E1 6BX

Tel: 020 7247 4013 **www.dennisseversbouse.co.uk**

Owner: Spitalfields Historic Buildings Trust **Contact:** Mick Pedroli

A time capsule furnished and decorated to tell the story of the Jervis family, Huguenot silk weavers from 1724–1919.

Location: MAP 20:P6, OS Ref. TQ335 820. ½m NE of Liverpool St. Station. E of Bishopsgate (A10), just N of Spitalfields Market.

Open/Admission: Every Mon evening (except BH), by Candelight, 'Silent Night'. Times vary with light of seasons, booking necessary. £12. First & third Suns, 2–4pm (last adm 3.15pm). £8. Mons following first & third Sun, 12–2pm. £5. 1 Nov–31 Mar, Sun, 12–4pm. Individual & group/corporate booking possible.

ALBERT MEMORIAL

Princes Gate, Kensington Gore SW7 2AN

Tel: Bookings - 020 7495 0916. Enquiries - 020 7495 5504

An elaborate memorial by George Gilbert Scott to commemorate the Prince Consort.

Location: MAP 20:J8, OS Ref. TQ266 798. Victoria Station 1½m, South Kensington Tube ½m.

Open: First Sun of the month, tours 1pm and 3pm. Tours last 45 mins.

Admission: Adult £5, Conc. £4.50.

APSLEY HOUSE

See page 59 for full page entry.

BANQUETING HOUSE

The Banqueting House, Horse Guards, Whitehall, London SW1A 2ER

Tel: General Enquiries: 0844 482 7777 **Functions:** 020 3166 6150 / 6151

Email: groupsandtraveltrade@hrp.org.uk **www.banqueting-house.org.uk**

Owner: Historic Royal Palaces

This revolutionary building, is the first in England to be designed in a Palladian style by Inigo Jones. The Banqueting House is most famous for one real life drama, the execution of Charles I.

Location: MAP 20:M8, OS Ref. TQ302 80, Underground: Westminster, Embankment and Charing Cross. Rail: Charing Cross. Boat: Embankment Pier.

Open: All year, Mon–Sat, 10am–5pm. Last admission 4.30pm. Closed 24 Dec–1 Jan, Good Friday and other public holidays. NB. Liable to close at short notice for Government functions.

Admission: Enquiry line for admission prices: 0844 482 7777.

Concerts. No photography inside. WCs. By arrangement.

Video and audio guide. Limited.

BLEWCOAT SCHOOL

23 Caxton Street, Westminster, London SW1H 0PY

Tel: 020 7222 2877

Owner: National Trust **Contact:** Janet Bowden

Built in 1709 at the expense of William Green, a local brewer, to provide an education for poor children. Used as a school until 1926, it is now the NT London Gift Shop and Information Centre.

Location: MAP 20:L9, OS Ref. TQ295 794. Near the junction with Buckingham Gate.

Open: All year: Mon–Fri, 10am–5.30pm. 6 Nov–18 Dec: Sat, 10am–4pm. Closed BHs.

For unique **Civil wedding** venues see our index at the end of the book.

BOSTON MANOR HOUSE

Boston Manor Road, Brentford TW8 9JX

Tel: 0845 456 2824 **E-mail:** info@cip.org.uk

Owner: Hounslow Cultural & Community Services

A fine Jacobean house built in 1623.

Location: MAP 19:B7, OS Ref. TQ168 784. 10 mins walk S of Boston Manor Station (Piccadilly Line) and 250yds N of Boston Manor Road junction with A4 Great West Road, Brentford.

Open: Apr–end Oct: Sat, Sun & BHs, 2.30–5pm. Park open daily.

Admission: Free.

BRUCE CASTLE MUSEUM

Haringey Libraries, Archives & Museum Service, Lordship Lane, London N17 8NU

Tel: 020 8808 8772 **Fax:** 020 8808 4118 **E-mail:** museum.services@haringey.gov.uk

Owner: London Borough of Haringey

A Tudor building. Sir Rowland Hill (inventor of the Penny Post) ran a progressive school at Bruce Castle from 1827.

Location: MAP 19:E6, OS Ref. TQ335 906. Corner of Bruce Grove (A10) and Lordship Lane, 600yds NW of Bruce Grove Station.

Open: All year: Wed–Sun & Summer BHs (except Good Fri), 1–5pm. Organised groups by appointment.

Admission: Free.

BUCKINGHAM PALACE

London SW1A 1AA

Tel: 020 7766 7300 **E-mail:** bookinginfo@royalcollection.org.uk

Owner: Official Residence of Her Majesty The Queen

Contact: Ticket Sales & Information Office

Buckingham Palace is the official London residence of Her Majesty The Queen and serves as both home and office. Its 19 State Rooms, which open for eight weeks a year, form the heart of the working palace. The garden walk offers superb views of the Garden Front of the Palace and the 19th century lake.

Location: MAP 20:L8, OS Ref. TQ291 796. Underground: Green Park, Victoria, St James's Park.

Open: Contact information office.

Admission: Contact information office.

Banqueting House

BURGH HOUSE

New End Square, Hampstead, London NW3 1LT

Tel: 020 7431 0144 **Buttery:** 0207 794 2905 **Fax:** 020 7435 8817

E-mail: info@burghhouse.org.uk **www.burghhouse.org.uk**

Owner: London Borough of Camden **Contact:** General Manager

A Grade I listed building of 1703 in the heart of old Hampstead with original panelled rooms, "barley sugar" staircase banisters and a music room. Child-friendly, refurbished Hampstead Museum, permanent and changing exhibitions. Prize-winning terraced garden. Regular programme of concerts, art exhibitions, and meetings. Receptions, seminars and conferences. Rooms for hire. Special facilities for schools visits. Wedding receptions and ceremonies.

Location: MAP 20:J2, OS Ref. TQ266 859. New End Square, E of Hampstead Underground station.

Open: All year: Wed–Sun, 12 noon–5pm. Sats by appointment only. Bank Hols, 2–5pm. (Open Good Friday and Easter Monday) Closed Christmas fortnight. Groups by arrangement. Buttery: Tue–Sun, 11am–5.30pm.

Admission: Free.

Ground floor & grounds. WC. Licensed buttery. By arrangement. None. By arrangement. Guide dogs only.

CAPEL MANOR GARDENS

BULLSMOOR LANE, ENFIELD EN1 4RQ

www.capelmanorgardens.co.uk

Tel: 08456 122122 **Fax:** 01992 717544

Owner: Capel Manor Charitable Organisation **Contact:** Customer Services

A beautiful 30 acre estate, first established in the late 13th century, Capel Manor provides a colourful & scented oasis surrounding a Georgian Manor House & Victorian Stables. Be inspired by prize winning themed, model & historical gardens including the latest additions the Old Manor House Garden (opened by her Majesty the Queen in June 2010) and the Family Friendly Garden (a 2010 Chelsea Flower Show Gold Medal Winner). Picnic by the lake or relax in the restaurant & finish with a visit to the gift shop. Free parking.

Location: MAP 19:E4, OS Ref. TQ344 997. Minutes from M25/J25. Tourist Board signs posted.

Open: Daily in summer: 10am–6pm. Last ticket 4.30pm. Check for winter times.

Admission: Adult £5.50, Child £2.50, Conc. £4.50, Family £13.50. Charges alter for special show weekends and winter months.

Grounds. WC. In grounds, on leads.

CAREW MANOR DOVECOTE

Church Road, Beddington SM6 7NH

Tel: 020 8770 4781 **Fax:** 020 8770 4777 **E-mail:** valary.murphy@sutton.gov.uk

www.sutton.gov.uk

Owner: London Borough of Sutton **Contact:** Ms V Murphy

An early 18th century octagonal brick dovecote with around 1200 nesting boxes and the original potence (circular ladder). Opened for tours with the adjacent late medieval Grade I listed Great Hall of Carew Manor.

Location: MAP 19:D9, OS Ref. TQ295 652. Just off A232 at entrance to Beddington Park.

Open: Organised tours only on selected Sundays. Ring or email for details.

Admission: Adult £4, Child £2.

Chelsea Physic Garden

CARLYLE'S HOUSE

24 Cheyne Row, Chelsea, London SW3 5HL

Tel: 020 7352 7087

Owner: National Trust **Contact:** The Custodian

Home of the writer Thomas Carlyle (1834–1881)

Location: MAP 20:K10, OS Ref. TQ272 777. Off the King's Road and Oakley Street, or off Cheyne Walk between Albert Bridge and Battersea Bridge on Chelsea Embankment.

CHAPTER HOUSE

East Cloisters, Westminster Abbey, London SW1P 3PA

Tel: 020 7654 4900 **E-mail:** customers@english-heritage.org.uk

www.english-heritage.org.uk/chapterhouseandpyxchamber

Owner: English Heritage **Managed by:** Dean & Chapter of Westminster

The Chapter House, built by the Royal masons c1250 and faithfully restored in the 19th century, contains some of the finest medieval sculpture to be seen and spectacular wall paintings. The building is octagonal, with a central column, and still has its original floor of glazed tiles.

Location: MAP 20:M8, OS Ref. TQ301 795.

Open: Throughout the year: 10am–4pm, Mon–Sun. Closed Good Fri, 24–26 Dec & 1 Jan. May be closed at short notice on state and religious occasions.

Admission: Free to EH members. Opening times and prices are valid until 31st March 2011, after this date details are subject to change please visit www.english-heritage.org.uk for the most up-to-date information.

CHELSEA PHYSIC GARDEN

66 Royal Hospital Road, London SW3 4HS

Tel: 020 7352 5646 **Fax:** 020 7376 3910 **E-mail:** enquiries@chelseaphysicgarden.co.uk

www.chelseaphysicgarden.co.uk

Owner: Chelsea Physic Garden Company **Managed by:** Dawn Kemp

Chelsea Physic Garden, founded in 1673, is London's oldest botanic garden and a unique living museum. Features include Europe's oldest pond rockery; pharmaceutical and perfumery beds; the Garden of World Medicine; a tropical plant greenhouse and over 5,000 different named plants. The Garden's renowned licensed cafe serves delicious homemade food.

Location: Bus: 170 from Victoria or Clapham Junction to Flood Street stop. Coach: Victoria Coach Station. Rail: Victoria or Imperial Wharf. Underground: Sloane Square or South Kensington. Boat: Cadogan Pier or Chelsea Harbour Pier.

Open: Apr-Oct: Suns & BHs 12–6pm. Weds, Thurs & Fris 12–5pm. Winter Openings Feb 5, 6, 12 & 13, 10am–4pm. Late Weds Openings Jul & Aug 12–10pm.

Admission: Adult £8, Students & Children aged 5-15 £5. Free for Under 5s. No min or max group size.

No bicycles, ball games or wheeled toys. Maximum of two Under 16s admitted per adult. Under 16s must be accompanied by an adult at all times. WCs. Licensed. By arrangement. Guide dogs only. Christmas Fair - 26 Nov 11am–4pm & 27 Nov 10am–4pm.

CHISWICK HOUSE & GARDENS

See page 60 for full page entry.

COLLEGE OF ARMS

Queen Victoria Street, London EC4V 4BT

Tel: 020 7248 2762 **Fax:** 020 7248 6448 **E-mail:** enquiries@college-of-arms.gov.uk

Owner: Corp. of Kings, Heralds & Pursuivants of Arms **Contact:** The Officer in Waiting

Mansion built in 1670s to house the English Officers of Arms and their records.

Location: MAP 20:O7, OS Ref. TQ320 810. On N side of Queen Victoria Street, S of St Paul's Cathedral.

Open: Earl Marshal's Court only; open all year (except BHs, State and special occasions) Mon–Fri, 10am–4pm. Group visits (up to 10) by arrangement only. Record Room: open for tours (groups of up to 20) by special arrangement in advance with the Officer in Waiting.

Admission: Free (groups by negotiation)

EASTBURY MANOR HOUSE

Eastbury Square, Barking, Essex IG11 9SN

Tel: 020 8724 1000 **Fax:** 020 8724 1003 **E-mail:** eastburyhouse@lbbd.gov.uk

www.barking-dagenham.gov.uk

Owner: National Trust **Contact:** Julie Packham

A fine example of a medium sized Tudor gentry house with attractive grounds. Intriguing Gunpowder Plot connections. Open to visitors all year. Heritage and arts activities and events. Available for education days, business conferences and Civil Wedding and Partnership ceremonies. Managed by the London Borough of Barking and Dagenham.

Location: MAP 19:F7, OS TQ457 838. In Eastbury Square off Ripple Road off A13. Bus: 287, 368 or 62. Underground: Upney (10 mins walk).

Open: All year: Mons & Tues and 1st & 2nd Sat of the month, 10am–4pm. However, closed on 1, 3 & 4 Jan, 25 Apr, 2 & 30 May, 29 Aug & 26 & 27 Dec.

Admission: Adult £3, Child £1, Conc. £1.50, Family £6. Groups (15+) by arrangement: £2.40pp. Free to NT Members.

WCs. Licensed. In Eastbury Square. On leads.

ELTHAM PALACE AND GARDENS

See page 61 for full page entry.

Fitzroy House

FENTON HOUSE

HAMPSTEAD GROVE, HAMPSTEAD, LONDON NW3 6SP

Tel/Fax: 020 7435 3471 **Infoline:** 01494 755563

E-mail: fentonhouse@nationaltrust.org.uk

Owner: National Trust **Contact:** The House Manager

A delightful late 17th century merchant's house which contains an outstanding collection of porcelain, needlework, pictures and furniture. The Benton Fletcher Collection of early keyboard instruments is also housed here. The walled garden has a formal lawn and walks, an orchard and vegetable garden.

Location: MAP 20:J2, OS Ref. TQ262 860. Visitors' entrance on W side of Hampstead Grove. Hampstead Underground station 300 yds.

Open: 5 Mar–30 Oct: Wed, Thur, Fri, Sat, Sun & BH Mons, 11am–5pm. (Open Good Friday). Some Thurs in June & July open at 2pm due to concerts, please check dates with property. Groups by appointment.

Admission: Adult £6.50, Child £3, Family £16, Groups (15+) £5.50. Joint ticket with 2 Willow Road, £9. Garden only: Adult £2. Garden Season Ticket £10. Free to NT Members.

Special Events: Summer concerts on Thurs lunchtimes and evenings, Apple Day end of Sept. Easter Egg Trail on Easter weekend.

No picnics in grounds. Partial. Licensed By arrangement. Demonstration tours. None. Guide dogs only. Send SAE for details.

FITZROY HOUSE

37 FITZROY STREET, FITZROVIA, LONDON W1T 6DX

www.fitzroyhouse.org

Tel/Fax: 020 7255 2422 **E-mail:** info@fitzroyhouse.org

Contact: Heritage Properties International **Contact:** Sarah Borburg

Built 1791, Fitzroy House was formerly inhabited by playwright George Bernard Shaw. Today it shows the life and work of L. Ron Hubbard, founder of Scientology, who worked there in the late 1950s. Steeped in 1950s memorabilia, the house displays a nostalgic collection of restored communications office equipment, complete with Adler typewriter, Grundig tape recorders, and Western Union Telefax.

Location: MAP 20:L6, OS Ref. TQ291 820. Underground: Warren St Underground.

Open: All year. Guided tours of the house between 11am–5pm by appointment.

Admission: Free admission. Coach parties welcome, teas served.

Morning Coffee and afternoon tea is served. Obligatory.

THE FOUNDLING MUSEUM

40 Brunswick Square, London WC1N 1AZ

Tel: 020 7841 3600 **Fax:** 020 7841 3601

Owner: The Foundling Museum

Site of London's first home for abandoned children. Established in 1739. The museum charts the history of the Foundling Hospital and its residents.

Location: MAP 20:M6, OS Ref. TQ303 822. Underground: Russell Square.

Open: Tues–Sat, 10am–5pm; Sun, 12 noon–5pm.

Admission: Adult £7.50, Child up to 16yrs Free, Conc. £5. Special rates for groups & schools.

FULHAM PALACE & MUSEUM

Bishop's Avenue, Fulham, London SW6 6EA

Tel: 020 7736 3233

Owner: London Borough of Hammersmith & Fulham & Fulham Palace Trust

Former home of the Bishops of London (Tudor with Georgian additions and Victorian Chapel). Set in gardens with a collection of rare trees. Museum, contemporary art gallery.

Location: MAP 20:I12, OS Ref. TQ240 761.

Open: Ring for details.

Admission: Palace & Gardens: Free.

GUNNERSBURY PARK & MUSEUM

Gunnersbury Park, London W3 8LQ

Tel: 020 8992 1612 **Fax:** 020 8752 0686 **E-mail:** gp-museum@cip.org.uk

Owner: Hounslow and Ealing Councils **Contact:** Lynn Acum

Built in 1802 and refurbished by Sydney Smirke for the Rothschild family.

Location: MAP 19:B7, OS Ref. TQ190 792. Acton Town Underground station. ¼m N of the junction of A4, M4 North Circular.

Open: Apr–Oct: daily: 11am–5pm. Nov–Mar: daily: 11am–4pm. Victorian kitchens summer weekends only. Closed Christmas Day & Boxing Day. Park: open dawn–dusk.

Admission: Free. Donations welcome.

HANDEL HOUSE MUSEUM

25 BROOK STREET, LONDON W1K 4HB

www.handelhouse.org

Tel: 020 7495 1685 **Fax:** 020 7495 1759 **E-mail:** mail@handelhouse.org

Owner: The Handel House Trust Ltd **Contact:** Gemma Morris

Handel House Museum is a beautifully restored Georgian townhouse where the famous composer George Frideric Handel lived for 36 years and composed timeless masterpieces such as *Messiah* and *Zadok the Priest*. The elegantly refurbished interiors create the perfect setting for 18th century fine art and furniture, evoking the spirit of Georgian London. Portraits and paintings of Handel and his contemporaries illustrate Handel's London life and the House is as vibrant with music as it was in Handel's day. Weekly Thursday evening recitals and regular weekend events are held in Handel's intimate music room (booking recommended).

Location: MAP 20:K7, OS Ref. TQ286 809. Central London, between New Bond St and Grosvener Square. Entrance in Lancashire Court. Bond Street Tube.

Open: All year, Tue–Sat, 10am–6pm (8pm Thur). Sun, 12 noon–6pm. Closed Mon. Groups by arrangement. Last entry 30 mins before closing.

Admission: Adult £5, Child £2 (Free on Sat), Conc. £4.50. The Art Fund cardholders Free.

No inside photography. By arrangement. Guide dogs only.

©NT/David Watson

©NT/Stephen Robson

HAM HOUSE & GARDEN

HAM ST, RICHMOND-UPON-THAMES, SURREY TW10 7RS

www.nationaltrust.org.uk/hamhouse

Tel: 020 8940 1950 **Fax:** 020 8439 8241 **E-mail:** hamhouse@nationaltrust.org.uk

Owner: National Trust **Contact:** The Property Manager

One of a series of grand houses and palaces alongside the River Thames, Ham House and Garden is an unusually complete survival of the 17th century. Rich in history and atmosphere, Ham was mainly created by the charismatic Elizabeth, Duchess of Lauderdale, who was deeply embroiled in the politics of the English Civil War and restoration of the monarchy. With lavish interiors unique historical features and outstanding art collections, Ham is a treasure trove waiting to be discovered. The gardens are a rare example of 17th century garden design.

Location: MAP 19:B8, OS Ref. TQ172 732. 1½ m from Richmond and 2m from Kingston. On the S bank of the River Thames, W of A307 at Petersham between Richmond and Kingston. Bus: TfL 371 (outside Richmond station) to Kingston, alight Ham Street by Royal Oak Pub, then ½ml walk. Rail/Tube: Richmond 1 ½ml by footpath, 2ml by road.

Open: House: 12 Feb–31 Mar: Guided tours of selected rooms only (40 min), no free flow visit. Tours start every half-hour. Entry by timed ticket. Max 20 tickets per tour. Book on arrival (not pre-bookable). Sat–Thur 11am–3.30pm. 2 Apr–30 Oct: Free flow visits only; Sat–Thur 12–4pm. 31 Oct–29 Nov: Guided tours, selected rooms only (40 min) Sat–Tue, 11.30am–3pm. Garden, Shop & Cafe: 1 Jan–11 Feb, daily, 11am–4pm; 12 Feb–30 Oct, daily, 11am–5pm; 31 Oct–18 Dec, daily, 11am–4pm.

***Admission:** House & Garden: 12 Feb–30 Oct Adult £10.90, Child £6.05, Family £27.90. 31 Oct–29 Nov Adult £9.10, Child £4.85, Family £23.05. Garden only: 1 Jan–11 Feb & 31 Oct–16 Dec Adult £1.85, Child £1.25, Family £4.90. 12 Feb–30 Oct Adult £3.65, Child £2.45, Family £9.75. *includes a voluntary donation of at least 10%; visitors can, however, choose to pay the standard prices which are displayed at the property and at www.nationaltrust.org.uk.

Special Events: Themed guided tours, open-air theatre and cinema, special Christmas events. For the first time in 2011 the garden, shop and café will be opening 7 days a week throughout the year. The house will be open 6 days a week throughout Spring and Summer.

WCs. Licensed. Licensed. By arrangement. Limited for coaches. Guide dogs only.

HONEYWOOD MUSEUM

Honeywood Walk, Carshalton SM5 3NX

Tel/Fax: 020 8770 4297 **E-mail:** lbshoneywood@btconnect.com

www.sutton.gov.uk www.friendsofhoneywood.co.uk

Owner: London Borough of Sutton **Contact:** The Curator

Local history museum in a 17th century listed building next to the picturesque Carshalton Ponds, containing displays on many aspects of the history of the London Borough of Sutton plus a changing programme of exhibitions and events on a wide range of subjects. Attractive garden at rear.

Location: MAP 19:D9, OS Ref. TQ279 646. On A232 approximately 4m W of Croydon.

Open: Wed–Fri, 11am–5pm. Sat, Suns & BH Mons, 10am–5pm. Closed for refurbishment. Re-opening Spring 2011. Please ring or check website before visiting.

Ground floor. WC. Limited. Guide dogs only.

Keats House

JEWEL TOWER

Abingdon Street, Westminster, London SW1P 3JX

Tel: 020 7222 2219 **E-mail:** customers@english-heritage.org.uk

www.english-heritage.org.uk/jeweltower

Owner: English Heritage **Contact:** Visitor Operations Team

Built c1365 to house the personal treasure of Edward III. One of two surviving parts of the original Palace of Westminster. Now houses an exhibition on 'Parliament Past and Present'. The second floor now includes new illustrated panels, telling the story of this small but important building.

Location: MAP 20:M8, OS Ref. TQ302 794. Opposite S end of Houses of Parliament (Victoria Tower).

Open: 1 Apr–31 Oct: daily, 10am–5pm. 1 Nov–31 Mar: daily, 10am–4pm. Closed 24–26 Dec & 1 Jan.

Admission: Adult £3.20, Child £1.60, Conc. £2.70. EH Members free. Group discount available. Opening times and prices are valid until 31st March 2011, after this date details are subject to change please see www.english-heritage.org.uk for the most up-to-date information.

DR JOHNSON'S HOUSE

17 Gough Square, London EC4A 3DE

Tel: 020 7353 3745 **E-mail:** curator@drjohnsonshouse.org

Owner: The Trustees

Fine 18th century house, once home to Dr Samuel Johnson, the celebrated literary figure, famous for his English dictionary.

Location: MAP 20:N7, OS Ref. TQ314 813. N of Fleet Street.

Open: Oct–Apr: Mon–Sat, 11am–5pm. May–Sept: Mon–Sat, 11am–5.30pm. Closed BHs.

Admission: Adult £4.50, Child £1.50 (under 10yrs Free), Conc. £3.50. Family £10. Groups: £3.50.

KENSINGTON PALACE

London W8 4PX

Tel Information line: 0844 482 7777 **Email:** groupsandtraveltrade@hrp.org.uk

Venue Hire and Corporate Hospitality: 020 3166 6104

www.kensington-palace.org.uk

Owner: Historic Royal Palaces

Generations of royal Women have shaped this stylish palace. Currently the palace is holding an Enchanted Palace interactive exhibit, and as a result some other areas are closed. Through the State Apartments there are stunning installations from leading and new fashion designers interwoven with the palace's own enchanting history. The birthplace and childhood home of Queen Victoria, the palace first became a royal residence for William and Mary in 1689. The famous Orangery was built in 1704 by Queen Anne, and George II's wife, Queen Caroline, another keen gardener, added further improvements.

Location: MAP 20:I8, OS Ref. TQ258 801 In Kensington Gardens. Underground: Queensway on Central Line, High Street Kensington on Circle & District Line.

Open: Nov–Feb: daily, 10am–6pm (last admission 5pm) Oct–Feb: daily, 10am–5pm (last admission 4pm) Closed 24–26 Dec.

Admission: Telephone Information Line for admission prices: 0844 482 7777. Advance Ticket Sales: 0844 482 7799. Group bookings 0844 482 7770. Quote Hudson's.

No photography indoors. Partial. WCs. By arrangement. Nearby. Please book, 0844 482 7777.

KEATS HOUSE

KEATS GROVE, HAMPSTEAD, LONDON NW3 2RR

www.cityoflondon.gov.uk/keatshousehampstead

Tel: 020 7332 3868 **E-mail:** keatshouse@cityoflondon.gov.uk

Owner: City of London **Contact:** The Manager

This Grade I listed Regency house is where the poet John Keats lived from 1818 to 1820 with his friend Charles Brown. Here he wrote *'Ode to a Nightingale'* and met and fell in love with Fanny Brawne. Suffering from tuberculosis, Keats left for Italy, where he died at the age of 25. Leaving his beloved Fanny in Hampstead, she wore his engagement ring until she died, now on display at the house. Their love story has been immortalised in the Jane Campion film, *Bright Star*, released in 2009.

The museum runs regular poetry readings, talks and events suitable for families throughout the year.

Location: MAP 20:K3, OS Ref. TQ272 856. Hampstead, NW3. Nearest Underground: Belsize Park & Hampstead.

Open: Keats House has recently reopened after the successful Magic Casements project funded by the Heritage Lottery Fund. Our opening hours are Easter–31 Oct, Tue–Sun, 1pm to 5pm. 1 Nov–Easter, Fri–Sun, 1pm–5pm. School parties and pre booked groups by arrangement. The house is also open on BH Mons.

Admission: Adults £5.00, Concessions £3.00 Children 16 and under are free. Tickets are valid for one year.

WC Ground floor & garden. None. Guide dogs only.

KENWOOD HOUSE

See page 62 for full page entry.

LITTLE HOLLAND HOUSE

40 Beeches Avenue, Carshalton SM5 3LW
Tel: 020 8770 4781 **Fax:** 020 8770 4777
E-mail: valary.murphy@sutton.gov.uk
www.sutton.gov.uk
Owner: London Borough of Sutton **Contact:** Ms V Murphy

The home of Frank Dickinson (1874–1961) artist, designer and craftsman, who dreamt of a house that would follow the philosophy and theories of William Morris and John Ruskin. Dickinson designed, built and furnished the house himself from 1902 onwards. The Grade II* listed interior features handmade furniture, metal work, carvings and paintings produced by Dickinson in the Arts and Crafts style.

Location: MAP 19:D9, OS Ref. TQ275 634. On B278 1m S of junction with A232.

Open: First Sun of each month & BH Suns & Mons (excluding Christmas & New Year), 1.30–5.30pm.

Admission: Free. Groups by arrangement, £4pp (includes talk and guided tour).

No photography in house. Ground floor. By arrangement. Guide dogs only.

© English Heritage

MARBLE HILL HOUSE

RICHMOND ROAD, TWICKENHAM TW1 2NL

www.english-heritage.org.uk/marblehillhouse

Tel: 020 8892 5115 **E-mail:** customers@english-heritage.org.uk
Owner: English Heritage **Contact:** Visitor Operations Team

This beautiful villa was built in 1724–29 for Henrietta Howard, mistress of George II. It contains an important collection of paintings and furniture, including pieces commissioned for the villa when it was built. A recent installation recreates the Chinese wallpaper hung in the Dining Room in 1751.

Location: MAP 19:B8, OS Ref. TQ174 736. A305, 600yds E of Orleans House.

Open: 1 Apr–31 Oct, Sat 10am–2pm; Sun & Bank Hols.10am–5pm. Guided tours at 12 noon on Sat; 11am & 2.30pm on Sun.
1 Nov–31 Mar Available for group tours - please call for details

Admission: Adult £5.00, Child £2.50, Conc. £4.30, Family £12.50. EH Members free. Group discount available. Opening times and prices are valid until 31st March 2011, after this date details are subject to change please see www.english-heritage.org.uk for the most up-to-date information.

On leads.

MORDEN HALL PARK

Morden Hall Road, Morden SM4 5JD
Tel: 020 8545 6850 **Fax:** 020 8417 8091
Owner: National Trust **Contact:** The Property Manager

Former deer park, waterways, meadows and wetlands.

Location: MAP 19:D8, OS Ref. TQ261 684. Off A24 and A297 S of Wimbledon, N of Sutton.

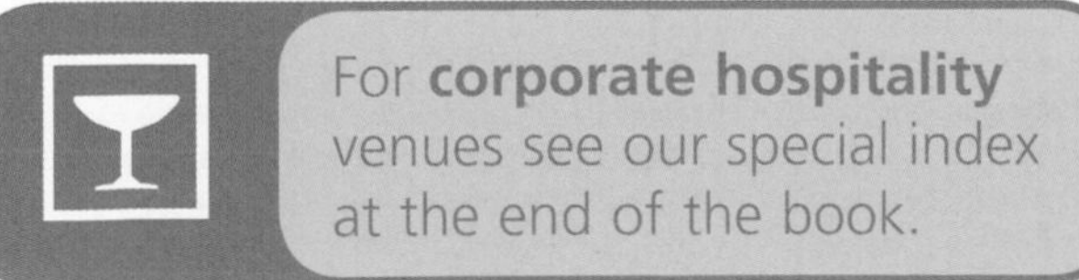

For **corporate hospitality** venues see our special index at the end of the book.

WILLIAM MORRIS GALLERY

Lloyd Park, Forest Road, Walthamstow, London E17 4PP
Tel: 020 8527 3782 **Fax:** 020 8527 7070
Owner: London Borough of Waltham Forest **Contact:** The Keeper

The William Morris Gallery is the only public Gallery devoted to William Morris - designer, craftsman, writer, socialist and conservationist - and displays an internationally important collection illustrating his life, achievements and influence. William Morris was born in Walthamstow in 1834. The Gallery is housed in the 18th century Water House, Morris' family home from 1848 to 1856.

Location: MAP 19:F6, OS Ref. SQ372 899. 15 mins walk from Walthamstow tube (Victoria line). 5–10 mins from M11/A406.

Open: Tue–Sat and first Sun each month, 10am–1pm and 2–5pm.

Admission: Free for all visitors but a charge is made for guided tours which must be booked in advance.

MYDDELTON HOUSE GARDENS

BULLS CROSS, ENFIELD, MIDDLESEX EN2 9HG

www.leevalleypark.org.uk

Tel: 08456 770 600
Owner: Lee Valley Regional Park Authority

Created by the famous plantsman and Fellow of the Royal Horticultural Society, E A Bowles, the gardens have year round interest. From the January snowdrops, through to springtime flowering daffodils, summer roses and autumn crocus, there's always something in the gardens to interest the visitor. National Collection of Bearded Iris.

Location: MAP 19:D4, OS Ref. TQ342 992. ¼m W of A10 via Turkey St. ¾m S M25/J25.

Open: Every day (except Christmas). Apr–Sept: 10am–4.30pm, Oct–Mar: 10am–3pm. Last admission 30 mins before closing.

Admission: Adult £3.30, Conc. £2.60. Prices subject to change April 2011. Separate charge for guided walks.

WCs. Please ring 01992 702 200. Limited for coaches.

NATIONAL MARITIME MUSEUM QUEEN'S HOUSE & ROYAL OBSERVATORY, GREENWICH

See page 63 for full page entry.

THE OCTAGON, ORLEANS HOUSE GALLERY

Riverside, Twickenham, Middlesex TW1 3DJ
Tel: 020 8831 6000 **Fax:** 020 8744 0501 **E-mail:** galleryinfo@richmond.gov.uk
Owner: London Borough of Richmond-upon-Thames **Contact:** The Curator

Stroll along a peaceful riverside road into secluded woodland gardens, to find a stunning 18th century interior design. Orleans House has a rich and vibrant history, from the baroque Octagon room, which was designed by renowned architect James Gibbs, to a main gallery which hosts five temporary exhibitions each year - ranging from the historical to the contemporary.

Location: MAP 19:B8, OS Ref. TQ168 734. On N side of Riverside, 700yds E of Twickenham town centre, 400yds S of Richmond Road. Vehicle access via Orleans Rd only.

Open: Tue–Sat, 1–5.30pm, Sun & BHs, 2–5.30pm. Garden: open daily, 9am–sunset.

Admission: Free.

© NTPL / Andrew Butler

© NTPL / Bill Batten

OSTERLEY PARK AND HOUSE

JERSEY ROAD, ISLEWORTH, MIDDLESEX TW7 4RB

www.nationaltrust.org.uk/osterley

Tel: 020 8232 5050 **Fax:** 020 8232 5080

E-mail: osterley@nationaltrust.org.uk

Owner: National Trust **Contact:** Visitor Experience & Marketing Manager

A spectacular mansion surrounded by gardens, park and farmland; Osterley is one of the last surviving country estates in London. Described as the 'the palace of palaces', Osterley was created in the late 18th century by Robert Adam for the Child family to entertain and impress their friends and clients and remains as impressive today.

Explore the dazzling interior with handheld audio visual guides, which bring the House to life in a completely new way. Outside the gardens are being restored to their 18th century glory offering a delightful retreat from urban life, perfect for picnics and leisurely strolls.

Location: MAP 19:B7, OS Ref. TQ146 780. On A4 between Hammersmith and Hounslow. Main gates at junction of Thornbury and Jersey Roads. If using SatNav, please enter 'Jersey Road' as well as 'TW7 4RB'. Bus: TfL H28, H91 to within 1 mile. Rail: Isleworth (1.5 miles). Tube: Osterley (Piccadilly Line - 1 mile).

Open: House: 23 Feb–27 Mar, Wed–Sun, 12–3.30pm (timed tours only). 30 Mar–30 Oct, Wed–Sun & BH, 12–4.30pm. 5 Nov–18 Dec, Sat & Sun, 12–3.30pm. Garden: 26 Feb–6 Mar, Sat & Sun, 12–3.30pm. 9 Mar–30 Oct, Wed–Sun & BH, 11am–5pm. Park & car park: All year, daily, 8am–7.30pm (closes 6pm in Winter). Café & Shop: 23 Feb–27 Mar, Wed–Sun, 11am–4pm. 30 Mar–30 Oct, Wed–Sun, 11am–5pm. 2 Nov–18 Dec, Wed–Sun, 12–4pm. Shop opens at 12.

***Admission:** House and Garden: Adult £9.20, Child £4.60, Family £23, Group (15+) £7.80. Garden: Adult £4, Child £2. Park: Free. Car Park: £3.50. Free to NT Members. *includes a voluntary 10% donation but visitors can choose to pay the standard prices displayed at the property and on the website.

Special Events: Please see website for event details.

No flash photography inside House. Partial. WCs. Licensed. Limited for coaches. In grounds.

PALACE OF WESTMINSTER

London SW1A 0AA

Tel: 020 7219 3000 / 0870 906 3773 **Info:** 020 7219 4272

Fax: 020 7219 5839 **Contact:** Information Office

The first Palace of Westminster was erected on this site by Edward the Confessor in 1042 and the building was a royal residence until a devastating fire in 1512. After this, the palace became the two-chamber Parliament for government – the House of Lords and the elected House of Commons. Following a further fire in 1834, the palace was rebuilt by Sir Charles Barry and decorated by A W Pugin.

Location: MAP 20:M8, OS Ref. TQ303 795. Central London, W bank of River Thames. 1km S of Trafalgar Square. Underground: Westminster.

Open: Aug–Sept (please ring for details). At other times by appointment.

Admission: Ring info line.

PITZHANGER MANOR-HOUSE

Walpole Park, Mattock Lane, Ealing W5 5EQ

Tel: 020 8567 1227 **Fax:** 020 8567 0595

E-mail: pmgallery&house@ealing.gov.uk **www.ealing.gov.uk/pmgalleryandhouse**

Owner: London Borough of Ealing **Contact:** Exhibition and Events Co-ordinator

Pitzhanger Manor-House, Ealing's flagship cultural venue, is a restored Georgian villa once owned and designed by the architect Sir John Soane in 1800. Rooms have been restored using Soane's highly individual ideas in design and decoration. The residence now also functions as a contemporary arts venue with a lively programme of events and exhibitions.

Location: MAP 19:B7, OS Ref. TQ176 805. Ealing, London.

Open: All year: Tue-Fri, 1-5pm. Sat, 11am-5pm. Summer Sunday Openings, please ring for details. Closed Christmas, Easter, New Year and BHs.

Admission: Free.

Art gallery and the ground floor of the house only. In grounds, on leads.

© NTPL / Andrew Butler

RED HOUSE

RED HOUSE LANE, BEXLEYHEATH DA6 8JF

Tel: 020 8304 9878 (Booking line: Tues–Sat, 9.30am–1.30pm)

Owner: National Trust

Commissioned by William Morris in 1859 and designed by Philip Webb, Red House is of enormous international significance in the history of domestic architecture and garden design. The garden was designed to "clothe" the house with a series of sub-divided areas that still clearly exist today. Inside, the house retains many of the original features and fixed items of furniture designed by Morris and Webb, as well as wall paintings and stained glass by Edward Burne-Jones.

Location: MAP 19:G8, OS Ref. TQ48 1750. Off A221 Bexleyheath. Visitors directions can be given on how to reach the property when booking. Nearest rail station Bexleyheath, 10 mins' walk.

Open: 2 Mar–30 Oct, Wed–Sun, 11am–5pm. 4 Nov–18 Dec, Fri–Sun only. Open Easter Sun, Good Fri, BH Mons. Ring 0208 304 9878 to book tours. Self guided viewing from 1.30pm, no need to book.

Admission: Adult £7.20, Child £3.60, Family £18.00. NT Members Free.

WC. Ground floor only. No parking on site. Disabled drivers can pre-book (limited parking). Parking at Danson Park (15 min walk). Parking charge at weekends and BHs. See Danson House (Kent section).

ST GEORGE'S CATHEDRAL, SOUTHWARK

Westminster Bridge Road, London SE1 7HY

Tel: 020 7928 5256 **Fax:** 020 7202 2189

E-mail: info@southwark-rc-cathedral.org.uk **Contact:** Canon James Cronin

Neo-Gothic rebuilt Pugin Cathedral bombed during the last war and rebuilt by Romily Craze in 1958.

Location: MAP 20:N9, OS Ref. TQ315 794. Near Imperial War Museum. ½m SE of Waterloo Stn.

Open: 8am–6pm, every day, except BHs. **Admission:** Free.

ST JOHN'S GATE

MUSEUM OF THE ORDER OF ST JOHN

ST JOHN'S GATE, CLERKENWELL, LONDON EC1M 4DA

www.sja.org.uk/museum

Tel: 020 7324 4005 **Fax:** 020 7336 0587 **E-mail:** museum@nhq.sja.org.uk

Owner: The Order of St John **Contact:** Pamela Willis

Tudor Gatehouse (built 1504), Priory Church and Norman Crypt. The remarkable history of the Knights Hospitaller is now revealed in new galleries showing our fine collections. Notable associations with Shakespeare, Hogarth, Dr Johnson, Dickens, David Garrick and many others. In Victorian times, St John Ambulance was founded here.

Location: MAP 20:N6, OS Ref. TQ317 821. St. John's Lane, Clerkenwell. Nearest Underground: Farringdon.

Open: New galleries open from Autumn 2010: Mon–Sat 10am–5pm. See website for further details.

Admission: Museum Galleries Free. Tours of the buildings: £5, OAP £4 (donation).

WCs. Guide dogs only. Reg. Charity No. 1077265

Supported by the National Lottery through the Heritage Lottery Fund.

ST PAUL'S CATHEDRAL *See page 64 for full page entry.*

SPENCER HOUSE *See page 65 for full page entry.*

STRAWBERRY HILL *See page 66 for full page entry.*

SYON PARK *See page 67 for full page entry.*

SIR JOHN SOANE'S MUSEUM

13 Lincoln's Inn Fields, London WC2A 3BP

Tel: 020 7405 2107 **Fax:** 020 7831 3957 **www.soane.org**

Owner: Trustees of Sir John Soane's Museum **Contact:** Julie Brock

The celebrated architect Sir John Soane built this in 1812 as his own house.

Location: MAP 20:M6, OS Ref. TQ308 816. E of Kingsway, S of High Holborn.

Open: Tue–Sat, 10am–5pm. First Tue of the month 6–9pm. Closed BHs & 24 Dec.

Admission: Free. Possible charge for first Tue and Sat tour. Groups must book.

SOUTHSIDE HOUSE

3 WOODHAYES ROAD, WIMBLEDON, LONDON SW19 4RJ

www.southsidehouse.com

Tel: 020 8946 7643 **E-mail:** info@southsidehouse.com

Owner: The Pennington-Mellor-Munthe Charity Trust **Contact:** The Administrator

Described by connoisseurs as an unforgettable experience, Southside House provides an enchantingly eccentric backdrop to the lives and loves of generations of the Pennington Mellor Munthe families. Maintained in traditional style, without major refurbishment, and crowded with the family possessions of centuries, Southside offers a wealth of fascinating family stories.

Behind the long façade are the old rooms, still with much of the original furniture and a superb collection of art and historical objects. John Pennington-Mellor's daughter, Hilda, married Axel Munthe, the charismatic Swedish doctor and philanthropist. The preservation of the house was left to their youngest son who led a life of extraordinary adventure during the Second World War. Malcolm Munthe's surviving children continue to care for the property.

The gardens are as fascinating as the house, with a series of sculptural "rooms" linked by water and intriguing pathways.

Location: MAP 20:D8, OS Ref. TQ234 706. On S side of Wimbledon Common (B281), opposite Crooked Billet Inn.

Open: Easter Sat–28 Sept: Weds, Sats, Suns & BH Mons. Closed during Wimbledon fortnight last week in June/first week in July. Guided tours on the hour 2, 3 & 4pm. Other times throughout the year by arrangement with the Administrator for groups of 15 or more.

Admission: Adult £6, Child £3 (must be accompanied by an adult), Conc. £4.50, Family £12.

No photography inside house. Unsuitable. Obligatory. Limited. In grounds, on leads.

SOMERSET HOUSE

SOMERSET HOUSE TRUST, SOUTH BUILDING, STRAND, LONDON WC2R 1LA

www.somersethouse.org.uk

Tel: 020 7845 6000 **Fax:** 020 7836 7613 **E-mail:** info@somersethouse.org.uk
Owner: Somerset House Trust **Contact:** Head of Visitor Services and Communications

Somerset House is a spectacular neo-classical building in the heart of London, sitting between the Strand and the River Thames. During summer months a 'grove' of 55 fountains dance in the courtyard, and in winter you can skate on London's favourite ice rink. Somerset House also hosts open-air concerts and films, contemporary art and design exhibitions, family workshops and free guided tours of spaces normally hidden to visitors.

Location: OS Ref. TQ308 809. In the West End of London, overlooking the Thames, by Waterloo Bridge. Entrances on Strand, Embankment and Waterloo Bridge. Underground: Temple, Embankment, Charing Cross, Covent Garden.

Open: Somerset House: Embankment level, 10am–6pm. Edmond J. Safra Fountain Court, 7.30am–11pm. River Terrace & Seamen's Hall, 8am–11pm. Embankment Galleries (during exhibitions): Open daily, 10am–6pm (last admission 5.30pm). The Courtauld Gallery: Open daily, 10am–6pm (last admission 5.30pm). Terrace Rooms (during exhibitions): Open daily, 10am–6pm (last admission 5.30pm). Rizzoli Bookshop at Somerset House: Open daily, 10am–6pm.

Admission: Embankment Galleries: Please see website for details. The Courtauld Gallery: Adults £6, Conc. £4.50, Full-time UK students/under 18s/ES40 holders Free, Mondays 10am–2pm (excl. public holidays) Free.

WC. Tea Room/Cafe. Licensed. Licensed. By arrangement. In grounds.

SUTTON HOUSE

2 & 4 HOMERTON HIGH STREET, HACKNEY, LONDON E9 6JQ

Tel: 020 8986 2264 **E-mail:** suttonhouse@nationaltrust.org.uk
Owner: National Trust **Contact:** The Custodian

A rare example of a Tudor red-brick house, built in 1535 by Sir Ralph Sadleir, Principal Secretary of State for Henry VIII, with 18th century alterations and later additions. Restoration revealed many 16th century details, even in rooms of later periods. Notable features include original linenfold panelling and 17th century wall paintings.

Location: MAP 20:P3, OS Ref. TQ352 851. At the corner of Isabella Road and Homerton High St.

Open: Historic rooms: 25 Jul–31 Aug; Mon, Tue, Wed, 10am–4.30pm. 3 Feb–16 Dec; Thur & Fri, 10am–4.30pm. 5 Feb–18 Dec; Sat & Sun, 12–4.30pm. Café & Shop: 25 Jul–31 Aug; Mon, Tue, Wed, 9am–5pm. 3 Feb–16 Dec; Thur & Fri, 9am–5pm. 5 Feb–18 Dec; Sat & Sun, 12–5pm. Open BH Mons & Good Fri.

Admission: Adult £3, Child £1, Family £6.60. Group £2.70. Free to NT Members.

Second-hand book shop. Ground floor only. WC. None.

TOWER OF LONDON

LONDON EC3N 4AB

www.tower-of-london.org.uk

Tel Information Line: 0844 482 7777 **Email:** groupsandtraveltrade@hrp.org.uk
Venue Hire and Corporate Hospitality: 020 3166 6207
Owner: Historic Royal Palaces

The ancient stones reverberate with dark secrets, priceless jewels glint in fortified vaults and pampered ravens strut the grounds. The Tower of London, founded by William the Conqueror in 1066–7, is Britain's most visited historic site. Despite a grim reputation as a place of torture and death, there are so many more stories to be told about the Tower, where an intriguing cast of characters have played their part. From 2010, Henry VIII: 'Fit For A King' - journey back with Henry through his historic reign at this spectacular exhibition of his armour and weapons brought together for the first time in modern history. Also 'Royal Beasts' an exciting new exhibition at the Tower, recalling its role as a royal menagerie.

Location: MAP 20:P7, OS Ref. TQ336 806, Underground: Tower Hill on Circle/District Line. Docklands Light Railway: Tower Gateway Station. Rail: Fenchurch Street Station and London Bridge Station. Bus: 15, 25, 42, 78, 100, D1, RV1. Riverboat: From Embankment Pier, Westminster or Greenwich to Tower Pier. London Eye to Tower of London Express.

Open: Summer: 1 Mar–31 Oct, Daily, Tues–Sat: 9am–6pm (last admission 5pm), Mons & Suns: 10am–6pm (last admission 5pm). Winter: 1 Nov–28 Feb, Tues–Sat: 9am–5pm, Mons & Suns: 10am–5pm (last admission 4pm). Closed 24–26 Dec and 1 Jan. Buildings close 30 minutes after last admission.

Admission: Telephone Information Line for admission prices: 0844 482 7777. Advance Ticket Sales: 0844 482 7799. Group bookings: 0844 482 7770. Quote Hudson's.

No photography in Jewel House. 020 3166 6311. Partial. WCs. Licensed Licensed Yeoman Warder tours are free and leave front entrance every ½ hr. None for cars. Coach parking nearby. To book 0844 482 7777.

© English Heritage Photo Library

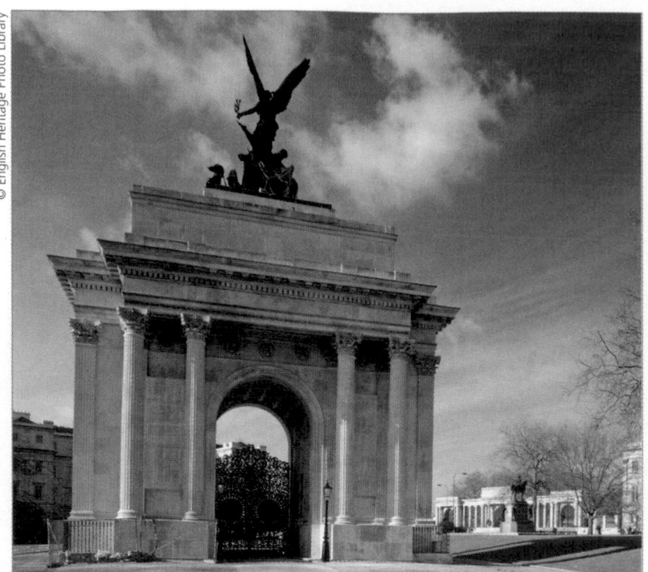

WELLINGTON ARCH

HYDE PARK CORNER, LONDON W1J 7JZ

www.english-heritage.org.uk/wellingtonarch

Tel: 020 7930 2726 **Venue Hire and Hospitality:** 020 7973 3292
E-mail: customers@english-heritage.org.uk
Owner: English Heritage **Contact:** Visitor Operations Team

Set in the heart of Royal London, Wellington Arch is a landmark for Londoners and visitors alike. George IV originally commissioned this massive monument as a grand outer entrance to Buckingham Palace. Visit the balconies just below the spectacular bronze sculpture for glorious views over London.

Location: MAP 20:L8, OS Ref. TQ285 798. Hyde Park Corner Tube Station.

Open: 1 Apr–31 Oct Wed–Sun & Bank Hols 10am–5pm. 1 Nov–31 Mar Wed–Sun 10am–4pm. Closed 24–26 Dec and 1 Jan. Last admission 1/2 hour before closing. The property may close at short notice, please ring in advance for details.

Admission: Adult £3.70, Child £1.90, Conc. £3.10. Groups (11+) 15% discount. Joint ticket available with Apsley House: Adult £7.40, Child £3.70, Conc. £6.30. EH Members free. Opening times and prices are valid until 31st March 2011, after this date details are subject to change please see www.english-heritage.org.uk for the most up-to-date information.

Mondays for groups only.

© English Heritage

THE 'WERNHER COLLECTION' AT RANGER'S HOUSE

CHESTERFIELD WALK, BLACKHEATH, LONDON SE10 8QX

www.english-heritage.org.uk/rangershouse

Tel: 020 8853 0035 **E-mail:** customers@english-heritage.org.uk
Owner: English Heritage **Contact:** House Manager

A truly hidden gem, in South East London's Greenwich Park, Ranger's House is home to the Wernher Collection - a sumptuous arrangement of glittering silver and jewels, paintings and porcelain. A wonderful day out for any art enthusiast, there are nearly 700 works on display.

Location: MAP 4:I2, OS Ref. TQ388 768. N of Shooters Hill Road.

Open: 1 Apr–30 Sep, Mon–Wed, entry by guided tours only at 11.30am and 2.30pm. Pre-booking advisable on 020 8853 0035. 1 Apr–30 Sep, Sun, 11am–5pm. 1 Oct–31 Mar Available for group tours - please call for details. The property may close at short notice, please ring in advance for details.

Admission: Adult £6.00, Child £3.00, Conc. £5.10. EH Members free. Group discount available. Opening times and prices are valid until 31st March 2011, after this date details are subject to change please see www.english-heritage.org.uk for the most up-to-date information.

WC.

THE TOWER BRIDGE EXHIBITION

Tower Bridge, London SE1 2UP
Tel: 0207 403 3761 **Fax:** 020 7357 7935
Owner: Corporation of London **Contact:** Emma Parlow

One of London's most unusual and exciting exhibitions is situated inside Tower Bridge. Enjoy spectacular views from the high level walkways.

Location: MAP 20:P8, OS Ref. TQ337 804. Adjacent to Tower of London, nearest Underground: Tower Hill.

Open: 1 Apr–30 Sep: 10am–5.30pm (last ticket). 1 Oct–31 Mar: 9.30am–5pm (last ticket). Closed 24–26 Dec.

Admission: Adult £7, Child £3, Conc. £5.

© Britainonview

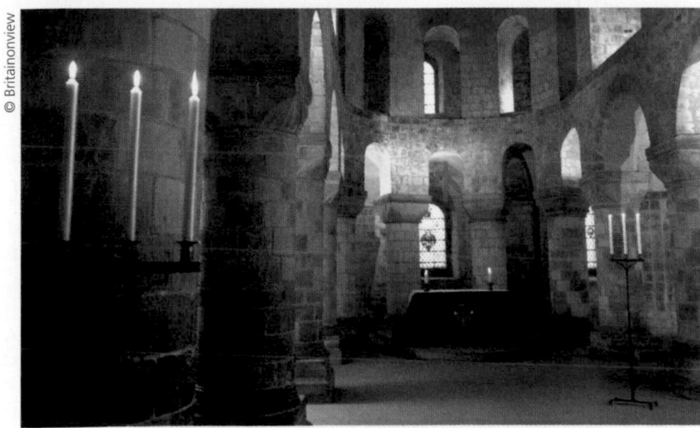

Tower of London

WESTMINSTER CATHEDRAL

Victoria, London SW1P 1QW
Tel: 020 7798 9055 **Fax:** 020 7798 9090 **www.westminstercathedral.org.uk**
Owner: Diocese of Westminster **Contact:** Revd Canon Christopher Tuckwell

The Roman Catholic Cathedral of the Archbishop of Westminster. Spectacular building in the Byzantine style, designed by J F Bentley, opened in 1903, famous for its mosaics, marble and music. Bell Tower viewing gallery has spectacular views across London.

Location: MAP 20:L9, OS Ref. TQ293 791. Off Victoria Street, between Victoria Station and Westminster Abbey.

Open: All year: 7am–7pm. Please telephone for times at Easter & Christmas.

Admission: Free. Tower lift/viewing gallery charge: Adult £5. Family (2+4) £11. Conc. £2.50

Ground floor. Booking required. None. Worksheets & tours. Guide dogs only.

WHITEHALL

1 Malden Road, Cheam SM3 8QD
Tel/Fax: 020 8643 1236 **E-mail:** whitehallcheam@btconnect.com
www.sutton.gov.uk www.friendsofwhitehallcheam.co.uk
Owner: London Borough of Sutton **Contact:** The Curator

A Tudor timber-framed house, c1500 with later additions, in the heart of Cheam Village conservation area. Displays on the history of the house and the people who lived here, plus nearby Nonsuch Palace, Cheam School and William Gilpin (Dr Syntax). Changing exhibition programme and special event days throughout the year. Attractive rear garden features medieval well from c1400. Tearoom features homemade cakes.

Location: MAP 19:C9, OS Ref. TQ242 638. Approx. 2m S of A3 on A2043 just N of junction with A232.

Open: Wed–Fri, 2–5pm; Sat 10am–5pm; Sun & BH Mons, 2–5pm. Tearoom closes 4.30pm.

Admission: Adult £1.60, Child (6-16yrs) 80p, under 5yrs Free. Groups by appt. Free admission to shop and tea room.

Ground floor. Guide dogs only.

West Dean Gardens

South East

Eight counties make up this region. In each you can find world-famous properties such as Windsor Castle, Blenheim Palace and Leeds Castle – and lesser known treasures such as Belmont, Broughton Castle and Great Dixter House and Gardens that give a deeper insight into britain's heritage and history both architectural and horticultural.

Stowe House, Buckinghamshire

Berkshire
Buckinghamshire
Hampshire
Kent
Oxfordshire
Surrey
Sussex
Isle of Wight

Loseley Park, Surrey

Minster Lovell Hall & Dovecote, Oxfordshire

Kingston Bagpuize House, Oxfordshire

■ **Owner**
The Crown Estate

■ **Contact**

The Savill Garden
Wick Lane
Englefield Green
Surrey TW20 0UU

Tel: 01784 435544
Fax: 01784 439746
E-mail: enquiries@theroyallandscape.co.uk

■ **Location**

MAP 3:G2
OS Ref. SU977 706

Sign posted off A30, M25 Junction 13 or M4 Junction 6.

Rail: Windsor Central or Egham.

■ **Opening Times**

Daily.

November–February: 10am–4:30pm.

March–October: 10am–6pm

Closed Christmas Eve and Christmas Day.

■ **Admission**

Nov 10–Feb 11

Adult	£6.00
Child under 6	Free
Child (6–16yrs)	£2.25
Seniors	£5.50
Groups (10+)	£4.95

Groups should pre-book.

Family ticket concessions available. For prices from March 2011, please telephone or email.

Guided tours available at additional cost.

Annual Memberships available from £40.

■ **Special Events**

A brief guide to some of the popular annual highlights:

February–March:
Camellias and daffodils.

April–May:
Azalea and rhododendrons. Easter events and Spring Gardens Week.

June–July:
Rose Garden, Hidden Gardens and the Dry Garden. Celebration of the Rose and Art Week.

August–September:
Herbaceous borders and Golden Jubilee Garden Open Air Theatre.

October–November:
Autumn Wood and The New Zealand Garden.

December–January:
Mahonia National Collection and a packed programme of Christmas festivities in the Savill Building. The Winter Garden.

See our website for updates about our exciting events programme.

The grand Herbaceous Border

THE SAVILL GARDEN

(WINDSOR GREAT PARK, BERKSHIRE)

www.theroyallandscape.co.uk

World-renowned 35 acres of ornamental gardens and woodland, including National Collections and rare international species, The Savill Garden provides a wealth of beauty and interest in all seasons.

Spring in The Savill Garden is heralded by hosts of daffodils, marvellous magnolias and the wonderful perfume of the varieties of rhododendrons and azaleas. Summer brings a contrast of colour, with the vibrancy of the grand Herbaceous Borders and the tranquil, pastel shades of the Golden Jubilee Garden. The glorious displays of autumn in the Garden are a joy to behold, before attention turns to the striking new additions to the Winter Garden.

The Rose Garden is truly an amazing sight with roses specially chosen for their scent and repeat flowering. As you approach, a blanket of highly perfumed scent envelops you along with the sight of 2,500 roses planted in unusual, interlocking crescents of borders. The contemporary design creates an intense sensory experience best enjoyed from the walkway, which appears to float above the Rose Garden.

The Queen Elizabeth Temperate House is another must-see element. The Temperate House provides an ideal environment to grow particularly tender plants, including examples of rhododendrons and mahonias from the National Collections. The Temperate House also showcases original and unusual seasonal plant displays which offer continuous floral interest and vitality throughout the year.

The Savill Building, with its award winning grid-shell roof fabricated from sustainable sources from forests within Windsor Great Park, offers excellent shopping, an art gallery, exhibitions and a restaurant, managed by Leith's. This impressive visitor centre is the gateway to The Royal Landscape and visitors to the Savill Building can also pick up information showing the extensive network of footpaths, picnic areas and cycle paths across The Royal Landscape including Valley Gardens and Virginia Water. Landmarks of The Royal Landscape include the 100ft Totem Pole, the 18th century ornamental waterfall, the Roman Ruins and the Obelisk.

The Savill Garden is open daily (except Christmas Eve and Christmas Day) between 10am and 6pm from March to October and 10am and 4.30pm during November to February. For more information, visit www.theroyallandscape.co.uk or call 01784 435544.

The new Rose Garden

The roof of The Savill Building

Film & photographic shoots.

Plant centre.

Grounds. WC.

Licensed.

For groups, by appointment.

Guide dogs only.

BASILDON PARK

BASILDON PARK, LOWER BASILDON, READING, BERKSHIRE RG8 9NR

www.nationaltrust.org.uk/basildonpark

Tel: 0118 984 3040 **E-mail**: basildonpark@nationaltrust.org.uk

Owner: National Trust **Contact:** The Administrator

This beautiful Palladian mansion stars as 'Netherfield' in the recent feature film adaptation of Jane Austen's classic novel *Pride and Prejudice*. It is an elegant, classical house designed in the 18th century by John Carr of York and set in rolling parkland in the Thames Valley. The house has rich interiors with fine plasterwork, pictures and furniture, and includes an unusual Octagon Room and decorative Shell Room. Basildon Park has connections with the East through its builder and was the home of a wealthy industrialist in the 19th century. Flower gardens, tearoom, shop, 400 acres of parkland with woodland walks.

Location: MAP 3:E2 OS Ref. SU611 782. 2½m NW of Pangbourne, W of A329, 7m from M4/J12.

Open: House: 9 Mar–30 Oct, 11am–5pm plus 1–18 Dec, 11am–3.30pm, daily except Mon & Tue (open BH Mons). Park, Gardens, Tearoom & Shop, as House, 10am-5pm, plus 9 Feb–6 Mar, 10am–3pm & 2 Nov–18 Dec, 11am–3.30pm, daily except Mon & Tue (open BH Mons).

***Admission:** House, Park & Garden: Adult £9.90 Child £5.00 Family £24.80. Groups (15+) by appointment. Free to NT Members. All information correct at time of going to print. *includes a voluntary 10% donation but visitors can choose to pay the standard prices displayed at the property and on the website.

In grounds. By appointment. On leads, in grounds only.

DORNEY COURT

NR WINDSOR, BERKSHIRE SL4 6QP

www.dorneycourt.co.uk

Tel: 01628 604638 **E-mail:** palmer@dorneycourt.co.uk

Owner/Contact: Mrs Peregrine Palmer

Just a few miles from the heart of bustling Windsor lies "one of the finest Tudor Manor Houses in England", Country Life. Grade I listed with the added accolade of being of outstanding architectural and historical importance, the visitor can get a rare insight into the lifestyle of the squirearchy through 550 years, with the Palmer family, who still live there today, owning the house for 450 of these years. The house boasts a magnificent Great Hall, family portraits, oak and lacquer furniture, needlework and panelled rooms. The adjacent 13th century Church of St James, with Norman font and Tudor tower can also be visited, as well as the adjoining Plant Centre in our walled garden where light lunches and full English cream teas are served in a tranquil setting throughout the day. Highly Commended by Country Life – The Nation's Finest Manor House – 2006.

Location: MAP 3:G2, OS Ref. SU926 791. 5 mins off M4/J7, 10mins from Windsor, 2m W of Eton.

Open: May–Jun, Mon–Fri inclusive. Bank holiday Sundays and Mondays in May. 1.30pm with last admissions at 4pm.

Admission: Adult: £7.50, Child (10yrs +) £5. Groups (10+) £6.50 when house is open to public. Private group rates at other times.

Film & photographic shoots. No stiletto heels. Garden centre.

Wedding receptions. Garden centre. Guide dogs only.

DONNINGTON CASTLE ⌗

Newbury, West Berkshire
Tel: 01424 775705 **E-mail:** customers@english-heritage.org.uk
www.english-heritage.org.uk/donningtoncastle
Owner: English Heritage
Built in the late 14th century, the twin-towered gatehouse of this heroic castle survives amid some impressive earthworks.
Location: MAP 3:D2, OS Ref. SU461 692. 1m N of Newbury off B4494.
Open: All year: Any reasonable time (exterior viewing only).
Admission: Free. Opening times and prices are valid until 31st March 2011, after this date details are subject to change please visit www.english-heritage.org.uk for the most up-to-date information.
On leads.

ETON COLLEGE

Windsor, Berkshire SL4 6DW
Tel: 01753 671177 **Fax:** 01753 671029 **www.etoncollege.com**
E-mail: r.hunkin@etoncollege.org.uk
Owner: Provost & Fellows **Contact:** Rebecca Hunkin
Eton College, founded in 1440 by Henry VI, is one of the oldest and best known schools in the country. The original and subsequent historic buildings of the Foundation are a part of the heritage of the British Isles and visitors are invited to experience and share the beauty of the ancient precinct which includes the magnificent College Chapel, a masterpiece of the perpendicular style.
Location: MAP 3:G2, OS Ref. SU967 779. Off M4/J5. Access from Windsor by footbridge only. Vehicle access from Slough 2m N.
Open: Daily during the school's holidays and Wednesdays, Fridays, Saturdays & Sundays during term time between March & early October: Times vary, please check with the Visits Office. Pre-booked groups welcome all year.
Admission: Guided tours only at 14.00hrs & 15.15hrs for interested individuals. Groups by appointment only. Rates vary according to type of tour.
Ground floor. WC. Limited. Guide dogs only.

SAVILL GARDEN

See page 80 for full page entry.

giftaid it Some properties will be operating the Gift Aid on Entry scheme at their admission points. Where the scheme is operating, visitors are offered a choice between paying the standard admission price or paying the 'Gift Aid Admission' which includes a voluntary donation of at least 10%. Gift Aid Admissions enable the charity to reclaim tax on the whole amount paid* - an extra 28% - potentially a very significant boost to property funds. Money raised from paying visitors in this way will go towards restoration projects at the property and will be very welcome.
Where shown, the admission prices are inclusive of the 10% voluntary donation where properties are operating the Gift Aid on Entry scheme, but both the standard admission price and the Gift Aid Admission will be displayed at the property and on their website.

*Gift Aid donations must be supported by a valid Gift Aid declaration and a Gift Aid declaration can only cover donations made by an individual for him/herself or for him/herself and members of his/her family.

SHAW HOUSE

CHURCH ROAD, SHAW, NEWBURY, BERKSHIRE RG14 2DR

www.shawhouse.org.uk

Tel: 01635 279279
E-mail: shawhouse@westberks.gov.uk
Owner: West Berkshire District Council
Built in 1581 by Newbury clothier Thomas Dolman, this fine Elizabethan building was recently restored through a £6million project. The stories and characters from Shaw House's varied past are bought to life in the exhibition. Family friendly 'Wheelie-do' activities throughout the house. Exciting events programme.
Location: MAP 3:D2, OS Ref. SU 47573 68363. Near Newbury.
Open: 12 Feb–31 Mar: Sat & Sun, 11am–4pm. 1 Apr–31 Jul: Sat & Sun, 11am-5pm. 1–31 Aug: Wed–Sun, 11am–5pm. 1 Sept–19 Dec: Sat & Sun, 11am–4pm. And some days in school holidays.
Admission: Adult £3.75, Child £1.90, Conc. £3.00, Family Ticket £9.90. Discounts apply for West Berkshire Residents Card Holders.
Partial. WCs. By arrangement. Limited. Guide dogs only.

WINDSOR CASTLE

Windsor, Berkshire SL4 1NJ
Tel: 020 7766 7304 **E-mail:** bookinginfo@royalcollection.org.uk
Owner: Official Residence of Her Majesty The Queen
Contact: Ticket Sales & Information Office
Windsor Castle, along with Buckingham Palace and the Palace of Holyroodhouse in Edinburgh, it is one of the official residences of Her Majesty The Queen. The magnificent State Rooms are furnished with some of the finest works of art from the Royal Collection.
Location: MAP 3:G2, OS Ref. SU969 770. M4/J6, M3/J3. 20m from central London.
Open: Contact information office.
Admission: Contact information office.

Windsor Castle

CHENIES MANOR HOUSE

www.cheniesmanorhouse.co.uk

Home of the MacLeod Matthews family, this 15th & 16th century Manor House with fortified tower is the original home of the Earls of Bedford, visited by Henry VIII and Elizabeth 1. Elizabeth was a frequent visitor, first coming as an infant in 1534 and as Queen she visited on several occasions, once being for a six week period. The Bedford Mausoleum is in the adjacent Church. The House contains tapestries and furniture mainly of the 16th and 17th centuries, hiding places and a collection of antique dolls. Art Exhibitions are held throughout the season in the newly restored 16th century Pavilion with its unusual cellars. The Manor is surrounded by five acres of enchanting gardens which have been featured in many publications and on television. It is famed for the spring display of tulips. From early June there is a succession of colour in the Tudor Sunken Garden, the White Garden, Herbaceous Borders and Fountain Court. The Physic Garden contains a wide selection of medicinal and culinary herbs.

In the Parterre is an ancient Oak and a complicated Yew Maze while the Kitchen Garden is in Victorian style with unusual vegetables and fruit. Attractive dried and fresh flower arrangements decorate the house.

Winner of the Historic Houses Association and Christie's Garden of the Year 2009 Award.

Delicious home made teas in the Garden Room.

Owners

Mrs E. MacLeod Matthews & Mr C. MacLeod Matthews

Contact

Chenies Manor House
Chenies
Buckinghamshire
WD3 6ER

Tel: 01494 762888
E-mail: macleodmatthews@btinternet.com

Location

MAP 7:D12
OS Ref. TQ016 984

N of A404 between Amersham & Rickmansworth M25–Ext 18, 3m

Opening Times

6 April–27 October, Wed & Thurs and BH Mons, 2–5pm. Last entry to House: 4.15pm.

Admission

House & Garden:

Adult	£6.50
Child	£4.00

Garden only:

Adult	£5.00
Child	£3.00

Groups (20+) by arrangement throughout the year.

Special Events

Bank Holidays, Easter 25 Apr–BH Mon, 2–5pm

Fun for Children, a special Easter Event. The first mention of the distribution of Eggs was at Chenies.

2 May BH Mon 2–5pm

"Tulip Festival", Bloms stunning Tulips throughout the House and Gardens.

30 May, BH Mon, 2–5pm

House & Garden open.

17 Jul Sun 10am–5pm

Famous Plant & Garden Fair (Manor opens from 2pm). Rare & exceptional plants, 70 Specialist Nurseries, Garden Books, Sculpture, Garden Accessories. Refreshments all day.

29 Aug BH Mon 2–5pm

Dahlia Festival.

26 & 27 Oct

Special opening for children Wednesday & Thursday 2–5pm. 'Spooks and Surprises' fun for Children.

■ **Owner**

Stowe House Preservation Trust

■ **Contact**

Visitor Services Manager
Stowe School
Buckingham
MK18 5EH

Tel: 01280 818229
Fax: 01280 818186
House only
E-mail: amcevoy@stowe.co.uk

■ **Location**

MAP 7:C10
OS Ref. SP666 366

From London, M1 to Milton Keynes, 1½ hrs or Banbury 1¼ hrs, 3m NW of Buckingham.

Bus: Buckingham 3m.

Rail: Milton Keynes 15m.

Air: Heathrow 50m.

■ **Opening Times**

House:
Easter & Summer School Holidays.
Wed–Sun 12noon–5pm (last admission 4pm), Guided tour at 2pm & also in term times, please check website or telephone for further details 01280 818166.

■ **Admission**

House (including optional tour)
Check website for admission prices.
www.shpt.org

Open to private groups (15–60 persons), all year round at discounted rates. Please telephone 01280 818229 to pre-book.

Visit both the Landscape Gardens and the House. For Landscape Gardens opening times telephone 01280 822850 or visit www.nationaltrust.org.uk/stowegardens
Joint tickets available.

Conference/Function

ROOM	MAX CAPACITY
Roxburgh Hall	350
Music Room	100
Marble Hall	200
State Dining Rm	200

STOWE HOUSE

www.shpt.org

Stowe owes its pre-eminence to the vision and wealth of two great owners. From 1715 to 1749 Viscount Cobham, one of Marlborough's Generals, continuously improved his estate, calling in the leading designers of the day to lay out the Gardens and commissioning several leading architects – Vanburgh, Gibbs, Kent and Leoni – to decorate them with garden temples. From 1750 to 1779 Earl Temple, his nephew and heir, continued to expand and embellish both the House and Gardens. As the estate was expanded, and political and military intrigues followed, the family eventually fell into debt, resulting in two great sales – 1848 when all the contents were sold and 1922 when the contents and the estate were sold off separately. The House is now part of a major public school, since 1923, and owned by Stowe House Preservation Trust, since 2000. Over the last four years, through the Trust, the House has under gone two phases of a six phase restoration – the North Front and Colonnades, the Central Pavilion and South Portico and the absolutely spectacular Marble Saloon, dating from the 1770s. Around the mansion is one of Britain's most magnificent and complete landscape gardens, taken over from the School by the National Trust in 1989. The Gardens have since undergone a huge, and continuing, restoration programme, and with the House restoration, Stowe is slowly being returned to its 18th century status as one of the most complete neo-classical estates in Europe.

Jerry Hardman-Jones / SHPT

- Indoor swimming pool, sports hall, tennis court, squash courts, astroturf, parkland, cricket pitches and golf course.
- International conferences, private functions, weddings, and prestige exhibitions. Catering on request.
- Visitors may alight at entrance, tel. 01280 818229 for details. Allocated parking. WC. 'Batricars' available (from NT – tel. 01280 818825).
- NT tearooms.
- Morning coffee, lunch and afternoon tea available at the House by pre-arrangement only, for up to 80.
- For parties of 15–60 at group rate. Tour time: house and garden 2½–4½ hrs, house only 1¼ hrs.
- Ample.
- In grounds on leads.
- Civil Wedding Licence.
- Available.
- House open to groups all year, tel for details.
- Please check website for 2011 events: www.stoweevents.co.uk

ASCOTT

Wing, Leighton Buzzard, Buckinghamshire LU7 0PS
Tel: 01296 688242 **Fax:** 01296 681904
Owner: National Trust **Contact:** Resident Agent
Houses fine art collections; extensive varied gardens.
Location: MAP 7:D11, OS Ref. SP891 230. ½ m E of Wing, 2m SW of Leighton Buzzard, on A418.

BOARSTALL DUCK DECOY

Boarstall, Aylesbury, Buckinghamshire HP18 9UX
Tel: 01280 822850
Owner: National Trust **Contact:** Assistant Property Manager – Stowe
17th c decoy in working order.
Location: MAP 7:B11, OS Ref. SP624 151. Midway between Bicester and Thame, 2m W of Brill.

BOARSTALL TOWER

Boarstall, Aylesbury, Buckinghamshire HP18 9UX
Tel: 01280 822850 (Mon–Fri)
Owner: National Trust **Contact:** Assistant Property Manager – Stowe
The stone gatehouse of a fortified house long demolished.
Location: MAP 7:B11, OS Ref. SP624 141. Midway between Bicester and Thame, 2m W of Brill.

BUCKINGHAM CHANTRY CHAPEL

Market Hill, Buckingham
Tel: 01280 822850 (Mon–Fri) **Fax:** 01280 822437
Owner: National Trust **Contact:** Assistant Property Manager – Stowe
15th c chapel now a secondhand book shop.
Location: MAP 7:B10, OS Ref. SP693 340. In narrow lane, NW of Market Hill.

CHENIES MANOR HOUSE

See page 83 for full page entry.

© NTPL

Boarstall Tower

CHILTERN OPEN AIR MUSEUM

Newland Park, Gorelands Lane, Chalfont St Giles, Buckinghamshire HP8 4AB
Tel: 01494 871117 **Fax:** 01494 872774
Owner: Chiltern Open Air Museum Ltd **Contact:** Phil Holbrook
A museum of historic buildings showing their original uses including a blacksmith's forge, stables, barns etc.
Location: MAP 3:G1, OS Ref. TQ011 938. At Newland Park 1½ m E of Chalfont St Giles, 4½ m from Amersham. 3m from M25/J17.
Open: Apr–Oct: daily. Please telephone for details.
Admission: Adult £7.50, Child (5–16yrs) £5, Child under 5yrs Free, OAP £6.50, Family (2+2) £22.20. Groups discount available on request.

© NTPL / Andreas von Einsiedel

© NT / Claydon House

CLAYDON

MIDDLE CLAYDON, NR BUCKINGHAM MK18 2EY

Tel: 01296 730349 **Fax:** 01296 738511 **Infoline:** 01494 755561
E-mail: claydon@nationaltrust.org.uk
Owner: National Trust **Contact:** The House Manager

Home of the Verney family for more than 400 years, the extraordinary interiors of Claydon House, built 1759–69, represent a veritable three-dimensional pattern book of 18th century decorative styles. Outstanding features include lavish wood carving in the Chinese Room and the fine grand staircase. Claydon has strong associations with Florence Nightingale, sister-in-law to Sir Harry Verney. Claydon is set within 21 hectares of unspoilt parkland with far-reaching views. The courtyard contains a second-hand bookshop and craft galleries, as well as a restaurant and tearoom (not NT). The gardens are open to visitors at an additional charge.

Location: MAP 7:C11, OS Ref. SP720 253. In Middle Claydon, 13m NW of Aylesbury, signposted from A413 and A41. 3½ m SW of Winslow.
Open: House: 12 Mar–2 Nov, daily except Thu & Fri (open Good Friday), 11am–5pm, last admission 4.30pm. Grounds, Garden, Bookshop, Church & facilities: As house, 12 noon–5pm.
Admission: Adult £6.65, Child £3.20, Family £16.40. Groups: Adult £6 (£1.50 extra for guided tour) Gardens: Separate charges apply, including NT Members, please call for details.
No photography. No pushchairs. No backpacks. No large bags. Second-hand books, pottery & art gallery. Partial. WCs. Licensed Licensed For groups only, by arrangement. Limited for coaches. In parkland only, on leads. For details visit www.nationaltrust.org.uk.

CLIVEDEN

Taplow, Maidenhead SL6 0JA
Tel: 01628 605069 **Infoline:** 01494 755562 **Fax:** 01628 669461
E-mail: cliveden@nationaltrust.org.uk
www.nationaltrust.org.uk/cliveden
Owner: National Trust **Contact:** Visitor Services Manager

A country retreat on a grand scale, Cliveden's magnificent gardens and breath-taking views over the River Thames have been admired for centuries. The beautiful gardens feature the celebrated parterre, season-long floral displays, distinctive topiary and an outstanding sculpture collection. The recreated yew tree Maze opens in May 2011.

Location: MAP 3:F1, OS Ref. SU915 851. 3m N of Maidenhead, M4/J7 onto A4 or M40/J4 onto A404 to Marlow and follow signs. Train: London Paddington to Burnham (3 miles). Taxi office at station. SatNav postcode SL1 8NS.

Open: Gardens & Shop: 19 Feb–30 Oct, daily 10am–5.30pm; 31 Oct–31 Dec*, daily 10am–4pm. Orangery Café: 19 Feb–30 Oct, daily 10am–5pm; 31 Oct–23 Dec, Sat–Sun, 10am–3.30pm. Coffee Shop: 19 Feb–30 Oct, daily 10am–5pm; 31 Oct–23 Dec, daily, 10am–3.30pm. House: 3 Apr–27 Oct. Thurs & Sun, 3–5.30pm. The house is now a hotel and admission is by timed ticket from the Information Centre only. Woodlands: 1 Jan–18 Feb, daily, 10am–4pm; Sat 19 Feb–30 Oct, daily 10am–5.30pm; 31 Oct–31 Dec*, daily, 10am–4pm. Some areas of the gardens may be closed for private events or when ground conditions are bad. *Estate closed 24–26 Dec. Shop closed 24–31 Dec.

Admission: Gift Aid Admission (standard). Grounds: Adult £9 (£8.15), Child £4.50 (£4.05), Family £22.50 (£20.45), Groups (must book) £7.65. House: Adult £1.50 extra, Child 75p extra.

WCs. Licensed. By arrangement. Limited for coaches. Assistance dogs welcome.

COWPER & NEWTON MUSEUM

Home of Olney's Heritage, Orchard Side, Market Place, Olney MK46 4AJ
Tel: 01234 711516 **E-mail:** cowpernewtonmuseum@btconnect.com
www.cowperandnewtonmuseum.org.uk
Owner: Board of Trustees **Contact:** Mrs A Pickard, House Manager

Once the home of 18th century poet and letter writer William Cowper and now containing furniture, paintings and personal belongings of both Cowper and his ex-slave trader friend, Rev John Newton (author of "Amazing Grace"). Attractions include two peaceful gardens and Cowper's restored summerhouse. Costume gallery, important collection of bobbin lace, and local history displays, from dinosaur bones to WW2. Visit website for our events.

Location: MAP 7:D9, OS Ref. SP890 512. On A509, 6m N of Newport Pagnell, M1/J14.

Open: 1 Mar–23 Dec: Tue–Sat & BH Mons, 10.30am–4.30pm. Closed on Good Fri.

Admission: Adult £4, Conc. £3.25, Child (5–16) £1, Under 5's Free, Family (2+2) £9, Groups (inc. introductory talk) £4.50, Guided Tour £5.50, Refreshments £1.50, Annual Family Membership £26.

No photography. Gardens. By arrangement. Guide dogs only.

FORD END WATERMILL

Station Road, Ivinghoe, Buckinghamshire
Tel: 01296 661997 **Contact:** John Wallis

The Watermill, a listed building, was recorded in 1616 but is probably much older.

Location: MAP 7:D11, OS Ref. SP941 166. 600 metres from Ivinghoe Church along B488 (Station Road) to Leighton Buzzard.

Open: Easter Mon–end Sept: two Suns each month & BHs, 2–5pm. Milling demonstrations some Sundays. Ring for details.

Admission: Adult £2, Child 50p (5–15yrs).

© NTPL / Matthew Antrobus

© NTPL / Andreas von Einsiedel

HUGHENDEN MANOR

HIGH WYCOMBE HP14 4LA

Tel: 01494 755573 **Infoline:** 01494 755565 **Fax:** 01494 474284
E-mail: hughenden@nationaltrust.org.uk
Owner: National Trust **Contact:** The General Manager

Discover the country hideaway and colourful private life of Benjamin Disraeli, the most unlikely Victorian Prime Minister. Follow in his footsteps where he would stroll in his German Forest, relax in his elegant garden, and dine with Queen Victoria in the atmospheric Manor. Uncover the top secret WWII story of Operation Hillside, how unconventional artists painted bombing maps for missions like the Dambusters raid. Experience Sergeant Hadfield's wartime living room. Then get tips for growing your own in our walled garden. Our new 'Fire and Ice' bunker has hands-on activities for all ages.

Location: MAP 3:F1, OS 165 Ref. SU866 955. 1½ m N of High Wycombe on the W side of the A4128. Bus: Arriva 300 High Wycombe to Aylesbury. Rail: High Wycombe train station 2 miles.

Open: Garden, shop & restaurant: 19–28 Feb & 1 Nov–31 Dec, daily, 11am–4pm, 1 Mar–31 Oct, daily, 11am–5.30pm. House: 19–28 Feb & 1 Nov–31 Dec, daily, 11am–3pm, 1 Mar–31 Oct, daily, 12–5pm. Park: Open all year. Admission by timed ticket on Bank Holidays and other busy days. Admission by guided tour only on weekdays during Feb and Nov. Special Christmas opening during December. Closed 25 Dec.

***Admission:** House & Garden: Adult £8.00, Child £4.10, Family £20. Garden only: Adult £3.20, Child £2.20. Park & Woodland Free. Groups: Adult £6.90. £1 off if arriving by public transport. Free to NT Members. *includes a voluntary 10% donation but visitors can choose to pay the standard prices displayed at the property and on the website.

Partial. WCs. Licensed For booked groups. Limited for cars. Guide dogs only.

LONG CRENDON COURTHOUSE

High St, Long Crendon, Buckinghamshire HP18 9AN
Tel: 01280 822850 (Mon–Fri) **E-mail:** stowegarden@nationaltrust.org.uk
Owner: National Trust **Contact:** Assistant Property Manager – Stowe
15th c building with exposed beams and early floorboards.
Location: MAP 7:B11, OS Ref. SP698 091. 3miles N of Thame.

JOHN MILTON'S COTTAGE

21 Deanway, Chalfont St Giles, Buckinghamshire HP8 4JH
Tel: 01494 872313 **E-mail:** info@miltonscottage.org
www.miltonscottage.org
Owner: Milton Cottage Trust **Contact:** Mr E A Dawson, Curator
Grade I listed 16th century cottage where John Milton lived and completed *'Paradise Lost'* and started *'Paradise Regained'*. Four ground floor museum rooms contain important first editions of John Milton's 17th century poetry and prose works. Amongst many unique items on display is the portrait of John Milton by Sir Godfrey Kneller. Well stocked, attractive cottage garden, listed by English Heritage.
Location: MAP 3:G1, OS Ref. SU987 933. 1/2 m W of A413. 3m N of M40/J2. S side of street.
Open: 1 Mar–31 Oct: Tue–Sun, 10am–1pm & 2–6pm (last entry 5pm). Closed Mons (open BH Mons). Coach parking by prior arrangement only.
Admission: Adult £5, under 15s £3, Groups (20+) £4.
Ground floor. Talk followed by free tour.

NETHER WINCHENDON HOUSE

Nether Winchendon, Nr Aylesbury, Buckinghamshire HP18 ODY
Tel: 01844 290101 **Fax:** 01844 290199
www.netherwinchendonhouse.com www.timelessweddingvenues.com
Owner/Contact: Mr Robert Spencer Bernard
Medieval and Tudor manor house. Great Hall. Dining Room with fine 16th century frieze, ceiling and linenfold panelling. Fine furniture and family portraits. Home of Sir Francis Bernard Bt (d1779), the last British Governor of Massachussetts Bay. Continuous family occupation since mid-16th century. House altered in late 18th century in the Strawberry Hill Gothick style. Interesting garden (5 acres) and specimen trees.
Location: MAP 7:C11, OS Ref. SP734 121. 2m N of A418 equidistant between Thame & Aylesbury.
Open: Wed 27 April–Mon 30 May (not Saturdays) 2.30–5.30pm. Tours only at 1/4 to the hour. Mon 29 Aug 2.30–5.30pm. Tours only at 1/4 to the hour.
Admission: Adult £8, OAP £5 (no concessions at weekends or BHs), Child (under 12) Free. HHA free (not on special groups). Parties by prior written agreement: £10 per person and a minimum charge of £300 per group, no concessions.
Please tel in advance. WC. By arrangement. Obligatory.

PITSTONE WINDMILL

Ivinghoe, Buckinghamshire
Tel: 01442 851227 **Group organisers:** 01296 668223 **Fax:** 01442 850000
Owner: National Trust
One of the oldest post mills in Britain restored by volunteers.
Location: MAP 7:D11, OS Ref. SP946 158. 1/2 m S of Ivinghoe, 3m NE of Tring. Just W of B488.

STOWE HOUSE

See page 84 for full page entry.

© NTPL / John Bethell

Cliveden

WADDESDON MANOR

Nr Aylesbury, Buckinghamshire HP18 0JH
Tel: 01296 653211 **Booking & Info:** 01296 653226 **Fax:** 01296 653212
Owner: National Trust
Built 19th c houses superb collection of art treasures.
Location: MAP 7:C11, OS Ref. SP740 169. Between Aylesbury & Bicester, off A41.

© NTPL / Andrew Butler

WEST WYCOMBE PARK

WEST WYCOMBE, HIGH WYCOMBE, BUCKINGHAMSHIRE HP14 3AJ
Tel: 01494 513569
Owner: National Trust **Contact:** The Head Guide
The fine Georgian landscape garden was created by infamous Sir Francis Dashwood, founder of the Dilettanti Society and Hellfire Club. The Palladian villa is among the most theatrical and Italianate in England. Lavishly decorated, it has featured in films and television series, including *Cranford* and *Foyle's War*. Stroll round the beautiful lake, streams and temples. Discover the stories behind the 2nd Baronet's notoriety. Enjoy the sumptuous decor of the Dashwood family home. A breathtaking visit.
Location: MAP 3:F1, OS Ref. SU828 947. At W end of West Wycombe S of the A40. Bus: Arriva 40 High Wycombe - Stokenchurch. Rail: High Wycombe train station 2.5 miles.
Open: House & Grounds: 29 May–31 Aug: daily except Fri & Sat, 2–6pm. Weekday entry by guided tour only every 20 mins (approx), last admission 5.15pm. Grounds only: 3 Apr–26 May: daily except Fri & Sat, 2–6pm.
Admission: Grounds only: Adult £4, Child £2.35. House & Grounds: Adult £8, Child £4, Family £20. Groups £6.60, Child £3.30. Reduced rate when arriving by public transport. Free to NT Members. Groups by arrangement. Note: The West Wycombe Caves and adjacent café are privately owned and NT members must pay admission fees.
Obligatory on weekdays. Limited for coaches. Guide dogs only.

WOTTON HOUSE

Wotton Underwood, Aylesbury, Buckinghamshire HP18 0SB
Tel: 01844 238363 **Fax:** 01844 238380 **E-mail:** david.gladstone@which.net
Owner/Contact: David Gladstone
The Capability Brown Pleasure Grounds at Wotton, currently undergoing restoration, are related to the Stowe gardens, both belonging to the Grenville family when Brown laid out the Wotton grounds between 1750 and 1767. A series of man-made features on the 3 mile circuit include bridges, follies and statues.
Location: MAP 7:B11, OS Ref. 468576, 216168. Either A41 turn off Kingswood, or M40/J7 via Thame. Rail: Haddenham & Thame 6m.
Open: 6 Apr–7 Sept: Weds only, 2–5pm. Also: 25 Apr, 30 May, 2 Jul, 6 Aug, 3 Sept: 2–5pm.
Admission: Adult £6, Child Free, Conc. £3. Groups (max 25).
Obligatory. Limited.

WYCOMBE MUSEUM

Priory Avenue, High Wycombe, Buckinghamshire HP13 6PX
Tel: 01494 421895 **E-mail:** museum@wycombe.gov.uk
Owner: Wycombe District Council **Contact:** Grace Wison
Set in historic Castle Hill House and surrounded by peaceful and attractive gardens.
Location: MAP 3:F1, OS Ref. SU867 933. Signposted off the A404 High Wycombe/Amersham road. The Museum is about 5mins walk from the town centre and railway station.
Open: Mon–Sat, 10am–5pm. Suns, 2–5pm. Closed BHs.
Admission: Free.

Owner
Lord Montagu

Contact
John Montagu Building
Beaulieu
Brockenhurst
Hampshire SO42 7ZN
Tel: 01590 612345
Fax: 01590 612624
E-mail: info@beaulieu.co.uk

Location
MAP 3:C6
OS Ref. SU387 025

M27 to J2, A326, B3054 follow brown signs.

Bus: Local service within the New Forest.

Rail: Stations at Brockenhurst 7m away.

Opening Times
Summer
May–September
Daily, 10am–6pm.

Winter
October–April
Daily, 10am–5pm.

Closed Christmas Day.

Admission
All year

Individual rates upon application.

Groups (15+)
Rates upon application.

Special Events
April 17
Boat Jumble

May 14–15
MotorMart Autojumble

June 4–5
Steam Revival

June 19
Hot Rod & Custom Car Show

June 26
Motorcycle Muster

September 10–11
International Autojumble

October 29
Fireworks Spectacular

All enquiries should be made to our Special Events Booking Office where advance tickets can be purchased. The contact telephone is 01590 612888.

Conference/Function

ROOM	SIZE	MAX CAPACITY
Brabazon (x3)	40' x 40'	85 (x3)
Domus	69' x 27'	150
Theatre		200
Palace House		60
Motor Museum		250

BEAULIEU

www.beaulieu.co.uk

The Beaulieu Estate has been owned by the same family since 1538 and is still the private home of the Montagus. Thomas Wriothesley, who later became the 1st Earl of Southampton, acquired the estate at the time of the Dissolution of the Monasteries when he was Lord Chancellor to Henry VIII.

Palace House, overlooking the Beaulieu River, was once the Great Gatehouse of Beaulieu Abbey with its monastic origins reflected in the fan vaulted ceilings of the 14th century Dining Hall and Lower Drawing Room. The rooms are decorated with furnishings, portraits and treasures collected by past and present generations of the family. Visitors can enjoy the fine gardens or take a riverside walk around the Monks' Mill Pond.

Beaulieu Abbey was founded in 1204 when King John gave the land to the Cistercians and although most of the buildings have now been destroyed, much of the beauty and interest remains. The former Monks' Refectory is now the local parish church and the Domus, which houses an exhibition and video presentation of monastic life, is home to beautiful wall hangings.

Beaulieu also houses the world famous National Motor Museum which traces the story of motoring from 1894 to the present day. 250 vehicles are on display including legendary world record breakers plus veteran, vintage and classic cars and motorcycles.

The modern Beaulieu is very much a family destination with many free and unlimited rides on a transportation theme to be enjoyed, including a mile long, high-level monorail and replica 1912 London open-topped bus.

BEAULIEU ...

Catering and Functions

Beaulieu also offers a comprehensive range of facilities for conferences, company days out, product launches, management training, corporate hospitality, promotions, film locations, exhibitions and outdoor events.

The National Motor Museum is a unique venue for drinks receptions, evening product launches and dinners or the perfect complement to a conference as a relaxing visit.

The charming 13th century Domus hall with its beautiful wooden beams, stone walls and magnificent wall hangings, is the perfect setting for weddings, conferences, dinners, buffets or themed evenings.

Palace House, the ancestral home of Lord Montagu is an exclusive setting for smaller dinners, buffets and receptions. With a welcoming log fire in the winter and the coolness of the courtyard fountain in the summer, it offers a relaxing yet truly 'stately' atmosphere to ensure a memorable experience for your guests whatever the time of year.

A purpose-built theatre, with tiered seating, can accommodate 200 people whilst additional meeting rooms can accommodate from 20 to 200 delegates. Bespoke marquees can also be erected in a charming parkland setting, for any event or occasion. With the nearby Beaulieu River offering waterborne activities and the Beaulieu Estate, with its purpose-built off road course, giving you the opportunity of indulging in a variety of country pursuits and outdoor management training, Beaulieu provides a unique venue for your conference and corporate hospitality needs.

For further information please call 01590 614769/87 or visit www.leithsatbeaulieu.co.uk

Allow 3 hrs or more for visits. Last adm. 40 mins before closing. Helicopter landing point. When visiting Beaulieu arrangements can be made to view the Estate's vineyards. Visits, which can be arranged between Apr–Oct, must be pre-booked at least one week in advance with Beaulieu Estate Office.

Palace House Shop and Kitchen Shop plus Main Reception Shop.

Disabled visitors may be dropped off outside Visitor Reception before parking. WC. Wheelchairs can be provided free of charge in Visitor Reception by prior booking.

The Brabazon restaurant seats 250.

Attendants on duty. Guided tours by prior arrangement for groups.

1,500 cars and 30 coaches. During the season the busy period is from 11.30am to 1.30pm. Coach drivers should sign in at Information Desk. Free admission for coach drivers plus voucher which can be exchanged for food, drink and souvenirs.

Professional staff available to assist in planning of visits. Services include introductory talks, films, guided tours, rôle play and extended projects. In general, educational services incur no additional charges and publications are sold at cost. Information available from Education at Beaulieu, John Montagu Building, Beaulieu, Hants SO42 7ZN.

In grounds, on leads only.

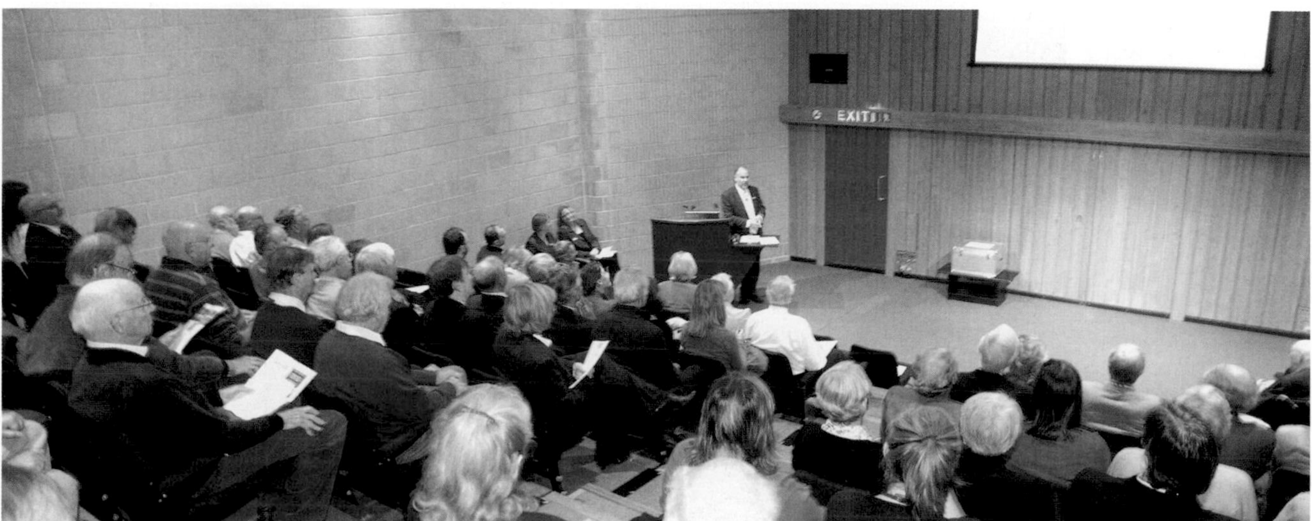

■ **Owner**
The National Museum of the Royal Navy

■ **Contact**
Giles Gould
Portsmouth
Historic Dockyard
HM Naval Base
Admiralty Road
Portsmouth
Hampshire PO1 3LA
Tel: 023 9272 7583
E-mail: giles.gould@nmrn.org.uk

■ **Location**
MAP 3:E6
OS Ref. SU632 002

■ **Opening Times**
Only closed Christmas Eve, Christmas Day and Boxing Day.

■ **Admission**
£19.50 per ticket,
Families £55 (2+2).

■ **Special Events**
Regular events held throughout the year.

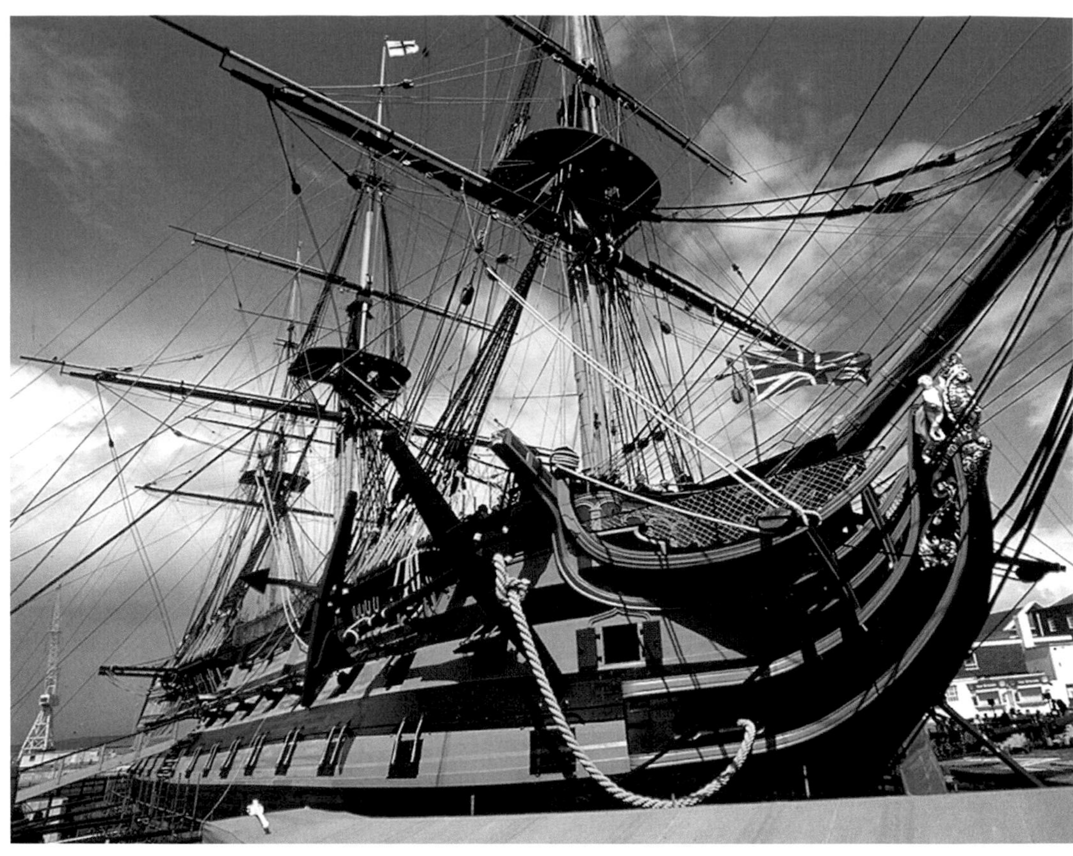

HMS VICTORY

www.hms-victory.com

You are invited to join with the National Museum of the Royal Navy and participate in an exclusive event that very few people have experienced since 1765.

Located in the heart of the Naval Base, and the oldest ship in commission in the world, HMS Victory reflects a heritage and prestige seldom found elsewhere.

HMS Victory is now available for privileged evening hire, and is able to accommodate up to 150 guests in a variety of spaces. The Quarterdeck, or Upper Gun Deck, will accommodate 150 for a reception, the Lower Gun Deck up to 90 for a dinner, and Nelson's Great Cabin up to 20.

Nelson's Great Cabin is the 'Jewel in the Crown' of what HMS Victory has to offer. You can have exclusive access to parts of the ship not open to the public and dine in exactly the spot that Nelson lived, dined and entertained over 200 years ago. This was where Nelson formulated his plans to defeat the French and Spanish fleets, giving rise to 'The Nelson Touch' and on that fateful morning of Monday 21st October 1805 where Nelson composed his famous and inspiring prayer.

The Lower Gun Deck allows guests the chance to dine at mess tables, where in the past the crew of Victory would have eaten their rations, slung between the 32-pounder guns. These were Victory's heaviest guns, each weighing in at 3.75 tons, including their carriage. HMS Victory is also open to visitors at certain times during the year. For full details please see our website.

Partial. WCs.

By arrangement.

No coaches.

Guide dogs only.

THE ABBEY CHURCH OF SS MARY AND ETHELFLAEDA

Church Lane, Romsey, Hants SO51 8EP

Tel: 01794 513125 **Email:** romsey.abbey@lineone.net

Website: www.romseyabbey.org.uk

Owner: Vicar and Church Wardens **Contact:** Debbie, Parish Secretary

This Parish Church is set in the centre of Romsey in peaceful grounds. Romsey Abbey is a magnificent predominantly Norman building with many unique features. Lord Louis Mountbatten is buried in the Abbey.

Location: MAP 3:C5. OS Ref: SU 353 212. M27/J3. Centre of Romsey.

Open: All year 8am–6pm. Times may vary for services and special events.

Admission: Free entry, suggested donations. Entry by ticket for some events, concerts etc.

By arrangement Limited. Coaches dropping off only Guide dogs only Open all year. €

JANE AUSTEN'S HOUSE MUSEUM

CHAWTON, ALTON, HAMPSHIRE GU34 1SD

www.jane-austens-house-museum.org.uk

Tel: 01420 83262 **E-mail:** enquiries@jahmusm.org.uk

Owner: Jane Austen Memorial Trust **Contact:** Ann Channon

17th century house where Jane Austen wrote or revised her six great novels. Contains many items associated with her and her family, documents and letters, first editions of the novels, pictures, portraits and furniture. Recreated Historic kitchen. Pleasant garden, suitable for picnics. Bakehouse with brick oven and wash tub, Jane's donkey carriage. Learning Centre.

Location: MAP 3:E4, OS Ref. SU708 376. Just S of A31, 1m SW of Alton, signposted Chawton.

Open: Jan/mid Feb: Sats & Suns, 10.30am–4.30pm. Mar–end May: daily, 10.30am–4.30pm. June–Aug: daily, 10am–5pm. Sept–end Dec: daily, 10.30am–4.30pm. Closed 25/26 December.

Admission: Fee charged.

Bookshop. Ground floor & grounds. WC. Opposite house. Opposite house. Guide dogs only.

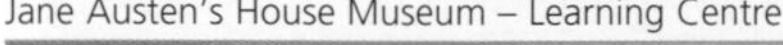

Jane Austen's House Museum – Learning Centre

AVINGTON PARK

WINCHESTER, HAMPSHIRE SO21 1DB

www.avingtonpark.co.uk

Tel: 01962 779260 **E-mail:** enquiries@avingtonpark.co.uk

Owner/Contact: Mrs S L Bullen

Avington Park, where Charles II and George IV both stayed at various times, dates back to the 11th century. The house was enlarged in 1670 by the addition of two wings and a classical Portico surmounted by three statues. The State rooms are magnificently painted and lead onto the unique pair of conservatories flanking the South Lawn. The Georgian church, St. Mary's, is in the grounds.

Avington Park is a privately owned stately home and is a most prestigious venue in peaceful surroundings. It is perfect for any event from seminars, conferences and exhibitions to wedding ceremonies and receptions, dinner dances and private parties. The Conservatories and the Orangery make a delightful location for summer functions, whilst log fires offer a welcome during the winter. Excellent caterers provide for all types of occasion, ranging from breakfasts and light lunches to sumptuous dinners. All bookings at Avington are individually tailor-made and only exclusive use is offered. Several rooms are licensed for Civil wedding ceremonies and a delightful fully-equipped apartment is available for short stays.

Location: MAP 3:D4, OS Ref. SU534 324. 4m NE of Winchester ½m S of B3047 in Itchen Abbas.

Open: May–Sept: Suns & BH Mons plus Mons in Aug, 2.30–5.30pm. Last tour 5pm. Other times by arrangement, coach parties welcome by appointment all year.

Admission: Adult £4.75, Child £2.

Conferences. Partial. WC. Obligatory.

In grounds, on leads. Guide dogs only in house.

BASING HOUSE

Redbridge Lane, Basing, Basingstoke RG24 7HB
Tel: 01256 467294
Owner: Hampshire County Council **Contact:** Alan Turton
Ruins, covering 10 acres, of huge Tudor palace. Recent recreation of Tudor formal garden.
Location: MAP 3:E3, OS Ref. SU665 526. 2m E from Basingstoke town centre. Signposted car parks are about 5 or 10 mins walk from entrance.
Open: Mar–Oct: Daily (closed Fri). 10am–5pm.
Admission: Adult £4.50, Child £3.50, Conc. £4.

BEAULIEU

See pages 88-89 for double page entry.

BISHOP'S WALTHAM PALACE

Bishop's Waltham, Hampshire SO32 1DH
Tel: 01489 892460 **E-mail:** customers@english-heritage.org.uk
www.english-heritage.org.uk/bishopswalthampalace
Owner: English Heritage **Contact:** Visitor Operations Team
The ruins of a medieval palace (with later additions) used by Bishops and senior clergy of Winchester as they travelled through their diocese. Winchester was the richest diocese in England; its properties were grandiose and extravagantly appointed. The ground floor of the Farmhouse is occupied by Bishop's Waltham Town Museum.
Location: MAP 3:D5, OS Ref. SU552 174. In Bishop's Waltham, 5 miles NE from M27/J8.
Open: Grounds: 1 May–30 Sep: Sun–Fri, 10am–5pm. Farmhouse: 1 May-30 Sep: Sat-Sun, 2pm-4pm.
Admission: Free. Opening times and prices are valid until 31st March 2011, after this date details are subject to change please visit www.english-heritage.org.uk for the most up-to-date information.

BROADLANDS

Romsey, Hampshire SO51 9ZD
Tel: 01794 529750 **www.broadlandsestates.co.uk**
Owner: Lord & Lady Brabourne
Broadlands, the historic home of the late Earl Mountbatten of Burma, is undergoing major remedial work over the next two years and will be closed to visitors throughout 2011. Outdoor events continue to be held, please see website for details.

CALSHOT CASTLE

Calshot, Fawley, Hampshire SO4 1BR
Tel: 02380 892023 or 02380 892077 **E-mail:** customers@english-heritage.org.uk
www.english-heritage.org.uk/calshotcastle
Owner: English Heritage **Contact:** Hampshire County Council
Henry VIII built this coastal fort in an excellent position, commanding the sea passage to Southampton. The fort houses an exhibition and recreated pre-World War I barrack room.
Location: MAP 3:D6, OS Ref. SU489 025. On spit 2 miles SE of Fawley off B3053.
Open: 1 Apr–30 Sep, daily 10.30am–4.30pm.
Admission: Adult £2.80, Child £2.00, Conc. £1.80, Family £7.00. EH Members Free. Group discount available. Opening times and prices are valid until 31st March 2011, after this date details are subject to change please visit www.english-heritage.org.uk for the most up-to-date information.
WCs. Partial.

ELING TIDE MILL

The Toll Bridge, Eling, Totton, Southampton, Hampshire SO40 9HF
Tel: 023 8086 9575 **E-mail:** info@elingtidemill.org.uk
Owner: Eling Tide Mill Trust Ltd & New Forest District Council
Contact: Mr David Blackwell-Eaton
Location: MAP 3:C5, OS Ref. SU365 126. 4m W of Southampton. ½m S of the A35.
Open: All year: Wed–Sun and BH Mons, 10am–4pm.
Admission: Adult £3, Child £1.75, Conc £2, Family £8.

© Colin Roberts

© Exbury Gardens

EXBURY GARDENS & STEAM RAILWAY

EXBURY, SOUTHAMPTON, HAMPSHIRE SO45 1AZ

www.exbury.co.uk

Tel: 023 8089 1203 **Fax:** 023 8089 9940
Owner: The Rothschild Family **Contact:** Estate Office
HHA/Christie's *Garden of the Year* 2001. A spectacular 200-acre woodland garden showcasing the world famous Rothschild Collection of rhododendrons, azaleas, magnolias, camellias, rare trees and plants. Enchanting river walk, ponds and cascades. Daffodil Meadow, Rock and Heather Gardens, exotic plantings and herbaceous borders ensure year-round interest. Superb autumn colour, with National Collection of *Nyssa* and *Oxydendrum*. The Steam Railway enchants visitors of all ages, passing through a Summer Garden, and featuring a bridge, tunnel and viaduct. Licensed for Civil weddings in three venues on site. Excellent Restaurant and Tearooms, and open air Tea Garden.

Location: MAP 3:D6, OS Ref. SU425 005. 20 mins Junction 2, M27 west. 11m SE of Totton (A35) via A326 & B3054 & minor road. In New Forest.
Open: 19 Mar–6 Nov: daily, 10am–5pm (dusk in Nov). Please call for details of Santa Steam Specials in December.
Admission: Adult £9, Child (3–15yrs) £2, OAP £8.50, Group £8, Family (2+3) £21; Railway +£3.50, Unlimited rides £4.50. Buggy tours + £3.50/£4. RHS Members Free Mar & Sept.
Licensed. By arrangement. In grounds, on leads. 19 Apr–31 May, The Glory of The Garden; 9 Oct–7 Nov, Festival of Autumn Colour; 1–2 Oct, Steam in the Gardens; 25–31 Oct, Exbury Ghost Train.

Exbury Gardens & Steam Railway

FORT BROCKHURST

Gunner's Way, Gosport, Hampshire PO12 4DS

Tel: 02392 581059 **E-mail:** customers@english-heritage.org.uk

www.english-heritage.org.uk/fortbrockhurst

Owner: English Heritage **Contact:** Visitor Operations Team

This 19th century fort was built to protect Portsmouth. Today it displays extraordinary objects found at sites across the region, including stonework, jewellery, textiles and furniture from various periods. Tours of the fort explain the exciting history of the site and the legend behind the ghostly activity in cell no.3.

Location: MAP 3:E6, OS196, Ref. SU596 020. Off A32, in Gunner's Way, Elson on N side of Gosport.

Open: The fort opens 11am–3pm on the 2nd Sat of every month, 1 Apr–30 Sep. The new Collections Resource Centre will also be open.

Admission: Free. Opening times and prices are valid until 31st March 2011, after this date details are subject to change please visit www.english-heritage.org.uk for the most up-to-date information.

WCs.

FURZEY GARDENS

Minstead, Lyndhurst, Hampshire SO43 7GL

Tel: 023 8081 2464 **Fax:** 023 8081 2297

Owner: Furzey Gardens Charitable Trust **Contact:** Maureen Cole

Informal garden established 1922.

Location: MAP 3:C5, OS Ref. SU273 114. Minstead village ½m N of M27/A31 junction off A337 to Lyndhurst.

Open: Gallery: Mar–Oct: daily, 10am–5pm. Gardens: All year.

Admission: Please contact property for prices.

For **corporate hospitality** venues see our special index at the end of the book.

GILBERT WHITE'S HOUSE & GARDEN & THE OATES COLLECTION

THE WAKES, HIGH STREET, SELBORNE, ALTON GU34 3JH

www.gilbertwhiteshouse.org.uk

Tel: 01420 511275 **E-mail:** info@gilbertwhiteshouse.org.uk

Owner: Oates Memorial Trust **Contact:** Duty Manager

Discover three fascinating stories of explorers of the Natural World… Gilbert White, 18th century naturalist. Explore his house and 25 acres of grounds. Captain Lawrence Oates, who travelled the epic journey to the South Pole in 1911-12 with Captain Scott. Frank Oates, 19th century explorer of Africa and the Americas.

Open: 1–30 Jan, Fri–Sun, 10.30am–4.30pm. 1 Feb–31 Mar, Tue–Sun, 10.30am–4.30pm. 1 Apr–30 Oct, Tue–Sun, 10.30am–5.15pm. 1 Nov–23 Dec, Tue–Sun, 10.30am–4.30pm. Plus BH Mons & Mons throughout Jun, Jul & Aug.

Admission: Adults £7.95, Conc. £6.95, Under 16 £2.50, Under 5 Free, Family Ticket (2 adults + 3 children) £18.50. Pre-booked group of 10 or more £5.95. Garden Only Ticket £5.50.

No photography in house. Partial. By arrangement.

Guide dogs only.

THE GREAT HALL & QUEEN ELEANOR'S GARDEN

CASTLE AVENUE, WINCHESTER SO23 8PJ

www.hants.gov.uk/greathall

Tel: 01962 846476 **Bookings:** Online

Owner: Hampshire County Council **Contact:** Custodian

The only surviving part of Henry III's medieval castle at Winchester, this 13th century hall was the centre of court and government life. The Round Table, closely associated with the legend of King Arthur, has hung here for over 700 years. Queen Eleanor's garden is a faithful representation of the medieval garden visited by Kings and Queens of England.

Location: MAP 3:D4, OS Ref. SU477 295. Central Winchester. SE of Westgate archway.

Open: Daily. Closed 25/26 Dec and for Civic events – see website for details.

Admission: Free. Donations appreciated towards the upkeep of the Great Hall.

By arrangement.

HINTON AMPNER

BRAMDEAN, ALRESFORD, HAMPSHIRE SO24 0LA

www.nationaltrust.org.uk

Tel: 01962 771305 **Fax:** 01962 793101

E-mail: hintonampner@nationaltrust.org.uk

Owner: National Trust **Contact:** The Property Manager

Best known for its fine garden, Hinton Ampner is an elegant country house with an outstanding collection of furniture, paintings and object d'art. House was remodelled after a fire in 1960. The garden is widely acknowledge as a masterpiece of 20th century design with formal and informal planting

Location: MAP 3:E4, OS Ref. SU597 275. M3/J9 follow signs to Petersfield. On A272, 1m W of Bramdean village, 8m E of Winchester.

Open: Garden, Shop & Tearoom: 19 Feb–30 Oct, Sat–Thur, 10am–5pm; 31 Oct–30 Nov, Sat–Wed, 10am–5pm; 3–11 Dec, daily, 11am–4pm. House: 19 Feb–30 Oct, Sat–Thur, 11am–5pm; 31 Oct–30 Nov, Sat–Wed, 11am–5pm; 3–11 Dec, daily, 11am–4pm.

Admission: House & Garden: Adult £8.25, Child (5–16yrs) £4.10 Garden only: Adult £7.00, Child (5–16yrs) £3.50, Free to NT Members. *includes a voluntary 10% donation but visitors can choose to pay the standard prices displayed at the property and on the website.

Special Events: Range of special events in the house and parkland throughout the year. Contact the property or National Trust website for details.

WCs. Licensed. By arrangement. Limited for coaches.

Guide dogs only.

HIGHCLERE CASTLE, GARDENS & EGYPTIAN EXHIBITION

HIGHCLERE CASTLE, NEWBURY, BERKSHIRE RG20 9RN

www.highclerecastle.co.uk

Tel: 01635 253210 24hr Info line: 01635 253204 **Fax:** 01635 255315

E-mail: theoffice@highclerecastle.co.uk

Owner: Earl of Carnarvon **Contact:** The Castle Office

Visit this spectacular Victorian Castle set in a 'Capability Brown' Park. The Gardens include a Monk's Garden, Secret Garden and a new Arboretum. Explore the new Egyptian Exhibition in the Castle Cellars; follow the Path to Discovery; which recreates the finding of Tutankhamun's tomb by Lord Carnarvon and Howard Carter.

Location: MAP 3:D3, OS Ref. SU445 587. M4/J13 – A34 south. M3/J8 – A303 – A34 north. Air: Heathrow M4 45 mins. Rail: Paddington – Newbury 45 mins.

Open: Easter Opening 2011: 17 Apr–3 May, every day. Bank Holiday 2011: Mon–Tue 30–31 May. Summer Opening 2011: 3 Jul–1 Sept, Sun–Thur. Information correct at time of publication but may be subject to change, please check before travelling.

Admission: Castle & Exhibition: Adult: £15, Child: £9, Conc. £13.50, Family (2+3/1+4) £40. Each element available separately; Group Rates available. Grounds & Gardens only; Adult £4, Child £1.

HOUGHTON LODGE GARDENS

STOCKBRIDGE, HAMPSHIRE, SO20 6LQ

www.houghtonlodge.co.uk

Tel: 01264 810502 **Fax:** 01264 810063 **E-mail:** info@houghtonlodge.co.uk

Owner/Contact: Captain & Mrs Martin Busk

A haven of peace above the tranquil beauty of the River Test. Grade II* Gardens with fine trees surround an enchanting and unique example of an 18th Century "Cottage Ornè". Chalk Cob walls enclose traditional Kitchen Garden with espaliers, herbs and heated greenhouses, hydroponicum and orchid collection. Gardens both formal and informal. Popular TV/Film location. For an additional £2.50 enjoy the 14 acres adjoining the garden which provide an experience of the natural world with meadow walks through the peaceful and unspoiled surroundings of the River Test and meet Tom, Dick and Harry, our new Alpacas. Licensed for Civil Weddings.

Location: MAP 3:C4, OS Ref. SU344 332. 1½m S of Stockbridge (A30) on minor road to Houghton village.

Open: 1 Mar–31 Oct, Thu–Tue, 10am–5pm. Weds & House by appointment only.

Admission: Adult £5, Children under 14 Free. Coach Tours and Groups welcome on any day by appointment only – special rates if booked in advance.

Self-service teas & coffees, home-made cakes. Obligatory, by arrangement.

In grounds, on short leads.

Hurst Castle

HMS VICTORY

See page 90 for full page entry.

HURST CASTLE ⌗

Keyhaven, Lymington, Hampshire SO41 0TP
Tel: 01590 642344 **E-mail:** customers@english-heritage.org.uk
www.english-heritage.org.uk/hurstcastle
Owner: English Heritage **Contact:** (Managed by) Hurst Castle Services

This was one of the most sophisticated fortresses built by Henry VIII, and later strengthened in the 19th and 20th centuries, to command the narrow entrance to the Solent. There is an exhibition in the castle, and two huge 38-ton guns form the fort's armaments.

Location: MAP 3:C7, OS196 Ref. SZ318 897. 1½ m walk on shingle spit from Milford-on-Sea.
Open: 1 Apr–30 Sep: daily, 10.30am–5.30pm, 1–31 Oct: daily, 10.30am-4pm.
Admission: Adult £3.60, Child £2.30, Conc. £3.30. EH Members free. Group discount available. Opening times and prices are valid until 31st March 2011, after this date details are subject to change please visit www.english-heritage.org.uk for the most up-to-date information.

WCs. On leads.

MEDIEVAL MERCHANT'S HOUSE ⌗

58 French Street, Southampton, Hampshire SO1 0AT
Tel: 02380 221503 **E-mail:** customers@english-heritage.org.uk
www.english-heritage.org.uk/medievalmerchantshouse
Owner: English Heritage **Contact:** Visitor Operations Team

The life of a prosperous merchant in the Middle Ages is vividly evoked in this recreated, faithfully restored 13th century townhouse.

Location: MAP 3:D5, OS Ref. SU419 112. 58 French Street. ¼m S of Bargate off Castle Way. 150yds SE of Tudor House.
Open: 1 Apr–30 Sep: Sun only, 12 noon–5pm.
Admission: Adult £4, Child £2, Conc. £3.40. EH Members free. Opening times and prices are valid until 31st March 2011, after this date details are subject to change please visit www.english-heritage.org.uk for the most up-to-date information.

Partial. Obligatory.

MOTTISFONT

Mottisfont, Nr Romsey, Hampshire SO51 0LP
Tel: 01794 340757 **Fax:** 01794 341492 **Recorded Message:** 01794 341220
Owner: National Trust **Contact:** General Manager

Historic estate home to Natural Collection of Old Fashioned Roses.

Location: MAP 3:C5, OS185 Ref. SU327 270. Off A3057 Romsey to Stockbridge road, 4½m N of Romsey. Also off B3084 Romsey to Broughton. Station: Dunbridge (U) ¾m.

Beaulieu – Palace House Interior

NETLEY ABBEY

Netley, Southampton, Hampshire SO31 5DG

Tel: 02392 378291 **www.english-heritage.org.uk/netleyabbey**

Owner: English Heritage **Contact:** Portchester Castle

A peaceful and beautiful setting for the extensive ruins of this 13th century Cistercian monastery converted in Tudor times for use as a house. Even in ruins, the abbey continues to be influential, inspiring Romantic writers and poets.

Location: MAP 3:D6, OS Ref. SU453 089. In Netley, 4 miles SE of Southampton, facing Southampton Water.

Open: 1 Apr–30 Sep: daily, 10am–6pm. 1 Oct–31 Mar '11: Sat & Sun, 10am–3pm. Closed 24–26 Dec & 1 Jan.

Admission: Free. Opening times and prices are valid until 31st March 2011, after this date details are subject to change please visit www.english-heritage.org.uk for the most up-to-date information.

NORTHINGTON GRANGE

New Alresford, Hampshire SO24 9TG

Tel: 01424 775705 **E-mail:** customers@english-heritage.org.uk

www.english-heritage.org.uk/northingtongrange

Owner: English Heritage **Contact:** 1066 Battle Abbey

Northington Grange and its landscaped park as you see it today, formed the core of the house as designed by William Wilkins in 1809. It is one of the earliest Greek Revival houses in Europe.

Location: MAP 3:E4, OS 185, SU562 362. 4 miles N of New Alresford off B3046 along farm track – 450 metres.

Open: Exterior only: 1 Apr–31 May: daily, 10am–6pm. 1 Jun–31 Jul: daily 10am–3pm. 1 Aug–30 Sep: daily, 10am–6pm. 1 Oct–31 Mar '11: daily, 10am–4pm. Closes 3pm Jun & Jul for opera evenings. Closed 24–26 Dec & 1 Jan.

Admission: Free. Opening times and prices are valid until 31st March 2011, after this date details are subject to change please visit www.english-heritage.org.uk for the most up-to-date information.

On leads.

PORTCHESTER CASTLE

Portsmouth, Hampshire PO16 9QW

Tel/Fax: 02392 378291 **E-mail:** customers@english-heritage.org.uk

www.english-heritage.org.uk/portchestercastle

Owner: English Heritage **Contact:** Visitor Operations Team

The rallying point of Henry V's expedition to Agincourt and the ruined palace of King Richard II. This grand castle has a history going back nearly 2,000 years and the most complete Roman walls in northern Europe. Exhibition telling the story of the castle and interactive audio tour.

Location: MAP 3:E6, OS196, Ref. SU625 046. On S side of Portchester off A27, M27/J11.

Open: 1 Apr–30 Sept: daily, 10am–6pm. 1 Oct–31 Mar '11: daily, 10am–4pm. Closed 24–26 Dec & 1 Jan.

Admission: Adult £4.50, Child £2.30, Conc. £3.80. Family £11.30. 15% discount for groups (11+). EH Members Free. Opening times and prices are valid until 31st March 2011, after this date details are subject to change please visit www.english-heritage.org.uk for the most up-to-date information.

WCs. Exhibition. On leads.

PORTSMOUTH CATHEDRAL

Portsmouth, Hampshire PO1 2HH

Tel: 023 9282 3300 **Fax:** 023 9229 5480

E-mail: rosemary.fairfax@portsmouthcathedral.org.uk **Contact:** Rosemary Fairfax

Maritime Cathedral founded in 12th century and finally completed in 1991. A member of the ship's crew of Henry VIII's flagship *Mary Rose* is buried in Navy Aisle.

Location: MAP 3:E6, OS Ref. SZ633 994. 1½ m from end of M275. Follow signs to Historic Ship and Old Portsmouth.

Open: Closes after eve service Sun. Open between services Sat & Sun and 10am weekdays. Sun service: 8am, 9.30am, 11am, 6pm. Weekday: 6pm (Choral on Tues and Fris in term time).

Admission: Donation appreciated.

SANDHAM MEMORIAL CHAPEL

Burghclere, Nr Newbury, Hampshire RG20 9JT

Tel/Fax: 01635 278394 **E-mail:** sandham@nationaltrust.org.uk

Owner: National Trust **Contact:** The Custodian

1920s chapel built for artist Stanley Spencer.

Location: MAP 3:D3, OS Ref. SU463 608. 4m S of Newbury, ½m E of A34.

ST AGATHA'S CHURCH

MARKET WAY, PORTSMOUTH PO1 4AD

Tel: 02392 837050

Owner: St Agatha's Trust **Contact:** Fr J Maunder (Tel/Fax: 01329 230330)

A grand Italianate basilica of 1894 enriched with marble, granite and carved stone. The apse contains Britain's largest sgraffito mural, by Heywood Sumner c1901. Fine furnishings, untouched by Vatican II, by Randoll Blacking, Sir Ninian Comper, Sir Walter Tapper, Martin Travers, Norman Shaw and others. Described by Pevsner as containing *"one of Portsmouth's few major works of art"*.

Location: MAP 3:D3, OS Ref. SU640 006. On route for Historic Ships. Near Cascades Centre car park.

Open: All year, Sats, 10am–4pm. Suns, 10am–2pm (High Mass 11am). Jun–Aug, Weds, 10.30am–3pm. Other times by appointment – 01329 230330.

Admission: No charge.

Available for hire – concerts, exhibitions & filming. Has featured in 'Casualty'. Partial. WCs. By arrangement. Limited.

STRATFIELD SAYE HOUSE

STRATFIELD SAYE, HAMPSHIRE RG7 2BZ

www.stratfield-saye.co.uk

Tel: 01256 882882 **Fax:** 01256 881466

Owner: The Duke of Wellington **Contact:** The Administrator

After the Duke of Wellington's victory against Napoleon at the Battle of Waterloo in 1815, the Duke chose Stratfield Saye as his country estate. The house provides a fascinating insight into how the 1st Duke lived and contains many of his possessions. It is still occupied by his descendents and is a family home rather than a museum. Over the last six years there has been an extensive programme of restoration and conservation. Of particular interest are many pieces of fine French furniture, porcelain and some rare examples of Print Rooms.

Location: MAP 3:E2, OS Ref. SU700 615. Equidistant from Reading (M4/J11) & Basingstoke (M3/J6) 1½m W of the A33.

Open: Thur 21–Mon 25 Apr (Easter). Thur 14 Jul–Mon 8 Aug.

Admission: Weekends: Adult £9.50, Child £5, OAP/Student £8.50. Weekdays: Adult £7, Child £4, OAP/Student £6. Groups by arrangement only.

WC. Obligatory. Guide dogs only.

Winchester Cathedral

WINCHESTER CATHEDRAL

1 The Close, Winchester SO23 9LS

Tel: 01962 857225 **Fax:** 01962 857201 **E-mail:** visits@winchester-cathedral.org.uk

www.winchester-cathedral.org.uk

Owner: The Dean and Chapter **Contact:** Group Visits Co-ordinator

Explore more than 1000 years of England's past. Walk in the footsteps of kings, saints, pilgrims, writers and artists in Europe's longest medieval Cathedral. Uncover the secrets of how a diver saved the Cathedral from collapse and learn why Jane Austen came to be buried in the nave. See the Winchester Bible, the finest of all the great 12th century manuscripts, illuminated in gold and lapis lazuli.

Location: MAP 3:D4, OS Ref. SU483 293. Winchester city centre.

Open: Daily 9am–5pm (12.30–3pm Sun). May vary for services.

Admission: Adult £6, Conc. £4.80. Student/Language Schools £3.50.

Licensed. In grounds, on leads. Fairs and markets, concerts and theatre, lectures tours and even an ice rink! See website for details.

TITCHFIELD ABBEY

Titchfield, Southampton, Hampshire PO15 5RA

Tel: 02392 378291 **E-mail:** customers@english-heritage.org.uk

www.english-heritage.org.uk/titchfieldabbey

Owner: English Heritage **Contact:** The Titchfield Abbey Association

Remains of a 13th century abbey overshadowed by the grand Tudor gatehouse. Reputedly some of Shakespeare's plays were performed here for the first time. Under local management of Titchfield Abbey Society.

Location: MAP 3:D6, OS Ref. SU542 067. ½m N of Titchfield off A27.

Open: 1 Apr–30 Sep: daily, 10am–5pm. 1 Oct–31 Mar '11: daily, 10am–4pm. Closed 24–26 Dec & 1 Jan.

Admission: Free. Opening times and prices are valid until 31st March 2011, after this date details are subject to change please visit www.english-heritage.org.uk for the most up-to-date information.

On leads.

©NT/David Watson

WINCHESTER CITY MILL

BRIDGE STREET, WINCHESTER

www.nationaltrust.org.uk/winchestercitymill

Tel/Fax: 01962 870057 **E-mail:** winchestercitymill@nationaltrust.org.uk

Owner: National Trust **Contact:** Anne Aldridge

Spanning the River Itchen and rebuilt in 1744 on an earlier medieval site, this corn mill has a chequered history. The machinery is completely restored making this building an unusual survivor of a working town mill. It has a delightful island garden and impressive mill races roaring through the building.

Location: MAP 3D:4, OS Ref. SU486 293. M3/J9 & 10. City Bridge near King Alfred's statue. 15 min walk from station.

Open: 2 Jan–4 Feb, Fri-Mon, 11am-4pm. 18 Feb–30 Nov, daily, 10am-5pm. 1-23 Dec, daily, 10.30am-4pm. Last Admission half an hour before closing.

Admission: *Gift Aid: Adult £4, Child £2, Family (2+2) £10. NT & H & IOW WLT members Free. * includes a voluntary 10% donation – but visitors can choose to pay the standard prices displayed at the property and on the NT website.

By arrangement. Nearby public car park.

THE VYNE

Sherborne St John, Basingstoke RG24 9HL

Tel: 01256 883858 **Infoline:** 01256 881337 **Fax:** 01256 881720

Owner: National Trust **Contact:** The Property Manager

16th c house gives insight to fads and fashions over five centuries. Full of history.

Location: MAP 3:E3, OS Ref. SU639 576. 4m N of Basingstoke between Bramley & Sherborne St John.

WOLVESEY CASTLE

College Street, Wolvesey, Winchester, Hampshire SO23 8NB

Tel: 02392 378291 **E-mail:** customers@english-heritage.org.uk

www.english-heritage.org.uk/wolveseycastleoldbishopspalace

Owner: English Heritage **Contact:** Portchester Castle

The fortified palace of Wolvesey was the chief residence of the Bishops of Winchester and one of the greatest medieval buildings in England. Wolvesey Castle was frequently visited by medieval and Tudor monarchs and was the scene of the wedding feast of Philip of Spain and Mary Tudor in 1554

Location: MAP 3:D4, OS Ref. SU484 291. ¾m SE of Winchester Cathedral, next to the Bishop's Palace; access from College Street.

Open: 1 Apr–30 Sep: daily, 10am–5pm. 1 Oct-31 Mar: Closed.

Admission: Free. Opening times and prices are valid until 31st March 2011, after this date details are subject to change please visit www.english-heritage.org.uk for the most up-to-date information.

On leads.

For rare and unusual plants visit the **plant sales** index at the end of the book.

■ **Owner**

National Trust

■ **Contact**

The Visitor Services Manager
Chartwell
Mapleton Road
Westerham
Kent TN16 1PS

Tel: 01732 868381
Fax: 01732 868193
E-mail: chartwell@nationaltrust.org.uk

■ **Location**

MAP 19:F11
OS Ref. TQ455 515

2m S of Westerham, forking left off B2026.

Bus: 246 from Bromley South, 401 from Sevenoaks (All services Suns & BHs only). Please check times.

■ **Opening Times**

12 Mar–3 Jul and 31 Aug–30 Oct, Wed–Sun & BHs, 11am–5pm.

5 Jul–23 Aug, Tues–Sun, 11am–5pm.

Last admission at 4.15pm

■ **Winter Opening**

Garden, Shop & Restaurant:
2 Nov–2 Jan 2012, Wed–Sun, 11am–4pm.
Closed 24 & 25 Dec.
Open BH Mons

■ ***Admission**

House, Garden & Studio	
Adult	£11.80
Child	£5.90
Family	£29.50
Pre-booked groups (minimum 15)	
Adult	£9.80
Child	£4.90
Garden & Studio only	
Adult	£5.90
Child	£2.95
Family	£14.75
Winter Gardens	
Adult	£4.50
Child	£2.00

*includes a voluntary donation but visitors can choose to pay the standard prices displayed at the property and on the website.

■ **Special Events**

Including school holiday activities, themed lunches and Christmas Market. Please see www.nationaltrust.org.uk for further details.

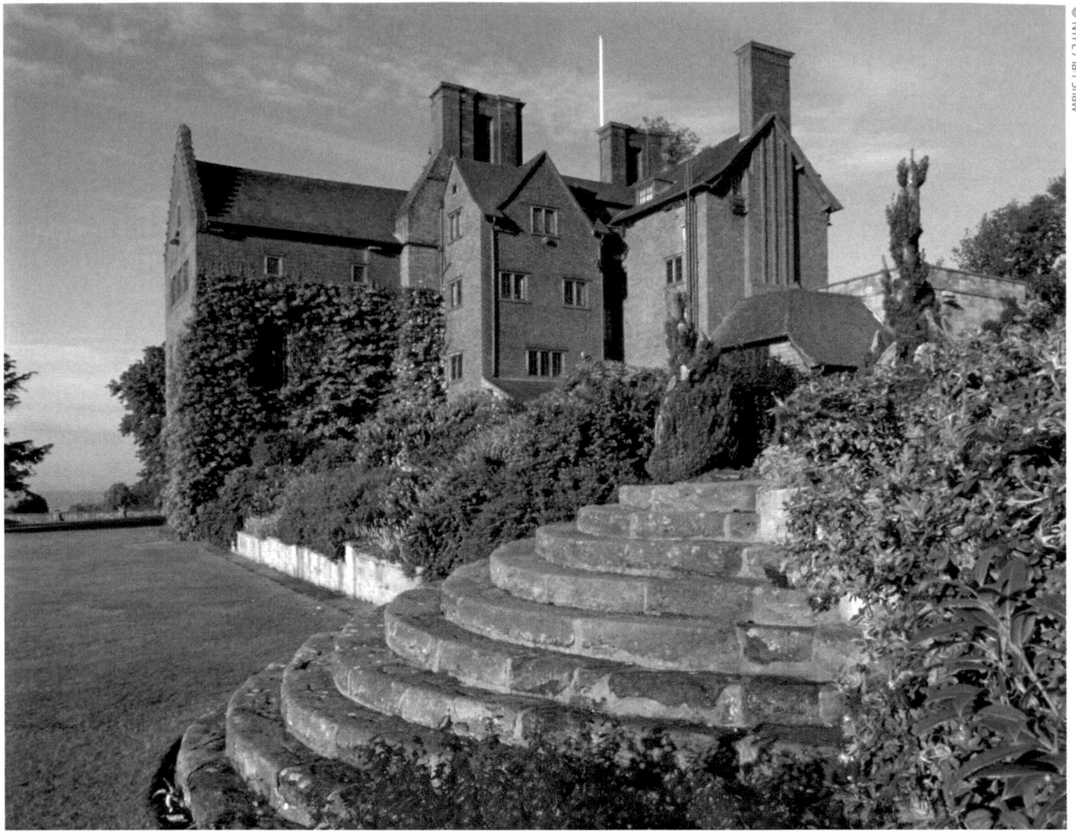

© NTPL / Ian Shaw

CHARTWELL

www.nationaltrust.org.uk/chartwell

The family home of Sir Winston Churchill from 1924 until the end of his life. He said of Chartwell, simply 'I love the place – a day away from Chartwell is a day wasted'. With magnificent views over the Weald of Kent it is not difficult to see why.

The rooms are left as they were in Sir Winston & Lady Churchill's lifetime with daily papers, fresh flowers grown from the garden and his famous cigars. Photographs and books evoke his career, interests and happy family life. Museum and exhibition rooms contain displays, sound recordings and superb collections of memorabilia, including gifts, uniforms and family photographs, and give a unique insight into Sir Winston's political career and personal life.

The garden studio contains Sir Winston's easel and paintbox, as well as many of his paintings. Terraced and water gardens descend to the lake, the gardens also include a golden rose walk, planted by Sir Winston and Lady Churchill's children on the occasion of their golden wedding anniversary, and the Marlborough Pavilion decorated with frescoes depicting the battle of Blenheim. Visitors can see the garden walls that Churchill built with his own hands, as well as the pond stocked with the golden orfe he loved to feed.

The Mulberry Room at the restaurant can be booked for meetings, conferences, lunches and dinners. Please telephone for details.

© NTPL / Andreas von Einsiedel

© NTPL / Ian Shaw

 Conference and function facilities.

 Partial. WCs.

 Licensed.

 By arrangement.

In grounds, on leads.

CHIDDINGSTONE CASTLE

www.chiddingstonecastle.org.uk

Chiddingstone Castle is located in the heart of the beautiful village of Chiddingstone, which dates from 1453. It lies between Sevenoaks and Tunbridge Wells and is conveniently located close to the M25 (Junction 5 – Sevenoaks or Junction 6 – Oxted). We welcome individuals, families and can accommodate pre-booked groups for guided tours (minimum 15 people). There is ample parking available and a beautifully restored Victorian Tearoom for delicious lunches and cream teas.

Set in 35 acres of unspoilt grounds with a growing Japanese theme, including a lake, waterfall, rose garden and woodland, this attractive country house originates from the 1550s when High Street House, as the Castle was known, was home to the Streatfeild family. Several transformations have since taken place and the present building dates back to 1805 when Henry Streatfeild extended and remodelled his ancestral home in the "castle style" which was then fashionable. Rescued from creeping dereliction in 1955 by the gifted antiquary Denys Bower, the Castle became home to his amazing and varied collections. With a genius for discovering masterpieces before they had been recognised, he amassed a stunning collection of Japanese armour, swords and lacquer as well as Egyptian antiquities, Buddhist artefacts, Jacobean manuscripts and paintings. Today, you can still enjoy Denys's eclectic collections as well as exhibitions devoted to both the castle and local history.

Children are encouraged to have a hands-on, fun approach in relation to the Castle's collections in our special craft and activity rooms. We are also proposing creating an exciting adventure playground during 2011 that will be themed to reflect the collections. Throughout the year we run a series of family activity days, such as the Japanese Festival in August and the Victorian and Egyptian days (visit our website for the programme for 2011). Pre-booking for these is not necessary and is included in our normal entrance price, or free to annual Family Pass holders.

- Museum, weddings, business and private functions, scenic gardens and lake, picnics. Fishing available.
- Well stocked gift shop.
- Available for special events. Licensed for Civil Ceremonies. Wedding receptions.
- Partial (grounds unsuitable). WC.
- A delightful tearoom and courtyard for lunches and cream teas.
- By arrangement.
- Ample for cars. Limited for coaches, please book.
- We welcome visits from schools who wish to use the collections in connection with classroom work.
- In grounds, on leads.

- Regular musical concerts – please refer to website for further details.

Owner

The Denys Eyre Bower Bequest, Registered Charitable Trust

Contact

Chiddingstone Castle
Nr Edenbridge
Kent TN8 7AD.

Tel: 01892 870347

E-mail: events@chiddingstonecastle.org.uk

Location

MAP 19:G12
OS Ref. TQ497 452

10m from Tonbridge, Tunbridge Wells and Sevenoaks.
4m Edenbridge.
Accessible from A21 and M25/J5.

London 35m.

Bus: Enquiries: Tunbridge Wells TIC 01892 515675.

Rail: Tonbridge, Tunbridge Wells, Edenbridge then taxi. Penshurst then 2m walk.

Air: Gatwick 15m.

Opening Times

Sunday, Monday, Tuesday, Wednesday & Bank Holidays from Sunday 27 March until Sunday 30 October.

New for 2011: We shall be open on Sundays throughout the winter season, excepting 2 January & 25 December (check the website for any unforeseen alterations to this).

Times: 11am to 5pm.

Last entry to house 4:15pm.

Admission

Adults £7, Children (5-13) £4. Parking and admission to Grounds £2.50 (per vehicle)

Victorian Tea Room and Gift Shop.

■ **Owner**
Cobham Hall

■ **Contact**
Enquiries
Cobham Hall
Cobham
Kent DA12 3BL

Tel: 01474 823371 /01474 825925
Fax: 01474 825906
E-mail: enquiries@cobhamhall.com

■ **Location**
MAP 4:K2
OS Ref. TQ683 689

Situated adjacent to the A2/M2. 1/2m S of A2, 4m W of Strood, 8m E of M25/J2 between Gravesend & Rochester. London 25m, Rochester 5m, Canterbury 30m.

Rail: Ebblesfleet 5.5m, Meopham 3m, Gravesend 5m. Taxi Ranks at all stations.

Air: Gatwick 1hr, Heathrow 1.5hrs, Stansted 1hr.

■ **Opening Times**
Please telephone to confirm or see website: www.cobhamhall.com.

Please note that mid-week opening times are restricted to pre-booked groups only. Pre-booked Parties (10+). The House is open on selected weekends.

House & Shop
House & Garden tours

House: 2–5pm (shop 2–5.30pm). Last tour at 4pm.

Garden
Closes at 6pm.

Cream Teas available 2–5pm.

■ **Admission**

Adult	£5.50
Conc.	£4.50
Self-guided tour of gardens only	£2.50

Historical/Conservation Tour of Grounds
(by arrangement)

Adult	£6.00
Conc.	£5.00

■ **Special Events**
See website: www.cobhamhall.com.

Conference/Function

ROOM	SIZE	MAX CAPACITY
Gilt Hall	41' x 34'	180
Wyatt Dining Room	49' x 23'	135
Oak Dining Rm	24' x 23'	75
Activities Centre	119' x 106'	300

COBHAM HALL

www.cobhamhall.com

Cobham Hall, a beautiful red brick Elizabethan, Jacobean, Carolean style mansion, is set in 150 acres of historic Grade II listed landscaped gardens and parkland and described as "one of the largest, finest and most important houses in Kent".

The renowned Gilt Hall, originally created in the 17th century, features a magnificent gilded plaster ceiling and wall decorations and houses one of the only two remaining working historic 18th century Snetzler Organs. The former seat to the Earls of Darnley, Cobham Hall was used for recuperating Australian Servicemen during the First World War, and was home to the 'Ashes', a personal gift to the cricket playing 8th Earl in 1883.

The gardens were landscaped for the 4th Earl of Darnley by Humphrey Repton and have recently been restored. They include a number of interesting architectural buildings and follies such as an Aviary, Pump House, an Ionic Temple, Repton's Seat built in memory of Humphrey Repton by his sons, and a Gothic Dairy.

The naturalesque gardens are without doubt beautiful throughout the year, and especially during the Spring, when they are clothed with snowdrops, celandines, narcissi and daffodils, including many nationally rare varieties.

Cobham Hall is licensed for Civil Ceremonies and is an ideal venue for weddings, conferences, private functions and large or small corporate events.

The Hall is now an independent boarding and day school for girls, attracting girls from the UK and around the World.

Conferences, business or social functions, 150 acres of parkland for sports, corporate events, open air concerts, sports centre, indoor swimming pool, art studios, music wing, tennis courts, helicopter landing area. Filming and photography. No smoking.

In-house catering team for private, corporate hospitality and wedding receptions. (cap. 120).

In areas. House tour involves 2 staircases, ground floor access for w/chairs.

Cream teas 2–5pm on open days. Other meals by arrangement.

Obligatory guided tours; tour time 1½hrs. Tours also arranged outside standard opening times.

By Agreement.

Ample. Pre-booked coach groups are welcome any time.

Guide dogs only.

18 single and 18 double with bathroom. 22 single and 22 double without bathroom. Dormitory's. Groups only.

DANSON HOUSE

www.dansonhouse.org.uk

In 1995 this Palladian villa by Robert Taylor was deemed the most significant building at risk in London. Following extensive restoration by English Heritage it has been returned to its former Georgian glory.

Completed in 1766, Danson was built for wealthy merchant Sir John Boyd. The house was designed to reflect its original purpose, that of a country house dedicated to entertainment. The sumptuous interior decoration tells stories that reveal the passion of Boyd for his wife and the love they shared.

The principal floor takes in the austere Entrance Hall that would have held Boyd's collection of souvenir sculpture from the Grand Tour. The exquisitely gilded Dining Room presents a set of wall paintings by Charles Pavillon. The octagonal Salon houses the only known portrait of Boyd in an original painting that has been reframed to the design of William Chambers. Chambers also made considerable changes to the house shortly after it was completed. The impressive Library is home to a George England organ, built for the house, and still in working order. Further displays relating to the history of the house and its inhabitants can be found on the bedroom level.

The principal floor is licensed for civil wedding ceremonies and can accommodate up to 65 guests. There is a programme of events throughout the whole year. Please telephone for details. Round off your visit with a light lunch and homemade cakes in the popular Breakfast Room, and indulge in our imaginatively stocked gift shop.

 Two.

 WCs.

 Licensed.

 By prior arrangement. Please telephone 020 8298 6951.

Limited for coaches. Parking here for The Red House see London section (15 mins walk).

For events and functions.

Owner

Bexley Heritage Trust

Contact

Miss Sarah Fosker
c/o Bexley Heritage Trust
Hall Place and Gardens
Bourne Road
Bexley
Kent DA5 1PQ

Tel: 020 8303 6699
Fax: 020 8304 6641
E-mail: info@dansonhouse.org.uk

www.bexleyheritagetrust.org.uk

Location

MAP 19:G8
OS Ref. TQ475 768

Signposted off the A2 and A221 Danson Park, Bexley, 5 minutes London-bound from M25 J/2.

Rail: Bexleyheath (15 min walk).

Bus: B15 bus to Danson Park.

Opening Times

1 Apr–31 Oct Wed, Thur, Sun & BH Mons. Additionally Tues Jun/Jul/Aug
11am–5pm. Last entry 4.15pm.

Pre-booked group guided tours (10+) year-round by arrangement. Please telephone: 020 8298 6951, E-mail: groupbookings@bexleyheritagetrust.org.uk

Admission

Adult	£6.00
Concessions	£5.00
English Heritage Members	£4.50
Child in family group	Free
Pre-arranged guided tours	£6.00 per person (including entry).

Please ring to check times and prices as these may vary.

Owner
English Heritage

Contact
Visitor Operations Team
Down House
Luxted Road
Downe
Kent BR6 7JT

Tel: 01689 859119
Fax: 01689 862755
E-mail: customers@english-heritage.org.uk

Location
MAP 19:F9
OS Ref, TQ431 611

In Luxted Road, Downe, off A21 near Biggin Hill.

Rail: From London Victoria or Charing Cross.

Bus: Orpington (& Bus R8) or Bromley South (& Bus 146). Bus R8 does not run on Sundays or BHs.

Opening Times
1 April–30 June: Wed–Sun & BHs, 11am–5pm.
1 July–31 August: daily, 11am–5pm (grounds open until 6pm).
1–31 October: Wed–Sun, 11am–5pm.
1 November–19 December: Wed–Sun, 11am–4pm.
20 December–31 January: Closed.
1 Feb–31 Mar: Wed–Sun,11am–4pm.

Admission

Adult	£9.30
Child	£4.70
Conc.	£7.90
Family (2+3)	£23.30

EH Members Free.

Groups (11+) 15% discount

Opening times and prices are valid until 31st March 2011, after this date details are subject to change please visit www.english-heritage.org.uk for the most up-to-date information.

Tour leader and coach driver have free entry.

Tearoom and shop on site.

© English Heritage

THE HOME OF CHARLES DARWIN ⌗

www.english-heritage.org.uk/darwin

A visit to the Home of Charles Darwin, Down House, is a fascinating journey of discovery for all the family. It was here that Charles Darwin worked on his scientific theories and wrote his groundbreaking theory, On the Origin of Species by Means of Natural Selection. Down House was also Darwin's home for 40 years and his family's influence can be felt throughout, remaining much as it did when they lived here.

See the armchair in which Darwin wrote his groundbreaking theory of evolution and wander the family rooms on the ground floor. His study is much the same as it was in his lifetime and is filled with belongings that give you an intimate glimpse into both his studies and everyday life.

On the first floor explore an exciting exhibition covering Darwin's life, his scientific work and the controversy it provoked. See manuscript pages from the Origin of the Species, Darwin's hat, microscope and notebooks, and a full scale replica of the cramped cabin he inhabited aboard HMS Beagle.

Outside, enjoy a stroll along the famous Sandwalk, then take time to explore the extensive gardens before sampling the delicious selection of home-made cakes in the tea room.

© English Heritage

© Richard Marsham

 WCs.

 Free.
 Limited.
 In grounds.

DOVER CASTLE

www.english-heritage.org.uk/dovercastle

Explore over 2,000 years of history at Dover Castle! Immerse yourself in the medieval world and royal court of King Henry II as you step inside the recently re-presented Great Tower. Meet the figures central to Henry II's royal court and on special days throughout the year interact with costumed characters as they bring to life the colour and opulence of medieval life.

Also journey deep into the White Cliffs as you tour the maze of Secret Wartime Tunnels. Through sight, sound and smells, re-live the wartime drama of a wounded pilot fighting for his life. From June 2011, discover what life would have been during the dark and dramatic days of the Dunkirk evacuation with exciting new audio-visual experiences.

Above ground, enjoy magnificent views of the White Cliffs from Admiralty Lookout and explore the Fire Command Post, re-created as it would have appeared 90 years ago in the last days of the Great War. Also see a Roman Lighthouse and Anglo-Saxon church, as well as an intriguing network of medieval underground tunnels, fortifications and battlements.

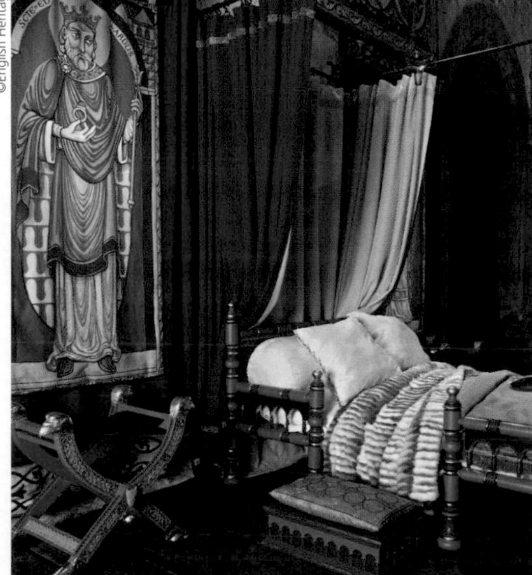

WCs. No flash photography within the Great Tower.

Two.

WCs.

Licensed.

Tour of tunnels: timed ticket system. Last tour 1 hr before closing.

Ample.

Free visits available for schools. Education centre. Pre-booking essential.

On leads.

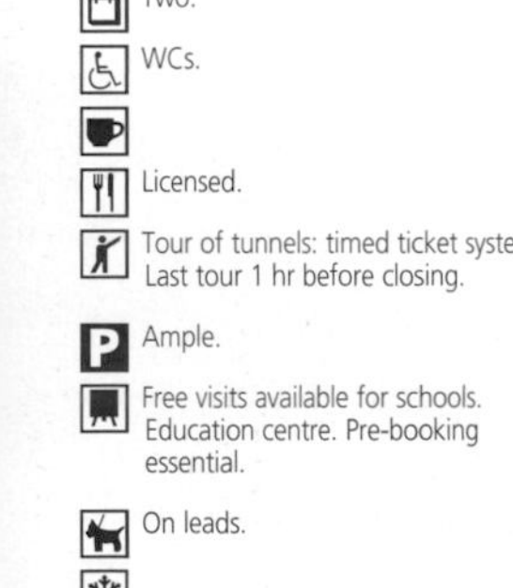

Owner

English Heritage

Contact

Visitor Operations Team
Dover Castle
Dover
Kent CT16 1HU

Tel: 01304 211067
E-mail: customers@english-heritage.org.uk

Location

MAP 4:O4
OS Ref. TR325 419

Easy access from A2 and M20. Well signed from Dover centre and east side of Dover.
2 hrs from central London.

Rail: London St. Pancras Intl (fast train); London Victoria; London Charing Cross.

Bus: 0870 6082608.

Opening Times

Summer

1 April–31 July: daily, 10am–6pm.
1–31 August: daily, 9.30am–6pm.
1–30 September: daily, 10am–6pm.
1–31 October: daily, 10am–5pm.
1 November–31 January 2011: Thur–Mon, 10am–4pm.
1 February–31 March: daily, 10am–4pm.
Closed 24–26 Dec & 1 Jan.
Note: Last admission ½ hr before closing.
Secret Wartime Tunnels tour – timed ticket system in operation; last tour 1 hour before closing.

*Admission

Adult	£13.90
Child	£7.00
Conc.	£11.80
Family (2+3)	£34.80

EH Members Free. Includes Secret Wartime Tunnels tour. Additional charges for members and non-members may apply on event days.

Groups: 15% discount for groups (11+). Free entry for tour leader and coach driver.

Opening times and prices are valid until 31st March 2011, after this date details are subject to change please visit www.english-heritage.org.uk for the most up-to-date information.

From October 2010 to June 2011, parts of the Secret Wartime Tunnels will be closed for the development of an exciting new visitor attraction. Tours of the Underground Hospital will continue to operate during this time. Please call the site for more information.

■ **Owner**

Bexley Heritage Trust

■ **Contact**

Mrs Janet Hearn-Gillham
Hall Place & Gardens
Bourne Road
Bexley
Kent DA5 1PQ

Tel: 01322 526574
Fax: 01322 522921
E-mail: info@hallplace.org.uk

Website www.bexleyheritagetrust.org.uk

■ **Location**

MAP 19:G8
OS Ref. TQ502 743

On the A2 less than 5m from the M25/J2 (London bound).

■ **Opening Times**

House:

January-March - open Wednesday-Sunday

April-November - open seven days a week.

December - open Tuesday-Saturday

Open 10am Monday-Saturday

Open 11am Sunday and Bank Holidays

Closed 4pm 1st November-31st March

Closed 4.45pm 1st April-31st October

(Last entry 30 minutes before closing.)

Visitor Centre:

Open seven days a week all year.

Open Monday-Saturday 10am

Open Sunday and Bank Holidays 11am

Closed 4.15pm 1st November-31st March

Closed 5pm 1st April-31st October

Tea Room last orders 30 minutes before Visitor Centre closes.

House and Visitor Centre closed Christmas Day, Boxing Day and New Year's Day. Christmas Eve and New Year's Eve closed 1pm.

Gardens:

Open throughout the year from 9am until dusk. Nursery shop with plants for sale. Gardens closed Christmas Day and New Year's Day.

■ **Admission**

Free. Charge may apply on special event days. Prearranged guided tours (10+) £6 per person. Please telephone 020.8298.6951, or e-mail groupbookings@bexleyheritagetrust.org.uk.

Please ring to check times and prices as these may vary.

HALL PLACE & GARDENS

www.hallplace.org.uk

A fine Grade I listed country house built in 1537 for Sir John Champneys, a wealthy merchant and former Lord Mayor of London. The house boasts a panelled Tudor Great Hall, overlooked by a minstrel's gallery, and various period rooms. The 17th century additions and improvements by Sir Robert Austen include a vaulted Long Gallery and splendid Great Chamber with a fine plaster ceiling.

Managed by Bexley Heritage Trust, this beautiful estate of 65 hectares stands on the banks of the River Cray at Bexley. Surrounding the house are award winning formal gardens with magnificent topiary, enclosed gardens and inspirational herbaceous borders. In the walled gardens there is a nursery selling plants grown in the Hall Place gardens, and a sub-tropical glasshouse where you can see ripening bananas in mid-winter.

The house has been recently restored and was fully open to the public for the first time in 2009. New displays include an introduction to the house's history, children's gallery of Tudor life, and exhibits from Bexley's extensive museum collection, as well as contemporary art exhibitions. The new visitor centre in the grounds offers a riverside tea room and a gift shop, as well as tourist information.

There is an extensive programme of events, art-based activities, concerts and theatre in the house and gardens. Several rooms are available to hire for meetings and events, including the Great Hall and Great Chamber, which are also licensed for civil wedding ceremonies. Bexley Heritage Trust runs a popular education and outreach service and organized activities during the school holidays.

Parts of the historic estate are occasionally used for filming and private hire. For this reason it is sometimes necessary to close certain areas of the house and gardens. We recommend that you call in advance of your visit before travelling a long distance or to see a particular feature.

House, lift & WC.

Licensed.

By arrangement (10+).

Guide dogs only.

HEVER CASTLE & GARDENS

www.hevercastle.co.uk

Hever Castle dates back to 1270, when the gatehouse, outer walls and the inner moat were first built. 200 years later the Bullen (or Boleyn) family added the comfortable Tudor manor house constructed within the walls. This was the childhood home of Anne Boleyn, Henry VIII's second wife and mother of Elizabeth I. There are many items relating to the Tudors, including two Books of Hours (prayer books) signed and inscribed by Anne Boleyn. The Castle was later given to Henry VIII's fourth wife, Anne of Cleves.

In 1903, the estate was bought by the American millionaire William Waldorf Astor, who became a British subject and the first Lord Astor of Hever. He invested an immense amount of time, money and imagination in restoring the castle and grounds. Master craftsmen were employed and the castle was filled with a fine collection of paintings, furniture and tapestries. The Miniature Model Houses exhibition, a collection of 1/12 scale model houses, room views and gardens, depicts life in English Country Houses.

Gardens

Between 1904–8 over 30 acres of formal gardens were laid out and planted; these have now matured into one of the most beautiful gardens in England. The unique Italian Garden is a four acre walled garden containing a magnificent collection of statuary and sculpture. The glorious Edwardian Gardens include the Rose Garden and Tudor Garden, a traditional yew maze and a 110 metre herbaceous border. There are several water features including a water maze and a 38 acre lake with rowing boats. There is also a Lake Walk, Adventure Play Area, Gift and Garden Shops, and a full calendar of special events throughout the season including Gardening, Jousting Tournaments and Christmas.

- Suitable for filming, conferences, corporate hospitality, weddings, product launches. Outdoor heated pool, tennis court and billiard room. No photography in house.
- Gift, garden & book.
- Exclusive use of Private Residence for Corporate Hospitality, Weddings and Golfing. Restaurants are also available for private functions and weddings.
- Access to gardens, ground floor only (no ramps into Castle), restaurants, gift, garden & book shops, and water maze. Wheelchairs available. WC.
- Two licensed restaurants. Supper provided during open air theatre season. Pre-booked lunches and teas for groups.
- Pre-booked tours in mornings. 21 Feb–24 Dec. Tour time 1 hr. Tours in French, German, Dutch, Italian and Spanish (min 20). Garden tours in English only (min 15). Audio tours.
- Free admission and refreshment voucher for driver and courier. Please book, group rates for 15+.
- Welcome (min 15). Private guided tours available (min 20). 1:6 ratio (up to 8 year olds: 1:10 9yrs+. Free preparatory visits for teachers during opening hours. Please book.
- In grounds, on leads.
- Private Residence.
- Call infoline: 01732 865224.

Owner

Hever Castle Ltd

Contact

Ann Watt
Hever Castle
Hever
Edenbridge
Kent TN8 7NG

Infoline: 01732 865224
Fax: 01732 866796
E-mail: mail@HeverCastle.co.uk

Location

MAP 19:G12
OS Ref. TQ476 450

Exit M25/J5 & J6 M23/J10 30 miles from central London, 1½m S of B2027 at Bough Beech, 3m SE of Edenbridge.

Rail: Hever Station 1m (no taxis), Edenbridge Town 3m (taxis).

Opening Times

21 February–2 January

Main Season
April–October, daily, 10.30am–5pm. Last exit 6pm.

Winter
March, November and December, please see website for details.

Admission

Individual	
Adult	£14.00
Senior	£12.00
Child	£8.00
Family	£36.00
Gardens only	
Adult	£11.50
Senior	£10.00
Child	£7.50
Family	£30.50
Group	
Adult	£11.50
Senior	£10.50
Student	£9.30
Child	£6.40
Gardens only	
Adult	£9.50
Senior	£9.00
Student	£7.90
Child	£6.10

Groups (15+)
Available on request.

Pre-booked private guided tours are available before opening, during season.

Conference/Function

ROOM	SIZE	MAX CAPACITY
Dining Hall	35' x 20'	70
Breakfast Rm	22' x 15'	12
Sitting Rm	24' x 20'	20
Pavilion	96' x 40'	250
Moat Restaurant	25' x 60'	75

■ **Owner**
National Trust

■ **Contact**
Property Manager
Knole
Sevenoaks
Kent TN15 0RP
Tel: 01732 462100
Info: 01732 450608
Fax: 01732 465528
E-mail: knole@nationaltrust.org.uk

■ **Location**
MAP 19:H10
OS Ref. TQ532 543

M25/J5. 25m SE of London. Just off A225 at S end of High Street, Sevenoaks, opposite St Nicholas' Church.

Rail: ½hr from London Charing Cross to Sevenoaks.

Bus: Arriva 402 Tunbridge Wells–Bromley North.

■ **Opening Times**
House:

12 March–30 October, Wed–Sun, inc Bank Hol Mons, 12pm–4pm.

Shop, Tearoom, Visitor Centre, Orangery & Courtyards:

1–11 March, Sat & Sun, 11am–4pm.

12 March–4 April, Wed–Sun, inc Bank Hol Mons, 10.30am–5pm.

5 April–2 October, Tues–Sun, inc Bank Hol Mons, 10.30am–5pm

3–30 October, Wed–Sun, inc Bank Hol Mons, 10.30am–5pm

Garden
5 April–27 September, Tuesdays only, 11am–4pm.

Last admission to house and garden is 30 mins before closing.

Christmas Shop, Tearoom & Courtyards:
2 Nov–23 Dec, Wed to Sun, 11am–4pm.

Park
Deer park has pedestrian access all year round.

■ ***Admission**

House	
Adult	£11.50
Child	£5.75
Family	£28.75
Groups (pre-booked 15+)	
Adult	£9.75
Garden	
Adult	£5.00
Child	£2.50
NT members Free.	
Parking	£5.00 per car
Park Free to pedestrians	

*includes a voluntary Gift Aid donation but visitors can choose to pay the standard prices displayed at the property and on the website.

■ **Special Events**
Please telephone or visit website for details.

© NTPL / Robert Truman

KNOLE

www.nationaltrust.org.uk/knole

Knole has been showing off to visitors for five centuries. It has fascinating links with Kings, Queens and the nobility, as well as literary links with Vita Sackville-West and Virginia Woolfe. Thirteen superb state-rooms are laid out much as they were in the 18th century to impress visitors by the wealth and status of the Sackville family, who continue to live at Knole. The house includes Royal Stuart furniture, paintings by Gainsborough, Van Dyck and Reynolds as well as many 17th century tapestries.

Knole is set at the heart of the only remaining medieval deer park in Kent, where Sika and Fallow deer roam freely amongst ancient oak, beech and chestnut trees.

Relax in the original Brew House with a cup of tea or enjoy a delicious lunch before browsing through the well-stocked shop full of local produce, exquisite gifts and its large collection of books. Visit the recently opened orangery, sit back, relax and look out over Lord Sackville's garden. Visitors can 'dip' into the Knole story in the new and innovative visitor centre. There is an extraordinary 3D model of the house as well as a comprehensive timeline, interactive interpretation and video room with its fascinating account of Knole's successive ownership.

Visit on a Tuesday between April and September and enjoy a leisurely stroll through Lord Sackville's private garden. The garden provides the most beautiful view of the house and allows visitors to observe the outside of the Orangery and the Chapel.

© NT / Knole / Melissa Hirst

© NTPL / Horst Kolo

Amateur outdoor photography welcomed.

Full range of NT goods and souvenirs of Knole.

Partial, WCs.

Licensed.

Guided tours for pre-booked groups, by arrangement. Short guides to the house available in French, Dutch & German.

Limited coach parking available.

Welcome. Contact Education Officer.

Guide dogs only.

Park open all year to pedestrians.

LEEDS CASTLE

www.leeds-castle.com

Set in 500 acres of beautiful parkland and gardens, Leeds Castle is one of the country's finest historic properties and is also one of the Treasure Houses of England.

A Norman fortress and a royal palace to the medieval and Tudor Kings and Queens of England, the development of Leeds Castle continued well into the 20th century. The last private owner, the Hon Olive, Lady Baillie, bought the castle in 1926, restored the castle and furnished its beautiful interiors.

The castle has a fine collection of paintings, tapestries and antiques and is also home to an unusual dog collar museum.

The park and grounds include the colourful and quintessentially English Culpeper Garden, the delightful Wood Garden, and the terraced Lady Baillie Garden with its views over the tranquil Great Water. Visit the Aviary, which houses approximately 100 rare and endangered species from around the world or get lost in the twist and turns of the yew Maze with its secret underground grotto. The Knights' Realm playground delights younger visitors and the 'World of Wings' free flying bird displays are a spectacular sight.

A highly popular and successful programme of special events is arranged throughout the year, details of which can be found on the website.

Residential conferences, exhibitions, sporting days, clay shooting off site, laser shooting, falconry, field archery, golf, croquet and helipad. Talks can be arranged for horticultural, viticultural, historical and cultural groups.

Corporate hospitality, large scale marquee events, wedding receptions, buffets and dinners.

Partial. WCs.

Licensed.

Licensed.

Guides in rooms. French, Spanish, Dutch and German speaking guides.

For hire in English, French, Spanish, German and Japanese.

Free parking.

Workshops, outside normal opening hours, private tours. Teacher's resource pack and worksheets.

Guide dogs only.

€

Owner

Leeds Castle Foundation

Contact

Leeds Castle
Maidstone
Kent ME17 1PL

Tel: 01622 765400
Fax: 01622 735616
E-mail: enquiries@leeds-castle.co.uk

Location

MAP 4:L3
OS Ref. TQ835 533

From London to A20/M20/J8, 40m, 1 hr. 7m E of Maidstone, ¼m S of A20.

Rail: South Eastern Trains available, London–Bearsted.

Opening Times

Summer
1 April–30 September
Daily, 10am–4.30pm (last adm).

Winter
1 October–31 March
Daily, 10am–3pm (last adm).

Castle & Grounds
Closed 16 July, 5 and 6 November and 25 December 2011.
Always check our website for up to date opening times before your visit.

Admission

Castle, Park & Gardens
Individuals (valid 1 year)*

Adult	£17.50
Child (4–15yrs)	£10.00
OAP/Student	£15.00
Visitor with disabilities (1 carer Free)	£15.00

Group 15+*

Adult	£12.00
Child (4–15yrs)	£8.50
OAP/Student	£11.50
Visitor with disabilities (1 carer Free)	£11.50

*2010 prices, subject to change.

A guidebook is published in English, French, Spanish, Italian and Japanese.

Please check website prior to your visit.

Special Events

A programme of special events are held throughout the year, please visit www.leeds-castle.com/events

Conference/Function

ROOM	SIZE	MAX CAPACITY
Fairfax Hall	19.8 x 6.7m	180
Gatehouse	9.8 x 5.2m	50
Terrace	8.9 x 15.4m	80
Castle Boardroom	9.7 x 4.8m	30
Castle Dining Rm	13.1 x 6.6m	70
Maiden's Tower	8 x 9m	120

■ **Owner**

Viscount De L'Isle

■ **Contact**

Penshurst Place
Penshurst
Nr Tonbridge
Kent TN11 8DG

Tel: 01892 870307
Fax: 01892 870866
E-mail: enquiries@penshurstplace.com

■ **Location**

MAP 19:H12
OS Ref. TQ527 438

From London M25/J5 then A21 to Hildenborough, B2027 via Leigh; from Tunbridge Wells A26, B2176.

Bus: Arriva 231, 233 from Tunbridge Wells and Edenbridge.

Rail: Charing Cross/ Waterloo–Hildenborough, Tonbridge or Tunbridge Wells; then bus or taxi.

■ **Opening Times**

19 Feb–27 Mar:
Sats & Suns only, 10.30am-4.30pm.

28 March–30 October, Daily, 10.30am-6pm.

House
Daily, 12 noon–4pm.

Grounds
Daily, 10.30am–6pm.
Last entry 5pm.

Shop
Open all year.

Winter
Open to Groups by appointment only (see Guided Tours).

■ **Admission Prices**

House & Gardens

Adult	£9.80
Child*	£6.20
Family (2+2)	£26.00
Groups (pre-booked 15+)	
Adult	£7.50
Child	£4.50

Garden only

Adult	£7.80
Child*	£5.80
Family (2+2)	£23.00

Garden Season Ticket £41.00

Garden Family Season Ticket (2+2), additional child £6.50 each. £67.00

House Tours (pre-booked 15+)

Adult	£9.50
Child	£5.00

Garden Tours (pre-booked 15+)

Adult	£9.50
Child	£5.00

House & Garden Tours

Adult	£15.00
Child (5–16 yrs)	£9.00

*under 5s Free.

■ **Special Events**

Weald of Kent Craft Show First May Bank Holiday and Second weekend in September Friday–Sunday.
Glorious Gardens Week First week in June.

Conference/Function

ROOM	SIZE	MAX CAPACITY
Sunderland Room	45' x 18'	100
Baron's Hall	64' x 39'	250
Buttery	20' x 23'	50

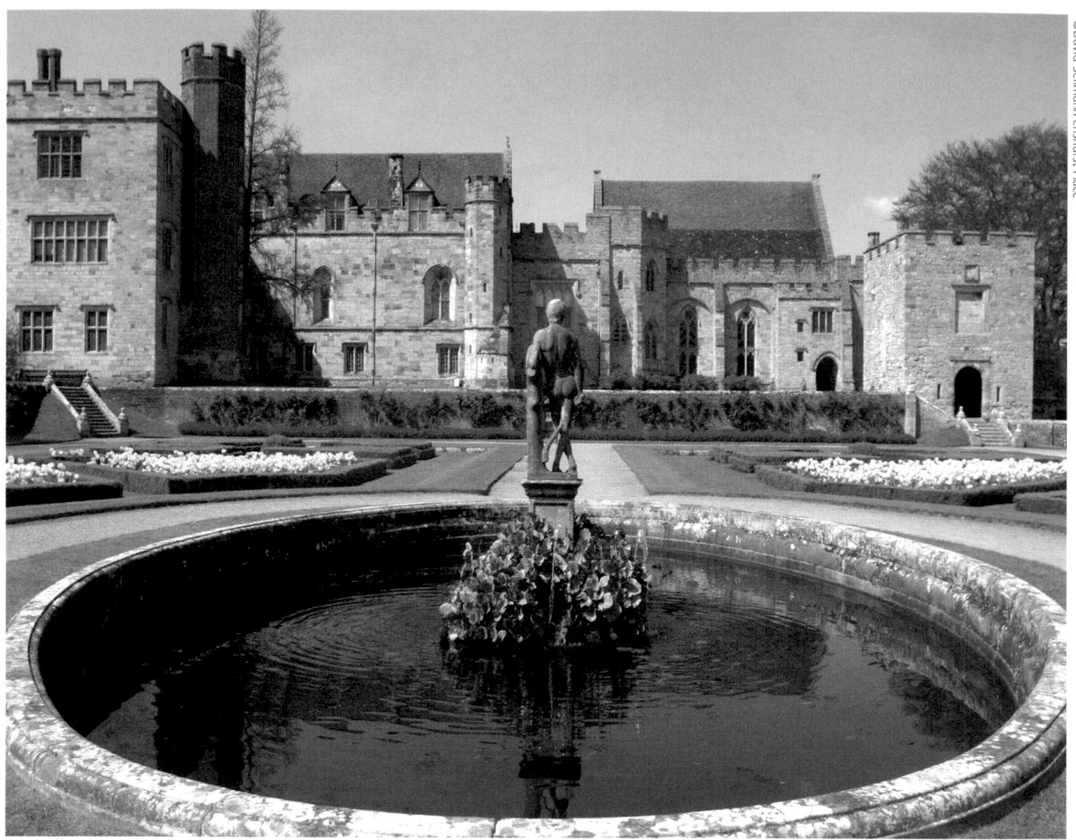

©David Sellman/Penshurst Place

PENSHURST PLACE & GARDENS

www.penshurstplace.com

Penshurst Place is one of England's greatest family-owned historic houses with a history going back six and a half centuries.

In some ways time has stood still at Penshurst; the great House is still very much a medieval building with improvements and additions made over the centuries but without any substantial rebuilding. Its highlight is undoubtedly the medieval Barons Hall, built in 1341, with its impressive 60ft-high chestnut-beamed roof.

A marvellous mix of paintings, tapestries and furniture from the 15th, 16th and 17th centuries can be seen throughout the House, including the helm carried in the state funeral procession to St Paul's Cathedral for the Elizabethan courtier and poet, Sir Philip Sidney, in 1587. This is now the family crest.

Gardens

The Gardens, first laid out in the 14th century, have been developed over successive years by the Sidney family who first came to Penshurst in 1552. A twenty-year restoration and re-planting programme under-taken by the 1st Viscount De L'Isle has ensured that they retain their historic splendour. He is commemorated with an Arboretum, planted in 1991. The gardens are divided by a mile of yew hedges into "rooms", each planted to give a succession of colour as the seasons change, with a major restoration project taking place on the Victorian double Herbaceous border 2009–11. There is also a Venture Playground, Woodland Trail, Toy Museum and a Gift Shop.

A variety of events in the park and grounds take place throughout the season.

Adventure playground & parkland & riverside walks. Wedding ceremonies and receptions, product launches, garden parties, photography, filming, fashion shows, receptions, archery, clay pigeon shooting, falconry, parkland for hire. Conference facilities. No photography in house.

Private banqueting, wedding receptions.

Partial. WCs.

Licensed.

Guided tours of House available by arrangement before the House opens to the public. Garden tours available 10.30am–4.30pm. Pre-booked freeflow (non-guided) visits available throughout opening hours.

Ample. Double decker buses to park from village.

All year by appointment, discount rates, education room and teachers' packs.

Guide dogs only.

POWELL-COTTON MUSEUM, QUEX HOUSE & GARDENS

www.quexpark.co.uk

The Powell-Cotton Museum at Quex Park was established in 1896 by Major Percy Horace Gordon Powell-Cotton (1866 -1940) to house natural history specimens and cultural objects collected on expeditions to Asia and Africa.

Major Powell-Cotton was a pioneer in the use of the diorama to display mounted mammals in representations of their natural habitats. The Powell-Cotton Museum natural history dioramas are outstanding examples, unique to the UK, stunning for their size, quality and imagery. Today they still excite the imagination of young and old alike.

The world-class natural history and ethnographical collections at the Museum support the study, understanding and simple enjoyment of the zoological, cultural and ecological diversity of Africa and the Indian sub-continent.

The 15th century Quex Estate was purchased by the financier John Powell in 1777 and the Regency-period Quex House was completed by his nephew in 1813. The house was remodelled and extended in the late 19th century. The beautiful gardens to be seen today were developed in Victorian times.

The Hannah Dining Suite caters as a fine dining, a la carte restaurant, serving home made dishes, using fresh local produce grown on Quex and surrounding areas. Visitors can enjoy lunch from a range of menus and can also take afternoon tea, The Hannah Dining Suite also specialises in catering for all corporate events, from team building and seminars to party's and weddings.

Also on site at Quex Park: the Quex Falconry, Quex Craft Village, Jungle Jims Indoor and Outdoor family entertainment centre, The Secret Garden Centre, Quex Maize Maze (summer only) and Quex Barn Farmshop and Restaurant.

Special Events

Events program throughout the year including outdoor concerts with internationally renowned artists, country fairs, Victorian themed events, children's storytelling, outdoor theatre, craft fayres, firework displays and seasonal events.

Please see our website for details: www.quexpark.co.uk

- Website available in French.
- Gift Shop and Craft Village on site.
- Plants grown in our Victorian greenhouses available for sale. Garden Centre with locally grown plants, shrubs and trees also on site.
- Residential conferences, sporting days, laser clay & pigeon shoots, falconry, field archery, croquet, helicopter pad. Talks can be arranged for horticultural, conservation, historical and cultural groups.
- Good Disabled Access.
- Light lunch, snack menu, traditional tea menu with home-made cakes. Picnics permitted in the gardens and picnic hampers available to order.
- Fine Dining for lunch and dinner (booking essential: 01843 844305). Fully Licensed. Restaurant also available for private functions, corporate hospitality and weddings. Groups welcome (seated capacity up to 100).
- Booking essential: 01843 842168.
- Free parking for coaches and cars.
- Workshops, School Visits and Tours. Teachers resource pack and worksheets available.
- Planned for 2011: Unique African Village, 4* self-catering Rondavels (room service available on request) For general enquiries please phone: 01843 482004.
- The Hall of Quex House offers a traditional setting for your Civil Wedding Ceremony, oak panelling, antique furniture and a magnificent carved staircase for the bride to make her entrance. One of our period rooms is available for the bride prior to the ceremony. Please see www.thehannahdiningsuite.co.uk for details.

Owner

Trustees of the Powell-Cotton Museum, Quex House & Gardens

Contact

Malcolm Harman,
Curator
Quex Park
Birchington
Kent CT7 0BH

Tel: 01843 842168
E-mail: enquiries@quexmuseum.org

Location

MAP 4:N2
OS Ref. TR308 683

½m from Birchington Church via Park Lane.

Opening Times

1 April–30 October 2011 (and February half term).

The Museum, Gardens, Restaurant & Tearooms
Tuesday–Sunday, 11am–5pm.

Quex House
2–4.30pm.

Winter Season
1 November–end March 2012

The Museum, Gardens, Restaurant & Tearooms
Sundays only, 1–3.30pm.

Quex House is closed through the winter season.

The Museum is open to schools and groups throughout the year.

Admission Prices

Museum, House & Gardens

Adults	£7.00
Seniors & Children up to 16 years	£5.00
Students	£4.00
Family (2+3)	£20.00
Carers for Disabled	Free
Under 5	Free

Gardens only

Adults	£2.00
Seniors & Children up to 16 years	£1.50
Students	£1.50
Carers for Disabled	Free
Under 5	Free

Groups of 20 or more

Adults	£6.00
Seniors & Children up to 16 years	£4.50

General introductory talk £25. Full guided tour £60.

Groups of 20 or more (outside normal hours)

Adults	£8.50
Seniors & Children up to 16 years	£6.50

Full guided tour £70.

(groups of 40 or more will be split and charged accordingly).

Winter Season

Museum

Adults	£5.00
Seniors & Children up to 16 years	£4.00
Students	£3.00
Family (2+3)	£14.00
Carers for Disabled	Free
Under 5	Free

Gardens only

Adults	£1.50
Seniors & Children up to 16 years	£1.00
Students	£1.00
Carers for Disabled	Free
Under 5	Free

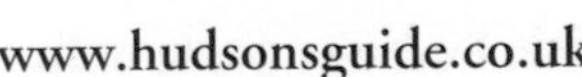

■ **Owner**
John St A Warde Esq

■ **Contact**
Mrs P A White
Administrator
Squerryes Court
Westerham
Kent TN16 1SJ
Tel: 01959 562345
Fax: 01959 565949
E-mail: enquiries
@squerryes.co.uk

■ **Location**
MAP 19:F11
OS Ref. TQ440 535

10 min from M25/J5 or 6 Off A25, ½m W from centre of Westerham

London 1–1½ hrs.

Rail: Oxted Station 4m. Sevenoaks 6m.

Air: Gatwick, 30 mins.

■ **Opening Times**

Summer
1 April–30 September, Wed, Sun & BH Mons, 12.30–5.00pm.
Last admission 4.30pm

Grounds
11.30am–5pm
Last admission 4.30pm.

NB. Pre-booked groups welcome any day except Saturday.

Winter
October–31 March
Closed.

■ **Admission**

House & Garden

Adult	£7.50
Child (under 16yrs)	£4.00
Senior	£7.00
Family (2+2)	£16.00

Groups (20+ booked)

Adult	£6.50
Child (under 16yrs)	£4.00

Wine Tasting Groups
(inc. House & Garden)

Adult	£9.50

New Exhibition
Edwardian Squerryes & Westerham
Please see website for details.

Garden only

Adult	£5.00
Child (under 16yrs)	£2.50
Senior	£4.50
Family (2+2)	£9.50

Groups (20+ booked)

Adult	£4.50
Child (under 16yrs)	£3.00

Conference/Function

ROOM	SIZE	MAX CAPACITY
Hall	32' x 32'	70
Green Dining Room	20' x 25' 6"	50

SQUERRYES COURT

www.squerryes.co.uk

Squerryes Court is a beautiful 17th century manor house which has been the Warde family home since 1731. It is surrounded by 10 acres of attractive and historic gardens which include a lake, restored parterres and an 18th century dovecote. Squerryes is 22 miles from London and easily accessible from the M25. There are lovely views and peaceful surroundings. Visitors from far and wide come to enjoy the atmosphere of a house which is still lived in as a family home.

There is a fine collection of Old Master paintings from the Italian, 17th century Dutch and 18th century English schools, furniture, porcelain and tapestries all acquired or commissioned by the family in the 18th century. General Wolfe of Quebec was a friend of the family and there are items connected with him in the Wolfe Room. The Tapestry Room has been re-decorated with the kind support of Farrow and Ball.

Gardens

These were laid out in the formal style but were re-landscaped in the mid 18th century. Some of the original features in the 1719 Badeslade print survive. The family have restored the formal garden using this print as a guide. The garden is lovely all year round with bulbs, wild flowers and woodland walks, azaleas, summer flowering herbaceous borders and roses.

- Suitable for conferences, product launches, filming, photography, outside events, garden parties. No photography in house. Picnics permitted by the lake.
- Small.
- 
- Wedding receptions (marquee).
- Limited access in house and garden. WCs.
- Lunches and light refreshments on open days. Licenced.
- For pre-booked groups (max 55), small additional charge. Tour time 1 hr. Wine tasting groups by arrangement 45 mins–1 hr. Additional charge.
- Limited for coaches.
- On leads, in grounds.

BELMONT HOUSE & GARDENS

BELMONT PARK, THROWLEY, FAVERSHAM ME13 0HH

www.belmont-house.org

Tel: 01795 890202 **Fax:** 01795 890042 **E-mail:** administrator@belmont-house.org

Owner: Harris (Belmont) Charity **Contact:** administrator@belmont-house.org

Belmont is an elegant 18th century house with views over the rolling Kentish North Downs. Its hidden gardens range from a Pinetum complete with grotto, a walled ornamental garden, a walled kitchen garden with Victorian greenhouse leading to a yew-lined walk to the family pets' graveyard.

Its very special collections echo its ownership by the Harris family since 1801 and include mementos of their travels and posts in India and Trinidad. The house was designed by Samuel Wyatt and includes many novel architectural details. In addition it has one of the most extensive collections of clocks in private hands in the country.

Location: MAP 4:M3, OS Ref. TQ986 564. 4½m SSW of Faversham, off A251.

Open: 31 Mar–30 Sept. House: Sats, Suns & BH Mons. Tours at 2.15pm, 2.45pm, 3.30pm. Group tours weekdays by appointment. Pre-booked specialist clock tours last Sat of month, Apr–Sept. Gardens are open all year round.

Admission: House & Garden: Adult £10, Child (12-16yrs) £6, Conc. £7, Family (2 adults 2 children) £30. Garden Only: Adult £5, Child (12-16yrs) £2.50, Conc. £4. Pre-booked Clock Tour (last Saturday of every month) £15.

No photography in house. Partial. WC. Obligatory.

Limited for coaches. In grounds on leads.

CHART GUNPOWDER MILLS

Chart Mills, Faversham, Kent ME13 7SE

Tel: 01795 534542 **E-mail:** ticfaversham@btconnect.com

Owner: Swale Borough Council **Contact:** Peter Garner

Oldest gunpowder mill in the world. Supplied gunpowder to Nelson for the Battle of Trafalgar, and Wellington at Waterloo.

Location: MAP 4:M3, OS Ref. TQ615 015. M2/J6. W of town centre, access from Stonebridge Way or South Road.

Open: Apr–Oct: Sat, Sun & BHs, 2–5pm, or by arrangement.

Admission: Free.

CHARTWELL

See page 98 for full page entry.

CHIDDINGSTONE CASTLE

See pages 99 for full page entry.

COBHAM HALL

See page 100 for full page entry.

DANSON HOUSE

See page 101 for full page entry.

THE HOME OF CHARLES DARWIN

See page 102 for full page entry.

For **special events** held throughout the year, see the index at the end of the book.

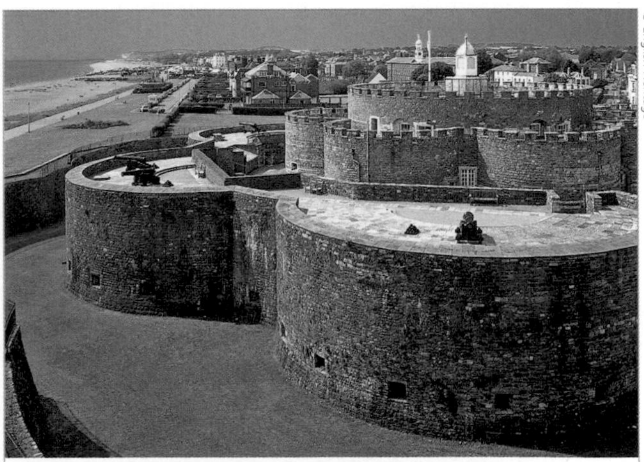

© English Heritage

DEAL CASTLE

VICTORIA ROAD, DEAL, KENT CT14 7BA

www.english-heritage.org.uk/dealcastle

Tel: 01304 372762 **Venue hire and Hospitality:** 01304 209889

E-mail: customers@english-heritage.org.uk

Owner: English Heritage **Contact:** Visitor Operations Team

Crouching low and menacing, the huge, rounded bastions of this austere fort, built by Henry VIII, once carried 119 guns. A fascinating castle to explore, with long, dark passages, battlements and a huge basement. The interactive displays and exhibition give an interesting insight into the castle's history.

Location: MAP 4:O3, OS Ref. TR378 522. SE of Deal town centre.

Open: 1 Apr–30 Sep: daily, 10am–6pm. 1 Oct–31 Mar: Closed.

Admission: Adult £4.50, Child £2.30, Conc. £3.80. Family £11.30. EH Members free. Group discount available. Opening times and prices are valid until 31st March 2011, after this date details are subject to change please visit www.english-heritage.org.uk for the most up-to-date information.

WCs. Exclusive private & corporate hospitality.

Coach parking on main road.

DODDINGTON PLACE GARDENS

Doddington, Nr Sittingbourne, Kent ME9 0BB

Tel: 01795 886101 **www.doddingtonplacegardens.co.uk**

Owner: Mr & Mrs Richard Oldfield **Contact:** Mrs Richard Oldfield

10 acres of landscaped gardens in an area of outstanding natural beauty.

Location: MAP 4:L3, OS Ref. TQ944 575. 4m N from A20 at Lenham or 5m SW from A2 at Ospringe, W of Faversham.

Open: Easter Sun–end Sept: Suns 2–5pm, BH Mons, 11am–5pm.

Admission: Adult £5, Child £1. Groups (10+) £4.50.

Limited. On leads.

DOVER CASTLE

See page 103 for full page entry.

DYMCHURCH MARTELLO TOWER

Dymchurch, Kent TN29 0TJ

Tel: 01304 211067 **E-mail:** customers@english-heritage.org.uk

www.english-heritage.org.uk/dymchurchmartellotower

Owner: English Heritage **Contact:** Dover Castle

Fully restored and re-equipped with its cannon, this is one of 103 ingeniously-designed artillery towers, built from 1805 at vulnerable points around the south and east coasts to resist threatened Napoleonic invasion.

Location: MAP 4:M4, OS189, Ref. TR102 294. In Dymchurch, access from High Street.

Open: Temporarily closed. External viewing only.

Admission: Free. Opening times and prices are valid until 31st March 2011, after this date details are subject to change please visit www.english-heritage.org.uk for the most up-to-date information.

© NTPL / Jerry Harpur

Emmetts Garden

EASTBRIDGE HOSPITAL OF ST THOMAS

25 High Street, Canterbury, Kent CT1 2BD

Tel: 01227 471688 **Fax:** 01227 781641 **E-mail:** info@eastbridgehospital.org.uk

www.eastbridgehospital.org.uk **Contact:** The Bursar

Medieval pilgrims' hospital with 12th century undercroft, refectory and chapel.

Location: MAP 4:N3, OS189, Ref. TR148 579. S side of Canterbury High Street.

Open: Hospital Mon–Sat 10am–5pm. Chapel Easter–end Sept Mon–Sat 2–4pm.

Admission: Ring for details.

© NTPL / Jerry Harpur

© NTPL / Jerry Harpur

EMMETTS GARDEN

IDE HILL, SEVENOAKS, KENT TN14 6AY

www.nationaltrust.org.uk/emmetts

Tel: 01732 868381 (Chartwell office) **Fax:** 01732 868193 **Info:** 01732 751509

E-mail: emmetts@nationaltrust.org.uk

Owner: National Trust

Contact: The Visitor Services Manager (Chartwell & Emmetts Garden, Mapleton Road, Westerham, Kent TN16 1PS)

Influenced by William Robinson, this charming and informal garden was laid out in the late 19th century, with many exotic and rare trees and shrubs from across the world. Wonderful views across the Weald of Kent – with the highest treetop in Kent. There are glorious shows of daffodils, bluebells, azaleas and rhododendrons, then acers and cornus in autumn, also a rose garden and rock garden.

Location: MAP 19:G11, OS Ref. TQ477 524. 1½m N of Ide Hill off B2042. M25/J5, then 4m.

Open: 12 Mar–30 Oct, Sat–Wed, 11am–5pm. Open BH Mons.

Admission: Adult £6.50, Child £1.70, Family (2+3) £14.70. Joint ticket with Quebec House: Adult £9.50. Group Adult £4.90. Gift Aid.

Special Events: Including family picnic day, school holiday activies and guided tours with the head gardener. Please see www.nationaltrust.org.uk for further details.

Partial, WCs. By arrangement. On leads.

GOODNESTONE PARK GARDENS

Goodnestone Park, Nr Wingham, Canterbury, Kent CT3 1PL

Tel/Fax: 01304 840107 **E-mail:** enquiries@goodnestoneparkgardens.co.uk

www.goodnestoneparkgardens.co.uk

Owner/Contact: Margaret, Lady FitzWalter

The garden is approximately 14 acres, set in 18th century parkland. A new gravel garden was planted in 2003. There are many fine trees, a woodland area and a large walled garden with a collection of old-fashioned roses, clematis and herbaceous plants, a new water feature has been installed in 2009. Jane Austen was a frequent visitor, her brother Edward having married a daughter of the house.

Location: MAP 4:N3, OS Ref. TR254 544. 8m ESE of Canterbury, 1½m E of B2046, at S end of village. The B2046 runs from the A2 to Wingham, the gardens are signposted from this road.

Open: Sun only 12noon–4pm from 13 Feb, Tues–Fri from 29 Mar–30 Sept 11am–5pm, Sun 12noon–5pm. Closed Sat and Mon except BH Mons. Groups welcome any day with prior notice.

Admission: Adult £5.50, Child (6–16 yrs) £1 (under 6 free), OAP £5.00, Student £3.00, Family ticket (2+2) £12.00, Groups (20+) £5.00. Groups out of opening hours £7.00.

Partial. Partial.

THE GRANGE

St Augustine's Road, Ramsgate, Kent CT11 9NY

Tel: 01628 825925 **E-mail:** bookings@landmarktrust.org.uk

www.landmarktrust.org.uk

Owner/Contact: The Landmark Trust

Augustus Pugin built this house in 1843–4 to live in with his family. It was at The Grange that Pugin produced the designs for the interiors of the House of Lords and the Medieval Court at the Great Exhibition but he reserved some of his finest and most characteristic flourishes for his own home. The Landmark Trust, a building preservation charity, has undertaken a major restoration of the building which is now available for holidays all year round. Full details of The Grange and 189 other historic and architecturally important buildings are featured in the Landmark Trust Handbook (£10 plus p&p refundable against a booking) and on the website.

Location: MAP 4:O2, OS Ref: TR3764

Open: Available for holidays for up to 8 people throughout the year. Parts of the ground floor are open to the general public by appointment on Wednesday afternoons and there are 8 Open Days a year. Contact the Landmark Trust for full details.

Admission: Free on Wednesday afternoons & Open Days and visits by appointment.

GROOMBRIDGE PLACE GARDENS

Groombridge Place, Groombridge, Tunbridge Wells, Kent TN3 9QG

Tel: 01892 861444 **Fax:** 01892 863996 **E-mail:** office@groombridge.co.uk

www.groombridge.co.uk

Owner: Groombridge Asset Management **Contact:** The Estate Office

Set in 200 acres, Groombridge features a series of magnificent, traditional walled gardens – set against the backdrop of a 17th century moated manor. Plus the ancient woodland of the "Enchanted Forest" where there's mystery, innovation and excitement for all ages. Packed programme of special events throughout the year. Visit our website for further details www.groombridge.co.uk

Location: MAP 4:J4, OS Ref. TQ534 375. Groombridge Place Gardens are located on the B2110 just off the A264. 4m SW of Tunbridge Wells and 9m E of East Grinstead. **Rail:** London Charing Cross to Tunbridge Wells 55mins. (Taxis). **Air:** Gatwick.

Open: Summer, Gardens: 2 Apr–30 Oct, daily, 10am–5.30pm (or dusk if earlier). The house is not open to the public.

Admission: Please visit our website www.groombridge.co.uk for up to date admission prices. *Child under 3yrs Free.

Film location Partial.WCs. Licensed. By arrangement. Limited for coached Guide dogs only. Please see our website for details of our special events www.groombridge.co.uk.

HALL PLACE & GARDENS

See page 104 for full page entry.

HEVER CASTLE & GARDENS

See page 105 for full page entry.

THE HISTORIC DOCKYARD CHATHAM

Chatham, Kent ME4 4TZ

Infoline: 01634 823800 **E-mail:** info@chdt.org.uk

Owner/Contact: Chatham Historic Dockyard Trust

Costumed guides help you discover over 400 years of maritime history.

Location: MAP 4:K2, OS Ref. TQ759 690. Signposted from M2/J1,3&4.

Open: 12 Feb–31 Oct; daily, 10am–4pm.

Admission: Adult £15; Child (5-15 yrs) £10.50; Conc. £12.50; (2010 prices).

HOLE PARK GARDENS

ROLVENDEN, CRANBROOK, KENT TN17 4JA

www.holepark.com

Tel: 01580 241344 / 241386 **Fax:** 01580 241882 **E-mail:** info@holepark.com

Owner/Contact: Edward Barham

A 15 acre garden with all year round interest, set in beautiful parkland with fine views. Trees, lawns and extensive yew hedges are a feature. Walled garden with mixed borders, pools and water garden. Natural garden with bulbs, azaleas, rhododendrons and flowering shrubs. Bluebell walk and autumn colours a speciality.

Location: MAP 4:L4, OS Ref. TQ830 325. 1m W of Rolvenden on B2086 Cranbrook road.

Open: Spring: 3 Apr–31 May, Open daily (including renowned bluebell season late Apr/early May). Summer: 1 Jun–27 Oct, Weds & Thurs. Autumn: 9, 16 & 23 Oct, Suns. All openings 11am–6pm and at all other times by appointment.

Admission: Adult £6, Child £1. Group visits with conducted tour of the gardens by the owner or head gardener a speciality. Please contact us for details.

WCs. By arrangement. Guide dogs only. Bluebell Spectacular late April to early May. €

IGHTHAM MOTE

Ightham Mote, Mote Road, Ivy Hatch, Sevenoaks, Kent TN15 0NT

Tel: 01732 810378 **Info:** 01732 811145 **Fax:** 01732 811029

Owner: National Trust **Contact:** The Property Manager

Moated manor house spanning nearly 700 years of history.

Location: MAP 19:H11, OS Ref. TQ584 535. 6m E of Sevenoaks off A25. 2½m S of Ightham off A227.

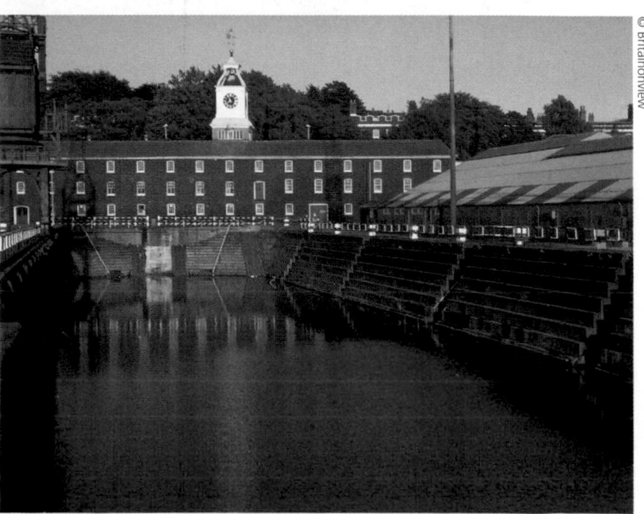

Chatham Dockyard

KNOLE

See page 106 for full page entry.

LEEDS CASTLE

See page 107 for full page entry.

LESNES ABBEY

Abbey Road, Abbey Wood, London DA17 5DL

Tel: 01322 526574

Owner: Bexley Council **Contact:** Lynda Weaver

The Abbey was founded in 1178 by Richard de Lucy as penance for his involvement in events leading to the murder of Thomas à Becket. Today only the ruins remain.

Location: MAP 19:G7, OS Ref. TQ479 788. In public park on S side of Abbey Road (B213), 500yds E of Abbey Wood Station, ¾m N of A206 Woolwich–Erith Road.

Open: Any reasonable time.

Admission: Free.

LULLINGSTONE CASTLE & WORLD GARDEN

Lullingstone, Eynsford, Kent DA4 0JA

Tel: 01322 862114 **Fax:** 01322 862115 **E-mail:** info@lullingstonecastle.co.uk

www.lullingstonecastle.co.uk

Owner/Contact: Guy Hart Dyke Esq

Fine State rooms, family portraits and armour in beautiful grounds. The 15th century gatehouse was one of the first ever to be made of bricks. This is also the site for the World Garden of Plants and for Lullingstone's Parish Church of St Botolph.

Location: MAP 19:G9, OS Ref. TQ530 644. 1m S Eynsford W side of A225. 600yds S of Roman Villa.

Open: Apr–Sept: World Garden Fris, Sats, Suns & BHs 12 noon–5pm. House open BH weekends at same times, and for special events 11am–5pm, and for Guided Groups of over 20 persons on Weds & Thurs by arrangement. Closed Good Fri.

Admission: Adult £7, Child £4, OAP £6.50, Family £18; Groups (20+): £8 pp plus £40 for a dedicated guide (Weds & Thurs only). HHA members free; 2 for 1 for English Heritage members.

No interior photography. Wheelchairs available upon request. WCs.

By arrangement. Limited for coaches. School packs available. Guide dogs only.

Lullingstone hosts a number of special events, the details of which are on the website.

LULLINGSTONE ROMAN VILLA

LULLINGSTONE LANE, EYNSFORD, KENT DA4 0JA

www.english-heritage.org.uk/lullingstone

Tel: 01322 863467 **E-mail:** customers@english-heritage.org.uk

Owner: English Heritage **Contact:** Visitor Operations Team

Recognised as a unique archaeological find, the villa has splendid mosaic floors and one of the earliest private Christian chapels. Step into the world of Roman Britain as a film and light show takes you back nearly 2,000 years. Marvel at the wall paintings and fascinating artefacts in the exhibition.

Location: MAP 19:G9, OS Ref. TQ529 651. ½m SW of Eynsford off A225, M25/J3. Follow A20 towards Brands Hatch. 600yds N of Castle.

Open: 1 Apr–30 Sep: daily, 10am–6pm. 1 Oct–30 Nov: daily, 10am–4pm. 1 Dec–31 Jan '11: Wed–Sun, 10am–4pm. 1 Feb–31 Mar: daily, 10am–4pm. Closed 24–26 Dec & 1 Jan.

Admission: Adult £5.90, Child £3, Conc £5, Family £14.80. EH Members Free. Group discount available. Opening times and prices are valid until 31st March 2011, after this date details are subject to change please visit www.english-heritage.org.uk for the most up-to-date information.

Lullingstone Roman Villa

MAISON DIEU

Ospringe, Faversham, Kent ME13 8NS

Tel: 01795 534542 **E-mail:** customers@english-heritage.org.uk

www.english-heritage.org.uk/maisondieu

Owner: English Heritage **Contact:** The Faversham Society

This forerunner of today's hospitals remains largely as it was in the 16th century with exposed beams and an overhanging upper storey. It now displays Roman artefacts from nearby sites.

Location: MAP 4:M3, OS Ref. TR002 608. In Ospringe on A2, ½m W of Faversham.

Open: 2 Apr–31 Oct: Sat–Sun & BHs, 2–5pm. Group visits at other times by appointment.

Admission: Adult £2, Child Free, Conc. £1. EH Members Free. Group discount available. Opening times and prices are valid until 31st March 2011, after this date details are subject to change please visit www.english-heritage.org.uk for the most up-to-date information.

WCs.

MILTON CHANTRY

New Tavern Fort Gardens, Gravesend, Kent DA12 2BH

Tel: 01474 321520 **E-mail:** customers@english-heritage.org.uk

www.english-heritage.org.uk/miltonchantry

Owner: English Heritage **Contact:** Gravesham Borough Council

A small 14th century building which housed the chapel of the leper hospital and the chantry of the de Valence and Montechais families and later became a tavern.

Location: MAP 4:K2, OS Ref.TQ653 743. In New Tavern Fort Gardens ¼m E of Gravesend off A226.

Open: 1 Apr–30 Sept: Sat–Sun & BHs, 12pm–5pm. Admission outside these times by appointment. Opening times subject to change, please call to avoid disappointment.

Admission: Free. Opening times and prices are valid until 31st March 2011, after this date details are subject to change please visit www.english-heritage.org.uk for the most up-to-date information.

MOUNT EPHRAIM GARDENS

Hernhill, Faversham, Kent ME13 9TX

Tel: 01227 751496 **Fax:** 01227 751011

www.mountephraimgardens.co.uk

Owner: William Dawes & Family **Contact:** Miss Claire Francis

In these enchanting 10 acres, terraces of fragrant roses lead to a small lake and woodland area. A new grass maze, Japanese-style rock garden, arboretum and many beautiful mature trees are other highlights. Peaceful, unspoilt atmosphere set in Kentish orchards.

Location: MAP 4:M3, OS Ref. TR065 598. In Hernhill village, 1m from end of M2. Signed from A2 & A299.

Open: Open Easter Sun–end Sept: Wed, Thu, Fri, Sat & Sun, 12 noon–5pm and BH Mons 11am–last entry 5pm. Groups Mar–Oct by arrangement.

Admission: Adult £5.00, Child (3–16) £2.50. Groups (10+): £4.50.

Partial. WCs. Licensed. Licensed. By arrangement. On leads. 1 & 2 May, Pat-A-Lamb Weekend, first BH weekend in May, make friends with cuddly lambs for the whole family to enjoy 11am–5pm; 15–26 June, Outdoor Shakespeare in the evenings performed by Kent Shakespeare Productions; Sunday 10 July, Cherry Day. Sample some the the best cherries in the county on a real family farm; 28 & 29 August, The Pantaloons present 'The Canterbury Tales' open air production; Sunday 11 September, 'Apple Sunday' Join in the apple harvest celebrations on the family far, including apple pressing demonstrations, orchard farm tours and a chance to sample and buy a wide range of apple varieties as well as pears, plums and cobnuts.

NURSTEAD COURT

Nurstead Church Lane, Meopham, Nr Gravesend, Kent DA13 9AD

Tel: 01474 812368 (guided tours); 01474 812121 (weddings & functions)

E-mail: info@nursteadcourt.co.uk **www.nursteadcourt.co.uk**

Owner/Contact: Mrs S Edmeades-Stearns

Nurstead Court is a Grade I listed manor house built in 1320 of timber-framed, crown-posted construction, set in extensive gardens and parkland. The additional front part of the house was built in 1825. Licensed weddings are now held in the house with receptions and other functions in the garden marquee.

Location: MAP 4:K2, OS Ref. TQ642 685. Nurstead Church Lane is just off the A227 N of Meopham, 3m from Gravesend.

Open: Every Wed & Thur in Sept, Oct 5 & Oct 6, 2–5pm. All year round by arrangement.

Admission: Adult £5, Child £2.50, OAP/Student £4. Group (max 54): £4.

Weddings & functions catered for. Licensed. WCs. By arrangement. Limited for coaches. On leads, in grounds.

David Winston, Period Piano Company

RESTORATION HOUSE

17–19 CROW LANE, ROCHESTER, KENT ME1 1RF

www.restorationhouse.co.uk

Tel: 01634 848520 **Fax:** 01634 880058

E-mail: robert.tucker@restorationhouse.co.uk

Owner: R Tucker & J Wilmot **Contact:** Robert Tucker

Unique survival of an ancient city mansion deriving its name from the stay of Charles II on the eve of The Restoration. Beautiful interiors with exceptional early paintwork related to decorative scheme 'run up' for Charles' visit. The house also inspired Dickens to situate 'Miss Havisham' here.

'Interiors of rare historical resonance and poetry', *Country Life*. Fine English furniture and pictures (Mytens, Kneller, Dahl, Reynolds and several Gainsboroughs). Charming interlinked walled gardens of ingenious plan in a classic English style. A private gem. 'There is no finer pre-Civil war town house in England than this' – Simon Jenkins, *The Times*.

Location: MAP 4:K2, OS Ref, TQ744 683. Historic centre of Rochester, off High Street, opposite the Vines Park.

Open: Sats 4 Jun & 9th Jul, 12–5pm. 2 Jun–30 Sept, Thur & Fri, 10am–5pm.

Admission: Adult £6.50 (includes 32 page illustrated guidebook), Child £3.25, Conc £5.50. Booked group (8+) tours: £7.50pp.

No stiletto heels. No photography in house. Garden by appointment.
1st, 2nd & 4th Thurs in month & other days by arrangement.
By arrangement. None. Guide dogs only.

OLD SOAR MANOR

Plaxtol, Borough Green, Kent TN15 0QX
Tel: 01732 810378 **Info Line:** 01732 811145 **E-mail:** oldsoarmanor@nationaltrust.org.uk
Owner: National Trust **Contact:** The Property Manager
A solar chamber over a barrel-vaulted undercroft is all that remains of a late 13th century knight's dwelling of c1290 which stood until the 18th century.
Location: MAP 4:K3, OS Ref.TQ619 541. 1m E of Plaxtol.
Open: 1 Apr–30 Sept: Sat–Thu, 10am–6pm. Daily except Fridays.
Admission: Free.

OWLETTS

The Street, Cobham, Gravesend, Kent DA12 3AP
Tel: 01372 453401 **Fax:** 01372 452023
Owner: National Trust **Contact:** The Property Manager
Former home of Sir Herbert Baker (architect).
Location: MAP 4:K2, OS Ref. TQ669 686. 1m south of A2 at west end of village. Limited car parking at property. Parking nearby in Cobham village.

PENSHURST PLACE & GARDENS

See page 108 for full page entry.

POWELL-COTTON MUSEUM, QUEX HOUSE & GARDENS.

See page 109 for full page entry

RECULVER TOWERS & ROMAN FORT

Reculver, Herne Bay, Kent CT6 6SS
Tel: 01227 740676 **E-mail:** customers@english-heritage.org.uk
Owner: English Heritage **Contact:** Reculver Country Park
This 12th century landmark of twin towers has guided sailors into the Thames estuary for seven centuries. Includes walls of a Roman fort, which were erected nearly 2,000 years ago.
Location: MAP 4:N2, OS Ref. TR228 693. At Reculver 3m E of Herne Bay by the seashore.
Open: Any reasonable time. External viewing only.
Admission: Free. Opening times and prices are valid until 31st March 2011, after this date details are subject to change please visit www.english-heritage.org.uk for the most up-to-date information.
WCs. On leads.

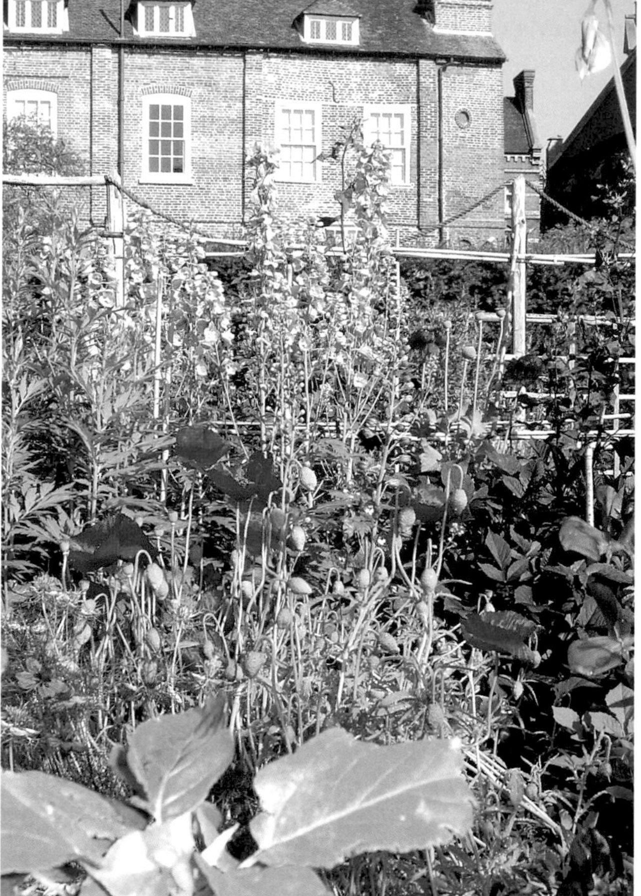

Restoration House

© The National Trust / J Rawlinson

QUEBEC HOUSE

WESTERHAM, KENT TN16 1TD

www.nationaltrust.org.uk/quebechouse

Tel: 01732 868381 (Chartwell office) **E-mail:** quebechouse@nationaltrust.org.uk
Owner: National Trust **Contact:** The Visitor Services Manager
This Grade I listed gabled house is situated in the centre of the beautiful village of Westerham. Many features of significant architectural and historical interest reflect its 16th century origins as well as changes made in the 18th and 20th centuries.

Quebec House was the childhood home of General James Wolfe, and rooms contain family and military memorabilia, prints and portraits. The Tudor Coach House contains an exhibition about the Battle of Quebec (1759) and the part played there by Wolfe, who led the British forces to victory over the French.

Location: MAP 19:F10, OS Ref. TQ449 541. At E end of village, on N side of A25, facing junction with B2026, Edenbridge Road.
Open: 12 Mar–30 Oct: House; Wed–Sun, 1–5pm. Garden & Exhibition; Wed–Sun, 12–5pm.
Admission: Adult £4.70, Child £1.70, Family (2+3) £11.00. Group: Adult £3.70. Joint ticket with Emmetts Garden £9.50. Gift Aid.
Special events: Including school holiday activities. Please see www.nationaltrust.org.uk for further details.
Partial. WCs. By arrangement In grounds.

RICHBOROUGH ROMAN FORT

Richborough, Sandwich, Kent CT13 9JW

Tel: 01304 612013 **E-mail:** customers@english-heritage.org.uk

www.english-heritage.org.uk/richborough

Owner: English Heritage **Contact:** Visitor Operations Team

This fort and township date back to the Roman landing in AD43. The fortified walls and the massive foundations of a triumphal arch which stood over 80 feet high still survive. The inclusive audio tour and the museum give an insight into life in Richborough's heyday as a busy township.

Location: MAP 4:O3, OS Ref. TR324 602. 1½m NW of Sandwich off A257.

Open: Amphitheatre: any reasonable time in daylight hours, access across grazed land from footpath, please call 01304 612013 for details. Fort: 1 Apr–30 Sept: daily, 10am–6pm. 1 Oct–31 Mar: closed.

Admission: Gardens: Adult £4.50, Child £2.30, Conc. £3.80. Family £11.30. EH Members Free. Group discount available. Opening times and prices are valid until 31st March 2011, after this date details are subject to change please visit www.english-heritage.org.uk for the most up-to-date information.

Museum. On leads.

RIVERHILL HIMALAYAN GARDENS

Sevenoaks, Kent TN15 0RR

Tel/Fax: 01732 458802 **E-mail:** sarah@riverhillgardens.co.uk

www.riverhillgardens.co.uk

Owner: The Rogers Family **Contact:** Mrs Rogers

Historic hillside gardens, privately owned by the Rogers family since 1840. Extensive views across the Weald of Kent. Spectacular rhododendrons, azaleas and specimen trees. Bluebell walk, Hedge Maze, Children's Hideout and Den Building Trail. Delicious coffee, light lunches and teas.

Location: MAP 4:J3, OS Ref. TQ541 522. 2m S of Sevenoaks on A225.

Open: 20 Mar–11 Sept 2011, Wed–Sun and BH Mondays, 10.30am–5pm. House open to pre-booked groups.

Admission: Adult £6.25, Child £3.95, Family £17.50, Senior Citizens £5.60. Adult Pre-booked Groups (20+) House & Garden £8.90, Garden only £5.60

Partial. By arrangement. Limited for coaches. See website for special events programme.

ROCHESTER CASTLE

The Lodge, Rochester-upon-Medway, Medway ME1 1SW

Tel: 01634 402276 **E-mail:** customers@english-heritage.org.uk

www.english-heritage.org.uk/rochestercastle

Owner: English Heritage (Managed by Medway Council)

Contact: Visitor Operations Team

Built in the 11th century. The keep is over 100 feet high and with walls 12 feet thick. Strategically placed astride the London Road, guarding an important crossing of the River Medway, this mighty fortress has a complex history of destruction and re-building.

Location: MAP 4:K2, OS Ref. TQ741 686. By Rochester Bridge. Follow A2 E from M2/J1 & M25/J2.

Open: 1 Apr–30 Sep: daily, 10am–6pm. 1 Oct–31 Mar: daily, 10am–4pm. Last admission 45 mins before closing. Closed 24–26 Dec & 1 Jan. Group discount available.

Admission: Adult £5, Child £3.50 Conc £3.50, Family £13.50. EH Members Free. Opening times and prices are valid until 31st March 2011, after this date details are subject to change please visit www.english-heritage.org.uk for the most up-to-date information.

WCs.

ROMAN PAINTED HOUSE

New Street, Dover, Kent CT17 9AJ

Tel: 01304 203279

Owner: Dover Roman Painted House Trust **Contact:** Mr B Philp

Discovered in 1970. Built around 200AD as a hotel for official travellers. Impressive wall paintings, central heating systems and the Roman fort wall built through the house.

Location: MAP 4:N4, OS Ref. TR318 414. Dover town centre. E of York St.

Open: Apr–Sept: 10am–5pm, except Mons. Suns 2–5pm. (may vary).

Admission: Adult £3, Students/Child/OAP £2.

SCOTNEY CASTLE

Lamberhurst, Tunbridge Wells, Kent TN3 8JN

Tel: 01892 893868 **Fax:** 01892 890110

Owner: National Trust **Contact:** Property Manager

Elizabethan style house (1837) with medieval ruins in valley.

Location: MAP 4:K4, OS Ref. TQ688 353. Signed off A21 1m S of Lamberhurst village.

SISSINGHURST CASTLE

SISSINGHURST, CRANBROOK, KENT TN17 2AB

www.nationaltrust.org.uk/sissinghurst

Tel: 01580 710700 **Infoline:** 01580 710701

E-mail: sissinghurst@nationaltrust.org.uk

Owner: National Trust **Contact:** The Administrator

Visit one of the world's most celebrated gardens. The creation of Vita Sackville-West and her husband Sir Harold Nicolson. Developed around the surviving parts of an Elizabethan mansion with a central red-brick prospect tower, the garden comprises a series of small, enclosed compartments, intimate in scale and romantic in atmosphere, providing outstanding design and colour throughout the season.

Location: MAP 4:L4, OS Ref. TQ807 383. 2m NE of Cranbrook, 1m E of Sissinghurst village (A262). Number 5 Arriva bus from Staplehurst train station.

Open: Garden: 12 Mar–30 Oct, Mon, Tues, Fri, Sat, Sun 10.30am–5pm; Closed Wed/Thur. Shop & Restaurant: As Garden. Vegetable Garden: 7 May–30 Sept, Mon, Tues, Fri, Sat, Sun, 10.30–5pm; Closed Wed/Thur. Late Night Opening: Until 8pm on Fri 27th May, Fri 3rd June, Fri 10th June, Fri 17th June, Fri 24th June.

***Admission:** Adult £11.00, Child £5.50, Family (2+3) £27.50, Groups £9.00. NT members free. *includes a voluntary donation but visitors can choose to pay the standard prices displayed at the property and on the website.

WCs. Licensed. Ample, £2 per car (NT Members free). Please book coaches in advance. Grounds only, on leads. Guide dogs only in Garden.

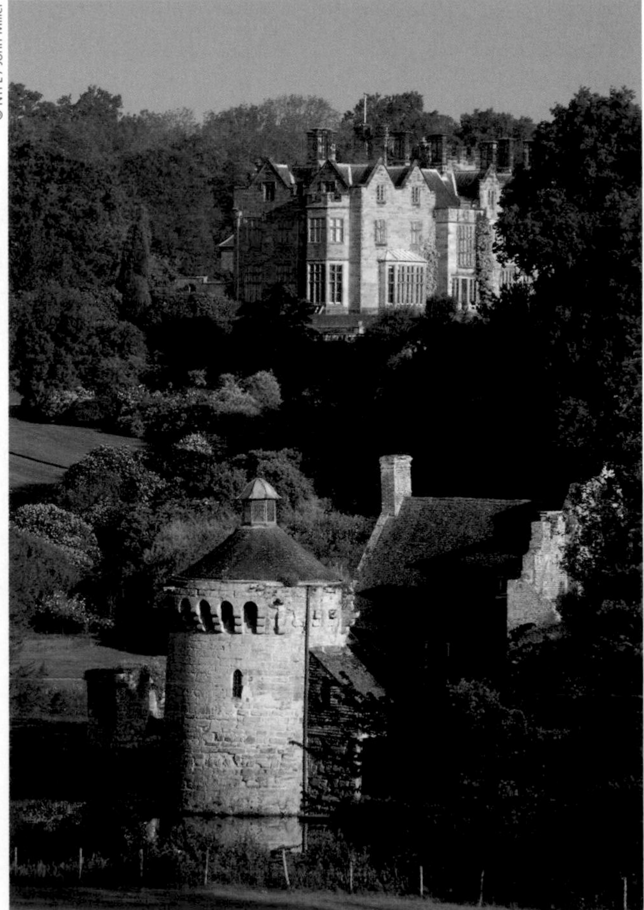

Scotney Castle

SOUTH FORELAND LIGHTHOUSE

The Front, St Margaret's Bay, Nr Dover CT15 6HP
Tel: 01304 852463 **Fax:** 01304 215484
www.nationaltrust.org.uk
Owner: National Trust **Contact:** Volunteer Co-ordinator

Historical Victorian Lighthouse part of White Cliffs of Dover.

Location: MAP 4:O3, OS138 Ref. TR359 433. 2m walk from White Cliffs car park, 1m walk from St Margaret's Village, short walk from bus stop Diamond route 15.

SQUERRYES COURT

See page 110 for full page entry.

ST AUGUSTINE'S ABBEY

Longport, Canterbury, Kent CT1 1TF
Tel: 01227 767345 **E-mail:** customers@english-heritage.org.uk
www.english-heritage.org.uk/staugustinesabbey
Owner: English Heritage **Contact:** Visitor Operations Team

The abbey, founded by St Augustine shortly after AD597, is part of a World Heritage Site. Take the free interactive audio tour which gives a fascinating insight into the abbey's history and visit the museum displaying artefacts uncovered during archaeological excavations of the site.

Location: MAP 4:N3, OS Ref. TR155 578. In Canterbury ½m E of Cathedral Close.

Open: 1 Apr–30 Jun: Wed–Sun, 10am–5pm. 1 Jul–31 Aug: daily, 10am–6pm. 1 Sep–31 Oct: Sat–Sun, 10am–5pm. 1 Nov–31 Mar '11: Sat & Sun, 10am–4pm. Closed 24–26 Dec & 1 Jan.

Admission: Adult £4.50, Child £2.30, Conc. £3.80. Family £11.30. 15% discount for groups (11+). EH Members Free. Opening times and prices are valid until 31st March 2011, after this date details are subject to change please visit www.english-heritage.org.uk for the most up-to-date information.

Free. Nearby. On leads.

ST JOHN'S COMMANDERY

Densole, Swingfield, Kent CT15 7HG
Tel: 01304 211067 **E-mail:** customers@english-heritage.org.uk
www.english-heritage.org.uk/stjohnscommandery
Owner: English Heritage **Contact:** Dover Castle

A medieval chapel built by the Knights Hospitallers. It has a moulded plaster ceiling, a remarkable timber roof and was converted into a farmhouse in the 16th century.

Location: MAP 4:N4, OS Ref. TR232 440. 2m NE of Densole on minor road off A260.

Open: Any reasonable time for exterior viewing. Internal viewing by appointment only, please call 01304 211067.

Admission: Free. Opening times and prices are valid until 31st March 2011, after this date details are subject to change please visit www.english-heritage.org.uk for the most up-to-date information.

Stoneacre

Squerryes Court

ST JOHN'S JERUSALEM

Sutton-at-Hone, Dartford, Kent DA4 9HQ
Tel: 01732 810378 **Fax:** 01732 811029
Owner: National Trust **Contact:** Property Manager

Site of former Knights Hospitaller Commandery chapel.

Location: MAP 4:J2, OS Ref. TQ557 701. 3m south of Dartford at Sutton-at-Hone, on east side of A225. Turn into entrance gate near Balmoral Road; parking at end of drive.

STONEACRE

Otham, Maidstone, Kent ME15 8RS
Tel/Fax: 01892 893842
Owner: National Trust **Contact:** The Tenant

Late 15th c yeoman's house, with great hall and crownpost.

Location: MAP 4:L3, OS Ref. TQ800 535. In narrow lane at N end of Otham village, 3m SE of Maidstone, 1m S of A20.

TEMPLE MANOR

Strood, Rochester, Kent ME2 2AH
Tel: 01634 338110 **E-mail:** customers@english-heritage.org.uk
www.english-heritage.org.uk/templemanor
Owner: English Heritage **Contact:** Medway Council

The 13th century manor house of the Knights Templar which mainly provided accommodation for members of the order travelling between London and the continent.

Location: MAP 4:K2, OS Ref. TQ733 685. In Strood (Rochester) off A228.

Open: 1 Apr–31 Oct: Sat & Sun, 11am–4pm. Closed 1 Nov–31 Mar. For group visits, please call 01634 402276.

Admission: Free. Opening times and prices are valid until 31st March 2011, after this date details are subject to change please visit www.english-heritage.org.uk for the most up-to-date information.

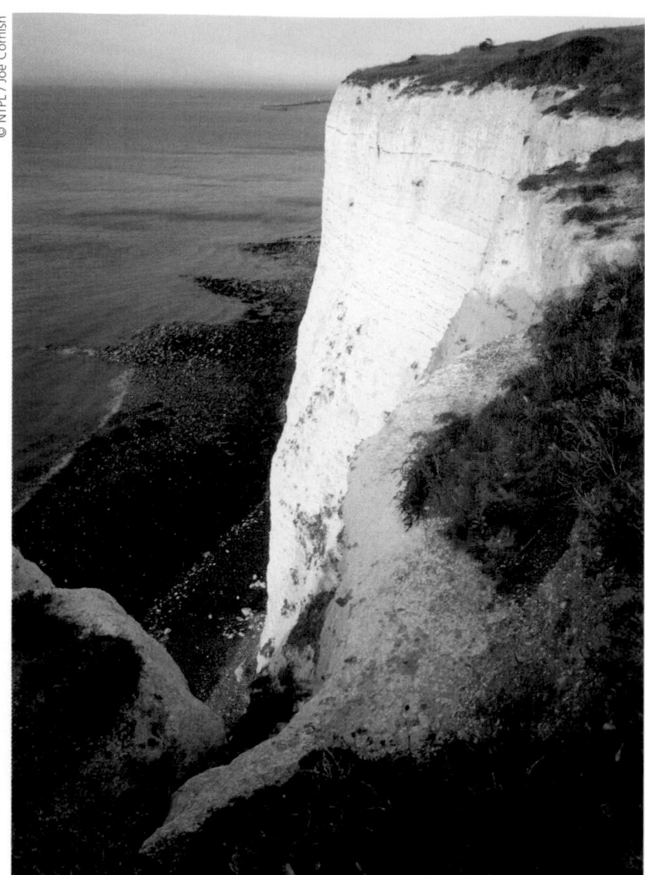

White Cliffs of Dover

UPNOR CASTLE ⌗

Upnor, Kent ME2 4XG

Tel: 01634 718742 **E-mail:** customers@english-heritage.org.uk

www.english-heritage.org.uk/upnorcastle

Owner: English Heritage **Contact:** Medway Council

Well preserved 16th century gun fort built to protect Queen Elizabeth I's warships. However in 1667 it failed to prevent the Dutch Navy which stormed up the Medway destroying half the English fleet.

Location: MAP 4:K2, OS Ref. TQ759 706. At Upnor, on unclassified road off A228. 2 miles NE of Strood.

Open: 1 Apr–31 Oct: daily 10am–6pm. Last admission 45 mins before closing. Closed 24–26 Dec & 1 Jan. May close early on Fri & Sat for weddings. Please call in advance to check.

Admission: Adult £5, Child/Conc £3.50, Family £13.50. EH Members Free. Group discount available. Opening times and prices are valid until 31st March 2011, after this date details are subject to change please visit www.english-heritage.org.uk for the most up-to-date information.

WCs.

WHITE CLIFFS OF DOVER

Upper Road, Langdon Cliffs, Nr Dover CT16 1HJ

Tel: 01304 202756 **Fax:** 01304 215484

www.nationaltrust.org.uk

Owner: National Trust **Contact:** Visitor Services

Visitor Centre offers great views and information about cliffs.

Location: MAP 4:O3, OS138 Ref. TR336 422. Follow White Cliffs brown signs from roundabout 1 m NE of Dover at junction of A2/A258.

WILLESBOROUGH WINDMILL

Mill Lane, Willesborough, Ashford, Kent TN24 0QG

Tel: 01233 661866

130 year old smock mill. Civil Wedding Licence.

Location: MAP 4:M4, OS Ref. TR031 421. Off A292 close to M20/J10. At E end of Ashford.

Open: Apr–end Sept; Sats, Suns & BH Mons, also Weds in Jul & Aug, 2–5pm or dusk if earlier.

Admission: Adult £3, Conc. £1.50.

WALMER CASTLE AND GARDENS ⌗

DEAL, KENT CT14 7LJ

www.english-heritage.org.uk/walmercastle

Tel: 01304 364288 **Venue Hire and Hospitality:** 01304 209889

E-mail: customers@english-heritage.org.uk

Owner: English Heritage **Contact:** Visitor Operations Team

A Tudor fort transformed into an elegant stately home. The residence of the Lords Warden of the Cinque Ports, who have included HM The Queen Mother, Sir Winston Churchill and the Duke of Wellington. Take the inclusive audio tour and see the Duke's rooms where he died over 150 years ago. Beautiful gardens including the Queen Mother's Garden, The Broadwalk with its famous yew tree hedge, Kitchen Garden and Moat Garden. Lunches and cream teas available in the delightful Lord Warden's tearooms.

Location: MAP 4:O3, OS Ref. TR378 501. S of Walmer on A258, M20/J13 or M2 to Deal.

Open: 1 Apr–30 Sept: daily, 10am–6pm. 1-31 Oct: Wed–Sun, 10am–4pm. 1 Nov–28 Feb: Closed. 1–31 Mar: Wed–Sun, 10am–4pm. Closed 9-11 July when Lord Warden is in residence.

Admission: Adult £7.00, Child £3.50, Conc. £6.00, Family £17.50. 15% discount for groups (11+). English Heritage members free. Opening times and prices are valid until 31st March 2011, after this date details are subject to change please visit www.english-heritage.org.uk for the most up-to-date information.

WCs. Private & corporate hire.

■ **Owner**

The Baring Family

■ **Contact**

Nigel Baring
Ardington House
Wantage
Oxfordshire OX12 8QA

Tel: 01235 821566
Fax: 01235 821151
E-mail: info@ardingtonhouse.com

■ **Location**

MAP 3:D1
OS Ref. SU432 883

12m S of Oxford,
12m N of Newbury,
2½m E of Wantage.

■ **Opening Times**

1 August–10 September, 2011, Mon–Fri, 11–2pm. (please phone to check if visiting on a Friday).

Excluding Bank Holidays.

■ **Admission**

House & Gardens

Adult	£5.00
Child	Free

ARDINGTON HOUSE

www.ardingtonhouse.com

Just a few miles south of Oxford stands the tranquil and entirely beautiful Ardington House. Surrounded by manicured lawns, terraced gardens, peaceful paddocks, parkland and its own romantic temple on an island, this Baroque house is the private home of the Barings. You will find it in the attractive village of Ardington, close to the Ridgeway on the edge of the Berkshire Downs.Built by the Strong brothers in 1720 with typical Georgian symmetry, the House is also famous for its Imperial Staircase. Leading from the Hall, the staircase is considered by experts to be one of the finest examples in Britain. Away from the crowds and the hustle of the workplace Ardington House provides a private and secluded setting. The calm, exclusive use environment allows for weddings, offsite board meetings, conference and workshops utilising the stylish, splendid complimentary marquee, gardens and grounds. There is a heated outdoor swimming pool, tennis court, croquet lawn and trout river. Close by is the ancient Ridgeway Path, a popular place for walking. Ardington House is licensed to hold Civil Wedding ceremonies. Poet Laureate Sir John Betjeman wrote of the homeliness and warmth of Ardington House, and the rooms have seen many special occasions and important visitors in the past with this tradition being continued.

The astonishing mixture of history, warmth and style you'll find at Ardington truly does place it in a class of its own.

- Conferences, product launches, films, weddings.
- Partial, WCs
- Licensed
- By arrangement. By members of the family.
- Free.
- Guide dogs only

Conference/Function

ROOM	MAX CAPACITY
Imperial Hall	
Theatre Style	80
U shape	30
Cabaret	40
Oak Room	
Theatre Style	40
U shape	20
Cabaret	30
Music Room	
Theatre Style	40
U shape	20
Cabaret	30

BLENHEIM PALACE

www.blenheimpalace.com

Blenheim Palace is home to the 11th Duke and Duchess of Marlborough and the birthplace of Sir Winston Churchill. Surrounded by over 2,000 acres of 'Capability' Brown landscaped parkland and the great lake, the Palace was created a World Heritage Site in 1987.

Conceived in 1705 by Sir John Vanbrugh, Blenheim Palace is a masterpiece of English Baroque architecture steeped in inspirational history. Visit the room where Sir Winston Churchill was born before taking a guided tour of the gilded State Rooms graced with priceless portraits, exquisite porcelain and the magnificent tapestries which were commissioned by John Churchill, 1st Duke of Marlborough, charting his famous victory over the French during in the Wars of the Spanish Succession.

A permanent visitor experience 'Blenheim Palace: The Untold Story' is open inside the Palace bringing to life enticing tales of the last 300 years, seen through the eyes of the household staff. Visitors can delve deeper in to the lives of the illustrious Marlborough family in the information rooms with touch screens and audio/visual units.

The Palace is surrounded by award winning Formal Gardens including the tranquil Secret Garden, the majestic Water Terraces, the fragrant Rose Garden, the Grand Cascade and Lake. An audio garden tour is available to hire. The Pleasure Gardens can be reached by a miniature train, which includes the Marlborough Maze, the Butterfly House and Adventure Playground, making it a great area for young children.

Admission

Friends of Blenheim Palace tickets available.

Palace, Garden & Park

Individual:
12 Feb–16 Dec

Adult	£19.00
Conc.	£15.00
Child*	£10.50
Family (2+2)	£50.00

Groups (15+)
Main Season:
12 Feb–20 Feb
1 Apr–30 Oct

Adult	£12.70
Conc.	£11.00
Child*	£6.90

Groups (15+)
Low Season:
21 Feb–31 Mar,
2 Nov–16 Dec

Adult	£10.75
Conc.	£9.60
Child*	£6.20

Park & Gardens

Individual:
12 Feb–16 Dec

Adult	£11.00
Conc.	£8.00
Child*	£5.50
Family	£28.00

Groups (15+)
Main Season:
12 Feb–20 Feb
1 Apr–30 Oct

Adult	£7.10
Conc.	£5.80
Child*	£3.40

Groups (15+)
Low Season:
21 Feb–31 Mar,
2 Nov–16 Dec

Adult	£5.65
Conc.	£4.50
Child*	£2.10

*(5–16yrs)

Private tours by appointment only, prices on request.

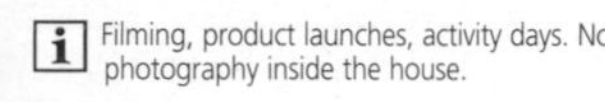

Filming, product launches, activity days. No photography inside the house.

Four shops.

Corporate Hospitality includes weddings, receptions, dinners, meetings and corporate events.

WCs.

Licensed.

Licensed.

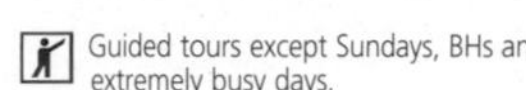

Guided tours except Sundays, BHs and extremely busy days.

Unlimited for cars and coaches.

Sandford Award holder since 1982. Teacher pre-visits welcome.

Dogs on leads in Park. Guide dogs only.

Full programme.

Owner

The Duke of Marlborough

Contact

Operations
Blenheim Palace
Woodstock OX20 1PX

Tel: 0800 849 6500
Fax: 01993 810570
E-mail: operations@blenheimpalace.com

Location

MAP 7:A11
OS Ref. SP441 161

From London, M40, A44 (1½ hrs), 8m NW of Oxford. London 63m Birmingham 54m.

Air: Heathrow 60m. Birmingham 50m.

Coach: From London (Victoria) to Oxford.

Rail: Oxford Station.

Bus: No.S3 from Oxford Station, Gloucester Green & Cornmarket.

Opening Times

Sat 12 Feb–Sun 30 Oct 2011, Daily.

Wed 2 Nov–Sun 16 Dec 2011, Wed–Sun.

Palace
10.30am–5.30pm
(last admission 4.45pm).

Palace and Formal Gardens
10.00am–5.30pm
(last admission 4.45pm).

Park
9am–6pm or dusk during autumn and winter months.

Except Christmas Day, all areas to be vacated by 6.00pm.

Open daily except Mondays & Tuesdays from 2 November.

Special Events

For full list of events please see Special Events Index at rear of book.

Conference/Function

ROOM	SIZE (m)	MAX CAPACITY
Orangery	36.25 x 7.1	250
Marlborough Room	14.3 x 7.1	120
Saloon	13.3 x 9.9	150
Great Hall	13.3 x 13.1	250
with Great Hall & Library		500
Long Library	45.7 x 5	500
Oudenarde Room	7.9 x 4.9	14
Ramillies Room	4.9 x 4.9	10
Malplaquet Room	4.9 x 4.9	12
Spencer Churchill Room	10 x 8	70
Courtyard	19.4 x 10.7	180

■ **Owner**

Lord Saye & Sele

■ **Contact**

Ms J. James
Broughton Castle
Broughton
Nr Banbury
Oxfordshire OX15 5EB

Tel: 01295 276070
E-mail: info@broughtoncastle.com

■ **Location**

MAP 7:A10
OS Ref. SP418 382

Broughton Castle is 2½m SW of Banbury Cross on the B4035, Shipston-on-Stour – Banbury Road. Easily accessible from Stratford-on-Avon, Warwick, Oxford, Burford and the Cotswolds. M40/J11.

Rail: From London/ Birmingham to Banbury.

■ **Opening Times**

Summer

Easter Sun & Mon, 1 May–15 September Weds, Suns & BH Mons, 2–5pm.

Also Thurs in July and August, 2–5pm.

Last admission – 4.30pm.

Open all year on any day, at any time, for group bookings – by appointment only.

■ **Admission**

Adult	£7.00
Child (5–15yrs)	£3.00
OAP/Student	£6.00
Garden only	£3.00
Groups	
Adult	£7.00
OAP	£7.00
Child (5–10yrs)	£3.00
Child (11–15yrs)	£4.00
Garden only	£4.00

(There is a minimum charge for groups – please contact admin for details.)

BROUGHTON CASTLE

www.broughtoncastle.com

Broughton Castle is essentially a family home lived in by Lord and Lady Saye & Sele and their family. The original medieval Manor House, of which much remains today, was built in about 1300 by Sir John de Broughton. It stands on an island site surrounded by a 3 acre moat. The Castle was greatly enlarged between 1550 and 1600, at which time it was embellished with magnificent plaster ceilings, splendid panelling and fine fireplaces. In the 17th century William, 8th Lord Saye & Sele, played a leading role in national affairs. He opposed Charles I's efforts to rule without Parliament and Broughton became a secret meeting place for the King's opponents. During the Civil War William raised a regiment and he and his four sons all fought at the nearby Battle of Edgehill. After the battle the Castle was besieged and captured. Arms and armour from the Civil War and other periods are displayed in the Great Hall. Visitors may also see the gatehouse, gardens and park together with the nearby 14th century Church of St Mary, in which there are many family tombs, memorials and hatchments.

Gardens

The garden area consists of mixed herbaceous and shrub borders containing many old roses. In addition, there is a formal walled garden with beds of roses surrounded by box hedging and lined by more mixed borders.

Photography allowed in house.

Partial.

Teas on Open Days. Groups may book morning coffee, light lunches and afternoon teas.

Available for booked groups.

Limited.

Guide dogs only in house. On leads in grounds.

Open all year for groups.

KINGSTON BAGPUIZE HOUSE

www.kingstonbagpuizehouse.com

A family home, this beautiful house originally built in the 1660s was remodelled in the early 1700s in red brick with stone facings with a cantilevered staircase.

New for 2011 see how Robert Mattock is establishing his significant collection of rare roses in the 2½ acre walled garden and park already notable for its important collection of rare cultivated plants and trees. See rare snowdrops during February; followed by a collection of magnolias in March and wisterias during late April; old garden and specie roses in May and June; herbaceous borders in July and autumn colour and rose hips in September.

The collection of Silk Road Hybrids in the new Mattock Rose Garden is being designed to illustrate how those roses that spread from China to Rome by 500 BC gave the western world roses that smell, and flower, so beautifully all summer long.

Connecting the history of the house, the history of the Mattock family and the long horticultural tradition of Kingston Bagpuize and its adjoining parishes is a new exhibition of old photographs, catalogues, horticultural tools and machinery. Specialist horticultural tools, books and equipment may be bought in our garden shop.

No photography in house.

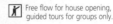

WCs.

Home-made teas and light refreshments. Light lunches for groups by appointment only.

Free flow for house opening, guided tours for groups only.

Guide dogs only. Dogs in car park area only.

Owner

Mrs Francis Grant

Contact

Virginia Grant
Kingston Bagpuize House
Abingdon
Oxfordshire OX13 5AX

Visitor Enquiries: 01865 820259

Corporate and Wedding Enquiries: 01865 820217

Fax: 01865 821659

E-mail: info@kingstonbagpuizehouse.com

Location

MAP 7:A12
OS Ref. SU408 981

In Kingston Bagpuize village, off A415 Abingdon to Witney road S of A415/A420 intersection. Abingdon 5m, Oxford 9m.

Opening Times

House and Gardens

15 May–7 July, Sunday–Thursday, Sundays, 11am–2pm, Weekdays 1–6pm.

Garden Only

6, 13, 20 & 27 February, 27 & 28 March, 25 & 26 April, 12-5pm.

18–29 September, Sunday–Thursday, Sundays 11am–2pm, Weekdays 1–6pm.

Admission

House and Garden:

Adult	£7.50
Child (4–15yrs)	£4.50
Groups per person including guide book, (by appointment only).	£7.50
Family (2+3)	£20.00

Gardens:

Adult	£5.00
Child (4–15yrs)	£3.00

Season tickets available on request.

This information is correct at the time of publication but may be subject to change. Please call our 24 hour telephone information line 01865 820259 to confirm before travelling.

Special Events

see www.kingstonbagpuizehouse.com.

Owner
Lord & Lady Camoys

Contact
The Administrator
Sue Gill
Stonor Park
Henley-on-Thames
Oxfordshire RG9 6HF

Tel: 01491 638587
E-mail: administrator@stonor.com

Location
MAP 3:E1
OS Ref. SU743 893

1 hr from London, M4/J8/9. A4130 to Henley-on-Thames.
On B480 NW of Henley. A4130/B480 to Stonor.
Rail: Henley-on-Thames Station 5m.

Opening Times
3 April–18 September Sundays and BH Mondays. Also Wednesdays, July and August only.

Gardens
1–5.30pm

House, Tea Room & Giftshop
2–5.30pm

Private Groups (20+): by arrangement Tuesday–Thursday, April–September

Last entry to the house 4.30pm.

Admission
House, Gardens, Chapel, Exhibition

Adults	£8.00
First Child (5–16)	£4.00
2 or more Children (5–16)	Free
Under 5s	Free

Gardens

Adults	£4.00
First Child (5–16)	£2.00
2 or more Children (5–16)	Free
Under 5s	Free

Groups

Adults	£9.00
Child (5–16)	£4.50

Includes guided tours.

Special Events
June 5
VW Owners' Rally.

August 26–29
Chilterns Craft Fair.

STONOR

www.stonor.com

Stonor is one of the very few houses in England that has remained in the same family from the earliest records to the present day and has been home to The Lord and Lady Camoys and the Stonor family for 850 years. The history of the house inevitably contributes to the atmosphere, at once unpretentious yet grand. A façade of warm brick with Georgian windows conceals much older buildings dating back to the 12th century and a 14th century Catholic Chapel sits on the south east corner. Stonor nestles in a fold of the beautiful wooded Chiltern Hills and has breathtaking views of the surrounding park where Fallow deer have grazed since medieval times.

It contains many family portraits, old Master drawings and paintings, Renaissance bronzes and tapestries, along with rare furniture and a collection of modern ceramics.

St Edmund Campion sought refuge at Stonor during the Reformation and printed his famous pamphlet 'Ten Reasons' here, in secret, on a press installed in the roof space. A small exhibition celebrates his life and work.

Mass has been celebrated since medieval times in the Chapel and is sited close by a pagan stone prayer circle. The painted and stained glass windows were executed by Francis Eginton, and installed in 1797. The Chapel decoration is that of the earliest Gothic Revival, begun in 1759, with additions in 1797. The Stations of the Cross seen in the lobby, were carved by Jozef Janas, a Polish prisoner of war in World War II and given to Stonor by Graham Greene in 1956.

The gardens offer outstanding views of the Park and valley and are especially beautiful in May and June, containing fine displays of daffodils, irises, peonies, lavenders and roses along with other herbaceous plants and shrubs.

- No photography in house.
- Unsuitable for physically disabled.
- Licensed.
- For 20–60.
- 100yds away.
- In Park on leads.
- See website or telephone for details.

Blenheim Palace

26A EAST ST HELEN STREET

Abingdon, Oxfordshire

Tel: 01865 242918 **E-mail:** info@oxfordpreservation.org.uk

www.oxfordpreservation.org.uk

Owner: Oxford Preservation Trust **Contact:** Mrs Debbie Dance

One of best preserved examples of a 15th century dwelling in the area. Originally a Merchant's Hall House with later alterations, features include a remarkable domestic wall painting, an early oak ceiling, traceried windows and fireplaces.

Location: MAP 7:A12, OS Ref. SU497 969. 300 yards SSW of the market place and Town Hall.

Open: By prior appointment.

Admission: Free.

ARDINGTON HOUSE

See page 120 for full page entry.

ASHDOWN HOUSE

Lambourn, Newbury RG17 8RE

Tel: 01793 762209

Owner: National Trust **Contact:** Coleshill Estate Office

Unusual building with a dolls'-house appearance.

Location: MAP 3:C1, OS Ref. SU282 820. 3½m N of Lambourn, on W side of B4000.

BLENHEIM PALACE

See page 121 for full page entry.

BROOK COTTAGE

Well Lane, Alkerton, Nr Banbury OX15 6NL

Tel: 01295 670303/670590 **Fax:** 01295 730362

Owner/Contact: Mrs David Hodges

4 acre hillside garden. Roses, clematis, water gardens, colour co-ordinated borders, trees, shrubs.

Location: MAP 7:A10, OS Ref. SP378 428. 6m NW of Banbury, ½m off A422 Banbury to Stratford-upon-Avon road.

Open: Easter Mon–end Oct: Mon–Fri, 9am–6pm. Evenings, weekends and all group visits by appointment.

Admission: Adult £5, OAP £4, Child Free.

BROUGHTON CASTLE

See page 122 for full page entry.

BUSCOT OLD PARSONAGE

Buscot, Faringdon, Oxfordshire SN7 8DQ

Tel: 01793 762209

Owner: National Trust **Contact:** Coleshill Estate Office

An early 18th century house of Cotswold stone on the bank of the Thames.

Location: MAP 6:P12, OS Ref. SU231 973. 2m from Lechlade, 4m N of Faringdon on A417.

BUSCOT PARK

BUSCOT, FARINGDON, OXFORDSHIRE SN7 8BU

www.buscotpark.com

Tel: Infoline 01367 240932 / Office 01367 240786 **Fax:** 01367 241794

E-mail: estbuscot@aol.com

Owner: National Trust (Administered on their behalf by Lord Faringdon)

Contact: The Estate Office

Family home of Lord Faringdon who continues to care for the property on behalf of the National Trust, together with the family art collection, the Faringdon Collection, which is displayed in the House. Consequently both the house and grounds remain intimate and idiosyncratic and very much a family home, allowing each generation to refresh and enliven the property for the enjoyment of both family and visitors. The Collection contains old master paintings and contemporary works in various media, as well as fine furniture and decorative art. The Pleasure Grounds include the renowned water garden designed by Harold Peto in 1904 and the Four Seasons Walled Garden created by the present Lord Faringdon.

Location: MAP 6:P12, OS Ref. SU239 973. Between Faringdon and Lechlade on A417.

Open: House, Grounds and Tearoom: 1 Apr–30 Sept: Wed–Fri, 2–6pm (last entry to house 5pm). Also open BH Mons and Good Fri, and the following weekends; 9/10, 23/24, 30 Apr; 1, 14/15, 28/29 May; 11/12, 25/26 Jun; 9/10, 23/24 Jul; 13/14, 27/28 Aug; 10/11, 24/25 Sept. Grounds only: 1 Apr–30 Sept, Mon & Tue, 2–6pm.

Admission: House & Grounds: Adult £8, Child £4. Grounds only: Adult £5, Child £2.50. NT members Free. Groups must book in writing, or by fax or e-mail. Disabled visitors may book single seater PMV in advance.

Occasional plant sales. Ample for cars, 2 coach spaces. May be exercised in overflow car park only.

CHASTLETON HOUSE

Chastleton, nr Moreton-in-Marsh, Oxfordshire GL56 0SU

Tel/Fax: 01608 674981 **Infoline:** 01494 755560

Owner: National Trust **Contact:** The Custodian

An atmospheric gem of a Jacobean country house.

Location: MAP 6:P10, OS Ref. SP248 291. 6m ENE of Stow-on-the-Wold. 1½ miles NW of A436. Approach only from A436 between the A44 (W of Chipping Norton) and Stow.

CHRIST CHURCH CATHEDRAL

The Sacristy, The Cathedral, Oxford OX1 1DP

Tel: 01865 276154

Contact: Tony Fox

12th century Norman Church, formerly an Augustinian monastery, given Cathedral status in 16th century by Henry VIII. Private tours available.

Location: MAP 7:A12, OS Ref. SP515 059. Just S of city centre, off St Aldates. Entry via Meadow Gate visitors' entrance on S side of college.

Open: Mon–Sat: 9am–5pm. Suns: 2–5pm.

Admission: Adult £6, Child under 5 & OAP Free.

DEDDINGTON CASTLE

Deddington, Oxfordshire

Tel: 01424 775705 **E-mail:** customers@english-heritage.org.uk

www.english-heritage.org.uk/deddingtoncastle

Owner: English Heritage, managed by Deddington Parish Council

Contact: 1066 Battle Abbey

Extensive earthworks marking the site of an 11th century motte and bailey castle.

Location: MAP 7:A10, OS Ref. SP472 316. S of B4031 on E side of Deddington, 17 miles N of Oxford on A423. 5 miles S of Banbury.

Open: Any reasonable time.

Admission: Free. Opening times and prices are valid until 31st March 2011, after this date details are subject to change please visit www.english-heritage.org.uk for the most up-to-date information.

On leads.

DITCHLEY PARK

Enstone, Oxfordshire OX7 4ER

Tel: 01608 677346 **www.ditchley.co.uk**

Owner: Ditchley Foundation **Contact:** Brigadier Christopher Galloway

The most important house by James Gibbs, with magnificent interiors by William Kent and Henry Flitcroft. For three centuries the home of the Lee family, restored in the 1930s by Ronald and Nancy (Lancaster) Tree, it was frequently used at weekends by Sir Winston Churchill during World War II.

Location: MAP 7:A11, OS Ref. SP391 214. 2m NE from Charlbury. 13 miles NW of Oxford – 4 miles on from Woodstock (Blenheim Palace).

Open: Visits only by prior arrangement with the Bursar, weekdays preferred.

Admission: £7.50 per person (minimum charge £60).

GREAT COXWELL BARN

Great Coxwell, Faringdon, Oxfordshire

Tel: 01793 762209 **E-mail:** greatcoxwellbarn@nationaltrust.org.uk

Owner: National Trust **Contact:** Coleshill Estate Office

A 13th century monastic barn, stone built with stone tiled roof, which has an interesting timber construction.

Location: MAP 3:C1, OS Ref. SU269 940. 2m SW of Faringdon between A420 and B4019.

Open: All year: daily at reasonable hours.

Admission: £1. Free to NT members.

KINGSTON BAGPUIZE HOUSE

See page 123 for full page entry.

For unique **Civil wedding** venues see our index at the end of the book.

GREYS COURT

ROTHERFIELD GREYS, HENLEY-ON-THAMES, OXFORDSHIRE RG9 4PG

Infoline: 01494 755564 **Tel:** 01491 628529 **E-mail:** greyscourt@nationaltrust.org.uk

Owner: National Trust **Contact:** The Property Operations Manager

This enchanting and intimate family home in a sixteenth century mansion, is set amidst a patchwork of colourful walled gardens, courtyard buildings including a Tudor donkey wheel and medieval walls and towers. Beyond lies an estate and beech woodlands set in the rolling Chiltern Hills.

Location: MAP 3:E1, OS Ref. SU725 834. 3m W of Henley-on-Thames, E of B481.

Open: House: 1 Apr–30 Oct, Wed–Sun, 1–5pm. Garden & Tearoom: 1 Apr–30 Oct, Wed–Sun, 11am–5pm. Last entry 4.30pm. Open BH Mons but closed Good Fri.

***Admission:** House & Garden: Adult £8.20, Child £5.40, Family £21.90. Group: Adult £7.10, Child £4.40. Garden Only: Adult £6, Child £3.20, Family £15.30. Group: Adult £5.20, Child £3. Groups must book in advance. Free to NT members. * Includes a voluntary donation but visitors can choose to pay the standard prices displayed at the property and on the website.

Grounds partial. WCs. In car park only, on leads.

Contact Property Operations Manager.

MINSTER LOVELL HALL & DOVECOTE

Witney, Oxfordshire

Tel: 01424 775705 **E-mail:** customers@english-heritage.org.uk

www.english-heritage.org.uk/minsterlovellhallanddovecote

Owner: English Heritage **Contact:** 1066 Battle Abbey

The ruins of Lord Lovell's 15th century manor house stand in a lovely setting on the banks of the River Windrush.

Location: MAP 6:P11, OS Ref. SP325 113. Adjacent to Minster Lovell Church; 3 miles W of Witney off A40.

Open: Any reasonable time. Dovecote – exterior only.

Admission: Free. Opening times and prices are valid until 31st March 2011, after this date details are subject to change please visit www.english-heritage.org.uk for the most up-to-date information.

On leads.

Greys Court

MAPLEDURHAM HOUSE

MAPLEDURHAM, READING RG4 7TR

www.mapledurham.co.uk

Tel: 0118 9723350 **Fax:** 0118 9724016 **E-mail:** enquiries@mapledurham.co.uk

Owner: The Mapledurham Trust **Contact:** Mrs Lola Andrews

Late 16th century Elizabethan home of the Blount family. Original plaster ceilings, great oak staircase, fine collection of paintings and a private chapel in Strawberry Hill Gothick added in 1797. 15th century watermill fully restored producing flour, semoline and bran.

Location: MAP 3:E3, OS Ref. SU670 767. N of River Thames. 4m NW of Reading, 1½ m W of A4074.

Open: Easter–Sept: Sats, Suns & BHs, 2–5.30pm. Last admission 5pm. Midweek parties by arrangement only. Mapledurham Trust reserves the right to alter or amend opening times or prices without prior notification.

Admission: Please call 01189 723350 for details.

Special Events: Various craft fairs, game fairs, corporate days, open air theatre and wedding receptions held in the grounds.

Partial.

MAPLEDURHAM WATERMILL

MAPLEDURHAM, READING RG4 7TR

www.mapledurhamwatermill.co.uk

Tel: 01189 723350 **Fax:** 01189 724016 **E-mail:** enquiries@mapledurham.co.uk

Owner: The Mapledurham Trust **Contact:** Mrs Lola Andrews

The last working watermill on the Thames still producing flour. It is a 600-year-old estate mill, powered by a wooden undershot waterwheel with parts of the original wooden structure still surviving inside the building. Sensitively repaired, visitors can see the milling process using French burr millstones.

Location: MAP 3:E3, OS Ref. SU670 767. N of River Thames. 4m NW of Reading, 1½ m W of A4074.

Open: Easter–Sept: Sats, Sundays & BH's 2–5.30pm. Midweek parties by arrangement only. Sunday afternoons in October.

Admission: Please call 01189 723350 for details.

Partial. WCs. By arrangement. In grounds.

MILTON MANOR HOUSE

MILTON, ABINGDON, OXFORDSHIRE OX14 4EN

www.miltonmanorhouse.com

Tel: 01235 831287 **Fax:** 01235 862321

Owner: Anthony Mockler-Barrett Esq **Contact:** Alex Brakespear

Dreamily beautiful mellow brick house, traditionally designed by Inigo Jones. Celebrated Gothic library and Catholic chapel. Lived in by the family; pleasant relaxed and informal atmosphere. Park with fine old trees, stables, walled garden and woodland walk. Picnickers welcome. Free Parking, refreshments and pony rides usually available.

Location: MAP 3:D1, OS Ref. SU485 924. Just off A34, village and house signposted, 9m S of Oxford, 15m N of Newbury. 3m from Abingdon and Didcot.

Open: Easter Sun & BH Mon; 1 May & BH Mon; then 15–31 May & 14–31 Aug. Guided tours of house: 2pm, 3pm & 4pm. For weddings/events etc. please contact the Administrator. Groups by arrangement throughout the year.

Admission: House & Gardens: Adult £7, Child £3.50. Garden & Grounds only: Adult £3, Child £1.50. Family tickets available for multiple visits throughout season. Garden & Grounds only (2+2): £30.

Grounds. Obligatory. Free. Guide dogs only.

PRIORY COTTAGES

1 Mill Street, Steventon, Abingdon, Oxfordshire OX13 6SP

Tel: 01793 762209

Owner: National Trust **Contact:** Coleshill Estate Office

Former monastic buildings, converted into two houses. South Cottage contains the Great Hall of the original priory.

Location: MAP 3:D1, OS Ref. SU466 914. 4m S of Abingdon, on B4017 off A34 at Abingdon West or Milton interchange on corner of The Causeway and Mill Street, entrance in Mill Street.

RICHARD JEFFERIES FARMHOUSE AND MUSEUM

Marlborough Road, Coate SN3 6AA

Tel: 01793 783040 **E-mail:** R.Jefferies_Society@tiscali.co.uk

Owner: Swindon Borough Council

Dating from the early 18th century, the Museum was the home of Richard Jefferies, nature writer, who is cited by historians as an authority upon agriculture and rural life in Victorian England. The main house is a Grade II listed building.

Location: Adjacent to the Sun Inn on Marlborough Road A4259 close to Coate Water Country Park.

Open: 1st, 3rd & 4th Sundays from May to end Sept 2–5pm. 2nd Wed throughout the year. 10am–4pm. Open at other times by request.

Admission: Free

ROUSHAM HOUSE

NR STEEPLE ASTON, BICESTER, OXFORDSHIRE OX25 4QX

www.rousham.org

Tel: 01869 347110 / 07860 360407 **E-mail:** ccd@rousham.org
Owner/Contact: Charles Cottrell-Dormer Esq

Rousham represents the first stage of English landscape design and remains almost as William Kent (1685–1748) left it. One of the few gardens of this date to have escaped alteration. Includes Venus' Vale, Townesend's Building, seven-arched Praeneste, the Temple of the Mill and a sham ruin known as the 'Eyecatcher'. The house was built in 1635 by Sir Robert Dormer. Excellent location for fashion, advertising, photography etc.

Location: MAP 7:A10, OS Ref. SP477 242. E of A4260, 12m N of Oxford, S of B4030, 7m W of Bicester.

Open: Garden: All year: daily, 10am–4.30pm (last adm). House: Pre-booked groups, May–Sept. (Mon–Thur)

Admission: Garden: £5. No children under 15yrs.

Partial.

STONOR *See page 124 for full page entry.*

Rousham House

SWALCLIFFE BARN

Swalcliffe Village, Banbury, Oxfordshire OX15 5DR

Tel: 01295 788278 **Contact:** Jeffrey Demmar

15th century half cruck barn, houses agricultural and trade vehicles which are part of the Oxford County Museum Services Collection. Exhibition of 2500 years' of Swalcliffe History.

Location: MAP 7:A10, OS Ref. SP378 378. 6m W of Banbury Cross on B4035.

Open: Easter–end Oct: Suns & BHs, 2–5pm.

Admission: Free.

WATERPERRY GARDENS

Waterperry, Nr Wheatley, Oxfordshire OX33 1JZ

Tel: 01844 339226 **Fax:** 01844 339883 **Email:** office@waterperrygardens.co.uk

www.waterperrygardens.co.uk

The estate at Waterperry is home to 8 acres of beautiful ornamental gardens, a quality plant centre and garden shop, gift barn, gallery, teashop and museum. There's also a year round programme of events and arts, crafts and gardening courses. Coach parties and groups welcome by arrangement.

Location: MAP 7:B12, OS Ref. SP610 068.

Open: Open every day except between Christmas and New Year and during Art in Action from 21–24 Jul 2011. Low season 10am–5pm. High season 10am–5.30pm.

Admission: Low season. Jan–Feb 2011 Adults and concessions £4.20. High season. March–October 2011 Adults £6.10. Concessions £4.80. Low season. Nov–Dec 2011. Adults and concessions £4.30. Children aged 16 and under free all year round.

WCs. Licensed. Licensed. By arrangement. Limited for coaches. Dogs not allowed in the gardens unless assistance dogs. Dogs must be on a lead elsewhere on the estate. Held throughout the year. Visit www.waterperrygardens.co.uk for details.

THE COLLEGES OF OXFORD UNIVERSITY

For further details contact:
Oxford Information Centre,
15–16 Broad Street, Oxford OX1 3AS
Tel: +44 (0)1865 252200
Email: tic@oxford.gov.uk
Fax: +44 (0)1865 240261
www.visitoxford.org

All Souls' College
High Street
Tel: 01865 279379
Founder: Archbishop Henry Chichele 1438
Open: Mon–Fri, 2–4pm (4.30pm in summer)

Balliol College
Broad Street
Tel: 01865 277777
Founder: John de Balliol 1263
Open: Daily, 1–5pm (or dusk)

Brasenose College
Radcliffe Square
Tel: 01865 277830
Founder: William Smythe, Bishop of Lincoln 1509
Open: Daily, 10–11.30am (tour groups only) & 2–4.30pm (5pm in summer)

Christ Church
St. Aldates
Tel: 01865 286573
Founder: Cardinal Wolsey/Henry VIII 1546
Open: Mon–Sat, 9am–5.30pm; Sun, 1–5.30pm (last adm 4.30pm)

Corpus Christi College
Merton Street
Tel: 01865 276700
Founder: Bishop Richard Fox 1517
Open: Daily, 1.30–4.30pm

Exeter College
Turl Street
Tel: 01865 279600
Founder: Bishop Stapleden of Exeter 1314
Open: Daily, 2–5pm

Green Templeton College
Woodstock Road
Tel: 01865 274770
Founder: Dr Cecil Green 1979
Open: By appointment only

Harris Manchester College
Mansfield Road
Tel: 01865 271011
Founder: Lord Harris of Peckham 1996
Open: Chapel only: Mon–Fri, 8.30am–5.30pm. Sat, 9am–12 noon

Hertford College
Catte Street
Tel: 01865 279400
Founder: TC Baring MP l740
Open: Daily, l0am–noon & 2pm–dusk

Jesus College
Turl Street
Tel: 01865 279700
Founder: Dr Hugh Price (Queen Elizabeth I) 1571
Open: Daily, 2–4.30pm

Keble College
Parks Road
Tel: 01865 272727
Founder: Public money 1870
Open: Daily, 2–5pm

Kellogg College
Banbury Road
Tel: 01865 61200
Founder: Kellogg Foundation 1990
Open: Mon–Fri, 9am–5pm

Lady Margaret Hall
Norham Gardens
Tel: 01865 274300
Founder: Dame Elizabeth Wordsworth 1878
Open: Gardens: 10am–5pm

Linacre College
St Cross Road
Tel: 01865 271650
Founder: Oxford University 1962
Open: By appointment only

Lincoln College
Turl Street
Tel: 01865 279800
Founder: Bishop Richard Fleming of Lincoln 1427
Open: Mon–Sat, 2–5pm; Sun, 11am–5pm

Magdalen College
High Street
Tel: 01865 276000
Founder: William of Waynefleete 1458
Open: Oct–Jun: 1–6pm/dusk (whichever is the earlier) and Jul–Sept: 12 noon–6pm

Mansfield College
Mansfield Road
Tel: 01865 270999
Founder: Free Churches 1995
Open: Mon–Fri, 9am–5pm

Merton College
Merton Street
Tel: 01865 276310
Founder: Walter de Merton l264
Open: Mon–Fri, 2–4pm; Sat & Sun, 10am–4pm

New College
New College Lane
Tel: 01865 279555
Founder: William of Wykeham, Bishop of Winchester 1379
Open: Daily, 11am–5pm (summer); 2–4pm (winter)

Nuffield College
New Road
Tel: 01865 278500
Founder: William Morris (Lord Nuffield) 1937
Open: Daily, 9am–5pm

Oriel College
Oriel Square
Tel: 01865 276555
Founder: Edward II/Adam de Brome 1326
Open: By arrangement with TIC

Pembroke College
St Aldates
Tel: 01865 276444
Founder: James I 1624
Open: By appointment only

The Queen's College
High Street
Tel: 01865 279120
Founder: Robert de Eglesfield 1341
Open: By arrangement with TIC

Somerville College
Graduate House, Woodstock Road
Tel: 01865 270600
Founder: Association for the Education of Women 1879
Open: 2–5.30pm

St. Anne's College
56 Woodstock Road
Tel: 01865 274800
Founder: Association for the Education of Women 1878
Open: 9am–5pm

St. Antony's College
62 Woodstock Road
Tel: 01865 284700
Founder: M. Antonin Bess 1948
Open: By appointment only

St. Catherine's College
Manor Road
Tel: 01865 271700
Founder: Oxford University 1964
Open: 9am–5pm

St. Edmund Hall
Queens Lane
Tel: 01865 279000
Founder: St. Edmund Riche of Abingdon c.l278
Open: Mon–Sun, Term time, 12 noon–4pm

St. Hilda's College
Cowley Place
Tel: 01865 276884
Founder: Miss Dorothea Beale l893
Open: By appointment only

St. Hugh's College
St. Margarets Road
Tel: 01865 274900
Founder: Dame Elizabeth Wordsworth 1886
Open: 10am–4pm

St. John's College
St. Giles
Tel: 01865 277300
Founder: Sir Thomas White 1555
Open: 1–5pm (or dusk)

St. Peter's College
New Inn Hall Street
Tel: 01865 278900
Founder: Rev. Christopher Charvasse 1928
Open: 10am–5pm

Trinity College
Broad Street
Tel: 01865 279900
Founder: Sir Thomas Pope 1554–5
Open: Mon–Fri 10am–noon and 2–4pm. Sat & Sun in term, 2–4pm; Sat & Sun in vacation 10am–12 noon and 2–4pm

University College
High Street
Tel: 01865 276602
Founder: Archdeacon William of Durham 1249
Open: Contact College for details

Wadham College
Parks Road
Tel: 01865 277900
Founder: Nicholas & Dorothy Wadham 1610
Open: Term time: daily, 1–4.15pm. Vacation: daily, 10.30–11.45am & 1–4.15pm

Wolfson College
Linton Road
Tel: 01865 274100
Founder: Oxford University 1966
Open: Daylight hours

Worcester College
Worcester Street
Tel: 01865 278300
Founder: Sir Thomas Cookes 1714
Open: Daily, 2–5pm

Christchurch College, Oxford

This information is intended only as a guide. Times are subject to change due to functions, examinations, conferences, holidays, etc. You are advised to check in advance opening times and admission charges which may apply at some colleges, and at certain times of the year. Visitors wishing to gain admittance to the Colleges (meaning the Courts, not to the staircases and students' rooms) are advised to contact the Tourist Information Office. It should be noted that Halls normally close for lunch (12 noon–2pm) and many are not open during the afternoon. Chapels may be closed during services. Libraries are not normally open, and Gardens do not usually include the Fellows' garden. Visitors, and especially guided groups, should always call on the Porters Lodge first. Groups should always book in advance. Dogs, except guide dogs are not allowed in any colleges.

■ **Owner**
National Trust

■ **Contact**
The Property Manager
Clandon Park &
Hatchlands Park
East Clandon
Guildford
Surrey GU4 7RT
Tel: 01483 222482
Fax: 01483 223176
E-mail: hatchlands@nationaltrust.org.uk

■ **Location**
MAP 19:A11

Clandon
OS Ref. TQ042 512
At West Clandon on the A247, 3m E of Guildford.
Rail: Clandon BR 1m.

Hatchlands
OS Ref. TQ063 516
E of East Clandon on the A246 Guildford–Leatherhead road.
Rail: Clandon BR 2 1/2m, Horsley 3m.

■ **Opening Times**
Clandon – House
13 March–30 October
Tue–Thur, Suns & BH Mons, Good Fri & Easter Sat
11am–5pm.

Garden
As house. 11am–5pm.

Queens Royal Surrey Regiment Museum
As house. 11am–5pm.

Hatchlands – House
1 April–30 October
Tue–Thur, Suns & BH Mon, Plus Fris in August.
2–5.30pm.

Park Walks
1 April–30 October
Daily 11am–6pm.

■ ***Admission**

Clandon	
House/Grounds	£8.60
Child	£4.20
Family	£23.10
Pre-booked Groups	
Adult	£7.00
Hatchlands	
House/Grounds	£7.00
Child	£3.60
Family	£18.90
Park Walks only	£4.00
Child	£2.00
Pre-booked Groups	
Adult	£5.95
Combined ticket	
Adult	£12.20
Child	£6.10
Family	£35.10

*includes a voluntary donation but visitors can choose to pay the standard prices displayed at the property and on the website.

Conference/Function

ROOM	SIZE	MAX CAPACITY
Marble Hall Clandon Pk	40' x 40'	160 seated 200 standing

© NTPL / John Miller

© NTPL / John Miller

CLANDON PARK & HATCHLANDS PARK

www.nationaltrust.org.uk/clandonpark

Clandon Park & Hatchlands Park were built during the 18th century and are set amidst beautiful grounds. They are two of England's most outstanding country houses and are only five minutes' drive apart.

Clandon Park is a grand Palladian Mansion, built c1730 for the 2nd Lord Onslow by the Venetian architect Giacomo Leoni. Clandon's interior is the most complete of his work to survive and is notable for its magnificent two-storied, white Marble Hall.

The Onslows have been active in the country's political history, being the only family ever to have produced three Speakers of the House of Commons. The last of these, Arthur Onslow, held the post from 1727 for over 30 years. Activity was not restricted to England; at the end of the 19th century the 4th Earl of Onslow served as Governor of New Zealand, whereupon the Maori meeting house came to be in the gardens at Clandon Park.

There is also an intimate sunken Dutch garden, at its best in May and June and a stunning bulb field flowering in spring.

Displayed inside the house is a superb collection of 18th century furniture, textiles and one of the finest collections of porcelain, including Meissen *Commedia Dell' Arte* figures.

Hatchlands Park was built in 1756 for Admiral Boscawen, hero of the Battle of Louisburg, and contains the earliest recorded decorations in an English country house by Robert Adam, whose ceilings appropriately feature nautical motifs.

The rooms are hung with the Cobbe Collection of Old Master paintings and portraits. The house is also home to the Cobbe Collection of keyboard instruments, the world's largest group of early keyboard instruments owned or played by famous composers such as Purcell, JC Bach, Mozart, Liszt, Chopin, Mahler and Elgar.

Hatchlands is set in a beautiful 430-acre Repton park, with a variety of way-marked walks offering vistas of open parkland and idyllic views of the house. The woodlands are a haven for wildlife and there is a stunning Bluebell wood in May.

There are frequent concerts on the instruments on the collection (for more details please contact: The Cobbe Collection Trust, 01483 211474, www.cobbecollection.co.uk).

© NTPL / Bill Batten

No photography.

For Clandon weddings and receptions tel: 01483 222502.

WCs. Hatchlands suitable. Clandon please tel for details.

Hatchlands: 01483 211120.

Licensed. Clandon: 01483 222502.

Clandon – by arrangement.

Children's quizzes available.

Hatchlands Parkland only.

Clandon only.

Tel: 01483 222482.

LOSELEY PARK

www.loseleypark.co.uk

Loseley Park, built in 1562 by Sir William More to entertain Queen Elizabeth I, is a fine example of Elizabethan architecture – its mellow stone brought from the ruins of Waverley Abbey now over 850 years old. The house is set amid magnificent parkland grazed by the Loseley Jersey herd. Many visitors comment on the very friendly atmosphere of the house. It is a country house, the family home of descendants of the builder.

Furniture, paintings and artefacts have been collected by the family since Loseley was built, including panelling from Nonsuch Palace, English and European furniture, a unique chalk fireplace and porcelain from the East. However, with all the history, it is still a family home.

Loseley Park is a stunning wedding venue with ceremonies in the Great Hall and receptions in the 17th century Tithe Barn. There are also flexible facilities for corporate and private functions. Highly rated film location. Christian Cancer/Parkinson's Disease Help Centre.

Garden

A magnificent Cedar of Lebanon presides over the front lawn. Parkland adjoins the lawn and a small lake adds to the beauty of Front Park. Walled Garden: Based on a Gertrude Jekyll design, the five gardens include the award-winning rose garden containing over 1,000 bushes, a magnificent vine walk, herb garden, colourful fruit and flower garden and the serene white garden. Other features include an organic vegetable garden and moat walk. HDRA Seed Library plants.

Lakeside walk. Picnic area. Chapel. Hire of gardens and grounds for corporate and private events. All group visits to be booked in advance. Group garden tours available. Lectures on history of house and contents by arrangement. South East Tourism Award Winner 2006, Runner-up 2008.

Corporate and private hire for special functions, conferences, meetings, civil ceremonies, wedding receptions, Elizabethan Banquets.

May alight at entrance to property. Access to all areas except house first floor. WCs.

Courtyard Tea Room & Garden Marquee serving light lunches, snacks and cream teas.

House tour obligatory: 40 mins. Group Garden tours available.

150 cars, 6 coaches. Summer overflow car park.

Guide dogs only.

100 max.

Tel or see website for details.

Owner

Mr Michael More-Molyneux

Contact

Sue Grant
Events Office
Loseley Park
Guildford
Surrey GU3 1HS

Tel: 01483 304440
Tel Events: 01483 405119/120
Fax: 01483 302036
E-mail: enquiries@loseleypark.co.uk

Location

MAP 3:G3
OS Ref. SU975 471

30m SW of London, leave A3 S of Guildford on to B3000. Signposted.

Bus: 1¼m from House.

Rail: Farncombe 2m, Guildford 3m, Godalming 4m.

Air: Heathrow 30m, Gatwick 30m.

Opening Times

Summer
Garden, Shop & Tearoom
May–September
Tues–Sun & BH Mons in May & August, 11am–5pm.

Loseley House
(guided tours)
May–August
Tues–Thurs, Suns & BH Mons in May & August, 1–5pm.

All Year (Private Hire)
Tithe Barn, Chestnut Lodge, House, Garden Marquee, Walled Garden and Grounds. Civil ceremonies and receptions. Lunches and dinners. Off-road 4x4 course and showground. Activity Days.

Admission

House & Gardens

Adult	£8.00
Child (5–16yrs)	£4.00
Conc.	£7.50
Child (under 5yrs)	Free
Family (2 + 3)	£20.00
Booked Groups (10+)	
Adult	£7.00
Child (5–16yrs)	£3.50
Garden tours	£3.00pp

Garden & Grounds only

Adult	£4.50
Child (5–16yrs)	£2.25
Conc.	£4.00
Family (2 + 3)	£12.00
Booked Groups (10+)	
Adult	£3.50
Child (5–16yrs)	£1.75

Conference/Function

ROOM	SIZE	MAX CAPACITY
Tithe Barn	100' x 18'	180
Marquee sites available		up to 4,000
Great Hall	70' x 40'	80
Drawing Rm	40' x 30'	50
Chestnut Ldg	42' x 20'	50
White Garden Marquee		70

■ **Owner**

Trustees of the Titsey Foundation.

■ **Contact**

Titsey
Oxted
Surrey RH8 0SD

Information Line: 01273 715359
Events Organiser: 01273 715356
Fax: 01273 779783
E-mail: kate.moisson@struttandparker.com

■ **Location**

MAP 19:F10
OS Ref. TQ406 551

■ **Opening Times**

Mid May–end of September: Wednesdays, Sundays, May & August Bank Holidays, 1–5pm. Garden Only Saturdays from 14 May–24 September.
The Church of St James is open from Easter Sunday–31 October each Wednesday, Saturday, Sunday and Bank Holidays.

■ **Admission**

House and Garden	£7.00
Garden Only	£4.50
Children under 16	£1.00
Woodland walks and open 365 days.	Free

Pre-booked tours

House and garden inc. guide per person	£8.50
Garden Only per person	£6.00
Garden Guide per group	£50

TITSEY PLACE

www.titsey.org

Dating from the 16th century, the Titsey Estate is one the largest surviving historic estates in Surrey. Nestling under the North Downs, Titsey Place, with its stunning garden, lakes, woodland walks, walled kitchen garden and park offering panoramic views, and enchants visitors. Enjoy the fine family portraits, furniture, a beautiful collection of porcelain and a marvelous set of four Canaletto pictures of Venice. After visiting the mansion house and grounds, why not relax in our tea room where light refreshments are available.

 Partial.

 Obligatory.

 Limited for coaches.

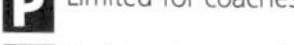 Guide dogs only.

BOX HILL

The Old Fort, Box Hill Road, Box Hill, Tadworth KT20 7LB

Tel: 01306 885502 **Fax:** 01306 875030

Owner: National Trust **Contact:** Head Warden

An outstanding area of woodland and chalk downland with wonderful walks and magnificent views across the weald. Long famous as a place for visitors and naturalists to enjoy as well as family picnics. Explore the Discovery Centre in the shop and 'Bee' amazed.

Location: MAP 19:C11, OS Ref. TQ171 519. 1m N of Dorking, 1.5m S of Leatherhead on A24.

Open: All year.

Admission: Free. Charge for car park, NT members Free.

Partial. WCs.

CLANDON PARK & HATCHLANDS PARK

See page 130 for full page entry.

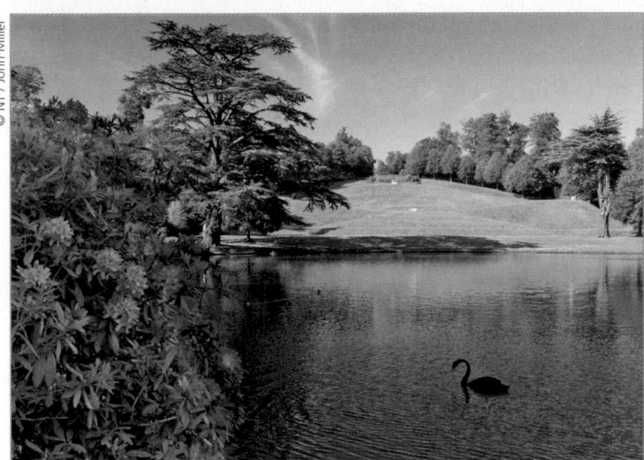

CLAREMONT LANDSCAPE GARDEN

PORTSMOUTH ROAD, ESHER, SURREY KT10 9JG

www.nationaltrust.org.uk/claremont

Tel: 01372 467806 **Fax:** 01372 476420 **E-mail:** claremont@nationaltrust.org.uk

Owner: National Trust **Contact:** The Property Manager

One of the earliest surviving English landscape gardens, restored to its former glory. Begun by Sir John Vanbrugh and Charles Bridgeman before 1720, the garden was extended and naturalised by William Kent. 'Capability' Brown also made improvements. Features include a lake, island with pavilion, grotto, turf amphitheatre, viewpoints and avenues.

Location: MAP 19:B9, OS Ref. TQ128 632. On S edge of Esher, on E side of A307 (no access from Esher bypass).

Open: Garden open throughout the year. Jan–end Mar, Nov–end Dec: daily except Mons: 10am–5pm or sunset if earlier. Apr–end Oct: daily: 10am–6pm. Closed 25 Dec.

***Admission:** Adult £6.80, Child £3.40. Family (2+2) £17 Groups (15+), £5.40. £1 tearoom voucher given if arriving by public transport. Coach groups must book; no coach groups on Sundays. *includes a voluntary donation but visitors can choose to pay the standard prices displayed at the property and on the website.

Special Events: Full events programme throughout the year. Please check website for details or send SAE for copy of Events Programme. Garden may close early in the event of bad weather (particularly high winds) and for certain events days in June & July. Please telephone property to check before travelling.

WCs. Licensed By arrangement. Limited for coaches. Guide dogs only. No dogs (Apr–Oct).

FARNHAM CASTLE

Farnham, Surrey GU9 0AG

Tel: 01252 721194 **Fax:** 01252 711283 **E-mail:** conf@farnhamcastle.com

Owner: The Church Commissioners **Contact:** Farnham Castle

Bishop's Palace built in Norman times by Henry of Blois. Tudor and Jacobean additions.

Location: MAP 3:F3, OS Ref. SU839 474. ½m N of Farnham town centre on A287.

Open: All year, except Christmas week: Weds, 2–4pm.

Admission: Adult £2.50, Child/Conc £1.50.

FARNHAM CASTLE KEEP

Castle Hill, Farnham, Surrey GU9 0JA

Tel: 01252 713393 **E-mail:** customers@english-heritage.org.uk

www.english-heritage.org.uk/farnhamcastlekeep

Owner: English Heritage **Contact:** Visitor Operations Team

The impressive motte, shell-keep, bailey wall and other defences of a castle founded in 1138 and redeveloped by Henry II after 1155. Long a residence of the wealthy Bishops of Winchester, the fortress itself was abandoned after Civil War service; later attendant buildings remain in private occupation.

Location: MAP 3:F3, OS Ref. SU837 473. ½m N of Farnham town centre on A287.

Open: 1 May–23 Dec: Mon–Fri, 9am–5pm (or dusk, whichever is earlier), Sat–Sun, 9am–4pm. 24 Dec–31 Jan: closed. 1 Feb–31 Mar: Mon–Fri, 9am–5pm, Sat–Sun, 9am–4pm.

Admission: Free. Opening times and prices are valid until 31st March 2011, after this date details are subject to change please visit www.english-heritage.org.uk for the most up-to-date information.

Partial.

GODDARDS

Abinger Common, Dorking, Surrey RH5 6TH

Tel: 01628 825925 **E-mail:** bookings@landmarktrust.org.uk

www.landmarktrust.org.uk

Owner: The Lutyens Trust, leased to The Landmark Trust **Contact:** The Landmark Trust

Built by Sir Edwin Lutyens in 1898–1900 and enlarged by him in 1910. Garden by Gertrude Jekyll. Given to the Lutyens Trust in 1991 and now managed and maintained by the Landmark Trust, a building preservation charity who let it for holidays. The whole house, apart from the library, is available for holidays. Full details of Goddards and 189 other historic and architecturally important buildings available for holidays are featured in The Landmark Handbook (price £10 plus p&p refundable against a booking) and on the website.

Location: MAP 19:B12, OS Ref. TQ120 450. 4½ m SW of Dorking on the village green in Abinger Common. Signposted Abinger Common, Friday Street and Leith Hill from A25.

Open: Available for holidays for up to 12 people. Other visits strictly by appointment. Must be booked in advance, including parking, which is very limited. Visits booked for Weds afternoons from the Wed after Easter until the last Wed of Oct, between 2.30–5pm. Only those with pre-booked tickets will be admitted. Visitors will have access to part of the garden and house only.

Admission: £4. Tickets available from Mrs Baker on 01306 730871, Mon–Fri, 9am & 6pm.

GREAT FOSTERS

Stroude Road, Egham, Surrey TW20 9UR

Tel: 01784 433822 **Fax:** 01784 472455 **E-mail:** enquiries@greatfosters.co.uk

www.greatfosters.co.uk

Owner: The Sutcliffe family **Contact:** Amanda Dougans

Grade II listed garden. Laid out in 1918 by W H Romaine-Walker in partnership with G H Jenkins, incorporating earlier features. The site covers 50 acres and is associated with a 16th century country house, reputed to be a former royal hunting lodge and converted into an hotel by the owners in 1931. The main formal garden is surrounded on three sides by a moat, thought to be of medieval origin, and is modelled on the pattern of a Persian carpet. The garden also includes an amphitheatre, lake and a sunken rose garden.

Location: MAP 3:G2, OS Ref. TQ015 694. M25 J/13, follow signs to Egham. Under motorway bridge, first left at roundabout (The Avenue). Left at the mini roundabout into Vicarage Rd. Right at next roundabout. Over M25, left into Stroude Rd. 500 yds on left.

Open: All year.

Admission: Free.

Partial. WC. Licensed. Guide dogs only.

Great Fosters

HAMPTON COURT PALACE

HAMPTON COURT PALACE, SURREY KT8 9AU

www.hrp.org.uk

Tel: 0844 482 7777
Venue Hire and Corporate Hospitailty: 02031 666505
Email: groupsandtraveltrade@hrp.org.uk **Web:** www.hrp.org.uk
Owner/Contact: Historic Royal Palaces

Henry VIII is most associated with this majestic palace, which he extended and developed in grand style after acquiring it from Cardinal Wolsey in the 1520s. The Tudor buildings that are among the most important in exisitence, but the elegance and romance of the palace owes much to the elegant Baroque buildings commissioned by William and Mary at the end of the 17th century. The palace is set in 60 acres of gardens, that include the famous Maze. The palace is decked out in splendour including a new Tudor Court garden. Visitors will revel in this moment of history that happened at Hampton Court in 1543.

Location: MAP 19:B9, OS Ref. TQ155 686. From M25/J15 and A312, or M25/J12 and A308, or M25/J10 and A307. Rail: From London Waterloo direct to Hampton Court (32 mins). 30 minutes from Waterloo, zone 6 travelcard.

Open: Mar–Oct: Daily, 10am–6pm (last admission 5.15pm). Nov–Feb: Daily, 10am–4.30pm (last admission 3.45pm). Closed 24–26 Dec.

Admission: Telephone Information Line for admission prices: 08444 827777. Advance Ticket Sales:08444 827799. Group Bookings 08444 827770, Quote Hudson's.

Information Centre. No photography indoors. Partial. WCs. Licensed. By arrangement Ample for cars, coach parking nearby. Rates on request 0844 482 7777. Guide dogs only

KEW GARDENS

Kew, Richmond, Surrey TW9 3AB
Tel: 020 8332 5655 **Fax:** 020 8332 5610 **E-mail:** info@kew.org **www.kew.org**
Contact: Visitor Information

Kew Gardens is a World Heritage Site. It is a mixture of stunning vistas, magnificent glasshouses and beautiful landscapes beside the River Thames. This once Royal residence represents nearly 250 years of historical gardens and today its 300 acres are home to over 40,000 types of plants from rainforest to desert. There is always something to see ... as the seasons change so does Kew.

Location: MAP 19:C7, OS Ref. TQ188 776. A307. Junc. A307 & A205 (1m Chiswick roundabout M4).

Open: All year: daily (except 24/25 Dec) from 9.30am. Closing time varies according to the season. Please telephone for further information.

Admission: 1 Nov '07–31 Mar '08: Adults £12.25, From 1 Apr: £13. Concessions available. Child (under 17) Free. Discounts for groups (10+). School groups: Free.

Licensed. Limited. Guide dogs only.

KEW PALACE, HISTORIC ROYAL PALACES

Kew Gardens, Kew, Richmond, Surrey TW9 3AB
Tel: Group Bookings 020 8332 5648 **E-mail:** groupsandtraveltrade@hrp.org.uk **www.hrp.org.uk** **Contact:** Visitor Information 0844 482 7777

Kew Palace and Queen Charlotte's Cottage. The most intimate of the five royal palaces, Kew was built as a private house but became a royal residence between 1728 and 1818. Both the palace and the nearby Queen Charlotte's cottage, built in 1770, are most closely associated with King George III and his family. Discover their story.

Location: MAP 19:C7, OS Ref. TQ188 776.193. A307. Junc A307 & A205 (1m Chiswick roundabout M4). Rail: 30 minutes from Waterloo, zone 6 travelcard.

Underground: District Line station nearby. Boat: From Kingston or central London.

Open: 10 Apr–27 Sept: daily, 10am–5pm, Last admission 4.15pm.

Admission: By joint ticket purchased through Kew Gardens.

WCs. Licensed. Licensed. By arrangement. Limited.

LOSELEY PARK

See page 131 for full page entry.

PAINSHILL PARK LANDSCAPE GARDEN

PORTSMOUTH ROAD, COBHAM, SURREY KT11 1JE

www.painshill.co.uk

Tel: 01932 868113 **Fax:** 01932 868001
E-mail: info@painshill.co.uk education@painshill.co.uk
Owner: Painshill Park Trust **Contact:** Visitor Operations Team

Discover 158 acres of magnificent 18th century landscape garden and 14 acre lake. Explore unusual follies, a unique crystal Grotto and enjoy spectacular views across Surrey. The landscape and plantings offer seasonal interest, and throughout the year you can enjoy entertaining events and talks.

Location: MAP 19:B10, OS Ref. TQ099 605. M25/J10/A3 to London. W of Cobham on A245. Signposted. Rail: Cobham/Stoke d'Abernon 2m. Bus: Route 515/515A.

Open: All Year (Closed Christmas Day & Boxing Day). Mar–Oct 10.30am-6pm or Dusk if earlier (last entry 4.30pm). Nov–Feb 10.30am to 4pm or Dusk if earlier (last entry 3pm).

Admission: Adult £6.60, Conc. £5.80, Child (5–16 yrs) £3.85, Family Ticket (2 Adults & 4 Children) £22.00, Under 5's & Disabled Carer: Free. Group rates available.

WCs. Film and photography location hire. Painshill Wine and Honey. Weddings, Private and Corporate. WCs. Accessible route. Free pre-booked wheelchair loan and guided buggy tours (Cap. Max 3). Licensed. Picnic area. Inc. German and French. Pre-book 10+ groups. English £2.50 pp. Free for disabled visitors. Free. Ample for Coaches and Cars. Coaches must book. Pre-book via Education Dept. On short leads. All year. Children's parties.

© NTPL / Nick Meers

POLESDEN LACEY

GREAT BOOKHAM, NR DORKING, SURREY RH5 6BD

www.nationaltrust.org.uk/polesdenlacey

Tel: 01372 452048 **Fax:** 01372 452023 **E-mail:** polesdenlacey@nationaltrust.org.uk

Owner: National Trust **Contact:** The Property Manager

Originally an elegant 1820s Regency villa in a magnificent landscape setting. The house was remodelled after 1906 by the Hon Mrs Ronald Greville, a well-known Edwardian hostess who used the house as a backdrop for her famous weekend house parties. Her collection of fine paintings, furniture, porcelain, Fabergé and silver are still displayed in the reception rooms and galleries. Extensive grounds (1,400 acre estate), walled rose garden, lawns and landscaped walks. Restaurant, coffee shop & gift shop open daily, located outside the pay perimeter.

Location: MAP 19:B11, OS Ref. TQ136 522. 5m NW of Dorking, 2m S of Great Bookham, off A246.

Open: House: 2 Mar–30 Oct; Wed–Sun, 11am–5pm. 3–18 Dec; Sat & Sun, 11am–4pm. House speak peak tours: 8 Jan–27 Feb & 5 Nov–27 Nov, Sat & Sun, 11am–4pm. Garden, restaurant, gift and garden shop & coffee shop: 1 Jan–18 Feb, daily, 10am–4pm. 19 Feb–30 Oct, daily, 10am–5pm. 31 Oct–31 Dec, daily, 10am–4pm. Car Park: Daily 7.30am–6.30pm or dusk if later. Open BH Mons. Weekends in Jan, Feb, Nov, Dec House open by guided tour. Closed 15 Mar, 24 & 25 Dec. Last admission is 30mins before closing.

Admission: House & Grounds: Adults £12, Child £6, Family £30, Group £10.20. Grounds only: Adult £7.40, Child £3.70, Family £18.50, Group £6.30.

Licensed. Grounds only. Tel: 01372 452048 for info.

RAMSTER GARDEN

Ramster, Chiddingfold, Surrey GU8 4SN

Tel: 01428 654167 **Email:** rosie@ramsterevents.com **www.ramsterweddings.co.uk**

Owner/Contact: Mrs R Glaister

The extensive woodland gardens at Ramster are famous for their rhododendrons, azaleas and carpets of bluebells, the woodland walks are a joy to explore in the spring. Ant Wood houses a national collection of hardy hybrid rhododendrons. The teahouse is open daily for drinks delicious cakes and sandwiches.

Location: MAP 3:G4, OS Ref. SU950 333. 1½ m S of Chiddingfold on A283.

Open: Ramster Garden and Tea House are open 1 April–19 June 2011, 10am–5pm.

Admission: Adult £5, Child (under 16) Free. Groups welcome by appointment.

Partial. WCs. By arrangement. On leads. Ramster Textile Art and Embroidery Exhibition 8–21 April 2011.

RHS GARDEN WISLEY

See main index.

RUNNYMEDE

Egham, Surrey

Tel: 01784 432891 **Fax:** 01784 479007

Owner: National Trust **Contact:** The Head Warden

An historic area alongside the River Thames where, in 1215, King John sealed Magna Carta, an event commemorated by the American Bar Association Memorial. The John F Kennedy Memorial was erected in 1965 to commemorate his life. The Commonwealth Air Forces Memorial is situated overlooking Runnymede and commemorates over 20,000 airmen and women with no known grave who died during World War II. Also here are the Fairhaven Lodges, designed by Lutyens, which host a summer art gallery and tearoom all year.

Location: MAP 3:G2, OS Ref. TQ007 720. 2m W of Runnymede Bridge, on S side of A308, M25/J13.

Open: All year. Riverside Car park (grass): Riverside open Apr–Sept only, daily, 10am–7pm. Tearoom & car park (hard standing): daily, all year, 8.30am–5pm (later in Summer).

Admission: Fees payable for parking (NT members Free), fishing & mooring.

Partial. On leads near livestock.

THE SAVILL GARDEN (WINDSOR GREAT PARK, BERKSHIRE)

See page 80 (Berkshire) for full page entry.

SHALFORD MILL

Shalford, Nr Guildford, Surrey GU4 8BS

Tel: 01483 561389

Owner: National Trust **Contact:** The Navigations Office

18th c watermill unaltered since ceasing operation in 1914.

Location: MAP 3:G3, OS Ref. TQ001 476.

TITSEY PLACE

See page 132 for full page entry.

Loseley Park

■ **Owner**

English Heritage

■ **Contact**

Visitor Operations Team
Battle
Sussex TN33 0AD

Tel: 01424 775705
E-mail: customers@english-heritage.org.uk

■ **Location**

MAP 4:K5
OS Ref. TQ749 157

Top of Battle High Street. Turn off A2100 to Battle.

■ **Opening Times**

1 April–30 September: daily, 10am–6pm.

1 October–31 March: daily 10am–4pm.

Closed 24–26 December & 1 January.

■ **Admission**

Adult	£7.00
Child	£3.50
Conc.	£56.00
Family	£17.50

English Heritage members Free. 15% discount for groups (11+).

Opening times and prices are valid until 31st March 2011, after this date details are subject to change please visit www.english-heritage.org.uk for the most up-to-date information.

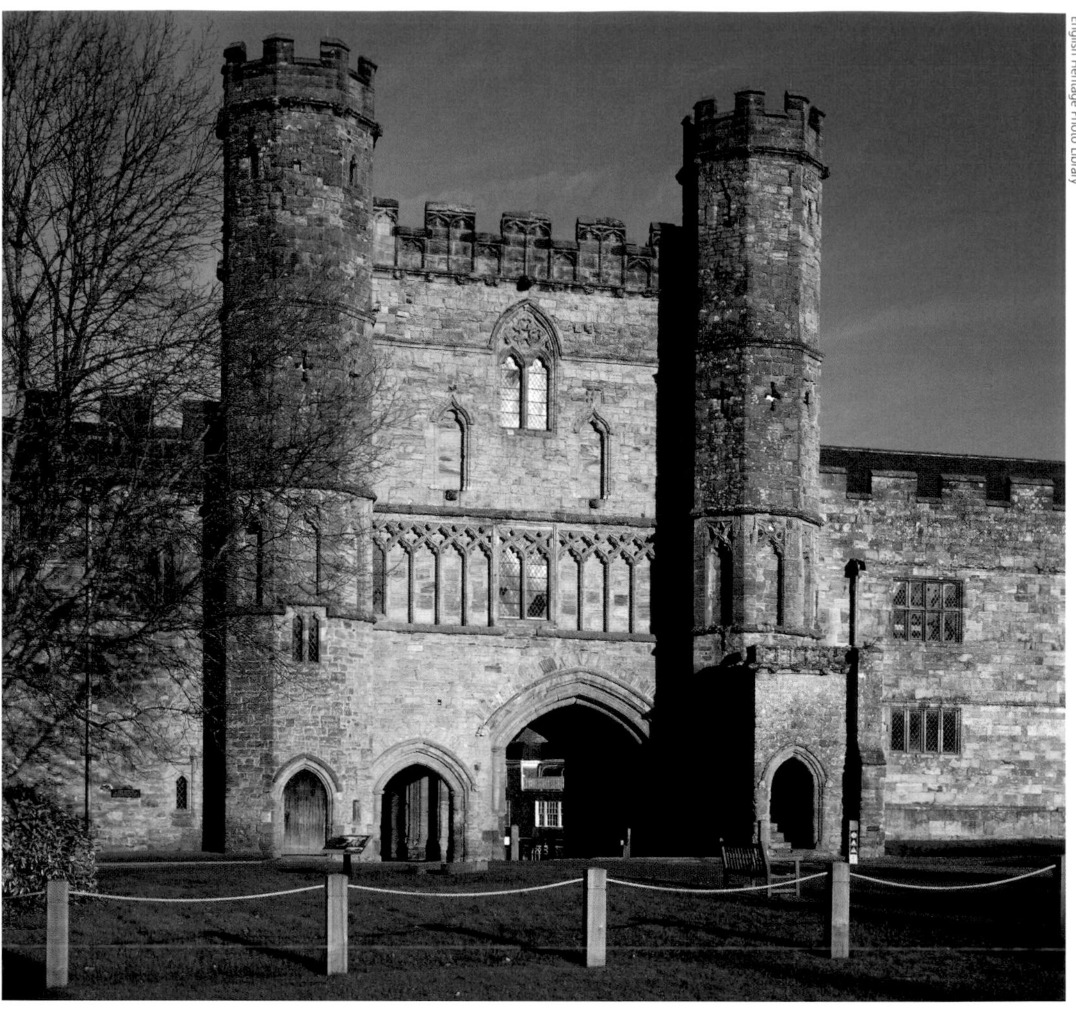

English Heritage Photo Library

1066 BATTLE OF HASTINGS, ABBEY AND BATTLEFIELD ⌗

www.english-heritage.org.uk/1066

Perhaps the most famous date in English History - 1066 is the year the Normans defeated the English at the Battle of Hastings. Visit the site of this momentous event and Battle Abbey, which was founded by William the Conqueror as penance for the bloodshed and as a memorial for the dead. Here, on the site of its high altar, you can stand at the very spot where King Harold of England fell.

An imaginative exhibition brings the background and impact of this renowned conflict to life, with interactive displays drawing a vivid picture from both English and Norman viewpoints. Listening points, graphic presentations, hands-on exhibits and touch-screen displays explore how life was on both sides of the battlefield. They also illustrate the impact this pivotal battle had on shaping English history.

The audio tour vividly describes and recreates the sounds of the battle on the very site where it took place. Listen to 'interviews' with soldiers, monks and key figures of the time as they retell the story of the Battle of Hastings.

Visit the monastic buildings which grew up around the battlefield as a result of its status as a symbol of Norman triumph. These include the impressive Great Gatehouse which is among the finest surviving monastic entrances in Britain.

The abbey museum explores the history of the abbey and includes artefacts found on site during excavations. Complete your visit with a cup of tea in the stylish café, which provides wonderful views of the historic gatehouse.

© English Heritage

© English Heritage

WCs.

Charge payable.

On leads.

ARUNDEL CASTLE & GARDENS

www.arundelcastle.org

A thousand years of history is waiting to be discovered at Arundel Castle in West Sussex. Dating from the 11th century, the Castle is both ancient fortification and stately home of the Dukes of Norfolk and Earls of Arundel.

Set high on a hill, this magnificent castle commands stunning views across the River Arun and out to sea. Climb the Keep, explore the battlements, wander in the grounds and recently restored Victorian gardens and relax in the garden of the 14th century Fitzalan Chapel.

In the 17th century during the English Civil War the Castle suffered extensive damage. The process of structural restoration began in earnest in the 18th century and continued up until 1900. The Castle was one of the first private residences to have electricity and central heating and had its own fire engine.

Inside the Castle over 20 sumptuously furnished rooms may be visited including the breathtaking Barons' Hall with 16th century furniture; the Armoury with its fine collection of armour and weaponry, and the magnificent Gothic library entirely fitted out in carved Honduras mahogany. There are works of art by Van Dyck, Gainsborough, Canaletto and Mytens; tapestries; clocks; and personal possessions of Mary Queen of Scots including the gold rosary that she carried to her execution.

There are special event days throughout the season, including opera, Shakespeare, jousting, and medieval re-enactments.

Do not miss the magnificent Collector Earl's garden based on early 17th century classical designs.

- No photography or video recording inside the Castle.
- Wide choice of distinctive and exclusive gifts.
- Many areas accessible. Visitors may alight at the Castle gates. Parking in the town car park. Passenger buggy available. WCs.
- Coffee shop.
- Licensed restaurant in Castle seats 120. Self-service. Serves morning coffee, lunch or afternoon tea.
- By prior arrangement. Tour time 1½–2 hrs. Tours available in various languages - please enquire.
- Ample car and coach parking in town car park. Free admission and refreshment voucher for coach driver.
- Items of particular interest include a Norman Motte & Keep, Armoury & Victorian bedrooms. Special rates for schoolchildren (aged 5–16) and teachers.
- Registered Assistance Dogs only
- For further information please visit our website, e-mail or telephone.

Owner

Arundel Castle Trustees Ltd

Contact

Bryan McDonald
Castle Manager
Arundel Castle
Arundel
West Sussex BN18 9AB

Tel: 01903 882173
Fax: 01903 884581
E-mail: bryan.mcdonald@arundelcastle.org

Location

MAP 3:G6
OS Ref. TQ018 072

Central Arundel, N of A27 Brighton 40 mins, Worthing 15 mins, Chichester 15 mins. From London A3 or A24, 1½ hrs. M25 motorway, 30m.

Bus: Bus stop 100 yds.

Rail: Station ½m.

Air: Gatwick 25m.

Opening Times

1 April–30 October 2011, Tuesday to Sunday.

Closed on Mondays.

Open Bank Holidays and Mondays in August.

Fitzalan Chapel, Gardens & Grounds
10am–5pm

Restaurant & Gift Shop
From 10.30am

Castle Keep
11.00am–4.30pm

Main Castle Rooms
12 noon–5pm
Last entry 4pm

Admission*

Gold Plus
Castle Rooms & Bedrooms, Castle Keep, Fitzalan Chapel, The Collector Earl's Garden, Gardens & Grounds: Adult £16, Child (5-16) £7.50, Conc. £13.50, Family (2+3 max) £39.00.

Gold
Castle Rooms, Castle Keep, Fitzalan Chapel, The Collector Earl's Garden, Gardens & Grounds: Adult £14, Child £7.50, Conc. £11.50, Family (2+3 max) £36.00.

Silver
Castle Keep, Fitzalan Chapel, The Collector Earl's Garden, Gardens & Grounds: Adult £9.00, Child £7.50

Bronze
Fitzalan Chapel, The Collector Earl's Garden, Gardens & Grounds: All £7.50.

Group rates available.

On special event days admission prices may vary.

For further information visit our website, email or telephone.

(*2010 prices)

■ **Owner**

National Trust

■ **Contact**

The Administrator
Bateman's
Burwash
Etchingham
East Sussex TN19 7DS

Tel: 01435 882302
Fax: 01435 882811
E-mail: batemans@nationaltrust.org.uk

■ **Location**

MAP 4:K5
OS Ref. TQ671 238

½ m S of Burwash off A265.

Rail: Etchingham 3m, then bus (twice daily).

Air: Gatwick 40m.

■ **Opening Times**

12 March–30 October: Sat–Wed, Good Fri & BH Mons, 11am–5pm. Last admission 4.30pm.

■ ***Admission**

House & Garden	
Adult	£8.60
Child	£4.30
Family (2+3)	£21.50
Groups	£7.50

*includes a voluntary donation but visitors can choose to pay the standard prices displayed at the property and on the website.

■ **Special Events**

Children's Fun Days.
Jacobean and WWI re-enactment weekends.
Lecture lunches.
Edwardian Christmas weekends.

© NTPL / Rupert Truman

BATEMAN'S

www.nationaltrust.org.uk/batemans

Built in 1634 and home to Rudyard Kipling for over 30 years, Bateman's lies in the richly wooded landscape of the Sussex Weald. Visit this Sussex sandstone manor house, built by a local ironmaster, where the famous writer lived from 1902 to 1936. See the rooms as they were in Kipling's day, including the study where the view inspired him to write some of his well-loved works including *Puck of Pook's Hill* and *Rewards and Fairies*. Find the mementoes of Kipling's time in India and illustrations from his famous Jungle Book tales of Mowgli, Baloo and Shere Khan.

Wander through the delightful Rose Garden with its pond and statues, with Mulberry and Herb gardens and discover the wild garden, through which flows the River Dudwell. Through the wild garden, you will find the Mill where you can watch corn being ground on most Saturday and Wednesday afternoons and one of the world's first water-driven turbines installed by Kipling to generate electricity for the house. In the garage, see a 1928 Rolls Royce, one of several owned by Kipling who was a keen early motorist.

Savour the peace and tranquillity of this beautiful property which Kipling described as *'A good and peaceable place' and of which he said 'we have loved it, ever since our first sight of it …'*.

There is a picnic glade next to the car park, or you can enjoy morning coffee, a delicious lunch or afternoon tea in the licensed tearoom where there is special emphasis on using local produce. The well-stocked gift shop offers the largest collection of Kipling books in the area.

© NTPL / Geoffrey Frosh

Partial. WCs.

Licensed.

Limited for coaches.

Guide dogs only.

CHARLESTON

www.charleston.org.uk

Situated in the heart of the South Downs, Charleston was from 1916 the home of the artists Vanessa Bell and Duncan Grant. Influenced by Post Impressionists such as Picasso and Cezanne, they took painting beyond the canvas, decorating walls, doors, furniture, ceramics and textiles, transforming the house itself into a work of art over the decades they spent here. Within the walled garden they created a summer haven overflowing with flowers and punctuated by sculptures, mosaics and ponds.

Charleston was a country retreat for Bloomsbury, the group of artists, writers and intellectuals that included Virginia and Leonard Woolf, John Maynard Keynes, E M Forster, Lytton Strachey, Roger Fry and Clive Bell. Today, Charleston contains the only complete example of the domestic decorative art of Bell and Grant anywhere in the world; alongside which hang their own easel paintings as well as works by the artists they knew and admired.

The Charleston shop stocks a range of original ceramics, painted furniture, textiles, clothes and books relating to Charleston and to Bloomsbury. The Outer Studio café provides light refreshment and the Charleston Gallery shows a changing programme of exhibitions.

The annual Charleston Festival is one of the UK's most successful independent literary events. Every May it presents a series of talks and lectures with an international cast of writers, performers and artists.

Charleston runs an exciting programme of events including walks, talks, discussions and workshops that use the collection as a catalyst for a wide range of creative activities to inform and inspire people about Bloomsbury and the arts.

 Filming and photography by arrangement.

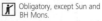

 Partial. Access leaflet. WC.

Obligatory, except Sun and BH Mons.

 Guide dogs only.

Owner

The Charleston Trust

Contact

Charleston
Firle
Nr Lewes
East Sussex BN8 6LL

Tel: 01323 811265
Fax: 01323 811628
E-mail: info@charleston.org.uk

Location

MAP 4:J6
OS Ref. TQ490 069

7m E of Lewes on A27 between Firle and Selmeston.

Opening Times

April–October.

Wed–Sat, guided tours only, 1–6pm (12–6pm in July and August). Last entry to the house 5pm.

Sun & BH Mons, 1–5.30pm. Last entry to the house 4.30pm.

Please check website for up to date information.

Admission

House & Garden

Adult	£9.00
Children	£5.00
Disabled	£5.00
OAPs	£8.00
Students / Those claiming benefits	£7.50
Family	£23.00
Conc. (Thur only)	£6.50
Themed tour	£10.00

Garden only

Adults	£3.00
Children	£1.50

Open by arrangement for groups
tel: 01323 811 626.

Owner

The Goodwood Estate Co.Ltd. (Earl of March and Kinrara).

Contact

Secretary to the Curator
Goodwood House
Goodwood
Chichester
West Sussex PO18 0PX

Tel: 01243 755048
01243 775537 (Weddings)
Recorded Info:
01243 755040
Fax: 01243 755005
E-mail: curator@goodwood.com or estatesalesofficeenquiries@goodwood.com

Location

MAP 3:F6
OS Ref. SU888 088

3½m NE of Chichester. A3 from London then A286 or A285. M27/A27 from Portsmouth or Brighton.

Rail: Chichester 3½m Arundel 9m.

Air: Heathrow 1½ hrs Gatwick ¾ hr.

Opening Times

Summer
20 March–26 September: Most Sundays and Mondays, 1–5pm (last entry 4pm).

1–31 August: Sundays–Thursdays, 1–5pm.

Please check Recorded Info 01243 755040.

Connoisseurs' Days
4 May & 6 September.

Special tours for booked groups only.

Closures
Closed for some special events and for two weekends between mid–June and mid–July for the Festival of Speed, in August for Vintage, and for one Sunday in September for the Revival Meeting.

Please ring Recorded Information on 01243 755040 to check these dates and occasional extra closures.

Admission

House

Adult	£9.50
Young Person (12–18yrs)	£4.00
Child (under 12yrs)	Free
Senior Citizen	£8.50
Family	£22.00

Booked Groups (20–200)	
Open Day (am)	£10.00
Open Day (pm)	£8.50
Connoisseur	£10.00

Special Events

Festival of Speed,
Glorious Goodwood Race–week,
Vintage,
Goodwood Revival.
Please visit our website for up-to-date information. www.goodwood.com.

Conference/Function

ROOM	SIZE	MAX CAPACITY
Ballroom	79' x 23'	180
6 other rooms available.		

GOODWOOD HOUSE

www.goodwood.com

Goodwood is one of England's finest sporting estates. At its heart lies Goodwood House, the ancestral home of the Dukes of Richmond and Gordon, direct descendants of King Charles II. Today, it is lived in by the present Duke's son and heir, the Earl of March and Kinrara, with his wife and family. Their home is open to the public on at least 60 days a year.

The art collection includes a magnificent group of British paintings from the 17th and 18th centuries, such as the celebrated views of London by Canaletto and superb sporting scenes by George Stubbs. The rooms are filled with fine English and French furniture, Gobelins tapestries and Sèvres porcelain. Special works of art are regularly rotated and displayed and the books can be viewed by written application to the Curator (there is a special charge for these viewings).

The summer exhibition in 2011, entitled 'The Horse', will look at the role horses have played in Goodwood's history. They are well represented in its art collection, from the great Wootton paintings of the 2nd Duke of Richmond's hunters to Dame Elizabeth Frink's lifesize bronze of a racehorse.

Goodwood is also renowned for its entertaining, enjoying a reputation for excellence. Goodwood's own organic farm provides food for the table in the various restaurants on the estate. With internationally renowned horseracing and motor sport events, the finest Downland golf course in the UK, its own Aerodrome and hotel, Goodwood offers an extraordinarily rich sporting experience.

Conference facilities. No photography. Highly trained guides. Shell House optional extra on Connoisseurs' Days.

Main shop at motor circuit.

Obligatory.

Ample.

In grounds, on leads. Guide dogs only in house.

Goodwood Hotel

Civil Wedding Licence. Telephone number for Weddings is 01243 775537 and email is estatesalesofficenquiries@goodwood.com.

GREAT DIXTER HOUSE & GARDENS

www.greatdixter.co.uk

Great Dixter, built c1450, is the birthplace of the late Christopher Lloyd, gardening author. Its Great Hall is the largest medieval timberframed hall in the country, restored and enlarged for Christopher's father (1910–12). The house was largely designed by the architect, Sir Edwin Lutyens, who added a 16th century house (moved from elsewhere) and knitted the buildings together with service accommodation and bedrooms above. The house retains most of the collections of furniture and other items put together by the Lloyds early in the 20th century, with some notable modern additions by Christopher.

The gardens feature a variety of topiary, pools, wild meadow areas and the famous Long Border and Exotic Garden. They featured regularly in "Country Life" from 1963, when Christopher was asked to contribute a series of weekly articles as a practical gardener – he never missed an issue in 42 years. There is a specialist nursery on site which offers an array of unusual plants of the highest quality, many of which can be seen in the fabric of the gardens. Light refreshments are available in the gift shop as well as tools, books and gifts.

The estate is 57 acres which includes ancient woodlands, meadows and ponds which have been consistently managed on a traditional basis. Coppicing the woodlands, for example, has provided pea sticks for plant supports and timber for fencing and repairs to the buildings.

There is a Friends programme available throughout the year. Friends enjoy invitations to events and educational courses as well as regular newsletters.

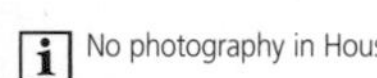

No photography in House.

Obligatory.

Limited for coaches.

Guide dogs only.

Owner

The Great Dixter Charitable Trust

Contact

Perry Rodriguez
Northiam
Rye
East Sussex TN31 6PH

Tel: 01797 252878
Fax: 01797 252879
E-mail: office@greatdixter.co.uk

Location

MAP 4:L5
OS Ref. TQ817 251.

Signposted off the A28 in Northiam.

Opening Times

1 April–30 October:
Tue–Sun, House 2–5pm.
Garden 11am–5pm.

Admission

House & Garden

Adult	£8.50
Child	£4.00

Gardens only

Adult	£7.00
Child	£3.50

Groups (25+) by appointment.

Specialist Nursery Opening times

April–October:
Mon–Fri, 9–5pm.
Sat 9–5pm
Sun 10–5pm.

Nov–end of March:
Mon–Fri 9–12.30pm, 1.30–4.30pm
Sat 9–12pm
Sun closed

■ **Owner**

National Trust

■ **Contact**

Nymans
Handcross
Haywards Heath
West Sussex
RH17 6EB
Tel: 01444 405250
E-mail: nymans@nationaltrust.org.uk

■ **Location**

MAP 4:I4
OS Ref. SU187:TQ265 294

At Handcross on B2114, 12 miles south of Gatwick, just off London–Brighton M23.

Bus: 273 Brighton–Crawley, 271 Haywards Heath–Crawley.

Rail: Balcombe 4 miles; Crawley 5 miles.

Air: Gatwick airport 12 miles

Ferry: Dieppe or L'Havre to Newhaven then 20 miles by road

■ **Opening Times**

Garden, woods, restaurant, shop & garden centre:
1 January–28 February, daily, 10am–4pm;
1 March–31 October, daily, 10am–5pm;
1 November–24 December, daily, 10am–4pm.

House
2 March–31 October: Wednesday–Monday, 11am–3pm.

■ ***Admission**

Adult	£9.50
Child	£5.00
Family	£24.00
Family (1 adult)	£14.50
Booked Groups (15+)	
Adult	£8.00
Child	£4.00

Free cup of tea or coffee in restaurant when arriving by green transport, including hybrid/electric cars.

*Includes a voluntary donation but visitors can choose to pay the standard prices displayed at visitor reception and on the website.

■ **Special Events**

We have an all year round programme of events including family activities, summer openair theatre, horticultural workshops, compost demonstrations, bat walks and photography workshops.

©NT/Nymans/Edward Shorthouse

NYMANS

www.nationaltrust.org.uk/nymans

In the late 1800s, an unusually creative family bought the Nymans estate in the picturesque High Weald landscape of Sussex to make a home in the country. Inspired by the setting and the soil, the Messels created one of the great gardens, with experimental designs and new plants from around the world. In their home they entertained family and friends, relaxing, strolling in the garden, playing and picnicking, and walking in the woods. We'd like you to feel free to enjoy Nymans in the way they did: you'll find garden games to play, picnic rugs and books to pick up, umbrellas when it's wet and garden temples to shelter in.

If you'd like to explore further than the garden and house, you can go for a walk in the woods among avenues, wild flowers and lakes. You can also take our new woodland buggy for a tour, designed for those who can't manage on foot. The woods really are delightful with lots to see, like the tallest tree in Sussex and the cascade waterfalls dug out by returning soldiers employed by the Messels after the First World War. You are welcome to walk your dogs in the woods and pick up a bag of charcoal made by our wardens for the shop.

Nymans is open every day, all year, because even in winter the garden's colours and scents change so much within a week. Rhododendron, Magnolia, Camellia and Azalea in spring, the renowned Summer Borders, the autumn colours and the scent of Daphne, the colour of Witch-hazel and the swathes of snowdrops in winter.

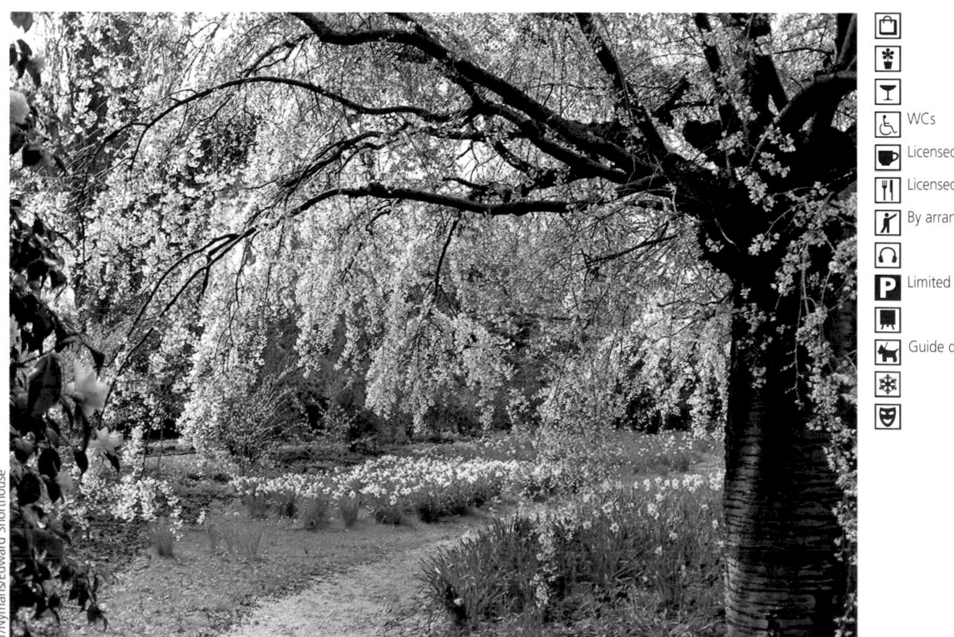

©NT/Nymans/Edward Shorthouse

WCs
Licensed
Licensed
By arrangement
Limited for coaches
Guide dogs only

© Marianne Majerus

PASHLEY MANOR GARDENS

www.pashleymanorgardens.com

A winner of HHA/Christie's Garden of the Year Award. The gardens offer a sumptuous blend of romantic landscaping, imaginative plantings and fine old trees, fountains, springs and large ponds. This is a quintessential English garden of a very individual character with exceptional views to the surrounding valleyed fields. Many eras of history are reflected here, typifying the tradition of the English Country House and its garden.

The gardens first opened in 1992 and were brought to their present splendour with the assistance of eminent landscape architect, the late Anthony du Gard Pasley. Different gardens have been created within the 11 acres allowing visitors to travel from blazing colour to cool creams, greens and golds.

The gardens are always evolving; it is hoped that they will be inspirational yet restful to the first-time visitor and will never disappoint those who return regularly.

Pashley prides itself on its delicious food. During warm weather, visitors can enjoy their refreshments on the terrace overlooking the moat or in the Jubilee Courtyard. Home-made soups, ploughman's lunches, fresh salad from the garden (whenever possible), home-made scones, delicious cakes, filter coffee, teas and fine wines are served from the Garden Room café. The new gift shop caters for every taste from postcards and local honey to hand-painted ceramics and tapestry cushions. A selection of plants and shrubs, many of which grow at Pashley, are available for purchase.

Permanent exhibition and sale of sculpture and botanical art.

Excellent location for corporate events, private parties and marquee wedding receptions.

© Leigh Clapp

Lilium 'Casablanca' and Sculpture by Helen Sinclair

© David Dixon

Wisteria on the side of the House

Partial. WCs.

Licensed.

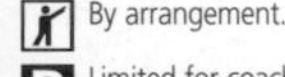

By arrangement.

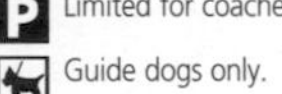

Limited for coaches.

Guide dogs only.

Owner

Mr & Mrs
James A Sellick

Contact

Pashley Manor
Ticehurst
Wadhurst
East Sussex TN5 7HE

Tel: 01580 200888
Fax: 01580 200102
E-mail: info@pashleymanorgardens.com

Location

MAP 4:K4
OS Ref. TQ707 291

On B2099 between A21 and Ticehurst Village.

Opening Times

2 April–29 September: Tues, Weds, Thurs, Sat, Bank Holiday Mons and Special Event days, 11am–5pm. October: Garden only Mon–Fri,10am–4pm.

Admission

Adult	£8.50
Children (6–16yrs)	£5.00
Groups (15+)	£8.00
Tulip Festival (no concessions)	£9.00
Season Ticket	£28.00

Coaches must book. Please telephone for details.

Special Events

27 April–8 May (inc.)
Tulip Festival

21–30 May (inc.)
Sculpture in Particular

17–19 June
Special Rose Weekend

24–26 June
Kitchen Garden Weekend

Mid July–Mid August
Lily Time

27–29 August
Sussex Guild Craft Show

Owner

National Trust

Contact

Jo Hopkins
Visitor Services &
Marketing Manager
Sheffield Park
East Sussex
TN22 3QX

Tel: 01825 790231
Fax: 01825 791264
E-mail: sheffieldpark@nationaltrust.org.uk

Location

MAP 4:I5

OS Ref. TQ415 240

Midway between East Grinstead and Lewes, 5m NW of Uckfield on E side of A275.

Bus: Please call Traveline on 0871 200 22 33 or log onto their website traveline.org.uk

Rail: Uckfield (6 miles), Haywards Heath (7 miles)

Opening Times

Garden

Closed Christmas Day.

Open all year, please call 01825 790231 or log onto our website for details of times.

Parkland

Open all year, dawn to dusk.

Admission

For 2011 prices, please call 01825 790231 or log onto our website.

Groups discount available (15+ prebooked)

NT, RHS Individual Members and Great British Heritage Pass holders Free.

Joint Ticket available with Bluebell Railway.

Special Events

Event programme throughout the year – please check our website.

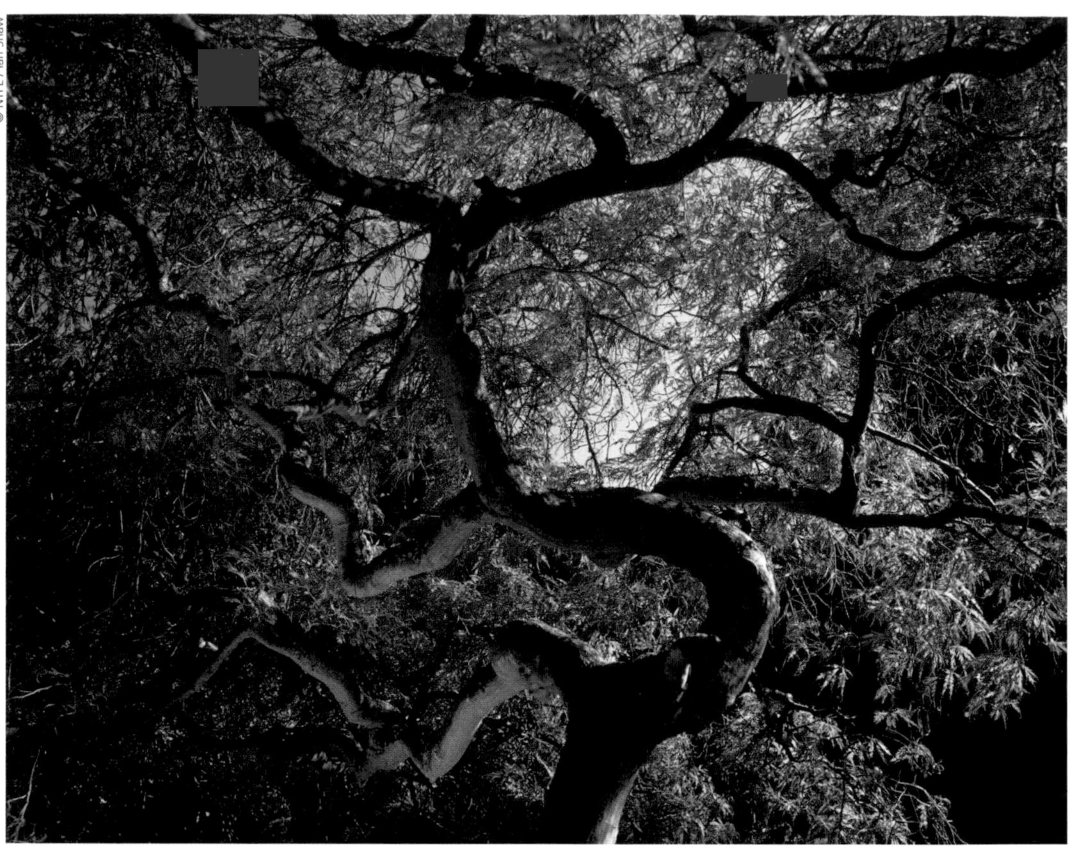

© NTPL / Ian Shaw

SHEFFIELD PARK & GARDEN

www.nationaltrust.org.uk/sheffieldpark

A magnificent 120 acre landscaped garden at the centre of which are the four lakes that mirror the unique planting and colour that each season brings. Swathes of delicate spring bulbs decorate the awakening garden, and there is an outstanding exhibition of colour in May with rhododendrons and the National Collection of Ghent Azaleas. Water lilies dress the lakes during the summer. Visitors to the garden during the summer months can enjoy a leisurely walk perhaps pausing to sit on a seat to enjoy the tranquil ambience. In the autumn the garden is transformed by trees planted specifically for their autumn colour including Nyssa sylvatica, Amelanchier and Acer palmatum. These and other fine specimen trees, particularly North American varieties, produce displays of gold, orange and crimson. The garden is open throughout the year and has something for all, whether a quiet stroll or a family gathering, allowing the children to participate in the many activities offered.

Whilst visiting the garden, take time to have a walk on South Park. 265 acres of beautiful countryside offering tranquil walks, stunning views and 'Parkland Playful Places', our new family trail with natural play areas to entertain the children. Special Events run throughout the year – please telephone for details.

© NT / Lisa Barnard

 WCs.

 By arrangement.

 Guide dogs only in garden. Dogs welcome on South Park.

© NTPL / Nadia Mackenzie

STANDEN

www.nationaltrust.org.uk/standen

Built in the 1890s for wealthy London solicitor, James Beale, and his large family, Standen has since become the icon of the Arts & Crafts Movement with its Morris & Co. interiors and Philip Webb architecture.

The story of this much loved home highlights the technological and social advances of the time, with its central heating, electric lighting and comfortable accommodation for servants, as well as the growing un-stuffiness of late Victorian family life.

The hillside garden, which served Mrs Beale's love of unusual plants as well as the family's dinner table, is now undergoing restoration which will see it re-established as one of the most important Arts & Crafts gardens in the country. In 2011 you can find out more about the history of the garden and its restoration by joining a free guided tour (please go to our website to find out times of the tours).

The atmosphere of a relaxed family home, originally used just for holidays and weekends, is still very much in evidence and you can experience Standen today as the Beales' guests would have done by relaxing on the sofa in the Morning Room, playing a game of Croquet in the garden, or adventuring into the surrounding Sussex countryside on one of the estate's many walks routes.

If you're inspired by the Arts & Crafts Movement at Standen you can buy your own piece of it in our Shop which sells a range of Morris & Co. inspired gifts as well as plants from the garden. Produce from our Kitchen Garden is used in the Barn Restaurant.

© NT / Chris Hill

© NTPL / John Miller

Owner

National Trust

Contact

The Property Manager
East Grinstead
West Sussex RH19 4NE

Tel: 01342 323029
Fax: 01342 316424
E-mail: standen@nationaltrust.org.uk

Location

MAP 4:I4
OS Ref. TQ389 356

2m S of East Grinstead, signposted from B2110.

Bus: Metrobus 84 East Grinstead – Crawley, request stop at end of Standen Drive (no service on Sunday or BH).

Opening Times

19 February–13 March; Sats & Suns, 11am–5.30pm (last entry to house 4pm).

16 March–30 October; Wed–Sun & BHs, 11am–5.30pm (last entry to house 4pm). Also Mons 11–25 April, 25 July–4 Sep, 24–30 October.

5 November–21 December; Sats & Suns (and Mon 19, Tue 20 & Wed 21 December), 11am–3pm (last entry to house 2.30pm).

*Admission

House & Garden

Adult	£9.00
Child	£4.50
Family	£22.50

Pre-booked groups: £7.80 (minimum 15) or £275 for exclusive tour of the house (one off fee for group).

*Includes a voluntary donation but visitors can choose to pay the standard prices displayed at the property and on the website.

Special Events

Children's crafts every Monday during the school holidays, regular contemporary Arts & Crafts selling exhibitions, lecture lunches, Christmas lunches.

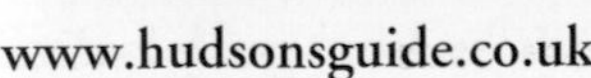

Owner

The Edward James Foundation

Contact

West Dean
Chichester
West Sussex
PO18 0RX

Tel Gardens: 01243 818210
Tel College: 01243 811301
Fax: 01243 811342
E-mail: enquiries@westdean.org.uk

Location

MAP 3:F5

OS Ref. SU863 128

SE of A286 Midhurst Road, 6m N of Chichester, 7m S of Midhurst.

Opening Times

Gardens
March–October:
daily, 10.30am–5pm
(last adm 4.30pm).

November–February:
daily, 10.30am–4pm.

Closed Jan 2011.

Admission

Summer

Adult	£7.50
Over 60s	£7
Child	£3.50
Family	£18

Groups

Adult	£7
Over 60s	£6.50

Winter

Adult	£4.75
Over 60s	£4.25
Child	£2.25
Family (2 Adults & 2 Children 5–15)	£11.50

Groups

Adult	£3.75
Over 60s	£3.50

Yearly Friends Memberships:

Single	£27.50
Single and Guest	£55
Family	£60

Some garden events will incur a supplementary charge.

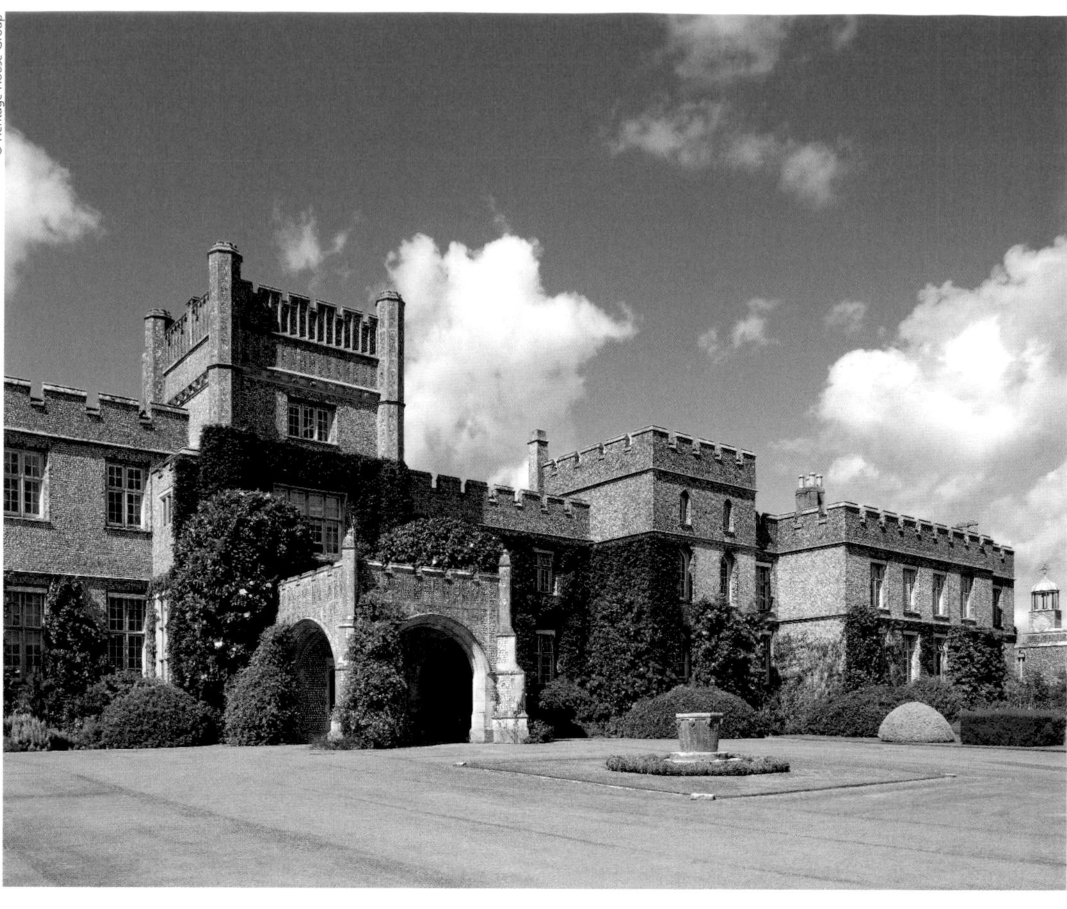

© Heritage House Group

WEST DEAN COLLEGE & GARDENS

www.westdean.org.uk

Situated within the 6,400 acre West Dean Estate, West Dean College and Gardens is at the heart of the newly designated South Downs National Park.

The 19th century flint-faced mansion was once home to Edward James, whose patronage of many emerging talents in the 1920s, 30s and 40s has ensured him a place within the history of art. Today, West Dean College is a centre for study of arts, crafts, conservation, writing, gardening, food and music, offering over 700 short courses and full-time graduate and post-graduate diplomas and MAs.

The Gardens are a showcase for variety in planting and excellence in presentation. Highlights include: the magnificent 90 metre-long Edwardian pergola; the restored Victorian walled kitchen garden and glasshouses featuring exotic fruits and vegetables; the Spring Garden with tranquil, winding rivers and intricate flint bridges; and the ever-popular picnic lawn. For breathtaking views of the Lavant Valley, enjoy the 2 ½ mile circular Parkland walk up to St Roche's arboretum. Also within the grounds are the Gardens Restaurant and Gift Shop.

West Dean College provides a stimulating and relaxing environment for meetings and conferences, creative breakout sessions can be incorporated into your event. The College, Gardens, Farms, Forests and Estate are available to hire for film locations or photo shoots.

© Heritage House Group

© Heritage House Group

Licensed.

Limited for coaches.
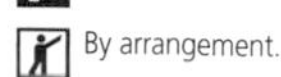
By arrangement.

Guide dogs only.

©NTPL/John Miller

ALFRISTON CLERGY HOUSE

THE TYE, ALFRISTON, POLEGATE, EAST SUSSEX BN26 5TL

Tel: 01323 870001 **Fax:** 01323 871318 **E-mail:** alfriston@nationaltrust.org.uk

Owner: National Trust **Contact:** The Property Manager

Step back into the Middle Ages with a visit to this 14th century thatched Wealden 'Hall House' which in 1896 was the first to be acquired by the National Trust. Explore the delightful cottage garden and idyllic setting with stunning views across the meandering River Cuckmere. NT shop on site.

Location: MAP 4:J6, OS Ref. TQ521 029. 4m NE of Seaford, just E of B2108.

Open: 26 Feb–9 Mar daily except Thur & Fri, 11am–4pm; 12 Mar–31 Jul daily except Thur & Fri, 10.30am–5pm; 1 Aug–28 Aug daily except Thur, 10.30am–5pm; 29 Aug–30 Oct daily except Thur & Fri 10.30am–5pm; 31 Oct–18 Dec daily except Thur & Fri 11am–4pm.

Admission: Adult £4.75, Child £2.40, Family (2+3) £11.90. Pre-booked groups £4.13.

No WCs. Parking in village car parks.

ANNE OF CLEVES HOUSE

52 SOUTHOVER HIGH STREET, LEWES, SUSSEX BN7 1JA

www.sussexpast.co.uk/anneofcleves

Tel: 01273 474610 **Fax:** 01273 486990 **E-mail:** anne@sussexpast.co.uk

Owner: Sussex Past **Contact:** Isobel Roberts

This atmospheric timber framed house was once owned by Anne of Cleves. Today you can explore the pretty Tudor garden, kitchen, and house which are furnished in period style, and give you a real sense of how people lived then. The building is also home to an eclectic local history museum including the Wealden Iron Gallery.

Location: MAP 4:I5, OS198 Ref. TQ410 096. S of Lewes town centre, off A27/A275/A26.

Open: 1 Mar–31 Oct, daily: Tues–Sat 10am–5pm; Sun, Mon & Bank Hols 11am–5pm. Special opening for half term Mon 14 Feb–Fri 18 Feb (and for events). Last admission 30 mins before closing time.

Admission: Adult £4.40, OAP/Student £3.90, Child £2.20, Family (2+2 or 1+4) £11.80, Disabled/carer £2.20. Groups (15+): Adult £4, OAP/Student £3.50, Child £2, Disabled/carer £2. Combined ticket with Lewes Castle: Adult £9.20, OAP/Student £8, Child £4.60, Family (2+2 or 1+4) £25, Disabled/carer £4.60. Groups (15+), Adult £8, OAP/Student £7, Child £4, Disabled/carer £4.

By arrangement. Limited (on road). Guide dogs only.

1066 BATTLE OF HASTINGS, ABBEY AND BATTLEFIELD

See page 136 for full page entry.

ARUNDEL CASTLE

See page 137 for full page entry.

ARUNDEL CATHEDRAL

Parsons Hill, Arundel, West Sussex BN18 9AY

Tel: 01903 882297 **Fax:** 01903 885335 **E-mail:** aruncath1@aol.com

Contact: Rev. Canon T. Madeley

French Gothic Cathedral, church of the RC Diocese of Arundel and Brighton built by Henry, 15th Duke of Norfolk and opened 1873.

Location: MAP 3:G6, OS Ref. TQ015 072. Above junction of A27 and A284.

Open: Summer: 9am–6pm. Winter: 9am–dusk. Mon, Tues, Wed, Fri, Sat: Mass 10am; Thurs: Mass 8.30am (at Convent of Poor Clares, Crossbush); Sat: Vigil Mass 6.15pm (at Convent of Poor Clares, Crossbush); Sun: Masses 9.30am and 11.15am. Shop open in the summer, Mon–Fri, 10am–4pm and after services and on special occasions and otherwise on request.

Admission: Free.

BATEMAN'S

See page 138 for full page entry.

BAYHAM OLD ABBEY

Lamberhurst, Sussex TN3 8DE

Tel/Fax: 01892 890381 **E-mail:** customers@english-heritage.org.uk

www.english-heritage.org.uk/bayhamoldabbey

Owner: English Heritage **Contact:** Visitor Operations Team

These riverside ruins are of a house of 'white' canons, founded c.1208 and preserved in the 18th century, when its surroundings were landscaped to create its delightful setting. Rooms in the Georgian Gothick dower house are also open to visitors.

Location: MAP 4:K4, OS Ref. TQ650 365. 1¾m W of Lamberhurst off B2169.

Open: 1 Apr–30 Sept: daily, 11am–5pm. 1 Oct–31 Mar: Closed.

Admission: Adult £4, Child £2, Conc. £3.40. English Heritage Members Free. Group discount available. Opening times and prices are valid until 31st March 2011, after this date details are subject to change please visit www.english-heritage.org.uk for the most up-to-date information.

On leads.

© Britainonview / Simon Kreitem

Arundel Castle

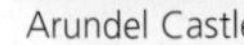

South-East – England

BORDE HILL GARDEN

Balcome Road, Haywards Heath, West Sussex RH16 1XP

Tel: 01444 450326 **E-mail:** info@bordehill.co.uk **www.bordehill.co.uk**

Contact: Susan Lewis

Award-winning heritage garden has enhanced colour and charm with new plantings throughout its distinctive 'rooms' including the Azalea Ring, Rose and Italian Gardens. Immense rare trees and shrubs inhabit the magical woodlands. With lakeside walks, and panoramic views, Borde Hill delights visitors and provides stunning backdrops for photography and film.

Location: MAP 4:I5

Open: 21 Mar–11 Sept & 22–30 Oct. Friends Weekend: 19–20 Mar.

Admission: Adults £8, Conc. £7, Group (pre-paid) £6.50, Child £4.75. Season Tickets: Adults £25, Child £15. Family Day Ticket £22. Annual Family Tickets: £65 (2 plus 2), £75 (2 plus 3). House Tour +£3.50.

WCs. Licensed. Licensed. Obligatory. On leads.

BOXGROVE PRIORY

Boxgrove, Chichester, West Sussex

Tel: 01424 775705 **E-mail:** customers@english-heritage.org.uk

www.english-heritage.org.uk/boxgrovepriory

Owner: English Heritage **Contact:** 1066 Battle Abbey

Remains of the Guest House, Chapter House and Church of this 12th century priory, which was the cell of a French abbey until Richard II confirmed its independence in 1383.

Location: MAP 3:G6, OS Ref. SU908 076. N of Boxgrove, 4 miles E of Chichester on minor road N of A27.

Open: Any reasonable time.

Admission: Free. Opening times and prices are valid until 31st March 2011, after this date details are subject to change please visit www.english-heritage.org.uk for the most up-to-date information.

BRAMBER CASTLE

Bramber, Sussex

Tel: 01424 775705 **E-mail:** customers@english-heritage.org.uk

www.english-heritage.org.uk/brambercastle

Owner: English Heritage **Contact:** 1066 Battle Abbey

The remains of a Norman castle gatehouse, walls and earthworks in a splendid setting overlooking the Adur Valley.

Location: MAP 3:H5, OS Ref. TQ185 107. On W side of Bramber village NE of A283.

Open: Any reasonable time.

Admission: Free. Opening times and prices are valid until 31st March 2011, after this date details are subject to change please visit www.english-heritage.org.uk for the most up-to-date information.

On leads.

CAMBER CASTLE

Camber, Nr Rye, East Sussex TN31 7RS

Tel: 01797 223862 **E-mail:** customers@english-heritage.org.uk

www.english-heritage.org.uk/cambercastle

Owner: English Heritage **Contact:** Rye Harbour Nature Reserve

A fine example of one of many coastal fortresses built by Henry VIII to counter the threat of invasion during the 16th century. Monthly guided walks of Rye Nature Reserve including Camber Castle: telephone for details.

Location: MAP 4:L5, OS189, Ref. TQ922 185. Across fields off A259, 1 mile S of Rye off harbour road.

Open: 1 Jul–30 Sep: Sat & Sun, 2–5pm (plus BH weekends Apr–Sep). Last entry 4.30pm. Opening times subject to change.

Admission: Adult £2, Accompanied children Free, Conc. £1. Friends of Rye Harbour Nature Reserve & EH Members Free. Group discount available. Opening times and prices are valid until 31st March 2011, after this date details are subject to change please visit www.english-heritage.org.uk for the most up-to-date information.

By arrangement.

For **accommodation** in the South East, see our special index at the end of the book.

© Britainonview / Tourism South East

Borde Hill Garden

CHARLESTON

See page 139 for full page entry.

CHICHESTER CATHEDRAL

CHICHESTER, W SUSSEX PO19 1RP

www.chichestercathedral.org.uk

Tel: 01243 782595 **Fax:** 01243 812499 **E-mail:** visitors@chichestercathedral.org.uk

Contact: Visitor Services Officer

In the heart of Chichester, this magnificent 900 year old Cathedral has treasures ranging from medieval stone carvings to world famous 20th century artworks. Open every day and all year with free entry. Free guided tours and special trails for children. Regular exhibitions, free weekly lunchtime concerts and a superb Cloisters Restaurant and Shop. A fascinating place to visit.

Location: MAP 3:F6, OS Ref. SU860 047. West Street, Chichester.

Open: Summer: 7.15am–7.00pm, Winter: 7.15am–6.00pm. All are welcome. Choral Evensong daily (except Wed) during term time.

Admission: Free entry. Donations greatly appreciated.

Private functions and conferences.

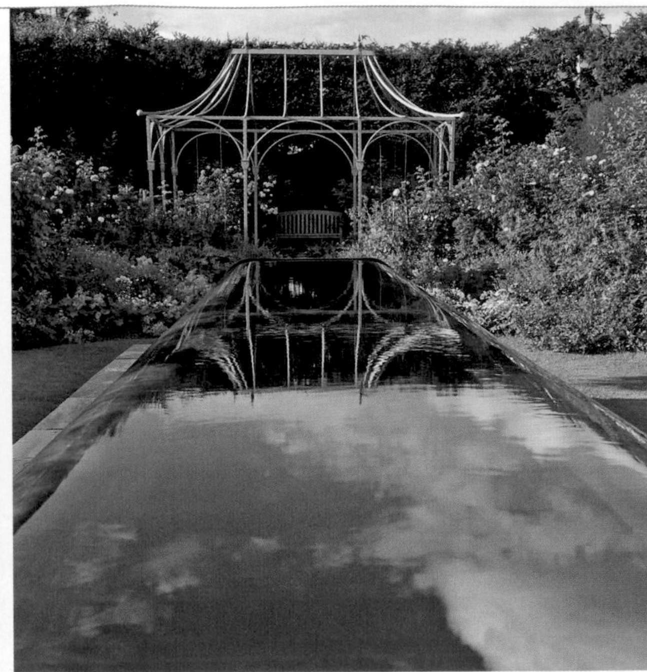

CLINTON LODGE GARDEN

FLETCHING, E SUSSEX TN22 3ST

Tel/Fax: 01825 722952 **e-mail:** garden@clintonlodge.com

Owner/Contact: Lady Collum

Clinton Lodge is named after one of Wellington's generals at Waterloo. The simple lawn and parkland beyond the gate reflect the 18th century facade. Beyond are double blue and white herbaceous borders between yew and box hedges, a cloister walk swathed in white roses, clematis and geraniums, a Herb Garden where hedges of box envelop herbs, seats are of turf, paths of camomile. A Pear Walk bursts with alliums or lilies, a Potager of flowers for cutting, old roses surround a magnificent water feature by William Pye, and much more. Private groups by appointment.

Location: MAP 4:I5, OS Ref. TQ428 238. In centre of village behind tall yew and holly hedge.

Open: NGS Open Days: Sun 8 May, Sun 5, Mon 20 Jun & Sun 26 Jun, Mon 4 & Mon 25 Jul, Mon 1 & Mon 8 Aug. Other days by appointment.

Admission: Entrance £5, Children free.

WCs. Unsuitable. By arrangement. Limited. Guide dogs only.

COWDRAY

RIVER GROUND STABLES, MIDHURST, W SUSSEX GU29 9AL

www.cowdray.org.uk

Tel: 01730 810781 **E-mail:** info@cowdray.org.uk

Owner: Cowdray Heritage Trust **Contact:** The Manager

As a major new attraction, Cowdray is one of the most important survivals of a Tudor nobleman's house. Set within the stunning landscape of Cowdray Park, the house was partially destroyed by fire in 1793. Explore the Tudor Kitchens, Buck Hall, Chapel, Gatehouse, Vaulted Storeroom and Cellars, Visitor Centre and Shop.

Location: MAP 3:F5, OS Ref. TQ891 216. E outskirts of Midhurst on A272.

Open: Mid Mar–end Oct. For days check website for details. 10.30am–4pm last admission. Groups all year round by arrangement.

Admission: Check website for details.

Partial. WCs. By arrangement. Nearby.

DENMANS GARDEN

Denmans Lane, Fontwell, West Sussex BN18 0SU

Tel: 01243 542808 **Fax:** 01243 544064 **E-mail:** denmans@denmans-garden.co.uk

www.denmans-garden.co.uk

Owner: John Brookes MBE & Michael Neve **Contact:** Mrs Claudia Murphy

A unique 20th century 4 acre garden designed for year round interest – through use of form, colour and texture – owned by John Brookes MBE, renowned garden designer and writer and Michael Neve. Beautiful plant centre, gift shop, garden shop and fully licensed multi award winning Garden Café.

Location: MAP 3:G6, OS197 Ref. SZ947 070. Off the A27 (westbound) between Chichester (6m) and Arundel (5m).

Open: Daily all year round. Garden: 9am–5pm. Plant centre: 9am–5pm. Café: 10am–5pm. Please check website for winter opening times.

Admission: Adult £4.95, Child (4–16) £3.95, OAP £4.75, Pre-booked groups (15+) £4.50. 2010 prices – please telephone or check website for current prices.

WC. Licensed. Licensed. Group menus on request. Guide dogs only.

Chichester Cathedral

©Jeremy Whitaker

FIRLE PLACE

FIRLE, LEWES, EAST SUSSEX BN8 6LP

www.firle.com

Tel: 01273 858307 (Enquiries) **Events:** 01273 858567
Fax: 01273 858188 **Restaurant:** 01273 858307 **E-mail:** gage@firleplace.co.uk
Owner: The Rt Hon Viscount Gage

Firle Place is the home of the Gage family and has been for over 500 years. Set at the foot of the Sussex Downs within its own parkland, this unique house originally Tudor, was built of Caen stone, possibly from a monastery dissolved by Sir John Gage, friend of Henry VIII. Remodelled in the 18th century it is similar in appearance to that of a French château. The house contains a magnificent collection of Old Master paintings, fine English and European furniture and an impressive collection of Sèvres porcelain collected mainly by the 3rd Earl Cowper from Panshanger House, Hertfordshire.

Events: The Great Tudor Hall can, on occasion, be used for private dinners, with drinks on the Terrace or in the Billiard Room. A private tour of the house can be arranged. Events are held in the Park and House during the year and wedding receptions can be held in the Park or Old Riding School. For all event enquiries, contact the Estate Office on 01273 858567.

Restaurant: Enjoy the licensed restaurant and tea terrace with views over the garden for luncheon and cream teas.

Location: MAP 4:J6, OS Ref. TQ473 071. 4m S of Lewes on A27 Brighton / Eastbourne Road.

Open: Easter & BH Sun/Mon. Jun–Sept: Wed, Thur, Sun & BHs, 2–4.30pm. Dates and times subject to change without prior notice. Last admission 4.15pm. Garden Open Days 23 and 24 April 2011.

Admission: Adult £7, Child £4, Conc. £6.

No photography in house. Ground floor & restaurant. Licensed. Tea Terrace. Wed & Thur. In grounds on leads.

FISHBOURNE ROMAN PALACE

SALTHILL ROAD, FISHBOURNE, CHICHESTER, SUSSEX PO19 3QR

www.sussexpast.co.uk/fishbourne

Tel: 01243 785859 **Fax:** 01243 539266 **E-mail:** adminfish@sussexpast.co.uk
Owner: Sussex Past **Contact:** Christine Medlock

The remains of a palatial Roman building constructed in the 1st century AD. View the stunning Roman mosaics and the replanted Roman garden. Visitors may join a tour of the Palace site as well as the popular Behind the Scenes Tour during which they are able to handle original artefacts and learn about their storage and conservation.

Location: MAP 3:F6, OS Ref. SU837 057. 1½m W of Chichester in Fishbourne village off A27/A259. 5 minutes walk from Fishbourne railway station.

Open: Jan 7 Dec Sun 10am-4pm; Feb-Nov Daily 10am-4pm.

Admission: Adult £7.60, Student/Senior Citizen £6.80, Child £4.

By arrangement. Guide dogs only.

GLYNDE PLACE

GLYNDE, Nr LEWES, EAST SUSSEX BN8 6SX

www.glyndeplace.co.uk

Tel/Fax: 01273 858224 **E-mail:** info@glynde.co.uk
Owners: Viscount & Viscountess Hampden **Contact:** The Estate Office

Glynde Place is a magnificent example of Elizabethan architecture commanding exceptionally fine views of the South Downs. Amongst the collections of 400 years of family living can be seen 17th and 18th century portraits of the Trevors, furniture, embroidery and silver.

Location: MAP 4:J5, OS Ref. TQ456 092. Sign posted off of A27, 4m SE of Lewes at top of village. Rail: Glynde is on the London/Eastbourne and Brighton/Eastbourne mainline railway. Air: Gatwick is 35 mins by car, or train via Lewes. Ferry: Newhaven - Calais.

Open: May–Aug: Weds, Suns & BHs, 2–5pm (last tour 4pm). Group bookings by appointment.

Admission: House & Garden: Adult £6, Child (under 12yrs) Free, Conc. £5. CPRE 2 for 1. Garden: Adult £3, Child (under 15yrs) Free, pensioners & students £2.

Special Events: Glynde Food & English Wine Festival.

No photography. Unsuitable. WCs. Obligatory. Free. Limited for coaches. Guide dogs only.

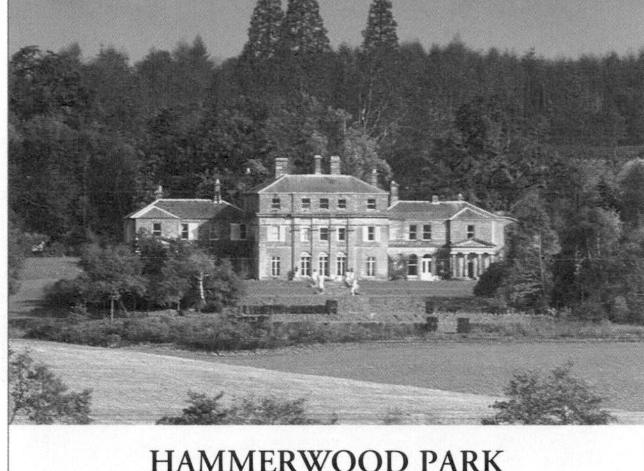

HAMMERWOOD PARK

EAST GRINSTEAD, SUSSEX RH19 3QE

www.hammerwoodpark.com

Tel: 01342 850594 **Fax:** 01342 850864 **E-mail:** latrobe@mistral.co.uk
Owner/Contact: David Pinnegar

Built in 1792 as an Apollo's hunting lodge by Benjamin Latrobe, architect of the Capitol and the White House, Washington DC. Owned by Led Zepplin in the 1970s, rescued from dereliction in 1982. Teas in the Organ Room; copy of the Parthenon frieze; and a derelict dining room still shocks the unwary. Guided tours (said by many to be the most interesting in Sussex) by the family. Also summer concerts.

Location: MAP 4:J4, OS Ref. TQ442 390. 3½ m E of East Grinstead on A264 to Tunbridge Wells, 1m W of Holtye.

Open: 1 June–end Sept: Wed, Sat & BH Mon, 2–5pm. Guided tour starts 2.05pm. Private groups: Easter–Jun. Coaches strictly by appointment. Small groups any time throughout the year by appointment.

Admission: House & Park: Adult £6, Child £2. Private viewing by arrangement.

Conferences. Obligatory. In grounds. B&B. €

GOODWOOD HOUSE *See page 140 for full page entry.*

GREAT DIXTER HOUSE & GARDENS *See page 141 for full page entry.*

© Britainonview / David Sellman

Great Dixter House & Gardens

GARDENS AND GROUNDS OF HERSTMONCEUX CASTLE

HAILSHAM, E SUSSEX BN27 1RN

www.herstmonceux-castle.com

Tel: 01323 833816 **Fax:** 01323 834499 **E-mail:** c_cullip@bisc.queensu.ac.uk
Owner: Queen's University, Canada **Contact:** C Cullip

This breathtaking 15th century moated Castle is set within 500 acres of parkland and gardens (including Elizabethan Garden) and is ideal for picnics and woodland walks. At Herstmonceux there is something for all the family.

Location: MAP 4:K5, OS Ref. TQ646 104. 2m S of Herstmonceux village (A271) by minor road. 10m WNW of Bexhill.

Open: 16 Apr–30 Oct: daily, 10am–6pm (last adm. 1 hour before closing). Closes 5pm from Oct.

Admission: Grounds & Gardens: Adults £6.00, Child under 15yrs & Students £3 (child under 5 Free), Conc. £4.95, Family £14. Group rates/bookings available.

Visitor Centre. Limited for Castle Tour. On leads.

HIGHDOWN GARDENS

Littlehampton Road, Goring-by-Sea, Worthing, Sussex BN12 6PE

Tel: 01903 501054

Owner: Worthing Borough Council **Contact:** Parks and Foreshore Manager

Unique gardens in disused chalk pit, begun in 1909.

Location: MAP 3:H6, OS Ref. TQ098 040. 3m WNW of Worthing on N side of A259, just W of the Goring roundabout.

Open: Apr–Sept: daily, 10am–6pm. Oct–Nov: Mon–Fri, 10am–4.30pm. Dec–Jan: Mon–Fri, 10am–4pm. Feb-Mar 10am–4.30pm.

Admission: Free.

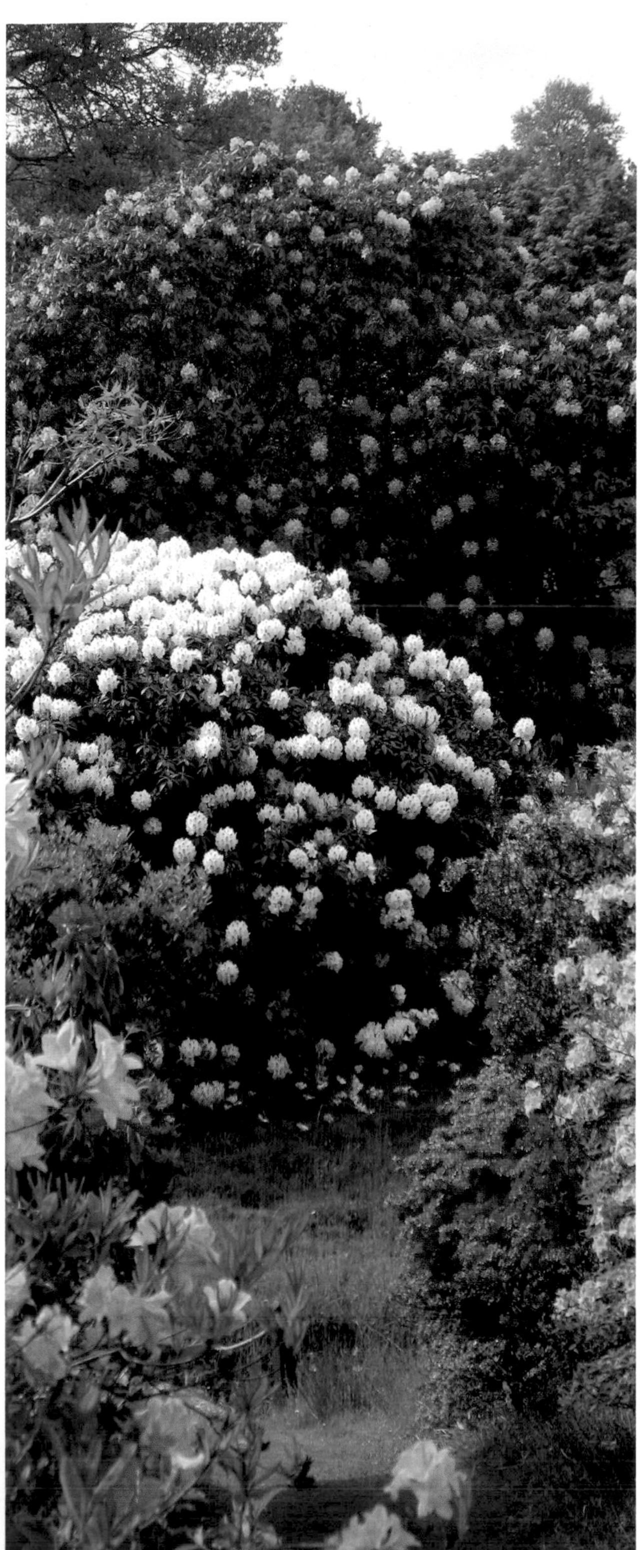

High Beeches Woodland & Water Gardens

David Sellman

HIGH BEECHES WOODLAND & WATER GARDENS

HIGH BEECHES LANE, HANDCROSS, SUSSEX RH17 6HQ

www.highbeeches.com

Tel: 01444 400589 **Fax:** 01444 401543 **E-mail:** gardens@highbeeches.com

Owner: High Beeches Gardens Conservation Trust (Reg. Charity)

Contact: Sarah Bray

Explore 27 acres of magically beautiful, peaceful woodland and water gardens. Daffodils, bluebells, azaleas, naturalised gentians and glorious autumn colours. Rippling streams, enchanting vistas. Four acres of natural wildflower meadows. Marked trails. Recommended by Christopher Lloyd. Enjoy lunches and teas in the tearoom and tea lawn in restored Victorian farm building.

Location: MAP 4:I4, OS Ref. TQ275 308. S side of B2110. 1m NE of Handcross.

Open: 19 Mar–31 Oct: daily except Weds, 1–5pm (last adm. 4.30pm). Coaches/guided tours anytime, by appointment only.

Admission: Adult £6.00, Child (under 14yrs) Free. Concession for groups (20+). Guided tours for groups £10pp.

Partial. WCs Tearoom fully accessible. Licensed Licensed. By arrangement. Limited for coaches Guide dogs only

LEWES CASTLE & BARBICAN HOUSE MUSEUM

169 HIGH STREET, LEWES, SUSSEX BN7 1YE

www.sussexpast.co.uk/lewescastle

Tel: 01273 486290 **Fax:** 01273 486990 **E-mail:** lamo@sussepast.co.uk

Owner: Sussex Past **Contact:** Front Desk

Lewes's imposing Norman castle offers magnificent views across the town and surrounding downland. Barbican House, towered over by the Barbican Gate, is home to an interesting museum of local history and archaeology. A superb scale model of Victorian Lewes provides the centrepiece of a 25 minute audio-visual presentation telling the story of the county town of Sussex. Lewes Castle reopened to the public on 2nd June 2009, after completion of a million-pound restoration project.

Location: MAP 4:I5, OS198 Ref. TQ412 101. Lewes town centre off A27/A26/A275.

Open: Castle & Barbican Museum open daily: Tues–Sat, 10am–5.30pm, Sun, Mon & Bank Hols 11am–5.30pm, except for Sat 24–Mon 26 Dec. Closed Mondays in January. Last admission to both 30 mins before closing time and Castle closes at dusk in winter.

Admission: Adult £6.40, OAP/Student £5.70, Child £3.20, Disabled/Carer £3.20 Family (2+2) (1+4) £17. Groups (15+): Adult £5.70, OAP/Student £5.10, Child £2.90, Disabled/Carer £2.90 Combined tickets with Anne of Cleves House: Adult £9.20, OAP/Student £8, Child £4.60, Family (2+2 or 1+4) £25, Disabled/carer £4.60. Groups (15+), Adult £8, OAP/Student £7, Child £4, Disabled/carer £4.

Unsuitable. By arrangement. Guide dogs only.

Pashley Manor Gardens

MICHELHAM PRIORY

UPPER DICKER, HAILSHAM, SUSSEX BN27 3QS

www.sussexpast.co.uk/michelham

Tel: 01323 844224 **Fax:** 01323 844030 **E-mail:** adminmich@sussexpast.co.uk

Owner: Sussex Past **Contact:** Chris Tuckett

Enter through the 14th century gatehouse and wander through beautiful gardens or tour the historic house. Furniture and artefacts trace the property's religious origins and its development over 800 years to a grand country house. Explore the medieval watermill, working forge, rope museum and dramatic Elizabethan Great Barn. Plenty of free parking, restaurant and gift shop plus special events.

Location: MAP 4:J5, OS Ref. TQ557 093. 8m NW of Eastbourne off A22/A27. 2m W of Hailsham.

Open: 1 Mar–30 Oct: Tues–Sun from 10.30am. Closed Mons except on Bank Holidays and in Aug. Closing Times: Mar & Oct, 4.30pm, Apr–Jul & Sept, 5pm, Aug, 5.30pm. Last admission 45 mins before closing time.

Admission: Adult £7, Student/OAP £6, Child £3.80, Disabled/Carer £3.80, Family (2+2) £18.40. Groups (15+): Adult/Student/OAP £5.70, Child £3.50, Disabled/Carer £3.80.

Licensed. By arrangement. Ample for cars & coaches. Guide dogs only.

MONK'S HOUSE

Rodmell, Lewes BN7 3HF

Tel: 01323 870001 (Property Office)

Owner: National Trust **Contact:** Property Office

A small weather-boarded house, the home of Leonard and Virginia Woolf until Leonard's death in 1969.

Location: MAP 4:I6, OS Ref. TQ421 064. 4 m E of Lewes, off former A275 in Rodmell village, near church.

Open: 2 Apr–30 Oct: Weds & Sats, 2–5.30pm. Last admission 5pm. Groups by arrangement with tenant.

Admission: Adult £4.20, Child £2.10, Family £10.50, Groups £3.50.

NYMAN'S

See page 142 for full page entry.

PALLANT HOUSE GALLERY

9 North Pallant, Chichester, West Sussex. PO19 1TJ

Tel: 01243 774557

Owner: Pallant House Gallery Trust **Contact:** Reception

Museum of the Year 2007, Pallant House Gallery houses one of the best collections of modern British art in the world alongside an exciting programme of temporary exhibitions.

Location: MAP 3:F6, OS Ref. SU861 047. City centre, SE of the Cross.

Open: Tue–Sat: 10am–5pm (Thur: 10am–8pm. Sun & BH Mons: 12.30–5pm).

Admission: Adult £7.50, Child (6–15yrs): £2.30, Students £4. Unemployed/Friends/Under 5s Free.

PARHAM HOUSE & GARDENS

PARHAM PARK, STORRINGTON, Nr PULBOROUGH, WEST SUSSEX RH20 4HS

www.parhaminsussex.co.uk

Tel: 01903 742021 **Info Line:** 01903 744888 Fax: 01903 746557
Email: enquiries@parhaminsussex.co.uk
Owner: Parham Park Trust **Contact:** Richard Pailthorpe

One of the top twenty in Simon Jenkins's book *"England's Thousand Best Houses"*, Parham is one of the country's finest Elizabethan examples. Idyllically set in the heart of a 17th century deer park, below the South Downs, the house contains a particularly important collection of needlework, paintings and furniture. The spectacular Long Gallery is the third longest in England. The award winning gardens include a four acre walled garden with stunning herbaceous borders, greenhouse, orchard, potager and herbiary. All the flowers used in the house are home grown. Parham has always been a much-loved family home. Now owned by a charitable trust, the house is lived in by Lady Emma Barnard, her husband James and their family.

Location: MAP 3: G5, OS Ref. TQ060 143. Midway between Pulborough & Storrington on A283. Equidistant from A24 &A29.

Open: 3 Apr–29 Sept. House: Wed, Thur, Sun and BH Mons from 2–5pm, also Aug, Tues and Fri. Gardens: Wed, Thur, Sun, BH Mons and Tues and Fri between May and Aug from 12noon–5pm. Open Sundays in October, last Sunday 16th.

Admission: Please contact property for details.

No photography in house. Partial. Licensed. By arrangement. In grounds, on leads. Special charges may apply. Please contact property for details.

PASHLEY MANOR GARDENS *See page 143 for full page entry.*

PETWORTH COTTAGE MUSEUM

346 High Street, Petworth, West Sussex GU28 0AU
Tel: 01798 342100 **E-mail:** petworthcottagemuseum@yahoo.co.uk
www.petworthcottagemuseum.co.uk
Owner: Petworth Cottage Trust **Contact:** Curator

A Leconfield Estate Cottage as if it were 1910, when Mary Cummings lived here. A nostalgic and educational reconstruction that takes account of living memories, Mary's Irish Catholic background and her work as a seamstress. The range is lit, the tea table is laid, the kettle is boiling.

Location: MAP 3:G5

Open: Apr–Oct: Tue–Sat & BH Mons, 2–4.30pm.

Admission: Adult £3, Child (under 14yrs) 50p. Group visits by arrangement.

PETWORTH HOUSE & PARK

Petworth House & Park, Church Street, Petworth, West Sussex GU28 0AE
Tel: 01798 342207 **Info:** 01798 343929 **Fax:** 01798 342963
Owner: National Trust **Contact:** The Administration Office

Late 17th c mansion with fine art collection. Set in 700 acre deer park.

Location: MAP 3:G5, OS Ref. SU976 218. In the centre of Petworth town (approach roads A272/A283/A285) Car park signposted.

PEVENSEY CASTLE

Pevensey, Sussex BN24 5LE
Tel/Fax: 01323 762604 **E-mail:** customers@english-heritage.org.uk
www.english-heritage.org.uk/pevensey
Owner: English Heritage **Contact:** Visitor Operations Team

Originally a 4th century Roman fort, Pevensey was where William the Conqueror landed in 1066 and established his first stronghold. The Norman castle includes remains of an unusual keep. An exhibition with artefacts found on site and an audio tour tells the story of the castle's 2,000 year history.

Location: MAP 4:K6, OS Ref. TQ645 048. In Pevensey off A259.

Open: 1 Apr–30 Sep: daily, 10am–6pm. 1–31 Oct, daily: 10am–4pm. 1 Nov–31 Mar '11: Sat & Sun, 10am–4pm. Closed 24–26 Dec & 1 Jan.

Admission: Adult £4.50, Child £2.30, Conc. £3.80. Family £11.30. 15% discount for groups of 11+. EH Members free. Opening times and prices are valid until 31st March 2011, after this date details are subject to change please visit www.english-heritage.org.uk for the most up-to-date information.

WC. Inclusive. On leads.

Cowdray

© NTPL / John Hammond

Petworth House (Chapel)

SACKVILLE COLLEGE

HIGH STREET, EAST GRINSTEAD, WEST SUSSEX RH19 3BX

www.sackvillecollege.co.uk

Tel: 01342 323414 **E-mail:** sackvillecollege@talktalkbusiness.net
Owner: Board of Trustees **Contact:** College Co-ordinator

Built in 1609 for Richard Sackville, Earl of Dorset, as an almshouse and overnight accommodation for the Sackville family. Feel the Jacobean period come alive in the enchanting quadrangle, the chapel, banqueting hall with fine hammerbeam roof and minstrel's gallery, the old common room and warden's study where "Good King Wenceslas" was composed. Chapel weddings by arrangement.

Location: MAP 4:I4, A22 to East Grinstead, College in High Street (town centre).

Open: 8 Jun–11 Sept: Wed–Sun, 2–5pm. Groups all year by arrangement.

Admission: Adult £3.50, Child £1. Groups: (10–60) no discount.

Large public car park adjacent to entrance. Partial. Obligatory. Limited. Guide dogs only. By arrangement.

SHEFFIELD PARK GARDEN *See page 144 for full page entry.*

STANDEN *See page 145 for full page entry.*

THE PRIEST HOUSE

NORTH LANE, WEST HOATHLY, SUSSEX RH19 4PP

www.sussexpast.co.uk/priest house

Tel: 01342 810479 **E-mail:** priest@sussexpast.co.uk
Owner: Sussex Past **Contact:** Antony Smith

Once a yeoman farmer's cottage, the 15th century timber-framed house, sits in the picturesque Wealden village of West Hoathly. Standing in a traditional cottage garden, it now contains country furniture, ironwork, textiles and domestic objects displayed in period rooms. The garden includes borders of perennials, shrubs, wild flowers and herbs. Guided tours available.

Location: MAP 4:J4, OS187 Ref. TQ362 325. In triangle formed by Crawley, East Grinstead and Haywards Heath, 4m off A22, 6m off M23.

Open: 1 Mar–31 Oct: Tue–Sat, 10.30am–5.30pm, Sun 12pm–5.30pm. Open on Bank Holiday Mondays and Mondays in August 10.30am–5.30pm.

Admission: Adult £3.50, Child £1.75, Conc. £3. Disabled/Carer £1.75. Garden only £1. Groups (15+) Adult £3.20, Child £1.60, Conc. £2.70. Disabled/Carer £1.75, Garden only £1.

Partial. By arrangement. Limited (on street). In grounds, on leads.

© Heritage House Group / Parham Park / Nick McCann

Parham House & Gardens

SAINT HILL MANOR

SAINT HILL ROAD, EAST GRINSTEAD, WEST SUSSEX RH19 4JY

www.sainthillmanor.org.uk

Tel: 01342 317057 **E-mail:** info@sainthillmanor.org.uk

Owner: Church of Scientology **Contact:** Elaine Mathieson Saint Hill Manor

Built in 1792 by Gibbs Crawfurd, Saint Hill Manor is one of Sussex's finest sandstone buildings, with breathtaking views of unspoiled countryside. Impressive features include the magnificent black Spanish marble pillars added by the Maharajah of Jaipur, and the delightful 100-foot Monkey Mural, painted by Winston Churchill's nephew. The final owner, author L Ron Hubbard, bought the Manor in 1959 and made it his family home, restoring much of the oak panelling and marble fireplaces. An impressive collection of Mr. Hubbard's published works is displayed in the library. There are 59 acres of grounds, lake and rose garden. Ideal for weddings and conferences.

Location: MAP 4:14, OS Ref. TQ383 359. 2 miles S of East Grinstead.

Open: All year. Guided tours of the house every afternoon 2–5 pm on the hour. Open in morning by arrangement. Gardens open all day.

Admission: Free of charge. Coach parties welcome, teas served.

Teas available. Obligatory. Group Visits Fair: Date TBC.

ST MARY'S HOUSE & GARDENS

BRAMBER, WEST SUSSEX BN44 3WE

www.stmarysbramber.co.uk

Tel/Fax: 01903 816205 **E-mail:** info@stmarysbramber.co.uk

Owners: Mr Peter Thorogood MBE and Mr Roger Linton MBE

Features in Simon Jenkins' book *'England's Thousand Best Houses'*. St. Mary's is an enchanting, medieval timber-framed house, with fine panelled interiors, including the unique Elizabethan 'Painted Room', giving an air of tranquillity and timelessness. Interesting displays of family memorabilia and rare Napoleonic collection. The formal gardens with amusing topiary, include an exceptional example of the prehistoric *Ginkgo Biloba*, magnificent *Magnolia Grandiflora* and mysterious ivy-clad Monks' Walk.

The five acres of grounds include the Victorian 'Secret' Garden with original fruit wall and pineapple pits, Rural Museum, Jubilee Rose Garden, Terracotta Garden, Woodland Walk and unusual circular Poetry Garden. In the heart of the South Downs National Park, St. Mary's is a house of fascination and mystery, with picturesque charm and atmosphere of friendliness and welcome.

Location: MAP 3:H6, OS Ref. TQ189 105. Bramber village off A283. From London 56m via M23/A23 or A24. Bus from Shoreham to Steyning, alight St Mary's, Bramber.

Open: May–end Sept: Suns, Thurs & BH Mons, 2–6pm. Last entry 5pm. Groups at other times by arrangement.

Admission: House & Gardens: Adult £7.50, Conc. £6.50, Child £4. Groups (25+) £7. Gardens Only: Adult £5, Conc. £4, Child, £2.50, Groups £4.50.

No photography in house. Partial. Obligatory for groups (max 60). Visit time 2½hrs. 30 cars, 2 coaches.

STANSTED PARK

STANSTED PARK, ROWLANDS CASTLE, HAMPSHIRE PO9 6DX

www.stanstedpark.co.uk

Tel: 023 9241 2265 **Fax:** 023 9241 3773 **E-mail:** enquiry@stanstedpark.co.uk

Owner: Stansted Park Foundation **Contact:** House and Events Manager

'One of the South's most beautiful stately homes'. The State Rooms and fully restored Servants' Quarters of Stansted House give the visitor a fascinating insight into the social history of an English Country House in its heyday in Edwardian times.

Location: MAP 3:F5, OS Ref. SU761 103. Follow brown heritage signs from A3 Rowlands Castle or A27 Havant. Rail: Havant (Taxi) or Rowlands Castle (2m walk).

Open: House & Chapel: Sun & BH from Easter Sun–end Sept: 1–4pm, Jun, Jul & Aug: Sun–Wed 1-4pm. Tea Room & Garden Centre open all year. Restricted access to grounds on Sats and during events. Stansted Park Light Railway runs through Arboretum.Tel: 02392 413324 for timetable. New Maze opening 2011.

Admission: House & Chapel: Adult £7, Child (5–15yrs) £3.50, Conc. £6, Family (2+3) £18. Groups/educational visits by arrangement other days.

Private & corporate hire. By arrangement. By arrangement. Guide dogs only. Grounds.

NT/Raymond Woodham

UPPARK HOUSE AND GARDEN

SOUTH HARTING, PETERSFIELD GU31 5QR

www.nationaltrust.org.uk/uppark

Tel: 01730 825415 **Fax:** 01730 825873 **E-mail:** uppark@nationaltrust.org.uk

Owner: National Trust **Contact:** Administrator

Marvel at the historic elegance of Uppark – with fine, late-Georgian interiors and collections of paintings, ceramics and textiles, extensive basement rooms, famous dolls house, Regency garden (stunning views to the sea), children's activities, shop and restaurant – there is everything for a perfect day out.

Location: MAP 3:F5, OS Ref 197 SU781 181. Between Petersfield & Chichester on B2146.

Open: 20 Mar–30 Oct: Sun–Thur; Grounds, Shop & Restaurant: 11.30am–5pm; House: 12.30–4.30pm. BH Suns, Mons & Good Friday, 11.30am–4.30pm. Print Room open 1st Wed of each Month.

***Admission:** Adult £8.80, Child £4.40, Family £22, Groups (15+) must book: £7.80.

*includes a voluntary donation but visitors can choose to pay the standard prices displayed at the property and on the website.

WCs Licensed By arrangement. Guide dogs only

© Heritage House Group

West Dean College & Gardens

WEST DEAN COLLEGE & GARDENS *See page 146 for full page entry.*

WILMINGTON PRIORY

Wilmington, Nr Eastbourne, East Sussex BN26 5SW

Tel: 01628 825925 **E-mail:** bookings@landmarktrust.org.uk

www.landmarktrust.org.uk

Owner: Leased to the Landmark Trust by Sussex Archaeological Society

Contact: The Landmark Trust

Founded by the Benedictines in the 11th century, the surviving, much altered buildings date largely from the 14th century. Managed and maintained by the Landmark Trust, which lets buildings for self-catering holidays. Full details of Wilmington Priory and 189 other historic and architecturally important buildings available for holidays are featured in The Landmark Trust Handbook (price £10 plus p&p refundable against a booking) and on the website.

Location: MAP 3:F5, OS Ref. TQ543 042. 600yds S of A27. 6m NW of Eastbourne.

Open: Available for self-catering holidays for up to 6 people throughout the year. Grounds, Ruins, Porch & Crypt: on 30 days between Apr–Oct. Whole property including interiors on 8 of these days. Other visits by appointment. Contact the Landmark Trust for details.

Admission: Free on Open Days and visits by appointment.

Owner
English Heritage

Contact
The House Administrator
Osborne House
Royal Apartments
East Cowes
Isle of Wight
PO32 6JX

Tel: 01983 200022
Fax: 01983 281380
E-mail: customers@english-heritage.org.uk

Venue Hire and Hospitality:
Tel: 01983 203055

Location
MAP 3:D6
OS Ref. SZ516 948

1 mile SE of East Cowes.

Ferry: Isle of Wight ferry terminals.

Red Funnel, East Cowes 1½ miles
Tel: 02380 334010.

Wightlink, Fishbourne 4 miles
Tel: 0870 582 7744

Opening Times
1 April–30 September
Daily: 10am–6pm (House closes 5pm, may close early for special events on occasional days in July & August).
Last admission 4pm.

1–31 October
Daily: 10am–4pm.

3 Nov–31 March,
Wed–Sun: 10am–4pm (pre-booked guided tours only. Last tour 2.30pm).
24–26 Dec & 1 Jan: closed.

Admission

Adult	£10.90
Child (5–15yrs)	£5.50
Child under 5yrs	Free
Conc.	£9.30
Family (2+3)	£27.30

Groups (11+) 15% discount. Tour leader and driver have free entry.

Opening times and prices are valid until 31st March 2011, after this date details are subject to change please visit www.english-heritage.org.uk for the most up-to-date information.

Conference/Function

ROOM	MAX CAPACITY
Durbar Hall	standing 80 seated 50
Upper Terrace	standing 250
Walled Gardens	standing 100
Marquee	Large scale events possible

© English Heritage

OSBORNE HOUSE ⌗

www.english-heritage.org.uk/osborne

Osborne House was the peaceful, rural retreat of Queen Victoria, Prince Albert and their family; they spent some of their happiest times here.

Step inside and marvel at the richness of the State Apartments including the Durbar Room with its lavish Indian décor. The Queen died at the house in 1901 and many of the rooms have been preserved almost unaltered ever since. The nursery bedroom remains just as it was in the 1870s when Queen Victoria's first grandchildren came to stay. Children were a constant feature of life at Osborne (Victoria and Albert had nine). Don't miss the Swiss Cottage, a charming chalet in the grounds built for teaching the royal children domestic skills.

Enjoy the beautiful gardens with their stunning views over the Solent and the fruit and flower Victorian Walled Garden.

© English Heritage

WCs. Suitable for filming, concerts, drama. No photography in the House. Children's play area.

Private and corporate hire.

Wheelchairs available, access to house via ramp and first floor via lift. WC.

Hot drinks, light snacks & waiter service lunches in the stunning terrace restaurant.

Open from Nov–Mar for pre-booked guided tours only. These popular tours allow visitors to see the Royal Apartments and private rooms at a quieter time of the year, and in the company of one of our expert guides.

Ample.

Visits free, please book. Education room available.

APPULDURCOMBE HOUSE ⌗

Wroxall, Shanklin, Isle of Wight PO38 3EW

Tel: 01983 852484 **E-mail:** customers@english-heritage.org.uk

www.english-heritage.org.uk/appuldurcombehouse

Owner: English Heritage **Contact:** Mr & Mrs Owen

The bleached shell of a fine 18th century Baroque style house standing in grounds landscaped by 'Capability' Brown. Once the grandest house on the Isle of Wight. An exhibition of photographs and prints depict the house and its history.

Location: MAP 3:D7, OS Ref. SZ543 800. ½mile W of Wroxall off B3327.

Open: 1 Apr–30 Sep: Sun–Fri, 10am–4pm; Sat, 10am–12pm. Last entry 1hr before closing. 1 Oct–31 Mar, Closed.

Admission: House: Adult £3.50, Child £2.50, Conc. £3.25, Family £12. EH members Free. Additional charge for the Falconry Centre. Group discount available. Opening times and prices are valid until 31st March 2011, after this date details are subject to change please visit www.english-heritage.org.uk for the most up-to-date information.

BEMBRIDGE WINDMILL

High Street, Bembridge, Isle of Wight PO35 5SQ

Correspondence to: NT Office, Strawberry Lane, Mottistone, Isle of Wight PO30 4EA

Tel: 01983 873945

Owner: National Trust **Contact:** The Custodian

Dating from around 1700, this is the only surviving windmill on the island and contains most of its original machinery. Four floors to explore plus small replica working model.

Location: MAP 3:E7, OS Ref. SZ639 874. ½m S of Bembridge off B3395.

Open: Mar–Oct, daily, 11am–5pm.

***Admission:** Adult £3, Child £1.50, Family £7.45. * includes a voluntary 10% donation but visitors can choose to pay the standard prices displayed at the property and on the website. Free to NT members. All school groups are conducted by a NT guide; special charges apply.

By arrangement. 100 yds. Guide dogs only.

© Britainonview / Martin Brent

Osborne House

BRIGHSTONE SHOP & MUSEUM

North St, Brighstone, Isle of Wight PO30 4AX

Tel: 01983 740689

Owner: National Trust **Contact:** The Manager

The traditional cottages contain a National Trust shop and Village Museum (run by Brighstone Museum Trust) depicting village life in the late 19th century.

Location: MAP 3:D7, OS Ref. SZ428 828. North Street, Brighstone, just off B3399.

Open: Jan–Dec. Times vary, ring for details.

Admission: Free.

Partial.

© English Heritage

© English Heritage

CARISBROOKE CASTLE ⌗

NEWPORT, ISLE OF WIGHT PO30 1XY

www.english-heritage.org.uk/carisbrooke

Tel: 01983 522107 **E-mail:** customers@english-heritage.org.uk

Owner: English Heritage **Contact:** Visitor Operations Team

The island's royal fortress and prison of King Charles I before his execution in London in 1648. See the famous Carisbrooke donkeys treading the wheel in the Well House as donkeys would have done in the 18th century. Visit the on-site Carisbrooke Museum and take an invigorating battlements walk. Enjoy a fascinating presentation reflecting 800 years of colourful history at the castle, brought to life using dramatic film and interactive exhibits. Don't miss the new Edwardian-style Princess Beatrice Garden, designed by TV and radio gardening presenter Chris Beardshaw.

Location: MAP 3:E7, OS196 Ref. SZ486 877. Off the B3401, 1¼ miles SW of Newport.

Open: 1 Apr–30 Sep: daily, 10am–5pm. 1 Oct–31 Mar 2010: daily, 10am–4pm. Closed 24–26 Dec & 1 Jan.

Admission: Adult £7, Child £3.50, Conc. £6, Family (2+3) £17.50. 15% discount for groups (11+). EH Members Free. Opening times and prices are valid until 31st March 2011, after this date details are subject to change please visit www.english-heritage.org.uk for the most up-to-date information.

WCs. Partial. WCs. Guide dogs only. Tel. for details.

MOTTISTONE MANOR GARDEN

Mottistone, Isle of Wight PO30 4ED
Tel: 01983 741302 **Fax:** 01983 741154
www.nationaltrust.org.uk
Owner: National Trust **Contact:** The Gardener

Set in a sheltered valley this magical garden is full of surprises with shrub filled banks, hidden pathways and colourful herbaceous borders. Surrounding an Elizabethan manor house (not open) this 20th century garden is experimenting with a Mediterranean-style planting scheme to take advantage of its southerly location.

Location: MAP 3:D7, OS Ref. SZ406 838. Car: Between Brighstone & Brook on B3399.

Open: Mar–Oct (Ring for details).

***Admission:** Garden: Adult £4, Child £2, Family £9.90 (2010 prices). Free to NT members. Extra charge for house. *Includes a voluntary 10% donation but visitors can choose to pay the standard prices displayed at the property and on the website.

Partial. WCs By arrangement. In grounds, on leads.

NEEDLES OLD BATTERY & NEW BATTERY

Alum Bay, Totland, Isle of Wight PO39 0JH
Tel: 01983 754772 **Fax:** 01983 741154
Owner: National Trust **Contact:** The Fort Manager

Built in 1862 this spectacularly sited cliff top fort overlooking the Needles contains exhibitions about its involvement in both World Wars. Two original gun barrels are displayed on the parade ground and a tunnel leads to a searchlight emplacement perched above the Needles Rocks. Rocket exhibition at Needles New Battery.

Location: MAP 3:C7, OS Ref. SZ300 848. Needles Headland W of Alum Bay (B3322)
Bus: Needles Tour Bus from Yarmouth or Alum Bay.

Open: Needles Old Battery: Mar–Oct every day, 10.30am–5pm. Needles New Battery: Mar–Oct, Sat, Sun & Tues, 11am–4pm. Closes in high winds; please telephone on day of visit to check.

***Admission:** Adult £4.85, Child £2.45, Family £12.10 (2010 prices). Free to NT members. Needles New Battery: Free. *Includes a voluntary 10% donation but visitors can choose to pay the standard prices displayed at the property and on the website.

No vehicular access. For disabled access please phone 01983 754772. WCs By appointment.

NEWTOWN OLD TOWN HALL

Newtown, Isle of Wight PO30 4PA
Tel: 01983 531785 **Fax:** 01983 741154
Owner: National Trust **Contact:** The Custodian

The small, now tranquil village of Newtown once sent two members to Parliament and the Town Hall was the setting for often turbulent elections. This historic building contains an exhibition depicting the exploits of "Ferguson's Gang", a mysterious group of anonymous benefactors. Regular art exhibtions.

Location: MAP 3:D7, OS Ref. SZ424 905. Between Newport and Yarmouth, 1m N of A3054.

Open: Mar–Oct. Times vary, ring for details.

Admission: Adult £2.20, Child £1.10, Family £5.50. Free to NT members.

Partial. WCs By arrangement No coaches. Guide dogs only.

NUNWELL HOUSE & GARDENS

Coach Lane, Brading, Isle of Wight PO36 0JQ
Tel: 01983 407240
Owner: Col J A Aylmer **Contact:** Col J A Aylmer

Nunwell has been a family home for five centuries and reflects much architectural and Island history. King Charles I spent his last night of freedom here. Jacobean and Georgian wings. Finely furnished rooms. Lovely setting with Channel views and five acres of tranquil gardens including walled garden. Family military collections.

Location: MAP 3:E7, OS Ref. SZ595 874. 1m NW of Brading. 3m S of Ryde signed off A3055.

Open: 29/30 May & 4 Jul–7 Sept: Mon–Wed, 1–5pm. House tours: 2 & 3.30pm (extra tours when needed). Groups welcome by arrangement throughout the year.

Admission: Adult £5, Pair of Adults £9.50 Child (under 10yrs) £1, OAP/Student £4.50. Garden only: Adult £3.

Obligatory. Guide dogs only.

OSBORNE HOUSE

See page 158 for full page entry.

YARMOUTH CASTLE

Quay Street, Yarmouth, Isle of Wight PO41 0PB
Tel: 01983 760678 **E-mail:** customers@english-heritage.org.uk
www.english-heritage.org.uk/yarmouthcastle
Owner: English Heritage **Contact:** Visitor Operations Team

This last addition to Henry VIII's coastal defences was completed in 1547, unusually for its kind, square with a fine example of an angle bastion. Exhibition displays artefacts and an atmospheric recreation of how the rooms were used in the 16th century. Magnificent picnic spot, with views over the Solent.

Location: MAP 3:C7, OS Ref. SZ354 898. In Yarmouth adjacent to car ferry terminal.

Open: 1 Apr–30 Sep: Sun–Thu, 11am–4pm.

Admission: Adult £3.80, Child £1.90, Conc. £3.20. EH Members Free. Group discount available. Opening times and prices are valid until 31st March 2011, after this date details are subject to change please visit www.english-heritage.org.uk for the most up-to-date information.

Mottistone Manor Garden

Osborne House

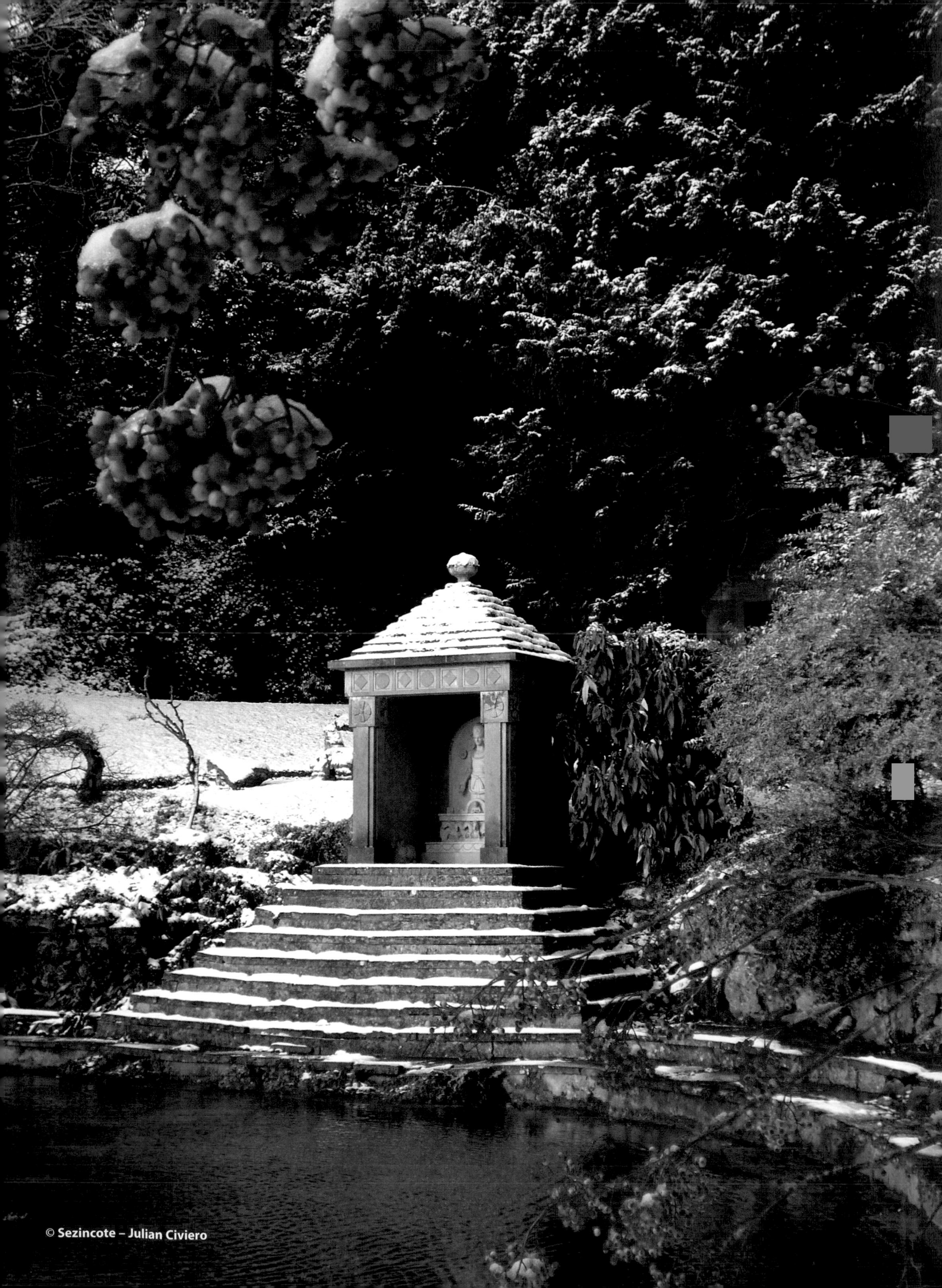

South West

The moorlands of Devon and Cornwall are among the most dramatic in Britain, contrasting with the unspoilt beaches. The temperate climate means gardens such as Abbotsbury Subtropical Gardens can grow exotic plants that wouldn't survive in other parts of the country. Compare this with the bustling terraces of Georgian Bath, or the fascinating wildlife at Longleat in Wiltshire.

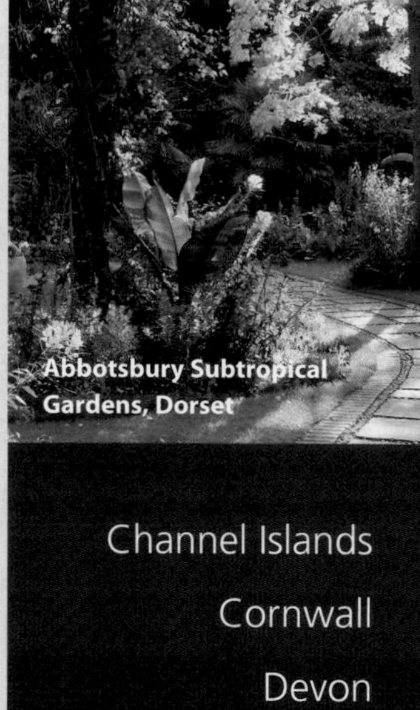

Abbotsbury Subtropical Gardens, Dorset

Channel Islands

Cornwall

Devon

Dorset

Gloucestershire

Somerset

Wiltshire

GLOCESTERSHIRE

WILTSHIRE

SOMERSET

DEVON

DORSET

CORNWALL

CHANNEL ISLANDS

Kingston Lacy ©NT/ Kingston Lacy, Dorset

Woodchester mansion, Gloucestershire

Hartland Abbey, Devon

■ **Owner**

The Seigneur de Sausmarez

■ **Contact**

Peter de Sausmarez
Sausmarez Manor
Guernsey
Channel Islands
GY4 6SG
Tel: 01481 235571/235655
Fax: 01481 235572
E-mail: sausmarezmanor@cwgsy.net

■ **Location**

Map 3:D10

2m S of St Peter Port, clearly signposted.

■ **Opening Times**

The Grounds:
Easter–End Oct
Daily: 10am–5pm

Guided tours of House
Easter–End Oct.
Mon–Thurs:
10.30 & 11.30am.
Additional 2pm tour during high season.

■ **Admission**

There is no overall charge for admission.

Sub Tropical Garden	£5.50
Sculpture Trail	£5.50
Pitch & Putt	£5.50
Putting	£2.00
House Tour	£7.00
Ghost Tour	£10.50
Train Rides	£2.00

Discounts for Children, Students, OAPs & Organised Groups.

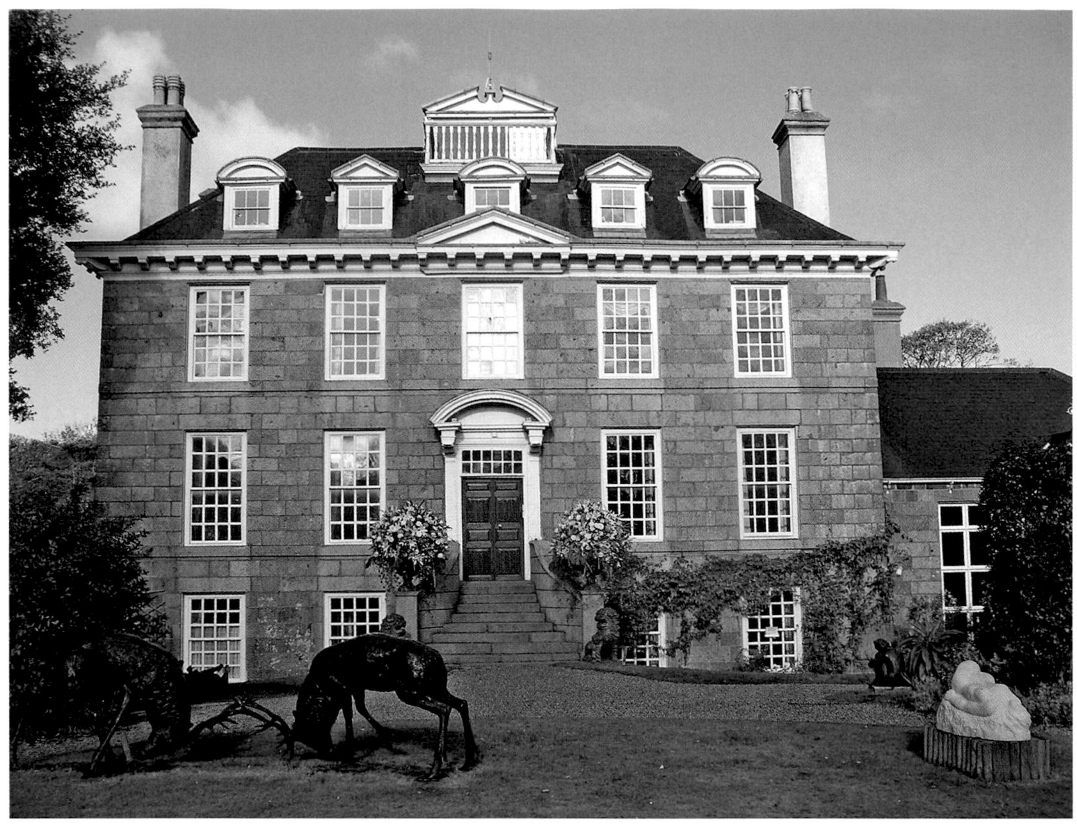

SAUSMAREZ MANOR

www.sausmarezmanor.co.uk www.artparks.co.uk

The home of the Seigneurs de Sausmarez since c1220 with a façade built at the bequest of the first Governor of New York.

An entertaining half day encompassing something to interest everyone. The family have been explorers, inventors, diplomats, prelates, generals, admirals, privateers, politicians and governors etc, most of whom left their mark on the house, garden or the furniture.

The sub-tropical woodland garden is crammed with such exotics as banana trees, tree ferns, ginger, 300 plus camellias, lilies, myriads of bamboos, as well as the more commonplace hydrangeas, hostas etc. The RHS recommends the gardens to its own members, as does 'The Good Garden Guide','1001 Gardens you must see before You Die' and the 'RHS Garden Finder'

The sculpture in the art park with its 200 or so pieces by artists from a dozen countries is the most comprehensive in Britain and rated 5th in the Daily Telegraph's top ten. The pitch and putt is a testing 500m 9 hole par 3. The Copper, and Silversmith demonstrates his ancient skills and is the remaining craftsman making the traditional copper Guernsey Milk Can. The two lakes are a haven for ornamental wildfowl and some of the sculpture.

The community Farmers' and Plantsmen's Market is every Saturday morning, selling local Fish, Crab/Lobster, Guernsey Beef and Veal, Sark Lamb and Butter, fresh locally grown vegetables and plants, home made Cakes, Jams, Pasties, Pate, Pies, Vegetarian Delights as well as gifts, Handcrafts & Toys, Island made Jewellery and herbal remedies, Crystals and Guernsey Cosmetics.

Partial.

Guided tours of House Easter–Oct.

Guide dogs only.

Two holiday flats are available see www.cottageguide.co.uk

€

BOCONNOC

www.boconnocenterprises.co.uk

'Let your ancestors speak through every stone and blade of grass.' At Boconnoc this is true. The 16th century Mohuns left a remarkable inscription in Boconnoc Church. Governor Pitt of Madras brought the Pitt Diamond back from India and with the proceeds bought Boconnoc from the Mohuns. Pitt's descendants were the two Prime Ministers and their cousin was Thomas Pitt, the creator of the Picturesque landscape at Boconnoc, which surrounds the extensive woodland gardens, with the newly planted Pinetum and collection of magnolias. Sir John Soane made additions to Boconnoc House and Stableyard and the second Lord Camelford created the Georgian Bath House near the Church, both of which stand above the undulating pasture, mature woodland and lake, below the Deer Park and Cricket Pitch. The restoration project on Boconnoc House is once again revealing the beauty of this interesting house. Talented local craftsmen have restored the rooms and these are now furnished from the Anthony Fortescue Furniture collection. Today Boconnoc is ideal for romantic weddings and house parties, offering peace, privacy, seclusion and magic. Boconnoc is a versatile location for films, fashion shoots, product launches, conferences and large events. Historical and garden groups are welcomed for day visits with guided tours and additional lectures. There is comfortable Stableyard accommodation as well as residential cottages and lodges to let.

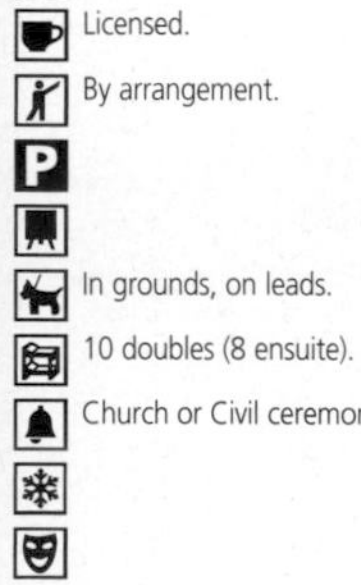

Owner

Anthony Fortescue Esq

Contact

Veryan Barneby
Events Organiser
The Estate Office,
Boconnoc, Lostwithiel,
Cornwall PL22 0RG

Tel: 01208 872507
Fax: 01208 873836
E-mail: adgfortescue@btinternet.com

Location

MAP 1:G8
OS Ref. 148 605

A38 from Plymouth, Liskeard or from Bodmin to Dobwalls, then A390 to East Taphouse.

Opening Times

House & Garden
1, 8, 15 & 22 May
Suns, 2–5pm.

Groups (15–100) by appointment all year with coffee, lunch and tea.

Admission

House	£4.00
Garden	£5.00
Children under 12 years	Free

Special Events

Sunday 6 March
Wedding Fair, 10am–4pm.

Tuesday 15 March
Red Cross Concert

Thursday 31 March
Floral Art Exhibition, 6–8pm.

Saturday 2– Sunday 3 March
Cornwall Garden Society Spring Flower Show.

Sunday 8 May
History Lecture in Church, 11.30am.

Wednesday 11 & Thursday 12 May
Spring Fair.

Sunday 15 May
St. John Ambulance Run
History Lecture in Church, 3pm.

Sunday 22 May
Precious Lives Dog Show.

Friday 24 June
Music in the Park.

Saturday & Sunday 2–3 July
Endurance Horse Ride.

Friday 22– Sunday 24 July
Steam Fair.

Saturday 10 September
Sheepdog trials.

Monday 3– Tuesday 4 October
Michaelmas Fair.

■ **Owner**

National Trust

■ **Contact**

Administrator
Kestle Mill
Nr Newquay
Cornwall TR8 4PG
Tel: 01637 875404
Fax: 01637 879300
E-mail: trerice@nationaltrust.org.uk

■ **Location**

MAP 1:E8
OS Ref. SW841 585

3m SE of Newquay via the A392 & A3058 (right at Kestle Mill). Or from A30–signs at Summercourt and Mitchell. Bus: Western Greyhound 527 Newquay - St Austell

■ **Opening Times**

5 March–30 October: Daily, 11am-5pm. (Garden, shop & tearoom 10.30am).
4 November–18 December, Fri-Sun, 11am-4pm.

■ ***Admission**

Adult	£7.70
Child	£3.90
Family	£19.10
1-Adult Family	£11.50
Pre-arranged Groups	£6.50

*includes a voluntary donation but visitors can choose to pay the standard prices displayed at Trerice and on the website.

TRERICE 

www.nationaltrust.org.uk

The intimate Elizabethan Manor at Trerice inspires visitors to discover relationships between a house, its people and its surrounding land told over many centuries. This atmospheric place is hidden away in a web of narrow lanes and still somehow caught in the spirit of its age.

Two of the largest rooms in this former Arundell family home, the Great Hall and Great Chamber are decorated with intriguing plasterwork ceilings and fireplaces. A replica handling collection of domestic items and games based of Tudor items enables everyone to get hands-on with the past. Long-gone threats of invasion and the need for security are brought to life by the replica armour which visitors can try on to feel the true weight of staying safe. There are many fine pieces of furniture, ceramics, glassware and a wonderful clock collection.

A range of agricultural buildings including the Great Barn and Hayloft match the house for size and presence, and now accommodate a tea-room and exhibition space.

The house and barn complex are surrounded by the gardens, which sit on a variety of terraces, with space to try kayling (Cornish bowls) and slap-cock, a fore-runner of badminton. There's an orchard with old varieties of south-west fruit trees and an experimental Tudor garden.

As new research uncovers the relationships and layers of history at Trerice, visitors will be able to discover more of the stories of this special Cornish Manor - with 500 years of mixed fortunes.

WCs.

Licensed.

Licensed.

Limited for coaches.

Guide dogs only.

Holiday flat.

ANTONY HOUSE & GARDEN & ANTONY WOODLAND GARDEN

Torpoint, Cornwall PL11 2QA
www.nationaltrust.org.uk
Antony House & Garden Tel: 01752 812191 **Owner:** National Trust
Antony Woodland Garden Tel: 01752 814210 **Owner:** Carew Pole Garden Trust
E-mail: antony@nationaltrust.org.uk

Superb 18th century house on the Lynher estuary, grounds landscaped by Repton. Formal garden with sculptures & National Collection of daylilies; woodland garden with magnolias, rhododendrons & National Collection of Camellia japonica.

Location: MAP 1:H9, OS Ref. SX418 564. 5m W of Plymouth via Torpoint car ferry, 2m NW of Torpoint.

Open: House: 29 Mar–26 May, Tue–Thur, 1–5pm. 31 May–30 Oct, Tues–Thur & Sun, 1–5pm. Garden, Shop & Tea-Room: 29 Mar–26 May, Tue–Thur, 11am–5pm. 31 May–29 Sept, Tues–Thur & Sat–Sun, 11am–5pm. 2–30 Oct, Tues–Thur & Sun, 11am–5pm. Woodland Garden: 1 Mar–30 Oct, daily except Mon & Fri, 11am–5pm. Open BH Mons, Good Friday & Easter Weekend.

Admission: House & Garden: £7.90, Child £5, Family £20.80, 1-Adult Family £12.90. Garden only: £4, Child £2. Group £6.60. Woodland Garden (not NT): Adult £5, Child Free. (NT members free only on days when the house is open). Joint Gardens-only tickets: Adult £8.

BOCONNOC

See page 165 for full page entry.

BURNCOOSE NURSERIES & GARDEN

Gwennap, Redruth, Cornwall TR16 6BJ
Tel: 01209 860316 **Fax:** 01209 860011 **E-mail:** burncoose@eclipse.co.uk
www.burncoose.co.uk
Owner/Contact: C H Williams

The Nurseries are set in the 30 acre woodland gardens of Burncoose.

Location: MAP 1:D10, OS Ref. SW742 395. 2m SE of Redruth on main A393 Redruth to Falmouth road between the villages of Lanner and Ponsanooth.

Open: Mon–Sat: 9am–5pm, Suns, 11am–5pm. Gardens and Tearooms open all year (except Christmas Day).

Admission: Nurseries: Free. Gardens: Adult/Conc. £2. Child Free. Group conducted tours: £3.50 by arrangement.

Grounds. WCs. By arrangement. In grounds, on leads.

CHYSAUSTER ANCIENT VILLAGE

Nr Newmill, Penzance, Cornwall TR20 8XA
Tel: 07831 757934 **E-mail:** customers@english-heritage.org.uk
www.english-heritage.org.uk/chysauster
Owner: English Heritage **Contact:** Visitor Operations Team

Set on a windy hillside, overlooking the wild and spectacular coast, explore this deserted Romano-Cornish village with a 'street' of nine well preserved houses, each comprising a number of rooms around an open court.

Location: MAP 1:C10, OS203 Ref. SW473 350. 2½m NW of Gulval off B3311.

Open: 1 Apr–31 Oct: daily, 10am–5pm (6pm Jul & Aug, 4pm Oct). Closed 1 Nov–31 Mar.

Admission: Adult £3.20, Child £1.60, Conc. £2.70, 15% discount for groups (11+). EH Members free. Opening times and prices are valid until 31st March 2011, after this date details are subject to change please visit www.english-heritage.org.uk for the most up-to-date information.

WC. No coaches. On leads.

COTEHELE

Cotehele, Saint Dominick, Saltash, Cornwall PL12 6TA
Tel: 01579 351346 **Fax:** 01579 351222
Owner: National Trust **Contact:** Charmian Saunders, General Manager

Fascinating estate on slopes of River Tamar.

Location: MAP 1:H8, OS Ref. SX422 685. 1m SW of Calstock by foot. 8m S of Tavistock, 4m E of Callington, 15m from Plymouth via the Tamar bridge at Saltash.

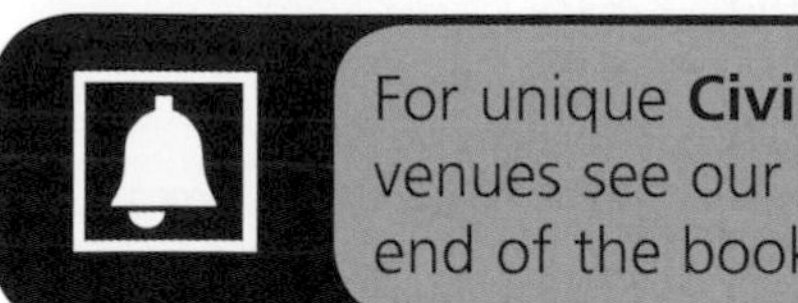

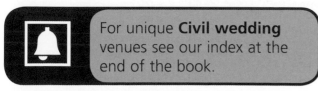

For unique **Civil wedding** venues see our index at the end of the book.

© NTPL / John Bethell

Antony House

CAERHAYS CASTLE & GARDEN

CAERHAYS, GORRAN, ST AUSTELL, CORNWALL PL26 6LY

www.caerhays.co.uk

Tel: 01872 501310 **Fax:** 01872 501870 **E-mail:** estateoffice@caerhays.co.uk
Owner: F J Williams Esq **Contact:** Cheryl Kufel

One of the very few Nash built castles still left standing – situated within approximately 60 acres of informal woodland gardens created by J C Williams, who sponsored plant hunting expeditions to China at the turn of the century. As well as guided tours of the house from March to May visitors will see some of the magnificent selection of plants brought back by the intrepid plant hunters of the early 1900s these include not only the collection of magnolias but a wide range of rhododendrons and the camellias which Caerhays and the Williams familly are associated with worldwide.

Location: MAP 1:F9, OS Ref. SW972 415. S coast of Cornwall – between Mevagissey and Portloe. 9m SW of St Austell.

Open: House: 14 Mar–30 May: Mon–Fri only (including BHs), 12 noon–4pm, booking recommended. Gardens: 14 Feb–5 Jun: daily (including BHs), 10am–5pm (last admission 4pm).

Admission: House: £7.50. Gardens: £7.50. House & Gardens: £12.00. Group tours: £8.50 by arrangement. Groups please contact Estate Office.

No photography in house. Partial. WC. Licensed. By arrangement. In grounds, on leads.

CAERHAYS CASTLE – THE VEAN

THE ESTATE OFFICE, CAERHAYS CASTLE, GORRAN, ST AUSTELL, CORNWALL PL26 6LY

www.thevean.co.uk

Tel: 01872 501310 **Fax:** 01872 501870 **E-mail:** manager@thevean.eclipse.co.uk
Owner: Mrs Lizzy Williams **Contact:** Sally Gammell

Staying at The Vean is like enjoying a house party where the owners have gone away for the weekend. The Vean is a luxury country house retreat, within the Caerhays Estate, that sleeps up to 16 people in its eight en-suite bedrooms. During the shooting season it is the shooting lodge for the guns at the Castle. The Vean is a restored former Georgian Rectory and is run with passion and a commitment to achieve the highest standards.

Location: MAP 1:F9, OS Ref. SW972 415. S coast of Cornwall – between Mevagissey and Portloe. 9m SW of St Austell.

Open: For bookings only. Licensed for Civil weddings.

Admission: Contact property for details.

Conferences & corporate breaks. Partial. Licensed. By arrangement. Ample for cars. In grounds, on leads. 8 x en-suite.

GLENDURGAN GARDEN

Mawnan Smith, Falmouth, Cornwall TR11 5JZ

Tel: 01326 252020 (opening hours) or 01872 862090 **Fax:** 01872 865808

Owner: National Trust

Fine trees, shrubs, water garden and laurel maze.

Location: MAP 1:D10, OS Ref. SW772 277. 4m SW of Falmouth, ½m SW of Mawnan Smith, on road to Helford Passage. 1m E of Trebah Garden. Accessible by ferry from Helford.

GODOLPHIN BLOWINGHOUSE

Blowinghouse Cottage, Godolphin Cross, Breage, Helston, Cornwall TR13 9RE

Tel: 01736 763218 **E-mail:** brian.portch@ndirect.co.uk

Owner/Contact: Mr & Mrs B J Portch

The Blowinghouse dates from the 16th century and was built as part of the Godolphin family tin mining works. The tin ingots weighed in excess of three hundredweight and were stamped with a cat's head that was the Godophin Mine logo.

Location: MAP 1:D10, OS Ref. SW508 521, Situated in the Godolphin Woods-National Trust opposite entrance to the Godolphin Manor House.

Open: Sunday, 7 Aug, 2011, 9.30am–4.30pm. Other times by appointment.

Admission: Free.

WCs. Limited. No coaches.

THE JAPANESE GARDEN & BONSAI NURSERY

St Mawgan, Nr Newquay, Cornwall TR8 4ET

Tel: 01637 860116 **Fax:** 01637 860887 **E-mail:** rob@thebonsainursery.com

Owner/Contact: Mr & Mrs Hore

Authentic Japanese Garden set in 1½ acres.

Location: MAP 2:E8, OS Ref. SW873 660. Follow road signs from A3059 & B3276.

Open: Open all year, daily. Closed Christmas Day–New Year's Day.

Admission: Ring for details.

KEN CARO GARDENS

Bicton, Nr Liskeard PL14 5RF

Tel: 01579 362446

Owner/Contact: Mr and Mrs K R Willcock

5 acre plantsman's garden with woods and picnic area. Total 12 acres.

Location: MAP 1:G8, OS Ref. SX313 692. 5m NE of of Liskeard. Follow brown sign off main A390 midway between Liskeard and Callington.

Open: Feb–Sept: daily, 10am–5.30pm.

Admission: Adult £4.50, Child £2.

LANHYDROCK

Lanhydrock, Bodmin, Cornwall PL30 5AD

Tel: 01208 265950 **Fax:** 01208 265959

Owner: National Trust **Contact:** General Manager

Grand house set in gardens, parkland and wood.

Location: MAP 1:F8, OS Ref. SX085 636. 2½ m SE of Bodmin, follow signposts from either A30, A38 or B3268.

Pentillie Castle & Estate

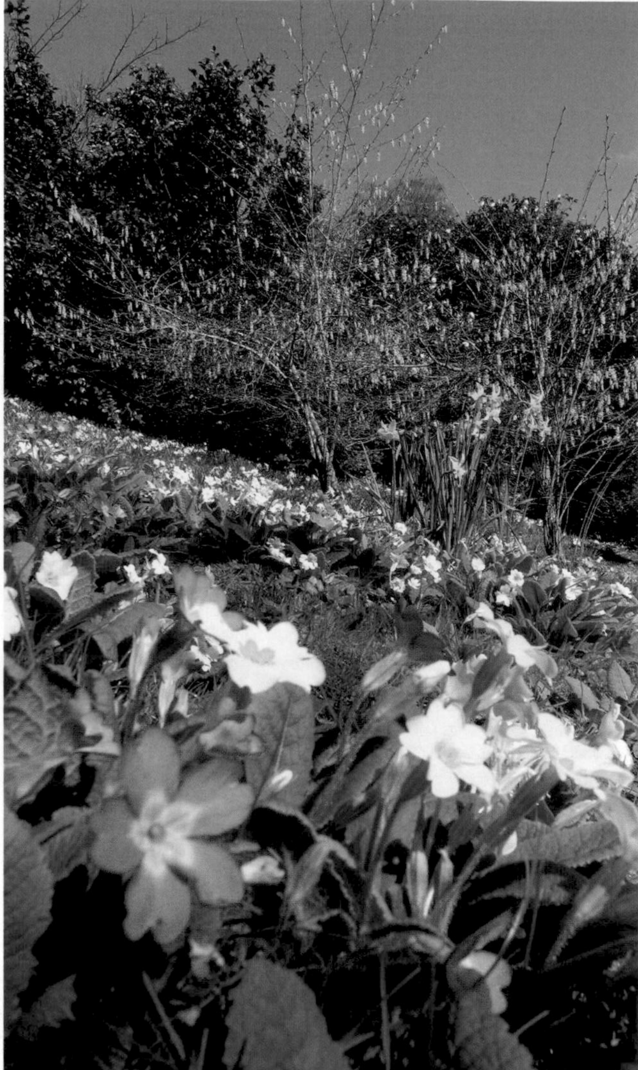

Caerhays Castle & Garden

LAUNCESTON CASTLE

Castle Lodge, Launceston, Cornwall PL15 7DR

Tel: 01566 772365 **Fax:** 01566 772396 **E-mail:** customers@english-heritage.org.uk

www.english-heritage.org.uk/launceston

Owner: English Heritage **Contact:** Visitor Operations Team

Set on the motte of the original Norman castle and commanding the town and surrounding countryside. The shell keep and tower survive of this medieval castle which controlled the main route into Cornwall. An exhibition shows the early history.

Location: MAP 1:H7, OS201 Ref. SX330 846. In Launceston.

Open: 1 Apr–30 Jun: daily, 10am–5pm. 1 Jul–31 Aug: daily, 10am–6pm. 1–30 Sep: daily, 10am–5pm. 1–31 Oct: daily, 10am–4pm. Closed 1 Nov–31 Mar.

Admission: Adult £3.20, Child £1.60, Conc. £2.70. 15% discount for groups (11+). EH members Free. Opening times and prices are valid until 31st March 2011, after this date details are subject to change please visit www.english-heritage.org.uk for the most up-to-date information.

Partial. NCP and coaches adjacent. Limited.

LAWRENCE HOUSE

9 Castle Street, Launceston, Cornwall PL15 8BA

Tel: 01566 773277

Owner: National Trust **Contact:** The Curator

A Georgian house given to the Trust to help preserve the character of the street, and now leased to Launceston Town Council as a museum and Mayor's Parlour.

Location: MAP 1:H7, OS Ref. SX330 848. Launceston.

Open: Mar–Oct: Mon–Fri, 10.30am–4.30pm and occasional Saturdays. Other times by appointment.

Admission: Free, but contributions welcome.

PENCARROW

BODMIN, CORNWALL PL30 3AG

www.pencarrow.co.uk

Tel: 01208 841369 **Fax:** 01208 841722 **E-mail:** info@pencarrow.co.uk
Owner: Molesworth-St Aubyn family **Contact:** Administrator

Owned, loved and lived in by the family. Georgian house and Grade II* listed gardens. Superb collection of portraits, furniture and porcelain. Marked walks through 50 acres of beautiful formal and woodland gardens, Victorian rockery, Italian garden, over 700 different varieties of rhododendrons, lake, Iron Age hill fort and icehouse.

Location: MAP 1:F8, OS Ref. SX040 711. Between Bodmin and Wadebridge. 4m NW of Bodmin off A389 & B3266 at Washaway.

Open: House: 3 Apr 2011–29 Sept 2011, Sun–Thur, 11am–4pm (last tour of the House at 3pm). Café & shop 11am–5pm. Gardens: 1 Mar–31 Oct, daily, 10am–5.30pm.

Admission: House & Garden: Adult £8.50, Child (5-16 years) £4, under 5's free. Family ticket (2 adults & 2 children) £22. Grounds only admission: Adult £4, Child (5-16 years) £1, under 5's free. Special rates available for pre-booked groups of 20 or more.

Shop, small children's play area, self-pick soft fruit. By arrangement. Licensed. Obligatory. Grounds only.

PENTILLIE CASTLE & ESTATE

ST MELLION, SALTASH, CORNWALL PL12 6QD

www.pentillie.co.uk

Tel: 01579 350044 **Fax:** 01579 212002 **E-mail:** contact@pentillie.co.uk
Owner: Ted and Sarah Coryton **Contact:** Sammie Coryton

Built by Sir James Tillie in the 17th century, historic Pentillie Castle is set within 2,000 acres of mature rolling woods and parkland overlooking the River Tamar. Now beautifully restored, the castle offers 5 star luxury accommodation and exclusive hire for weddings and corporate guests. Other activities available on request.

Location: MAP 1:H8, OS Ref. SX040 645. 7m West of Plymouth. Take the A38 into Cornwall. At the 1st roundabout turn right onto the A388. Drive 3.1m before turning right at Paynters Cross. Entrance within 100metres of main road.

Open: Gardens open 20 Mar, 3 Apr, 1/2 May; 11am–4pm. Snowdrop Walk 20 Feb (numbers limited). Bluebell Walk 17 May (numbers limited). Dates may be subject to change. Please phone or visit website. Private group tours and lunches available on request.

Admission: Gardens £6. House £3. Children under 12 free. Snowdrop and bluebell walks £25 inc lunch.

Special Events: Summer events including outdoor theatre. See website for more details.

Visit website for more information. WCs. Licensed. Licensed. By arrangement. Guide dogs only. By appointment only.

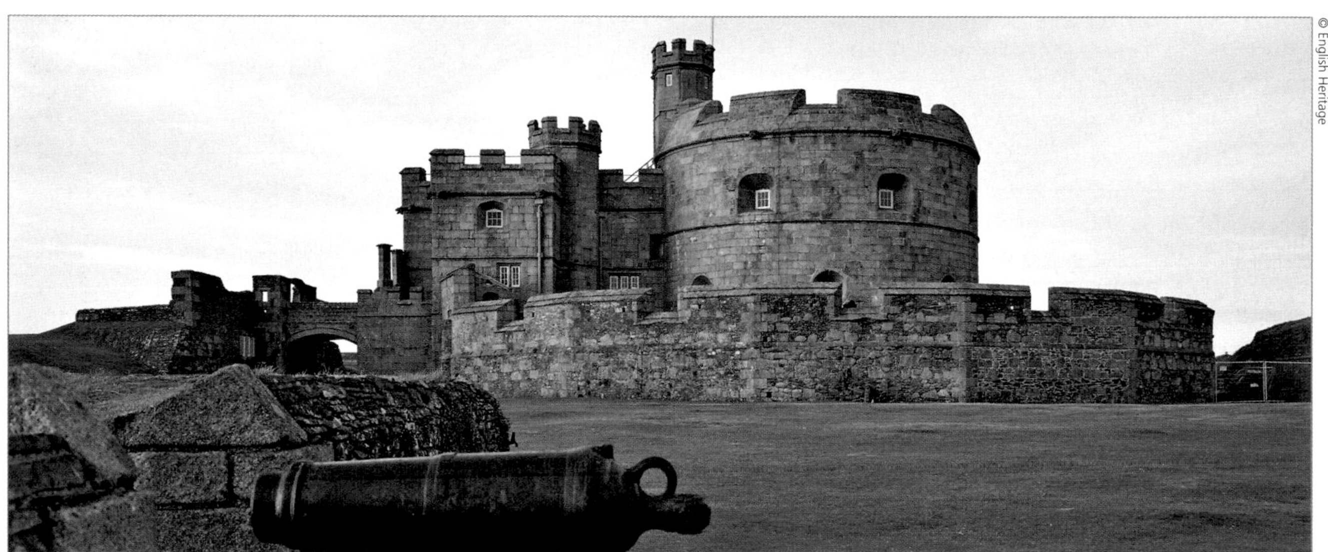

PENDENNIS CASTLE

FALMOUTH, CORNWALL TR11 4LP

www.english-heritage.org.uk/pendennis

Tel: 01326 316594 **E-mail:** pendennis.castle@english-heritage.org.uk
Venue and Hire Hospitality: 01326 310106
Owner: English Heritage **Contact:** Visitor Operations Team

At the mouth of the River Fal estuary, Pendennis and its neighbour, St Mawes form the Cornish end of costal castles built by Henry VIII to counter threat of invasion from France and Spain. Thereafter Pendennis was frequently adapted to face new enemies over 400 years, right through to World War II.

Pendennis today stands as a landmark, with fine sea views and excellent site facilities including a hands-on discovery centre, exhibitions, a museum, guardhouse, shop and tearoom. It is also an excellent venue for special events throughout the year.

Location: MAP 1:E10, OS Ref. SW824 318. On Pendennis Head.

Open: 1 Apr–30 Jun: daily, 10am–5pm (closes 4pm Sat). 1 Jul–31 Aug: daily, 10am–6pm (closes 4pm Sat). 1–30 Sep: daily 10am–5pm (closes 4pm Sat). 1 Oct–31 Mar: daily, 10am–4pm. The Keep will close for 1 hour at lunch on Saturdays if an event is booked. Closed 24 –26 Dec & 1 Jan.

Admission: Adult £6.00, Child £3.00, Conc. £5.10, Family £15.00. 15% discount for groups (11+). EH members Free. Opening times and prices are valid until 31st March 2011, after this date details are subject to change please visit www.english-heritage.org.uk for the most up-to-date information.

WC. Partial. No coaches. In grounds only. 0870 333 1187 €

© Noel Chanan

PORT ELIOT

ST. GERMANS, SALTASH, CORNWALL PL12 5ND

www.porteliot.co.uk

Tel: 01503 230211 **Fax:** 01503 230112 **E-mail:** info@porteliot.co.uk

Owner: The Earl of St Germans **Contact:** Port Eliot Estate Office

Port Eliot is an ancient, hidden gem, set in stunning fairytale grounds which nestle beside a secret estuary in South East Cornwall. It has the rare distinction of being a Grade I Listed house, park and gardens. This is due in part to the work of Sir John Soane, who worked his magic on the house and Humphrey Repton, who created the park and garden.

Explore the treasures in the house. Gaze at masterpieces by Reynolds and Van Dyck. Decipher the Lenkiewicz Round Room Riddle Mural. Still a family home, you will be beguiled by the warm atmosphere.

Location: MAP 1:H8, OS Ref. SX359 578. Situated in the village of St Germans on the Rame Peninsula in South East Cornwall. Parking signposted off B3249 (Tideford Cricket Ground/ Port Eliot).

Open: 14 Mar–7 Jul. Daily except Friday. Open 2–6pm. Last admission to the house at 5pm.

Admission: House & Garden: *Adult £7, Children (under 16) Free. Group (20+): Adult £6, *also vistors by public transport £6.00. Grounds only: Adult £4, Children (under 16) Free.

Special Events: In July, Port Eliot Festival is an annual celebration of words, music, imagination, laughter, exploration and above all - fun in one of the most beautiful and secret gardens in England.

No photography. WCs. On leads.

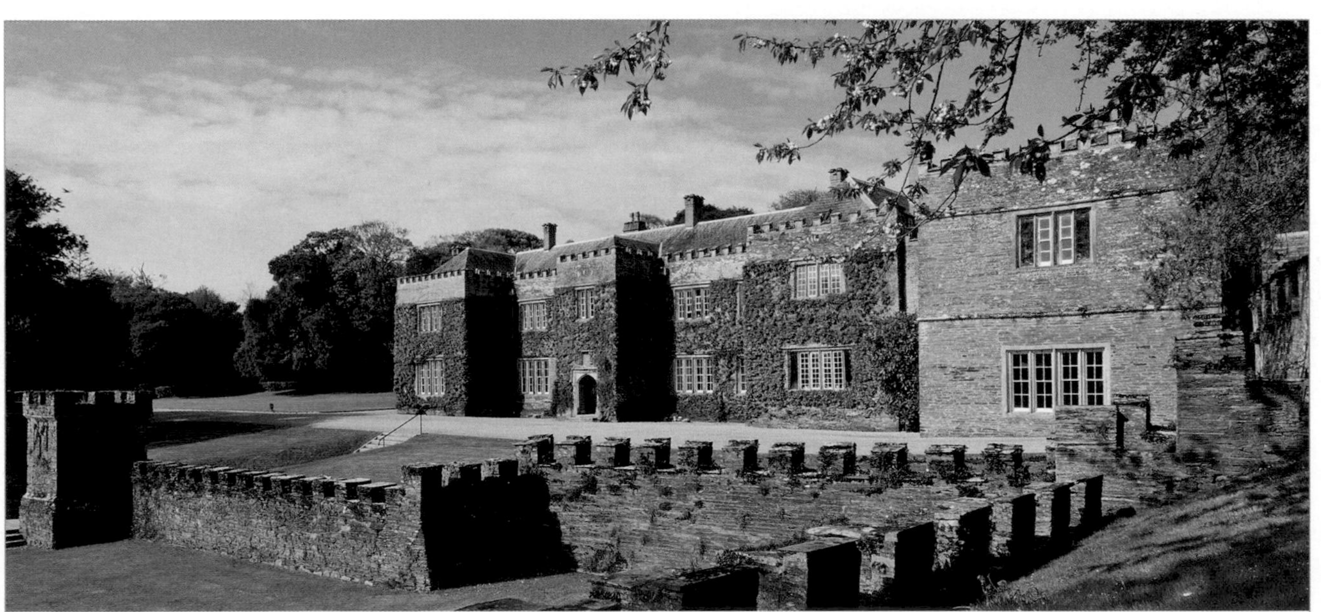

PRIDEAUX PLACE

PADSTOW, CORNWALL PL28 8RP

www.prideauxplace.co.uk

Tel: 01841 532411 **Fax:** 01841 532945 **E-mail:** office@prideauxplace.co.uk

Owner/Contact: Peter Prideaux-Brune Esq

Tucked away above the busy port of Padstow, the home of the Prideaux family for over 400 years, is surrounded by gardens and wooded grounds overlooking a deer park and the Camel estuary to the moors beyond. The house still retains its 'E' shape Elizabethan front and contains fine paintings and furniture. Now a major international film location, this family home is one of the brightest jewels in Cornwall's crown. The historic garden is undergoing major restoration work and offers some of the best views in the county. A cornucopia of Cornish history under one roof.

Location: MAP 1:E7, OS Ref. SW913 756. 5m from A39 Newquay/Wadebridge link road. Signposted by Historic House signs.

Open: Easter Sun 24–28 Apr, 15 May–6 Oct. Daily except Fris & Sats. Grounds & Tearoom: 12.30–5pm. House Tours: 1.30–4pm (last tour).

Admission: House & Grounds: Adult £8, Child £2. Grounds only: Adult £3.50, Child £1. Groups (15+) discounts apply.

By arrangement. Partial, ground floor & grounds. Fully licensed. Obligatory. By arrangement. On leads. By arrangement. Open Air Theatre, Open Air Concerts, Car Rallies, Art Exhibitions, Charity Events.

© EHPL / Skyscan

© NTPL / John Millar

St Michael's Mount

RESTORMEL CASTLE ⌗

LOSTWITHIEL, CORNWALL PL22 0EE

www.english-heritage.org.uk/restormel

Tel: 01208 872687 **E-mail:** customers@english-heritage.org.uk

Owner: English Heritage **Contact:** Visitor Operations Team

Perched on a high mound, surrounded by a deep moat, the huge circular keep of this splendid Norman castle survives in remarkably good condition. It is still possible to make out Restormel's Keep Gate, Great Hall and even the kitchens and private rooms.

Location: MAP 1:F8, OS200 Ref. SX104 614. 1½m N of Lostwithiel off A390.

Open: 1 Apr–30 Jun: daily, 10am–5pm. 1 Jul–31 Aug: daily, 10am–6pm. 1–30 Sep: daily, 10am–5pm. 1–31 Oct: daily, 10am–4pm. Closed 1 Nov–31 Mar.

Admission: Adult £3.20, Child £1.60, Conc. £2.70. 15% discount for groups (11+). EH Members free. Opening times and prices are valid until 31st March 2011, after this date details are subject to change please visit www.english-heritage.org.uk for the most up-to-date information.

WC. Limited for coaches.

ST CATHERINE'S CASTLE ⌗

Fowey, Cornwall

Tel: 01326 310109 **E-mail:** customers@english-heritage.org.uk

Owner: English Heritage **Contact:** Visitor Operations Administrator

A small fort built by Henry VIII to defend Fowey harbour, with fine views of the coastline and river estuary.

Location: MAP 1:F9, OS200 Ref. SX118 508. 1½m SW of Fowey along footpath off A3082.

Open: Any reasonable time, daylight only.

Admission: Free. Opening times and prices are valid until 31st March 2011, after this date details are subject to change please visit www.english-heritage.org.uk for the most up-to-date information.

© NT / St Michael's Mount

© NT / St Michael's Mount

ST MICHAEL'S MOUNT

MARAZION, Nr PENZANCE, CORNWALL TR17 0HT

www.stmichaelsmount.co.uk www.nationaltrust.org.uk

Tel: 01736 710507 (710265 tide information) **Fax:** 01736 719930

E-mail: mail@stmichaelsmount.co.uk

Owner: National Trust **Contact:** Clare Sandry, Manor Office, Marazion, Cornwall TR17 0EF

This beautiful island has become an icon for Cornwall and has magnificent views of Mount's Bay from its summit. There the church and castle, whose origins date from the 12th century, have at various times acted as a Benedictine priory, a place of pilgrimage, a fortress, a mansion house and now a magnet for visitors from all over the world. Following the Civil War, the island was acquired by the St Aubyn family who still live in the castle today.

Location: MAP 1:C10, OS Ref. SW515 300. 4m E of Penzance. At Marazion there is access on foot over causeway at low tide. In the main season, the property is reached at high tide by a short evocative boat trip. Sensible shoes are advised as causeway and paths are cobbled and uneven and there is a steep climb to the castle.

Open: Castle: 27 Mar–30 Oct, Sun–Fri, 10.30am–5pm (1 Jul–31 Aug, 10.30am–5.30pm). Last admission 45 mins before castle closing time, but allow plenty of time before this to reach the island. In winter, guided tours only, telephone in advance. Garden: May & Jun: Mon–Fri; Jul–Oct: Thur & Fri, 10.30am–5pm (until 5.30pm Jul & Aug). Church Service: Whit Sunday–end Sept (also Christmas Day, Good Fri & Easter Sun): Sun, 11.15am. All visits subject to weather and tides. For specialist events please check the website.

Admission: Adult £7, Child (under 17) £3.50, Family £17.50, 1-Adult Family £10.50. Booked groups £6.00, Garden: Adult £3.50, Child £1.50. Combined Adult £8.75, Child £4.25, Family £21.75, 1-Adult Family £13.00. Groups £7.50.

Parking on mainland (not NT). Dogs not permitted in the castle or gardens. Partial. Licensed. Licensed. by arrangement. Tel for details. On mainland, including coach parking (not NT.) Guide dogs only.

© English Heritage

ST MAWES CASTLE

ST MAWES, CORNWALL TR2 5DE

www.english-heritage.org.uk/stmawes

Tel/Fax: 01326 270526 **Venue Hire and Hospitality:** 01326 310106
E-mail: stmawes.castle@english-heritage.org.uk
Owner: English Heritage **Contact:** Visitor Operations Team

St Mawes Castle is among the best-preserved of Henry VIII's coastal artillery fortresses, and the most elaborately decorated of them all. Situated on the edge of St Mawes village, this fine example of Tudor military architecture offers views over the little boat-filled harbour and the splendid surrounding coastline.

Location: MAP 1:E10, OS204 Ref. SW842 328. W of St Mawes on A3078.

Open: 1 Apr–30 Jun: Sun–Fri, 10am–5pm. 1 Jul–31 Aug: Sun–Fri, 10am–6pm. 1–30 Sep: Sun–Fri, 10am–5pm. 1–31 Oct: daily, 10am–4pm. 1 Nov–31 Mar: Fri–Mon, 10am–4pm. Closed Sat. May close 4pm on Sun & Fri for private events. Closed 24–26 Dec & 1 Jan.

Admission: Adult £4.20, Child £2.10, Conc. £3.60. 15% discount for groups (11+). EH members Free. Opening times and prices are valid until 31st March 2011, after this date details are subject to change please visit www.english-heritage.org.uk for the most up-to-date information.

01326 310106 Partial. Limited.
Grounds only. 0870 333 1187

© EHPL / Skyscan

TINTAGEL CASTLE

TINTAGEL, CORNWALL PL34 0HE

www.english-heritage.org.uk/tintagel

Tel/Fax: 01840 770328 **E-mail:** tintagel.castle@english-heritage.org.uk
Owner: English Heritage **Contact:** Visitor Operations Team

Set spectacularly on the wild Cornish coast, Tintagel Castle is a place of magic where the legend of King Arthur was born. Explore the extensive ruins of a medieval castle, enjoy the dramatic costal views, then relax in our Beach Café which serves a delicious selection of refreshments.

Location: MAP 1:F7, Landranger Sheet 200 Ref. SX048 891. On Tintagel Head, ½m along uneven track from Tintagel.

Open: 1 Apr–30 Sep: daily, 10am–6pm. 1–31 Oct: daily, 10am–5pm. 1 Nov–31 Mar: daily, 10am–4pm. Closed 24–26 Dec & 1 Jan.

Admission: Adult £5.20, Child £2.60, Conc. £4.40. Family £13.00. 15% discount for groups (11+). EH members Free. Opening times and prices are valid until 31st March 2011, after this date details are subject to change. Please visit www.english-heritage.org.uk for the most up-to-date information.

WC. No vehicles. Parking (not EH) in village only.

For **accommodation** in the South West, see our special index at the end of the book.

TINTAGEL OLD POST OFFICE

Tintagel, Cornwall PL34 0DB
Tel: 01840 770024 or 01208 265200
Owner: National Trust **Contact:** The Custodian
Small 14th c House of great antiquity, charm and interest.
Location: MAP 1:F7, OS Ref. SX056 884. In the centre of Tintagel.

TRELISSICK GARDEN

Feock, Truro, Cornwall TR3 6QL
Tel: 01872 862090 **Fax:** 01872 865808
www.nationaltrust.org.uk
Owner: National Trust **Contact:** Administrator
Tranquil garden and estate.
Location: MAP 1:E10, OS Ref. SW837 396. 4m S of Truro on B3289 above King Harry Ferry.

TRENGWAINTON GARDEN

Penzance, Cornwall TR20 8RZ
Tel: 01736 363148 **Fax:** 01736 367762
Owner: National Trust **Contact:** Administrator
Varied and interesting garden with stunning views over Mount's Bay.
Location: MAP 1:B10, OS Ref. SW445 315. 2m NW of Penzance, ½m W of Heamoor on Penzance–Morvah road (B3312), ½m off St. Just road (A3071).

TRERICE

See page 166 for full page entry.

TREWITHEN

Tel: 01726 883647 **Fax:** 01726 882301 **E-mail:** info@trewithengardens.co.uk
www.trewithengardens.co.uk
Owner: A M J Galsworthy **Contact:** The Estate Office

Trewithen is an historic estate near Truro, Cornwall. Owned and lived in by the same family for 300 years, it is both private home and national treasure. The woodland gardens are outstanding – with 24 champion trees and famously rare and highly prized plants. Tours of the house prove equally memorable.

Location: MAP 1:E9. Grampound Road, near Truro, Cornwall

Open: House: Mon & Tues from April–July & August BH Monday. 2–4pm. Garden: Mon–Sat from March–Sept & Sundays Mar–May only. 10am–4.30pm.

Admission: House guided tour: Adult £7.50 (Groups 20+ £5) Children under 12 Free. Garden entry: Adult £7.50 (Groups 20+ £5) Children under 12 Free. Combined: Adult £12 (Groups 20+ £8) Children under 12 Free. Guided garden tours available (groups up to 25 £50 & 25+ £70) & with head gardener (Groups 15–20 £150).

No photography in house. Partial. WC. By arrangement.
Limited for coaches. In grounds, on leads.

© NTPL / Andrew Butler

Trelissick Garden

■ Owner

The Hon. John Rous

■ Contact

Visitor Centre
Clovelly
Nr Bideford
N Devon EX39 5TA

Tel: 01237 431781
Fax: 01237 431644
E-mail: visitorcentre@clovelly.co.uk

■ Location

OS Ref. SS248 319

On A39 10 miles W of Bideford, 15 miles E of Bude. Turn off at 'Clovelly Cross' roundabout and follow signs to car park.

Air: Exeter & Plymouth Airport both 50 miles.

Rail: Barnstaple 19 miles.

Bus: from Bideford.

■ Opening Times

High season:
9am–6pm.

Low season:
10am–4.30pm.

■ Admission

Adult	£5.95
Child (7–16yrs)	£3.75
Child (under 7yrs)	Free
Family (2+2)	£15.90
Group Rates (20+)	
Adult	£4.95
Child	£3.50

The entrance fee covers parking and other facilities provided by Clovelly Estate. As well as admission to the audio-visual film, Fisherman's Cottage, and Kingsley Museum, your fee contributes to the ongoing maintenance of the village, itself part of a private estate.

Prices correct at time of going to press.

■ Special Events

Easter
Red Letter Days

May
Celebration of Ales & Ciders

July
Clovelly Maritime Festival
Woolsery Agricultural Show
Lundy Row

August
Lifeboat Day
Clovelly Gig Regatta

September
Lobster & Crab Feast

November
Clovelly Herring Festival

December
Christmas Lights

CLOVELLY

www.clovelly.co.uk

From Elizabethan days until today, Clovelly Village has been in private ownership, which has helped preserve its original atmosphere. The main traffic-free street, known as 'up-a-along' and 'down-a-long', tumbles its cobbled way down to the tiny harbour, which is protected by an ancient stone breakwater. It is a descent through flower-strewn cottages broken only by little passageways and winding lanes that lead off to offer the prospect of more picturesque treasures.

The New Inn, which is 400 years old, is halfway down the street, and another, the Red Lion, is right on the quayside. Both Inns have long histories and an atmosphere rarely found in the modern world. In addition you'll find the Visitor Centre, a range of gift shops, a café and an audio-visual theatre in which visitors are treated to a history of the village. Just below is the Stable Yard with a pottery and silk workshop. There are beautiful coastal and woodland walks.

Access is restricted to pedestrians only via the Visitor Centre with a Land Rover taxi service for those unable to walk.

Rubber soled, low heel shoes are recommended.

Partial.

Licensed.

Licensed.

By arrangement.

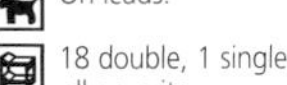
On leads.

18 double, 1 single, all en suite.

Civil Wedding Licence

HARTLAND ABBEY

www.hartlandabbey.com

Hartland Abbey is a fascinating house. Built across a narrow, wooded valley leading to an Atlantic cove a mile away, Henry VIII gifted the Abbey to The Keeper of his Wine Cellar, whose descendants live here today. Not only can visitors experience the stunning interiors, collections, beautiful gardens and walks but the Abbey exudes the warmth and friendliness only found in a family home cherished for generations. Close family connections to Poltimore House and Clovelly Court nearby are evident.

Amongst the impressive interiors spanning Mediaeval, Queen Anne, Georgian, Regency and Victorian periods you can see the three main Reception Rooms, the fabulous Alhambra Corridor by Sir George Gilbert Scott and the Gothic Library by Meadows with its fireplace by Batty Langley. Important paintings by artists including Reynolds and Gainsborough, furniture, porcelain, early photographs, a museum of documents from 1160 and changing displays of family memorabilia fascinate visitors.

Much of the 50 acres of gardens and woodland walks had been lost since the First World War but since restoration began in 1996 once again there are beautiful paths through bulbs, rhododendrons, azaleas, camellias and hydrangeas; the Bog Garden and Fernery, by Gertrude Jekyll, thrive again. In the three 18th century Walled Gardens climbers, herbaceous, tender perennials and vegetables delight and glasshouses protect stunning plants for display in the house.

Walk through carpets of primroses, historic daffodils, bluebells and wildflowers to the newly restored (2011) Summerhouse in the woods, the Gazebo and Blackpool Mill with its beautiful beach and cottage, home to the Dashwood family in Jane Austen's 'Sense and Sensibility' and the location for Rosamunde Pilcher's 'The Shell Seekers'. Donkeys, black sheep and peacocks roam. Children's Quiz. Five stunning wedding venues available. Holiday cottages to rent. Hartland Abbey adjoins the SW Coastal Footpath in an area of Outstanding Natural Beauty. Free parking. Gift Shop. 1 mile from Hartland Quay and St. Nectan's Church, the 'Cathedral of North Devon'.

Wedding receptions.

Partial. WC.

By arrangement.

In grounds, on leads.

■ Owner

Sir Hugh Stucley Bt

■ Contact

The Administrator
Hartland Abbey
Nr. Bideford
North Devon
EX39 6DT

Tel: 01237 441264/234
01884 860225
Fax: 01237 441264
01884 861134
E-mail: ha_admin@btconnect.com

■ Location

MAP 1:G5
OS Ref. SS240 249

15m W of Bideford, 15m N of Bude off A39 between Hartland and Hartland Quay on B3248.

■ Opening Times

House
6, 13 February, 20 March (11am–4pm).

1 April–20 May, Wed, Thur, Sun & BHs inc. Good Friday.

20 May–2 October Sun–Thurs, 2–5pm. Last adm. 4.30pm.

Gardens, Grounds & Beachwalk
6, 13 February, 20 March (11am–4pm).

1 April–2 October, Daily except Sats, 11.30am–5pm.

Tea Room
Light lunches and cream teas 11.30am–5pm (House open days only).

■ Admission

House, Gardens, Grounds & Beachwalk

Adult	£10.00
Child (5–15ys)	£3.50
Family	£23.00

Gardens, Grounds & Beachwalk only

Adult	£5.00
Child (5–15ys)	£2.00
Family	£12.00

Groups and coaches
Concessions to groups of 20+. Open to coaches at other dates and times. Booking essential.
Large car park adjacent to the house.

■ Special Events

6 & 13 February (11am–4pm)
Snowdrop Sundays.

20 March (11am–4pm)
Daffodil Day.

3 April
Regis Car Tour.

Good Friday 22 & Easter Monday 25 April
Bluebell Days.

1 & 2 May
Bluebell Days.

19 June
Atlantic Coast Express MG Car Rally (arrival pm).

17–21 June
Flower Festival.

25 & 26 June
Country Fair Weekend (see website).

A LA RONDE

Summer Lane, Exmouth, Devon EX8 5BD
Tel: 01395 265514
Owner: National Trust **Contact:** Assistant Property Manager
Unique 16-sided house completed c1796.
Location: MAP 2:L7, OS Ref. SY004 834. 2m N of Exmouth on A376.

ANDERTON HOUSE

Goodleigh, Devon EX32 7NR
Tel: 01628 825925 **E-mail:** bookings@landmarktrust.org.uk
www.landmarktrust.org.uk
Owner/Contact: The Landmark Trust
Anderton House is a Grade II* listed building of an exceptional modern design by Peter Aldington of Aldington and Craig. It was commissioned in 1969 as a family home and is highly evocative of its time, retaining the contemporary features and materials. Anderton House is cared for by The Landmark Trust, a building preservation charity who let it for holidays. Full details of Anderton House and 189 other historic and architecturally important buildings are featured in the Landmark Trust Handbook (price £10 plus p&p refundable against a booking) and on the website.
Location: MAP 2:I14, OS Ref. SS603 343. In village.
Open: Available for holidays for up to 5 people throughout the year. Two Open Days a year. Other visits by appointment. Contact Landmark Trust for details.
Admission: Free on Open Days and visits by appointment.

ARLINGTON COURT

Nr Barnstaple, North Devon EX31 4LP
Tel: 01271 850296 **Fax:** 01271 851108
Owner: National Trust **Contact:** Ana Chylak – Property Manager
Intimate Victorian House full of treasures in 3,000-acre estate.
Location: MAP 2:I4, OS180 Ref. SS611 405. 7m NE of Barnstaple on A39.

BRADLEY

Newton Abbot, Devon TQ12 6BN
Tel: 01803 843235 **E-mail:** bradley@nationaltrust.org.uk
Owner: National Trust
Small medieval manor house set in woodland and meadows.
Location: MAP 2:K8, OS Ref. SX848 709. On Totnes road A381. ¾ m SW of Newton Abbot.

BRANSCOMBE MANOR MILL, THE OLD BAKERY & FORGE

Branscombe, Seaton, Devon EX12 3DB
Tel: Manor Mill – 01752 346585 Old Bakery – 01297 680333 Forge – 01297 680481
Owner: National Trust
Manor Mill, still in working order and recently restored, is a water-powered mill which probably supplied the flour for the bakery.
Location: MAP 2:M7, OS Ref. SY198 887. In Branscombe ½ m S off A3052 by steep, narrow lane.

BUCKFAST ABBEY

Buckfastleigh, Devon TQ11 0EE
Tel: 01364 645500 **Fax:** 01364 643891 **E-mail:** education@buckfast.org.uk
Owner: Buckfast Abbey Trust **Contact:** The Warden
The original monastery at Buckfast was formed during the reign of King Cnut in 1018.
Location: MAP 2:J8, OS Ref. SX741 674. ½m from A38 Plymouth – Exeter route.
Open: Church: Weekdays 9am–6pm. Grounds: All year: Suns noon–6pm.
Admission: Free.

BUCKLAND ABBEY

Yelverton, Devon PL20 6EY
Tel: 01822 853607 **Fax:** 01822 855448
Owner: National Trust **Contact:** Jon Cummins – Visitor Services Manager
Former 13th c monastery became home of Sir Francis Drake 1581.
Location: MAP 2:I8, OS201 Ref. SX487 667. 6m S of Tavistock; 11m N of Plymouth off A386.

© English Heritage

BERRY POMEROY CASTLE

TOTNES, DEVON TQ9 6LJ

www.english-heritage.org.uk/berrypomeroy

Tel: 01803 866618 **E-mail:** customers@english-heritage.org.uk
Owner: The Duke of Somerset **Contact:** Visitor Operations Team
A romantic late medieval castle, dramatically sited half-way up a wooded hillside, looking out over a deep ravine and stream. It is unusual in combining the remains of a large castle with a flamboyant courtier's mansion. Reputed to be one of the most haunted castles in the country.
Location: MAP 2:J8, OS202 Ref. SX839 623. 2½m E of Totnes off A385. Entrance gate ½m NE of Berry Pomeroy village, then ½m drive. Narrow approach, unsuitable for coaches.
Open: 1 Apr–30 Jun: daily, 10am–5pm 1 Jul–31 Aug: daily, 10am–6pm. 1–30 Sep: daily, 10am–5pm. 1–31 Oct: daily, 10am–4pm. 1 Nov–31 Mar: Closed.
Admission: Adult £4.50, Child £2.30, Conc £3.80. 15% discount for groups (11+). EH members Free. Opening times and prices are valid until 31st March 2011, after this date details are subject to change please visit www.english-heritage.org.uk for the most up-to-date information.
No access for coaches. Guide dogs only.

CADHAY

OTTERY ST MARY, DEVON EX11 1QT

www.cadhay.org.uk

Tel: 01404 813511
Owner: Mr R Thistlethwayte **Contact:** Jayne Covell
Cadhay is approached by an avenue of lime-trees, and stands in an extensive garden, with herbaceous borders and yew hedges, with excellent views over the original medieval fish ponds. The main part of the house was built in about 1550 by John Haydon who had married the de Cadhay heiress. He retained the Great Hall of an earlier house, of which the fine timber roof (about 1420–1460) can be seen. An Elizabethan Long Gallery was added by John's successor at the end of the 16th century, thereby forming a unique courtyard with statues of Sovereigns on each side, described by Sir Simon Jenkins as one of the 'Treasures of Devon'.
Location: MAP 2:L6, OS Ref. SY090 962. 1m NW of Ottery St Mary. From W take A30 and exit at Pattesons Cross, follow signs for Fairmile and then Cadhay. From E, exit at the Iron Bridge and follow signs as above.
Open: May–Sept, Fridays 2pm–5pm. Also: late May + Summer BH Sat-Sun-Mon. Last tour 4.15pm.
Admission: Guided tours: Adult £7, Child £3. Gardens: Adults £3, Child £1. Parties of 15+ by prior arrangement.
Ground floor & grounds. Obligatory. Guide dogs only.

© National Trust / David Cripps

© National Trust / John Such

CASTLE DROGO

DREWSTEIGNTON, EXETER EX6 6PB

www.nationaltrust.org.uk

Tel: 01647 433306 **Fax:** 01647 433186 **E-mail:** castledrogo@nationaltrust.org.uk

Owner: National Trust **Contact:** Catherine Maddern, Visitor Services Manager

Extraordinary granite and oak castle, designed by Sir Edwin Lutyens, which combines the comforts of the 20th century with the grandeur of a Baronial castle. Elegant dining and drawing rooms and fascinating kitchen and scullery. Terraced formal garden with colourful herbaceous borders and rose beds. Panoramic views over Dartmoor and delightful walks in the dramatic Teign Gorge.

Location: MAP 2:J7, Landranger Sheet 191. SX724 902. 5m S of A30 Exeter–Okehampton road.

Open: Castle: 21–27 Feb, daily, 11am–4pm; 12 Mar–30 Oct, daily, 11am–5pm; 5 Nov–11 Dec, Sat & Sun, 11am–4.30pm; 17–23 Dec, daily, 11am–4.30pm. Last admission 1/2 hour before closing. Garden, Shop, Cafe & Visitor Centre: 1 Jan–11 Mar, daily, 11am–4pm; 12 Mar–30 Oct, daily, 9am–5.30pm (Cafe open from 8.30am); 31 Oct–23 Dec, daily, 11am–5pm (or dusk if earlier).

***Admission:** House & Garden: Adult £9.10, Child £4.60, Family £22.70, 1-Adult Family £13.60. Group: £7.70. Garden only: Adult £5.75, Child £3.15, Group £4.90. *includes a voluntary donation but visitors can choose to pay the standard prices displayed at the property and on the website.

Partial. WCs. By arrangement. In grounds

CHAMBERCOMBE MANOR

Ilfracombe, Devon EX34 9RJ

Tel: 01271 862624 **www.chambercombemanor.co.uk**

Owner: Chambercombe Trust **Contact:** Angela Powell

Guided tours of Norman Manor House which is mentioned in Domesday Book. Hear the legend of Chambercombe and visit Haunted Room. Set in 16 acres of woodland and landscaped gardens. Lady Jane Tea Rooms offering light lunches and cream teas.

Location: MAP 2:I3, OS Ref. SS539 461. East of Ilfracombe between A399 and B3230, follow brown historic house signs. Private car park at end of Chambercombe Lane.

Open: Easter–end Oct: Mon–Fri, 10.30am–5pm; Sun, 1–5pm. Last tour 3.30pm.

Admission: Adult £7, Child/Conc. £5, Family £22, under 5s free. Group (max 50) discount – apply to Manor.

No photography in house. Partial. Obligatory. Limited for coaches. On leads, in grounds.

CLOVELLY

See page 174 for full page entry.

COLETON FISHACRE

Brownstone Road, Kingswear, Dartmouth TQ6 0EQ

Tel: 01803 752466 **Tea-room:** 01803 752984 **Fax:** 01803 753017

Owner: National Trust **Contact:** Administrator

Lutyens-style house built 1920s with 30 acre garden.

Location: MAP 2:K9, OS202 Ref. SX910 508. 3m E of Kingswear, follow brown tourist signs.

COMPTON CASTLE

Marldon, Paignton TQ3 1TA

Tel: 01803 843235

Owner: National Trust **Contact:** Administrator

Fortified manor house built by Gilbert family (between 14th-16th c).

Location: MAP 2:K8, OS180 Ref. SX865 648. At Compton, 3m W of Torquay signed at Marldon. Coaches must approach from A381 Totnes Road at Ipplepen.

© NTPL / James Mortimer

Castle Drogo

CULVER HOUSE

LONGDOWN, EXETER, DEVON EX6 7BD

www.culver.biz

Tel: 01392 811885 **Fax:** 01392 811817 **E-mail:** info@culver.biz

Owner/Contact: Charles Eden Esq

Culver was built in 1836, but redesigned by the great Victorian architect, Alfred Waterhouse in a mock Tudor style. The distinctive interior of the house makes it a favoured location for functions and Culver was featured in BBC1's 'Down to Earth'. It has also been used by German and American film crews.

Location: MAP 2:J7, OS Ref. SX848 901. 5m W of Exeter on B3212.

Open: Not open to the public. Available for corporate hospitality.

Admission: Please telephone for booking details.

CUSTOM HOUSE

THE QUAY, EXETER EX2 4AN

Tel: 01392 665521 **E-mail:** exeter.arch@exeter.gov.uk

Owner: Exeter City Council

The Custom House, located on Exeter's historic Quayside, was constructed from 1680–1682. It is the earliest substantial brick building in Exeter and was used by HM Customs and Excise until 1989. The building has an impressive sweeping staircase and spectacular ornamental plaster ceilings.

Location: MAP 2:K6, OS Ref. SX919 921. Exeter's historic Quayside.

Open: 1 Apr–31 Oct: Guided tour programme, telephone 01392 265203.

Admission: Free.

Partial. Obligatory. Guide dogs only.

Fursdon House

© English Heritage

DARTMOUTH CASTLE

CASTLE ROAD, DARTMOUTH, DEVON TQ6 0JN

www.english-heritage.org.uk/dartmouth

Tel: 01803 833588 **Fax:** 01803 834445
E-mail: dartmouth.castle@english-heritage.org.uk
Owner: English Heritage **Contact:** Visitor Operations Team

One of the most picturesquely-sited forts in England, for six hundred years Dartmouth Castle has guarded the narrow entrance to the Dart Estuary and the busy, vibrant port of Dartmouth. A fascinating complex of defences dating back to 1388, today the castle is remarkably intact with excellent hands-on exhibitions.

Location: MAP 2:K9, OS202 Ref. SX887 503. 1m SE of Dartmouth off B3205, narrow approach road.

Open: 1 Apr–30 Jun: daily, 10am–5pm. 1 Jul–31 Aug: daily, 10am–6pm. 1–30 Sep: daily, 10am–5pm. 1–31 Oct: daily, 10am–4pm. 1 Nov–31 Mar: Sat–Sun, 10am–4pm. Closed 24–26 Dec & 1 Jan.

Admission: Adult £4.50, Child £2.30, Conc. £3.80. 15% discount for groups (11+). EH members Free. Opening times and prices are valid until 31st March 2011, after this date details are subject to change please visit www.english-heritage.org.uk for the most up-to-date information.

WC (not EH). Limited (charged, not EH).

DOCTON MILL & GARDEN

Spekes Valley, Hartland, Devon EX39 6EA
Tel/Fax: 01237 441369
Owner/Contact: John Borrett

Garden for all seasons in 8 acres of sheltered wooded valley, plus working mill.

Location: MAP 1:G5, OS Ref. SS235 226. 3m Hartland Quay. 15m N of Bude. 3m W of A39, 3m S of Hartland.

Open: Mar–Oct: 10am–6pm.

Admission: Adult £4, Child (under 16 yrs) Free, OAP £3.75.

DOWNES

Crediton, Devon EX17 3PL
Tel: 01363 775142
Owner: Trustees of the Downes Estate Settlement **Contact:** Amanda Boulton

Downes is a Palladian Mansion dating originally from 1692. As the former home of General Sir Redvers Buller, the house contains a large number of items relating to his military campaigns. The property is now predominantly a family home with elegant rooms hung with family portraits, and a striking main staircase.

Location: MAP 2:K6, OS Ref. SX852 997. Approx a mile from Crediton town centre.

Open: 18 Apr–19 Jul and Aug BH, Mons & Tues. Guided tours 2.15 & 3.30pm. Open to groups (15+) at other times between 18 Apr–19 Jul, by prior appointment.

Admission: Adult £6, Child (5–16yrs) £3, Child (under 5yrs) Free. Groups (15+) £5.

Obligatory.

THE ELIZABETHAN GARDENS

Plymouth Barbican Assoc. Ltd, New St, The Barbican, Plymouth PL1 2NA
Tel/Fax: 01822 611027/612983 **E-mail:** avdalo@dsi.pipex.com
Owner: Plymouth Barbican Association Limited **Contact:** Mr Anthony P Golding

Very small series of four enclosed gardens laid out in Elizabethan style in 1970.

Location: MAP 1:H8, OS Ref. SX477 544. 3 mins walk from Dartington Glass (a landmark building) on the Barbican.

Open: Mon–Sat, 9am–5pm. Closed Christmas.

Admission: Free.

© Britainonview

Exeter Cathedral

EXETER CATHEDRAL

Exeter, Devon EX1 1HS
Tel: 01392 285983 (Visitors' Officer) **Fax:** 01392 285986
E-mail: visitors@exeter-cathedral.org.uk
Owner: Dean & Chapter of Exeter **Contact:** Visitors' Officer

Fine example of decorated gothic architecture. Longest unbroken stretch of gothic vaulting in the world.

Location: MAP 2:K6, OS Ref. SX921 925. Central to the City – between High Street and Southernhay. Groups may be set down in South Street.

Open: All year: Mon–Sat, 9am–4.45pm.

Admission: Adults £5, Conc £3.

FINCH FOUNDRY

Sticklepath, Okehampton, Devon EX20 2NW
Tel: 01837 840046
Owner: National Trust

19th century water-powered forge, which produced agricultural and mining hand tools.

Location: MAP 2:I6, OS Ref. SX641 940. 4m E of Okehampton off the A30.

FURSDON HOUSE

CADBURY, Nr THORVERTON, EXETER, DEVON EX5 5JS

www.fursdon.co.uk

Tel: 01392 860860 **Fax:** 01392 860126 **E-mail:** admin@fursdon.co.uk
Owner: Mr E D Fursdon **Contact:** Mrs C Fursdon

The Fursdons have lived here for more than 750 years and the house, greatly modified in the 18th century, is at the heart of a small estate within a wooded and hilly landscape. Family memorabilia is displayed including a letter to Grace Fursdon from King Charles during the Civil War as well as exceptional examples of costume and textiles. An almost secret terraced and walled garden with shrubs, roses and herbs has extensive views to Dartmoor. Woodland and Meadow Garden now included. Two private wings offer quality self catering accommodation.

Location: MAP 2:K6, OS Ref. SS922 046. 1½m S of A3072 between Thorverton & Crediton, 9m N of Exeter turning off A396 to Thorverton. Narrow lanes!

Open: House: BH Mons except Christmas. Jun, Jul & Aug, Suns & Weds. Guided tours at 2.30 & 3.30pm. Garden: as house 2–5pm. Tea Room. Groups welcome by prior arrangement.

Admission: House and Garden: Adult £7, Child (10–16yrs) £4, Child (under 10yrs) Free. Garden only: £4.

Conferences. No photography or video. Partial. Obligatory. Guide dogs only. Self-catering.

GREAT FULFORD

DUNSFORD, NR EXETER, DEVON EX6 7AJ

Tel: 01647 24205 **Fax:** 01647 24401 **E-mail:** francis@greatfulford.co.uk

Owner/Contact: Francis Fulford

The ancient home of the Fulford family since circa 1190. Built round a courtyard it is mainly early Tudor. There is a superb panelled Great Hall and a marvellous 17th century Great Staircase. Other rooms in the 'gothic' taste by James Wyatt when the house was remodelled in 1805.

Location: MAP 2:J7, OS Ref. SX790 917. In the centre of Devon. 10 miles west of Exeter. South of the A30 between the villages of Cheriton Bishop and Dunsford.

Open: All year by appointment only for parties or groups containing a minimum of 10 persons.

Admission: £7.50 per person.

Obligatory.

© Terry Squires

HALDON BELVEDERE (LAWRENCE CASTLE)

HIGHER ASHTON, NR DUNCHIDEOCK, EXETER, DEVON EX6 7QY

www.haldonbelvedere.co.uk

Tel/Fax: 01392 833668 **E-mail:** enquiries@haldonbelvedere.co.uk

Owner: Devon Historic Buildings Trust **Contact:** Ian Turner

18th century Grade II* listed triangular tower with circular, corner turrets. Built in memory of Major General Stringer Lawrence, father of the Indian Army. Restored in 1995 to illustrate the magnificence of its fine plasterwork, gothic windows, mahogany flooring and marble fireplaces. Breathtaking views of the surrounding Devon countryside.

Location: MAP 2:K7, OS Ref. SX875 861. 7m SW of Exeter. Exit A38 at Exeter racecourse for 2½m.

Open: Easter–Sept: Suns & BHs, 2–5pm.

Admission: Adult £2, Child Free.

Partial, WCs. Obligatory. By arrangement. Limited for coaches. Guide dogs only.

GREENWAY

Greenway Road, Galmpton, Churston Ferrers, Devon TQ5 0ES

Tel: 01803 842382

Owner: National Trust **Contact:** Administrator

Once holiday home of Agatha Christie still set in the 1950s.

Location: MAP 2:K8, OS Ref. SX876 548.

© Hartland Abbey

Hartland Abbey

HARTLAND ABBEY

See page 175 for full page entry.

HEMYOCK CASTLE

Hemyock, Cullompton, Devon EX15 3RJ

Tel: 01823 680745

Owner/Contact: Mrs Sheppard

Former medieval moated castle, displays show site's history as fortified manor house, castle and farm.

Location: MAP 2:L6, OS Ref. ST135 134. M5/J26, Wellington then 5m S over the Blackdown Hills.

Open: BH Mons 2–5pm. Other times by appointment. Groups & private parties welcome.

Admission: Adult £1, Child 50p. Group rates available.

KILLERTON

Broadclyst, Exeter EX5 3LE

Tel: 01392 881345

Owner: National Trust **Contact:** Denise Melhuish – Assistant Property Manager

18thc house (with costume museum), garden surrounded by parkland.

Location: MAP 2:K6,OS Ref. SS977 001. Off Exeter – Cullompton Rd (B3181). M5 N'bound J30, M5 S'bound J28

KNIGHTSHAYES COURT

Bolham, Tiverton, Devon EX16 7RQ

Tel: 01884 254665

Owner: National Trust **Contact:** Penny Woollams – Property Manager

Victorian, gothic house with fine garden.

Location: MAP 2:K5, OS Ref. SS960 151. 2m N of Tiverton (A396) at Bolham.

Hartland Abbey

LOUGHWOOD MEETING HOUSE

Dalwood, Axminster, Devon EX13 7DU

Tel/Fax: 01752 346585

Owner: National Trust

Around 1653 the Baptist congregation of the nearby village of Kilmington constructed this simple thatched building dug into the hillside. It still contains the original box pews.

Location: MAP 2:M6, OS Ref. SY253993. 4m W of Axminster.

Open: All year, daily.

Admission: Free.

MARKER'S COTTAGE

Broadclyst, Exeter, Devon EX5 3HR

Tel: 01392 881345 (Killerton House for information)

Owner: National Trust **Contact:** The Custodian

Thatched, medieval cob house containing a cross-passage screen.

Location: MAP 2:K6, OS Ref. SX985 973. ¼m E of B3181 in village of Broadclyst.

MARWOOD HILL GARDEN

Barnstaple, Devon EX31 4EB

Tel: 01271 342528 **Email:** info@marwoodhillgarden.co.uk

www.marwoodhillgarden.co.uk

Owner: Dr John Snowden **Contact:** Mrs Patricia Stout

20 acre garden with 3 small lakes. Extensive collection of camellias, bog garden. National collection of astilbes.

Location: MAP 2:I4, OS Ref. SS545 375. 4m N of Barnstaple. ½m W of B3230. Signs off A361 Barnstaple – Braunton road.

Open: 1 Mar–31 Oct, daily, 10am–5pm.

Admission: Adult £5.50, Child 12-16 £2.50, Child under 12 Free. Pre-booked group of 10+ £5.

Partial. WCs. By arrangement. Limited. On leads.

OKEHAMPTON CASTLE

Okehampton, Devon EX20 1JA

Tel: 01837 52844 **E-mail:** customers@english-heritage.org.uk

www.english-heritage.org.uk/okehampton

Owner: English Heritage **Contact:** Visitor Operations Team

The ruins of the largest castle in Devon stand above a river surrounded by splendid woodland. There is still plenty to see, including the Norman motte and the jagged remains of the Keep. There is a picnic area and lovely woodland walks.

Location: MAP 2:I6, OS Ref. SX584 942. 1m SW of Okehampton town centre off A30 bypass.

Open: 1 Apr–30 Jun: daily, 10am–5pm. 1 Jul–31 Aug: daily, 10am–6pm. 1–30 Sep: daily, 10am–5pm. Closed 1 Oct–31 Mar.

Admission: Adult £3.50, Child £1.80, Conc. £3. 15% discount for groups (11+). EH members Free. Opening times and prices are valid until 31st March 2011, after this date details are subject to change please visit www.english-heritage.org.uk for the most up-to-date information.

OVERBECK'S

Sharpitor, Salcombe, South Devon TQ8 8LW

Tel: 01548 842893

Owner: National Trust **Contact:** Property Manager

Edwardian house and unusual and exotic garden.

Location: MAP 2:J10, OS Ref. SX728 374. 11/2m SW of Salcombe. Signposted from Salcombe (single track lanes).

POWDERHAM CASTLE

KENTON, Nr EXETER, DEVON EX6 8JQ

www.powderham.co.uk

Tel: 01626 890243 **Fax:** 01626 890729 **E-mail:** castle@powderham.co.uk

Owner: The Earl of Devon **Contact:** Mr Simon Fishwick – Estate Director

A splendid castle built in 1391 by Sir Philip Courtenay, remaining in the same family and currently home to the 18th Earl of Devon. Set in a tranquil deer park alongside the Exe estuary, its stunning location offers glorious views for miles around. Guided tours showcase the Castle's majestic rooms and stunning interiors, while fascinating stories bring its intriguing history to life. The courtyard tea room offers a selection of delicious cakes and home cooked meals. Gift shop, plant centre, friendly animals and children's play area.

Location: MAP 2:K7, OS Ref. SX965 832. 6m SW of Exeter, 4m S M5/J30. Access from A379 in Kenton village. Bus: No 2 Bus stops outside. Rail: Starcross Station – 2m. Ferry: Starcross Ferry – 2m.

Open: 1 Apr–30 Oct: Sun–Fri, 11am–4.30pm/5.30pm in summer (Last guided tour 1hr before closing and 2.30pm on Fri). Available for private hire all year.

Admission: Adult £9.50, Child (3–14yrs) £7.50, Senior £8.50, Family: £26.50. Groups (15+) special rates available. (2010 prices).

Available for private hire all year round. Partial. Licensed. Licensed. Included. 1hr. Free. Guide dogs only.

RHS GARDEN ROSEMOOR

See main index.

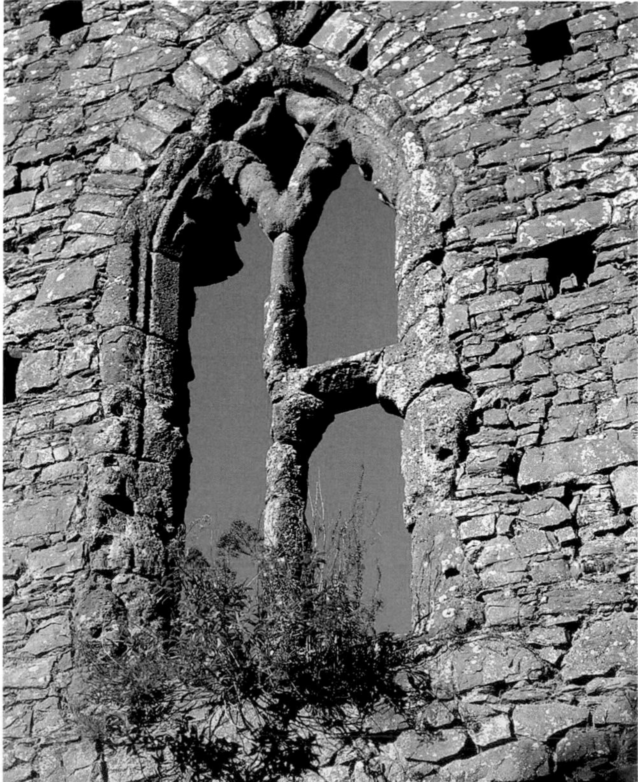

Tiverton Castle

SALTRAM

Plympton, Plymouth, Devon PL7 1UH

Tel: 01752 333500 **Fax:** 01752 336474

Owner: National Trust **Contact:** Administrator

18-19th c house and garden. Magnificent interior decoration.

Location: MAP 2:I9, OS Ref. SX520 557.

SAND

SIDBURY, SIDMOUTH EX10 0QN

Tel: 01395 597230 **E-mail:** info@SandSidbury.co.uk **www.SandSidbury.co.uk**

Contact: Mr & Mrs Huyshe-Shires

Sand is one of East Devon's hidden gems. The beautiful valley garden extends to 6 acres and is the setting for the lived-in Tudor house, the c15th Hall House, and the c16th Summer House. The family, under whose unbroken ownership the property has remained since 1560, provide guided house tours.

Location: MAP 2:L7, OS Ref. SY146 925. Well signed, 400 yards off A375 between Honiton and Sidmouth.

Open: House, garden & tearoom: Suns & Mons in June and on Bank Holidays, 24/25 Apr, 1/2 May, 29/30 May, 5/6, 12/13, 19/20, 26/27 June & 28/29 Aug; other dates as advertised on our website. Open 2–6pm. Last admission 5pm. Groups by appointment throughout the year.

Admission: House & Garden: Adult £7, Child/Student £1. Garden only: Adult £3, accompanied Child (under 16) Free.

No photography in house. Partial. Obligatory. Limited for coaches. On leads. Open air Shakespeare, see website for details.

SHUTE BARTON

Shute, Axminster, Devon EX13 7PT

Tel: 01752 346585 **www.nationaltrust.org.uk**

Owner: National Trust

One of the most important surviving non-fortified manor houses of the Middle Ages.

Location: MAP 2:M6, OS Ref. SY253 974. 3m SW of Axminster, 2m N of Colyton, 1m S of A35.

Open: 4 weekends 15 May–17 Oct 11am–5pm only. Tel. for dates.

Admission: Adult £3.20, Child £1.60. No group reductions.

Powderham Castle

TAPELEY PARK & GARDENS

Instow, Bideford, Devon EX39 4NT

Tel: 01271 860897 **Fax:** 01271 342371

Owner: Tapeley Park Trust

Extensive gardens and park.

Location: MAP 1:H4, OS Ref. SS478 291. Between Bideford and Barnstaple near Instow. Follow brown tourist signs from the A39 onto B3233.

Open: Sun–Fri 10am–5pm.

Admission: Adult £4, Child £2.50, OAP £3.50.

TIVERTON CASTLE

TIVERTON, DEVON EX16 6RP

www.tivertoncastle.com

Tel: 01884 253200/255200 **Fax:** 01884 254200 **E-mail:** tiverton.castle@ukf.net

Owner: Mr and Mrs A K Gordon **Contact:** Mrs A Gordon

Part Grade I Listed, part Scheduled Ancient Monument, few buildings evoke such an immediate feeling of history. All ages of architecture from medieval to modern. Fun for children - try on Civil War armour; ghost stories, secret passages, beautiful walled gardens, including working kitchen garden. Interesting furniture, pictures. Comfortable holiday accommodation.

Location: MAP 2:K5, OS Ref. SS954 130. Just N of Tiverton town centre.

Open: Easter–end Oct: Sun, Thur, BH Mon, 2.30–5.30pm. Last admission 5pm. Open to groups (12+) by prior arrangement at any time.

Admission: Adult £6, Child (7–16yrs) £2.50, Child under 7 Free. Garden only: £1.50.

Partial. By arrangement. 4 Apartments, 1 Cottage.

TOTNES CASTLE

Castle Street, Totnes, Devon TQ9 5NU

Tel/Fax: 01803 864406 **E-mail:** customers@english-heritage.org.uk

www.english-heritage.org.uk/totnes

Owner: English Heritage **Contact:** Visitor Operations Team

By the North Gate of the hill town of Totnes you will find a superb motte and bailey castle, with splendid views across the roof tops and down to the River Dart. It is a symbol of lordly feudal life and a fine example of Norman fortification.

Location: MAP 2:J8, OS202 Ref. SX800 605. In Totnes, on hill overlooking the town. Access in Castle St off W end of High St.

Open: 1 Apr–30 Jun: daily 10am–5pm. 1 Jul–31 Aug: daily, 10am–6pm. 1–30 Sep: daily, 10am–5pm. 1–31 Oct: daily, 10am–4pm. Closed 1 Nov–31 Mar.

Admission: Adult £3.20, Child £1.60, Conc. £2.70. 15% discount for groups (11+). EH members Free. Opening times and prices are valid until 31st March 2011, after this date details are subject to change please visit www.english-heritage.org.uk for the most up-to-date information.

Partial. Charged, 64 metres (70 yds), not EH.

See which properties offer **educational facilities** or **school visits** in our index at the end of the book.

■ Owner

The Hon
Mrs Townshend DL

■ Contact

Shop Manager
Abbotsbury
Weymouth
Dorset DT3 4LA

Tel: 01305 871387
E-mail: info@abbotsbury-tourism.co.uk

■ Location

MAP 2:N7
OS Ref. SY564 851

Off A35 nr Dorchester, on B3157 between Weymouth & Bridport.

■ Opening Times

Mar–Nov: daily, 10am–6pm.

Winter: daily, 10am–4pm. (Closed Christmas and New Year.)

Last admission 1 hr before closing.

■ Admission

Adult	£10.00
Child	£7.00
OAP	£9.50

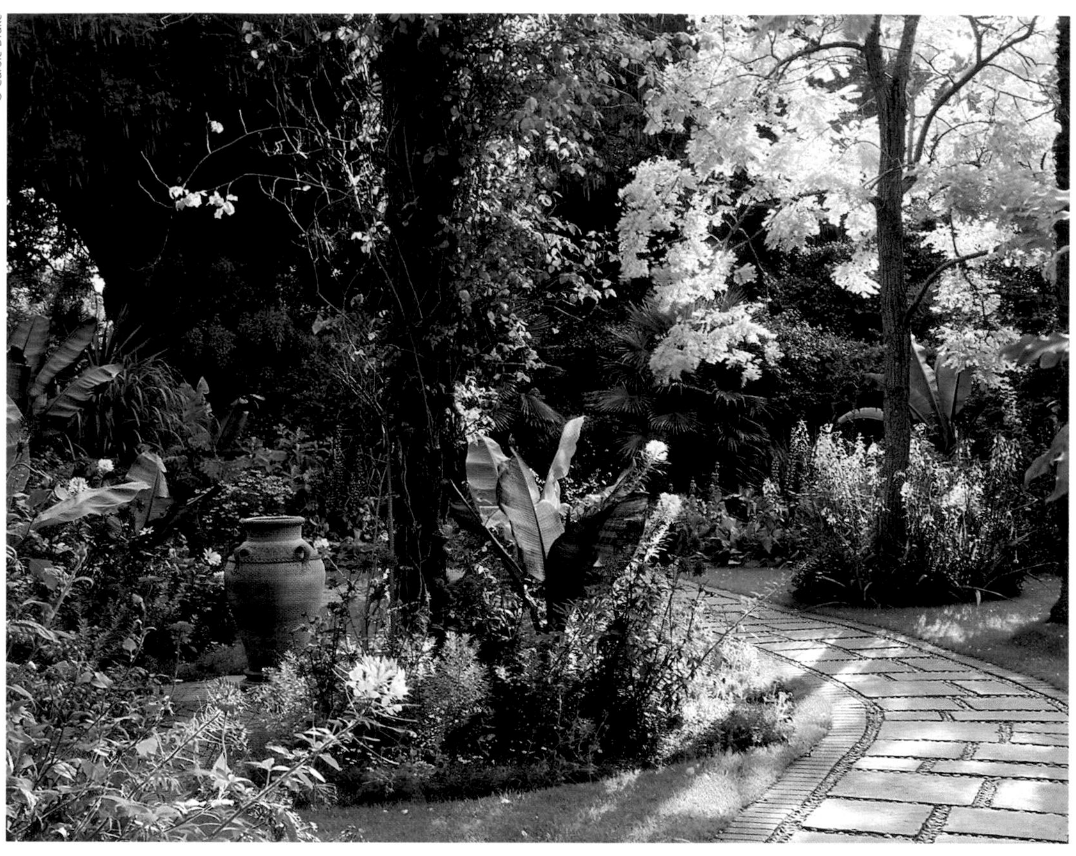
© Carole Drake

ABBOTSBURY SUBTROPICAL GARDENS

www.abbotsburygardens.co.uk www.abbotsburyplantsales.co.uk

Established in 1765 by the first Countess of Ilchester. Developed since then into a 20-acre Grade I listed, magnificent woodland valley garden.

World famous for its camellia groves, magnolias, rhododendron and hydrangea collections. In summer it is awash with colour.

Since the restoration after the great storm of 1990 many new and exotic plants have been introduced. The garden is now a mixture of formal and informal, with charming walled garden and spectacular woodland valley views.

Facilities include a Colonial Restaurant for lunches, snacks and drinks, a plant centre and quality gift shop. Events such as Shakespeare and concerts are presented during the year. The floodlighting of the garden at the end of October should not be missed.

Voted "Our Favourite Garden" by readers of *The Daily Telegraph*.

"One of the finest gardens I have ever visited" *Alan Titchmarsh BBC Gardeners World magazine Sept 2008.*

Plants also for sale online.

Partial.

Licensed.

By arrangement.

Free.

In grounds, on leads.

Civil Wedding Licence

■ **Owner**

Mr & Mrs Julian Kennard

■ **Contact**

Carolyn Clay
Forde Abbey
Chard
Somerset TA20 4LU

Tel: 01460 220231
E-mail: info@fordeabbey.co.uk

■ **Location**

MAP 2:N6
OS Ref. ST358 041

Just off the B3167
4m SE of Chard.

■ **Opening Times**

House
1st April–30 October
Tue–Fri, Sun & BH Mons
12 noon–4pm (last admission)

Gardens
Daily all year:
10am–4.30pm (last admission)

■ **Admission**

For current admission prices phone 01460 221290.

FORDE ABBEY & GARDENS

www.fordeabbey.co.uk

Forde Abbey is a treasure in an area already known for its outstanding beauty. More than 900 years of history are encapsulated in this elegant former Cistercian monastery and its 30 acres of award-winning gardens. In the peaceful solitude of its secluded position it is possible to imagine just how it looked to its previous owners: monks going about their daily round of work and prayer, prosperous parliamentary gentlemen discussing the Cavalier threat, gifted philosophers debating the imponderable, elegant Victorian ladies fanning themselves by the fireside and country gentlemen going about their work on the estate.

Set on the banks of the River Axe, this beautiful home contains many treasures including the Mortlake Tapestries, woven from cartoons painted for the Sistine Chapel by Raphael. The intricacy of their original design is matched by the story behind these particular tapestries involving Civil war, rebellion and loyalty rewarded.

The garden has been described by Alan Titchmarsh as "one of the greatest gardens of the West Country" and includes a mature arboretum, rockery, bog garden, working kitchen garden, sloping lawns and a cascade of lakes surrounding the Centenary Fountain, the highest powered fountain in England. The fruits of the garden and estate can be sampled in the Undercroft Tearoom with a wide selection of homemade lunches and cakes. A gift shop, plant centre, forge and pottery exhibition add to the day.

Enjoy England Awards for Excellence Silver Winner 2008

South West Tourism's Small Visitor Attraction of the Year 2006 & 2007

Available for wedding receptions. No photography in house.

Partial.

Licensed.

Licensed.

By arrangement.

On leads, in grounds.

ATHELHAMPTON HOUSE & GARDENS

DORCHESTER, DT2 7LG

www.athelhampton.co.uk

Tel: 01305 848363 **Email:** enquiry@athelhampton.co.uk

Owner: Patrick Cooke Esq **Contact:** Owen Davies, Laura Dean or Natalie Gillham

Topiary restaurant open as House & Gardens. Bookings taken for Sunday Carvery. Athelhampton's facilities are available for private visits & entertaining outside our opening hours throughout the year. We hold wedding Ceremonies & Receptions on Fridays and Saturdays. Please contact Owen Davies, Catering Manager.

Location: MAP 2:P6, OS Ref. SY771 942. Off A35 (T) at Puddletown Northbrook junction, 5m E of Dorchester. Nearest rail station Dorchester.

Open: 1 Mar–31 Oct, Sun–Thur (Open Sundays Nov–Feb), 10.30am–5pm/dusk. Last admission 4.30pm.

Admission: House & Gardens: Adult £9.50, Senior £9.00, Child (under 16 accompanied by an adult) Free, Disabled £6.50, Student £6.50. Groups (12+) Adult £7.90 (£6.90 with pre-booked catering order). See our website for special offers and up-to-date admission charges.

By arrangement.

ABBOTSBURY SUBTROPICAL GARDENS

See page 184 for full page entry.

BROWNSEA ISLAND

Poole Harbour, Dorset BH13 7EE

Tel: 01202 707744 **Fax:** 01202 701635

Owner: National Trust **Contact:** NT Office

Atmospheric island of heath and woodland with wide variety of wildlife. The island is dramatically located at the entrance to Poole harbour, offering spectacular views across to Studland and the Purbeck Hills. Its varied and colourful history includes use as a coastguard station, Victorian pottery, Edwardian country estate, daffodil farm, and as a decoy in the Second World War. In 1907 it was the site of Baden-Powell's experimental camp from which Scouting and Guiding evolved. Home to important populations of red squirrels and seabirds, the island provides a safe and relaxing place for walks and picnics, ideal for families to explore.

Location: MAP 3:A7, OS Ref. SZ032 878. In Poole Harbour. Boats run from Poole Quay and Sandbanks every 30 mins.

Open: Mar–Oct, daily 10am–5pm. Boat service from Sandbanks only, full boat service from Poole Quay and Sandbanks from end of Mar.

***Admission:** Adult £5.50, Child: £2.70, Family (2+3) £13.70, Family (1+3) £8.20. (2010 prices). *Price includes voluntary gift aid donation: visitors can however, choose to pay the standard admission charges which are displayed on the island and at www.nationaltrust.org.uk

Abbotsbury Subtropical Gardens

CHURCH OF OUR LADY & ST IGNATIUS

North Chideock, Bridport, Dorset DT6 6LF

Tel: 01308 488348 **E-mail:** amyasmartelli40@hotmail.com

Owner: The Weld Family Trust **Contact:** Mrs G Martelli

The Church, dedicated to Our Lady Queen of Martyrs and St Ignatius, was built on the site of an existing chapel-barn in 1872 by Charles Weld of Chideock Manor. It is one of the gems of English Catholicism and is designed in the Italian Romanesque style. It is a pilgrimage centre of the Chideock martyrs who are depicted in portraits over the nave. 19th century wall paintings by the Weld family can be seen in the original barn-chapel (now priest's sacristry) by arrangement. The church is also a shrine to Our Lady and has been a centre of Catholicism since penal times. A Museum of village life is on view in the adjoining cloister.

Location: MAP 2:N6, OS Ref. SY419 937. A35 from Bridport into Chideock. Right at St Giles' Church. Continue towards North Chideock for ½m. The Church is on the right.

Open: All year: 10am–4pm.

Admission: Donations welcome.

Moveable ramp in Church Porch. Limited.

CLAVELL TOWER

Kimmeridge, near Wareham, Dorset

Tel: 01628 825925 **E-mail:** bookings@landmarktrust.org.uk

www.landmarktrust.org.uk

Owner/Contact: The Landmark Trust

Clavell Tower was built in 1830 by Reverend John Richards Clavell of Smedmore as an observatory and folly. It was designed by Robert Vining with four storeys and a distinctive Tuscan colonnade. Also known as the Tower of the Winds, it has a special place in literary history. Thomas Hardy often took his first love, Eliza Nicholl, there and used it as a frontispiece for his Wessex Poems. The Tower was also the inspiration for PD James' novel, The Black Tower. It was derelict from the 1930s and remained so up until 2007 when it was painstakingly rebuilt 25 metres inland by the Landmark Trust, safeguarding it from the cliff erosion and further neglect. Full details of Clavell Tower and 189 other historical and architecturally important buildings are featured in the Landmark Trust Handbook (price £10 plus p&p refundable against a booking) and on the website.

Location: Map 2:A7, OS Ref. SY909 786

Open: Available for holidays for up to 2 people throughout the year. Two Open Days a year. Other visits by appointment. Contact the Landmark Trust for details.

Admission: Free on Open Days and visits by appointment.

© NT / Peter Preen

CLOUDS HILL

WAREHAM, DORSET BH20 7NQ

www.nationaltrust.org.uk

Tel: 01929 405616 **Email:** westdorset@nationaltrust.org.uk
Owner: National Trust **Contact:** The Visitor Reception Assistant

A tiny isolated brick and tile cottage, bought in 1929 by T E Lawrence (Lawrence of Arabia) as a retreat. The austere rooms inside are much as he left them and reflect his complex personality and close links with the Middle East. An exhibition details Lawrence's extraordinary life.

Location: (194:SY824 909) 1m N of Bovington Tank Museum (King George V Road), Station: Wool 3½m; Moreton (U) 3½m. Road: 9m E of Dorchester, 1½m E of Waddock crossroads (B3390), 4m S of A35 Poole–Dorchester.

Open: 17 Mar–30 Oct 2011, Thurs–Mons, 12 noon–5pm or dusk if earlier; no electric light. Groups wishing to visit at other times must telephone in advance.

Admission: £4.50, Child £2

No WC. No coaches. Small groups.

© NT / Peter Preen

HARDY'S BIRTHPLACE

HIGHER BOCKHAMPTON, DORCHESTER, DORSET DT2 8QJ

www.nationaltrust.org.uk

Tel: 01305 262366
Owner: National Trust **Contact:** Visitor Reception Assistant

A small cob and thatch cottage where the novelist and poet Thomas Hardy was born in 1840, and from where he would walk to school every day in Dorchester, six miles away. It was built by his great-grandfather and is little altered. Since the family left the interior has been furnished by the Trust (see also Max Gate). His early novels *Under the Green Wood Tree* and *Far From the Madding Crowd* were written here. Charming cottage garden.

Location: MAP 2:P6, OS Ref. SY728 925. 3m NE of Dorchester, 1/2m S of A35. 800+ Metres walk through the woods from car park.

Open: 14 Mar–31 October: Thur–Mon, 11am–5pm.

Admission: Adult £4.75, Child £2.20.

No WC. Partial. No coach parking.

CORFE CASTLE

Wareham, Dorset BH20 5EZ
Tel: 01929 481294 **Fax:** 01929 477067
Owner: National Trust **Contact:** Visitor Services and Enterprises Manager

The once important stronghold now a majestic ruin.

Location: MAP 3:A7, OS Ref. SY959 824. On A351 Wareham–Swanage Rd. NW of the village.

EDMONDSHAM HOUSE & GARDENS

Cranborne, Wimborne, Dorset BH21 5RE
Tel: 01725 517207
Owner/Contact: Mrs Julia E Smith

Charming blend of Tudor and Georgian architecture with interesting contents. Organic walled garden, 6 acre garden with unusual trees and spring bulbs. 12th century church nearby.

Location: MAP 3:A5, OS Ref. SU062 116. Off B3081 between Cranborne and Verwood, NW from Ringwood 9m, Wimborne 9m.

Open: House & Gardens: All BH Mons & Weds in Apr & Oct 2–5pm. Gardens: Apr–Oct, Suns & Weds 2–5pm.

Admission: House & Garden: Adult £5, Child £1 (under 5yrs Free). Garden only: Adult £2.50, Child 50p. Garden Season Ticket (incl. children) £10. Groups by arrangement, teas for groups.

Pre-booked (max 50). Obligatory. Car park only. (max 50).

FORDE ABBEY & GARDENS

See page 185 for full page entry.

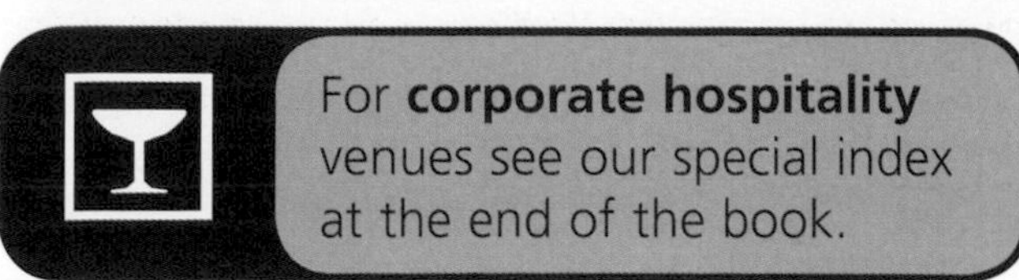
For **corporate hospitality** venues see our special index at the end of the book.

Forde Abbey & Gardens

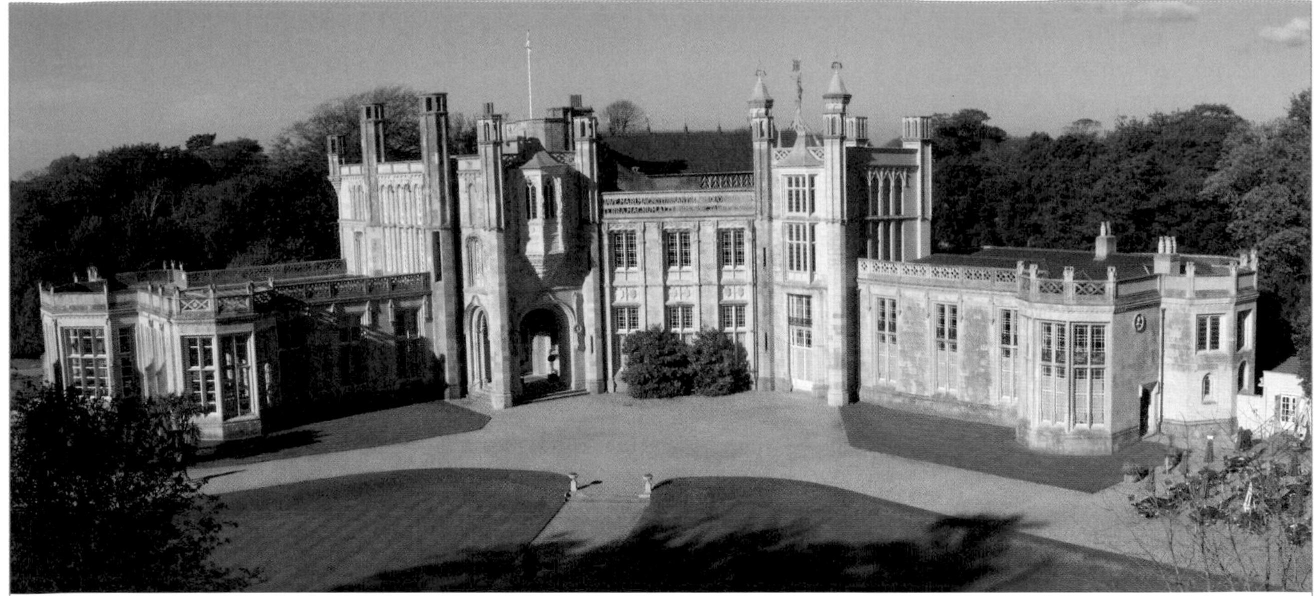

HIGHCLIFFE CASTLE

ROTHESAY DRIVE, HIGHCLIFFE-ON-SEA, CHRISTCHURCH BH23 4LE

www.highcliffecastle.co.uk

Tel: 01425 278807 **Fax:** 01425 280423 **E-mail:** enquiries@highcliffecastle.co.uk

Owner: Christchurch Borough Council **Contact:** David Hopkins

Built in the 1830s for Lord Stuart de Rothesay in the Romantic/Picturesque style and incorporating French medieval stonework and stained glass. The rooms in this Grade I listed building remain mostly unrepaired and now house a Heritage Centre and Gift Shop. They also provide a unique setting for changing exhibitions, featuring local and national artists. Programme of concerts and outdoor events. The refurbished Dining Room is available for wedding receptions, banquets and corporate use. Internal Guided Tours incorporating the upper floors. Cliff-top grounds. Access to Christchurch Coastal Path and beach.

Location: MAP 3:B6, OS Ref. SZ200 930. Off the A337 Lymington Road, between Christchurch and Highcliffe-on-Sea.

Open: 1 Feb–23 Dec: daily, 11am–5pm. Last admission 4.30 (4pm Fri/Sat). Grounds: All year: daily from 7am. Limited access for coaches. Tearooms closed Christmas Day.

Admission: Adult £2.95, accompanied U16 free. Group (10+) rates available. Guided tours of unrestored areas: Adult £3.95, accompanied U16 free. Grounds: Free. (May be unsuitable for people with mobility problems – please ring for details).

Wedding receptions. WC. 10am–5pm. By arrangement.
Limited. Parking charge. By arrangement. In grounds, on leads.

© NTPL / James Mortimer

Kingston Lacy

HIGHER MELCOMBE

Melcombe Bingham, Dorchester, Dorset DT2 7PB
Tel: 01258 880251
www.highermelcombemanor.co.uk
Owner/Contact: Mr M C Woodhouse
Consists of the surviving wing of a 16th century house with its attached domestic chapel. A fine plaster ceiling and linenfold panelling. Conducted group tours by owner.
Location: MAP 2:P6, OS Ref. ST749 024. 1km W of Melcombe Bingham.
Open: May–Sept by appointment.
Admission: Adult £4.
Unsuitable. By written appointment only. Limited. Guide dogs only
Accommodation Civil Wedding Licence.

KINGSTON LACY

Kingston Lacy, Wimborne Minster, Dorset BH21 4EA
Tel: 01202 883402 **Fax:** 01202 882402
www.nationaltrust.org.uk
Owner: National Trust **Contact:** The Property Manager
Elegant Country mansion with fine art collection.
Location: MAP 3:A6, OS Ref. ST980 019. On B3082 – Blandford / Wimborne road, 1½m NW of Wimborne Minster.

KNOLL GARDENS & NURSERY

Stapehill Road, Hampreston, Wimborne BH21 7ND
Tel: 01202 873931 **Fax:** 01202 870842 **E-mail:** enquiries@knollgardens.co.uk
Owner: J & J Flude & N R Lucas **Contact:** Mr John Flude
Nationally acclaimed 6 acre gardens, with 6000+ named plants.
Location: MAP 3:B6, OS Ref. SU059 001. Between Wimborne & Ferndown. Exit A31 Canford Bottom roundabout, B3073 Hampreston. Signposted 1½m.
Open: May–Oct: Tue–Sun, 10am–5pm. Nov–Apr: Wed–Sat, 10am–4pm. Closed Jan. Opens 2 Feb.
Admission: Adult £5.50, Child (5–15yrs) £4, Conc £4.75.

© Patrick Cooke

MAPPERTON

BEAMINSTER, DORSET DT8 3NR

www.mapperton.com

Tel: 01308 862645 **Fax:** 01308 861082 **E-mail:** office@mapperton.com
Owner/Contact: The Earl & Countess of Sandwich
'The Nation's Finest Manor House' – *Country Life*. Jacobean mainly 1660s manor overlooking an Italianate upper garden with orangery, topiary and formal borders descending to fish ponds and shrub gardens. All Saints Church forms south wing opening to courtyard and stables. Area of Outstanding Natural Beauty with fine views of Dorset hills and woodlands.
Location: MAP 2:N6, OS Ref. SY503 997. 1m S of B3163, 2m NE of B3066, 2m SE Beaminster, 5m NE Bridport.
Open: House: 11 Jul–12 Aug, Mon–Fri, plus 30 May & 29 Aug, 2–4.30pm, last admission 4pm. Garden & All Saints Church: 1 Apr–31 Oct: daily (exc. Sat) 11am–5pm. Café: Apr–Sept: daily (exc. Sat) 11am–5.30pm, for lunch and tea. Tel: 01308 863348.
Admission: Gardens: Adult £5.00, Child (under 18yrs) £2.50, under 5yrs Free. House: £4.50. Group tours by appointment. House and Gardens combined £9.00 for groups over 20.
Partial. Licensed. By arrangement.
Limited for coaches. Guide dogs only.

LULWORTH CASTLE & PARK

EAST LULWORTH, WAREHAM, DORSET BH20 5QS

www.lulworth.com

Tel: 0845 4501054 **Fax:** 01929 400563 **E-mail:** office@lulworth.com
Owner: The Weld Estate
Surrounded by beautiful parkland with views of the Jurassic Coast this 17th century hunting lodge was destroyed by fire in 1929 and has been externally restored and internally consolidated by English Heritage. Steeped in history the Castle has remained in the same family since 1641. Features include a gallery on the Weld family, reconstructed kitchen, dairy and laundry rooms and a wine cellar. The Chapel is reputed to be one of the finest pieces of architecture in Dorset and houses an exhibition on vestments and recusant silver.
Location: MAP 3:A7, OS Ref. SY853 822. In E Lulworth off B3070, 3m NE of Lulworth Cove.
Open: Castle & Park: All year, Sun–Fri (but closed 9–21 Jan inc, 28 Jul–1 Aug inc, 24 & 25 Dec. Open Sat 23 Apr, 28 May & 17 Sept). See website for extensive list of Special Events.
Admission: Off peak: Adults £8.50, Senior £7, Child (4–15) £4, Family (2+3) £25, Family (1+3) £16.50, Under 4's Free. Festival rates: 1&2 May, 28 May–3 Jun, 24 Jul-29 Aug (exc. Camp Bestival), 17 & 18 Sept: Adults £11, Conc. £10, Child (4–15) £6, Family (2+3) £34, Family (1+3) £23, Under 4's Free. Groups (10+) receive 10% discount. Season tickets available.
Concerts, corporate & private hire/events by arrangement. Partial. WC. Licensed. By arrangement. Free. Meal voucher & free access for coach drivers. In grounds, on leads. Not permitted in buildings except Guide Dogs. 5 holiday cottages, tel: 01929 400100. See website.

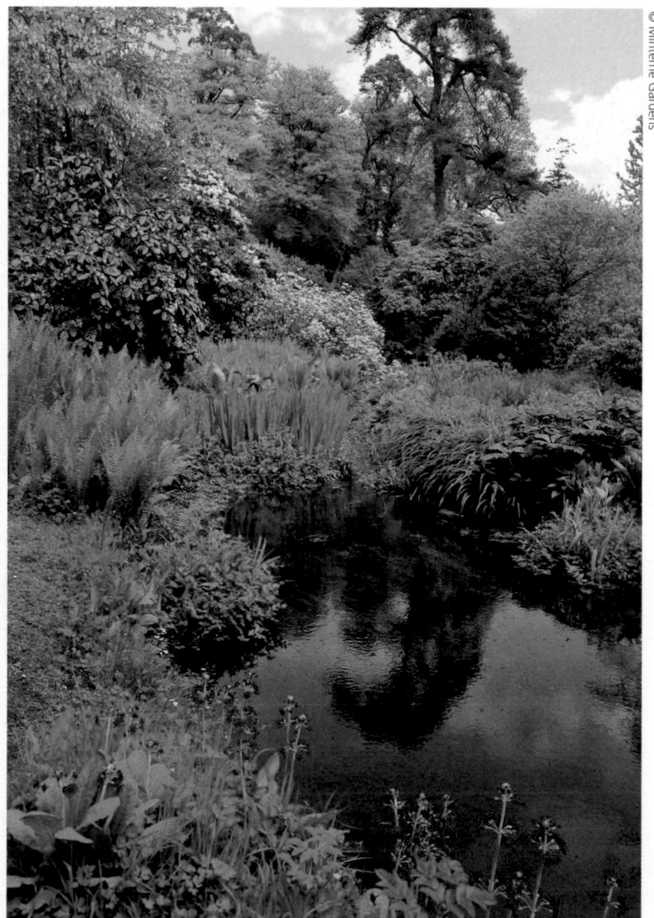
© Minterne Gardens

Minterne Gardens

© NTPL / Andrew Butler

Max Gate

MAX GATE

Alington Avenue, Dorchester, Dorset DT1 2AB

Tel: 01305 262538

www.nationaltrust.org.uk

Owner: National Trust **Contact:** The Tenant

Novelist Thomas Hardy designed and lived here 1885–1928.

Location: MAP 2:P7, OS Ref. SY704 899. 1m E of Dorchester just N of the A352 to Wareham. From Dorchester follow A352 signs to the roundabout named Max Gate (at Jct. of A35 Dorchester bypass). Turn left and left again into cul-de-sac outside Max Gate.

MILTON ABBEY CHURCH

Milton Abbas, Blandford, Dorset DT11 0BZ

Tel: 01258 880215

Owner: Diocese of Salisbury **Contact:** Chris Fookes

Abbey church dating from 14th century.

Location: MAP 2:P6, OS Ref. ST798 024. 3½m N of A354. Between Dorchester/Blandford Road.

Open: Abbey Church: daily 10.30am–5pm. Groups by arrangement please.

Admission: By donation except Easter & mid-Jul–end Aug.

MINTERNE GARDENS

MINTERNE MAGNA, Nr DORCHESTER, DORSET DT2 7AU

www.minterne.co.uk

Tel: 01300 341370 **Fax:** 01300 341747 **E-mail:** enquiries@minterne.co.uk

Owner/Contact: The Hon Henry and Mrs Digby

Landscaped in the manner of 'Capability' Brown in the 18th century, Minterne's unique garden has been described by Simon Jenkins as *'a corner of paradise.'* Wander peacefully through 20 wild woodland acres where magnolias, rhododendrons and eucryphias provide a new vista at each turn, with small lakes, streams and cascades. Minterne also hosts private house tours, dinners, seminars, weddings and events, ensuring that guests leave with cherished memories of those special occasions.

Location: MAP 2:O6, OS Ref. ST660 042. On A352 Dorchester/Sherborne Rd, 2m N of Cerne Abbas.

Open: 1 Mar–9 Nov: daily, 10am–6pm.

Admission: Adult £5, accompanied children under 12 free.

Unsuitable. By arrangement. Free. Picnic tables in car park.

In grounds on leads.

© English Heritage

PORTLAND CASTLE

CASTLETOWN, PORTLAND, WEYMOUTH, DORSET DT5 1AZ

www.english-heritage.org.uk/portland

Tel: 01305 820539 **Fax:** 01305 860853 **Email:** customers@english-heritage.org.uk

Owner: English Heritage **Contact:** Visitor Operations Staff

Discover one of Henry VIII's finest coastal fortresses, perfectly preserved in a waterfront location overlooking Portland harbour. Explore the Tudor kitchen and gun platform, see the superb battlement views and enjoy lunch in the Captain's Tearoom. An audio tour, included with admission, brings the castle's long history to life.

Location: MAP 2:O7, OS Ref. SY684 743. Overlooking Portland harbour.

Open: 1 Apr–30 Jun: daily, 10am–5pm. 1 Jul–31 Aug: daily, 10am–6pm. 1–30 Sep: daily, 10am–5pm. 1–31 Oct: daily, 10am–4pm. Closed 1 Nov–31 Mar.

Admission: Adult £4.20, Child £2.10, Conc. £3.60. Family £10.50 .15% discount for groups (11+). EH members Free. Opening times and prices are valid until 31st March 2011, after this date details are subject to change please visit www.english-heritage.org.uk for the most up-to-date information.

Special Events: Check the English Heritage website for details of special events.

Partial. By arrangement. Limited for coaches.

Guide dogs only

SANDFORD ORCAS MANOR HOUSE

Sandford Orcas, Sherborne, Dorset DT9 4SB

Tel: 01963 220206

Owner/Contact: Sir Mervyn Medlycott Bt

Tudor manor house with gatehouse, fine panelling, furniture, pictures. Terraced gardens with topiary and herb garden. Personal conducted tour by owner.

Location: MAP 2:O5, OS Ref. ST623 210. 2½m N of Sherborne, Dorset 4m S of A303 at Sparkford. Entrance next to church.

Open: Easter Mon, 10am–5pm. May & Jul–Sept: Suns & Mons, 2–5pm.

Admission: Adults £5, Child £2.50. Groups (10+): Adult £4, Child £2.

Unsuitable. Obligatory. In grounds, on leads. Parking available

© Britainonview / Jerry Harpur

Athelhampton Gardens

SHERBORNE CASTLE

SHERBORNE, DORSET DT9 5NR

www.sherbornecastle.com

Tel: 01935 812072 **Fax:** 01935 816727 **E-mail:** enquiries@sherbornecastle.com

Owner: Mr & Mrs John Wingfield Digby **Contact:** The Custodians

Built by Sir Walter Raleigh in 1594, Sherborne Castle has been the home of the Digby family since 1617. Prince William of Orange was entertained here in 1688, and George III visited in 1789. Splendid interiors and collections of art, furniture and porcelain are on view in the Castle. Lancelot 'Capability' Brown created the lake in 1753 and gave Sherborne the very latest in landscape gardening, with magnificent vistas of the surrounding parklands. Today, over 30 acres of beautiful lakeside gardens and grounds are open for public viewing.

Location: MAP 2:O5, OS Ref. ST649 164. ¾m SE of Sherborne town centre. Follow brown signs from A30 or A352. ½m S of the Old Castle.

Open: Castle, Gardens, Shop & Tearoom: 1 Apr–30 Oct: daily except Mon & Fri (open BH Mons), 11am–4.30pm last admission. (On Sats, Castle interior from 2pm). Groups (15+) by arrangement during normal opening hours.

Admission: (2011 prices) Castle & Gardens: Adult £9.50, Child (0–15yrs) Free (max 4 per adult), Senior £9. Groups (15+): Adult/Senior £8.50, Child (0–15yrs) £3.50. Private views (15+): Adult/Senior £10.50, Child £5. Gardens only: Adult/Senior £5, Child (0–15yrs) Free (max 4 per adult), no concessions or group rates for gardens only.

Partial. Licensed. By arrangement. Ample for cars.

In grounds, on leads.

Minterne

© Britainonview

Mapperton

SHERBORNE OLD CASTLE

Castleton, Sherborne, Dorset DT9 3SA

Tel/Fax: 01935 812730 **Email:** customers@english-heritage.org.uk

www.english-heritage.org.uk/sherborne

Owner: English Heritage **Contact:** Visitor Operations Staff

The ruins of this early 12th century castle are a testament to the 16 days it took Cromwell to capture it during the Civil War, after which it was abandoned. A gatehouse, some graceful arcading and decorative windows survive.

Location: MAP 2:O5, OS Ref. ST647 167. ½m E of Sherborne off B3145. ½m N of the 'new' 1594 Castle.

Open: 1 Apr–30 Jun: daily, 10am–5pm. 1 Jul–31 Aug: daily, 10am–6pm. 1–30 Sept: daily, 10am–5pm. 1–31 Oct: daily, 10am–4pm. Closed 1 Nov–31 Mar.

Admission: Adult £3.20, Child £1.60, Conc. £2.70. 15% discount for groups of 11+. Joint ticket with Sherborne Castle grounds, £6.50. EH members Free. Opening times and prices are valid until 31st March 2011, after this date details are subject to change please visit www.english-heritage.org.uk for the most up-to-date information.

Partial. Limited for coaches. Guide dogs only

STOCK GAYLARD HOUSE

Stock Gaylard, Sturminster Newton, Dorset DT10 2BG

Tel: 01963 23215 **E-mail:** langmeadj@stockgaylard.com

www.stockgaylard.com

Owner: Mrs J Langmead **Contact:** Mrs J Langmead

A Georgian house overlooking an ancient deer park with the parish church of St Barnabas in the garden. The grounds and principal rooms of the house are open to the public for 28 days a year.

Location: MAP 2:P5, OS Ref. ST722 130. 1 mile S of the junction of the A357 and the A3030 at the Lydlinch Common.

Open: 23 Apr–2 May, 22–30 Jun & 22–30 Sept, 2–5pm. Large parties & coaches by appointment on Tue & Wed. Access to the Park by arrangement, please telephone for information.

Admission: Adult £5.00.

Special Events: Stock Gaylard Oak Fair, 28th August, 2010

Partial. Obligatory In grounds. Guide dogs only

WHITE MILL

Sturminster Marshall, Nr Wimborne, Dorset BH21 4BX

Tel: 01258 858051

Owner: National Trust **Contact:** The Custodian

Rebuilt in 1776 on a site marked as a mill in the Domesday Book, this substantial corn mill was extensively repaired in 1994 and still retains its original elm and applewood machinery (now too fragile to be operative).

Location: MAP 3:A6, OS Ref. ST958 006. On River Stour ½m NE of Sturminster Marshall. From the B3082 Blandford to Wimborne Rd, take road to Sturminster Marshall. Mill is 1m on right. Car park nearby.

Open: end Mar–end Oct: Sats, Suns & BH Mons, 12 noon–5pm. Admission by guided tour only (last tour 4pm).

Admission: Adult £3, Child £2. Groups by arrangement.

WOLFETON HOUSE

Nr DORCHESTER, DORSET DT2 9QN

Tel: 01305 263500

E-mail: kthimbleby.wolfeton@gmail.com

Owner: Capt N T L L T Thimbleby **Contact:** The Steward

A fine medieval and Elizabethan manor house lying in the water-meadows near the confluence of the rivers Cerne and Frome. It was much embellished around 1580 and has splendid plaster ceilings, fireplaces and panelling of that date. To be seen are the Great Hall, Stairs and Chamber, Parlour, Dining Room, Chapel and Cyder House. The medieval Gatehouse has two unmatched and older towers. There are good pictures and furniture.

Location: MAP 2:O6, OS Ref. SY678 921. 1½m from Dorchester on the A37 towards Yeovil. Indicated by Historic House signs.

Open: June–end Sept: Mons, Weds & Thurs, 2–5pm. Groups by appointment throughout the year.

Admission: £6.

By arrangement. Ground floor. By arrangement. By arrangement.

© Forde Abbey

Forde Abbey

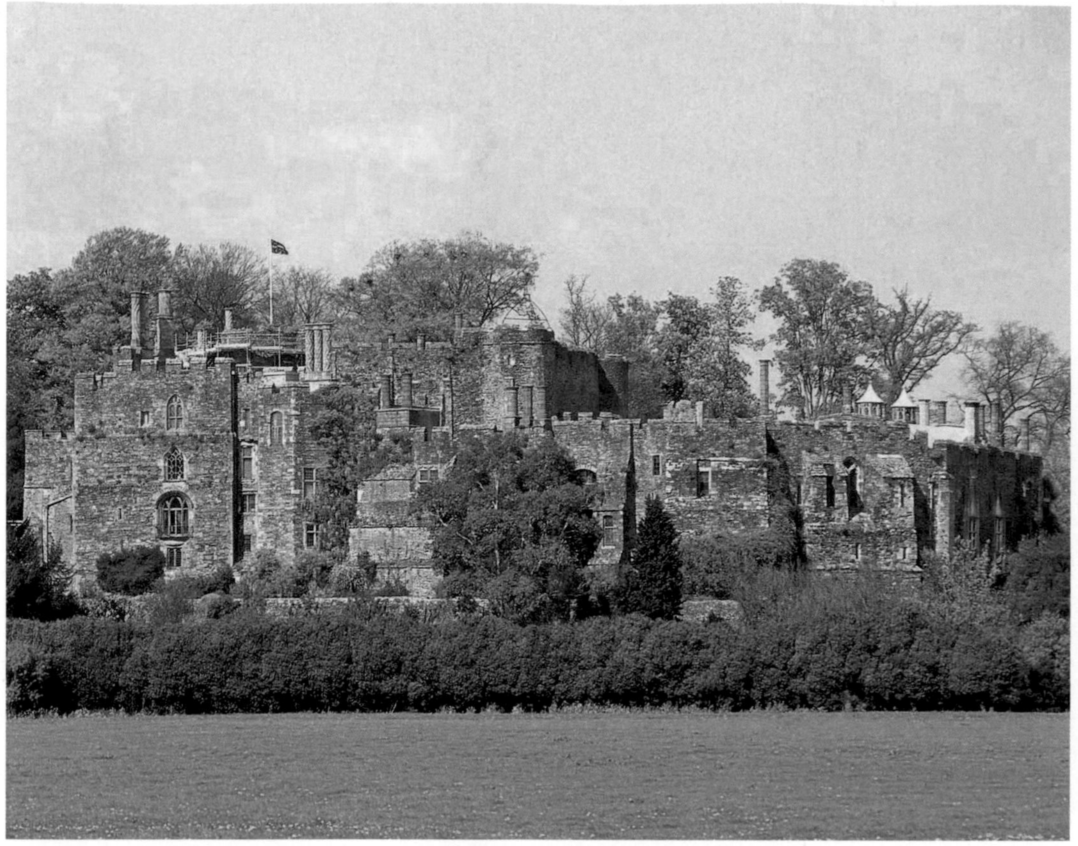

BERKELEY CASTLE

www.berkeley-castle.com

Berkeley Castle is one of the most remarkable buildings in the Country and possibly the most outstanding example of Medieval domestic architecture in Britain.

English history has been lived out within the walls of the Castle and the most remarkable thing is that for nine centuries, the building, the Berkeley Family, the archives, the contents and the Estate have all survived together. The Castle is now the oldest building in the Country to be inhabited by the same family who built it.

Scene of the brutal murder of Edward II in 1327 (visitors can see his cell and the nearby dungeon) and besieged by Cromwell's troops in 1645, the Castle is steeped in history but twenty-four generations of Berkeleys have gradually transformed a Norman fortress into the lovely home it is today.

The State Apartments contain magnificent collections of furniture, rare paintings by primarily English and Dutch masters, and tapestries. Part of the world-famous Berkeley silver is on display in the Dining Room. Many other rooms are equally interesting including the Great Hall where it is said that the Earl of Suffolk's Jester, Dicky Pearce, died in mysterious circumstances in the 1720s, and his epitaph can be found on a tomb in the Churchyard.

In addition to the fantastic guided tours provided by the experienced guides, visitors can stroll along the beautiful Elizabethan garden terraces with ornamental lily pond, Elizabeth I's bowling green, and sweeping lawns. Also during the summer, visitors can enjoy the Tropical Butterfly House located in the Walled Garden.

No photography inside the Castle.

Wedding receptions and corporate entertainment.

Partial.

Licensed.

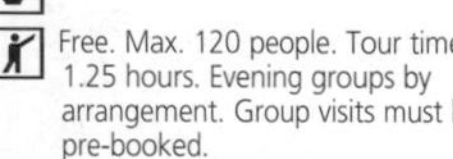

Free. Max. 120 people. Tour time: 1.25 hours. Evening groups by arrangement. Group visits must be pre-booked.

Cars 150yds from Castle, 15 coaches 250yds away. Free.

Welcome. General and social history and architecture.

Guide dogs only.

Owner

Mr R J G Berkeley

Contact

The General Manager
Berkeley Castle
Berkeley
Gloucestershire
GL13 9BQ

Tel: 01453 810332
Fax: 01453 512995
E-mail: info@berkeley-castle.com

Location

MAP 6:M12
OS Ref. ST685 990

SE side of Berkeley village. Midway between Bristol & Gloucester, 2m W off the A38.

From motorway M5/J14 (5m) or J13 (9m).

Opening Times

Open from Sunday 3 April–Sunday 30 October 2011

Open Thursdays & Sundays & Bank Holidays in April (including Good Friday & Easter Saturday), May, June, September & October 2011

Open Sundays–Thursdays during School Holidays (incl. all of July)

10–25 April 2011 (Easter)

29 May–5 June 2011 (Whitsun Half-Term)

3 July–4 September 2011 (Summer)

23–30 October 2011 (October Half-Term)

Opening Hours
11.00am–5.30pm
(Last admission 4.30pm)

Admission

Global Ticket including Castle & Gardens

Adult	£9.50
Child (5–16yrs)	£5.00
Child (under 5s)	Free
OAP	£7.50
Family (2+2)	£24.00

Groups (25+ pre-booked)

Adult	£9.00
Child (5-16yrs)	£4.00
OAP	£7.00

Gardens only

Adult	£4.00
Child	£2.00

Special Events

Special Events programme throughout the year. Music & theatrical evenings. Outdoor theatre, steam rally, car show, country show, medieval festival. Activities for children during school holidays.

Conference/Function

ROOM	MAX CAPACITY
Great Hall	150
Long Drawing Rm	100

■ Owner

Mr David Lowsley-Williams

■ Contact

D Lowsley-Williams
or Caroline
Lowsley-Williams
Chavenage
Tetbury
Gloucestershire
GL8 8XP

Tel: 01666 502329
Fax: 01666 504696
E-mail: info@chavenage.com

■ Location

MAP 3:A1
OS Ref. ST872 952

Less than 20m from M4/J16/17 or 18. 1¾m NW of Tetbury between the B4014 & A4135. Signed from Tetbury. Less than 15m from M5/J13 or 14. Signed from A46 (Stroud–Bath road).

Rail: Kemble Station 7m.

Taxi: Martin Cars 01666 503611.

Air: Bristol 35m. Birmingham 70m. Grass airstrip on farm.

■ Opening Times

Summer
May–September, Thur, Sun, 2–5pm.
Last admission 4pm.
Also Easter Sun, Mon & BH Mondays.

NB. Will open on any day and at other times by prior arrangement for groups.

Winter
October–March
By appointment only for groups.

■ Admission

Tours are inclusive in the following prices.

Summer

Adult	£7.00
Child (5–16 yrs)	£3.50

Winter
Groups only
(any date or time)
Rates by arrangement.

Concessions:
By prior arrangement, concessions may be given to groups of 40+ and also to disabled and to exceptional cases.

Conference/Function

ROOM	SIZE	MAX CAPACITY
Ballroom	70' x 30'	120
Oak Room	25 'x 20'	30

CHAVENAGE

www.chavenage.com

Chavenage is a wonderful Elizabethan house of mellow grey Cotswold stone and tiles which contains much of interest for the discerning visitor.

The approach aspect of Chavenage is virtually as it was left by Edward Stephens in 1576. Only two families have owned Chavenage; the present owners since 1891 and the Stephens family before them. A Colonel Nathaniel Stephens, MP for Gloucestershire during the Civil War was cursed for supporting Cromwell, giving rise to legends of weird happenings at Chavenage since that time.

There are many interesting rooms housing tapestries, fine furniture, pictures and relics of the Cromwellian period. Of particular note are the Main Hall, where a contemporary screen forms a minstrels' gallery and two tapestry rooms where it is said Cromwell was lodged.

Recently Chavenage has been used as a location for TV and film productions including a Hercule Poirot story *The Mysterious Affair at Styles*, many episodes of the sequel to *Are you Being Served* called *Grace & Favour*, episodes of *The House of Elliot, Casualty*, *Berkeley Square* and *Cider with Rosie*. In 2005 it was one of the homes Jeremy Musson visited in the BBC's *The Curious House Guest*. Chavenage has recently doubled as Candleford Manor in the BBC costume drama *Lark Rise to Candleford*. Scenes from the series *Bonekickers* and *Tess of the D'Urbervilles* were shot at Chavenage in 2008.

Chavenage is especially suitable for those wishing an intimate, personal tour, usually conducted by the owner or his family, or for groups wanting a change from large establishments. Meals for pre-arranged groups have proved hugely popular. It also provides a charming venue for wedding receptions, small conferences and other functions.

Suitable for filming, photography, corporate entertainment, activity days, seminars, receptions and product launches.

Occasional.

Corporate entertaining. Private drinks parties, lunches, dinners, anniversary parties and wedding receptions.

Partial. WC.

Lunches, teas, dinners and picnics by arrangement.

By owner. Large groups given a talk prior to viewing. Couriers/group leaders should arrange tour format prior to visit.

Up to 100 cars. 2–3 coaches (by appointment). Coaches access from A46 (signposted) or from Tetbury via the B4014, enter the back gates for coach parking area.

Chairs can be arranged for lecturing.

In grounds on leads. Guide dogs only in house.

Chavenage

BERKELEY CASTLE

See page 193 for full page entry.

BLACKFRIARS PRIORY

Ladybellegate Street, Gloucester GL1 2HS
Tel: 0117 9750700 **Email:** customers@english-heritage.org.uk
www.english-heritage.org.uk/blackfriars
Owner: English Heritage **Contact:** The South West Regional Office

One of the most complete surviving friaries in England, later converted into a Tudor house and cloth factory. Most of the original 13th century church remains and a rare scissor-braced roof in the dormitory.

Location: MAP 6:N11, OS Ref. SO830 186. In Blackfriars Lane, off Ladybellegate St, Gloucester, off Southgate Street.

Open: Temporarily closed to the public until March 2011. After this date please contact the South West Regional Office for 2011 opening times.

Admission: Adult £3.50, EH members £3, Child Free. Opening times and prices are valid until 31st March 2011, after this date details are subject to change please visit www.english-heritage.org.uk for the most up-to-date information.

Obligatory. Nearby, not EH, charged. Guide dogs only.

BOURTON HOUSE GARDEN

BOURTON-ON-THE-HILL, GLOUCESTERSHIRE, GL56 9AE

www.bourtonhouse.com

Tel: 01386 700754 **E-mail:** admin@bourtonhouse.com
Owner: Mr R Quintus **Contact:** Mrs Christine Walford

The Cotswolds best kept secret! An award-winning three acre garden featuring wide herbaceous borders with stunning plant and colour combinations; imaginative topiary including topiary walk, knot garden and parterre; water features; a unique Shade House and many creatively planted pots. The unusual, rare and exotic make this garden a plantsman's delight.

Location: MAP 6:P10, OS Ref. SP180 324. 1¾ m W of Moreton-in-Marsh on A44.

Open: Apr–Oct, Wed–Fri, 10am–5pm.

Admission: Adult £6, Under 16 Free.

Partial. By arrangement. Limited for coaches.

CHAVENAGE

See page 194 for full page entry.

CHEDWORTH ROMAN VILLA

Yanworth, Nr Cheltenham, Gloucestershire GL54 3LJ
Tel: 01242 890256 **Fax:** 01242 890909
www.nationaltrust.org.uk
Owner: National Trust **Contact:** The Visitor Services Manager

Discover one of the largest Romano-British sites in the country. First excavated in 1864.

Location: MAP 6:O11, OS Ref. SP053 135. 3m NW of Fossebridge on Cirencester–Northleach road (A429) via Yanworth or from A436 via Withington. Coaches must approach from Fossebridge.

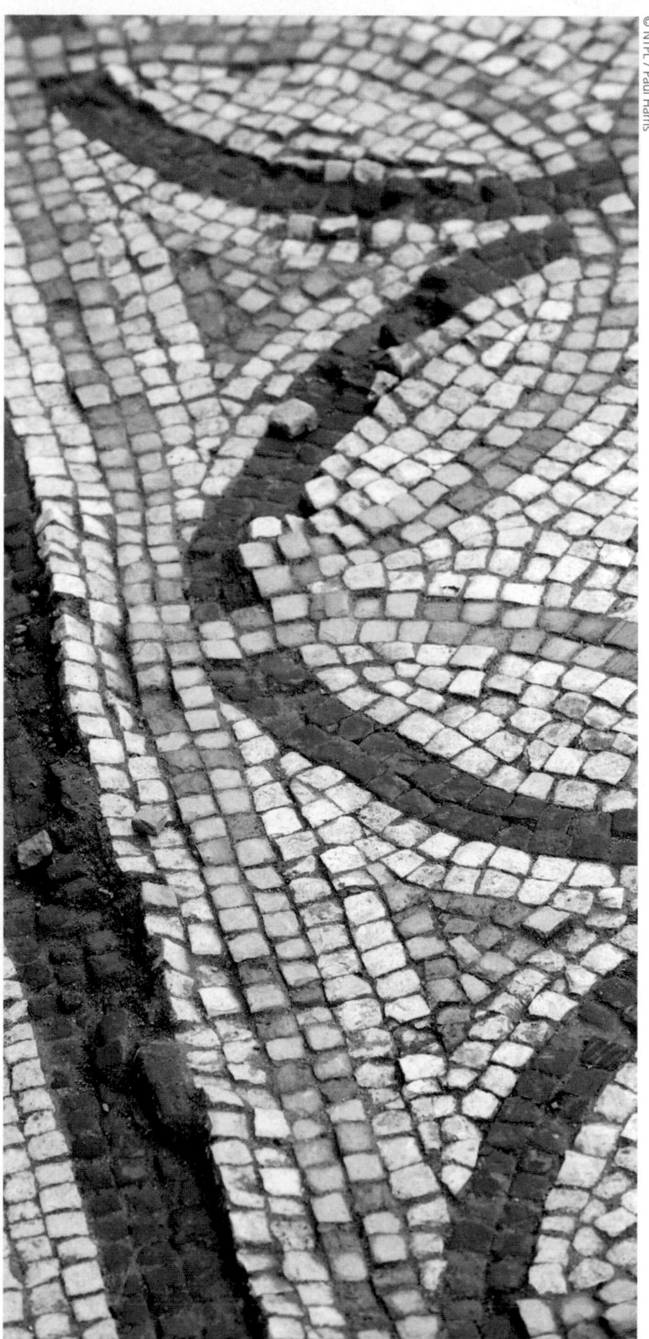

Chedworth Roman Villa

For **special events** held throughout the year, see the index at the end of the book.

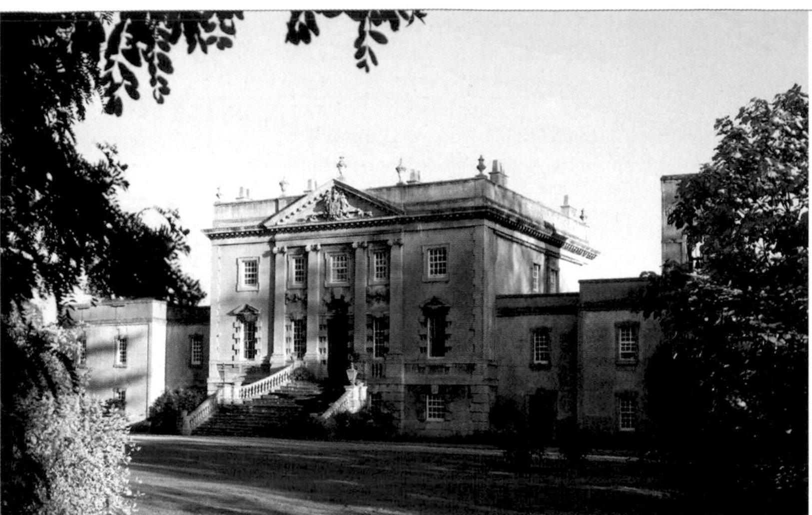

FRAMPTON COURT, THE ORANGERY AND FRAMPTON MANOR

FRAMPTON-ON-SEVERN, GLOUCESTERSHIRE GL2 7EP

www.framptoncourtestate.co.uk

Tel: 01452 740268 **Fax:** 01452 740698

E-mail: events@framptoncourtestate.co.uk

Owner: Mr & Mrs Rollo Clifford **Contact:** Janie Clifford, Frampton Manor

The Cliffords have lived in Frampton since the 11th century. Frampton Court, built in 1731, has a superb panelled interior housing period furniture, china and 19th century 'Frampton Flora' water-colours. Bed and breakfast and house parties available.

The 18th century 'Strawberry Hill gothic' Orangery sits – breath-takingly – at the end of the ornamental canal in the garden at Frampton Court, and is now a self-catering holiday house. Half-timbered Frampton Manor is said to be the birth-place of 'Fair Rosamund' Clifford, mistress of Henry II. The walled garden is a plantsman's delight. The 16th century Wool Barn is contemporary with the main part of the house. A whole day is recommended for tours of both houses and gardens.

Location: MAP 6:M12, OS Ref. SO750 078. In Frampton, ¼m SW of B4071, 3m SW of M5/J13.

Open: Frampton Court and Frampton Manor by appointment for groups (10+). Frampton Manor Garden: Mon & Fri 2.30–5pm, 18 Apr–22 Jul.

Admission: Frampton Court House & Garden: £8. Manor, Garden & Wool Barn: £8. Garden only: £4. Wool Barn only £2.

Filming, parkland for hire. Pan Global Plants in walled garden (01452 741641). Wedding receptions. Partial. WC Frampton Manor. For groups by arrangement in the Wool Barn at Frampton Manor. Usually by family members. For both houses at Frampton Manor. House parties and B&B at Frampton Court contact Gillian Keightley 01452 740267; self-catering holidays at The Orangery 01452 740698. By arrangement. Frampton Country Fair 11 Sep 2011.

GLOUCESTER CATHEDRAL

Cathedral Office, College Green, Gloucester GL1 2LR

Tel: 01452 508211 **Fax:** 01452 300469

E-mail: lin@gloucestercathedral.org.uk **www.gloucestercathedral.org.uk**

Contact: Mrs L Henderson

Daily worship and rich musical tradition continue in this abbey church founded 1300 years ago. It has a Norman nave with massive cylindrical pillars, a magnificent east window with medieval glass and glorious fan-vaulted cloisters. You can also find the tombs of King Edward II and Robert, Duke of Normandy.

Location: MAP 6:M11, OS Ref. SO832 188. Off Westgate Street in central Gloucester.

Open: Open: Daily 7.30am (term time closed 8.45am–9.15am) to 6pm. Sun 11.45am–2.45pm.

Admission: £5 donation requested.

Partial. WC. By arrangement. None. In grounds, on leads.

© Britainonview

Hailes Abbey

HAILES ABBEY

Nr Winchcombe, Cheltenham, Gloucestershire GL54 5PB

Tel/Fax: 01242 602398 **E-mail:** customers@english-heritage.org.uk

www.english-heritage.org.uk/hailes

Owner: English Heritage & National Trust **Contact:** Visitor Operations Staff

Seventeen cloister arches and extensive excavated remains in lovely surroundings of an abbey founded by Richard, Earl of Cornwall, in 1246. Let the audio tour bring this Cistercian Abbey to life and see sculptures, stonework and other site finds in the museum.

Location: MAP 6:O10, OS Ref. SP050 300. 2m NE of Winchcombe off B4632.

Open: 1 Apr–30 Jun: daily, 10am–5pm. 1 Jul–31 Aug: daily, 10am–6pm. 1–30 Sep: daily 10am–5pm. 1–31 Oct: daily, 10am–4pm. Closed 1 Nov–31 Mar 2011.

Admission: Adult £4, Child £2, Conc. £3.40. EH Members Free. NT members Free, but charge for audio tour (£1) and special events. Group discount available. Opening times and prices are valid until 31st March 2011, after this date details are subject to change please visit www.english-heritage.org.uk for the most up-to-date information.

By arrangement. Limited for coaches. On leads.

HIDCOTE MANOR GARDEN

Hidcote Bartrim, Nr Chipping Campden, Gloucestershire GL55 6LR

Tel: 01386 438333 **Fax:** 01386 438817

Owner: National Trust **Contact:** Visitor Services Manager

Delightful and interesting garden created in early 20th c.

Location: MAP 6:O9, OS Ref. SP176 429. 4m NE of Chipping Campden, 1m E of B4632 off B4081. At Mickleton ¼ m E of Kiftsgate Court. Coaches are not permitted through Chipping Campden High Street.

For rare and unusual plants visit the **plant sales** index at the end of the book.

© Stephen Randall Photography

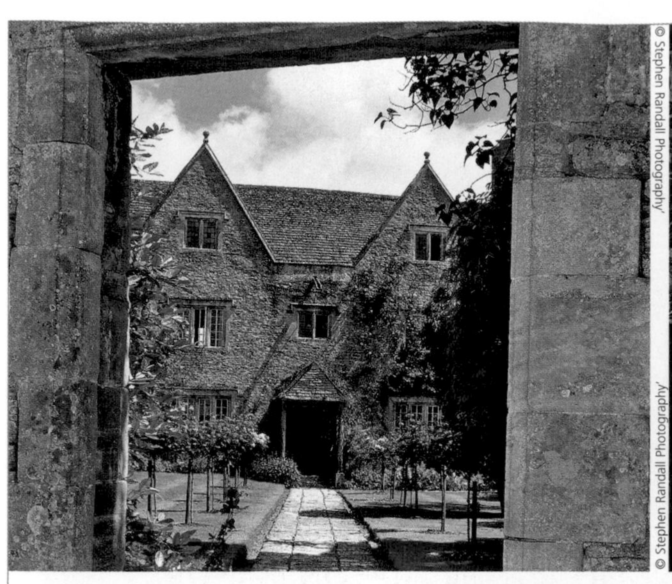

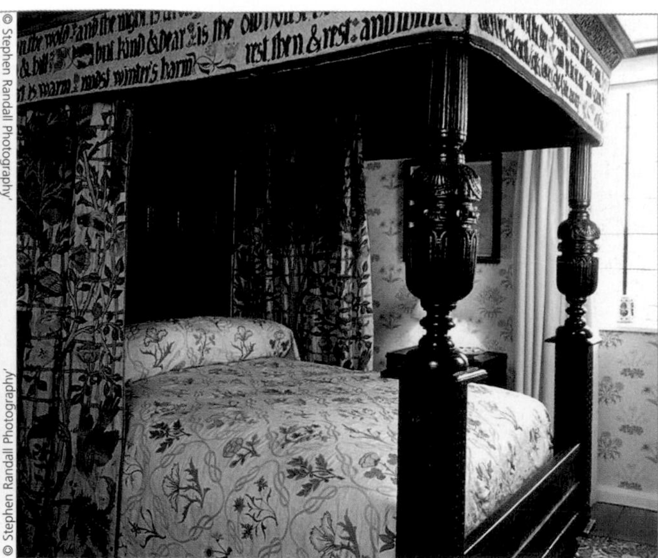

KELMSCOTT MANOR

KELMSCOTT, NR LECHLADE, GLOUCESTERSHIRE GL7 3HJ

www.kelmscottmanor.org.uk

Tel: 01367 252486 **Fax:** 01367 253754 **E-mail:** admin@kelmscottmanor.org.uk

Owner: Society of Antiquaries of London **Contact:** Jane Milne

Kelmscott Manor, a Grade I listed Tudor farmhouse adjacent to the River Thames, was William Morris' summer residence from 1871 until his death in 1896. Morris loved Kelmscott Manor, which seemed to him to have 'grown up out of the soil'. Its beautiful gardens with barns, dovecote, meadow and stream provided a constant source of inspiration. The house contains an outstanding collection of the possessions and work of Morris, his family and associates, including furniture, textiles, pictures, carpets and ceramics.

Location: MAP 6:P12, OS Ref. SU252 988. At SE end of the village, 2m due E of Lechlade, off the Lechlade – Faringdon Road.

Open: House and Garden Apr–Oct: Wednesdays and Saturdays, 11am – 5pm (Ticket office opens 10.30am). Last admission to the house, 4.30pm. No advance bookings on public open days. House has limited capacity; timed ticket system operates.

Group visits Apr–Oct: Thursdays. Must be booked in advance.

Admission: Adult £9, Child/Student £4.50. Garden only: £2.50. Carer accompanying disabled person Free.

Special Events: Please see the website

No photography in house. WCs. Licensed. Licensed. By arrangement. 10 mins walk. Limited for coaches. Guide dogs only.

© Britainonview

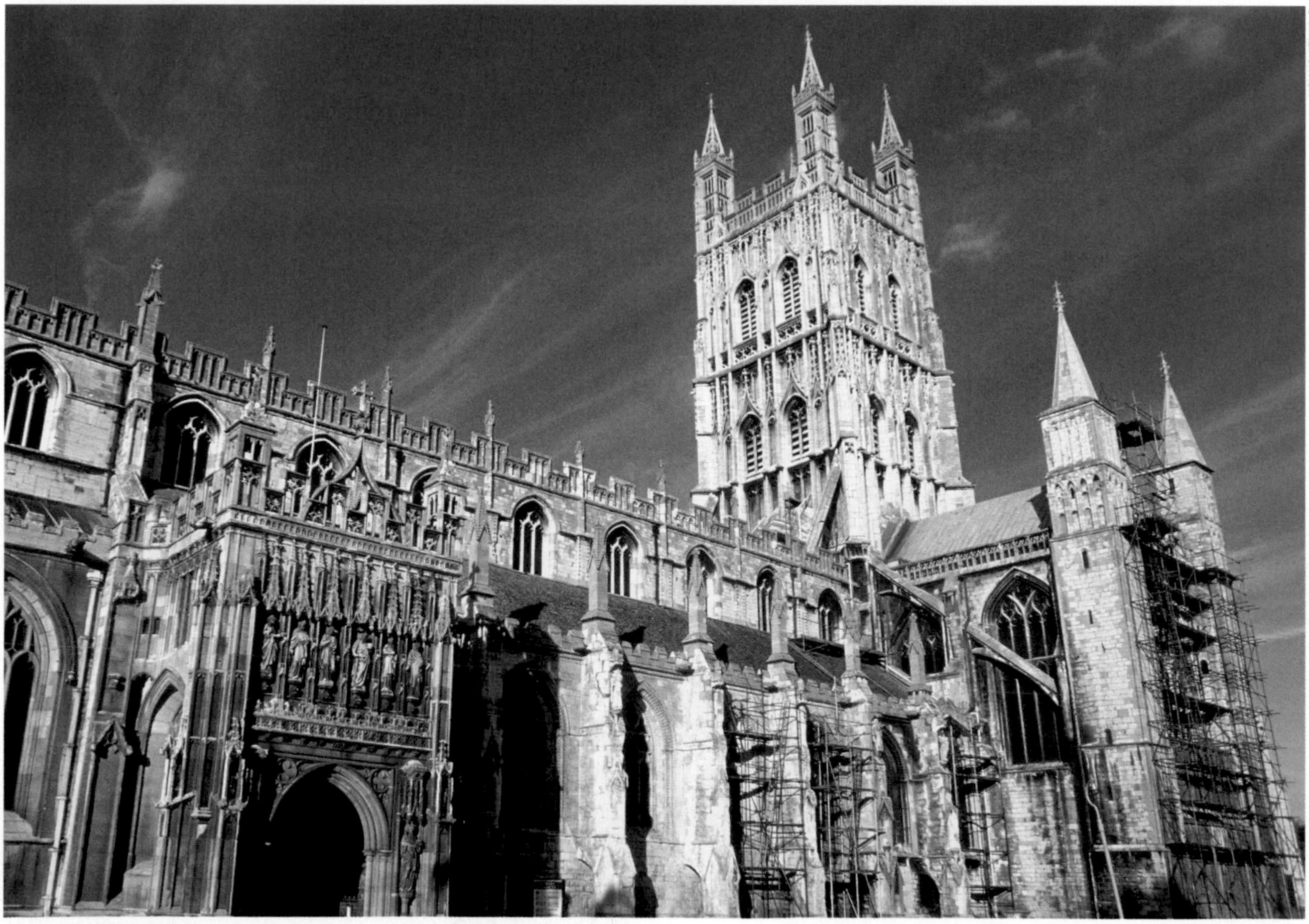

Gloucester Cathedral

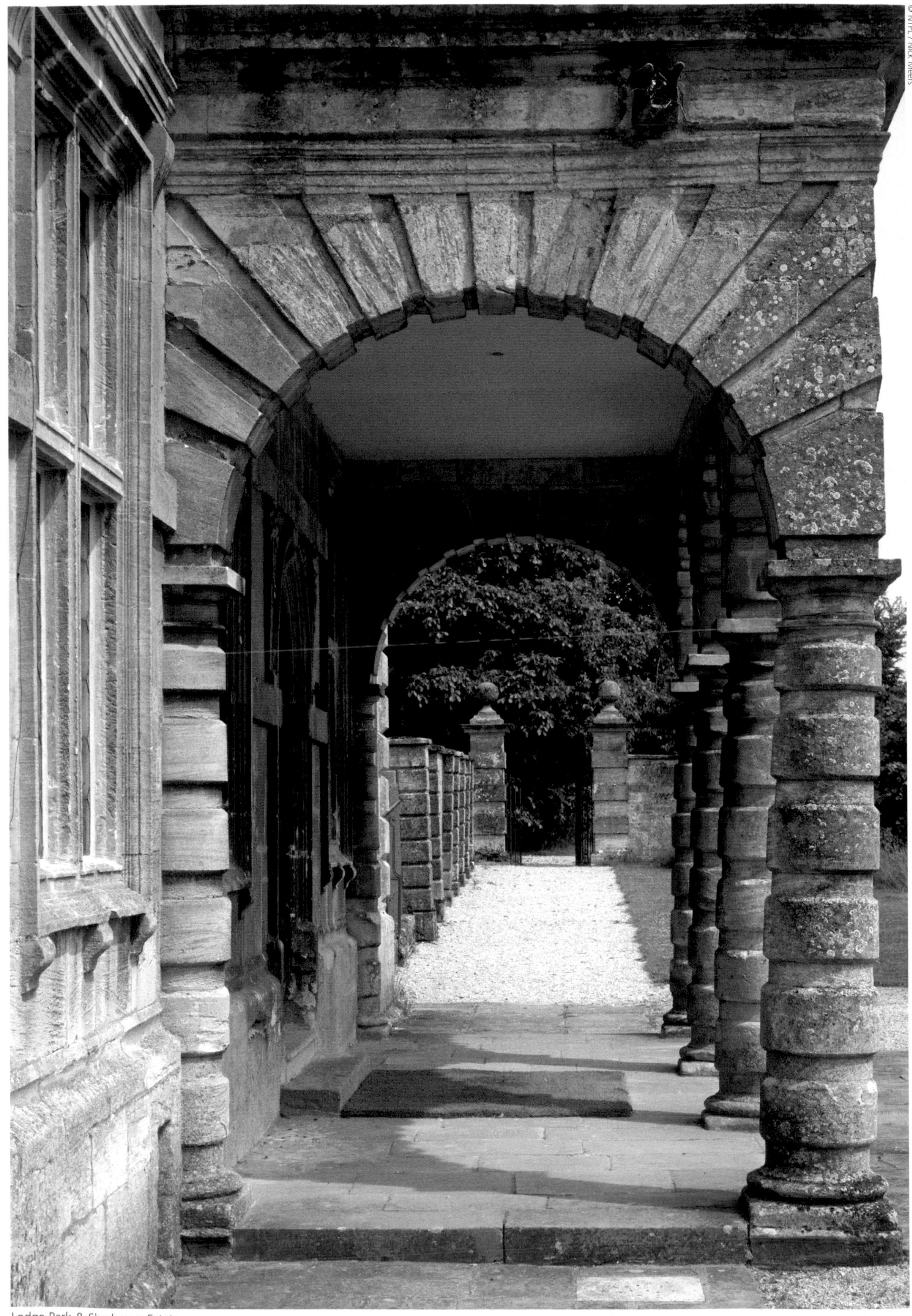

Lodge Park & Sherborne Estate

KIFTSGATE COURT GARDENS

CHIPPING CAMPDEN, GLOUCESTERSHIRE GL55 6LN

www.kiftsgate.co.uk

Tel/Fax: 01386 438777 **E-mail:** info@kiftsgate.co.uk

Owner: Mr and Mrs J G Chambers **Contact:** Mr J G Chambers

Magnificently situated garden on the edge of the Cotswold escarpment with views towards the Malvern Hills. Many unusual shrubs and plants including tree peonies, abutilons, specie and old-fashioned roses. Winner HHA/Christie's Garden of the Year Award 2003.

Location: MAP 6:O9, OS Ref. SP173 430. 4m NE of Chipping Campden. ¼ m W of Hidcote Garden.

Open: May, Jun, Jul, Sat–Wed, 12 noon–6pm. August, Sat–Wed, 2pm–6pm. Apr & Sept, Sun, Mon & Wed, 2pm–6pm.

Admission: Adult: £7.00, Child £2.50. Groups (20+) £6.00.

Partial. Limited for coaches. Guide dogs only.

PAINSWICK ROCOCO GARDEN

PAINSWICK, GLOUCESTERSHIRE GL6 6TH

www.rococogarden.org.uk

Tel: 01452 813204 **Fax:** 01452 814888 **E-mail:** info@rococogarden.org.uk

Owner: Painswick Rococo Garden Trust **Contact:** P R Moir

Unique 18th century garden restoration situated in a hidden 6 acre Cotswold combe. Charming contemporary buildings are juxtaposed with winding woodland walks and formal vistas. Famous for its early spring show of snowdrops. Anniversary maze.

Location: MAP 6:N11, OS Ref. SO864 106. ½ m NW of village of Painswick on B4073.

Open: 10 Jan–31 Oct: daily, 11am–5pm.

Admission: Adult £6, Child £3, OAP £5. Family (2+2) £16. Free introductory talk for pre-booked groups (20+).

Partial. WC. Licensed. In grounds, on leads.

LODGE PARK & SHERBORNE ESTATE

Aldsworth, Nr Cheltenham, Gloucestershire GL54 3PP

Tel: 01451 844130 **Fax:** 01451 844131 **Email:** lodgepark@nationaltrust.org.uk

www.nationaltrust.org.uk/lodgepark

Owner: National Trust **Contact:** Visitor Services Manager

Lodge Park is a unique survival of a 17th century Grandstand, Deer Course and Park. The interior has been reconstructed to its original form and is the first project of its kind undertaken by the Trust relying totally on archaeological evidence. The park was designed by Charles Bridgeman in 1725.

Location: MAP 6:O11, OS Ref. SP146 123. 3m E of Northleach, approach only from A40. Sherborne Park walks start from Ewe Pen car park. Approach from A40 towards Sherborne village.

Open: Grandstand & Deer Park: Mid Mar–End Oct: Fri–Sun & BH Mon, 11am–4pm. Property occasionally closes for weddings. Please tel. to confirm opening times. Sherborne Park open all year round, walks start from the Ewe Pen car park near Sherborne village.

Admission: Adult £5.25, Child £3, Family £13.50. (*2010 prices).

Video shows during the day. Civil ceremonies & receptions. WCs. By arrangement. Limited for coaches. Guide dogs only. Reenactment events, outdoor theatre, concerts, children's trails and family events throught the year. More information on www.nationaltrust.org.uk/lodgepark.

NEWARK PARK

Ozleworth, Wotton-Under-Edge, Gloucestershire GL12 7PZ

Tel: 01453 842644 **Fax: 01453 845308** **Infoline:** 01793 817666

www.nationaltrust.org.uk

Owner: National Trust **Contact:** Michael Claydon

Tudor hunting lodge converted into castellated country house.

Location: MAP 2:P1, OS Ref172. ST786 934. 1½ m E of Wotton-under-Edge, 1¾ m S of Junction of A4135 & B4058, follow signs for Ozleworth, House signposted from main road.

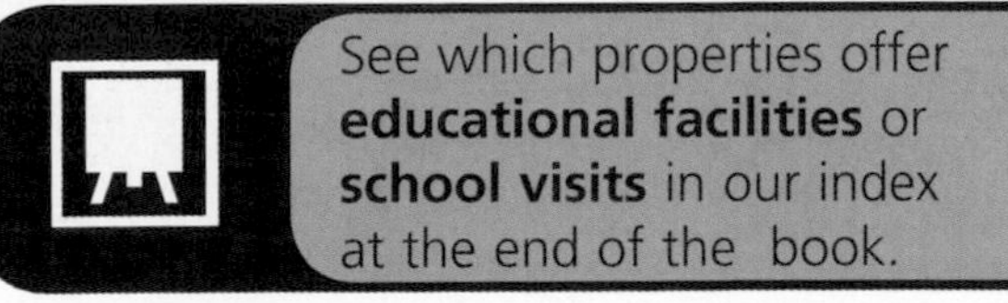

See which properties offer **educational facilities** or **school visits** in our index at the end of the book.

© NTPL / Matthew Antrobus

Newark Park

RODMARTON MANOR

CIRENCESTER, GLOUCESTERSHIRE GL7 6PF

www.rodmarton-manor.co.uk

Tel: 01285 841253
E-mail: sarahpoperodmarton@yahoo.co.uk
Owner: Mr & Mrs Simon Biddulph **Contact:** Sarah Pope

A Cotswold Arts and Crafts house, one of the last great country houses to be built in the traditional way and containing beautiful furniture, ironwork, china and needlework specially made for the house. The large garden complements the house and contains many areas of great beauty and character including the magnificent herbaceous borders, topiary, roses, rockery and kitchen garden. Available as a film location and for small functions.

Location: MAP 6:N12, OS Ref. ST943 977. Off A433 between Cirencester and Tetbury.

Open: House & Garden: Easter Monday & May–Sept (Weds, Sats & BHs), 2–5pm (Not guided tours). Garden only, for snowdrops,: 6, 13 & 17 and 20 Feb: from 1.30pm. Groups please book. Individuals need not book. Guided tours of the house (last about 1hr) may be booked for groups (15+) at any time of year (minimum group charge of £120 applies). Groups (5+) may book guided or unguided tours of the garden at other times.

Admission: House & Garden: £8, Child (5–15yrs) £4. Garden only: £5, Child (5–15yrs) £1. Guided tour of Garden: Entry fee plus £40 per group.

Colour guidebook & postcards on sale. Available for filming. No photography in house. WCs in garden. Garden & ground floor. Open days and groups by appointment. By arrangement. Guide dogs only.

SEZINCOTE

MORETON-IN-MARSH, GLOUCESTERSHIRE GL56 9AW

www.sezincote.co.uk

Tel: 01386 700444
Owner/Contact: Dr E Peake

Exotic oriental water garden by Repton and Daniell. Large semi-circular orangery. House by S P Cockerell in Indian style was the inspiration for Brighton Pavilion.

Location: MAP 6:P10, OS Ref. SP183 324. 2½m SW of Moreton-in-Marsh. Turn W along A44 to Broadway and left into gateway just before Bourton-on-the-Hill (opposite the gate to Batsford Park, then 1m drive.

Open: Garden: Thurs, Fris & BH Mons, 2–6pm (dusk if earlier) throughout the year except Dec. House: Open as Garden but closed Oct–April. Groups at any time by written appointment. Tea and cake in Orangery when house open.

Admission: House: Adult £10 (guided tour). Garden: Adult £5, Child £1.50 (under 5yrs Free).

Gravel paths. Café. Obligatory. Guide dogs only.

SNOWSHILL MANOR

Snowshill, Nr Broadway, Gloucestershire WR12 7JU
Tel: 01386 852410 **Fax:** 01386 842822
Owner: National Trust **Contact:** The Property Manager

Manor house with stunning garden. View the huge collection of varied items.

Location: MAP 6:O10, OS Ref. SP096 339. 2½ m SW of Broadway.

Woodchester Mansion

STANWAY HOUSE & WATER GARDEN

STANWAY, CHELTENHAM, GLOS GL54 5PQ

www.stanwayfountain.co.uk

Tel: 01386 584528 **Fax:** 01386 584688 **E-mail:** stanwayhse@btconnect.com

Owner: The Earl of Wemyss and March **Contact:** Debbie Lewis

"As perfect and pretty a Cotswold manor house as anyone is likely to see" (Fodor's Great Britain 1998 guidebook). Stanway's beautiful architecture, furniture, parkland and village are now complemented by the restored 18th century water garden and the magnificent fountain – 300 feet – making it the tallest garden fountain and gravity fountain in the world. Teas available. Beer for sale. Wedding reception venue.

Location: MAP 6:O10, OS Ref. SP061 323. N of Winchcombe, just off B4077.

Open: House & Garden: June–Aug: Tue & Thur, 2–5pm. Private tours by arrangement at other times.

Admission: Adult £7, Child £2.00, OAP £5.00. Garden only: Adult £4.50, Child £1.50, OAP £3.50.

Film & photographic location. Wedding receptions. By arrangement. In grounds on leads.

ST MARY'S CHURCH

Kempley, Gloucestershire GL18 2AT

Tel: 0117 9750700 **E-mail:** customers@english-heritage.org.uk

www.english-heritage.org.uk/stmarys

Owner: English Heritage **Contact:** The South West Regional Office

A delightful Norman church with superb wall paintings from the 12th–14th centuries which were only discovered beneath whitewash in 1871.

Location: MAP 6:M10, OS Ref. SO670 313. On minor road. 1 mile N of Kempley off B4024; 6 miles NE of Ross-on-Wye.

Open: 1 Mar–31 Oct: daily, 10am–6pm. Telephone for appointment in winter.

Admission: Free. Opening times and prices are valid until 31st March 2011, after this date details are subject to change please visit www.english-heritage.org.uk for the most up-to-date information.

SUDELEY CASTLE

Winchcombe , Gloucestershire GL54 5JD

Tel: 01242 602308 **Fax:** 01242 602959 **E-mail:** enquiries@sudeley.org.uk

www.sudeleycastle.co.uk

Owner: Lady Ashcombe, Henry and Mollie Dent-Brocklehurst **Contact:** Kevin Jones

Award-winning gardens and medieval ruins surround Sudeley Castle, nestled in the Cotswold Hills. Fascinating exhibitions explore Sudeley's royal connections spanning over 1000 years; Katherine Parr is entombed in St Mary's Church within the grounds. Tours of the private apartments are available on Tuesdays, Wednesdays and Thursdays.

Location: MAP 6:O10, OS Ref. SP032 277. 8m NE of Cheltenham, at Winchcombe off B4632. From Bristol or Birmingham M5/J9. Take A46 then B4077 towards Stow-on-the-Wold. Bus: Castleways to Winchcombe. Rail: Cheltenham Station 8m. Air: Birmingham or Bristol 45m.

Open: March–October, daily, 10.30am–5pm.

Admission: Adult £7.20, Child (5-15yrs) £4.20, Children under 5 Free, Conc. £6.20, Family (2+2) £20.80. Group discounts 10+.

Connoisseur Tours of the private apartments Tue, Wed & Thur only.

Corporate & private events, wedding receptions. Licensed. By arrangement.

Guide dogs only.

© Adrian Mason

Chavenage

TYTHE BARN

Tanhouse Farm, Churchend, Frampton-on-Severn, Gloucestershire GL2 7EH

Tel: 01452 741072 **E-mail:** cottages@tanhouse-farm.co.uk

Owner/Contact: Michael Williams

Tythe Barn Grade II* c1650 recently restored in conjunction with English Heritage. Barn incorporating cow shed, the exceptional length and width of the timber framed structure upon a low stone plinth with box framing and undaubed wattle panels marks it out from other contemporary farm buildings.

Location: MAP 6:M12, OS Ref. SP014 206. Southern end of Frampton-on-Severn, close to church.

Open: By arrangement all year 10am–4pm.

Admission: Free.

Partial. Obligatory. By arrangement. Limited. None for coaches.

WESTBURY COURT GARDEN

Westbury-on-Severn, Gloucestershire GL14 1PD

Tel: 01452 760461

Owner: National Trust **Contact:** The Head Gardener

Dutch water garden with canals and yew hedges.

Location: MAP 6:M11, OS Ref. SO718 138. 9m SW of Gloucester on A48.

WHITTINGTON COURT

Cheltenham, Gloucestershire GL54 4HF

Tel: 01242 820556 **Fax:** 01242 820218

Owner: Mr & Mrs Jack Stringer **Contact:** Mrs J Stringer

Elizabethan manor house. Family possessions including ceramics, antique and modern glass, fossils and fabrics.

Location: MAP 6:N11, OS Ref. SP014 206. 4m E of Cheltenham on N side of A40.

Open: 23 Apr–8 May & 13–29 Aug: 2–5pm.

Admission: Adult £5, Child £1, OAP £4.

WOODCHESTER MANSION

NYMPSFIELD, STONEHOUSE, GLOUCESTERSHIRE GL10 3TS

www.woodchestermansion.org.uk

Tel: 01453 861541 **Fax:** 01453 861337 **E-mail:** office@woodchestermansion.org.uk

Operated by: Woodchester Mansion Trust Ltd.

Location: MAP 6:M12, OS Ref. SO809 013. Near Nympsfield off the B4066 Stroud-Dursley road.

Hidden in a wooded valley near Stroud is one of the most intriguing houses in the country. Woodchester Mansion was started in the mid-1850s, but abandoned incomplete. It offers a unique insight into traditional building techniques. The Trust's repair programme includes courses in stone masonry and building conservation.

Open: Easter–Oct: Suns & 1st Sat of every month & BH weekends inc. Mon. Jul–Aug: Sat & Sun.

Admission: Adult £5.50, Child (under 14 yrs) Free, Conc £4.50. Group rates available.

Obligatory. Limited.

Berkeley Castle

■ **Owner**

Sir Benjamin Slade Bt

■ **Contact**

The Events Team
North Newton
Nr Taunton
Somerset TA7 0BU

Tel: 01278 661076
Fax: 01278 661074
E-mail: info@maunselhouse.co.uk

■ **Location**

MAP 2:M4
OS Ref. ST302 303

Less than 20m Bridgwater 4m, Bristol 20m, Taunton 7m, M5/J24, A38 to North Petherton. 2½m SE of A38 at North Petherton via North Newton.

■ **Opening Times**

Monday-Friday 9am-5pm. Pre-booked only.

Coaches & groups welcome by appointment.

Caravan rally field available.

■ **Admission**

Price on application.

Conference/Function

ROOM	SIZE	MAX CAPACITY
Ballroom	70' x 30'	120
Oak Room	25 'x 20'	30

MAUNSEL HOUSE

www.maunselhouse.co.uk

Maunsel House is a magnificent 13th century Manor set in 100 acres of stunning parkland at the heart of a sprawling 2,000 acre Estate, comprising of farms, lakes, woodlands, walnut groves, orchards, Somerset wetlands, cottages and ancient barns.

The ancestral seat of the Slade family and home of the 7th baronet Sir Benjamin Slade, the house can boast such visitors as Geoffrey Chaucer who wrote part of the Canterbury Tales whilst staying here.

The beautiful grounds and spacious rooms provide both privacy and a unique atmosphere for any special event. Available for weddings, we are licensed for civil ceremonies outside in the antique bandstand or inside in the large regency ballroom, the wedding breakfast can be under the garlanded pergola in the walled garden or in the ballroom surrounded by old masters on the walls. There are thirteen luxurious bedrooms, many with four poster beds crowned by the Kings Room which holds the great bed of Maunsel, an Elizabethan four poster 8'6" wide and 6' long.

There are four picturesque cottages on the estate, all within walking distance of the House offering a further fourteen bedrooms, the cottages are available for additional accommodation for the weddings and holiday breaks.

Maunsel is also available for house hire, celebration parties, conferences, film shooting and photo shoots.

Please contact the events team for further information.

Functions.

Partial.

In grounds, on leads.

NO 1 ROYAL CRESCENT

BATH BA1 2LR

www.bath-preservation-trust.org.uk

Tel: 01225 428126 Fax: 01225 481850
E-mail: no1museum@bptrust.org.uk
Owner: Bath Preservation Trust **Contact:** Victoria Barwell – Curator

No. 1 Royal Crescent is a magnificently restored and authentically furnished Georgian Town House. From the elegant drawing room to the splendidly equipped Georgian kitchen, it creates a vivid picture of fashionable life in 18th century Bath.

Location: MAP 2:P2, OS Ref. ST746 653. M4/J18. A46 to Bath. ¼m NW of city centre.

Open: 19 Feb–10 Dec, Tues–Sun, 10.30am–5pm. BH Mons. Closes 4pm in Nov. Open Good Fri. Last admission 30 mins before closing. Evening tours and other times by arrangement.

Admission: Adult £6, Child (5–16yrs) £2.50, Conc £5, Family £12. Groups: £4.

Unsuitable. The Royal Crescent & Bath centre.

BARRINGTON COURT

Barrington, Ilminster, Somerset TA19 0NQ
Tel: 01460 241938 **Info:** 01460 242614
www.nationaltrust.org.uk
Owner: National Trust **Contact:** Visitor Services Manager

Tudor manor house with enchanting formal garden and Kitchen Garden.

Location: MAP 2:N5, OS Ref. ST395 181. In Barrington village, 5m NE of Ilminster, on B3168.

BECKFORD'S TOWER & MUSEUM

Lansdown Road, Bath BA1 9BH
Tel: 01225 460705 **Fax:** 01225 481850 **E-mail:** beckford@bptrust.org.uk
Owner: Bath Preservation Trust **Contact:** The Administrator

Built in 1827 for eccentric William Beckford and recently restored by Bath Preservation Trust. The tower is a striking feature of the Bath skyline.

Location: MAP 2:P2, OS Ref. ST735 676. Lansdown Road, 2m NNW of city centre.

Open: Easter weekend–end of Oct: Sats, Suns & BH Mons, 10.30am–5pm.

Admission: Adult £3, Child £1.50, Conc. £2, Family £8.

BREAN DOWN

Brean, North Somerset
Tel: 01934 844518 **www.nationaltrust.org.uk**
Owner: National Trust **Contact:** Administrator

Brean Down, rich in wildlife and history, is one of the most striking landmarks of the Somerset coastline, extending 1½m into the Bristol Channel. A Palmerston Fort built in 1865 and then re-armed in World War II, provides a unique insight into Brean's past.

Location: MAP 2:M3, OS Ref. ST290 590. Between Weston-super-Mare and Burnham-on-Sea about 8m from M5/J22. Rail: Highbridge 5m.

Open: All year.

Admission: Free. Donations welcome.

The cliffs are extremely steep. Please stay on the main paths and wear suitable footwear. (Not NT.) Partial. WC in café. (Not NT.) Guided walks. On leads.

Barrington Court

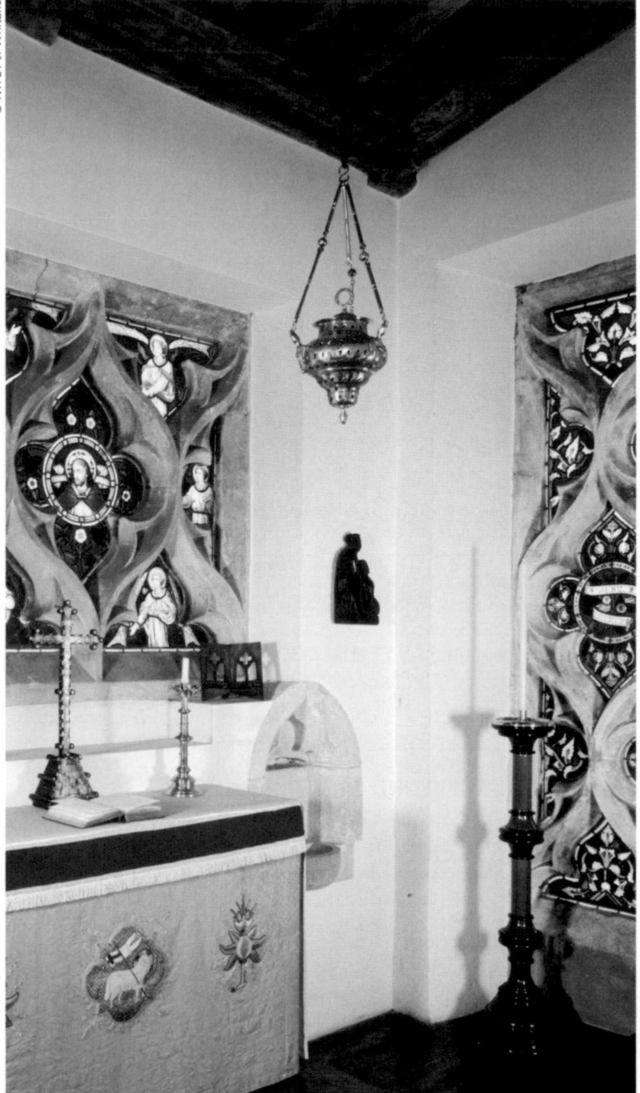

Clevedon Court

CLEVEDON COURT

Tickenham Road, Clevedon, North Somerset BS21 6QU

Tel/Fax: 01275 872257 **E-mail:** clevedon.court@nationaltrust.org.uk

Owner: National Trust **Contact:** The Administrator

Outstanding manor house, with much 14th century work remaining, set in a beautifully landscaped 18th century terraced garden. Home to the Elton family since 1709. Visitors will see striking examples of Eltonware pottery and a fascinating collection of Nailsea glass.

Location: MAP 2:N2, OS ref: 172:ST4237161 1.5m E of Clevedon, on Bristol road (B3130) signposted from M5, exit 20.

Open: 3 Apr–29 Sept, 2–5pm (entry to house by timed ticket, on a first come, first served basis, car park opens 1.15pm). Open Wed, Thur, Sun & BH Mons.

Admission: Gift Aid (Standard Admission prices in bracket): £7 (£6.30), Child £3.30 (£3). Garden only: Adult £3.30 (£3).

COLERIDGE COTTAGE

35 Lime Street, Nether Stowey, Bridgwater, Somerset TA5 1NQ

Tel: 01278 732662

Owner: National Trust **Contact:** The Visitor Services Manager, Dunster Castle

The home of Samuel Taylor Coleridge 1797–1800.

Location: MAP 2:M4, OS Ref. ST191 399. At W end of Lime St, opposite the Ancient Mariner pub, 8m W of Bridgwater.

THE BUILDING OF BATH MUSEUM

The Countess of Huntingdon's Chapel, The Vineyards, The Paragon, Bath BA1 5NA

Tel: 01225 333895 **Fax:** 01225 445473 **E-mail:** enquiries@bathmuseum.co.uk

Owner: Bath Preservation Trust **Contact:** The Administrator

Discover the essence of life in Georgian Bath.

Location: MAP 2:P2, OS Ref. ST751 655. 5 mins walk from city centre. Bath M4/J18.

Open: Feb–Nov: Tue–Sun & BH Mons, 10.30am–5pm (last adm. 4.30pm).

Admission: Adult £4, Child £1.50, Conc. £3.

CLEEVE ABBEY

Washford, Nr Watchet, Somerset TA23 0PS

Tel: 01984 640377 **Email:** customers@english-heritage.org.uk

www.english-heritage.org.uk/cleeve

Owner: English Heritage **Contact:** Visitor Operations Staff

There are few monastic sites where you will see such a complete set of cloister buildings, including the refectory with its magnificent timber roof. This Cistercian abbey was built in the 13th century and its fine collection of heraldic tiles is the subject of an ongoing high profile research project.

Location: MAP 2:L4, OS Ref. ST047 407. In Washford, ¼m S of A39.

Open: 1 Apr–30 Jun: daily, 10am–5pm. 1 Jul–31 Aug: daily, 10am–6pm. 1–30 Sep: daily, 10am–5pm. 1–31 Oct: daily, 10am–4pm. Closed 1 Nov–31 Mar '11.

Admission: Adult £4, Child £2, Conc. £3.40. 15% discount for groups (11+). EH Members free. Opening times and prices are valid until 31st March 2011, after this date details are subject to change please visit www.english-heritage.org.uk for the most up-to-date information.

Partial. By arrangement. Limited for coaches. In grounds.

COTHAY MANOR & GARDENS

GREENHAM, WELLINGTON, SOMERSET TA21 0JR

www.cothaymanor.co.uk

Tel: 01823 672283 **E-mail:** cothaymanor@btinternet.com

Owner/Contact: Mr & Mrs Alastair Robb

The magical, romantic, gardens of Cothay surround what is said to be the most perfect example of a small classic medieval manor. Many garden rooms, each a garden in itself, are set off a 200yd yew walk. In addition there is a bog garden with azaleas, and drifts of primuli, fine trees, cottage garden, courtyards, and river walk. A plantsman's paradise. The manor is open to groups throughout the year.

Location: MAP 2:L5, OS Ref. ST085 212.

Open: Garden: 1st Sunday in April until end Sept: Tues, Weds, Thurs, Suns, & BHs, 11am–5pm, last entry 4pm. On Sundays we open the manor for the general public with two guided groups, one at 11.45am, and the other at 2.45pm. Groups (20+) by appointment throughout the year.

Admission: Please go to our website for details: www.cothaymanor.co.uk.

No photography in house. Not in house.

For **accommodation** in the South West, see our special index at the end of the book.

Hestercombe Gardens

DODINGTON HALL

Nr Nether Stowey, Bridgwater, Somerset TA5 1LF

Tel: 01278 741400

Owner: Lady Gass **Contact:** P Quinn (occupier)

Small Tudor manor house on the lower slopes of the Quantocks. Great Hall with oak roof. Semi-formal garden with roses and shrubs.

Location: MAP 2:L4, OS Ref. ST172 405. ½m from A39, 11m W of Bridgwater, 7m E of Williton.

Open: 5–15 June, 2–5pm.

Admission: Donations to Dodington Church.

No inside photography. Unsuitable. Limited. No coach parking. Guide dogs only.

DUNSTER CASTLE

Dunster, Nr Minehead, Somerset TA24 6SL

Tel: 01643 821314 **Fax:** 01643 823000

Owner: National Trust **Contact:** Visitor Services Manager

17th c house with fine oak staircase and plasterwork.

Location: MAP 2:K4, OS Ref. SS995 435. In Dunster, 3m SE of Minehead.

DUNSTER WORKING WATERMILL

Mill Lane, Dunster, Nr Minehead, Somerset TA24 6SW

Tel: 01643 821759

Owner: National Trust **Contact:** The Tenant

Built on the site of a mill mentioned in the Domesday Survey of 1086.

Location: MAP 2:K4, OS Ref. SS995 435. On River Avill, beneath Castle Tor, approach via Mill Lane or Castle gardens on foot.

For unique **Civil wedding** venues see our index at the end of the book.

ENGLISHCOMBE TITHE BARN

Rectory Farmhouse, Englishcombe, Bath BA2 9DU

Tel: 01225 425073 **E-mail:** jennie.walker@ukonline.co.uk

Contact: Jennie Walker

An early 14th century cruck-framed Tithe Barn built by Bath Abbey.

Location: MAP 2:P2, OS172 Ref. ST716 628. Adjacent to Englishcombe Village Church. 1m SW of Bath.

Open: BHs, 2–6pm. Other times by appointment.

Admission: Free.

FAIRFIELD

Stogursey, Bridgwater, Somerset TA5 1PU

Tel: 01278 732251

Owner: Lady Acland-Hood Gass **Contact:** Fairfield Estate

Elizabethan and medieval house. Occupied by the same family (Acland-Hoods and their ancestors) for over 800 years. Woodland garden. Views of Quantocks and the sea. House described in Simon Jenkins' book 'England's Thousand Best Houses'.

Location: MAP 2:L4, OS Ref. ST187 430. 11m W of Bridgwater, 8m E of Williton. From A39 Bridgwater/Minehead turn North. House 1m W of Stogursey on road to Stringston.

Open: 13 Apr–30 May & 8–22 Jun: Wed–Fri and Bank Holiday Mondays (not open on Good Friday, 22 Apr). Guided house tours at 2.30 & 3.30pm. Groups also at other times by arrangement. Garden also open for NGS and other charities on dates advertised in Spring. Advisable to contact to confirm dates.

Admission: £5 in aid of Stogursey Church.

No inside photography. Obligatory. No coach parking.

Guide dogs only.

FARLEIGH HUNGERFORD CASTLE

Farleigh Hungerford, Bath, Somerset BA2 7RS

Tel/Fax: 01225 754026 **E-mail:** customers@english-heritage.org.uk

www.english-heritage.org.uk/farleighhungerford

Owner: English Heritage **Contact:** Visitor Operations Staff

Extensive ruins of a 14th century castle with a splendid chapel containing rare medieval wall paintings, stained glass and the fine tomb of Sir Thomas Hungerford, builder of the castle. Displays in the Priest's House and a complimentary audio tour tell of the castle's sinister past.

Location: MAP 2:P3, OS173, ST801 577. In Farleigh Hungerford 3½m W of Trowbridge on A366. 9 miles SE of Bath.

Open: 1 Apr–30 Jun: daily, 10am–5pm. 1 Jul–31 Aug: daily 10am–6pm. 1–30 Sep: daily, 10am–5pm. 1–31 Oct: daily, 10am–4pm. 1 Nov–31 Mar: Sat & Sun, 10am–4pm. Closed 24–26 Dec & 1 Jan.

Admission: Adult £3.80, Child £1.90, Conc. £3.20. 15% discount for groups of 11+. EH Members free. Opening times and prices are valid until 31st March 2011, after this date details are subject to change please visit www.english-heritage.org.uk for the most up-to-date information.

Partial. By arrangement. Limited for coaches.

THE GEORGIAN HOUSE

7 Great George Street, Bristol, Somerset BS1 5RR

Tel: 0117 921 1362

Owner: City of Bristol Museums & Art Gallery **Contact:** Karin Walton

18th century townhouse restored to its former glory.

Location: MAP 2:O2, OS172 ST582 730. Bristol.

Open: Easter–Oct Wed–Sun 10.30am–4pm.

Admission: Free.

GLASTONBURY ABBEY

Abbey Gatehouse, Magdalene Street, Glastonbury BA6 9EL

Tel: 01458 832267 **Fax:** 01458 836117 **E-mail:** info@glastonburyabbey.com

www.glastonburyabbey.com

Owner: Glastonbury Abbey Estate **Contact:** Francis Thyer

"Unique", "Peaceful", "Such atmosphere", "A hidden gem". Come and discover this wonderful place for yourself. From March to October hear, from our enactors, how the monks used to live and some of the history of this once great Abbey. See website for events. Outdoor Summer Café.

Location: MAP 2:N4, OS Ref. ST499 388. 50 yds from the Market Cross, in the centre of Glastonbury. M5/J23, then A39.

Open: Open: Daily except Christmas Day. Summer 9am–6pm. Winter 10am–4.30pm.

Admission: Adult £5.50, Child (5-15 yrs) £3.50, Conc. £5, Family (2+2) £16.

Summer only.

GLASTONBURY TOR

Nr Glastonbury, Somerset

Tel: 01934 844518

Owner: National Trust **Contact:** The Regional Office

The dramatic and evocative Tor dominates the surrounding countryside and offers spectacular views over Somerset, Dorset and Wiltshire. At the summit of this very steep hill an excavation has revealed the plans of two superimposed churches of St Michael, of which only the 15th century tower remains.

Location: MAP 2:N4, OS Ref. ST512 386. Signposted from Glastonbury town centre, from where seasonal park-and-ride (not NT) operates.

Open: All year.

Admission: Free.

Park & ride from town centre Apr–Sept. Also free at Rural Life Museum. Tel 01458 831197. On leads only.

GLASTONBURY TRIBUNAL

Glastonbury High Street, Glastonbury, Somerset BA6 9DP

Tel: 01458 832954 **Email:** customers@english-heritage.org.uk

www.english-heritage.org.uk/glastonburytribunal

Owner: English Heritage **Contact:** The TIC Manager

A well preserved medieval town house, reputedly once used as the courthouse of Glastonbury Abbey. Now houses Glastonbury Tourist Information Centre and the Glastonbury Lake Village Museum.

Location: MAP 2:N4, OS182 Ref. ST499 390. In Glastonbury High Street.

Open: Mon–Thur, 10am–4pm, Fri–Sat, 10am–4.30pm, Sun, closed. 25–26 Dec & 1 Jan: closed. Opening hours may be extended during peak season.

Admission: Museum: Adult £2.50, Conc £2, Senior £1.50, Child £1, EH Members free. Group discount available. Opening times and prices are valid until 31st March 2011, after this date details are subject to change please visit www.english-heritage.org.uk for the most up-to-date information.

Partial. Charge. Guide dogs only.

HESTERCOMBE GARDENS

CHEDDON FITZPAINE, TAUNTON, SOMERSET TA2 8LG

www.hestercombe.com

Tel: 01823 413923 **Fax:** 01823 413747 **E-mail:** info@hestercombe.com

Owner: Hestercombe Gardens Trust **Contact:** The Administration Office

Exquisite Georgian landscape garden designed by Coplestone Warre Bampfylde, Victorian terrace/shrubbery, and Edwardian Lutyens/Jekyll formal gardens together make up 50 acres of woodland walks, temples, terraces, pergolas, lakes and cascades. Licensed Restaurant/ Coffee Shop & Courtyard. Conference and wedding venue, Shop/Plant Centre. Beautifully restored 17th century watermill, seasonal Mill Tea Garden.

Location: MAP 2:M5, OS Ref. ST241 287. 4m NE from Taunton, 1m NW of Cheddon Fitzpaine.

Open: All year: daily, 10am–6pm (last admission 5pm). Groups & coach parties by arrangement.

Admission: Adult £8.90, Conc. £8.30, Children £3.30, Family Saver £22 (2 adults and up to 4 children), Guided tours from £12.

Partial. WC. Licensed. Licensed. By arrangement. Limited for coaches. On short leads

HOLNICOTE ESTATE

Selworthy, Minehead, Somerset TA24 8TJ

Tel: 01643 862452 **Fax:** 01643 863011 **E-mail:** holnicote@nationaltrust.org.uk

Owner: National Trust **Contact:** The Estate Office

The Holnicote Estate covers 5042ha (12,500 acres) of Exmoor National Park. The Estate also covers 4 miles of coastline between Porlock Bay and Minehead. There are over 100 miles of footpaths to enjoy through the fields, woods, moors and villages.

Location: MAP 2:K3, OS Ref. SS920 469. Off A39 Minehead–Porlock, 3m W of Minehead. Station: Minehead 5m.

Open: Estate Office: All year: Mon–Fri, 8.30am–5pm, Closed Bank Hols. Estate: open all year.

Admission: Free.

(Not NT.)

KENTSFORD

Washford, Watchet, Somerset TA23 0JD

Tel: 01984 631307

Owner: Wyndham Estate **Contact:** Mr R Dibble

Location: MAP 2:L4, OS Ref. ST058 426.

Open: House open only by written appointment with Mr R Dibble. Gardens: 6 Mar–28 Aug: Tues & BHs.

Admission: House: £3, Gardens: Free.

Gardens only. Limited. In grounds, on leads.

KING JOHN'S HUNTING LODGE

The Square, Axbridge, Somerset BS26 2AP

Tel: 01934 732012 **www.nationaltrust.org.uk**

Owner/Contact: National Trust

An early Tudor merchant's house, extensively restored in 1971. Note: the property is run as a local history museum by Axbridge & District Museum Trust in co-operation with Sedgemoor District Council, County Museum's Service and Axbridge Archaeological & Local History Society.

Location: MAP 2:N3, OS Ref. ST431 545. In the Square, on corner of High Street, off A371.

Open: 2 April–30 Sept 2010: 1–4pm daily. 1 Oct–31 Dec: open first Sat of month 10–4pm, to coincide with Farmers' Market.

Admission: Free. Donations welcome.

Ground floor. By arrangement.

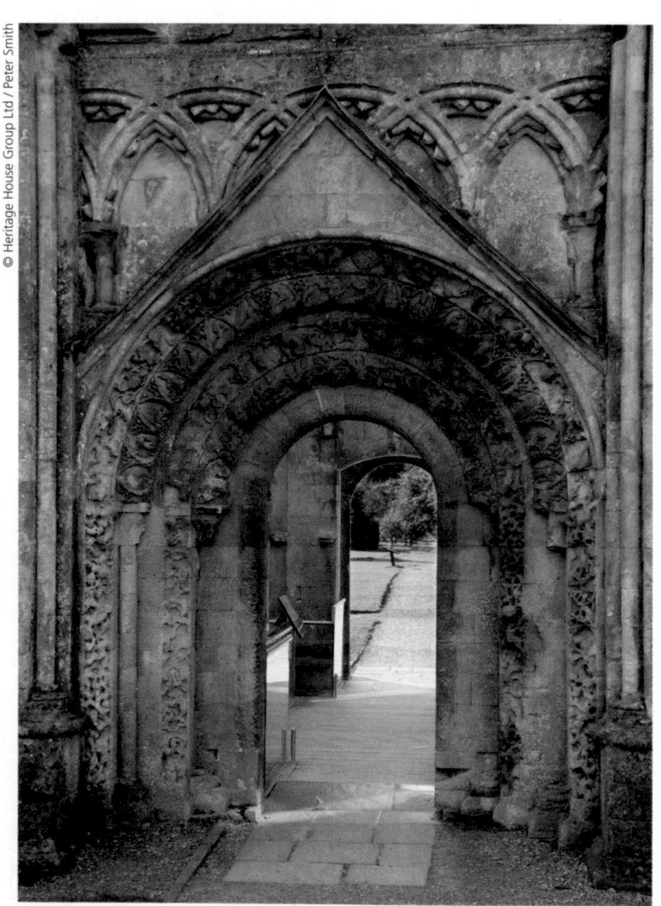

Glastonbury Abbey

LOWER SEVERALLS

Crewkerne, Somerset TA18 7NX
Tel: 01460 73234 **E-mail:** mary@lowerseveralls.co.uk
Owner/Contact: Mary Pring
2½ acre garden, developed over the last 25 years including herb garden, mixed borders and island beds with innovative features.
Location: MAP 2:N5, OS Ref. ST457 112. 1½m NE of Crewkerne, between A30 & A356.
Open: Mar–Sept: Tue, Wed, Fri & Sat, 10am–5pm. Closed Aug.
Admission: Adult £3, Child (under 16yrs) Free.

LYTES CARY MANOR

Nr Charlton Mackrell, Somerset TA11 7HU
Tel: 01458 224471
Owner: National Trust **Contact:** Visitor Services Manager
Manor House with Arts & Crafts style garden.
Location: MAP 2:O5, OS Ref. ST529 269. 1m N of Ilchester bypass A303, signposted from Podimore roundabout at junction of A303. A37 take A372.

MAUNSEL HOUSE

See page 203 for full page entry.

MILTON LODGE GARDENS

Old Bristol Road, Wells, Somerset BA5 3AQ
Tel: 01749 672168 **www.miltonlodgegardens.co.uk**
Owner/Contact: S Tudway Quilter Esq
"The great glory of the gardens of Milton Lodge is their position high up on the slopes of the Mendip Hills to the north of Wells ... with broad panoramas of Wells Cathedral and the Vale of Avalon", (Lanning Roper). Charming, mature, Grade II listed terraced garden dating from 1909. Replanned 1962 with mixed shrubs, herbaceous plants, old fashioned roses and ground cover; numerous climbers; old established yew hedges. Fine trees in garden and in 7-acre arboretum across old Bristol Road.
Location: MAP 2:O3, OS Ref. ST549 470. ½m N of Wells from A39. N up Old Bristol Road. Free car park first gate on left.
Open: Garden & Arboretum: Easter–end Oct: Tues, Weds, Suns & BHs, 2–5pm. Parties & coaches by prior arrangement.
Admission: Adult £5, Children under 14 Free.
Unsuitable.

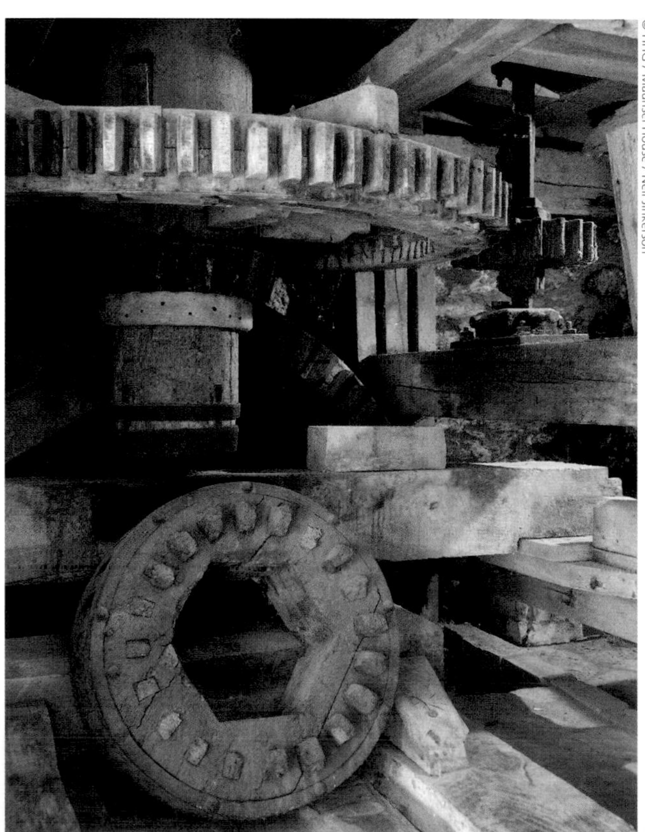
© HHG / Maunsel House / Neil Jinkerson
Maunsel House

MONTACUTE HOUSE

Montacute, Somerset TA15 6XP
Tel: 01935 823289 **Fax:** 01935 826921 **E-mail:** montacute@nationaltrust.org.uk
www.nationaltrust.org.uk
Owner: National Trust **Contact:** The Administrator
A glittering Elizabethan house, adorned with elegant chimneys, carved parapets and other Renaissance features, including contemporary plasterwork, chimney pieces and heraldic glass. The magnificent state rooms, including a long gallery which is the largest of its type in England, are full of fine 17th and 18th century furniture and Elizabethan and Jacobean portraits from the National Portrait Gallery.
Location: MAP 2:N5, OS Ref. ST499 172. In Montacute village, 4m W of Yeovil, on S side of A3088, 3m E of A303.
Open: House & Garden: 12 Mar–30 Oct: daily except Tue, 11am–5pm. Last entry to house 4.30pm.
Partial. Braille guide. WC. Licensed. Christmas lunches in Dec (must book). In park, on leads.

MUCHELNEY ABBEY

Muchelney, Langport, Somerset TA10 0DQ
Tel: 01458 250664 **Fax:** 01458 253842 **Email:** customers@english-heritage.org.uk
www.english-heritage.org.uk/muchelney
Owner: English Heritage **Contact:** Visitor Operations Staff
Well-preserved ruins of the cloisters, with windows carved in golden stone, and abbot's lodging of the Benedictine abbey, which survived by being used as a farmhouse after the Dissolution. Tactile displays and interactive video illustrate monastic life.
Location: MAP 2:N5, OS193 Ref. ST428 248. In Muchelney 2m S of Langport.
Open: 1 Apr–30 Jun: daily, 10am–5pm. 1 Jul–31 Aug: daily, 10am–6pm. 1–30 Sep: daily, 10am–5pm. 1–31 Oct: daily, 10–4pm. Closed 1 Nov–31 Mar.
Admission: Adult £4, Child £2, Conc. £3.40. 15% discount for groups (11+). EH Members free. Opening times and prices are valid until 31st March 2011, after this date details are subject to change please visit www.english-heritage.org.uk for the most up-to-date information.
Partial. By arrangement. In grounds.

NUNNEY CASTLE

Nunney, Somerset BA11 4LQ
Tel: 0117 9750700 **Email:** customers@english-heritage.org.uk
www.english-heritage.org.uk/nunneycastle
Owner: English Heritage **Contact:** Visitor Operations Staff
A small 14th century moated castle with a distinctly French style. Its unusual design consists of a central block with large towers at the angles.
Location: MAP 2:P3, OS183 Ref. ST737 457. In Nunney 3½m SW of Frome, 1m N of the A361.
Open: Any reasonable time.
Admission: Free. Opening times and prices are valid until 31st March 2011, after this date details are subject to change please visit www.english-heritage.org.uk for the most up-to-date information.
Partial. Limited for cars. No coaches. On leads.

ORCHARD WYNDHAM

Williton, Taunton, Somerset TA4 4HH
Tel: 01984 632309
Owner: Wyndham Estate **Contact:** Wyndham Estate Office
English manor house. Family home for 700 years encapsulating continuous building and alteration from the 14th to the 20th century.
Location: MAP 2:L4, OS Ref. ST072 400. 1m from A39 at Williton.
Open: Telephone for details.
Admission: Telephone for details.
Obligatory & pre-booked. Limited. No coach parking. In grounds, on leads.

PRIEST'S HOUSE

Muchelney, Langport, Somerset TA10 0DQ
Tel: 01458 253771 (Tenant)
Owner: National Trust **Contact:** The Administrator
A late medieval hall house with large gothic windows, originally the residence of priests serving the parish church across the road. Lived-in and recently repaired.
Location: MAP 2:N5, OS Ref. ST429 250. 1m S of Langport.

ROBIN HOOD'S HUT

Halswell, Goathurst, Somerset TA5 2EW

Tel: 01628 825925 **E-mail:** bookings@landmarktrust.org.uk

www.landmarktrust.org.uk

Owner/Contact: The Landmark Trust

Robin Hood's Hut is an 18th century garden building with two distinct faces. On one side it is a small rustic cottage, with thatched roof and bark clad door while on the other is an elegant pavilion complete with umbrello (or stone canopy). In the 1740s, Charles Kemeys Tynte began to transform the landscape around Halswell House into one of the finest Georgian gardens in the south west. He built several follies including Robin Hood's Hut in 1767. It is cared for by The Landmark Trust, a building preservation charity who let it for holidays. Full details of Robin Hood's Hut and 189 other historic and architecturally important buildings are featured in the Landmark Trust Handbook (price £10 plus p&p refundable against a booking) and on the website.

Location: MAP 2:M4, OS Ref. ST255 333.

Open: Available for holidays for up to 2 people throughout the year. Other visits by appointment. Please contact the Landmark Trust for details.

Admission: Free on Open Days and visits by appointment.

STEMBRIDGE TOWER MILL

High Ham, Somerset TA10 9DJ

Tel: 01935 823289

Owner: National Trust **Contact:** The Administrator

The last thatched windmill in England, dating from 1822 and in use until 1910.

Location: MAP 2:N4, OS Ref. ST432 305. 2m N of Langport, ½m E of High Ham.

Open: Mar–Oct, daily. Ring for details.

Admission: Ring for details.

STOKE-SUB-HAMDON PRIORY

North Street, Stoke-sub-Hamdon, Somerset TA4 6QP

Tel: 01935 823289

Owner/Contact: National Trust

A complex of buildings, begun in the 14th century for the priests of the chantry of St Nicholas, which is now destroyed. The Great Hall is open to visitors.

Location: MAP 2:N4, OS Ref. ST473 174. ½m S of A303. 2m W of Montacute between Yeovil and Ilminster.

Open: Mar–Sept: daily, 11am–5pm or dusk if earlier. Not suitable for coaches.

Admission: Free.

TINTINHULL GARDEN

Farm Street, Tintinhull, Somerset BA22 9PZ

Tel: 01935 823289

Owner: National Trust **Contact:** The Administrator

A delightful formal garden, created in the 20th century around a 17th century manor house. Small pools, varied borders and secluded lawns are neatly enclosed within walls and clipped hedges and there is also an attractive kitchen garden.

Location: MAP 2:O5, OS Ref. ST503 198. 5m NW of Yeovil, ½m S of A303, on E outskirts of Tintinhull.

Open: Mar–Oct: Wed–Sun (open BH Mon), 11am–5pm (Tearoom 11am–4.30pm) or dusk if earlier.

Grounds. Braille guide. Limited.

TREASURER'S HOUSE

Martock, Somerset TA12 6JL

Tel: 01935 825015

Owner/Contact: National Trust

A small medieval house, recently refurbished by The Trust. The two-storey hall was completed in 1293 and the solar block is even earlier.

Location: MAP 2:N5, OS Ref. ST462 191. 1m NW of A303 between Ilminster and Ilchester.

Open: Mar–Sept: Sun–Tue, 2–5pm. Only medieval hall, wall paintings and kitchen are shown.

Admission: Adult £3.60, Child £1.80. Not suitable for groups.

TYNTESFIELD

Wraxall, North Somerset BS48 1NX

Tel: 01275 461900 **E-mail:** tyntesfield@nationaltrust.org.uk

www.nationaltrust.org.uk/tyntesfield

Owner/Contact: National Trust

This extraordinary Victorian estate is ready to explore all year round. The house is a Gothic revival extravaganza with 200ha of surrounding formal gardens, kitchen garden and extensive woodland. This year a new visitor centre is open for the first time with a restaurant, shop, exhibition space and play area.

Location: MAP 2:N2, OS Ref. ST506 715. Off B3128.

Open: 28 Feb–30 Oct, House & Chapel, 11am–5pm; 5–27 Nov, House & Chapel weekend tours (Sat & Sun) only, 11am–3pm; 28 Feb–31 Dec (closed 25 Dec), Gardens & Estate, 10am–6pm (closes 5pm (or dusk if earlier) Jan, Feb, Nov, Dec); Shop, Restaurant & Café, 10am–4.30pm (between 1 Apr–30 Sept shop open until 5.30pm). Christmas opening: House, gardens and visitor facilities open 10am–3pm, 3/4, 10/11, 17/18 Dec for Christmas events only. Last admission to house one hour before closing. Entry cannot be guarenteed on busy days.

Admission: (Gift Aid prices in brackets) House, Chapel & Gardens: Adult £12.20 (£13.50), Child £6.00 (£6.75), Family £30.40 (£33.75). Gardens only: Adult £9 (£10), Child £4.50 (£5), Family £22.50 (£25). Discount for group admission (minimum 15 people, by appointment).

WCs. By arrangement. Guide dogs only.

WELLS CATHEDRAL

Cathedral Green, Wells, Somerset BA5 2UE

Tel: 01749 674483 **Fax:** 01749 832210

Owner: The Chapter of Wells **Contact:** Mr John Roberts

Fine medieval Cathedral. The West Front with its splendid array of statuary, the Quire with colourful embroideries and stained glass, Chapter House and 1392 astronomical clock should not be missed.

Location: MAP 2:O3, OS Ref. ST552 458. In Wells, 20m S from both Bath & Bristol.

Open: Apr–Sept: 7am–7pm; Oct–Mar: 7am–6pm.

Admission: Suggested donation: Adult £5.50, Child/Student £2.50, OAP £4. Photo permit £3.

WOODLANDS CASTLE

Ruishton, Taunton, Somerset TA3 5LU

Tel: 01823 444955 **Fax:** 01823 444019 **E-mail:** info@woodlandscastle.co.uk

www.woodlandscastle.co.uk

Owner: Sir Benjamin Slade **Contact:** Gemma Halliwell

Woodlands Castle is a beautiful period house in 12 acres of private grounds situated on Junction 25 of the M5. Woodlands is available for private functions from weddings and conferences to barbecues, birthdays and wakes. Ample free parking. Accommodation within walking distance.

Location: MAP 2:M5, OS Ref. ST258 248.

Open: All year to private bookings only.

Admission: No admission.

Partial. Licensed. Licensed. By arrangement. Ample for cars. Limited for coaches. In grounds.

© NTPL / Steve Stephens

Tyntesfield

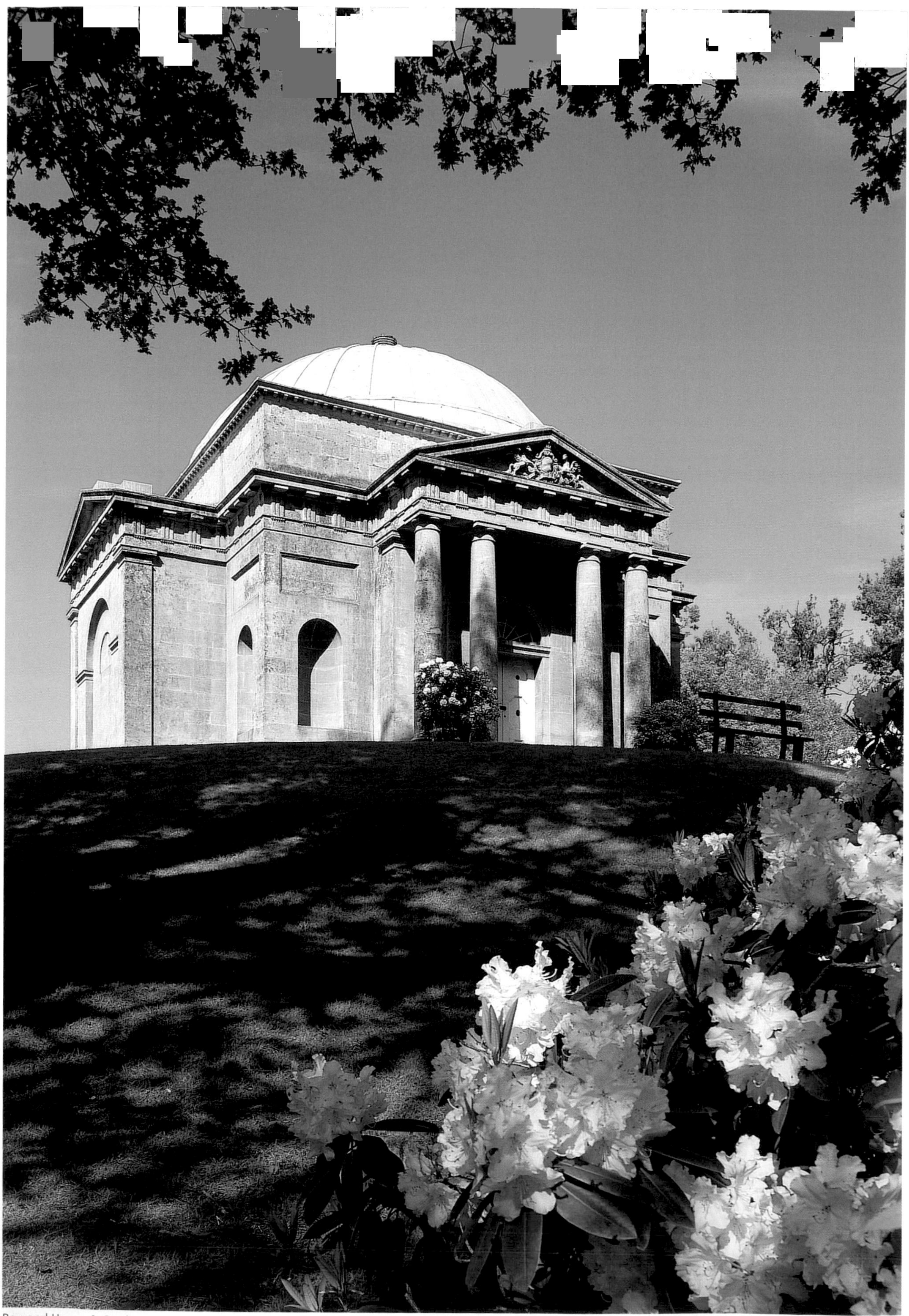

Bowood House & Gardens

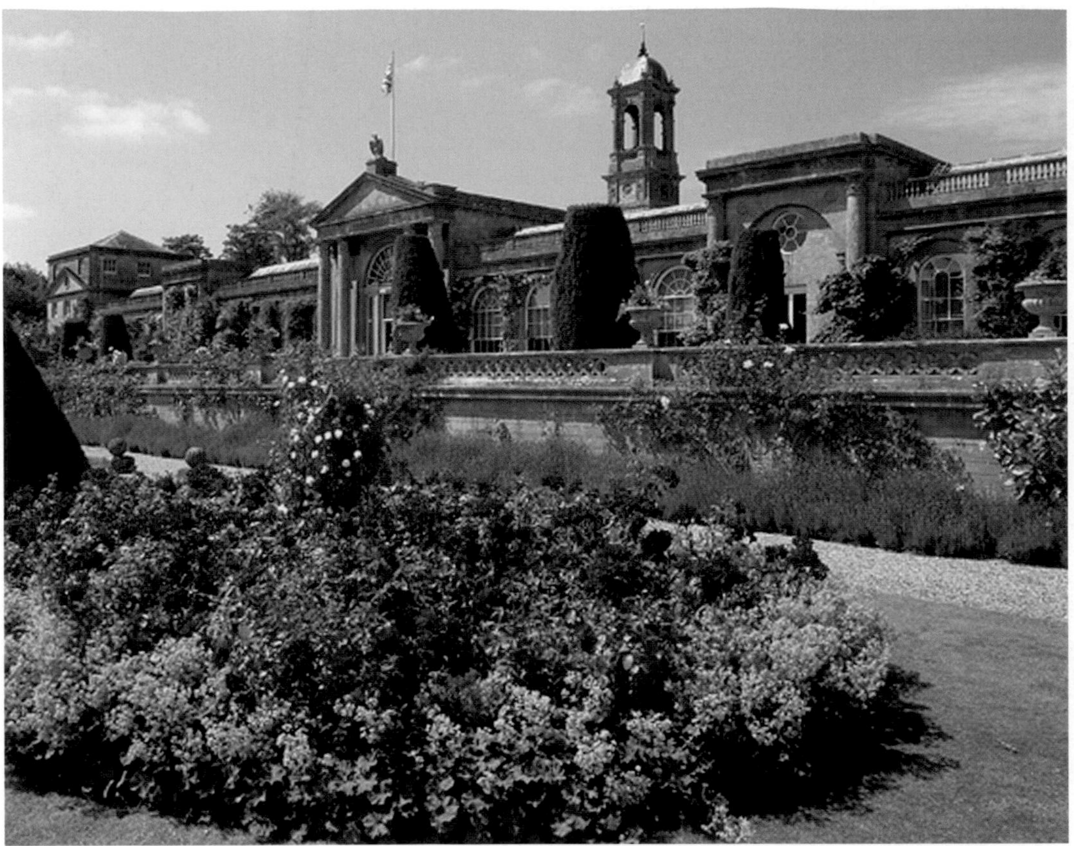

BOWOOD HOUSE & GARDENS

www.bowood-house.co.uk

Bowood is the family home of the Marquis and Marchioness of Lansdowne. Begun c1720 for the Bridgeman family, the house was purchased by the 2nd Earl of Shelburne in 1754 and completed soon afterwards. Part of the house was demolished in 1955, leaving a perfectly proportioned Georgian home, over half of which is open to visitors. Robert Adam's magnificent Diocletian wing contains a splendid library, the laboratory where Joseph Priestley discovered oxygen gas in 1774, the orangery, now a picture gallery, the Chapel and a sculpture gallery in which some of the famous Lansdowne Marbles are displayed.

Among the family treasures shown in the numerous exhibition rooms are Georgian costumes, including Lord Byron's Albanian dress; Victoriana; Indiana (the 5th Marquess was Viceroy 1888–94); and superb collections of watercolours, miniatures and jewellery.

The House is set in one of the most beautiful parks in England. Over 2,000 acres of gardens and grounds were landscaped by 'Capability' Brown between 1762 and 1768, and are embellished with a Doric temple, a cascade, a pinetum and an arboretum. The Rhododendron Gardens are open for six weeks from late April to early June. All the walks have seats.

Receptions, film location, 2,000 acre park, 40 acre lake, 43 bedroom hotel, Spa and 18-hole golf course.

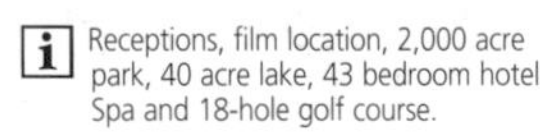

Visitors may alight at the House before parking. WCs.

Self-service snacks, teas etc.

The Restaurant (waitress service, capacity 85). Groups that require lunch or tea should book in advance.

On request, groups can be given introductory talk, or for an extra charge, a guided tour. Guide sheets in French, German, Dutch, Spanish & Japanese.

Parking for 1,000 cars, unlimited for coaches, 400 yds from house. Allow 2–3 hrs to visit house, gardens and grounds.

Special guide books. Picnic areas. Adventure playground.

Working assistance dogs only.

Sunday 12th June 2011 Bowood Dog Show.

Owner

The Marquis of Lansdowne

Contact

The Administrator
Bowood House and Gardens
Calne
Wiltshire SN11 0LZ

Tel: 01249 812102
Fax: 01249 281751
E-mail: houseandgardens@bowood.org

Location

MAP 3:A2
OS Ref. ST974 700

From London M4 J17 off the A4 in Derry Hill village, midway between Calne and Chippenham. Swindon 17m, Bristol 26m, Bath 16m.

Bus: to the gate, 1½ m through the park to the House.

Rail: Chippenham Station 5m.

Taxi: AA Taxis, Chippenham 657777.

Air: Heathrow Airport 80m.

Opening Times

House & Garden
Friday 1 April–
Sunday 30th October.
Daily, 11am–6pm.
Last admission 5pm (or 1hr earlier after the autumn clock change).

Rhododendron Walks
Off the A342 Chippenham to Devizes road, midway between Derry Hill and Sandy Lane.

Open daily for 6 weeks during the flowering season, usually from late April to early June, 11am–6pm.

We recommend visitors telephone or visit the website to check the progress of the flowering season.

Admission

House & Garden	
Adult	£9.50
Junior	£7.50
Child	£5.00
Senior Citizen	£8.00
Family (2+2)	£28.50
Groups (20+)	
Adult	£8.50
Junior	£6.50
Child	£4.00
Senior Citizen	£7.00
Rhododendron Walks	
Adult	£6.00
Senior Citizen	£5.50
Adult Combined Ticket	£13.50
Senior Citizen combined ticket	£11.50
Season Tickets (no early discount)	
Adult	£41.00
Senior Citizen	£36.00
Junior	£35.00
Child	£26.00
Family	£125.00

■ Owner
Marquess of Bath

■ Contact
Longleat
Warminster
Wiltshire BA12 7NW
Tel: 01985 844400
Fax: 01985 844885
E-mail: enquiries@longleat.co.uk
www.longleat.co.uk

■ Location
MAP 2:P4
OS Ref. ST809 430

Just off the A36 between Bath–Salisbury (A362 Warminster–Frome). 2hrs from London following M3, A303, A36, A362 or M4/J18, A46, A36.

Rail: Warminster (5m) on Cardiff/Portsmouth line. Westbury (12m) on Paddington/Penzance line. Taxis at Warminster & Westbury Stations.

Air: Bristol 30m.

■ Opening Times
All attractions open daily from Saturday 19 February–Sunday 30 October 2011 inclusive.

Longleat House also offers 'behind the scenes' VIP Tours for Groups in 'closed periods'. Subject to availability, pre booking essential.

Please see www.longleat.co.uk for details.

■ Admission
Prices unavailable at time of going to print. Please see www.longleat.co.uk for details.

Conference/Function

ROOM	SIZE	MAX CAPACITY
Great Hall	8 x 13m	120
Banqueting Suite	2 x (7 x 10m)	50
Green Library	7 x 13m	70

LONGLEAT

www.longleat.co.uk

Set within 900 acres of 'Capability' Brown landscaped parkland, Longleat House is regarded as one of the best examples of high Elizabethan architecture in Britain and widely acknowledged as one of the most beautiful stately homes open to the public.

The House was built by Sir John Thynne between 1568 and 1580 as a prodigy House, visited by Elizabeth I in 1574, and now the home of the 7th Marquess of Bath, Alexander Thynn.

Inspired by various Italian interiors, including the Ducal Palace in Venice, the ceilings are renowned for their ornate paintings and abundance of gilt, made by the firm of John Dibblee Crace in the 1870s and 1880s. The furniture collection includes English pieces from as early as the 16th century and fine French furniture of the 17th and 18th centuries.

Lord Bath's paintings, The Murals, are unique to Longleat as they have been created by Lord Bath himself. Incorporating a mixture of oil paints and sawdust, these private works of art offer an insight into Lord Bath's personality and beliefs. Tours can be booked at the Front Desk of Longleat House on the day of your visit, subject to availability.

Longleat House offers "free flow" tours for the majority of the visitor season with guides posted in most of the rooms. If you'd prefer a more intimate visit, then the award-winning VIP Tours are ideal. Running from November through to March, these tours give visitors a chance to look behind closed doors and see parts of the House not usually accessible to the general public.

Longleat House VIP Tours are subject to availability and must be pre-booked. Please see www.longleat.co.uk for details.

Rooms in Longleat House can be hired for conferences, gala dinners and product launches. Extensive parkland for company fun days, marquee based gala dinners and product promotions. Film location.

Please see www.longleat.co.uk or request a Map and Access leaflet at the time of enquiry for full details.

Out of main season. Please see www.longleat.co.uk for details.

Ample.

Welcome with 1 teacher free entry per 8 children. Talks and packs available on request. Pre-booking essential. Education sheets. Specialists in Vocational Studies.

Service Dogs only. Please see www.longleat.co.uk for full details.

Please see www.longleat.co.uk for details.

STOURHEAD

www.nationaltrust.org.uk

Often referred to as "Paradise", Stourhead is an exquisite example of an English landscape garden. It was once described by Horace Walpole as 'one of the most picturesque scenes in the world'.

Visitors can discover the inspiration behind Henry Hoare II's world famous garden, laid out between 1741 and 1780, and enjoy breathtaking views all year round.

The garden is dotted with Classical temples including the Pantheon and the Temple of Apollo, which provide dramatic backdrops to the majestic lake, secluded valley and mature woodland replete with exotic trees.

Stourhead House is an 18th century Palladian Mansion home to the beautifully restored Pope's Cabinet, furniture by the younger Chippendale and a magnificent collection of paintings. It is situated at the top of the gardens surrounded by lawns and parkland.

The Stourhead Estate extends east to King Alfred's Tower, a triangular folly 21/2 miles from the House which affords stunning views across three counties, and is the perfect place for picnics.

Visitors can also enjoy breathtaking walks across Whitesheet Hill's chalk downs, and explore open countryside where native wildlife, including woodland birds, badgers, deer and wildflowers, can be seen.

The Restaurant offers fresh new flavours and local produce, there is an extensive Gift Shop and Plant Centre, and there are many opportunities to get involved with Stourhead's exciting Events Programme.

The Estate also comprises The Spread Eagle Inn, First View Art Gallery and Stourhead Farm Shop (all non NT).

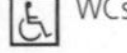
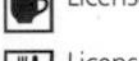
WCs.

Licensed.
Licensed.
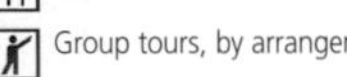
Group tours, by arrangement.
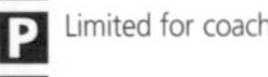
Limited for coaches.

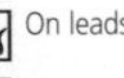
On leads.

Owner
National Trust

Contact
The Estate Office
Stourton
Nr Warminster
BA12 6QD

Tel: 01747 841152
Fax: 01747 842005
E-mail: stourhead@nationaltrust.org.uk

Location
MAP 2:P4
OS Ref. ST780 340

At Stourton off the B3092, 3m NW of A303 (Mere), 8m S of A361 (Frome).

Rail: Gillingham 6½m; Bruton 7m.

Bus: South West Coaches 80 Frome to Stourhead on Sat; First 58/0A.

Opening Times
House
12 Mar–30 Oct: Fri–Tue, 11am–5pm. Last admission 4.30pm.

Garden
All year: daily, 9am–7pm or dusk if earlier.

King Alfred's Tower
12 Mar–30 Oct: daily, 11am–5pm. or dusk if earlier. Last admission: 4.30pm.

Restaurant
All year, daily (closed 25 December), Mar & Oct: 10am–5.30pm; Nov–Feb: 10am–4.30pm.

Shop & Plant Centre
All year, daily, (closed 25 December) Mar & Oct: 10am–5pm; Apr–Sept: 10am–6pm; Nov–Feb: 10am–4pm.

Farm Shop
(closed 24 Dec–1 Jan) 2 Jan–28 Mar: 10am–4pm; 29 Mar–24 Oct: 10am–6pm; 25 Oct–23 Dec: 10am–5pm.

*Admission
House & Garden

Adult	£13.40*
Child	£6.70*
Family	£31.90*
Groups (15+)	£11.50

House OR Garden

Adult	£8.10*
Child	£4.40*
Family	£19.20*
Groups (15+)	£7.00

NT Members FREE

NB. Groups must book.

*includes a 10% voluntary donation but visitors can however choose to pay the standard admission prices displayed at the property and on the website.

Special events
please contact us or visit the website for details of our full events programme.

■ Owner
The Earl of Pembroke

■ Contact
The Estate Office
Wilton, Salisbury SP2 0BJ

Tel: 01722 746720
Fax: 01722 744447
E-mail: tourism@wiltonhouse.com

■ Location
MAP 3:B4
OS Ref. SU099 311

3m W of Salisbury along the A36.

■ Opening Times

Summer
House
22 April–1 September & 4 September: Sundays–Thursdays. BH Sats 23 & 30 April, 28 May & 27 August 11.30am–4.30pm, last admission 3.45pm.

Dining Room
30 April–2 May, 28–30 May, 3 July–4 August, Suns–Thurs inclusive, 27–29 August.

Grounds & Restaurant
10 April–4 September, daily. Subsequent weekends in September, 11am–5pm, last admission 4pm.

Winter
At all other times, the House and Grounds are closed except for bespoke tours and groups by prior arrangement.

Closures
This information is correct at the time of publication, but may be subject to change. Please check recorded information on 01722 746720 or visit our website.

■ Admission

House & Grounds*

Adult	£15.00
Child (5–15)	£8.00
Concession	£12.00
Family	£36.00

*includes admission to Dining Room when open.

Grounds

Adult	£5.50
Child (5–15)	£4.00
Concession	£5.00
Family	£16.50

Group Admission

Adult	£12.00
Child	£6.00
Concession	£9.50
Guided Tour	£6.00

Membership
From £20.00

WILTON HOUSE

www.wiltonhouse.com

Wilton House has been the ancestral home of the Earl of Pembroke and his family for 460 years. In 1544, Henry VIII gave the Abbey and lands of Wilton to Sir William Herbert who had married Anne Parr, sister of Katherine, sixth wife of King Henry.

The Clock Tower, in the centre of the east front, is reminiscent of the part of the Tudor building which survived a fire in 1647. Inigo Jones and John Webb were responsible for the rebuilding of the house in the Palladian style whilst further alterations were made by James Wyatt from 1801.

The chief architectural features are the magnificent 17th century state apartments (including the famous Single and Double Cube rooms) and the 19th century cloisters. The House was the recipient of the 2010 HHA/Sotheby's Restoration Award for the recent restoration of several ground floor rooms including the Dining Room.

The House contains one of the finest art collections in Europe, with over 230 original paintings on display including works by Van Dyck, Rubens, Joshua Reynolds and Brueghel.

Wilton House is set in magnificent landscaped parkland, bordered by the River Nadder which is the setting for the Palladian Bridge. A large adventure playground provides hours of fun for younger visitors.

Film location, fashion shows, product launches, equestrian events, garden parties, antiques fairs, concerts, vehicle rallies. No photography in house. French, German, Spanish, Italian, Japanese and Dutch information.

Adjacent garden centre

Exclusive banquets.

Visitors may alight at the entrance. WCs.

Licensed.

By arrangement. £6. Tours in French, German and Spanish.

200 cars and 12 coaches. Free coach parking. Group rates (min 15), drivers' meal voucher.

National Curriculum KS1/2.
Free preparatory visit for teachers.
Sandford Award Winner 2002 & 2008

Guide dogs only.

4–6 March 2011 Antiques Fair
Please see our website for full details.

©NTPL / David Noton

©NT / David Norton

AVEBURY MANOR & GARDEN, AVEBURY STONE CIRCLE & ALEXANDER KEILLER MUSEUM

AVEBURY, NR MARLBOROUGH, WILTSHIRE SN8 1RF

www.nationaltrust.org.uk/avebury

Tel: 01672 539250 **E-mail:** avebury@nationaltrust.org.uk

Owner: National Trust **Contact:** The Visitor Services Manager

Avebury Manor & Garden: A much–altered house of monastic origin, the present buildings date from the early 16th century, with notable 18th century alterations and Edwardian renovation by Colonel Jenner. The garden comprises tranquil 'rooms', featuring topiary and a succession of seasonal colour and contrast. The Manor House has recently returned to the National Trust management after 15 years of tenanted occupancy. Many previously unseen rooms are now open to the public, including the former bedroom and dressing room of the charismatic Alexander Keiller. If there is prolonged wet weather it may be necessary to close the house and garden.

Avebury Stone Circle: One of Britain's finest, most impressive circles stands proud amidst the rolling Wiltshire landscape, steeped in 6,000 years of history.

Alexander Keiller Museum Barn & Stables Galleries: The investigation of Avebury Stone Circle was largely the work of archaeologist and 'marmalade millionaire' Alexander Keiller in the 1930s. He put together one of the most important prehistoric archaeological collections, which can be seen in the Stables Gallery. The 'Story of the Stones', the people who strove to reveal the true significance of Avebury's Stone Circle and the development of the Avebury landscape, are depicted through interactive displays in the spectacular Barn Gallery, a 17th century thatched threshing barn.

Location: MAP 3:B2, OS Ref. SU101 701 (Avebury Manor). OS Ref. SU102 699 (Stone Circle). OS Ref. SU100 699 (Alexander Keiller Museum). 7m W of Marlborough, 1m N of the A4 on A4361 & B4003.

Open: Avebury Manor: 1 Apr–31 Oct 2011, 11am–5pm everyday (House and Garden). Opening arrangements subject to change, visit website for details. **Stone Circle:** Open all year – Car Park open 9.15am–6.30pm, Apr–Oct. 9.15am–4.30pm, Nov–Mar. Pay and Display – NT and EH Members Free. **Alexander Keiller Museum Galleries:** 1 Jan–31 Mar, Daily, 10am–4.30pm. 1 Apr–31 Oct, Daily, 10am–6pm and 1 Nov–31 Dec, Daily, 10am–4.30pm. **Shop and Circle Restaurant:** 1 Jan–31 Mar Daily 10.30am–4pm, 1 Apr–31 Oct Daily 10am–5.30pm, 1 Nov–31 Dec Daily 10.30am–4pm. Musuem, Galleries, Shop and restaurant closed 24–26 Dec 2010.

Admission: Avebury Manor & Garden: Adult £4.90 and Child £2.45. **Stone Circle:** Free. **Alexander Keiller Museum Barn & Stables Galleries:** *Gift Aid Admission: Adults £4.90, Children £2.45, Family (2+2) £13.45, Family (1+3) £8.70.

Alexander Keiller Museum & Shop. Avebury Manor: ground floor with assistance & grounds; Alexander Keiller Museum: fully accessible. WCs. Braille guide. Avebury, licensed. Pay & display. No dogs in house, guide dogs only in garden (Avebury Manor). On leads in Stone Circle and museum galleries. Stone Circle.

© Britainonview

Bowood House & Gardens

BOWOOD HOUSE & GARDENS

See page 211 for full page entry.

BRADFORD-ON-AVON TITHE BARN

Bradford-on-Avon, Wiltshire BA15 2EF

Tel: 0117 975 0700 **Email:** customers@english-heritage.org.uk

www.english-heritage.org.uk/bradford-on-avontithebarn

Owner: English Heritage **Contact:** South West Regional Office

A magnificent medieval stone-built barn with a slate roof and wooden beamed interior.

Location: MAP 2:P2, OS Ref. ST824 604. ½m S of town centre, off B3109.

Open: Daily, 10.30am–4pm. Closed 25 Dec.

Admission: Free. Opening times and prices are valid until 31st March 2011, after this date details are subject to change please visit www.english-heritage.org.uk for the most up-to-date information.

Partial. Limited. Charged. Guide dogs only

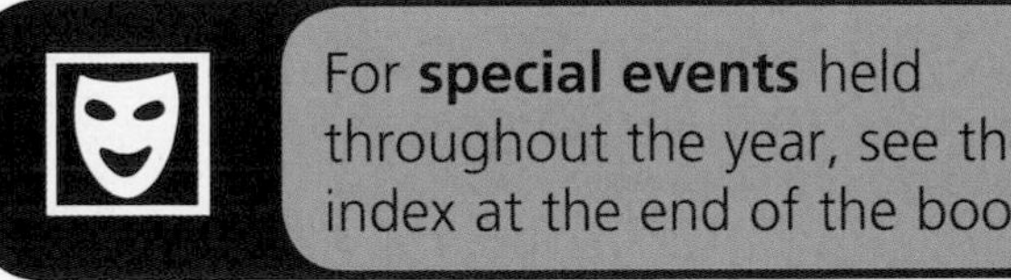

For **special events** held throughout the year, see the index at the end of the book.

CORSHAM COURT

CORSHAM, WILTSHIRE SN13 0BZ

www.corsham-court.co.uk

Tel/Fax: 01249 712214 / 701610 **E-mail:** staterooms@corsham-court.co.uk

Owner: J Methuen-Campbell Esq **Contact:** The Curator

Corsham Court, a splendid Elizabethan house dating from 1582, was acquired in 1745 to display Sir Paul Methuen's celebrated collection of 16th and 17th century Old Master paintings. This internationally renowned collection includes important works by Van Dyck, Carlo Dolci, Filippo Lippi, Salvator Rosa, Reynolds and Romney.

Capability Brown was employed during the 1760's to enlarge the house, creating the magnificent Picture Gallery and suite of State Rooms. These rooms still retain their original silk wall-hangings and furniture designed by Chippendale, Johnson, Cobb and the Adam brothers.

Surrounding the Court are the delightful gardens and parkland which were initially designed by Brown and later completed by Humphry Repton. The gardens are particularly admired for the collection of magnolias, specimen trees and spring bulbs.

Location: MAP 3:A2, OS Ref. ST874 706. Car: Signposted from the A4, approx 4m W of Chippenham. Bus: Bath to Chippenham. Rail: Chippenham Station 6m.

Open: Spring / Summer: 20 March – 30 September. Daily, except Mons & Fris but including Bank Holidays 2–5.30pm. Last admission 5pm. Winter: 1 October – 19 March (closed December).Weekends only 2–4.30pm. Last admission 4pm. NB: Open throughout the year by appointment for groups. For further details and special viewings of the the collection, see our website.

Admission:.House & Garden: Adult £7.00, Child (5–15yrs) £3.00, OAP £6.00. Groups (includes guided tour) Adult £6.00. Garden only: Adult £2.50, Child (5–15yrs) £1.50, OAP £2.00.

No photography in house. WCs Max 45. If requested the owner may meet the group. Bookings for morning tours are preferred. Tour time 1hr. 120 yards from the house. Coaches may park in Church Square. Coach parties must book in advance. No camper vans, no caravans. Available: rate negotiable. A guide will be provided.

GREAT CHALFIELD MANOR & GARDENS

Nr Melksham, Wiltshire SN12 8NH

Tel: 01225 782239 **Email:** greatchalfieldmanor@nationaltrust.org.uk

Owner: National Trust **Contact:** Mr & Mrs R. Floyd

Charming 15th century manor with Arts and Crafts gardens c1910.

Location: MAP 3:A2, OS Ref. ST860 631. 3m SW of Melksham off B3107 via Broughton Gifford Common, sign for Atworth. Rail: Bradford-on-Avon 3m, Chippenham 10m.

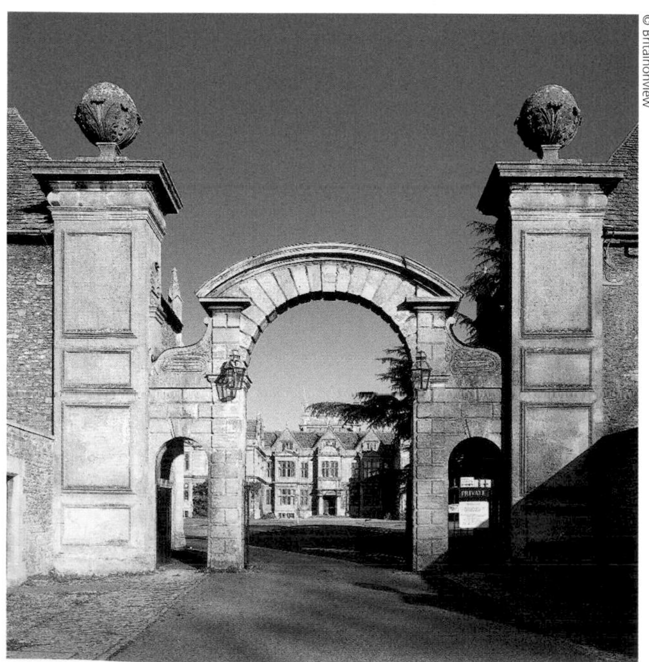

© Britainonview

Corsham Court

© Skyscan. Taken from the book 'Historic Family Homes & Gardens from the Air'.

HAMPTWORTH LODGE

HAMPTWORTH, LANDFORD, SALISBURY, WILTSHIRE SP5 2EA

www.hamptworthestate.co.uk

Tel: 01794 390700 **Fax:** 01794 390644

E-mail: kate@hamptworthestate.co.uk

Contact: N D Anderson Esq/Miss K Anderson

Jacobean style manor house standing in mature deciduous woodland within the northern perimeter of the New Forest National Park. Grade II* with period furniture including clocks. The Great Hall has an unusual roof truss construction. There is a collection of prentice pieces and the Moffatt collection of contemporary copies of Tudor furniture. One room has late 17th century leather wall coverings. Henry Willis organ. Available for events.

Location: MAP 3:C5, OS Ref. SU227 195. 10m SE of Salisbury on road linking Downton on A338. (Salisbury to Ringwood road) to Landford on A36 (Salisbury to Southampton road).

Open: House and Garden: 11–14 Apr, 3–6 May, 9–12 May, 13–16 Jun, 25–30 Jul, 1–6 Aug. 2.15pm–last admission 4.15pm. Private Groups and coaches only by prior appointment from 1 Apr–31 Oct only.

Admission: Adult £6, Child (under 5yrs) Free.

Ground floor & grounds. Obligatory.

LACOCK ABBEY, FOX TALBOT MUSEUM & VILLAGE

Lacock, Chippenham, Wiltshire SN15 2LG

Tel: 01249 730459 (Visitor Reception) **Fax:** 01249 730501 (Estate Office)

www.nationaltrust.org.uk

Owner: National Trust **Contact:** The General Manager

Founded in 1232 and converted to country house c1540.

Location: MAP 3:A2, OS Ref. ST919 684. In the village of Lacock, 3m N of Melksham, 3m S of Chippenham just E of A350.

LONGLEAT

See page 212 for full page entry.

© Jane Gifford

LYDIARD PARK

LYDIARD TREGOZE, SWINDON, WILTSHIRE SN5 3PA

www.lydiardpark.org.uk

Tel: 01793 770401 **Fax:** 01793 770968 **E-mail:** lydiardpark@swindon.gov.uk

Owner: Swindon Borough Council **Contact:** The Keeper

Lydiard Park is the ancestral home of the Viscounts Bolingbroke. This beautifully restored Palladian house contains the family's furnishings and portraits, exceptional plasterwork, rare 17th century window and room devoted to the 18th century society artist Lady Diana Spencer. The faithfully restored 18th century ornamental Walled Garden is a beautiful and tranquil place to stroll, with seasonal displays of flowers and unique garden features. Exceptional monuments, including the Golden Cavalier, in the adjacent church.

Location: MAP 3:B1, OS Ref. SU104 848. 4m W of Swindon, 1½ m N of M4/J16.

Open: House & Walled Garden: Tues–Sun, 11am–5pm (4pm Nov–Feb). Grounds: all day, closing at dusk. Victorian Christmas decorations in December.

Admission: House & Walled Garden: Adult £4.50, Senior Citizen £4, Child £2.25. Pre-booked groups: Adult £4, Senior Citizen £3.50. Opening times and prices may change April 2011 – please telephone to confirm.

No photography in house. Open all year, but groups must book. By arrangement. In grounds on leads.

© NTPL / Andrew Butler

Great Chalfield Manor

© NTPL / Arnhel de Serra

Lacock Abbey

THE MERCHANT'S HOUSE

132 HIGH STREET, MARLBOROUGH, WILTSHIRE SN8 1HN

www.themerchantshouse.co.uk

Tel/Fax: 01672 511491 **E-mail:** manager@merchantshousetrust.co.uk

Owner: Marlborough Town Council, leased to The Merchant's House (Marlborough) Trust **Contact:** Michael Gray

Situated in Marlborough's world-famous High Street, The Merchant's House is one of the finest middle-class houses in England. Its well-preserved Panelled Chamber was completed in 1656. Both the Dining Room and Great Staircase display recently uncovered 17th century wall paintings which have aroused much expert interest. Latest attraction is our 17th century formal garden.

Location: MAP 3:B2, OS Ref. SU188 691. N side of High Street, near Town Hall.

Open: Easter–end Sept: Fris & Sats, guided tours 11am, 12noon, 2pm, 3pm. Booked groups at other times by appointment.

Admission: Adult £5, Child 50p. Booked groups (10-40): Adult £4, Child 50p.

Photography only by arrangement. Outside house, also in Hillier's Yard. Guide dogs only.

© NTPL / Peter Cook

MOMPESSON HOUSE

CATHEDRAL CLOSE, SALISBURY, WILTSHIRE SP1 2EL

www.nationaltrust.org.uk

Tel: 01722 335659 **Infoline:** 01722 420980 **Fax:** 01722 321559
E-mail: mompessonhouse@nationaltrust.org.uk
Owner: National Trust **Contact:** The Property Manager

Elegant,spacious house in the Cathedral Close, built 1701. Featured in award-winning film Sense and Sensibility. Magnificent plasterwork and fine oak staircase.Good period furniture and the Turnbull collection of 18th century drinking glasses. The delightful walled garden has a pergola and traditional herbaceous borders.Garden Tea Room serves light refreshments.

Location: MAP 3:B4, OS Ref. SU142 297. On N side of Choristers' Green in Cathedral Close, near High Street Gate. Rail: Salisbury Station ½ mile.

Open: 12 Mar–30 Oct: Sat–Wed, 11am–5pm. Last admission 4.30pm. Open Good Fri.

***Admission:** Adult £5.75, Child £2.90, Family (2+3) £14.40, Groups £4.75. Garden only: £1. Reduced rate when arriving by public transport. *includes a voluntary donation but visitors can choose to pay the standard prices displayed at the property and on the website.

Special Events: Regular croquet on the lawn, for all ages and stages.

WCs. By arrangement. Guide dogs only.

NEWHOUSE

Redlynch, Salisbury, Wiltshire SP5 2NX
Tel: 01725 510055
Owner: George & June Jeffreys **Contact:** Mrs Jeffreys

A brick, Jacobean 'Trinity' House, c1609, with two Georgian wings and a basically Georgian interior. Home of the Eyre family since 1633.

Location: MAP 3:B5, OS184, SU218 214. 9m S of Salisbury between A36 & A338.

Open: 1 Mar–8 Apr, Mon–Fri & 29 Aug: 2–5pm.

Admission: Adult £5.00, Child £3.00, Conc. £5.00. Groups (15+): Adult £4.00, Child £3.00, Conc. £4.00.

No photography in house, except at weddings. By arrangement.
Limited for coaches. Guide dogs only.

NORRINGTON MANOR

Alvediston, Salisbury, Wiltshire SP5 5LL
Tel: 01722 780 259
Owner/Contact: Mr & Mrs J Sykes

Built in 1377 it has been altered and added to in every century since, with the exception of the 18th century. Only the hall and the 'undercroft' remain of the original. It is currently a family home and the Sykes are only the third family to own it.

Location: MAP 3:A5, OS Ref. ST966 237. Signposted to N of Berwick St John and Alvediston road (half way between the two villages).

Open: By appointment in writing.

Admission: A donation to the local churches is asked for.

Unsuitable. By arrangement. Limited for cars, none for coaches.

For **corporate hospitality** venues see our special index at the end of the book.

© NTPL / Nadia Mackenzie

Mompesson House

© English Heritage

OLD SARUM ⌗

CASTLE ROAD, SALISBURY, WILTSHIRE SP1 3SD

www.english-heritage.org.uk/oldsarum

Tel: 01722 335398 **E-mail:** customers@english-heritage.org.uk

Owner: English Heritage **Contact:** Visitor Operations Team

High above the Salisbury Plain stands the mighty hill fort of Old Sarum, the former site of the city of Salisbury. The Romans, Saxons and Normans have all left their mark on this site. Discover where the Norman cathedral once stood, and enjoy magnificent views over the surrounding countryside.

Location: MAP 3:B4, OS184, SU138 327. 2m N of Salisbury off A345.

Open: 1 Apr–30 Jun: daily, 10am–5pm. 1 Jul–31 Aug: daily, 9am–6pm. 1–30 Sep: daily, 10am–5pm. 1–31 Oct: daily, 10am–4pm. 1 Nov–31 Jan: daily, 11am–3pm. 1–28 Feb: daily, 11am–4pm. 1–31 Mar: daily, 10am–4pm. Closed 24–26 Dec & 1 Jan.

Admission: Adult £3.50, Child £1.80, Conc. £3. 15% discount for groups (11+). EH Members Free. Opening times and prices are valid until 31st March 2011, after this date details are subject to change please visit www.english-heritage.org.uk for the most up-to-date information.

Special Events: See English Heritage website for details of special events.

WCs. Partial. By arrangement. Limited for coaches. On leads.

© English Heritage

OLD WARDOUR CASTLE ⌗

NR TISBURY, WILTSHIRE SP3 6RR

www.english-heritage.org.uk/oldwardour

Tel/Fax: 01747 870487 **E-mail:** customers@english-heritage.org.uk

Owner: English Heritage **Contact:** Visitor Operations Team

In a picture-book setting, the unusual hexagonal ruins of this 14th century castle stand on the edge of a beautiful lake, surrounded by landscaped grounds which include an elaborate rockwork grotto.

Location: MAP 3:A5, OS184, ST939 263. Off A30 2m SW of Tisbury.

Open: 1 Apr–30 Jun: daily, 10am–5pm. 1 Jul–31 Aug: daily, 10am–6pm. 1–30 Sep: daily, 10am–5pm. 1–31 Oct: daily, 10am–4pm. 1 Nov–31 Mar: Sat–Sun, 10am–4pm. Closed 24–26 Dec & 1 Jan.

Admission: Adult £3.80, Child £1.90, Conc. £3.20. 15% discount for groups (11+). EH Members Free. Opening times and prices are valid until 31st March 2011, after this date details are subject to change please visit www.english-heritage.org.uk for the most up-to-date information.

Special Events: See the English Heritage website for details of special events.

WCs. Partial. Limited for coaches. On leads.

© Longleat

Longleat – The Great Hall

© Robert Coles

THE PETO GARDEN AT IFORD MANOR

BRADFORD-ON-AVON, WILTSHIRE BA15 2BA

www.ifordmanor.co.uk

Tel: 01225 863146 **Fax:** 01225 862364

Owner/Contact: Mrs E A J Cartwright-Hignett

This unique Grade I Italian-style garden is set on a romantic hillside beside the River Frome. Designed by the Edwardian architect Harold A Peto, who lived at Iford Manor from 1899–1933, the garden has terraces, colonnades, a cloister, casita, statuary, evergreen planting and magnificent rural views. Renowned for its tranquility and peace, the Peto Garden won the 1998 HHA/Christie's *Garden of the Year* Award.

Location: MAP 2:P3, OS Ref. ST800 589. 7m SE of Bath via A36, signposted Iford. 1½m SW of Bradford-on-Avon via Westwood on B3109.

Open: Apr & Oct: Suns only & Easter Mon, 2–5pm. May–Sept: Tue–Thur, Sats, Suns & BH Mons, 2–5pm. Children under 10yrs welcome weekdays only for safety reasons.

Admission: Adult £5, Conc. £4.50. Groups (10+) welcome outside normal opening hours, by arrangement only, £5.

Partial. WCs. Teas (May–Sep: Sats, Suns & BHs, 2.30–5pm). Open to non-garden visitors. By arrangement. Limited for coaches. On leads, in grounds.

Wilton House

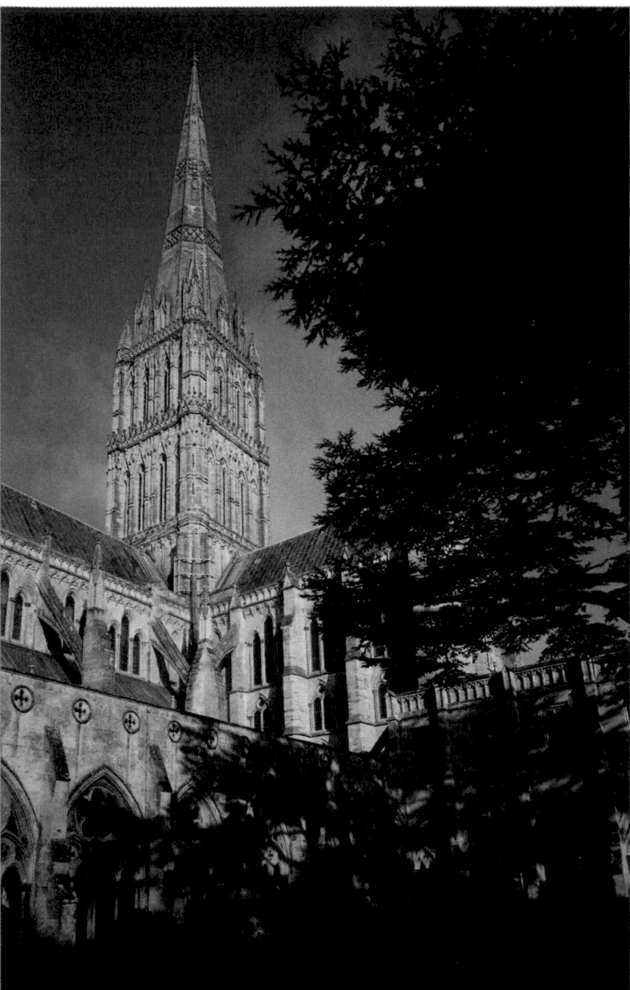

SALISBURY CATHEDRAL

33 THE CLOSE, SALISBURY SP1 2EJ

www.salisburycathedral.org.uk

Tel: 01722 555120 **Fax:** 01722 555116 **E-mail:** visitors@salcath.co.uk

Owner: The Dean & Chapter **Contact:** Visitor Services

Be inspired by the peace and beauty of one of Britain's finest medieval cathedrals, Salisbury Cathedral offers a warm welcome to all who visit. Set within eight acres of lawn and surrounded by historic buildings and museums within the spectacular Cathedral Close, the Cathedral is unique in being built almost entirely in one architectural style - Early English Gothic. Britain's tallest spire (123m / 404ft) was added a generation later.

Inside the Cathedral discover nearly 800 years of history including the finest preserved original Magna Carta (1215), Europe's oldest working clock (1386) and most stunning font (2008). Boy and girl choristers sing daily services. Explore the roof spaces on a tower tour, climbing 332 steps to the base of the spire, and admire the magnificent views across Salisbury.

New this year – the Cathedral's beautiful new flowing water font, designed by sculptor William Pye, and a new West Front statue of Canon Ezra, a 20th Century Sudanese martyr.

Location: MAP 3:B4, OS Ref. SU143 295. S of City. M3, A303, A30 from London or A36.

Open: All year daily: 7.15am–6.15pm.

Admission: Donation suggested. Event & Tower require ticket purchase.

Licensed. Tower tour: 90 mins–Book in advance. In city centre. In grounds, on leads.

STOURHEAD

See page 213 for full page entry.

STOURTON HOUSE FLOWER GARDEN

Stourton, Warminster, Wiltshire BA12 6QF

Tel: 01747 840417

Owner/Contact: Mrs E Bullivant

Four acres of peaceful, romantic, plantsman's garden. Rare daffodils, camellias, rhododendrons, roses, hydrangeas and wild flowers.

Location: MAP 2:P4, OS Ref. ST780 340. A303, 2m NW of Mere next to Stourhead car park. Follow blue signs.

Open: Apr–end Nov: Weds, Thurs, Suns, and BH Mons, 11am–6pm.

Admission: Adult £4, Child £1.

WILTON HOUSE

See page 214 for full page entry.

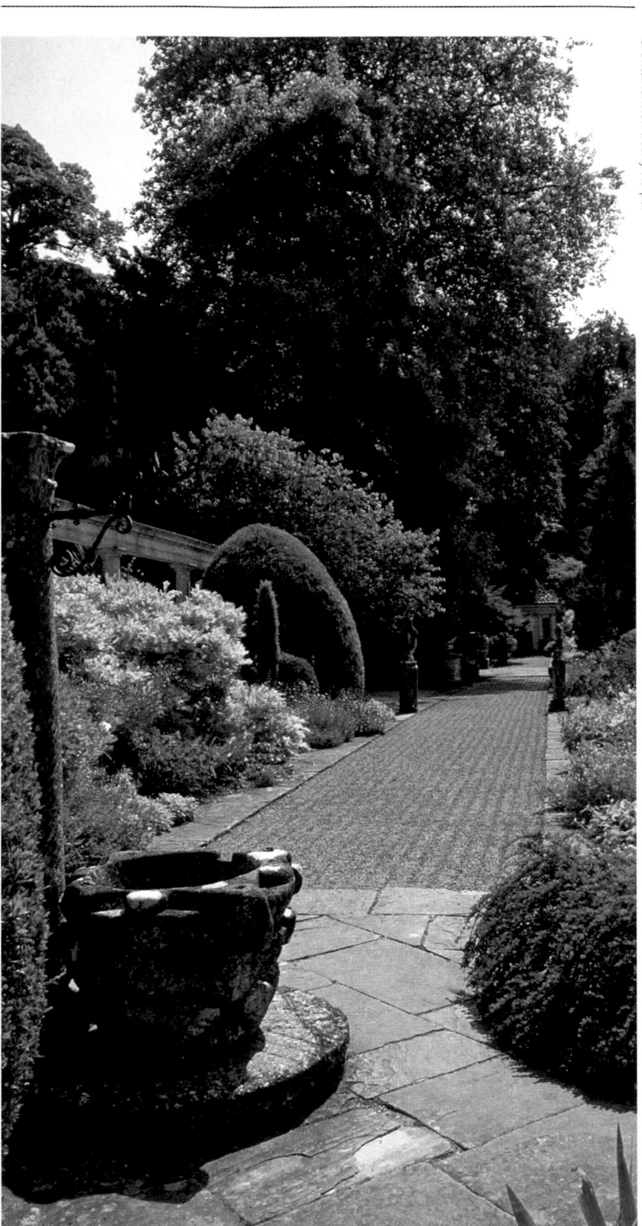

The Peto Garden at Iford Manor

STONEHENGE ⌗

AMESBURY, WILTSHIRE SP4 7DE

www.english-heritage.org.uk/stonehenge

Tel: 0870 3331181 (Customer Services) **Email:** customers@english-heritage.org.uk

Owner: English Heritage

The great and ancient stone circle of Stonehenge is unique; an exceptional survival from a prehistoric culture now lost to us. The monument evolved between 3,000BC and 1,600BC and is aligned with the rising and setting of the sun at the solstices, but its exact purpose remains a mystery. To this day Stonehenge endures as a source of inspiration and fascination and, for many, a place of worship and celebration. Discover the history and legends which surround this awe-inspiring site with a complimentary audio tour available in 10 languages (subject to availability).

Location: MAP 3:B4, OS Ref. SU122 422. 2m W of Amesbury on junction of A303 and A344 / A360.

Open: 1 Apr–31 May: daily 9.30am–6pm. 1 Jun–31 Aug: daily, 9am–7pm. 1 Sep–15 Oct: daily, 9.30am–6pm. 16 Oct–15 Mar: daily, 9.30am–4pm. 16–31 Mar: 9.30am–6pm. Closed 24/25 Dec. 26 Dec & 1 Jan, 10am–4pm. Opening times from 20–22 June may be subject to change due to Summer Solstice. Please call 0870 333 1181 before you visit. Recommended last admission time no later than 30 minutes before the advertised closing time. Stonehenge will close promptly 20 minutes after the advertised closing time. When weather conditions are bad, access may be restricted and visitors may not be able to use the walkway around the stone circle.

Admission: Adult £6.90, Child £3.50, Conc £5.90, Family (2+3) £17.30. Groups (11+) 10% discount. NT/EH Members Free. Opening times and prices are valid until 31st March 2011, after this date details are subject to change please visit www.english-heritage.org.uk for the most up-to-date information.

Guide dogs only.

Wilton House

Walsingham Abbey, Norfolk

Eastern Region

East Anglia has magical coastal areas ranging from The Wash in Norfolk down to the Essex marshes. The half timbered houses in Suffolk villages such as Lavenham contrast with the Norfolk flint found further north. Among the major properties that welcome visitors are Sandringham, the country home of HM The Queen, Woburn Abbey and Hatfield House; but off the beaten track find time for Copped Hall or The Manor, Hemingford Grey.

Hatfield House, Hertfordshire

Bedfordshire
Cambridgeshire
Essex
Hertfordshire
Norfolk
Suffolk

NORFOLK
CAMBRIDGESHIRE
SUFFOLK
BEDFORDSHIRE
ESSEX
HERTFORDSHIRE

Holkham Hall, Norfolk

Glemham Hall, Suffolk

Audley End, Essex
© English Heritage

■ **Owner:**
The Duke and Duchess of Bedford & The Trustees of the Bedford Estates

■ **Contact**
Woburn Abbey
Woburn
Bedfordshire MK17 9WA

Tel: 01525 290333
Fax: 01525 290271
E-mail: admissions@woburnabbey.co.uk

■ **Location**
MAP 7:D10
OS Ref. SP965 325

On A4012, midway between M1/J13, 3m, J14, 6m and the A5 (turn off at Hockliffe). London approx. 1hr by road (43m).

Rail: London Euston to Leighton Buzzard, Bletchley/Milton Keynes. Kings Cross Thameslink to Flitwick.

Air: Luton 14m. Heathrow 39m.

■ **Opening Times**
Woburn Abbey
15 April–2 October 2011, daily.

Gardens & Deer Park
All year: Daily
10am–5pm.
(except 24–26 December).

■ **Admission**
Woburn Abbey, Grounds, Deer Park & Car Park
Please telephone or visit our website for details.

Group rates available.

Conference/Function

ROOM	SIZE	MAX CAPACITY
Sculpture Gallery	128' x 24'	300 250 (sit-down)
Lantern Rm	44' x 21'	60
Long Harness Room	35' x 21'	80

WOBURN ABBEY

www.woburn.co.uk

Set in a beautiful 3,000 acre deer park, Woburn Abbey has been the home of the Russell Family for nearly 400 years, and is now occupied by the 15th Duke of Bedford and his family.

Admired as one of the world's finest private collections of art, there are many famous paintings by Cuyp, Gainsborough, Reynolds and Van Dyck. The Abbey houses the largest private collection in the world of Venetian views painted by Canaletto in one room (photograph below).

The tour of the Abbey covers three floors, including the vaults, with 18th century furniture, silver and gold collections, a wide range of porcelain and many items treasured by the Russell family throughout the centuries on display. Amongst the highlights are a selection of pieces from the Sevres dinner service presented to the 4th Duke by King Louis XV.

The Deer Park is home to ten species of deer, including the Père David, descended from the Imperial Herd of China, which was saved from extinction at Woburn and is now the largest breeding herd of this species outside china. In 1985 the 14th Duke gave 22 Père David deer to the People's Republic of China and herds are now well established in their natural environment and numbers several thousand.

Wobum Abbey specialises in banqueting, conferences, receptions and company days; and the Sculpture Gallery overlooking the Private Gardens provides a splendid setting for weddings and wedding receptions for groups of 20 to over 1,000.

2011 will see a number of events in the Park including Craft Fairs and a variety of musical and open air theatrical performances.

Suitable for fashion shows, product launches and company 'days out'. Use of parkland and garden. No photography in House.

Conferences, exhibitions, banqueting, luncheons, dinners in the Sculpture Gallery, Lantern & Long Harness rooms.

Group bookings in the Sculpture Gallery and the Duchess' Tea Room.

Licensed.

By arrangement, max groups of 8. Tours in French, German & Italian available. Guide book and audio guide available (additional charge). Special interest tours can be arranged.

Please telephone for details.

In park on leads, and guide dogs in house.

The Inn at Woburn.

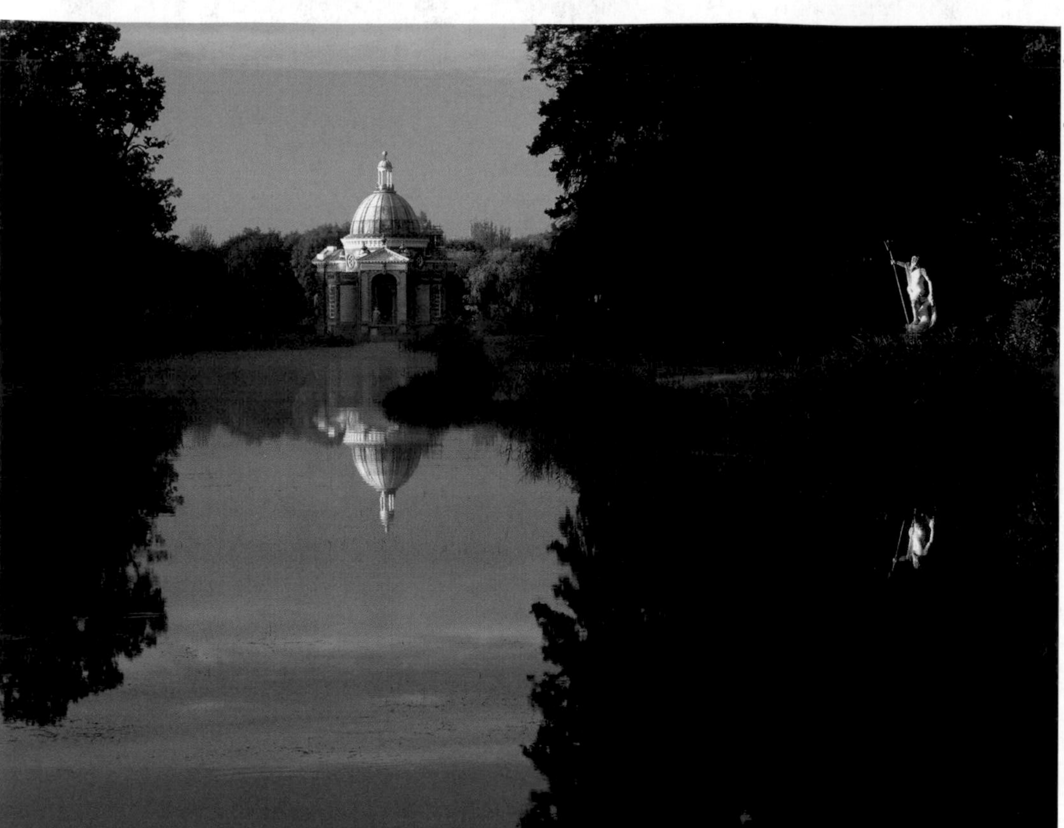
© English Heritage

WREST PARK ⌗

www.english-heritage.org.uk/wrest

Unseen and unknown for decades, the 'Sleeping Beauty' of English gardens wakes from its slumbers in July 2011 after a revitalisation project which will see its attractions and facilities transformed. Wrest Park will boast a new visitor centre in its Walled Garden - complete with introductory exhibition, shop, children's play area and café.

Wrest Park is unique in allowing visitors to see the evolution of garden styles over the 18th and 19th centuries. The De Grey family, owners from the middle ages until the early 20th century, commissioned famous designers over 250 years. Whereas in other gardens previous designs were lost in the pursuit of new gardening vogues, each generation at Wrest Park respected the vision of their predecessors.

In July 2011 Wrest Park will reopen with extended opening times and a greater programme of events. Improved access will lead visitors to the newly-restored Italian and Rose gardens and the amazing classical and Baroque garden buildings. They include the 18th century Pavilion by Thomas Archer, focal point of the extensive grounds at the end of a long stretch of water. Other buildings include a French-style Orangery and the 18th century Bowling Green House.

Inside the mansion, inspired by 18th century Parisian architecture, exciting new exhibitions tell the story of the estate, its evolution and its personalities. Selected rooms can be viewed, including the restored Countess' Sitting Room, shown as it would have been in the mid-19th century.

Please note no photography or stiletto heels in the house.

© English Heritage

© English Heritage

WCs. Picnickers welcome. Buggies available.

On leads.

■ Owner:

English Heritage

■ Contact

Visitor Operations Team
Silsoe
Luton
Bedfordshire MK45 4HS

Tel: 01525 860152
E-mail: customers@english-heritage.org.uk

■ Location

MAP 7:E10
OS Ref 153. TL093 356

¾m E of Silsoe off A6, 10m S of Bedford.

■ Opening Times

1 April–30 June:
Sat–Sun & BHs, 10am–6pm.

1 July–31 August:
Thu–Mon, 10am–6pm.

1–30 September:
Sat–Sun, 10am–6pm.

1–31 October:
Sat–Sun, 10am–5pm.

Last admission 1hr before closing. The house may be closed if an event is booked. The gardens may also close early. Please call to check.

■ Admission

Adult	£5.50
Child	£2.80
Conc.	£4.70
Family	£13.80

Group discounts.

EH members Free.

Opening times and prices are valid until 31st March 2011, after this date details are subject to change please visit www.english-heritage.org.uk for the most up-to-date information.

BUSHMEAD PRIORY ⌗

Colmworth, Bedford, Bedfordshire MK44 2LD

Tel: 01525 860000 **E-mail:** customers@english-heritage.org.uk

www.english-heritage.org.uk/bushmeadpriory

Owner: English Heritage **Contact:** Visitor Operations Team

A rare survival of the medieval refectory of an Augustinian priory, with its original timber-framed roof almost intact and containing interesting wall paintings and stained glass.

Location: MAP 7:E9, OS Ref. TL115 607. On unclassified road near Colmworth; off B660, 2m S of Bolnhurst. 5m W of St. Neots (A1).

Open: 1 May–31 Aug. Entry by pre-booked guided tours on first Sat of the month only. Telephone: 01525 860000 to book.

Admission: Adult £5.30, Child £2.70, Conc. £4.50. Group discount. EH members Free. Opening times and prices are valid until 31st March 2011, after this date details are subject to change please see www.english-heritage.org.uk for the most up-to-date information.

Picnickers welcome.

DE GREY MAUSOLEUM ⌗

Flitton, Bedford, Bedfordshire

Tel: 01525 860094 (Key-keeper) **E-mail:** customers@english-heritage.org.uk

www.english-heritage.org.uk/degreymausoleum

Owner: English Heritage **Contact:** Mrs Stimson

A remarkable treasure-house of sculpted tombs and monuments from the 16th to 19th centuries dedicated to the de Grey family of nearby Wrest Park.

Location: MAP 7:D10, OS Ref. TL059 359. Attached to the church on unclassified road 1½m W of A6 at Silsoe.

Open: Weekends only. Contact the keykeeper in advance. Mrs Stimson, 3 Highfield Rd, Flitton. Tel: 01525 860094.

Admission: Free. Opening times and prices are valid until 31st March 2011, after this date details are subject to change please see www.english-heritage.org.uk for the most up-to-date information.

HOUGHTON HOUSE ⌗

Ampthill, Bedford, Bedfordshire

Tel: 01223 582700 (Regional Office) **E-mail:** customers@english-heritage.org.uk

www.english-heritage.org.uk/houghtonhouse

Owner: English Heritage **Contact:** East of England Regional Office

Reputedly the inspiration for the 'House Beautiful' in John Bunyan's Pilgrim's Progress, it was built around 1615 for Mary, Dowager Countess of Pembroke. A mixture of Jacobean and Classical styles: the ground floors of two Italianate loggias survive, possibly the work of Inigo Jones. Download an audio tour from the website.

Location: MAP 7:E9, OS Ref. TL039 394. 1m NE of Ampthill off A421, 8m S of Bedford.

Open: Any reasonable time.

Admission: Free. Opening times and prices are valid until 31st March 2011, after this date details are subject to change please visit www.english-heritage.org.uk for the most up-to-date information.

Picnickers welcome.

MOGGERHANGER PARK

Park Road, Moggerhanger, Bedfordshire MK44 3RW

Tel: 01767 641007 **Fax:** 01767 641515

E-mail: enquiries@moggerhangerpark.com **www.moggerhangerpark.com**

Owner: Moggerhanger House Preservation Trust **Contact:** Mrs Carrie Irvin

Award Winning Georgian Grade I listed Country House designed by Sir John Soane, recently restored, in 33 acres of Humphry Repton designed parkland and woodland. Moggerhanger House has 3 executive conference suites and 2 function rooms, making an ideal venue for conferences, promotions, corporate entertainment, family functions and weddings.

Location: MAP 7:E9, OS Ref. TL048 475. On A603, 3m from A1 at Sandy, 6m from Bedford.

Open: House Tours: See website or telephone for current information. Grounds, Tearooms & Visitors' Centre: Open all year.

Admission: Please telephone 01767 641007.

Special Events: Snowdrops Jan/Feb. Bluebells April/May. Summer theatre, concerts, craft fairs – see website for current information.

No photography. No smoking. WCs. Licensed. Licensed.
By arrangement. Limited for coaches. On leads.

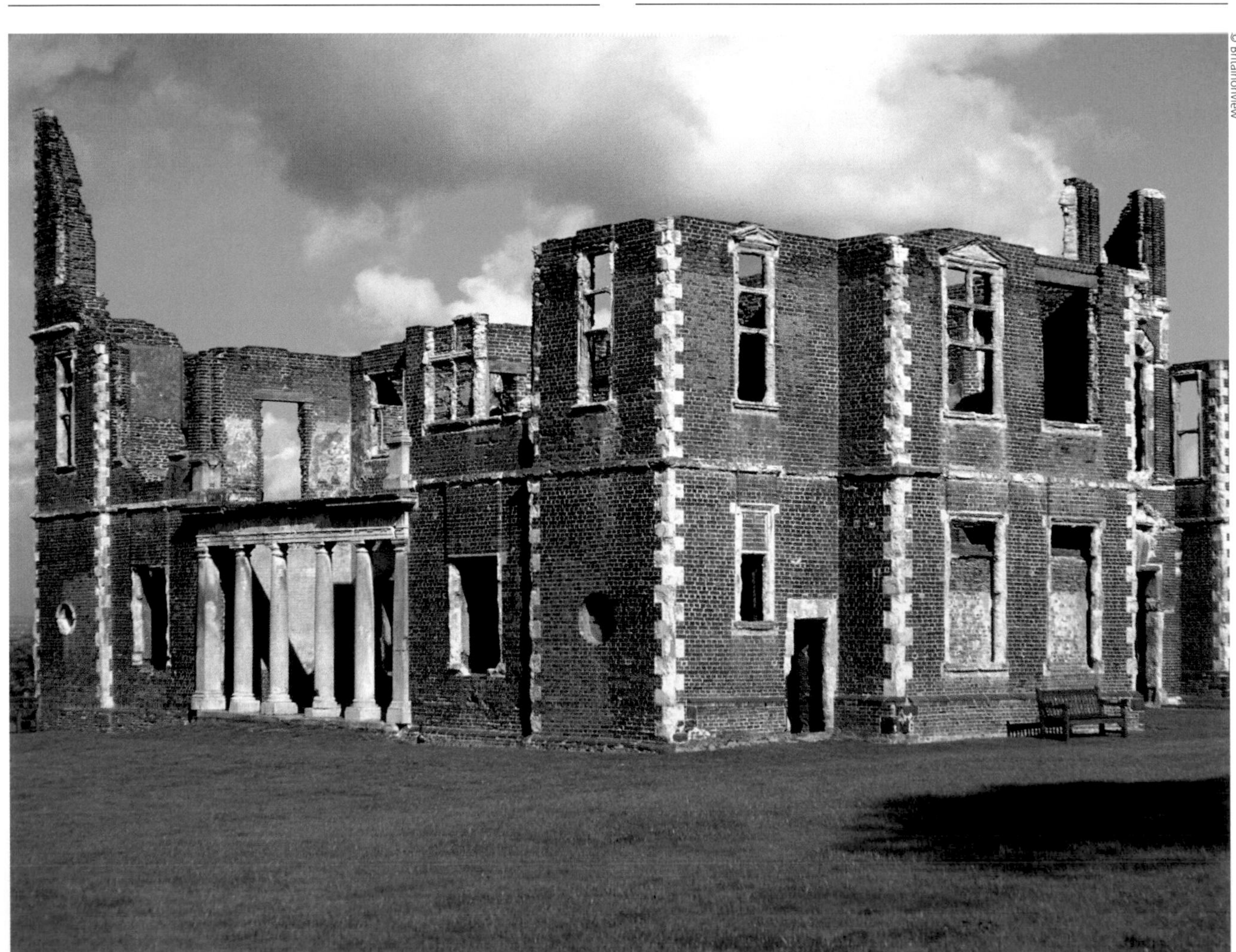

© Britainonview

Houghton House

© Britainonview / Grant Pritchard

Wrest Park

QUEEN ANNE'S SUMMERHOUSE

Shuttleworth, Old Warden, Bedfordshire SG18 9DU
Tel: 01628 825925 **Email:** bookings@landmarktrust.org.uk
www.landmarktrust.org.uk
Owner/Contact: The Landmark Trust

The outstanding fine brickwork of this foursquare folly makes it likely to date from the early eighteenth century, as its name suggests. Surrounded by the flora and forna of a beautiful woodland, with the model village of Old Warden just down the drive, this is a magical spot. The Landmark Trust, a building preservation charity, has undertaken a major restoration of the building which is now available for holidays all year round. Full details of Queen Anne's Summerhouse and 189 other historic and architecturally important buildings are featured in the Landmark Trust Handbook (£10 plus p&p refundable against a booking) and on the website.

Location: MAP 7:E10, OS Ref. TL144436.
Open: Available for holidays for up to 2 people throughout the year. Six Open Days a year and visits by appointment. Contact the Landmark Trust for details.
Admission: Free on Open Days and visits by appointment.

SWISS GARDEN

OLD WARDEN PARK, BEDFORDSHIRE

www.shuttleworth.org

Tel: 01767 627927
Operated By: The Shuttleworth Trust

The Swiss Garden, Old Warden Park, Bedfordshire, created in the 1820s by Lord Ongley, is a late Regency garden and an outstanding example of the Swiss picturesque. The Swiss Cottage provides the main element for this unusual and atmospheric garden. It provides the principal aspect for a number of contrived vistas which lead the eye towards this attractive thatched structure. Interesting things to see in the garden are: a grotto and fernery, a thatched tree shelter, an Indian Pavilion, two ponds and many fine specimens of shrubs and conifers, plus some remarkable trees.

Location: MAP 7:E9, OS Ref. TL150 447. 1½m W of Biggleswade A1 roundabout, signposted from A1 and A600.
Open: Mar–Oct: 9.30am–5pm; Nov–Feb: 9.30am–4pm. Closed Christmas week.
Admission: Adult £5, Child Free, Conc. £4. Special rates for groups, tours & private hire.
Catering. Refreshments adjacent.

TURVEY HOUSE

Turvey, Bedfordshire MK43 8EL
Tel/Fax: 01234 881244 **E-mail:** danielhanbury@hotmail.com
Owner: The Hanbury Family **Contact:** Daniel Hanbury

A neo-classical house set in picturesque parkland bordering the River Great Ouse. The principal rooms contain a fine collection of 18th and 19th century English and Continental furniture, pictures, porcelain, *objets d'art* and books. Walled Garden.

Location: MAP 7:D9, OS Ref. SP939528. Between Bedford and Northampton on A428.
Open: 9, 30 Apr. 2, 3, 5, 7, 17, 19, 21, 28, 30, 31 May. 2, 4, 14, 16, 18, 28, 30 Jun. 2, 12, 14, 16, 26, 28, 30 Jul. 27, 29 Aug, 2–5pm. Last Admission 4.30pm.
Admission: Adult £6, Child £3.
No photography in house. Partial. Obligatory.
Ample for cars, none for coaches.

WOBURN ABBEY

See page 224 for full page entry.

WREST PARK

See page 225 for full page entry.

© Woburn Abbey / Heritage House Group / Peter Smith

Woburn Abbey

© NT / Richard Todd

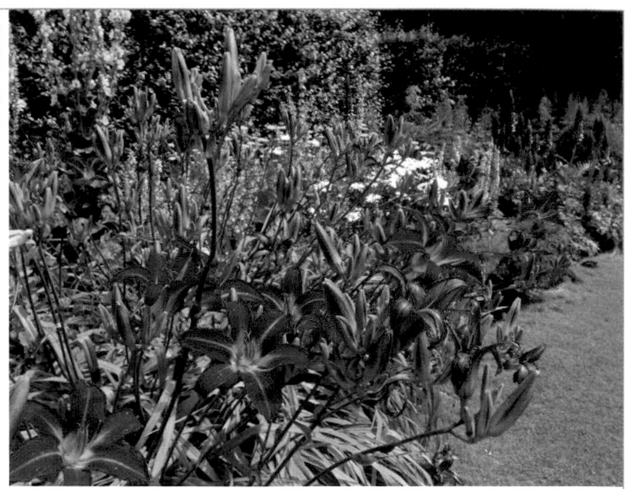

© Brian & Nina Chapple

ANGLESEY ABBEY, GARDENS & LODE MILL

QUY ROAD, LODE, CAMBRIDGESHIRE CB25 9EJ

www.nationaltrust.org.uk/angleseyabbey

Tel: 01223 810080 **Fax:** 01223 810088 **E-mail:** angleseyabbey@nationaltrust.org.uk

Owner: National Trust **Contact:** Administrator

A passion for tradition and style inspired one man to transform a run-down country house and desolate landscape. Step into his elegant home and encounter the luxuries enjoyed by guests. Experience the warmth and comfort and be amazed at rare and fabulous objects. Lord Fairhaven was a generous host, delighting in entertaining guests and a life occupied with horse racing and shooting. The 114 acre garden, with its working watermill, wildlife discovery area and statuary offers inspiration and planting for all seasons. Explore the borders, meadow and avenues bursting with vibrant colour, delicious scent and the simple pleasures of nature.

Location: MAP 7:G8, OS Ref. TL533 622. 6m NE of Cambridge on B1102, signs from A14 jct35.

Open: House: 2 Mar–30 Oct, Wed–Sun, 11am–5pm; Garden, Restaurant, Shop & Plant Centre: 28 Feb–30 Oct, Mon–Sun, 10.30am–5.30pm; Lode Mill: 2 Mar–30 Oct, Wed–Sun, 11am–4pm. Winter: Garden, Restaurant, Shop & Plant Centre: 1 Jan–27 Feb & 31 Oct–31 Dec, Mon–Sun, 10.30am – 4.30pm; Picture Galleries: 1 Jan–16 Jan & 16 Nov–31 Dec, Wed–Sun, 11am–3.30pm; Lode Mill: 1 Jan–27 Feb & 2 Nov–31 Dec, Wed–Sun, 11am–3pm. House open BH Mons. Closed Christmas Eve, Christmas Day and Boxing Day. Groups must book, no groups on BHs. Snowdrop season: 24 Jan–27 Feb.

***Admission:** House, Garden & Mill: Adult £10.50, Child £5.25, Family £26.25, Family (1 adult) £15.75. Groups: Adult £8.90, child £4.45. Garden & Mill (+Picture Galleries in the winter): Adult £6.25, Child £3.10, Family £15.60, Family (1 adult) £9.35. Groups: Adult £5.30, Child £2.60 *includes a voluntary donation of at least 10% which will be put towards the restoration and upkeep of this property. Visitors can choose to pay the standard prices displayed at the entrance and on the website.

Special Events: From garden study mornings to live theatre, children's fun days and wildlife watchings, there are events to suit everyone all year round.

WCs. Licensed. By arrangement. Guide dogs only.

©Nigel Luckhurst

CAMBRIDGE UNIVERSITY BOTANIC GARDEN

1 BROOKSIDE, CAMBRIDGE CB2 1JE

www.botanic.cam.ac.uk

Tel: 01223 336265 **Fax:** 01223 336278 **E-mail:** enquiries@botanic.cam.ac.uk

Owner: University of Cambridge **Contact:** Enquiries Desk

Opened in 1846 by John Henslow, teacher and mentor of Charles Darwin, this heritage-listed garden displays over 8000 plant species in a beautifully-designed landscape. Important collections include species tulips, geraniums and lavenders, and the finest arboretum in the East of England. The Garden also boasts the magnificent Glasshouses, recently restored to their original glory, which are planted with flamboyant tropical plants, extraordinary cacti and other plants requiring winter protection. Delicate alpines on the Rock Garden, Lake and Water Gardens teeming with aquatic life, and fabulous herbaceous plantings throughout make for a great day out whilst model gardens including the Dry Garden and Winter Garden provide year-round inspiration for the keen gardener.

Location: MAP 7:G9, OS Ref. TL453 573. 3/4 m S of Cambridge city centre; new Brookside Gate entrance on corner of Trumpington Road (A1309) and Bateman Street. Station Road Gate at the corner of Hills Road (A1307) and Station Road is 10mins walk from railway station with direct services to London, Birmingham and the north-west, and Norwich.

Open: Apr–Sept: daily, 10am–6pm; closes 5pm in Autumn & Spring and 4pm in winter. Closed over Christmas and New Year, please telephone for details.

Admission: Adult £4, Child (under 16yrs) Free, Conc. £3.50. Groups must book. Please use Trumpington Park & Ride, now open daily, and alight Bateman Street stop.

By arrangement. Street/Pay & Display. Schools and leisure groups must book. Guide dogs only.

DENNY ABBEY & THE FARMLAND MUSEUM

Ely Road, Chittering, Waterbeach, Cambridgeshire CB25 9PQ

Tel: 01223 860489 **E-mail:** customers@english-heritage.org.uk

www.english-heritage.org.uk/dennyabbey

Owner: English Heritage/Managed by the Farmland Museum Trust

Contact: Visitor Operations Team

What at first appears to be an attractive stone farmhouse is actually the remains of a 12th century Benedictine abbey which, at different times, also housed the Knights Templar and Franciscan nuns. Founded by the Countess of Pembroke. Family-friendly activities include hands-on interactives.

Location: MAP 7:G8, OS Ref. TL495 684. 6m N of Cambridge on the E side of the A10.

Open: 1 Apr–31 Oct: Mon–Fri, 12 noon–5pm. Sat, Sun & BHs 10.30am–5pm.

Admission: Museum & Abbey: Adult £4.00, Child £2.00, Child under 5 Free, Conc. £3.00, Family £10.00. The Abbey is free to members but there is a small charge for the Museum: Adult £2.80, Child £1.00, Conc £2.00, Family £6.00. Opening times and prices are valid until 31st March 2011, after this date details are subject to change please visit www.english-heritage.org.uk for the most up-to-date information.

Farmland museum. Picnickers welcome. WC. On leads.

DOCWRA'S MANOR GARDEN

Shepreth, Royston, Hertfordshire SG8 6PS

Tel: 01763 261473 **Information:** 01763 260677

Owner: Mrs Faith Raven **Contact:** Peter Rocket

Extensive garden around building dating from the 18th century.

Location: MAP 7:F9, OS Ref. TL393 479. In Shepreth via A10 from Royston.

Open: All year: Weds & Fris, 10am–4pm & 1st Sun in month from Apr–Oct: 2–4pm.

Admission: £4.

For **accommodation** in the Eastern Region, see our special index at the end of the book.

ELTON HALL

Nr PETERBOROUGH PE8 6SH

www.eltonhall.com

Tel: 01832 280468 **Fax:** 01832 280584 **E-mail:** office@eltonhall.com

Owner: Sir William Proby Bt, CBE **Contact:** The Administrator

Sir Peter Proby rose to prominence during the reign of Elizabeth I and by the early 17th century had acquired land at Elton. His grandson, Sir Thomas, was the first member of the family to establish himself at Elton Hall and he built a charming Restoration house attached to the medieval buildings. Succesive generations, who later became the Earls of Carysfort, have added to the house greatly, both architecturally and artistically. The house has many fine paintings and furniture. The library is one of the best in private hands and includes Henry VIII's prayer book. Since 1983 the garden has been energetically restored and includes finely clipped topiary, a stunning new flower garden, Millennium Orangery and Box Walk.

Location: MAP 7:E7, OS Ref. TL091 930. Close to A1 in the village of Elton, off A605 Peterborough – Oundle Road.

Open: Late May bank holiday (Sun & Mon); June & Jul : Weds, Thur. Aug: Wed, Thur, Sun & BH Mon, 2–5pm. Private groups by arrangement Apr–Sept.

Admission: House & Garden: £8, Conc. £7. Garden only: Adult £5.50, Conc. £5. Accompanied child under 16 Free.

No photography in house. Garden suitable. Obligatory. Guide dogs in gardens only.

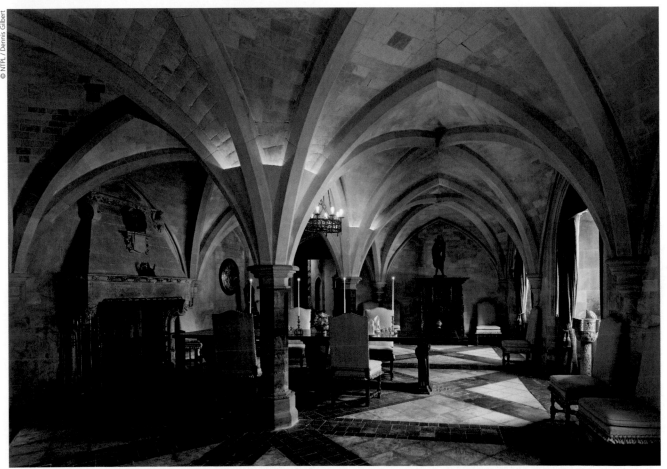

© NTPL / Dennis Gilbert

Anglesey Abbey

Ely Cathedral

ELY CATHEDRAL

The Chapter House, The College, Ely, Cambridgeshire CB7 4DL

Tel: 01353 667735 ext.261 **Fax:** 01353 665658

Contact: Sally-Ann Ford (Visits & Tours Manager)

A wonderful example of Romanesque architecture. Octagon and Lady Chapel are of special interest. Superb medieval domestic buildings surround the Cathedral. Stained Glass Museum. Brass rubbing. Octagon and West Tower tours peak season.

Location: MAP 7:G7, OS Ref. TL541 803. Via A10, 15m N of Cambridge City centre.

Open: Summer Daily 7am–7pm. Winter Mon–Sat 7.30am–6pm, Sun 7.30am–5pm.

Admission: Adult £6, Child Free. Extra for Museum and Tower.

KIMBOLTON CASTLE

Kimbolton, Huntingdon, Cambridgeshire PE28 0EA

Tel: 01480 860505 **Fax:** 01480 861763

www.kimbolton.cambs.sch.uk/thecastle

Owner: Governors of Kimbolton School **Contact:** Mrs N Butler

A late Stuart house, an adaptation of a 13th century fortified manor house, with evidence of Tudor modifications. The seat of the Earls and Dukes of Manchester 1615–1950, now a school. Katharine of Aragon died in the Queen's Room – the setting for a scene in Shakespeare's Henry VIII. 18th century rebuilding by Vanbrugh and Hawksmoor; Gatehouse by Robert Adam; the Pellegrini mural paintings on the Staircase, in the Chapel and in the Boudoir are the best examples in England of this gifted Venetian decorator. New Heritage Room.

Location: MAP 7:E8, OS Ref. TL101 676. 7m NW of St Neots on B645.

Open: 6 Mar & 6 Nov, 1–4pm.

Admission: Adult £5, Child £2.50, OAP £4. Groups by arrangement throughout the year, including evenings, special rates apply.

Unsuitable. By arrangement. On leads in grounds.

LONGTHORPE TOWER

Thorpe Rd, Longthorpe, Cambridgeshire PE1 1HA

Tel: 01536 203230 **E-mail:** customers@english-heritage.org.uk

www.english-heritage.org.uk/longthorpetower

Owner: English Heritage **Contact:** Visitor Operations Team

The finest example of 14th century domestic wall paintings in northern Europe including the Wheel of Life, the Nativity and King David. The Tower that contains the paintings, is part of a fortified manor house.

Location: MAP 7:E6, OS Ref. TL163 983. 2m W of Peterborough just off A47.

Open: 1 Apr–30 Sep: Pre-booked guided tours on first Sun of the month only. Tel 01536 203230 during office hours to book.

Admission: Adult £5.30, Child £2.70, Conc. £4.50. Group discount. EH members Free. Opening times and prices are valid until 31st March 2011, after this date details are subject to change please see www.english-heritage.org.uk for the most up-to-date information.

Picnickers welcome. By arrangement.

ISLAND HALL

GODMANCHESTER, CAMBRIDGESHIRE PE29 2BA

www.islandhall.com

Tel: (Groups) 01480 459676 (Individuals via *Invitation to View*) 01206 573948

E-mail: cvp@cvpdesigns.com

Owner: Mr Christopher & Lady Linda Vane Percy **Contact:** Mr C Vane Percy

An important mid 18th century mansion of great charm, owned and restored by an award-winning interior designer. This family home has lovely Georgian rooms, with fine period detail, and interesting possessions relating to the owners' ancestors since their first occupation of the house in 1800. A tranquil riverside setting with formal gardens and ornamental island forming part of the grounds in an area of Best Landscape. Octavia Hill wrote *"This is the loveliest, dearest old house, I never was in such a one before."*

Location: MAP 7:F8, OS Ref. TL244 706. Centre of Godmanchester, Post Street next to free car park. 1m S of Huntingdon, 15m NW of Cambridge A14.

Open: Groups by arrangement: All year round. Individuals via *Invitation to View*.

Admission: Groups: (40+) Adult £6.50, (20–40) Adult £7. Under 20 persons, min charge £110 per group (sorry but no children under 13yrs).

See website for more details. Home made teas.

THE MANOR, HEMINGFORD GREY

HUNTINGDON, CAMBRIDGESHIRE PE28 9BN

www.greenknowe.co.uk

Tel: 01480 463134 **E-mail:** diana_boston@hotmail.com

Owner: Mrs D S Boston **Contact:** Diana Boston

Built about 1130 and one of the oldest continuously inhabited houses in Britain. Made famous as 'Green Knowe' by the author Lucy Boston. Her patchwork collection is also shown. Four acre garden, laid out by Lucy Boston, surrounded by moat, with topiary, old roses, award winning irises and herbaceous borders.

Location: MAP 7:F8, OS Ref. TL290 706. Off A14, 3m SE of Huntingdon. 12m NW of Cambridge. Access is by a small gate on the riverside footpath. Bus: No. 5 Cambridge - Huntingdon bus stops in Hemingford Grey. Coach: Off A14, 3m SE of Huntingdon. 12m NW of Cambridge. Please contact us for coach drop off and parking information. Rail: Nearest station Huntingdon (on Kings Cross line), then bus or taxi.

Open: House: All year (except May), to individuals or groups by prior arrangement. In May guided tours will be daily at 2pm (booking advisable). Garden: All year, daily, 11am–5pm (4pm in winter).

Admission: House & Garden: 1 May–31 July: Adult £7, Child £2, OAP £5.50. Rest of year: Adult £6, Child £2, OAP £4.50. Garden only: 1 May–31 July: Adult £4, Child Free, OAP £3.50. Rest of year: Adult £3, Child Free, OAP £2.50

No photography in house. Partial. By prior arrangement. Obligatory. Cars: Disabled only. Coaches: Nearby. On leads.

OCTAVIA HILL'S BIRTHPLACE HOUSE

8 South Brink, Wisbech, Cambridgeshire PE13 1JB

Tel/Fax: 01945 476358 **E-mail:** info@octaviahill.org

www.octaviahill.org

Owner: Octavia Hill Birthplace Museum Trust **Contact:** Mr Peter Clayton

A Grade II* listed Georgian house, in which Octavia Hill, social reformer and cofounder of the National Trust was born. Features for 2011 include a Victorian Chamber of Horrors, a history of social housing room, a National Trust room, Victorian tea room, garden and shop.

Location: MAP 7:G6, OS Ref. TF459 096. On S bank of River Nene, in Wisbech.

Open: All year by arrangement. 16 Mar–31 Oct, Mon–Wed, Sat & Sun, 1–4.30pm (last admission 4pm).

Admission: Adult £3.50, Child £1.50, Family (2+2) £8, Groups, Conc. & NT members £2.50.

WC. Obligatory. 2 coach bays nearby. Guide dogs only.

OLIVER CROMWELL'S HOUSE

29 St Mary's Street, Ely, Cambridgeshire CB7 4HF

Tel: 01353 662062 **Fax:** 01353 668518 **E-mail:** tic@eastcambs.gov.uk

Owner: East Cambridgeshire District Council

The former home of the Lord Protector, now Ely TIC.

Location: MAP 7:G7, OS Ref. TL538 803. N of Cambridge, ¼m W of Ely Cathedral.

Open: 1 Nov–31 Mar: Mon–Fri & Sun, 11am–4pm; Sats, 10am–5pm. 1 Apr–31 Oct: daily, 10am–5pm.

Admission: Adult £4.50, Child £3.10, Conc. £4, Family (2+3) £13.

Properties that **open all year** appear in the special index at the end of the book.

©NTPL / Andreas von Einsiedel

PECKOVER HOUSE & GARDEN

NORTH BRINK, WISBECH, CAMBRIDGESHIRE PE13 1JR

www.nationaltrust.org.uk

Tel/Fax: 01945 583463 **E-mail:** peckover@nationaltrust.org.uk

Owner: National Trust **Contact:** The Property Secretary

Peckover House is an oasis hidden away in an urban environment. A classic Georgian merchant's townhouse, it was lived in by the Peckover family for 150 years and reflects their Quaker lifestyle. The gardens are outstanding - two acres of sensory delight, complete with orangery, summer houses, croquet lawn.

Location: MAP 7:G6, OS Ref. TF458 097. On N bank of River Nene, in Wisbech B1441. Rail: 12m from March (Cambs) & Downham Market stations.

Open: House & Garden: 12 Mar–30 Oct, Sat–Wed 1–5pm. Garden: As house, plus 19 Feb–6 Mar, Sat & Sun 12–3pm. Seven day opening in Easter holidays, Whitsun week, Wisbech Rose Fair week and October Half-Term. Also open for Christmas 10–14 Dec 12–7pm.

Admission: Adult £6.60, Child £3.30, Family £16.50. Groups discount (min 15 people)- book in advance with Property Secretary. **Special Events:** Call for leaflet.

No picnics in grounds, no photography in House. PMV available for loan in grounds. Free garden tours most days. Partial. WCs Licensed. By arrangement. Signposted. Guide dogs only.

PETERBOROUGH CATHEDRAL

Cathedral Office, Minster Precincts, Peterborough PE1 1XS

Tel: 01733 355300 **Fax:** 01733 355316

E-mail: andrew.watson@peterborough-cathedral.org.uk

www.peterborough-cathedral.org.uk

Contact: Andrew Watson

'An undiscovered gem.' With magnificent Norman architecture a unique 13th century nave ceiling, the awe-inspiring West Front and burial places of two Queens to make your visit an unforgettable experience. Exhibitions tell the Cathedral's story. Tours by appointment, of the cathedral, tower, Deanery Garden or Precincts. Group catering available – advance booking necessary. Cathedral gift shop and light refreshments at Coffee Shop. Business meeting facilities.

Location: MAP 7:E6, OS Ref. TL194 986. 4m E of A1, in City Centre.

Open: All year: Mon–Fri, 9am–6.30pm (restricted access after 5.30pm because of Evensong). Sat, 9am–5pm. Sun: services from 7.30am; visitors: 12 noon–5pm.

Admission: No fixed charge – donations are requested.

Visitors' Centre. By arrangement. None. Guide dogs only. See website for details.

© NTPL / Andreas von Einsiedel

Peckover House

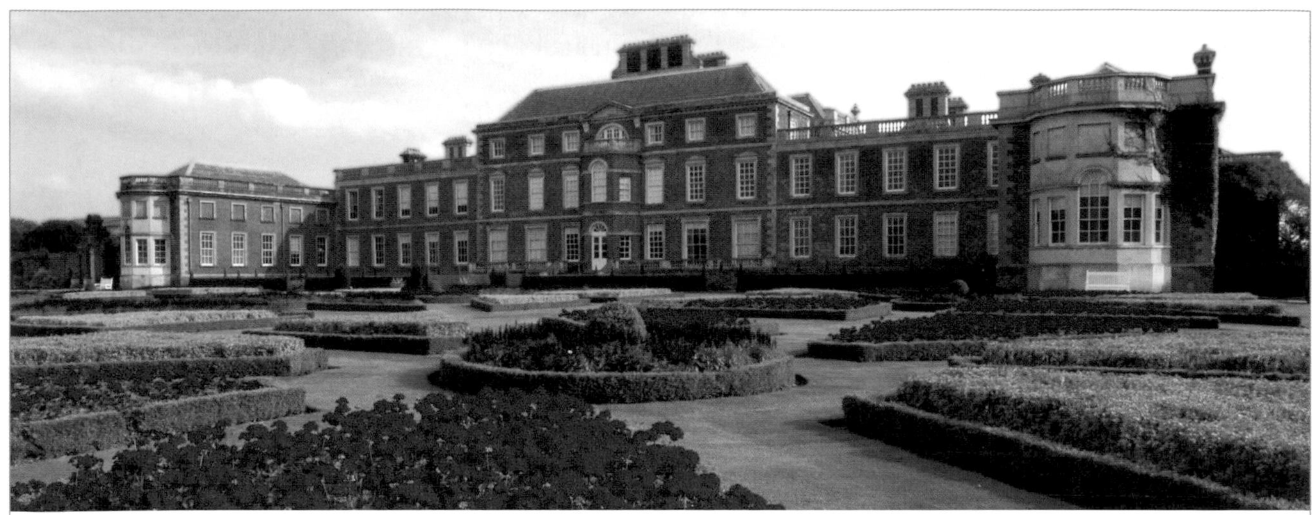

© NT / Fisheye Images

WIMPOLE HALL & HOME FARM

ARRINGTON, ROYSTON, CAMBRIDGESHIRE SG8 0BW

www.nationaltrust.org.uk www.wimpole.org

Tel: 01223 206000 **Fax:** 01223 207838 **E-mail:** wimpolehall@nationaltrust.org.uk

Owner: National Trust **Contact:** General Manager

A unique working estate still guided by the seasons, an impressive mansion at its heart, with beautiful interiors by Gibbs, Flitcroft and Soane. Uncover the stories of the people who have shaped Wimpole; soak up the atmosphere; take in the spectacular views and find your own special place. Stroll through the Pleasure Grounds to the Walled Garden, bursting with seasonal produce and glorious herbaceous borders. At Home Farm contrast the traditional farmyard, with the noisy modern piggery and cattle sheds. Ask our Stockman about our rare breeds and learn more about your food and our farming.

Location: MAP 7:F9, OS154. TL336 510. 8m SW of Cambridge (A603), 6m N of Royston (A1198). Rail: Shepreth 5ml. Royston with a taxi rank 8ml.

Open: Hall: 19 Feb–20 Jul & 3 Sept–30 Oct, Sat–Wed; 23 Jul–1 Sept, Sat–Thur, 11am–5pm. Hall open Sat–Thur during local school hols and also Good Friday 11am–5pm. Farm, Garden, Shop & Restaurant: 19 Feb–30 Oct Daily 10.30am–5pm. Garden, Shop & Restaurant: 1 Jan–16 Feb, 31 Oct–24 Dec, Sat–Wed, 11am–4pm; 27 Dec–4 Jan, Daily 11am–4pm. Farm: 1 Jan–16 Feb, 5 Nov–24 Dec, Sat–Sun 11am–4pm; 27 Dec–1 Jan, Daily 11am–4pm. Park: dawn–dusk, daily, all year.

***Admission:** Hall: Adult £9.80, Child £5.45. Joint ticket with Home Farm: Adult £14.70, Child £8, Family £38.20. Garden: £4.10. Group rates (not Suns or BH Mons). Farm & Garden: Adult £8, Child (3yrs & over) £5.50, Family £25.20. Discount for NT members. *includes a voluntary donation but visitors can choose to pay the standard prices displayed at the property and on the website.

Partial. WCs Licensed. By arrangement. Limited for coaches. Guide dogs only.

© NTPL / Andreas von Einsiedel

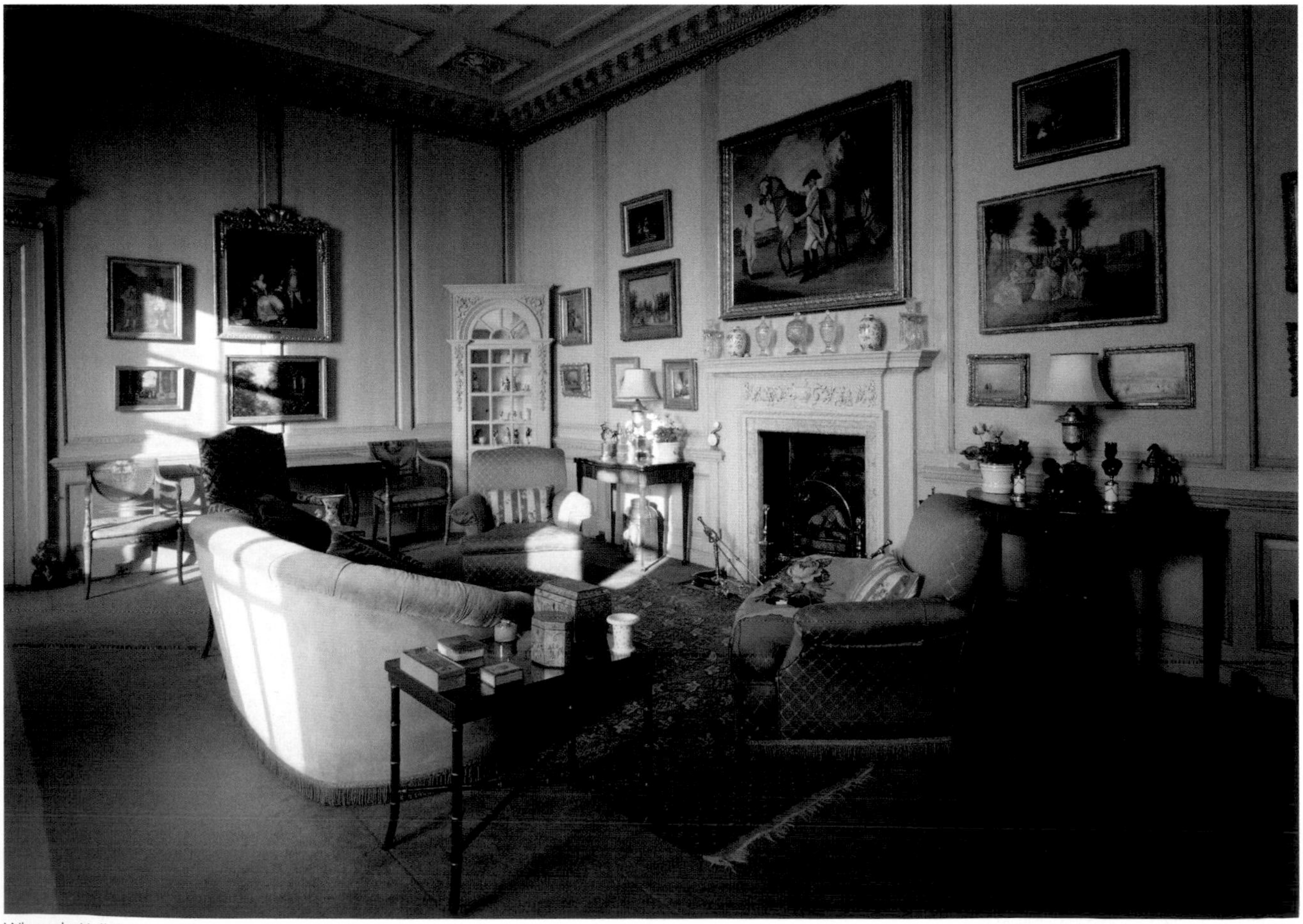

Wimpole Hall & Home Farm

For further details contact:
(general enquiries): +44 (0)1223 337733

Christ's College
St Andrew's Street,
Cambridge CB2 3BU
Tel: 01223 334900
Website: www.christs.cam.ac.uk/admissn
Founder: Lady Margaret Beaufort
Founded: 1505

Churchill College
Madingley Road, Cambridge CB3 0DS
Tel: 01223 336000
Website: www.chu.cam.ac.uk
Founded: 1960

Clare College
Trinity Lane, Cambridge CB2 1TL
Tel: 01223 333200
Website: www.clare.cam.ac.uk
Founded: 1326

Clare Hall
Herschel Road, Cambridge CB3 9AL
Tel: 01223 332360
Website: www.clarehall.cam.ac.uk
Founded: 1965

Corpus Christi College
King's Parade, Cambridge CB2 1RH
Tel: 01223 338000
Website: www.corpus.cam.ac.uk
Founded: 1352

Darwin College
Silver Street, Cambridge CB3 9EU
Tel: 01223 335660
Website: www.dar.cam.ac.uk
Founded: 1964

Downing College
Regent Street, Cambridge CB2 1DQ
Tel: 01223 334800
Website: www.dow.cam.ac.uk
Founded: 1800

Emmanuel College
St Andrew's Street, Cambridge CB2 3AP
Tel: 01223 334200
Website: www.emma.cam.ac.uk
Founded: 1584

Fitzwilliam College
Huntingdon Road, Cambridge CB3 0DG
Tel: 01223 332000
Website: www.fitz.cam.ac.uk
Founded: 1966

Girton College
Huntingdon Road, Cambridge CB3 0JG
Tel: 01223 338999
Website: www.girton.cam.ac.uk
Founded: 1869

Gonville & Caius College
Trinity Street, Cambridge CB2 1TA
Tel: 01223 332400
Website: www.cai.cam.ac.uk
Founded: 1348

Homerton College
Hills Road, Cambridge CB2 2PH
Tel: 01223 507111
Website: www.homerton.cam.ac.uk
Founded: 1976

Hughes Hall
Wollaston Road, Cambridge CB1 2EW
Tel: 01223 334897
Website: www.hughes.cam.ac.uk
Founded: 1885

Jesus College
Jesus Lane, Cambridge CB5 8BL
Tel: 01223 339339
Website: www.jesus.cam.ac.uk
Founded: 1496

King's College
King's Parade, Cambridge CB2 1ST
Tel: 01223 331100
Website: www.kings.cam.ac.uk
Founded: 1441

Lucy Cavendish College
Lady Margaret Road, Cambs CB3 0BU
Tel: 01223 332190
Website: www.lucy-cav.cam.ac.uk
Founded: 1965

Magdalene College
Magdalene Street, Cambridge CB3 0AG
Tel: 01223 332100
Website: www.magd.cam.ac.uk
Founded: 1428

New Hall
Huntingdon Road, Cambridge CB3 0DF
Tel: 01223 762100
Website: www.newhall.cam.ac.uk
Founded: 1954

Newnham College
Grange Road, Cambridge CB3 9DF
Tel: 01223 335700
Website: www.newn.cam.ac.uk
Founded: 1871

Pembroke College
Trumpington Street, Cambs CB2 1RF
Tel: 01223 338100
Website: www.pem.cam.ac.uk
Founded: 1347

Peterhouse
Trumpington Street, Cambs CB2 1RD
Tel: 01223 338200
Website: www.pet.cam.ac.uk
Founder: The Bishop of Ely
Founded: 1284

Queens' College
Silver Street, Cambridge CB3 9ET
Tel: 01223 335511
Website: www.quns.cam.ac.uk
Founder: Margaret of Anjou, Elizabeth Woodville
Founded: 1448

Ridley Hall
Ridley Hall Road, Cambridge CB3 9HG
Tel: 01223 741080
Website: www.ridley.cam.ac.uk
Founded: 1879

Robinson College
Grange Road, Cambridge CB3 9AN
Tel: 01223 339100
Website: www.robinson.cam.ac.uk
Founded: 1979

St Catharine's College
King's Parade, Cambs CB2 1RL
Tel: 01223 338300
Website: www.caths.cam.ac.uk
Founded: 1473

St Edmund's College
Mount Pleasant, Cambridge CB3 0BN
Tel: 01223 336086
Website: www.st-edmunds.cam.ac.uk
Founded: 1896

St John's College
St John's Street, Cambridge CB2 1TP
Tel: 01223 338600
Website: www.joh.cam.ac.uk
Founded: 1511

Selwyn College
Grange Road, Cambridge CB3 9DQ
Tel: 01223 335846
Website: www.sel.cam.ac.uk
Founded: 1882

Sidney Sussex College
Sidney Street, Cambridge CB2 3HU
Tel: 01223 338800
Website: www.sid.cam.ac.uk
Founded: 1596

Trinity College
Trinity Street, Cambridge CB2 1TQ
Tel: 01223 338400
Website: www.trin.cam.ac.uk
Founded: 1546

Trinity Hall
Trinity Lane, Cambridge CB2 1TJ
Tel: 01223 332500
Website: www.trinhall.cam.ac.uk
Founded: 1350

Wesley House
Jesus Lane, Cambridge CB5 8BJ
Tel: 01223 350127 / 367980
Website: www.wesley.cam.ac.uk

Wescott House
Jesus Lane, Cambridge CB5 8BP
Tel: 01223 741000
Website: www.ely.anglican.org/westcott

Westminster & Cheshunt
Madingley Road Cambridge CB3 0AA
Tel: 01223 741084
Website: www.westminstercollege.co.uk

Wolfson College
Grange Road, Cambridge CB3 9BB
Tel: 01223 335900
Website: www.wolfson.cam.ac.uk
Founded: 1965

Visitors wishing to gain admittance to the Colleges (meaning the Courts, not to the staircases & students' rooms) are advised to contact the Tourist Office for further information. It should be noted that Halls normally close for lunch (12–2pm) and many are not open during the afternoon. Chapels may be closed during services. Libraries are not normally open, and Gardens do not usually include the Fellows' garden. Visitors, and especially guided groups, should always call on the Porters Lodge first.

■ **Owner**
English Heritage

■ **Contact**
Visitor Operations Team
Audley End House
Audley End
Saffron Walden
Essex CB11 4JF

Tel: 01799 522842
Fax: 01799 521276
E-mail: customers@english-heritage.org.uk

■ **Location**
MAP 7:G10
OS Ref. TL525 382

1m W of Saffron Walden on B1383, M11/J8 & J10.

Rail: Audley End 1¼ m.

■ **Opening Times**

House
1 Apr–30 Sept, Wed–Sun & BHs, 11am–5pm

1–31 Oct, Wed–Sun, 11am–4pm.

1 Nov–31 Mar, House closed. Last entry 1 hour before closing.

Gardens & Service Wing
1 Apr–30 Sep, Wed–Sun, 10am–6pm. 1–31 Oct, Wed–Sun, 10am–5pm.

1 Nov–19 Dec, Sat–Sun, 10am–4pm.

20 Dec–31 Jan closed. 1–13 Feb, Sat–Sun, 10am–4pm.

14–28 Feb, Wed–Sun, 10am–4pm. 1–31 Mar, Wed–Sun, 10am–5pm.

Guided Tours House
1–30 Apr, Wed–Sun (except Easter).

1 May–16 Jul, Wed–Fri (except 2-4 June).

1 Sep–22 Oct, Wed–Sun.

■ **Admission**

House & Gardens

Adult	£11.90
Child (5–15yrs)	£6.00
Child (under 5yrs	Free
Conc.	£10.10
Family (2+3)	£29.80

Service Wing & Gardens

Adult	£8.30
Child (5–15yrs)	£4.20
Child (under 5yrs	Free
Conc.	£7.10
Family (2+3)	£20.80

Groups
(11+) 15% discount.

EH Members free.

Opening times and prices are valid until 31 March 2011, after this date please visit www.english-heritage.org.uk. for the latest information.

© English Heritage

AUDLEY END ⌗

www.english-heritage.org.uk/audleyend

See what's new at Audley End House and enjoy a great day out at one of England's grandest stately homes.

With the doors of our restored historic stables opened, visitors can now enjoy a day out with a difference, as the daily routine of a Victorian stable yard is brought to life. Complete with resident horses and a costumed groom, the stables experience includes an exhibition where you can find out about the workers who lived on the estate in the 1880s, the tack house and the Audley End fire engine. There is also a new children's play area and café which are ideal for family visitors.

Every great house needed an army of servants and the restored Victorian Service Wing shows a world "below stairs" that was never intended to be seen. Immerse yourself in the past as you visit the kitchen, scullery, pantry and laundries with film projections, introductory wall displays and even original food from the era. The cook, Mrs Crocombe, and her staff can regularly be seen trying out new recipes and going about their chores.

Audley End House is itself a magnificent house, built to entertain royalty. Among the highlights is a stunning art collection including works by Masters Holbein, Lely and Canaletto.

Its pastoral parkland is designed by "Capability" Brown and there is an impressive formal garden to discover. Don't miss the working Organic Kitchen Garden with its glasshouses and vinery growing original Victorian varieties of fruit and vegetables.

© English Heritage

© English Heritage

Open air concerts and other events. WCs.

Service Yard and Coach House Shops.

Partial.

By arrangement for groups.

Coaches to book in advance. Free entry for coach drivers and tour guides.

School visits free if booked in advance. Contact the Administrator or tel 01223 582700 for bookings.

On leads only.

LAYER MARNEY TOWER

Nr COLCHESTER, ESSEX CO5 9US

www.layermarneytower.co.uk

Layer Marney Tower is a wonderful Tudor building of soft red brick and buff coloured terracotta, set within delightful gardens and parkland. In many respects the apotheosis of the Tudor gatehouse, Layer Marney Tower soars over the surrounding countryside offering spectacular views to those who climb the ninety nine steps to the top.

Built in the reign of Henry VIII by Henry, 1st Lord Marney, Layer Marney Tower is the tallest Tudor gatehouse in Great Britain and was intended to surpass the rival work being undertaken by Cardinal Wolsey at Hampton Court. Henry Marney died in 1523 before his ambition was realized and the death of his son John just two years later brought an end to the building work. By then the gatehouse and principal range were completed, as well as the stable block, some outbuildings and the parish church.

Layer Marney Tower has some of the finest terracotta work in the country, probably executed by Flemish craftsmen trained by Italian masters. The terracotta is used on the battlements, windows and, most lavishly of all, the tombs of Henry and John Marney. Much repair work has recently been undertaken to the upper parts of the gatehouse. Visitors may now wander through the recently restored tower rooms as they make their way up to the new viewing platform on the roof. The new lavatory block is a delight – worth a visit in its own right.

There are fine outbuildings, including the Long Gallery with its magnificent oak roof and the medieval barn, the principal timbers of which date to about 1450. The gardens follow a relatively formal Edwardian layout, with herbaceous borders, broad paths and plentiful roses that flourish in the heavy Essex clay.

One of the countries most desirable wedding venues, Layer Marney Tower is also used for conferences, banquets, trade shows, presentations and many corporate functions. During the year there are many special events ranging from plays to lantern tours to kite festivals.

No photography inside the house. Suitable for conferences, business and social functions. Park and woodland for sports, corporate events, open air concerts, team building, balloon festivals and helicopter landing. Film location. Wedding ceremonies and receptions throughout the year.

Partial. WC.

Licensed

Banquets and pre-booked meals only

By arrangement – about 1½ hrs.

Cars & Coaches

On a lead.

Self catering cottage, 2 beds.

By appointment for groups and special events.

Owner/Contact

Mr Nicholas Charrington

Tel: 01206 330784
E-mail: info@layermarneytower.co.uk

Location

MAP 8:J11,
OS Ref. TL929 175.

7m SW of Colchester, signed off B1022.

Opening Times

12noon–5pm:
April, May, June and September,
Weds & Suns

July & August
Sun–Thurs

Admission

Adults £6.00
Children (3–15) £4.00
Family ticket £18.00

Group visits and guided tours throughout the year, by arrangement.

Guided tours £10.00 per person, minimum charge for a group – £200.00

Group visits £5.00 person, minimum group size 20.

Invitation to View

Personal tours by the owners – see www.invitationtoview.co.uk for info and booking.

Special Events

See website www.layermarneytower.co.uk for details.

AUDLEY END

See page 234 for full page entry.

BOURNE MILL

Bourne Road, Colchester, Essex CO2 8RT

Tel: 01206 572422

Owner: National Trust **Contact:** The Custodian

Originally a fishing lodge built in 1591. It was later converted into a fulling mill with a 4 acre mill pond, then became a corn mill. Working waterwheel.

Location: MAP 8:J11, OS Ref. TM006 238. 1m S of Colchester centre, in Bourne Road, off the Mersea Road B1025.

Open: Limited opening Jun–Aug.

Admission: Ring for details.

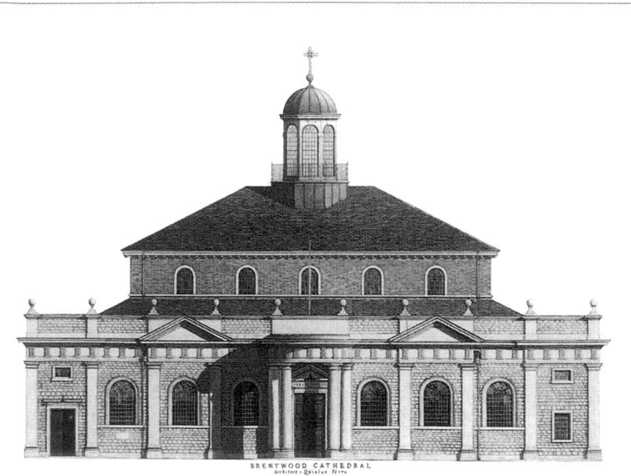

BRENTWOOD CATHEDRAL

INGRAVE ROAD, BRENTWOOD, ESSEX CM15 8AT

Tel: 01277 232266 **E-mail:** bishop@dioceseofbrentwood.org

Owner: Diocese of Brentwood **Contact:** Rt Rev Thomas McMahon

The new (1991) Roman Catholic classical Cathedral Church of St Mary and St Helen incorporates part of the original Victorian church. Designed by distinguished classical architect Quinlan Terry with roundels by Raphael Maklouf. Architecturally, the inspiration is early Italian Renaissance crossed with the English Baroque of Christopher Wren. The north elevation consists of nine bays each divided by Doric pilasters. This is broken by a huge half-circular portico. The Kentish ragstone walls have a natural rustic look, which contrasts with the smooth Portland stone of the capitals and column bases. Inside is an arcade of Tuscan arches with central altar with the lantern above.

Location: MAP 4:J1, OS Ref. TQ596 938. A12 & M25/J28. Centre of Brentwood, opposite Brentwood School.

Open: All year, daily.

Admission: Free.

Limited. None for coaches.

CHELMSFORD CATHEDRAL

New Street, Chelmsford, Essex CM1 1TY

Tel: 01245 294489 **E-mail:** office@chelmsfordcathedral.org.uk

Contact: Mrs Bobby Harrington

15th century building became a Cathedral in 1914. Extended in 1920s, major refurbishment in 1980s and in 2000 with contemporary works of distinction and splendid new organs in 1994 and 1996.

Location: MAP 7:H12, OS Ref. TL708 070. In Chelmsford.

Open: Sun 7.30am–12.30pm & 2–7pm. Mon–Sat 7.45am–6pm.

Admission: No charge but donation invited.

For rare and unusual plants visit the **plant sales** index at the end of the book.

COGGESHALL GRANGE BARN

Grange Hill, Coggeshall, Colchester, Essex CO6 1RE

Tel: 01376 562226

Owner: National Trust **Contact:** The Custodian

One of Europe's oldest timber-framed buildings with a cathedral-like interior. Exhibition of local woodcarving and tools.

Location: MAP 8:I11, OS Ref. TL848 223. Signposted off A120 Coggeshall bypass. West side of the road southwards to Kelvedon.

Open: Apr–Oct: Thurs, Fri, Sat, Suns & BH Mons, 1–5pm.

Admission: Adult £2.70, Child £1.20.

WCs Coaches must book. In Grounds.

COLCHESTER CASTLE MUSEUM

14 Ryegate Road, Colchester, Essex CO1 1YG

Tel: 01206 282939 **Fax:** 01206 282925

Owner: Colchester & Ipswich Museum Sevice **Contact:** Museum Resource Centre

The largest Norman Castle Keep in Europe with fine archaeological collections on show. Hands-on & interactive display brings history to life.

Location: MAP 8:J11, OS Ref. TL999 253. In Colchester town centre, off A12.

Open: All year: Mon–Sat, 10am–5pm, also Suns, 11am–5pm.

Admission: Adult £5.70, Child (5–15yrs)/Conc. £3.60. Child under 5yrs Free. Saver ticket: £15. Prices may increase from April 2011.

© Peter Gamble

COPPED HALL

CROWN HILL, EPPING, ESSEX CM16 5HS

www.coppedhalltrust.org.uk

Tel: 020 7267 1679 **E-mail:** Coxalan1@aol.com

Owner: The Copped Hall Trust **Contact:** Alan Cox

Mid 18th century Palladian mansion under restoration. Situated on ridge overlooking excellent landscaped park. Ancillary buildings including stables and small racquets court. Former elaborate gardens being rescued from abandonment. Large early 18th century walled garden – adjacent to site of 16th century mansion where *'A Midsummer Night's Dream'* was first performed. Ideal film location.

Location: MAP 7:G12, OS Ref. TL433 016. 4m SW of Epping, N of M25.

Open: Ticketed events and special open days. See website for dates. By appointment only for groups (20+).

Admission: Gardens Only £3.50. Open Days £5. Guided Tour Days £7.

Partial. In grounds on leads. Concerts, plays and study days.

FEERINGBURY MANOR

Coggeshall Road, Feering, Colchester, Essex CO5 9RB

Tel: 01376 561946

Owner/Contact: Mrs Giles Coode-Adams

Location: MAP 8:I11, OS Ref. TL864 215. 1¼m N of A12 between Feering & Coggeshall.

Open: From 1st Thur in Apr to last Fri in Jul: Thur & Fri only, 8am–4pm.

Admission: Adult £4, Child Free. In aid of National Gardens Scheme.

Copped Hall

HARWICH REDOUBT FORT

Main Road, Harwich, Essex
Tel/Fax: 01255 503429 **E-mail:** info@harwich-society.co.uk
www.harwich-society.co.uk
Owner: The Harwich Society **Contact:** Mr A Rutter
180ft diameter circular fort built in 1808 to defend the port against Napoleonic invasion. Being restored by Harwich Society and part is a museum. Eleven guns on battlements.
Location: MAP 8:K10, OS Ref. TM262 322. Rear of 29 Main Road. CO12 3LT.
Open: 1 May–31 Aug: daily, 10am–4pm. Sept–Apr: Suns only, 10am–4pm. Groups by appointment at any time.
Admission: Adult £3, Child Free (no unaccompanied children).
€

INGATESTONE HALL

HALL LANE, INGATESTONE, ESSEX CM4 9NR

www.ingatestonehall.com

Tel: 01277 353010 **Fax:** 01245 248979 **Email:** house@ingatestonehall.co.uk
Owner: The Lord Petre **Contact:** The Administrator
16th century mansion, with 11 acres of grounds (formal garden and wild walk), built by Sir William Petre, Secretary of State to four Tudor monarchs, which has remained in his family ever since. Furniture, portraits and memorabilia accumulated over the centuries – and two Priests' hiding places.
Location: MAP 7:H12, OS Ref. TQ654 986. Off A12 between Brentwood & Chelmsford. Take Station Lane at London end of Ingatestone High Street, cross level-crossing and continue for ½ m to SE.
Open: 24 Apr–28 Sept: Wed, Suns & BH Mons (not Weds in June), 12noon–5pm.
Admission: Adult £6, Child £2.50 (under 5yrs Free), Conc. £5. (Groups of 20+ booked in advance: Adult £5, Child £1.50, Conc. £4.)
No photography in house. Partial, WCs. By arrangement.
Guide dogs only.

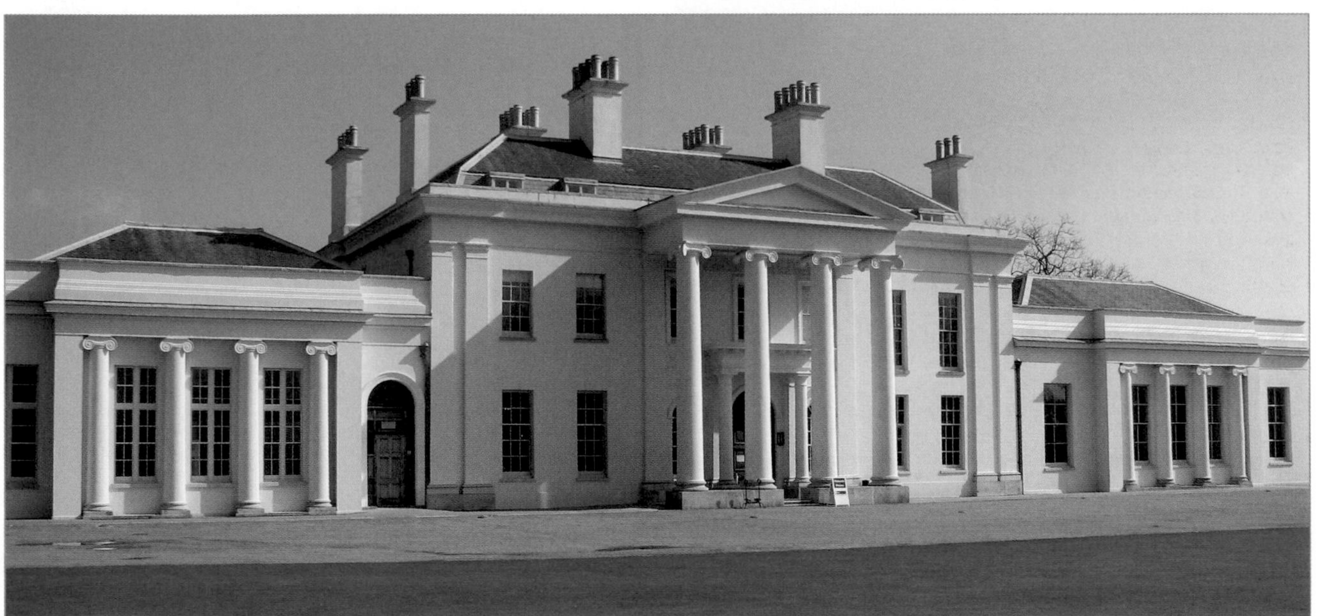

HYLANDS HOUSE & ESTATE

HYLANDS PARK, LONDON ROAD, CHELMSFORD CM2 8WQ

www.chelmsford.gov.uk/hylands

Tel: 01245 605500 **Fax:** 01245 605510
E-mail: hylands@chelmsford.gov.uk
Owner: Chelmsford Borough Council **Contact:** Ceri Lowen
Hylands House is a beautiful Grade 11* listed building, set in 574 acres of historic landscaped parkland. Built c1730, the original House was a Queen Anne style mansion. Subsequent owners modernised and enlarged the property. The Stables Visitor Centre, incorporates a Gift Shop, Café, Artist Studios and a Second-hand Bookshop. Visitors can also enjoy the beautiful Pleasure Gardens and the tranquil One World Garden.

Location: MAP 7:H12, OS Ref. TL681 054. 2m SW of Chelmsford. Signposted on A414 from J15 of A12, near Chelmsford.
Open: House: Suns & Mons, 10am–5pm Apr–Sept, Sun only 10am–4pm Oct–Mar, Closed 25 Dec. Stables Visitor Centre and Park: Daily. Guided Tours, Talks and Walks are available by arrangement.
Admission: House: Adult £3.60, Conc. £2.60, accompanied children under 16's Free. Visitor Stables Centre and Park: Free.
Visitor Centre. Daily. By arrangement. By arrangement.
In grounds. Guide dogs only in house.

LAYER MARNEY TOWER

See page 235 for full page entry.

MISTLEY TOWERS

Colchester, Essex

Tel: 01206 393884 / 01223 582700 (Regional Office)

E-mail: customers@english-heritage.org.uk

www.english-heritage.org.uk/mistleytowers

Owner: English Heritage **Contact:** The Keykeeper (Mistley Quay Workshops)

The remains of one of only two churches designed by the great architect Robert Adam. Built in 1776. It was unusual in having towers at both the east and west ends.

Location: MAP 8:K10, OS Ref. TM116 320. On B1352, 1½m E of A137 at Lawford, 9m E of Colchester.

Open: Key available from Mistley Quay Workshops, 01206 393884.

Admission: Free. Opening times and prices are valid until 31st March 2011, after this date details are subject to change please see www.english-heritage.org.uk for the most up-to-date information.

Picnickers welcome.

PAYCOCKE'S

West Street, Coggeshall, Colchester, Essex C06 1NS

Tel: 01376 561305

www.nationaltrust.org.uk

Owner: National Trust **Contact:** The Custodian

Merchant's house built c1500. Stunning woodcarving and panelling.

Location: MAP 8:I11, OS Ref. TL848 225. Signposted off A120.

Open: Mar–Oct.

Admission: Adult £3.40, Child £1.70.

No WC, nearest one at Coggeshall Grange Barn. By arrangement NT's at the Coggeshall Grange Barn. Guide dogs only.

Paycocke's

PRIOR'S HALL BARN

Widdington, Newport, Essex

Tel: 01223 582700 (Regional Office) **E-mail:** customers@english-heritage.org.uk

www.english-heritage.org.uk/priorshallbarn

Owner: English Heritage **Contact:** East of England Regional Office

One of the finest surviving medieval barns in south-east England and representative of the group of aisled barns centred on north-west Essex.

Location: MAP 7:G10, OS Ref. TL538 319. In Widdington, on unclassified road 2m SE of Newport, off B1383.

Open: 1 Apr–30 Sep: Sat & Sun, 10am–6pm.

Admission: Free. Opening times and prices are valid until 31st March 2011, after this date details are subject to change please see www.english-heritage.org.uk for the most up-to-date information.

Picnickers welcome.

RHS GARDEN HYDE HALL

See main index.

TILBURY FORT

No. 2 Office Block, The Fort, Tilbury, Essex RM18 7NR

Tel: 01375 858489 **E-mail:** customers@english-heritage.org.uk

www.english-heritage.org.uk/tilburyfort

Owner: English Heritage **Contact:** Visitor Operations Team

The best and largest example of 17th century military engineering in England, commanding the Thames. Learn more about the fascinating history of Tilbury Fort with a new interpretation scheme in the North East Bastion magazine passages.

Location: MAP 4:K2, OS Ref. TQ651 754. ½m E of Tilbury off A126. Near Port of Tilbury.

Open: 1 Apr–31 Oct: daily, 10am–5pm. 1 Nov–31 Mar: Thur–Mon, 10am–4pm. 24–26 Dec & 1 Jan: Closed.

Admission: Adult £4.20, Child £2.10, Under 5s Free. Conc. £3.60. Family £10.50. EH Members/OVP Free. Group discount available. Opening times and prices are valid until 31st March 2011, after this date details are subject to change please visit www.english-heritage.org.uk for the most up-to-date information.

Picnickers welcome. WCs. Partial. On leads.

WALTHAM ABBEY GATEHOUSE & BRIDGE

Waltham Abbey, Essex

Tel: 01992 702200 / 01223 582700 (Regional Office)

E-mail: customers@english-heritage.org.uk

www.english-heritage.org.uk/walthamabbeygatehouse

Owner: English Heritage **Contact:** East of England Regional Office (01223 582700)

The late 14th century abbey gatehouse, part of the north range of the cloister and the medieval 'Harold's Bridge' of one of the great monastic foundations of the Middle Ages.

Location: MAP 7:G12, OS Ref. TL381 008. In Waltham Abbey off A112. Just NE of the Abbey church.

Open: Any reasonable time.

Admission: Free. Opening times and prices are valid until 31st March 2011, after this date details are subject to change please see www.english-heritage.org.uk for the most up-to-date information.

Picnickers welcome.

HATFIELD HOUSE

www.hatfield-house.co.uk

In 2011, Hatfield House will be celebrating its 400th anniversary. There will be a series of special events throughout the year. One of the highlights will be a major exhibition in the West Garden of Henry Moore's sculptures. Entitled 'Moore at Hatfield', it will be the largest collection of Henry Moore's monumental works ever exhibited in the grounds of a historic house.

Hatfield House is the home of the 7th Marquess of Salisbury and the House has been in the Cecil family since it was built. The House is steeped in Elizabethan and Victorian political history and contains many fascinating objects, textiles, furnishings and armour collected by the family. Lady Salisbury and her team have created many new borders and additions to the famous Garden which is delightful at any time of year. The Kitchen has recently been restored to show preparations for Queen Victoria's visit in 1846, giving a fascinating insight into life in a grand house at this time.

In the Park, there is a new adventure play area which features a large scale model of the House. Work is underway on Lawn Farm, which will be home to many traditional breed animals and is sure to be popular with visitors.

The area around the gift shop, Stable Yard, has been given a new look and there are now exclusive retailers offering antiques, collectables, jewellery, plants and gifts.

The West Garden

The Marble Hall

No photography in house. 5m of marked trails, children's play area. Film enquiries welcome.

Stable yard shopping complex

Weddings, functions: tel 01707 262055. Banquets held in the Old Palace.

WCs. Parking next to house. Lift.

Seats 150. Pre-booked lunch and tea for groups 20+. Tel: 01707 262030.

Group tours available by prior arrangement.

Ample. Hardstanding for coaches.

Resource books, play area & nature trails. Living History days throughout the school year: tel 01707 287042.

In park only, on leads.

€

Owner

The 7th Marquess of Salisbury

Contact

Director – Visitors & Events
Hatfield House
Hatfield
Hertfordshire AL9 5NQ
Tel: 01707 287010
Fax: 01707 287033
E-mail: visitors@hatfield-house.co.uk

Location

MAP 7:F11
OS Ref. TL 237 084

21m N of London, M25/J23 7m, A1(M)/J4, 2m.

Bus: Local services from St Albans and Hertford.

Rail: From Kings Cross every 30 mins. Station is opposite entrance to Park.

Air: Luton (30 mins). Stansted (45 mins).

Opening Times

Easter Sat–end September

House
Wed–Sun & BHs.
12 noon–5pm. (Last admission 4pm).

Park, West Garden, Exhibition, Restaurant & Shops
Tues–Sun & BHs.
11am–5.30pm.

East Garden
Weds only.
11am–5.30pm.

Admission

Henry Moore, West Garden & Park	
Adult	£12.50
Child	£8.00
Concessions	£11.50
Hatfield House, Henry Moore, West Garden & Park	
Adult	£18.50
Child	£11.50
Concessions	£17.50
House Supplement	
Adult	£6.00
Child	£3.50
House & Park	
Adult	£9.00
Child	£5.50
Park only	
Adult	£3.00
Child	£2.00
East Garden	
(Wednesdays)	£4.00 extra

Special Events

5–9 May
Living Crafts.

5–7 August
Art in Clay.

19–21 August
Hatfield House Country Show.

Please see website for details of events programme.

■ **Owner**

The Hon Henry Lytton Cobbold

■ **Contact**

The Estate Office
Knebworth House
Knebworth
Hertfordshire SG3 6PY

Tel: 01438 812661
Fax: 01438 811908

E-mail: info@knebworthhouse.com

■ **Location**

OS Ref. TL230 224

Direct access off the A1(M) J7 Stevenage, SG1 2AX, 28m N of London, 15m N of M25/ J23.

Rail: Stevenage Station 2m (Kings Cross).

Air: Luton Airport 15m

Taxi: 01438 811122.

■ **Opening Times**

Open daily: 9–25 April, 28 May–5 June, 2 July–31 August. Weekends & BHs: 26 March–3 April, 30 April–22 May, 11-26 June, 3–25 September.

Park, Playground & Gardens

11am–5pm, (last ticket sold 4.15pm)

House & Indian Exhibition

12 noon–5pm, (last tour 4.00pm).

■ **Admission**

Including House	
Adult	£10.50
Child*/Conc	£10.00
Family Day Ticket (4 persons)	£37.00
Groups (20+)	
Adult	£9.50
Child*/Conc	£9.00
Excluding House	
All Persons	£8.00
Family Day Ticket (4 persons)	£28.00
Groups (20+)	
All persons	£7.00

*4–16 yrs, under 4s Free.

Special Events

Check website for details.

Conference/Function

ROOM	SIZE	MAX CAPACITY
Banqueting Hall	25' x 39'	100
Dining Parlour	21' x 36'	50
Library	21' x 32'	40
Manor Barn	25' x 70'	180
Lodge Barn	30' x 75'	180
Garden Terrace Barn	35' x 40'	30

KNEBWORTH HOUSE

www.knebworthhouse.com

Home of the Lytton family since 1490, and still a lived-in family house. Transformed in early Victorian times by Edward Bulwer-Lytton, the author, poet, dramatist and statesman, into the unique high gothic fantasy house of today, complete with turrets, griffins and gargoyles. Historically home to Constance Lytton, the Suffragette, and her father, Robert Lytton, the Viceroy of India who proclaimed Queen Victoria Empress of India at the Great Delhi Durbar of 1877. Visited by Queen Elizabeth I, Charles Dickens and Sir Winston Churchill. The interior contains various styles including the magnificent Jacobean Banqueting Hall, a unique example of the 17th century change in fashion from traditional English to Italian Palladian. The high gothic State Drawing Room by John Crace contrasts with the Regency elegance of Mrs Bulwer-Lytton's bedroom and the 20th century designs of Sir Edwin Lutyens in the Entrance Hall, Dining Parlour and Library.

25 acres of beautiful gardens, simplified by Lutyens, including pollarded lime avenues, formal rose garden, maze, Gertrude Jekyll herb garden and the walled kitchen garden. The Dinosaur Trail with 72 life-size dinosaurs set grazing through the Wilderness Walk within the Formal Gardens. 250 acres of gracious parkland, with herds of red and sika deer, includes children's giant adventure playground and miniature railway.

World famous for its huge open-air rock concerts, and used as a film location for The King's Speech, The Great Ghost Rescue, St Trinian's 2, Miss Marple and Poirot amongst others.

Suitable for conferences and banquets, product launches, weddings, commercial photography, filming, exhibitions, garden shows, concerts and festivals.

Partial. WCs. Parking. Ground floor accessible.

Licensed tearoom. Special rates for advance bookings, menus on request.

Obligatory.

Ample.

National Curriculum based school activity days.

Guide dogs only in House. Park, on leads.

Licensed Knebworth House, Garden Gazebo & Manor Barn.

Telephone for details.

ASHRIDGE

Ringshall, Berkhamsted, Hertfordshire HP4 1LT

Tel: 01442 851227 **Fax:** 01442 850000 **E-mail:** ashridge@nationaltrust.org.uk

Owner: National Trust **Contact:** The Visitor Centre

The Ashridge Estate comprises over 5000 acres of woodlands, commons and downland. At the northerly end of the Estate the Ivinghoe Hills are an outstanding area of chalk downland supporting a rich variety of plants and insects.

Location: MAP 7:D11 OS Ref. SP970 131. Between Northchurch & Ringshall, just off B4506.

Open: Visitor Centre & Shop: 13 Feb–19 Dec daily, 10am–5pm. Monument: 3 Apr–31 Oct: Sats, Suns & BHs 12 noon–last admission 4.30pm. Tearoom: 1 Jan–31 Dec: daily, 10am–5pm. Tearoom opening hours may vary. Tearoom closes at 4pm 1 Jan–1 Apr and 1 Nov–31 Dec.

Admission: Monument: £1.70, Child 85p. Free to NT members.

Visitor Centre. Vehicles available. Limited for coaches.

In grounds, on leads.

BENINGTON LORDSHIP GARDENS

Stevenage, Hertfordshire SG2 7BS

Tel: 01438 869668 **Fax:** 01438 869622 **E-mail:** garden@beningtonlordship.co.uk

www.beningtonlordship.co.uk

Owner: Mr R R A Bott **Contact:** Mr or Mrs R R A Bott

7 acre garden overlooking lakes in a timeless setting. Features include Norman keep and moat, Queen Anne manor house, James Pulham folly, formal rose garden, renowned herbaceous borders, walled vegetable garden, grass tennis court and verandah. Spectacular display of snowdrops in February. All location work welcome.

Location: MAP 7:F11, OS Ref. TL296 236. In village of Benington next to the church. 4m E of Stevenage.

Open: Gardens only: Snowdrops: 5 Feb–27 Feb, daily, 12 noon–4pm. Easter & May BH weekends: Suns, 2–5pm. Mons, 12 noon–5pm. Floral Festival, 12 noon–6pm, 25/26 Jun. Chilli Festival, 10am–5pm, 28/29 Aug (admission £5). By request all year, please telephone. Coaches must book.

Admission: Adult £4 (Suns in Feb £4.50), Child under 12 Free.

February. Partial. By arrangement. Limited.

BERKHAMSTED CASTLE

Berkhamsted, St Albans, Hertfordshire

Tel: 01223 582700 (Regional Office) **www.english-heritage.org.uk/berkhamsted**

Owner: English Heritage **Contact:** East of England Regional Office

The extensive remains of a large 11th century motte and bailey castle which held a strategic position on the road to London.

Location: MAP 7:D12, OS Ref. SP996 083. Adjacent to Berkhamsted rail station.

Open: Summer: daily, 10am–6pm. Winter: daily, 10am–4pm. Closed 25 Dec & 1 Jan.

Admission: Free. Opening times and prices are valid until 31st March 2011, after this date details are subject to change please see www.english-heritage.org.uk for the most up-to-date information.

Picnickers welcome.

CROMER WINDMILL

Ardeley, Stevenage, Hertfordshire SG2 7QA

Tel: 01438 861662/01763 271305

Owner: Hertfordshire Building Preservation Trust

Guardians: Simon Bennett/Robin Webb

Hertfordshire's last surviving post mill restored to working order. Ample parking, disabled access to video. Gifts and refreshments.

Location: MAP 7:F10, OS Ref. TL305 286. 4m E of Stevenage B1037. 2m NE of Walkern.

Open: Mid May–Mid-Sept: Sun & BH Mons, 2nd & 4th Sat, 2.30–5pm.

Admission: Adult £2, Child 25p.

Ample.

See which properties offer **educational facilities** or **school visits** in our index at the end of the book.

© Britainonview

St Albans Cathedral

Thinking of a short break or weekend away?
See Historic Places to Stay

GORHAMBURY

St Albans, Hertfordshire AL3 6AH
Tel: 01727 854051 **Fax:** 01727 843675
Owner: The Earl of Verulam **Contact:** The Administrator
Late 18th century house by Sir Robert Taylor. Family portraits from 15th–21st centuries.
Location: MAP 7:E11, OS Ref. TL114 078. 2m W of St Albans. Access via private drive off A4147 at St Albans.
Open: May–Sept: Thurs, 2–5pm (last entry 4pm).
Admission: House & Gardens: Adult £7.50, Child £4, Conc £6.50. Visitors join guided tours. Special groups by arrangement (Thurs preferred). (*2010 prices/opening times).
Partial. Obligatory.

HATFIELD HOUSE

See page 239 for full page entry.

HERTFORD MUSEUM

18 Bull Plain, Hertford SG14 1DT
Tel: 01992 582686
Owner: Hertford Museums Trust **Contact:** Helen Gurney
Local museum in 17th century house, altered by 18th century façade, with recreated Jacobean knot garden.
Location: MAP 7:F11, OS Ref. TL326 126. Town centre.
Open: Tue–Sat, 10am–5pm.
Admission: Free.

KNEBWORTH HOUSE

See page 240 for full page entry.

THE NATURAL HISTORY MUSEUM AT TRING

Akeman Street, Tring, Hertfordshire HP23 6AP
Tel: 020 7942 6171 **Fax:** 020 7942 6150
Owner: The Natural History Museum **Contact:** General Organiser
The museum was opened to the public by Lord Rothschild in 1892. It houses his private natural history collection. Over 4,000 species of animal in a Victorian setting.
Location: MAP 7:D11, OS Ref. SP924 111. S end of Akeman Street, ¼m S of High Street.
Open: All year, daily: Mon–Sat, 10am–5pm, Suns, 2–5pm. Closed 24–26 Dec.
Admission: Free.

OLD GORHAMBURY HOUSE

St Albans, Hertfordshire
Tel: 01223 582700 (Regional Office) **E-mail:** customers@english-heritage.org.uk
www.english-heritage.org.uk/oldgorhamburyhouse
Owner: English Heritage **Contact:** East of England Regional Office
The decorated remains of this Elizabethan mansion, particularly the porch of the Great Hall, illustrate the impact of the Renaissance on English architecture.
Location: MAP 7:E11, OS Ref. TL110 077. On foot by permissive 2m path. By car, drive to Gorhambury Mansion and walk across the gardens (1 May–30 Sep).
Open: By foot: All year (except 1 Jun and Sat 1 Sept–1 Feb), 8.30am–5.30pm.
By car: 1 May–30 Sep, Thur, 2–5pm.
Admission: Free. Opening times and prices are valid until 31st March 2011, after this date details are subject to change please visit www.english-heritage.org.uk for the most up-to-date information.
Picnickers welcome.

SCOTT'S GROTTO

Ware, Hertfordshire S912 9SQ
Tel: 01920 464131
Owner: East Hertfordshire District Council **Contact:** J Watson
One of the finest grottos in England built in the 1760s by Quaker Poet John Scott.
Location: MAP 7:F11, OS Ref. TL355 137. In Scotts Rd, S of the A119 Hertford Road.
Open: Apr–Sept: Sat & BH Mon, 2–4.30pm. Also by appointment.
Admission: Suggested donation of £1 for adults. Children Free. Please bring a torch.

SHAW'S CORNER

Ayot St Lawrence, Welwyn, Hertfordshire AL6 9BX
Tel/Fax: 01438 820307
www.nationaltrust.org.uk
Owner: National Trust **Contact:** The House Manager
Home and garden of playwright George Bernard Shaw.
Location: MAP 7:E11, OS Ref. TL194 167. At SW end of village, 2m NE of Wheathampstead, approximately 2m N from B653. A1(M)/J4, M1/J10.

ST ALBANS CATHEDRAL

St Albans, Hertfordshire AL1 1BY
Tel: 01727 860780 **Fax:** 01727 850944 **E-mail:** mail@stalbanscathedral.org.uk
www.stalbanscathedral.org.uk
Owner: Dean and Chapter of St Albans **Contact:** Susan Keeling, Visitors' Officer
Magnificent Norman abbey church built with recycled Roman bricks from the nearby city of Verulanium, the setting for the Shrine (1308) of Alban, Britain's first Christian martyr. Series of 12th–13th century wall paintings, painted Presbytery ceiling (1280), wooden watching loft (1400) and the tomb of Humphrey, Duke of Gloucester (1447).
Location: MAP 7:E12. OS Ref. TL145 071. Centre of St Albans.
Open: Daily, 9am–5.45pm.
Admission: Free, donations welcomed.
WCs. Licenced. By prior arrangement. In grounds, on leads.

Shaw's Corner

HOLKHAM HALL

www.holkham.co.uk

Set in a 3,000 acre deer park this elegant 18th century Palladian style mansion, based on designs by William Kent, was built by Thomas Coke 1st Earl of Leicester and is home to his descendants. It reflects Coke's natural appreciation of classical art developed during his Grand Tour. Built from local yellow brick, with its pedimented portico, square corner towers and side wings, it has been little altered over the years, and has been described by Sir Nikolaus Pevsner as "The most classically correct house in Britain".

'The Marble Hall' is a spectacular introduction to this vast and imposing house, with its 50ft pressed plaster dome ceiling and walls of English alabaster, not marble as its name implies. Stairs from the hall lead to magnificent state rooms with superb collections of ancient statuary, original furniture, tapestries and paintings by Rubens, Van Dyck, Claude, Gaspar Poussin and Gainsborough.

In an adjacent courtyard is a range of impressive buildings which were the original stables, brew and malt houses, former laundry for the hall and a building that once housed the huge machines generating electricity. Nowadays they are home to a spacious gift shop and our café serving delicious, local produce. The Bygones Museum occupies the historical stable block, displaying over 4,000 items ranging from kitchenware and toys to steam engines and vintage cars. Opposite, the History of Farming Exhibition highlights how a great estate such as Holkham works and has evolved, explaining 'Coke of Norfolk's' role in the great Agricultural Revolution of the 18th century.

There is parkland to explore and wildlife to discover. Cycles can be hired and boat trips on the lake are available. An exciting 5 year project is underway to sensitively restore the 6½ acre walled gardens, originally laid out by Samuel Wyatt in the late 1700s. The impressive glasshouses have been restored with the help of English Heritage and visitors can see the work, as it develops, to restore the fabric of the gardens and bring them back to all their glory. At the north entrance of the park lies Holkham village, with the estate's own hotel 'The Victoria', a selection of shops and a tearoom. Directly opposite lies the entrance to the award-winning Holkham beach and national nature reserve, renowned for its endless golden sands and panoramic vista.

- Grounds for shows, weddings, product launches, rallies and filming. Photography allowed in hall. Central ticket office for admission & events tickets. Cycle hire available.
- Gift shop in the park.
- In gift shop and at walled gardens.
- Hall & grounds.
- Access to first floor in the hall is suitable for most manual wheelchairs. Elsewhere, full disabled access.
- Stables Café, licensed, local produce and homemade cakes.
- The Victoria Hotel at Holkham and The Globe Inn, Wells-next-the-Sea.
- Private guided tours of hall are available by arrangement when the hall is not open to the public. Please tel for details.
- Unlimited for cars, 12+ coaches. Parking charges.
- Bygones Museum, History of Farming Exhibition, Walled Gardens, Nature Trail and quiz.
- No dogs in hall, on leads in grounds.
- Victoria Hotel at Holkham and Globe Inn, Wells-next-the-Sea, managed in partnership with Adnams, Southwold.
- Weddings and Civil Partnerships.
- Outdoor Theatre Productions, Marble Hall & Open-Air Concerts.

Owner

Trustees of the Holkham Estate. Home of the Coke family.

Contact

Marketing Manager
Laurane Herrieven
Holkham Estate Office
Wells-next-the-Sea
Norfolk NR23 1AB

Tel: 01328 710227
Fax: 01328 711707
E-mail: enquiries@holkham.co.uk

Location

MAP 8:I4
OS Ref. TF885 428

From London 120m
Norwich 35m
King's Lynn 30m.

Rail: Norwich Station 35m King's Lynn Station 30m.

Air: Norwich Airport 32m.

Opening Times

Hall

1 April–31 October,
12noon–4pm, Sun, Mon & Thurs.

Bygones Museum, History of Farming Exhibition, Gift Shop, Stables Café

1 April–31 October,
10am–5pm every day.

Boat Trips

11am–5pm.

1–30 April & 1–31 October, Sun, Mon & Thurs.

1 May–30 September Sat, Sun, Mon, Tues & Thurs.

25 minute trips, weather permitting.

Walled Gardens

1 April–31 October,
12noon–4pm every day.

The Libraries, Chapel & Strangers' Wing form part of the private accommodation and are open at the family's discretion.

Admission

Holkham Hall	
Adult	£9.00
Child (5–16yrs)	£4.50
Bygones Museum	
Adult	£4.00
Child (5–16yrs)	£2.00
Hall & Museum	
Adult	£11.00
Child (5–16yrs)	£5.50
Family (2+2)	£28.00

Groups (20+) 10% discount, organiser free entry, coach driver's refreshment voucher.

Private Guided Tours £20.00
Price per person, min 12 people.

History of Farming	Free
Walled Gardens	Free
Boat trips on the lake	
Adult	£3.50
Child (5–16yrs)	£2.50

Cycle Hire
For rates and availability visit www.cyclenorfolk.co.uk

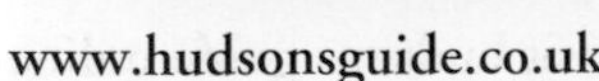

BINHAM PRIORY

Binham-on-Wells, Norfolk

Tel: 01328 830362 / 01223 582700 (Regional Office)
E-mail: customers@english-heritage.org.uk
www.english-heritage.org.uk/binhampriory
Owner: English Heritage (Managed by Binham Parochial Church Council)
Contact: East of England Regional Office

Extensive remains of a Benedictine priory, of which the original nave of the church is still in use as the parish church, displaying a screen with medieval saints overpainted with Protestant texts.

Location: MAP 8:J4, OS Ref. TF982 399. ¼m NW of village of Binham-on-Wells, on road off B1388.

Open: Binham Priory (monastic ruins): Any reasonable time. Priory Church: Summer, daily, 10am-6pm. Winter, daily, 10am-4pm.

Admission: Free. Opening times and prices are valid until 31st March 2011, after this date details are subject to change please see www.english-heritage.org.uk for the most up-to-date information.

Picnickers welcome.

BIRCHAM WINDMILL

Snettisham Road, Great Bircham, Norfolk PE31 6SJ

Tel: 01485 578393
Owner/Contact: Mr & Mrs S Chalmers

One of the last remaining complete windmills. Tearoom, bakery, windmill museum, gift shop, cycle hire, regular events and holiday cottage.

Location: MAP 8:I4, OS Ref. TF760 326. ½m W of Bircham. N of the road to Snettisham.

Open: Easter–end Sept: Daily 10am–5pm.

Admission: Adult £3.75, Child £2, OAP £3.

Holkham Hall

BURGH CASTLE

Breydon Water, Great Yarmouth, Norfolk

Tel: 01223 582700 (Regional Office) **E-mail:** customers@english-heritage.org.uk
www.english-heritage.org.uk/burghcastle
Owner: English Heritage **Contact:** East of England Regional Office

Impressive walls, with projecting bastions, of a Roman fort built in the late 3rd century as one of a chain to defend the coast against Saxon raiders.

Location: MAP 8:M6, OS Ref. TG475 046. At far W end of Breydon Water, on unclassified road 3m W of Great Yarmouth. SW of the church.

Open: Any reasonable time. Managed by Norfolk Archaeological Trust.

Admission: Free. Opening times and prices are valid until 31st March 2011, after this date details are subject to change please see www.english-heritage.org.uk for the most up-to-date information.

Picnickers welcome.

BLICKLING HALL

BLICKLING, NORWICH, NORFOLK NR11 6NF

www.nationaltrust.org.uk

Tel: 01263 738030 **Fax:** 01263 738035 **E-mail:** blickling@nationaltrust.org.uk
Owner: National Trust **Contact:** The General Manager

Built in the early 17th century and one of England's great Jacobean houses. Blickling is famed for its spectacular long gallery, superb library and fine collections of furniture, pictures and tapestries.

Location: MAP 8:K5, OS133 Ref. TG178 286. 1½m NW of Aylsham on B1354. Signposted off A140 Norwich (15m) to Cromer.

Open: House: 19 Feb–24 Jul & 14 Sept–30 Oct, Wed–Sun & BH Mons, 11am–5pm. 25 Jul–11 Sept, Wed–Mon, 11am–5pm. Garden, Shop, Restaurant & Bookshop: 2 Jan–18 Feb, Thur–Sun, 11am–4pm. 19 Feb–30 Oct, daily, 10am–5.30pm. 2 Nov–31 Dec, Wed–Sun, 11am–4pm. Plant Centre: 12 Mar–30 Oct, daily, 10am–5.30pm. Cycle Hire: 9 Apr–30 Oct, Sat–Sun and daily during local school holidays 10am–5.30pm. Park: daily, open all year. Tours of the hall available Mon & Tues, 19 Feb–30 Oct at 1, 2 & 3pm. All other days 10.45am. Spaces limited, please call for details.

***Admission:** Hall & Gardens: Adult £10.75, Child £5.25, Family £29, Family (1 adult, 3 children) £21. Group £9.10. Garden only: Adult £7.25, Child £3.65, Family £21.50 , Family (1 adult, 3 children) £14.70. Group £6.20. *includes a voluntary donation but visitors can choose to pay the standard prices displayed at the property and on the website.

Cycle hire available in Orchard, ring for details. Open as garden. WCs. Licensed. By arrangement. In park, on leads.

CAISTER CASTLE CAR COLLECTION

Caister-on-sea, Great Yarmouth, Norfolk NR30 5SN

Tel: 01572 787649

Owner/Contact: Mr J Hill

Large collection of historic motor vehicles from 1893 to recent. Moated Castle built by Sir John Falstaff in 1432. Car park free.

Location: MAP 8:M6, OS Ref. TG502 122. Take A1064 out of Caister-on-sea towards Filby, turn left at the end of the dual carriageway.

Open: Mid May–End Sept: Sun–Fri (closed Sats), 10am–4.30pm.

Admission: Contact property for details.

No photography. Partial. WCs.

CASTLE ACRE PRIORY

Stocks Green, Castle Acre, King's Lynn, Norfolk PE32 2XD

Tel: 01760 755394 **E-mail:** customers@english-heritage.org.uk

www.english-heritage.org.uk/castleacrepriory

Owner: English Heritage **Contact:** Visitor Operations Team

Explore the romantic ruins of this 12th century Cluniac priory, set in the picturesque village of Castle Acre. The impressive Norman façade, splendid prior's lodgings and chapel, and delightful recreated medieval herb garden should not be missed.

Location: MAP 8:I5, OS Ref. TF814 148. ¼m W of village of Castle Acre, 5m N of Swaffham.

Open: 1 Apr–30 Jun: daily, 10am–5pm. 1 Jul–31 Aug: daily, 10am–6pm. 1 Sep–30 Sep: daily, 10am–5pm. 1 Oct–31 Mar: Thu–Mon, 10am–4pm. Closed 24–26 Dec & 1 Jan. EH Members/OVP free.

Admission: Adult £5.30, Child £2.70, Conc. £4.50. Family £13.30. Group discount available. Opening times and prices are valid until 31st March 2011, after this date details are subject to change please see www.english-heritage.org.uk for the most up-to-date information.

Picnickers welcome. Partial. Limited for coaches. On leads.

CASTLE RISING CASTLE

CASTLE RISING, KING'S LYNN, NORFOLK PE31 6AH

Tel: 01553 631330 **Fax:** 01553 631724

Owner: Lord Howard **Contact:** The Custodian

Possibly the finest mid-12th century Keep left in England: it was built as a grand and elaborate palace. It was home to Queen Isabella, grandmother of the Black Prince. Still in surprisingly good condition, the Keep is surrounded by massive ramparts up to 120 feet high. Picnic area, adjacent tearoom. Audio tour.

Location: MAP 7:H5, OS Ref. TF666 246. Located 4m NE of King's Lynn off A149.

Open: 1 Apr–1 Nov: daily, 10am–6pm (closes at dusk if earlier in Oct). 2 Nov–31 Mar: Wed–Sun, 10am–4pm. Closed 24–26 Dec.

Admission: Adult £4, Child £2.50, Conc. £3.30, Family £12 (2 adults & 2 children, each additional child £2). 15% discount for groups (11+). Prices include VAT. Opening times and prices are subject to change.

Picnic area. Grounds. WC.

CLIFTON HOUSE

Queen Street, King's Lynn, Norfolk PE30 1HT

E-mail: anna@kingstaithe.com **www.cliftonhouse.org.uk**

Owner/Contact: Anna Keay and Simon Thurley

Magnificent grade-one listed merchant's house being restored as a family home. Features include 13th century tiled floors – the largest of their kind in England – and a 14th century vaulted undercroft. Remodelled by Henry Bell in 1700, the interiors date from 1500 to 1740. The spectacular Elizabethan tower contains original wall paintings.

Location: MAP 8:H5, OS Ref. TF615 198.

Open: Sun 17 Jul & Sun 24 Jul, 12–4pm. By pre-booked guided tour throughout the year - see website for details.

Admission: Adult admission on open days: £3.50.

Partial. By arrangement.

FELBRIGG HALL

Felbrigg, Norwich, Norfolk NR11 8PR

Tel: 01263 837444 **Fax:** 01263 837032

www.nationaltrust.org.uk

Owner: National Trust **Contact:** The Property Manager

Fine 17th c house with restored Walled Garden and parkland.

Location: MAP 8:K4, OS133 Ref. TG193 394. Nr Felbrigg village, 2m SW of Cromer.

GREAT YARMOUTH ROW HOUSES & GREYFRIARS' CLOISTERS

South Quay, Great Yarmouth, Norfolk NR30 2RQ

Tel: 01493 857900 **E-mail:** customers@english-heritage.org.uk

www.english-heritage.org.uk/greatyarmouthrowhouses

Owner: English Heritage **Contact:** Visitor Operations Team

Two immaculately presented 17th century Row Houses, a type of building unique to Great Yarmouth. Row 111 House was almost destroyed by bombing in 1942/3 and contains items rescued from the rubble. Old Merchant's House boasts magnificent plaster-work ceilings and displays of local architectural fittings.

Location: MAP 8:M6, OS134, TG525 072. In Great Yarmouth, make for Historic South Quay, by riverside and dock, ½ m inland from beach. Follow signs to dock and south quay.

Open: 1 Apr–30 Sept: daily, 12 noon–5pm.

Access to Greyfriars' Cloisters is by pre-arrangement only, contact 01493 857900.

Admission: Adult £4.20. Child £2.10, Conc. £3.60, Family £10.50. EH Members Free. Group discount available. Opening times and prices are valid until 31st March 2011, after this date details are subject to change please visit www.english-heritage.org.uk for the most up-to-date information.

Picnickers welcome. Museum.

HOLKHAM HALL

See page 243 for full page entry.

Felbrigg Hall

© NTPL / Nick Meers

GRIME'S GRAVES – PREHISTORIC FLINT MINE ⌗

LYNFORD, THETFORD, NORFOLK IP26 5DE

www.english-heritage.org.uk/grimesgraves

Tel: 01842 810656 **E-mail:** customers@english-heritage.org.uk

Owner: English Heritage **Contact:** Visitor Operations Team

This is the only Neolithic flint mine open to visitors in Britain. This lunar landscape was first named Grim's Graves by the Anglo-Saxons. It was not until 1870 that they were identified as flint mines dug over 5,000 years ago.

An interactive exhibition illustrates the history of the site, and visitors (over 5 yrs old) can enter one excavated mine shaft to see the jet-black flint.

Set amid the distinctive Breckland heath landscape, this is also a Site of Special Scientific Interest and a habitat for rare fauna. NB: Visitors are advised to wear sensible flat shoes.

Location: MAP 8:I7, OS 144, TL818 898. 7m NW of Thetford off A134.

Open: 1–31 Mar: Thu–Mon, 10am–5pm. 1 Apr–30 Jun: daily, 10am–5pm. 1 Jul–31 Aug: daily, 10am–6pm. 1 Sep–30 Sep: daily 10am–5pm, 1–31 Oct, Thu–Mon 10am–5pm, 1 Nov–28 Feb closed. Last visit to site 30 mins before close. No entry to the mines for children under 5 yrs.

Admission: Adult £3.20, Child £1.60 (Child under 5yrs free), Conc. £2.70, Family £8. EH Members/OVP free. Group discount available. Opening times and prices are valid until 31st March 2011, after this date details are subject to change please visit www.english-heritage.org.uk for the most up-to-date information.

Picnickers welcome. Partial. Limited. On leads.

HOUGHTON HALL

HOUGHTON, KING'S LYNN, NORFOLK PE31 6UE

www.houghtonhall.com

Tel: 01485 528569 **Fax:** 01485 528167 **E-mail:** info@houghtonhall.com

Owner: The Marquess of Cholmondeley **Contact:** Susan Cleaver

Houghton Hall is one of the finest examples of Palladian architecture in England. Built in the 18th century by Sir Robert Walpole, Britain's first prime minister. Original designs by James Gibbs & Colen Campbell, interior decoration by William Kent. The House has been restored to its former grandeur, containing many of its original furnishings. The spectacular award-winning 5-acre walled garden is divided into areas devoted to fruit and vegetables, elegant herbaceous borders, and a formal rose garden with over 150 varieties – full of colour throughout the summer. The unique Model Soldier Collection contains over 20,000 models arranged in various battle formations. Contemporary Sculptures in the Gardens.

Location: MAP 8:I5, OS Ref. TF792 287. 13m E of King's Lynn, 10m W of Fakenham 1½m N of A148.

Open: Easter Sun 24 Apr–29 Sept: Weds, Thurs, Suns & BH Mons. Park, Walled Garden, Soldier Museum, Restaurant & Gift Shop: 11.30am–5.30pm (last admission 5pm). House: 1.30–5pm (last admission 4.30pm).

Admission: 2010 Prices: Adult £8.80, Child (5–16) £3.50, Family (2+2) £22. Everything but the House: Adult £6, Child £2.50, Family (2+2) £15. Group (20+) discounts available, please tel for details.

Licensed. Licensed. By arrangement.

On leads, in grounds.

KIMBERLEY HALL

Wymondham, Norfolk NR18 0RT

Tel: 01603 759447 **Fax:** 01603 758244 **E-mail:** events@kimberleyhall.co.uk

www.kimberleyhall.co.uk

Owner/Contact: R Buxton

Magnificent Queen Anne house built in 1712 by William Talman for Sir John Wodehouse, an ancestor of P G Wodehouse. Towers added after 1754 and wings connected to the main block by curved colonnades in 1835. Internal embellishments in 1770s include some very fine plasterwork by John Sanderson and a 'flying' spiral staircase beneath a coffered dome. The park, with its picturesque lake, ancient oak trees and walled gardens was laid out in 1762 by 'Capability' Brown.

Location: MAP 8:K6, OS Ref. TG091 048. 10m SW of Norwich, 3m from A11.

Open: House & Park not open to the public. Grounds, certain rooms and extensive cellars, together with 3,500 sq.ft of refurbished function space over two floors in the west wing are available for corporate hospitality and weddings (licensed for Civil ceremonies and partnerships) as well as product launches, film and fashion shoots. Tipis within walled garden available for hire.

Admission: Please telephone for details.

MANNINGTON GARDENS & COUNTRYSIDE

MANNINGTON HALL, NORWICH NR11 7BB

www.manningtongardens.co.uk

Tel: 01263 584175 **Fax:** 01263 761214

Owner: The Lord & Lady Walpole **Contact:** Lady Walpole

The gardens around this medieval moated manor house feature a wide variety of plants, trees and shrubs in many different settings. Throughout the gardens are thousands of roses especially classic varieties. The Heritage Rose and 20th Century Rose Gardens have roses in areas with designs reflecting their date of origin from the 15th century to the present day.

Location: MAP 8:K5, OS Ref. TG144 320. Signposted from Saxthorpe crossroads on the Norwich–Holt road B1149. 1½m W of Wolterton Hall.

Open: Gardens: May–Sept: Suns 12–5pm. Jun–Aug: Wed–Fri, 11am–5pm, and at other times by prior appointment. Walks: daily from 9am. Medieval Hall open by appointment. Grounds & Park open all year.

Admission: Adult £5, Child (under 16yrs) Free, Conc. £4. Groups by arrangement.

Grounds. WCs. Licensed. By arrangement.

£2 car park fee (walkers only). In park only. Park. €

NORWICH CATHEDRAL

12 The Close, Norwich NR1 4DH

Tel: 01603 218300 **Fax:** 01603 766032 **E-mail:** reception@cathedral.org.uk

www.norwichcathedral.org.uk

Contact: Susan Brown

A fine example of Romanesque architecture featuring the world's largest collection of medieval roof bosses, England's second tallest spire and largest cloister. Visitors encounter a true learning experience in the recently completed Hostry – the Visitors and Education Centre which houses a classroom, conference facilities and a digital interpretative exhibition space.

Location: MAP 8:K6, OS Ref. TG 235 087. South side of Norwich City Centre. A11 from London.

Open: Mon–Sat 7.30am–6.30pm, Sun 11.45am–3.30pm.

Admission: Suggested donation: Adult £5, Conc £4, Family £12. Group rates available.

Partial. WCs. Licensed. Licensed. By arrangement. Limited. No coaches. Guide dogs only.

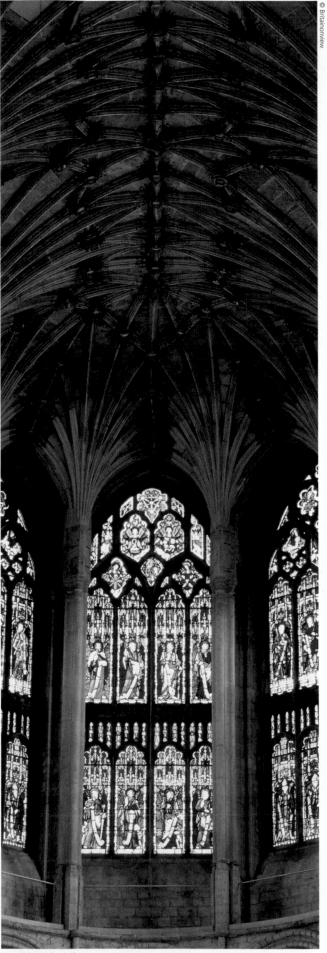

© Britainonview

Norwich Cathedral

© NTPL / Nick Daly

OXBURGH HALL

OXBOROUGH, KING'S LYNN, NORFOLK PE33 9PS

www.nationaltrust.org.uk

Tel: 01366 328258 **Fax:** 01366 328066 **E-mail:** oxburghhall@nationaltrust.org.uk
Owner: National Trust **Contact:** The Property Secretary

No-one ever forgets their first sight of Oxburgh. A romantic moated manor house, it was built by the Bedingfeld family in the 15th century and they have lived here ever since. Inside, the family's Catholic history is revealed, complete with a secret priest's hole which you can crawl inside. See the astonishing needlework by Mary, Queen of Scots, and the private chapel, built with reclaimed materials. Outside, you can enjoy the panoramic views from the Gatehouse roof and follow the woodcarving trails in the gardens and woodlands. The late winter drifts of snowdrops and aconites are not to be missed.

Location: MAP 8:I6, OS143, TF742 012. At Oxborough, 7m SW of Swaffham on S side of Stoke Ferry road. Rail: 10miles from Downham Market station.

Open: House: 26 Feb–30 Oct, 11am–5pm (closes 4pm in Feb, Mar & Oct; Daily in Easter holidays, Whitsun week and August. Garden: As House plus 8 Jan–6 Mar and 5 Nov–18 Dec 11am–4pm weekends only.

Admission: House & Garden: Adult £8.20, Child £4.10, Family £20.50. Garden & Estate only: Adult £4.30, Child £2.15, Family £10.75. Groups discount (min 15) – must book in advance with the Property Secretary. Admission includes a voluntary 10% Gift Aid donation but visitors can choose to pay the standard prices displayed at the property and on the website.

Special Events: Ask for leaflet.

No picnics or dogs allowed in Garden; no photography in House. Free garden tours daily. Souvenir guides, gift shop, second-hand bookshop. Partial. WCs. Licensed. By arrangement. Limited for Coaches. Guide dogs only Send SAE for details.

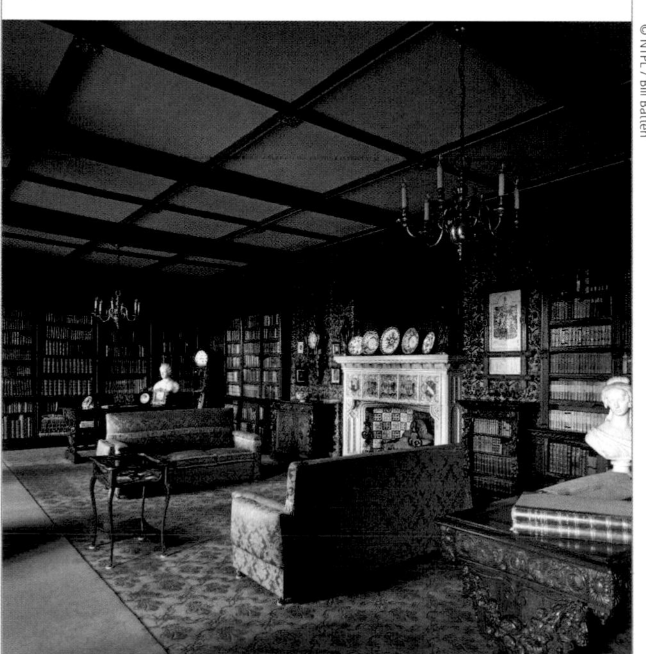
© NTPL / Bill Batten

RAVENINGHAM GARDENS

RAVENINGHAM, NORWICH, NORFOLK NR14 6NS

www.raveningham.com

Tel: 01508 548152 **Fax:** 01508 548958
E-mail: info@raveningham.com
Owner: Sir Nicholas Bacon Bt **Contact:** Diane Hoffman

Superb herbaceous borders, 18th century walled kitchen garden, Victorian glasshouse, herb garden, Edwardian rose garden, contemporary sculptures, 14th century church and much more.

Location: MAP 8:L7, OS Ref. TM399 965. Between Norwich & Lowestoft off A146 then B1136.

Open: Easter–Aug BH: Thur, 11am–4pm. BH Suns & Mons, 2–5pm. Snowdrops, Agapanthus, Rose and Vegetable weekends - see website.

Admission: Adult £4, Child (under 16yrs) Free, OAP £3. Groups by prior arrangement.

Teas only on Suns & BH Mons.

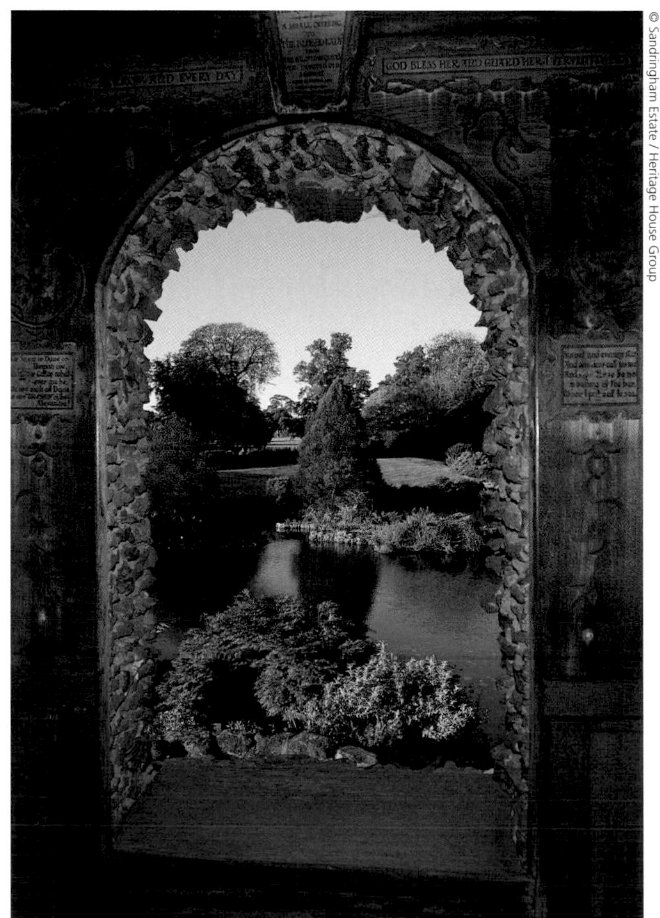
© Sandringham Estate / Heritage House Group

Sandringham

© NTPL / Nadia Mackenzie

Oxburgh Hall

SANDRINGHAM

THE ESTATE OFFICE, SANDRINGHAM, NORFOLK PE35 6EN

www.sandringhamestate.co.uk

Tel: 01553 612908 **Fax: 01485 541571 E-mail:** visits@sandringhamestate.co.uk

Owner: H M The Queen **Contact:** The Public Enterprises Manager

Sandringham House, the charming Norfolk retreat of Her Majesty The Queen, is set in 60 acres of beautiful gardens. All the main ground floor rooms used by The Royal Family, full of their treasured ornaments, portraits and furniture and still maintained in the style of King Edward VII and Queen Alexandra, are open to the public. Don't miss the fascinating Museum and the charming parish church, to round off an absorbing day. There are also 600 acres of the Country Park open to all, with tractor tours running daily. Guided garden tours available; land train shuttle service inside the gardens.

Location: MAP 7:H5, OS Ref. TF695 287 8m NE of King's Lynn on B1440 off A148.

Rail: King's Lynn. **Air:** Norwich.

Open: 23 April–late July & early August–30 October.

Admission: House, Museum & Gardens, Adult £11, Child £5.50, Conc. £9, Family, £27.50. Museum & Gardens, Adult £7.50, Child £4, Conc. £6.50, Family £19. Groups (20+), Adult £10, Child £5 Conc. £8.

No photography in house. Plant Centre. Visitor Centre only. Licensed. Licensed. By arrangement. Private evening tours. Ample. Guide dogs only.

ST GEORGE'S GUILDHALL

29 King Street, King's Lynn, Norfolk PE30 1HA

Tel: 01553 765565 **www.west-norfolk.gov.uk**

Owner: National Trust **Contact:** The Administrator

The largest surviving English medieval guildhall. The building is now converted into a theatre and arthouse cinema. Many interesting features survive.

Location: MAP 7:H5, OS132, TF616 202. On W side of King Street close to the Tuesday Market Place.

Open: All year Mon–Fri 10am–2pm.

Admission: Free.

Pay and Display

SHERINGHAM PARK

Upper Sheringham, Norfolk NR26 8TL

Tel: 01263 820550 **E-mail:** sheringhampark@nationaltrust.org.uk

www.nationaltrust.org.uk

Owner: National Trust **Contact:** Visitor Centre

One of Humphry Repton's most outstanding achievements, the landscape park contains fine mature woodlands, and the large woodland garden is particularly famous for its spectacular show of rhododendrons and azaleas (mid May–June). There are stunning views of the coast and countryside from the viewing towers and many delightful waymarked walks. Programme of special events.

Location: MAP 8:K4, OS133, TG135 420. 2m SW of Sheringham, access for cars off A148 Cromer–Holt road; 5m W of Cromer, 6m E of Holt.

Open: Park open all year, daily, dawn–dusk.

Admission: Pay & Display: Cars £4.50 (NT members Free–display members' sticker in car). Coaches Free must book in advance.

Partial. WC. Easter–end Sept, daily. Sats/Suns all year. Coaches free but must book in advance. In grounds, on leads.

STODY LODGE

Stody, Melton Constable, Norfolk NR24 2EW

Tel: 01263 860572 **Fax:** 01263 861179 **E-mail:** aggie.slater@stodyestate.co.uk

www.stodyestate.co.uk

Owner: Mrs Adel Macnicol **Contact:** Aggie Slater

Spectacular gardens having one of the largest concentrations of Rhododendrons and Azaleas in East Anglia. Created in the 1920s the gardens also feature many ornamental trees, shrubs, late daffodils and bluebells, herbaceous borders, expansive lawns and magnificient yew hedges. Lovely walk through to woodland gardens. Picnic area, teas, parking.

Location: MAP 8:J5, OS Ref. TG067 339. Off B1354. Signed from Melton Constable on Holt Road.

Open: May only, Sundays in May & Bank Holiday Monday 30 May 2011, 2–5pm.

Admission: Adult £4.50, Children under 12 Free.

Partial. WCs. In grounds, on leads.

WALSINGHAM ABBEY GROUNDS & SHIREHALL MUSEUM

Little Walsingham, Norfolk NR22 6BP

Tel: 01328 824432 **Fax:** 01328 820098 **E-mail:** jackie@walsingham-estate.co.uk

www.walsinghamabbey.com

Owner: Walsingham Estate Company **Contact:** Jackie Seals

Set in the picturesque medieval village of Little Walsingham, a place of pilgrimage since the 11th century, the grounds contain the remains of the famous Augustinian Priory with attractive gardens and river walks. The Shirehall Museum includes a Georgian magistrates' court and displays on the history of Walsingham.

Location: MAP 8:J4, OS Ref. TF934 367. B1105 N from Fakenham–5m.

Open: 2 Apr–30 Oct: daily, 10am–4.30pm. Also daily during snowdrop season (February) 10am–4pm. Other times, please telephone for details.

Admission: Adult £3.50, Conc. £2.50.

No commercial photography. Partial. WCs. By arrangement. On leads.

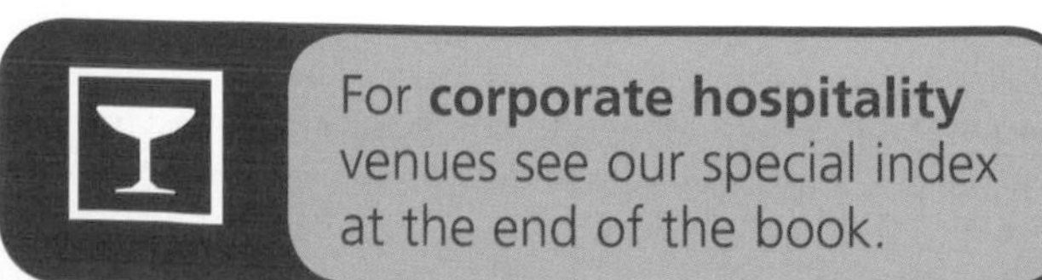
For **corporate hospitality** venues see our special index at the end of the book.

WOLTERTON PARK

NORWICH, NORFOLK NR11 7LY

www.manningtongardens.co.uk

Tel: 01263 584175/768444 **Fax:** 01263 761214 **E-mail:** admin@walpoleestate.co.uk

Owner: The Lord and Lady Walpole **Contact:** The Lady Walpole

18th century Hall. Portrait collection annual exhibitions. Historic park with lake.

Location: MAP 8:K5, OS Ref. TG164 317. Situated near Erpingham village, signposted from Norwich–Cromer Rd A140.

Open: Park: daily from 9am. Hall: 29 Apr–28 Oct: Fridays, 2–5pm (last entry 4pm) by appointment and various events.

Admission: £5. £2 car park fee only for walkers. (Groups by application: from £4.)

Small. Partial. WC. In park, on leads. Park. €

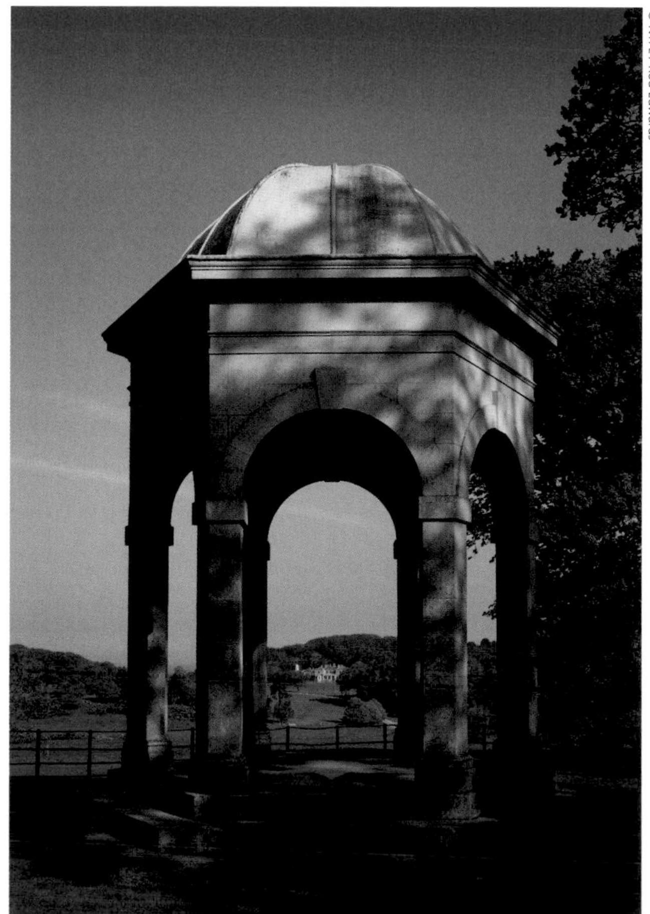

© NTPL / Rod Edwards

Sheringham Park

EUSTON HALL

Euston, Nr Thetford, Norfolk IP24 2QP

Tel: 01842 766366 (Estate Office) **Fax:** 01842 766764

Email: admin@euston-estate.co.uk **www.eustonhall.co.uk**

Owner: The Duke of Grafton **Contact:** Mrs L Campbell

Home of the Dukes of Grafton for over 300 years. The Hall contains a unique collection of paintings of the Court of Charles II. Formal gardens and walks through the Pleasure Grounds, designed by diarist John Evelyn, can still be enjoyed today. Admission also includes access to 18th century watermill and 'Wren' style church which stand in the grounds. Tea Room and Gift Shop.

Location: MAP 8:J8, OS Ref. TL897 786. 12m north of Bury St Edmunds, on A1088. 2m E of A134.

Open: 16 Jun–15 Sept, Thurs. Also Sun 7 Aug & Sun 4 Sept. 2.30–5pm. Please check opening times before your visit.

Admission: Adult £7, Child £3, OAP £6. Groups (12+) £6 pp.

Access to ground floor of house, tea room, shop and WCs. Guide dogs only.

FLATFORD BRIDGE COTTAGE

Flatford, East Bergholt, Colchester, Essex CO7 6UL

Tel: 01206 298260 **Fax:** 01206 297212

Email: flatfordbridgecottage@nationaltrust.org.uk **www.nationaltrust.org.uk**

Owner: National Trust **Contact:** Visitor Services

In the heart of the beautiful Dedham Vale, the hamlet of Flatford is the location for some of John Constable's most famous paintings. Find out more about Constable at the exhibition in Bridge Cottage. Next door is the riverside tea-room and gift shop. Note: No public access to Flatford Mill.

Location: MAP 8:J10, OS Ref. TM077 332. On N bank of Stour, 1m S of East Bergholt B1070. Rail: Manningtree 2miles by footpath

Open: 2 Jan–28 Feb: Sats & Suns only, 11am–3.30pm. 2–31 Mar: Wed–Sun, 11am–4pm. 1–30 Apr: daily, 11am–5pm. 1 May–30 Sept: daily, 10.30am–5.30pm. 1–31 Oct: daily, 11am–4.30pm. 2 Nov–23 Dec: Wed–Sun, 11am–3.30pm. Closed Christmas & New Year.

Admission: Guided walks (when guide available) £3, accompanied child Free.

Car park is not NT. WCs. Licensed By arrangement. Charge applies. Limited parking for coaches. Guide dogs only.

© Freston Tower / Landmark Trust

Freston Tower

© English Heritage

© English Heritage

FRAMLINGHAM CASTLE

FRAMLINGHAM, SUFFOLK IP13 9BP

www.english-heritage.org.uk/framlingham

Tel: 01728 724189 **E-mail:** customers@english-heritage.org.uk

Owner: English Heritage **Contact:** Visitor Operations Team

Framlingham is a magnificent 12th century castle. From the continuous curtain wall linking 13 towers, there are excellent panoramic views of the town and the charming reed-fringed Mere. Visitors can experience life at Framlingham Castle through the ages with our introductory exhibition, themed trails and variety of indoor and outdoor games. Entry also includes access to the Lanman Trust's Museum of local history.

Location: MAP 8:L8, OS Ref. TM287 637. In Framlingham on B1116. NE of town centre.

Open: 1 Apr–30 Jun: daily, 10am–5pm. 1 Jul–31 Aug: daily, 10am–6pm. 1 Sep–31 Oct: daily, 10am–5pm. 1 Nov–31 Mar: Thu–Mon, 10am–4pm. Closed 24–26 Dec & 1 Jan. The property may close early if an event is booked, please ring in advance for details.

Admission: Adult £6. Child £3, Children under 5 Free. Conc. £5.10, Family £15. EH Members/OVP Free. Group discount available. Opening times and prices are valid until 31st March 2011, after this date details are subject to change please visit www.english-heritage.org.uk for the most up-to-date information.

Picnickers welcome. Partial. WCs. Limited for coaches. On leads.

Glemham Hall

FRESTON TOWER

Nr Ipswich, Suffolk IP9 1AD

Tel: 01628 825925 **E-mail:** bookings@landmarktrust.org.uk

www.landmarktrust.org.uk

Owner/Contact: The Landmark Trust

An Elizabethan six-storey tower overlooking the estuary of the River Orwell. The tower was built in 1578 by a wealthy Ipswich merchant called Thomas Gooding, perhaps to celebrate the recent grant of his coat of arms. Freston Tower is cared for by The Landmark Trust, a building preservation charity who let it for holidays. Full details of Freston Tower and 189 other historic and architecturally important buildings are featured in the Landmark Trust Handbook (price £10 plus p&p refundable against a booking) and on the website.

Location: MAP 8:K9, OS Ref. TM177 397.

Open: Available for holidays for up to 4 people throughout the year. Open Days on 8 days a year. Other visits by appointment. Please contact the Landmark Trust for details.

Admission: Free on Open Days and visits by appointment.

GLEMHAM HALL

LITTLE GLEMHAM, WOODBRIDGE, SUFFOLK IP13 0BT

www.glemhamhall.co.uk

Tel: 01728 746704 **Fax:** 01728 747236 **E-mail:** events@glemhamhall.co.uk

Owner: Philip & Raewyn Hope-Cobbold

Contact: Louise Codd – Events Manager

Built around 1560, the Hall remained in the Glemham family until 1700 when it passed to the Norths (Earls of Guilford). Dudley North's wife Catherine was daughter of Elihu Yale, founder of the famous American University. The Cobbold's acquired the Hall in 1923. Old English: Gleam (happy) + ham (village) + Parva (small) hence Little Glemham.

Location: MAP 8:L9, OS Ref. TM212 GR347 592. Heritage signs off A12 between Woodbridge & Saxmundham.

Open: Various months/days/times throughout the year (see website).

Admission: Adult £15, Child under 13 Free, Groups min 10 max 30.

Partial.WC. Obligatory, by arrangement. Cars & coaches ample.

GAINSBOROUGH'S HOUSE

46 GAINSBOROUGH ST, SUDBURY, SUFFOLK CO10 2EU

www.gainsborough.org

Tel: 01787 372958 **Fax:** 01787 376991 **E-mail:** mail@gainsborough.org

Owner: Gainsborough's House Society **Contact:** Rosemary Woodward

Gainsborough's House is the birthplace museum of Thomas Gainsborough (1727–1788), one of the greatest painters in the history of British art. More of his paintings, drawings and prints are on display here at any one time than anywhere else in the world. The collection encompasses Gainsborough's whole career, from early portraits or landscapes painted in Suffolk in the 1750s to later works from his London period of the 1770s and 80s. A varied programme of exhibitions of both historic British and contemporary art are organised throughout the year. The historic house dates back to the 16th century with an attractive walled garden.

Location: MAP 8:I10, OS Ref. TL872 413. 46 Gainsborough St, Sudbury town centre.

Open: All year: Mon–Sat, 10am–5pm. Closed: Suns, Good Fri and Christmas to New Year.

Admission: Adult £4.50, Child/Student £2.00, Conc £3.60, Family Ticket £10. Tues, 1–5pm: Free.

No photography. WCs. None.

HADLEIGH GUILDHALL

Hadleigh, Suffolk IP7 5DT

Tel: 01473 822544

Owner: Hadleigh Market Feoffment Charity **Contact:** Jane Haylock

Fine timber framed guildhall, one of the least known medieval buildings in Suffolk.

Location: MAP 8:J9, OS Ref. TM025 425. S side of churchyard.

Open: By arrangement for Tours of 10 or more. Ring for details.

Admission: £2.50 per person.

HAUGHLEY PARK

Stowmarket, Suffolk IP14 3JY

Tel: 01359 240701 **www.haughleyparkbarn.co.uk**

Owner/Contact: Mr & Mrs Robert Williams

Mellow red brick manor house of 1620 set in gardens, park and woodland. Original five-gabled east front, north wing re-built in Georgian style, 1820. 6 acres of well tended gardens including walled kitchen garden. 17th century brick and timber barn restored as meeting rooms. Woodland walks with bluebells (special Sun opening), lily-of-the-valley (May), rhododendrons and azaleas.

Location: MAP 8:J8, OS Ref. TM005 618. 4m W of Stowmarket signed off A14.

Open: Garden only: May–Sept: Tues & last Sun in Apr & 1st Sun in May, 2–5.30pm. Barn bookable for lectures, dinners, weddings etc (capacity 160).

Admission: Garden: £3. Child under 16 Free.

Picnics allowed. Bluebell Sun. Bluebell Sun. On leads only.

For **special events** held throughout the year, see the index at the end of the book.

HELMINGHAM HALL GARDENS

HELMINGHAM, SUFFOLK IP14 6EF

www.helmingham.com

Tel: 01473 890799 **Fax:** 01473 890776 **E-mail:** events@helmingham.com

Owner: The Lord & Lady Tollemache **Contact:** Events Office

Grade 1 listed gardens, redesigned by Lady Tollemache (a Chelsea Gold Medallist) set in a 400 acre deer park surrounding a moated Tudor Hall. Visitors are enchanted by the stunning herbaceous borders within the walled kitchen garden, the herb, knot, rose and wild gardens. Coach bookings are warmly welcomed and there are a variety of exciting events throughout the season.

Location: MAP 8:K9, OS Ref. TM190 578. B1077, 9m N of Ipswich, 5m S of Debenham.

Open: Gardens only 1st May–18th September 2011 (12–5pm Tuesdays, Wednesdays, Thursdays, Sundays).

Admission: Adults £6, Child (5-15yrs) £3. Groups (30+) £5.00.

Grounds. WCs. By arrangement. Pre-booking required. On leads. Please contact us for details.

©NT/Fisheye Images

ICKWORTH HOUSE, PARK & GARDENS

HORRINGER, BURY ST EDMUNDS IP29 5QE

www.nationaltrust.org.uk/ickworth

Tel: 01284 735270 **Fax:** 01284 735175 **E-mail:** ickworth@nationaltrust.org.uk

Owner: National Trust **Contact:** Property Administrator

One of the most unusual houses in East Anglia. The huge Rotunda of this 18th century Italianate house dominates the landscape. Inside are collections of Georgian silver, Regency furniture, Old Master paintings and family portraits. **NEW**: Servants' quarters and finishing kitchen open to the public in Summer 2011.

Location: MAP 8:I9, OS155 Ref. TL816 611. In Horringer, 3m SW of Bury St Edmunds on W side of A143.

Open: House: 28 Feb–30 Oct, Fri–Tue, 11am–5pm. Park: Open all year, daily, 8am-8pm or dusk if earlier. Gardens: 1 Jan–27 Feb daily, 11am–4pm. 28 feb–30 Oct, daily, 10am–5pm. 31 Oct-31 Dec daily, 10am-4pm. West Wing Shop & Restaurant: 1 Jan–27 Feb, Fri–Tue, 11am–4pm. 28 feb-30 Oct, Thur–Tue, 10am–5pm. 31 Oct-31 Dec, Thur-Tue, 10am-4pm. Open all BH Mons, Good Friday & 1 Jan & every day in local school holidays. Property closed 14 Apr, 2 Jun & 24, 25, 26 Dec.

***Admission:** Gift Aid Admission (Standard Admission prices in brackets) House, park & gardens: £9.15 (£8.30), child £3.65 (£3.30), family £21.90 (£19.90). Park & garden only: £4.65 (£4.20), child £1.15 (£1), family £10.40 (£9.45). House upgrade: £4.50 (£4.05), child £2.50 (£2.25), family £11.50 (£10.45). *2010 prices

By arrangement. Limited for coaches.

KENTWELL HALL & GARDENS

LONG MELFORD, SUFFOLK CO10 9BA

www.kentwell.co.uk

Tel: 01787 310207 **Fax:** 01787 379318 **E-mail:** info@kentwell.co.uk

Owner: Patrick Phillips Esq QC **Contact:** The Estate Office

A beautiful mellow redbrick Tudor Mansion, surrounded by a broad moat, with rare service building of c1500. Interior 'improved' by Thomas Hopper in 1820s. Still a lived-in family home.

Restoration - Famed for long-time, long term, ongoing works in House & Gardens.

Gardens – Over 30 years' endeavour has resulted in gardens which are a joy in all seasons. Moats, massed spring bulbs, mature trees, delightful walled garden, with potager, herbs and ancient espaliered fruit trees. Much topiary from massive ancient yews to the unique 'Pied Piper' story.

Re-Creations – renowned for the award-winning Re-Creations of Tudor Life. Also occasional Re-Creations of WW2 Life and now too of Victorian Life. Re-Creations take place on selected weekends from April to December.

Corporate – House and upgraded 2500 sq ft Function Room for conferences, dinners, banquets of all sizes and Corporate Activity Days of originality.

Schools – Perhaps the biggest, most original and stimulating educational programme in the region enjoyed by about 20,000 schoolchildren each year.

Filming – Much used for medieval and Tudor periods for its wide range of perfectly equipped locations inside and out and access to Kentwell's 700 Tudors as extras.

Scaresville – Award-winning Scariest Halloween Event 15–31 October.

Location: MAP 8:I9, OS Ref. TL864 479. Off the A134. 4m N of Sudbury.

Open: For full details see our website or call for Opening Leaflet.

Admission: Charges apply according to the Event (if any) on. Call for details.

No photography in house. Conferences, dinners, Tudor feasts for groups of 40 or more. Car rallies. Home-made food. Including themed ceremonies. Open-air theatre, opera and concert season Jul–Aug.

© NTPL / Martin Charles

Melford Hall

LEISTON ABBEY

Leiston, Suffolk

Tel: 01223 582700 (Regional Office) **E-mail:** customers@english-heritage.org.uk

www.english-heritage.org.uk/leistonabbey

Owner: English Heritage **Contact:** The East of England Regional Office

The remains of this abbey for Premonstratensian canons, including a restored chapel, are amongst the most extensive in Suffolk.

Location: MAP 8:M8, OS Ref. TM445 642. 1m N of Leiston off B1069.

Open: Any reasonable time.

Admission: Free. Opening times and prices are subject to change; please check the English Heritage website for up-to-date information.

Picnickers welcome.

LANDGUARD FORT

Felixstowe, Suffolk IP11 3TX

Tel: 07749 695523 **E-mail:** customers@english-heritage.org.uk

www.english-heritage.org.uk/landguardfort

Owner: English Heritage **Contact:** Visitor Operations Team (Managed by Languard Fort Trust)

Impressive 18th c fort with later additions built on a site originally fortified by Henry VIII, and in use until after World War II. Guided tours and audio tours of the fort are supplemented by a DVD presentation of the site's history and by guided tours of the substantial outside batteries.

Location: MAP 8:L10, OS Ref. TM284 318. 1m S of Felixstowe town centre – follow brown tourist signs to Landguard Point and Nature Reserve from A14.

Open: 27 Mar–31 May: daily, 10am–5pm. 1 Jun–30 Sep: daily, 10am–6pm. 1 Oct– 31 Oct: daily, 10am–5pm. Last admission 1 hour before closing. An average tour takes 1.5 hours. Please call 07749 695523 to book Battery & group tours.

Admission: Adult £3.50, Child £1, Conc. £2.50. Prices may vary on event days. Free entry for children under 5yrs and wheelchair users. No unaccompanied children. EH Members Free. Group discount available. Opening times and prices are valid until 31st March 2011, after this date details are subject to change please see www.english-heritage.org.uk for the most up-to-date information.

Picnickers welcome. Contact David Morgan for details of tours of the outer batteries and charges for special events.

LITTLE HALL

Market Place, Lavenham, Sudbury, Suffolk CO10 9QZ

Tel: 01787 247019 **Fax:** 01787 248341 **E-mail:** info@littlehall.org.uk

www.littlehall.org.uk

Owner: Suffolk Building Preservation Trust Ltd **Contact:** Jeremy Wagener

A beautifully presented 14th c. hall house in the heart of historic Lavenham. A warm, friendly, furnished building with a pretty walled garden and courtyard. Its fascinating history mirrors the rise and fall of Lavenham's woollen-cloth trades and its eventful 20th c. Restoration by the Gayer-Anderson brothers.

Location: MAP 8:J9, TL915 942. 6m NNE of Sudbury.

Open: Wed, Thur, Sat & Sun, 2–5.30pm. Bank Holidays, 11am–5.30pm. Last entry 4.30pm. Groups by arrangement throughout year.

Admission: Adults £3, Accompanied Children Free, Concessions for CPRE & SPS Members, Groups £2.50 (Schools 50p).

No photography. Partial. Optional, Always available (free) Guide dogs only. Groups only. See website.

© Lavenham Photographic Studios

LAVENHAM: THE GUILDHALL OF CORPUS CHRISTI

THE MARKET PLACE, LAVENHAM, SUDBURY CO10 9QZ

www.nationaltrust.org.uk

Tel: 01787 247646 **E-mail:** lavenhamguildhall@nationaltrust.org.uk

Owner: National Trust **Contact:** Jane Gosling

With its numerous timber-framed houses and magnificent church, a visit to picturesque Lavenham is a step back in time. The sixteenth-century Guildhall is the ideal place to begin with its exhibitions on the woollen cloth industry, agriculture and local history bringing to life the fascinating stories behind this remarkable village.

Location: MAP 8:J9, OS155, TL915 942. 6m NNE of Sudbury. Village centre. A1141 & B1071.

Open: 5–27 Mar, Wed–Sun, 11am–4pm; 28 Mar–30 Oct, daily, 11am–5pm; 5–27 Nov, Sat & Sun, 11am–4pm. Closed Good Friday. Parts of the building may be closed occasionally for community use.

Admission: Adult £4.50, Child £1.90, Family £10.90, Groups: Adult £3.80, Child £1.40. School parties by arrangement.

Program of special talks, tours and events throughout year. Contact the property for an event calendar.

©NT/Fisheye Images

MELFORD HALL

LONG MELFORD, SUDBURY, SUFFOLK CO10 9AA

www.nationaltrust.org.uk

Tel: 01787 379228 **Info:** 01787 376395 **E-mail:** melford@nationaltrust.org.uk

Owner: National Trust **Contact:** Josephine Waters

For over two centuries Melford Hall has been the much loved family home of the Hyde Parkers. The interior charts their changing tastes and fashions and the stories about visits by Beatrix Potter and family life at Melford show that a home is far more than just bricks and mortar.

Location: OS Ref. TL867 462. In Long Melford off A134, 14m S of Bury St Edmunds, 3m N of Sudbury.

Open: 2–17 Apr, Sat–Sun, 23 Apr-2 Oct, Wed–Sun, 8–30 Oct, Sat–Sun. Also open on Bank Holiday Mondays. All 1.30–5pm.

Admission: House & Garden: Adult £6.60, Child (under 16yrs) £3.30, Family £16.50. Groups (15+): Adult £5.50, Child £2.75. Garden Only: Adult £3.30, Child (u16) £1.65, Family £8.25.

Special Events: Range of special events in the house and parkland throughout the year. Contact the property or National Trust website for details.

No flash photography in house. WCs. Limited parking for coaches Guide dogs only.

© English Heritage

ORFORD CASTLE ⌗

ORFORD, WOODBRIDGE, SUFFOLK IP12 2ND

www.english-heritage.org.uk/orford

Tel: 01394 450472 **E-mail:** customers@english-heritage.org.uk

Owner: English Heritage **Contact:** Visitor Operations Team

It has a warren of passageways and chambers to be explored, with a winding staircase right to the top where you can enjoy spectacular views of Orford Ness.

Location: MAP 8:M9, OS169, TM419 499. In Orford on B1084, 20m NE of Ipswich.

Open: 1 Apr–30 Jun: daily, 10am–5pm. 1 Jul–31 Aug: daily, 10am–6pm. 1 Sep–30 Sept: daily, 10am–5pm. 1 Oct–31 Mar: Thur–Mon, 10am–4pm. Closed 24–26 Dec & 1 Jan.

Admission: Adult £5.30, Child £2.70, Under 5s Free, Conc. £4.50, Family £13.30. EH Members/OVP Free. Group discount available. Opening times and prices are valid until 31st March 2011, after this date details are subject to change please see www.english-heritage.org.uk for the most up-to-date information.

© Britainonview

Kentwell Hall & Gardens

OTLEY HALL

OTLEY, IPSWICH, SUFFOLK IP6 9PA

www.otleyhall.co.uk

Tel: 01473 890264 **Fax:** 01473 890803 **E-mail:** enquiries@otleyhall.co.uk

Owner: Dr Ian & Mrs Catherine Beaumont **Contact:** Louise Rutterford

A stunning medieval Moated Hall (Grade I) frequently described as "one of England's loveliest houses". Noted for its richly carved beams, superb linenfold panelling and 16th century wall paintings, Otley Hall was once owned by the Gosnold family and is still a family home. Bartholomew Gosnold voyaged to the New World in 1602 and named Cape Cod and Martha's Vineyard. Gosnold returned in 1607 and founded the Jamestown colony, the first English-speaking settlement in the US. The unique 10-acre gardens include historically accurate Tudor re-creations and were voted among the top 10 gardens to visit in Great Britain.

Location: MAP 8:K9, OS Ref. TM207 563. 7m N of Ipswich, off the B1079.

Open: BH Suns (1 & 29 May, 28 Aug), 1–5pm. Afternoon teas available. Groups and individuals welcome all year by appointment for private guided tours.

Admission: BHs: Adult £6, Child £3.

Special Events: Otley Hall is open to the public three times per year on the bank holiday Sundays in May and August. The House and grounds are available for wedding ceremonies and receptions where we offer exclusive access to the venue on the wedding day. For more information please visit our website.

Partial. Licensed. By arrangement.

ST EDMUNDSBURY CATHEDRAL

Angel Hill, Bury St Edmunds, Suffolk IP33 1LS

Tel: 01284 748720 **Fax:** 01284 768655 **Email:** cathedral@stedscathedral.org

www.stedscathedral.co.uk

Owner: The Church of England **Contact:** Sarah Friswell

The striking Millennium Tower, completed on 2005, is the crowning glory of St Edmundsbury Cathedral. Built from English limestone, brick and lime mortar, the 150ft Lantern Tower, along with new chapels, cloisters and North Transept, completes nearly fifty years of development in a style never likely to be repeated.

Location: OS Ref. TL857 642. Bury St Edmunds town centre.

Open: All year: daily 8.30am–6pm.

Admission: Donation invited.

SAXTEAD GREEN POST MILL

Post Mill Bungalow, Saxtead Green, Woodbridge, Suffolk IP13 9QQ

Tel: 01728 685789 **E-mail:** customers@english-heritage.org.uk

www.english-heritage.org.uk/saxteadgreenpostmill

Owner: English Heritage **Contact:** Visitor Operations Team

The finest example of a Suffolk Post Mill. Still in working order, you can climb the wooden stairs to the various floors, full of fascinating mill machinery. Ceased production in 1947.

Location: MAP 8:L8, OS Ref. TM253 645. 2½m NW of Framlingham on A1120.

Open: 1 Apr–30 Sep: Fri–Sat & BHs, 12 noon–5pm.

Admission: Adult £3.50, Child £1.80, Conc. £3.00. EH Members Free. Group discount available. Opening times and prices are valid until 31st March 2011, after this date details are subject to change please visit www.english-heritage.org.uk for the most up-to-date information.

Picnickers welcome. Museum.

SOUTH ELMHAM HALL

HALL LANE, ST CROSS, HARLESTON, NORFOLK IP20 0PZ

www.southelmham.co.uk www.batemansbarn.co.uk

Tel: 01986 782526 **Fax:** 01986 782203 **E-mail:** enquiries@southelmham.co.uk

Owner/Contact: John Sanderson

A Grade I listed medieval manor house set inside moated enclosure. Originally built by the Bishop of Norwich around 1270. Much altered in the 16th century. Self guided trail through former deer park to South Elmham Minster, a ruined Norman chapel with Saxon origins.

Location: MAP 8:L7, OS30 Ref. TM778 324. Between Harleston and Bungay from the A143 take the B1062.

Open: Minster, Walks (Café: 1 May–30 Sept: Sundays & BH Mons). 1 Oct–30 Apr: Suns only, 10am–5pm. Hall: Guided tours only: 1 May–30 Sept: Thurs, (pre-tour lunches can be booked) 2pm, Sun & BH Mons, 3pm.

Admission: House: Adult £6.50, Child £3. Groups (15-50): Adult £4.50, Child £2.50. Walks (free).

WC. Licensed. Obligatory. On leads.

SOMERLEYTON HALL & GARDENS

SOMERLEYTON, LOWESTOFT, SUFFOLK NR32 5QQ

www.somerleyton.co.uk

Tel: 08712 224244 (office) **Fax:** 01502 732143

E-mail: carolyn.ashton@somerleyton.co.uk

Owner: Hon Hugh Crossley **Contact:** Carolyn Ashton

Originally Jacobean the Hall was extensively re-modelled in 1844, guided tours of the state rooms are available on all open days. The 12 acres of fabulous landscaped gardens include the famous yew hedge maze, 300ft pergola, Vulliamy tower clock, Paxton glasshouses and walled, formal and arboreal gardens.

Location: MAP 8:M8, OS134 Ref. TM493 977. 5m NW of Lowestoft on B1074, 7m SW of Great Yarmouth off A143.

Open/Admission: Please visit www.somerleyton.co.uk or call the estate office on 01502 734901 for 2011 opening dates and admission prices.

No photography in house. Receptions/functions/conferences/weddings. Obligatory.

St Edmundsbury Cathedral

© Somerleyton Hall / Heritage House Group

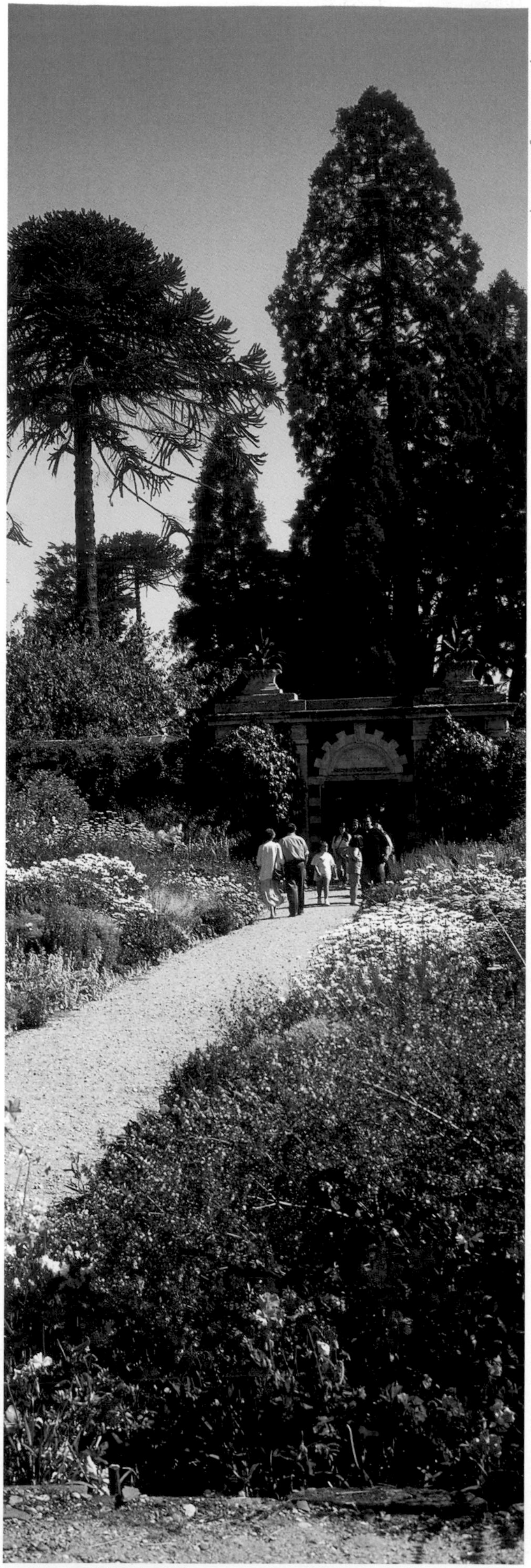

Somerleyton Hall & Gardens

© NT / Sutton Hoo / Fisheye Images

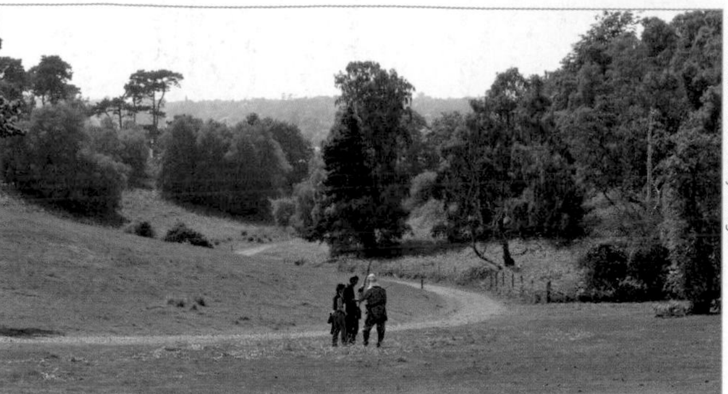

SUTTON HOO

WOODBRIDGE, SUFFOLK IP12 3DJ

www.nationaltrust.org.uk/suttonhoo

Tel: 01394 389700 **Fax:** 01394 389702 **E-mail:** suttonhoo@nationaltrust.org.uk

Owner: National Trust **Contact:** The Property Secretary

Hauntingly beautiful site, home to one of the world's greatest archaeological discoveries. Walk around the ancient mounds and discover the incredible story of the royal Anglo-Saxon ship burial. Enjoy beautiful period interiors of Mrs Pretty's Country House. Site includes exhibition hall, café, shop, site walks. Special events all year.

Location: MAP 8:L9, OS Ref. TM288 487. Off B1083 Woodbridge to Bawdsey road. Follow signs from A12. Rail: Melton station 1/2 mile.

Open: Exhibition Hall, House, Shop & Café: 1 Jan–20 Feb, Sat & Sun, 11am–4pm; 21–27 Feb, Mon–Sun, 11am–4pm; 2 Mar–3 April, Wed–Sun, 10.30am–5pm; 4 Apr–30 Oct, Mon–Sun, 10.30am–5pm; 5 Nov–18 Dec, Sat & Sun, 11am–4pm; 26 Dec–31 Dec, Mon–Sat, 11am–4pm. Open bank holidays, closed 25 Dec. Estate walks open daily all year 9am–6pm (except for some Thur, Nov–Jan 2012).

***Admission:** Adult £7.20, Child £3.75. Family £18.20. Groups £6.25. Discount for visitors arriving by cycle or on foot. NT members free. *Includes a voluntary donation but visitors can choose to pay the standard prices displayed at the property and on the website.

WCs. Licensed. Licensed. By arrangement. Limited for Coaches. Dogs on leads welcome in the grounds. Programme of events, tel for details.

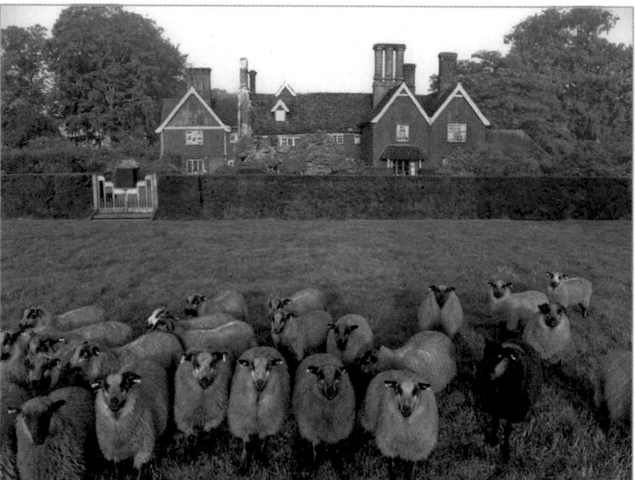

WYKEN HALL GARDENS

STANTON, BURY ST EDMUNDS, SUFFOLK IP31 2DW

www.wykenvineyards.co.uk

Tel: 01359 250287 **Fax:** 01359 253821

Owner: Sir Kenneth & Lady Carlisle **Contact:** Mr Alan North

Wyken is an Elizabethan manor house surrounded by a romantic, plantlovers' garden with maze, knot and herb garden and rose garden featuring old roses. A walk through ancient woodlands leads to award-winning Wyken Vineyards. The 16th century barn houses the Vineyard Restaurant featured in Michelin and Good Food Guides, and the Leaping Hare Country Store, described in *Country Living* as 'a model of what a shop should be.'

Location: MAP 8:J8, OS Ref. TL963 717. 9m NE of Bury St. Edmunds 1m E of A143. Follow brown tourist signs to Wyken Vineyards from Ixworth.

Open: 5 Jan–24 Dec: daily, 10am–6pm. Garden: 1 Apr–1 Oct: daily except Sat, 2–6pm. Open for dinner from 7pm Fri & Sat (advisable to book).

Admission: Gardens: Adult £3.50, Child (under 12yrs) Free, Conc. £3. Groups by appointment.

Suitable. WC. Licensed. No dogs in garden.

Haddon Hall, Tapestry detail

East Midlands

This is a part of Britain that is sadly often overlooked, but merits further investigation. Visit Rockingham Castle, with its dramatic views over five counties. Further north, Chatsworth and Haddon Hall are two very different examples of stately homes. Contrast them with the charming manor house of Eyam Hall and the stunning gardens of Coton Manor.

Belvoir Castle, Leicestershire

Derbyshire

Leicestershire & Rutland

Lincolnshire

Northamptonshire

Nottinghamshire

NOTTINGHAMSHIRE
DERBYSHIRE
LINCOLNSHIRE
LEICESTERSHIRE & RUTLAND
NORTHAMPTONSHIRE

Burghley House, Lincolnshire

Clumber Park, Nottinghamshire
©NT/ J Unell

Kelmarsh Hall, Northamptonshire

■ Owner

Trustees of the Chatsworth Settlement. Home of the Devonshire family

■ Contact

The Booking Office
Chatsworth
Bakewell
Derbyshire DE45 1PP

Tel: 01246 565300
Fax: 01246 583536
E-mail: visit@chatsworth.org

■ Location

MAP 6:P2
OS Ref. SK260 703

From London 3 hrs M1/J29, signposted via Chesterfield.

3m E of Bakewell, off B6012, 10m W of Chesterfield.

Rail: Chesterfield Station, 11m.

Bus: Chesterfield – Baslow, 1½m.

■ Opening Times

House, garden and farmyard open daily, from mid March to 23 December. The park is open every day and the shopping and food areas open from 10 January 2011.

■ Admission

The admission prices for the house, garden and farmyard are listed on our website at www.chatsworth.org. Discounted day tickets can be purchased online.

Conference/Function

ROOM	SIZE	MAX CAPACITY
Hartington Rm.		80
Burlington Rm.		80
Racing Rm.		22

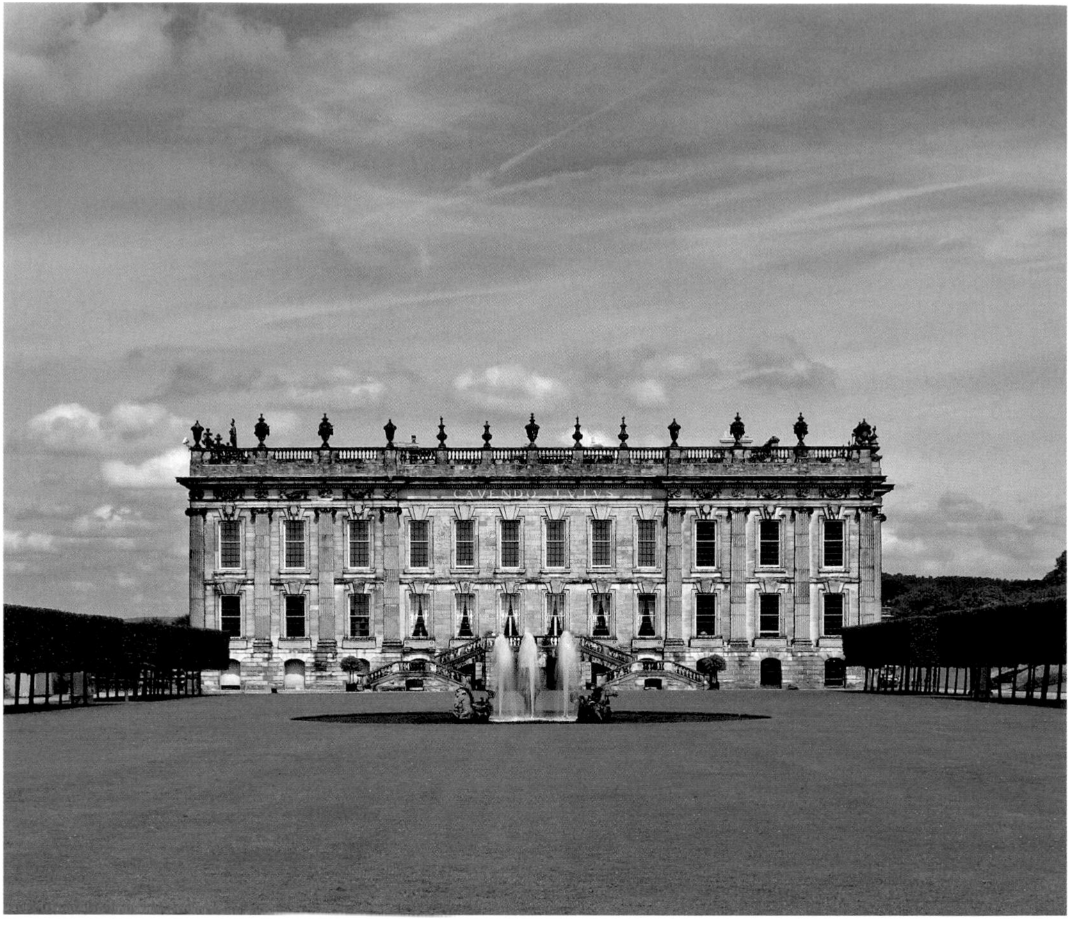

CHATSWORTH

www.chatsworth.org

The home of the Duke and Duchess of Devonshire is one of the country's greatest Treasure Houses, renowned for the quality of its art, landscape and hospitality. Home of the Cavendish family since the 1550s, it has evolved through the centuries to reflect the tastes, passions and interests of succeeding generations. Today Chatsworth contains works of art that span 4000 years, from ancient Roman and Egyptian sculpture, and masterpieces by Rembrandt, Reynold and Veronese, to work by outstanding modern artists, including Lucian Freud, Edmund de Waal, Sean Scully and David Nash. The garden is famous for its rich history, historic and modern waterworks and sculptures, the Victorian rock garden and the maze. Younger visitors also enjoy the working farmyard and woodland adventure playground and the 1000 acre park is open for walks, picnics and play.

2011 continues to offer great things for our visitors. There will be an entirely new exhibition celebrating the life of the 6th Duke of Devonshire. Visitors will also witness the Queen of Scots and Leicester Apartments being restored to Regency bedrooms over the course of the year. In addition there will be an exhibition curated by the Duke and Duchess themselves, of their favourite things from the Collection. All this and work on the Masterplan continues with the major conservation of the house.

Our programme of events sees the return of the spring festival of Tulips, International Horse Trials, Country Fair and a new Festival of Innovation. The season ends with a visual celebration of traditional Christmas carols entitled "Deck the Halls".

- 5 gift shops, farm shop and pantry.
- Rooms available for conferences and private functions. Contact Head of Catering.
- WCs and full house access.
- Cafes and food to go.
- (Max 300); home-made food. Menus on request. Licensed.
- Daily tours (small charge). Private tours of house or greenhouses and Behind the Scenes Days, by arrangement only (extra charges apply). Groups please pre-book.
- New adult and child audio tours, in English.
- Cars 100 yds, Coaches drop off at house.
- Guided tours, packs, and new self-guiding materials. Free preliminary visit recommended.
- On leads.
- Holiday cottages.

HADDON HALL

www.haddonhall.co.uk

Haddon Hall sits on a rocky outcrop above the River Wye near the market town of Bakewell. Looking much as is would have done in Tudor times. There has been a dwelling here since the 11th century but the house we see today dates mainly from the late 14th century with major additions in the following 200 years and some alterations in the early 17th century including the creation of the Long Gallery.

William the Conqueror's illegitimate son Peverel, and his descendants, held Haddon for 100 years before it passed to the Vernon family. In the late 16th century the estate passed through marriage to the Manners family, in whose possession it has remained ever since.

When the Dukedom of Rutland was conferred on the Manners family in 1703 they moved to Belvoir Castle, and Haddon was left deserted for 200 years. This was Haddon's saving grace as the Hall thus escaped the major architectural changes of the 18th and 19th centuries ready for the great restoration at the beginning of the 20th century by the 9th Duke of Rutland. Henry VIII's elder brother Arthur, who was a frequent guest of the Vernons, would be quite familiar with the house as it stands today.

Haddon Hall is a popular location for film and television productions. Recent films include *Pride & Prejudice* and the BBC dramatisation of *Jane Eyre*.

Gardens

Magnificent terraced gardens with over 150 varieties of rose and clematis, provide colour and scent throughout the summer.

Haddon Hall is ideal as a film location due to its authentic and genuine architecture requiring little alteration. Suitable locations are also available on the Estate.

Unsuitable, WCs.

Licensed.

Special tours £11.50pp for groups of 15, 7 days' notice.

Ample. 450 yds from house. £1.50 per car.

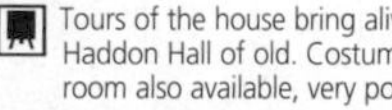

Tours of the house bring alive Haddon Hall of old. Costume room also available, very popular!

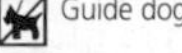

Guide dogs only.

Owner

Lord Edward Manners

Contact

Janet Blackburn
Estate Office
Haddon Hall
Bakewell
Derbyshire DE45 1LA

Tel: 01629 812855
Fax: 01629 814379
E-mail: info@haddonhall.co.uk

Location

MAP 6:P2
OS Ref. SK234 663

From London 3 hrs
Sheffield ½ hr
Manchester 1 hr
Haddon is on the E side of A6 1½m S of Bakewell. M1/J29.

Rail: Chesterfield Station, 12m.

Bus: Chesterfield Bakewell.

Opening Times

Summer

Easter: 22–26 April inc. Apr (except 2, 3 & 4) & Oct: Sat–Mon; May–Sept: Daily, 12 noon–5pm (closed 2 & 3 July). Last admission 4pm. Christmas: 3–12 December, 10.30am–4pm (last admission 3.30pm).

Admission

Summer	
Adult	£9.50
Child (5–15yrs)	£5.50
Conc	£8.50
Family (2+3)	£27.50
Regular Visitor Pass	£18.00
Groups (15+)	
Adult	£8.50
Child (5–15yrs)	£4.50
Conc	£7.50
Parking	£1.50

Special Events

Regular programme of special events - check website for details.

Owner
National Trust

Contact
Victoria Flanagan
Property Manager
Kedleston Hall
Derby DE22 5JH

Tel: 01332 842191
Fax: 01332 844059
Email: kedlestonhall@nationaltrust.org.uk

Location
MAP 6:P4
OS ref. SK312 403

5 miles NW of Derby, signposted from the roundabout where the A38 crosses A52 Derby ring road

Opening Times
House
19 February–30 October: Sat–Wed, 12noon–5pm, last entry 4.15pm. Open Good Friday.

19 February–20 March: House will be shown by guided tour only.

Pleasure Grounds
19 February–30 October: daily, 10am–6pm.

Park
19 February–30 October: daily, 10am–6pm.

3 November–17 February 2012: daily, 10am–4pm, with occasional day closures.

Restaurant & Shop
19 February–30 October, Sat–Wed, 11am–5pm; plus 28 July–26 August, Thu/Fri, 11am–3pm; 5 November–12 February 2012, Sat/Sun 11am–3pm.

Admission
Hall (Gift Aid)

Adult	£9.90
Child	£4.90
Family	£24.80

Garden & Park (Gift Aid)

Adult	£4.40
Child	£2.20
Family	£11.10

Groups Hall

Adult	£7.60
Child	£3.95

Groups Park & Garden

Adult	£3.70
Child	£1.80

Winter charge £1 per adult & 50p per child

Conference/Function

ROOM	SIZE	MAX CAPACITY
Caesars' Hall	40' x 60'	120 dining 150 reception 100 delegates theatre style
Saloon		Civil Weddings only – seats 110
Restaurant		90 dining split in 2 rooms

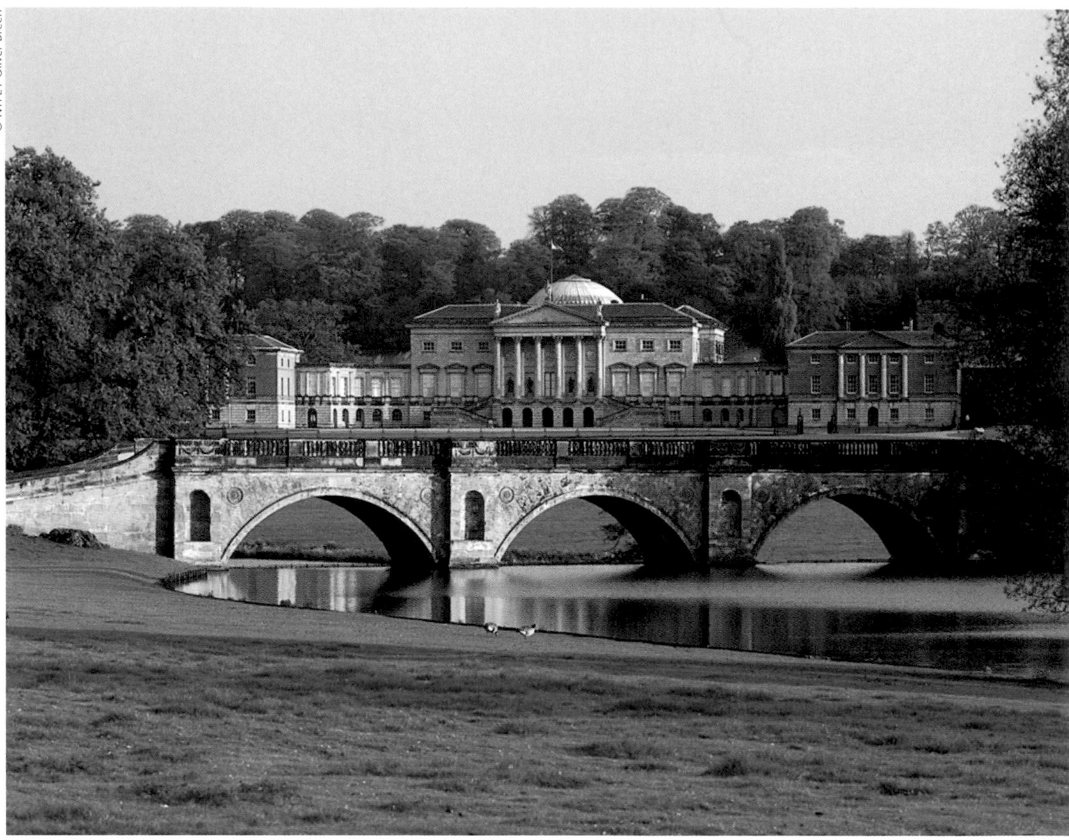
© NTPL / Oliver Breen

KEDLESTON HALL

www.nationaltrust.org.uk/kedleston

Kedleston was built between 1759 and 1765 for the Curzon family who have lived in the area since the 12th century. The hall boasts the most complete and least altered sequence of Robert Adam interiors in England, with the magnificent State rooms retaining much of their great collections of paintings and furniture. The Adam influence can be seen across the 18th century pleasure grounds and 800 acre park. Since 1987 the National Trust has undertaken a programme of work to return these interiors to their original appearance so that visitors can re-live the experience of coming to see a 'palace of the arts'. The Eastern Museum houses a remarkable collection, collected by Lord Curzon when he was Viceroy of India (1899–1905). Kedleston has a year wide programme of special events and can be used for corporate events and civil wedding ceremonies please ring the property or visit the website for more details.

New for 2011

See Caesars Hall brought to life as an Edwardian reception to the house. Relax in deep chairs and enjoy the warming log fires. Use our trail to follow in the footsteps of *The Duchess* film (Keira Knightley) in which Kedleston was used as a key location.

See artist silversmith, Theresa Nguyen, demonstrating contemporary silversmithing techniques as part of an exhibition by the Goldsmiths' company entitled 'Studio Silver Today', telling a story of the Company and the career of Theresa Nguyen. Each Saturday between 5th March and 29th October 2011, the artist will be in residence producing a beautiful contemporary tumbler, which when finished will be placed in a prize draw for the public to win.

© The Worshipful Company of Goldsmiths / Clarissa Bruce

'Parissa' centrepiece, 2009 by Theresa Nguyen

© The Worshipful Company of Goldsmiths / Clarissa Bruce

'Alcove' centrepiece, 2008 by Theresa Nguyen

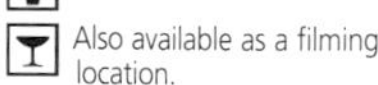
We welcome photography, but for the enjoyment of all our visitors, we ask visitors not to use tripods or flash.

Also available as a filming location.

WCs.

Licensed.

Must be booked in advance.

Limited for coaches.

Guide dogs only.

Please call us on 01332 842191 to be sent an events programme.

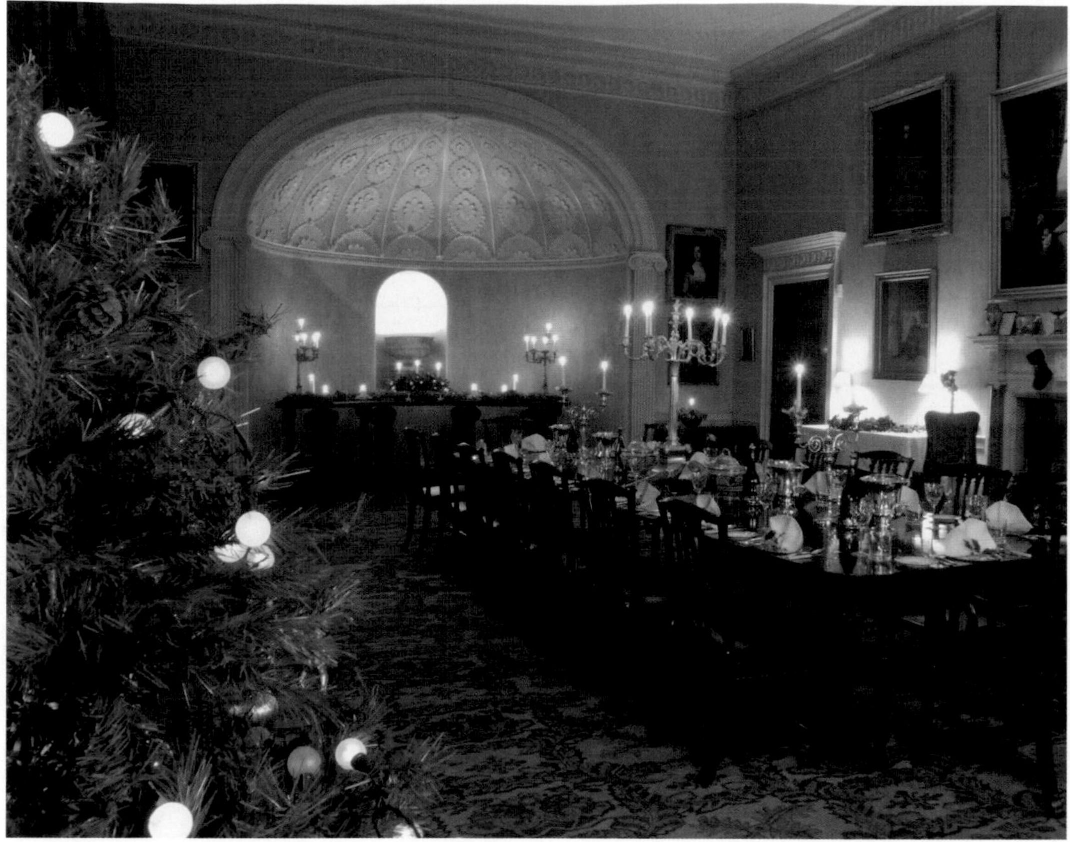

RENISHAW HALL AND GARDENS

www.renishaw-hall.co.uk

Renishaw Hall has been home to the Sitwell family for over 400 years. Its present owner, Alexandra, inherited the Estate from her late father Sir Reresby Sitwell and she now lives there with her husband and children. Renishaw Hall is set in eight acres of formal Italianate gardens featuring marble statues and shaped yew hedges alongside large English herbaceous borders and ornamental ponds dominated by an impressive fountain. Beyond the gardens are the mature park and woodlands stretching down to the lakes. Throughout the year the woods blossom with snowdrops, daffodils, camellias and spectacular carpets of bluebells in late spring.

The Georgian Stables house the Sitwell Museum and Gallery along with the resident artist and studio. The Gallery Café offers an exceptional menu of snacks, lunch and home-made scones and cakes. The Shop is stocked with many interesting designs, gardening and literary inspired gifts as well as Renishaw Hall Regional and Sparkling wines.

The Hall is available for exclusive hire as a film location. Civil Weddings are held in the grand Georgian Red Dining Room. The Hall is open for guided group tours and the guided public tours are now organised every Friday, of the Season, at 2.30 pm. Booking is essential.

There are trails throughout the grounds for children as well as a willow tunnel and maze. Well behaved dog-owners are welcome with their dogs. A full day is recommended for your visit to make the most of all that Renishaw has to offer. The Hall is particularly popular at Christmas, Bluebell fortnight and during June and July when the peonies and roses are at their most beautiful.

Gallery Cafe, Gift Shop, resident artist and facilities are available during garden opening.

WCs.

Licensed.

Licensed.

By arrangement.

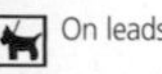

On leads.

Owner

Sitwell Estate

Contact

The Administrator
Renishaw
Nr Sheffield
Derbyshire
S21 3WB

Tel: 01246 432310
Fax: 01246 430760
E-mail: enquiries@renishaw-hall.co.uk

Location

MAP 7:A2
OS Ref. SK435 786

On A6135 3m from M1/J30, equidistant from Sheffield and Chesterfield.

Opening Times

2011 Season
Friday 1 April–30 September.
Wednesday through to Sunday and BH Mondays.
10.30am to 4.30pm.

Please note Renishaw Hall is only open to the general public when prebooking onto a guided tour on Friday at 2.30pm.

Hall Tours are also available for private groups by prior arrangement Wednesday, Thursday and Friday.

Admission

Admissions to gardens, museum & gallery.

Adults	£6.00
Conc.	£5.00
Children	£3.00
Children (under 5)	Free
Car Parking Fee	£1.00

Season Tickets available.

Optional information (HHA and RHS members welcome free to gardens, museum and gallery.) When available, guided garden tours and hall tours are £6 per person.

A full Christmas and event programme runs throughout the year, please see the website for details.

Special Events

Plant Fairs, Food Fairs, Music, Film and theatre events. Full gardens and walks programme. Special exhibitions and artist in residence.

■ **Owner**
Sir Richard FitzHerbert Bt

■ **Contact**
Isobel James
Ashbourne
Derbyshire
DE6 1RA
Tel: 01335 352200
E-mail: events@tissingtonhall.co.uk

■ **Location**
MAP 6:P3
OS Ref. SK175 524

4m N of Ashbourne off A515 towards Buxton.

■ **Opening Times**
Easter Week: Monday 25 April–Friday 29 April, 12–3pm.

2–5 June, Thurs–Sun inclusive, 12–3pm.

19 Jul–26 Aug, Tues–Fri inclusive, 12–3pm.

Mon 29 August, 12–3pm.

■ **Admission**

Hall & Gardens:	
Adult	£8.50
Child (10–16yrs)	£4.00
Conc.	£7.00
Gardens only:	
Adult	£3.50
Child (10–16yrs)	£2.00
Conc.	£3.50

Group visits from Womens Institutes, Garden Societies and History Groups are welcome throughout the year and are our speciality.

Please contact the numbers for further details.

■ **Special Events**
Sir Richard & his Guiding Team are available to speak or lecture at History Society or WI meetings etc., throughout the year. Please contact the Office for details.

2-8 June 2011 & 17-23 May 2012

Well Dressings

Annual week-long event with six village wells decorated in a fabulous montage of flowers, moss and twigs, depicting scenes from the Bible.

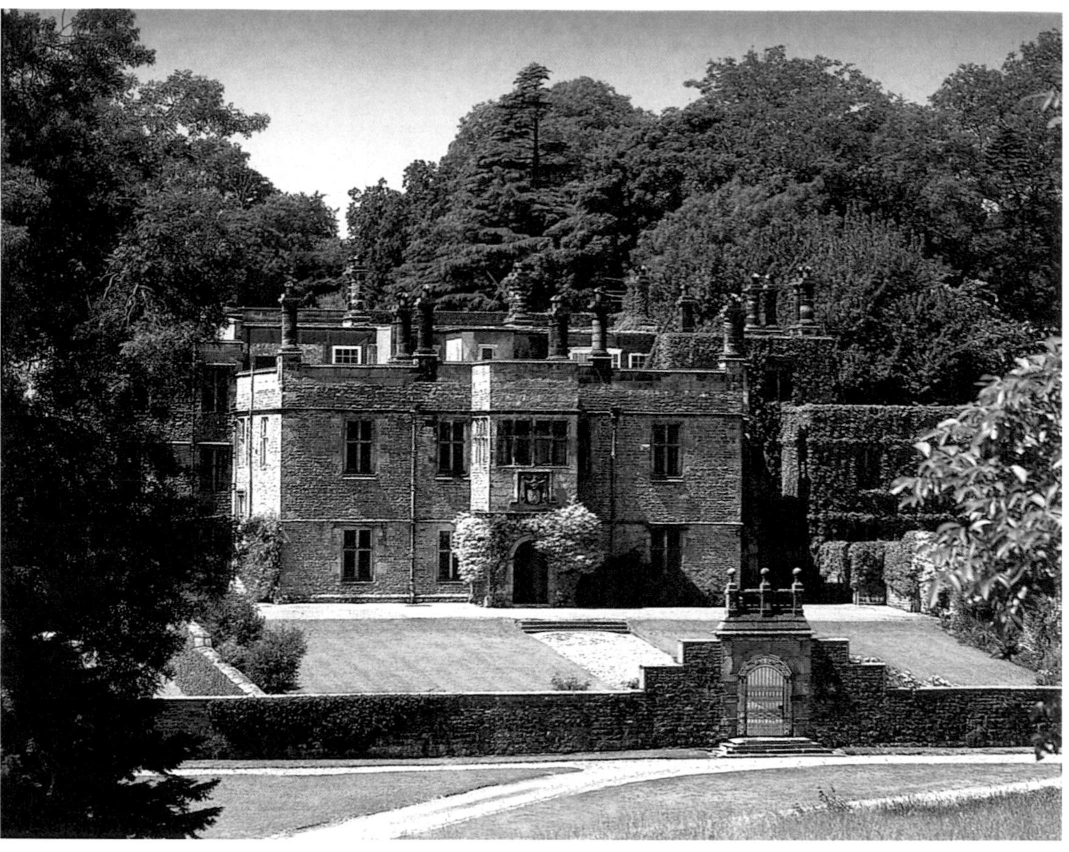

TISSINGTON HALL

www.tissingtonhall.co.uk

Tissington Hall was built in 1609 by Francis FitzHerbert and has been in the hands of the same family ever since, one of only 300 homes in the country that boast such a lengthy patronage of one family. Presently Sir Richard, 9th Baronet resides there with his family. The Hall stands at the centre of the model Estate village which is an attraction in itself with its award-winning tearooms, local butchery, candle workshop, B&Bs and other attractions. Close to the eponymous Tissington Trail (the old railway line between Ashbourne and Buxton, now a popular cycling path) Tissington stands at the southern edge of the Peak District National Park, and acts as a springboard for the other heritage attractions in the area.

Tissington Hall itself contains fine old masters, Chippendale furniture, a handsome 3000 volume library and all the effects of a much-loved family home. Open on published days throughout the summer. Private tours for groups are most welcome all year round as are enquiries for functions, parties and weddings, all of which can make use of the fabulous gardens and 5 acre arboretum. Recently the Estate has added two holiday cottages to its portfolio (which can be booked through www.statelyholidaycottages.co.uk) which act as a great base for exploring the wider Peak District.

No photography in house.

Licensed.

Obligatory.

Limited.

Guide dogs only.

© English Heritage / Jonathan Bailey

© English Heritage / Peter Richardson

BOLSOVER CASTLE

CASTLE STREET, BOLSOVER, DERBYSHIRE S44 6PR

www.english-heritage.org.uk/bolsover

Tel: 01246 822844 **E-mail:** customers@english-heritage.org.uk

Owner: English Heritage **Contact:** Visitor Operations Team

An enchanting and romantic spectacle, situated high on a wooded hilltop dominating the surrounding landscape. Built on the site of a Norman castle, this is largely an early 17th c mansion. The 'Little Castle', houses intricate carvings, panelling and wall painting. See the restored interiors of the Little Castle including the only remaining copies of Titian's Caesar Paintings, and the Venus Fountain and statuary. There is also an impressive 17th c indoor Riding House built by the Duke of Newcastle. Interesting interpretation facilities include Audio/Visual and scale model of Little Castle. (Bolsover is now available for Civil weddings, receptions and corporate hospitality.)

Location: MAP 7:A2, OS120, SK471 707. Signposted from M1/J29A, 6m from Mansfield. In Bolsover 6m E of Chesterfield on A632.

Open: 1 Apr–31 Oct: daily, 10am–5pm (closes 4pm Fri & Sat). 1 Nov–31 Mar: Thu–Mon, 10am–4pm. Closed 24–26 Dec & 1 Jan. Part of the castle may close for 1 hour if an event is booked. Please call to check.

Admission: Adult £7.40, Child £3.70, Conc. £6.30, Family £18.50. 15% discount for groups (11+). EH members Free. Opening times and prices are valid until 31st March 2011, after this date details are subject to change please visit www.english-heritage.org.uk for the most up-to-date information.

Picnickers welcome.

CALKE ABBEY

Ticknall, Derbyshire DE73 7LE

Tel: 01332 863822 **Fax:** 01332 865272

Owner: National Trust **Contact:** The Property Administrator

Baroque mansion, little restored. Walled and pleasure gardens and orangery.

Location: MAP 7:A5, OS128, SK356 239. 10m S of Derby, on A514 at Ticknall.

CHATSWORTH

See page 260 for full page entry.

© Chatsworth Estate / David Vintner

Chatsworth

CATTON HALL

CATTON, WALTON-ON-TRENT, SOUTH DERBYSHIRE DE12 8LN

www.catton-hall.com

Tel: 01283 716311 **Fax:** 01283 712876 **E-mail:** r.neilson@catton-hall.com

Owner/Contact: Robin & Katie Neilson

Catton, built in 1745, has been in the hands of the same family since 1405 and is still lived in by the Neilsons as their private home. This gives the house, with its original collection of 17th and 18th century portraits, pictures and antique furniture, a unique, relaxed and friendly atmosphere. With its spacious reception rooms, luxurious bedrooms and delicious food and wine, Catton is centrally located for residential or non-residential business meetings/seminars, product launches and team-building activities, as well as for accommodation for those visiting Birmingham, the NEC, the Belfry, the Potteries and Dukeries – or just for a weekend celebration of family and friends. The acres of parkland alongside the River Trent are ideal for all types of corporate and public events.

Location: MAP 6:P5, OS Ref. SK206 154. 2m E of A38 at Alrewas between Lichfield & Burton-on-Trent (8m from each). Birmingham NEC 20m.

Open: By prior arrangement all year for corporate hospitality, shooting parties, wedding receptions, private groups. (Groups all year by prior arrangement).

Conference facilities. By arrangement. By arrangement for groups.

4 x four posters, 5 twin, all en-suite.

EYAM HALL

EYAM, HOPE VALLEY, DERBYSHIRE S32 5QW

www.eyamhall.co.uk

Tel: 01433 631976 **E-mail:** info@eyamhall.co.uk
Owner: Mr R H V Wright **Contact:** Mrs N Wright

This beautiful, unspoilt Jacobean manor house was built by the Wright family in 1671 and is still their much loved family home. The guided tour tells the story of generations of Wrights with portraits, tapestries, costumes and family possessions. The walled garden is included in the tour. The former home farm is now a working craft centre and licensed restaurant.

Location: MAP 6:P2, OS119, SK216 765. Approx 10m from Sheffield, Chesterfield and Buxton, Eyam is off the A623 between Chesterfield and Chapel en le Frith. Eyam Hall is in the centre of the village past the church.

Open: House and Garden: Sun 3 Apr–Mon 2 May & Wed 3–Wed 31 Aug, Wed, Thurs, Sun & BH Mon, 12noon–4pm. Craft Centre: All year except Jan, Tues–Sun.

Admission: House & Garden: Adult £6.25, Child £4, Conc. £5.75. Group discounts.

Craft Centre, Free. Partial. Licensed. Obligatory. Free. In grounds, on leads. Guide dogs only in house.

HADDON HALL

See page 261 for full page entry.

HARDSTOFT HERB GARDEN

Chesterfield Road, Hardstoft, Chesterfield S45 8AH
Tel: 01246 854268
Owner: Mr Stephen Raynor/L M Raynor **Contact:** Mr Stephen Raynor

Consists of two display gardens with information boards and well labelled plants.

Location: MAP 7:A3, OS Ref. SK436 633. On B6039 between Holmewood & Tibshelf, 3m from J29 on M1.

Open: Gardens, Mar-Sep: Wed–Sun and BH Mon, 10am–5pm.

Admission: Adult £1, Child Free.

© NTPL / Robert Morris

Hardwick Estate – Stainsby Mill

© Haddon Hall

Haddon Hall

© English Heritage

HARDWICK OLD HALL

DOE LEA, NR CHESTERFIELD, DERBYSHIRE S44 5QJ

www.english-heritage.org.uk/hardwickoldhall

Tel: 01246 850431 **E-mail:** customers@english-heritage.org.uk
Owner: National Trust, managed by English Heritage
Contact: Visitor Operations Team

This large ruined house, finished in 1591, still displays Bess of Hardwick's innovative planning and interesting decorative plasterwork. Graphic panels focus on the rich interiors Bess created. The views from the top floor over the country park and 'New' Hall are spectacular.

Location: MAP 7:A3, OS120, SK463 638. 7½m NW of Mansfield, 9½m SE of Chesterfield, off A6175, from M1/J29.

Open: 1 Apr-31 Oct: Wed–Sun, 10am–5pm. Closed 1 Nov–31 Mar.

Admission: Adult £4.50, Child £2.30, Conc. £3.80, Family £11.30. 15% discount for groups (11+). NT members free, but small charge at events. EH members Free. Tickets for the New Hall (NT) and joint tickets for both properties available at extra cost. Opening times and prices are valid until 31st March 2011, after this date details are subject to change please see www.english-heritage.org.uk for the most up-to-date information.

Picnickers welcome. WC. Free with admission.

KEDLESTON HALL

See page 262 for full page entry..

© NT / Giraffe Photography

© NT / Giraffe Photography

HARDWICK ESTATE

DOE LEA, CHESTERFIELD, DERBYSHIRE S44 5QJ

www.nationaltrust.org.uk/hardwick

Tel: 01246 850430 **Fax:** 01246 858424 **Shop/Restaurant:** 01246 858409

E-mail: hardwickhall@nationaltrust.org.uk

Owner: National Trust **Contact:** Support Service Assistant

Hardwick Hall: One of the most splendid houses in England. Built by the extraordinary Bess of Hardwick in the 1590's, and unaltered since: yet its huge windows and high ceilings make it feel strikingly modern. Rich tapestries, plaster friezes and alabaster fireplaces colour the rooms. Walled courtyards enclose fine gardens, orchards and a herb garden. The Parkland has circular walks, fishing ponds and rare breed animals.

Hardwick Hall is now licensed for civil wedding ceremonies (Apr-Oct) and offers a marquee for receptions.

Location: MAP 7:A3, OS120, SK456 651. 7.5m NW of Mansfield, 9½m SE of Chesterfield: approach from M1/J29 via A6175 From M1/J29 take A6175, signposted to Clay Cross then first left and left again to Stainsby Mill.

Hardwick Estate – Stainsby Mill is a 19th century water-powered corn mill in working order. Freshly milled flour for sale.

Location: MAP 7:A3, OS120, SK455 653. From M1/J29 take A6175, signposted to Clay Cross then first left and left again to Stainsby Mill.

Open: Hall: 23 Feb–30 Oct, Wed–Sun, BH Mon and Good Friday; 12 noon–4.30pm. Gardens, Shop and Restaurant: same days as the Hall; 11am–5pm, plus 25 Jul–4 Sept, Mon–Sun; 11am–5pm. Christmas opening: 3–18 Dec, weekends only; 11am–3pm.

Stainsby Mill: 23 Feb–30 Oct, Wed–Sun; 10am–4pm. Christmas Opening: 3–18 Dec, weekends only; 11am–3pm. Boxing Day & 1 Jan 2012 11am–3pm.

***Admission:** House & Garden: Adult £11, Child £5.50, Family £27.45. Garden only: Adult £5.55, Child £2.80, Family £13.90. Groups (15+) Adult £9.50. Stainsby Mill: Adult £3.65, Child £1.80, Family £9.15. *Includes a voluntary donation but visitors can choose to pay the standard prices displayed at the property and on the website.

Special Events: Derbyshire Food Fair - 21 & 22 May 2011. Elizabethan Weekend - 24 & 25 September 2011.

Dogs welcome in the Parkland only, on leads. Partial. WCs. Licensed. By arrangement. Limited for coaches. Guide dogs only.

© Renishaw Hall

Renishaw Hall

MELBOURNE HALL & GARDENS

MELBOURNE, DERBYSHIRE DE73 8EN

www.melbournehall.com

Tel: 01332 862502 **Fax:** 01332 862263

Owner: Lord & Lady Ralph Kerr **Contact:** Mrs Gill Weston

This beautiful house of history, in its picturesque poolside setting, was once the home of Victorian Prime Minister William Lamb. The fine gardens, in the French formal style, contain Robert Bakewell's intricate wrought iron arbour and a fascinating yew tunnel. Upstairs rooms available to view by appointment.

Location: MAP 7:A5, OS Ref. SK389 249. 8m S of Derby. From London, exit M1/J24.

Open: Hall: Aug only (not first 3 Mons) 2–5pm. Last admission 4.15pm. Gardens: 1 Apr–30 Sept: Weds, Sats, Suns, BH Mons, 1.30–5.30pm. Additional open days possible in August, please telephone for details.

Admission: Hall: Adult £3.50, Child £2, OAP £3. Gardens: Adult £3.50, Child/OAP £2.50. Hall & Gardens: Adult £5.50, Child £3.50, OAP £4.50.

Crafts. No photography in house. Partial. Obligatory in house Tue–Sat. Limited. No coach parking. Guide dogs only.

PEVERIL CASTLE

Market Place, Castleton, Hope Valley S33 8WQ

Tel: 01433 620613 **E-mail:** customers@english-heritage.org.uk

www.english-heritage.org.uk/peveril

Owner: English Heritage **Contact:** Visitor Operations Team

This is one of the earliest Norman castles to be built in England. The Castle walkway opens up new areas and breathtaking views of the Peak District. The Visitor Centre has displays which tell the story of Peveril as the focal point of the Royal Forest of the Peak.

Location: MAP 6:O2, OS110, SK150 827. S side of Castleton, 15m W of Sheffield on A6187.

Open: 1 Apr–31 Oct: daily, 10am–5pm. 1 Nov–31 Mar: Thu–Mon, 10am–4pm. Closed 24–26 Dec & 1 Jan.

Admission: Adult £4.20, Child £2.10, Conc. £3.60, Family £10.50. 15% discount for groups (11+). EH members Free. Opening times and prices are valid until 31st March 2011, after this date details are subject to change please visit www.english-heritage.org.uk for the most up-to-date information.

Picnickers welcome. WCs.

RENISHAW HALL & GARDENS

See page 263 for full page entry.

SUTTON SCARSDALE HALL

Chesterfield, Derbyshire

Tel: 01604 735400 (Regional Office) **E-mail:** customers@english-heritage.org.uk

www.english-heritage.org.uk/suttonscarsdalehall

Owner: English Heritage **Contact:** East Midlands Regional Office

The dramatic hilltop shell of a great early 18th century baroque mansion.

Location: MAP 7:A2, OS Ref. SK441 690. Between Chesterfield & Bolsover, 1½m S of Arkwright Town.

Open: Summer: daily, 10am–6pm; rest of year: daily, 10am–4pm. Closed 24–26 Dec & 1 Jan.

Admission: Free. Opening times and prices are valid until 31st March 2011, after this date details are subject to change please visit www.english-heritage.org.uk for the most up-to-date information.

Picnickers welcome.

TISSINGTON HALL

See page 264 for full page entry.

Tissington Hall

BELVOIR CASTLE

www.belvoircastle.co.uk

Belvoir Castle, home of the Duke and Duchess of Rutland, commands a magnificent view over the Vale of Belvoir. The name Belvoir, meaning beautiful view, dates back to Norman times, when Robert de Todeni, Standard Bearer to William the Conqueror, built the first castle on this superb site. Destruction caused by two Civil Wars and by a catastrophic fire in 1816 have breached the continuity of Belvoir's history. The present building owes much to the inspiration and taste of Elizabeth, 5th Duchess of Rutland and was built after the fire.

Inside the Castle are notable art treasures including works by Poussin, Holbein, Rubens, and Reynolds, Gobelin and Mortlake tapestries, Chinese silks, furniture, fine porcelain and sculpture.

Gardens

A remarkable survival of English garden history that are being sensitively restored to their former glory. The Duchess's Garden, opened to all day visitors in 2005, contain a collection of Victorian daffodils planted sympathetically with primroses and bluebells, against a background of rhododendrons and azaleas. There are also rare specimen trees, many the largest of their type in the British Isles.

Belvoir Castle is available for exclusive hire as a film location and for conferences, weddings and special events. It is also possible to put on events in conjunction with the open season.

Suitable for exhibitions, product launches, conferences, filming. Guide books £4.

Banquets, private room available.

Ground floor and restaurant accessible. Please telephone for advice. WC.

Licensed. Groups catered for (100 max).

Weekdays only, twice daily. Tour time: 1¼ hrs.

Ample.

Guided tours. Teacher's pack. Education room. Picnic area.

Guide dogs only.

Belvoir Castle is a day out for all the family and hosts different events including Napoleonic wars re-enactments. Tel for details.

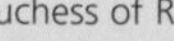

Owner

Their Graces The Duke & Duchess of Rutland

Contact

Sallyann Jackson
Castle Opening Office
Belvoir Castle
Grantham
Leicestershire NG32 1PE

Tel: 01476 871023
Fax: 01476 870443
E-mail: info@belvoircastle.com

Location

MAP 7:C4
OS Ref. SK820 337

A1 from London 110m Grantham Junction York 100m. Leicester 30m Grantham 7m. Nottingham 20m.

Air: East Midlands & Robin Hood Airports. Helicopter Landing Pad.

Rail: Grantham Stn 7m

Bus: Melton Mowbray – Vale of Belvoir via Castle Car Park.

Taxi: Grantham Taxis 01476 563944 / 563988.

Opening Times

Castle & Gardens:
Please see website or telephone 01476 871002

Admission

Castle and Gardens

Adult	£10.00
Child (5–16yrs)	£6.00
Conc.	£9.00
Family (2+3)	£28.00

Gardens only

Adult	£5.00
Child (5–16yrs)	£3.00
Conc.	£4.00
Family (2+3)	£15.00

Groups

Adult	£9.00
Conc.	£8.00
Schools	£5.00

SEASON TICKETS

Castle and Gardens

Adult	£20.00
Child (5–16yrs)	£12.00
Conc.	£18.00
Family (2+3)	£56.00

Gardens only

Adult	£10.00
Child (5–16yrs)	£6.00
Conc.	£8.00
Family (2+3)	£30.00

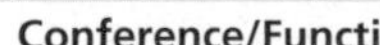

Conference/Function

ROOM	SIZE	MAX CAPACITY
State Dining Room	52' x 31'	130
Old Kitchen	45' x 22'	100
Ballroom		90
Guards Room		175
Stewards Restaurant		100

■ **Owner**

Mr & Mrs N Fothergill

■ **Contact**

Sarah Maughan
Stanford Hall
Lutterworth
Leicestershire
LE17 6DH

Tel: 01788 860250
Fax: 01788 860870
E-mail: s.maughan@stanfordhall.co.uk

■ **Location**

MAP 7:B7
OS Ref. SP587 793

M1/J18 6m,M1/J19 (from/to the N only) 2m, M6 exit/access at A14/M1(N)J 2m, A14 2m. Follow Historic House signs.

Rail: Rugby Stn 7½ m.

Air: Birmingham Airport 27m.

Taxi: George's Taxis 01455 559000.

■ **Opening Times**

Special two week easter opening- Sunday 17 April to Monday 2 May 2011. Other open days in conjunction with park events.
Please see our website or telephone for details.

House open any day or evening (except Saturdays) for pre-booked groups.

■ **Admission**

House & Grounds

Adult	£6.00
Child (5–15yrs)	£2.50
Private Group Tours (20+)	
Adult	£6.50
Child (5–15yrs)	£2.50
Grounds only	
Adult	£3.50
Child (5–15yrs)	£1.50

Conference/Function

ROOM	SIZE	MAX CAPACITY
Ballroom	39' x 26'	100
Old Dining Rm	30' x 20'	20
Crocodile Room	39' x 20'	60

STANFORD HALL

www.stanfordhall.co.uk

Stanford has been the home of the Cave family, ancestors of the present owner, since 1430. In the 1690s, Sir Roger Cave commissioned the Smiths of Warwick to pull down the old Manor House and build the present Hall, which is an excellent example of their work and of the William and Mary period.

As well as over 5000 books, the handsome Library contains many interesting manuscripts, the oldest dating from 1150. The splendid pink and gold Ballroom has a fine coved ceiling with four *trompe l'oeil* shell corners. Throughout the house are portraits of the family and examples of furniture and objects which they collected over the centuries. There is also a collection of Royal Stuart portraits, previously belonging to the Cardinal Duke of York, the last of the male Royal Stuarts. An unusual collection of family costumes is displayed in the Old Dining Room, which also houses some early Tudor portraits and a fine Empire chandelier.

The Hall and Stables are set in an attractive Park on the banks of Shakespeare's Avon. There is a walled Rose Garden behind the Stables. An early ha-ha separates the North Lawn from the mile-long North Avenue.

- Craft centre (most Suns). Corporate days, clay pigeon shoots, filming, photography, small conferences. Parkland, helicopter landing area, lecture room, Blüthner piano. Caravan site.
- Lunches, dinners & wedding receptions.
- Visitors may alight at the entrance. WC.
- Teas, lunch & supper. Groups must book (70 max.)
- Tour time: ¾ hr in groups of approx 25.
- 1,000 cars and 6–8 coaches. Free meals for coach drivers, coach parking on gravel in front of house.
- In Park, on leads.
- Accommodation available.
- Concerts/Theatre in the Ballroom or Park.

ASHBY DE LA ZOUCH CASTLE

South Street, Ashby de la Zouch, Leicestershire LE65 1BR

Tel: 01530 413343 **E-mail:** customers@english-heritage.org.uk

www.english-heritage.org.uk/ashbydelazouchcastle

Owner: English Heritage **Contact:** Visitor Operations Team

The impressive ruins of this late medieval castle are dominated by a magnificent tower, over 80 feet high, which was split in two during the Civil War. Panoramic views. Explore the tunnel linking the kitchens to the Hastings Tower. New interpretation and audio tour.

Location: MAP 7:A7, OS128, SK363 167. In Ashby de la Zouch, 12m S of Derby on A511. SE of town centre.

Open: 1 Apr–30 Jun: Thu–Mon, 10am–5pm. 1 Jul–31 Aug: daily, 10am–5pm. 1 Sep–31 Oct: Thu–Mon, 10am–5pm. 1 Nov–31 Mar: Thur–Mon, 12 noon–4pm. Closed 24–26 Dec & 1 Jan.

Admission: Adult £4.20, Child £2.10, Conc. £3.60, Family £10.50. 15% discount for groups (11+). EH Members free. Opening times and prices are valid until 31st March 2011, after this date details are subject to change please visit www.english-heritage.org.uk for the most up-to-date information.

Picnickers welcome. WC. Free with admission. Restricted.

BELVOIR CASTLE

See page 269 for full page entry.

BRADGATE PARK & SWITHLAND WOOD COUNTRY PARK

Bradgate Park, Newtown Linford, Leics LE6 0HE

Tel: 0116 2362713

Owner: Bradgate Park Trust **Contact:** M H Harrison

Includes the ruins of the brick medieval home of the Grey family and childhood home of Lady Jane Grey. Also has a medieval deer park.

Location: MAP 7:B6, OS Ref. SK534 102. 7m NW of Leicester, via Anstey & Newtown Linford. Country Park gates in Newtown Linford. 1¼ m walk to the ruins.

Open: All year during daylight hours.

Admission: No charge. Car parking charges.

DONINGTON-LE-HEATH MANOR HOUSE

Manor Road, Donington-le-Heath, Leicestershire LE67 2FW

Tel: 01530 831259 / 0116 2658326

Owner/Contact: Leicestershire County Council

Medieval manor c1280 with 16th–17th century alterations.

Location: MAP 7:A6, OS Ref. SK421 126. ½ m SSW of Coalville. 4½ m W of M1/J22, by A511.

Open: Feb-Dec: daily, 11am–4pm. Jan: Sat & Sun only, 11am–4pm.

Admission: Free.

Properties that **open all year** appear in the special index at the end of the book.

KIRBY MUXLOE CASTLE

Kirby Muxloe, Leicestershire LE9 2DH

Tel: 01162 386886 **E-mail:** customers@english-heritage.org.uk

www.english-heritage.org.uk/kirbymuxloecastle

Owner: English Heritage **Contact:** Visitor Operations Team

Picturesque, moated, brick built castle begun in 1480 by William Lord Hastings. Recently reopened after extensive conservation work.

Location: MAP 7:B6, OS140, SK524 046. 4m W of Leicester off B5380.

Open: 1 May–31 Aug: Sat, Sun & BHs, 10am–5pm.

Admission: Adult £3.20, Child £1.60, Conc. £2.70. EH Members free. Group discount available. Opening times and prices are valid until 31st March 2011, after this date details are subject to change please visit www.english-heritage.org.uk for the most up-to-date information.

Picnickers welcome.

LYDDINGTON BEDE HOUSE

Blue Coat Lane, Lyddington, Uppingham, Rutland LE15 9LZ

Tel: 01572 822438 **E-mail:** customers@english-heritage.org.uk

www.english-heritage.org.uk/lyddingtonbedehouse

Owner: English Heritage **Contact:** Visitor Operations Team

Located in this picturesque 'Cotswold' village of honey coloured stone cottages and public houses lies the splendid former 'palace' of the powerful medieval Bishops of Lincoln. In the 1600s the building was converted into an almshouse.

Location: MAP 7:D6, OS141, SP875 970. In Lyddington, 6m N of Corby, 1m E of A6003.

Open: 1 Apr–31 Oct: Thu–Mon, 10am–5pm.

Admission: Adult £4.20, Child £2.10, Conc. £3.60, Family £10.50. 15% group discount (11+). EH Members free. Opening times and prices are valid until 31st March 2011, after this date details are subject to change please visit www.english-heritage.org.uk for the most up-to-date information.

Picnickers welcome.

STANFORD HALL

See page 270 for full page entry.

STAUNTON HAROLD CHURCH

Staunton Harold Church, Ashby-de-la-Zouch, Leicestershire, LE65 1RW

Tel: 01332 863822 **Fax:** 01332 865272 **E-mail:** calkeabbey@nationaltrust.org.uk

www.nationaltrust.org.uk

Owner: National Trust **Contact:** Calke Abbey

One of the very few churches to be built during the Commonwealth, erected by Sir Robert Shirley, an ardent Royalist. The interior retains its original 17th century cushions and hangings and includes fine panelling and painted ceilings.

Location: MAP 7:A5, OS Ref. SK379 208. 5m NE of Ashby-de-la-Zouch, W of B587.

Open: Apr–Oct, Sat & Sun, Jun–Aug, Wed–Sun, 1–4.30pm.

Admission: £1 donation.

By arrangement.

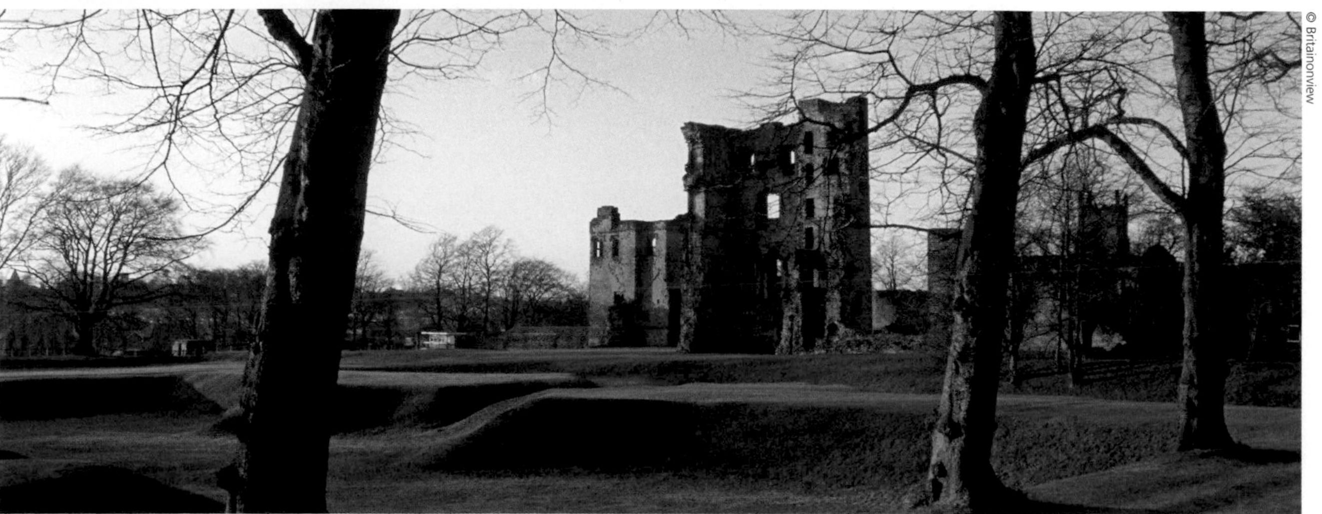

© Britainonview

Ashby De La Zouch Castle

■ Owner
National Trust

■ Contact
Support Services Team
Grantham
Lincolnshire NG32 2LS
Tel: 01476 566116
Fax: 01476 542980
E-mail: belton@nationaltrust.org.uk

■ Location
MAP 7:D4
OS Ref. SK929 395

3m NE of Grantham on A607, Signed off the A1.

■ Opening Times
House
5–13 March:
Sat–Sun, 12.30–4pm;
16 Mar–30 Oct, Wed–Sun, 11–5pm
(Last entry 30 mins before closing).
Basement only 11am–3.30pm (days as house). Open BH Mons.

Garden, Park, Restaurant & Shop:
5–27 Feb: Sat–Sun,
12 noon–4pm;
5 Mar–30 Oct Mon–Sun, 11–5.30pm; 4 Nov–18 Dec, Sat–Sun, 12noon–4pm.

■ *Admission

Adult	£11.00
Child	£6.75
Family	£29.00
Garden, Park & Playground:	
Adult	£9.00
Child	£5.00
Family	£23.00
Garden & Park (Winter):	
Adult	£3.50
Child	£2.25

*Includes a voluntary Gift Aid donation but visitors can choose to pay the standard prices displayed at the property and on the website.

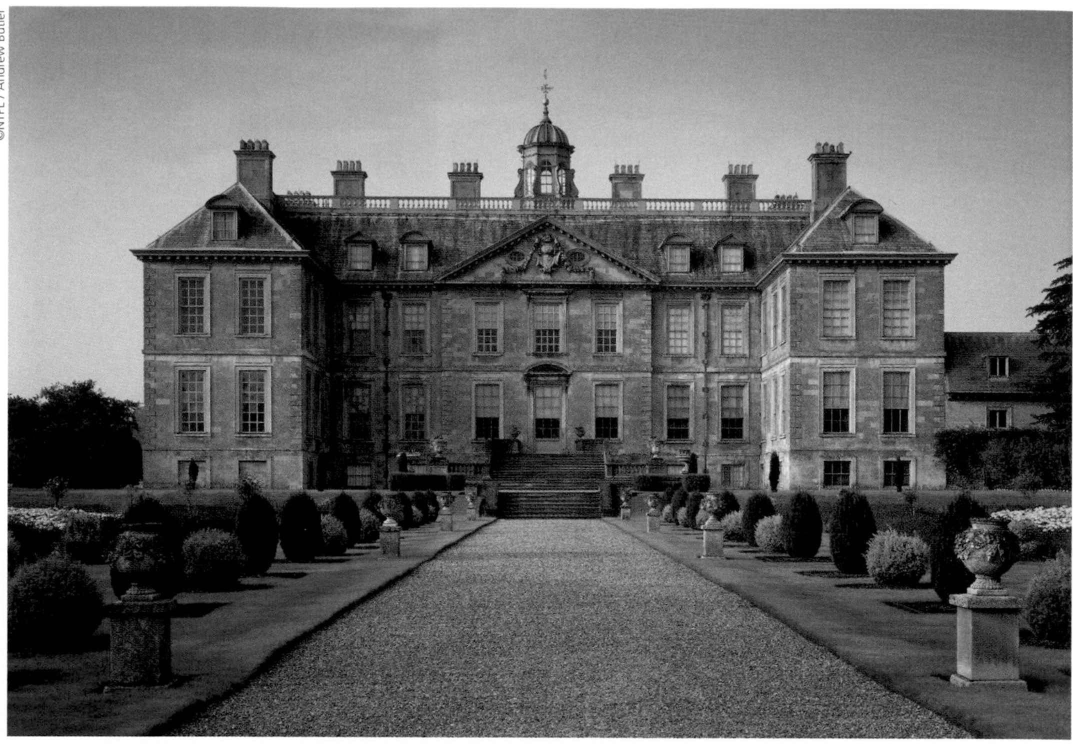

©NTPL / Andrew Butler

BELTON HOUSE

www.nationaltrust.org.uk/belton

The perfect English country house, set in its own extensive deer park, Belton was designed to impress. Built in the late 17th century by 'Young' Sir John Brownlow, with family fortunes founded in law, it is one of the finest examples of Restoration architecture and was, for centuries, the scene of lavish hospitality. Opulent décor, stunning silverware, wonderful woodcarvings, imposing paintings – including many old masters – and personal mementos convey wealth, but also a family atmosphere. The Brownlow family had many royal connections and Edward VIII was a frequent visitor before his abdication. Open Basements (11am – 3pm during main season) provide a fascinating glimpse into life below stairs at a large country house.

Belton House featured in the BBC's adaptation of 'Pride and Prejudice' with Colin Firth and Jennifer Erhle, whilst the sundial, featuring the figure of Time, by Cibber, inspired 'The Moondial' Helen Cresswell's children's book and the subsequent BBC series of the same name.

Delightful gardens, luxuriantly planted Orangery and lakeside walks are a pleasure to explore all year round. Snowdrops, daffodils and bluebells provide a succession of springtime colour in the informal woodland gardens. Lavender, roses and orange blossom give wonderful fragrance through the summer months. Ruby red 'Bishop of Llandaff' dahlias add rich autumn colour. The recently restored boathouse by the lakeshore is a testament to traditional craftsmanship and a delightful feature in this tranquil location.

The Stables Restaurant (self service) features local produce including our award-winning Belton venison, reared on the estate, in season. A wide range of souvenirs can be found in the well-stocked Gift Shop whilst the Plant & Garden Shop provides year-round inspiration.

For families, we have the largest Children's Adventure Playground in Lincolnshire and the 'Moondial Express' miniature train. The Discovery Centre in the Estate Yard offers a variety of hands-on activities at weekends. (Both open March – Oct).

Belton's varied events programme includes Theatre in the Garden, Easter and Halloween Trails, Garden Tours, Costumed Talks and special exhibitions. Please tel 01476 566116 for details.

Fine church (not NT) with many family monuments.

© NT / Rika Gordon

i Adventure playground opens 5 March 2011

Partial. Please telephone for arrangements.

Licensed.

P

Civil Wedding Licence.

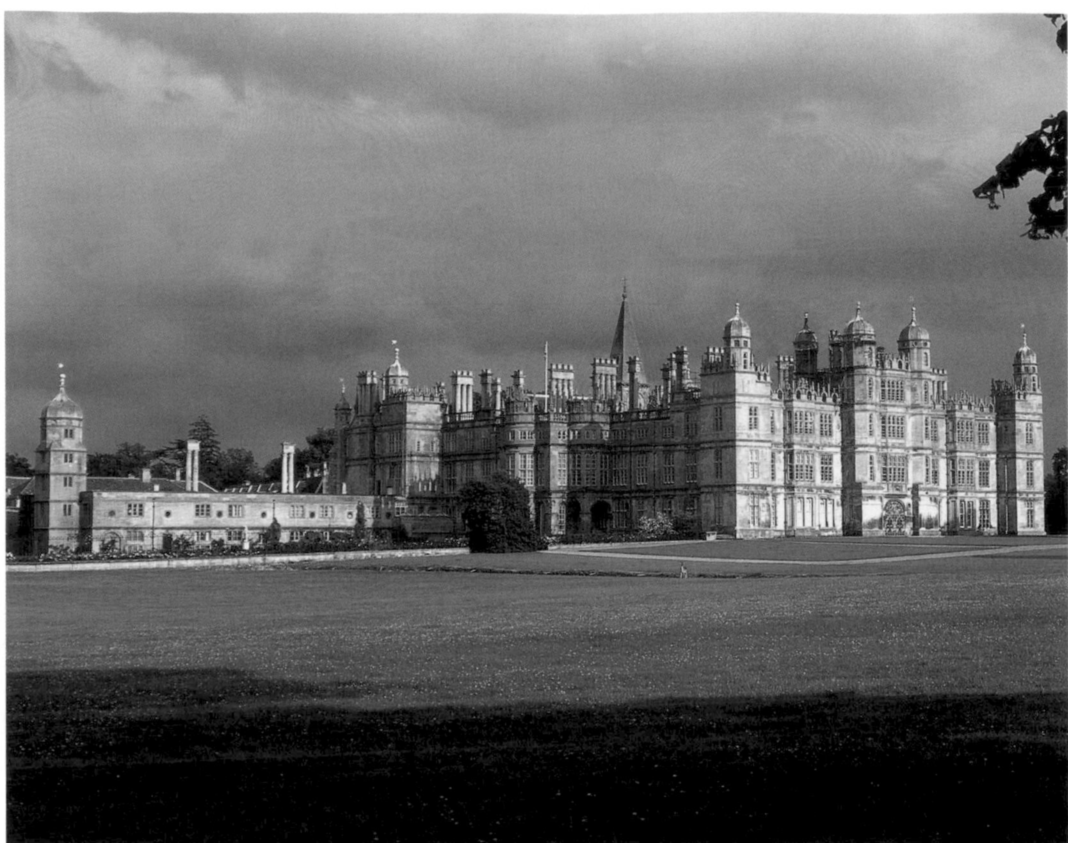

BURGHLEY HOUSE

www.burghley.co.uk

Burghley House, home of the Cecil family for over 400 years, was built as a country seat during the latter part of the 16th century by Sir William Cecil, later Lord Burghley, principal adviser and Lord Treasurer to Queen Elizabeth.

The House was completed in 1587 and there have been few alterations to the architecture since that date thus making Burghley one of the finest examples of late Elizabethan design in England. The interior was remodelled in the late 17th century by John, 5th Earl of Exeter who was a collector of fine art on a huge scale, establishing the immense collection of art treasures at Burghley. Burghley is truly a 'Treasure House', containing one of the largest private collections of Italian art, unique examples of Chinese and Japanese porcelain and superb items of 18th century furniture. The remodelling work of the 17th century means that examples of the work of the principal artists and craftsmen of the period are to be found at Burghley: Antonio Verrio, Grinling Gibbons and Louis Laguerre all made major contributions to the beautiful interiors.

Park and Gardens

The house is set in a 300-acre deer park landscaped by 'Capability' Brown. A lake was created by him and delightful avenues of mature trees feature largely in his design. The park is home to a large herd of Fallow deer, established in the 16th century. Opened in 2007, the Gardens of Surprise incorporates the existing Contemporary Sculpture Garden, containing many specimen trees and shrubs, and the new Elizabethan Garden, over an acre of yew mazes, revolving Caesars' heads and spurting fountains. The private gardens around the house are open in April for the display of spring bulbs.

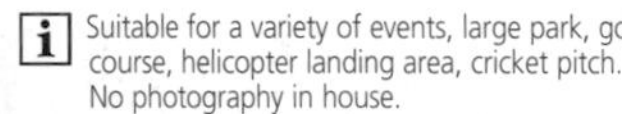

Suitable for a variety of events, large park, golf course, helicopter landing area, cricket pitch. No photography in house.

Visitors may alight at entrance. WC. Chair lift to Orangery Restaurant, house tour has two staircases one with chairlift.

Restaurant/tearoom. Groups can book in advance.

Available.

Ample. Free refreshments for coach drivers.

Welcome. Guide provided.

No dogs in house. In park on leads.

Civil Wedding Licence.

Owner

Burghley House Preservation Trust Ltd

Contact

The House Manager
Burghley House
Stamford
Lincolnshire PE9 3JY

Tel: 01780 752451
Fax: 01780 480125
E-mail: burghley@burghley.co.uk

Location

MAP 7:E7
OS Ref. TF048 062

Burghley House is 1m SE of Stamford. From London, A1 2hrs.

Visitors entrance is on B1443.

Rail: London – Peterborough 1hr (GNER). Stamford Station 1½m, regular service to Peterborough.

Taxi: Direct Line: 01780 481481.

Opening Times

Summer

House & Gardens
19 March–30 October (closed 1–4 September): Daily (Gardens only on Fridays), 11am–5pm, (last admission 4.30pm).

South Gardens
April: Daily (except Fridays), 11am–4pm.

Park
All year. Admission is free except on event days.

Admission

House & Gardens	
Adult	£12.20
Child (3–15yrs)	£6.00
Conc.	£10.80
Family	£31.50
Groups (20+)	
Adult	£10.50
School (up to 14yrs)	£6.00
Gardens of Surprise only	
Adult	£7.00
Child (3–15yrs)	£4.50
Conc.	£5.80
Family	£21.50

We are a charitable trust, by paying an extra 10% we can claim back the tax paid on this and use it for the benefit of the house and collections.

Conference/Function

ROOM	SIZE	MAX CAPACITY
Great Hall	70' x 30'	150
Orangery	100' x 20'	120

■ **Owner**

Grimsthorpe and Drummond Castle Trust Ltd. A Charity Registered in England & Wales (507478) and in Scotland (SCO39364).

■ **Contact**

Ray Biggs
Grimsthorpe Estate Office
Grimsthorpe
Bourne, Lincolnshire
PE10 0LY

Tel: 01778 591205
Fax: 01778 591259
E-mail: ray@grimsthorpe.co.uk

■ **Location**

MAP 7:D5
OS Ref. TF040 230

4m NW of Bourne on A151, 8m E of Colsterworth Junction of A1.

■ **Opening Times**

Castle
April & May:
Suns, Thurs & BH Mons.

June–September:
Sun–Thur. 1–5pm
(last admission 4pm).

Park & Gardens
As Castle,
11am–6pm
(last admission 5pm).

Groups: Apr–Sept: by arrangement.

■ **Admission**

Castle, Park & Garden

Adult	£10.00
Child	£4.00
Conc.	£9.00
Family (2+3)	£24.00

Park & Gardens

Adult	£5.00
Child	£2.00
Conc.	£4.00
Family (2+3)	£12.00

Special charges may be made for special events. Group rates on application.

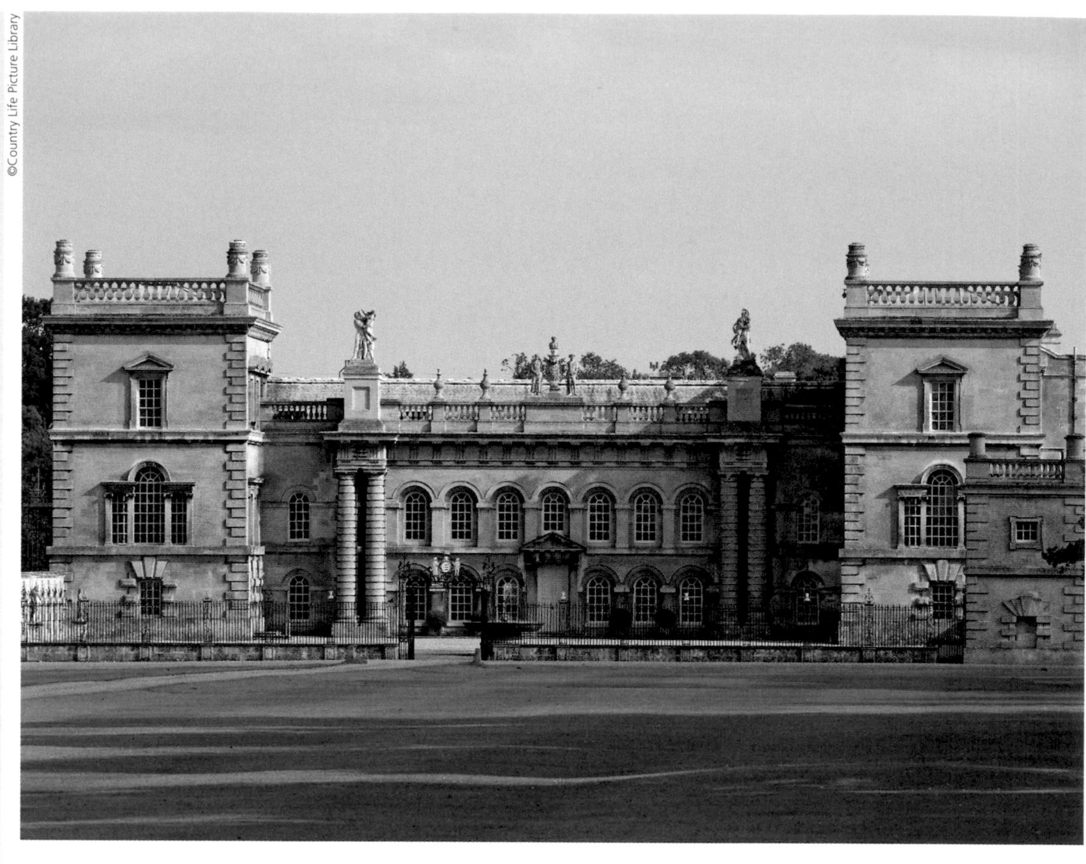
©Country Life Picture Library

GRIMSTHORPE CASTLE, PARK & GARDENS

www.grimsthorpe.co.uk

Home of the Willoughby de Eresby family since 1516. Examples of 13th century architecture and building styles from the Tudor period. The dramatic 18th century North Front is Sir John Vanbrugh's last major work. State Rooms and picture galleries with magnificent contents including tapestries, furniture and paintings. Unusual collection of thrones, fabrics and objects from the old House of Lords, associated with the family's hereditary Office of Lord Great Chamberlain.

The Grounds and Gardens

3,000 acre landscaped park with lakes, ancient woods, woodland walk with all-weather footpath, adventure playground. Family cycle trail and cycle hire shop. Park tours in a vehicle with the Ranger.

Unusual ornamental vegetable garden and orchard, created in the 1960s by the Countess of Ancaster and John Fowler. Intricate parterres lined with box hedges. Herbaceous border with yew topiary framing views across to the lake. Woodland garden.

Groups can explore the park from the comfort of their own coach by booking a one-hour, escorted park tour, with opportunities to discover more about the site of the Cistercian Abbey, the ancient deer parks, historic woodland and extensive series of early tree-lined avenues, Special study days can be booked including 'How Grimsthorpe Works in the 21st Century' and 'Garden Evolution' days. See website for full programme details.

©Country Life Picture Library

- No photography in house.
- Conferences (up to 40), inc catering.
- Partial. WC.
- Licensed.
- Obligatory except Suns.
- Ample.
- In grounds, on leads.

AUBOURN HALL

LINCOLN LN5 9DZ

Tel: 01522 788224 **Fax:** 01522 788199 **E-mail:** estate.office@aubournhall.co.uk

Owner: Mr & Mrs Christopher Nevile **Contact:** Andrew Widd, Head Gardener.

Early 17th century house by John Smythson. Important staircase and panelled rooms. 10 acre garden.

Location: MAP 7:D3, OS Ref. SK928 628. 6m SW of Lincoln. 2m SE of A46.

Open: Garden: Open for Events, Groups and Garden visits. Please contact the property for details.

Admission: Please contact property for details.

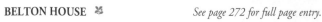

BELTON HOUSE *See page 272 for full page entry.*

BURGHLEY HOUSE *See page 273 for full page entry.*

© Heritage House Group

Burghley House

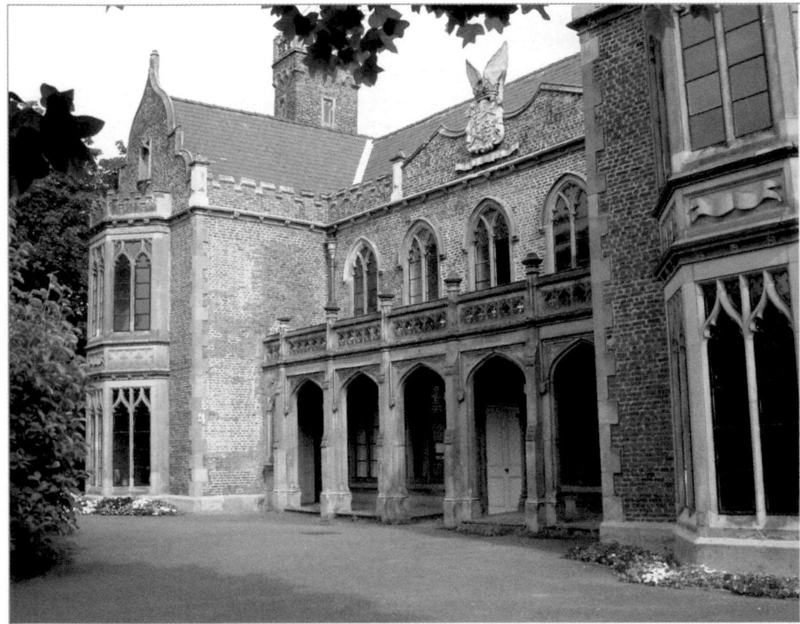

AYSCOUGHFEE HALL MUSEUM & GARDENS

CHURCHGATE, SPALDING, LINCOLNSHIRE PE11 2RA

www.ayscoughfee.org

Tel: 01775 764555 **E-mail:** museum@sholland.gov.uk

Owner: South Holland District Council **Contact:** Museum Manager

Ayscoughfee Hall, a magnificent Grade II* listed building, was built in the 1450s. The Hall is set in extensive landscaped grounds which include, amongst other impressive features, a memorial designed by Edwin Lutyens. The building and gardens combined reflect the splendour of the Medieval, Georgian and Victorian ages.

The Hall has been fully restored and a number of important and rare features uncovered. The Museum explains the history of the Hall, and features the lives of the people who lived there and in the surrounding Fens.

Location: MAP 7:F5, OS Ref. TF249 223. E bank of the River Welland, 5 mins walk from Spalding town centre.

Open: House: 10.30am–4pm Wed–Sun throughout the year (we are also open on BH Mons). Gardens: 8am until dusk Mon–Sat, 10am until dusk Sun.

Admission: Free.

WCs. Guide dogs only.

DODDINGTON HALL & GARDENS

LINCOLN LN6 4RU

www.doddingtonhall.com

Tel: 01522 812510 **Fax:** 01522 687213 **E-mail:** info@doddingtonhall.com
Owner: Mr & Mrs J J C Birch **Contact:** The Estate Office

Romantic Smythson mansion which stands today as it was built in 1595 with its mellow walled gardens and gatehouse. Never sold since it was built, Doddington is still very much a family home and its contents reflect over 400 years of unbroken family occupation. There is an elegant Georgian interior with fine collections of porcelain, paintings and textiles. The five acres of beautiful gardens contain a superb layout of box-edged parterres filled with bearded Iris in midsummer, sumptuous borders that provide colour in all seasons, and a wild garden with a marvellous succession of spring bulbs and flowering shrubs set amongst mature trees. Exclusive private group visits with guided tours a speciality. Please call the Estate Office to discuss your requirements. Award winning facilities for disabled visitors, include sensory tours of house and gardens for the Visually Impaired; free use of electric buggy and panaoramic tour of upper floors – please call for details. Free audioguides and children's activity trail. Civil weddings and receptions at Doddington Hall and in The Littlehouse next door. Newly resurrected working walled Kitchen Garden.

Farm shop with kitchen garden and local produce plus café serving delicious, seasonal and freshly cooked teas and lunches. Open seven days a week, reservations advisable for lunch.

Location: MAP 7:D2, OS Ref. SK900 710. 5m W of Lincoln on the B1190, signposted off the A46.

Open: Gardens only: 13 Feb–17 Apr & thoughout Oct: Suns only 11am–4pm. House & Gardens: 24 Apr (Easter Day)–28 Sep, every Wed, Sun & BH Mon 1pm–5pm (gardens open 11am). Last admission 4.15pm (Guided party tours of both House & Gardens welcome at other times by prior arrangement).

Admission: House & Gardens: Adult £8.50, Child £4.25, Family £22 (2+4, U4 free). House & Gardens Season Ticket £25 (single adult); £40 (2 adults), £45 (2+4). Group visits (20 or more): (Guided tours) private tour of House + free wander in Gardens, £8.50pp; private garden tour with Head Gardener, £7.25pp; private House + garden tour, £14.50pp. Groups (20 or more): (Self-guided tours) Gardens, £4.50pp, House + Gardens £7pp.

No photography in Hall. No stilettos. Gardens & ground floor. WC. In farm shop & café. Groups must book. By arrangement. Free. Guide dogs only.

EASTON WALLED GARDENS

THE GARDENS OFFICE, EASTON, GRANTHAM, LINCOLNSHIRE NG33 5AP

www.eastonwalledgardens.co.uk

Tel: 01476 530063 **Fax:** 01476 530063 **E-mail:** info@eastonwalledgardens.co.uk
Owner: Sir Fred & Lady Cholmeley **Contact:** Landy Hosli

In 1901 President Franklin Roosevelt described these gardens as a *'Dream of Nirvana … almost too good to be true'*. 50 years later, the house was pulled down and the gardens abandoned. 100 years later see the ongoing revival of these magnificent gardens. Funded privately and with the support of visitors, this garden experience is like no other. Alongside the recovery of these 400 year old gardens are: fantastic snowdrops, David Austin Roses and Sweet Pea Collections, a cut flower garden, cottage garden and pictorial meadow plantings. Teas and light lunches are served overlooking the garden. Groups can book out of hours if wished.

Location: MAP 7:D5, OS Ref. SK938 274. 1m from A1 (between Stamford and Grantham) North of Colsterworth, onto B6403 and follow signs.

Open: 12–20 Feb for snowdrops: 11am–4pm; Wed, Thurs, Fri, Suns & BH Mons. Mar–Oct, Suns in Nov for xmas shopping. Sweet Pea Week 3–10 Jul: daily 11am–4pm. For other events and extended opening times please see our website.

Admission: Adult £6, Child £1.50.

Partial. WCs. By arrangement. Guide dogs only.

FULBECK MANOR

Fulbeck, Grantham, Lincolnshire NG32 3JN

Tel: 01400 272231 **Fax:** 01400 273545 **E-mail:** fane@fulbeck.co.uk
Owner/Contact: Mr Julian Francis Fane

Built c1580. 400 years of Fane family portraits. Open by written appointment. Guided tours by owner approximately 1¼ hours. Tearooms at Craft Centre, 100 yards, for light lunches and teas.

Location: MAP 7:D3, OS Ref. SK947 505. 11m N of Grantham. 15m S of Lincoln on A607. Brown signs to Craft Centre & Tearooms and Stables.

Open: By written appointment.

Admission: Adult £6. Groups (10+) £5.

No photography. Partial. WCs. Obligatory. Ample for cars. Limited for coaches. Guide dogs only.

GAINSBOROUGH OLD HALL

Parnell Street, Gainsborough, Lincolnshire DN21 2NB

Tel: 01427 612669 / 01522 782040 **E-mail:** customers@english-heritage.org.uk
www.english-heritage.org.uk/gainsborougholdhall
Owner: English Heritage **Contact:** Lincolnshire County Council

A large medieval manor house with a magnificent Great Hall and suites of rooms. A collection of historic furniture and a re-created medieval kitchen are on display.

Location: MAP 7:C1, OS121, SK815 895. In centre of Gainsborough, opposite library.

Open: 1 Mar-31 Oct, Mon-Fri, 10am-5pm, Sat-Sun 11am-5pm.1 Nov-28 Feb, Mon-Fri, 10am-4pm, Sat 11am-4pm, Sun closed. 20 Dec-3 Jan closed.

Admission: Admission charge applies, contact site for details.

Picnickers welcome. WC.

GRIMSTHORPE CASTLE, PARK & GARDENS

See page 274 for full page entry.

LEADENHAM HOUSE

Leadenham House, Lincolnshire LN5 0PU

Tel: 01400 273256 **Fax:** 01400 272237 **Email:** leadenhamhouse@googlemail.com

Owner: Mr P Reeve **Contact:** Mr and Mrs P Reeve

Late eighteenth century house in park setting.

Location: MAP 7:D3, OS Ref. SK949 518. Entrance on A17 Leadenham bypass (between Newark and Sleaford).

Open: 4–8, 11–15 Apr, 3–6, 9–13, 16–20, 24 & 25 May, Spring & Aug BHs. All 2–5pm.

Admission: £4.00. Please ring door bell. Groups by prior arrangement only.

No photography. Obligatory. Limited for cars & coaches. Guide dogs only.

LINCOLN CATHEDRAL

Lincoln LN2 1PZ

Tel: 01522 561600 **Fax:** 01522 561634 **Contact:** Communications Office

One of the finest medieval buildings in Europe.

Location: MAP 7:D2, OS Ref. SK978 718. At the centre of Uphill, Lincoln.

Open: All year: Jun–Aug, 7.15am–8pm. Winter, 7.15am–6pm. Sun closing 6pm in Summer & 5pm in Winter.

Admission: £6, Child (5–16yrs) £1, Child (under 5s) Free, Conc. £4.75, No charge for services.

LINCOLN MEDIEVAL BISHOPS' PALACE

Minster Yard, Lincoln LN2 1PU

Tel/Fax: 01522 527468 **E-mail:** customers@english-heritage.org.uk

www.english-heritage.org.uk/lincolnmedievalbishopspalace

Owner: English Heritage **Contact:** Visitor Operations Team

Constructed in the late 12th century, the medieval bishops' palace was once one of the most important buildings in England. Built on hillside terraces, it has views of the cathedral and the Roman, medieval and modern city. See a virtual tour of the Palace and explore the grounds.

Location: MAP 7:D2, OS121 Ref. SK981 717. S side of Lincoln Cathedral, in Lincoln.

Open: 1 Apr–31 Oct: daily, 10am–5pm. 1 Nov–31 Mar: Thu–Mon, 10am–4pm. Closed 24–26 Dec & 1 Jan.

Admission: Adult £4.20, Child £2.10, Conc. £3.60, Family £10.50. 15% discount for groups (11+). EH Members free. Opening times and prices are valid until 31st March 2011, after this date details are subject to change please visit www.english-heritage.org.uk for the most up-to-date information.

Picnickers welcome.

MARSTON HALL

Marston, Grantham NG32 2HQ

Tel/Fax: 07812 356237 **E-mail:** johnthorold@aol.com

Owner/Contact: J R Thorold

The ancient home of the Thorold family. The building contains Norman, Plantaganet, Tudor and Georgian elements through to the modern day. Marston Hall is undergoing continuous restoration some of it which may be disruptive. Please telephone in advance of intended visits.

Location: MAP 7:D4, OS Ref. SK893 437. 5m N of Grantham and about 1m E of A1.

Open: 26, 27 & 28 Feb, 19, 20, 21, 22 & 23 Mar, 22, 23, 24, 25 & 26 Apr, 2 & 30 May, 18, 19 & 20 Jun, 9, 10, 11 & 12 Jul, 27, 28 & 29 Aug, 10, 11 & 12 Sept.

Admission: Adult £4, Child £1.50. Groups must book.

No photography.

SIBSEY TRADER WINDMILL

Sibsey, Boston, Lincolnshire PE22 0SY

Tel: 07718 320449 **E-mail:** customers@english-heritage.org.uk

www.english-heritage.org.uk/sibseytrader

Owner: English Heritage **Contact:** Ian Ansell

An impressive old mill built in 1877, with its machinery and six sails still intact. Flour milled on the spot can be bought here. The award-winning tearoom sells produce made from the Mill's organic stoneground flour.

Location: MAP 7:F3, OS Ref. TF345 511. ½m W of village of Sibsey, off A16, 5m N of Boston.

Open: 1 Mar–30 Apr: Sat & BHs, 10am–6pm; Sun, 11am–6pm. 1 May–30 Sept: Sat & BHs, 10am–6pm; Sun, 11am–6pm & Tue 10am - 6pm. 1 Oct–31 Oct: Sat & BHs, 10am–6pm; Sun, 11am–6pm. 1 Nov–28 Feb: Sat, 11am–5pm (Mill only). Closed 25 Dec–1 Jan.

Admission: Adult £2.50, Child £1 (under 5yrs Free), Conc. £2. Members OVP Free. EH Members free. Opening times and prices are valid until 31st March 2011, after this date details are subject to change please visit www.english-heritage.org.uk for the most up-to-date information.

Picnickers welcome. WC.

For unique **Civil wedding** venues see our index at the end of the book.

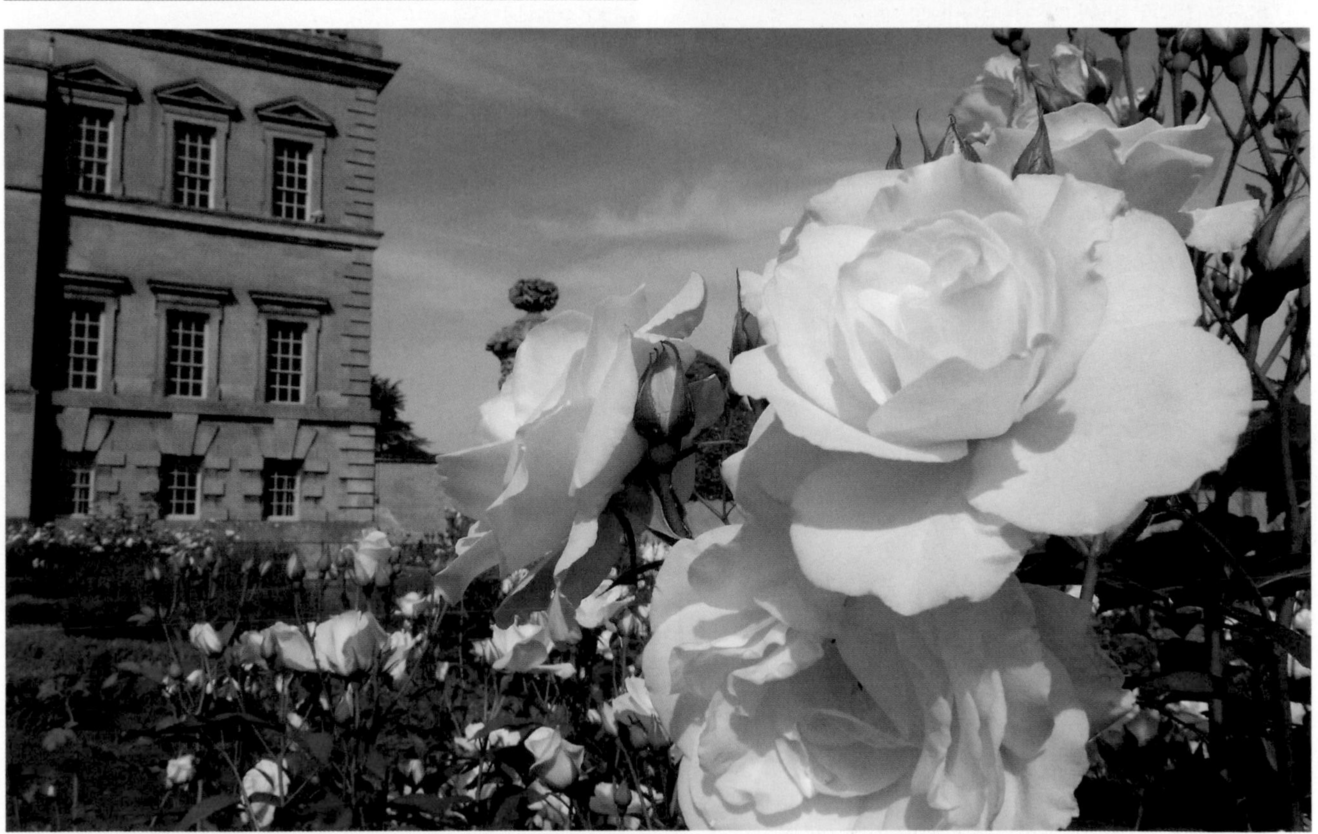

Grimsthorpe Castle Park & Gardens

© NTPL / Andrew Butler

© NT / SCrow

TATTERSHALL CASTLE

SLEAFORD ROAD, TATTERSHALL, LINCOLNSHIRE LN4 4LR

www.nationaltrust.org.uk/tattershall

Tel: 01526 342543 **Fax:** 01526 348826 **E-mail:** tattershallcastle@nationaltrust.org.uk

Owner: National Trust **Contact:** Visitor Services Manager

A vast fortified tower built c1440 for Ralph Cromwell, Lord Treasurer of England. The Castle is an national example of an early brick building, with a tower rising 130ft, rescued from dereliction and restored by Lord Curzon 1911–14. Explore all 6 floors, from basements to the battlements.

Location: MAP 7:E3, OS122 Ref. TF209 575. On S side of A153, 12m NE of Sleaford, 10m SW of Horncastle.

Open: 5 Mar–13 Mar, weekends only, 11am–4pm; 14 Mar–30 Mar, Open 5 days a week, 11am–4pm, closed Thurs & Fri; 2 Apr–28 Sept, Open 5 days a week, 11am–5pm, closed Thurs & Fri; 1 Oct–30 Oct, Open 5 days a week, 11am–4pm, closed Thurs & Fri; 5 Nov–18 Dec, weekends only, 11am–4pm; last entry 30 min before closing; open 1pm some Sat's if hosting wedding, please ring to confirm 01526 342543.

***Admission:** Adult £5.50, Child £3, Family £14. Group discounts. *includes a voluntary donation but visitors can choose to pay the standard prices displayed at the property and on the website.

Special Events: Property offers a host of events and activities throughout the year. Check out the website for the latest details. Or follow us on Facebook! www.nationaltrust.org.uk/tattershall.

Open Good Friday from 11am–5pm. Free audio guide available up to one hr before closing. Shop serves light refreshments, hot & cold drinks and ice-creams. Family friendly. Picnic anywhere in the grounds. Partial. WCs. Free. Limited for coaches. Guide dogs only.

WALCOT HALL

Nr Alkborough, North Lincolnshire DN15 9JT

Tel/Fax: 01724 720266 **E-mail:** WalcotHallEstate@gmail.com

www.WalcotHallEstate.com

Owner: Walcot Hall Estate **Contact:** Carol Davies

Grade II listed, Georgian hall built in 1726 with canted bays at either end and an imposing doric portico. Originally the family seat of Goulton-Constables. Set in glorious parkland in the North Lincolnshire countryside with five acres of beautifully landscaped gardens.

Location: MAP 11:D11, OS Ref. SE872 872. 15 mins SW of Humber Bridge & 15 mins N of M181. 45 mins from Robin Hood/Doncaster & Humberside international airports.

Open: Not open to the general public. Available for exclusive hire for film locations, corporate events, weddings and special events.

Limited for coaches.

© Doddington Hall

Doddington Hall

© NTPL / Nick Meers

WOOLSTHORPE MANOR

WATER LANE, WOOLSTHORPE BY COLSTERWORTH, GRANTHAM NG33 5PD

www.nationaltrust.org.uk

Tel: 01476 860338 **Fax:** 01476 862826

E-mail: woolsthorpemanor@nationaltrust.org.uk

Owner: National Trust **Contact:** The Visitor Services Manager

Isaac Newton, scientist, Master of the Royal Mint and President of the Royal Society, was born in this modest 17th century manor house in 1642 and developed his theories about light and gravity here. Visit the apple tree, explore his ideas in the Science Discovery Centre, see the short film.

Location: MAP 7:D5, OS130 Ref. SK924 244. 7m S of Grantham, ½ m NW of Colsterworth, 1m W of A1.

Open: House & Grounds: 5–13 Mar, Sat–Sun, 11am–5pm; 16 Mar–30 Oct, Wed–Sun, 11am–5pm; Open BH Mons and Good Fri 11am–5pm.

***Admission:** Adult £6.40, Child £3.20, Family £16, reduction for groups which must book in advance. *includes a voluntary donation but visitors can choose to pay the standard prices displayed at the property and on the website.

Special Events: Groups: Free-flow visits during opening hours, Special Interest Tours out of hours.

Partial. WCs. By arrangement. Limited for coaches. Guide dogs only.

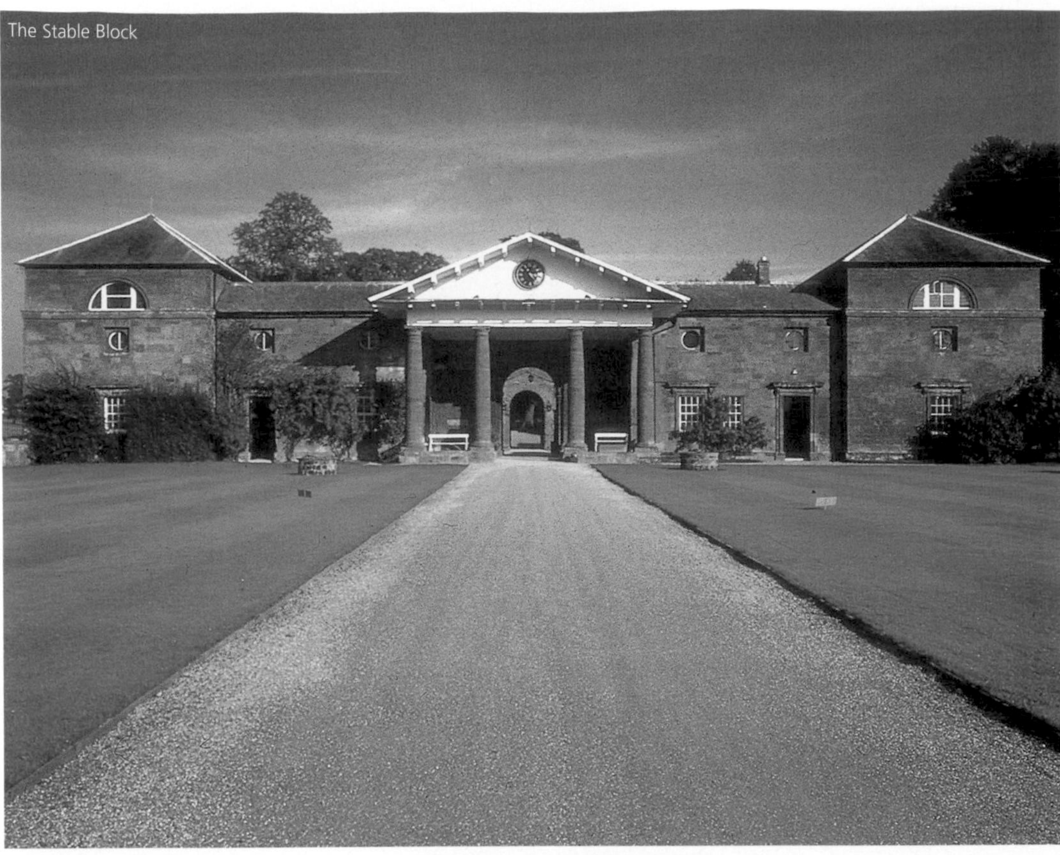
The Stable Block

ALTHORP

www.althorp.com

The history of Althorp is the history of a family. The Spencer's have lived and died here for over five centuries and nineteen generations.

Since the death of Diana, Princess of Wales, Althorp has become known across the world, but before that tragic event, connoisseurs had heard of this most classic of English stately homes on account of the magnificence of its contents and the beauty of its setting.

Althorp contains a fascinating variety of pictures, furniture and ceramics, a result of one family's uninterrupted occupancy for over 500 years. Enjoy the work of Van Dyck, Rubens, Gainsborough and Reynolds in one of Europe's finest private collections of the decorative arts.

Next to the mansion at Althorp lies the honey-coloured stable block, a truly breathtaking building which at one time accommodated up to 100 horses and 40 grooms. The stables are now the setting for the Exhibition celebrating the life of Diana, Princess of Wales.

All visitors are invited to view the House, Exhibition and Grounds as well as the Round Oval where Diana, Princess of Wales is laid to rest.

The Picture Gallery

Information leaflet issued to all ticket holders who book in advance. No indoor photography with still or video cameras. House and grounds available for private hire, events and specialist set location filming.

WCs.

By arrangement.

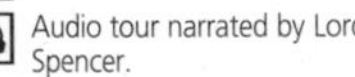
Audio tour narrated by Lord Spencer.

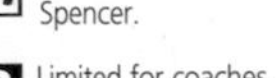
Limited for coaches.

Guide dogs only.

Owner

The Rt Hon The 9th Earl Spencer

Contact

Althorp
Northampton NN7 4HQ

Tel: 01604 770107
Fax: 01604 770042

Book online
www.althorp.com

E-mail: mail@althorp.com

Location

MAP 7:C9
OS Ref. SP682 652

From the M1/J16, 7m J18, 10m. Situated on A428 Northampton – Rugby. London on average 85 mins away.

Rail: 5m from Northampton station. 14m from Rugby station.

Opening Times

Summer

July and August, daily, 11am–5pm. (excluding 31 August.)
Last admission 4pm.

Winter

Closed.

Admission

House & Grounds

Contact for admission prices and group rates.

Carers accompanying visitors with disabilities are admitted free.

Please check website for up to date information.

■ **Owner**

His Grace The Duke of Buccleuch & Queensberry, KBE

■ **Contact**

Charles Lister
House Manager
Boughton House
Kettering
Northamptonshire
NN14 1BJ

Tel: 01536 515731
Fax: 01536 417255
E-mail: llt@boughtonhouse.org.uk

■ **Location**

MAP 7:D7
OS Ref. SP900 815

3m N of Kettering on A43/J7 from A14. Signposted through Geddington.

■ **Opening Times**

House
1–2 May
1 August–1 September
Daily, 2–5pm.
Last entry 4pm.
Self guided tour normally in operation. Entry by guided tour only on Mons & Fris, except on BH Mons.

Daily by appointment throughout the year for Groups – contact for details.

Grounds
1 May–31 July, daily, 1pm–5pm. Closed Saturdays.

1 August–1 September, daily, 12 noon–5pm.

■ **Admission**

House & Grounds

Adult	£10.00
Child	£7.00
Family (2+2)	£25.00

Grounds

Adult	£6.00
Child	£2.00
Family (2+2)	£14.00

Wheelchair visitors Free. HHA Friends are admitted Free 1–2 May, 1 August–1 September.

Conference/Function

ROOM	MAX CAPACITY
Great Hall	100
Stewards Hall	40
Lecture	120
Seminar Rm	25

BOUGHTON HOUSE

www.boughtonhouse.org.uk

Boughton, a Tudor manor house transformed into a vision of Louis XIV's Versailles has been the Northamptonshire home of the Duke and Duchess of Buccleuch and their Montagu ancestors since 1528. The house displays a staggering collection of fine art including paintings, furniture, porcelain, weapons, and textiles.

The 18th century Designed Landscape, originally created to provide vistas, avenues, water features and formality is presently being restored. In 2007, the Duke commissioned Kim Wilkie to design a striking new landform – "Orpheus" which both complements and enhances the older landscape created by his ancestors.

For information on the group visits programme, events or education services, please contact The House Manager.

Our website gives considerable information on Boughton, together with full details of our schools' educational facilities (Sandford Award winner 1988, 1993, 1998, 2003 and 2008).

"I never desired anything so earnestly as to go to Boughton to see my Lord, the Good Company and learning in its full lustre." Charles de Saint Evremond, the French soldier, poet and essayist writing in 1700 about the home of his good friend, Ralph Montagu.

Parkland available for film location and other events. Stableblock room contains 100 seats. No inside photography. No unaccompanied children. Browse our website for a 'virtual' tour of the house.

Access to ground floor and all facilities. Virtual tour of first floor.

Tearoom seats 80, groups must book. Licensed.

By arrangement.

Heritage Education Trust Sandford Award winner 1988, 1993, 1998, 2003 & 2008.

No dogs in house and garden, welcome in Park on leads.

By arrangement.

DEENE PARK

www.deenepark.com

A most interesting house, occupied and developed by the Brudenell family since 1514, from a medieval manor around a courtyard into a Tudor and Georgian mansion. Visitors see many rooms of different periods, providing an impressive yet intimate ambience of the family home of many generations. The most flamboyant member of the family to date was the 7th Earl of Cardigan, who led the charge of the Light Brigade at Balaklava and of whom there are many historic relics and pictures on view.

Mr Edmund Brudenell, the current owner, has taken considerable care in restoring the house after the Second World War. The gardens have also been improved during the last thirty years or so, with long, mixed borders of shrubs, old-fashioned roses and flowers, together with a parterre designed by David Hicks and long walks under fine old trees by the water.

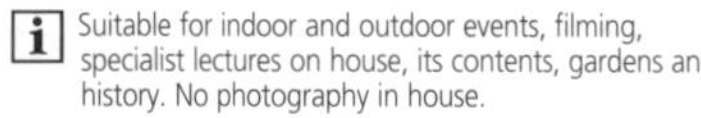
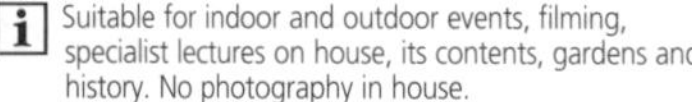

- Suitable for indoor and outdoor events, filming, specialist lectures on house, its contents, gardens and history. No photography in house.
- Including buffets, lunches and dinners.
- Partial. Visitors may alight at the entrance, access to ground floor and garden.
- Special rates for groups, bookings can be made in advance, menus on request.
- By arrangement.
- Tours inclusive of admittance, tour time 90 mins. Owner will meet groups if requested.
- Unlimited for cars, space for 3 coaches 10 yds from house.
- In car park only.
- Residential conference facilities by arrangement.

Owner

E Brudenell Esq

Contact

The Administrator
Deene Park
Corby
Northamptonshire
NN17 3EW

Tel: 01780 450278
Fax: 01780 450282
E-mail: admin@deenepark.com

Location

MAP 7:D7
OS Ref. SP950 929

6m NE of Corby off A43. From London via M1/J15 then A43, or via A1, A14, A43 – 2 hrs.

From Birmingham via M6, A14, A43, 90 mins.

Rail: Corby Station 10 mins and Kettering Station 20 mins.

Opening Times

Open Easter Sun & Mon, Suns and BH Mons from May to end August & Weds in May & 1 June 2–5pm.
Last admission 4pm.

Refreshments available in the Old Kitchen.

Open at other times by arrangement for groups.

Admission

Public Open Days
House & Gardens

Adult	£8.00
Child (10–14yrs)	£4.00
Conc.	£7.00

Gardens only

Adult	£5.50
Child (10–14yrs)	£2.50

Groups (20+) by arrangement:

Weekdays	£7.00
	(Min £140)
Weekends & BHs	£8.00
	(Min £160)

Child up to 10yrs free with an accompanying adult.

Special Events

13 & 20 February
Snowdrop Sundays (Gardens Only), 11am–4pm

27 March
Daffodil Day (Gardens Only), 11am–4pm

15 June
Head Gardener's Tour with Supper
Booking Essential, 6pm

For more information about these and other events please visit our website.

Conference/Function

ROOM	MAX CAPACITY
Great Hall	150
Tapestry Rm	75
East Room	18

■ **Owner**

The Kelmarsh Trust

■ **Contact**

Estelle Chapman
Kelmarsh
Northampton
NN6 9LY

Tel: 01604 686543
E-mail: enquiries@kelmarsh.com

■ **Location**

OS Ref. SP736 795

⅓ m N of A14–A508 jct 2. Rail & Bus: Mkt Harborough.

■ **Opening Times**

Hall and Gardens open 24 April–29 September 2011.

Gardens: Tues, Weds Thurs & Suns, 11am–5pm. Plus Bank Holiday Suns and Mons: April, May & August, 11am–5pm.

Hall: Guided tours of Hall & Croome Collection are available on Thurs, 12noon–4pm. Plus Bank Holiday Suns and Mons: April, May & August, 12noon–4pm.

■ **Admission**

House or Croome tour:

Adults	£6.00
Child	£4.00
Conc.	£5.50

Gardens

Adults	£5.00
Child	£3.50
Conc.	£4.50

Garden season tickets are available.

Conference/Function

ROOM	SIZE	MAX CAPACITY
The Great Hall	8.8 x 8.4m	80
The Saloon	7.2 x 11.2m	100
The Ballroom	7.6 x 11m	112
The Dining Room	5.9 x 7.5m	20

KELMARSH HALL

www.kelmarsh.com

Built in the Palladian style to a James Gibbs design, 18th century Kelmarsh Hall is set in beautiful gardens with views over the surrounding parkland.

The former home of society decorator, Nancy Lancaster, renowned for working with John Fowler and acclaimed for creating the 'English Country House Style', Kelmarsh still reflects the essence of her panache and flair.

On the first floor of the Hall the Croome Exhibition can be seen, showcasing furniture and paintings on loan from Croome Court in Worcestershire and home to the Earls of Coventry.

The award winning gardens that visitors see at Kelmarsh today are largely inspired by Nancy Lancaster. She extended her interior style of shabby chic charm into the gardens and drafted in the garden designer of her day, Norah Lindsay.

Around the Hall, the landscape architect Geoffrey Jellicoe laid out a formal terrace and horse chestnut avenues leading down to the lake.

From the sophisticated pastels of the sunken garden through to the showier shades of the 30 metre long border, the garden leads you on a tour around the perimeter of a triangular walled kitchen garden. This secret heart is a newly restored space filled with traditional fruit and vegetables, cut flower beds and a restored vinery.

Kelmarsh Hall, gardens and parkland can be hired exclusively for weddings, corporate events and private parties. We are experienced at providing bespoke events throughout the year, for any number of people.

Please visit our website, www.kelmarsh.com, for our programme of special events throughout the year.

LAMPORT HALL & GARDENS

www.lamporthall.co.uk

Home of the Isham family from 1560 to 1976. The 17th and 18th century façade is by John Webb and the Smiths of Warwick. The Hall contains an outstanding collection of furniture, china and paintings including portraits by Van Dyck, Kneller and Lely and other important works of art, many brought back from a Grand Tour in the 17th century. The Library contains books dating back to the 16th century and the Cabinet Room houses rare Italian cabinets. The first floor includes a replicated 17th century bedchamber and a photographic record of Sir Gyles Isham, a Hollywood actor, who initiated the restoration. Refreshments are served in the Victorian dining room. The gardens owe much to the 10th Baronet who, in the mid 19th century, created the famous rockery and populated it with the first garden gnomes. He also made a small Italian garden with a shell fountain, planted herbaceous borders and wisteria, which still thrives today. Other features include an 18th century box bower and a 17th century cockpit. The newly restored 2 acre walled garden, which opened in 2010, now houses one of the largest cutting gardens in England and brings the total area of gardens to over 5 acres. Many of the plants used in the cutting garden were sourced from Piet Oudolf's Dutch nursery. The Lamport Hall Preservation Trust was formed in 1974 by Sir Gyles to complete the restoration work initiated by him and completed in 2007.

No photography in house, Available for filming.

Partial.

Licensed.

Licensed.

Obligatory other than Fair Days.

Limited for coaches.

On leads.

Groups only.

Owner

Lamport Hall Trust

Contact

Executive Director
Lamport Hall
Northamptonshire
NN6 9HD

Tel: 01604 686272
Fax: 01604 686224
E-mail: admin@lamporthall.co.uk

Location

MAP 7:C8
OS Ref. SP759 745

Entrance on A508. 8m N of Northampton, 3m S of A14 J2.

Bus:
Limited Stagecoach from Northampton and Leicester.

Opening Times

House open for guided tours at 2.15 & 3pm Wed & Thu, from April 27 to October 6 and non guided tours on Bank Hol Suns & Mons from Easter Sunday and some event days inc October 8/9. Private tours at other times by arrangement, minimum charge £200 for house & garden & £100 for garden only.

Admission

House & Garden,

Adult	£7.50
Child (11–16yrs)	£2.50
OAP	£7.00

Gardens only

Adult	£4.00
Child (11–16yrs)	£2.00
OAP	£3.50

Special Events

April 24/25
Easter Sunday and Monday – Antiques and Collectors Fair

May 28/29/30 Bank Holiday Weekend
Festival of Country Life

August 28/29
Bank Holiday Sunday and Monday Antiques and Collectors Fair

October 8/9
Autumn Gift and Craft Fair

Please see website for up-to-date list of educational courses, theatre, music and other events.

Conference/Function

ROOM	SIZE	MAX CAPACITY
Victorian Dining Room	7.5 x 9.5m	80
High Room	5.9 x 9.2m	60
Oak Room	6.1 x 8.2m	70

Complete stable yard and buildings available for fairs, exhibitions, corporate use, etc.

■ **Owner**
James Saunders Watson

■ **Contact**
Andrew Norman
Operations Manager
Rockingham Castle
Rockingham
Market Harborough
Leicestershire
LE16 8TH
Tel: 01536 770240
Fax: 01536 771692
E-mail: estateoffice@
rockinghamcastle.com

■ **Location**
MAP 7:D7
OS Ref. SP867 913.

1m N of Corby on A6003. 9m E of Market Harborough. 14m SW of Stamford on A427.

■ **Opening Times**
17 April–to the end of May: Suns & BH Mons.

June–September:
Tues, Suns & BH Mon.
12 noon–5pm

Grounds open at 12 noon

Castle opens at 1pm.

Last entry 4.30pm.

■ **Admission**

House & Grounds

Adult	£9.00
Senior Citizen	£8.00
Child (5–16yrs)	£5.00
Family ticket (2+2)	£23.00

Grounds only
Including Gardens, Salvin's Tower, Gift Shop and Licensed Tea Room.

Adult & Child	£5.00

(Not available when special events are held in grounds.)

Groups (min 20 visitors)

Adult (on open days)	£8.00
Adult (private guided tour)	£10.00
Child (5–16yrs)	£4.75

School groups (min 20 visitors)

Adult	£8.00
Children	£4.75

(1 Adult Free with every 15 children). Groups and school parties can be accommodated on most days by arrangement.

■ **Special Events**

April 24 & 25
Easter Sunday & Monday

June 12
Jousting & Medieval Living History Village

July 10
Falconry & Owl Day

August 28 & 29
Vikings! Of Middle England

November 21–25
Christmas at Rockingham Castle

ROCKINGHAM CASTLE

www.rockinghamcastle.com

Rockingham Castle stands on the edge of an escarpment giving dramatic views over five counties and the Welland Valley below. Built by William the Conqueror, the Castle was a royal residence for 450 years. In the 16th century Henry VIII granted it to Edward Watson and for 450 years it has remained a family home. The predominantly Tudor building, within Norman walls, has architecture, furniture and works of art from practically every century including, unusually, a remarkable collection of 20th century pictures. Charles Dickens was a regular visitor to the Castle and based Chesney Wolds in Bleak House on Rockingham. Surrounding the Castle are some 18 acres of gardens largely following the foot print of the medieval castle. The vast 400 year old "Elephant Hedge" bisects the formal 17th century terraced gardens. The circular yew hedge stands on the site of the motte and bailey and provides shelter for the Rose Garden. Outside of which stands the newly planted 'Room Garden' created by Chelsea gold medal winner Robert Myers, using Yew hedging, shrubs and herbaceous planting. Below the Castle is the beautiful 19th century "Wild Garden" replanted with advice from Kew Gardens during the early 1960s. Included in the gardens are many specimen tress and shrubs including the remarkable Handkerchief Tree.

No photography in Castle.

Partial. WCs.

Licensed.

Licensed.

By arrangement.

Limited for coaches.

On leads.

78 DERNGATE: THE CHARLES RENNIE MACKINTOSH HOUSE & GALLERIES

82 Derngate, Northampton NN1 1UH www.78derngate.org.uk

Tel: 01604 603407 **E-mail:** info@78derngate.org.uk

Owner: 78 Derngate Northampton Trust **Contact:** House Manager

Winner Enjoy England Gold Award for Best Small Visitor Attraction 2009. 78 Derngate was remodelled by the world-famous architect and designer, Charles Rennie Mackintosh, in his iconic modernist style. Free entry to the Gallery Upstairs, restaurant, shop and contemporary craft. Truely is a must-see venue.

Location: MAP 7:C9, OS Ref. SP759 603. In the heart of Northampton close to the rear of the Royal & Derngate Theatres. Follow Derngate out of the centre of town.

Open: 1 Feb–18 Dec 2011, Tues–Sun & BH Mons: 10am–5pm. Group and school bookings are also available.

Admission: Adult £6, Conc. £5.50. Family (2+2): £15. Groups (15+) £5pp.

No indoor photography. Partial. WCs. Licensed. Licensed. By arrangement. None. Guide dogs only.

ALTHORP

See page 279 for full page entry.

BOUGHTON HOUSE

See page 280 for full page entry.

CANONS ASHBY

Canons Ashby, Daventry, Northamptonshire NN11 3SD

Tel: 01327 861900 **Fax:** 01327 861909

Owner: National Trust **Contact:** The Property Manager

Elizabethan manor house with later alterations. Formal garden.

Location: Map 7:B9, OS Ref. SP577 506. Access from M40/J11, or M1/J16. Signposted from A5, 3m S of Weedon crossroads. Then 7m to SW.

CASTLE ASHBY GARDENS

Castle Ashby, Northampton NN7 1LQ

Tel: 01604 695200 **E-mail:** markbrooks@castleashby.co.uk

www.castleashbygardens.co.uk

Contact: Mark Brooks – Head Gardener / Peter Cox – Assistant Head Gardener

Castle Ashby House is the ancestral home of the 7th Marquis of Northampton. The house is set amidst a 10,000 acre working estate with an extensive 25 acres of gardens which are open to the public 365 days a year. A children's playground with a wide selection of rare breed animals can also be found within the gardens and now include a tea room, plant centre and gift shop.

Location: Castle Ashby is situated off the A428 between Northampton and Bedford, and is also accessible from the A45.

Open: 1 Apr–30 Sept, 10am–5.30pm. 1 Oct–31 Mar, 10am–4.30pm.

Admission: Adults: £5, OAP/children over 10 £4.50, Family £16, and children under 10 free.

Disabled Access Guide tours available. Booking required. Length of visit: 2-3 hours.

© Althorp

Althorp

© Coton Manor Garden

Coton Manor Garden

COTON MANOR GARDEN

NR GUILSBOROUGH, NORTHAMPTONSHIRE NN6 8RQ

www.cotonmanor.co.uk

Tel: 01604 740219 **Fax:** 01604 740838

E-mail: pasleytyler@cotonmanor.co.uk

Owner: Ian & Susie Pasley-Tyler **Contact:** Sarah Ball

Traditional English garden laid out on different levels surrounding a 17th century stone manor house. Many herbaceous borders, with extensive range of plants, old yew and holly hedges, rose garden, water garden and fine lawns set in 10 acres. Also wild flower meadow and bluebell wood.

Location: Map 7:B8, OS Ref. SP675 716. 9m NW of Northampton, between A5199 (formerly A50) and A428.

Open: 1 Apr–1 Oct: Tue–Sat & BH weekends; also Suns Apr–May: 12 noon–5.30pm.

Admission: Adult £6, Child £2, Conc. £5.50. Groups: £5.

Partial. WCs. Licensed. Licensed. By arrangement.

COTTESBROOKE HALL & GARDENS

COTTESBROOKE, NORTHAMPTONSHIRE NN6 8PF

www.cottesbrookehall.co.uk

Tel: 01604 505808 **Fax:** 01604 505619 **E-mail:** enquiries@cottesbrooke.co.uk

Owner: Mr & Mrs A R Macdonald-Buchanan **Contact:** The Administrator

This magnificent Queen Anne house dating from 1702 is set in delightful rural Northamptonshire. The Hall's beauty is matched by the magnificence of the gardens and views and by the excellence of the picture, furniture and porcelain collections it houses. The Woolavington collection of sporting pictures at Cottesbrooke is possibly one of the finest of its type in Europe and includes paintings by Stubbs, Ben Marshall and many other artists renowned for works of this genre, from the mid 18th century to the present day. Portraits, bronzes, 18th century English and French furniture and fine porcelain are also among the treasures of Cottesbrooke Hall. In the formal gardens a huge 300-year-old cedar sets off the magnificent double herbaceous borders, pools and lily-ponds. In midsummer, visitors enjoy the splendid array of planters, a sight not to be missed. The Wild Garden is a short walk across the Park and is planted along the course of a stream with its small cascades and arched bridges. Previously winner of the HHA/Christie's *Garden of the Year Award*. Nominated as one of the best gardens in the world in *"1001 Gardens you must see before you die"*.

Location: MAP 7:B8, OS Ref. SP711 739. 10m N of Northampton near Creaton on A5199 (formerly A50). Signed from Junction 1 on the A14.

Open: May–end of Sept. May & Jun: Wed & Thur, 2–5.30pm. Jul–Sept: Thur, 2–5.30pm. Open BH Mons (May–Sept), 2–5.30pm. The first open day is bank holiday Monday 2nd May 2011.

Admission: House & Gardens: Adult £8, Child £3.50, Conc £6.50. Gardens only: Adult £5.50, Child £2.50, Conc £4.50. RHS members receive free access to gardens. Group & private bookings by arrangement.

No photography in house. Filming & outside events. Gardens. WC. Parking. Home-made cakes. Hall guided tours obligatory.

Haddonstone Show Gardens

DEENE PARK

See page 281 for full page entry.

ELEANOR CROSS

Geddington, Kettering, Northamptonshire

Tel: 01604 735400 (Regional Office) **E-mail:** customers@english-heritage.org.uk

www.english-heritage.org.uk/eleanorcrossgeddington

Owner: English Heritage **Contact:** East Midlands Regional Office

One of a series of famous crosses, of elegant sculpted design, erected by Edward I to mark the resting places of the body of his wife, Eleanor, when brought for burial from Harby in Nottinghamshire to Westminster Abbey in 1290.

Location: MAP 7:D7, OS Ref. SP896 830. In Geddington, off A43 between Kettering and Corby.

Open: Any reasonable time.

Admission: Free. Opening times and prices are valid until 31st March 2011, after this date details are subject to change please visit www.english-heritage.org.uk for the most up-to-date information.

Picnickers welcome.

HADDONSTONE SHOW GARDENS

The Forge House, Church Lane, East Haddon, Northampton NN6 8DB

Tel: 01604 770711 **Fax:** 01604 770027

E-mail: info@haddonstone.co.uk **www.haddonstone.com**

Owner: Haddonstone Ltd **Contact:** Marketing Director

See Haddonstone's classic garden ornaments in the beautiful setting of the walled manor gardens including: urns, troughs, fountains, statuary, bird baths, sundials and balustrading – even an orangery. The garden is on different levels with shrub roses, conifers, clematis and climbers. The Jubilee garden features a pavilion, temple and Gothic grotto. As featured on BBC *Gardeners' World*.

Location: MAP 7:B8, OS Ref. SP667 682. 7m NW of Northampton off A428. Signposted.

Open: Mon–Fri, 9am–5.30pm. Closed weekends, BHs & Christmas period.

Admission: Free. Groups by appointment only. Not suitable for coach groups.

By arrangement. Limited. Guide dogs only.

HOLDENBY

HOLDENBY, NORTHAMPTON NN6 8DJ

www.holdenby.com

Tel: 01604 770074 **Fax:** 01604 770962 **E-mail:** office@holdenby.com

Owner: James Lowther **Contact:** Caroline Houghton/Amanda Askew, Commercial Managers

Once the largest private house in England and subsequently the palace and prison of King Charles I, Holdenby has a special atmosphere all of its own. Its elegant rooms and acres of gardens and parkland make it a magnificent venue for corporate events, dinners and meetings, as well as an ideal location for films and TV. Visitors to the gardens can enjoy fascinating flying displays of birds from our famous Falconry Centre, while couples continue to choose Holdenby as an enchanting venue for weddings. Holdenby is six times winner of the Sandford Award for Heritage Education.

Location: MAP 7:B8, OS Ref. SP693 681. M1/J15a. 7m NW of Northampton off A428 & A5199.

Open: Gardens & Falconry: May–Aug, Suns & BH Mons, Easter Sun & Mon 1–5pm. Gardens only: Apr & Sep, 1–5pm. House: 7/8 May 2011, 28/29 Aug 2011.

Admission: With Falconry Centre: Adult £5, Child £3.50, Conc. £4.50, Family (2+3) £15; Gardens only: Adult £3, Child £2, Conc. £2.50, Family (2+3) £8. Different prices on event days. Groups must book.

Children's play area. By arrangement. Limited for coaches. 6 times Sandford Award Winner. On leads. Holdenby Garden & Home Show 7/8th May 2011, Northamptonshire Food Show @ Holdenby 28/29 August 2011.

Kelmarsh Hall

KELMARSH HALL

See page 282 for full page entry.

© English Heritage

KIRBY HALL

DEENE, CORBY, NORTHAMPTONSHIRE NN17 3EN

www.english-heritage.org.uk/kirbyhall

Tel: 01536 203230 **E-mail:** customers@english-heritage.org.uk

Owner: The Earl of Winchilsea & Nottingham (Managed by English Heritage)

Contact: Visitor Operations Team

Kirby Hall is one of England's greatest Elizabethan and 17th century Houses. The partial ruins contain exceptional decoration, full of renaissance detail. The Great Hall and state rooms remain in tact, restored to authentic 17th and 18th century style decor. The 'cutwork' gardens boast beautiful statues, seating and topiary.

Location: MAP 7:D7 OS Ref. SP926 927. On unclassified road off A43, Corby to Stamford road, 4m NE of Corby. 2m W of Deene Park.

Open: 1 Apr–30 Jun: Thur–Mon, 10am–5pm. 1 Jul–31 Aug: daily, 10am–5pm. 1 Sep–31 Oct: Thu–Mon, 10am–5pm. 1 Nov–31 Mar: Thur–Mon, 12noon–4pm. Closed 24–26 Dec & 1 Jan. May close early for private events. Please call ahead to check.

Admission: Adult £5.30, Child £2.70, Conc. £4.50, Family £13.30. 15% discount for groups (11+). EH Members Free. Opening times and prices are valid until 31st March 2011, after this date details are subject to change please visit www.english-heritage.org.uk for the most up-to-date information.

Picnickers welcome. WC. Free with admission.

LAMPORT HALL & GARDENS

See page 283 for full page entry.

LYVEDEN NEW BIELD

Nr Oundle, Northamptonshire PE8 5AT

Tel: 01832 205358 **Fax:** 01832 205158

E-mail: lyveden@nationaltrust.org.uk **www.nationaltrust.org.uk**

Owner: National Trust **Contact:** Mark Bradshaw

An incomplete Elizabethan garden house and moated garden. Begun in 1595 by Sir Thomas Tresham to symbolise his Catholic faith, Lyveden remains virtually unaltered since work stopped when Tresham died in 1605. Fascinating Elizabethan architectural detail; remains of one of the oldest garden layouts; set amongst beautiful open countryside.

Location: MAP 7:D7, OS141, SP983 853. 4m SW of Oundle via A427, 3m E of Brigstock, off Harley Way. NT car park 100m from property.

Open: House & Garden: 1 Feb–31 Oct, Sat & Sun, 11am–4pm, 1 Mar–31 Oct, Wed–Sun, 10.30am–5pm. 1 Jul–31 Aug, daily 10.30am–5pm.

***Admission:** Adult £5.00, Child Free. *includes a voluntary donation but visitors can choose to pay the standard prices displayed at the property and on the website.

On leads.

ROCKINGHAM CASTLE

See page 284 for full page entry.

RUSHTON TRIANGULAR LODGE

Rushton, Kettering, Northamptonshire NN14 1RP

Tel: 01536 710761 **E-mail:** customers@english-heritage.org.uk

www.english-heritage.org.uk/rushton

Owner: English Heritage **Contact:** Visitor Operations Team

This extraordinary building, completed in 1597, symbolises the Holy Trinity. It has three sides, 33 ft wide, three floors, trefoil windows and three triangular gables on each side.

Location: MAP 7:C7 OS141, SP830 831. 1m W of Rushton, on unclassified road 3m from Desborough on A6.

Open: 1 Apr–31 Oct: Thu–Mon, 11am–4pm.

Admission: Adult £3.20, Child £1.60, Conc. £2.70. EH Members Free. Group discount available. Opening times and prices are valid until 31st March 2011, after this date details are subject to change please see www.english-heritage.org.uk for the most up-to-date information.

Picnickers welcome. Nearby lay-by.

SOUTHWICK HALL

Nr Oundle, Peterborough PE8 5BL

Tel: 01832 274064 **www.southwickhall.co.uk**

Owner: Christopher Capron **Contact:** G Bucknill

A family home since 1300, retaining medieval building dating from 1300, with Tudor rebuilding and 18th century additions. Exhibitions: Victorian and Edwardian Life, collections of agricultural and carpentry tools and local archaeological finds.

Location: MAP 7:E7, OS152, TL022 921. 3m N of Oundle, 4m E of Bulwick.

Open: BH Suns & Mons: 24–25 Apr; 1–2 May; 29–30 May; 28–29 Aug: 2–5pm. The Sunday of The Heritage Open Days: Sept 2011 2–5pm under the scheme.

Admission: House & Grounds: Adult £6, Child £3. To be confirmed.

Partial. WC. By arrangement. In grounds on leads.

STOKE PARK PAVILIONS

Stoke Bruerne, Towcester, Northamptonshire NN12 7RZ

Tel: 01604 862329 or 07768 230325

Owner/Contact: A S Chancellor Esq

The two Pavilions, dated c1630 and attributed to Inigo Jones, formed part of the first Palladian country house built in England by Sir Francis Crane. The central block, to which the Pavilions were linked by quadrant colonnades, was destroyed by fire in 1886. The grounds include extensive gardens and overlooks former parkland, now being restored.

Location: MAP 7:C10, OS Ref. SP740 488. 7m S of Northampton.

Open: Aug: daily, 3–6pm. Other times by appointment only.

Admission: Adult £3, Child £1.50.

Grounds. Limited. In grounds, on leads.

WAKEFIELD LODGE

Potterspury, Northamptonshire NN12 7QX

Tel: 01327 811395 **Fax:** 01327 811051

Owner/Contact: Mrs J Richmond-Watson

Georgian hunting lodge with deer park

Location: MAP 7:C10, OS Ref. SP739 425. 4m S of Towcester on A5. Take signs to farm shop for directions.

Open: House: 18 Apr–31 May: Mon–Fri (closed BHs), 12noon–4pm. Appointments by telephone. Access walk open Apr & May.

Admission: £5.

No photography. Unsuitable for wheelchairs. Obligatory. Guide dogs only.

WESTON HALL

Towcester, Northamptonshire NN12 8PU

Tel: 01295 768212 **E-mail:** susanna.sitwell@uwclub.net

Owner/Contact: Mrs Sitwell

This is a small Northamptonshire manor house with an interesting collection much of which is associated with the literary Sitwell family.

Location: MAP 7:B10, OS Ref. SP592 469, five miles west of Towcester.

Open: Throughout the year by prior written appointment. Heritage Open Days 12-13 Sept.

Admission: £8. No charge on Heritage Open Days.

No photography. Obligatory. Limited. On leads.

CLUMBER PARK

CLUMBER PARK, WORKSOP, NOTTINGHAMSHIRE S80 3AZ

www.clumber-park.org.uk

Tel: 01909 544917 **Fax:** 01909 500721 **Email:** clumberpark@nationaltrust.org.uk

Owner: National Trust **Contact:** Visitor Enquiries Point

Once the country estate of the Dukes of Newcastle, today Clumber offers freedom to discover a haven for wildlife within glimpses of its grand past – from the 'cathedral in miniature' and pleasure ground to the Walled Kitchen Garden where you can experience sights, scents and a taste of the past.

Location: MAP 7:B2, OS120 Ref SK625 745. 4.5m SE of Worksop, 6½m SW of Retford, just off A1/A57 via A614. 11m from M1/J30.

Open: Parkland and visitor facilities (Café, Shop, Plant Sales, The Clumber Story): throughout the year, daily. Walled Kitchen Garden: 12 Mar–30 Oct, daily. Chapel: as Visitor Facilities except 12 Jan–28 Mar when closed for conservation cleaning. Discovery and Exhibition Centre: as Visitor Facilities from Easter. Cycle Hire Centre: Jan–26 March, Sat, Sun & school holidays, 27 Mar–29 Oct, daily, 30 Oct–31 Dec, Sat, Sun & school holidays. See website or contact property for details.

Admission: Vehicle £5.50. Walled Kitchen Garden: Adults £3, children free. NT members free.

Special Events: Clumber holds a packed events programme throughout the year from open-air concerts to our ever-popular Christmas at Clumber. See website or contact property for details.

Licensed. WCs, level or ramped access to all buildings and grounds. Licensed. Special interest tours, including The Clumber Wildlife Safari, A Delve into Clumber's Past and A Taste of Tradition, are available for an additional fee. Booking essential. Around the Walled Kitchen Garden. Separate coach parking. Must be on leads in Walled Kitchen Garden, Pleasure Grounds and grazing areas.

HODSOCK PRIORY GARDENS

Blyth, Nr Worksop, Nottinghamshire S81 0TY

Tel: 01909 591204 **www.snowdrops.co.uk**

Owner: Sir Andrew & Lady Buchanan **Contact:** George Buchanan

"A magical sight you will never forget". Myriads of flowers in the 5-acre garden plus a half mile walk through the woodland with sheets of snowdrops. Banks of *hellebores*, carpets of pink *cyclamen*, ribbons of golden *aconites*, blue *irises*, the red, orange, green, black and white stems of *Acers*, *Cornus* and *Willows* and the heady fragrance of *sarcococca*. There is a clearly marked trail, with plenty of seats. Shortcuts are signed for those who prefer a shorter walk.

Location: MAP 7:B1, OS Ref. SK612 853. W of B6045 Worksop/Blyth road, 1m SW of Blyth, less than 2m from A1.

Open: Every day in February, 10am–4pm.

Admission: Adult £5, accompanied Child (6–16yrs) £1.

Heritage shop.

HOLME PIERREPONT HALL

Holme Pierrepont, Nr Nottingham NG12 2LD

Tel/Fax: 0115 933 2371 **www.holmepierreponthall.com**

Owner: Mr & Mrs Robin Brackenbury **Contact:** Robert Brackenbury

This charming 16th century manor house set in thirty acres of Park and gardens with a carved Charles II Staircase, family portraits and furniture is still lived in by descendents of the Pierrepont family. The Ball Room, Drawing Room and Long Gallery are available for functions on an exclusive basis. Filming welcome.

Location: MAP 7:B4, OS Ref. SK628 392. 5m ESE of central Nottingham. Follow signs to the National Water Sports Centre and continue for 1½m.

Open: The house is open every Sunday, Monday & Tuesday from 1 Feb–29 Mar 2011, 2–5pm. Also Hellebore Sunday, 6 Mar & Tulip Sun, 10 Apr 2011.

Admission: House & Garden: Adult £5, Child £1.50. Gardens only: Adult £3, Child £1.

No photography or video recording in house when open to the public. Groups welcome by appointment. Business and charity functions, wedding receptions, dinners, seminars and conferences. Please ring for details. In grounds on leads.

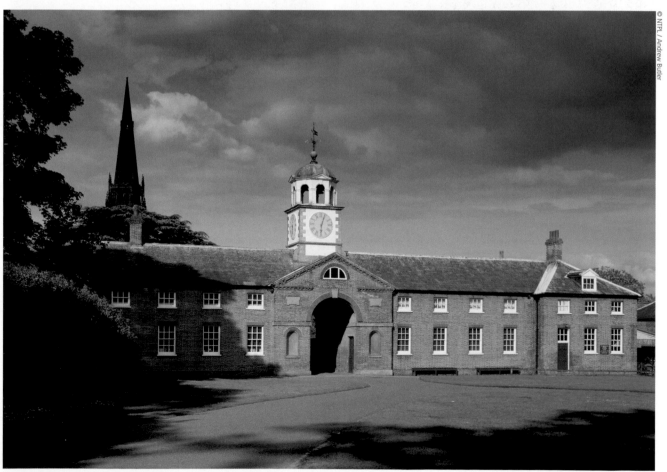

Clumber Park

NEWSTEAD ABBEY HISTORIC HOUSE & GARDENS

Newstead Abbey Park, Nottinghamshire NG15 8NA

Tel: 01623 455900 **Fax:** 01623 455904

www.mynottingham.gov.uk/newsteadabbey

Owner: Nottingham City Council **Contact:** Gillian Crawley

Historic home of the poet, Lord Byron, set in extensive formal gardens and parkland of 300 acres. See Byron's private apartments, period rooms and the medieval cloisters. The West Front of the Priory Church is a stunning local landmark.

Location: MAP 7:B3, OS Ref. SK540 639. 12m N of Nottingham 1m W of the A60 Mansfield Rd.

Open: House: 1 Apr–30 Sept: 12 noon–5pm, last adm. 4pm. Grounds: All year: 9am–6pm or dusk except for the last Friday in November and 25 Dec/1 Jan.

Admission: Please check website or ring the Abbey for admission prices.

By arrangement. On leads.

© Britaonview

Newstead Abbey

NOTTINGHAM CASTLE

Off Friar Lane, Nottingham NG1 6EL

Tel: 0115 9153700 **Fax:** 0115 9153653 **E-mail:** castle@ncmg.org.uk

www.mynottingham.gov.uk/nottinghamcastle

Owner: Nottingham City Council

17th century ducal mansion built on the site of the original medieval Castle. A vibrant museum and art gallery housing international collections and 15 centuries of Nottingham history plus exhibitions of contemporary and historical art. Tour the underground caves system. Special events take place throughout the year, please visit www.nottinghamcity.gov.uk/whatson.

Location: MAP 7:B4, OS Ref. SK569 395. Just SW of the city centre on hilltop.

Open: Tues–Sun 10am–5pm (4pm during winter). Closed 24–26 Dec & 1 Jan.

Admission: Joint admission with The Museum of Nottingham Life. Please call the castle on 0115 915 3700 for 2011 prices.

WCs. Caves.

PAPPLEWICK HALL

PAPPLEWICK, NOTTINGHAMSHIRE NG15 8FE

www.papplewickhall.co.uk

Tel: 0115 9632623 **E-mail:** mail@papplewickhall.co.uk

Owner/Contact: Mr & Mrs J R Godwin-Austen

A beautiful classic Georgian house, built of Mansfield stone, set in parkland, with woodland garden laid out in the 18th century. The house is notable for its very fine plasterwork, and elegant staircase. Grade I listed.

Location: MAP 7:B3, OS Ref. SK548 518. Half way between Nottingham & Mansfield, 3m E of M1/J27. A608 & A611 towards Hucknall. Then A6011 to Papplewick and B683 N for ½m.

Open: 1st, 3rd & 5th Wed in each month 2–5pm, and by appointment.

Admission: Adult £5. Groups (10+): £4.

No photography. Obligatory. Limited for coaches. In grounds on leads.

© English Heritage Photo Library

Rufford Abbey

RUFFORD ABBEY

Rufford, Newark, Nottinghamshire NG22 9DF

Tel: 01623 821338 **E-mail:** customers@english-heritage.org.uk

www.english-heritage.org.uk/ruffordabbey

Owner: English Heritage **Contact:** Nottinghamshire County Council

The remains of a 17th century country house; built on the foundations of a 12th century Cistercian Abbey, set in Rufford Country Park.

Location: MAP 7:B3, OS120, SK645 646. 2m S of Ollerton off A614.

Open: All year, daily, from 10am–5pm. Closed 25 Dec. Please call for full opening times and other site facilities.

Admission: Free – parking charge applies. Opening times and prices are valid until 31st March 2011, after this date details are subject to change please see www.english-heritage.org.uk for the most up-to-date information.

Picnickers welcome. WC.

THRUMPTON HALL

THRUMPTON, NOTTINGHAM NG11 0AX

www.thrumptonhall.com

Tel: 07590818045 **E-mail:** enquiries@thrumptonhall.com

Owner: Miranda Seymour **Contact:** Debbie Knox

Magnificent lakeside Jacobean house, built in 1607. Priest's hiding hole, carved Charles II staircase, panelled saloon, Byron memorabilia. Large lawns separated from landscaped park by ha-ha. Personal tours are led by family members. Dining room with capacity for 50 silver service or buffet for 100. Beautiful lakeside Pavilion for up to 250. Free access for coach drivers.

Location: MAP 7:A5, OS Ref. SK508 312. 7m S of Nottingham, 3m E M1/J24, 1m from A453, 4m from East Midlands Airport.

Open: By appointment throughout the year. Groups of (20+) 10.30am–6pm.

Admission: Adult £10, Child £3.50.

Wedding receptions, conferences, events. Ground floor & grounds. WC. Unlimited. In grounds, on leads.

WINKBURN HALL

Winkburn, Newark, Nottinghamshire NG22 8PQ

Tel: 01636 636465 **Fax:** 01636 636717

Owner/Contact: Richard Craven-Smith-Milnes Esq

A fine William and Mary house.

Location: MAP 7:C3, OS Ref. SK711 584. 8m W of Newark 1m N of A617.

Open: Throughout the year by appointment only.

Admission: £6.

WOLLATON HALL & DEER PARK

Wollaton, Nottingham, Nottinghamshire NG8 2AE

Tel: 0115 915 3900 **E-mail:** wollaton@ncmg.org.uk

www.mynottingham.gov.uk/wollatonhall

Owner: Nottingham City Council **Contact:** The Manager

A stunning Elizabethan, Grade I listed building. Sat on a hillside with beautiful views a 500 acre historic deer park, it is home to red and fallow deer. Historic house runs a variety of tours plus houses a Natural History Museum. Events held regularly – please visit www.mynottingham.gov.uk/whatson

Location: MAP 7:B4, OS Ref. SK532 392. Wollaton Park, Nottingham. 3m W of city centre.

Open: All year, daily.

Admission: Free. Car parking charge of £2 per car applies. Admission payable for some events and tours.

Special Events: Armed Forces weekend - June. Splendour pop festival - July. Children's/family events - Summer. Spooky Ghost Tours - Oct/Nov. Magical christmas markets - December.

WCs. By arrangement. In grounds.

See which properties offer **educational facilities** or **school visits** in our index at the end of the book.

Hodsock Priory Gardens

Eastnor Castle © HHG – Peter Smith of Newbery Smith Photography

Heart of England

Shakespeare's birthplace of Stratford-upon-Avon justly receives thousands of visitors each year, but travel further west too, into the gloriously unspoilt counties of Herefordshire and Worcestershire. Surrounded by the Malvern Hills, the fairytale Eastnor Castle has something to interest all visitors, whilst the fully restored Trentham Gardens offer something for everybody including "Barfuss Park" – Britain's first barefoot walk.

Ludlow Castle, Shropshire

Herefordshire

Shropshire

Staffordshire

Warwickshire

West Midlands

Worcestershire

STAFFORDSHIRE

SHROPSHIRE

WEST MIDLANDS

WORCESTERSHIRE

WARWICKSHIRE

HEREFORDSHIRE

Selly Manor, West Midlands

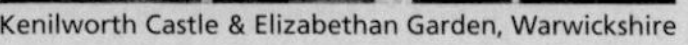

Kenilworth Castle & Elizabethan Garden, Warwickshire

■ **Owner**

Mr J Hervey-Bathurst

■ **Contact**

Castle Office
Eastnor Castle
Nr Ledbury
Herefordshire HR8 1RL

Tel: 01531 633160
Fax: 01531 631776
E-mail: enquiries@eastnorcastle.com

■ **Location**

MAP 6:M10
OS Ref. SO735 368

2m SE of Ledbury on the A438 Tewkesbury road. Alternatively M50/J2 & from Ledbury take the A449/A438.

Tewkesbury 20 mins, Malvern 20 mins, Gloucester 25 mins, Hereford 25 mins, Worcester 30 mins, Cheltenham 30 mins, B'ham 1 hr, London 2¼ hrs.

Taxi: Richard James 07836 777196.

■ **Opening Times**

Easter Weekend: Fri 22, Sat 23, Sun 24 & BH Mon 25 April.
May Bank Holiday Weekends: Sun 1/Mon 2 & Sun 29/Mon 30 May.
Every Sunday from 5 June–25 September.
Sun–Thurs from 17 July–31 August.

■ **Admission**

Summer

Castle & Grounds

Adult	£8.75
Child (5–15yrs)	£5.75
OAP	£7.75
Family (2+3)	£23.25

Grounds only

Adult	£5.75
Child (5–15yrs)	£3.75
OAP	£4.75
Family (2+3)	£15.25

Groups (20+)	
Guided	£10.75
Freeflow	£7.25
Schools	£6.25

Privilege Pass

Valid for 1 year and includes all Castle special events (apart from theatre productions)

Adult	£22.00
Child (5–15yrs)	£14.00
OAP	£19.50
Family (2+3)	£58.00

■ **Special Events**

See website for further details.

Conference/Function

ROOM	SIZE	MAX CAPACITY
Great Hall	16 x 8m	150
Dining Rm	11 x 7m	80
Gothic Rm	11 x 7m	80
Octagon Rm	9 x 9m	50

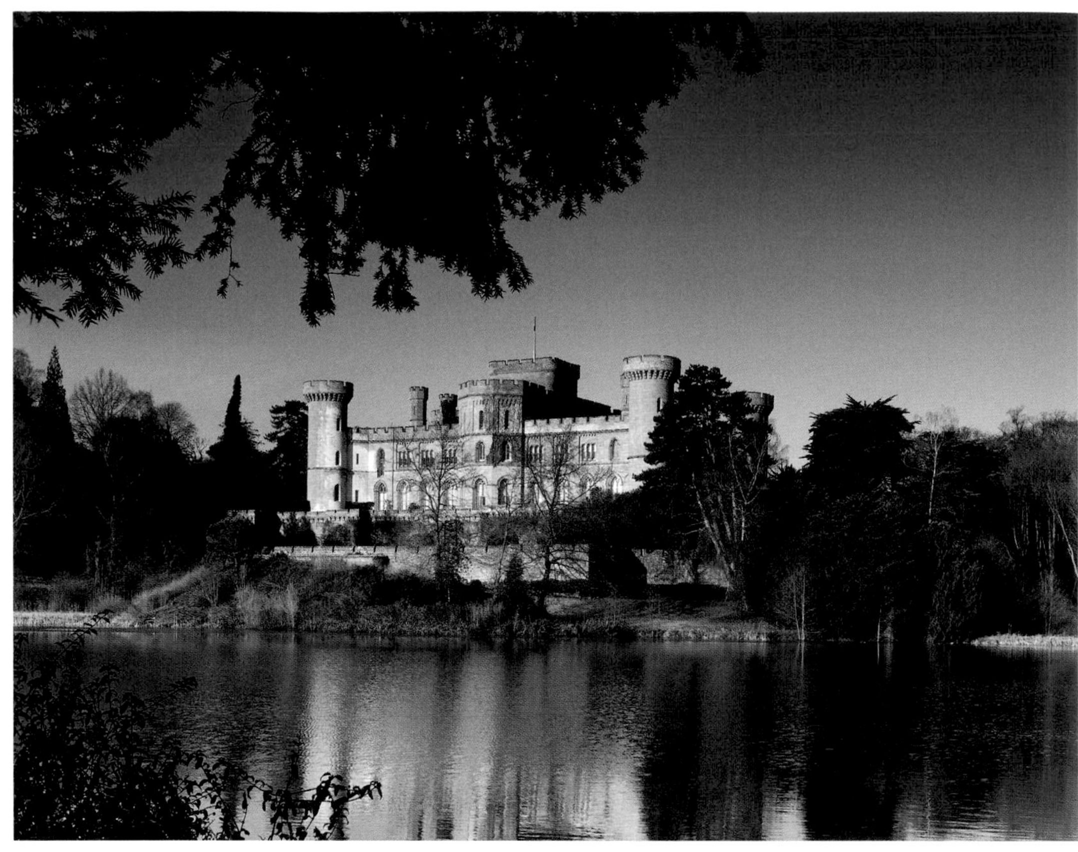

EASTNOR CASTLE

www.eastnorcastle.com

In the style of a medieval Welsh-border fortress, Eastnor Castle was built in the early 19th century by John First Earl Somers and is a good example of the great Norman and Gothic revival in architecture of that time. The Castle is dramatically situated in a 5000 acre estate in the Malvern Hills and remains the family home of the Hervey-Bathursts, his direct descendants.

This fairytale home is as dramatic inside as it is outside. A vast, 60' high Hall leads to a series of State Rooms including a Gothic Drawing Room designed by Pugin, with its original furniture, and a Library in the style of the Italian Renaissance, with views across the Lake. The Hervey-Bathursts have lovingly restored the interiors and many of the Castle's treasures which have been buried away in the cellars and attics since the Second World War – early Italian Fine Art, medieval armour, 17th century Venetian furniture, Flemish tapestries and paintings by Van Dyck, Reynolds, Romney and Watts and early photographs by Julia Margaret Cameron.

Gardens

Castellated terraces descend to a 21 acre lake with a restored lakeside walk. The arboretum holds a famous collection of mature specimen trees. There are spectacular views of the Malvern hills across a 300 acre deer park, once part of a mediaeval chase and now designated a Site of Special Scientific Interest.

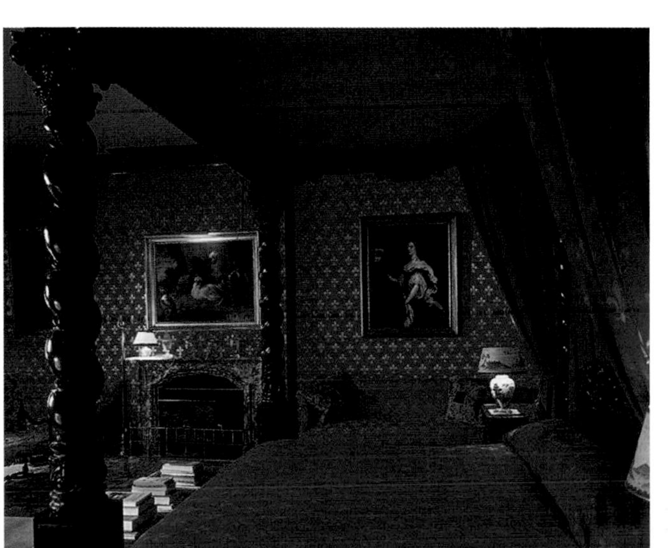

Knight's maze, tree trail, children's adventure playground, junior assault course. Corporate events – off-road driving, country pursuits, outside adventure days, private dinners, exclusive hire, public events.

Gift shop open on public open days, also on-line shop.

Exclusive use for weddings, private and corporate events. Product launches, TV and feature films, concerts and charity events.

Wheelchair stairclimber to main State rooms. DVD tour of first floor rooms. Visitors may alight at the Castle. Priority parking.

Licensed.

By arrangement, Mons & Tues all year, outside normal opening hours.

Ample 10–200 yds from Castle. Coaches phone in advance to arrange parking & catering. Tearoom voucher for drivers/courier.

Guides available.

On leads.

Exclusive use accommodation.

Exclusive use for weddings.

ABBEY DORE COURT GARDEN

Abbey Dore, Herefordshire HR2 0AD

Tel/Fax: 01981 240419

Owner/Contact: Mrs C L Ward

A peaceful 6 acre plant and bird lovers' garden with many contrasting areas. These include formal purple, gold and silver borders, an interesting walled garden, many herbaceous borders and a river walk leading to a further 5 acre meadow with unusual trees. Small nursery of herbaceous perennials.

Location: MAP 6:K10, OS Ref. SO387 309. 3 m W of A465 midway between Hereford and Abergavenny.

Open: Apr–Sept: Visitors welcome any day but must telephone first. Groups by arrangement.

Admission: Adult £3.50, Child £1. (May vary).

BERRINGTON HALL

Berrington Hall, Nr Leominster, Herefordshire HR6 0DW

Tel: 01568 615721 **Fax:** 01568 613263

Owner: National Trust **Contact:** The Property Manager

Austere exterior belies the lavishness of the interior.

Location: MAP 6:L8, OS137 SP510 637. 3m N of Leominster, 7m S of Ludlow on W side of A49.

EASTNOR CASTLE

See page 294 for full page entry.

For **accommodation** in the Heart of England, see our special index at the end of the book.

© English Heritage

GOODRICH CASTLE

ROSS-ON-WYE HR9 6HY

www.english-heritage.org.uk/goodrich

Tel: 01600 890538 **Email:** customers@english-heritage.org.uk

Owner: English Heritage **Contact:** Visitor Operations Team

Dramatically set on a rocky outcrop with stunning views over the Wye Valley, Goodrich Castle gives a fascinating insight into life in a medieval castle. Climb to the battlements for wonderful views and learn about the murder holes built into the castle walls. Finally, relax in our delightful castle café.

Location: MAP 6:L11, OS162 Ref. SO577 200. 5m S of Ross-on-Wye, off A40.

Open: 1 Apr–30 Jun: daily, 10am–5pm. 1 Jul–31 Aug: daily, 10am–6pm. 1 Sep–31 Oct: daily, 10am–5pm. 1 Nov–28 Feb '11: Wed–Sun, 10am–4pm. 1–31 Mar: Wed–Sun, 10am–5pm. Closed 24–26 Dec & 1 Jan.

Admission: Adult £5.50, Child £2.80, Conc. £4.70, Family £13.80. 15% discount for groups (11+). EH Members Free. Opening times and prices are valid until 31st March 2011, after this date details are subject to change please visit www.english-heritage.org.uk for the most up-to-date information.

WC. Guidebooks. Hazardous. Ovp. Family learning resources available. On leads.

HELLENS

MUCH MARCLE, LEDBURY, HEREFORDSHIRE HR8 2LY

Tel: 01531 660504

Owner: Pennington-Mellor-Munthe Charity Trust **Contact:** The Administrator

Built as a monastery and then a stone fortress in 1292 by Mortimer, Earl of March, with Tudor, Jacobean and Stuart additions and lived in ever since by descendants of the original builder. Visited by the Black Prince, Bloody Mary and the 'family ghost'. Family paintings, relics and heirlooms from the Civil War and possessions of the Audleys, Walwyns and Whartons as well as Anne Boleyn. Also beautiful 17th century woodwork carved by the 'King's Carpenter', John Abel. All those historical stories incorporated into guided tours, revealing the loves and lives of those who lived and died here. Goods and chattels virtually unchanged.

Location: MAP 6:M10, OS Ref. SO661 332. Off A449 at Much Marcle. Ledbury 4m, Ross-on-Wye 4m.

Open: 24 Apr–2 Oct: Wed, Thur, Sun & BH Mons. Guided tours only at 2pm, 3pm & 4pm. Other times by arrangement with the Administrator.

Admission: Adult £6, Child £3, Concession £4.50, Family £12.

No photography inside house. Partial. Obligatory.

In grounds, on leads.

Hereford Cathedral

HEREFORD CATHEDRAL

Mappa Mundi and Chained Library Exhibition. Hereford HR1 2NG

Tel: 01432 374202 **Fax:** 01432 374220 **E-mail:** visits@herefordcathedral.org

Contact: The Visits Manager **www: herefordcathedral.org**

Built on a place of worship used since Saxon times, Hereford Cathedral contains some of the finest examples of architecture from Norman times to the present day. The Mappa Mundi & Chained Library Exhibition houses the spectacular medieval map of the world and the Cathedral's unique Chained Library.

Location: MAP 6:L10, OS Ref. SO510 398. Hereford city centre on A49.

Open: Cathedral: Daily, 7.30am–Evensong. Exhibition: Easter–Oct: Mon–Sat, 10am–4.30pm. Nov–Easter: Mon–Sat, 10am–3.30pm. Sundays subject to change, please telephone to check before you visit.

***Admission:** Admission only for Mappa Mundi and Chained Library Exhibition: Adult £4.50, Child under 5yrs Free, Conc. £3.50. Family (2+3) £10. *2010 prices.

HERGEST CROFT GARDENS

KINGTON, HEREFORDSHIRE HR5 3EG

www.hergest.co.uk

Tel: 01544 230160 **Fax:** 01544 232031 **E-mail:** gardens@hergest.co.uk

Owner: E J Banks **Contact:** Mrs Melanie Lloyd

From spring bulbs to autumn colour, Hergest Croft is a garden for all seasons. Four distinct gardens with over 5,000 rare shrubs and trees are sure to delight everyone. Rhododendrons in Park Wood and azaleas in the Azalea Garden are spectacular in spring. The large Kitchen Garden contains long colourful herbaceous borders, the Rose Garden, Spring Border and unusual vegetables. Autumn colour is superb.

Location: MAP 6:J9, OS Ref. SO281 565. On W side of Kington. ½ m off A44, left at Rhayader end of bypass. Turn right and the car park is ½ m on right. Signposted from bypass.

Open: March: Sats & Suns. 2 Apr–30 Oct: daily, 12noon–5.30pm. Season tickets and groups by arrangement throughout the year.

Admission: Adult £6, Child (under 16yrs) Free. Pre-booked groups (20+) £5. Season ticket £25.

Special Events: Flower Fair, Mon 2 May 10.30am–5pm. Plant Fair, Sun 16 Oct 10.30am–4.30pm. Contact website for other events.

Rare plants. Partial. WCs. By arrangement On leads. Guide Dogs only.

KINNERSLEY CASTLE

Kinnersley, Herefordshire HR3 6QF

Tel: 01544 327407 **E-mail:** katherina@kinnersleycastle.co.uk

www.kinnersleycastle.co.uk

Owner/Contact: Katherina Garratt-Adams

Marches castle renovated around 1580. Still a family home; many interesting owners with unusual connections. Fine plasterwork solar ceiling. Organic gardens with specimen trees including one of Britain's largest gingkos.

Location: MAP 6:K9, OS Ref. SO3460 4950. Situated on A4112 Leominster to Brecon road, castle driveway lies behind village sign approaching from the north.

Open: Contact local Tourist Information Office or check Kinnersley Castle website end of March.

Admission: Adult £4.50. Child £2. Concs. & Groups over 8: £3.50.

No indoor photography. Coach parties by arrangement. Partial. Obligatory. Ample for cars. Limited for coaches.

© Britainonview

Hergest Croft Gardens

LANGSTONE COURT

Llangarron, Ross on Wye, Herefordshire HR9 6NR

Tel: 01989 770254

Owner/Contact: R M C Jones Esq

Mostly late 17th century house with older parts. Interesting staircases, panelling and ceilings.

Location: MAP 6:L11, OS Ref. SO534 221. Ross on Wye 5m, Llangarron 1m.

Open: 20 May–31 Aug: Wed & Thur, 11am–2.30pm, also spring & summer BHs.

Admission: Free.

LONGTOWN CASTLE ⌗

Abbey Dore, Herefordshire

Tel: 01299 896636 **E-mail:** customers@english-heritage.org.uk

www.english-heritage.org.uk/longtowncastle

Owner: English Heritage **Contact:** Visitor Operations Team

An unusual cylindrical keep, perched atop a large earthen motte, built c1200, with walls 15ft thick. There are magnificent views of the nearby Black Mountains.

Location: MAP 6:K10, OS161 Ref. SO321 291. 4m WSW of Abbey Dore.

Open: Any reasonable time.

Admission: Free. Opening times and prices are valid until 31st March 2011, after this date details are subject to change please visit www.english-heritage.org.uk for the most up-to-date information.

On leads.

OLD SUFTON

Mordiford, Hereford HR1 4EJ

Tel: 01432 870268/850328 **Fax:** 01432 850381 **E-mail:** jameshereford@waitrose.com

Owner: Trustees of Sufton Heritage Trust **Contact:** Mr & Mrs J N Hereford

A 16th century manor house which was altered and remodelled in the 18th and 19th centuries and again in this century. The original home of the Hereford family (see Sufton Court) who have held the manor since the 12th century.

Location: MAP 6:L10, OS Ref. SO575 384. Mordiford, off B4224 Mordiford– Dormington road.

Open: By written appointment to Sufton Court or by fax or email.

Admission: Adult £3, Child 50p.

Partial. Obligatory. Small school groups. No special facilities.

ROTHERWAS CHAPEL ⌗

Herefordshire, Rotherwas Chapel

Tel: 01299 896636 **E-mail:** customers@english-heritage.org.uk

www.english-heritage.org.uk/rotherwas

Owner: English Heritage **Contact:** Visitor Operations Team

This Roman Catholic chapel, dating from the 14th and 16th centuries, is testament to the past grandeur of the Bodenham family and features an interesting mid-Victorian side chapel and High Altar.

Location: MAP 6:L10, OS149 Ref. SO536 383. 1.5m SE of Hereford on B4399, left into Chapel Road.

Open: Any reasonable time. Key keeper located at nearby filling station.

Admission: Free. Opening times and prices are valid until 31st March 2011, after this date details are subject to change please visit www.english-heritage.org.uk for the most up-to-date information.

SUFTON COURT

Mordiford, Hereford HR1 4LU

Tel: 01432 870268/850328 **Fax:** 01432 850381 **E-mail:** jameshereford@waitrose.com

Owner: J N Hereford **Contact:** Mr & Mrs J N Hereford

Sufton Court is a small Palladian mansion house. Built in 1788 by James Wyatt for James Hereford. The park was laid out by Humphrey Repton whose 'red book' still survives. The house stands above the rivers Wye and Lugg giving impressive views towards the mountains of Wales.

Location: MAP 6:L10, OS Ref. SO574 379. Mordiford, off B4224 on Mordiford– Dormington road.

Open: 17–30 May & 16–29 Aug: 2–5pm. Guided tours: 2, 3 and 4pm.

Admission: Adult £5, Child 50p.

Obligatory. Only small coaches. Small school groups. No special facilities.

In grounds, on leads.

© Britainonview / Joanna Henderson

Eastnor Castle

■ **Owner**

National Trust

■ **Contact**

The Property Administrator
Attingham Park
Shrewsbury
Shropshire
SY4 4TP

Infoline: 01743 708123
Tel: 01743 708162
Fax: 01743 708155
E-mail: attingham @nationaltrust.org.uk

■ **Location**

MAP 6:L6
OS Ref. 127 SJ837 083

4m SE of Shrewsbury on N side of B4380 in Atcham village.

■ **Opening Times**

Mansion
12 March–30 October: Daily 11am–1pm guided tours only.
1–5.30pm free flow.
Last admission 4.30pm.

Weekend Winter Tours:
8 January–6 March & 5–27 November
Sat and Sun 11am–2pm.

Mansion Christmas opening:
10–23 December, 11am–4.30pm.
Last admission 3.30pm

Park, Walled Garden and Café:
Daily except Christmas Day, 9am–6pm (5pm or dusk if earlier in Jan, Feb, Nov, Dec).

■ **Admission**

NT Members and under 5s free.

House & Grounds	
Adult	£9.90
Child	£5.80
Family	£22.00
Park & Walled Garden	
Adult	£4.50
Child	£2.40
Family	£11.40
Groups discount: 15%	

Admission price includes voluntary Gift Aid donation.
Gift Aid is not included in Group prices.

©NTPL / Matthew Antrobus

ATTINGHAM PARK

www.nationaltrust.org.uk/attinghampark

Attingham Park reflects the Regency splendour of England with richly furnished rooms and is surrounded by beautiful parkland, designed by the renowned Humphry Repton, complete with walled garden and deer park which is home to a herd of fallow deer.

Over five generations of Berwicks lived at Attingham but their legacy is both astounding and enduring. The Lord Berwicks left a Georgian mansion with intricate decoration, Regency furniture and art, luxurious stables and a walled garden, deer park and estate in the fertile valley of the River Severn. But physical structures are only part of the story – Attingham has been the setting for romantic love and despair, for astutely accumulated fortunes, followed by flamboyant overspending and bankruptcy, decay and desertion. It has seen times of careful repair and enforced economies, of expansion and decline, of innovation and restoration. It is a story of love and neglect, of changing fortunes, revival and rediscovery.

©NTPL / David Levenson

More recently Attingham has experienced some stunning developments inside the mansion and the walled garden as part of the Attingham Re-discovered project of conservation and restoration. Mansion highlights include the atmospheric Dining Room, set for an evening banquet, and the contrasting decoration of the delicate feminine Boudoir with the rich, opulent textiles of the masculine Octagon Room. Bringing the walled garden back to life is an exciting prospect. The glasshouses and the vinery have been repaired and the gardeners' bothay has been restored and is once more the head gardener's office as well as a demonstration potting area with interpretation about the history of the garden and its features.

Situated in 500 acres of wonderful parkland Attingham boasts magnificent walks along the River Tern and through the Deer Park that take in picturesque views of the Wrekin and Shropshire Hills.

Attingham hosts a diverse events programme throughout the year, both inside the house and in the Park.

Attingham Re-discovered conservation and restoration programme. Conservation in Action demonstrations and tours. Range of walks around the park. Attingham Estate produce including venison and vegetables from the walled garden for sale when in season. No photography or filming in house. No unaccompanied children.

Includes plants grown by volunteers.

Grounds accessible. House partial access including Lower Ground and Ground Floor that include main show rooms. WC. Mobility scooters and wheelchairs available to loan.

Mansion Tearooms and Carriage House Café. Licensed.

Available from 11am. Can be booked upon arrival. Private Guided Tours for coach parties / social groups must be pre-booked.

P

Large range of guided and self-guide educational tours on offer. Pre-booking essential.

Dogs welcome. Must be on leads in designated areas in park. Only assistance dogs permitted in house.

Full range of special events. Please see website for details.

South-Side of the House

WESTON PARK

www.weston-park.com

Weston Park is a magnificent Stately Home and Parkland situated on the Shropshire / Staffordshire border. The former home of the Earls of Bradford, the park is now held in trust for the nation by the Weston Park Foundation.

Built in 1671 by Lady Elizabeth Wilbraham, this warm and welcoming house boasts internationally important paintings, including work by Van Dyck, Gainsborough and Stubbs, furniture and objets d'art, providing continued interest and enjoyment for all its visitors.

Step outside to enjoy the 1,000 acres of glorious Parkland, take one of a variety of woodland and wildlife walks, all landscaped by the legendary 'Capability' Brown in the 18th century.

Relax in the Stables Coffee Bar with coffee, sandwiches and homemade cake. With the exciting Woodland Adventure Playground, Orchard and Deer Park, as well as the Miniature Railway, there is so much for children to do.

The Granary Farm Shop stocks the best in locally produced food and drink and the Art Gallery stages a series of exciting changing exhibitions throughout the year.

The Granary Grill, Bar & Restaurant sizzles up lunch and dinner seven days a week and is open all year round.

The Drawing Room

Granary Farm Shop

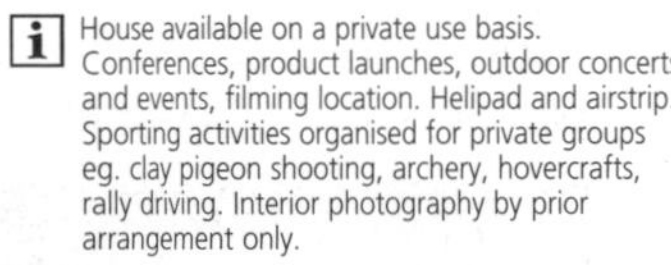
House available on a private use basis. Conferences, product launches, outdoor concerts and events, filming location. Helipad and airstrip. Sporting activities organised for private groups eg. clay pigeon shooting, archery, hovercrafts, rally driving. Interior photography by prior arrangement only.

Gift Shop.

Full event organisation service. Residential parties, special dinners, wedding receptions. Dine and stay arrangements in the house on selected dates.

House and part of the grounds. WCs.

Licensed.

The Stables provides light snacks. Licensed. Granary Grill, Bar & Restaurant.

By arrangement.

Ample free parking.

Award-winning educational programme available during all academic terms. Private themed visits aligned with both National Curriculum and QCA targets.

In grounds, on leads.

Weston Park offers 28 delightful bedrooms with bathrooms (25 doubles & 3 singles) 17 en suite.

Owner

The Weston Park Foundation

Contact

Kate Thomas
Weston Park
Weston-under-Lizard
Nr Shifnal
Shropshire TF11 8LE

Tel: 01952 852100
Fax: 01952 850430
E-mail: enquiries@weston-park.com

Location

MAP 6:N6
OS Ref. SJ808 107

Birmingham 40 mins. Manchester 1 hr. Motorway access M6/J12 or M54/J3 and via the M6 Toll road J11A. House situated on A5 at Weston-under-Lizard.

Rail: Nearest Railway Stations:Wolverhampton, Stafford or Telford.

Air: Birmingham, West Midlands, Manchester.

Opening Times

Open daily from Saturday 28 May–Sunday 4 Sept. Except 17–24 Aug. House is closed on Saturdays.

Admission

House, Park & Gardens

Adult	£8.00
Child (3–14yrs)	£5.50
OAP	£7.00
Family (2+3 or 1+4)	£20.00

Park & Gardens

Adult	£5.00
Child (3–14yrs)	£3.00
OAP	£4.50

Groups (Parks & Gardens)

Adult	£4.00
Child (3–14yrs)	£3.00
OAP	£4.00
House admission	+ £2.00

Granary Farm Shop & Art Gallery

Free entry
Open all year round

Granary Grill, Bar & Restaurant

Open daily, all year round, for lunch and dinner.

NB. Admission prices are correct at the time of going to print. Visitors are advised to telephone to confirm opening times and admission prices.

Conference/Function

ROOM	SIZE	MAX CAPACITY
Dining Rm	52' x 23'	90
Orangery	56'1" x 22'4"	120
Music Rm	55' x 17'	60
The Hayloft	32' x 22'	40
Doncaster	49' x 18'7"	80

SHROPSHIRE

ACTON BURNELL CASTLE

Acton Burnell, Shrewsbury, Shropshire
Tel: 01926 852078 **Email:** customers@english-heritage.org.uk
www.english-heritage.org.uk/actonburnellcastle
Owner: English Heritage **Contact:** Visitor Operations Administrative Assistant
The red sandstone shell of a semi-fortified tower house, built between 1284-93 by Bishop Burnell, Edward I's Chancellor. Parliaments were twice held here, in 1283 and 1285.
Location: MAP 6:L6, OS126, SJ534 019. In Acton Burnell, on unclassified road 8m S of Shrewsbury.
Open: Any reasonable time.
Admission: Free. Opening times and prices are valid until 31st March 2011, after this date details are subject to change please visit www.english-heritage.org.uk for the most up-to-date information.
On leads.

ATTINGHAM PARK

See page 298 for full page entry.

BENTHALL HALL

Benthall, Nr Broseley, Shropshire TF12 5RX
Tel: 01952 882159
www.nationaltrust.org.uk
Owner: National Trust **Contact:** The Custodian
A 16th century stone house with mullioned windows and moulded brick chimneys.
Location: MAP 6:M6, OS Ref. SJ658 025. 1m NW of Broseley (B4375), 4m NE of Much Wenlock, 1m SW of Ironbridge.

BUILDWAS ABBEY

Iron Bridge, Telford, Shropshire TF8 7BW
Tel: 01952 433274 **Email:** customers@english-heritage.org.uk
www.english-heritage.org.uk/buildwas
Owner: English Heritage **Contact**: Visitor Operations Team
Extensive remains of a Cistercian abbey built in 1135, set beside the River Severn against a backdrop of wooded grounds. The remains include the church which is almost complete except for the roof.
Location: MAP 6:M6, OS127, SJ643 043. On S bank of River Severn on A4169, 2m W of Ironbridge.
Open: 1 Apr–30 Sep: Wed–Sun & BH Mons, 10am–5pm.
Admission: Adult £3.20, Child £1.60, Conc. £2.70. EH Members free. Group discount available. Opening times and prices are valid until 31st March 2011, after this date details are subject to change please visit www.english-heritage.org.uk for the most up-to-date information.
Guidebooks. Hazardous. Ovp. On leads.

Benthall Hall

CLUN CASTLE

Clun, Ludlow, Shropshire
Tel: 01299 896636 **Email:** customers@english-heritage.org.uk
www.english-heritage.org.uk/cluncastle
Owner: English Heritage **Contact:** Visitor Operations Team
Remains of a four-storey keep and other buildings of this border castle are set in outstanding countryside, near the Welsh border. New information panels tell the story of the castle and the nearby town. Built in the 11th century.
Location: MAP 6:J7, OS137, SO299 809. In Clun, off A488, 18m W of Ludlow.
Open: Any reasonable time.
Admission: Free. Opening times and prices are valid until 31st March 2011, after this date details are subject to change please visit www.english-heritage.org.uk for the most up-to-date information.
Hazardous. Picnic area. Guidebooks (available from Stokesay Castle) On leads.

COMBERMERE ABBEY

Whitchurch, Shropshire SY13 4AJ
Tel: 01948 662880 **Fax:** 01948 871604
E-mail: estate@combermereabbey.co.uk **www.combermereabbey.co.uk**
Owner: Mrs S Callander Beckett **Contact:** Administrator
Combermere Abbey, its large mere and 1000 acre park began as a Cistercian monastery, remodelled as a Tudor manor house and in 1820 as a Gothic house. Group tours include the restored Walled Gardens, The Glasshouse and Fruit Tree Maze. Excellent accommodation is available on the Estate.
Location: MAP 6:L4, OS Ref. SJ599 434. 5m E of Whitchurch, off A530. Manchester, Liverpool and Birmingham airports 1hr.
Open: 22 Mar–26 May: Tues, Weds & Thurs only for tours, 12 noon, 2 & 4pm. Advance bookings necessary. Group visits (20–60) by arrangement. Available for corporate hospitality, meetings, location shoots, wedding and naming ceremonies in The Glasshouse. Please look at What's On/Abbey section on website for full events schedule.
Admission: On open days: Adult £5, Child (under 15yrs) £3. Group tours: £10 per person inclusive of refreshments.
Special Events: Combermere Abbey Annual Bluebell Walk and Open Gardens – Sunday May 15th 2011. 1–4.30pm. Refreshments, plant sale and estate produce stall. Dogs welcome. For the month of May 2011, Bluebell Guided Walks for groups of 20 or more (weekdays only) pre-booking essential – call the Estate Office for further information.
No photography. Partial. Obligatory. By arrangement
Limited for coaches. Guide dogs only. For groups.

COUND HALL

Cound, Shropshire SY5 6AH
Tel: 01743 761721 **Fax:** 01743 761722
Owner: Mr & Mrs D R Waller **Contact:** Mrs J Stephens
Queen Anne red brick Hall.
Location: MAP 6:L6, OS Ref. SJ560 053.
Open: 15–19 August 2011, 10am–4pm.
Admission: Adult £4.50, Child £2.30, Conc. £3.40, Family £11.30.
No photography. Limited.

DUDMASTON ESTATE

Quatt, Bridgnorth, Shropshire WV15 6QN
Tel: 01746 780866 **Fax:** 01746 780744
Owner: National Trust **Contact:** The House & Visitor Services Manager
Covers 3500 acres with Dudmaston Hall and gardens.
Location: MAP 6:M7, OS Ref. SO748 888. 4m SE of Bridgnorth on A442.

HAUGHMOND ABBEY

Upton Magna, Uffington, Shrewsbury, Shropshire SY4 4RW
Tel: 01743 709661 **Email:** customers@english-heritage.org.uk
www.english-heritage.org.uk/haughmond
Owner: English Heritage **Contact:** Visitor Operations Team
Extensive remains of a 12th century Augustinian abbey, including the Chapter House which retains its late medieval timber ceiling, and including some fine medieval sculpture. Pictorial interpretation boards guide the visitor, and an introductory exhibition displays archaeological finds.
Location: MAP 6:L5, OS126, SJ542 152. 3m NE of Shrewsbury off B5062.
Open: 1 Apr–30 Sept: Wed–Sun & BH Mons, 10am–5pm.
Admission: Adult £3.20, Child £1.60, Conc. £2.70. EH Members free. Group discount available. Opening times and prices are valid until 31st March 2011, after this date details are subject to change please visit www.english-heritage.org.uk for the most up-to-date information.
Guidebooks. Museum. Hazardous. Ovp. On leads.

HODNET HALL GARDENS

Hodnet, Market Drayton, Shropshire TF9 3NN

Tel: 01630 685786 **Fax:** 01630 685853

E-mail: secretary@heber-percy.freeserve.co.uk **www.hodnethallgardens.org**

Owner: Mr and the Hon Mrs A Heber-Percy **Contact:** Secretary

The 60+ acres are renowned as amongst the finest in the country. Forest trees provide a wonderful backdrop for formal gardens planted to give delight during every season, with extensive woodland walks amongst wild flowers and unusual flowering shrubs along the banks of a chain of ornamental pools.

Location: MAP 6:L5, OS Ref. SJ613 286. 12m NE of Shrewsbury on A53; M6/J15, M54/J3.

Open: 10 & 17 Apr. 24–25 Apr (Easter). 1–2 May (Bank Hol) & 8, 15, 22 & 29–30 (Bank Hol). 5 (Plant Hunters Fair), 12 & 19 (NGS Day) Jun. 3, 17 & 27 Jul. 7, 14, 17 & 28–29 August (Bank Hol). 11 & 25 Sept.

Admission: Adult £5. Children £2.50.

Groups of 25+ at other times by appointment. Partial. WCs. Educational package linked to Key Stages 1 & 2 of National Curriculum. On leads.

IRON BRIDGE

Ironbridge, Shropshire

Tel: 01926 852078 **Email:** customers@english-heritage.org.uk

www.english-heritage.org.uk/ironbridge

Owner: English Heritage **Contact:** Regional Head Office

The world's first iron bridge and Britain's best known industrial monument. Cast in Coalbrookdale by local ironmaster, Abraham Darby, it was erected across the River Severn in 1779. Iron Bridge is a World Heritage Site. Visit the recently refurbished Toll House on the Bridge, with interpretation displays.

Location: MAP 6:M6, OS127, SJ672 034. In Ironbridge, adjacent to A4169.

Open: Any reasonable time.

Admission: Free. Opening times and prices are valid until 31st March 2011, after this date details are subject to change please visit www.english-heritage.org.uk for the most up-to-date information.

LANGLEY CHAPEL

Acton Burnell, Shrewsbury, Shropshire

Tel: 01926 852078 **Email:** customers@english-heritage.org.uk

www.english-heritage.org.uk/langleychapel

Owner: English Heritage **Contact:** Visitor Operations Team

A delightful medieval chapel; tranquilly set all alone in the charming countryside. Its atmospheric interior contains a perfect set of 17th century timber furnishings including a musicians' pew.

Location: MAP 6:L6, OS126, SJ538 001. 11.5m S of Acton Burnell, on an unclassified road off the A49, 9 1/2m S of Shrewsbury.

Open: 1 Mar–31 Oct: daily, 10am–5pm; 1 Nov–28 Feb '11: daily, 10am-4pm, closed 24-26 Dec & 1 Jan.

Admission: Free. Opening times and prices are valid until 31st March 2011, after this date details are subject to change please visit www.english-heritage.org.uk for the most up-to-date information.

LILLESHALL ABBEY

Oakengates, Shropshire

Tel: 01926 852078 **Email:** customers@english-heritage.org.uk

www english-heritage.org.uk/lilleshallabbey

Owner: English Heritage **Contact:** Visitor Operations Team

Extensive ruins of an abbey of Augustinian canons including remains of the 12th and 13th century church and the cloister buildings. Surrounded by green lawns and ancient yew trees.

Location: MAP 6:M6, OS127, SJ738 142. On unclassified road off the A518, 4m N of Oakengates.

Open: 1 Apr–30 Sept: daily, 10am–5pm. 1 Oct–31 Mar: Closed.

Admission: Free. Opening times and prices are valid until 31st March 2011, after this date details are subject to change please visit www.english-heritage.org.uk for the most up-to-date information.

On leads.

Iron Bridge

Ludlow Castle

Castle House

LUDLOW CASTLE

CASTLE SQUARE, LUDLOW, SHROPSHIRE SY8 1AY

www.ludlowcastle.com

Tel: 01584 873355 **E-mail:** info@ludlowcastle.com

Owner: The Earl of Powis & The Trustees of the Powis Estates

Contact: Helen J Duce (Custodian)

This magnificent ruin, the heart of Ludlow, a medieval market town, dates from 1086. Extended over the centuries to a fortified Royal Palace and seat of the government for the Council of Wales and the Marches; privately owned by the Earls of Powis since 1811. In Castle House, the Castle Tea Rooms serve fresh locally-sourced foods. The Beacon Rooms are available for corporate events, exhibitions and Civil weddings. Three self-catering holiday apartments (each for four persons), finished to the highest standards, are the ideal accommodation for a stay in Ludlow. Tel: 01584 873355/874465 for more details.

Location: MAP 6:L8, OS Ref. SO509 745. Shrewsbury 28m, Hereford 26m. A49 centre of Ludlow.

Open: Jan & Dec: Sat & Sun, 10am–4pm, Feb–Mar & Oct–Nov: daily, 10am–4pm. Apr–Sept: daily, 10am–5pm (7pm Aug). Daily 26 Dec–1 Jan. Last adm. 30mins before closing. Closed Christmas Day.

Admission: Adult £5.00, Child £2.50, Conc. £4.50, Family £13.50. 10% reduction for groups (10+).

Partial. WCs Licensed. Licensed. By arrangement. None. In grounds, on leads. Rated 4*-5* enjoyEngland.com

© Britainonview

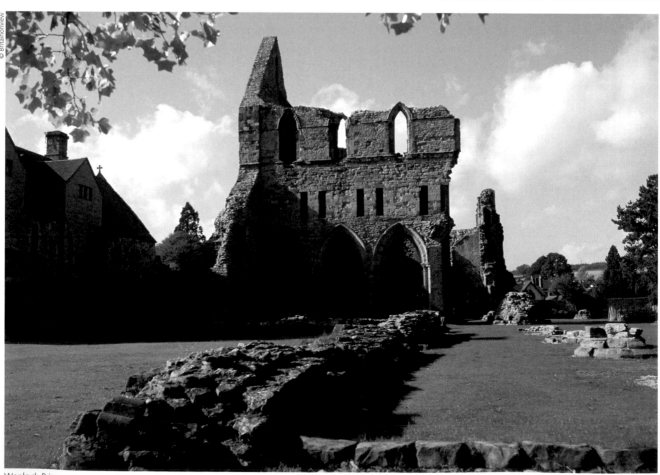

Wenlock Priory

LONGNER HALL

Uffington, Shrewsbury, Shropshire SY4 4TG

Tel: 01743 709215

Owner: Mr R L Burton **Contact:** Mrs R L Burton

Designed by John Nash in 1803, Longner Hall is a Tudor Gothic style house set in a park landscaped by Humphry Repton. The home of one family for over 700 years. Longner's principal rooms are adorned with plaster fan vaulting and stained glass.

Location: MAP 6:L6, OS Ref. SJ529 110. 4m SE of Shrewsbury on Uffington road, ¼m off B4380, Atcham.

Open: Apr–Sept: Tues & BH Mons, 2–5pm. Tours at 2pm & 3.30pm. Groups at any time by arrangement.

Admission: Adult £5, Child/OAP £3.

No photography in house. Partial. Obligatory. Limited for coaches. By arrangement. Guide dogs only.

MAWLEY HALL

CLEOBURY MORTIMER DY14 8PN

www.mawley.com

Tel: 0208 298 0429 **Fax:** 0208 303 0717 **E-mail:** administration@mawley.com

Owner: R Galliers-Pratt Esq **Contact:** Mrs R Sharp

Built in 1730 and attributed to Francis Smith of Warwick, Mawley is set in 18th century landscaped parkland with extensive gardens and walks down to the River Rea. Magnificent plasterwork and a fine collection of English and Continental furniture and porcelain.

Location: MAP 6:L8, OS137, SO688 753. 1m N of Cleobury Mortimer on the A4117 and 7m W of Bewdley.

Open: 11 Apr–14 Jul: Mons & Thurs, 3–5pm and throughout the year by appointment.

Admission: Adult £10, Child/OAP £6. Outside set opening dates and times all visitors £10.

By arrangement. In grounds, on leads.

MORETON CORBET CASTLE

Moreton Corbet, Shrewsbury, Shropshire

Tel: 01926 852078 **Email:** customers@english-heritage.org.uk

www.english-heritage.org.uk/moretoncorbetcastle

Owner: English Heritage **Contact:** Visitor Operations Team

A ruined medieval castle with the substantial remains of a splendid Elizabethan mansion, captured in 1644 from Charles I's supporters by Parliamentary forces. New information panels illustrate the 500 year history of the castle.

Location: MAP 6:L5, OS126, SJ561 231. In Moreton Corbet off B5063, 7m NE of Shrewsbury.

Open: Any reasonable time.

Admission: Free. Opening times and prices are valid until 31st March 2011, after this date details are subject to change please visit www.english-heritage.org.uk for the most up-to-date information.

Guidebooks available from Buildwas & Haughmond Abbeys.

MORVILLE HALL

Bridgnorth, Shropshire WV16 5NB

Tel: 01746 780838

Owner: National Trust **Contact:** Dr & Mrs C Douglas

An Elizabethan house of mellow stone, converted in the 18th century and set in attractive gardens.

Location: MAP 6:M7, OS Ref. SO668 940. Morville, on A458 3m W of Bridgnorth.

Open: By written appointment only with the tenants.

Admission: £3.50. NT members Free.

PREEN MANOR GARDENS

Church Preen, Church Stretton, Shropshire SY6 7LQ

Tel: 01694 771207

Owner/Contact: Mrs P Trevor-Jones

Six acre garden on site of Cluniac monastery, with walled, terraced, wild, water, kitchen and chess gardens. 12th century monastic church.

Location: MAP 6:L6, OS Ref. SO544 981. 10m SSE of Shrewsbury. 7m NE of Church Stretton, 6m SW of Much Wenlock.

Open: Dates vary under NGS. Ring for details.

Admission: Adult £3.50, Child 50p. (May change).

SHIPTON HALL

Much Wenlock, Shropshire TF13 6JZ

Tel: 01746 785225 **Fax:** 01746 785125

Owner: Mr J N R Bishop **Contact:** Mrs M J Bishop

Built around 1587 by Richard Lutwyche who gave the house to his daughter Elizabeth on her marriage to Thomas Mytton. Shipton remained in the Mytton family for the next 300 years. The house has been described as *'an exquisite specimen of Elizabethan architecture set in a quaint old fashioned garden, the whole forming a picture which as regards both form and colour, satisfies the artistic sense of even the most fastidious'*. The Georgian additions by Thomas F Pritchard include some elegant rococo interior decorations. There is some noteworthy Tudor and Jacobean panelling. Family home. In addition to the house visitors are welcome to explore the gardens, the dovecote and the parish church which dates back to Saxon times.

Location: MAP 6:L7, OS Ref. SO563 918. 7m SW of Much Wenlock on B4378. 10m W of Bridgnorth.

Open: Easter–end Sept: Thurs, 2.30–5.30pm. Also Suns and Mons of BH, 2.30–5.30pm. Last admission 5.00pm. Groups of 20+ at any time of day or year by prior arrangement.

Admission: Adult £5, Child (under 14yrs) £2.50. 10% Discount for groups (20+).

Unsuitable. By arrangement for groups (20+). Obligatory. Guide dogs only.

SHREWSBURY ABBEY

Shrewsbury, Shropshire SY2 6BS

Tel: 01743 232723 **Fax:** 01743 240172

Contact: Gillian Keates

Benedictine Abbey founded in 1083, tomb of Roger de Montgomerie and remains of tomb of St Winefride, 7th century Welsh saint. The Abbey was part of the monastery and has also been a parish church since the 12th century.

Location: MAP 6:L6, OS Ref. SJ499 125. Signposted from Shrewsbury bypass (A5 and A49). 500yds E of town centre, across English Bridge.

Open: All year. Mon–Sat 10.30am–2.30pm, Sun 11.30am–2.30pm.

Admission: Donation. For guided tours, please contact Abbey.

SHREWSBURY CASTLE & THE SHROPSHIRE REGIMENTAL MUSEUM

Castle Street, Shrewsbury SY1 2AT

Tel: 01743 358516 **E-mail:** shrewsburymuseum@shropshire.gov.uk

www.shrewsburymuseums.com

Owner: Shropshire Council **Contact:** Tim Jenkins

Norman Castle with 18th century work by Thomas Telford. The main hall houses The Shropshire Regimental Museum and displays on the history of the castle. Free admission to attractive floral grounds. Open-air theatre, music and events throughout the summer.

Location: MAP 6:L6, OS Ref. SJ495 128. Town centre, adjacent BR and bus stations.

Open: Please contact for 2011 details or visit the website.

Admission: Museum: Prices under review. Grounds: Free.

No photography. Partial. None. Guide dogs only.

SHREWSBURY MUSEUM & ART GALLERY (ROWLEY'S HOUSE)

Barker Street, Shrewsbury, Shropshire SY1 1QH
Tel: 01743 281205 **E-mail:** shrewsburymuseum@shropshire.gov.uk
www.shrewsburymuseums.com
Owner: Shropshire Council **Contact:** Tim Jenkins

Impressive 16th/17th century timber-framed building and attached 17th century brick mansion with displays of natural history, geology, archaeology, social history, fine and decorative arts. Also special exhibitions including contemporary art.

Location: OS Ref. SJ490 126.

Open: Please contact for 2011 details or visit the website.

Admission: Free.

No photography. Ground floor only. Adjacent public. Guide dogs only.

Clun Castle

For **special events** held throughout the year, see the index at the end of the book.

STOKESAY CASTLE ⌗

Nr CRAVEN ARMS, SHROPSHIRE SY7 9AH

www.english-heritage.org.uk/stokesaycastle

Tel: 01588 672544 **Email:** customers@english-heritage.org.uk
Owner: English Heritage **Contact:** Visitor Operations Team

Nestling in a green valley in the heart of Shropshire, Stokesay is England's most delightful fortified medieval manor. This beautiful house dates to the 11th century with a great hall that has remained unaltered since 1291. An audio tour will help to bring the history of the castle to life.

Location: MAP 6:K7, OS148, SO446 787. 7m NW of Ludlow off A49.

Open: 1 Apr–30 Sep: daily, 10am–5pm. 1–31 Oct: Wed–Sun, 10am–5pm. 1 Nov–28 Feb '11: Thur–Sun, 10am–4pm. 1–31 Mar: Wed–Sun, 10am–5pm. Closed 24–26 Dec & 1 Jan. Please note: castle may close early for functions. Please call to check.

Admission: Adult £5.50, Child £2.80, Conc. £4.70, Family £13.80. 15% discount for groups (11+). EH Members free. Opening times and prices are valid until 31st March 2011, after this date details are subject to change please visit www.english-heritage.org.uk for the most up-to-date information.

Guidebooks. Hazardous. Ovp. Family learning resources available.

STOKESAY COURT

ONIBURY, CRAVEN ARMS, SHROPSHIRE SY7 9BD

www.stokesaycourt.com

Tel: 01584 856238 **E-mail:** info@stokesaycourt.com
Owner/Contact: Ms Caroline Magnus

Unspoilt and secluded, Stokesay Court is an imposing late Victorian mansion with Jacobean style façade, magnificent interiors and extensive grounds containing a grotto, woodland and interconnected pools. Set deep in the beautiful rolling green landscape of South Shropshire near Ludlow, the house and grounds featured as the Tallis Estate in the award winning film 'Atonement'.

Location: MAP 6:K7, OS148, SO444 786. A49 Between Ludlow and Craven Arms.

Open: Guided tours all year for booked groups (20+). Groups (up to 60) can be accommodated. Tours for individuals take place on dates advertised on website. Booking essential. Tours are usually taken by the owner.

Admission: Adult £15pp to include light refreshments (full catering service available on request).

No stilettos. No photography in house. Partial. WCs. Obligatory. Guide dogs only. €

Stokesay Court

WENLOCK GUILDHALL

Much Wenlock, Shropshire TF13 6AE

Tel: 01952 727509

Owner/Contact: Much Wenlock Town Council

16th century half-timbered building has an open-arcade market area.

Location: MAP 6:L6, OS Ref. SJ624 000. In centre of Much Wenlock, next to the church.

Open: Apr–Oct: Mon–Sat, 10.30am–1pm & 2–4pm. Suns: 2–4pm.

Admission: Adult £1 (including guide), Child Free.

WENLOCK PRIORY

Much Wenlock, Shropshire TF13 6HS

Tel: 01952 727466 **Email:** customers@english-heritage.org.uk

www.english-heritage.org.uk/wenlockpriory

Owner: English Heritage **Contact:** Visitor Operations Team

The remains of this medieval monastery are set on the edge of beautiful Much Wenlock. The priory's grandeur can be traced in the ruins of its 13th century church, ornate Norman chapter house and rare monk's wash house. These majestic ruins are set in green lawns and topiary.

Location: MAP 6:L6, OS127, SJ625 001. In Much Wenlock.

Open: 1–30 Apr: Wed–Sun & BH Mons, 10am–5pm. 1 May–31 Aug: daily, 10am–5pm. 1 Sep–31 Oct: Wed–Sun, 10am–5pm. 1 Nov–28 Feb '11: Thur–Sun, 10am–4pm. 1–31 Mar: Wed–Sun & BH Mons, 10am–5pm. Closed 24–26 Dec & 1 Jan.

Admission: Adult £3.80, Child £1.90, Conc. £3.20. EH Members free. Group discount available. Opening times and prices are valid until 31st March 2011, after this date details are subject to change please visit www.english-heritage.org.uk for the most up-to-date information.

WC. Baby changing facilities. Gardens. Guidebooks. Ovp. On leads.

WESTON PARK

See page 299 for full page entry.

WROXETER ROMAN CITY

Wroxeter, Shrewsbury, Shropshire SY5 6PH

Tel: 01743 761330 **Email:** customers@english-heritage.org.uk

www.english-heritage.org.uk/wroxeter

Owner: English Heritage **Contact:** Visitor Operations Team

The part-excavated centre of the fourth largest city in Roman Britain, originally home to some 6,000 men and several hundred houses. Impressive remains of the 2nd century municipal baths. There is a site museum in which many finds are displayed, including those from work by Birmingham Field Archaeological Unit.

Location: MAP 6:L6, OS126, SJ565 087. At Wroxeter, 5m E of Shrewsbury, on B4380.

Open: 1 Apr–31 Oct: daily, 10am–5pm. 1 Nov–28 Feb '11: Wed–Sun, 10am–4pm. 1–31 Mar: daily, 10am–5pm. Closed 24–26 Dec & 1 Jan.

Admission: Adult £4.40, Child £2.20, Conc. £3.70, Family £11.00. EH Members free. Group discount available. Opening times and prices are valid until 31st March 2011, after this date details are subject to change please visit www.english-heritage.org.uk for the most up-to-date information.

WC. Museum. Hazard. Ovp. On leads.

See which properties offer **educational facilities** or **school visits** in our index at the end of the book.

THE ANCIENT HIGH HOUSE

Greengate Street, Stafford ST16 2JA

Tel: 01785 619131 **Fax:** 01785 619132 **E-mail:** ahh@staffordbc.gov.uk

www.staffordbc.gov.uk/heritage

Owner: Stafford Borough Council **Contact:** Mark Hartwell

Over four hundred years of history are waiting to be discovered within the walls of Stafford's Ancient High House – England's largest timber-framed town house and one of the finest Tudor buildings in the country. Now fully restored, the superb period room settings reflect its fascinating story.

Location: MAP 6:N5, OS Ref. SJ922 232. Town centre.

Open: All year: Tues–Sat, 10am–4pm.

Admission: Free. Check for events, charges may apply.

Unsuitable. By arrangement. School tours by arrangement.

Guide dogs only.

BIDDULPH GRANGE GARDEN

Grange Road, Biddulph, Staffordshire ST8 7SD

Tel: 01782 517999 **Fax:** 01782 510624 **E-mail:** biddulph.grange@nationaltrust.org.uk

www.nationaltrust.org.uk

Owner: National Trust **Contact:** The Garden Office

Amazing Victorian garden created by Darwin contemporary and correspondent James Bateman as an extension of his beliefs, scientific interests and collection of plants. Visit the Italian terrace, Chinese inspired garden, dahlia walk and the oldest surviving golden larch in Britain brought from China by the great plant hunter Robert Fortune.

Location: MAP 6:N3, OS Ref. SJ891 592. E of A527, 3½m SE of Congleton, 8m N of Stoke-on-Trent.

Open: 21–27 Feb, 10.30am–3.30pm, daily. 3–28 Mar, 10.30am–5.30pm, Thurs–Mon. 1 Apr–31 Oct, 10.30am–5.30pm, daily. 4 Nov–19 Dec, 10.30am–3.30pm, Fri–Mon.

Admission: Adults £7.35 (£6.68), Child £3.70 (£3.36), Family (2+3) £18.40 (£16.72), Groups (15+ people) £6.20. Gift aid prices displayed with standard admission in brackets. Winter admission prices apply from 4 Nov–19 Dec.

© English Heritage

BOSCOBEL HOUSE & THE ROYAL OAK

BISHOP'S WOOD, BREWOOD, STAFFORDSHIRE ST19 9AR

www.english-heritage.org.uk/boscobel

Tel: 01902 850244 **E-mail:** customers@english-heritage.org.uk

Owner: English Heritage **Contact:** Visitor Operations Team

This 17th century hunting lodge played a vital part in Charles II's escape from the Roundheads. See a descendant of the Royal Oak and 'priest-hole' in the attic, which both sheltered the fugitive future King from Cromwell's troops in 1651. Then explore Boscobel's more recent past as a Victorian farm.

Location: MAP 6:N6, OS127, SJ838 082. On unclassified road between A41 & A5. 8m NW of Wolverhampton.

Open: 1 Apr–31 Oct: Wed–Sun & BH Mons, 10am–5pm. Last entry 1hr before closing.

Admission: Adult £5.50, Child £2.80, Conc. £4.70, Family £13.80. EH Members free. Group discount available. Opening times and prices are valid until 31st March 2011, after this date details are subject to change please visit www.english-heritage.org.uk for the most up-to-date information.

Exhibition. Guidebooks. Pinic Area. Hazardous. Ovp.

© NTPL / Andrew Butler

Biddulph Grange Garden

© The Trentham Estate

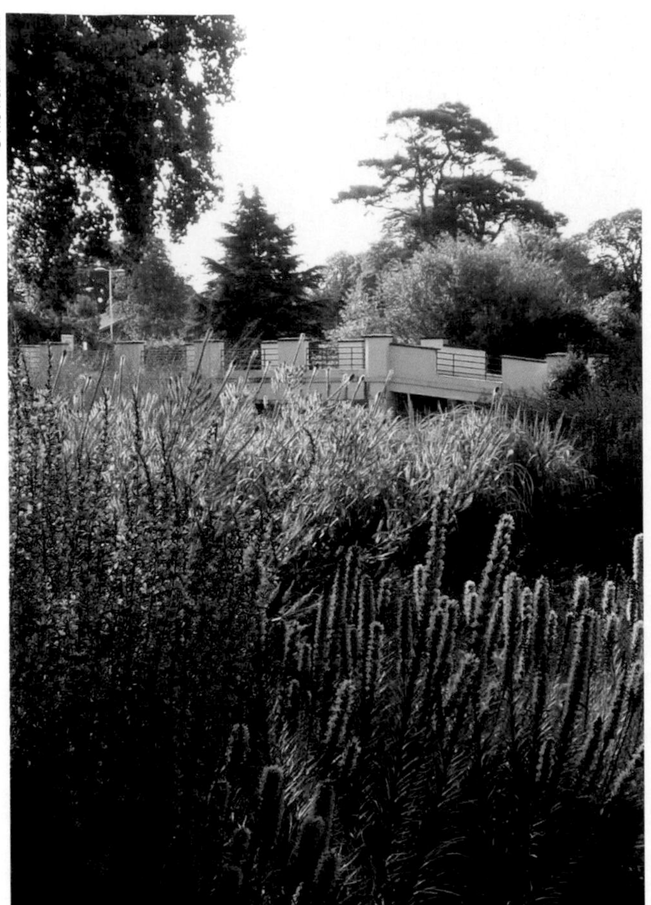

The Trentham Estate

CASTERNE HALL

Ilam, Nr Ashbourne, Derbyshire DE6 2BA

Tel: 01335 310489 **E-mail:** mail@casterne.co.uk **www.casterne.co.uk**

Owner/Contact: Charles Hurt

Manor house in beautiful location, a seat of the Hurt family for 500 years.

Location: MAP 6:O3, OS Ref. SK123 523. From Ilam take first turning on left N of village and continue past 'Casterne Farms only' sign.

Open: 22 Jun–29 July: weekdays only for tour at 2pm only.

Admission: £5.

Partial. Obligatory. Limited for coaches. Guide dogs only. €

giftaid it Some properties will be operating the Gift Aid on Entry scheme at their admission points. Where the scheme is operating, visitors are offered a choice between paying the standard admission price or paying the 'Gift Aid Admission' which includes a voluntary donation of at least 10%. Gift Aid Admissions enable the charity to reclaim tax on the whole amount paid* – an extra 28% – potentially a very significant boost to property funds. Money raised from paying visitors in this way will go towards restoration projects at the property and will be very welcome.
Where shown, the admission prices are inclusive of the 10% voluntary donation where properties are operating the Gift Aid on Entry scheme, but both the standard admission price and the Gift Aid Admission will be displayed at the property and on their website.

*Gift Aid donations must be supported by a valid Gift Aid declaration and a Gift Aid declaration can only cover donations made by an individual for him/herself or for him/herself and members of his/her family.

CHILLINGTON HALL

CODSALL WOOD, WOLVERHAMPTON, STAFFORDSHIRE WV8 1RE

www.chillingtonhall.co.uk

Tel: 01902 850236 **E-mail:** info@chillingtonhall.co.uk

Owner/Contact: Mr & Mrs J W Giffard

Home of the Giffards since 1178. Built during 18th century by Francis Smith of Warwick and John Soane. Park designed by 'Capability' Brown. Smith's Staircase, Soane's Saloon and the Pool (a lake of 70 acres) are splendid examples of the days of the Georgian landowner.

Location: MAP 6:N6, OS Ref. SJ864 067. 2m S of Brewood off A449. 4m NW of M54/J2. SAT NAV. (off) Port Lane Brewood.

Open: House: Mon–Thur, 11 Apr–26 May, 2–5pm. Last entry 4pm. Grounds: As House. Parties by separate arrangement.

Admission: Adult £6, Child £3. Grounds only: half price.

Partial. Obligatory. In grounds, on leads. €

THE DOROTHY CLIVE GARDEN

WILLOUGHBRIDGE, MARKET DRAYTON, SHROPSHIRE TF9 4EU

www.dorothyclivegarden.co.uk

Tel: 01630 647237 **Fax:** 01630 647902 **E-mail:** info@dorothyclivegarden.co.uk

Owner: The Willoughbridge Garden Trust **Contact:** Administrator

Stephen Lacey noted in The Garden under the title of 'The Season Starts Here' (RHS, March 2009); 'This 4.8ha (12 acre) hillside garden displays an extensive and discerningly chosen collection of perennials and bulbs around handsome scree and waterfall features. Highlights include the Quarry Garden's rhododendron and azalea collection'. The garden is quite simply a treasure trove for the plant enthusiast and a delightful discovery for the discerning garden visitor. Glorious, framed views to the surrounding countryside punctuate the garden at regular intervals; whilst a network of criss-crossing paths provide for a stimulating and fun walk.

Location: MAP 6:M4, OS Ref. SJ753 400. A51, 2m S of Woore, 3m from Bridgemere.

Open: Sat 19 Mar–Sun 25 Sept 2011, every day. 10am–5.30pm (last admissions at 4.30pm).

Admission: Adult £6, OAP £5, Child (u19) Free. Pre-booked Groups (20+) £4.50 per person.

Special Events: For all special fund-raising events visit the website at www.dorothyclivegarden.co.uk

Dogs on leads welcome. Wheelchairs available free of charge. WCs

By arrangement. On leads.

ERASMUS DARWIN HOUSE

Beacon Street, Lichfield, Staffordshire WA13 7AD

www.erasmusdarwin.org

Tel: 01543 306260 **Fax:** 01543 306261 **E-mail:** enquiries@erasmusdarwin.org

Owner: Erasmus Darwin Foundation **Contact:** Alison Wallis

Grandfather of Charles Darwin and a founder member of the Lunar Society, Erasmus Darwin (1731–1802) was a leading doctor, scientist, inventor and poet. This elegant Georgian house was his home and contains an exhibition of his life, theories and inventions. There is also an 18th century herb garden.

Location: MAP 6:P5, OS Ref. SK115 098. Situated at the West end of Lichfield Cathedral Close.

Open: Apr–Oct, Tues–Sun, 11am–5pm. Nov–Mar, Thur–Sun, 12–4.30pm. Check website or phone for details.

Admission: Adult £3, Conc. £2, Child £1.

WCs. By arrangement. Disabled only. Guide dogs only.

THE HEATH HOUSE

Tean, Stoke-on-Trent, Staffordshire ST10 4HA

Tel: 01538 723944 **E-mail:** ben.philips@theheathhouse.co.uk

Owner: Mr John Philips **Contact:** Mr Ben Philips

The Heath House is an early Victorian mansion designed and built 1836–1840 in the Tudor style for John Burton Philips. The collection of paintings is a rare survival and has remained undisturbed since its acquisition. It is still a Philips family home. Large attractive formal garden.

Location: MAP 6:O4, OS Ref. SK030 392. A522 off A50 at Uttoxeter 5m W, at Lower Tean turn right.

Open: Easter Monday & August BH Mons & 2 May–2 Jun Sun–Thur inc 2.30 to 5pm. Tours begin at 2.30. Teas by prior arrangement £3. Please telephone in advance to confirm visiting times.

Admission: £6. No Conc. No reductions for groups.

No photography or video recording. WCs. Obligatory.

IZAAK WALTON'S COTTAGE

Worston Lane, Shallowford, Nr Stone, Stafford ST16 0PA

Tel/Fax: 01785 760278

E-mail: iwc@staffordbc.gov.uk **www.staffordbc.gov.uk/heritage**

Owner: Stafford Borough Council **Contact:** Mark Hartwell

Stafford's rural heritage is embodied in the charming 17th century cottage owned by the celebrated author of *The Compleat Angler*. Izaak Walton's Cottage gives a fascinating insight into the history of angling and the life of a writer whose work remains 'a unique celebration of the English countryside.'

Location: MAP 6:N5, OS Ref. SJ876 293. M6/J14, A5013 towards Eccleshall, signposted on A5013.

Open: May–Aug: Sun, 1–5pm.

Admission: Free. Check for events, charges may apply.

Partial. WCs. Limited for cars. Guide dogs only.

MOSELEY OLD HALL

Fordhouses, Wolverhampton WV10 7HY

Tel: 01902 782808 **www.nationaltrust.org.uk**

Owner: National Trust **Contact:** The Property Manager

Brick encased Elizabethan timber-framed house.

Location: MAP 6:N6, OS Ref. SJ932 044. 4m N of Wolverhampton between A449 and A46.

STAFFORD CASTLE & VISITOR CENTRE

Newport Road, Stafford ST16 1DJ

Tel/Fax: 01785 257698 **E-mail:** staffordcastle@staffordbc.gov.uk

www.staffordbc.gov.uk/heritage

Owner: Stafford Borough Council **Contact:** Mark Hartwell

Stafford Castle has dominated the Stafford landscape for over 900 years. William the Conqueror first built Stafford Castle as a fortress to subdue the local populace. The visitor centre – built in the style of a Norman guardhouse – features an audio-visual area that brings its turbulent past to life.

Location: MAP 6:N5, OS Ref. SJ904 220. On N side of A518, 1½m WSW of town centre.

Open: Apr–Oct: Wed–Sun, 11am–4pm (open BHs). Nov–Mar: Sat & Sun, 11am–4pm.

Admission: Free (admission charges may apply for events).

By arrangement. Visitor centre – Guide dogs only.

THE TRENTHAM ESTATE

STONE ROAD, TRENTHAM, STAFFORDSHIRE ST4 8AX

www.trentham.co.uk

Tel: 01782 646646 **Fax:** 01782 644536 **Email:** enquiry@trentham.co.uk
Owner: St Modwen Properties **Group Booking contact:** Jackie Grice.
Tel: 01782 645215 **Email:** jgrice@trentham.co.uk

Winners of the 2010 European Award for Historic Garden Restoration. Enjoy Trentham Gardens where vast perennial plantings by renowned garden designers and Chelsea gold-medal winners Tom Stuart-Smith and Piet Oudolf, present breath-taking vistas throughout the seasons. Enjoy the lake, woodlands and the country's first barefoot walk. There's something for everyone at Trentham.

Location: MAP 6:N4, OS Ref. SJ864 408, SAT NAV: ST4 8JG. 5 minute drive M6/J15. 45 minutes from Birmingham & Manchester.

Open: Summer: Apr–Oct: daily, 9am–6pm. Exit by 8pm. Winter: Nov–Mar: daily, 10am–3pm. Exit by 4pm. Trentham Gardens are open every day except Christmas Day.

Admission: Summer: Adult £7.75, Child (5-15) & Conc. £6.50, Families (2+3) £26.50 (1+3) £18.75, Disabled/Carer £3.85, Under 5's free; maximum 3 under 5s per full paying adult. Discounts apply for groups of 12 or more, pre-paid and booked in advanced, please telephone 01782 645215 for more information.

Special Events: Summer Music Festival, family activities and seasonal events.

Shopping & several restaurants on site. Wheelchair loan available. Licensed. By arrangement. Free Parking. Coach parking, drop-off, meet & greet available. On leads.

© Boscobel House & The Royal Oak

Boscobel House & The Royal Oak

WALL ROMAN SITE (LETOCETUM)

Watling Street, Nr Lichfield, Staffordshire WS14 0AW
Tel: 01926 852078 **E-mail:** customers@english-heritage.org.uk
www.english-heritage.org.uk/wallromansiteletocetum
Owner: English Heritage **Contact:** Visitor Operations Team

The remains of a staging post alongside Watling Street. The foundations of an inn and bathhouse can be seen, and many of the excavated finds are displayed in the on-site museum.

Location: MAP 6:O6, OS139, SK098 066. Off A5 at Wall, nr Lichfield.

Open: Site: 1 Mar–31 Oct: daily, 10am–5pm, 1 Nov-28 Feb '11: daily, 10am-4pm, 24-26 Dec & 1 Jan: closed. Museum: 4-5 Apr, 24-25 Apr, 2-3 May, 29-31 May, 26-27 Jun, 24-25 Jul, 28-30 Aug, 25-26 Sep, 30-31 Oct: 11am-4pm, 1 Nov-28 Feb '11: closed.

Admission: Free. Opening times and prices are valid until 31st March 2011, after this date details are subject to change please visit www.english-heritage.org.uk for the most up-to-date information.

Picnic area.

© NTPL / Andreas von Einsiedel

Moseley Old Hall

WHITMORE HALL

WHITMORE, NEWCASTLE-UNDER-LYME ST5 5HW

Tel: 01782 680478 **Fax:** 01782 680906
Owner: Mr Guy Cavenagh-Mainwaring **Contact:** Mr Michael Cavenagh-Thornhill

Whitmore Hall is a Grade I listed building, designated as a house of outstanding architectural and historical interest, and is a fine example of a small Carolinian manor house (1676), although parts of the hall date back to a much earlier period. The hall has beautifully proportioned light rooms, curving staircase and landing. There are some good family portraits to be seen with a continuous line, from 1624 to the present day. It has been the family seat, for over 900 years, of the Cavenagh-Mainwarings who are direct descendants of the original Norman owners. The interior of the hall has recently been refurbished and is in fine condition. The grounds include a beautiful home park with a lime avenue leading to the house, as well as landscaped gardens encompassing an early Victorian summer house. One of the outstanding features of Whitmore is the extremely rare example of a late Elizabethan stable block, the ground floor is part cobbled and has nine oak-carved stalls.

Location: MAP 6:M4, OS Ref. SJ811 413. On A53 Newcastle–Market Drayton Road, 3m from M6/J15.

Open: 1 May–31 Aug: Tues, Weds, 2–5pm (last tour 4.30pm).

Admission: Adult £5, Child 50p.

Ground floor & grounds.

Afternoon teas for booked groups (15+), May–Aug.

■ **Owner**

The Viscount Daventry

■ **Contact**

Events Secretary
Arbury Hall
Nuneaton
Warwickshire CV10 7PT

Tel: 024 7638 2804
Fax: 024 7664 1147
E-mail: info@arburyestate.co.uk

■ **Location**

MAP 7:A7
OS Ref. SP335 893

London, M1, M6/J3 (A444 to Nuneaton), 2m SW of Nuneaton. 1m W of A444. Nuneaton 5 mins. Birmingham City Centre 20 mins. London 2 hrs, Coventry 20 mins.

Bus: Nuneaton 3m.

Rail: Nuneaton Station 3m.

Air: Birmingham International 17m.

■ **Opening Times**

All year
For corporate events.

Pre-booked visits to the Hall and Gardens for groups of 25+ from Easter to the end of September.

Hall & Gardens open 2–5pm on BH weekends only (Suns & Mons) Easter–September.

■ **Admission**

Summer
Hall & Gardens

Adult	£7.50
Child (up to 14 yrs)	£4.50
Family (2+2)	£19.00

Gardens Only

Adult	£5.50
Child (up to 14 yrs.)	£4.00

Groups/Parties (25+)
By arrangement.

Conference/Function

ROOM	SIZE	MAX CAPACITY
Dining Room	35' x 28'	80
Saloon	35' x 30'	70
Stables Tearooms	31' x 18'	70

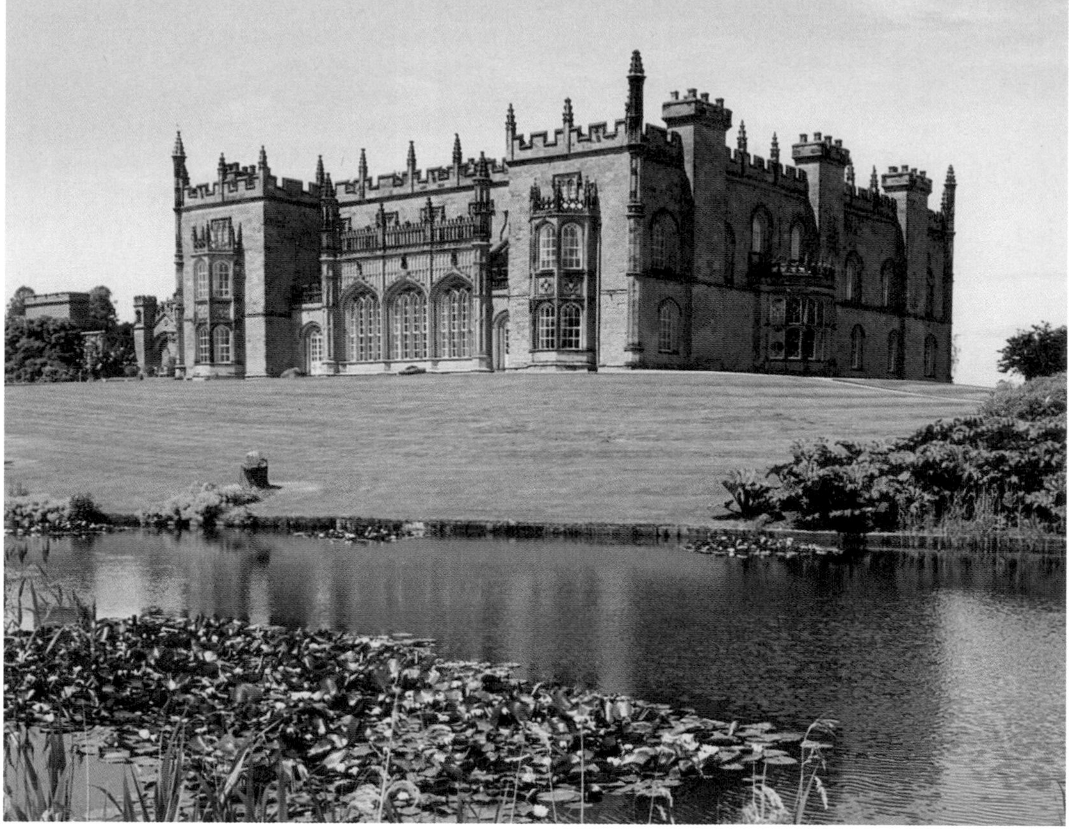

ARBURY HALL

www.arburyestate.co.uk

Arbury Hall has been the seat of the Newdegate family for over 450 years and is the ancestral home of Viscount Daventry. This Tudor/Elizabethan House was gothicised by Sir Roger Newdegate in the 18th century and is regarded as the 'Gothic Gem' of the Midlands. The principal rooms, with their soaring fan vaulted ceilings and plunging pendants and filigree tracery, stand as a most breathtaking and complete example of early Gothic Revival architecture and provide a unique and fascinating venue for corporate entertaining, product launches, receptions, fashion shoots and activity days.

Exclusive use of this historic Hall, its gardens and parkland is offered to clients. The Hall stands in the middle of beautiful parkland with landscaped gardens of rolling lawns, lakes and winding wooded walks. Spring flowers are profuse and in June rhododendrons, azaleas and giant wisteria provide a beautiful environment for the visitor. George Eliot, the novelist, was born on the estate and Arbury Hall and Sir Roger Newdegate were immortalised in her book 'Scenes of Clerical Life'.

Corporate hospitality, film location, small conferences, product launches and promotions, marquee functions, clay pigeon shooting, archery and other sporting activities, grand piano in Saloon, helicopter landing site. No cameras or video recorders indoors.

Exclusive lunches and dinners for corporate parties in dining room, max. 50, buffets 80.

WCs.

Obligatory. Tour time: 1hr.

200 cars and 3 coaches 250 yards from house. Follow tourist signs. Approach map available for coach drivers.

Welcome, must book. School room available.

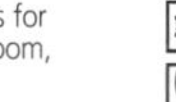

Guide dogs only.

KENILWORTH CASTLE ⌗

& ELIZABETHAN GARDEN

www.english-heritage.org.uk/kenilworth

A vast medieval fortress which became an Elizabethan palace, Kenilworth Castle is one of Britain's largest and most impressive historic sites.

Spanning more than five centuries, Kenilworth's varied buildings and architectural styles reflect its long connection with successive English monarchs. Geoffrey de Clinton, Henry I's treasurer, began the massive Norman keep at the core of the fortress in the 1120s, and subsequent monarchs and noblemen all left their mark on the romantic ruin that still captivates visitors today.

Kenilworth's greatest period of fame was during the Elizabethan era as the home of Robert Dudley, the great love of Queen Elizabeth I. Dudley created an ornate palace at Kenilworth to impress his beloved queen, which included a spectacular garden, created specially for her final visit in 1575. Due to extensive redevelopments to the site, this magnificent garden has been authentically re-created and is now astounding visitors once more.

As part of the multi-million pound English Heritage investment in Kenilworth Castle, Leicester's Gatehouse is displayed with the chambers on its lower floors re-created as they might have appeared when the gatehouse was last inhabited in the 1930s. The top floor houses an exhibition that tells the story of Elizabeth's relationship with Dudley, and her four visits to Kenilworth.

No visit to the castle is complete without a visit to the castle tearoom, housed in the impressively timbered Tudor stables. The stables also feature an fascinating interactive display on the castle's history.

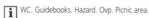

WC. Guidebooks. Hazard. Ovp. Picnic area.

P

Exhibition. Family learning resources available.

On leads.

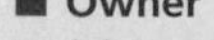

■ Owner

English Heritage

■ Contact

Visitor Operations Team
Kenilworth, Warwickshire
CV8 1NE

Tel: 01926 852 078
E-mail: customers@english-heritage.org.uk

■ Location

MAP 6:P8
OS140, SP278 723

In Kenilworth off A46, W end of town.

■ Opening Times

1 April–31 October: daily, 10am–5pm.

1 November–28 February 2011, daily, 10am–4pm.

1–31 March: daily, 10am–5pm.

Closed 24–26 December & 1 January.

Gatehouse may close early for private events.

■ Gift Aid Admission*

Adult	£7.60
Child	£3.80
Conc.	£6.50
Family	£19.00

15% discount for groups (11+).

EH Members Free.

Opening times and prices are valid until 31st March 2011, after this date details are subject to change please visit www.english-heritage.org.uk for the most up-to-date information.

■ **Owner**
The Marquess of Hertford

■ **Contact**
Alcester
Warwickshire B49 5NJ
Tel: 01789 762090
Fax: 01789 764791
E-mail: ragley
@ragleyhall.com

■ **Location**
MAP 6:O9
OS Ref. SP073 555
Off A46/A435 1m SW of Alcester, From London 100m, M40 via Oxford and Stratford-on-Avon.

■ **Opening Times**
Please see website for details.

■ **Admission**
Please see website for details.

RAGLEY HALL & GARDENS

www.ragleyhall.com

Ragley Hall was designed in 1680 and remains the family home of the Marquess and Marchioness of Hertford, managing to retain its family charm despite the thousands of people who visit each year.

The Palladian House is a well preserved example of a Regency interior with magnificent baroque plasterwork and is set in beautiful formal gardens and 400 acres of parkland. Highlights include the impressive Red Saloon which remains exactly as it was designed by James Wyatt in 1780 and the breathtaking mural 'The Temptation' by Graham Rust.

Ragley's beautiful gardens include a modern Rose Garden, Spring Bulb Bank and Alpine Garden all of which provide visitors with a contemporary and colourful vista as they stroll through Ragley's grounds. Ragley is also home to the Jerwood sculptures, an impressive and diverse collection of 20th & 21st century pieces which are displayed throughout the gardens and Woodland Walk. The working stables house a collection of 19th century carriages and are also home to the new Jerwood Studio which gives information on all of the pieces in the collection.

The Adventure Playground and picturesque Lakeside Picnic area makes Ragley a great day out for the whole family. Ragley can provide private guided tours of the House and Gardens for groups of twenty or more and also offer a range of packages to include refreshments from two course lunches in a private dining room to cream teas on the terrace.

No video in the house.

Visitors may alight at entrance. Parking. WCs. Lifts. Electric scooter for visiting the gardens may be available. Please enquire.

Drinks and light snacks available from Bodger's Cabin at the Adventure Playground and from Hooke's Cafe when the House is open.

By arrangement.

Coach drivers admitted free. Please advise of group visits.

Education programme & outdoor classroom. Contact education officer.

In grounds, on leads.

Mary Arden's Farm

Shakespeare's Birthplace

Anne Hathaway's Cottage

THE SHAKESPEARE HOUSES

www.shakespeare.org.uk

Five beautifully preserved Tudor Houses and Gardens telling the complete Shakespeare story and all directly linked with William Shakespeare and his family. Each house has a unique story to tell and together they provide a unique experience of the dramatist's life and times.

Shakespeare's Birthplace

Start this fascinating journey with an introduction to William Shakespeare through a Life, Love & Legacy exhibition before visiting this wonderful Tudor town house where the world's most famous playwright was born and grew up. See where prominent writers including Charles Dickens and Thomas Hardy have left their mark and watch demonstrations of the traditional craft practiced by Shakespeare's father, John, in the Glover's workshop. Meet your favourite Shakespeare characters in the garden with live impromptu performances from Shakespeare Aloud! Stroll round the traditional English garden, which features many plants and herbs mentioned in Shakespeare's plays, and remember your visit with a purchase from the gift shop.

Mary Arden's Farm – A Real Working Tudor Farm

Visit the childhood home of Shakespeare's mother and see the farm's history brought to life. Step back into the 1570s and encounter the authentic sights, sounds and smells of a working farm in Shakespeare's day. Our Tudor costumed residents will invite you to get involved and help with the day-to-day running of the farm and try out traditional rural skills. See our rare breed pigs, cattle, goats and handsome horses. Fun activities make Mary Arden's Farm a perfect family day out complete with adventure playground, willow tunnels, picnic point, shop, café and free car parking.

Anne Hathaway's Cottage – The Most Romantic Shakespeare House.

Discover and fall in love with this beautiful English thatched cottage and family home of Shakespeare's wife, Anne Hathaway and see where he wooed her. Stroll through and admire the award winning cottage garden which overflows with old-fashioned plants, orchards and traditional vegetables. Sit in the romantic Willow Cabin and be inspired by Shakespeare's sonnets. Visit the Shakespeare Sculpture and Tree Garden and wander through the enchanting Woodland Walk.

Hall's Croft – The Jacobean Doctor's House

Explore the elegant house with its lavish rooms once owned by Shakespeare's daughter Susanna and wealthy physician husband John Hall. Examine the fascinating collection of apothecary's equipment, books and medical instruments of the day. Relax in the tranquil gardens and savour the fragrant herb beds, like those used by John Hall in his remedies.

Nash's House & New Place – Where the Shakespeare Story Ended.

Experience a live archaeological dig at New Place, Shakespeare's final home, and take in the period splendour of Nash's House, once owned by Shakespeare's granddaughter. See archaeological experts carry out excavations at the site of New Place to try and gain an understanding of how the world's greatest dramatist spent his last years in Stratford-upon-Avon. Dig for Shakespeare will continue throughout 2011.

The Shakespeare Houses and Gardens are owned and cared for by The Shakespeare Birthplace Trust which is an independent charity. Every admission to the Shakespeare Houses and purchase in the gift shops supports the work of the Trust enabling the preservation of the houses and gardens for future generations.

City Sightseeing guided bus tour service connecting the town houses with Anne Hathaway's Cottage and Mary Arden's Farm. No photography inside houses.

Gifts are available at all five Shakespeare properties.

Plants are available for sale at Anne Hathaway's Cottage, Mary Arden's Farm and Hall's Croft.

Available, tel for details.

Partial. WCs.

Mary Arden's Farm

Hall's Croft

By special arrangement.

The Trust provides a free coach terminal for delivery and pick-up of groups, maximum stay 30 mins at Shakespeare's Birthplace. Parking at Anne Hathaway's Cottage and Mary Arden's.

Available for all houses. For information 01789 201804.

Guide dogs only.

Please check our website for further details.

■ Owner

The Shakespeare Birthplace Trust

■ Contact

The Shakespeare Birthplace Trust
Henley Street
Stratford-upon-Avon
CV37 6QW

Tel: 01789 204016 (General enquiries)
Tel: 01789 201806/201836 (Group Visits)
Fax: 01789 263138
E-mail: info@shakespeare.org.uk
groups@shakespeare.org.uk

■ Location

MAP 6:P9
OS Refs:
Birthplace – SP201 552
New Place – SP201 548
Hall's Croft – SP200 546
Hathaway's – SP185 547
Arden's – SP166 582

Rail: Direct service from London (Marylebone)

2 hrs from London
45 mins from Birmingham by car.

4m from M40/J15 and well signed from all approaches.

■ Opening Times

The Shakespeare Houses are open daily throughout the year except Christmas Day and Boxing Day.

1 November–31 March: Last entry 4pm

Feb Half-Term (19–27), 1 April–31 October: Last entry 5pm

July & August: Last entry 6pm at Shakespeare's Birthplace only.

Please note that Mary Arden's Farm is open from 1 April–31 October.

■ Admission

Tickets to the Shakespeare Houses are valid for a full year, with unlimited entry. So for the price of one ticket, you can enjoy days out at the Shakespeare Houses all year round –for free!

Visit the website for further details.

■ **Owner**

Stoneleigh Abbey Ltd

■ **Contact**

Estate Office
Stoneleigh Abbey
Kenilworth
Warwickshire CV8 2LF

Tel: 01926 858535
Fax: 01926 850724
E-mail: enquire@stoneleighabbey.org

■ **Location**

MAP 6:P8
OS Ref. SP318 712

Off A46/B4115, 2m W of Kenilworth. From London 100m, M40 to Warwick.

Rail: Coventry station 5m, Leamington Spa station 5m.

Air: Coventry Airport 3m Birmingham International 17m.

■ **Opening Times**

Good Fri–end October

Tue–Thur, Suns & BHs: House tours at 11am, 1pm & 3pm.

Grounds: 10am–5pm.

■ **Admission**

House Tour & Grounds

Adult	£7.00
1 Child Free with each adult	
Additional Child	£3.00
OAP	£6.50

Discounts for Groups (20+).

Jane Austen Tours

Sundays and Wednesdays, 1pm	£7.00
Grounds only	£3.00

Parking

Car parking is free of charge to purchasers of tickets for a guided tour or admission to the grounds.

Groups are welcome during the published opening times or at other times by arrangement. Please telephone.

(2010 opening times/ prices).

Conference/Function

ROOM	SIZE	MAX CAPACITY
Saloon	14 x 9m	100
Gilt Hall	7 x 7m	60
Servants' Hall	14 x 8m	100
Riding School	12 x 33m	490
Conservatory	19 x 6m	100

STONELEIGH ABBEY

www.stoneleighabbey.org

Stoneleigh Abbey was founded in the reign of Henry II and after the Dissolution was granted to the Duke of Suffolk. The estate then passed into the ownership of the Leigh family who remained for 400 years. The estate is now managed by a charitable trust.

Visitors will experience a wealth of architectural styles spanning more than 800 years: the magnificent State rooms and chapel of the 18th century Baroque West Wing contain original pieces of furniture including a set of library chairs made by William Gomm in 1763; a medieval Gatehouse; the Gothic Revival-style Regency Stables. Jane Austen was a distant relative of the Leigh family and in her description of 'Sotherton' in *Mansfield Park* she recalls her stay at Stoneleigh Abbey. Parts of *Northanger Abbey* also use Stoneleigh for inspiration.

The River Avon flows through the estate's 690 acres of grounds and parkland which displays the influences of Humphry Repton and other major landscape architects. In June 1858 Queen Victoria and Prince Albert visited Stoneleigh Abbey – during their stay Queen Victoria planted an oak tree. In 2003 HRH Prince Charles visited Stoneleigh to mark the completion of the restoration of the Abbey and during his visit he also planted an English oak tree.

Stoneleigh Abbey has been the subject of a major restoration programme funded by the Heritage Lottery Fund, English Heritage and the European Regional Development Fund.

Available for public and commercial hire.

House only. WCs.

Obligatory.

Schools welcome.

ARBURY HALL

See page 310 for full page entry.

BADDESLEY CLINTON

Baddesley Clinton, Warwickshire B93 0DQ

Tel: 01564 783294 **Fax:** 01564 782706 **Email:** baddesleyclinton@nationaltrust.org.uk

www.nationaltrust.org.uk

Owner: National Trust **Contact:** Property Administrator

A 500 year old moated medieval manor house with hidden secrets! The house and interiors reflect its heyday in the Elizabethan era, when it was a haven for persecuted Catholics – there are three priest holes. The intimate gardens incorporate stewponds, small lake, walled garden, lakeside walk and nature trail.

Location: MAP 6:P8, OS Ref. SP199 715. ¾ m W of A4141 Warwick/Birmingham road at Chadwick End.

Open: 1 Feb–31 Dec, Tue–Sun & BH Mons, 11am–5pm.

Admission: Prices tbc. Please visit www.nationaltrust.org.uk.

WCs. Licensed. By arrangement. Guide dogs only.

CHARLECOTE PARK

Charlecote Park, Warwick CV35 9ER

Tel: 01789 470277 **Fax:** 01789 470544

Owner: National Trust **Contact:** Visitor Services Manager

House with fascinating history built 16c with subsequent extensive renovations.

Location: MAP 6:P9, OS151, SP263 564. 1m W of Wellesbourne, 5m E of Stratford-upon-Avon.

For unique **Civil wedding** venues see our index at the end of the book.

COMPTON VERNEY

COMPTON VERNEY, WARWICKSHIRE CV35 9HZ

www.comptonverney.org.uk

Tel: 01926 645500 **Fax:** 01926 645501 **E-mail:** info@comptonverney.org.uk

Owner: Compton Verney House Trust **Contact:** Ticketing Desk

Set within a Grade I listed mansion remodelled by Robert Adam in the 1760s, Compton Verney offers a unique art gallery experience. Relax and explore the 120 acres of 'Capability' Brown landscaped parkland, discover a collection of internationally significant art, enjoy free tours and a programme of popular events.

Location: MAP 7:A9, OS Ref. SP312 529. 9m E of Stratford-upon-Avon, 10 mins from M40/J12, on B4086 between Wellesbourne and Kineton. Rail: Nearest station is Banbury or Leamington Spa. Air: Nearest airport Birmingham International.

Open: 26 Mar–11 Dec: Tues–Sun & BH Mons, 11am–5pm. Last entry to Gallery 4.30pm. Groups welcome, please book in advance.

Admission: Please call for details. Group discounts are available.

Special Events: 2011 exhibitions: 26 Mar–5 Jun, Alfred Wallis and Ben Nicholson. 25 July–2 October, Stanley Spencer and the English garden. 'Capability' Brown and the landscapes of middle England. 22 October-11 December call for details. Special events during the school holidays (Easter, May Bank Holiday, May Half Term, Summer Holidays, October Half Term and Christmas) please call or visit www.comptonverney.org.uk for details or sign up to our e-bulletin.

No photography in the Gallery. WCs. Licensed. Licensed. By arrangement. Ample. Guide dogs only.

Baddesley Clinton

© NTPL / Robert Morris

COUGHTON COURT

ALCESTER, WARWICKSHIRE B49 5JA

www.nationaltrust.org.uk

Tel: 01789 400777 **Fax:** 01789 765544 **E-mail:** coughtoncourt@nationaltrust.org.uk

Contact: National Trust

Home to the Throckmorton family for 600 years, this finest of Tudor houses stands testament to a family's courage to maintain their beliefs. From high favour and fortunes to fear, oppression and danger following the Reformation, the Throckmortons were leaders in a dangerous age, and helped to bring about Catholic Emancipation in the nineteenth century. Coughton is still very much a family home with an intimate feel: the Throckmorton family live here and continue to manage the stunning gardens, which they have created.

Location: MAP 6:O9, OS Ref. SP080 604, Located on A435, 2m N of Alcester, 8m NW of Stratford-upon-Avon, 18m from Birmingham City Centre.

Open: House: 12–28 Mar, Sat–Sun, 1 Apr–30 Jun, Wed–Sun, 1 Jul–31 Aug, Tue–Sun, 1–30 Sep, Wed–Sun, 1 Oct–6 Nov, Thu–Sun, 11am–5pm. 3–11 Dec, Daily for Winter Festival 12–6pm. Open BH Mons. Closed Good Friday & closed Sat 12 Jun & Sat 10 Jul. Admission is by timed ticket at weekends and on busy days. Garden, shop and Restaurant: As house, 11am–5.30pm.

Walled Garden: As house 11.30am–4.45pm but closed Mar, Thur & Fri in Oct, Dec.

***Admission:** House and Garden £9.70, Child (5–16), £4.90, Family £24.50, Groups (15+) £8.00. Winter Festival: Adult £3.50, Child £1.50 (House and Gardens partially open). Gardens only: Adult £6.50, Child £3.25, Family £16.25, Groups (15+) £5.50. Walled Garden: NT members £2 (included in admission price for non-members). *includes a voluntary donation but visitors can choose to pay the standard prices displayed at the property and on the website. Not included in group prices.

Special Events: There is an exciting events programme that includes walks, outdoor theatre, Christmas Wassail and a Christmas Festival. For further details please call the property or see website.

New for 2011: House represented telling some of the unique and fascinating stories. Mighty Mission Quiz for children. Outdoor Adventure Packs for families. Children's play area. Ice Cream Parlour and Secondhand Bookshop. No indoor photography with flash. Private dinners can be provided by prior arrangement in restaurant. Ground floor of house, gardens & restaurant. WC. Licensed. Licensed. Capacity: 70 inside, Covered Courtyard 50. Free introductory talks available most days. Guide dogs only.

COUGHTON COURT GARDENS

ALCESTER, WARWICKSHIRE B49 5JA

www.coughtoncourt.co.uk

Garden Tours: 01789 762542 **Fax:** 01789 764369

E-mail: office@throckmortons.co.uk

Contact: Throckmorton family

Heralded by the RHS as one of the finest gardens in Britain, the beautiful 25 acres of grounds include a walled garden, lake, riverside walk and bog garden, colour themed gardens, daffodils and orchards and fruit gardens. The Rose Labyrinth, designed by daughter Christina Williams, boasts spectacular displays of roses and received an **Award of Garden Excellence from the World Federation of Rose Societies** – a first for the UK. It is also the first private garden to be awarded a Gilt Medal from The Daffodil Society for an outstanding contribution to daffodils. A newly designed garden featuring the rare Throckmorton daffodils opened in 2009. Plants for sale are grown by the family.

Location / Open / Admission: see above.

Partial. WCs. Licensed. Licensed. Guide dogs only.

©Coughton Court

©Coughton Court

© NTPL / Angelo Hornak

FARNBOROUGH HALL

BANBURY, OXFORDSHIRE OX17 1DU

www.nationaltrust.org.uk

Tel: 01295 690002 (information line)

Owner: National Trust

This honey-coloured stone house has been home of the Holbech family for 300 years. It has exquisite plasterwork and treasures collected during the Grand Tour. The house is surrounded by a fine landscape garden, including a terraced walk with fine views, ornamented with temples.

Location: MAP 7:A9, OS151, SP430 490. 6m N of Banbury, ½ m W of A423.

Open: House & Terrace Walk: 2 Apr–28 Sept: Weds & Sats, 2–5.30pm. Also 1 & 2 May: Last admission 5pm.

Admission: House & Terrace Walk: Adult £5.60, Child £3.00, Family £14.20.

Partial. Limited Guide dogs only.

© NTPL / Matthew Antrobus

Farnborough Hall

© Britainonview

Kenilworth Castle

THE HILLER GARDEN

Dunnington Heath Farm, Alcester, Warwickshire B49 5PD

Tel: 01789 491342 **Fax:** 01789 490439

Owner: A H Hiller & Son Ltd **Contact:** Mr Jeff Soulsby

2 acre garden of unusual herbaceous plants and over 200 rose varieties.

Location: MAP 6:O9, OS Ref. SP066 539. 1½ m S of Ragley Hall on B4088 (formerly A435).

Open: All year: daily. Nov–Mar 10am–5pm. Apr–Oct 10am–6pm. Closed 25 & 26 Dec.

Admission: Free.

HONINGTON HALL

SHIPSTON-ON-STOUR, WARWICKSHIRE CV36 5AA

Tel: 01608 661434 **Fax:** 01608 663717

Owner/Contact: Benjamin Wiggin Esq

This fine Caroline manor house was built in the early 1680s for Henry Parker in mellow brickwork, stone quoins and window dressings. Modified in 1751 when an octagonal saloon was inserted. The interior was also lavishly restored around this time and contains exceptional mid-Georgian plasterwork. Set in 15 acres of grounds.

Location: MAP 6:P9, OS Ref. SP261 427. 10m S of Stratford-upon-Avon. 1½ m N of Shipston-on-Stour. Take A3400 towards Stratford, then signed right to Honington.

Open: By appointment for groups (10+).

Admission: Telephone for details.

Obligatory.

KENILWORTH CASTLE *See page 311 for full page entry.*

LORD LEYCESTER HOSPITAL

HIGH STREET, WARWICK CV34 4BH

www.lordleycester.com

Tel: 01926 491422

Owner: The Governors **Contact:** The Master

This magnificent range of 14th and 15th century half-timbered buildings was adapted into almshouses by Robert Dudley, Earl of Leycester, in 1571. The Hospital still provides homes for ex-Servicemen and their wives. The Guildhall, Great Hall, chantry Chapel, Brethren's Kitchen and galleried Courtyard are still in everyday use. The regimental museum of the Queen's Own Hussars is housed here. The historic Master's Garden was featured in BBC TV's Gardener's World, and the Hospital buildings in many productions including, most recently, "Dr Who" and David Dimbleby's "How We Built Britain".

Location: OS Ref. 280 648. 1m N of M40/J15 on the A429 in town centre. Rail: 10 minutes walk from Warwick station.

Open: All year: Tue–Sun & BHs (except Good Fri & 25 Dec), 10am–5pm (4pm in winter). Garden: Apr–Sept: 10am–4.30pm.

Admission: Adult £4.90, Child £3.90, Conc. £4.40. Garden only £2. 5% discount for adult groups (20+).

Partial. WCs. By arrangement. Limited for cars. No coaches. Guide dogs only.

© Simon Hadley / Throckmorton Estates

Coughton Court Gardens

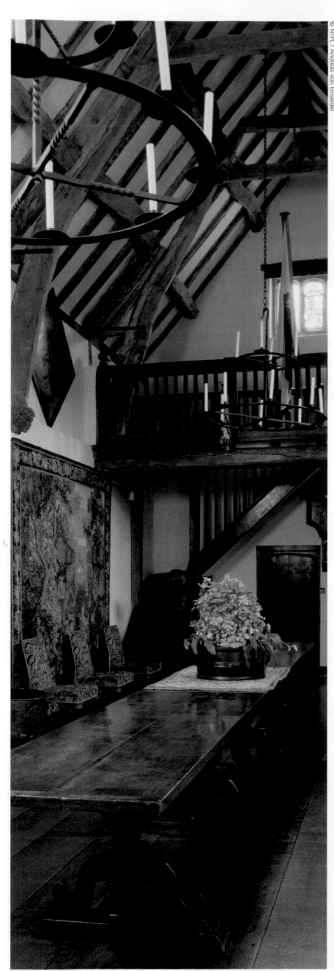

Packwood House

PACKWOOD HOUSE

Packwood House, Lapworth, Solihull B94 6AT
Tel: 01564 783294 **Fax:** 01564 782706 **E-mail:** packwood@nationaltrust.org.uk
www.nationaltrust.org.uk

Owner: National Trust **Contact:** The Estate Office

Packwood House is originally 16th century; its interiors were extensively restored between the world wars by Graham Baron Ash to create a fascinating 20th century evocation of domestic Tudor architecture. It contains a fine collection of 16th century textiles and furniture. The gardens are renowned for the herbaceous borders and a famous collection of yews.

Location: MAP 6:O8. OS Ref. SP174 722. 2m E of Hockley Heath (on A3400), 11m SE of central Birmingham.

Open: 1 Feb 2011–31 Oct, Tues–Sun, 11am–5pm with last entry 4.30pm.

Admission: Adult £8.70, Child £4.80, Family £22.20, Groups £7.00, Guided tours (out of hours) £14.00. Garden only: Adult £5, Child £3, Family £13. Combined Ticket with Baddesley Clinton: Adult £13.65, Child £6.90, Family £34.15. Gardens only: Adult £7.30, Child £3.70, Family £18.30. *includes a voluntary donation but visitors can choose to pay the standard prices displayed at the property and on the website. This does not apply to group prices.

WCs. By arrangement. Guide dogs only. Parkland only.

RAGLEY HALL & GARDENS

See page 312 for full page entry.

RYTON GARDENS

Wolston Lane, Ryton on Dunsmore, Coventry, Warwickshire CV8 3LG
Tel: 024 7630 3517 **Fax:** 024 7663 9229 **E-mail:** enquiry@gardenorganic.org.uk
www.gardenorganic.org.uk

Owner: Garden Organic **Contact:** Justine Williams

The home of UK's leading organic growing charity – Garden Organic. Ten acres of organic grounds, comprising 30 individual demonstration gardens showcasing organic ornamentals to fruit and veg growing, earth friendly pest and disease control, and tips on how to compost. Organic café, restaurant, plant sales and shop on site.

Location: OS Ref. SP4074.

Open: 7 days, 9am–5pm, excluding Christmas Day & Boxing Day.

Admission: Adult £6.60 incl. giftaid, £6 excl. giftaid (includes one free child). Conc. £6 incl. giftaid, £5.45 excl. giftaid. Child £3.30, under 5's free.

WCs. Licensed. Licensed. By arrangement. Guide dogs only.

THE SHAKESPEARE HOUSES

See page 313 for full page entry

STONELEIGH ABBEY

See page 314 for full page entry.

UPTON HOUSE & GARDENS

Upton House & Gardens, Banbury, Oxfordshire OX15 6HT
Tel: 01295 670266 **Fax:** 01295 671144

Owner: National Trust **Contact:** The Visitor Services Manager

Country home of 1930s millionaire.

Location: MAP 7:A9, OS Ref. SP371 461. On A422, 7m NW of Banbury. 12m SE of Stratford-upon-Avon.

The Shakespeare Houses – Mary Arden Farm

For **special events** held throughout the year, see the index at the end of the book.

Birmingham Botanical Gardens

© NTPL / Robert Morris

BACK TO BACKS

55–63 HURST STREET, BIRMINGHAM B5 4TE

www.nationaltrust.org.uk/backtobacks

Tel: 0121 666 7671 (Booking line open Tues–Fri, 10am–4pm; Sat/Sun, 10am–12 noon)
E-mail: backtobacks@nationaltrust.org.uk
Owner: National Trust **Contact:** House & Visitor Services Manager

Take an exciting step back into Birmingham's industrial past by visiting the last remaining courtyard of Back to Back houses in Birmingham. Visitors are taken back in time to the start of the 1840s when Court 15 was both a home and workplace for its many inhabitants. Four houses have been restored to reflect the different time periods and lives of the people who lived there. Experience the sights, sounds and smells of the 1930s sweetshop and see what life was like for George Saunders, a tailor from St Kitts, who came to live and work in Birmingham in the 1950s.

Location: MAP 6:O7, OS Ref. SP071 861. In the centre of Birmingham next to the Hippodrome Theatre, within easy walking distance of bus and railway stations.

Open: 2 Feb–23 Dec, Tues–Sun, 10am–5pm. Admission is by timed ticket and guided tour only. Advance booking strongly advised. Open BH Mons, closed following Tues. Please note: during term time property will normally be closed for use by school groups on Tues, Weds, & Thurs mornings 10am–1pm. Last tour times vary due to light levels, please check with the property.

***Admission:** Gift Aid admission Adult £6, Child £3, Family £15 *includes a voluntary donation but visitors can choose to pay the standard prices displayed at the property and on the website. (2010 prices).

Partial, WCs. Obligatory. Guide dogs only.

BIRMINGHAM BOTANICAL GARDENS AND GLASSHOUSES

WESTBOURNE ROAD, EDGBASTON, BIRMINGHAM, B15 3TR

www.birminghambotanicalgardens.org.uk

Tel: 0121 454 1860 **Fax:** 0121 454 7835
E-mail: admin@birminghambotanicalgardens.org.uk
Owner: Birmingham Botanical & Horticultural Society

Tropical, Mediterranean and Arid Glasshouses contain a wide range of exotic and economic flora. 15 acres of beautiful gardens with the finest collection of plants in the Midlands. Home of the National Bonsai Collection. Children's adventure playground, aviaries, gallery and sculpture trail. An independent educational charity.

Location: MAP 6:N7, OS Ref. SP048 855. 2m W of city centre. Follow signs to Edgbaston then brown tourist signs.

Open: Daily: 9am–Dusk (7pm latest except pre-booked groups). Suns opening time 10am. Closed Christmas Day.

Admission: Adult £7.50, Family £22. Groups, Conc. £4.75, Children under 5 FREE.

Guide dogs only.

COVENTRY CATHEDRAL

1 Hill Top, Coventry CV1 5AB
Tel: 024 7652 1200 **Fax:** 024 7652 1220
E-mail: information@coventrycathedral.org.uk
Owner: Dean & Canons of Coventry Cathedral **Contact:** The Visits Secretary

The remains of the medieval Cathedral, bombed in 1940, stand beside the new Cathedral by Basil Spence, consecrated in 1962. Modern works of art include a huge tapestry by Graham Sutherland, a stained glass window by John Piper and a bronze sculpture by Epstein. 'Reconciliation' statue by Josefina de Vasconcellos.

Location: MAP 6:P7, OS Ref. SP336 790. City centre.

Open: Cathedral: All year: Mon–Sat 9am–5pm. Sun 12–3.45pm. Groups must book in advance.

Admission: Free – donations welcomed.

KINVER EDGE AND THE HOLY AUSTIN ROCK HOUSES

Compton Road, Kinver, Nr Stourbridge, Staffs DY7 6DL
Tel: 01384 872553
Owner: National Trust **Contact:** The Custodian

Cave houses inhabited until the 1950s.

Location: MAP 7:A8, OS Ref. SO834 835 GB. 4m W of Stourbridge, 4m N of Kidderminster.

© Britainonview / Daniel Bosworth

Coventry Cathedral

© NTPL / Andreas von Einsiedel

Wightwick Manor

SELLY MANOR

MAPLE ROAD, BOURNVILLE, WEST MIDLANDS B30 2AE

www.bvt.org.uk/sellymanor

Tel/Fax: 0121 472 0199 **E-mail:** sellymanor@bvt.org.uk

Owner: Bournville Village Trust **Contact:** Gillian Ellis

A beautiful half-timbered manor house in the heart of the famous Bournville village. The house has been lived in since the 14th century and was rescued from demolition by George Cadbury. It houses furniture dating back several centuries and is surrounded by a delightful typical Tudor garden.

Location: MAP 6:O7, OS Ref. SP045 814. N side of Sycamore Road, just E of Linden Road (A4040). 4m SSW of City Centre.

Open: All year: Tue–Fri, 10am–5pm. Apr–Sept: Sats, Suns & BHs, 2–5pm. Closed Mons.

Admission: Adult £3.50, Child £1.50, Conc. £2.50, Family £9.50.

Partial. WC. By arrangement. Limited. In grounds, on leads.

WIGHTWICK MANOR & GARDENS

Wightwick Bank, Wolverhampton, West Midlands WV6 8EE

Tel: 01902 761400 **Email:** wightwickmanor@nationaltrust.org.uk

www.nationaltrust.org.uk

Owner: National Trust **Contact:** The Property Manager

Begun in 1887, the house is a notable example of the influence of William Morris, with many original Morris wallpapers and fabrics. Also of interest are pre-Raphaelite pictures, Kempe glass and De Morgan ware. The 17 acre Victorian/Edwardian garden designed by Thomas Mawson has formal beds, pergola, yew hedges, topiary and terraces, woodland, two pools and kitchen garden.

Location: MAP 6:N6, OS Ref. SO869 985. 3m W of Wolverhampton, off the A454.

Open: 16 Feb–30 Jun & 1 Sept–31 Oct: Wed–Sun. 1 Jul–31 Aug: Mon–Sun. 4 Nov–18 Dec: Fri–Sun. (last entry 4.30pm). Admission by timed ticket. (Taster Tour: 11am–12.30pm, access limited.) Guided groups through ground floor, freeflow upstairs (min. tour time approx. 1 hr). No guided tours on first Thur & Sat of the month – freeflow through the house from 12.30. Open BH Mons ground floor only. Garden, tea-room and shop also open seven days a week 1 Jul–31 Aug.

***Admission:** Adult £8.70, Child £4.30. Garden only: £4.30, Child £2.10. *includes a voluntary donation but visitors can choose to pay the standard prices displayed at the property and on the website.

Special Events: Full calendar of events throughout the year.

No internal Photography. No Sharp Heeled Shoes. Partial. WCs. Obligatory. 400 yds. Guide dogs only.

CROOME PARK

Near High Green, Worcestershire WR8 9DW
Tel: 01905 371006 **Fax:** 01905 371090
Owner: National Trust **Contact:** House & Visitor Services Manager
'Capability' Brown's first complete landscape.
Location: MAP 6:N9, OS150, SO878 448. 9m S of Worcester. Signposted from A38 and B4084.

THE GREYFRIARS

Worcester WR1 2LZ
Tel: 01905 23571
Owner: National Trust **Contact:** House and Visitor Services Manager
Timber-framed house built c1480 with later additions.
Location: MAP 6:N9, OS150, SO852 546. Friar Street, in centre of Worcester.

HANBURY HALL

Droitwich, Worcestershire WR9 7EA
Tel: 01527 821214 **Fax:** 01527 821251
Owner: National Trust **Contact:** The Property Manager
Completed 1701 and famed for fine ceilings and staircase.
Location: MAP 6:N8, OS150, SO943 637. 4½m E of Droitwich, 4m SE M5/J5.

Thinking of a short break or weekend away?
See Historic Places to Stay

Harvington Hall

HARVINGTON HALL

HARVINGTON, KIDDERMINSTER, WORCESTERSHIRE DY10 4LR

www.harvingtonhall.com

Tel: 01562 777846 **Fax:** 01562 777190
E-mail: harvingtonhall@btconnect.com **Contact:** The Hall Manager
Owner: Roman Catholic Archdiocese of Birmingham
Description: Harvington Hall is a moated, medieval and Elizabethan manor house. Many of the rooms still have their original Elizabethan wall paintings and the Hall contains the finest series of priest hides in the country. A full programme of events throughout the year including outdoor plays and music, living history weekends, candlelight tours and a pilgrimage is available.
Location: MAP 6:N8, OS Ref. SO877 745. On minor road, ½ m NE of A450/A448 crossroads at Mustow Green. 3m SE of Kidderminster.

Open: Mar & Oct: Sats & Suns; Apr–Sept: Wed–Sun & BH Mons (closed Good Fri), 11.30am–4pm. Also open throughout the year for pre-booked groups and schools. Occasionally the Hall may be closed for a private function, please ring for up to date information.

Admission: Adult £7.50, Child (5-16) £5, OAP £6.50, Family (2 adults & 3 children) £21. Garden and Malt House Visitor Centre: £3.

Partial. WCs Obligatory Limited for coaches.
Guide dogs only.

LEIGH COURT BARN

Worcester

Tel: 01299 896636 **Email:** customers@english-heritage.org.uk

www.english-heritage.org.uk/leighcourtbarn

Owner: English Heritage **Contact:** Visitor Operations Administrative Assistant

Magnificent 14th century timber-framed barn built for the monks of Pershore Abbey. It is the largest of its kind in Britain.

Location: MAP 6:M9,OS150 Ref. SO783 535. 5m W of Worcester on unclassified road off A4103.

Open: 1 Apr–30 Sept: Thur–Sun & BH Mons, 10am–5pm.

Admission: Free. Opening times and prices are valid until 31st March 2011, after this date details are subject to change please visit www.english-heritage.org.uk for the most up-to-date information.

MADRESFIELD COURT

Madresfield, Malvern WR13 5AJ

Tel: 01684 579947 **E-mail:** helen.madresfield@yahoo.com

Owner: The Trustees of Madresfield Estate **Contact:** Mrs Helen Sommerville

Elizabethan and Victorian house with medieval origins. Fine contents. Extensive gardens and arboretum.

Location: MAP 6:M9, OS Ref. SO809 474. 6m SW of Worcester. 1½ m SE of A449. 2m NE of Malvern.

Open: Pre-booked guided tours: 6 Apr–2 Jul: mostly Wed & Thur, also Sats 16 Apr, 21 May, 11 Jun & 2 Jul: 10.45am & 2.30pm. Numbers are restricted and prior booking, by telephone to Mrs Helen Sommerville, is strongly recommended to avoid disappointment.

Admission: £10.

Partial, WCs Obligatory.

LITTLE MALVERN COURT

Nr Malvern, Worcestershire WR14 4JN

Tel: 01684 892988 **Fax:** 01684 893057

Owner: Trustees of the late T M Berington **Contact:** Mrs T M Berington

Prior's Hall, associated rooms and cells, c1480, of former Benedictine Monastery. Formerly attached to, and forming part of the Little Malvern Priory Church which may also be visited. It has an oak-framed roof, 5-bay double-collared roof, with two tiers of cusped windbraces. Library. Collections of religious vestments, embroideries and paintings. Gardens: 10 acres of former monastic grounds with spring bulbs, blossom, old fashioned roses and shrubs. Access to Hall only by flight of steps.

Location: MAP 6:M9, OS Ref. SO769 403. 3m S of Great Malvern on Upton-on-Severn Road (A4104).

Open: 20 Apr–21 Jul: Weds & Thurs, 2.15–5pm. 20 Mar for NGS: 2–5pm. Last admission 4.15pm.

Admission: House & Garden: Adult £6.00, Child £2.00, Garden only: Adult £5.00, Child £1.00. Groups must book, max 30.

Garden (partial).

ROSEDENE

Dodford, Worcestershire B61 9BU

Tel: 01527 821214

Owner: National Trust **Contact:** Property Manager

Mid 19th century Chartist cottage with organic vegetable garden and orchard.

Location: MAP 6:N8, OS Ref. SO393 273. 3½ m NW of Bromsgrove off A448.

Properties that **open all year** appear in the special index at the end of the book.

SPETCHLEY PARK GARDENS

SPETCHLEY PARK, WORCESTER WR5 1RS

www.spetchleygardens.co.uk

Tel: 01453 810303 **Fax:** 01453 511915 **E-mail:** hb@spetchleygardens.co.uk

Owner: Spetchley Gardens Charitable Trust **Contact:** Mr RJ Berkeley

A garden that inspired Elgar and helped WWII airmen recuperate must have something special. This lovely 30 acre private garden contains a large collection of trees, shrubs and plants, many rare or unusual. A garden full of secrets, every corner reveals some new vista, some treasure of the plant world. The exuberant planting and the peaceful walks make this an oasis of beauty, peace and quiet. Relax in the wonderful atmosphere of the old laundry tearoom and enjoy a traditional English tea or walk in the nearby deer park full of red and fallow deer.

Location: MAP 6:N9, OS Ref. SO895 540. 3m E of Worcester on A44. Leave M5/J6/J7.

Open: 21 Mar–30 Sept: Wed–Sun & BHs, 11am–6pm. Oct: Sats & Suns, 11am–4pm. (last admission 1hr before closing).

Admission: Adult £6, Child (under 16yrs) Free. Conc. £5.50. Groups (25+): Adult £5.50. Adult Season Ticket £25.

Special Events: Please consult website.

Available for filming. WCs. By arrangement. Limited for coaches. Guide dogs only.

Harvington Hall

THE TUDOR HOUSE MUSEUM

16 Church Street, Upton-on-Severn, Worcestershire WR8 0HT

Tel: 01684 592447

Owner: Mrs Lavender Beard **Contact:** Mrs Wilkinson

Upton past and present, exhibits of local history.

Location: MAP 6:N10, OS Ref. SO852 406. Centre of Upton-on-Severn, 7m SE of Malvern by B4211.

Open: Apr–Oct: Daily 2–5pm, including Bank Holidays. Winter: Suns only, 2–4pm.

Admission: Adult £1, Conc. 50p, Family £2.

giftaid it Some properties will be operating the Gift Aid on Entry scheme at their admission points. Where the scheme is operating, visitors are offered a choice between paying the standard admission price or paying the 'Gift Aid Admission' which includes a voluntary donation of at least 10%. Gift Aid Admissions enable the charity to reclaim tax on the whole amount paid* - an extra 28% - potentially a very significant boost to property funds. Money raised from paying visitors in this way will go towards restoration projects at the property and will be very welcome.
Where shown, the admission prices are inclusive of the 10% voluntary donation where properties are operating the Gift Aid on Entry scheme, but both the standard admission price and the Gift Aid Admission will be displayed at the property and on their website.

*Gift Aid donations must be supported by a valid Gift Aid declaration and a Gift Aid declaration can only cover donations made by an individual for him/herself or for him/herself and members of his/her family.

© English Heritage

© English Heritage

WITLEY COURT & GARDENS ⌗

GREAT WITLEY, WORCESTER WR6 6JT

www.english-heritage.org.uk/witleycourt

Tel: 01299 896636 **E-mail:** customers@english-heritage.org.uk

Owner: English Heritage **Contact:** Visitor Operations Team

A hundred years ago, Witley Court was one of England's great country houses, hosting many extravagant parties. Today it is a spectacular ruin, the result of a devastating fire in 1937.

The vast and rambling remains of the 19th century mansion are surrounded by magnificent landscaped gardens. After a long period of decline, recent major restoration has brought the spectacular gardens back to life.

There are also many woodland walks to enjoy in the North Park, which features trees and shrubs acquired from around the world.

Attached to Witley Court is Great Witley Church, with its amazing Italianate Baroque interior.

Location: MAP 6:M8, OS150, SO769 649. 10m NW of Worcester off A443.

Open: 1 Apr–30 Jun: daily, 10am–5pm. 1 Jul–31 Aug: daily, 10am–6pm. 1 Sep–31 Oct: daily, 10am–5pm. 1 Nov–28 Feb '11: Wed–Sun, 10am–4pm. 1–31 Mar: Wed–Sun, 10am–5pm. Closed 24–26 Dec & 1 Jan.

Admission: Adult £6, Child £3, Conc. £5.10, Family £15. 15% discount for groups (11+). EH Members Free. Opening times and prices are valid until 31st March 2011, after this date details are subject to change please visit www.english-heritage.org.uk for the most up-to-date information.

Visitor welcome point. Guidebooks. Hazard. Ovp. Family learning resources available. On leads. Holiday cottage available to let.

York Minster Quire Screen

Yorkshire and the Humber

York contains reminders of its medieval origins but is as well known for its elegant Jacobean and Georgian architecture. Within easy reach are grand palaces such as Castle Howard and Harewood House, but there are also more modest gems to be seen such as Sion Hill Hall, and the gardens at RHS Harlow Carr are amongst the finest in Britain.

YORKSHIRE

Richmond Castle

Wentworh Castle Gardens

Scarborough Castle

Ripley Castle

Scampston Hall

Ripley Castle

BRODSWORTH HALL & GARDENS ⌗

www.english-heritage.org.uk/brodsworthhall

Explore the changing fortunes of a wealthy Victorian family through the stories of a house and the memories of a home at Brodsworth Hall. This is no glossily restored showpiece, frozen in a single period of manicured grandeur, the hall was 'Conserved as found' and is a mansion which has grown comfortably old over 120 years, and reveals a country house as it really was: still reflecting its original opulence but well-used, patched up in places and full of unexpected family curios.

Built in the Italianate style of the 1860s by the fabulously wealthy Charles Sabine Augustus Thellusson, the hall served as the family home for over 120 years. The pillared, sculpture-lined and sumptuously furnished 'grand rooms' on the ground floor recall the house's Victorian heyday. The Thellusson family's sporting interests, horse racing and yachtting, are reflected throughout the house. Sporting successes also include the magnificent silver Goodwood Cup, won by a family racehorse in 1835

In contrast to the house, the extensive gardens have been wonderfully restored to their original horticultural splendour as 'a collection of grand gardens in miniature'. Restoration work continues to reveal new features, along with visitas last enjoyed before World War 1. Explore the enghanted Grove with paths, banks and bridges winding over and under each other revealing an array of different views, which reflect the desires and apsorations of Victorian gentry. No matter what time of year visited the gardens at Brodsworth Hall are a delight in any season.

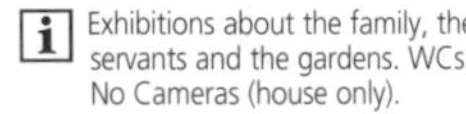

Exhibitions about the family, the servants and the gardens. WCs. No Cameras (house only).

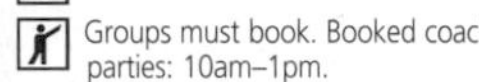

Groups must book. Booked coach parties: 10am–1pm.

220 cars and 3 coaches. Free.

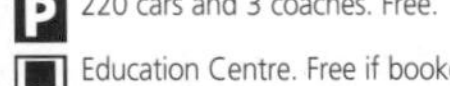

Education Centre. Free if booked in advance.

Gardens, Tearoom and Servants' Wing only.

■ Owner

English Heritage

■ Contact

Visitor Operations Team
Brodsworth Hall
Brodsworth
Nr Doncaster
Yorkshire DN5 7XJ

Tel: 01302 722598
Fax: 01302 337165

E-mail: brodsworth.hall@english-heritage.org.uk

■ Location

MAP 11:B12
OS Ref. SE506 070

In Brodsworth, 5m NW of Doncaster off A635. Use A1(M)/J37.

Rail: South Elmsall 4m; Moorthorpe 4.5m; Doncaster 5.5m.

■ Opening Times

Summer

House
1 April–30 September
Tue–Sun & BHs, 1–5pm.

1–31 October
Sat–Sun, 12 noon–4pm.

Gardens & Tearoom
1 April–31 October
Tue–Sun & BHs, 10am–5.30pm.

Gardens, Tearoom, Shop & Servants' Wing

1 November–31 March
Sat–Sun, 10am–4pm.

Closed 24–26 December & 1 January.

Last admission ½ hr before closing.

■ Admission

House & Gardens

Adult	£8.70
Child (5–15yrs)	£4.40
Child (under 5yrs)	Free
Conc.	£7.40

Groups (11+) 15% discount.

Gardens only

Adult	£5.30
Child (5–15yrs)	£2.70
Child (under 5yrs)	Free
Conc.	£4.50

EH members Free

Free admission for tour leaders and coach drivers.

Opening times and prices are valid until 31st March 2011, after this date details are subject to change please visit www.english-heritage.org.uk for the most up-to-date information.

■ Special Events

Snow drop festival during February half term.

Owner

The Hon Simon Howard

Contact

Visitor Services
Castle Howard
York, North Yorks
YO60 7DA

Tel: 01653 648333
Fax: 01653 648529
E-mail: house@castlehoward.co.uk

Location

MAP 11:C8
OS Ref. SE716 701

Approaching from S, A64 to Malton, on entering Malton, take Castle Howard road via Coneysthorpe village. Or from A64 following signs to Castle Howard via the Carrmire Gate 9' wide by 10' high.

York 15m (20 mins), A64. From London: M1/J32, M18 to A1(M) to A64, York/Scarborough Road, 3½ hrs.

Train: London Kings Cross to York 1hr. 50 mins. York to Malton Station 30 mins.

Bus: Service and tour buses from York Station.

Opening Times

House: 12 March–30 October & 26 November–18 December. Daily, 11am–4pm (last admission).

Gardens: All year except Christmas Day, daily from 10am.

Stable Courtyard: (Gift Shops, Farm Shop, Chocolate Shop, Plant Centre, Café): All year, daily, 10am–5pm, free admission.

Access to Pretty Wood Pyramid 1 July–31 August.

Special tours to newly restored rooms in the house are available by arrangement.

For more information please contact Castle Howard Estate Office on 01653 648444.

Admission

Annual Passes available

Summer
House & Garden

Adult	£13.00
Child (5–16yrs)	£7.50
Under 5yrs	Free
Conc.	£11.00

Garden only

Adult	£8.50
Child (5–16yrs)	£6.00
Under 5yrs	Free
Conc.	£8.00

Winter (when the house is closed) Gardens only

Adult	£6.00
Child (5–16yrs)	£3.00
Under 5yrs	Free

Conference/Function

ROOM	SIZE	MAX CAPACITY
Long Gallery	197' x 24'	200
Grecian Hall	40' x 40'	70

CASTLE HOWARD

www.castlehoward.co.uk

In a dramatic setting between two lakes with extensive gardens and impressive architecture, Castle Howard is undoubtedly one of Britain's finest private residences. Built by Sir John Vanbrugh in 1699 for Charles Howard, third Earl of Carlisle, Castle Howard remains the home of the Howard family.

With its impressive painted and gilded dome reaching 80ft, Castle Howard has collections of antique furniture; porcelain and sculpture, while the famous Holbein portraits of Henry VIII and the Duke of Norfolk dominate its fabulous collection of paintings.

The High South apartments, so disastrously destroyed by fire in 1940, are now open to the public for the first time. During the recent re-filming of *Brideshead Revisited* these bare rooms were converted into a film set and today visitors can witness this extraordinary transformation, with props and painted scenery, and see exhibitions that tell the story of the fire, and how Evelyn Waugh's famous novel came to be filmed not just once, but twice, at Castle Howard.

Designed on a heroic scale, the 1000 acres of gardens are dotted with statues and fountains, and include memorable sights such as The Temple of the Four Winds, the Mausoleum and New River Bridge. The walled garden has collections of old and modern roses, plus ornamental vegetable garden and Ray Wood, acknowledged by the Royal Botanical Collection, Kew, as a "rare botanical jewel" has a unique collection of rare trees, shrubs, rhododendrons, magnolias and azaleas.

Attractions include a changing programme of exhibition and events, plus a choice of shops and cafés. Families can also experience the new adventure playground and childrens activities.

- Filming, product launches, activity days. Suitable for helicopter landing. Photography allowed in the House for personal use only. Commercial photography with prior permission only.
- Choice of six shops including farm shop, plant centre, chocolate shop, bookshop and two gift shops. Free admission to Stable Courtyard shops and cafés.
- Plant Centre & Tearoom open daily all year with free admission.
- Hospitality includes dinners, meetings, corporate events and wedding receptions.
- Car parking, toilets, ramped pathways and doors, wheelchair lift inside the House.
- Choice of four cafés to suit all the family.
- Private group lunches and afternoon teas in the Grecian Hall. Menus upon request.
- Free outdoor guided tours for visitors Mar–Nov. Private tours & lectures available for special interest groups.
- Plentiful free parking, including disabled.
- School parties welcome. Preferential rates available. Teacher pre-visits.
- Dogs on leads welcome. Registered assistance dogs in house only.
- Holiday homes sales, plus camping and caravanning at the Lakeside Holiday Park.
- Temple of the Four Winds.
- Gardens open all year except Christmas Day.
- Full programme for all the family.

© NTPL / Andrew Butler

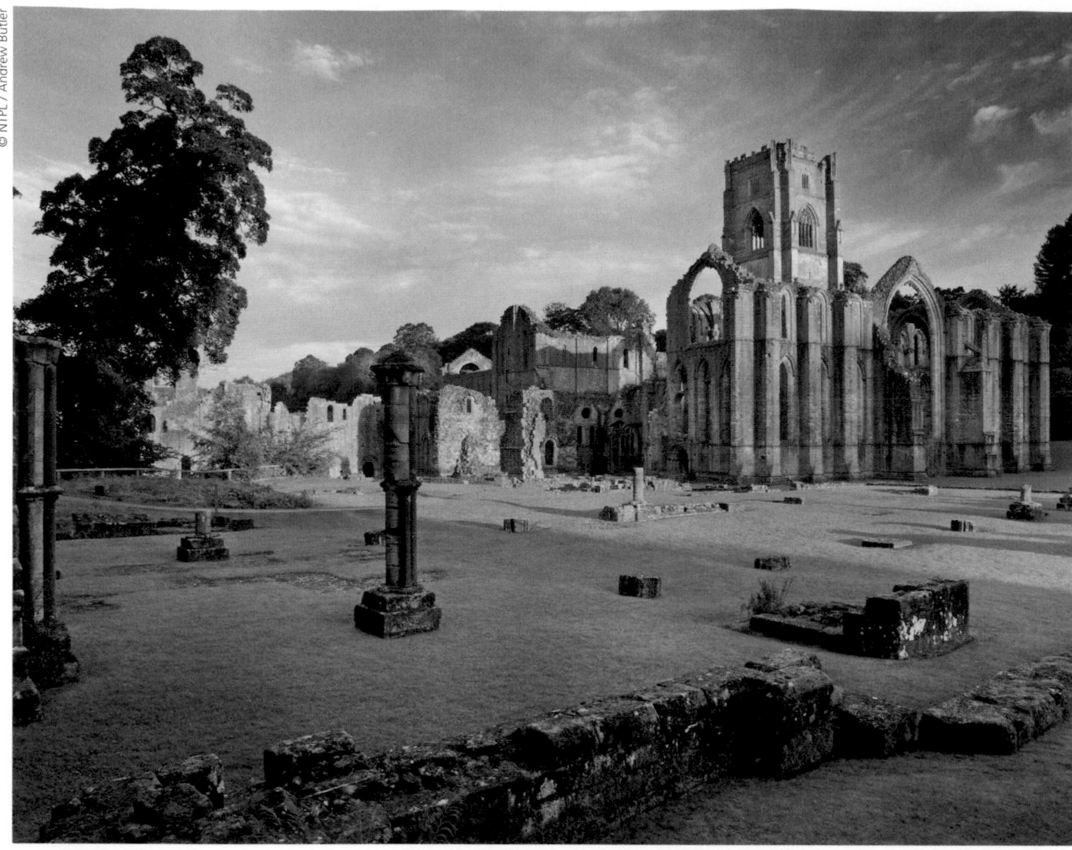

FOUNTAINS ABBEY & STUDLEY ROYAL

www.fountainsabbey.org.uk

One of the most remarkable sites in Europe, sheltered in a secluded valley, Fountains Abbey and Studley Royal, a World Heritage Site, encompasses the spectacular remains of a 12th century Cistercian abbey with one of the finest surviving monastic watermills in Britain, an Elizabethan mansion, and one of the best surviving examples of a Georgian water garden. Elegant ornamental lakes, avenues, temples and cascades provide a succession of unforgettable eye-catching vistas in an atmosphere of peace and tranquillity. St Mary's Church, built by William Burges in the 19th century, provides a dramatic focal point to the medieval deer park with over 500 wild deer. Exhibitions, events, activities and guided tours throughout the year.

© NTPL / Andrew Butler

Events held throughout the year. Exhibitions. Seminar facilities. Outdoor concerts, meetings, activity days, walks.

Two shops.

Dinners.

WCs.

Licensed.

Licensed.

Free, but seasonal. Groups (please book on 01765 643197), please use Visitor Centre entrance.

Audio tour £2.00.

Drivers must book groups.

On leads.

Fountains Hall, an Elizabethan Mansion is an ideal setting for weddings. For details or a Wedding pack tel: 01765 643198.

Owner

National Trust

Contact

National Trust
Fountains Abbey
and Studley Royal
Ripon
North Yorkshire
HG4 3DY

Tel: 01765 608888
E-mail: info@fountainsabbey.org.uk

Location

MAP 10:P8
OS Ref. SE275 700

Abbey entrance: 4m W of Ripon off B6265. 8m W of A1.

Rail: Harrogate 12m.

Bus: Regular season service Traveline: 0871 200 2233 for details.

Opening Times

April–September
Daily: 10am–5pm.

October–March
Daily: 10am–4pm or dusk if earlier.

Closed 24/25 December, & Fridays from Nov–Jan.

Deer Park: All year, daily during daylight (closed 24/25 December).

*Admission

Adult	£9.00
Child (5–16yrs)	£4.85
Family	£23.00
Groups (15+)	
Adult	£7.70
Groups (31+)	
Adult	£7.45

Group discount applicable only with prior booking.

Group visits and disabled visitors, please telephone in advance, 01765 643197.

Includes a voluntary donation but visitors can choose to pay the standard prices displayed at the property and on the website. Does not apply to group prices.

NT, EH Members & Under 5s Free.

The Abbey is owned by the National Trust and maintained by English Heritage. St Mary's Church is owned by English Heritage and managed by the National Trust.

■ **Owner**

Mr Richard Compton

■ **Contact**

The Administrator
Newby Hall
Ripon
North Yorkshire
HG4 5AE

Tel: 01423 322583
Information Hotline: 0845 450 4068
Fax: 01423 324452
E-mail: via www.newbyhall.com

■ **Location**

MAP 11:A8
OS Ref. SE348 675

Midway between London and Edinburgh, 4m W of A1, towards Ripon. S of Skelton 2m NW of (A1) Boroughbridge. 4m SE of Ripon.

Taxi: Ripon Taxi Rank 01765 601283.

Bus: On Ripon–York route.

***SatNav users:** please use postcode **HG4 5AJ**

■ **Opening Times**

Summer

House*
1 April–25 September.
April, May, June & September:
Tues–Sun & BH Mons;
July–August: Daily
12 noon–5pm.
Last admission 4pm.
*Areas of the House can be closed to the public from time to time, please check website for details.

Garden
Dates as House,
11am–5.30pm.
Last admission 5pm.

Winter
October–end March
Closed.

■ **Admission (2010 Prices)**

House & Garden

Adult	£12.00
Child/Disabled	£9.50
OAP	£11.00
Group (15+)	
Adult/Conc	£10.50
Child/Disabled	£8.00
Family (2+2)	£40.00
Family (2+3)	£43.00

Garden only

Adult	£8.50
Child/Disabled	£7.00
OAP	£7.50
Group (15+)	
Adult	£7.00
Child (4–16yrs)	£6.00
Family (2+2)	£30.00
Family (2+3)	£36.00

Conference/Function

ROOM	SIZE	MAX CAPACITY
Grantham Room	90' x 20'	150

NEWBY HALL & GARDENS

www.newbyhall.com

The home of Richard and Lucinda Compton, Newby Hall is one of England's renowned Adam houses. In the 1760s William Weddell, an ancestor of the Comptons, acquired a magnificent collection of Ancient Roman sculpture and Gobelins tapestries. He commissioned Robert Adam to alter the original Wren designed house and Thomas Chippendale to make furniture. The result is a perfect example of the Georgian 'Age of Elegance' with the atmosphere and ambience of a family home.

Gardens

25 acres of stunning award-winning gardens contain rare and beautiful shrubs and plants, including a National collection of the Genus Cornus (Dogwoods). Newby's famous double herbaceous borders, framed by great bastions of yew hedges, make the perfect walkway to the River Ure. Formal gardens such as the Autumn and Rose Garden, the tranquillity of Sylvia's Garden and the Tropical Garden make Newby an inspiring and exciting place to explore. Walking through the curved pergolas leads to the Victorian Rock garden, which is an enchanting magical space for all ages. The gardens feature an exciting children's adventure garden and miniature railway. From 1st June there is an annual exhibition of contemporary sculptures in the mature woodland.

- Allow a full day for viewing house and gardens. Suitable for filming and for special events, craft and country fairs, vehicle rallies etc, promotions and lectures. No indoor photography.
- 'The Shop @ Newby Hall' – Modern British Art and Craftsmanship.
- Wedding receptions & special functions.
- WCs.
- Licensed.
- Licensed.
- Obligatory.
- Ample. Hard standing for coaches.
- Welcome. Rates on request. Grantham Room for use as wet weather base subject to availability. Woodland discovery walk, adventure gardens and train rides on 10¼" gauge railway.
- Guide Dogs only.

RIPLEY CASTLE

www.ripleycastle.co.uk

Ripley Castle has been the home of the Ingilby family for twenty-six generations and Sir Thomas and Lady Ingilby, together with their five children, continue the tradition. The guided tours are amusing and informative, following the lives and loves of one family for 700 years and how they have been affected by events in English history. The Old Tower dates from 1555 and houses splendid armour, books, panelling and a Priest's Secret Hiding Place, together with fine paintings, china, furnishings and chandeliers collected by the family over the centuries.

The extensive Victorian Walled Gardens have been transformed and are a colourful delight through every season. In the Spring you can appreciate 150,000 flowering bulbs which create a blaze of colour through the woodland walks, and also the National Hyacinth Collection whose scent is breathtaking. The restored Hot Houses have an extensive tropical plant collection, and in the Kitchen Gardens you can see an extensive collection of rare vegetables from the Henry Doubleday Research Association.

Ripley village on the Castle's doorstep is a model estate village with individual charming shops, an art gallery, delicatessen and Farmyard Museum.

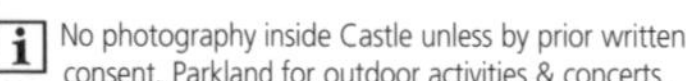

No photography inside Castle unless by prior written consent. Parkland for outdoor activities & concerts.

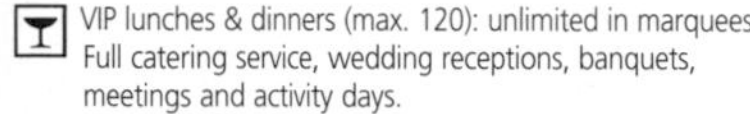

VIP lunches & dinners (max. 120): unlimited in marquees. Full catering service, wedding receptions, banquets, meetings and activity days.

5/7 rooms accessible. Gardens accessible (not Tropical Collection). WCs. Parking 50 yds.

The Castle Tearooms (seats 54) in Castle courtyard. Licensed. Pub lunches or dinner at hotel (100 yds). Groups must book.

Obligatory. Tour time 75 mins.

290 cars – 300 yds from Castle entrance. Coach park 50 yds. Free.

Welcome by arrangement, between 10.30am–7.30pm.

Guide dogs only.

Boar's Head Hotel (AA***) 100 yds. Owned and managed by the estate.

Owner

Sir Thomas Ingilby Bt

Contact

Tours: Jenny Carter
Meetings/Dinners:
Rebecca Riordan
Ripley Castle
Ripley, Harrogate
North Yorkshire
HG3 3AY

Tel: 01423 770152
Fax: 01423 771745
E-mail: enquiries@ripleycastle.co.uk

Location

MAP 10:P9
OS Ref. SE283 605

W edge of village. Just off A61, 3½ m N of Harrogate, 8m S of Ripon. M1 18m S, M62 20m S.

Rail: London–Leeds/York 2hrs. Leeds/York–Harrogate 30mins.

Taxi: Blueline taxis Harrogate (01423) 503037.

Opening Times

Castle
Easter–end September: Daily.
October, November & March: Tues, Thurs, Sat & Sun.
10.30am–3pm.

December–February: Sats & Suns.
10.30am–3pm.

Gardens
All year, daily (except Christmas Day and Boxing Day), 10am–5pm (winter 4.30pm).

Admission

All Year
Castle & Gardens

Adult	£8.50
Child (5–16yrs)	£5.50
Child under 5yrs	Free
OAP	£8.00
Groups (20+)	
Adult	£7.50
Child (5–16yrs)	£5.00

Gardens only

Adult	£6.00
Child (5–16yrs)	£4.00
OAP	£5.50
Groups (20+)	
Adult	£6.00
Child (5–16yrs)	£3.50
Child under 5yrs	Free

Special Events

Check website or ring for details.

Conference/Function

ROOM	SIZE	MAX CAPACITY
Morning Rm	27' x 22'	80
Large Drawing Rm	30' x 22'	80
Library	31 x 19'	70
Tower Rm	33' x 21'	70
Map Rm	19' x 14'	20
Dining Rm	23' x 19'	20
Long Gallery	19' x 6.5'	150
Amcotts Suite	10.2' x 6.6' 7.3' x 6'	120

■ Contact

Judith Parker
Skipton Castle
Skipton
North Yorkshire
BD23 1AW

Tel: 01756 792442
Fax: 01756 796100
E-mail: info@skiptoncastle.co.uk

■ Location

MAP 10:O9
OS Ref. SD992 520

In the centre of Skipton, at the N end of High Street.

Skipton is 20m W of Harrogate on the A59 and 26m NW of Leeds on A65.

Rail: Regular services from Leeds & Bradford.

■ Opening Times

All year
(closed 25 December)

Mon–Sat: 10am–6pm
Suns: 12 noon–6pm
(October–February 4pm).

■ Admission

Adult	£6.50
Child (0–4yrs)	Free
Child (5–17yrs)	£3.90
OAP	£5.90
Student (with ID)	£5.90
Family (2+3)	£20.50
Groups (15+)	
Adult	£5.50
Child (0–17yrs)	£3.90

Includes illustrated tour sheet in a choice of nine languages, plus free badge for children.

Groups welcome: Guides available for booked groups at no extra charge.

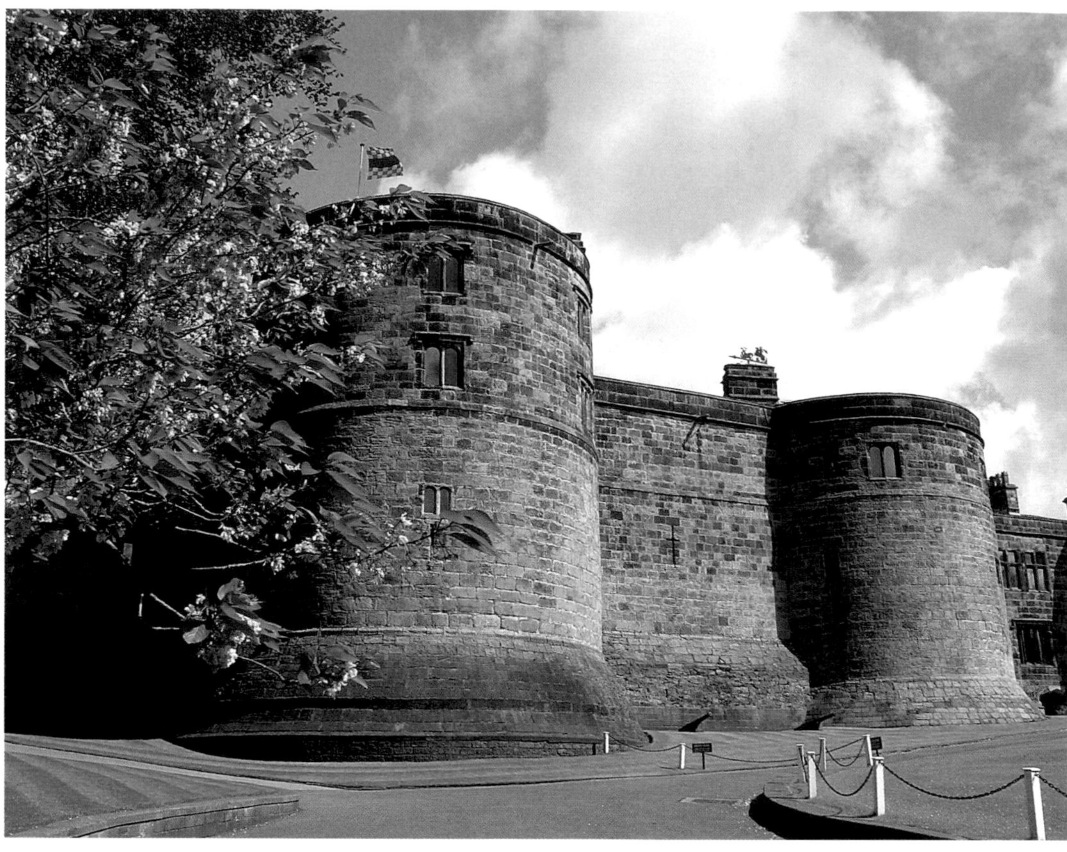

SKIPTON CASTLE

www.skiptoncastle.co.uk

Guardian of the gateway to the Yorkshire Dales for over 900 years, this unique fortress is one of the most complete and well-preserved medieval castles in England. Standing on a 40-metre high crag, fully-roofed Skipton Castle was founded around 1090 by Robert de Romille, one of William the Conqueror's Barons, as a fortress in the dangerous northern reaches of the kingdom.

Owned by King Edward I and Edward II, from 1310 it became the stronghold of the Clifford Lords withstanding successive raids by marauding Scots. During the Civil War it was the last Royalist bastion in the North, yielding only after a three-year siege in 1645. 'Slighted' under the orders of Cromwell, the castle was skilfully restored by the redoubtable Lady Anne Clifford and today visitors can climb from the depths of the Dungeon to the top of the Watch Tower, and explore the Banqueting Hall, the Kitchens, the Bedchamber and even the Privy!

Every period has left its mark, from the Norman entrance and the Medieval towers, to the beautiful Tudor courtyard with the great yew tree planted by Lady Anne in 1659. Here visitors can see the coat of arms of John Clifford, the infamous 'Bloody' Clifford of Shakespeare's Henry VI, who fought and died in the Wars of the Roses whereupon the castle was possessed by Richard III. Throughout the turbulent centuries of English history, the Clifford Lords fought at Bannockburn, at Agincourt and in the Wars of the Roses. The most famous of them all was George Clifford, 3rd Earl of Cumberland, Champion to Elizabeth I, Admiral against the Spanish Armada and conqueror of Puerto Rico in 1598.

In the castle grounds visitors can see the Tudor wing built as a royal wedding present for Lady Eleanor Brandon, niece of Henry VIII, the beautiful Shell Room decorated in the 1620s with shells and Jamaican coral and the ancient medieval chapel of St John the Evangelist. The Chapel Terrace, with its delightful picnic area, has fine views over the woods and Skipton's lively market town.

Unsuitable.

Tearoom. Indoor and outdoor picnic areas.

Obligatory.

Large public coach and car park off nearby High Street. Coach drivers' rest room at Castle.

Welcome. Guides available. Teachers free.

In grounds on leads.

ALDBOROUGH ROMAN SITE

Main Street, Aldborough, Boroughbridge, North Yorkshire YO51 9ES
Tel: 01423 322768 **E-mail:** customers@english-heritage.org.uk
www.english-heritage.org.uk/aldborough
Owner: English Heritage **Contact:** Visitor Operations Team
Aldborough was the 'capital' of the Romanised Brigantes, the largest tribe in Britain. One corner of the defences is laid out amid a Victorian arboretum, and two mosaic pavements can be viewed in their original positions. The site's fascinating museum has an outstanding collection of Roman finds.
Location: MAP 11:A8, OS Ref. SE405 662. Located in Aldborough 0.75m SE of Boroughbridge on a minor road off B6265; within 1 mile junction of A1 and A6055. Rail: Cattal 7.5m
Open: 1 Apr–30 Sept: Sat–Sun & BHs, 11am–5pm.
Admission: Adult £3.20, Child £1.60, Conc. £2.70. 15% discount for groups (11+). EH members Free. Opening times and prices are valid until 31st March 2011, after this date details are subject to change please visit www.english-heritage.org.uk for the most up-to-date information.
WC. On leads.

ASKE HALL

Richmond, North Yorkshire DL10 5HJ
Tel: 01748 822000 **Fax:** 01748 826611 **E-mail:** office@aske.co.uk
www.aske.co.uk
Owner: Earl of Ronaldshay **Contact:** Mandy Blenkiron
A predominantly Georgian collection of paintings, furniture and porcelain in house which has been the seat of the Dundas family since 1763.
Location: MAP 10:P6, OS Ref. NZ179 035. 4m SW of A1 at Scotch Corner, 2m from the A66, on the B6274.
Open: 8 & 9 Sept (Heritage Open Days). Tours 10.00, 12.00 & 14.00, limited to 15 max. Booking advisable and ID will be required (passport, driving licence etc). For further details contact Mandy Blenkiron.
Admission: Free.
No photography Partial Obligatory. Limited.

BAGSHAW MUSEUM

Wilton Park, Batley, West Yorkshire WF17 0AS
Tel: 01924 326155 **Fax:** 01924 326164
Owner: Kirklees Culture & Leisure Services **Contact:** Amanda Daley
A Victorian Gothic mansion set in Wilton Park.
Location: MAP10:P11, OS Ref. SE235 257. From M62/J27 follow A62 to Huddersfield. At Birstall, follow tourist signs.
Open: All year, 11am–5pm, Mon–Fri. 12noon–5pm, Sat–Sun.
Admission: Free.

BENINGBROUGH HALL & GARDENS

Beningbrough, North Yorkshire YO30 1DD
Tel: 01904 472027
Owner: National Trust **Contact:** Visitor Services Manager
Imposing 18th century house with new interpretation galleries with the National Portrait Gallery.
Location: MAP 11:B9, OS Ref. SE516 586. 8m NW of York, 3m W of Shipton, 2m SE of Linton-on-Ouse, follow signposted route.

For unique **Civil wedding** venues see our index at the end of the book.

BOLTON ABBEY

SKIPTON, NORTH YORKSHIRE BD23 6EX

www.boltonabbey.com

Tel: 01756 718009 **Fax:** 01756 710535 **E-mail:** tourism@boltonabbey.com
Owner: Chatsworth Settlement Trustees **Contact:** Visitor Manager
Set in the heart of the Yorkshire Dales on the banks of the River Wharfe, this historic estate is the Yorkshire home of the Duke and Duchess of Devonshire and a magnet for visitors drawn to its breathtaking landscape and excellent facilities.
Explore the ruins of the Priory and discover a landscape full of history and legend. Wander along the woodland and riverside paths or cross the exposed heights of heather moorland.
Enjoy local produce in the excellent restaurants, tea rooms and cafés. Indulge in a little retail therapy in the gift and food shops. Or simply relax and enjoy a picnic whilst the children play.
Location: MAP 10:O9, OS Ref. SE074 542. On B6160, N from the junction with A59 Skipton–Harrogate road, 23m from Leeds.
Open: All year from 9am.
Admission: Please see www.boltonabbey.com for the most up-to-date information.
Licensed. Licensed. By arrangement. Devonshire Arms Country House Hotel & Devonshire Fell Hotel nearby.

Burton Agnes Hall & Gardens

BROCKFIELD HALL

Warthill, York YO19 5XJ

Tel: 01904 489362 **E-mail:** simon@brockfieldhall.co.uk

www.brockfieldhall.co.uk

Owner: Mr & Mrs Simon Wood **Contact:** Simon Wood

A fine late Georgian house designed by Peter Atkinson, assistant to John Carr of York, for Benjamin Agar Esq. Begun in 1804, its outstanding feature is an oval entrance hall with a fine cantilevered stone staircase curving past an impressive Venetian window. It is the family home of Mr and Mrs Simon Wood. Mrs Wood is the daughter of the late Lord and of Lady Martin Fitzalan Howard. He was the brother of the 17th Duke of Norfolk and son of the late Baroness Beaumont of Carlton Towers, Selby. There are some interesting portraits of her old Roman Catholic family, the Stapletons, and some good English furniture. Permanent exhibition of paintings by Staithes Group Artists (by appointment outside August).

Location: MAP 11:C9, OS Ref. SE664 550. 5m E of York off A166 or A64.

Open: 31 July & 2–31 August inclusive except Mons (open BH Mon), 1–4pm. Conducted tours at 13.00, 14.00 and 15.00.

Admission: Adult £6, Child £2.

No photography inside house. Partial. By arrangement.
In grounds, on leads.

BRODSWORTH HALL & GARDENS

See page 329 for full page entry.

BROUGHTON HALL

SKIPTON, YORKSHIRE BD23 3AE

www.broughtonhall.co.uk
www.aldourie.co.uk www.utopia.co.uk

Tel: 01756 799608 **Fax:** 01756 700357 **E-mail:** tempest@broughtonhall.co.uk

Owner: The Tempest Family **Contact:** The Estate Office

The Tempest family have been in the area since 1097. The Grade I listed Hall was built in 1597 and has fine furniture and portraits. Set within 3000 acres with parkland, Italianate gardens and stunning conservatory, it is an ideal venue for enterprise and living. Close by is the award winning Broughton Hall Business Park which is the home of 51 companies and with first class meeting room and food facilities within the Utopia building.

Location: MAP 10:N9, OS Ref. SD943 507. On A59, 2m W of Skipton.

Open: Group tours by arrangement.

Admission: £8.

BURTON AGNES HALL & GARDENS

DRIFFIELD, EAST YORKSHIRE YO25 4NB

www.burtonagnes.com

Tel: 01262 490324 **Fax:** 01262 490513 **E-mail:** office@burtonagnes.com

Owner: Burton Agnes Hall Preservation Trust Ltd **Contact:** Mr Simon Cunliffe-Lister

A lovely Elizabethan Hall containing treasures collected by the family over four centuries, from the original carving and plasterwork to modern and Impressionist paintings. The Hall is surrounded by lawns and topiary yew. The award winning gardens contain a maze, potager, jungle garden, campanula collection and colour gardens incorporating giant game boards. Children's corner.

Location: MAP 11:E9, OS Ref. TA103 633. Off A614 between Driffield and Bridlington.

Open: Gardens, shops & café: Snowdrops 5–27 Feb, daily, 11am–4pm. Hall & gardens, shops and café: 1 Apr–31 Oct, daily 11am–5pm. Christmas opening: 14 Nov–22 Dec, daily, 11am–5pm.

Admission: Hall & Gardens: Adult £8, Child £4, OAP £7.50. Gardens only: Adult £5, Child £3, OAP £4.50. 10% reduction for groups of 30+.

Gift Shop, Farm Shop and Home and Garden Shop. Ground floor & grounds. Café. Ice-cream parlour. In grounds, on leads.

BURTON CONSTABLE

SKIRLAUGH, EAST YORKSHIRE HU11 4LN

www.burtonconstable.com

Tel: 01964 562400 **Fax:** 01964 563229 **Email:** helendewson@btconnect.com

Owner: Burton Constable Foundation **Contact:** Mrs Helen Dewson

One of the most fascinating country houses surviving with its historic collections, Burton Constable is a large Elizabethan mansion surrounded by extensive parkland. The interiors of faded splendour are filled with fine furniture, paintings and sculpture, a library of 5,000 books and a remarkable 18th century 'Cabinet of Curiosities'.

Location: MAP 11:E10 OS Ref TA 193 369. Beverley 14m, Hull 10m. Signed from Skirlaugh.

Open: Easter Sat–27 Oct, Sat–Thur inc. Hall: 1–5pm (last admission 4pm). 19 Nov–4 Dec, Sat–Thur inc. Hall: 1–4pm (last admission 3pm). Grounds & Tea Room: 12.30–5pm. Please telephone to confirm opening times.

Admission: Hall & Grounds: Adult £6.75, Child £3.50, OAP £6.25, Family £17 (2 adults & 4 children), Groups 15+ £5.75 each. Grounds only: Adult £3, Child £1.50, Family £8. Season Ticket £16 (2 adults & 4 children).

Photography allowed in house. WCs. Guide dogs only.

BYLAND ABBEY

Coxwold, Thirsk, North Yorkshire YO61 4BD

Tel: 01347 868614 **E-mail:** byland.abbey@english-heritage.org.uk

www.english-heritage.org.uk/byland

Owner: English Heritage **Contact:** Visitor Operations Team

Once one of the greatest monasteries in England, Byland inspired the design of church buildings throughout the north. An outstanding example of early gothic architecture, it inspired the design of the famous York Minster rose window. The Abbey's collection of medieval floor tiles is a testament to its earlier magnificence.

Location: MAP 11:B8, OS Ref. SE549 789. 2m S of A170 between Thirsk and Helmsley, NE of Coxwold village. Rail: Thirsk 10m

Open: 1 Apr–30 Jun: Wed–Mon, 11am–6pm. 1 Jul–31 Aug: Daily, 11am–6pm. 1–30 Sep: Wed–Mon, 11am–5pm.

Admission: Adult £4.20, Child £2.10, Conc. £3.60. 15% discount for groups (11+). Opening times and prices are valid until 31st March 2011, after this date details are subject to change please visit www.english-heritage.org.uk for the most up-to-date information.

WC. Limited for coaches. On leads.

CANNON HALL MUSEUM, PARK & GARDENS

Cawthorne, Barnsley, South Yorkshire S75 4AT

Tel: 01226 790270 **E-mail:** cannonhall@barnsley.gov.uk **www.barnsley.gov.uk**

Owner: Barnsley Metropolitan Borough Council **Contact:** The Museum Manager

Set in 70 acres of historic parkland and gardens, Cannon Hall now contains collections of fine furniture, old master paintings, stunning glassware and colourful pottery, much of which is displayed in period settings. Plus 'Charge', the Regimental museum of the 13th/18th Royal Hussars (QMO) and the Light Dragoons. Events and education programme and an ideal setting for conferences and Civil wedding ceremonies.

Location: MAP 10:P12, OS Ref. SE272 084. 6m NW of Barnsley of A635. M1/J38.

Open: Please call for opening times.

Admission: Free except for some events. Charge for car parking.

Partial. WC. Weekends & school holidays. Pre-booked. In grounds, on leads.

CASTLE HOWARD

See page 330 for full page entry.

CAWTHORNE VICTORIA JUBILEE MUSEUM

Taylor Hill, Cawthorne, Barnsley, South Yorkshire S75 4HQ

Tel: 01226 790545 / 790246

Owner: Cawthorne Village **Contact:** Mrs Mary Herbert

A quaint and eccentric collection in a half-timbered building. Museum has a ramp and toilet for disabled visitors. School visits welcome.

Location: MAP 10:P12, OS Ref. SE285 080. 4m W of Barnsley, just off the A635.

Open: Palm Sun–end Oct: Sats, Suns & BH Mons, 2–5pm. Groups by appointment throughout the year.

Admission: Adult 50p, Child 20p.

CLIFFE CASTLE

Keighley, West Yorkshire BD20 6LH

Tel: 01535 618231

Owner: City of Bradford Metropolitan District Council **Contact:** Daru Rooke

Victorian manufacturer's house of 1878 with tall tower and garden. Now a museum.

Location: MAP 10:O10, OS Ref. SE057 422. ¾ m NW of Keighley off the A629.

Open: All year: Tues–Sat & BH Mons, 10am–5pm. Suns, 12 noon–5pm. Closed Good Friday and 25/26 Dec.

Admission: Free.

© English Heritage

CLIFFORD'S TOWER

TOWER STREET, YORK YO1 9SA

www.english-heritage.org.uk/cliffords

Tel: 01904 646940 **E-mail:** customers@english-heritage.org.uk

Owner: English Heritage **Contact:** Visitor Operations Team

Cliffords Tower is a must see attraction for any one that is planning a visit to York, with sweeping panoramic views of York and the surrounding countryside. Once the central stronghold of York Castle, the tower has survived turbulent centuries of fire, siege and attempted demolition.

Location: MAP 21, OS Ref. SE 605 515. York city centre.

Open: 1 Apr–30 Sep: daily, 10am–6pm; 1–31 Oct: daily, 10am–5pm. 1 Nov–31 Mar: daily, 10am–4pm. Closed 24–26 Dec & 1 Jan.

Admission: Adult £3.50, Child £1.80, Conc. £3. Family ticket £8.80. 15% discount available for groups (11+). Opening times and prices are valid until 31st March 2011, after this date details are subject to change please visit www.english-heritage.org.uk for the most up-to-date information.

Special Events: Throughout the holiday periods you can explore the part Clifford's Tower played in the history of England with special hidden history guided tours.

Unsuitable. Charged.

CONISBROUGH CASTLE

Castle Hill, Conisbrough, South Yorkshire DN12 3BU
Tel: 01709 863329 **E-mail:** conisbrough.castle@english-heritage.org.uk
www.english-heritage.org.uk/conisbrough
Owner: English Heritage **Contact:** The Administrator

One of Yorkshire's best surviving examples of medieval military architecture, with a reinstated roof and floors; this 12th century castle is a spectacular structure. Built of magnesium limestone, it is the only example of its kind in Europe, and was one of the inspirations for Sir Walter Scott's classic novel, Ivanhoe.

Location: MAP 7:A1, OS Ref. SK515 989. Located NE of Conisbrough town center off A630 4.5 miles SW of Doncaster. Rail: Conisbrough 0.5m.

Open: 1 Apr–30 Jun: Sat–Wed, 10am–5pm. 1 Jul–31 Aug: daily, 10–5pm. 1–30 Sep: Sat–Wed 10am–5pm. 1 Oct–31 Mar: Sat–Wed, 10am–4pm. (last admission 4.20pm). Closed 24–26 Dec & 1 Jan.

Admission: Adult £4.20, Child £2.10, Conc. £3.60, Family £10.50. Opening times and prices are valid until 31st March 2011, after this date details are subject to change please visit www.english-heritage.org.uk for the most up-to-date information.

Partial. Partial. On leads.

Fairfax House

CONSTABLE BURTON HALL GARDENS

LEYBURN, NORTH YORKSHIRE DL8 5LJ

www.constableburtongardens.co.uk

Tel: 01677 450428 **Fax:** 01677 450622
Owner/Contact: M C A Wyvill Esq

A delightful terraced woodland garden of lilies, ferns, hardy shrubs, roses and wild flowers, attached to a beautiful Palladian house designed by John Carr (not open). Garden trails and herbaceous borders. Stream garden with large architectural plants and reflection ponds. Impressive spring display of daffodils and tulips.

Location: MAP 10:P7, OS Ref. SE164 913. 3m E of Leyburn off the A684.

Open: Garden only: 20 Mar–26 Sept: daily, 9am–6pm.

Admission: Adult £4, Children under 16 years 50p. OAP £3.50.

Partial, WC. Group tours of house & gardens by arrangement.
Limited for coaches. In grounds, on leads.

Skyscan/William Cross

DUNCOMBE PARK

HELMSLEY, NORTH YORKSHIRE YO62 5EB

www.duncombepark.com

Tel: 01439 770213 **Fax:** 01439 771114 **E-mail:** info@duncombepark.com
Owner/Contact: Hon. Jake Duncombe

The sweeping grass terraces, towering veteran trees, and classical temples are described by historian Christopher Hussey as 'the most spectacularly beautiful among English landscape conceptions of the 18th century'. Beside superb views over the Rye valley, visitors will discover woodland walks, ornamental parterres, and a 'secret garden' at the Conservatory.

Location: MAP 11:B7, OS Ref. SE604 830. Entrance just off Helmsley Market Square, signed off A170 Thirsk–Scarborough road.

Open: Garden Only: 1 Jun–30 Aug, Wed–Sun, 10.30am–5pm. Last admission 4pm. The garden may close for private events and functions – please check website for information.

Admission: Gardens & Parkland: Adult £5, Conc £4.50, Child (5–16yrs) £3, Child under 5yrs Free, Groups (15+) £4, Group guided tour £5. Parkland: Adult £3, Child (10–16yrs) £2, Child under 10yrs Free.

Wedding receptions, conferences, corporate hospitality, country walks, nature reserve, orienteering, film location, product launches, vehicle rallies. Banqueting facilities. For 15+ groups only. In park on leads only.

FAIRFAX HOUSE

FAIRFAX HOUSE, CASTLEGATE, YORK YO1 9RN

www.fairfaxhouse.co.uk

Tel: 01904 655543 **Fax:** 01904 652262 **E-mail:** info@fairfaxhouse.co.uk

Owner: York Civic Trust **Contact:** Hannah Phillip

Fairfax House is a classical architectural masterpiece and one of the finest Georgian townhouses in England. Originally owned by the Fairfax family, its richly decorated interior was designed by York's most distinguished architect, John Carr. After extensive adaptation in the 20th century as a cinema, Fairfax House was fully restored by York Civic Trust in 1983/84. Today it is home to the Noel Terry collection of Georgian furniture, clocks and decorative arts, described by Christie's as one of the finest collections formed in the 20th century. It perfectly complements the house, bringing it to life and creating a special lived-in atmosphere.

Location: MAP 11:B9, OS Ref. SE605 515. In centre of York between Castle Museum and Jorvik Centre.

Open: 12 Feb–31 Dec, Mon–Thur: 11am–5pm. Fri: Guided tours only 11am and 2pm. Sat: 11am–5pm. Sun: 1.30–5pm. Last admission 4.30pm. Closed 1 Jan–11 Feb & 24–26 Dec.

Admission: Gift Aid Adult £6, Gift Aid Conc. £5, Children under 16 Free with full paying adult. Groups from £4.50 pp. Min payment 10 persons.

Suitable for filming. No photography in house. Max. 28 seated. Groups up to 50.

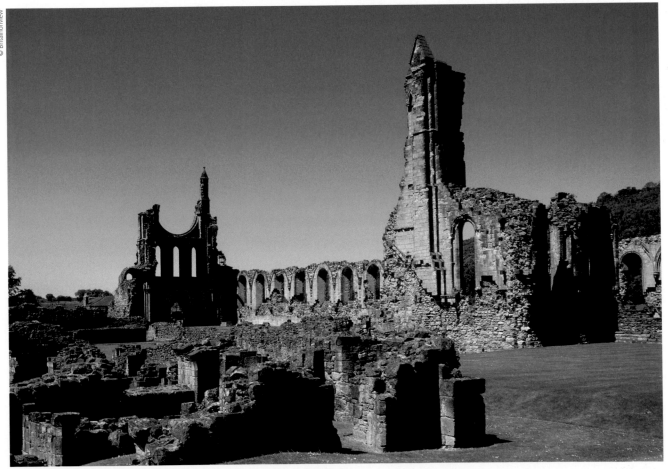

Byland Abbey

FOUNTAINS ABBEY & STUDLEY ROYAL

See page 331 for full page entry.

THE GEORGIAN THEATRE ROYAL

Victoria Road, Richmond, North Yorkshire DL10 4DW

Tel: 01748 823710 **Box Office:** 01748 825252

E-mail: admin@georgiantheatreroyal.co.uk

Owner: Georgian Theatre Royal Trust **Contact:** Trish Hoines

The most complete Georgian playhouse in Britain. Built in 1788 by actor/manager, Samuel Butler and restored to its Georgian grandeur in 2003.

Location: MAP 10:P6, OS Ref. NZ174 013. 4m from the A1 (Scotch Corner) on the A6108.

Open: All year: Mon–Sat. Guided tours only: On the hour, 10am–4pm.

Admission: Donation £3.50. Child £1.50.

giftaid it Some properties will be operating the Gift Aid on Entry scheme at their admission points. Where the scheme is operating, visitors are offered a choice between paying the standard admission price or paying the 'Gift Aid Admission' which includes a voluntary donation of at least 10%.
Gift Aid Admissions enable the charity to reclaim tax on the whole amount paid* - an extra 28% - potentially a very significant boost to property funds. Money raised from paying visitors in this way will go towards restoration projects at the property and will be very welcome.
Where shown, the admission prices are inclusive of the 10% voluntary donation where properties are operating the Gift Aid on Entry scheme, but both the standard admission price and the Gift Aid Admission will be displayed at the property and on their website.

*Gift Aid donations must be supported by a valid Gift Aid declaration and a Gift Aid declaration can only cover donations made by an individual for him/herself or for him/herself and members of his/her family.

© Britainonview

Harewood House

HAREWOOD HOUSE

HAREWOOD, LEEDS, WEST YORKSHIRE LS17 9LG

www.harewood.org

Tel: 0113 2181010 **Fax:** 0113 2181002 **E-mail:** info@harewood.org

Owner: The Earl of Harewood **Contact:** Harewood House Trust

Home to the Queen's cousin, the Earl of Harewood, Harewood is renowned for its 'Capability' Brown landscapes, magnificent architecture and outstanding art collections. Designed by John Carr, the House features exquisite interiors by Robert Adam, furnishings by Thomas Chippendale, world-class art, including J M W Turner, Gainsborough, Sir Joshua Reynolds and Renaissance masterpieces.

'Below Stairs' includes many items from HRH Princess Mary, (Lord Harewood's mother) the Princess Royal's life, as well as providing a fascinating glimpse into the hidden world of the servants' domain.

Harewood's stunning gardens include a Himalayan Garden, Walled Garden and Parterre Terrace. Harewood plays hosts to many special events, and features a strong exhibition programme. Visit www.harewood.org for details.

Location: MAP 10:P10 OS Ref. SE311 446: A1 N or S to Wetherby. A659 via Collingham, Harewood is on A61 between Harrogate and Leeds. Easily reached from A1, M1, M62 and M18. Half an hour from York, 15 mins from centre of Leeds or Harrogate. Bus: No. 36 from Leeds or Harrogate. Rail: Leeds Station 7m. Air: Leeds Bradford Airport 7m.

Open: Please see our website for specific opening times, go online www.harewood.org/tickets-times or call 0113 218 1010.

Admission: Adults from £7.50–£14.30, Children from £4.50–£7.25, Seniors from £6.50–£13.25, Family from £25–£44.

Marquees can be accommodated, concerts and product launches. No photography in the House. Ideal for corporate entertaining including drinks receptions, buffets and wedding receptions. Specific rooms available. WCs. Licensed. Licensed Lectures by arrangement. Daily free talks. Audio tour of house available. Cars 400 yds from house. 50+ coaches 500 yds from house. Drivers to verify in advance. Sandford Award for Education. Dogs on leads in grounds, guide dogs only in house.

HELMSLEY CASTLE

CASTLEGATE, HELMSLEY, NORTH YORKSHIRE YO62 5AB

www.english-heritage.org.uk/helmsley

Tel/Fax: 01439 770442 **E-mail:** helmsley.castle@english-heritage.org.uk

Owner: English Heritage **Contact:** Visitor Operations Team

Explore 900 years of life at Helmsley Castle which boasts some amazing medieval architecture. Discover how the castle evolved from a medieval fortress, to a luxurious Tudor mansion, to a Civil War stronghold and a romantic Victorian ruin. Take an audio tour and see original artefacts excavated from the site.

Location: MAP 11:B7, OS Ref. SE611 836. In Helmsley town.

Open: 1 Apr–30 Sep: daily, 10am–6pm. 1–31 Oct: Thu–Mon, 10am–5pm. 1 Nov–28 Feb, Thu–Mon, 10am–4pm. 1–31 Mar: Thu–Mon, 10am–5pm. Closed 24–26 Dec & 1 Jan.

Admission: Adult £4.70, Child £2.40, Conc £4.00, Family £11.80. 15% discount for groups (11+). Opening times and prices are valid until 31st March 2011, after this date details are subject to change please visit www.english-heritage.org.uk for the most up-to-date information.

Tourist information located within Castle Visitor Centre. Charged. On leads.

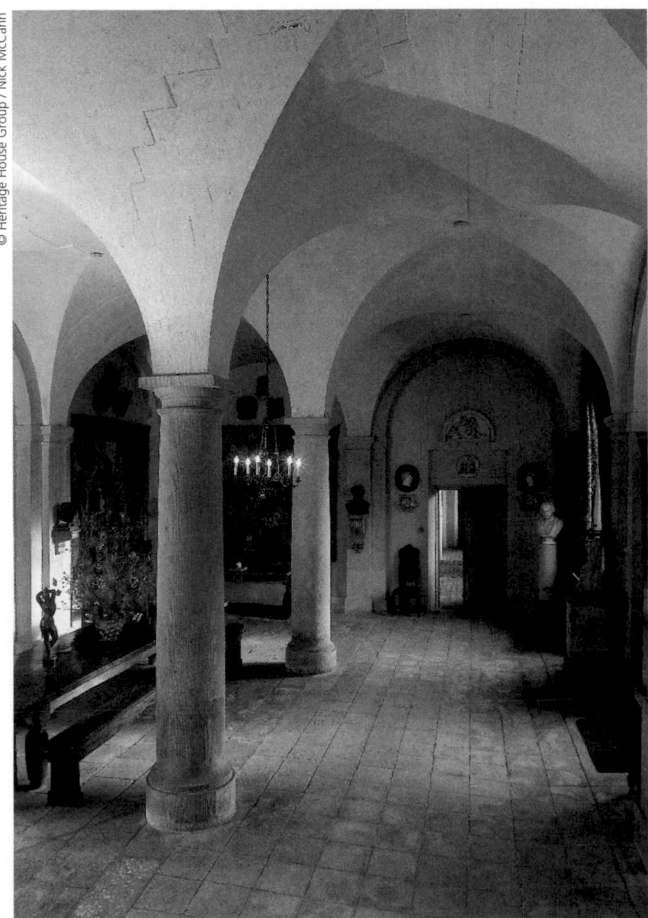

Hovingham Hall

HELMSLEY WALLED GARDEN

Cleveland Way, Helmsley, North Yorkshire YO62 5AH

Tel/Fax: 01439 771427

Owner: Helmsley Walled Garden Ltd **Contact:** Paul Radcliffe/Lindsay Tait

A 5 acre walled garden under restoration. Orchid house and vinery restored. Plant sales area and vegetarian café.

Location: MAP 11:B7, OS Ref. SE611 836. 25m N of York, 15m from Thirsk. In Helmsley follow signs to Cleveland Way.

Open: 1 Apr–31 Oct: daily, 10.30am–5pm.

Admission: Adult £4, Child Free, Conc. £3.

HOVINGHAM HALL

YORK, NORTH YORKSHIRE YO62 4LU

www.hovingham.co.uk

Tel: 01653 628771 **Fax:** 01653 628668 **E-mail:** office@hovingham.co.uk

Owner: William Worsley **Contact:** Mrs Lamprey

This attractive Palladian family home, in its beautiful parkland setting, was designed and built by Thomas Worsley, Surveyor General to King George III. It is still lived in by his descendants and was the childhood home of Katharine Worsley, the Duchess of Kent. Hovingham Hall is unique in being entered through a huge riding school and features halls with vaulted ceilings and a beautiful collection of pictures and furniture. The house has attractive gardens with magnificent Yew hedges and the cricket ground in front of the house is reputed to be the oldest private cricket ground in England.

Location: MAP 11:C8, OS Ref. SE666 756. 18m N of York on Malton/Helmsley Road (B1257).

Open: 1 Jun–28 Jun inclusive 12.30pm to 4.30pm (last tour 3.30pm).

Admission: Adult £8.00, Conc. £7.50, Child £3. Gardens only: £4.

No photography in house. Partial. Obligatory. Limited. Guide dogs only.

JERVAULX ABBEY

Ripon, North Yorkshire HG4 4PH

Tel: 01677 460226 / 460391

Owner/Contact: Mr I S Burdon

Extensive ruins of a former Cistercian abbey.

Location: MAP 10:P7, OS Ref. SE169 858. Beside the A6108 Ripon–Leyburn road, 5m SE of Leyburn and 5m NW of Masham.

Open: Daily during daylight hours.

Admission: Adult £2, Child £1.50 in honesty box at Abbey entrance.

Thinking of a short break or weekend away?
See Historic Places to Stay

KIPLIN HALL

Nr SCORTON, RICHMOND, NORTH YORKSHIRE DL10 6AT

www.kiplinhall.co.uk

Tel: 01748 818178 **E-mail:** info@kiplinhall.co.uk
Owner: Kiplin Hall Trustees **Contact:** The Administrator

Unusual Jacobean House built by George Calvert, founder of Maryland, USA. 'Gothic' Drawing Room wing added in the 1820s, later converted into a Jacobean-style Library designed by W. E. Nesfield. Visitors are now welcomed into a charming Victorian home, furnished with an eclectic mix of furniture, paintings, portraits and personalia, including many Arts and Crafts items, collected by the Calverts, Crowes, Carpenters and Talbots – the families who owned Kiplin between 1620 and 1968. The gardens and pleasure grounds are undergoing restoration. Visitors are delighted by the extent and beauty of the landscape.

Location: MAP 11:A7, OS Ref. SE274 976. Between Richmond and Northallerton, approx. 5 miles east of the A1, on the B6271 Scorton – Northallerton road.

Open: Hall, Gardens and Grounds: 3 Apr–28 Sept, Sun, Mon, Tues & Wed, 2–5pm; Good Fri and Easter Sat 2–5pm; Christmas Weekend, Fri 2 Dec–Sun 4 Dec, 11am–5pm. Gardens and Grounds: Sun, Mon, Tues & Wed, 1 Feb–30 Oct, 10am–4pm (until 6pm 3 Apr–30 Sept).

Admission: Hall, Gardens & Grounds: Adult £7, Conc. £6, Child £3, family (2+3) £18. Larger groups by arrangement. Gardens and Grounds only, including woodland and lakeside walks: Adult £4, Conc. £3, Child £1, family (2+3) £9.

Partial. WCs. By arrangement. In grounds, on leads. Assistance dogs only in house.

KIRKHAM PRIORY

Kirkham, Whitwell-on-the-Hill, North Yorkshire YO60 7JS
Tel: 01653 618768 **E-mail:** kirkham.priory@english-heritage.org.uk
www.english-heritage.org.uk/kirkhampriory
Owner: English Heritage **Contact:** Visitor Operations Team

The ruins of this Augustinian priory include a magnificent carved gatehouse, declaring to the world the Priory's association with the rich and powerful. Discover the stories of a monk's life and the Priory's involvement in WWII including a secret visit by the then Prime Minister Winston Churchill.

Location: MAP 11:C8, OS Ref. SE736 658. 5m SW of Malton on minor road off A64.

Open: 1 Apr–31 Jul: Thur–Mon, 10am–5pm. 1–31 Aug: daily, 10am–5pm. 1–30 Sep: Thu–Mon, 10am–5pm.

Admission: Adult £3.20, Child £1.60, Conc. £2.70. 15% discount for groups (11+). Opening times and prices are valid until 31st March 2011, after this date details are subject to change please visit www.english-heritage.org.uk for the most up-to-date information.

WC. Limited for coaches. On leads.

KNARESBOROUGH CASTLE & MUSEUM

Knaresborough, North Yorkshire HG5 8AS
Tel: 01423 556188 **Fax:** 01423 556130
Owner: Duchy of Lancaster **Contact:** Diane Taylor

Ruins of 14th century castle standing high above the town. Local history museum housed in Tudor Courthouse. Gallery devoted to the Civil War.

Location: MAP 11:A9, OS Ref. SE349 569. 5m E of Harrogate, off A59.

Open: Good Friday–5 Oct: daily, 10.30am–5pm.

Admission: Adult £2.90, Child £1.60, OAP £1.90, Family £7.50.

LEDSTON HALL

Hall Lane, Ledston, Castleford, West Yorkshire WF10 2BB
Tel: 01423 523423 Fax: 01423 521373 **E-mail:** helen.bridges@carterjonas.co.uk
Contact: Helen Bridges

17th century mansion with some earlier work.

Location: MAP 11:A11, OS Ref. SE437 289. 2m N of Castleford, off A656.

Open: Exterior only: May–Aug: Mon–Fri, 9am–4pm. Other days by appointment.

Admission: Free.

LOTHERTON HALL & GARDENS

Aberford, Leeds, West Yorkshire LS25 3EB
Tel: 0113 2813259
Owner: Leeds City Council **Contact:** Michael Thaw

Edwardian house with fine collections. Gardens and deer park.

Location: MAP 11:B10, OS92, SE450 360. 2½ m E of M1/J47 on B1217 the Towton Road.

MANSION HOUSE

ST HELEN'S SQUARE, YORK YO1 9QL

www.mansionhouseyork.co.uk

Tel: 01904 552036 **Fax:** 01904 551052 **E-mail:** mansionhouse@york.gov.uk
Owner: City of York Council **Contact:** Richard Pollitt

The Mansion House is one of York's great historic treasures and the oldest surviving mayoral residence in the country. The beauiful simplicity of the hallway gives way to the magnificent grandeur of the stateroom. The extensive civic collection ranges from silver chamber pots to medieval ceremonial swords.

Location: MAP 21, SE601 518 situated in St Helen's Square, close to the post office and to York Minster.

Open: House tours: 11am, 12.30pm & 2pm every Thur, Fri & Sat from Mar–Dec (no need to book in advance). Open all year for pre booked groups. For House, Silver & Connoisseur Tours, contact property for details.

Admission: House tours: Adult £5, Child (up to 16) Free, Conc £4. Pre-booked house tours 10% discount for groups 10+ (Fri & Sat). *Silver Tours £8.50, *Behind the scenes Tour £8.50 *Connoisseur Tours £12.95. *Includes refreshments.

No photography. Obligatory Guide dogs only.

© York Gate Garden

York Gate Garden

MARKENFIELD HALL

NR RIPON, NORTH YORKSHIRE HG4 3AD

www.markenfield.com

Tel: 01765 692303 **Fax:** 01765 607195

E-mail: info@markenfield.com

Owner: Lady Deirdre Curteis **Contact:** The Administrator

"This wonderfully little-altered building is the most complete surviving example of the medium-sized 14th century country house in England" John Martin Robinson *The Architecture of Northern England*. Tucked privately away down a mile-long winding drive, Markenfield is one of the most astonishing and romantic of Yorkshire's medieval houses: fortified, completely moated, and still privately owned. Winner of the HHA and Sotheby's Finest Restoration Award 2008.

Location: MAP 10:P8, OS Ref. SE294 672. Access from W side of A61. 2½ miles S of the Ripon bypass.

Open: 1–14 May & 19 June–2 Jul: daily, 2–5pm. Groups all year round by appointment.

Admission: Adult £4, Conc £3. Booked groups £5 per person (min charge £80).

MIDDLEHAM CASTLE

Castle Hill, Middleham, Leyburn, North Yorkshire DL8 4QG

Tel: 01969 623899 **E-mail:** middleham.castle@english-heritage.org.uk

www.english-heritage.org.uk/middleham

Owner: English Heritage **Contact:** Visitor Operations Team

Once the childhood and favourite home of Richard III, where he learnt the military skills and the courtly manners appropriate for a future king. The massive keep, one of the largest in England, was both a defensive building and a self-contained residence for the Lords of this fortress palace.

Location: MAP 10:O7, OS Ref. SE128 876. At Middleham, 2m S of Leyburn on A6108. Rail: Leyburn (Wensleydale Railway) 2m

Open: 1 Apr–30 Sept: daily, 10am–6pm. 1 Oct–31 Mar: Sat–Wed, 10am–4pm. Closed 24–26 Dec & 1 Jan.

Admission: Adult £4.20, Child £2.10, Conc. £3.60. 15% discount for groups (11+). Opening times and prices are valid until 31st March 2011, after this date details are subject to change please visit www.english-heritage.org.uk for the most up-to-date information.

Exhibition. Partial. On leads.

MOUNT GRACE PRIORY

Staddlebridge, Nr Northallerton, North Yorkshire DL6 3JG

Tel: 01609 883494 **E-mail:** mountgrace.priory@english-heritage.org.uk

www.english-heritage.org.uk/mountgracepriory

Owner: English Heritage **Contact:** Visitor Operations Team

Set amid woodland, this enchanting monastery is the best preserved Carthusian priory in Britain. Discover how the monks lived 600 years ago in the reconstructed monk's cell and herb plot. The gardens, re-modelled in the Arts & Crafts style, are a haven for the famous 'Priory Stoats'.

Location: MAP11:A7, OS Ref. SE449 985. 12m N of Thirsk, 6m NE of Northallerton on A19. Rail: Northallerton 6m

Open: 1 Apr–30 Sept: Thur–Mon, 10am–6pm. 1 Oct–31 Mar: Thur–Sun, 10am–4pm. Closed 24–26 Dec & 1 Jan. Please note on the days there are summer evening theatre events, the site will open at 12pm.

Admission: Adult £4.70, Child £2.40, Conc. £4, Family £11.80. 15% discount for groups (11+). NT Members Free, (except on event days). Opening times and prices are valid until 31st March 2011, after this date details are subject to change please visit www.english-heritage.org.uk for the most up-to-date information.

WCs.

NATIONAL CENTRE FOR EARLY MUSIC

St Margaret's Church, Walmgate, York YO1 9TL

Tel: 01904 632220 **Fax:** 01904 612631 **E-mail:** info@ncem.co.uk **www.ncem.co.uk**

Owner: York Early Music Foundation **Contact:** Mrs G Baldwin

The National Centre for Early Music is based in the medieval church of St Margaret's York. The church boasts a 12th century Romanesque doorway and a 17th century brick tower of considerable note. The Centre hosts concerts, music education activities, conferences, recordings and events.

Location: MAP 21, OS Ref. SE609 515. Inside Walmgate Bar, within the city walls, on the E side of the city.

Open: Mon–Fri, 10am–4pm. Also by appointment. Access is necessarily restricted when events are taking place.

Admission: Free, donations welcome.

Obligatory. By arrangement. Limited. No coaches.

Kiplin Hall

NEWBURGH PRIORY

COXWOLD, NORTH YORKSHIRE YO61 4AS

Tel: 01347 868372

Owner/Contact: Sir George Wombwell Bt

Originally 1145 with major alterations in 1568 and 1720, it has been the home of the Earls of Fauconberg and of the Wombwell family since 1538. Tomb of Oliver Cromwell (3rd daughter Mary married Viscount Fauconberg) is in the house. Extensive grounds contain a water garden, walled garden, topiary yews and woodland walks.

Location: MAP 11:B8, OS Ref. SE541 764. 4m E of A19, 18m N of York, ½ m E of Coxwold.

Open: 3 Apr–29 Jun Wed & Sun + Easter Mon BH + Mon 30 May. House: 2.30–4.45pm. Garden: 2–6pm. Tours every 1/2 hour, take approximately 50–60mins. Booked groups by arrangement.

Admission: House & Gardens: Adult £6. Child £1.50. Gardens only: Adult £3, Child Free. Special tours of private apartment Sun only 3–24 Apr & Easter Mon £5pp.

No photography in house. Partial. Obligatory. Limited for coaches. In grounds, on leads. And wedding receptions.

© NT / Kippa Matthews

NOSTELL PRIORY & PARKLAND

DONCASTER ROAD, WAKEFIELD, WEST YORKSHIRE WF4 1QE

www.nationaltrust.org.uk

Tel: 01924 863892 **E-mail:** nostellpriory@nationaltrust.org.uk

Owner: National Trust **Contact:** Visitor Services Manager

Set in over 350 acres of parkland, Nostell Priory is one of Yorkshire's jewels. It is an architectural treasure by James Paine with later additions by Robert Adam, and an internationally renowned Chippendale Collection.

Location: MAP 11:A11, OS Ref. SE403 175. 6m SE of Wakefield, off A638.

Open: Parkland: 2 Jan–31 Dec, daily, 9am–7pm. House: 11am–1pm for guided tours at 11.15am, 11.45am & 12.15pm. 26 Feb–30 Oct, Wed–Sun, 1–5pm; 3–4 Dec, Sat & Sun, 1–4pm; 7–11 Dec, Wed–Sun, 1–4pm (7 & 8 Dec 5–8pm). Shop & Tearoom: 26 Feb–30 Oct, daily, 10am–5.30pm; 31 Oct–31 Dec, daily, 10am–4pm. Gardens: 26 Feb–30 Oct, Wed–Sun, 11am–5.30pm; 5 Nov–31 Dec, Sat & Sun, 11am–4pm. School holidays, Open daily, 11am–4.30pm. Rose garden may be closed on occasions for private functions. Closed 25 Dec.

***Admission:** Parkland: Free. House & Garden: Adult £9.50, Child £4.50, Family (2+3) £22. Garden: Adult £6, Child £3, Family £14.75. Group (standard admission) Adult £7, Child £3.50. *Includes a voluntary donation but visitors can choose to pay the standard prices displayed at the property and on the website.

Baby facilities. WCs. By arrangement. Limited for coaches. On leads.

NORTON CONYERS

Nr RIPON, NORTH YORKSHIRE HG4 5EQ

Tel/Fax: 01765 640333 **E-mail:** norton.conyers@btinternet.com

Owner: Sir James and Lady Graham **Contact:** Lady Graham

Visited by Charlotte Brontë, Norton Conyers is an original of 'Thornfield Hall'. House and garden have belonged to the Grahams since 1624. The charming and historically important mid-eighteenth century walled garden retains its original design. Herbaceous borders flanked by yew hedges lead to central pavilion with attached peach-house (still in use). Small sales area specialising in unusual hardy plants. PYO fruit, and cut peonies, in season.

Location: MAP 11:A8, OS Ref. SF319 763. 4m NW of Ripon. 3½ m from the A1.

Open: House will be closed for repairs during 2011. Garden: 1/2 & 29/30 May; Sun & Mon 5 Jun–8 Aug, also 28/29 Aug; daily 6–9 Jul. All 2–5pm; last admissions 4.40pm. Groups by appointment. (In addition garden is usually open on Mondays and Saturdays throughout the year; please ring for confirmation).

Admission: Individual admission to garden is free; donations are very welcome. A charge is made when the garden is open for charity; teas are served at these openings. Charges for groups by arrangement (min. 10, max 60).

Pavilion is available for functions: seats up to 20. By arrangement. Ample for cars. Limited for coaches. On leads.

© Heritage House Group Ltd

Newby Hall - The Ante Room

NEWBY HALL & GARDENS

See page 332 for full page entry.

NUNNINGTON HALL

Nunnington, North Yorkshire YO62 5UY
Tel: 01439 748283
Owner: National Trust **Contact:** The Property Manager

17th century manor house with magnificent oak-panelled hall, nursery, haunted room, and attics, with their fascinating Carlisle collection of miniature rooms fully furnished to reflect different periods.

Location: MAP 11:C8, OS Ref. SE670 795. In Ryedale, 4½ m SE of Helmsley, 1½ m N of B1257.

ORMESBY HALL

Ladgate Lane, Ormesby, Middlesbrough TS7 9AS
Tel: 01642 324188
Owner: National Trust **Contact:** Mr P Burton

A mid 18th century house with opulent decoration inside, including fine plasterwork by contemporary craftsmen.

Location: MAP 11:B6, OS Ref. NZ530 167. 3m SE of Middlesbrough.

PARCEVALL HALL GARDENS

Skyreholme, Skipton, North Yorkshire BD23 6DE
Tel:/Fax: 01756 720311 **E-mail:** parcevallhall@btconnect.com
Owner: Walsingham College (Yorkshire Properties) Ltd.
Contact: Phillip Nelson (Head Gardener)
Location: MAP 10:O8, OS Ref. SE068 613. E side of Upper Wharfedale, 1½ m NE of Appletreewick. 12m NNW of Ilkley by B6160 and via Burnsall.
Open: 1 Apr–31 Oct: 10am–6pm.
Admission: Adult £5.50, Child £2.50.

PICKERING CASTLE

Castlegate, Pickering, North Yorkshire YO18 7AX
Tel/Fax: 01751 474989 **E-mail:** pickering.castle@english-heritage.org.uk
www.english-heritage.org.uk/pickering
Owner: English Heritage **Contact:** Visitor Operations Team

Pickering Castle is set in an attractive market town. Built by William the Conqueror the splendid 13th century Castle was used as a royal hunting lodge, holiday home and stud farm by a succession of medieval kings. Explore the walls, towers and mote and climb the steps to the motte.

Location: MAP 11:C7, OS Ref. SE998 845. In Pickering, 15m SW of Scarborough. Rail: Malton 9m, Pickering (N York Moors Railway) 0.5m
Open: 1 Apr–30 Jun: Thu–Mon, 10am–5pm. 1 Jul–31 Aug: Daily, 10am–5pm. 1–30 Sep: Thu–Mon, 10am–5pm.
Admission: Adult £3.70, Child £1.90, Conc. £3.10, Family £9.30. 15% discount for groups (11+). Opening times and prices are valid until 31st March 2011, after this date details are subject to change please visit www.english-heritage.org.uk for the most up-to-date information.

WCs. Partial. Limited. On leads.

PLUMPTON ROCKS

Plumpton, Knaresborough, North Yorkshire HG5 8NA
Tel: 01289 386360
Owner: Edward de Plumpton Hunter **Contact:** Robert de Plumpton Hunter

Grade II* listed garden extending to over 30 acres including an idyllic lake, dramatic millstone grit rock formation, romantic woodland walks winding through bluebells and rhododendrons. Declared by English Heritage to be of outstanding interest. Painted by Turner. Described by Queen Mary as *'Heaven on earth'*.

Location: MAP 11:A9, OS Ref. SE355 535. Midway between Harrogate and Wetherby on the A661, 1m SE of A661 junction with the Harrogate southern bypass.
Open: Mar–Oct: Sat, Sun & BHs, 11am–6pm.
Admission: Adult £2.50, Child/OAP £1.50. (2010 prices, subject to change).

Unsuitable. Limited for coaches. In grounds, on leads.

RHS GARDEN HARLOW CARR

See main index.

© Britainonview

Pickering Castle

© English Heritage

RICHMOND CASTLE

TOWER ST, RICHMOND, NORTH YORKSHIRE DL10 4QW

www.english-heritage.org.uk/richmond

Tel/Fax: 01748 822493 **E-mail:** customers@english-heritage.org.uk
Owner: English Heritage **Contact:** Visitor Operations Team

Built shortly after 1066 on a rocky promontory high above the River Swale, this is the best preserved castle of such scale and age in Britain. The magnificent keep, with breathtaking views, is reputed to be the place where the legendary King Arthur sleeps.

Location: MAP 10:P6, OS Ref. NZ172 007. In Richmond.
Open: 1 Apr–30 Sep: daily, 10am–6pm. 1 Oct–31 Mar: Thur–Mon, 10am–4pm. Closed 24–26 Dec & 1 Jan.
Admission: Adult £4.50, Child £2.30, Conc. £3.80 15% discount for groups (11+). Opening times and prices are valid until 31st March 2011, after this date details are subject to change please visit www.english-heritage.org.uk for the most up-to-date information.

Interactive exhibition. WCs. On leads.

© English Heritage

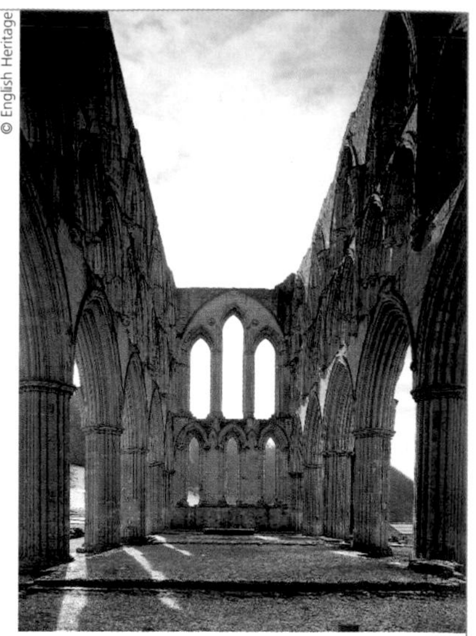
© English Heritage

RIEVAULX ABBEY ⌗

RIEVAULX, Nr HELMSLEY, NORTH YORKSHIRE YO62 5LB

www.english-heritage.org.uk/rievaulx

Tel: 01439 798228 **E-mail:** rievaulx.abbey@english-heritage.org.uk

Owner: English Heritage **Contact:** Visitor Operations Team

Rievaulx was the first Cistercian Abbey to be founded in the North of England in the 12th century by St Bernard of Clairvaux. Set in a beautiful tranquil valley, it is the most atmospheric and complete of all the ruined abbeys in the region.

"Everywhere peace, everywhere serenity, and a marvellous freedom from the tumult of the world", these words still describe Rievaulx today; written over eight centuries ago by, St Aelred.

An exhibition "The Work of God and Man" explores the agricultural, industrial, spiritual and commercial history of Rievaulx. The tearoom offers delicious Yorkshire fare; made with fresh local produce.

Location: MAP 11:B7, OS Ref. SE577 850. In Rievaulx; 2¼m N of Helmsley on minor road off B1257.

Open: 1 Apr–30 Sep: daily, 10am–6pm. 1–31 Oct: Thu–Mon, 10am–5pm. 1 Nov–31 Mar 2010: Thu–Mon, 10am–4pm. Closed 24–26 Dec & 1 Jan.

Admission: Adult £5.30, Child £2.70, Conc. £4.50. 15% discount for groups (11+). Opening times and prices are valid until 31st March 2011, after this date details are subject to change please visit www.english-heritage.org.uk for the most up-to-date information.

WCs. Audio tours (also available for the visually impaired, those with learning difficulties and in French and German). Pay and display parking, refundable to EH members and paying visitors upon admission. On leads.

RIEVAULX TERRACE & TEMPLES

Rievaulx, Helmsley, North Yorkshire YO62 5LJ

Tel: 01439 798340 (winter 01439 748283)

Owner: National Trust **Contact:** The Property Manager

A ½m long grass-covered terrace and adjoining woodlands with vistas over Rievaulx Abbey and the Rye valley. There are two mid-18th century temples. Note: no access to the property Nov–end Mar.

Location: MAP 11:B7, OS Ref. SE579 848. 2½m NW of Helmsley on B1257. E of the Abbey.

Open: Feb–Oct, daily, 11am–5pm.

***Admission:** Adult £5.25, Child (under 17yrs) £2.90, Family (2+3) £12.60. (2010 prices). Groups (15+): £4.40. NT Members Free. *includes a voluntary donation but visitors can choose to pay the standard prices displayed at the property and on the website.

Grounds. Batricar available. In grounds, on leads.

RIPLEY CASTLE

See page 333 for full page entry.

RIPON CATHEDRAL

Ripon, North Yorkshire HG4 1QR

Tel: 01765 604108 (information on tours etc.) **Contact:** Canon Keith Punshon

One of the oldest crypts in Europe (672). Marvellous choir stalls and misericords (500 years old). Almost every type of architecture. Treasury.

Location: MAP 10:P8, OS Ref. SE314 711. 5m W signposted off A1, 12m N of Harrogate.

Open: All year: 8am–6pm.

Admission: Donations: £3. Pre-booked guided tours available.

For rare and unusual plants visit the **plant sales** index at the end of the book.

© Britainonview

Ripon Cathedral

ROCHE ABBEY ⌗

Maltby, Rotherham, South Yorkshire S66 8NW

Tel: 01709 812739 **E-mail:** roche.abbey@english-heritage.org.uk

www.english-heritage.org.uk/rocheabbey

Owner: English Heritage **Contact:** Visitor Operations Team

Beautifully set in a valley landscaped by 'Capability' Brown in the 18th century. It has one of the most complete ground plans of any English Cistercian monastery, laid out as excavated foundations. The most striking feature of this abbey is the Gothic transepts which still survive to their original height.

Location: MAP 7:B1, OS Ref. SK544 898. 1.5m S of Maltby off A634. Rail: Conisbrough 7m.

Open: 1 Apr–30 Sept: Thur–Sun & BHs, 11am–4pm.

Admission: Adult £3.20, Child £1.60, Conc. £2.70. 15% discount for groups (11+). Opening times and prices are valid until 31st March 2011, after this date details are subject to change please visit www.english-heritage.org.uk for the most up-to-date information.

WCs. Limited.

RYEDALE FOLK MUSEUM

Hutton le Hole, York, North Yorkshire YO62 6UA

Tel: 01751 417367 **E-mail:** info@ryedalefolkmuseum.co.uk

Owner: The Crosland Foundation

13 historic buildings showing the lives of ordinary folk from earliest times to the present day.

Location: MAP 11:C7, OS Ref. SE705 902. Follow signs from Hutton le Hole. 3m N of Kirkbymoorside.

Open: Daily 10am–5.30pm (last adm. 4.30pm). Oct–Mar 10am–dusk.

Admission: Adult £5.50, Child £4. Family (2+2) £15.

See which properties offer **educational facilities** or **school visits** in our index at the end of the book.

© English Heritage Photo Library

SCARBOROUGH CASTLE ⌗

CASTLE ROAD, SCARBOROUGH, NORTH YORKSHIRE YO11 1HY

www.english-heritage.org.uk/scarborough

Tel: 01723 372451 **E-mail:** scarborough.castle@english-heritage.org.uk

Owner: English Heritage **Contact:** Visitor Operations Team

Overlooking the town of Scarborough, the castle has witnessed 3000 years of turbulent history from the Bronze Age to WWII. Gain fascinating insights into the past with an exhibition in the Master Gunner's house and see intriguing artefacts from the site. Viewing platforms offer panoramic views of the coast.

Location: MAP 11:E7, OS Ref. TA050 892. Castle Road, E of the town centre. Rail: Scarborough 1m.

Open: 1 Apr–30 Sep: daily, 10am–6pm. 1 Oct–31 Mar: Thur–Mon, 10am–4pm. Closed 24–26 Dec & 1 Jan.

Admission: Adult £4.70, Child £2.40, Conc. £4.00, Family £11.80. 15% discount for groups (11+). Opening times and prices are valid until 31st March 2011, after this date details are subject to change please visit www.english-heritage.org.uk for the most up-to-date information.

WCs. Inclusive. Limited. (pre-booked parking only for disabled visitors, otherwise located in town centre). On leads.

©Tim Imrie-Tait/Country Life Picture Library

SCAMPSTON HALL

SCAMPSTON, MALTON, NORTH YORKSHIRE YO17 8NG

www.scampston.co.uk

Tel: 01944 759111 **Fax:** 01944 758700 **E-mail:** info@scampston.co.uk

Owner: Sir Charles Legard Bt **Contact:** The Administrator

Scampston is among the best examples of the English country house, combining fine architecture with a wealth of art treasures and set in 18th century 'Capability' Brown parkland. The double award winning house was featured in 'Hidden Treasure Houses' on FIVE in 2006. Guided tours around this family home are often led by the owner. Restaurant, disabled facilities and shop in The Walled Garden (see separate entry).

Location: MAP 11:D8, OS Ref. SE865 755. 4m E of Malton, off A64.

Open: 17 May–31 Jul (exc. 8–10 July), Tue–Fri & Suns & BH Mons. 1–3.45pm. All visits by guided tour. Tours at 1pm, 2pm & 3pm.

Admission: House, Front Garden & Cascade Circuit Walk inc. Children's Play Area: Adults £6, Child (5-16yrs) £3, Under 5s Free. Combined ticket inc. Walled Garden: Adults £11, Child (5-16yrs) £5.50. Groups (15+) by appointment.

HHA Members & Friends free admission to house only.

THE WALLED GARDEN AT SCAMPSTON

SCAMPSTON HALL, MALTON, NORTH YORKSHIRE YO17 8NG

www.scampston.co.uk

Tel: 01944 759111 **Fax:** 01944 758700 **E-mail:** info@scampston.co.uk

Owner: Sir Charles Legard Bt **Contact:** The Administrator

A contemporary garden with striking perennial meadow planting, as well as traditional spring/autumn borders, created by internationally acclaimed designer and plantsman Piet Oudolf. Described in *The Times* as "a gem". The garden is complemented by an excellent restaurant. "It's bold and beautiful – a must if you are heading to Yorkshire" *Toparius*.

Location: MAP 11:D8, OS Ref. SE865 755. 4m E of Malton, off A64.

Open: 12 Apr–30 Oct, daily (closed Mons except BHs), 10am–5pm, last adm. 4.30pm.

Admission: Walled Garden: Adult £6, Child (5–16) £3, Under 5s Free. Front Garden & Cascade Circuit Walk inc. Children's Play Area: Adult £3, Child (5–16) £1.50. Groups welcome by arrangement. See separate house listing for combined entry prices/dates. Please note: HHA membership does not give access to the Walled Garden.

© Britainonview

York Minster

SHIBDEN HALL

Lister's Road, Halifax, West Yorkshire HX3 6XG

Tel: 01422 352246 **Fax:** 01422 348440 **Email:** shibden.hall@calderdale.gov.uk

www.calderdale.gov.uk

Owner: Calderdale MBC **Contact:** Valerie Stansfield

A half-timbered 15th century manor house, the home of Anne Lister, set in a newly restored historic landscaped park. Oak furniture, 17th century aisled barn containing carriages and a folk museum, make Shibden an intriguing place to visit.

Location: MAP 10:O11, OS Ref. SE106 257. 1½ m E of Halifax off A58.

Open: 1 Mar–30 Nov: Mon–Sat, 10am–5pm (last admission 4.15pm), Sun, 12 noon–5pm (last admission 4.15pm). Dec–Feb: Mon–Sat, 10am–4pm, Sun, 12 noon–4pm (last admission 3.15pm).

Admission: Adult £3.50, Child/Conc. £2.50, Family £10. Prices subject to change April 2010.

Ground floor & grounds. Restaurant by the lake. By arrangement. In grounds on leads. Special events.

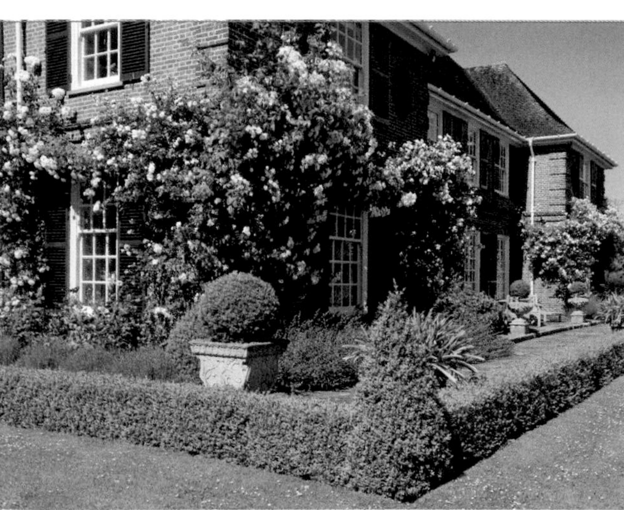

SION HILL

KIRBY WISKE, THIRSK, NORTH YORKSHIRE YO7 4EU

www.sionhillhall.co.uk

Tel: 01845 587206 **Fax:** 01845 587486 **E-mail:** sionhill@btconnect.com

Owner: H W Mawer Trust **Contact:** R M Mallaby

Sion Hill was designed in 1912 by the renowned York architect Walter H Brierley, 'the Lutyens of the North', receiving an award from the Royal Institute of British Architects as being of 'outstanding architectural merit'. The house is furnished with a fine collection of antique furniture, paintings, ceramics and clocks.

Location: MAP 11:A7, OS Ref. SE373 844. 6m S of Northallerton off A167, signposted. 4m W of Thirsk, 6m E of A1 via A61.

Open: April to October. Please contact the house for dates, times and booking arrangements. Admission strictly by pre-booked ticket.

Admission: £10 per person to include guided tour and admission to the grounds.

No photography in the house. Partial. WC. By arrangement. Ample for cars and coaches. Guide dogs only.

SLEDMERE HOUSE

SLEDMERE, DRIFFIELD, EAST YORKSHIRE YO25 3XG

www.sledmerehouse.com

Tel: 01377 236637 **Fax:** 01377 236500 **Email:** info@sledmerehouse.com

Owner: Sir Tatton Sykes **Contact:** The House Secretary

At the heart of the Yorkshire Wolds, Sledmere House is the home of Sir Tatton Sykes, 8th Baronet. Built in 1751 and enlarged by Sir Christopher Sykes, 2nd Baronet, in the 1780s and sympathetically restored after a serious fire in 1911. The house exudes 18th century elegance with each room containing decorative plasterwork by Joseph Rose Junior, and examples of the finest craftsmen of the period, including Chippendale, Hepplewhite & Sheraton. A tour of the house culminates in the magnificent Library which overlooks the 'Capability' Brown landscaped park. Award Winning Garden including Octagonal Walled Garden & Parterre, Wagoners' Special Reserve Military Museum, In-House Children's Quiz, Adventure Playground, The Terrace Café & Gift Shop, The Triton Gallery, Park Walks, unspoilt Model Estate Village, Famous pipe organ played Weds & Suns 1.30pm–3.30pm.

Location: MAP 11:D9, OS Ref. SE931 648. Off the A166 between York & Bridlington. Scenic drive from York, Bridlington & Scarborough, 7 miles NW of Driffield.

Open: Fri 22 Apr–Sun 25 Sept, Tues–Fri & Sun, BH Sat & Mon. Garden & Grounds, Shop, Terrace Café: Open 10am–5pm. House: Open 11am–4pm. The Triton Gallery: Open 11am–4pm.

Admission: House & Gardens: Adult £8, Conc. £7.50, Child £3, (Groups of 15+ £6.50pp), Family Ticket £18 (2 Adults & 2 Children 5–16). Gardens & Park: Adult £5, Child £2, RHS members £4.50 (Gardens & Grounds only).

No photography in house. Licensed. By arrangement. In grounds on leads. Guide dogs in house.

SKIPTON CASTLE

See page 334 for full page entry.

ST PETER'S CHURCH & BURIED LIVES! EXHIBITION

Beck Hill, Barton upon Humber DN18 5EX

Tel: 01652 632516 or 01302 722598 **E-mail:** customers@english-heritage.org.uk

www.english-heritage.org.uk/stpeterschurch

Owner: English Heritage **Contact:** Visitor Operations Team

With a history spanning a millennium, St Peter's is both an architectural and archaeological treasure. The thousand-year architecture includes a working Anglo-Saxon bell-tower and some surprising gargoyles. An exhibition includes the UK's largest resource for historic bone analysis from excavations of 2800 burials dating back over 900 years.

Location: MAP 11:E11, OS Ref TA03 3219. In Barton upon Humber town centre. Rail: Barton upon Humber 0.5m

Open: 1 Apr–30 Sep, Sat–Sun & BHs, 11am–3pm

Admission: Adult £3, Child £1.50, Conc. £2.60. Opening times and prices are valid until 31st March 2011, after this date details are subject to change please visit www.english-heritage.org.uk for the most up-to-date information.

By arrangement.

Skipton Castle

STOCKELD PARK

WETHERBY, NORTH YORKSHIRE LS22 4AW

www.stockeldpark.co.uk

Tel: 01937 586101 **Fax:** 01937 580084 **Email:** enquiries@stockeldpark.co.uk
Owner: Mr and Mrs P G F Grant **Contact:** Mr P Grant

A gracious Palladian mansion by James Paine (1763), featuring a magnificent cantilevered staircase in the central oval hall. Surrounded by beautiful gardens and set in 18th century landscaped parkland at the heart of a 2000 acre estate. Popular for filming and photography. Home of The Christmas Adventure www.thechristmasadventure.com

Location: MAP 11:A9, OS Ref. SE376 497. York 12m, Harrogate 5m, Leeds 12m.

Open: Privately booked events and tours only. Please contact the Estate Office: 01937 586101.

Admission: Prices on application.

Special Events: Outdoor Activities during Summer and Winter months, October Half Term Activities, Halloween Events, Guy Fawkes Firework Display, Children in Need 1000 Lantern Launch, Santa's Grotto, Fresh Christmas Tree Sale and The Christmas Adventure.

WCs. Licensed. Licensed. By arrangement Limited for coaches.

SUTTON PARK

SUTTON-ON-THE-FOREST, NORTH YORKSHIRE YO61 1DP

www.statelyhome.co.uk

Tel: 01347 810249 **Fax:** 01347 811239
E-mail: suttonpark@statelyhome.co.uk
Owner: Sir Reginald & Lady Sheffield **Contact:** Administrator

The Yorkshire home of Sir Reginald and Lady Sheffield. Early Georgian architecture. Magnificent plasterwork by Cortese. Rich collection of 18th century furniture, paintings and porcelain, put together with great style to make a most inviting house. Award winning gardens attract enthusiasts from home and abroad. Yorkshire in Bloom Award 2008.

Location: MAP 11:B9, OS Ref. SE583 646. 8m N of York on B1363 York–Helmsley Road.

Open: House: Apr–Sep: Wed, Sun & BHs, 1.30–5pm (last tour 4pm). Gardens: Apr–Sep: daily, 11am–5pm. Tearoom: Apr–Sep: Wed–Sun, 11am–5pm. Private groups any other day by appointment. House open Oct–Mar for private parties (15+) only.

Admission: House & Garden: Adult £6.50, Child £4, Conc. £5.50. Private Groups (15+): £7. Gardens only: Adult £3.50, Child £1.50, Conc. £3. Coaches £3. Caravans: £9.00 per unit per night. Electric hookup: £11.00 per unit per night.

Special Events: Specialist Plant Fair 10th April 2011.

No photography. Lunches & dinners in Dining Room. Partial. WCs. Licensed. Obligatory. Limited for coaches.

TEMPLE NEWSAM

LEEDS LS15 0AE

www.leeds.gov.uk/templenewsamhouse

Tel: 0113 2647321 **E-mail:** temple.newsam.house@leeds.gov.uk
Owner: Leeds City Council **Contact:** Bobbie Robertson

One of the great country houses of England, this Tudor-Jacobean mansion was the birthplace of Lord Darnley, husband of Mary Queen of Scots and home to the Ingram family for 300 years. Rich in newly restored interiors, paintings, furniture (including Chippendale), textiles, silver and ceramics; an ever-changing exhibitions programme, audio-tours, family activities and children's trails are also on offer along with one of the largest working rare breed farms in Europe. Temple Newsam sits within 1500 acres of grand and beautiful 'Capability' Brown parkland with formal and wooded gardens as well as national plant collections.

Location: MAP 10:P10, OS Ref. SE358 321. 4m E of city centre B6159 or 2m from M1 junction 46. SAT NAV: LS15 0AE.

Open: British Summer Time, Tues–Sun & BHs. House 10.30am–5pm, Farm 10am–5pm. Greenwich Mean Time, Tues–Sun & BHs. House 10.30am–4pm, Farm 10am–4pm. Last admission ¾ hour before closing. Estate and Gardens open free, dawn to dusk.

Admission: Please call or check website for current charges. Special group package and rates available. Free parking or patrolled car park £3.60. Pre-booked coach parking free.

THORNTON ABBEY AND GATEHOUSE

Ulceby DN39 6TU

Tel: 01469 541445 **E-mail:** thornton.abbey@english-heritage.org.uk
www.english-heritage.org.uk/thornton
Owner: English Heritage **Contact:** Visitor Operations Team

The enormous fortified Gatehouse of Thornton Abbey is the finest surviving in Britain, trumpeting the prosperity of what was once one of the wealthiest Augustinian monasteries. Built in the nervous years following the Peasants' Revolt of 1381, it is thought to have protected the Abbey's treasures and his guests.

Location: MAP 11:E11, OS Map 284 Ref TA118 189. 18m NE of Scunthorpe on a road N of A160. 7m SE of Humber Bridge, on a road E of A1077. Rail: Thornton Abbey 0.25m.

Open: 1 Apr–30 Jun: Wed–Sun & BHs, 10am–5pm. 1 Jul–31 Aug: daily, 10am–5pm. 1 Sep–31 Mar, Fri–Sun, 10am–4pm. Closed 24–26 Dec & 1 Jan.

Admission: Adult £4.20, Child £2.10, Conc. £3.60. Opening times and prices are valid until 31st March 2011, after this date details are subject to change please visit www.english-heritage.org.uk for the most up-to-date information.

Partial. On leads.

TREASURER'S HOUSE

Minster Yard, York, North Yorkshire YO1 7JL

Tel: 01904 624247
Owner: National Trust **Contact:** The Property Manager

Named after the Treasurer of York Minster and built over a Roman road, the house is not all that it seems!

Location: MAP 21, OS Ref. SE604 523. The N side of York Minster. Entrance on Chapter House St.

WASSAND HALL

SEATON, HULL, EAST YORKSHIRE HU11 5RJ

www.wassand.co.uk

Tel: 01964 534488 **Fax:** 01964 533334 **E-mail:** reorussell@lineone.net

Owner/Contact: R E O Russell – Resident Trustee

Fine Regency house 1815 by Thomas Cundy the Elder. Beautifully restored walled gardens, woodland walks, Parks and vistas over Hornsea Mere, part of the Estate since 1580. The Estate was purchased circa 1520 by Dame Jane Constable and has remained in the family to the present day, Mr Rupert Russell being the great nephew of the late Lady Strickland-Constable. The house contains a fine collection of 18/19th century paintings, English and Continental silver, furniture and porcelain. Wassand is very much a family home and retains a very friendly atmosphere. Homemade afternoon teas are served in the conservatory on Open Days.

Location: MAP 11:F9, OS Ref. TA174 460. On the B1244 Seaton–Hornsea Road. Approximately 2m from Hornsea.

Open: 27–30 May; 9–13, 24–28 Jun; 8 & 9 (Sunday the 10th – Concert - House closed), 29–31 Jul; 1 & 2, 5, (6 Aug not open – House & Gardens closed), 7–8, 26–29 Aug. 2–5pm.

Admission: Hall, all grounds & walks: Adult £5.50, OAP £5, Child (11–15yrs) £3, Child (under 10) Free. Hall: Adult £3.50, OAP £3, Child (11–15yrs) £1.50, Child (under 10) Free. Grounds & Garden: Adult £3.50, OAP £3, Child (11–15yrs) £3, Child (under 10) Free. Guided tours and groups by arrangment – POA.

Limited. By arrangement. Ample for cars, limited for coaches.

In grounds, on leads.

Sledmere House

WENTWORTH CASTLE GARDENS

LOWE LANE, STAINBOROUGH, BARNSLEY, SOUTH YORKSHIRE S75 3ET

Tel: 01226 776040 **Fax:** 01226 776042

Owner: Wentworth Castle Trust **Contact:** Vicky Martin – Director

The only Grade 1 listed landscape in South Yorkshire. This historic 18th century 500-acre parkland estate features 26 listed monuments, including a castle, follies and a magnificent 60-acre formal garden containing 100,000 bulbs as well as 3 National Collections – Rhododendrons, Camellias and Magnolias. Shop, Café, Adventure Playground. Tours by arrangement.

Location: MAP 10:P12, OS Ref. SE320 034. 5 mins from M1/J37.

Open: All year daily (except Christmas Day): Apr–Sept 10am–5pm, Oct–Mar 10am–4pm.

Admission: (2010 Prices) Garden, Parkland & Playground: Adult £4.75, Conc. £3.75, Child (5–16yrs) £2.75.Guided tours £2.50 extra. Parkland only: Free (£3 car park charge).

WHITBY ABBEY ⌗

WHITBY, NORTH YORKSHIRE YO22 4JT

www.english-heritage.org.uk/whitbyabbey

Tel: 01947 603568 **E-mail:** customers@english-heritage.org.uk

Owner: English Heritage **Contact:** Visitor Operations Team

The dramatic ruins of this once magnificent abbey stand high on the headland over the town of Whitby, on the Yorkshire coast.

Founded by St Hilda in AD657, Whitby Abbey soon acquired great influence, before being ransacked by the invading Viking army. It was to be 200 years before the monastic tradition was revived, but yet again the Abbey was plundered, this time following the dissolution.

Inspired by detailed archaeological investigation of the site, an interactive visitor centre provides visitors with a chance to discover the Abbey's rich history from St Hilda to Dracula.

Location: MAP 11:D6, OS Ref. NZ904 115. On cliff top E of Whitby. Rail: Whitby 0.5m

Open: 1 Apr–30 Sep: daily, 10am–6pm. 1 Oct–31 Mar: Thur–Mon, 10am–4pm. Closed 24–26 Dec & 1 Jan.

Admission: Adult £5.80, Child £2.90, Conc. £4.90, Family £14.50. 15% discounts for groups (11+). EH members Free. Opening times and prices are valid until 31st March 2011, after this date details are subject to change please visit www.english-heritage.org.uk for the most up-to-date information.

[i] WCs. From the Whitby harbour area, the Abbey can only be directly reached on foot via the 199 'Abbey steps' (or Caedmon's Trod). Alternatively, a well-signposted road leads from the town outskirts to the cliff-top Abbey. [P] Parking not managed by English Heritage. Charge payable. On leads.

WILBERFORCE HOUSE

25 High Street, Hull, East Yorkshire HU1 1NQ

Tel: 01482 613902 **Fax:** 01482 613710

Owner: Hull City Council **Contact:** S R Green

Birthplace of slavery abolitionist William Wilberforce. Reopened 2007 following £1.6 million redevelopment. Displays chart the history of slavery, the abolition campaign and slavery today.

Location: MAP 11:E11, OS Ref. TA102 286. High Street, Hull.

Open: Mon–Sat, 10am–5pm, Sun 1.30–4.30pm.

Admission: Free.

WORTLEY HALL

Wortley, Sheffield, South Yorkshire S35 7DB

Tel: 0114 2882100 **Fax:** 0114 2830695

Owner: Labour, Co-operative & Trade Union Movement **Contact:** Marc Mallender

15 acres of formal Italianate gardens surrounded by 11 acres of informal pleasure grounds.

Location: MAP 6:P1, OS Ref. SK313 995. 10kms S of Barnsley in Wortley on A629.

Open: Gardens: Daily 10am–4pm.

Admission: Donation.

YORK MINSTER

Deangate, York YO1 7HH

Tel: 01904 557216 **Fax:** 01904 557218 **E-mail:** visitors@yorkminster.org

Owner: Dean and Chapter of York **Contact:** Stephen Hemming

Large gothic church housing the largest collection of medieval stained glass in England.

Location: MAP 21, OS Ref. SE603 522. Centre of York.

Open: All year: Mon–Sat, 9am–5pm, Sun: 12 noon–3.45pm.

Admission: Adult £8, Child (under 16yrs) Free, Conc. £7.

YORK GATE GARDEN

BACK CHURCH LANE, ADEL, LEEDS, WEST YORKSHIRE LS16 8DW

www.perennial.org.uk/yorkgate

Tel: 0113 2678240

Owner: Perennial **Contact:** The Garden Co-ordinator

Inspirational one acre garden widely recognized as one of Britain's finest small gardens. A series of smaller gardens with different themes and in contrasting styles are linked by a succession of delightful vistas. Striking architectural features play a key role throughout the garden which is also noted for its exquisite detailing.

Location: MAP 10:P10, OS Ref. 275 403. 2¼m SE of Bramhope. ½m E of A660.

Open: Apr–Sept: Thur & Sun, 2–5pm. BH weekends (Apr, May & Aug) Sun & Mon, 11am–5pm. See website for other dates.

Admission: Adult £4, Child (16yrs & under) Free.

[i] Groups must book. Not suitable. By arrangement. Guide dogs only.

Rode Hall & Gardens, Kitchen Garden

North West

Cheshire has two strikingly different faces; the East, more industrial and more rugged where it adjoins the Peak District National Park, and the West, the flatter 'Cheshire Plain', more densely farmed and with easily recognisable red brick buildings. On the edge of the Lake District is Levens Hall and to the west is Muncaster Castle and its fascinating Owl Centre.

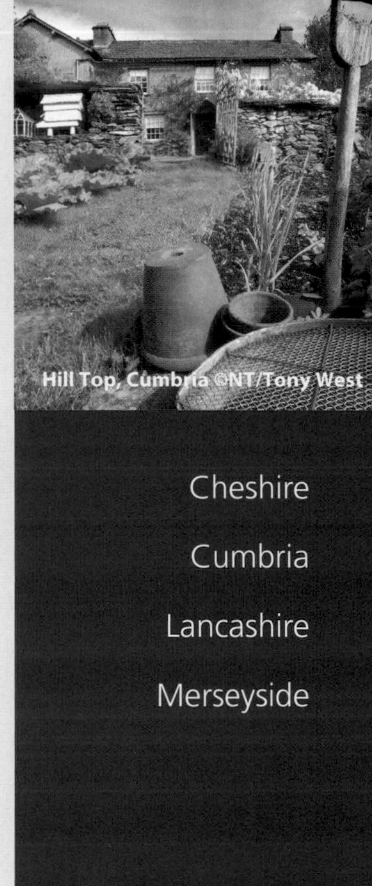

Hill Top, Cumbria ©NT/Tony West

CUMBRIA

LANCASHIRE

MERSEYSIDE

CHESHIRE

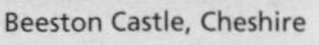
Beeston Castle, Cheshire

■ **Owner**

Mrs C J C Legh

■ **Contact**

The Hunting Lodge
Adlington Hall
Macclesfield
Cheshire
SK10 4LF

Tel: 01625 827595
Fax: 01625 820797
E-mail: enquiries@adlingtonhall.com

■ **Location**

MAP 6:N2
OS Ref. SJ905 804

5m N of Macclesfield, A523, 13m S of Manchester. London 178m.

Rail: Macclesfield & Wilmslow stations 5m.

Air: Manchester Airport 8m.

■ **Opening Times**

July, August & September
Sunday 3 July to Sunday 4 September inclusive. Tuesdays, Wednesdays & Sundays, 2.00–5.00pm.

■ **Admission**

House & Gardens	
Adult	£8.00
Child	£4.00
Student	£4.00
Gardens only	
Adult	£5.00
Child	FREE
Student	FREE
Groups of 20+	£7.50

Conference/Function

ROOM	SIZE	MAX CAPACITY
Great Hall	11 x 8m	80
Dining Rm	10.75 x 7m	80
Courtyard	27 x 17m	200
Hunting Lodge		130

ADLINGTON HALL

www.adlingtonhall.com

Adlington Hall, the home of the Leghs of Adlington from 1315 to the present day, was built on the site of a Hunting Lodge which stood in the Forest of Macclesfield in 1040. Two oaks, part of the original building, remain with their roots in the ground and support the east end of the Great Hall, which was built between 1480 and 1505.

The Hall is a manor house, quadrangular in shape, and was once surrounded by a moat. Two sides of the Courtyard and the east wing were built in the typical 'Black and White' Cheshire style in 1581. The south front and west wing (containing the Drawing Room and Dining Room) were added between 1749 and 1757 and are built of red brick with a handsome stone portico with four Ionic columns on octagonal pedestals. Between the trees in the Great Hall stands an organ built by 'Father' Bernard Smith (c1670-80). Handel subsequently played on this instrument and, now fully restored, it is the largest 17th century organ in the country.

Gardens

The Gardens have been laid out over many centuries. A lime walk planted in 1688 leads to a Regency rockery that surrounds the unique Shell Cottage. The Wilderness, a Rococo styled landscape garden of the Georgian period contains many follies such as the chinoserie T'Ing House, Pagoda bridge and a classical Temple to Diana. Newly created formal gardens around the house include an old fashioned rose garden yew maze and a flower parterre and water garden.

Suitable for corporate events, product launches, business meetings, conferences, concerts, fashion shows, garden parties, rallies, clay-pigeon shooting, filming and weddings.

The Great Hall and Dining Room are available for corporate entertaining. Catering can be arranged.

Visitors may alight at entrance to Hall. WCs.

By arrangement.

For 100 cars and 4 coaches, 100 yds from Hall.

By prior appointment.

ARLEY HALL & GARDENS

www.arleyhallandgardens.com

Owned by the same family for over 500 years, Arley is a delightful estate. The award-winning gardens, recently voted in the top 50 in Europe and in Britain's top 10, have been created gradually over 250 years with each generation of the family making its own contribution. The result is a garden of great atmosphere, interest and vitality, which blends strong elements of design from earlier centuries with modern ideas in both planting and design. Arley is, therefore, a wonderful example of the idea that the best gardens are living, changing works of art. Outstanding features are the renowned double herbaceous border (c1846), the Quercus Ilex and pleached Lime Avenues, Victorian Rootree, walled gardens, yew hedges and shrub rose collection. The family tradition continues today with the current Viscount Ashbrook, who over the last 30 years has created the less formal Grove and Woodland Walk, where 300 varieties of rhododendron grow amongst a collection of rare trees and shrubs in a delightful tranquil setting. One of Cheshire's most charming stately homes, the Hall (Grade II*) was built by the present Viscount Ashbrook's great, great grandfather, Rowland Egerton-Warburton between 1832 and 1885 and is a fine example of the Victorian Jacobean style. Each room is given its own individual character by the elaborate plasterwork, wood panelling, family portraits and porcelain. From the grandeur of the Gallery to the intimacy of the Library the Hall exudes charm. The Emperor's Room was even home to Prince Louis Napoleon, later Napoleon III of France, in the winter of 1847–48. Arley won the title of 2009 'Small Visitor Atraction of the Year' in the North West and with its new, purpose built conference facility 'Olympia' is also a wonderful, exclusive venue for weddings, corporate functions and private parties.

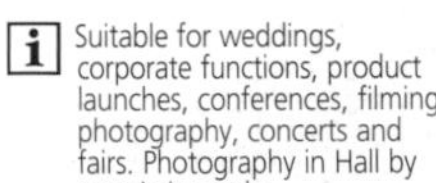

Suitable for weddings, corporate functions, product launches, conferences, filming, photography, concerts and fairs. Photography in Hall by permission only.

Open while the Garden is open.

Comprehensive set of menus available for entertaining in the Hall and Tudor Barn.

Partial access to the Hall, full access to Gardens, WCs.

Licensed Tudor Barn Restaurant.

Welcomed by arrangement.

Free

In the grounds on leads.

Owner

Viscount & Viscountess Ashbrook

Contact

Estate Manager – Garry Fortune
The Estate Office
Arley
Nr Northwich
Cheshire CW9 6NA

Tel: 01565 777353
Fax: 01565 777465
E-mail: enquiries@arleyhallandgardens.com
Arley Weddings: www.arleyweddings.com

Location

MAP 6:M2
OS Ref. SJ675 809

5m W Knutsford, 5m from M6/J19 & 20 and M56/J9 & 10.

Opening Times

2 April–30 October (November weekends only)

Gardens: Tuesday–Sunday & BHs, 11am–5pm.

Hall: Tues, Suns & BHs, 12noon–4.30pm.

Admission

Gardens	
Adult	£7.00
Child (5–16yrs)	£2.50
Senior	£6.50
Family (2+2)	£16.50
Groups:	
Adult	£6.50
Concession	£6.00
Children	£2.00
Hall	
Adult	£3.00
Child (5–12yrs)	£2.00
Senior	£2.50
Groups:	
Adult	£2.50
Season tickets	
Individual	£30.00
Joint	£50.00
Family (2+3)	£70.00

Special Events

February
Wedding Fair

March
Mothers Day Celebrations

April
Spring Plant Fair
Bluebell Walks

June
Arley Garden Festival

October
Halloween Murder Mystery Evening

December
Christmas Floral Extravaganza

■ **Owner**
Sir William and Lady Bromley-Davenport

■ **Contact**
Christine Mountney
Hall Manager
Capesthorne Hall
Siddington
Macclesfield
Cheshire SK11 9JY
Weddings and Corporate enquiries
Tel: 01625 861221
Fax: 01625 861619
E-mail: info@capesthorne.com

■ **Location**
MAP 6:N2
OS Ref. SJ840 727

5m W of Macclesfield. 30 mins S of Manchester on A34. Near M6, M63 and M62.

Air: Manchester International 20 mins.

Rail: Macclesfield 5m (2 hrs from London).

Taxi: 01625 533464.

■ **Opening Times**
Summer
April–Oct Suns, Mons & BHs.
Hall 1.30–4pm. Last admission 3.30pm.
Gardens & Chapel 12 noon–5pm.
Groups welcome by appointment. Caravan Park also open Easter–end October. Corporate enquiries: March–December.

■ **Admission**
Sundays & BHs only
Hall, Gardens & Chapel

Adult	£7.00
Child (5–16yrs)	£3.50
OAP	£6.00
Family*	£16.00

*Parents and children aged up to 16yrs in the same car.

Gardens & Chapel only

Adult	£4.50
Child (5–16yrs)	£2.50
OAP	£3.50

Transfers from Gardens & Chapel to Hall

Adult/OAP	£3.50
Child (5–16yrs)	£2.00

Mondays only: Hall, Chapel & Gardens

Car (up to 4 pass.)	£10.00
Additional person	£2.50
Minibus (up to 12 pass)	£35.00
Coach (up to 50 pass)	£70.00

Caravan Park
Closed for 2011 season

■ **Special Events**
See www.capesthorne.com

CAPESTHORNE HALL

www.capesthorne.com

Capesthorne Hall, set in 100 acres of picturesque Cheshire parkland, has been touched by nearly 1,000 years of English history – Roman legions passed across it, titled Norman families hunted on it and, during the Civil War, a Royalist ancestress helped Charles II to escape after the Battle of Worcester. The Jacobean-style Hall has a fascinating collection of fine art, marble sculptures, furniture and tapestries. Originally designed by the Smiths of Warwick it was built between 1719 and 1732. It was altered by Blore in 1837 and partially rebuilt by Salvin in 1861 following a disastrous fire.

The present Squire is William Bromley-Davenport, Lord Lieutenant of Cheshire, whose ancestors have owned the estate since Domesday times when they were appointed custodians of the Royal Forest of Macclesfield.

In the grounds near the family Chapel the 18th century Italian Milanese Gates open onto the herbaceous borders and maples which line the beautiful lakeside gardens. But amid the natural spectacle and woodland walks, Capesthorne still offers glimpses of its man-made past ... the remains of the Ice House, the Old Boat House and the curious Swallow Hole.

Facilities at the Hall can be hired for corporate occasions and family celebrations including Civil Wedding ceremonies.

i Available for corporate functions, meetings, product launches, promotions, exhibitions, presentations, seminars, activity days, Civil Weddings and receptions, family celebrations, still photography, clay shooting, car rallies, garden parties, barbecues, concerts, antique, craft, country and game fairs. No photography in Hall.

Catering can be provided for groups (full menus on request). Function rooms available for wedding receptions, corporate hospitality, meetings and other special events. 'The Butler's Pantry' serves light refreshments.

Guided tours available for pre-booked parties (except Sunday and Monday).

P 100 cars/20 coaches on hard-standing and unlimited in park, 50 yds from house.

For rare and unusual plants visit the **plant sales** index at the end of the book.

ADLINGTON HALL *See page 354 for full page entry.*

ARLEY HALL AND GARDENS *See page 355 for full page entry.*

BEESTON CASTLE

CHAPEL LANE, BEESTON, TARPORLEY, CHESHIRE CW6 9TX

www.english-heritage.org.uk/beestoncastle

Tel: 01829 260464 **Email:** beeston.castle@english-heritage.org.uk

Owner: English Heritage **Contact:** Visitor Operations Team

Standing majestically on a sheer rocky crag, Beeston offers perhaps the most stunning views of any castle in England as well as fantastic woodland walks in the castle grounds. Its 4,000 year history spans Bronze Age settlement to Iron Age hill fort, to impregnable royal fortress.

Location: MAP 6:L3, OS Ref. SJ537 593. 11m SE of Chester on minor road off A49, or A41. 2m SW of Tarporley.

Open: 1 Apr–30 Sept: daily, 10am–6pm. 1 Oct–31 Mar: Thur–Mon, 10am–4pm. Closed 24–26 Dec & 1 Jan.

Admission: Adult £5.30, Child £2.70, Conc. £4.50. 15% discount for groups (11+). EH members Free. Opening times and prices are valid until 31st March 2011, after this date details are subject to change please visit www.english-heritage.org.uk for the most up-to-date information.

Exhibition. WCs. Partial. The car park is not owned by English Heritage. There is a parking charge of £2. On leads.

BRAMALL HALL

Bramhall Park, Bramhall, Stockport, Cheshire SK7 3NX

Tel: 0161 485 3708 **Fax:** 0161 486 6959 **Email:** bramallhall@stockport.gov.uk

www.bramallhall.org.uk

Owner: Stockport Metropolitan Borough Council **Contact:** Caroline Egan, House Manager

Bramall Hall is a magnificent black and white timber-framed Tudor manor house with Victorian additions, spanning six centuries and set in 70 acres of parkland. It gives a unique insight into the families and servants who have lived and worked there. A great afternoon out.

Location: OS Ref. SJ890 864. 3/4m N of Bramhall centre, off A5102

Open: 1 Apr–31 Oct: Tues–Thurs 1–5pm, Fri & Sat 1–4pm, Sun 1–5pm, BHs 11am–5pm. 1 Nov–31 Mar: Sat & Sun only 1–4pm, BHs 11am–4pm. Telephone for Christmas openings. Guided Tours 1.15pm and 2.15pm. Self guided tours other times.

Admission: Adult £4.05, Conc. & under 16s £3.05, Stockport Leisure Key and under 5s Free.

No photography inside the Hall. Partial, WCs. By arrangement. Ample for cars, limited for coaches. Dogs allowed in the grounds on leads. Guide dogs only in the house.

CAPESTHORNE HALL *See page 356 for full page entry.*

CHESTER CATHEDRAL

St. Werburgh Street, Chester, Cheshire

Tel: 01244 324756 **Fax:** 01244 341110 **E-mail:** visits@chestercathedral.com

www.chestercathedral.com

Owner: Church of England

Chester Cathedral opens a window onto a rich and varied story of monks, kings and craftsmen. 1000 years of history but a living thriving centre of community and Christian worship. A wonderful shop and unique 13th century Refectory Café complement this magnificent National Treasure in the Heart of Chester.

Location: MAP 6:K2, OS Ref. SJ406 665. Chester city centre.

Open: Mon–Sat: 9am–5pm. Sun 1–4.30pm.

Admission: Adult £5, Child (5–16) £2.50, Senior Citizens/Groups £4.

CHESTER ROMAN AMPHITHEATRE

Vicars Lane, Chester, Cheshire CH1 1QX

Tel: 01244 402009 **Email:** customers@english-heritage.org.uk

www.english-heritage.org.uk/chester

Owner: Managed by English Heritage and Chester City Council

Contact: Chester City Council

The largest Roman amphitheatre in Britain. Excavations carried out over 2004/05 indicate that there were two stone-built amphitheatres, one very similar to those in Pompeii, emphasising the great importance of Chester during the Roman era.

Location: MAP 6:K2, OS Ref. SJ408 662. On Vicars Lane beyond Newgate, Chester.

Open: Any reasonable time.

Admission: Free. Opening times and prices are valid until 31st March 2011, after this date details are subject to change please visit www.english-heritage.org.uk for the most up-to-date information.

Capesthorne Hall

Thinking of a short break or weekend away?
See Historic Places to Stay

CHOLMONDELEY CASTLE GARDEN

MALPAS, CHESHIRE SY14 8AH

www.cholmondeleycastle.com

Tel: 01829 720383 **Fax:** 01829 720877 **E-mail:** dilys@cholmondeleycastle.co.uk

Owner: The Marchioness of Cholmondeley **Contact:** The Secretary

Extensive ornamental gardens dominated by a romantic Castle built in 1801 of local sandstone. Visitors can enjoy the beautiful Temple Water Garden, Ruin Water Garden and memorial mosaic designed by Maggy Howarth. Rose garden and many mixed borders. Lakeside picnic area, children's play areas, farm animals, llamas, children's corner, chickens and free flying aviary birds. Private chapel in the park.

Location: MAP 6:L3, OS Ref. SJ540 515. Off A41 Chester/Whitchurch Rd. & A49 Whitchurch/ Tarporley Road. 7m N of Whitchurch.

Open: Sun 3 April–Sun 25 Sept 2011, 11am–5pm, Wed, Thur, Sun & Bank hols. Autumn Tints, Sun 9 & Sun 23 Oct. (The castle is only open to groups by prior arrangement on limited days).

Admission: Adult £5, Child £2, (reduction for groups to gardens of 25+).

Limited. WCs. In grounds, on leads only.

DORFOLD HALL

ACTON, Nr NANTWICH, CHESHIRE CW5 8LD

Tel: 01270 625245 **Fax:** 01270 628723

Owner/Contact: Richard Roundell

Jacobean country house built in 1616 for Ralph Wilbraham. Family home of Mr & Mrs Richard Roundell. Beautiful plaster ceilings and oak panelling. Attractive woodland gardens and summer herbaceous borders.

Location: MAP 6:L3, OS Ref. SJ634 525. 1m W of Nantwich on the A534 Nantwich–Wrexham road.

Open: Apr–Oct: Tue only and BH Mons, 2–5pm.

Admission: Adult £6, Child £3.

Obligatory. Limited. Narrow gates with low arch prevent coaches.

In grounds on leads.

DUNHAM MASSEY

Altrincham, Cheshire WA14 4SJ

Tel: 0161 941 1025 **Fax:** 0161 929 7508 **E-mail:** dunhammassey@nationaltrust.org.uk

www.nationaltrust.org.uk

Owner: National Trust **Contact:** Visitor Services

An elegant Georgian mansion with a sumptuous Edwardian interior filled with fabulous collections of paintings, furniture and Huguenot silver. Enjoy the great plantsman's garden full of native favourites and exotic treasures and Georgian Orangery. Experience the creation of Britain's largest Winter Garden. Wander around the ancient deer park.

Location: MAP 6:M1, OS Ref. SJ735 874. 3m SW of Altrincham off A56. M6/J19. M56/J7. Station Altrincham (BR & Metro) 3m.

Open: House: 26 Feb–30 Oct, 11am–5pm, Mon–Wed, Sat & Sun. Taster Tours: 11.00 & 11.30am (restricted numbers, allocated upon arrival), last admission 4.30pm. Open Good Friday. Garden: 1 Jan–25 Feb & 31 Oct–31 Dec, 11am–4pm, Mon–Sun; 26 Feb–30 Oct, 11am–5.30pm, Mon–Sun. Winter closure at 4 or dusk if earlier. Park: Open all year, 9am–5pm, Mon–Sun. Mar–Oct Gates remain open till 7.30pm. Property closed, including park, 25 Dec. Also closed 23 Nov for staff training. Restaurant/Shop: 1 Jan–25 Feb & 31 Oct–31 Dec, 10.30am–4pm, Mon–Sun; 26 Feb–30 Oct, 10.30am–5pm, Mon–Sun. Mill: 26 Feb–30 Oct, 12noon–4pm, Mon–Wed, Sat & Sun. White Cottage: 27 Feb–30 Oct, 2–5pm, Last Sunday of the month only – all visits must be booked on 0161 928 0075 or by email to dunmasswhite@nationaltrust.org.uk.

***Admission:** House & Garden: Adult £10, Child £5, Family (2+3 max) £25, Group £8.50. Garden only: Adult £7, Child £3.50, Family £17.50. Group £5.95. Reduced rate when arriving by public transport. *includes a voluntary 10% donation but visitors can choose to pay the standard prices displayed at the property and on the website.

Photography is permitted in the house, please no flash. Partial. WC. Batricars. Licensed. Optional. No extra charge. £5 per car. In grounds, on leads.

For unique **Civil wedding** venues see our index at the end of the book.

GAWSWORTH HALL

MACCLESFIELD, CHESHIRE SK11 9RN

www.gawsworthhall.com

Tel: 01260 223456 **Fax:** 01260 223469 **E-mail:** gawsworthhall@btinternet.com

Owner: Mr and Mrs T Richards **Contact:** Mr T Richards

Fully lived-in Tudor half-timbered manor house with Tilting Ground. Former home of Mary Fitton, Maid of Honour at the Court of Queen Elizabeth I, and the supposed 'Dark Lady' of Shakespeare's sonnets. Fine pictures, sculpture, furniture and beautiful grounds adjoining a medieval church.

Location: MAP 6:N2, OS Ref. SJ892 697. 3m S of Macclesfield on the A536 Congleton to Macclesfield road.

Open: Daily 2-5pm in July and August, other times see www.gawsworthhall.com

Special Events: Open-air theatre with covered grandstand, performances in July and August. Yuletide decorations by Barry Grey in December.

Admission: Adult £7, Child £4. Groups (20+): £6.

Partial. WCs. Licensed Licensed By arrangement In grounds

HOLMSTON HALL BARN

Little Budworth, Tarporley, Cheshire CW6 9AY

Tel: 01829 760366/07778 510287

Owner/Contact: Mr Richard Hopkins

Newly restored 15th century oak framed barn. Sandstone base and floors, with twelve exterior oak doors.

Location: MAP 6:L3, OS Ref. SJ607 626. Off A49. 2m from Eaton village.

Open: All year by appointment only.

Admission: Free.

© NTPL / Andreas von Einsiedel

Little Moreton Hall

© NTPL / Andreas von Einsiedel

Dunham Massey

© NTPL / Rupert Truman

LITTLE MORETON HALL

CONGLETON, CHESHIRE CW12 4SD

www.nationaltrust.org.uk

Tel: 01260 272018

Owner: National Trust **Contact:** The Property Administrator

Begun in 1504 and completed 100 years later, Little Moreton Hall is regarded as the finest example of a timber-framed moated manor house in the country.

Location: MAP 6:N3, OS Ref. SJ833 589. 4m SW of Congleton on E side of A34.

Open: 26 Feb–13 Mar, Sat & Sun, 11am–4pm; 16 Mar–30 Oct, Wed–Sun (& BH Mon), 11am–5pm; 5 Nov–18 Dec, Sat & Sun, 11am–4pm.

***Admission:** Adult £7.40, Child £3.70, Family £18.50. Groups: £6.30 (must book).

*includes a voluntary donation but visitors can choose to pay the standard prices displayed at the property and on the website.

Partial. WCs. Licensed. Limited for coaches. Guide dogs only.

© NTPL / Arnhel de Serra

© NTPL / Alan Novelli

LYME PARK

DISLEY, STOCKPORT, CHESHIRE SK12 2NX

www.nationaltrust.org.uk

Tel: 01663 762023 **Fax:** 01663 765035

Owner: National Trust **Contact:** The Visitor Experience Manager

On the edge of the Peak District nestling within sweeping moor land Lyme Park is a magnificent estate. Its wild remoteness and powerful beauty contrast with one of the most famous country house images in England - the backdrop to where Darcy meets Elizabeth in Pride and Prejudice. Discover a colourful family history from rescuing the Black Prince, sailing into exile with the Duke of Windsor, to the writing of the hit series Upstairs Downstairs. Enjoy hearing visitors play the piano as you discover impressive tapestries and beautifully furnished rooms, or escape to the park and feel miles from anywhere.

Location: MAP 6:N2, OS Ref. SJ965 825. Off the A6 at Disley. 61/2m SE of Stockport. M60 J1.

Open: House: 26 Feb–30 Oct, 11am–5pm, Mon, Tue, Fri–Sun. Park: open all year, 8am–6pm, Mon–Sun. Garden: 26 Feb–30 Oct, 11am–5pm, Mon–Sun; Please call for winter opening times.

***Admission:** House & Gardens: Adult £9.50, Child £4.75, Family £23. Garden only: Adult £6, Child £3. House only: Adult £6.25, Child £3.15. Park only: Car £5, Motorbike £3, Coach £20. Booked coach groups visiting house and garden park admission free. NT members free. *includes a voluntary donation but visitors can choose to pay the standard prices displayed at the property and on the website.

No photography in house. Licensed. Licensed. By arrangement.

NESS BOTANIC GARDENS

Ness, Neston, Cheshire CH64 4AY

Tel: 0151 353 0123 **Fax:** 0151 353 1004

Owner: University of Liverpool **Contact:** Dr E J Sharples

Leading garden in the North West for rhododendrons and azaleas.

Location: MAP 6:J2, OS Ref. SJ302 760 (village centre). Off A540. 10m NW of Chester. 1½m S of Neston.

Open: Feb–Oct 10am–5pm, Nov–Jan 10am–4.30pm.

Admission: Adult £6.50, Conc. £5.50, Child: (under 5yrs) Free, (5-16yrs) £3, Family ticket £18.

NORTON PRIORY MUSEUM & GARDENS

Tudor Road, Manor Park, Runcorn WA7 1SX

Tel: 01928 569895 **E-mail:** info@nortonpriory.org **www.nortonpriory.org**

Owner/Contact: The Norton Priory Museum Trust

An award winning museum, excavated medieval ruins, spectacular St Christopher statue, Walled Garden, extensive woodland and sculpture trail.

Location: MAP 6:K1, OS Ref. SJ545 835. 3m from M56/J11. 2m E of Runcorn.

Open: All year Daily 12 noon–4 pm (Walled garden closed Nov–Mar).

Admission: Adult £5.20. Child/Conc. £3.70. Family £13.40. Groups £3.40, (as from Apr '08).

Wheelchairs, braille guide, audio tapes & WC. By arrangement.

In grounds, on leads.

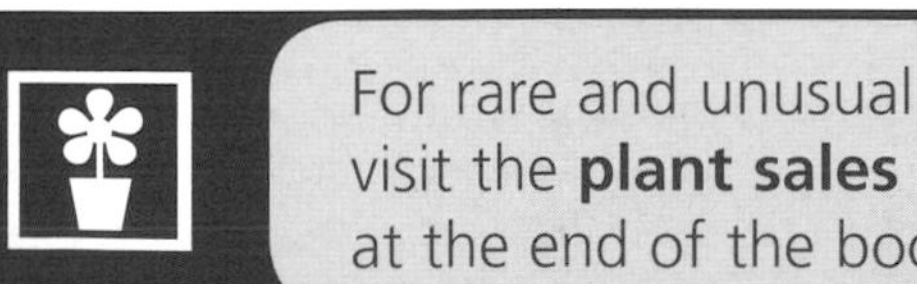

PEOVER HALL

OVER PEOVER, KNUTSFORD WA16 9HW

Tel: 01565 632358

Owner: Randle Brooks **Contact:** I Shepherd

An Elizabethan house dating from 1585. Fine Carolean stables. Mainwaring Chapel, 18th century landscaped park. Large garden with topiary work, and walled gardens.

Location: MAP 6:M2, OS Ref. SJ772 734. 4m S of Knutsford off A50 at Whipping Stocks Inn.

Open: May–Aug: Carolean Stables & Gardens, Mon & Thu except BHs, 2–5pm. Tours of the House at 2.30 & 3.30pm.

Admission: House, Carolean Stables & Gardens: Adult £5. Carolean Stables & Gardens only: Adult £4. Accompanied children free.

Mon & Thur. Obligatory.

Lyme Park

QUARRY BANK MILL & STYAL ESTATE

Styal, Wilmslow SK9 4LA

Tel: 01625 527468 **Fax:** 01625 539267

Owner: National Trust **Contact:** Visitor Services Manager

Full atmosphere of Industrial revolution.

Location: MAP 6:N1, OS Ref. SJ835 835. 1.5m N of Wilmslow off B5166. 2.5m from M56/J5. Styal Shuttle Bus.

RODE HALL

CHURCH LANE, SCHOLAR GREEN, CHESHIRE ST7 3QP

www.rodehall.co.uk

Tel: 01270 873237 **Fax:** 01270 882962

E-mail: enquiries@rodehall.co.uk

Owner/Contact: Sir Richard Baker Wilbraham Bt

The Wilbraham family have lived at Rode since 1669; the present house was constructed in two stages, the earlier two storey wing and stable block around 1705 and the main building was completed in 1752. Later alterations by Lewis Wyatt and Darcy Braddell were undertaken in 1812 and 1927 respectively. The house stands in a Repton landscape and the extensive gardens include a woodland garden, with a terraced rock garden and grotto, which has many species of rhododendrons, azaleas, hellebores and climbing roses following snowdrops and daffodils in the early spring. The formal rose garden was designed by W Nesfield in 1860; there is a large walled kitchen garden and a new Italian garden. The icehouse in the park has recently been restored.

Location: MAP 6:M3, OS Ref. SJ819 573. 5m SW of Congleton between the A34 and A50. Kidsgrove railway station 2m NW of Kidsgrove.

Open: 5 Apr–28 Sept: Weds & BHs and by appointment. Garden only: Tues & Thurs, 2–5pm. Snowdrop Walk: 29 Jan–13 March daily except Mons 12 noon–4pm.

Admission: House & Garden: Adult £6, Conc £5. Garden only and snowdrop walk: Adult £4, Conc £3.

Home-made teas. On leads.

Norton Priory

TABLEY HOUSE

KNUTSFORD, CHESHIRE WA16 0HB

www.tableyhouse.co.uk

Tel: 01565 750151 **Fax:** 01565 653230 **E-mail:** tableyhouse@btconnect.com

Owner: The University of Manchester **Contact:** The Administrator

The finest Palladian House in the North West, Tabley a Grade I listing, was designed by John Carr of York for the Leicester family. Set in landscaped parkland it contains one of the first collections of English paintings, including works of art by Turner, Reynolds, Lawrence and Lely. Furniture by Chippendale, Bullock and Gillow and fascinating family memorabilia adorn the rooms. Interesting Tea Room and 17th century Chapel adjoin.

Location: MAP 6:M2, OS Ref. SJ725 777. M6/J19, A556 S on to A5033. 2m W of Knutsford.

Open: House: Apr–end Oct: Thurs–Suns & BHs, 2–5pm. Tea Room: All year Thurs–Suns, 11am–6pm. (Tea Room tel: 07804 378504).

Admission: Adult £4. Child/Student £1.50. Groups by arrangement.

Please telephone for easiest access. Civil Wedding Licence plus Civil Naming Ceremonies & Re-affirmation of Vows.

© NTPL / Stephen Robson

Tatton Park

TATTON PARK

Knutsford, Cheshire WA16 6QN

Tel: 01625 374400 **Info:** 01625 374435 **Fax:** 01625 374403

www.nationaltrust.org.uk

Owner: National Trust (Managed by Cheshire East County Council)

Gardens extending over 50 acres include Japanese, walled and formal.

Location: MAP 6:M2, OS Ref. SJ745 815. From M56/J7 follow signs. From M6/J19, signed on A56 & A50.

WOODHEY CHAPEL

Faddiley, Nr Nantwich, Cheshire CW5 8JH

Tel: 01270 524215

Owner: The Trustees of Woodhey Chapel **Contact:** Mr Robinson, The Curator

Small private chapel built in 1690, now restored.

Location: MAP 6:L3, OS Ref. SJ573 528. Proceeding W from Nantwich on A534, turn left 1m W of the Faddiley – Brindley villages onto narrow lane, keep ahead at next turn, at road end obtain key from farmhouse.

Open: Apr–Oct: Sats & BHs, 2–5pm, or apply for key at Woodhey Hall.

Admission: Donation box.

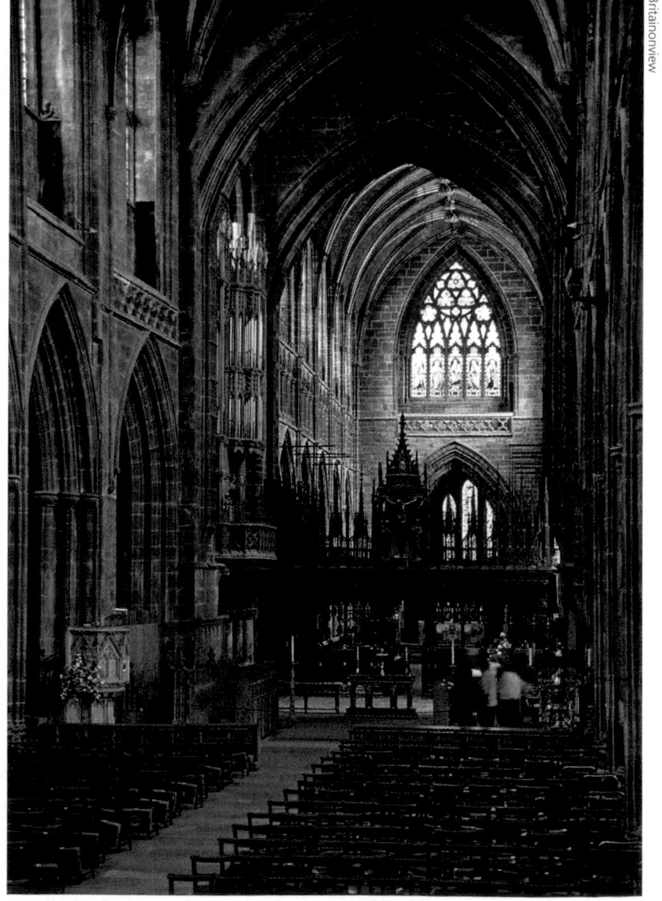

© Britainonview

Chester Cathedral

DALEMAIN

www.dalemain.com

Dalemain is a fine mixture of medieval, Tudor and early Georgian architecture. The imposing Georgian façade strikes the visitor immediately but in the cobbled courtyard the atmosphere of the north country Tudor manor is secure. The 12th century Norman Pele Tower is the oldest part of Dalemain. The manor house has evolved through the centuries and the early Georgian pink ashlar facade completed in 1744 was the last significant addition. The present owner's family have lived at Dalemain since 1679 and have collected a wide variety of china, furniture and family portraits. Don't miss Mrs Mouse's House on the back stairs!

The Gardens have developed during the passing generations of owners and are for all to enjoy. There are 5 acres of richly planted herbaceous borders with and intriguing and unusual combination of flowers set against the picturesque splendour of the Lakeland Fells and Parkland. Highlights are the Rose Walk with over 100 old-fashioned roses and ancient apple trees of named varieties, magnificent Abies Cephalonica and Tulip Tree. Tudor Knot Garden. Wild Garden with a profusion of flowering shrubs and wild flowers and in early summer the breathtaking display of blue Himalayan Poppies. Giantess Earth Sculpture and newly developed Stumpery in Lobs's Wood, a woodland garden.

Jane Hasell-McCosh is the founder of The World's Original Marmalade Festival which is held in February each year and hosts the prize giving for Competitions for Amateur and Artisan Marmalade Makers. www.marmaladefestival.com

No photography in house. Moorings available on Ullswater. Phone for event enquiries

Partial WCs.

Licensed.

Licensed.

Obligatory, 1hr tours. German and French translations. Garden tour for groups extra.

Parking for coaches 50 yds.

Guide dogs only.

■ Owner

Robert Hasell-McCosh Esq

■ Contact

Jennifer Little
House Administrator
Penrith, Cumbria
CA11 0HB
Tel: 017684 86450
Fax: 017684 86223
E-mail: admin@dalemain.com

■ Location

MAP 10:L5
OS Ref. NY477 269.

On A592 1m S of A66. 4m SW of Penrith. From London, M1, M6/J40: 5 hrs. From Edinburgh, A73, M74,M6/J40: 2½ hrs.

■ Opening Times

Gardens & Tearoom:
30 Jan–31 Mar & 30 Oct–15 Dec: Sun–Thur. 11am–3pm.

Gardens, Tearoom & Gift Shop:
3 Apr–27 Oct: Sun–Thur. 10.30am–5pm (4pm in Oct). House opens 11.15am–4pm (3pm in Oct). Groups (12+) please book.

■ Admission

House & Garden:

Adult	£9.50
Accompanied Children under 16	Free

Gardens only:

Adult	£6.50
Accompanied Children under 16	Free

Group prices on application.

■ Special Events

Details tbc.

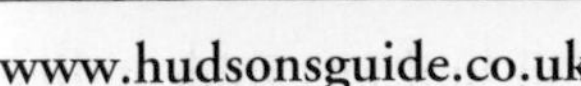

■ **Owner**
Lord Cavendish of Furness

■ **Contact**
Sarah Ross
Holker Hall and Gardens
Cark-in-Cartmel
Grange-over-Sands
Cumbria LA11 7PL

Tel: 015395 58328
E-mail: info@holker.co.uk

■ **Location**
MAP 10:K8
OS Ref. SD359 773

Close to Morecambe Bay, 5m W of Grange-over-Sands by B5277. From Kendal, A6, A590, B5277, B5278: 16m. Motorway: M6/J36.

■ **Open**
Hall:
12–27 February: daily, 11am–4pm.

3 April–30 October: Sunday–Friday, closed Saturday, 11am–4pm.

Gardens:
12–27 February: daily, 10.30am–4pm.

3 April–30 October: Sunday–Friday, closed Saturday, 10.30am–5.30pm.

Cafe, gift shop & food hall:
12 February–24 December, daily, from 10.30am.

■ **Admission**

House & Gardens	
Adult	£10.00
Concession	£9.00
Child (age 6-15 years)	£5.50
Under 6 years	FOC
Family (2 adults & 2–4 children)	£27.50
Gardens & Park	
Adult	£6.50
Concession	£5.50
Child (age 6-15 years)	£3.50
Under 6 years	FOC
Family (2 adults & 2–4 children)	£16.50

Group Rates
Available for groups of 10 or more:

Hall & Gardens:	
Adult	£6.70
Concession	£6.25
Gardens & Park:	
Adult	£4.70
Concession	£4.25

■ **Special Events**
Friday 3–Sunday 5 June
Holker Garden Festival

Saturday 3–Wednesday 21 December
Christmas at Holker

Details of the full events programme (including outdoor theatre) and online tickets are available on the website www.holker.co.uk

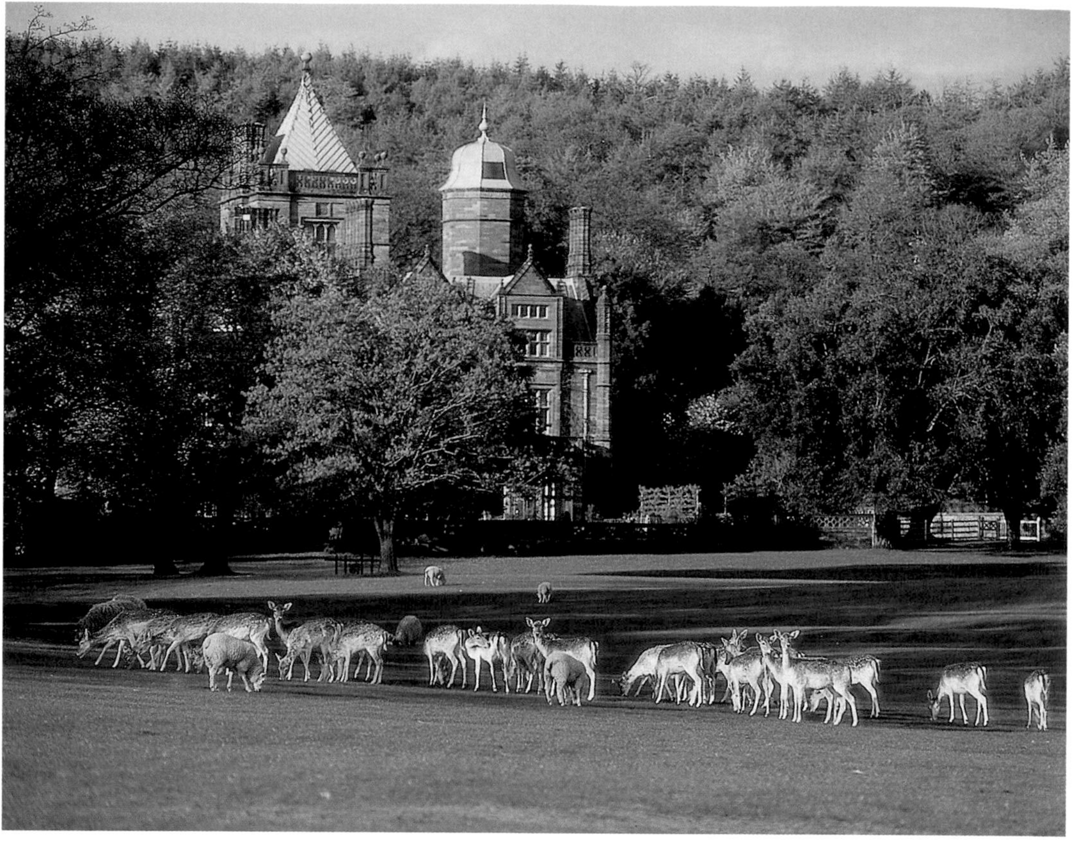

HOLKER HALL & GARDENS

www.holker.co.uk

Holker is the family home of Lord and Lady Cavendish, who extend a warm welcome to visitors of all ages. This beautiful historic house, surrounded by formal and woodland gardens and gently undulating deer park, is perfectly situated between the Lakeland hills and the expanse of Morecambe Bay.

The hall itself is a magnificent Victorian Mansion in the neo-Elizabethan gothic style. Although largely rebuilt in the 1870's following a disastrous fire, its origins date back to the early 1600's. Steeped in history, it contains superb examples of local craftsmanship, fine art and furnishings. The absence of ropes or barriers allows true visitor engagement and a refreshing feeling of freedom and warmth.

The gardens offer a wonderful sensory experience. They are a living reflection of the imagination and care of the owners and gardeners who have tended them over the centuries. Highlights and unique features include the National Collection of Styracaceae, exquisitely sculptured yew and box hedging, ancient trees, glades of rhododendrons, the mystical labyrinth, the slate sundial, the stunning cascade water feature, and the 400 year old Great Holker Lime. The inspirational planting schemes provide beauty and interest throughout the seasons.

Holker's Courtyard Cafe serves delicious homemade food, sourced from the Holker Estate and the local area. The food hall stocks estate produce and the best from Lakeland producers, as well as fine foods and gifts from further afield. The gift shop offers an array of lovely and unusual items, and plants from local nurseries including Holker's own.

No photography in house.
Holker Food Hall – produce from the Estate.
WCs and access to all areas except first floor of the Hall. Carers FOC.
Licensed.
Menus using Estate produce according to season
For groups, by arrangement.
75 yds from Hall.
By arrangement.
On leads (restrictions apply).

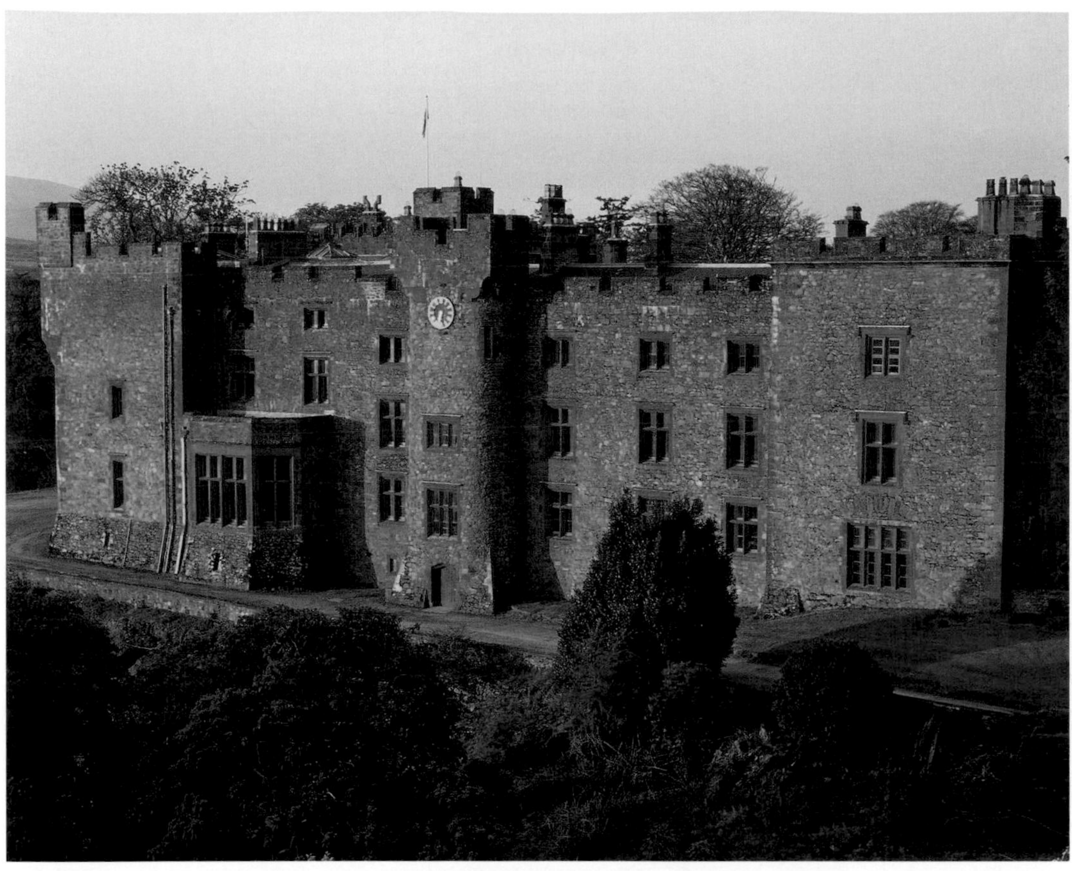

©Brian Sherwen

MUNCASTER CASTLE

GARDENS & OWL CENTRE

www.muncaster.co.uk

Described by Ruskin as the 'Gateway to Paradise', Muncaster is set in 77 acres of historic woodland Grade 2 listed gardens of the Lake District National Park and is, uniquely, also the start of the famous 'Hadrian's Wall Country'.

With the Georgian Terrace (c.1780), 12th century Church and home to the World Owl Centre (with more than 200 birds on display), the Gardens also house one of Europe's largest collection of rhododendron's amongst the rich and diverse planting of this stunning landscape.

With influences dating back to Roman times, the Castle, (the jewel in the crown at Muncaster) is an iconic landmark in our local history. Since 1208 Muncaster has been the family home of the Pennington family and is still a lived in family home to this day. The impressive library, beautiful barrel-vaulted drawing room and exquisite dining room are a real treasure trove of furniture, tapestries, silver, porcelain and interesting stories. Muncaster's beautiful setting is perfect for weddings, team building events, conferences as well as parties and private dining experiences.

4* Guest B&B accommodation is available at the Coachman's Quarters within the Castle Gardens or at the 3* luxurious Pennington Hotel in Ravenglass. The Pennington was formerly a coaching inn and has been recently rennovated in a modern and comfortable style. 3 holiday cottages are also available providing the ideal base for your short break or family holiday.

Whether to relax, wonder, relish or enjoy, your experience will be as unique and personal as the service.

© Mike McKenzie

- Church. Garden parties, film location, clay pigeon shooting. No photography inside the Castle.
-
-
- For wedding receptions, catering, & functions, tel: 01229 717614.
- WCs.
- Licensed.
- Licensed.
- Private tours with a personal guide (family member possible) can be arranged at additional fee.
- Individual audio tour (40mins) included in price.
- 500 cars 800 yds from Castle; coach park available at centre of estate, all parking free.
- Guides available. Historical subjects, horticulture, conservation, owl tours.
- On leads.

Owner

Mrs Phyllida Gordon-Duff-Pennington

Contact

Steve Bishop
Muncaster Castle
Ravenglass
Cumbria CA18 1RQ

Tel: 01229 717614
Fax: 01229 717010
E-mail: info@muncaster.co.uk

Location

MAP 10:J7
OS Ref. SD103 965
SAT NAV – CA18 1RD

From S – M6/J36, A590, A595
From NE – M6/J40, A66, A595
From Carlisle (N) A595

On the A595 1m S of Ravenglass, 19m S of Whitehaven.

From Chester 2.5 hrs, Edinburgh 3.5 hrs, Manchester 2.5 hrs.

Rail: Ravenglass (on Barrow-in-Furness-Carlisle Line) 1½ m.

Air: Manchester 2½ hrs.

Opening Times

Full Season
Last Sunday in March–last Sunday in October Gardens & World Owl Centre open daily 10.30am–6pm,(dusk if earlier). Castle open Sunday–Friday 12–4.30pm.

Winter Season
11am–4pm (dusk if earlier).

Castle open reduced hours, please see website or call for details.

Closed in January.

Open for groups, conferences and weddings by appointment.

Darkest Muncaster
Explore the hauntingly beautiful illuminated gardens by night and light, see website or call for more details.

'Meet the Birds'
Daily at 2.30pm, Full season only.
'Heron Happy Hour' daily 4.30pm (winter 3.30pm).

Admission

Castle, Gardens, Owl Centre & Meadow Vole Maze
Please see www.muncaster.co.uk for details.

Gardens, Owl Centre & Meadow Vole Maze
Please see www.muncaster.co.uk for details.

Special discounts groups (12+).

Special Events

See our website www.muncaster.co.uk for details.

Conference/Function

ROOM	MAX CAPACITY
Drawing Room	100
Dining Room	50
Family Dining Rm	60
Great Hall	100
Old Laundry	120
Library	48
Guard Room	30
Marquee	200

ACORN BANK GARDEN & WATERMILL

Temple Sowerby, Penrith, Cumbria CA10 1SP
Tel: 01768 361893 **E-mail:** acornbank@nationaltrust.org.uk
www.nationaltrust.org.uk
Owner: National Trust **Contact:** The Custodian

Seventeenth century walls enclose a herb garden with over 250 varieties of medicinal and culinary plants and orchards with traditional fruit trees surrounded by mixed borders. Beyond the walls, paths lead through woodland to a partially restored watermill. House not open. Tearoom serving delicious seasonal food.

Location: Gate: MAP 10:M5, OS Ref. NY612 281. Just N of Temple Sowerby, 6m E of Penrith 1m from A66.

Open: 26 Feb–6 Mar, weekends; 12 Mar–30 Oct, daily except Mon & Tue, 10am–5pm. Last admission 4.30pm. Tearoom 11am–4.30pm.

***Admission:** Adult £4.40, Child £2.20, Family £11. *includes a voluntary 10% donation but visitors can choose to pay the standard prices displayed at the property and on the website.

Special events: Apple Day 16 Oct, seperate charge including NT members.

Limited. On leads.

BEATRIX POTTER GALLERY

Main Street, Hawkshead, Cumbria LA22 0NS
Tel: 01539 436355 **Fax:** 01539 436187
Owner: National Trust **Contact:** Ticket Office/House Steward

Changing exhibition of original watercolours and sketches by the children's author.

Location: MAP 10:K7, OS Ref. SD352 982. 5m SSW of Ambleside. In the Square. Parking 300yards (pay and display, not NT). Tel. 01539 445161 for complete bus and ferry timetable.

Thinking of a short break or weekend away?
See Historic Places to Stay

BRANTWOOD

Coniston, Cumbria LA21 8AD
Tel: 01539 441396 **Fax:** 01539 441263 **E-mail:** enquiries@brantwood.org.uk
www.brantwood.org.uk
Owner: The Brantwood Trust

Brantwood, the former home of John Ruskin, is the most beautifully situated house in the Lake District. Explore Brantwood's estate and gardens or experience contemporary art in the Severn Studio. Brantwood's bookshop, the Jumping Jenny restaurant and Coach House Craft Gallery combine for a perfect day out.

Location: MAP 10:K7, OS Ref. SD313 959. 2½m from Coniston village on the E side of Coniston Water.

Open: Mid Mar–mid Nov: daily, 11am–5.30pm. Mid Nov–mid Mar: Wed–Sun, 11am–4.30pm.

Admission: Adult £6.30, Child £1.35, Student £5.00, Family (2+3) £13.15. Garden only: Adult £4.50, Family (2+3) £8.60. Groups: Adult £5.95, Child £1.35, Student £4.50. Gift Aid admission available.

No photography in the house. Licensed. Licensed. Licensed. By arrangement. Ample. Limited for coaches. in grounds, on leads.

BROUGH CASTLE

Brough, Cumbria

Please call 0870 3331181 for details of opening times and charges
E-mail: customers@english-heritage.org.uk
www.english-heritage.org.uk/broughcastle
Owner: English Heritage **Contact:** Visitor Operations Manager

This ancient site dates back to Roman times. The 12th century keep replaced an earlier stronghold destroyed by the Scots in 1174.

Location: MAP 10:M6, OS Ref. NY791 141. 8m SE of Appleby S of A66. South part of the village.

Open: 1 Apr–30 Sep: daily, 10am–5pm. 1 Oct–31 Mar: daily, 10am–4pm. Closed 24–26 Dec & 1 Jan.

Admission: Free. Opening times and prices are valid until 31st March 2011, after this date details are subject to change please visit www.english-heritage.org.uk for the most up-to-date information.

BLACKWELL, THE ARTS & CRAFTS HOUSE

BOWNESS ON WINDERMERE, CUMBRIA LA23 3JT

www.blackwell.org.uk

Tel: 015394 46139 **Fax:** 015394 88486 **E-mail:** info@blackwell.org.uk
Owner: Lakeland Arts Trust **Contact:** Blackwell

Blackwell, completed in 1900, is the largest and most important surviving example of work by architect Mackay Hugh Baillie Scott. Designed as a holiday retreat for Sir Edward Holt, the house survives in a truly remarkable state of preservation retaining many original decorative features. Visitors are encouraged to sit and soak up the atmosphere in Blackwell's fireplace inglenooks and are free to enjoy the house as it was originally intended, without roped-off areas. The period rooms are furnished with Arts & Crafts furniture and decorative arts, which are complemented by exhibitions of historical applied arts and contemporary craft.

Location: MAP 10:K7, OS Ref. SD400 945. 11/2 m S of Bowness just off the A5074 on the B5360. Rail: Windermere. Air: Manchester.

Open: Open Daily 10.30am–5pm (Closing 4pm Nov–Mar). 14 Jan–31 Dec 2011. If you are planning to see a specific event please check our website.

Admission: Adult £7, Gift Aid it for £7.70. Child £4, Gift Aid it for £4.40. Family £18, Gift Aid it for £19.80.

No photography inside house. No picnic areas at Blackwell. Partial. WCs. Licensed. Free for cars, coaches by appointment. Guide dogs only.

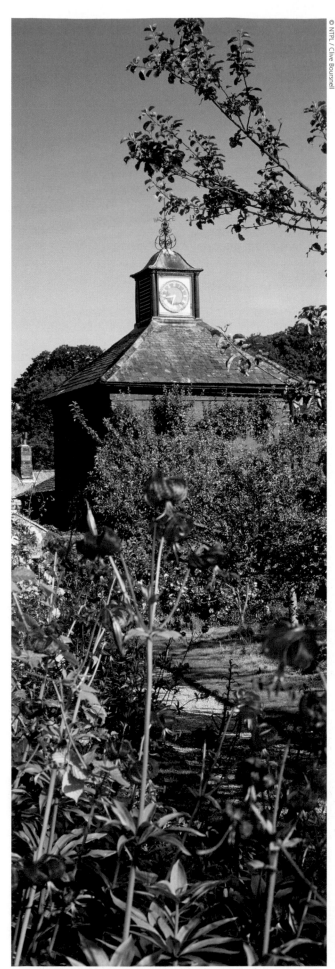

Acorn Bank Garden & Watermill

BROUGHAM CASTLE

Penrith, Cumbria CA10 2AA

Tel: 01768 862488 **E-mail:** customers@english-heritage.org.uk

www.english-heritage.org.uk/broughamcastle

Owner: English Heritage **Contact:** Visitor Operations Team

Come to the gentle banks of the River Eamont and discover the intriguing story of Lady Anne Clifford. Visit the exhibition highlighting her remarkable life at these impressive 13th century ruins.

Location: MAP 10:L5, OS Ref. NY537 290. 1½ m SE of Penrith, between A66 & B6262.

Open: 1 Apr–30 Sep: daily, 10am–5pm.

Admission: Adult £3.70, Child £1.90, Conc. £3.10. Family £9.30. 15% discount for groups (11+). EH members Free. Opening times and prices are valid until 31st March 2011, after this date details are subject to change please visit www.english-heritage.org.uk for the most up-to-date information.

WCs.

CARLISLE CASTLE

CARLISLE, CUMBRIA CA3 8UR

www.english-heritage.org.uk/carlisle

Tel: 01228 591922 **Email:** customers@english-heritage.org.uk

Owner: English Heritage **Contact:** Visitor Operations Team

One of Britain's best border castles, dating back over 900 years, this was a flashpoint of Anglo-Scottish border warfare, beating off sieges and serving as a grim prison for many generations of captives including Mary, Queen of Scots. Exhibition on Bonnie Prince Charlie and the Jacobite Rising.

Location: MAP 10:K3, OS Ref. NY396 562. In Carlisle town, at N end of city centre.

Open: 1 Apr–30 Sep: daily, 9.30am–5pm. 1 Oct–31 Mar: daily, 10am–4pm. Closed 24–26 Dec & 1 Jan.

Admission: Adult £4.80, Child £2.40, Conc £4.10. 15% discount for groups (11+). EH members Free. Opening times and prices are valid until 31st March 2011, after this date details are subject to change please visit www.english-heritage.org.uk for the most up-to-date information.

Obligatory. Disabled parking only.

CARLISLE CATHEDRAL

Carlisle, Cumbria CA3 8TZ

Tel: 01228 548151 **Fax:** 01228 547049 **Contact:** Ms C Baines

Fine sandstone Cathedral, founded in 1122. Medieval stained glass.

Location: MAP 10:K3, OS Ref. NY399 559. Carlisle city centre, 2m from M6/J43.

Open: Mon–Sat: 7.30am–6.15pm, Suns, 7.30–5pm.

Admission: Donation.

For unique **Civil wedding** venues see our index at the end of the book.

CONISHEAD PRIORY & BUDDHIST TEMPLE

A5087 Coast Road, Ulverston, Cumbria LA12 9QQ

Tel: 01229 584029 **Fax:** 01229 580080 **E-mail:** visits@manjushri.org

www.manjushri.org

Owner: New Kadampa Tradition **Contact:** Geoffrey Roe

Gothic mansion on Morecambe Bay. Reception rooms with decorative ceilings, vaulted great hall, amazing stained glass, grand staircase, 48m cloister corridor. Now international Buddhist Centre with unique Temple. Café, Gift shop. Guided tours explain the healing work since 1160. Simon Jenkins says: *"There is no house in England like Conishead"*.

Location: MAP 10:K8, OS Ref. SD305 757. 2m S of Ulverston on A5087 Coast Road. Bus: Service 11 from Ulverston. Rail: 2m from Ulverston Station.

Open: See website or phone for details. 5 Mar–11 Dec. Temple & Shop open Sat, Sun & Bank Hols, 12noon–5pm. Mon–Fri 2–5pm. Café & Guided Tours on Sat, Sun & Bank Hols only. Except when closed for Buddhist Festivals.

Admission: Free. Guided Tours £3, Children Free.

WCs. Limited for coaches. Guide dogs only.

DALEMAIN

See page 363 for full page entry.

For **corporate hospitality** venues see our special index at the end of the book.

©The Wordsworth Trust

DOVE COTTAGE, AND THE WORDSWORTH MUSEUM

GRASMERE, CUMBRIA LA22 9SH

www.wordsworth.org.uk

Tel: 01539 435544 **Fax:** 01539 435748 **E-mail:** enquiries@wordsworth.org.uk

Owner: The Wordsworth Trust **Contact:** Bookings Officer

Situated in the heart of the Lake District, Dove Cottage is the beautifully preserved home of William Wordsworth. Visitors can take a guided tour of the cottage then discover more about the poet at the award-winning Wordsworth Museum next door. On site café/restaurant and shop.

Location: MAP 10:K6, OS Ref. NY342 070. Immediately S of Grasmere village on A591. Main car/coach park next to Restaurant.

Open: All year: daily, 9.30am–5.30pm (last admission 5pm). Closed 24–26 Dec & early Jan–early Feb. Winter opening hours apply Nov-Feb.

Admission: Adult £7.50, Child £4.50, Family and group rates available. Prices are subject to change without notice.

No photography. Partial. WC. Obligatory for Dove Cottage. Guide dogs only.

FURNESS ABBEY

Barrow-in-Furness, Cumbria LA13 0PJ

Tel: 01229 823420 **E-mail:** customers@english-heritage.org.uk

www.english-heritage.org.uk/furnessabbey

Owner: English Heritage **Contact:** Visitor Operations Staff

Set in the peaceful 'Valley of Nightshade' are the beautiful red sandstone remains of the wealthy abbey founded in 1123 by Stephen, later King of England. This abbey first belonged to the Order of Savigny and later to the Cistercians. There is a museum and exhibition.

Location: MAP 10:J8, OS Ref. SD218 717. 1½ m N of Barrow-in-Furness off A590.

Open: 1 Apr–30 Sep: Thu–Mon, 10am–5pm. 1 Oct–31 Mar: Sat–Sun, 10am–4pm. Closed 24–26 Dec & 1 Jan.

Admission: Adult £3.70, Child £1.90, Conc. £3.10. 15% discount for groups (11+). EH members Free. Opening times and prices are valid until 31st March 2011, after this date details are subject to change please visit www.english-heritage.org.uk for the most up-to-date information.

WC. Inclusive.

HARDKNOTT ROMAN FORT

Ravenglass, Cumbria

Tel: 0161 242 1400 **E-mail:** customers@english-heritage.org.uk

www.english-heritage.org.uk/hardknottromanfort

Owner: English Heritage **Contact:** The North West Regional Office

This fort, built between AD120 and 138, controlled the road from Ravenglass to Ambleside.

Location: MAP 10:J6, OS Ref. NY218 015. At the head of Eskdale. 9m NE of Ravenglass, at W end of Hardknott Pass.

Open: Any reasonable time. Access may be hazardous in winter.

Admission: Free. Opening times and prices are valid until 31st March 2011, after this date details are subject to change please visit www.english-heritage.org.uk for the most up-to-date information.

HERON CORN MILL & MUSEUM OF PAPERMAKING

Beetham Trust, Waterhouse Mills, Beetham, Milnthorpe LA7 7AR

Tel: 015395 65027 **Fax:** 015395 65033 **E-mail:** info@heronmill.org

Owner: Heron Corn Mill Beetham Trust **Contact:** Audrey Steeley

A fascinating visitor attraction. An 18th century corn mill and museum of papermaking offers hand-made paper demonstrations and art workshops for visitors.

Location: MAP 10:L8, OS Ref. SD497 800. At Beetham. 1m S of Milnthorpe on the A6.

Open: Wed–Sun & Bank Hol Mons, 11am–4pm.

Admission: Please telephone for details.

© Britainonview

Furness Abbey

Dalemain

For rare and unusual plants visit the **plant sales** index at the end of the book.

HILL TOP

Near Sawrey, Ambleside, Cumbria LA22 0LF

Tel: 01539 436269 opt 5 **Fax:** 01539 436811

Owner: National Trust **Contact:** Administrator

17th c cottage and garden used by Beatrix Potter writer and illustrator.

Location: MAP 10:K7, OS Ref. SD370 955. 2m S of Hawkshead, in hamlet of Near Sawrey.

HOLEHIRD GARDENS

Patterdale Road, Windermere, Cumbria LA23 1NP

Tel: 01539 446008

Owner: Lakeland Horticultural Society **Contact:** The Hon Secretary/Publicity Officer

Over 10 acres of hillside gardens overlooking Windermere, including a wide variety of plants, specimen trees and shrubs, extensive rock and heather gardens, a walled garden, alpine houses and herbaceous borders. The all year garden also is home to the national collections of Astilbe, Hydrangea and Polystichum ferns. Managed and maintained entirely by volunteers.

Location: MAP 10:K7, OS Ref. NY410 008. On A592, ¾m N of junction with A591. ½ m N of Windermere. 1m from Townend.

Open: All year: dawn till dusk. Groups strictly by arrangement. Reception: Apr–Oct, 10am–5pm.

Admission: Free. Donation appreciated.

HOLKER HALL & GARDENS

See page 364 for full page entry.

HUTTON-IN-THE-FOREST

PENRITH, CUMBRIA CA11 9TH

www.hutton-in-the-forest.co.uk

Tel: 017684 84449 **Fax:** 017684 84571 **E-mail:** info@hutton-in-the-forest.co.uk

Owner: Lord Inglewood **Contact:** Leah Cameron

The home of Lord Inglewood's family since 1605. Built around a medieval pele tower with 17th, 18th and 19th century additions. Fine collections of furniture, paintings, ceramics and tapestries. Outstanding grounds with terraces, topiary, walled garden, dovecote and woodland walk through magnificent specimen trees.

Location: MAP 10:L5, OS Ref. NY460 358. 6m NW of Penrith & 2½ m from M6/J41 on B5305.

Open: 17 Apr–2 Oct 2011. Wed, Thur, Sun, BH Mon, 12.30–4pm. Tearoom as House 11am–4.30pm. Gardens & Grounds: 31 Mar–31 Oct 2011, daily except Sat, 11am–5pm.

Admission: Please see www.hutton-in-the-forest.co.uk or telephone 017684 84449 for details

Picnic area. Gift stall. By arrangement. Partial. WCs Licensed. Obligatory (except Jul/Aug & BHs). In grounds.

LANERCOST PRIORY

Brampton, Cumbria CA8 2HQ

Tel: 01697 73030 **E-mail:** customers@english-heritage.org.uk

www.english-heritage.org.uk/lanercostpriory

Owner: English Heritage **Contact:** Visitor Operations Team

This Augustinian priory was founded c1166. The nave of the church, which is intact and in use as the local parish church, contrasts with the ruined chancel, transepts and priory buildings.

Location: MAP 10:L3, OS Ref. NY556 637. 2m NE of Brampton. 1m N of Naworth Castle.

Open: 1 Apr–30 Sep: daily, 10am–5pm. 1–31 Oct: Thu–Mon, 10am–4pm.

Admission: Adult £3.20, Child £1.60, Conc. £2.70, Groups (11+): 15% discount. EH members Free. Opening times and prices are valid until 31st March 2011, after this date details are subject to change please visit www.english-heritage.org.uk for the most up-to-date information.

Limited for coaches.

© Britainonview

Holker Hall

MIREHOUSE

KESWICK, CUMBRIA CA12 4QE

www.mirehouse.com

Tel: 017687 72287 **E-mail:** info@mirehouse.com

Owner: James Fryer-Spedding **Contact**: Janaki Spedding

Melvyn Bragg described Mirehouse as *'Manor from Heaven'*. Simon Jenkins in *The Times* said *'It is the Lake District with its hand on its heart'*. Literary house linked with Tennyson and Wordsworth. Live piano music and children's history trail in house. Natural playgrounds, serene bee garden and lakeside walk.

Location: MAP 10:J5, OS Ref. NY235 284. Beside A591, 3½ m N of Keswick. Good bus service.

Open: Apr–Oct: Gardens & Tearoom: daily, 10am–5pm. House: Suns & Weds (also Fris in Aug), 2–5pm (4.30pm last entry). Groups (15+) welcome by appointment.

Admission: House & Garden: Adult £6.50, Child £3.00, Family (2+4) £18.00. Gardens only: Adult £3, Child £1.50.

No photography in house. By arrangement.

LEVENS HALL

LEVENS HALL, KENDAL, CUMBRIA LA8 0PD

www.levenshall.co.uk

Tel: 015395 60321 **Fax:** 015395 60669 **E-mail:** houseopening@levenshall.co.uk

Owner: C H Bagot **Contact:** The Administrator

Levens Hall is an Elizabethan mansion built around a 13th century pele tower. The much loved home of the Bagot family, with fine panelling, plasterwork, Cordova leather wall coverings, paintings by Rubens, Lely and Cuyp, the earliest English patchwork and Wellingtoniana combine with other beautiful objects to form a fascinating collection.

The world famous Topiary Gardens were laid out by Monsieur Beaumont from 1694 and his design has remained largely unchanged to this day. Over 90 individual pieces of topiary, some over nine metres high, massive beech hedges and colourful seasonal bedding provide a magnificent visual impact.

Location: MAP 10:L7, OS Ref. SD495 851. 5m S of Kendal on the A6. Exit M6/J36.

Open: 10 April–13 Oct, Sun–Thurs (closed Fris & Sats). Garden, Tea Room, Gift Shop & Plant Centre 10am–5pm. House 12 noon–4.30pm (last entry 4pm). Groups (20+) please book.

Admission: House & Gardens or Gardens Only. Please see www.levenshall.co.uk for details. Group Rates on application.

No indoor photography. Gift shop Partial. WC. Electric buggy hire. DVD of interior of house. Licensed By arrangement. Free on-site parking. Assistance dogs only.

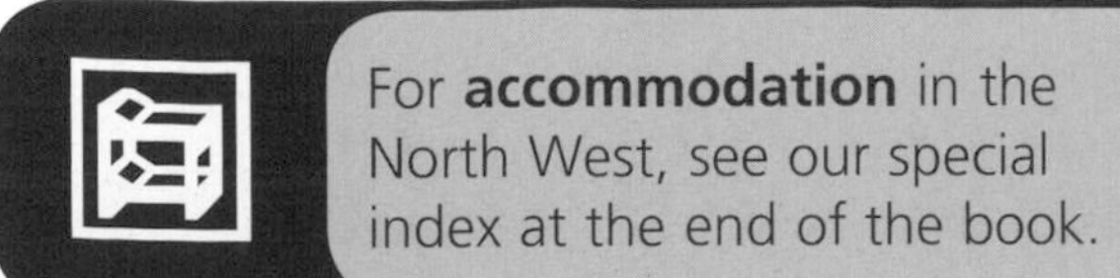

For accommodation in the North West, see our special index at the end of the book.

MUNCASTER CASTLE, GARDENS & OWL CENTRE

See page 365 for full page entry.

PENRITH CASTLE

Penrith, Cumbria

Tel: 0161 242 1400 **E-mail:** customers@english-heritage.org.uk

www.english-heritage.org.uk/penrithcastle

Owner: English Heritage **Contact:** The North West Regional Office

This mainly 15th century castle, set in a park on the edge of the town, was built to defend Penrith against repeated attacks by Scottish raiders.

Location: MAP 10:L5, OS Ref. NY513 299. Opposite Penrith railway station. W of the town centre. Fully visible from the street.

Open: Park: Summer: 7.30am–9pm; Winter: 7.30am–4.30pm.

Admission: Free. Opening times and prices are valid until 31st March 2011, after this date details are subject to change please visit www.english-heritage.org.uk for the most up-to-date information.

WC.

SIZERGH CASTLE & GARDEN

Sizergh, Nr Kendal, Cumbria LA8 8AE

Tel: 01539 560951

Owner: National Trust **Contact:** Property Administrator

Imposing house in beautiful gardens.

Location: MAP 10:L7, OS Ref. SD498 878. 3½m S of Kendal, NW of the A590/A591 interchange.

© Levens Hall

Levens Hall

STOTT PARK BOBBIN MILL

Low Stott Park, Nr Newby Bridge, Cumbria LA12 8AX

Tel: 01539 531087 **E-mail:** customers@english-heritage.org.uk

www.english-heritage.org.uk/stottpark

Owner: English Heritage **Contact:** Visitor Operations Team

Built in 1835, this mill was vital to the spinning and weaving industry in Lancashire. A remarkable opportunity to see demonstrations of the machinery and techniques of the Industrial Revolution. Free guided tours.

Location: MAP 10:K7, OS Ref. SD372 881. 1½m N of Newby Bridge off A590.

Open: 1 Apr–31 Oct: Mon–Fri, 11am–5pm. Last tour begins ½hr before closing.

Admission: Adult £4.80, Child £2.40, Conc £4.10, Family £12.00. Groups: discount for groups (11+). EH members Free. Opening times and prices are valid until 31st March 2011, after this date details are subject to change please visit www.english-heritage.org.uk for the most up-to-date information.

Obligatory. Free.

TOWNEND

Troutbeck, Windermere, Cumbria LA23 1LB

Tel: 015394 32628 **Fax:** 015394 32628 **E-mail:** townend@nationaltrust.org.uk

www.nationaltrust.org.uk/townend

Owner: National Trust **Contact:** The Custodian

The Brownes of Townend were just an ordinary farming family, but their home and belongings bring to life over 400 years of extraordinary stories. Townend contains carved woodwork, books, papers, furniture and fascinating implements of the past which were accumulated by the Browne family who lived here from before 1626 until 1943.

Location: MAP 10:K6, OS Ref. NY407 023. 3m SE of Ambleside at S end of Troutbeck village. 1m from Holehird, 3m N of Windermere.

Open: 12 Mar–30 Oct, Wed–Sun. Entry by guided tour at 11am & 12 noon, places limited and available on a first come first served basis. Self-guided opening 1–5pm with last admission 30 mins before closing.

***Admission:** Adult £5.00, Child £2.50, Family £12.50. No reduction for groups which must be pre-booked. *Includes a voluntary donation but visitors can choose to pay the standard prices displayed at the property and on the website.

Partial. By arrangement. Limited.

THE WATERMILL

Little Salkeld, Penrith, Cumbria CA10 1NN

Tel: 01768 881523 **E-mail:** organicflour@aol.com

www.organicmill.co.uk

Owner: Nick and Ana Jones **Contact:** Nick Jones 01768 881047

Traditional 18th century Cumbrian watermill producing stoneground organic and biodynamic flours. Milltours. Tearoom. Millshop. Mail order service. Online shop. Breadmaking, baking courses. Childrens workshops. Near Long Meg Stone Circle, Lacy Caves, River Eden.

Location: MAP 10:L5, OS Ref. NY566 362. 7m from Penrith M6 (J40) in Eden Valley.

Open: Daily 10.30am–5pm. Closed Christmas to mid-Jan.

Admission: £2. Guided tour £3.50.

WORDSWORTH HOUSE AND GARDEN

Main Street, Cockermouth, Cumbria CA13 9RX

Tel: 01900 824805 **Opening Info:** 01900 820884

E-mail: wordsworthhouse@nationaltrust.org.uk

www.nationaltrust.org.uk www.wordsworthhouse.org.uk

Owner: National Trust **Contact:** The Custodian

This Georgian townhouse was the birthplace of William Wordsworth. Imaginatively presented as his family home in the 1770s, it offers a lively and participative visit with costumed living history and hands-on rooms. The garden, with terraced walk, has been restored to its 18th century appearance. Talks and tours available for groups.

Location: MAP 10:J5, OS Ref. NY118 307. Main Street, Cockermouth.

Open: 12 Mar–30 Oct: Sat–Thur, 11am–5pm. Last entry 4pm. Shop: 4–15 Jan: Tue–Sat, 10am–4pm; 12 Mar–30 Oct: Mon–Sun, 10am–5pm; 31 Oct–23 Dec, Mon–Sat, 10am–4.30pm.

***Admission:** Adult £6.50, Child £3.25, Family £16.25. Pre-booked groups (15+): Adult £5.70, Child £2.50. Group out of hours £9. *Includes a voluntary donation but visitors can choose to pay the standard prices displayed at the property and on the websites.

Special Events: Extensive events programme including talks, tours, concerts and school holiday activities. Also wedding photography packages. See websites for details.

WCs. By arrangement only. Guide dogs only.

■ Owner

Chorley Council

■ Contact

Curator
Astley Park, Off Hallgate, Chorley, PR7 1NP
Tel: 01257 515151
E-mail: astley.hall@chorley.gov.uk

■ Location

MAP 10:L11
OS Ref. SD574 183

Car: Junction 8 on M61. Signposted from A6

Bus: From Chorley Interchange regular services

Rail: Regular services from Manchester, Preston and London

■ Opening Times

Hall and Coach House Gallery: April–November, Fri–Sun, 12.00pm-5pm (last admission 4pm). Ring to check in advance as opening times may vary.

Cafe Ambio: April–November, Mon-Sun 9am-5.30pm

Grounds and Park/Walled Garden: Open all year round daily.

■ Admission

Free admission. Charges for guided tours available on request.

■ Special Events

We have an annual programme of events including outdoor theatre, music events and antique fairs as well as 2 art galleries with changing exhibitions.

More details can be found on our website.

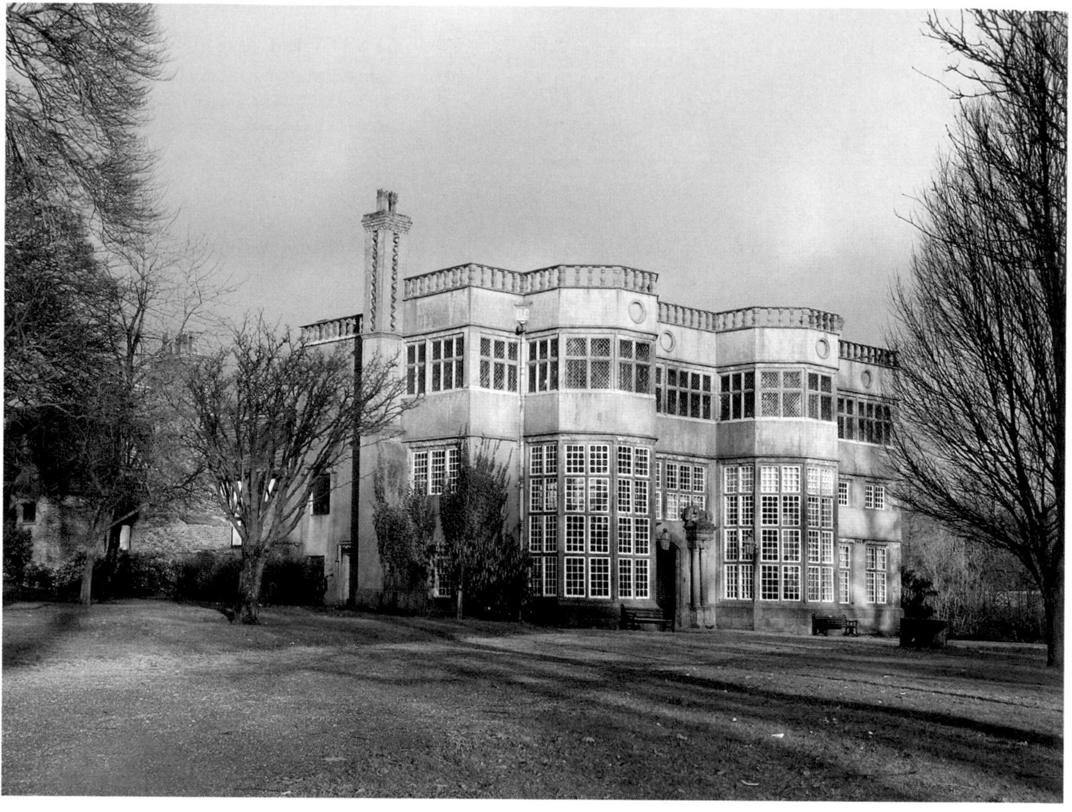

ASTLEY HALL & PARK

www.chorley.gov.uk/astleyhall

Chorley's famous Astley Hall Museum and Gallery is often referred to as the 'Jewel in Chorley's crown' and features in Simon Jenkins book 'Britain's Best 1,000 Houses'.

The history of the Hall itself is full of intrigue, with stories of plotting and religious turmoil. It dates back to Elizabethan times with changes and additions over the centuries, all helping make a visit to the Hall a fascinating and enjoyable experience. This grade 1 listed building truly is the jewel in Chorley's crown, with stunning plaster work and architectural features. As the town's museum and art gallery it is also home to items of local historical interest.

Interiors include sumptuous plaster ceilings, fine 17th century oak furniture and tapestries. The Hall is spread over three floors; upstairs particularly of note are the Cromwell bedroom which has unusually enriched panelling and a plaster overmantel dating from the 16th century. A Priest's hole can be found and 'Cromwell's bed' in the Oak Room reveals an exquisite inlay on the canopy and floral carving on the headboard. The top floor houses the Long Gallery, and reveals the longest shovel-board in existence at 23 feet long, with twenty legs.

Situated within hundreds of acres of historic, recently restored parkland, which is home to outdoor theatre and music events, there is a walled garden and Grade II listed Coach House which houses two art galleries, offering exciting and changing exhibitions and Café Ambio.

Astley Hall can be hired for exclusive use, small conferences, evening events and weddings.

No photography in period rooms. Hall not accessible to wheelchair users above ground floor level.

WCs.

Licensed.

Licensed.

By arrangement.

Limited for coaches.

In grounds.

Browsholme Hall

ASTLEY HALL & PARK

See page 372 for full page entry.

BLACKBURN CATHEDRAL

Cathedral Close, Blackburn, Lancashire BB1 5AA
Tel: 01254 503090 **Fax:** 01254 689666 **Contact:** Pauline Rowe
www.blackburncathedral.com

On an historic Saxon site in town centre. The 1826 Parish Church dedicated as the Cathedral in 1926 with new extensions to give a spacious and light interior. Of special interest is '*The Journey*', a contemporary version of *The Stations of the Cross*, by Penny Warden commisioned by the Cathedral in 2005. The Cathedral is also noted for its outstanding music and significant contributions to the work of cultural understanding both locally and nationally.

Location: MAP 10:M11, OS Ref. SD684 280. 9m E of M6/J31, via A59 and A677. Town centre.
Open: Daily 9am–5pm.
Admission: Free. Donations invited.

BROWSHOLME HALL

CLITHEROE, LANCASHIRE BB7 3DE

www.browsholme.com

Tel: 01254 827166 **E-mail**: info@browsholme.com
Owner: The Parker Family **Contact:** Rebecca Clarke, Events Manager

Built in 1507 and the ancestral Home of the Parker Family, this remarkable Tudor Hall has a major collection of oak furniture and portraits, arms and armour, stained glass and many unusual antiquities from the Civil war to a fragment of a Zeppelin. Browsholme, pronounced 'Brusom', lies in the Forest of Bowland, and is set in unspoilt parkland in the style of Capability Brown. The façade still retains the 'H' shape of the original house with later Queen Anne and Regency additions when the house was refurbished by Thomas Lister Parker a noted antiquarian and patron of artists such as Turner and Northcote. In 2010 a 17th c 'tithe barn' was restored for refreshments, concerts, theatre, events and wedding ceremony and receptions.

Location: MAP 10:M10, OS Ref. SD683 452. 5m NW of Clitheroe off B6243.
Open: 2–5pm 1st Sunday in Mar–Oct with farmers market, Easter BH Sunday & Monday, Spring BH Sun & Mon. Every day 24–31 Jul & 21–31 Aug but not inc Fri or Sat. Sunday 4 December Xmas special. Groups welcome at all times by appointment.
Admission: Adult £6, OAP & Groups £5.50, Child (under 16) £1.50, Grounds only £2.

GAWTHORPE HALL

Padiham, Nr Burnley, Lancashire BB12 8UA
Tel: 01282 771004 **Fax:** 01282 776663
www.nationaltrust.org.uk
Owner: National Trust, managed by Lancashire County Council
Contact: Property Office

Gawthorpe was the home of the Shuttleworths and the Shuttleworth Textile collection is on display.

Location: MAP 10:N10, OS Ref. SD806 340. M65/J8. On E outskirts of Padiham, ¾ m to house on N of A671. Signed to Clitheroe, then signed from 2nd set of traffic lights.

HALL I'TH'WOOD

off Green Way, off Crompton Way, Bolton BL1 8UA
Tel: 01204 332370
Owner: Bolton Metropolitan Borough Council **Contact:** Liz Shaw

Late medieval manor house with 17/18th century furniture, paintings and decorative art.

Location: MAP 10:M12, OS Ref. SD724 116. 2m NNE of central Bolton. ¼m N of A58 ring road between A666 and A676 crossroads.
Open: Times vary, please ring for details.
Admission: Adult £2, Child/Conc. £1, Family £5.

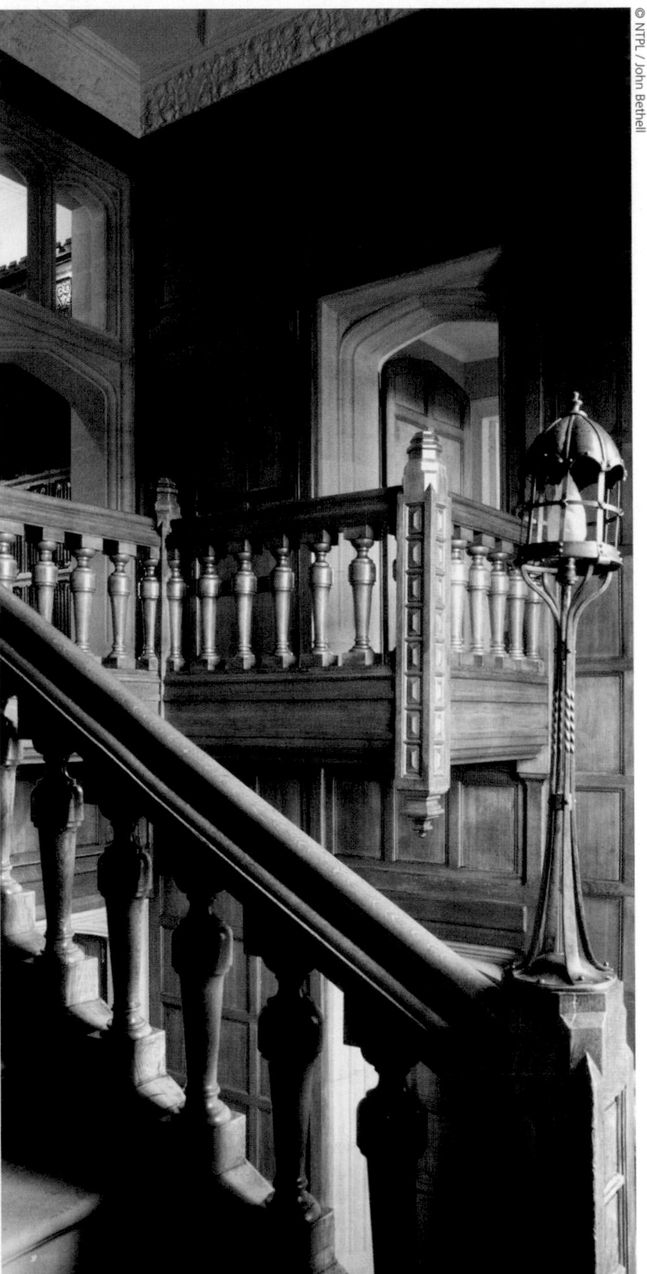

Gawthorpe Hall

HEATON PARK

PRESTWICH, MANCHESTER M25 2SW

www.heatonpark.org.uk

Tel: 0161 773 1085 **Fax** 0161 798 0107 **E-mail:** heatonpark@manchester.gov.uk
Owner: Manchester City Council **Contact:** Graham Wightman

Heaton Park has been in public ownership since 1902 when the 5th Earl of Wilton sold it to the Manchester Corporation. The landscape surrounding the house was designed by William Emes and modified by John Webb and has recently been restored in partnership with the HLF, together with four of the park's historic buildings. The magnificent James Wyatt house was built for Sir Thomas Egerton in 1772, and is one of Manchester's most impressive and important buildings. The principal rooms have been beautifully restored and are used to display furniture, paintings and other decorative arts appropriate to the late 18th century.

Location: MAP 6:N1, OS Ref. SD833 044. NW Manchester, close to M60/J19. Main entrance off St Margaret's Road, off Bury Old Road – A665.

Open: House: Aug–Sep, Thur–Sun & BH Mons, 11am–5.30pm. Park: all year, daily, 8am–dusk.

Admission: Free.

No photography in house, no dogs in buildings. Partial. WCs. By arrangement. Ample for cars, but limited for coaches. In grounds, on leads. Double x 2.

Leighton Hall

Len Grant

HOGHTON TOWER

HOGHTON, PRESTON, LANCASHIRE PR5 0SH

www.hoghtontower.co.uk

Tel: 01254 852986 **Fax:** 01254 852109 **E-mail:** mail@hoghtontower.co.uk

Owner: Sir Bernard de Hoghton Bt **Contact:** Office

Hoghton Tower, home of 14th Baronet, is one of the most dramatic looking houses in northern England. Three houses have occupied the hill site since 1100 with the present house re-built by Thomas Hoghton between 1560–1565. Rich and varied historical events including the Knighting of the Loin 'Sirloin' by James I in 1617.

Location: MAP 10:L11, OS Ref. SD622 264. M65/J3. Midway between Preston & Blackburn on A675.

Open: Jul, Aug & Sept: Mon–Thur, 11am–4pm. Suns, 1–5pm. BH Suns & Mons excluding Christmas & New Year. Group visits by appointment all year.

Admission: Gardens & House tours: Adult £6, Child/Conc. £5, Family £18. Gardens, Shop & Tearoom only: £3. Children under 5yrs Free. Private tours by arrangement (25+) £6, OAP £5.

Conferences, wedding receptions. Unsuitable. Obligatory.

© Britainonview

Blackburn Cathedral

LEIGHTON HALL

CARNFORTH, LANCASHIRE LA5 9ST

www.leightonhall.co.uk

Tel: 01524 734474 **Fax** 01524 720357 **E-mail:** info@leightonhall.co.uk

Owner: Richard Gillow Reynolds Esq **Contact:** Mrs C S Reynolds

Leighton Hall is one of the most beautifully sited houses in the British Isles, situated in a bowl of parkland, with the whole panorama of the Lakeland Fells rising behind. The Hall's neo-gothic façade was superimposed on an 18th century house, which, in turn, had been built on the ruins of the original medieval house. The present owner is descended from Adam d'Avranches who built the first house in 1246. The whole house is, today, lived in by the Reynolds family whose emphasis is put on making visitors feel welcome in a family home. Mr Reynolds is also descended from the founder of Gillow and Company of Lancaster. Connoisseurs of furniture will be particularly interested in the many 18th century Gillow pieces, some of which are unique. Fine pictures, clocks, silver and objéts d'art are also on display. Birds of Prey Flying Display at 3.30pm on open days.

Gardens: The main garden has a continuous herbaceous border with rose covered walls, while the Walled Garden contains flowering shrubs, a herb garden and an ornamental vegetable garden with a caterpillar maze. Beyond is the Woodland Walk where wild flowers abound from early spring.

Location: MAP 10:L8, OS Ref. SD494 744. 9m N of Lancaster, 10m S of Kendal, 3m N of Carnforth. 1½ m W of A6. 3m from M6/A6/J35, signed from J35A.

Open: May–Sep, Tue–Fri (also BH Sun & Mon, Suns in Aug) 2–5pm. Booked groups (25+) at any time, all year by arrangement.

Admission: Adult £7.50, Child (5–12 Years) £4.95, Family £22.50, Conc. £6.50, Garden only £4.50. Booked groups (25+): Inside Leighton £6, Tea & Tour £12.50, Candelit Tour £12.50, Educational visits for Schools £4.95.

No photography in house. Unusual plants for sale. Partial. WCs. Obligatory. Ample for cars and coaches. In Park, on leads.

© NTPL / Andreas von Einsiedel

Rufford Old Hall

STONYHURST COLLEGE

STONYHURST, CLITHEROE, LANCASHIRE BB7 9PZ

www.stonyhurst.ac.uk

Tel: 01254 826345 **Fax:** 01254 827040 **Email:** domestic-bursar@stonyhurst.ac.uk

Owner: Stonyhurst College **Contact:** Frances Ahearne

One of the largest buildings in the North West, this magnificent 16th century estate is home to a famous Catholic co-educational boarding and day school. Tours include Chapels, Library, school-rooms and historical apartments. Extensive grounds and parking. Day/evening groups by prior arrangement. Tea/gift shop.

Location: MAP 10:M10. Stonyhurst College, Hurst Green, Lancs.

Open: 25 Jul–29 Aug (inc Aug BH), open daily except Fri, 1–4.30pm.

Admission: Adult £6.50, Conc. £5.50, Child (4–14) £5, Child (Under 4) Free, Family (2 Adults, 2 Children) £20. Groups welcome.

No photography. By arrangement. In grounds, on leads.

MANCHESTER CATHEDRAL

Manchester M3 1SX

Tel: 0161 833 2220 **Fax:** 0161 839 6218 **www.manchestercathedral.org**

In addition to regular worship and daily offices, there are frequent professional concerts, day schools, organ recitals, guided tours and brass-rubbing. The cathedral contains a wealth of beautiful carvings and has the widest medieval nave in Britain.

Location: MAP 6:N1, OS Ref. SJ838 988. Manchester.

Open: Daily. Visitor Centre: Mon–Sat, 9am–4.30pm.

Admission: Donations welcome.

Visitor Centre. Dogs are not permitted except for guide dogs.

MARTHOLME

Great Harwood, Blackburn, Lancashire BB6 7UJ

Tel: 01254 886463

Owner: Mr & Mrs T H Codling **Contact:** Miss P M Codling

Part of medieval manor house with 17th century additions and Elizabethan gatehouse.

Location: MAP 10:M10, OS Ref. SD753 338. 2m NE of Great Harwood off A680 to Whalley.

Open: May 1–3, 7–8, 27–31. June 1–5. Aug 26–30. Sep 2–5, 16–19.

Admission: £5. Groups welcome by appointment.

RUFFORD OLD HALL

Rufford, Nr Ormskirk, Lancashire L40 1SG

Tel: 01704 821254 **Fax:** 01704 823813

www.nationaltrust.org.uk

Owner: National Trust **Contact:** The Property Manager

Fine 16th century building and attractive gardens.

Location: MAP 10:L11, OS Ref. SD463 160. 7m N of Ormskirk, in Rufford village E of A59.

SAMLESBURY HALL

Preston New Road, Samlesbury, Preston PR5 0UP

Tel: 01254 812010 **Fax:** 01254 812174

Owner: Samlesbury Hall Trust **Contact:** Mrs S Jones - Director

Built in 1325, the hall is an attractive black and white timbered manor house set in extensive grounds. Weddings and events welcome. Antiques and crafts all year.

Location: MAP 10:L11, OS Ref. SD623 305. N side of A677, 4m WNW of Blackburn.

Open: All year: daily except Sats: 11am–4.30pm.

Admission: Adult £3, Child £1.

SMITHILLS HALL HISTORIC HOUSE

Smithills Dean Road, Bolton BL7 7NP

Tel: 01204 332377 **E-mail:** smithills@bolton.gov.uk

Owner: Bolton Metropolitan Borough Council **Contact:** Liz McNabb

14th century manor house with Tudor panelling. Stuart furniture. Stained glass.

Location: MAP 10:M12, OS Ref. SD699 119. 2m NW of central Bolton, ½m N of A58 ringroad.

Open: Apr–Oct: Tue–Fri & Sun, 12 noon–5pm. Last adm. 4pm.

Admission: Adult £3, Conc. £2, Family (2+3) £7.75.

© Leighton Hall / Heritage House Group

Leighton Hall

TOWNELEY HALL ART GALLERY & MUSEUMS

BURNLEY BB11 3RQ

www.towneleyhall.org.uk

Tel: 01282 424213 **Fax:** 01282 436138
Owner: Burnley Borough Council **Contact:** Mr. Ken Darwen
House dates from the 14th century with 17th and 19th century modifications. Collections include oak furniture, 18th and 19th century paintings. There is a Museum of Local History.
Location: MAP 10:N10, OS Ref. SD854 309. ½m SE of Burnley on E side of Todmorden Road (A671).
Open: All year: daily except Fri's, 12 noon–5pm. Closed Christmas–New Year.
Admission: Small charge. Guided tours: To be booked for groups.
WC.

TURTON TOWER

Tower Drive, Chapeltown Road, Turton BL7 0HG
Tel: 01204 852203 **Fax:** 01204 853759 **E-mail:** turtontower@mus.lancscc.gov.uk
Owner: The Trustees of Turton Tower (run by Lancashire County Museums Service)
Contact: Fiona Jenkins
Country house based on a medieval tower, extended in the 16th, 17th and 19th centuries.
Location: MAP 10:M11, OS Ref. SD733 153. On B6391, 4m N of Bolton.
Open: Mar–Oct, Wed–Sun 12–5pm.
Admission: Adult £4, Child Free, Conc. £3.

WARTON OLD RECTORY

Warton, Carnforth, Lancashire
Tel: 0161 242 1400 **Email:** customers@english-heritage.org.uk
www.english-heritage.org.uk/wartonoldrectory
Owner: English Heritage **Contact:** The North West Regional Office
A rare medieval stone house with remains of the hall, chambers and domestic offices.
Location: MAP 10:L8, OS Ref. SD499 723. At Warton, 1m N of Carnforth on minor road off A6.
Open: 1 Apr–30 Sept: daily, 10am–6pm. 1 Oct–31 Mar: daily 10am–4pm. Closed 24–26 Dec & 1 Jan.
Admission: Free. Opening times and prices are valid until 31st March 2011, after this date details are subject to change please visit www.english-heritage.org.uk for the most up-to-date information.

For unique **Civil wedding** venues see our index at the end of the book.

© Britainonview

Manchester Cathedral

CROXTETH HALL & COUNTRY PARK

Liverpool, Merseyside L12 0HB

Tel: 0151 233 6910 **Fax:** 0151 228 2817

Owner: Liverpool City Council **Contact:** Mrs Irene Vickers

Ancestral home of the Molyneux family. 500 acres country park. Regular events.

Location: MAP 6:K1, OS Ref. SJ408 943. 5m NE of Liverpool city centre.

Open: Apr–Oct (Hall may be closed for functions).

Admission: Hall, Farm & Garden: Adult £5.50, Conc. £3.50.

LIVERPOOL CATHEDRAL

Liverpool, Merseyside L1 7AZ

Tel: 0151 709 6271 **Fax:** 0151 702 7292

Owner: The Dean and Chapter **Contact:** Eryl Parry

Sir Giles Gilbert Scott's greatest creation. Built last century from local sandstone with superb glass, stonework and major works of art, it is the largest cathedral in Britain.

Location: MAP 6:K1, OS Ref. SJ354 893. Central Liverpool, ½m S of Lime Street Station.

Open: All year: daily, 8am–6pm. Tower daily 10am–4.30pm.

Admission: Cathedral: Donation. Charge to visit Tower.

LIVERPOOL METROPOLITAN CATHEDRAL OF CHRIST THE KING

Metropolitan Cathedral, Mount Pleasant, Liverpool L3 5TQ

Tel: 0151 709 9222 **Fax:** 0151 708 7274 **Email:** enquiries@metcathedral.org.uk

www.liverpoolmetrocathedral.org.uk

Owner: Roman Catholic Archdiocese of Liverpool

Modern circular cathedral with spectacular glass by John Piper and numerous modern works of art. Extensive earlier crypt by Lutyens. Grade II* listed.

Location: MAP 6:K1, OS Ref. SJ356 903. Central Liverpool, ½m E of Lime Street Station.

Open: 7.30am–6pm (closes 5pm Suns in Winter).

Admission: Donation.

Except crypt. WCs. By arrangement. Ample for cars.

Guide dogs only.

MEOLS HALL

Churchtown, Southport, Merseyside PR9 7LZ

Tel: 01704 228326 **Fax:** 01704 507185 **E-mail:** events@meolshall.com

www.meolshall.com

Owner: The Hesketh Family **Contact:** Pamela Whelan

17th century house with subsequent additions. Interesting collection of pictures and furniture. Tithe Barn available for wedding ceremonies and receptions all year.

Location: MAP 10:K11, OS Ref. SD365 184. 3m NE of Southport town centre in Churchtown. SE of A565.

Open: 14 Aug–14 Sept: daily, 2–5pm.

Admission: Adult £4, Child £1. Groups welcome but Afternoon Tea is only available for bookings of 25+.

Wedding ceremonies and receptions now available in the Tithe Barn.

SPEKE HALL GARDEN & ESTATE

The Walk, Speke, Liverpool L24 1XD

Tel: 0151 427 7231 **Fax:** 0151 427 9860 **Info Line:** 0844 800 4799

Owner: National Trust **Contact:** The Property Manager

Superb half-timbered Tudor house, with rich Victorian interiors, fine gardens and estate. Close to Liverpool – but with room to breathe.

Location: MAP 6:K1, OS Ref. SJ419 825. North bank of the Mersey, 6m SE of city centre. Follow signs for Liverpool John Lennon airport.

World He

LIVE

Liver Building
1908–11 Listed Grade I
The head offices of the Royal Liver Friendly Society were designed by Aubrey Thomas. It is notable as one of Britain's first multi-storey reinforced concrete framed buildings. The clock towers are mounted with copper Liver Birds which to many are the very identity of Liverpool.

Cunard Building
1913–1916 Grade II*
This substantial building was built as the offices of the Cunard Shipping Company to the designs of Willink and Thicknesse. Its proportions give it the form of an Italian palazzo. The portraits of races from around the world symbolise the global operations of the company.

Leeds and Liverpool Canal Locks
Circa 1848 Grade II
The canal had been in partial use since 1774 and was completed through to Leeds in 1816; a direct link to the docks was formed in 1848. The four locks were designed by Hartley, and are the only all-granite canal locks in the country. The brick viaduct carried the Liverpool and Bury Railway. The canal has been extended to the Albert Dock.
www.britishwaterways.co.uk /liverpoolcanallink/index.php

The Dock Wall
Its purpose was to control rather than prevent access from the town into the docks, and the monumental gateways with their heavy wooden gates sliding in iron guide rails effectively made the docks into a fortress-like stronghold. The design of the various gate piers demonstrates a fascinating progressi from Foster's early classical style to Hartley's whimsical turrets.

St George's Hall
1840–55 Grade I
A design competition for a new musical venue for Liverpool was held and won by young architect Harvey Lonsdale Elmes. The Hall is built in Grecian style externally with a Roman interior. It contains the lavish Great Hall, with its Minton tiled floor and great organ, and the more intimate Small Concert Room, much visited by Charles Dickens. The Crown and Civil courts at either end were introduced following a further competition. The Hall re-opened in April 2007 following a £23m refurbishment to restore its concert room and create a Heritage visitor centre.

World Museum Liverpool and Central Library
1857–60 Grade II*
The completion of the magnificent new hall on St George's Plateau set the pattern for other civic projects on adjacent land. The Liverpool Improvements Act was passed and a competition was opened in 1855 for a new museum and public library. Local MP William Brown donated £6,000, and the street was renamed in his honour. The building is now home to the internationally important collections of World Museum Liverpool.

ge City
OOL

UNESCO seeks to encourage the identification, protection and preservation of the cultural and natural heritage around the world that is considered to be of outstanding universal value to humanity. Sites that meet the strict criteria of eligibility established by UNESCO are inscribed onto the World Heritage List.

Liverpool – Maritime Mercantile City was nominated by the UK government as "The supreme example of a commercial port at the time of Britain's greatest global influence" and was inscribed as a World Heritage Site by UNESCO's World Heritage Committee in July 2004. The status is a great honour as it acknowledges that Liverpool's architectural and technological heritage is of international significance and should rank alongside Stonehenge, the Taj Mahal and the Pyramids of Egypt.

'ort of Liverpool Building

ompleted 1907 Grade II*

ne domed head office of the 'lersey Docks and Harbour oard was designed by Briggs, Volstenholme and Thorneley in 901. Features include cast iron ates and gate piers decorated with aritime symbols and lamp holders the form of naval monuments.

George's Dock Tunnel Ventilation Building and Offices

1931–1934 Grade II

This stylised obelisk, reminiscent of ancient Egypt, was designed by Sir Basil Mott and J A Brodie, with Herbert J Rowse, to serve the Mersey Road Tunnel. It has statues of Night and Day, symbols of the never-closing Mersey Tunnel and a black marble memorial to the workers who died in its construction.

Memorial to Heroes of the Engine Room (Titanic Memorial)

Circa 1916 Grade II

The memorial was originally intended to be for the engineers who stayed at their posts on 15th April 1912 when the Titanic sank. Its dedication was broadened to include all maritime engine room fatalities incurred during the performance of duty. The figures are naturalistic, the detail of their work-clothes being carefully studied.

Albert Dock's Warehouses

Albert Dock's warehouses form England's largest group of Grade I Listed Buildings. Jesse Hartley used well-established techniques adapted from textile mill methods. He introduced new solutions, such as the amazing stressed-skin iron roof. Raising of goods from the quaysides was performed with the first hydraulic cargo-handling installation. Today the dock is home to Tate Liverpool, Merseyside Maritime Museum and numerous bars and restaurants

Stanley Dock Warehouses

Stanley Dock opened in 1848, and between 1852–55 it was equipped with import warehouses. The complex includes: The North Stanley Warehouse 1852–5 Grade II*,The South Stanley Warehouse 1852–5 Grade II, The Stanley Dock Tobacco Warehouse The Hydraulic Tower 1852–55 Grade II, two entrances from Great Howard Street and two from Regent Road.

iverpool Town Hall

rade I

verpool's finest Georgian building, the result of three building ampaigns. The original design was y John Wood of Bath, and was built 1749–54. Additions and alterations ere designed by James Wyatt nd carried out by the elder John oster in 1789–92. Following a fire of 795, it was reconstructed the work ontinuing until 1820.

India Building

1924–31 Grade II

This immense office block was built for the Blue Funnel Line and designed by Herbert J Rowse with Briggs, Wostenholme and Thorneley. It has stripped classical facades; Italian Renaissance detail is restricted to the top and bottom storeys. The building was badly damaged in the war, and restored under Rowse's supervision.

Martin's Building

1927–32 Grade II*

Originally Martin's Bank, designed by Rowse it is monumental and American influenced. The stylish top lit banking hall, with its Parisian jazz moderne fittings, survives well, as does the boardroom. Sculpture and carvings by Herbert Tyson Smith with Edmund Thompson and George Capstick celebrate maritime themes and commerce.

Oriel Chambers

1864 Grade I

Designed by Peter Ellis, the use of oriel windows was driven by a desire to provide good daylight. The oriels themselves are framed in the thinnest sections of iron. In its day, the building aroused much opposition. It is only recently that its futuristic qualities have become appreciated.

Bluecoat Chambers

Opened 1718 Grade I

Bluecoat Chambers was originally built as a charity school in 1717 in the Queen Anne style and in 1928 became one of the UK's first arts centres. The main is round headed with a broken pediment above containing a cartouche of the arms of Liverpool. To the rear is a landscaped garden. After a £12.5m refurbishment the building reopened in 2008 complete with a new wing. www.thebluecoat.org.uk

'he Walker Art Gallery

pened 1877 Grade II*

nown as the 'national gallery of the orth', the Walker was designed y architects Sherlock and Vale and amed after its principal benefactor, lderman Sir Andrew Barclay Valker, at that time Lord Mayor of iverpool. A classical portico is the entrepiece of the exterior, which cludes friezes of scenes from the ty's history, and is surmounted by a ersonification of Liverpool. www.liverpoolmuseums.org.uk valker/

Croxteth Hall

Originally built in 1575, the Croxteth Hall you see today is an Edwardian Country house with beautiful surroundings including a country park. The Hall and its outbuilding are a Grade II* Listed Building, as are 3 other buildings; another 15 on the estate are Grade II. The ancestral home of the Molyneux family (Earls of Sefton) until 1972, it is two miles from Aintree racecourse, which the family had owned and developed. For more information please visit www.croxteth.co.uk

Sudley House

This Grade II late Regency/Victorian red Liverpool sandstone mansion, believed to be the work of Thomas Harrison, was completed in 1824 for Nicholas Robinson, Lord Mayor of Liverpool in 1828–9. Today Sudley House contains the only surviving Victorian merchant art collection in Britain still hanging in its original location. For more information visit www.sudleyhouse.org.uk

Speke Hall

Built in 1530 Speke Hall was central to a 2,500 acre farm until it passed to the National Trust in 1944. This Grade I listed half-timbered Tudor house is set on the banks of the River Mersey with extensive views across to the mountains of North Wales. The Hall's atmospheric interior spans many periods – from its fine Tudor Great Hall and priest hole, to smaller more intimate rooms furnished by Speke's Victorian occupants. For information visit www.nationaltrust.org.uk

Lowlands

Built by renowned Liverpool architect Thomas Haigh as his residence in 1846, Grade II-listed Lowlands (13 Haymans Green, West Derby, Liverpool L12 7JG) is the home of the West Derby Community Association. Italianate stucco-faced mansion set in rare city woodland garden. Lowlands hosts many public events and has function rooms available for hire.

For further information visit: visitliverpool.com

Raby Castle, pagoda detail

North East

Rugged and Roman – the North East region of Britain offers the visitor a wealth of history going back to the Roman occupation. As well as visiting the magnificent fortress castles at Alnwick, Bamburgh and Chillingham, time should be set aside to explore The Lady Waterford Murals at Ford, with its 1860 biblical murals.

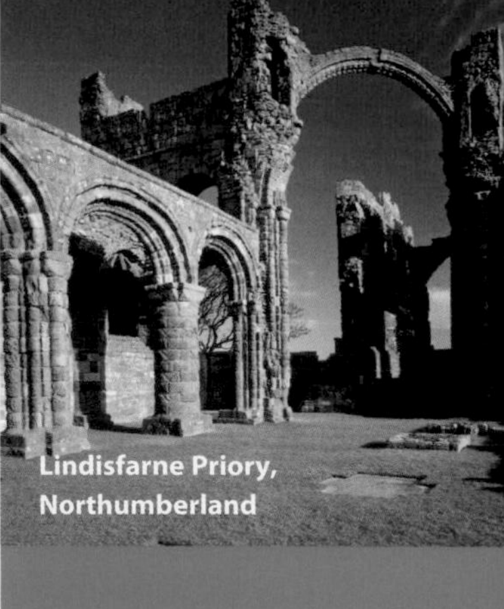

Lindisfarne Priory, Northumberland

Co. Durham

Northumberland

Tyne & Wear

NORTHUMBERLAND

TYNE & WEAR

CO. DURHAM

Chillingham Castle, Northumberland

Newcastle Castle Keep, Tyne & Wear

Alnwick Castle, Northumberland

Durham Cathedral

RABY CASTLE

www.rabycastle.com

The magnificent Raby Castle has been home to Lord Barnard's family since 1626, when it was purchased by his ancestor, Sir Henry Vane the Elder, the eminent Statesman and Politician. The Castle was built mainly in the 14th century by the Nevill family on a site of an earlier Manor House. The Nevills continued to live at Raby until 1569, when after the failure of the Rising of the North, the Castle and its land were forfeited to the Crown.

A particular highlight of the Castle is the magnificent Barons Hall, where 700 knights met to plot The Rising of the North. Architect John Carr raised the floor level by 3 metres when constructing a carriageway below in the Entrance Hall and later William Burn extended the room by 17 metres over his elaborate Octagon Drawing Room (pictured). Today it houses an impressive Meissen bird collection. Other Raby treasures include fine furniture and artworks with paintings by Munnings, Reynolds, Van Dyck, Batoni, Teniers, Amigoni and Vernet.

There is a large Deer Park with two lakes and a beautiful walled garden with formal lawns, yew hedges and an ornamental pond. The 18th century Stable block contains a horse-drawn carriage collection including the State Coach last used by the family for the Coronation of Edward VII in 1902. Parts of the Stables have been converted into a Gift Shop and Tearooms, where the former stalls have been incorporated to create an atmospheric setting.

Film locations, product launches, corporate events, fairs and concerts. Raby Estates venison and game sold in tearooms. Soft fruit when in season. No photography or video filming is permitted inside. Colour illustrated guidebook and DVD on sale. Christmas Shop and Santa's Grotto in Stable Yard throughout December.

Partial. WC. Castle DVD viewing area.

Licensed.

By arrangement for groups (20+) or min charge. VIP & Standard Castle Tours available. Tour time 1½ hrs.

P

By arrangement (20+), weekday am. Primary & Junior £4; Secondary £4.50.

Guide dogs welcome. All dogs welcome in Park on leads.

Varied programme throughout the summer.

Owner

The Lord Barnard

Contact

Clare Owen /
Rachel Milner
Raby Castle
Staindrop
Darlington
Co. Durham DL2 3AH

Tel: 01833 660202
Fax: 01833 660169
E-mail: admin@rabycastle.com

Location

MAP 10:O5
OS Ref. NZ129 218

On A688, 1m N of Staindrop. 8m NE of Barnard Castle, 12m WNW of Darlington.

Rail: Darlington Station, 12m.

Air: Durham Tees Valley Airport, 20m.

Opening Times

Castle
Easter weekend, May, June & September, Sun–Wed. July & August: Daily except Sats. (Open BH Sats), 1–5pm.

Park & Gardens
As Castle, 11am–5.30pm.

Admission

Castle, Park & Gardens

Adult	£9.50
Child (5–16yrs)	£4.00
OAP/Student	£8.50

Family discounts available.

Groups (12+)

Adult	£7.50

Park & Gardens

Adult	£6.00
Child (5+)	£2.50
Conc.	£5.00

Groups (12+)

Adult	£4.50

Season Tickets available.

VIP Private Guided Tours (20+)*
(incl. reception, tea/coffee in entrance hall) Easter–Sept, Mon–Fri mornings. £11.00

Standard Guided Tours (20+)*
(Easter–Sept, Mon–Fri.
Adult £8.50

*Please book in advance.

Free RHS access to Park & Gardens.

AUCKLAND CASTLE DEER HOUSE ⌗

Bishop Auckland, Durham DL14 7NR

Tel: 0191 2691200 **E-mail:** customers@english-heritage.org.uk

www.english-heritage.org.uk/aucklandcastledeerhouse

Owner: English Heritage **Contact:** The North East Regional Office

A charming building erected in 1760 in the Park of the Bishops of Durham so that the deer could shelter and find food.

Location: MAP 10:P5, OS Ref. NZ216 304. In Bishop Auckland Park, just N of town centre on A68. About 500 yds N of the castle.

Open: Park: 1 Apr–30 Sept: daily, 10am–6pm 1 Oct–31 Mar: daily, 10am–4pm. Closed 24–26 Dec & 1 Jan.

Admission: Free. Opening times and prices are valid until 31st March 2011, after this date details are subject to change please see www.english-heritage.org.uk for the most up-to-date information.

On leads.

BARNARD CASTLE ⌗

Barnard Castle, Castle House, Durham DL12 8PR

Tel: 01833 638212 **E-mail:** Barnard.Castle@english-heritage.org.uk

www.english-heritage.org.uk/barnardcastle

Owner: English Heritage **Contact:** Visitor Operations Team

Barnard Castle is spectacularly set on a high rock above the river tees. Taking its name from its 12th century founder Bernard de Balliol, this huge and imposing fortress was later developed by the Beauchamp family and Richard III. Richard's boar emblem is carved above a window in the inner ward.

Location: MAP 10:O5, OS92, NZ049 165. In Barnard Castle Town.

Open: 1 Apr–30 Sept: daily, 10am–6pm. 1 Oct–31 Mar: Sat & Sun, 10am–4pm. Closed 24–26 Dec & 1 Jan.

Admission: Adult £4.20, Child £2.10, Conc. £3.60. 15% discount for groups (11+). EH members Free. Opening times and prices are valid until 31st March 2011, after this date details are subject to change please see www.english-heritage.org.uk for the most up-to-date information.

i WCs in town. A 'sensory garden' of scented plants and tactile objects. On leads.

BINCHESTER ROMAN FORT

Bishop Auckland, Co. Durham

Tel: 01388 663089 / 0191 3834212 (outside opening hours)

Owner: Durham County Council **Contact:** Deborah Anderson

Once the largest Roman fort in Co Durham, the heart of the site has been excavated.

Location: MAP 10:P5, OS92 Ref. NZ210 312. 1½ m N of Bishop Auckland, signposted from A690 Durham–Crook and from A688 Spennymoor–Bishop Auckland roads.

Open: Easter–30 Sept: daily, 11am–5pm.

Admission: Adult £2.50, Child/Conc. £1.

CROOK HALL & GARDENS

Sidegate, Durham DH1 5SZ

Tel: 0191 3848028

Owner: Keith & Maggie Bell **Contact:** Mrs Maggie Bell

Medieval manor house set in rural landscape on the edge of Durham city.

Location: MAP 10:P4, OS Ref. NZ274 432. ½ m N of city centre.

Open: Easter weekend, Apr-Sept: daily except Fri & Sat, 11am–5pm.

Admission: Adult £6, Conc. £5.50, Child. £5, Family £18.

DERWENTCOTE STEEL FURNACE ⌗

Newcastle, Durham NE39 1BA

Please call 0191 269 1200 (Mon–Fri) for opening details

E-mail: customers@english-heritage.org.uk

www.english-heritage.org.uk/derwentcotesteelfurnace

Owner: English Heritage **Contact:** The North East Regional Office

Built in the 18th century, it is the earliest and most complete authentic steel-making furnace to have survived.

Location: MAP 10:O3, OS Ref. NZ130 566. 10m SW of Newcastle N of the A694 between Rowland's Gill and Hamsterley.

Open: Please call for details.

Admission: Free. Opening times and prices are valid until 31st March 2011, after this date details are subject to change please see www.english-heritage.org.uk for the most up-to-date information.

P

Auckland Castle

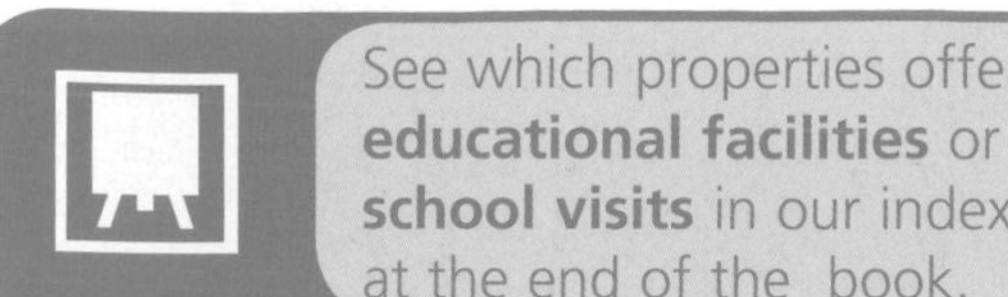
See which properties offer
educational facilities or
school visits in our index
at the end of the book.

DURHAM CASTLE

Palace Green, Durham DH1 3RW

Tel: 0191 3343800 **Fax:** 0191 3343801 **Contact:** Mrs Julie Marshall

Durham Castle, founded in the 1070s, with the Cathedral is a World Heritage Site.

Location: MAP 10:P4, OS Ref. NZ274 424. City centre, adjacent to Cathedral.

Open: Daily. Guided tours only, please ring for details.

Admission: Adult £5, OAP £3, Family (2+2) £12.

DURHAM CATHEDRAL

Durham DH13 3EH

Tel: 0191 3864266 **Fax:** 0191 3864267 **E-mail:** enquiries@durhamcathedral.co.uk

www.durhamcathedral.co.uk

Contact: Miss A Heywood

A World Heritage Site. Norman architecture. Burial place of St Cuthbert and the Venerable Bede.

Location: MAP 10:P4, OS Ref. NZ274 422. Durham city centre.

Open: Mon–Sat, 9.30am–6pm (8pm summer). Sun 12.30–5.30pm.

Admission: Free but donations very welcome. Charge for exhibitions.

EGGLESTONE ABBEY ⌗

Durham

Tel: 0191 2691200 **E-mail:** customers@english-heritage.org.uk

www.english-heritage.org.uk/egglestoneabbey

Owner: English Heritage **Contact:** The North East Regional Office

The charming ruins of a small monastery set in a bend of the River Tees. Much of the 13th century church and a range of living quarters remain.

Location: MAP 10:O6, OS Ref. NZ062 151. 1m S of Barnard Castle on minor road off B6277.

Open: Daily, 10am–6pm.

Admission: Free. Opening times and prices are valid until 31st March 2011, after this date details are subject to change please see www.english-heritage.org.uk for the most up-to-date information.

On leads.

ESCOMB CHURCH

Escomb, Bishop Auckland DL14 7ST

Tel: 01388 602861

Owner: Church of England **Contact:** Mrs D Denham

Saxon church dating from the 7th century built of stone from Binchester Roman Fort.

Location: MAP 10:P5, OS Ref. NZ189 302. 3m W of Bishop Auckland.

Open: Summer: 9am–8pm. Winter: 9am–4pm. Key available from 26 Saxon Green, Escomb.

Admission: Free.

FINCHALE PRIORY ⌗

Finchdale Priory, Brasside, Newton Hall DH1 5SH

Tel: 0191 269 1200 **E-mail:** customers@english-heritage.org.uk

www.english-heritage.org.uk/finchalepriory

Owner: English Heritage **Contact:** The North East Regional Office

These beautiful 13th century priory remains are located beside the curving River Wear.

Location: MAP 10:P4, OS Ref. NZ296 471. 3m NE of Durham.

Open: Any reasonable time.

Admission: Free. Opening times and prices are valid until 31st March 2011, after this date details are subject to change please visit www.english-heritage.org.uk for the most up-to-date information.

WC. (charge) on S side of river.

RABY CASTLE

See page 383 for full page entry.

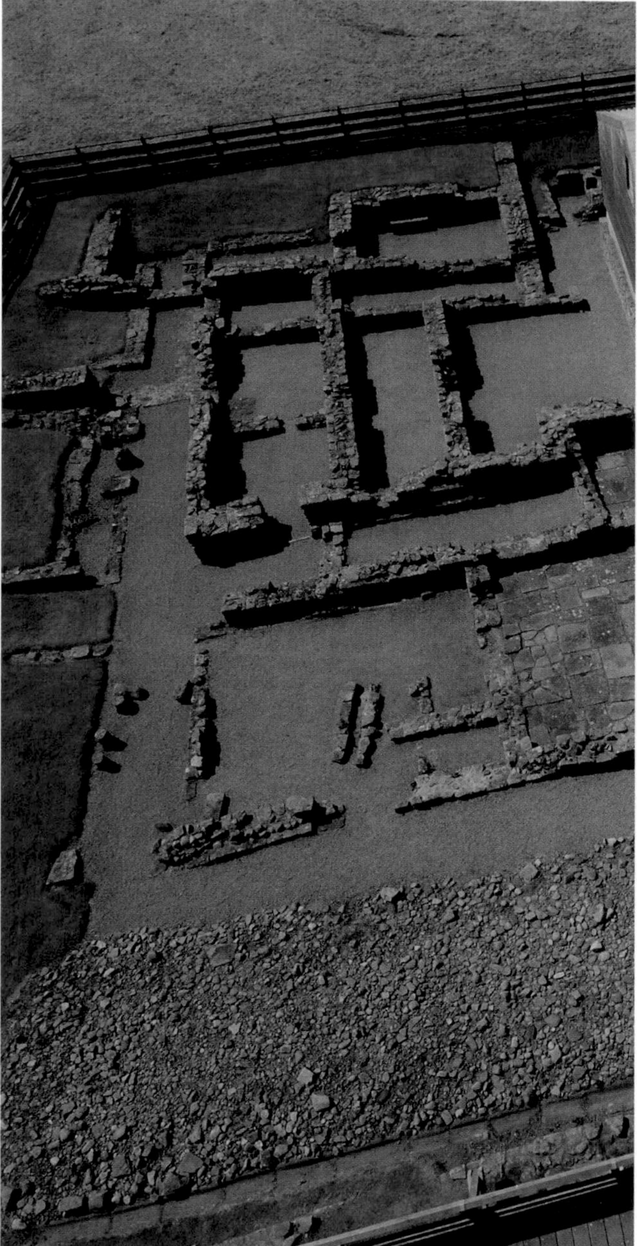

Binchester Roman Fort

ROKEBY PARK

Barnard Castle, Co. Durham DL12 9RZ

Tel: 01609 748612 **E-mail:** admin@rokebypark.com

www.rokebypark.com

A Palladian Country House c1730 with unique print room, period furniture and paintings.

Location: MAP 10:O6, OS ref NZ 080 142. 3m SE of Barnard Castle, N of A66.

Open: 2 May, 30 May–6 Sept: Mons & Tues, 2–5 pm (last admission 4.30 pm). Groups by appointment.

Admission: Adult £6.75. Children under 16 Free. Over 60s £5.75. Students £4.50. Groups £5.75 on open days, by arrangement on other days.

No photography in house. Ground floor only, no WC. By arrangement.

THE WEARDALE MUSEUM & HIGH HOUSE CHAPEL

Ireshopeburn, Co. Durham DL13 1EY

Tel: 01388 517433 **E-mail:** dtheatherington@ormail.co.uk

Contact: D T Heatherington

Small folk museum and historic chapel. Includes 1870 Weardale cottage room, John Wesley room and local history displays.

Location: MAP 10:N4, OS Ref. NZ872 385. Adjacent to 18th century Methodist Chapel.

Open: Easter & May–Oct: Wed–Sun & BH, 2–5pm. Aug: daily, 2–5pm.

Admission: Adult £2, Child 50p.

Owner

His Grace the Duke of Northumberland

Contact

Alnwick Castle
Estate Office
Alnwick
Northumberland
NE66 1NQ

Tel: 01665 511172
Group bookings: 01665 511184
Fax: 01665 511169
E-mail: enquiries@alnwickcastle.com

Location

MAP 14:M11
OS Ref. NU187 135

In Alnwick 1½ m W of A1.
From London 6hrs, Edinburgh 2hrs, Chester 4hrs, Newcastle 40mins North Sea ferry terminal 30mins.

Bus: From bus station in Alnwick.

Rail: Alnmouth Station 5m. Kings Cross, London 3½hrs.

Air: Newcastle 40mins.

Opening Times

1 April–30 October
Daily, 10am–6pm.
Last admission to State Rooms 4.30pm).

Admission*

Adult	£13.00
Child (5–15yrs)	£6.30
Child (under 5yrs)	Free
Conc.	£11.00
Family	£34.60
Booked Groups (14+)	£9.60

*prices are subject to change.

Seasonal and two day combined tickets with The Alnwick Garden are available.

Conference/Function

ROOM	SIZE	MAX CAPACITY
The Guest Hall	100' x 30'	250

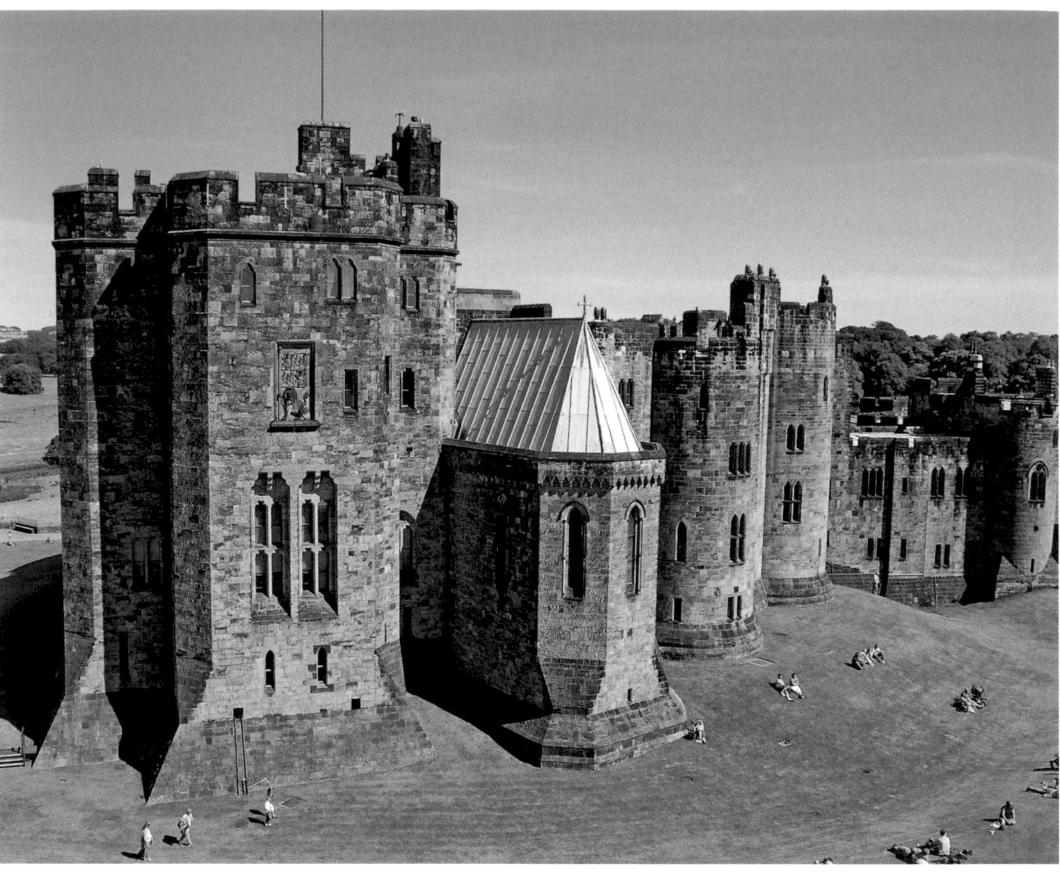

ALNWICK CASTLE

www.alnwickcastle.com

Set in a stunning landscape designed by 'Capability' Brown, Alnwick Castle is the family home of the Duke of Northumberland. Owned by his family since 1309, this beautiful castle, originally built to defend England from the Scots, now appeals to visitors of all ages from across the world.

Considered to be one of the finest castles in England, and known as the 'Windsor of the North', this has been the home of the Percy family for nearly 700 years. In the 1760s it was transformed from a fortification into a family home for the First Duke and Duchess. Today Alnwick Castle is an attraction of real significance, with lavish State Rooms, superb art treasures, fun activities and entertainment, all set in a beautiful landscape.

Visitors walking through the gates, set in massive stone walls, enter one of the most stunning castles in Europe. The Keep sits magnificently in the spacious grounds, with its medieval towers housing the castle's 14th century dungeon and the entrance to the remarkable State Rooms. The refurbished and restored dining room is worth a visit. Beautifully silked walls, a hand-woven carpet and intricate carved ceiling are among the delights. Important ceramics of the Meissen, Chelsea and Paris factories are impressively displayed in the china gallery.

Within the grounds are the museums and towers that tell the story of the Northumberland Fusiliers from 1674 to the present day, local archaeology of the area, the Percy Tenantry Volunteers and an exhibition on siege craft.

Adding to the magic of this castle is an interactive and fun activity area where children can enter the exciting and enchanting world of knights and dragons. They can learn how to become a Knight or Lady of Alnwick then take the ultimate challenge to win their spurs by facing the monster which rules the kingdom in Dragon's Quest.

Conference facilities, events, fairs and exhibitions. Film location hire. No photography inside the castle. No unaccompanied children.

Wedding receptions.

Partial. Parking.

Coffee, light lunches and teas.

Shared with Alnwick Gardens.

Guidebook and worksheet, special rates for children and teachers.

Guide dogs only.

© English Heritage

BELSAY HALL, CASTLE & GARDENS ⌗

www.english-heritage.org.uk/belsay

With so much to see and do, a trip to Belsay is one of the best value days out in north east England.

Explore the grand medieval castle, later extended to include a magnificent Jacobean mansion and don't miss the stunning views from the top of the tower.

Then it's on to Belsay Hall, an architectural masterpiece with a fabulous 'Pillar Hall'. A true labour of love, the design was inspired by a honeymoon trip to Greece.

Last but not least, there are the huge grounds, packed with an impressive array of shrubs and flowers. See the seasons change in the Grade 1 gardens, with a carpet of Snowdrops in Spring, Rhododendrons and giant Lillies during the Summer, a stunning display of colours in Autumn and even more Rhododendrons in the Winter. The unique Quarry Gardens carry an air of mystery, and not just in the plant species growing there. Tours with the Head Gardener are availble throughout the year, call ahead for details.

The Middleton family created this whole property over seven centuries, and there are facsinating stories at every turn; from the family move from the castle to the hall on Christmas Day 1817, to the pioneering plantsman who introduced exotic species to the Quarry Garden.

Level paths and short grass make the gardens suitable for wheelchairs, and there are plenty of seats around. The tearoom, in the original Victorian kitchens, provides a perfect setting for a break during your visit.

© English Heritage

© English Heritage

Owner

English Heritage

Contact

Visitor Operations Team
Belsay
Nr Ponteland
Northumberland
NE20 0DX

Tel: 01661 881636
E-mail: customers@english-heritage.org.uk

Location

MAP 10:O2
OS 87. NZ086 785

In Belsay 14m (22.4 km) NW of Newcastle on SW of A696. 7m NW of Ponteland. Nearest airport and station is Newcastle.

Opening Times

1 April–30 September: daily, 10am–6pm.

1–31 October: daily, 10am–4pm.

1 November–31 March: Thur–Mon, 10am–4pm.

Closed 24–26 December and 1 January.

Admission

Adult	£6.80
Child (5–15yrs)	£3.40
Conc.	£5.80
Family	£17.00

15% discount for groups (11+).

Opening times and prices are valid until 31st March 2011, after this date details are subject to change please visit www.english-heritage.org.uk for the most up-to-date information.

■ **Owner**

Sir Humphry Wakefield Bt

■ **Contact**

Administrator
Chillingham Castle
Northumberland
NE66 5NJ

Tel: 01668 215359
Fax: 01668 215463
E-mail: enquiries@chillingham-castle.com

■ **Location**

MAP 14:L11
OS Ref. NU062 258

45m N of Newcastle between A697 & A1.
2m S of B6348 at Chatton.
6m SE of Wooler.

Rail: Alnmouth or Berwick.

■ **Opening Times**

Summer
Easter–31 October
Closed Sats, Castle, Garden & Tearoom,
12 noon–5pm.

Winter
October–April: Groups & Coach Tours any time by appointment. All function activities available.

■ **Admission**

Summer

Adult	£7.00
Children	£3.50
Conc.	£5.50
Family Ticket	£18.00

(2 adults and 2 children under 16)

CHILLINGHAM CASTLE

www.chillingham-castle.com

Only 20 minutes from the seaside. Rated **4-star** in Simon Jenkins' *England's Thousand Best Houses* and **First** of *The 50 Best Castles in Britain & Ireland* in the Independent.

This remarkable castle, the home of Sir Humphry Wakefield Bt, with its alarming dungeons has, as now and since the 1200s, been continuously owned by one family line and their relations. You will see active restoration of complex masonry, metalwork and ornamental plaster as the great halls and state rooms are gradually brought back to life with tapestries, arms and armour as of old and even a torture chamber.

At first a 12th century stronghold, Chillingham became a fully fortified castle in the 14th century (see the original 1344 Licence to Crenellate). Wrapped in the nation's history it occupied a strategic position as a fortress during Northumberland's bloody border feuds, often besieged and at many times enjoying the patronage of royal visitors. In Tudor days there were additions but the underlying medieval character has always been retained. The 18th and 19th centuries saw decorative extravagances including the lake, garden and grounds laid out by Sir Jeffrey Wyatville, fresh from his triumphs at Windsor Castle. These contrast with the prehistoric Wild Cattle in the park beyond (a separate tour).

Gardens

With romantic grounds, the castle commands breathtaking views of the surrounding countryside. As you walk to the lake you will see, according to season, drifts of snowdrops, daffodils or bluebells and an astonishing display of rhododendrons. This emphasises the restrained formality of the Elizabethan topiary garden, with its intricately clipped hedges of box and yew. Lawns, the formal gardens and woodland walks are all fully open to the public.

Conference/Function

ROOM	MAX CAPACITY
King James I Room	
Great Hall	100
Minstrels' Hall	60
2 x Drawing Room	
Museum	
Tea Room	35
Lower Gallery	
Upper Gallery	

 Corporate entertainment, lunches, drinks, dinners, wedding ceremonies and receptions.

Partial.

By arrangement.

Avoid Lilburn route, coach parties welcome by prior arrangement.

 Self catering apartments.

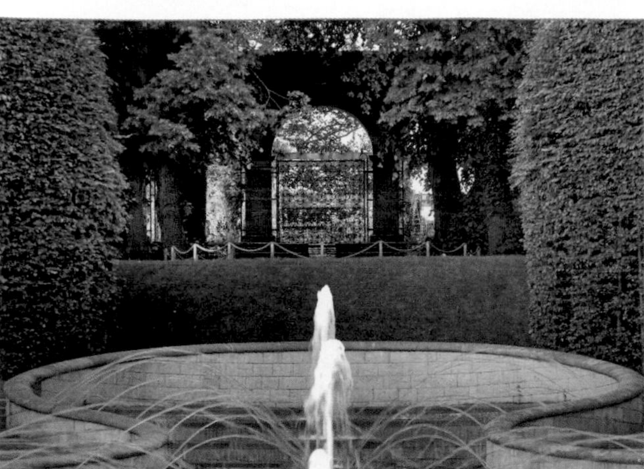

THE ALNWICK GARDEN

DENWICK LANE, ALNWICK, NORTHUMBERLAND NE66 1YU

www.alnwickgarden.com

Tel: 01665 511350 **Fax:** 01665 511351 **email:** info@alnwickgarden.com

Owner: The Alnwick Garden Trust

Experience the making of one of the most unusual and spectacular public gardens of the 21st century, The Alnwick Garden. This exciting new garden, with the Grand Cascade as its centrepiece, as well as the fascinating Poison Garden and enormous Treehouse, mixes the unique and the beautiful in an enchanting landscape.

Location: MAP 14:M11, OS Ref. NU192 132. Just off the A1 at Alnwick, Northumberland.

Open: High Season: 1 Apr–30 Oct plus vacation, 10am–6pm. Low Season: 1 Nov–28 Feb except vacation, 10am–4pm. Closed 25 Dec.

Admission*: High Season: Adult £9.90, Conc. £7.90, Child 1p, Group (14+) £7.40. Low Season: Adult £5.20, Conc. £4.20, Child 1p. Group (14+) £3.90. (*prices are subject to change).

Licensed. By arrangement. Cars & coaches. Guide dogs only. See website for details.

ALNWICK CASTLE

See page 386 for full page entry.

AYDON CASTLE

Corbridge, Northumberland NE45 5PJ

Tel: 01434 632450 **E-mail:** customers@english-heritage.org.uk

www.english-heritage.org.uk/aydoncastle

Owner: English Heritage **Contact:** Visitor Operations Team

One of the finest fortified manor houses dating back from the late 13th century. Set in an area of outstanding natural beauty its survival, intact, can be attributed to its conversion to a farmhouse in the 18th century.

Location: MAP 10:O3, OS Ref. NZ001 663. 1m NE of Corbridge, on minor road off B6321 or A68.

Open: 1 Apr–30 Sept: Thur–Mon, 10am–5pm.

Admission: Adult £3.70, Child £1.90, Conc. £3.10. 15% discount for groups (11+). EH Members free. Opening times and prices are valid until 31st March 2011, after this date details are subject to change please visit www.english-heritage.org.uk for the most up-to-date information.

WC.

Alnwick Castle

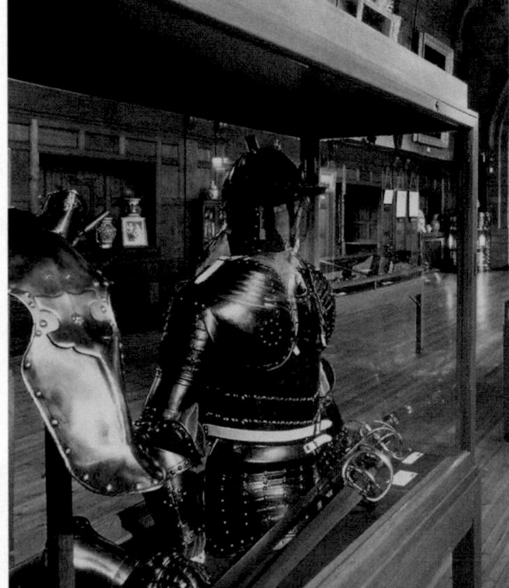

BAMBURGH CASTLE

BAMBURGH, NORTHUMBERLAND NE69 7DF

www.bamburghcastle.com

Tel: 01668 214515 **E-mail:** administrator@bamburghcastle.com

Owner: Trustees Lord Armstrong dec'd. **Contact:** The Administrator

Welcome to the Royal Seat of the Kings of Northumbria and the Armstrong family home since 1894. These formidable stone walls have witnessed dark tales of royal rebellion, bloody battles, spellbinding legends and millionaire benefactors. With fourteen public rooms and over 3000 artefacts, including arms and armour, porcelain, furniture and artwork. The Armstrong and Aviation artefacts Museum houses artefacts spanning both World Wars as well as others relating to Lord Armstrongs ship building empire on the Tyne. Each summer sees live archaeology on the country's most important Anglo-Saxon excavation. Have a go yourself in the test pit!

Location: MAP 14:M10, OS Ref. NU184 351. 42m N of Newcastle-upon-Tyne. 20m S of Berwick-upon-Tweed. 6m E of Belford by B1342 from A1 at Belford. Taxi: Parks Taxi 01665 306124. Bus: Bus service 200 yards. Rail: Berwick-upon-Tweed 20m. Air: Newcastle-upon-Tyne 1 hour.

Open: 19 Feb–31 Oct, Daily, 10am–5pm. Last entry 4pm. 1 Nov–18 Feb Weekends Only, 11am–4.30pm. Last entry 3.30pm.

Admission: Adult £8.50, Child (5–15yrs) £4, OAP £7.50. Groups (Over 15 people): Adult £6.80, Child (5–15yrs) £3.20, OAP £6. For group bookings, phone 01668 214208.

No Flash Photography in the State Rooms. Partial. WCs. Licensed. By arrangement at any time, min charge out of hours £150. 100 cars, coaches park on tarmac drive at entrance. Welcome. Guide provided if requested. Guide dogs only. See Website for a programme of re-enactments and concerts.

BELSAY HALL, CASTLE & GARDENS

See page 387 for full page entry.

BERWICK-UPON-TWEED BARRACKS & MAIN GUARD

The Parade, Berwick-upon-Tweed, Northumberland TD15 1DF

Tel: 01289 304493 **E-mail:** customers@english-heritage.org.uk

www.english-heritage.org.uk/daysout/properties/berwick-upon-tweed-barracks-and-main-guard

Owner: English Heritage **Contact:** Visitor Operations Team

Among the earliest purpose built barracks, these have changed very little since 1717. They house an exhibition 'By Beat of Drum', which recreates scenes such as the barrack room from the life of the British infantryman, the King's Own Scottish Borderers Regimental Museum, the Gymnasium Gallery and the Berwick Museum.

Location: MAP 14:L9, OS Ref. NU001 531. On the Parade, off Church Street, Berwick town centre.

Open: Barracks: 1 Apr–30 Sept: Wed–Sun & Bank Hol Mon, 10am–5pm. Main Guard: Please call for details.

Admission: Adult £3.70, Child £1.90, Conc. £3.10. 15% discount for groups (11+). Opening times and prices are valid until 31st March 2011, after this date details are subject to change please visit www.english-heritage.org.uk for the most up-to-date information.

In town. On leads. Main Guard.

BERWICK-UPON-TWEED CASTLE & RAMPARTS

Berwick-upon-Tweed, Northumberland TD15 1DF

Tel: 0191 269 1200 **E-mail:** customers@english-heritage.org.uk

www.english-heritage.org.uk/berwickcastle

Owner: English Heritage **Contact:** The North East Regional Office

A remarkably complete system of town fortifications consisting of gateways, ramparts and projecting bastions built in the 16th century.

Location: MAP 14:L9, OS Ref. NT993 534. Surrounding Berwick town centre on N bank of River Tweed.

Open: Any reasonable time.

Admission: Free. Opening times and prices are valid until 31st March 2011, after this date details are subject to change please visit www.english-heritage.org.uk for the most up-to-date information.

Ramparts.

BRINKBURN PRIORY

Long Framlington, Morpeth, Northumberland NE65 8AR

Tel: 01665 570628 **E-mail:** customers@english-heritage.org.uk

www.english-heritage.org.uk/brinkburnpriory

Owner: English Heritage **Contact:** Visitor Operations Staff

Completely roofed and restored, this beautiful 12th century church of the Augustinian priory of Brinkburn survives. Picturesquely set by a bend in the River Coquet, it is reached by a scenic 10-minute walk from the car park.

Location: MAP 14:L12, OS Ref. NZ116 983. 4½ m SE of Rothbury off B6344 5m W of A1.

Open: 1 Apr–30 Sept: Thur–Mon, 11am–4pm.

Admission: Adult £3.20, Child £1.60, Conc. £2.70. 15% discount for groups (11+). EH Members free. Opening times and prices are valid until 31st March 2011, after this date details are subject to change please visit www.english-heritage.org.uk for the most up-to-date information.

On leads.

© Bamburgh Castle

Bamburgh Castle

CAPHEATON HALL

NEWCASTLE-UPON-TYNE NE19 2AB

Tel/Fax: 01830 530159 **E-mail:** elizab-s@hotmail.co.uk

Owner: W Browne-Swinburne **Contact:** Eliza Browne-Swinburne

One of the most fascinating houses in Northumberland, Capheaton was designed by Robert Trollope in 1668 for the Swinburne family. Described by Pevsner as 'one of the most interesting houses of its date and character in England'. Outstanding working kitchen garden with extensive soft fruit glasshouses, conservatory and landscaped park.

Location: MAP 10:O2, OS Ref. NZ038 805. 17m NE of Newcastle off A696.

Open: Open by appointment.

Admission: £8.00 per adult, Min number 10.

Licensed. Obligatory. In grounds, on leads. Bed & Breakfast Accommodation available

© Britainonview

Cragside

The Alnwick Garden

CHESTERS ROMAN FORT & MUSEUM

CHOLLERFORD, Nr HEXHAM, NORTHUMBERLAND NE46 3EU

www.english-heritage.org.uk/chesters

Tel: 01434 681379 **E-mail:** customers@english-heritage.org.uk

Owner: English Heritage **Contact:** Visitor Operations Team

The best visible remains of a Roman cavalry fort in Britain, including remains of the bath house on the banks of the River Tyne. The museum houses a fascinating collection of Roman finds retrieved by the local antiquarian John Clayton.

Location: MAP 10:N2, OS87, NY913 701. ¼m W of Chollerford on B6318.

Open: 1 Apr–30 Sept: daily, 10am–6pm. 1 Oct–31 Mar: daily, 10am–4pm. Closed 24–26 Dec and 1 Jan.

Admission: Adult £4.80, Child £2.40, Conc. £4.10. 15% discount for groups (11+). EH Members free. Opening times and prices are valid until 31st March 2011, after this date details are subject to change please visit www.english-heritage.org.uk for the most up-to-date information.

CHILLINGHAM CASTLE

See page 388 for full page entry.

CHIPCHASE CASTLE

Wark, Hexham, Northumberland NE48 3NT

Tel: 01434 230203 **Fax:** 01434 230740

Owner/Contact: Mr J R Elkington

The castle overlooks the River North Tyne and is set in formal and informal gardens. One walled garden is used as a nursery specialising in unusual perennial plants.

Location: MAP 10:N2, OS Ref. NY882 758. 10m NW of Hexham via A6079 to Chollerton. 2m SE of Wark.

Open: Castle: 1–28 Jun, 3–5pm daily. Tours by arrangement at other times.
Castle Gardens & Nursery: Easter–31 Aug, Thur–Sun & BH Mons, 10am–5pm.

Admission: Castle £6, Garden £4, concessions available. Nursery Free.

Unsuitable. Obligatory for house only.

CORBRIDGE ROMAN TOWN

Corbridge, Northumberland NE45 5NT

Tel: 01434 632349 **E-mail:** customers@english-heritage.org.uk

www.english-heritage.org.uk/corbridge

Owner: English Heritage **Contact:** Visitor Operations Team

This once prosperous garrison town was a vital supply base for troops. A fascinating series of excavated remains including a fountain house with an aqueduct and the best preserved granaries in Britain.

Location: MAP 10:N3, OS Ref. NY983 649. ½m NW of Corbridge on minor road, signposted for Corbridge Roman Site.

Open: 1 Apr–30 Sept: daily, 10am–5.30pm (last adm. 5pm). 1–31 Oct: daily, 10am–4pm. 1 Nov–31 Mar: Sat & Sun, 10am–4pm. Closed 24–26 Dec and 1 Jan.

Admission: Adult £4.80, Child £2.40, Conc. £4.10. 15% discount for groups (11+). EH Members free. Opening times and prices are valid until 31st March 2011, after this date details are subject to change please visit www.english-heritage.org.uk for the most up-to-date information.

Inclusive. Limited for coaches.

CRAGSIDE

Rothbury, Morpeth, Northumberland NE65 7PX

Tel: 01669 620333 **www.nationaltrust.org.uk**

Owner: The National Trust **Contact:** Assistant to General Manager

Revolutionary home of Lord Armstrong, Victorian inventor and landscape genius, Cragside sits on a rocky crag high above the Debdon Burn. Crammed with ingenious gadgets, it was the first house in the world to be lit with hydro-electricity.

Location: MAP 14:L12, OS Ref. NU073 022. ½m NE of Rothbury on B6341.

Open: House: 19-27 Feb & 5-6 Mar (ground floor only), Tues-Sun, 12-4pm; 12 Mar–15 Apr, 1–5pm Tues–Fri, 11am–5pm Sat & Sun; 16 Apr–2 May, Tues–Sun, 11am–5pm; 3 May–27 May, 1–5pm Tues–Fri, 11am–5pm Sat & Sun; 28 May–5 Jun, Tues–Sun, 11am–5pm; 7 Jun–22 Jul, 1–5pm Tues–Fri, 11am–5pm Sat & Sun; 23 Jul–11 Sept, Tues–Sun, 11am–5pm; 13 Sept–21 Oct, 1–5pm Tues–Fri, 11am–5pm Sat & Sun; 22-30 Oct, Tues–Sun, 11am–5pm. last admission 1 hour before closing). Gardens, Estate, Gift Shop & Tea Room: 19-27 Feb & 5-6 Mar, Tues-Sun, 11am-4pm (last admission 3pm); 12 Mar–30 Oct, Tues–Sun, 10am–7pm (last admission 5pm, 7pm close or sunset if earlier); 2 Nov–18 Dec, Wed–Sun, 11am–4pm.

Admission: House, Gardens & Estate: Adult £14.60*, Child (5–17 yrs) £7.35*, Family (2+3) £36.50*, Group (+15) £11. Estate & Gardens: Adult £9.45*, Child (5-17 yrs) £4.80*, Family (2+3) £22.70*, Groups (15+) £7.15. Winter Opening; Gardens, Estate, Gift Shop & Tea Room (House closed): Adult £4.60*, Child (5-17 yrs) £2.10*, Family (2+3) £10.90*, Groups (15+) £3.60. *Admission Price includes voluntary donation of 10% Gift Aid.

In grounds, on leads.

DUNSTANBURGH CASTLE

Grieves Garage, Embleton, Northumberland NE66 3TT

Tel: 01665 576231 **E-mail:** customers@english-heritage.org.uk

www.english-heritage.org.uk/dunstanburghcastle

Owner: National Trust **Guardian:** English Heritage

Contact: Visitor Operations Team

Reached by a beautiful coastal walk, this wonderful 14th century castle can be admired from afar in its dramatic setting. Built on the most magnificent scale and rivalling any castle of its day, it stands on a remote headland. The surviving ruins include the gatehouse and curtain walls.

Location: MAP 14:M11, OS75, NU257 219. 8m NE of Alnwick.

Open: 1 Apr–30 Sept: daily, 10am–5pm. 1–31 Oct: daily 10am–4pm. 1 Nov–31 Mar: Thur–Mon, 10am–4pm. Closed 24–26 December and 1 Jan.

Admission: Adult £3.80, Child £1.90, Conc. £3.20. 15% discount for groups (11+). EH and NT Members free. Opening times and prices are valid until 31st March 2011, after this date details are subject to change please visit www.english-heritage.org.uk for the most up-to-date information.

In Craster village, 1½m walk. A charge is payable.

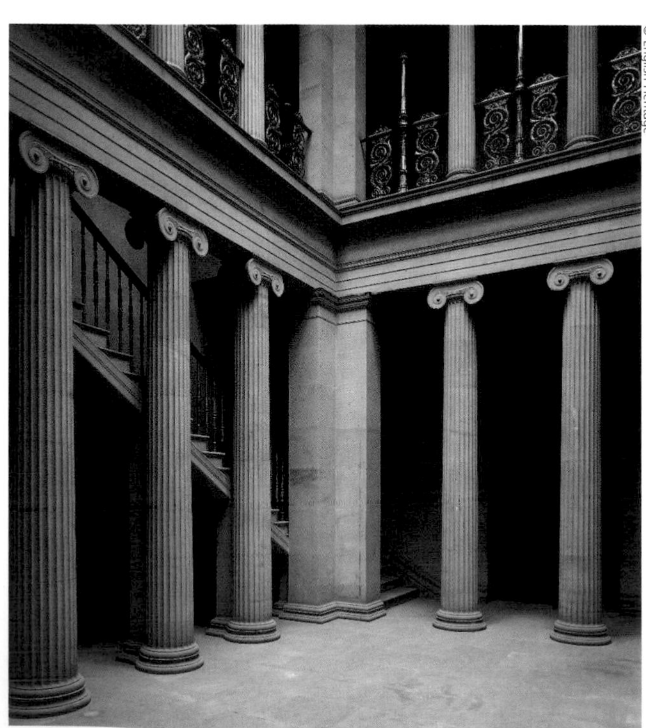

© English Heritage

Belsay Pillar Hall

EDLINGHAM CASTLE

Edlingham, Alnwick, Northumberland

Tel: 0191 269 1200 **E-mail:** customers@english-heritage.org.uk

www.english-heritage.org.uk/edlinghamcastle

Owner: English Heritage **Contact:** The North East Regional Office

The riverside ruins, principally the solar tower of a manor house, progressively fortified against the Scots during the 14th century.

Location: MAP 14:L11, OS Ref. NU116 092. At E end of Edlingham village, on minor road off B6341 6m SW of Alnwick.

Open: Any reasonable time.

Admission: Free. Opening times and prices are valid until 31st March 2011, after this date details are subject to change please visit www.english-heritage.org.uk for the most up-to-date information.

ETAL CASTLE

Cornhill-on-Tweed, Northumberland TD12 4TN

Tel: 01890 820332 **E-mail:** customers@english-heritage.org.uk

www.english-heritage.org.uk/etalcastle

Owner: English Heritage **Contact:** Visitor Operations Team

A 14th century castle located in the picturesque village of Etal. Award-winning exhibition tells the story of the Battle of Flodden and the Anglo-Scottish border warfare.

Location: MAP 14:K10, OS75, NT925 393. In Etal village, 10m SW of Berwick.

Open: 1 Apr–30 Sept: daily, 11am–4.30pm.

Admission: Adult £3.70, Child £1.90, Conc. £3.10, Family £9.30. 15% discount for groups (11+). EH Members free. Opening times and prices are valid until 31st March 2011, after this date details are subject to change please visit www.english-heritage.org.uk for the most up-to-date information.

WC in village. Inclusive.

© English Heritage

HOUSESTEADS ROMAN FORT

Nr HAYDON BRIDGE, NORTHUMBERLAND NE47 6NN

www.english-heritage.org.uk/housesteads

Tel: 01434 344363 **E-mail:** customers@english-heritage.org.uk

Owner: The National Trust **Guardian:** English Heritage

Contact: Visitor Operations Team

The most complete example of a Roman fort in Britain and one of the most popular sites on Hadrian's Wall. Excavations have revealed gateways, the turreted curtain wall, three visible barrack blocks and the famous and well-preserved latrines.

Location: MAP 10:M3, OS Ref. NY790 687. Bardon Mill 4m.

Open: 1 Apr–30 Sept: daily, 10am–6pm. 1 Oct–31 Mar: daily, 10am–4pm. Closed 24–26 Dec and 1 Jan.

Admission: Adult £4.80, Child £2.40, Conc. £4.10. Free entry to EH & NT members. Group discount available. Opening times and prices are valid until 31st March 2011, after this date details are subject to change please visit www.english-heritage.org.uk for the most up-to-date information.

500 metres from site. Charge.

THE LADY WATERFORD HALL & MURALS

Ford, Berwick-upon-Tweed TD15 2QA
Tel: 01890 820503 **Fax:** 01890 820384
Owner: Ford & Etal Estates **Contact:** Dorien Irving

Commissioned in 1860 the walls of this beautiful building are decorated with beautiful murals depicting Bible stories.

Location: MAP 14:K10, OS Ref. NT945 374. On the B6354, 9m from Berwick-upon-Tweed, midway between Newcastle-upon-Tyne and Edinburgh, close to the A697.

Open: Mar–Oct: daily, 11am–5pm.

Admission: Adult £2, Child £1.50. Prices subject to change.

Some properties will be operating the Gift Aid on Entry scheme at their admission points. Where the scheme is operating, visitors are offered a choice between paying the standard admission price or paying the 'Gift Aid Admission' which includes a voluntary donation of at least 10%. Gift Aid Admissions enable the charity to reclaim tax on the whole amount paid* - an extra 28% - potentially a very significant boost to property funds. Money raised from paying visitors in this way will go towards restoration projects at the property and will be very welcome.

Where shown, the admission prices are inclusive of the 10% voluntary donation where properties are operating the Gift Aid on Entry scheme, but both the standard admission price and the Gift Aid Admission will be displayed at the property and on their website.

*Gift Aid donations must be supported by a valid Gift Aid declaration and a Gift Aid declaration can only cover donations made by an individual for him/herself or for him/herself and members of his/her family.

LINDISFARNE CASTLE

Holy Island, Berwick-upon-Tweed, Northumberland TD15 2SH
Tel: 01289 389244 **www.nationaltrust.org.uk**
Owner: The National Trust **Contact:** Property Manager

Built in 1550 to protect Holy Island harbour from attack, the castle was restored and converted into a private house for Edward Hudson by Sir Edwin Lutyens in 1903.

Location: MAP 14:L9, OS Ref. NU136 417. On Holy Island, ¾m E of village, 6m E of A1 across causeway. Usable at low tide.

Open: 19-27 Feb, 12 Mar–30 Oct: closed Mondays (except BHs but open everday in Aug): Alternate weekends throughout winter: 29-31 Dec. Times vary depending on tides but will be either 10am-3pm or 12-5pm. Please telephone for details.

***Admission:** Adult £7.20, Child £3.60, Family £18. Garden only: Adult £1.50, Child Free. Out of hours tours (20+) by arrangement £10.20, NT members £3. *includes a voluntary donation but visitors can choose to pay the standard prices displayed at the property

NT Shop (in Main St).

© NTPL / Arnhel de Serra

Lindisfarne Castle

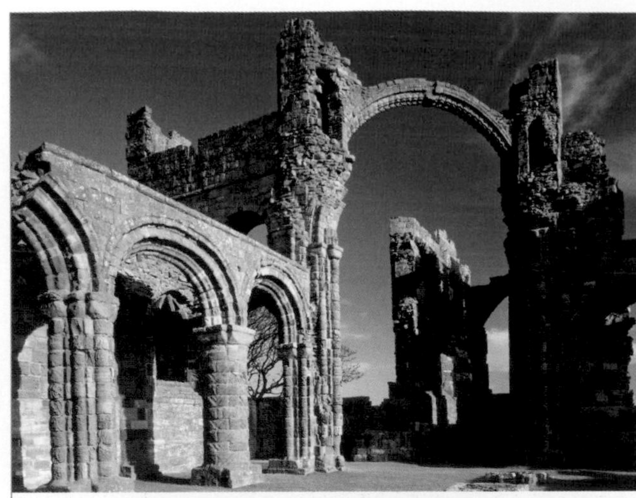

© English Heritage

LINDISFARNE PRIORY

HOLY ISLAND, NORTHUMBERLAND TD15 2RX

www.english-heritage.org.uk/lindisfarne

Tel: 01289 389200 **E-mail:** customers@english-heritage.org.uk
Owner: English Heritage **Contact:** Visitor Operations Team

Famed as the home and original burial ground of St Cuthbert, this site was one of the most important centres of early Christianity in Anglo-Saxon England. Indulge in the stunning coastal views and atmospheric ruins, then visit the museum for fascinating insight into the lives of the priory's former residents.

Location: MAP 14:L9, OS Ref. NU126 417. On Holy Island, check tide times.

Open: 1 Apr–30 Sept daily, 9.30am–5pm. 1–31 Oct daily, 9.30am–4pm, 1 Nov–31 Jan, Sat–Mon, 10am–2pm. 1 Feb–31 Mar, daily 10am–4pm. Closed 24–26 Dec & 1 Jan. Access to the island is affected by high tide, please check the tide times before setting out.

Admission: Adult £4.50, Child £2.30, Conc. £3.80. 15% discount for groups (11+). Opening times and prices are valid until 31st March 2011, after this date details are subject to change please visit www.english-heritage.org.uk for the most up-to-date information.

Charge.

© Britainonview

Preston Tower

Alnwick Castle

MELDON PARK

MELDON PARK, MORPETH, NORTHUMBERLAND NE61 3SW

www.meldonpark.co.uk

Tel: 01670 772341 **Fax:** 01670 772357

E-mail: michelle@flyingfox.co.uk / james@flying-fox.co.uk

Owner: James Cookson **Contact:** James Cookson / Michelle Foggo (Administrator)

Meldon Park is a traditional rural estate west of Morpeth, Northumberland. Entry is free to the working kitchen garden and surrounding wild garden. The cafe and shop sell home grown produce. Meg's walk meanders through parkland by the river Wansbeck. Group tours of the house and gardens can be arranged.

Location: MAP 10:P2, OS Ref. NZ 107 855.

Open: Summer opening: Mon–Sun, 10am–5pm. Winter opening may vary – phone for details 01670 772341.

Admission: Free admission to Walled Garden. House & Garden tours £12 per person by arrangement. £2.50 per adult on Meg's Walk, children free, no dogs allowed.

Partial. Licensed. Licensed. By arrangement. Limited for coaches. Guide dogs only.

NORHAM CASTLE

Norham, Northumberland TD15 2JY

Tel: 01289 304493 **E-mail:** customers@english-heritage.org.uk

www.english-heritage.org.uk/norhamcastle

Owner: English Heritage **Contact:** Visitor Operations Team

Commanding a vital ford over the River Tweed, this was one of the strongest of the Border castles. Built c1160 it was the most often attacked by the Scots.

Location: MAP 14:K9, OS75, NT906 476. 6m SW of Berwick ,on minor road off B6470 (from A698).

Open: Sat–Sun & BHs, 10am–5pm. Admission is limited.

Admission: Free. Opening times and prices are valid until 31st March 2011, after this date details are subject to change please visit www.english-heritage.org.uk for the most up-to-date information.

On leads.

PRESTON TOWER

Chathill, Northumberland NE67 5DH

Tel: 01665 589227 **www.prestontower.co.uk**

The Tower was built by Sir Robert Harbottle in 1392 and is one of the few survivors of 78 pele towers listed in 1415. The tunnel vaulted rooms remain unaltered and provide a realistic picture of the grim way of life under the constant threat of "Border Reivers". Two rooms are turnished in contemporary style and there are displays of historic and local information. Visitors are welcome to walk in the grounds which contain a number of interesting trees and shrubs. A woodland walk to the natural spring from which water is now pumped up to the Tower for the house and cottages.

Location: MAP 14:M11, OS Ref. NU185 253. Follow Historic Property signs on A1 7m N of Alnwick.

Open: All year daily, 10am–6pm, or dusk, whichever is earlier.

Admission: Adult £2, Child 50p, Conc. £1.50. Groups £1.50.

Grounds.

PRUDHOE CASTLE ⌗

Prudhoe, Northumberland NE42 6NA
Tel: 01661 833459 **E-mail:** customers@english-heritage.org.uk
www.english-heritage.org.uk/prudhoecastle
Owner: English Heritage **Contact:** Visitor Operations Team

Extensive remains of a much besieged fortress perched on a tree-covered hill overlooking the River Tyne. Visit the keep, great hall and towered walls, enclosing a fine Georgian mansion.

Location: MAP 10:O3, OS88 Ref. NZ091 634. In Prudhoe, on minor road off A695.

Open: 1 Apr–30 Sept: Thur–Mon, 10am–5pm.

Admission: Adult £4.20, Child £2.10, Conc. £3.60. 15% discount for groups (11+). Opening times and prices are valid until 31st March 2011, after this date details are subject to change please visit www.english-heritage.org.uk for the most up-to-date information.

WC.

SEATON DELAVAL HALL

The Avenue, Seaton Sluice, Northumberland NE26 4QR
Tel: 0191 237 9100 **E-mail:** seatondelavalhall@nationaltrust.org.uk
www.nationaltrust.org.uk/seatondelavalhall
Owner: National Trust

Seaton Delaval Hall was designed by Sir John Vanbrugh for Admiral George Delaval. It has formal gardens with colourful borders and is much more than an architectural masterpiece. A new National Trust property, please note that there may be some ongoing building works.

Location: Just off the A190, close the A19 and 5m from the A1.

Open: Jan–Mar, Fri–Mon, 11am–3pm; Apr–Oct, Fri–Mon, 11am–5pm; Nov–Dec, Fri–Mon, 11am–3pm. Closed 23–26 Dec.

Admission: Adult £5, Child £2.25, Family £12.50. Groups by arrangement only.

WALLINGTON

Cambo, Morpeth, Northumberland NE61 4AR
Tel: 01670 773600 **www.nationaltrust.org.uk**
Owner: National Trust **Contact:** The Estate Office

17th c house with magnificent interior.

Location: MAP 10:O2, OS Ref. NZ030 843. Near Cambo, 6m NW of Belsay (A696).

© English Heritage Photo Library

WARKWORTH CASTLE ⌗

WARKWORTH, ALNWICK, NORTHUMBERLAND NE65 0UJ

www.english-heritage.org.uk/warkworth

Tel: 01665 711423 **E-mail:** customers@english-heritage.org.uk
Owner: English Heritage **Contact:** Visitor Operations Team

The magnificent cross-shaped keep dominates one of the largest, strongest and most impressive fortresses in northern England. This was once home to the powerful Percy family, whose lion badge can still be seen around the castle today. Almost complete, the keep dates mainly from the end of the 14th century.

Location: MAP 14:M12, OS Ref. NU247 058. 7½m S of Alnwick on A1068.

Open: 1 Apr–30 Sept: daily, 10am–5pm. 1–31 Oct: daily, 10am–4pm. 1 Nov–31 Mar: Sat–Mon, 10am–4pm. Closed 24–26 Dec and 1 Jan.

Admission: Castle: Adult £4.50, Child £2.30, Conc. £3.80, Family £11.30. 15% discount for groups (11+). EH Members free. Opening times and prices are valid until 31st March 2011, after this date details are subject to change please visit www.english-heritage.org.uk for the most up-to-date information.

WC. Partial. Inclusive. On leads.

WARKWORTH HERMITAGE ⌗

Warkworth, Northumberland NE65 0UJ
Tel: 01665 711423 **E-mail:** customers@english-heritage.org.uk
www.english-heritage.org.uk/warkworth
Owner: English Heritage **Contact:** Visitor Operations Team

Half a mile upstream by boat from Warkworth castle lies the medieval Hermitage and chapel of a solitary holy man.

Location: MAP 14:M12, OS Ref. NU242 060. 7½ m SE of Alnwick on A1068.

Open: 1 Apr–30 Sept: Weds, Suns & BHs, 11am–5pm.

Admission: Adult £3.20, Child £1.60, Conc. £2.70. EH Members free. Group discount available. Opening times and prices are valid until 31st March 2011, after this date details are subject to change please visit www.english-heritage.org.uk for the most up-to-date information.

At Castle. On leads.

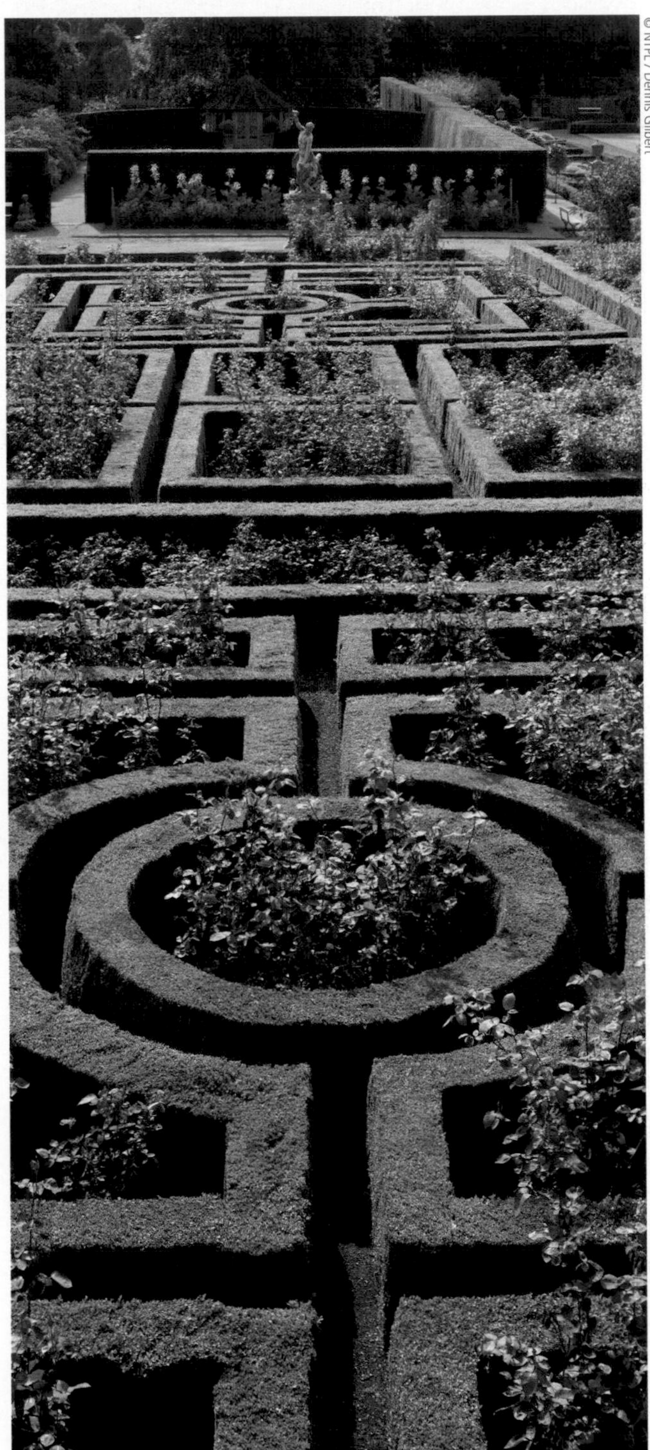

© NTPL / Dennis Gilbert

Seaton Delaval Hall

ARBEIA ROMAN FORT

Baring Street, South Shields, Tyne & Wear NE33 2BB
Tel: 0191 456 1369 **Fax:** 0191 427 6862
Owner: South Tyneside Metropolitan Borough Council **Contact:** The Curator
Managed by: Tyne & Wear Museums

More than 1,500 years on, the remains at Arbeia represent the most extensively excavated example of a military supply base anywhere in the Roman Empire. Museum includes weapons, jewellery and tombstones.

Location: MAP 11:A3, OS Ref. NZ365 679. Near town centre and Metro Station.
Open: Apr–Oct: Mon–Sat, 10am–5pm, Suns, 1–5pm. Closed 1 Nov–31 Mar.
Admission: Free.

BEDE'S WORLD MUSEUM

Church Bank, Jarrow, Tyne & Wear NE32 3DY
Tel: 0191 489 2106 **Fax:** 0191 428 2361 **E-mail:** visitor.info@bedesworld.co.uk
Managed by: Bede's World **Contact:** Visitor Services

Discover the world of the Venerable Bede, who lived and worked at the monastery of Wearmouth-Jarrow 1300 years ago.

Location: MAP 11:A3, OS Ref. NZ339 652. Just off A19, S end of Tyne Tunnel. 300yds N of St Paul's.
Open: Jan–Dec Mon–Sat, 10am–5pm, Suns, 12 noon–5pm. Closed over Christmas.
Admission: Adult £5.50, Child/Conc. £3.50, Family (2+2) £12.50. Groups by arrangement.

BESSIE SURTEES HOUSE ⌗

41–44 Sandhill, Newcastle, Tyne & Wear NE1 3JF
Tel: 0191 269 1200 **E-mail:** customers@english-heritage.org.uk
www.english-heritage.org.uk/bessiesurteeshouse
Owner: English Heritage **Contact:** Reception

These two five-storey 16th and 17th century merchants' houses are fine examples of Jacobean domestic architecture, with splendid period interiors. Best known as the scene of the elopement of Bessie with John Scott, later Lord Chancellor of England. An exhibition illustrating the history of the houses is on the first floor.

Location: MAP 10:P3, OS Ref. NZ252 638. Riverside.
Open: All year: Mon–Fri: 10am–4pm. Closed BHs & 24 Dec–7 Jan.
Admission: Free. Opening times and prices are valid until 31st March 2011, after this date details are subject to change please visit www.english-heritage.org.uk for the most up-to-date information.

WC.

GIBSIDE

Nr Rowlands Gill, Burnopfield, Newcastle upon Tyne NE16 6BG
Tel: 01207 541820 **E-mail:** gibside@nationaltrust.org.uk
www.nationaltrust.org.uk/gibside
Owner: National Trust **Contact:** Visitor Services Team

Among the North's finest landscape parks, Gibside is an 18th century 'forest' garden, created by wealthy coal baron George Bowes, ancestor of the Queen Mother. Gibside is a haven for wildlife with stunning Derwent Valley views, miles of woodland and riverside walks, a spectacular Palladian Chapel and exciting Stables Discovery Centre.

Location: MAP 10:P3, OS Ref. NZ172 583. 6m SW of Gateshead, 20m NW of Durham. Entrance on B6314 between Burnopfield and Rowlands Gill.
Open: Gardens, Walks & Stables: 1 Jan–28 Feb: daily, 10am–4pm. 1 Mar–31 Oct: daily, 10am–6pm. 1 Nov–31 Dec: daily, 10am–4pm. Chapel: 1 Jan–28 Feb: weekends, 10am–3.30pm. 1 Mar–31 Oct: daily, 10am–5pm. 1 Nov–31 Dec: weekends, 10am–3.30pm. Gift Shop, Farm Shop & Tearoom: 1 Jan–28 Feb: daily, 11am–4pm. 1 Mar–31 Oct: daily, 11am–5pm. 1 Nov–31 Dec: daily, 11am–4pm. Closed 24 & 25 Dec.
***Admission:** Adult £6.50, Child £4, Family (2 adults + children) £18.50, Family (1 adult + children) £13. Booked groups £5.20. *Includes a Gift Aid donation but visitors can choose to pay the standard prices displayed at the property and on website.

WCs. Licensed. Licensed. By arrangement. Limited for coaches. On leads. Events every weekend, from family activities to farmers market.

Properties that **open all year** appear in the special index at the end of the book.

NEWCASTLE CASTLE KEEP

CASTLE KEEP, CASTLE GARTH, NEWCASTLE-UPON-TYNE NE1 1RQ

www.castlekeep-newcastle.org.uk

Tel: 0191 232 7938
Owner: Newcastle City Council **Contact:** Tony Ball

The Castle Keep was built by Henry II between 1168–1178 and is one of the finest surviving examples of Norman Keep in the country. It stands within a site which also contains an early motte and bailey castle built by Robert Curthose, the son of William the Conqueror. It is managed by the Society of Antiquaries of Newcastle-upon-Tyne, the second oldest antiquarian society in the world.

Location: MAP 10:P3, OS Ref. NZ251 638. City centre between St Nicholas church and the High Level bridge.
Open: Daily Mon–Sat 10am–5pm, Sun 12–5pm, Last admission 4.15pm. Closed 25/26 Dec & 1 Jan.
Admission: Adult £4, Senior/Student £3, U-18s free when accompanied by an adult.

Partial. By arrangement. On street. Guide dogs only.

SEGEDUNUM ROMAN FORT, BATHS & MUSEUM

Buddle Street, Wallsend, NE28 6HR
Tel: 0191 236 9347 **Fax:** 0191 295 5858

Explore life on the Roman frontier as it was 1,800 years ago, at the most completely excavated fort on Hadrian's Wall. See reconstructions of a section of the Wall together with an impressive Roman military bath house building.

Location: MAP 11:A3, OS Ref. N2 301 660.
Open: 1 Apr–31 Oct: daily, 10am–5pm. 1 Nov–31 Mar: daily, 10am–3pm.
Admission: Adults £4.35, Child (16 and under) Free. Conc. £2.10.

SOUTER LIGHTHOUSE

Coast Road, Whitburn, Sunderland, Tyne & Wear SR6 7NH
Tel: 0191 529 3161
www.nationaltrust.org.uk
Owner: National Trust **Contact:** The House Manager

Built 1871, the first to be powered by alternating electric current.

Location: MAP 11:A3, OS Ref. NZ408 641. 2½m S of South Shields on A183. 5m N of Sunderland.

© NTPL / Joe Cornish

Washington Old Hall

Gibside

ST PAUL'S MONASTERY

Jarrow, Tyne & Wear

Tel: 0191 489 7052 **E-mail:** customers@english-heritage.org.uk

www.english-heritage.org.uk/stpauls

Owner: English Heritage **Contact:** The Regional Office – 0191 269 1200

The home of the Venerable Bede in the 7th and 8th centuries, partly surviving as the chancel of the parish church. It has become one of the best understood Anglo-Saxon monastic sites.

Location: MAP 11:A3, OS Ref. NZ339 652. In Jarrow, on minor road N of A185. 300yds S of Bede's World.

Open: Monastery ruins: Any reasonable time.

Admission: Free. Opening times and prices are valid until 31st March 2011, after this date details are subject to change please visit www.english-heritage.org.uk for the most up-to-date information.

TYNEMOUTH PRIORY & CASTLE

North Pier, Tynemouth, Tyne & Wear NE30 4BZ

Tel: 0191 257 1090 **E-mail:** customers@english-heritage.org.uk

www.english-heritage.org.uk/tynemouth

Owner: English Heritage **Contact:** Visitor Operations Team

Set on a steep headland, Tynemouth has always been as much a fortress as a religious site, playing its role in the Civil War and both World Wars. The Life in the Stronghold exhibition tells the story of the 2000 year history, from its original beginnings as an Anglo-Saxon settlement.

Location: MAP 11:A2, OS Ref. NZ373 694. In Tynemouth near North Pier.

Open: 1 Apr–30 Sept: daily, 10am–5pm. 1 Oct–31 Mar: Thur–Mon, 10am–4pm. Open daily during October and February Half Term holidays. Closed 24–26 Dec & 1 Jan. Gun Battery: Access limited, please ask site staff for details.

Admission: Adult £4.20, Child £2.10, Conc. £3.60, Family £10.50. 15% discount for groups (11+). EH Members free. Opening times and prices are valid until 31st March 2011, after this date details are subject to change please visit www.english-heritage.org.uk for the most up-to-date information.

By arrangement.

WASHINGTON OLD HALL

The Avenue, Washington Village, Washington, Tyne & Wear NE38 7LE

Tel: 0191 416 6879

www.nationaltrust.org.uk

Owner: National Trust **Contact:** The Manager

17th c house was the medieval home of George Washington's ancestors.

Location: MAP 11:A3, OS Ref. NZ312 566. In Washington on E side of The Avenue. 5m W of Sunderland (2m from A1), S of Tyne Tunnel, follow signs for Washington then A1231.

Souter Lighthouse

Edinburgh Castle © Historic Scotland

Scotland

First time visitors to Scotland can only scratch the surface of its cultural and social history. Edinburgh Castle is, of course, Scotland's most famous castle but there are so many others which merit a visit: fairytale Dunrobin on the east coast, Dunvegan on the Isle of Skye and Cawdor, home of the Thanes of Cawdor from the 14th century.

Cawdor Castle, Nairn

Borders

South West Scotland, Dumfries & Galloway, Ayrshire & the Isle of Arran

Edinburgh City, Coast Countryside

Greater Glasgow & the Clyde Valley

Perthshire, Angus & Dundee & The Kingdom of Fife

West Highlands & Islands, Loch Lomond, Stirling & Trossachs

Grampian Highlands, Aberdeen & The North East Coast

Highlands & Skye

Outer Islands, Western Isles, Orkney & Shetland

WESTERN ISLES

HIGHLANDS & SKYE

GRAMPIAN HIGHLANDS

PERTHSHIRE /FIFE

WEST HIGHLANDS & ISLANDS

GREATER GLASGOW

EDINBURGH

BORDERS

SOUTH WEST SCOTLAND

le Kennedy & Gardens, Dumfries & Galloway

Inveraray Castle, West Highlands
© HHG/Nick McCann

Dumfries House, Ayrshire

■ Owner

The Lord Palmer

■ Contact

The Lord and Lady Palmer
Manderston
Duns
Berwickshire
Scotland TD11 3PP

Tel: 01361 883450
Secretary: 01361 882636
Fax: 01361 882010
E-mail: palmer@manderston.co.uk

■ Location

MAP 14:K9
OS Ref. NT810 544

From Edinburgh 47m, 1hr.
1½ m E of Duns on A6105.

Bus: 400 yds.

Rail: Berwick Station 12m.

Taxi: 07970 221821.

Airport: Edinburgh or Newcastle both 60m or 80 mins.

■ Opening Times

Summer
12 May–25 September
Thurs & Sun, 1.30–5pm
Last entry 4.15pm.
Gardens: 11.30am–dusk.

BH Mons, late May & late August. Gardens open until dusk.

Groups welcome all year by appointment.

Winter
September–May
Group visits welcome by appointment.

■ Admission

House & Grounds

Adult	£9.00
Child (under 12yrs)	Free
Conc.	£9.00
Groups (15+)	£8.50

(£9.00 outside opening days).

Grounds only including Stables & Marble Dairy £5.00

On days when the house is closed to the public, groups viewing by appointment will have personally conducted tours. The Gift Shop will be open. On these occasions reduced party rates (except for school children) will not apply. Group visits (15+) other than open days are £8.50pp. Snaffles Tearoom open on Open Days or by arrangement.

Conference/Function

ROOM	SIZE	MAX CAPACITY
Dining Rm	22' x 35'	100
Ballroom	34' x 21'	150
Hall	22' x 38'	130
Drawing Rm	35' x 21'	150

MANDERSTON

www.manderston.co.uk

Manderston, together with its magnificent stables, stunning marble dairy and 56 acres of immaculate gardens, forms an ensemble which must be unique in Britain today.

The house was completely rebuilt between 1903 and 1905, with no expense spared. Visitors are able to see not only the sumptuous State rooms and bedrooms, decorated in the Adam manner, but also all the original domestic offices, in a truly 'upstairs downstairs' atmosphere. Manderston boasts a unique and recently restored silver staircase.

There is a special museum with a nostalgic display of valuable tins made by Huntly and Palmer from 1868 to the present day. Winner of the AA/NPI Bronze Award UK 1994.

Gardens

Outside, the magnificence continues and the combination of formal gardens and picturesque landscapes is a major attraction unique amongst Scottish houses. The stables, still in use, have been described by *Horse and Hound* as 'probably the finest in all the wide world'.

Manderston has often been used as a film location, most recently it was the star of Channel 4's *'The Edwardian Country House'*.

- Corporate & incentives venue. Ideal retreat: business groups, think-tank weekends. Fashion shows, air displays, archery, clay pigeon shooting, equestrian events, garden parties, shows, rallies, filming, product launches and marathons. Two airstrips for light aircraft, approx 5m, grand piano, billiard table, pheasant shoots, sea angling, salmon fishing, stabling, cricket pitch, tennis court, lake. Nearby: 18-hole golf course, indoor swimming pool, squash court. No photography in house.
- Available. Buffets, lunches and dinners. Wedding receptions.
- Special parking available outside the House.
- Snaffles Tearoom – home made lunches, teas, cakes and tray bakes. Can be booked in advance, menus on request.
- Included. Available in French. Guides in rooms. If requested, the owner may meet groups. Tour time 1¼ hrs.
- 400 cars 125yds from house, 30 coaches 5yds from house. Appreciated if group fees are paid by one person.
- Welcome. Guide can be provided. Biscuit Tin Museum of particular interest.
- Grounds only, on leads.
- 6 twin, 4 double.

TRAQUAIR

www.traquair.co.uk

Traquair, situated amidst beautiful scenery and close by the River Tweed, is the oldest inhabited house in Scotland – visited by twenty-seven kings. Originally a Royal hunting lodge, it was owned by the Scottish Crown until 1478 when it passed to a branch of the Royal Stuart family whose descendants still live in the house today. Nearly ten centuries of Scottish political and domestic life can be traced from the collection of treasures in the house. It is particularly rich in associations with the Catholic Church in Scotland, Mary Queen of Scots and the Jacobite Risings.

Visitors are invited to enjoy the house, extensive grounds, maze, craft workshops, 1745 Cottage Restaurant and the famous Traquair House Brewery housed in the eighteenth century wing and producing the world famous Traquair House Ales.

Traquair is a unique piece of living history welcoming visitors from all over the world, providing a magical and romantic setting for weddings, hosting a wide range of summer events and a superb venue for corporate groups. You can even stay at Traquair House. There are three spacious double bedrooms furnished with antique furniture, canopied beds, private bathrooms and central heating. They are all available on a bed and breakfast basis.

No photography in house.

Exclusive lunches/dinners (max 30) in the Dining Room.

Licensed.

Licensed.

By arrangement. Apr & outside opening hours.

Coaches please book.

On leads.

3 en-suites. B&B.

Owner

Catherine Maxwell Stuart, 21st Lady of Traquair

Contact

Ms C Maxwell Stuart
Innerleithen
Peeblesshire EH44 6PW
Tel: 01896 830323
Fax: 01896 830639
E-mail: enquiries@traquair.co.uk

Location

MAP 13:H10
OS Ref. NY330 354

On B709 near junction with A72. Edinburgh 1hr, Glasgow 1½ hrs, Carlisle 1½ hrs, Newcastle 1½ hrs.

Opening Times

Daily 9 April–31 Oct. Weekends only in Nov.

Apr, May & Sept: 12 noon–5pm; Jun, Jul & Aug: 10.30am–5pm; Oct: 11am–4pm; Nov: 11am–3pm.

Guided tours for groups may be arranged outside normal opening hours. These can be conducted by an experienced guide or by the owner, Catherine Maxwell Stuart, 21st Lady of Traquair for an additional charge. Groups may also like to book a free introductory talk.

Traquair Experiences
Lunches, dinners, receptions, coffee and shortbread, ale tasting and even ghost tours may all be arranged in the house. See information on group tours.

Admission

House & Grounds

Adult	£7.60
Child	£4.10
Senior	£6.90
Family(2+3)	£21.20
Groups (20+)	
Adult	£6.60
Child	£3.60
Senior	£6.10
Grounds only	
Adult	£4.00
Concessions	£2.50
Guide book	£4.25

Special Events

April 24
Easter Egg Extravaganza
May 28/29
Medieval Fayre
August 6/7
Traquair Fair
October 28/29
Halloween Experience
November 26/27
Christmas Opening

Conference/Function

ROOM	SIZE	MAX CAPACITY
Dining Room	33' x 16'	34 seated
Drawing Rm	27' x 24'	50/60 receptions

Bowhill House & Country Estate, Morning Room

ABBOTSFORD

Abbotsford, Melrose, Roxburghshire TD6 9BQ

Tel: 01896 752043 Fax: 01896 752916 **Email:** jacquie.wright@scottsabbotsford.co.uk

www.scottsabbotsford.co.uk

Owners: The Abbotsford Trust **Contact:** Jacquie Wright

Abbotsford, situated on the banks of the River Tweed, west of Melrose, is the house built and lived in by Sir Walter Scott, the 19th century novelist, and author of timeless classics such as Waverley, Rob Roy, Ivanhoe and The Lady of the Lake. Visitors are able to see Sir Walter's Study, internationally renowned Library, Entrance Hall, Drawing Room, Armoury, Dining Room and Chapel (built after his death). Gift Shop. Tearoom, Walled Garden. Woodland and River Walks.

Location: MAP 14:I10, OS Ref. NT508 342. 2 miles from Melrose and Galashiels. Edinburgh 35 miles, Glasgow & Newcastle approx 70 miles. Major routes: A1, A68 and A7.

Open: Opening times vary, please call for details.

Admission: Adult £7. Child £3.50. Garden £3.50. Group Adult £5.50. Group Child £3.50. Student £4.

No photography in house. Obligatory for groups.

In grounds, on leads. Nov–Feb by arrangement (groups only Mon–Fri).

BOWHILL HOUSE & COUNTRY ESTATE

BOWHILL, SELKIRK TD7 5ET

www.bowhill.org

Tel: 01750 22204 **Fax:** 01750 23893 **E-mail:** bht@buccleuch.com

Owner: The Duke of Buccleuch & Queensberry KBE

Contact: Buccleuch Heritage Trust

Rich history and beautiful landscape combine at the Scottish Borders home of the Duke of Buccleuch & Queensberry KBE providing an unique opportunity to enjoy culture and countryside at its best. Outstanding collection of art, silverware, porcelain and French furniture. Country Park with lochs, rivers and woodland walks.

Location: MAP 13:H10, OS Ref. NT426 278. 3m W of Selkirk off A708 Moffat Road, A68 from Newcastle, A7 from Carlisle or Edinburgh.

Open: House: May Bank Holiday Weekends and every day Jul & Aug – please call for times. Country Estate: 2–17 Apr daily; then weekends & Bank Holidays in Apr, May & Jun; Jul & Aug daily, 10am–5pm. Educational & private groups at other times by request.

Admission: House & Country Park: Adult £8, Child (3–16yrs) £3.50, OAP £7.

Country Park only: Adults £3.50, Child £2.50, under 3's free, Family tickets available.

Special Events: Please visit our website for event details.

WCs. Licensed. For groups. Tour time 1hr. Limited for coaches.

On leads.

AYTON CASTLE

AYTON, EYEMOUTH, BERWICKSHIRE TD14 5RD

www.aytoncastle.co.uk

Tel: 018907 81212 or 018908 70248 **Fax:** 018908 70238

Owner: D H Liddell-Grainger of Ayton **Contact:** Lady de la Rue

Built in 1846 by the Mitchell-Innes family and designed by the architect James Gillespie Graham. Over the last ten years it has been fully restored and is now a family home. It is a unique restoration project and the quality of the original and restored workmanship is outstanding. The castle stands on an escarpment surrounded by mature woodlands containing many interesting trees and has been a film-making venue due to this magnificent setting.

Location: MAP 14:K8, OS Ref. NT920 610. 7m N of Berwick-on-Tweed on Route A1.

Open: 28 May–29 Aug, Sat & Sun only 2–5pm. Weekdays by appointment only for groups and parties.

Admission: Adult £7.50, Child (under 10yrs) £3, Conc. £4.75

Partial. Obligatory. In grounds, on leads.

Ayton Castle

DAWYCK BOTANIC GARDEN

Stobo, Peeblesshire EH45 9JU

Tel: 01721 760254 **Fax:** 01721 760214 **E-mail:** dawyck@rbge.org.uk

Contact: The Curator

Renowned historic arboretum. Amongst mature specimen trees – some over 40 metres tall – are a variety of flowering trees, shrubs and herbaceous plants. Explore the world's first Cryptogamic Sanctuary and Reserve for 'non-flowering' plants.

Location: MAP 13:G10, OS Ref. NT168 352. 8m SW of Peebles on B712.

Open: Feb–Nov: daily, 10am–6pm (closes 4pm Feb & Nov, 5pm Mar & Oct). Last admission 1 hr before closing.

Admission: Adult £4, Child £1, Conc. £3.50, Family £9. Group discounts & membership programme available.

DRYBURGH ABBEY

St Boswells, Melrose TD6 0RQ

Tel: 01835 822381 **www.historic-scotland.gov.uk**

Owner: Historic Scotland **Contact:** The Monument Manager

Remarkably complete ruins of Dryburgh Abbey by the River Tweed. The chapter house reveals plaster and paintwork dating back to its inception.

Location: MAP 14:I10, OS Ref. NT591 317. 8m SE of Melrose on the B6404, turn left onto the B6356. 1.5m N of St Boswells.

Open: 1 Apr–30 Sept: daily, 9.30am–5.30pm. 1 Oct–31 Mar: daily, 9.30am–4.30pm. Last ticket 30 mins before closing.

Admission: Adult £4.70, Child £2.80, Conc. £3.80 (2010 prices).

Picnic area. Bicycle rack. Limited for coaches. On leads. €

FERNIEHIRST CASTLE

JEDBURGH, ROXBURGHSHIRE TD8 6NX

www.ferniehirst.com

Tel: 01835 862201 **Fax:** 01835 863992

Owner: The Ferniehirst Trust **Contact:** Mr Bob Lawson (Curator)

Ferniehirst is a Border fortress, with features surviving from the 15th century. The ancestral home of Clan Kerr. The undercroft has survived these long centuries. Now housing the Clan Kerr display, a must-see room for all associated with Clan Kerr. Guided Tours Only.

Location: MAP 14:J11, OS Ref. NT653 181. 2m S of Jedburgh on the A68.

Open: July: Tue–Sun, 11am–4pm. (Closed Mons.)

WCs. Guided tours only, groups by arrangement. Ample for cars and coaches. In grounds, on leads.

FLOORS CASTLE

KELSO, ROXBURGHSHIRE, SCOTLAND TD5 7SF

www.floorscastle.com

Tel: 01573 223333 **Fax:** 01573 226056 **E-mail:** cnewton@floorscastle.com

Owner: His Grace the Duke of Roxburghe **Contact:** Charlotte Newton

Explore the spectacular state rooms with outstanding collections of paintings, tapestries and furniture. Find hidden treasures like the collections of porcelain and oriental ceramics. Enjoy the picturesque grounds and gardens including the beautiful walled gardens. Stop at the Courtyard Restaurant and enjoy a morning coffee or delicious lunch.

Location: MAP 14:J10, OS Ref. NT711 347. From South A68, A698. From North A68, A697/9 In Kelso follow signs. Bus: Kelso Bus Station 1m. Rail: Berwick 20m.

Open: Summer: 22 Apr–31 Oct, daily, 11am–5pm. Last admission 4.30pm. Winter: November–March, Closed to the general public, available for events. Please check our website for details.

Admission: Castle, Grounds & Gardens: Adult £8, Child* (5–16yrs) £4, Seniors £7. Groups (20+) Adult £7, Child* (5–16yrs) £4, Seniors £6. Grounds & Gardens: Adult £4, Child* (5–16yrs) £1.50, Seniors £3.50. Groups (20+) Adult £4, Child* (5–16yrs) £1, Seniors £3.50.*Under 5yrs Free.

Special Events: Snowdrop Festival, Easter Eggstravaganza, Floors Castle Horse Trials, Massed Pipe Bands Day. Please check our website for details.

Gala dinners, conferences, product launches, 4 x 4 driving, incentive groups, highland games and other promotional events. Extensive park, helicopter pad, fishing, clay pigeon and pheasant shooting. No photography inside the castle. Exclusive lunches & dinners. Partial. WCs. Licensed. Licensed. By arrangement. Unlimited for cars, 100 yds away, coach park 150 yds. Coaches can be driven to the entrance. Lunch or tea for coach drivers. Welcome, guide provided. Playground facilities. On leads, in grounds.

HALLIWELL'S HOUSE MUSEUM

Halliwell's Close, Market Place, High Street, Selkirk

Tel: 01750 20096 **Fax:** 01750 23282

Owner: Scottish Borders Council **Contact:** Brian Appleby

Re-creation of buildings, formerly used as a house and ironmonger's shop.

Location: MAP 14:I10, OS Ref. NT472 286. In Selkirk town centre.

Open: 2 Apr–30 Sept, Mon–Sat: 10am–5pm, Sun: 11am–3pm. 1–31 Oct, Mon–Sat: 10am–4pm. Sun: 11am–3pm. Please telephone in advance to confirm opening times.

Admission: Free.

HERMITAGE CASTLE

Liddesdale, Newcastleton TD9 0LU

Tel: 01387 376222 **www.historic-scotland.gov.uk**

Owner: In the care of Historic Scotland **Contact:** Monument Manager

An eerie fortress at the heart of the bloodiest events in the history of the Borders. Mary Queen of Scots made her famous ride here to visit her future husband.

Location: MAP 10:L1, OS Ref. NY497 961. In Liddesdale, 5.5 m NE of Newcastleton, B6399.

Open: 1 Apr–30 Sept: daily, 9.30am–5.30pm. Last ticket 30 mins before closing.

Admission: Adult £3.70, Child £2.20, Conc. £3.00 (2010 prices).

Picnic area. Limited for coaches. On leads. €

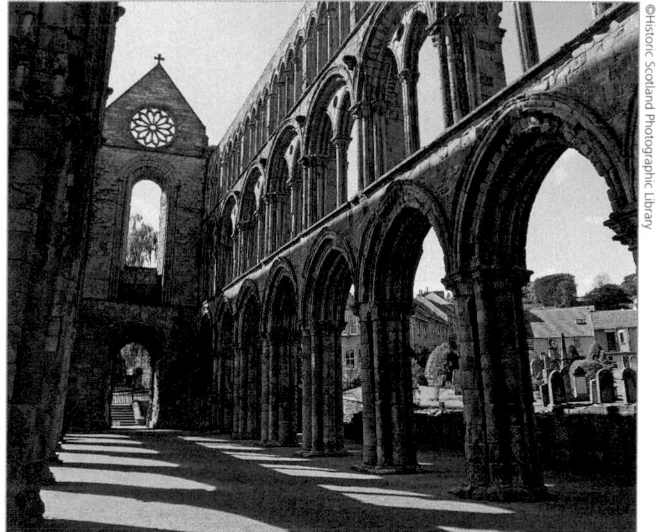

©Historic Scotland Photographic Library

JEDBURGH ABBEY

4/5 ABBEY BRIDGEND, JEDBURGH TD8 6JQ

www.historic-scotland.gov.uk

Tel: 01835 863925

Owner: In the care of Historic Scotland **Contact:** Monument Manager

Founded by David I c1138 for Augustinian Canons. The abbey is mostly in the Romanesque and early Gothic styles and is remarkably complete. The award winning visitor centre contains the priceless 12th century 'Jedburgh Comb' and other artefacts found during archaeological excavations.

Location: MAP 14:J11, OS Ref. NT650 205. In Jedburgh on the A68.

Open: Apr–Sept: daily, 9.30am–5.30pm. Oct–Mar: daily, 9.30am–4.30pm. Last ticket 30 mins before closing.

Admission: Adult £5.20, Child £3.10, Conc. £4.20 (2010 prices).

WCs. Limited for coaches. Free when booked.

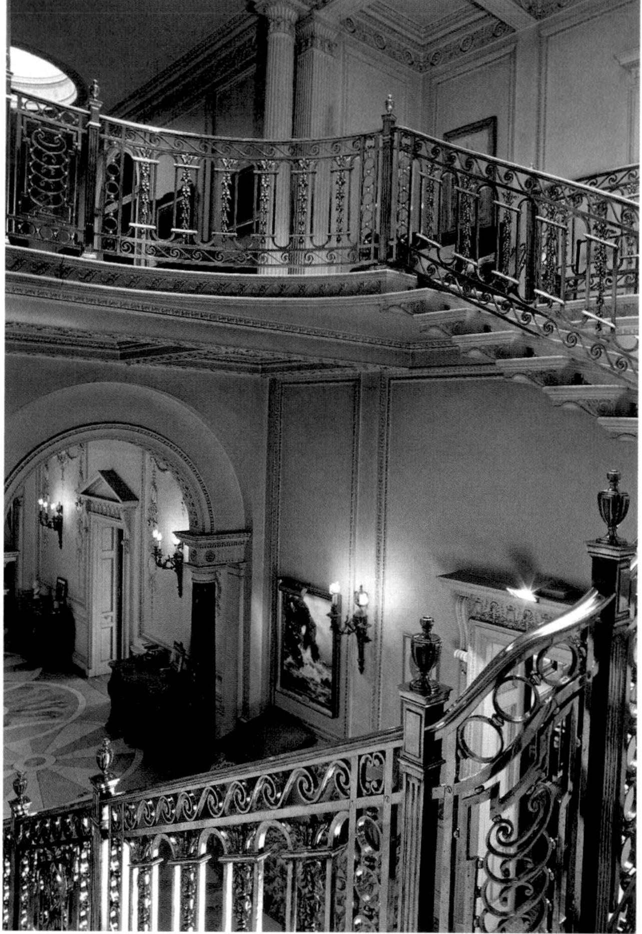

© Britainonview

Manderston

MANDERSTON *See page 400 for full page entry.*

Mellerstain House

MELLERSTAIN HOUSE

MELLERSTAIN, GORDON, BERWICKSHIRE TD3 6LG

www.mellerstain.com

Tel: 01573 410225 **Fax:** 01573 410636 **E-mail:** enquiries@mellerstain.com

Owner: The Earl of Haddington **Contact:** The Administrator

One of Scotland's great Georgian houses and a unique example of the work of the Adam family; the two wings built in 1725 by William Adam, the large central block by his son, Robert 1770-78. Rooms contain fine plasterwork, colourful ceilings and marble fireplaces. The library is considered to be Robert Adam's finest creation. Many fine paintings and period furniture.

Location: MAP 14:J10, OS Ref. NT648 392. From Edinburgh A68 to Earlston, turn left 5m, signed.

Open: Easter weekend, 1 May–30 Jun & 1–30 Sept: Suns, Weds & BH Mons. 1 Jul–31 Aug: Sun, Mon, Wed & Thurs. Oct: Suns only. House: 12.30–5pm. Last ticket 4.15pm. Groups any time by appointment. Tearoom & gardens: 11.30am–5pm.

Admission: See our website or call us.

Special Events: Mellerstain Summer Art Exhibition. Details on our website.

No photography or video cameras. Partial. By arrangement. In grounds, on leads. Guide dogs only in house.

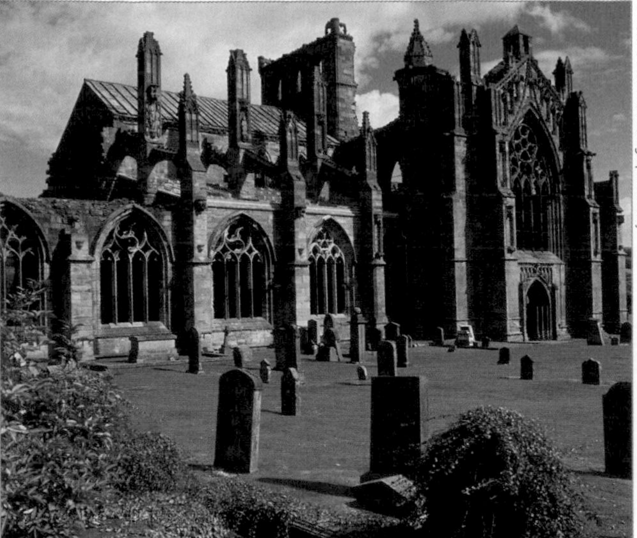

©Historic Scotland Photographic Library

MELROSE ABBEY

MELROSE, ROXBURGHSHIRE TD6 9LG

www.historic-scotland.gov.uk

Tel: 01896 822562

Owner: Historic Scotland **Contact:** Monument Manager

The abbey was founded about 1136 by David I and at one time was probably the richest in Scotland. Richard II's English army largely destroyed it in 1385 but it was rebuilt and the surviving remains are mostly 14th century. Burial place of Robert the Bruce's heart. Local history displays.

Location: MAP 14:I10, OS Ref. NT548341. In the centre of Melrose off the A68 or A7.

Open: Apr–Sept: daily, 9.30am–5.30pm. Oct–Mar: daily, 9.30am–4.30pm. Last ticket 30 mins before closing.

Admission: Adult £5.20, Child £3.10, Conc. £4.20 (2010 prices).

Limited for coaches. Pre-booked visits free. On leads. €

© Britainonview

Paxton House Gallery

OLD GALA HOUSE

Scott Crescent, Galashiels TD1 3JS

Tel: 01750 20096 **Fax:** 01750 23282

Owner: Scottish Borders Council

Dating from 1583, the former house of the Lairds of Gala. Particularly memorable is the painted ceiling dated 1635.

Location: MAP 14:I10, OS Ref. NT492 357. S of town centre, signed from A7.

Open: Apr, May & Sept: Tue–Sat, 10am–4pm. Jun–Aug: Mon–Sat, 10am–4pm, Sun, 1–4pm. Oct: Tue–Fri, 1–4pm, Sat, 10am–4pm. Please telephone in advance to confirm up to date opening times.

Admission: Free.

PAXTON HOUSE, GALLERY & COUNTRY PARK

BERWICK-UPON-TWEED TD15 1SZ

www.paxtonhouse.com

Tel: 01289 386291 **E-mail:** info@paxtonhouse.com

Owner: The Paxton Trust **Contact:** Reception

Palladian country house built 1758. designed by John Adam. 12 period rooms, magnificent Picture Gallery - outstation of the National Galleries of Scotland, working Georgian kitchen. Grounds, gardens, riverside and woodland walks, red squirrel hide and salmon net fishing museum. Gift shop, tearoom serving home cooked lunches. Ellem Fishing Club exhibition.

Location: MAP 14:K9, OS Ref. NT931 520. 3m west off the A1 Berwick-upon-Tweed bypass on B6461. Rail: Berwick upon Tweed.

Open: 1 Apr–31 Oct: House: 11am–5pm. Last house tour 4pm.
Grounds: 10am–sunset. Open to groups/schools all year by appointment.

Admission: Adult £7.50, Child £3.50, Family £20. Concession £7. Groups (pre-arranged, 12+). Adult £6.00, Child £3.00. Grounds only: Adult £4, Child £2, Family £11.

No photography in House. Conferences, weddings. WCs. Obligatory. In grounds. Music Festival 15–24 July 2011.

SMAILHOLM TOWER

Smailholm, Kelso TD5 7PG

Tel: 01573 460365 **www.historic-scotland.gov.uk**

Owner: Historic Scotland **Contact:** The Monument Manager

Set on a high rocky knoll this well preserved 16th century tower houses an exhibition of tapestries and costume dolls depicting characters from Sir Walter Scott's Minstrelsy of the Scottish Borders.

Location: MAP 14:J10, OS Ref. NT638 347. Near Smailholm Village, 6m W of Kelso on A6089 then follow the B6397 before turning on to the B6404.

Open: 1 Apr–30 Sept: daily, 9.30am–5.30pm. Oct-Mar 9.30am–4.30pm, Sat & Sun only. Last ticket 30 mins before closing.

Admission: Adult £3.70, Child £2.20, Conc. £3.00 (2010 prices).

Limited for coaches. € Audio tour.

TRAQUAIR

See page 401 for full page entry.

■ **Owner**

His Grace the Duke of Buccleuch & Queensberry KBE

■ **Contact**

Claire Oram
Drumlanrig Castle
Thornhill
Dumfriesshire
DG3 4AQ

Tel: 01848 331555
Fax: 01848 331682
E-mail: enquiries@drumlanrig.com

■ **Location**

MAP 13:E12
OS Ref. NX851 992

18m N of Dumfries, 3m NW of Thornhill off A76. 16m from M74 at Elvanfoot. Approx. 1½ hrs by road from Edinburgh, Glasgow and Carlisle.

■ **Opening Times**

Summer
Castle
1 April–31 August: daily, 11am–4pm (last entry).

Gardens & Country Estate
1 April–23 October: daily, 10am–5pm.

Winter
By appointment only.

■ **Admission***

Please call or visit our website for admission charges.

*All visitors to the Castle must sign the visitor book as a condition of entry.

Conference/Function

ROOM	SIZE	MAX CAPACITY
Visitors' Centre	6m x 13m	50

DRUMLANRIG CASTLE

www.drumlanrig.com

Drumlanrig is perhaps the most rewarding and romantic of Scotland's great houses with its magnificent rooms and spectacular collections of silver, porcelain, French furniture and art – including Rembrandt's *Old Woman Reading*.

Beyond the house, the gardens extend to over 70 acres and include great formal parterres, dells, rockeries and charming summer houses as well as many impressive trees and a collection of rare shrubs from China.

Around the estate, the possibilities are endless. Walk, cycle or mountain-bike on miles of clearly marked paths and off-road trails, spot wildlife (including red squirrels) or visit the unique Scottish Cycle Museum, with its extensive collection of vintage bicycles.

In our stableyard you'll find craft workshops, local food producers and an education and visitor centre. There's a great gift shop full of top quality foods, whiskies and souvenirs, a thrilling Adventure Playground, bike hire from Rik's Bike Shed, guided walks and Landrover tours, fishing and other country sports. And when you need a break from all that activity, you can enjoy some delicious home cooking at The Castle Kitchen Tearoom. There's so much to do at Drumlanrig, you'll be longing to return.

No photography inside the Castle.

Suitable. WC. Please enquire about facilities before visit.

Licensed.

Snacks, lunches and teas during opening hours.

Adjacent to the Castle.

Children's quiz and worksheets. Ranger-led activities, including woodlands and forestry. Adventure playground. School groups welcome throughout the year by arrangement.

In Country Park on leads.

DUMFRIES HOUSE

www.dumfries-house.org.uk

Dumfries House – a Georgian Gem. Nestling within 2,000 acres of scenic Ayrshire countryside in south-west Scotland, this beautiful Palladian mansion house has been described as an 18th century time-capsule with many of its principal rooms extremely well preserved and some of their exquisite contents virtually unchanged for nearly 250 years.

Commissioned by William Crichton Dalrymple, the 5th Earl of Dumfries, the House was designed by renowned 18th century architect brothers John, Robert and James Adam and built between 1754 and 1759. Recognised as one of the Adam brothers' masterpieces it remained unseen by the public since it was built 250 years ago until it opened its doors as a visitor attraction in June 2008. The former home of the Marquises of Bute, it was saved for the nation at the eleventh hour by a consortium of organisations and individuals brought together by HRH The Prince Charles, Duke of Rothesay.

The house holds the most important collection of works from Thomas Chippendale's 'Director' period. It is widely recognised that Scotland was a testing ground for Thomas Chippendale's early rococco furniture and the Dumfries House collection is regarded as his key project in this area. Dumfries House also holds the most comprehensive range of pieces by Edinburgh furniture makers Alexander Peter, William Mathie and Francis Brodie. Indeed, the Scottish furniture together with the Chippendale collection is of outstanding worldwide historical significance.

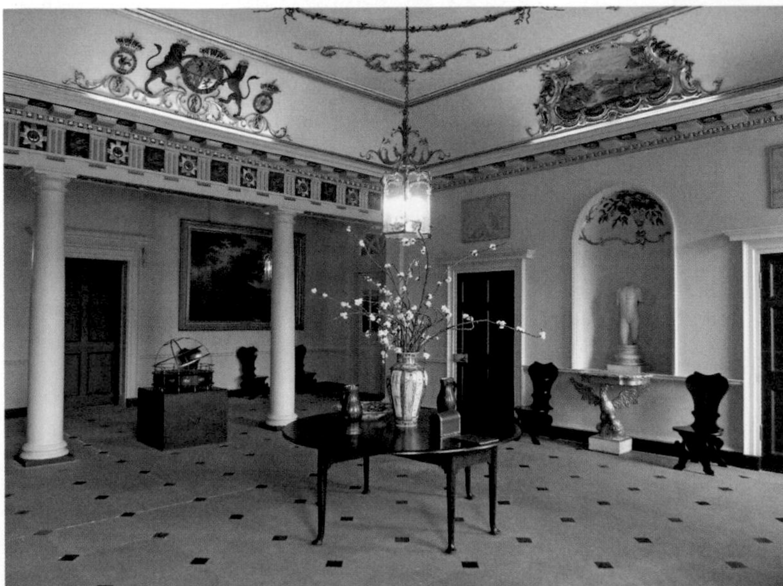

- Pre-booking of tours is recommended (Online at www.dumfries-house.org.uk or via the booking line 01290 551111). Tour times may vary.
- Unsuitable. WCs.
- Obligatory.
- Cars ample. Coaches ample.
- In grounds. Guide dogs only in the house.
- Grounds only.

Owner

The Great Steward of Scotland's Dumfries House Trust

Contact

The Administrator
Dumfries House
Cumnock
Ayrshire
Scotland
KA18 2NJ

Tel: 01290 425959
(Booking Line
01290 551111)
Fax: 01290 425464
E-mail: info@dumfries-house.org.uk

Location

MAP 10:I2
OS Ref. NS539 200

Car: Cumnock, East Ayrshire. Sat Nav KA18 2LN. Visitors Entrance on Barony Road (B7036).

Rail: Auchinleck.

Air: Prestwick.

Opening Times

1 April to 30 September: 11.00am to 3.00pm for guided tours only. Closed every Tuesday & Wednesday and on other days for private functions. Please check with the property before travelling any distance.

Admission

Adult	£10.00
Child (5–16yrs)	£5.00
Child (under 5)	Free
Art Fund members	Free
Historic Scotland members	£7.50

Special Events

Grounds available all year.

House may close for private functions.

Please check with the property before travelling any distance.

Special Events information available at www.dumfries-house.org.uk

House available for private functions and corporate events. Minister license for weddings.

ARDWELL GARDENS

Ardwell, Nr Stranraer, Dumfries and Galloway DG9 9LY
Tel: 01776 860227
Owner: Mr Francis Brewis **Contact:** Mrs Terry Brewis
The gardens include a formal garden, wild garden and woodland.
Location: MAP 9:D4, OS Ref. NX102 455. A716 10m S of Stranraer.
Open: 1 Mar–30 Sept: daily, 10am–5pm.
Admission: Adult £3, Children under 14 free.

AUCHINLECK HOUSE

Ochiltree, Ayrshire
Tel: 01628 825925
E-mail: bookings@landmarktrust.org.uk **www.landmarktrust.org.uk**
Owner/Contact: The Landmark Trust
One of the finest examples of an 18th century Scottish country house, the importance of which is further enhanced by its association with James Boswell, author of The Life of Samuel Johnson. The house has been restored by the Landmark Trust and is let for holidays for up to 13 people. Full details of Auchinleck House and 189 other historic and architecturally important buildings are featured in the Landmark Trust Handbook (price £10 plus p&p refundable against booking) and on the website.
Location: MAP 13:C11, OS Ref. NS507 230.
Open: Available for holidays for up to 13 people throughout the year. Parts of the house are open to the public Easter–Oct: Wed afternoons. Grounds: dawn–dusk in the Spring & Summer season. Contact the Landmark Trust for details.
Admission: By appointment only. Tickets £3 from 01628 825920.
In grounds, on leads.

BARGANY GARDENS

Girvan, Ayrshire KA26 9QL
Tel: 01465 871249 **Fax:** 01465 871282 **E-mail:** bargany@btinternet.com
Owner: Mr John Dalrymple Hamilton **Contact:** Mrs Sally Anne Dalrymple Hamilton
Lily pond, rock garden and a fine collection of hard and softwood trees.
Location: MAP 9:E1, OS Ref. NX851 992. 18m N of Dumfries, 3m NW of Thornhill off A76. 16m from M74 at Elvanfoot.
Open: May: daily, 10am–5pm.
Admission: Adult: £2, Child Free. Buses by arrangement.

BRODICK CASTLE

Isle of Arran KA27 8HY
Tel: 0131 243 9300
Owner: The National Trust for Scotland
Castle built on the site of a Viking fortress with interesting contents.
Location: MAP 12:P10, OS Ref. NX684 509. Off A711 /A755, in Kirkcudbright, at 12 High St.

©Historic Scotland
Maclellans Castle

BURNS COTTAGE

Alloway, Ayrshire KA7 4PY
Tel: 01292 441215 **Fax:** 01292 441750
Contact: J Manson
Thatched cottage, birthplace of Robert Burns in 1759, with adjacent museum.
Location: OS Ref. NS335 190. 2m SW of Ayr. Two separate sites, 600yds apart.
Open: 3 Jan–31 Mar, daily 10am–5pm; 1 Apr–31 Oct, daily 10am–5.30pm; 1 Nov–31 Dec, daily 10am–5pm (closed 25/26 Dec).
Admission: Adult £4, Child/OAP £2.50, Family £10.

Thinking of a short break or weekend away?
See Historic Places to Stay

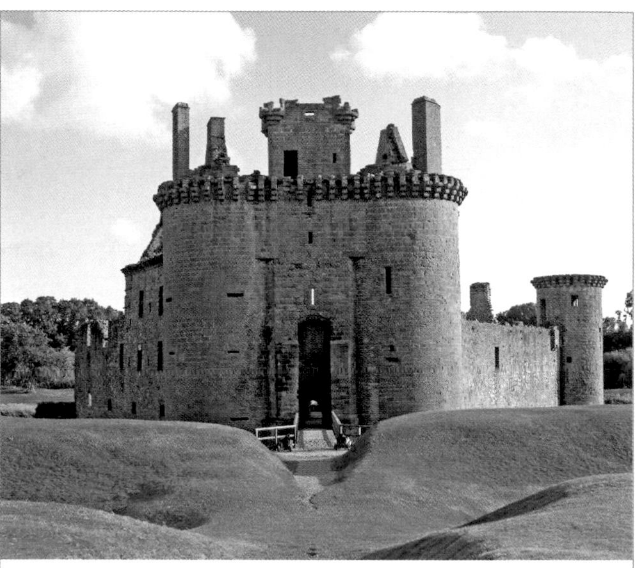

CAERLAVEROCK CASTLE

GLENCAPLE, DUMFRIES DG1 4RU

www.historic-scotland.gov.uk

Tel: 01387 770244
Owner: In the care of Historic Scotland **Contact:** The Monument Manager
Caerlaverock Castle is an impressive medieval stronghold which sits on a triangular site surrounded by moats. The castle's remarkable features include the twin-towered gatehouse and the Renaissance Nithsdale lodging. Today visitors can enjoy a siege warfare exhibition, a children's adventure park and a nature trail leading to an earlier castle.
Location: MAP 10:I3, OS NY025 656. 8m SE of Dumfries on the B725.
Open: Apr–Sept: daily, 9.30am–5.30pm; Oct–Mar: daily, 9.30am–4.30pm. Last ticket sold 30 mins before closing.
Admission: Adult £5.20, Child £3.10, Conc. £4.20 (2010 prices).
WCs. Limited for coaches. Free if pre-booked. On leads. €

CARDONESS CASTLE

Gatehouse of Fleet, DG7 2EH
Tel: 01557 814427 **www.historic-scotland.gov.uk**
Owner: Historic Scotland **Contact:** The Monument Manager
A well preserved ruin of a six storey tower house dating back to the 15th century. Standing on a rocky platform above the Water of Fleet the castle was the ancient home of the McCulloch clan. Very fine fireplaces and excellent views over Fleet Bay.
Location: MAP 9:G3, OS Ref. NX591 553. 1m SW of Gatehouse of Fleet on the A75.
Open: 1 Apr–30 Sept: daily, 9.30am–5.30pm. 1 Oct–31 Mar 9.30am–4.30pm weekends only. Last ticket 30 mins before closing.
Admission: Adult £3.70, Child £2.20, Conc. £3.00 (2010 prices).
Picnic Area Limited for coaches. On leads. €

CASTLE KENNEDY & GARDENS

STAIR ESTATES, REPHAD, STRANRAER, DUMFRIES AND GALLOWAY DG9 8BX

www.castlekennedygardens.co.uk

Tel: 01776 702024 / 01581 411225 **Fax:** 01776 706248
E-mail: info@castlekennedygardens.co.uk
Owner/Contact: The Earl and Countess of Stair

Famous 75 acre gardens situated between two large natural lochs. Ruined Castle Kennedy at one end overlooks a beautiful herbaceous walled garden; Lochinch Castle is at the other. Close proximity to the gulf-stream provides an impressive collection of rare trees, including spectacular Champion Trees (largest of their type) and exotic shrubs. Snowdrop walks, daffodils, rhododendron and magnolia displays, tree trails and children's activities make this a 'must visit' through-out the year.

Location: MAP 9:D3, OS Ref. NX109 610. 3m E of Stranraer on A75.

Open: Gardens and Tearoom: 1 Apr-30 Sept: daily 10am-5pm. Feb, Mar & Oct: Weekends only. Gardens open all year.

Admission: Adult £4, Child £1, OAP £3.

Partial Teas and light lunches with home baking. On leads Childrens activities

CASTLE OF ST JOHN

Stranraer, Dumfries and Galloway
Tel: 01776 705088 **Fax:** 01776 705835
Owner: Dumfries & Galloway Council **Contact:** John Picken

A much altered 16th century L-plan tower house, now a museum.

Location: MAP 9:D3, OS Ref. NX061 608. In Stranraer, towards centre, ¼m short of the harbour.

Open: Please telephone in advance to confirm up to date opening times.

Admission: Free.

CRAIGDARROCH HOUSE

Moniaive, Dumfriesshire DG3 4JB
Tel: 01848 200202
Owner/Contact: Mrs Carin Sykes

Built by William Adam in 1729, over the old house dating from 14th century (earliest records). The marriage home of Annie Laurie, the heroine of 'the world's greatest love-song', who married Alexander Fergusson, 14th Laird of Craigdarroch, in 1720 and lived in the house for 33 years.

Location: MAP 9:G1, OS Ref. NX741 909. S side of B729, 2m W of Moniaive, 19m WNW of Dumfries.

Open: Jul: daily, 2–4pm. Please note: no WCs.

Admission: £2.

CRAIGIEBURN GARDEN

Craigieburn House, Nr Moffat, Dumfriesshire DG10 9LF
Tel: 01683 221250
Owner/Contact: Janet Wheatcroft

A plantsman's garden with a huge range of rare and unusual plants surrounded by natural woodland.

Location: MAP 13:G12, OS Ref. NT117 053. NW side of A708 to Yarrow & Selkirk, 2½m E of Moffat.

Open: Easter–Oct: Tue–Sun.

Admission: Adult £2.50, Child Free (charges support Sherpa school in Nepal).

Dumfries House

CROSSRAGUEL ABBEY

Maybole, Strathclyde, KA19 5HQ

Tel: 01655 883113 **www.historic-scotland.gov.uk**

Owner: In the care of Historic Scotland **Contact:** Monument Manager

Founded in the early 13th century by the Earl of Carrick. Remarkably complete remains include church, cloister, chapter house and much of the domestic premises.

Location: MAP 13:B11, OS Ref. NS275 083. 2m S of Maybole on the A77.

Open: 1 Apr–30 Sept: daily, 9.30am–5.30pm. Last ticket 30 mins before closing.

Admission: Adult £3.70, Child £2.20, Conc. £3.00 (2010 prices).

Picnic area. Partial Limited for coaches On leads. €

CULZEAN CASTLE

Maybole KA19 8LE

Tel: 0131 243 9300

Owner: The National Trust for Scotland

Romantic 18th century Robert Adam clifftop mansion.

Location: MAP 13:B11, OS Ref. NS240 100. 12m SW of Ayr, on A719, 4m W of Maybole.

DALGARVEN MILL MUSEUM

Dalgarven, Dalry Road, Nr Kilwinning, Ayrshire KA13 6PL

Tel/Fax: 01294 552448 **E-mail:** admin@dalgarvenmill.org.uk

Owner: Dalgarven Mill Trust **Contact:** The Administrator

Museum of Ayrshire Country Life and Costume.

Location: MAP 13:B9, OS Ref. NS295 460. On A737 2m from Kilwinning.

Open: All year: Summer: Easter–end Oct: Tue–Sat, 10am–5pm, Suns, 11am–5pm. Winter: Tue–Fri, 10am–4pm, Sat 10am–5pm, Sun, 11am–5pm.

Admission: Charges. Groups (10+) must book.

DEAN CASTLE COUNTRY PARK

Dean Road, Kilmarnock, East Ayrshire KA3 1XB

Tel: 01563 522702 **Fax:** 01563 572552

Owner: East Ayrshire Council **Contact:** Andrew Scott-Martin

Set in 200 acres of Country Park. Visits to castle by guided tour only.

Location: MAP 13:C10, OS Ref. NS437 395. Off A77. 1¼m NNE of town centre.

Open: Country Park: All year: dawn–dusk. Please telephone 01563 578155 for Castle opening details.

Admission: Free (group charge on application).

DRUMLANRIG CASTLE

See page 406 for full page entry.

DUMFRIES HOUSE

See page 407 for full page entry.

DUNDRENNAN ABBEY

Dundrennan, Dumfries and Galloway, DG6 4QH

Tel: 01557 500262 **www.historic-scotland.gov.uk**

Owner: Historic Scotland **Contact:** Monument Manager

This 12th century Cistercian abbey stands in a small and secluded valley and was founded by David I. Mary Queen of Scots spent her last night on Scottish soil here in 1568.

Location: MAP 9:G4, OS Ref. NX749 475. 6.5 m SE of Kirkcudbright on the A711.

Open: 1 Apr–30 Sept: daily, 9.30am–5.30pm. 1 Oct–31 Mar: 9.30am–4.30pm, weekends only. Last ticket 30 mins before closing.

Admission: Adult £3.20, Child £1.90, Conc. £2.70 (2010 prices).

Limited parking for coaches On leads. €

GLENLUCE ABBEY

Glenluce, Dumfries and Galloway, DG8 0AF

Tel: 01581 300541 **www.historic-scotland.gov.uk**

Owner: Historic Scotland **Contact:** The Monument Manager

Glenluce Abbey, founded around 1192 by Roland, Lord of Galloway, is set in the secluded valley of the Water of Luce. Its remains include a 16th century chapter house with fine architectural features and wonderful acoustics. The abbey's museum of monastic life houses a fascinating collection of artefacts.

Location: MAP 9:D3, OS Ref. NX185 587. 2m NW of Glenluce village off the A75.

Open: 1 Apr–30 Sept: daily 9.30am–5.30pm. Last ticket 30 mins before closing.

Admission: Adult £3.20, Child £1.90, Conc. £2.70 (2010 prices).

Limited for coaches. On leads. €

GLENMALLOCH LODGE

Newton Stewart, Dumfries and Galloway

Tel: 01628 825925

E-mail: bookings@landmarktrust.org.uk **www.landmarktrust.org.uk**

Owner/Contact: The Landmark Trust

Glenmalloch Lodge represents the aristocratic philanthropy that characterised the Victorian Age at its best. It lies in the middle of a wild glen, framed by wide views of the surrounding hills, with the Solway Firth just a mile or so away. The cottage was built originally not as a lodge, but rather as a picturesque schoolhouse through the philanthropy of Harriet, Countess of Galloway, some time before 1842. It has been restored by the Landmark Trust, and is now let for holidays. Full details of Glenmalloch Lodge and 189 other historical and architecturally important buildings are featured in the Landmark Trust Handbook (price £10 plus p&p refundable against a booking) and on the website.

Location: MAP 9:F3, OS Ref. NX423 682.

Open: Available for holidays for up to 2 people throughout the year. Other visits by appointment. Contact the Landmark Trust for details.

GLENWHAN GARDENS

Dunragit, Stranraer, Wigtownshire DG9 8PH

Tel/Fax: 01581 400222 **E-mail:** tess@glenwhan.freeserve.co.uk

www.glenwhangardens.co.uk

Contact: Tessa Knott

Beautiful 12 acre garden overlooking Luce Bay and the Mull of Galloway. Licensed tearoom, groups catered for.

Location: MAP 9:D3, OS Ref. NX150 580. N side of A75, 6m E of Stranraer.

Open: Mar–Oct, daily, 10am–5.30pm. Large parties are advised to book well in advance!.

Admission: Adult £4.50, Child £1.50, Conc. £3.50, Family £10 or by Honesty Box in October.

Unlicensed.

KELBURN CASTLE & COUNTRY CENTRE

FAIRLIE, BY LARGS, AYRSHIRE KA29 0BE

www.kelburncountrycentre.com

The most colourful Castle in Scotland. Country Park and Castle tours: Earl of Glasgow

Tel: 01475 568685 **Fax:** 01475 568121 **E-mail:** admin@kelburncountrycentre.com

Functions in the Castle: **Tel:** 01475 568595 **E-mail:** maggie@kelburncastle.com

Owner: The Earl of Glasgow

Kelburn is the home of the Earls of Glasgow and has been in the Boyle family for over 800 years. It is notable for its waterfalls, historic gardens, romantic glen and unique trees. Recently the Castle has been the venue of a major art grafiti project. The Country Centre includes exhibitions, gift shop, licensed café, riding school, falconry centre, ranger events programme, stockade, indoor playbarn, pet's corner and Scotland's most unusual attraction – The Secret Forest. The Castle is open for guided tours in July and August and available for weddings, conferences, dinner parties and other functions all the year round.

Open: Country Centre: Easter–Oct: daily. Castle: July & Aug. Open by arrangement for groups at other times of the year.

Admission: Country Centre: Adult £7.50, Child/Conc. £5, Family £25. Groups (10+): Adult, £4.50, Conc. £3.50. Castle: £1.75 extra pp.

Partial. Licensed. July & August. By arrangement at other times of the year. In grounds on leads.

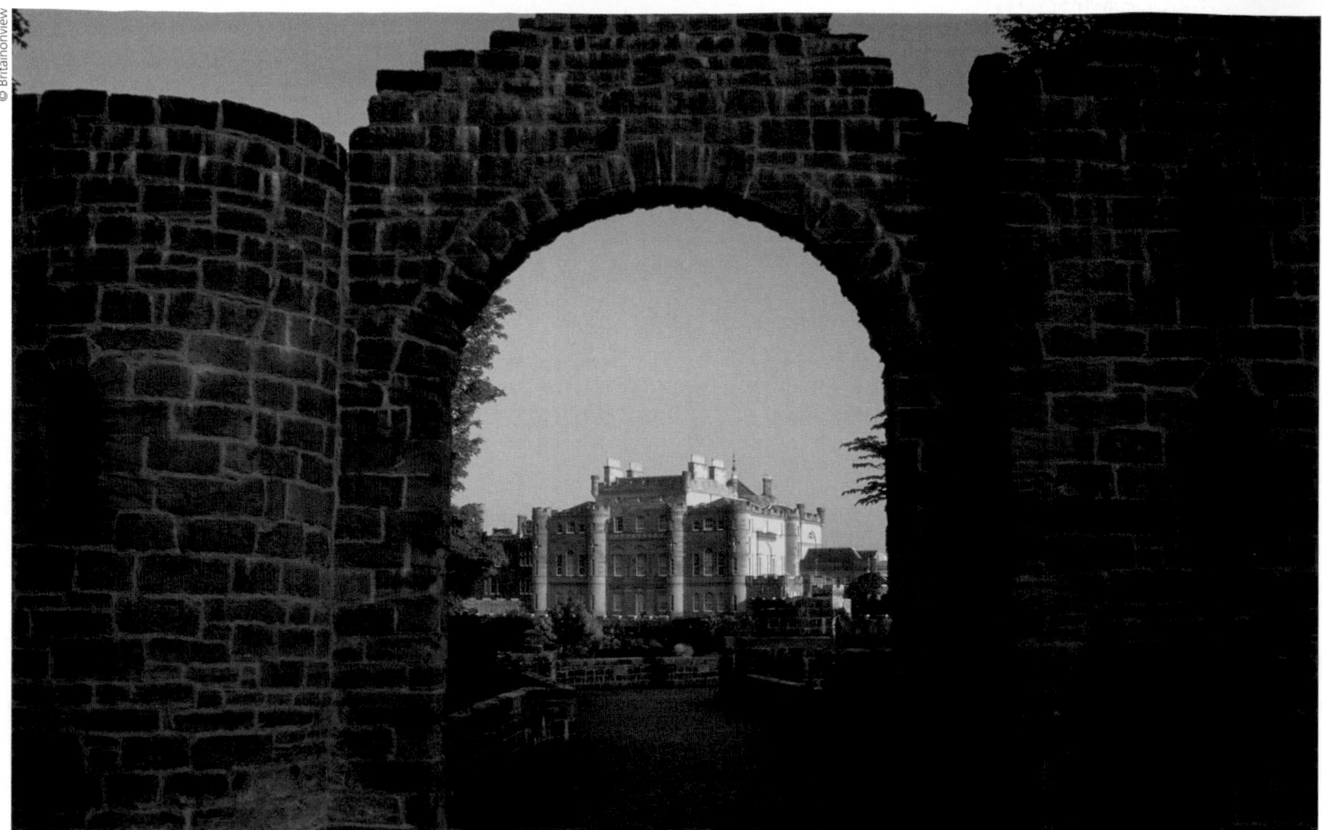

Culzean Castle

MACLELLAN'S CASTLE

Kirkcudbright, DG6 4JD

Tel: 01557 331856 **www.historic-scotland.gov.uk**

Owner: In the care of Historic Scotland **Contact:** Monument Manager

Named after Sir Thomas MacLellan of Bombie, a former provost of Kirkcudbright. This 16th century castle demonstrates the change from heavily defended tower houses to more domestic designs. The Great Hall's fireplace has a rare "laird's lug" through which the master of the house could eavesdrop on guests.

Location: MAP 9:G4, OS Ref. NX683 511. Centre of Kirkcudbright on the A711.

Open: 1 Apr–30 Sept: daily, 9.30am–5.30pm. Last ticket 30 mins before closing.

Admission: Adult £3.70, Child £2.20, Conc. £3.00 (2010 prices).

Closes for lunch. On leads. €

NEW ABBEY CORN MILL

New Abbey Village, DG2 8BU

Tel: 01387 850260 **www.historic-scotland.gov.uk**

Owner: Historic Scotland **Contact:** The Monument Manager

This carefully renovated 18th century water-powered oatmeal mill is in full working order. Regular demonstrations are given for visitors in the summer to show how oatmeal was produced.

Location: MAP 10:I3, OS Ref. NX962 663. 7m S of Dumfries on the A710.

Open: 1 Apr–30 Sept: daily, 9.30am–5.30pm. 1–31 Oct: daily, 9.30am–4.30pm. Nov-Mar: 9.30am–4.30pm, closed Thurs & Fri. Last ticket 30 mins before closing.

Admission: Adult £4.20, Child £2.50, Conc. £3.40 (2010 prices).

Closes for lunch. By arrangement. Limited. No coaches. €

RAMMERSCALES

Lockerbie, Dumfriesshire DG11 1LD

Tel: 01387 810229 **Fax:** 01387 810940 **E-mail:** malcolm@rammerscales.co.uk

www.rammerscales.co.uk

Owner/Contact: Mr M A Bell Macdonald

Georgian house, with extensive library and fine views over Annandale.

Location: MAP 10:I2, OS Ref. NY080 780. W side of B7020, 3m S of Lochmoben.

Open: Last week in Jul, 1st three weeks in Aug: daily (excluding Sat), 2–5pm. Bus tours by appointment.

Admission: Adult £5, Conc. £2.50.

SWEETHEART ABBEY

New Abbey Village, DG2 8BU

Tel: 01387 850397 **www.historic-scotland.gov.uk**

Owner: Historic Scotland **Contact:** The Monument Manager

Founded in 1273 by Lady Devorgilla of Galloway in memory of her husband John Balliol. On her death, she was buried next to her husband's embalmed heart and the monks named their abbey in memory of her. The graceful ruin nestles between Criffel Hill and the Solway Firth.

Location: MAP 10:I3, OS Ref. NX965 663. In New Abbey Village, on A710.

Open: 1 Apr–30 Sept: daily, 9.30am–5.30pm. Oct daily, 9.30am–4.30pm. 1 Nov–31 Mar 9.30am–4.30pm, closed Thurs & Fri. Last ticket 30 mins before closing.

Admission: Adult £3.00, Child £1.80, Conc. £2.50 (2010 prices).

Limited parking for coaches On leads. €

THREAVE CASTLE

Castle Douglas, DG7 1TJ

Tel: 07711 223101 **www.historic-scotland.gov.uk**

Owner: In the care of Historic Scotland **Contact:** Monument Manager

Built by Archibald the Grim in the late 14th century, Threave Castle was an early stronghold of the Black Douglases. Around its base is an artillery fortification built before 1455 when the castle was besieged by James II. Ring the bell and the custodian will come to ferry you over.

Location: MAP 9:H3, OS Ref. NX739 623. 3m W of Castle Douglas on the A75.

Open: 1 Apr–30 Sept: daily, 9.30am to last outward sailing at 4.30pm. Oct daily 9.30am to last outward sailing at 3.30pm.

Admission: Adult £4.20, Child £2.50, Conc. £3.40 (2010 prices). Price includes a ferry trip.

Limited parking for coaches.

WHITHORN PRIORY & MUSEUM

Whithorn, DG8 8PY

Tel: 01988 500700 **www.historic-scotland.gov.uk**

Owner: In the care of Historic Scotland **Contact:** Monument Manager

The site of the first Christian church in Scotland. Founded as 'Candida Casa' by St Ninian in the early 5th century it later became the cathedral church of Galloway. Visitors can now see the collection of early Christian carved crosses in a newly refurbished museum.

Location: MAP 9:F4, OS Ref. NX445 403. At Whithorn on the A746.

Open: 1 Apr–31 Oct: daily, 10.30am–5pm.

Admission: Adult £4.50, Child £2.25, Conc. £3.00 (2010 prices).

WCs Limited parking for coaches €

■ Owner
The Earl of Rosebery

■ Contact
The Administrator
Dalmeny House
South Queensferry
Edinburgh EH30 9TQ

Tel: 0131 331 1888
Fax: 0131 331 1788
E-mail: events@dalmeny.co.uk

■ Location
MAP 13:G8
OS Ref. NT167 779

From Edinburgh A90, B924, 7m N, A90 1/2m.

On south shore of Firth of Forth.

Bus: From St Andrew Square to Chapel Gate 1m from House.

Rail: Dalmeny station 3m.

Taxi: Hawes Cars 0131 331 1077.

■ Opening Times
Summer
29 May–26 July
Sun–Tue, 2–5pm.
Entry by Guided Tours only. Tours are 2.15pm & 3.30pm.

Winter
Open at other times by appointment only.

■ Admission
Summer

Adult	£6.00
Child (10–16yrs)	£4.00
OAP	£5.00
Student	£5.00
Groups (20+)	£5.00

DALMENY HOUSE

www.dalmeny.co.uk

Dalmeny House rejoices in one of the most beautiful and unspoilt settings in Great Britain, yet it is only seven miles from Scotland's capital, Edinburgh, fifteen minutes from Edinburgh airport and less than an hour's drive from Glasgow. It is an eminently suitable venue for group visits, business functions, and special events, including product launches. Outdoor activities, such as off-road driving, can be arranged.

Dalmeny House, the family home of the Earls of Rosebery for over 300 years, boasts superb collections of porcelain and tapestries, fine paintings by Gainsborough, Raeburn, Reynolds and Lawrence, together with the exquisite Mentmore Rothschild collection of 18th century French furniture. There is also the Napoleonic collection, assembled by the 5th Earl of Rosebery, Prime Minister, historian and owner of three Derby winners.

The Hall, Library and Dining Room will lend a memorable sense of occasion to corporate receptions, luncheons and dinners. A wide range of entertainment can also be provided, from a clarsach player to a floodlit pipe band Beating the Retreat.

Fashion shows, product launches, archery, clay pigeon shooting, shows, filming, background photography, and special events. Lectures on House, contents and family history. Helicopter landing area.

Conferences and functions, buffets, lunches, dinners.

WCs.

Obligatory. Special interest tours can be arranged outside normal opening hours.

60 cars, 3 coaches. Parking for functions in front of house.

In grounds.

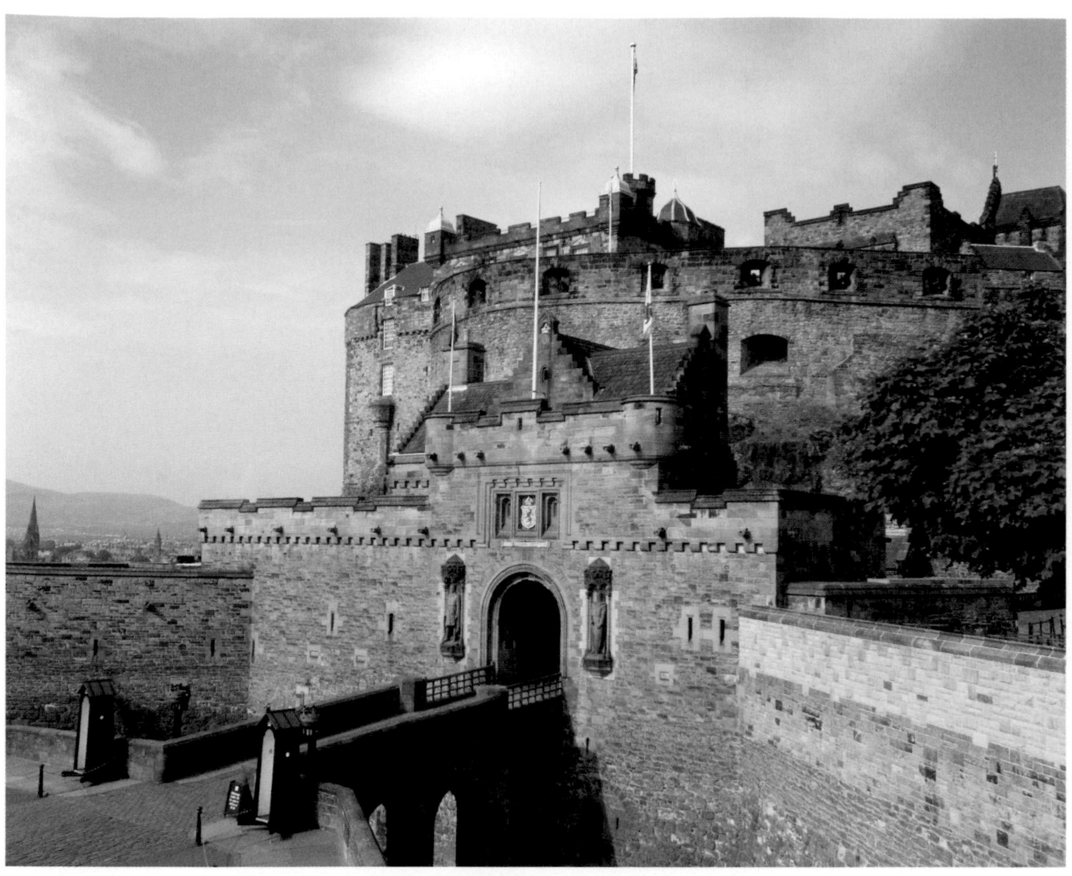

EDINBURGH CASTLE

www.edinburghcastle.gov.uk

Edinburgh Castle, built on the 340 million-year-old remains of an extinct volcano, dominates the skyline of Scotland's capital city just as it has dominated the country's history.

The 'stronghold of Eidyn' was first recorded before 600AD, and by the Middle Ages, it had become a mighty fortification and the favoured residence of Scotland's kings and queens. In 1140, it became the first recorded meeting place of the assembly now known as the Scottish Parliament. And in 1566, it was the birthplace of the only child of Mary Queen of Scots; a son who grew up to unite the crowns of Scotland and England.

The castle boasts a wealth of attractions including: The Honours of Scotland - the nation's crown jewels; The Stone of Destiny - the coronation stone of the ancient kings of Scots; The Great Hall, Laich Hall, King's Dining Room and St Margaret's Chapel - remarkable medieval rooms and buildings where royalty and great nobles wined, dined and worshipped; The Prisons of War Experience – showing what 18th century prison life was like for military prisoners held here; The National War Memorial - commemorating those who have died in conflict from World War I onwards; Mons Meg - a huge medieval siege gun; The One O'clock Gun - fired daily, except the Sabbath and certain holidays, as a time signal; The Dog Cemetery – the last resting place of regimental mascots and officers' pets.

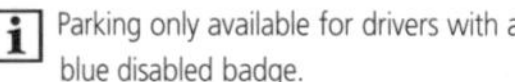

Parking only available for drivers with a blue disabled badge.

Private evening hire.

WCs.

In 8 languages.

€

Owner

Historic Scotland

Contact

Monument Manager
Castle Hill, Edinburgh
EH1 2NG

Tel: 0131 225 9846

Location

MAP 21
OS NT252 736

At the top of the Royal Mile in Edinburgh.
Rail: Edinburgh Waverley Station.

Opening Times

April–September: daily, 9.30am–6pm.

October–March, daily, 9.30am–5pm.

Last ticket 45 mins before closing.

Open New Year's Day 11am–5pm. Closed Christmas Day and Boxing Day.

Admission

Prices range from:

Adult	£12.00–£14.00
Child	£6.50–£7.50
Conc.	£9.20–11.20

(2010 prices)

Buy tickets on-line to beat the queues!

Visit www.edinburghcastle.gov.uk for details.

Owner

Hopetoun House Preservation Trust

Contact

Piers de Salis
Hopetoun House
South Queensferry
Edinburgh
West Lothian EH30 9SL

Tel: 0131 331 2451
Fax: 0131 319 1885
E-mail: marketing@hopetoun.co.uk

Location

MAP 13:F7
OS Ref. NT089 790

2½m W of Forth Road Bridge.

12m W of Edinburgh (25 mins. drive).

34m E of Glasgow (50 mins. drive).

Opening Times

Summer
Easter – End September: Daily, 10.30am–5pm. Last admission 4pm.

Winter
By appointment only for Groups (20+).

Admission

House & Grounds

Adult	£8.00
Child (5–16yrs)*	£4.25
Conc/Student	£7.00
Family (2+2)	£22.00
Additional Child	£3.00
Groups	£7.00

Grounds only

Adult	£3.70
Child (5–16yrs)*	£2.20
Conc/Student	£3.20
Family (2+2)	£10.00
Groups	£3.20

School Visits

Child	£5.50
Teachers	Free

*Under 5yrs Free.

Winter group rates on request.

Admission to Tearoom Free.

Special Events

November 25–27
Christmas Shopping Fair

Conference/Function

ROOM	SIZE	MAX CAPACITY
Ballroom	92' x 35'	300
Tapestry Rm	37' x 24'	100
Red Drawing Rm	44' x 24'	100
State Dining Rm	39' x 23'	20
Stables	92' x 22'	200

HOPETOUN HOUSE

www.hopetoun.co.uk

Hopetoun House is a unique gem of Europe's architectural heritage and undoubtedly 'Scotland's Finest Stately Home'. Situated on the shores of the Firth of Forth, it is one of the most splendid examples of the work of Scottish architects Sir William Bruce and William Adam. The interior of the house, with opulent gilding and classical motifs, reflects the aristocratic grandeur of the early 18th century, whilst its magnificent parkland has fine views across the Forth to the hills of Fife. The house is approached from the Royal Drive, used only by members of the Royal Family, notably King George IV in 1822 and Her Majesty Queen Elizabeth II in 1988.

Hopetoun is really two houses in one, the oldest part of the house was designed by Sir William Bruce and built between 1699 and 1707. It shows some of the finest examples in Scotland of carving, wainscotting and ceiling painting. In 1721 William Adam started enlarging the house by adding the magnificent façade, colonnades and grand State apartments which were the focus for social life and entertainment in the 18th century.

The house is set in 100 acres of rolling parkland including fine woodland walks, the red deer park, the spring garden with a profusion of wild flowers, and numerous picturesque picnic spots.

Hopetoun has been home of the Earls of Hopetoun, later created Marquesses of Linlithgow, since it was built in 1699 and in 1974 a charitable trust was created to preserve the house with its historic contents and surrounding landscape for the benefit of the public for all time.

Private functions, special events, antiques fairs, concerts, Scottish gala evenings, conferences, wedding ceremonies and receptions, grand piano, helicopter landing. No smoking or flash photography in house.

Receptions, gala dinners.

Partial.

Licensed.

By arrangement.

Close to the house for cars and coaches. Book if possible, allow 1–2hrs for visit (min).

Special tours of house and/or grounds for different age/ interest groups.

No dogs in house, on leads in grounds.

AMISFIELD MAINS

Nr Haddington, East Lothian EH41 3SA
Tel: 01875 870201 **Fax:** 01875 870620
Owner: Wemyss and March Estates Management Co Ltd **Contact:** M Andrews
Georgian farmhouse with gothic barn and cottage.
Location: MAP 14:I8, OS Ref. NT526 755. Between Haddington and East Linton on A199.
Open: Exterior only: By appointment, Wemyss and March Estates Office, Longniddry, East Lothian EH32 0PY.
Admission: Please contact for details.

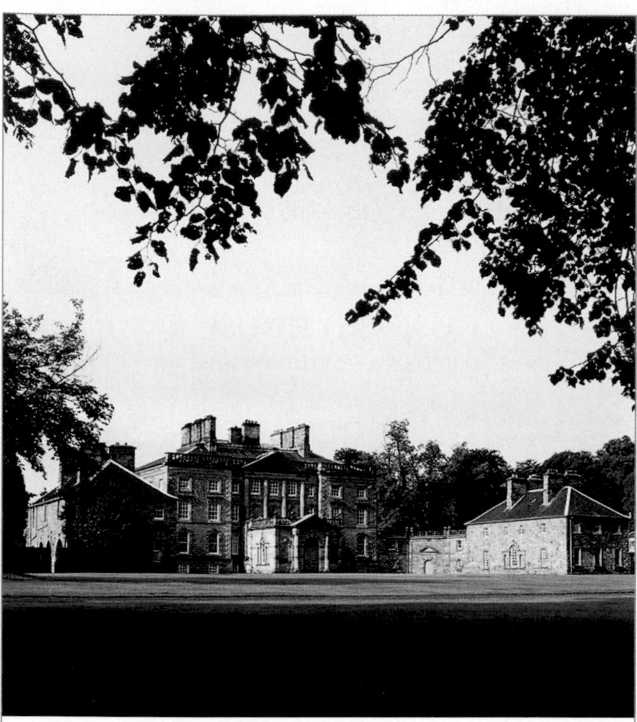

ARNISTON HOUSE

GOREBRIDGE, MIDLOTHIAN EH23 4RY

www.arniston-house.co.uk

Tel/Fax: 01875 830515 **E-mail:** info@arniston-house.co.uk
Owner: Mrs A Dundas-Bekker **Contact:** Mrs H Dundas
Magnificent William Adam mansion started in 1726. Fine plasterwork, Scottish portraiture, period furniture and other fascinating contents. Beautiful country setting beloved by Sir Walter Scott.
Location: MAP 13:H9, OS Ref. NT326 595. Off B6372, 1m from A7, Temple direction.
Open: May & Jun: Tue & Wed; 1 Jul–11 Sept: Tue, Wed & Sun, guided tours at 2pm & 3.30pm. Pre-arranged groups (10–50) accepted all year.
Admission: Adult £6, Child £3, Conc. £5.
No inside photography. Partial. WCs. Obligatory. Ample for cars. Limited for coaches. On leads.

BEANSTON

Nr Haddington, East Lothian EH41 3SB
Tel: 01875 870201 **Fax:** 01875 870620
Owner: Wemyss and March Estates Management Co Ltd **Contact:** M Andrews
Georgian farmhouse with Georgian orangery.
Location: MAP 14:I8, OS Ref. NT546 763. Between Haddington and East Linton on A199.
Open: Exterior only: By appointment, Wemyss and March Estates Office, Longniddry, East Lothian EH32 0PY.
Admission: Please contact for details.

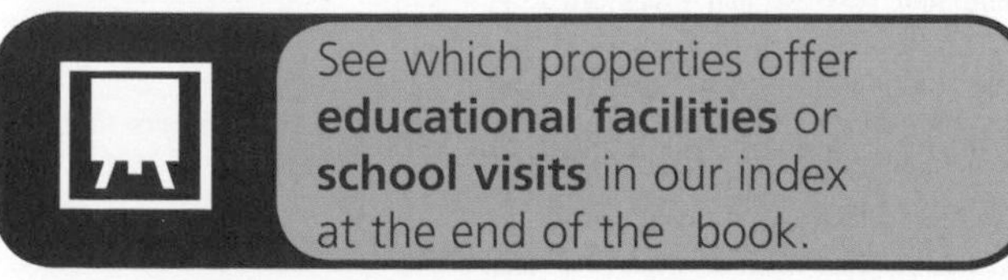

BLACKNESS CASTLE

Blackness EH49 7NH
Tel: 01506 834807 **www.historic-scotland.gov.uk**
Owner: Historic Scotland **Contact:** The Monument Manager
One of Scotland's most important strongholds. Built in the 14th century and strengthened in the 16th century as an artillery fortress, it has been a royal castle, prison armaments depot and film location for Hamlet. It stands on a promontory in the Firth of Forth.
Location: MAP 13:F7, OS Ref. NT055 803. 4m NE of Linlithgow on the Firth of Forth, off the A904.
Open: 1 Apr–30 Sept: daily, 9.30am–5.30pm, 1 Oct–31 Mar 9.30am–4.30pm. Nov–Mar, closed Thurs & Fri. Last ticket 30 mins before closing.
Admission: Adult £4.20, Child £2.50, Conc. £3.40 (2010 prices).
Limited for coaches. On leads. €

CRAIGMILLAR CASTLE

Edinburgh EH16 4SY
Tel: 0131 661 4445 **www.historic-scotland.gov.uk**
Owner: Historic Scotland **Contact:** The Monument Manager
Mary, Queen of Scots fled to Craigmillar after the murder of Rizzio. This well preserved medieval castle was built around an L-plan tower house. It also inlcudes a courtyard, gardens and a range of private rooms linked to the hall of the old tower.
Location: MAP 13:H8, OS Ref. NT286 708. 2½m SE of Edinburgh off the A7.
Open: 1 Apr–30 Sept: daily, 9.30am–5.30pm. 1 Oct–31 Mar 9.30am–4.30pm, Nov–Mar closed Thurs & Fri. Last ticket 30 mins before closing.
Admission: Adult £4.20, Child £2.50, Conc. £3.40 (2010 prices).
Picnic area. bicycle racks Partial. WCs. No coaches. On leads. €

CRICHTON CASTLE

Pathhead EH37 5XA
Tel: 01875 320017 **www.historic-scotland.gov.uk**
Owner: Historic Scotland **Contact:** The Monument Manager
Built as the lordly residence of the Crichtons, the castle later became home to the earls of Bothwell. This large and sophisticated castle has a spectacular Italian style façade added by the Earl of Bothwell in the 16th century. Mary Queen of Scots attended a wedding here.
Open: 1 Apr–30 Sept: daily, 9.30am–5.30pm. Last ticket 30 mins before closing.
Admission: Adult £3.70, Child £2.20, Conc. £3.00 (2010 prices).
Closes for lunch Limited for coaches. On lead. €

DALMENY HOUSE

See page 412 for full page entry.

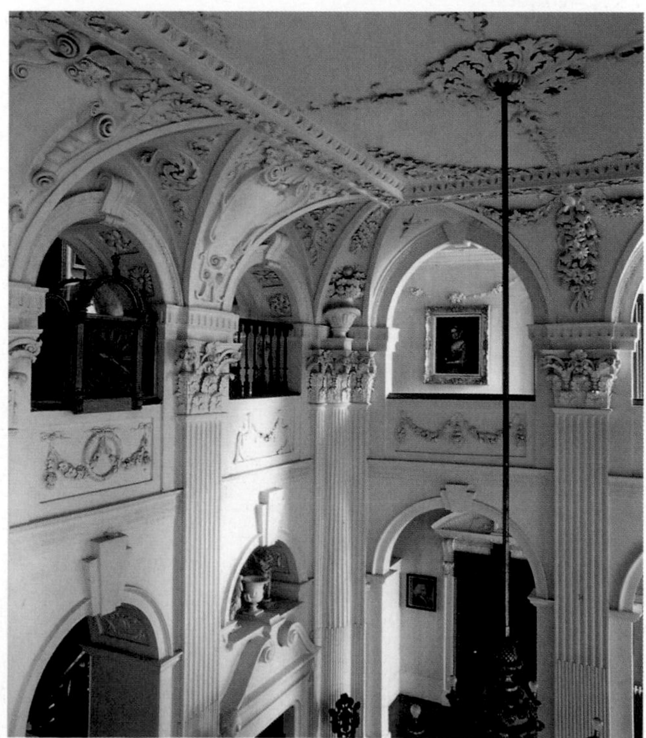
Arniston House

DIRLETON CASTLE & GARDENS

DIRLETON, EAST LOTHIAN EH39 5ER

www.historic-scotland.gov.uk

Tel: 01620 850330

Owner: In the care of Historic Scotland **Contact:** The Monument Manager

The oldest part of this romantic castle dates from the 13th century, when it was built by the De Vaux family. The renowned gardens, first laid out in the 16th century, now include a magnificent Arts and Crafts herbaceous border (the longest in the world) and a re-created Victorian Garden.

Location: MAP 14:I7, OS Ref. NT516 839. In Dirleton, 3m W of North Berwick on the A198.

Open: Apr–Sept: daily, 9.30am–5.30pm. Oct–Mar: daily, 9.30am–4.30pm. Last ticket 30 mins before closing.

Admission: Adult £4.70, Child £2.80, Conc. £3.80 (2010 prices).

Limited for coaches. Free if booked. On leads €

GOSFORD HOUSE

LONGNIDDRY, EAST LOTHIAN EH32 0PX

Tel: 01875 870201

Owner/Contact: The Earl of Wemyss

In 1791 the 7th Earl of Wemyss, aided by Robert Adam, built one of the grandest houses in Scotland, with a "paradise" of lakes and pleasure grounds in the "Beautiful style" in its lee. New wings, including the celebrated Marble Hall were added in 1891 by William Young. The house has a fine collection of paintings and furniture.

Location: MAP 14:I7, OS Ref. NT453 786. Off A198 2m NE of Longniddry.

Open: 4 Aug–15 Sep: Thurs–Sun, 1–4pm.

Admission: Adult £6, Child £1.

In grounds, on leads.

DUNGLASS COLLEGIATE CHURCH

Cockburnspath

Tel: 0131 668 8600 **www.historic-scotland.gov.uk**

Owner: Historic Scotland

Founded in 1450 for a college of canons by Sir Alexander Hume. A handsome crossshaped building with vaulted nave, choir and transepts.

Location: MAP 14:J8, OS67 NT766 718. 1m NW of Cockburnspath off the A1.

Open: All year.

Admission: Free.

EDINBURGH CASTLE

See page 413 for full page entry.

GEORGIAN HOUSE

7 Charlotte Square, Edinburgh EH2 4DR

Tel: 0131 243 9300

Owner: The National Trust for Scotland

A good example of the neo-classical 'palace front'. Three floors are furnished as they would have been around 1796. There is an array of china and silver, pictures and furniture, gadgets and utensils.

Location: MAP 21, OS Ref. NT247 738. In Charlotte Square.

GLADSTONE'S LAND

477b Lawnmarket, Royal Mile, Edinburgh EH1 2NT

Tel: 0131 243 9300

Owner: The National Trust for Scotland

Gladstone's Land was the home of a prosperous Edinburgh merchant in the 17th century. Decorated and furnished to give visitors an impression of life in Edinburgh's Old Town some 300 years ago.

Location: MAP 21, OS Ref. NT255 736. In Edinburgh's Royal Mile, near the castle.

HAILES CASTLE

East Linton

Tel: 0131 668 8600 **www.historic-scotland.gov.uk**

Owner: In the care of Historic Scotland

Beautifully-sited ruin incorporating a fortified manor of the 13th century. It was extended in the 14th and 15th centuries. There are two vaulted pit prisons.

Location: MAP 14:I8, OS Ref. NT575 758. 1.5 m SW of East Linton off the A1.

Open: All year.

Admission: Free.

No coaches. On leads.

HARELAW FARMHOUSE

Nr Longniddry, East Lothian EH32 0PH

Tel: 01875 870201 **Fax:** 01875 870620

Owner: Wemyss and March Estates Management Co Ltd **Contact:** M Andrews

Early 19th century 2-storey farmhouse built as an integral part of the steading. Dovecote over entrance arch.

Location: MAP 14:I8, OS Ref. NT450 766. Between Longniddry and Drem on B1377.

Open: Exteriors only: By appointment, Wemyss and March Estates Office, Longniddry, East Lothian EH32 0PY.

Admission: Please contact for details.

HOPETOUN HOUSE

See page 414 for full page entry.

HOUSE OF THE BINNS

Linlithgow, West Lothian EH49 7NA

Tel: 0131 243 9300

Owner: The National Trust for Scotland

17th century house, home of the Dalyells, one of Scotland's great families, since 1612.

Location: MAP 13:F7, OS Ref. NT051 786. Off A904, 15m W of Edinburgh. 3m E of Linlithgow.

LENNOXLOVE HOUSE

HADDINGTON, EAST LOTHIAN EH41 4NZ

www.lennoxlove.com

Tel: 01620 828614 **Fax:** 01620 825112 **Email:** ken-buchanan@lennoxlove.com
Owner: Lennoxlove House Ltd **Contact:** Kenneth Buchanan, General Manager
Service, Style and Seclusion. House to many of Scotland's finest artefacts, including the Death Mask of Mary, Queen of Scots, furniture and porcelain collected by the Douglas, Hamilton and Stewart families. Open to the public and available for events, the House lends itself perfectly to intimate parties offering 11 luxury suites for an overnight stay.
Location: MAP 14:I8, OS Ref. NT515 721. 18m E of Edinburgh, 1m S of Haddington.
Open: Easter-Oct: Weds, Thurs & Suns, 1.30-4pm. Guided Tours.

LINLITHGOW PALACE

LINLITHGOW, WEST LOTHIAN EH49 7AL

www.historic-scotland.gov.uk

Tel: 01506 842896
Owner: Historic Scotland **Contact:** The Monument Manager
The magnificent remains of a great royal palace set in a picturesque park, beside Linlithgow Loch. A favoured residence of the Stewart monarchs, James V and his daughter Mary, Queen of Scots were born here. Bonnie Prince Charlie stayed here during his bid to regain the British crown.
Location: MAP 13:F8, OS Ref. NT003 774. In the centre of Linlithgow off the M9.
Open: Apr–Sept: daily, 9.30am–5.30pm. Oct–Mar: daily, 9.30am–4.30pm. Last ticket 45 mins before closing.
Admission: Adult £5.20, Child £3.10, Conc. £4.20. (2010 prices).
Partial. WCs. Limited, Cars only. On leads €

NEWLISTON

Kirkliston, West Lothian EH29 9EB
Tel: 0131 333 3231
Owner/Contact: Mrs Caroline Maclachlan
Late Robert Adam house. 18th century designed landscape, rhododendrons, azaleas and water features. On Sundays there is a ride-on steam model railway from 2–5pm.
Location: MAP 13:G8, OS Ref. NT110 735. 8m W of Edinburgh, 3m S of Forth Road Bridge, off B800.
Open: 1 May–4 Jun: Wed–Sun, 2–6pm. Also by appointment.
Admission: Adult £3, Conc. £2.
In grounds, on leads.

PALACE OF HOLYROODHOUSE

Edinburgh EH8 8DX
Tel: 0131 556 5100 **E-mail:** bookinginfo@royalcollection.org.uk
Owner: Official Residence of Her Majesty The Queen
Contact: Ticket Sales & Information Office
The Palace of Holyroodhouse, the official residence in Scotland of Her Majesty The Queen, stands at the end of Edinburgh's Royal Mile against the spectacular backdrop of Arthur's Seat. The Royal Apartments are used by The Queen for State ceremonies and official entertaining. They are finely decorated with magnificent works of art from the Royal Collection.
Location: MAP 21, OS Ref. NT269 739. Central Edinburgh, end of Royal Mile.
Open: Contact information office.
Admission: Contact information office.

PRESTON MILL

East Linton, East Lothian EH40 3DS
Tel: 0131 243 9300
Owner: The National Trust for Scotland **Contact:** Property Manager
For centuries there has been a mill on this site and the present one operated commercially until 1957.
Location: MAP 14:I7, OS Ref. NT590 770. Off the A1, in East Linton, 23m E of Edinburgh.

Palace of Holyrood House

RED ROW

Aberlady, East Lothian
Tel: 01875 870201 **Fax:** 01875 870620
Owner: Wemyss & March Estates Management Co Ltd **Contact:** M Andrews
Terraced Cottages.
Location: MAP 14:I7, OS Ref. NT464 798. Main Street, Aberlady, East Lothian.
Open: Exterior only. By appointment, Wemyss & March Estates Office, Longniddry, East Lothian EH32 0PY.
Admission: Please contact for details.

ROYAL BOTANIC GARDEN EDINBURGH

20A Inverleith Row, Edinburgh EH3 5LR
Tel: 0131 552 7171 **Fax:** 0131 248 2901 **E-mail:** info@rbge.org.uk
Contact: Press Office
Scotland's premier garden. Discover the wonders of the plant kingdom in over 70 acres of beautifully landscaped grounds.
Location: MAP 21, OS Ref. NT249 751. Off A902, 1m N of city centre.
Open: Daily (except 25 Dec & 1 Jan): open 10am, closing: Nov–Feb: 4pm; Mar & Oct: 6pm; Apr–Sept: 7pm.
Admission: Free, with an admission charge on the Glasshouses.

THE ROYAL YACHT BRITANNIA

Ocean Terminal, Leith, Edinburgh EH6 6JJ
Tel: 0131 555 5566 **Fax:** 0131 555 8835
Email: enquiries@tryb.co.uk **www.royalyachtbritannia.co.uk**
Owners: The Royal Yacht Britannia Trust **Contact:** Julia Stephenson
Britain's last Royal Yacht; home to the Royal Family from 1953 to 1997. Learn about *Britannia's* history prior to boarding in the fascinating Visitor Centre. Enjoy a complimentary audio tour of 5 decks, available in 21 languages. Discover the heart and soul of this very special royal residence.
Location: MAP 13:H7, OS Ref. NT264 769. 2 miles from Edinburgh city centre, in historic port of Leith.
Open: Year round – 10.00am to last admission 3.30pm. Extended hours in summer.
Admission: Adult £11.50, Senior £9.75, Child £7.50, Group discount for 15 or more.
WCs. Licensed Guide dogs only.

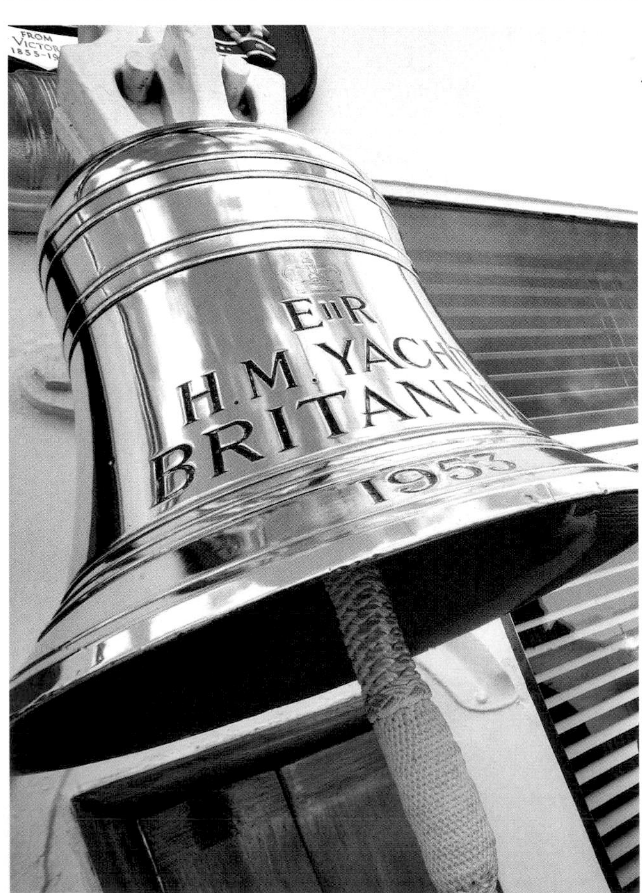

© The Royal Yacht Britannia

The Royal Yacht Britannia

ST MARY'S EPISCOPAL CATHEDRAL

Palmerston Place, Edinburgh EH12 5AW
Tel: 0131 225 6293 **Fax:** 0131 225 3181
Contact: Cathedral Secretary
Neo-gothic grandeur in the classical new town. Designed by G Gilbert Scott.
Location: MAP 21, OS Ref. NT241 735. 1/2 m W of west end of Princes Street.
Open: Mon–Fri, 7.30am–6pm; Sat & Sun, 7.30am–5pm. Sun services: 8am, 10.30am & 3.30pm. Services: Weekdays, 7.30am, 1.05pm & 5.30pm; Thurs, 11.30am, Sat, 7.30am.
Admission: Free.

SCOTTISH NATIONAL PORTRAIT GALLERY

1 Queen Street, Edinburgh EH2 1JD
Tel: 0131 624 6200
Unique visual history of Scotland.
Location: MAP 21, OS Ref. NT256 742. At E end of Queen Street, 300yds N of Princes Street.
Open: All year to permanent collection: daily, 10am–5pm (Thurs closes 7pm).
Closed 25 & 26 Dec. Open 1 Jan, 12 noon–5pm.
Admission: Free. (There may be a charge for special exhibitions.)

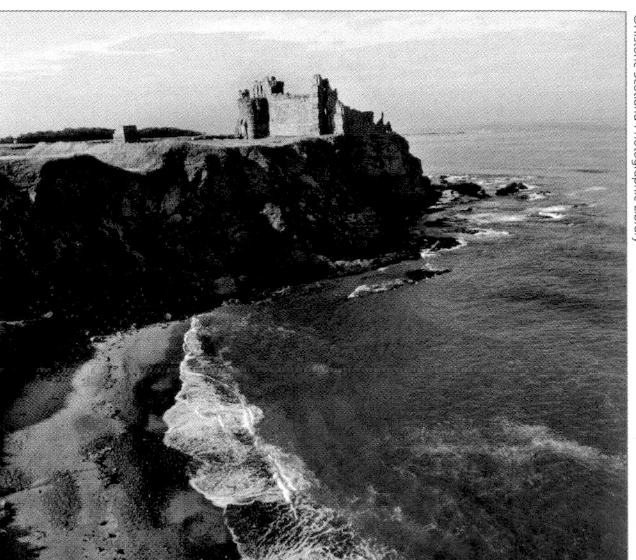
©Historic Scotland Photographic Library

TANTALLON CASTLE

BY NORTH BERWICK, EAST LOTHIAN EH39 5PN

www.historic-scotland.gov.uk

Tel: 01620 892727
Owner: In the care of Historic Scotland **Contact:** The Monument Manager
Set atop cliffs, looking out to the Bass Rock, this formidable castle was a stronghold of the powerful Douglas family. The castle has earthwork defences and a massive 80-foot high 14th century curtain wall and has endured frequent sieges.
Location: MAP 14:I7, OS67 NT595 850. 3m E of North Berwick off the A198.
Open: 1 Apr–30 Sept: daily, 9.30am–5.30pm. 1–31 Oct, 9.30am–4.30pm. 1 Nov–31 Mar 9.30am–4.30pm, closed Thurs & Fri. Last ticket 30 mins before closing.
Admission: Adult £4.70, Child £2.80, Conc. £3.80. (2010 prices).
Limited for coaches. Booked school visits free. On leads. €

TRINITY HOUSE MARITIME MUSEUM

99 Kirkgate, Edinburgh EH6 6BJ
Tel: 0131 554 3289 **www.historic-scotland.gov.uk**
Owner: Historic Scotland **Contact:** The Monument Manager
This fine Georgian mansion contains a treasure trove of maritime artefacts including paintings by Henry Raeburn. The site has been home to the Incorporation of Masters and Mariners since the Middle Ages. Many of the artefacts were donated by Leith sailors who travelled the world in centuries gone by.
Location: MAP 13:G8, OS Ref. NT269 760, 99 Kirkgate, Leith, Edinburgh.
Open: Pre-booked visits Tues-Fri. Call 0131 554 3289 to book (max 10-15 people per tour). Guided tours available on Saturdays at 1pm, 2pm and 3pm.
Admission: Free, donations welcome.
By arrangement. Max 10–15 people.

Hopetoun House

BURRELL COLLECTION

Pollok Country Park, 2060 Pollokshaws Road, Glasgow G43 1AT

Tel: 0141 287 2550 **Fax:** 0141 287 2597

Owner: Glasgow Museums

An internationally renowned, outstanding collection of art.

Location: MAP 13:C8, OS Ref. NS555 622. Glasgow 15 min drive.

Open: All year: Mon–Thur & Sats, 10am–5pm, Fri & Sun, 11am–5pm. Closed 25/26 Dec, 31 Dec (pm) & 1/2 Jan.

Admission: Free. Small charge may apply for temporary exhibitions.

COREHOUSE

Lanark, ML11 9TQ

Tel: 01555 663126

Owner: Colonel D A S Cranstoun of that Ilk TD **Contact:** Estate Office

Designed by Sir Edward Blore and built in the 1820s, Corehouse is a pioneering example of the Tudor Architectural Revival in Scotland.

Location: MAP 13:E9, OS Ref. NS882 416. On S bank of the Clyde above the village of Kirkfieldbank.

Open: 1–21 May & 10–21 Sept: Sat-Wed. Guided tours: weekdays: 1 & 2pm, weekends: 2 & 3pm. Closed Thurs & Fri.

Admission: Adult £6, Child (under 14yrs)/OAP £3.

Partial. Obligatory. Limited. In grounds.

CRAIGNETHAN CASTLE

Lanark, Strathclyde, ML11 9PL

Tel: 01555 860364 **www.historic-scotland.gov.uk**

Owner: Historic Scotland **Contact:** The Monument Manager

In a picturesque setting overlooking the River Nethan and defended by a wide and deep ditch. The castle's defences include an unusual caponier, a stone vaulted artillery chamber, unique in Britain.

Location: MAP 13:E9, OS Ref. NS815 463. 5.5m WNW of Lanark off the A72.

Open: 1 Apr–30 Sept: daily, 9.30am–5.30pm. 1 Oct–31 Mar 9.30am–4.30pm, Nov–Mar weekends only. Last ticket 30 mins before closing time.

Admission: Adult £3.70, Child £2.20, Conc. £3.00 (2010 prices).

Picnic area. Bicycle Rack. No coaches. €

© Britainonview

Tenement House

GLASGOW CATHEDRAL

Castle Street, Glasgow, G4 0QZ

Tel: 0141 552 6891 **www.historic-scotland.gov.uk**

Owner: Historic Scotland **Contact:** The Monument Manager

The only Scottish mainland medieval cathedral to have survived the Reformation complete. Built over the tomb of St Kentigern. Notable features in this splendid building are the elaborately vaulted crypt, the stone screen of the early 15th century and the unfinished Blackadder Aisle.

Location: MAP 13:D8, OS Ref. NS603 656. In Glasgow, off the M8, J15 next to the Royal Infirmary.

Open: 1 Apr–30 Sept: Mon–Sat, 9.30am–5.30pm, Sun 1–5pm. 1 Oct–31 Mar: Mon–Sat, 9.30am–4.30pm, Sun 1–4.30pm. Last entry 45 mins before closing.

Admission: Free.

MOTHERWELL HERITAGE CENTRE

High Road, Motherwell ML1 3HU

Tel: 01698 251000

Owner: North Lanarkshire Council **Contact:** The Manager

VisitScotland 4-star attraction. Technopolois multi-media display tells the story of the area from the Romans, through the days of heavy industry, to the present time. Exhibition gallery, shop and tower viewing platform. A local studies and family history research room has census, newspaper and other databases on-line. Staff assistance available.

Location: MAP 13:E9, OS Ref. NS750 570. In High Road, 200yds N of A723 (Hamilton Road).

Open: All year, 10am–5pm. Sun, 12 noon–5pm (closed 25/26 Dec & 1/2 Jan and every Mon & Tues).

Admission: Free.

NEW LANARK WORLD HERITAGE SITE

New Lanark Mills, Lanark, S Lanarkshire ML11 9DB

Tel: 01555 661345 **Fax:** 01555 665738 **E-mail:** visit@newlanark.org

www.newlanark.org

Owner: New Lanark Trust **Contact:** Trust Office

Surrounded by native woodlands and close to the famous Falls of Clyde, this cotton mill village was founded in 1785 and became famous as the site of Robert Owen's radical reforms. Now beautifully restored as both a living community and attraction, the fascinating history of the village is interpreted in an award-winning Visitor Centre. There is a Roof Garden and Viewing Platform giving panoramic views of the historic village and surrounding woodland. Accommodation is available in the New Lanark Mill Hotel and Waterhouses, a stunning conversion from an original 18th century mill. New Lanark is now a World Heritage Site.

Location: MAP 13:E9, OS Ref. NS880 426. 1m S of Lanark.

Open: All year: daily, 10.00am–5pm (11am–5pm Oct–March). Closed 25 Dec & 1 Jan.

Admission: Visitor Centre: Adult £6.95, Child/Conc. £5.95. Groups: 1 free/10 booked.

Conference facilities. Partial. WC. Visitor Centre wheelchair friendly. By arrangement. 5 min walk. In grounds, on leads.

NEWARK CASTLE

Port Glasgow, Strathclyde, PA14 5NH

Tel: 01475 741858 **www.historic-scotland.gov.uk**

Owner: Historic Scotland **Contact:** The Monument Manager

The oldest part of the castle is a tower built soon after 1478 with a detached gatehouse, by George Maxwell. The main part was added in 1597–99 in a most elegant style. Enlarged in the 16th century by his descendent, the wicked Patrick Maxwell who murdered two of his neighbours.

Location: MAP 13:B8, OS Ref. NS329 744. In Port Glasgow on the A8 at Newark roundabout.

Open: 1 Apr–30 Sept: daily, 9.30am–5.30pm. Last ticket 30 mins before closing.

Admission: Adult £3.70, Child £2.20, Conc. £3.00 (2010 prices).

Closes for lunch. Limited for coaches. €

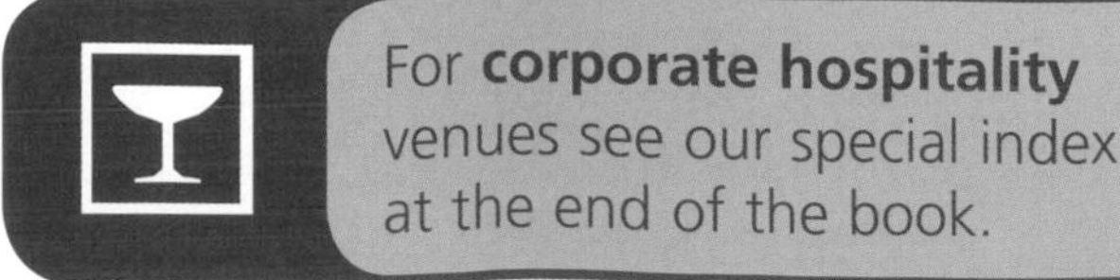

New Lanark World Heritage Site

POLLOK HOUSE

Pollok Country Park, Pollokshaws Road, Glasgow G43 1AT

Tel: 0131 243 9300

Owner: The National Trust for Scotland

The house contains an internationally famed collection of paintings as well as porcelain and furnishings appropriate to an Edwardian house.

Location: MAP 13:C8, OS Ref. NS550 616. In Pollok Country Park, off M77/J1, follow signs for Burrell Collection.

ST MARY'S EPISCOPAL CATHEDRAL

300 Great Western Road, Glasgow G4 9JB

Tel: 0141 339 6691 **Fax:** 0141 334 5669 **Email:** office@thecathedral.org.uk

Contact: The Office

Newly restored, fine Gothic Revival church by Sir George Gilbert Scott, with outstanding contemporary murals by Gwyneth Leech. Regular concerts and exhibitions.

Location: MAP 13:D8, OS Ref. NS578 669. ¼m after the Dumbarton A82 exit from M8 motorway.

Open: All year. Mon–Fri, 9.15–10am. Thur, 5.30–7.30pm. Sat, 9.30–10am.
Sun services: 8.30am, 10.30am & 6.30pm. Please telephone in advance to confirm up to date opening times.

Admission: Free

SUMMERLEE INDUSTRIAL MUSEUM

Heritage Way, Coatbridge, North Lanarkshire ML5 1QD

Tel: 01236 638460

Owner: North Lanarkshire Council **Contact:** The Manager

Summerlee, the Scottish museum of industrial life, is a VisitScotland 4-star attraction. It is based around the site of the former Summerlee Ironworks and a branch of the Monklands Canal. The museum has recently reopened after a major Heritage Lottery Fund supported redevelopment. The main exhibition hall has been cleared and rebuilt with new displays, interactive features, children's activities and new shop and café.

Location: MAP 13:D8, OS Ref. NS729 655. 600yds NW of Coatbridge town centre.

Open: All year 10am–5pm (Oct–Mar to 4pm). Closed 25/26 Dec & 1/2 Jan.

TENEMENT HOUSE

145 Buccleuch Street, Glasgow G3 6QN

Tel: 0131 243 9300

Owner: The National Trust for Scotland

A typical Victorian tenement flat of 1892, and time capsule of the first half of the 20th century.

Location: MAP 13:D8, OS Ref. NS583 662. Garnethill (three streets N of Sauchiehall Street, near Charing Cross), Glasgow.

Owner
Blair Charitable Trust

Contact
Administration Office
Blair Castle
Blair Atholl
Pitlochry
Perthshire PH18 5TL

Tel: 01796 481207
Fax: 01796 481487
E-mail: bookings@blair-castle.co.uk

Location
MAP 13:E3
OS Ref. NN880 660

Car: Just off the main Perth/Inverness road (A9), 35 miles north of Perth. Approximately 90 minutes drive from Edinburgh and Glasgow.

Bus: Elizabeth Yule Service 87 (end March to early Nov), or Stagecoach 83 service from Perth.

Rail: Blair Atholl Station 1m. Serviced by main London Euston to Inverness line.

Opening Times
Summer:
1 April–28 October, Daily, 9.30am–5.30pm (Last admission to castle tour 4.30pm)

Winter:
1 November–31 March, Tues & Sats, 9.30am–2.30pm (last admission 1.30pm).

Limited opening between Christmas & New Year. Please check website for details.

Admission
House & Grounds

Adult	£9.25
Child (5–16yrs)	£5.65
Senior	£7.95
Student (with ID)	£7.95
Family	£25.00
Disabled	£2.85

Groups* (12+) (Please book)

Adult	£7.00
Child(5–16yrs)	£5.15
Primary School	£4.05
Senior/Student	£7.00
Disabled	£2.55

Grounds only
(inc. Restaurant, Gift Shop & WC)

Adult	£5.10
Child (5–16yrs)	£2.40
Senior/Student	£5.10
Family	£12.50
Disabled	Free
Scooter Hire	£3.85

Groups* (12+) (Please book)

Adult	£4.20
Child (5–16yrs)	£2.30
Primary School	£2.30
Senior/Student	£4.20
Disabled	Free

*Group rates only apply when all tickets are bought by the Driver, Courier or Group leader at one time. Advance booking, particulary when guides are requested, is strongly recommended.

All prices are inclusive of VAT at the current rate.

Conference/Function

ROOM	SIZE	MAX CAPACITY
Ballroom	88' x 36'	400 or 220 dining
State Dining Room	36' x 26'	150 or 16–50 dining
Banvie Hall	55' x 32'	150

BLAIR CASTLE

www.blair-castle.co.uk

Nestling like a white jewel in the dramatic Highland Perthshire landscape, Blair Castle has a centuries old history as a strategic stronghold at the gateway to the Grampians and the route north to Inverness.

Famous as the last castle to be held under siege in 1746, Blair Castle is the ancient seat of the Dukes and Earls of Atholl and the home of the Atholl Highlanders, Europe's only remaining private army. More than 30 rooms are on display, full of treasures and alive with the characters and personalities of their former occupants. Highlights of the visit include: the magnificent ballroom bedecked with 175 pairs of antlers; the superb China Room featuring more than 1700 individual pieces and an ornamental Victorian armoury housing a targe used at the Battle of Culloden. There are also paintings by Sir Edwin Landseer, fine mortlake tapestries and plasterwork by Thomas Clayton.

Gardens & Grounds

Blair Castle is at the hub of a breath-taking historic landscape most of which was laid out in the 18th century and features a beautiful 9 acre walled garden with landscaped ponds, a peaceful wooded grove home to some of the countries tallest trees, a ruined Celtic kirk; a red deer park and a whimsical gothic folly. Children will also enjoy the castle's woodland adventure playground.

- Photography allowed in Ballroom only.
- Licensed Gift Shop.
- Civil and religious weddings may be held in the castle and receptions for up to 220 guests can be held in the ballroom. Banquets, dinners and private functions are welcome.
- Partial, WCs.
- Licensed.
- Licensed.
- For group bookings, guides may be available in English and other languages. Tour time 50mins. Illustrated guide books (English, German, French and Italian) available. Special interest tours also available.
- 200 cars, 20 coaches. Coach drivers/couriers free, plus meal and shop voucher and information pack.
- Nature walks, deer park, ranger service, pony trekking and children's woodland adventure playground.
- Guide dogs only.
- Civil Wedding Licence.
- Regular winter opening.
- Atholl Highlanders' Parade Saturday 28 May, Highland Games Sunday 29 May, Blair Castle International Horse Trials and Country Fair 18-21 August, Nov–Dec Christmas Castle, Feb Snowdrop Festival.

■ **Owner**

Grimsthorpe & Drummond Castle Trust
A registered charity (SCO39364) (507478)

■ **Contact**

The Caretaker
Drummond Castle Gardens
Muthill
Crieff
Perthshire PH7 4HZ

Tel: 01764 681433
Fax: 01764 681642
E-mail: thegardens@drummondcastle.sol.co.uk

■ **Location**

MAP 13:E5
OS Ref. NN844 181

2m S of Crieff off the A822.

■ **Opening Times**

Easter weekend,
1 May–31 October:
Daily, 1–6pm.
Last admission 5pm.

■ **Admission**

Adult	£5.00
Child	£2.00
Conc.	£4.00

Groups (20+)
10% discount.

DRUMMOND CASTLE GARDENS

www.drummondcastlegardens.co.uk

Scotland's most important formal gardens, among the finest in Europe. A mile of beech-lined avenue leads to a formidable ridge top tower house. The magnificent Italianate parterre is revealed from a viewpoint at the top of the terrace, celebrating the saltaire and family heraldry that surrounds the famous multiplex sundial by John Milne, master mason to Charles I. First laid out in the early 17th century by John Drummond, 2nd Earl of Perth and renewed in the early 1950s by Phyllis Astor, Countess of Ancaster.

The gardens contain ancient yew hedges and two copper beech trees planted by Queen Victoria during her visit in 1842. Shrubberies are planted with many varieties of maple and other individual ornamental trees including purple-leaf oaks, whitebeam, weeping birch and a tulip tree, *Liriodendron tulipifera*. The tranquility of the gardens makes them the perfect setting to stroll amongst the well-manicured plantings or sit and absorb the atmosphere of this special place.

Partial. WCS.

By arrangement.

Limited parking available for coaches.

On leads.

■ Owner

The Earl of Strathmore & Kinghorne

■ Contact

General Manager
Estates Office
Glamis By Forfar
Angus DD8 1RJ

Tel: 01307 840393
Fax: 01307 840733
E-mail: enquiries@glamis-castle.co.uk

■ Location

MAP 13:H4
OS Ref. NO386 480

Situated just off the A94. From Edinburgh M90, A94, 81miles. From Glasgow M90, A94, 93miles. From Aberdeen A90, A94, 50 miles.

Air: Nearest: Dundee: Aberdeen: Edinburgh: Glasgow.

Bus: www.stagecoachbus.com Bus no. 20 from Seagate Station Dundee and no. 124 from Forfar to Glamis.

Ferry: Nearest Ferry Port, Rosyth.

Rail: Dundee Station 12m.

Taxi: K Cabs 01575 573744.

■ Opening Times

2 April–End December, daily, 10am–6pm. Last admission 4.30pm. (November–December, 10.30am–4.30pm. Last admission 3pm)

Extended opening July–August.

Groups & Private Tours are welcome in January–March, by prior arrangement.

■ Admission

Castle & Grounds:	
Adult	£9.50
Child (5–16yrs)	£7.00
Concession	£8.75
Grounds, Shops, Restaurant and Exhibition only:	
Adult	£5.50
Child (5–16yrs)	£3.50
Concession	£5.00
Groups (20+)	
Adult	£8.50
Child (5–16yrs)	£6.00
Senior/Student	£7.75

Drivers and group leaders are admitted free of charge and issued with meal/refreshment voucher.

■ Special Events

Special Events in 2011: Easter at Glamis - April

Scottish Transport Extravaganza - July

A Grand Scottish Prom - August

Scotland's Countryside Festival - September

Halloween at Glamis - October

Winter programme of events - November - December

www.glamis-castle.co.uk

Conference/Function

ROOM	SIZE	MAX CAPACITY
Dining Room	84 sq.m	90
Restaurant	140 sq.m	100
16th Century Kitchens		40

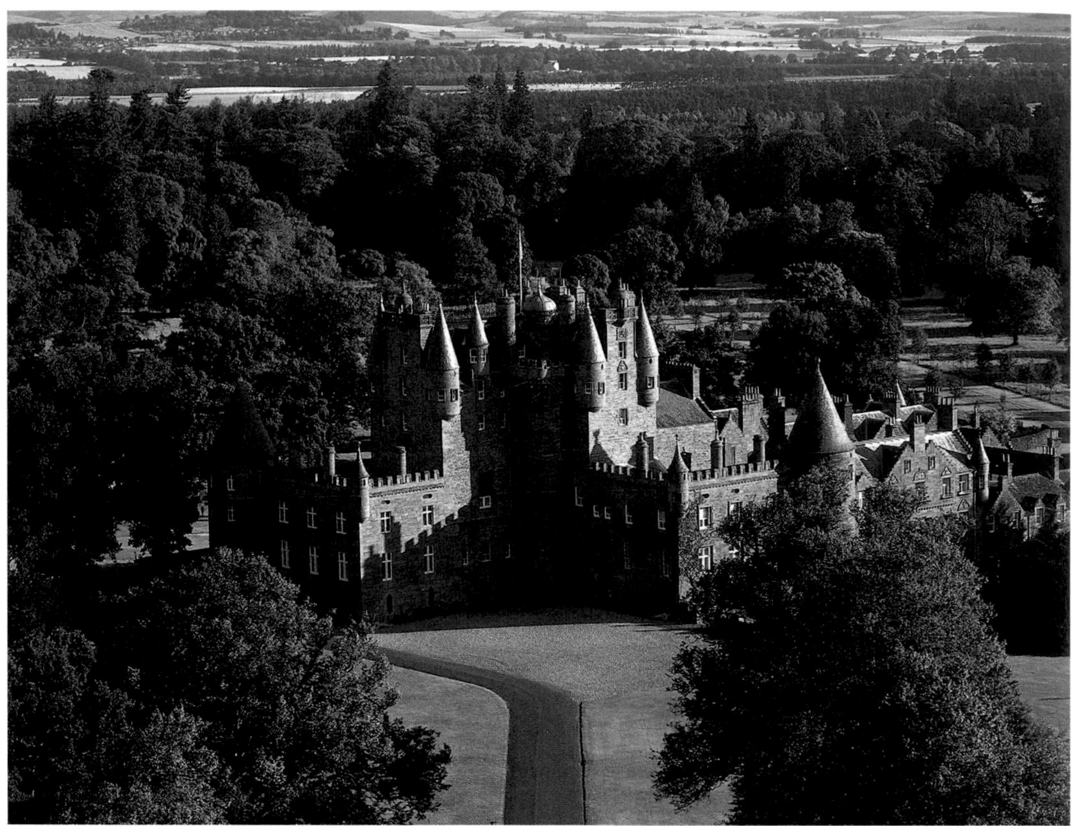

GLAMIS CASTLE

www.glamis-castle.co.uk

Glamis Castle is the family home of the Earls of Strathmore and Kinghorne and has been a royal residence since 1372. It was the childhood home of Her Majesty Queen Elizabeth The Queen Mother, the birthplace of Her Royal Highness The Princess Margaret and the legendary setting of Shakespeare's play Macbeth. Although the Castle is open to visitors it remains a family home, lived in and loved by the Strathmore family. The Castle, a five-storey 'L' shaped tower block, was originally a royal hunting lodge. It was remodelled in the 17th century and is built of pink sandstone. It contains the Great Hall, with its magnificent plasterwork ceiling dated 1621, a beautiful family Chapel constructed inside the Castle in 1688, an 18th century billiard room housing what is left of the extensive library once at Glamis, a 19th century dining room containing family portraits and the Royal Apartments which have been used by Her Majesty Queen Elizabeth The Queen Mother. The Castle stands in an extensive park, landscaped towards the end of the 18th century, and contains the beautiful Italian Garden and the Pinetum which reflect the peace and serenity of the Castle and grounds.

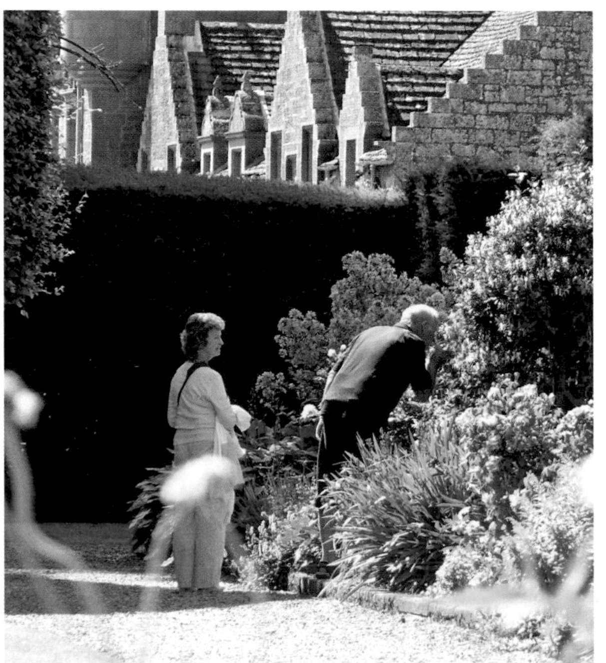

Weddings, fashion shoots, archery, equestrian events, shows, rallies, filming, product launches, highland games, Royal memorials, Christmas programme of events Nov–Dec. Photography allowed during special events and private tours.

Shopping pavilion.

The State Rooms are available for grand dinners, lunches and wedding receptions.

WCs

Licensed

All visits are guided, tour time 50–60 mins. Tours leave frequently throughout the day. Tours in French, German, Italian and Spanish by appointment at no additional cost. Three exhibitions.

500 cars and 20 coaches 200 yds from castle. Coach drivers and couriers admitted free and receive meal/refreshment voucher.

One teacher free for every 10 children. Nature trail, family exhibition rooms, dolls' house, play park. Glamis Heritage Education Centre in Glamis village. Children's guide book. Garden Trail.

On leads.

By appointment Jan–Mar.

€

SCONE PALACE & GROUNDS

www.scone-palace.co.uk

Scone Palace is the home of the Earl and Countess of Mansfield and is built on the site of an ancient abbey. 1500 years ago it was the capital of the Pictish kingdom and the centre of the ancient Celtic church. In the intervening years, it has been the seat of parliaments and crowning place of Scottish kings, including Macbeth, Robert the Bruce and Charles II. The State Rooms house a superb collection of objets d'art, including seventeenth and eighteenth century ivories, mostly collected by the fourth Earl of Mansfield. Notable works of art are also on display, including paintings by Sir David Wilkie, Sir Joshua Reynolds, and Johann Zoffany. The Library boasts one of Scotland's finest collections of porcelain, including Sèvres, Ludwigsburg and Meissen, whilst the unique 'Vernis Martin' papier mâché may be viewed in the Long Gallery. An audio visual presentation explores centuries of Scone's history.

Gardens

The grounds of the Palace house magnificent collections of shrubs, with woodland walks through the Wild Garden containing David Douglas' original fir and the unique Murray Star Maze. A pavilion dedicated to Douglas and other Scottish plant hunters has recently been constructed. A Wildlife Trail way-marked by cartoon character 'Cyril the Squirrel' encourages younger visitors to become nature detectives. There are Highland cattle and peacocks to admire and an adventure play area for children. The 100 acres of mature Policy Parks, flanked by the River Tay, are available for a variety of events, including corporate and private entertaining.

- Receptions, fashion shows, war games, archery, clay pigeon shooting, equestrian events, garden parties, shows, rallies, filming, shooting, fishing, floodlit tattoos, product launches, highland games, parkland, cricket pitch, helicopter landing, croquet, racecourse, polo field, firework displays, adventure playground. No photography in state rooms.
- Gift shop & food shop.
- Grand dinners in state rooms (inc. buffets & cocktail parties).
- All state rooms on one level, accessible by wheelchair, as are restaurants.
- Licensed. Teas, Lunches & Dinners, can be booked (menus upon request). Special rates for groups
- Available for private hire.
- By Arrangement. Guides in each room. Private tours in French, German, Italian and English by appointment only.
- 300 cars and 15 coaches (coaches – booking preferable). Couriers and coach drivers free meal and admittance.
- Welcome.
- By Appointment.
- Please telephone or see website for details.

Owner

The Earl of Mansfield

Contact

The Administrator
Scone Palace
Perth PH2 6BD

Tel: 01738 552300
Fax: 01738 552588
E-mail: visits@scone-palace.co.uk

Location

MAP 13:G5
OS Ref. NO114 266

From Edinburgh Forth Bridge M90, A93 1hr.

Bus: Regular buses from Perth.

Rail: Perth Station 3m.

Motorway: M90 from Edinburgh.

Taxi: 01738 636777.

Opening Times

Summer

1 April–31 October. Gates open at 9.30am–last admission 5.00pm, Mon–Fri & Sun.

9.30am–last admission 4.00pm, Sat.

Grounds Only open each Friday during Winter, 10am–4pm.

Evening and Winter tours by appointment.

Please check our website for details of Winter Events.

Admission

Admission prices correct at time of going to print:

Palace & Grounds	
Adult	£9.00
Conc.	£7.90
Child (5–16yrs)	£6.00
Family	£26.00
Groups (20+)	
Adult	£7.90
Conc.	£6.75
Child (5–16yrs)	£5.50
Grounds only	
Adult	£5.10
Conc.	£4.50
Child (5–16yrs)	£3.50

Under 5s Free
Private Tour £45 supplement.

Special Events

2011 Events Include:

1, 2 & 3 July: The Scottish Game Fair.

For details of our 2011 event programme please visit www.scone-palace.co.uk

Conference/Function

ROOM	SIZE	MAX CAPACITY
Long Gallery	140' x 20'	200
Queen Victoria's Rm	20' x 20'	20
Drawing Rm	48' x 25'	80
Balvaird Rm	29' x 22'	50/60
Tullibardine Rm	19' x 23'	40/50

ABERDOUR CASTLE AND GARDENS

Aberdour, Fife, KY3 0SL

Tel: 01383 860519 **www.historic-scotland.gov.uk**

Owner: Historic Scotland **Contact:** Monument Manager

This 12th century fortified residence was extended by the Douglas family. The gallery on the first floor gives an idea of how it was furnished at the time. The castle has a 14th century tower extended in the 16th and 17th centuries, a delightful walled garden and a circular dovecote.

Location: MAP 13:G7, OS Ref. NT193 854. In Aberdour 8m E of the Forth Bridge on the A921.

Open: 1 Apr–30 Sept: daily, 9.30am–5.30pm. 1 Oct–31 Mar: 9.30am–4.30pm. Nov–Mar, closed Thurs & Fri. Last ticket 30 mins before closing.

Admission: Adult £4.20, Child £2.50, Conc. £3.40 (2010 prices).

Obligatory. Parking on site for disabled visitors only. Other parking available at the nearby railway station. On leads. €

ARBROATH ABBEY

Arbroath, Tayside, DD11 1EG

Tel: 01241 878756 **www.historic-scotland.gov.uk**

Owner: Historic Scotland **Contact:** The Monument Manager

The substantial ruins of a Tironensian monastery. Arbroath Abbey holds a very special place in Scottish history due to its association with the 'Declaration of Arbroath'. In this document Scotland's nobles swore their independence from England in 1320. The visitor centre includes an exhibition on the declaration.

Location: MAP 14:J4, OS Ref. NO644 414. In Arbroath town centre on the A92.

Open: 1 Apr–30 Sept: daily 9.30am–5.30pm. 1 Oct–31 Mar: daily, 9.30am–4.30 pm. Last ticket 30 mins before closing.

Admission: Adult £4.70, Child £2.80, Conc. £3.80 (2010 prices).

WCs. On leads. €

BALCARRES

Colinsburgh, Fife KY9 1HN

Tel: 01333 340520

Owner: Balcarres Heritage Trust **Contact:** Lord Balniel

16th century tower house with 19th century additions by Burn and Bryce. Woodland and terraced gardens.

Location: MAP 14:I6, OS Ref. NO475 044. ½m N of Colinsburgh.

Open: Woodland & Gardens: 1 Mar–30 Sept, 2–5pm. House not open except by written appointment and 1–30 Apr, excluding Sun.

Admission: Adult £7. Garden only: £4.50.

Partial. By arrangement.

© Blair Castle

Blair Castle

BALGONIE CASTLE

Markinch, Fife KY7 6HQ

Tel: 01592 750119 **Fax:** 01592 753103 **E-mail:** sbalgonie@yahoo.co.uk

Owner/Contact: The Laird of Balgonie

14th century tower, additions to the building up to 1702. Still lived in by the family. 14th century chapel for weddings.

Location: MAP 13:H6, OS Ref. NO313 006. ½ m S of A911 Glenrothes–Leven road at Milton of Balgonie on to B921.

Open: Telephone for information.

Admission: Telephone for information.

BALHOUSIE CASTLE (BLACK WATCH MUSEUM)

Hay Street, North Inch Park, Perth PH1 5HR

Tel: 0131 310 8530

Owner: MOD **Contact:** Major Proctor

Regimental museum housed in the castle.

Location: MAP 13:G5, OS Ref. NO115 244. ½ m N of town centre, E of A9 road to Dunkeld.

Open: Apr–Oct, Mon–Sat, 9.30am–5pm. Sunday 10am–3.30pm (except Easter Sunday). Nov–Mar, Mon–Sat, 9.30am–5pm. The Museum is closed during the Festive period - please contact the Museum for details.

Admission: Free.

BRANKLYN GARDEN

Dundee Road, Perth PH2 7BB

Tel: 01738 625535

Owner: The National Trust for Scotland

Small garden with an impressive collection of rare and unusual plants.

Location: MAP 13:F5, OS Ref. NO125 225. On A85 at 116 Dundee Road, Perth.

BLAIR CASTLE

See page 422 for full page entry.

BRECHIN CASTLE

Brechin, Angus DD9 6SG

Tel: 01356 624566 **E-mail:** mandyferries@dalhousieestates.co.uk

www.dalhousieestates.co.uk

Owner: Dalhousie Estates **Contact:** Mandy Ferries

Dating from 1711 the Castle contains many family pictures and artefacts. Beautiful gardens.

Location: MAP 14:J3, OS Ref. NO593 602. Off A90 on A935.

Open: 28 May–26 Jun: guided tours only, 2 & 3.15pm.

Admission: Adult £6. Child under 12yrs Free.

No photography. Unsuitable. Obligatory.

BROUGHTY CASTLE

Broughty Ferry, Dundee DD5 2TF

Tel: 01382 436916

Owner: Historic Scotland **Contact:** The Monument Manager

A delightful castle originating from the 15th century and spectacularly positioned overlooking the Tay estuary. It was adapted over the centuries to reflect advances in warfare and defence. The castle houses a museum with fascinating displays on changing life, times and people of Broughty Ferry and about its wildlife.

Location: MAP 14:F4, OS Ref. NO464 304. On the shores of the River Tay at Broughty Ferry, Dundee off the A930.

Open: Please telephone the site for opening times.

Admission: Please telephone the site for details.

The museum is run by Dundee City Council. Visit www.dundeecity.gov.uk/broughtycastle

CASTLE CAMPBELL

Dollar Glen, Central District

Tel: 0131 243 9300

Owner: The National Trust for Scotland **Contact:** Historic Scotland

Known as 'Castle Gloom' this spectacularly sited 15th century fortress was the lowland stronghold of the Campbells. Stunning views from the parapet walk.

Location: MAP 13:F6, OS Ref. NS961 993. At head of Dollar Glen, 10m E of Stirling on the A91.

Scone Palace, The Ambassador's Room

CHARLETON HOUSE

Colinsburgh, Leven, Fife KY9 1HG

Tel: 01333 340249 Fax: 01333 340583

Location: MAP 14:I6, OS Ref. NO464 036. Off A917. 1m NW of Colinsburgh. 3m NW of Elie.

Open: Sept: daily, 12 noon–3pm. Admission every ½hr with guided tours only.

Admission: £12.

Obligatory.

CORTACHY ESTATE

Cortachy, Kirriemuir, Angus DD8 4LX

Tel: 01575 570108 **Fax:** 01575 540400

E-mail: office@airlieestates.com **www.airlieestates.com**

Owner: Trustees of Airlie Estates **Contact:** Estate Office

Countryside walks including access through woodlands to Airlie Monument on Tulloch Hill with spectacular views of the Angus Glens and Vale of Strathmore. Footpaths are waymarked and colour coded.

Location: MAP 13:H3, OS Ref. N0394 596. Off the B955 Glens Road from Kirriemuir.

Open: Woodland Walks: all year. Gardens: 22–25 Apr (Easter); 2 May & 16 May–5 Jun; 1 & 29 Aug. Castle not open. 10am–4pm. Last admission 3.30pm.

Admission: Please contact estate office for details.

Suitable. Limited.

CULROSS PALACE

Tel: 0131 243 9300

Owner: The National Trust for Scotland **Contact:** Property Manager

Relive the domestic life of the 16th and 17th centuries at this Royal Burgh fringed by the River Forth. Enjoy too the Palace, dating from 1597 and the medieval garden.

Location: MAP 13:F7, OS Ref. NS985 860. Off A985. 12m W of Forth Road Bridge and 4m E of Kincardine Bridge, Fife.

DRUMMOND CASTLE GARDENS

See page 423 for full page entry.

DUNFERMLINE ABBEY & PALACE

Dunfermline, Fife, KY12 7PE

Tel: 01383 739026 **www.historic-scotland.gov.uk**

Owner: In the care of Historic Scotland **Contact:** The Monument Manager

The remains of the Benedictine abbey founded by Queen Margaret in the 11th century. The foundations of her church are under the 12th century Romanesque-style nave. Robert the Bruce was buried in the choir. Substantial parts of the abbey buildings remain, including the vast refectory.

Location: MAP 13:G7, OS Ref. NT090 873. In Dunfermline off the M90.

Open: All year 1 Apr–30 Sept: daily, 9.30am–5.30pm. Oct daily, 9.30am–4.30pm. Nov–Mar: Mon–Sat, 9.30am–4.30pm. Closed Thurs pm, Fri and Sun am. Closed for lunch 12.30pm–1.30pm. Last ticket 30 mins before closing.

Admission: Adult £3.70, Child £2.20, Conc. £3.00 (2010 prices).

€

DUNNINALD

Montrose, Angus DD10 9TD

Tel: 01674 672031 **Fax:** 01674 674860

E-mail: visitorinformation@dunninald.com **www.dunninald.com**

Owner: EBJ Stansfeld **Contact:** Mrs M Stansfeld

This house, the third Dunninald built on the estate, was designed by James Gillespie Graham in the gothic Revival style, and was completed for Peter Arkley in 1824. It has a fine walled garden and is set in a planned landscape dating from 1740. It is a family home.

Location: MAP 14:J3, OS Ref. NO705 543 2m S of Montrose, between A92 and the sea.

Open: 30 June–31 Jul, daily, 1–5pm, Garden from 12 noon. (Closed Mondays).

Admission: Adult £6, Child (under 12) Free, Conc. £5. Garden only: £4.

No photography in house. Unsuitable. Obligatory.

In grounds, on leads. €

EDZELL CASTLE AND GARDEN

Edzell, Angus, DD9 7UE

Tel: 01356 648631 **www.historic-scotland.gov.uk**

Owner: Historic Scotland **Contact:** The Monument Manager

The beautiful walled garden was created by Sir David Lindsay in 1604. The 'Pleasance', a delightful garden, has walls decorated with sculptured stone panels. The towerhouse dates from late 15th century. Mary Queen of Scots held a council meeting here in 1562 as her army marched north against the Gordons.

Location: MAP 14:I2, OS Ref. NO585 691. At Edzell, 6m N of Brechin on B966.

Open: 1 Apr–30 Sept: daily, 9.30am–5.30pm. 1 Oct–31 Mar: 9.30am–4.30pm, Nov-Mar closed Thur & Fri. Last ticket 30 mins before closing.

Admission: Adult £4.70, Child £2.80, Conc. £3.80 (2010 prices).

Picnic Area. Closes for lunch. WCs. Limited for coaches. On leads. €

ELCHO CASTLE

Perth, PH2 8QQ

Tel: 01738 639998 **www.historic-scotland.gov.uk**

Owner: Historic Scotland **Contact:** The Monument Manager

This handsome and complete fortified mansion of 16th century date has three projecting towers. The original wrought-iron grilles to protect the windows are still in place. Located on the River Tay, the castle is rich in bird life.

Location: MAP 13:G5, OS Ref. NO164 211. 5m NE of Bridge of Earn off the A912 and close to Rhynd.

Open: 1 Apr–30 Sept: daily, 9.30am–5.30pm. Last ticket 30 mins before closing.

Admission: Adult £3.20, Child £1.90, Conc. £2.70 (2010 prices).

Picnic area. No coaches. €

FALKLAND PALACE

Falkland KY15 7BU

Tel: 0131 243 9300

Owner: The National Trust for Scotland

Built between 1502 and 1541, the Palace is a good example of Renaissance architecture. Surrounded by gardens, laid out in the 1950s.

Location: MAP 13:G6, OS Ref. NO253 075. A912, 11m N of Kirkcaldy.

GLAMIS CASTLE

See page 424 for full page entry.

GLENEAGLES

Auchterarder, Perthshire PH3 1PJ

Tel: 01764 682388

Owner: Gleneagles 1996 Trust **Contact:** Martin Haldane of Gleneagles

Gleneagles has been the home of the Haldane family since the 12th century. The 18th century pavilion is open to the public by written appointment.

Location: MAP 13:F6, OS Ref. NS931 088. ¾m S of A9 on A823. 2½m S of Auchterarder.

Open: By written appointment only.

HILL OF TARVIT MANSIONHOUSE

Cupar, Fife KY15 5PB

Tel: 0131 243 9300

Owner: The National Trust for Scotland

House rebuilt in 1906 by Sir Robert Lorimer, the renowned Scottish architect, for a Dundee industrialist, Mr F B Sharp.

Location: MAP 13:F6, OS Ref. NO379 118. Off A916, 2½m S of Cupar, Fife.

HOUSE OF DUN

Montrose, Angus DD10 9LQ

Tel: 0131 243 9300

Owner: The National Trust for Scotland

Georgian house, overlooking the Montrose Basin, designed by William Adam and built in 1730 for David Erskine, Lord Dun.

Location: OS Ref. NO670 599. 3m W Montrose on A935.

HUNTINGTOWER CASTLE

Perth, PH1 3JL

Tel: 01738 627231 **www.historic-scotland.gov.uk**

Owner: In the care of Historic Scotland **Contact:** The Monument Manager

The splendid painted ceilings are especially noteworthy in this castle, once owned by the Ruthven family. Scene of a famous leap between two towers by a daughter of the house who was nearly caught in her lover's room. The castle is now home to two colonies of bats.

Location: MAP 13:F5, OS Ref. NO084 252. 3m NW of Perth off the A85 to Crieff.

Open: 1 Apr–30 Sept: daily, 9.30am–5.30pm. Oct daily, 9.30am–4.30pm. 1 Nov–31 Mar 9.30am–4.30pm, closed Thur & Fri. Last ticket 30 mins before closing.

Admission: Adult £4.20, Child £2.50, Conc. £3.40 (2010 prices).

Closes for lunch. Picnic area. WCs. By arrangement. No coaches. On leads. €

INCHCOLM ABBEY AND ISLAND

Inchcolm, Fife

Tel: 01383 823332 **www.historic-scotland.gov.uk**

Owner: In the care of Historic Scotland **Contact:** The Monument Manager

Known as the 'Iona of the East'. This is the best preserved group of monastic buildings in Scotland, founded in 1123. Includes a 13th century octagonal chapter house.

Location: MAP 13:H7, OS Ref. NT190 826. On Inchcolm in the Firth of Forth. Reached by ferry from South Queensferry (30 mins), or Newhaven (45 mins). Tel. 0131 331 5000 or 0870 118 1866 for times/charges.

Open: Depending on the availability of the ferry service: 1 Apr–30 Sept, daily, 9.30am–5.30pm. 1–31 Oct, 9.30am–4.30pm. Last ticket 30 mins before closing.

Admission: Adult £4.70, Child £2.80, Conc. £3.80 (2010 prices). Additional charge for ferries.

Visitor Centre. Picnic area. On leads. €

KELLIE CASTLE & GARDEN

Pittenweem, Fife KY10 2RF

Tel: 0131 243 9300

Owner: The National Trust for Scotland

Good example of domestic architecture in Lowland Scotland dates from the 14th century and was sympathetically restored by the Lorimer family in the late 19th century.

Location: MAP 14:I6, OS Ref. NO519 051. On B9171, 3m NW of Pittenweem, Fife.

LOCHLEVEN CASTLE

Loch Leven, Kinross, KY13 8UF

Tel: 01577 862670 **www.historic-scotland.gov.uk**

Owner: Historic Scotland **Contact:** The Monument Manager

Mary Queen of Scots endured nearly a year of imprisonment in this 14th century tower before her dramatic escape in May 1568. During the First War of Independence it was held by the English, stormed by Wallace and visited by Bruce.

Location: MAP 13:G6, OS Ref. NO138 018. On an island in Loch Leven reached by ferry from Kinross off the M90.

Open: Apr–Sept: 9.30am to last outward sailing at 4.30pm. Oct: daily 9.30am to last outward sailing at 3.30pm.

Admission: Adult £4.70, Child £2.80, Conc. £3.80 (2010 prices). Prices include boat trip.

Picnic area. Limited for coaches. On leads. €

MEGGINCH CASTLE

Errol, Perthshire PH2 7SW

Tel: 01821 642222 **Email:** catherine.herdman@gmail.com

Owner: Mr Giles Herdman & The Hon Mrs Drummond-Herdman

15th century castle, 1,000 year old yews, flowered parterre, topiary, double walled kitchen garden, astrological garden, heritage orchard. Early 19th century courtyard with Pagoda dovecote, part used as a location for the film *Rob Roy*.

Location: MAP 13:G5, OS Ref. NO241 245. 8m E of Perth on A90.

Open: Scottish Gardens Scheme. By Appointment. Gardens Only.

Admission: Contact property for details.

Partial. By arrangement. Limited for coaches. In grounds, on leads.

MONZIE CASTLE

Crieff, Perthshire PH7 4HD

Tel: 01764 653110

Owner/Contact: Mrs C M M Crichton

Built in 1791. Destroyed by fire in 1908 and rebuilt and furnished by Sir Robert Lorimer.

Location: MAP 13:E5, OS Ref. NN873 244. 2m NE of Crieff.

Open: 14 May–12 Jun: daily, 2–4.30pm. By appointment at other times.

Admission: Adult £5, Child £1. Group rates available, contact property for details.

ST ANDREWS CASTLE

THE SCORES, ST ANDREWS KY16 9AR

www.historic-scotland.gov.uk

Tel: 01334 477196

Owner: Historic Scotland **Contact:** Monument Manager

The main residence of the bishops of St Andrews. Explore the fascinating 16th century siege mine and counter-mine, rare examples of medieval siege techniques. There is also a bottle dungeon hollowed out of solid rock.

Location: MAP 14:I5, OS Ref. NO512 169. In St Andrews on the A91.

Open: Apr–Sept: daily, 9.30am–5.30pm. Oct–Mar: daily, 9.30am–4.30pm. Last ticket 30 mins before closing.

Admission: Adult £5.20, Child £3.10, Conc. £4.20 (2010 prices). 10% discount for groups (11+). Joint ticket with St Andrews Cathedral available.

WCs. Free if booked. €

ST ANDREWS CATHEDRAL

St Andrews, Fife, KY16 9QL

Tel: 01334 472563 **www.historic-scotland.gov.uk**

Owner: Historic Scotland **Contact:** The Monument Manager

Once the largest cathedral in Scotland, the remains still give a vivid impression of its impressive scale. See the associated domestic ranges of the priory and climb St Rule's Tower for spectacular views.

Location: MAP 14:I5, OS Ref: NO5143 167. In St Andrews on the A91.

Open: 1 Apr–30 Sept: daily, 9.30am–5.30pm. 1 Oct–31 Mar: daily, 9.30am–4.30pm. Last ticket 30 mins before closing.

Admission: Adult £4.20, Child £2.50, Conc. £3.40 (2010 prices). Joint entry ticket with St Andrews Castle available.

On leads. €

SCONE PALACE & GROUNDS

See page 425 for full page entry.

STOBHALL

Stobhall, Cargill, Perthshire PH2 6DR

Tel: 01821 640332 **www.stobhall.com**

Owner: Viscount Strathallan

Original home of the Drummond chiefs from the 14th century. Romantic cluster of small-scale buildings around a courtyard in a magnificent situation overlooking the River Tay, surrounded by formal and woodland gardens. 17th century painted ceiling in Chapel depicts monarchs of Europe and North Africa on horse (or elephant) back.

Location: MAP 13:G4, OS Ref. NO132 343. 7m N of Perth on A93.

Open: 2–31 Jul: Tues–Sun, (closed Mons). Open by tour only. Tours at 2, 3 & 4pm of the Chapel, Drawing Room and Folly. Explore the garden at leisure after the tour. Library by prior appointment.

Admission: Adult £4, Child £2. Large group visits must be booked.

Partial. Obligatory. Limited. Coaches please book. Guide dogs only.

STRATHTYRUM HOUSE & GARDENS

St Andrews, Fife

Tel: 01334 473600 **E-mail:** info@strathtyrumhouse.com

www.strathtyrumhouse.com

Owner: The Strathtyrum Trust **Contact:** Henry Cheape

Location: MAP 14:I5, OS Ref: NO490 172. Entrance from the St Andrews/Guardbridge Road which is signposted when open.

Open: 2–6 May, 6–10 Jun, 4–8 Jul, 1–5 Aug, 5–9 Sept: 2–4pm. Guided tours at 2 & 3pm.

Admission: Adult £5, Child + Conc. £2.50.

2pm and 3pm. Free. Guide dogs only.

TULLIBOLE CASTLE

Crook of Devon, Kinross KY13 0QN

Tel: 01577 840236 **E-mail:** visit@tulbol.demon.co.uk **www.tulbol.demon.co.uk**

Owner: Lord & Lady Moncreiff **Contact:** Lord Moncreiff

Recognised as a classic example of the Scottish tower house. Completed in 1608, the Moncreiff family have lived here since 1747. The Castle is in a parkland setting with ornamental fishponds (moat), a roofless lectarn doocot, with a short walk to a 9th century graveyard and a ruined church.

Location: MAP 13:F6, OS Ref. NO540 888. Located on the B9097 1m E of Crook of Devon.

Open: Last week in Aug–30 Sept: Tue–Sun, 1–4pm. Admission every ½ hr with guided tours only.

Admission: Adult £3.50, Child/Conc. £2.50. Free as part of "Doors Open Day" (last weekend of Sept).

Unsuitable. Obligatory. Ample for cars but limited for coaches.

Guide dogs only. 1 x twin, 1 bed holiday cottage.

Thinking of a short break or weekend away?
See Historic Places to Stay

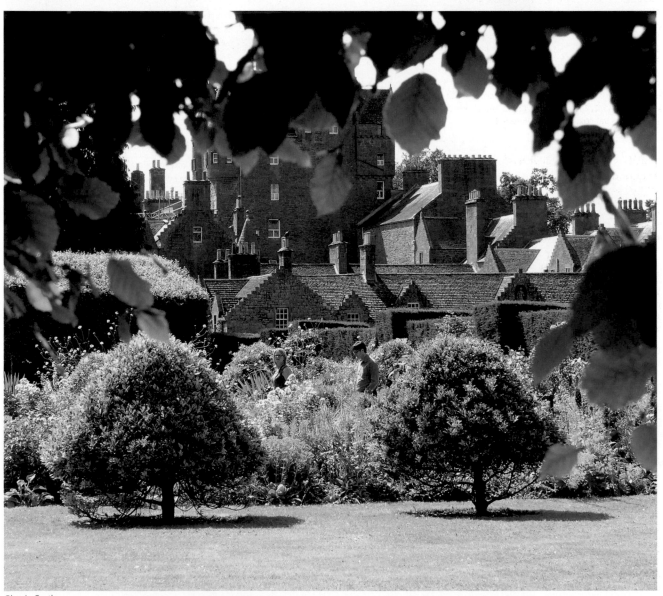

Glamis Castle

■ **Owner**

Duke of Argyll

■ **Contact**

Argyll Estates
Inveraray Castle
Inveraray
Argyll PA32 8XE

Tel: 01499 302203
Fax: 01499 302421
E-mail: enquiries@inveraray-castle.com

■ **Location**

MAP 13:A6
OS Ref. NN100 090

From Edinburgh 2½–3hrs via Glasgow.

Just NE of Inveraray on A83. W shore of Loch Fyne.

Bus: Bus route stopping point within ½m.

■ **Opening Times**

Summer
1 April–31 October: 7 Days 10am–5.45pm. Last admission 5pm.

Winter
Closed.

■ **Admission**

Castle & Gardens

Adult	£9.20
	(£7.40)
Senior Citizen	£7.60
	(£6.10)
Student (on production of student card)	£7.60 (£6.10)
Child (under 16yrs)	£6.20
	(£5.00)
Family (2 adults & 2 or more children)	£25.50
School Group	£3.50 each

A 20% discount is allowed on groups of 20 or more persons (as shown in brackets).

Pre-booking available.

■ **Special Events**

Check website www.inveraray-castle.com for details of forthcoming events.

©Inveraray Castle/Heritage House Group/Nick McCann

INVERARAY CASTLE & GARDEN

www.inveraray-castle.com

The ancient Royal Burgh of Inveraray lies about 60 miles north west of Glasgow by Loch Fyne in an area of spectacular natural beauty. The ruggedness of the highland scenery combines with the sheltered tidal loch, beside which nestles the present Castle built between 1745 and 1790.

The Castle is home to the Duke and Duchess of Argyll. The Duke is head of the Clan Campbell and his family have lived in Inveraray since the early 15th century. Designed by Roger Morris and decorated by Robert Mylne, the fairytale exterior belies the grandeur of its gracious interior. The Clerk of Works, William Adam, father of Robert and John, did much of the laying out of the present Royal Burgh, which is an unrivalled example of an early planned town.

Visitors enter the famous Armoury Hall containing some 1,300 pieces including Brown Bess muskets, Lochaber axes, 18th century Scottish broadswords, and can see preserved swords from the Battle of Culloden. The fine State Dining Room and Tapestry Drawing Room contain magnificent French tapestries made especially for the Castle, fabulous examples of Scottish, English and French furniture and a wealth of other works of art. The unique collection of china, silver and family artifacts spans the generations which are identified by a genealogical display in the Clan Room.

©Inveraray Castle/Heritage House Group/Nick McCann

No photography. Guide books in French, Italian and German translations.

Partial. WCs.

Licensed.

Available for up to 100 people at no additional cost. Groups please book. Tour time: 1 hr.

100 cars. Car/ coach park close to Castle.

£3.50 per child. A guide can be provided. Areas of interest include a woodland walk.

Guide dogs only.

ANGUS'S GARDEN

Barguillean, Taynuilt, Argyll, West Highlands PA35 1HY
Tel: 01866 822335 **Fax:** 01866 822539
Contact: Sean Honeyman
Memorial garden of peace, tranquillity and reconciliation.
Location: MAP 12:P5, OS Ref. NM978 289. 4m SW on Glen Lonan road from A85.
Open: All year: daily, 9am–5pm (dusk during summer months).
Admission: Adult £2, Child Free.

ARDENCRAIG GARDENS

Ardencraig, Rothesay, Isle of Bute, West Highlands PA20 9BP
Tel: 01700 505339 **Fax:** 01700 502492
Owner: Argyll and Bute Council **Contact:** Allan Macdonald
Walled garden, greenhouses, aviaries. Woodland walk from Rothesay 1 mile (Skippers Wood.)
Location: MAP 13:A8, OS Ref. NS105 645. 2m from Rothesay.
Open: May–Sept: Mon–Fri, 10am–3.30pm, Sat & Sun, 1–4.30pm.
Admission: Free.

ARGYLL'S LODGING

Argyll's Lodging, Castle Wynd, Stirling FK8 1EG
Tel: 01786 450000
www.historic-scotland.gov.uk
Owners: Historic Scotland **Contact:** Monument Manager
An attractive townhouse decorated with rich materials and colours as it would have been during the 9th Earl of Argyll's occupation around 1680. During its restoration hidden secrets were revealed including a section of 17th century trompe l'oeil panelling in the dining room, created by painter David McBeath.
Location: MAP 13:E7, OS Ref. NS793 938. In Stirling's historic old town just below Stirling Castle off the M9. Rail: Stirling Train Station. Air: Edinburgh or Glasgow airport.
Open: Guided tours leave from Stirling Castle. Call 01786 450000 for times.
Admission: Included with entry to Stirling Castle.
Access is by guided tour only. Evening receptions/dinners. WCs. Obligatory. Parking for cars and coaches available on Stirling Castle esplanade. Free pre-booked school visits scheme.

BALLOCH CASTLE COUNTRY PARK

Balloch, Dunbartonshire G83 8LX
Tel: 01389 737000
Contact: West Dunbartonshire Council
A 200 acre country park on the banks of Loch Lomond.
Location: MAP 13:C7, OS Ref. NS390 830. SE shore of Loch Lomond, off A82 for Balloch or A811 for Stirling.
Open: All year: dawn–dusk.
Admission: Free.

BENMORE BOTANIC GARDEN

Dunoon, Argyll PA23 8QU
Tel: 01369 706261 **Fax:** 01369 706369
Contact: The Curator
A botanical paradise. Enter the magnificent avenue of giant redwoods and follow trails through the Formal Garden and hillside woodlands with its spectacular outlook over the Holy Loch and the Eachaig Valley.
Location: MAP 13:A7, OS Ref. NS150 850. 7m N of Dunoon on A815.
Open: 1 Mar–31 Oct: daily, 10am–6pm. Closes 5pm in Mar & Oct.
Admission: Adult £5, Child £1, Conc. £4, Family £10. Group discounts available.

BONAWE HISTORIC IRON FURNACE

Taynuilt, Argyll PA35 1JQ
Tel: 01866 822432
www.historic-scotland.gov.uk
Owner: Historic Scotland **Contact:** The Monument Manager
Set in stunning surroundings beside Loch Etive, the ironworks were founded in 1753 by Cumbrian iron masters. It is the most complete remaining charcoal fuelled ironworks in Britain. Displays bring to life the industrial heritage of the area and illustrate how iron was once made here.
Location: MAP 12:P4, OS Ref. NN010 318. By the village of Taynuilt off the A85.
Open: 1 Apr–30 Sept: daily, 9.30am–5.30pm. Last ticket 30 mins before closing.
Admission: Adult £4.20, Child £2.50, Conc. £3.40 (2010 prices).
Picnic area. Closes for lunch. No coaches. On leads. €

© Britainonview

Castle Stalker

CASTLE STALKER

Portnacroish, Appin, Argyll PA38 4BA

Tel: 01631 730354 & 07789 597442 **www.castlestalker.com**

Owner: The Allward Family **Contact:** Messrs R & A Allward

Early 15th century tower house and seat of the Stewarts of Appin. Set on an islet 400 yds off the shore of Loch Linnhe. Reputed to have been used by James IV as a hunting lodge. Restored by the late Lt Col Stewart Allward and now retained by his family.

Location: MAP 12:P3, OS Ref. NM930 480. Approx. 20m N of Oban on the A828. On islet ¼m offshore.

Open: 16–20 May, 30 May–3 June, 11–15 July, 29 Aug–2 Sept, 26–30 Sept. Telephone for appointments. Times variable depending on tides and weather.

Admission: Adult £10, Child £5.

Not suitable for coach parties. Unsuitable Obligatory No coaches.

DOUNE CASTLE

Doune FK16 6EA

Tel: 01786 841742 **www.historic-scotland.gov.uk**

Owner: Earl of Moray (leased to Historic Scotland) **Contact:** Monument Manager

A formidable 14th century courtyard castle, built for the Regent Albany. The striking keep-gatehouse combines domestic quarters including the splendid Lord's Hall with its carved oak screen, musicians' gallery and double fireplace.

Location: MAP 13:D6, OS Ref. NN727 009. In Doune, 10m NW of Stirling off the A84.

Open: 1 Apr–30 Sept: daily, 9.30am–5.30pm. 1 Oct–31 Mar 9.30am–4.30pm, Nov–Mar closed Thurs & Fri. Last ticket 30 mins before closing.

Admission: Adult £4.20, Child £2.50, Conc. £3.40 (2010 prices).

Picnic area. WCs. Limited for coaches. On leads. €

For **special events** held throughout the year, see the index at the end of the book.

Duart Castle

DUART CASTLE

ISLE OF MULL, ARGYLL PA64 6AP

www.duartcastle.com

Tel: 01680 812309 **E-mail:** duart.guide@btinternet.com

Owner/Contact: Sir Lachlan Maclean Bt

Duart is a fortress, one of a line of castles stretching from Dunollie in the east to Mingary in the north, all guarding the Sound of Mull. The earliest part of the castle was built in the 12th century, the keep was added in 1360 by the 5th Chief Lachlan Lubanach and the most recent alterations were completed in 1673. The Macleans were staunchly loyal to the Stuarts. After the rising of 1745 they lost Duart and their lands were forfeited. Sir Fitzroy Maclean, 25th Chief, restored the Castle in 1910. Duart remains the family home of the Chief of the Clan Maclean.

Location: MAP 12:O4, OS Ref. NM750 350. Off A849 on the east point of the Isle of Mull.

Open: Castle & tea room open from 3rd April Sun–Thur 11am–4pm. Open daily from 1st May (including shop) 10.30am–5.30pm. Castle closes 18th Oct (tea room & shop close 11th Oct).

Admission: Adult: £5.30, Child (3–14) £2.65, Conc. £4.80, Family (2+2) £13.25.

Unsuitable. By arrangement. In grounds, on leads.

DUMBARTON CASTLE

Dumbarton, Strathclyde, G82 1JJ

Tel: 01389 732167 **www.historic-scotland.gov.uk**

Owner: Historic Scotland **Contact:** The Monument Manager

Dumbarton was the centre of the ancient kingdom of Strathclyde from the 5th century until 1018. Situated on a volcanic rock overlooking the Firth of Clyde, Dumbarton Castle was an important royal refuge sheltering both David II and Mary Queen of Scots.

Location: MAP 13:C8, OS Ref. NS 404 743. In Dumbarton off the A82.

Open: 1 Apr–30 Sept: daily, 9.30am–5.30pm. 1 Oct–31 Mar 9.30am–4.30pm, Nov–Mar closed Thurs & Fri. Last ticket 30 mins before closing.

Admission: Adult £4.20, Child £2.50, Conc £3.40 (2010 prices).

Picnic Area. Bicycle Rack. No coaches. €

DUNBLANE CATHEDRAL

Dunblane, FK15 0AQ

Tel: 01786 823388 **www.historic-scotland.gov.uk**

Owner: Historic Scotland **Contact:** The Monument Manager

One of Scotland's noblest medieval churches. The lower part of the tower is Romanesque but the larger part of the building is of the 13th century. It was restored in 1889–93 by Sir Rowand Anderson.

Location: MAP 13:E6, OS Ref. NN782 014. In Dunblane just off the B8033 close to Dunblane Station. Rail: Dunblane Station.

Open: 1 Apr–30 Sept: daily, 9.30am–5.30pm, Sundays open 2–5.30pm. 1 Oct–31 Mar 9.30am–4.30pm, Sundays open 2–4.30pm. Closed for lunch daily 12.30–1.30pm. Last ticket 30 mins before closing.

Admission: Free, donations welcome.

Partial. By arrangement.

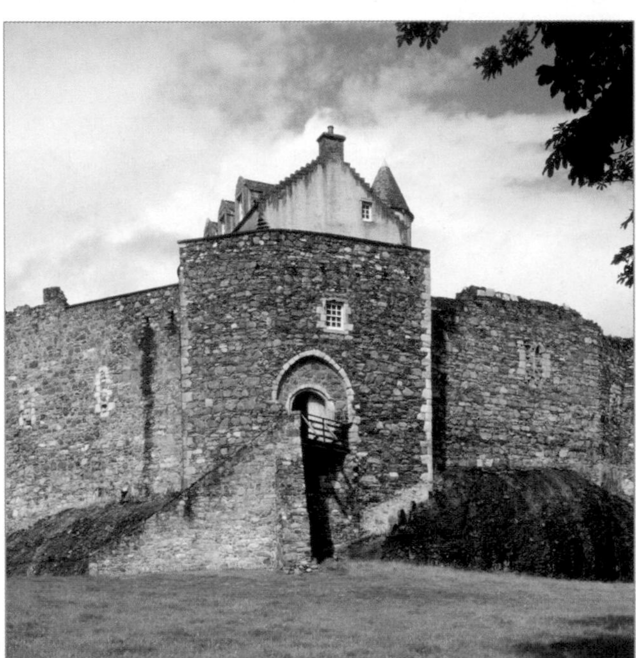

©Historic Scotland Photographic Library

DUNSTAFFNAGE CASTLE & CHAPEL

BY OBAN, ARGYLL PA37 1PZ

www.historic-scotland.gov.uk

Tel: 01631 562465

Owner: In the care of Historic Scotland **Contact:** The Monument Manager

A fine 13th century castle built on a rock overlooking the Firth of Lorn. Captured by Robert the Bruce in 1309, it remained in royal possession for some years. The castle was briefly the prison of Flora Macdonald in 1746. Close by are the remains of the chapel.

Location: MAP 12:P4, OS49 NM882 344. Near Dunbeg 3m N of Oban off A85.

Open: 1 Apr–30 Sept: daily, 9.30am–5.30pm. 1–31 Oct, 9.30am–4.30pm. 1 Nov–31 Mar 9.30am–4.30pm, closed Thurs & Fri. Last ticket 30 mins before closing.

Admission: Adult £3.70, Child £2.20, Conc. £3.00 (2010 prices). 10% discount for groups (11+).

Limited for coaches. Free pre-booked school visits.

On leads. €

HILL HOUSE

Upper Colquhoun Street, Helensburgh G84 9AJ

Tel: 0131 243 9300

Owner: The National Trust for Scotland

Charles Rennie Mackintosh set this 20th century masterpiece high on a hillside overlooking the Firth of Clyde. Mackintosh also designed furniture, fittings and decorative schemes to complement the house.

Location: MAP 13:B7, OS Ref. NS300 820. Off B832, between A82 & A814, 23m NW of Glasgow.

INCHMAHOME PRIORY

Port of Menteith, FK8 3RA

Tel: 01877 385294 **www.historic-scotland.gov.uk**

Owner: Historic Scotland **Contact:** The Monument Manager

A beautifully situated Augustinian priory on an island in the Lake of Menteith founded in 1238 with much of the building surviving. The five year old Mary, Queen of Scots was sent here for safety in 1547.

Location: MAP 13:C6, OS Ref. NN574 005. On an island in Lake of Menteith. Reached by ferry from Port of Menteith, 8m S of Callander off A81.

Open: Open Apr–Sept, 9.30am–5.30pm, last outward sailing at 4.30pm. 1–31 Oct, 9.30am–4.30pm, last outward sailing at 3.30pm.

Admission: Adult £4.70, Child £2.80, Conc. £3.80 (2010 prices). Charge includes ferry trip.

Picnic area. Limited for coaches. On leads. €

INVERARAY CASTLE

See page 430 for full page entry.

Torosay Castle & Gardens

IONA ABBEY & NUNNERY

Iona, Argyll, PA76 6SQ

Tel/Fax: 01681 700512 **www.historic-scotland.gov.uk**

Owner: In the care of Historic Scotland **Contact:** The Monument Manager

One of Scotland's most historic and venerated sites, Iona Abbey is a celebrated Christian centre and the burial place for many Scottish kings. The abbey and nunnery grounds house a superb collection of Christian carved stones and crosses, dating back to 600AD. Includes the Columba Centre and Fionnphort exhibition.

Location: MAP 12:L5, OS Ref. NM287 244. Ferry service from Fionnphort, Mull.

Open: All year, depending on the ferries. Apr–Sept: daily, 9.30am–5.30pm. Oct–Mar: daily, 9.30am–4.30pm. Last ticket 30 mins before closing.

Admission: Adult £4.70, Child £2.80, Conc. £3.80 (2010 prices).

On leads. €

KILCHURN CASTLE

Loch Awe, Dalmally, Argyll

Tel: 0131 668 8600 **www.historic-scotland.gov.uk**

Owner: Historic Scotland **Contact:** The Monument Manager

A square tower, built by Sir Colin Campbell of Glenorchy c1550. Much enlarged in 1693 it incorporates the first purpose-built barracks in Scotland. The picturesque castle ruins have spectacular views along Loch Awe.

Location: MAP 13:A5, OS Ref. NN133 276. At the NE end of Loch Awe, 2.5m W of Dalmally off the A85.

Open: Summer only, Apr–Sept.

Admission: Free.

ROTHESAY CASTLE

Rothesay, Isle of Bute, PA20 0DA

Tel: 01700 502691 **www.historic-scotland.gov.uk**

Owner: In the care of Historic Scotland **Contact:** The Steward

A favourite residence of the Stuart kings, this is a wonderful example of a 13th century circular castle of enclosure with 16th century forework containing the Great Hall. Attacked by Vikings in its earlier days.

Location: MAP 13:A8, OS Ref. NS088 646. In Rothesay, Isle of Bute. Ferry from Wemyss Bay on the A78.

Open: 1 Apr–30 Sept: daily, 9.30am–5.30pm. 1–31 Oct: daily, 9.30am–4.30pm. Nov–Mar 9.30am–4.30pm, closed Thurs & Fri. Last ticket 30 mins before closing.

Admission: Adult £4.20, Child £2.50, Conc. £3.40 (2010 prices).

Closes for lunch. By arrangement. On leads. €

ST BLANE'S CHURCH, KINGARTH

Kingarth, Isle of Bute

Tel: 0131 668 8600 **www.historic-scotland.gov.uk**

Owner: In the care of Historic Scotland

This 12th century Romanesque chapel stands on the site of a 12th century Celtic monastery. A charming, tranquil spot.

Location: MAP 13:A9, OS Ref. NS090 535. At the south end of the Isle of Bute.

Open: All year: daily.

Admission: Free.

No coaches. On leads.

TOROSAY CASTLE & GARDENS

Craignure, Isle of Mull PA65 6AY

Tel: 01680 812421 **E-mail:** torosay@aol.com **www.torosay.com**

Owner/Contact: Mr Chris James

Torosay Castle was completed in 1858 by eminent architect David Bryce in the Scottish Baronial style, and remains a much loved family home. There are 12 acres of superb gardens, including three Italianate Terraces and the Statue Walk, and less formal woodland water gardens, rockery, Oriental and Alpine gardens, with a large collection of rare and tender plants, all offset by dramatic mountain and seascapes. The Castle offers family history, portraits, scrapbooks and antiques in an informal and relaxed atmosphere.

Location: MAP 12:O4, OS Ref. NM730 350. 1½m SE of Craignure by A849.

Open: At the time of going to press, Torosay Castle has been offered for sale, and its future is not settled. For up to date information on access to Torosay Castle & Gardens, please visit the website www.torosay.com.

Children's adventure playground. WC. Holiday cottages. €

MOUNT STUART

ISLE OF BUTE PA20 9LR

www.mountstuart.com

Tel: 01700 503877 **Fax:** 01700 505313 **E-mail:** contactus@mountstuart.com

Owner: Mount Stuart Trust **Contact:** Mount Stuart Office

Spectacular High Victorian gothic house, ancestral home of the Marquess of Bute. Splendid interiors, art collection and architectural detail. Set in 300 acres of stunning woodlands, mature Victorian pinetum, arboretum and exotic gardens.

Location: MAP 13:A9, OS Ref. NS100 600. SW coast of Scotland, 5m S of Rothesay. Local bus service to the Visitor Centre, frequent ferry service from Wemyss Bay, Renfrewshire and Colintraive, Argyll.

Open: Seasonal opening hours – please call for further information.

No photography. Licensed. Licensed. Ample. Guide dogs only. Exclusive.

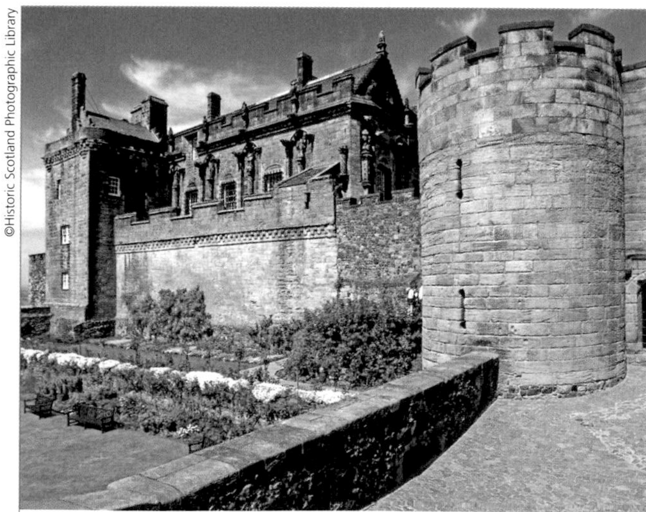

©Historic Scotland Photographic Library

STIRLING CASTLE

CASTLE WYND, STIRLING FK8 1EJ

www.stirlingcastle.gov.uk

Tel: 01786 450000

Owner: Historic Scotland **Contact:** Monument Manager

High on a volcanic rock overlooking Bannockburn, Stirling Castle was a mighty fortress and luxurious royal residence. Easter 2011 sees the reopening of the Renaissance palace which was the childhood home of Mary, Queen of Scots. Visitors can also see the royal kitchens, Chapel Royal and Scotland's largest medieval Great Hall.

Location: MAP 13:E7, OS Ref. NS790 941. At the top of Castle Wynd in Stirling's historic old town. Off the M9 junction 9 or 10.

Open: Apr–Sept: 9.30am–6pm. Oct–Mar: 9.30am–5pm. Last ticket 45 mins before closing.

Admission: Adult £9.00 Child £5.40, Conc. £7.20 (2010 prices). Admission includes a guided tour of Argyll's Lodgings.

Private hire. WCs. Obligatory. Limited for coaches. €

Iona Abbey

ALTYRE ESTATE

Altyre Estate, Forres, Moray IV36 2SH

Tel: 01309 672265 **Fax:** 01309 672270 **E-mail:** office@altyre.com

Contact: Sir Alastair Gordon Cumming

Altyre Estate comprises architecturally interesting buildings including Italianate farm buildings, standing stones and access to areas of natural and ornithological interest. Altyre Estate may interest scientific groups, students, and the general public.

Location: MAP 16:P8, OS Ref. NJ028 552. Details given on appointment.

Open: Visitors are welcome by appointment, please telephone for information.

Admission: Free.

BALFLUIG CASTLE

Alford, Aberdeenshire AB33 8EJ

Tel: 020 7624 3200

Owner/Contact: Mark Tennant of Balfluig

Small 16th century tower house, restored in 1967. Its garden and wooded park are surrounded by farmland.

Location: OS Ref. NJ586 151. Alford, Aberdeenshire.

Open: Please write to M I Tennant Esq, 30 Abbey Gardens, London NW8 9AT. Occasionally let by the week for holidays. Graded *** by VisitScotland, see www.visitscotland.com/balfluigcastle

Unsuitable. 1 single, 4 double.

BALMORAL CASTLE (GROUNDS & EXHIBITIONS)

Balmoral, Ballater, Aberdeenshire AB35 5TB

Tel: 013397 42534 **Fax:** 013397 42034 **E-mail:** info@balmoralcastle.com

www.balmoralcastle.com

Owner: Her Majesty The Queen **Contact:** Garry Marsden

Scottish home to The Royal Family. Ballroom, grounds and exhibitions, large café seating 120, quality gift shop. Excellent for coaches and groups. Holiday cottages, salmon fishing, Land Rover safaris and activity holidays.

Location: MAP 13:G1, OS Ref. NO256 951. Off A93 between Ballater and Braemar. 50m W of Aberdeen.

Open: 1 Apr–31 Jul: daily, 10am–5pm, last admission 4.30pm. Nov & Dec: Guided tours available – ring for details.

Admission: Adult £8.70, Seniors/Students £7.70, Children (5–16yrs) £4.60, Family (2 adults & up to 4 children) £23 (Audio tour included). Discounts for groups (20+).

BALVENIE CASTLE

Dufftown, AB55 4DH

Tel: 01340 820121 **www.historic-scotland.gov.uk**

Owner: Historic Scotland **Contact:** The Monument Manager

Picturesque ruins of 13th century moated stronghold originally owned by the Comyns. Visited by Edward I in 1304 and by Mary Queen of Scots in 1562. Occupied by Cumberland in 1746.

Location: MAP 17:B9, OS Ref. NJ326 408. At Dufftown on A941.

Open: 1 Apr–30 Sept: daily, 9.30am–5.30pm. Last ticket 30 mins before closing.

Admission: Adult £3.70, Child £2.20, Conc. £3.00 (2010 prices).

Partial. WCs. In grounds. €

BRODIE CASTLE

Forres, Moray IV36 0TE

Tel: 0131 243 9300

Owner: The National Trust for Scotland

The lime harled building is a typical 'Z' plan tower house with ornate corbelled battlements and bartizans, with 17th & 19th century additions.

Location: MAP 16:P8, OS Ref. NH980 577. Off A96 4½m W of Forres and 24m E of Inverness.

CAIRNESS HOUSE

Lonmay, Fraserburgh, Aberdeenshire AB43 8XP

Tel: 01346 582078 **Email:** info@cairnesshouse.com **www.cairnesshouse.com**

Owners: Mr J Soriano-Ruiz / Mr K H Khairallah **Contact:** Property Manager

Cairness is Scotland's most extraordinary neoclassical house, recently brought back to life in a major restoration. Its exquisite interiors include the earliest Egyptian room in Britain, full of mysterious symbols. The house now contains one of the finest collections of furniture and paintings in the North East.

Location: MAP 17:F8, OS Ref. NK038 609. Off A90, 4m SE of Fraserburgh, ½m W of B9033 about 2m S of St Comb's.

Open: Groups and special visits all year by prior arrangement.

Admission: Adult £7.50, tours with tea: £9.50. For special tours, lunches etc, please apply for details and rates. Minimum number for groups: 15.

No photography. No smoking. Obligatory. Limited.

© Balmoral Castle

Balmoral Castle

Cairness House

CASTLE FRASER & GARDEN

Sauchen, Inverurie AB51 7LD

Tel: 0131 243 9300

Owner: The National Trust for Scotland

Begun in 1575, the two low wings contribute to the scale and magnificence of the towers rising above them, combining to make this the largest and most elaborate of the Scottish castles built on the 'Z' plan.

Location: MAP 17:D11, OS Ref. NJ723 125. Off A944, 4m N of Dunecht & 16m W of Aberdeen.

CORGARFF CASTLE

Strathdon, AB36 8YP

Tel: 01975 651460 **www.historic-scotland.gov.uk**

Owner: Historic Scotland **Contact:** The Monument Manager

A 16th century tower house converted into a barracks for Hanoverian troops in 1748. Corgarff Castle is surrounded by a distinctive star-shaped perimeter wall dating back to the 18th century.

Location: MAP 17:A11, OS Ref. NJ255 086. 8m W of Strathdon on A939.

Open: 1 Apr–30 Sept: daily, 9.30am–5.30pm. 1 Oct–31 Mar 9.30am–4.30pm Sat & Sun only. Last ticket 30 mins before closing.

Admission: Adult £4.70, Child £2.80, Conc. £3.80 (2010 prices).

Limited. €

CRAIG CASTLE

Rhynie, Huntly, Aberdeenshire AB54 4LP

Tel: 01464 861705 **Fax:** 01464 861702

Owner: Mr A J Barlas **Contact:** The Property Manager

The Castle is built round a courtyard and consists of a 16th century L-shaped Keep, a Georgian house (architect John Adam) and a 19th century addition (architect Archibald Simpson of Aberdeen). The Castle was a Gordon stronghold for 300 years. It has a very fine collection of coats-of-arms.

Location: MAP 17:C10, OS Ref. NJ472 259. 3m W of Rhynie and Lumsden on B9002.

Open: May–Sept: Wed & every 2nd weekend in each month, 2–5pm.

Admission: Adult £5, Child £1.

Unsuitable. By arrangement. Limited for coaches. Guide dogs only.

CRAIGSTON CASTLE

Turriff, Aberdeenshire AB53 5PX

Tel: 01888 551228 **E-mail:** wu-gen01@craigston.co.uk

Owner: William Pratesi Urquhart **Contact:** The Housekeeper

Built in 1607 by John Urquhart Tutor of Cromarty, Craigston bears the marks of a client's brief rather than an architect's whim, which seems to belong to that strange slightly Gothic world. Few changes have been made to its exterior in its 400 years. A sculpted balcony unique in Scottish architecture depicts a piper, two grinning knights and David and Goliath. The interior dates from the early 19th century. Remarkable carved oak panels of Scottish kings' biblical heroes, mounted in doors and shutters of the early 17th century.

Location: MAP 17:D8, OS Ref. NJ762 550. On B9105, 4½m NE of Turriff.

Open: 11–26 Jun, 6–14 Aug: daily 1–4pm. Guided house tours: 1pm, 2pm & 3pm. Groups by appointment throughout the year.

Admission: Adult £6, Child £2, Conc. £4. Groups: Adult £5, Child/School £1.

Unsuitable. Obligatory. In grounds on leads.

CRATHES CASTLE & GARDEN

Banchory AB31 3QJ

Tel: 0131 243 9300

Owner: The National Trust for Scotland

The building of the castle began in 1553 and took 40 years to complete. Just over 300 years later, Sir James and Lady Burnett began developing the walled garden.

Location: MAP 17:D12, OS Ref. NO733 969: On A93, 3m E of Banchory and 15m W of Aberdeen.

CRUICKSHANK BOTANIC GARDEN

St Machar Drive, Aberdeen AB24 3UU

Tel: 01224 272704 **Fax:** 01224 272703

Owner: University of Aberdeen **Contact:** R B Rutherford

Extensive collection of shrubs, herbaceous and alpine plants and trees. Rock and water gardens.

Location: MAP 17:E11, OS Ref. NJ938 084. In old Aberdeen. Entrance in the Chanonry.

Open: Oct–Mar, Mon–Fri, 9am–4.30pm. Closed at weekends, Closed 24 Dec–5 Jan. Apr & Sept, Open every day 9am–6.30pm. May & Aug, Open every day 9am–8.30pm. Jun & Jul, Open every day 9am–9.30pm.

Admission: Free.

DALLAS DHU HISTORIC DISTILLERY

Forres, IV36 2RR

Tel: 01309 676548 **www.historic-scotland.gov.uk**

Owner: In the care of Historic Scotland **Contact:** The Monument Manager

A completely preserved time capsule of the distiller's craft. Wander at will through this fine old Victorian distillery then enjoy a dram. Visitor centre, shop and audio-visual theatre.

Location: MAP 16:P8, OS Ref. NJ035 566. 1m S of Forres off the A940.

Open: 1 Apr–30 Sept: daily, 9.30am–5.30pm, 1 Oct–31 Mar 9.30am–4.30pm, Nov–Mar closed Thurs & Fri. Last ticket 30 mins before closing.

Admission: Adult £5.20, Child £3.10, Conc. £4.20 (2010 prices).

WCs. By arrangement. Limited for coaches. €

DAVID WELCH WINTER GARDENS – DUTHIE PARK

Polmuir Road, Aberdeen, Grampian Highlands AB11 7TH

Tel: 01224 585310 **Fax:** 01224 210532 **E-mail:** wintergardens@aberdeencity.gov.uk.

www.aberdeencity.gov.uk

Owner: Aberdeen City Council **Contact:** Alan Findlay

One of Europe's largest indoor gardens with many rare and exotic plants on show from all around the world.

Location: MAP 17:E11, OS Ref. NJ97 044. Just N of River Dee, 1m S of city centre.

Open: All year: daily from 9.30pm.

Admission: Free.

DELGATIE CASTLE

TURRIFF, ABERDEENSHIRE AB53 5TD

www.delgatiecastle.com

Tel/Fax: 01888 563479 **E-mail:** joan@delgatiecastle.com

Owner: Delgatie Castle Trust **Contact:** Mrs Joan Johnson

"Best Visitor Experience" Award Winner. Dating from 1030 the Castle is steeped in Scottish history yet still has the atmosphere of a lived in home. It has some of the finest painted ceilings in Scotland, Mary Queen of Scots' bed-chamber, armour, Victorian clothes, fine furniture and paintings are displayed. Widest turnpike stair of its kind in Scotland. Clan Hay Centre. 17th best place in Britain for afternoon tea.

Location: MAP 17:D9, OS Ref. NJ754 506. Off A947 Aberdeen to Banff Road.

Open: Daily, 10am–5pm. Closed Christmas & New Year weeks.

Admission: Adult £6, Child/Conc. £4, Family £16. Groups (10+): £4.

No photography. Ground floor. WC. Home-baking and lunches. By arrangement. 6 x houses for self catering.

DRUM CASTLE & GARDEN

Drumoak, by Banchory AB31 3EY

Tel: 0131 243 9300

Owner: The National Trust for Scotland

Owned for 653 years by one family, the Irvines. The combination over the years of a 13th century square tower, a very fine Jacobean mansion house and the additions of the Victorian lairds make Drum Castle unique among Scottish castles.

Location: MAP 17:D12, OS Ref. NJ796 004. Off A93, 3m W of Peterculter and 10m W of Aberdeen.

DRUMMUIR CASTLE

Drummuir, by Keith, Banffshire AB55 5JE

Tel: 01542 810332 **Fax:** 01542 810302

Owner: The Gordon-Duff Family **Contact:** Alison Noakes

Castellated Victorian Gothic-style castle built in 1847 by Admiral Duff. 60ft high lantern tower with fine plasterwork. Family portraits, interesting artefacts and other paintings.

Location: MAP 17:B9, OS Ref. NJ372 442. Midway between Keith (5m) and Dufftown, off the B9014.

Open: Sat 27 Aug–Sun 25 Sept 2011: daily, 2–5pm (last tour 4.15pm).

Admission: Adult £2, Child £1.50. Pre-arranged groups: Adult £2, Child £1.50.

Obligatory. In grounds on leads.

DUFF HOUSE

Banff AB45 3SX

Tel: 01261 818181 **Fax:** 01261 818900

Contact: The Manager

One of the most imposing and palatial houses in Scotland, with a strong classical façade and a grand staircase leading to the main entrance.

Location: MAP 17:D8, OS Ref. NJ691 634. Banff. 47m NW of Aberdeen on A947.

Open: Apr–Oct: daily, 11am–5pm. Nov–Mar: Thur–Sun, 11am–4pm.

Admission: Adult £6.55, Conc. £5.45, Family £16.70. Groups (10+): £5. Free admission to shop, tearoom, grounds & woodland walks.

ELGIN CATHEDRAL

Elgin, IV30 1HU

Tel: 01343 547171 **www.historic-scotland.gov.uk**

Owner: Historic Scotland **Contact:** The Monument Manager

Once one of the most beautiful Scottish cathedrals, known as the Lantern of the North. This magnificent ruin has many outstanding features including one of the country's finest octagonal chapter houses. See the bishop's home at Spynie Palace, 2m N. of the town.

Location: MAP 17:A8, OS Ref. NJ223 630. In Elgin on the A96.

Open: 1 Apr–30 Sept: daily, 9.30am–5.30pm. Oct daily, 9.30am–4.30pm. Nov–Mar 9.30am–4.30pm closed Thurs & Fri. Last ticket 30 mins before closing.

Admission: Adult £4.70, Child £2.80, Conc. £3.80 (2010 prices). Joint entry ticket available with Spynie Palace.

€

FYVIE CASTLE

Turriff, Aberdeenshire AB53 8JS

Tel: 0131 243 9300

Owner: The National Trust for Scotland

The five towers of the castle bear witness to the five families who have owned it. Fyvie Castle has a fine wheel stair and a collection of arms and armour and paintings.

Location: MAP 17:D9, S Ref. NJ763 393. Off A947, 8m SE of Turriff, and 25m N of Aberdeen.

HADDO HOUSE

Tarves, Ellon, Aberdeenshire AB41 0ER

Tel: 0131 243 9300

Owner: The National Trust for Scotland

Designed by William Adam in 1731 for William, 2nd Earl of Aberdeen. Much of the interior is 'Adam Revival' carried out about 1880 for John, 7th Earl and 1st Marquess of Aberdeen and his Countess, Ishbel.

Location: MAP 17:E10, OS Ref. NJ868 348. Off B999, 4m N of Pitmedden, 10m NW of Ellon.

HUNTLY CASTLE

Huntly, AB54 4SH

Tel: 01466 793191 **www.historic-scotland.gov.uk**

Owner: Historic Scotland **Contact:** The Monument Manager

Known also as Strathbogie Castle, this glorious ruin stands in a beautiful setting on the banks of the River Deveron. Famed for its fine heraldic sculpture and inscribed stone friezes.

Location: MAP 17:C9, OS Ref. NJ532 407. In Huntly off the A96. N side of the town.

Open: 1 Apr–30 Sept: daily, 9.30am–5.30pm. 1–31 Oct daily, 9.30am–4.30pm. 1 Nov–31 Mar, 9.30am–4.30pm closed Thurs & Fri. Last ticket 30 mins before closing.

Admission: Adult £4.70, Child £2.80, Conc £3.80 (2010 prices).

Partial. WCs. On leads. €

KILDRUMMY CASTLE

Alford, Aberdeenshire, AB33 8RA

Tel: 01975 571331 **www.historic-scotland.gov.uk**

Owner: Historic Scotland **Contact:** The Monument Manager

Though ruined, the best example in Scotland of a 13th century castle with a curtain wall, four round towers, hall and chapel of that date. The seat of the Earls of Mar, it was dismantled after the first Jacobite rising in 1715.

Location: MAP 17:C11, OS Ref. NJ455 164. 10m SW of Alford on the A97.

Open: 1 Apr–30 Sept: daily, 9.30am–5.30pm. Last ticket 30 mins before closing.

Admission: Adult £3.70, Child £2.20, Conc. £3.00 (2010 prices).

Limited for coaches. By arrangement. Limited for coaches. On leads. €

KILDRUMMY CASTLE GARDEN

Kildrummy, Aberdeenshire

Tel: 01975 571203 / 563451 **Contact:** Alastair J Laing

Ancient quarry, shrub and alpine gardens renowned for their interest and variety. Water gardens below ruined castle.

Location: MAP 17:C11, OS Ref. NJ455 164. On A97 off A944 10m SW of Alford. 16m SSW of Huntly.

Open: Apr–Oct: daily, 10am–5pm.

Admission: Adult £3.50, Child Free.

LEITH HALL

Huntly, Aberdeenshire AB54 4NQ

Tel: 0131 243 9300

Owner: The National Trust for Scotland **Contact:** The Property Manager

This mansion house, built around a courtyard was the home of the Leith family for almost 300 years.

Location: MAP 17:C10, OS Ref. NJ541 298. B9002, 1m W of Kennethmont, 7m S of Huntley.

LICKLEYHEAD CASTLE

Auchleven, Insch, Aberdeenshire AB52 6PN

Tel: 01651 821276

Owner: The Leslie family **Contact:** Mrs C Leslie

A beautifully restored Laird's Castle, Lickleyhead was built by the Leslies c1450 and extensively renovated in 1629 by John Forbes of Leslie, whose initials are carved above the entrance. It is an almost unspoilt example of the transformation from 'Chateau-fort' to 'Chateau-maison' and boasts many interesting architectural features.

Location: MAP 17:C10, OS Ref. NJ628 237. Auchleven is 2m S of Insch on B992. Twin pillars of castle entrance on left at foot of village.

Open: 2–6, 9–13 May and 6–10 June: 12 noon–2pm. Also Sats only during high season 2 July–3 Sept: 12 noon–2pm.

Admission: Free.

Unsuitable. Limited. No coaches. In grounds, on leads.

PITMEDDEN GARDEN

Ellon, Aberdeenshire AB41 0PD

Tel: 0131 243 9300

Owner: The National Trust for Scotland

The centrepiece of this property is the Great Garden which was originally laid out in 1675 by Sir Alexander Seton, 1st Baronet of Pitmedden.

Location: MAP 17:E10, OS Ref. NJ885 280. On A920 1m W of Pitmedden village & 14m N of Aberdeen.

PLUSCARDEN ABBEY

Nr Elgin, Moray IV30 8UA

Tel: 01343 890257 **Fax:** 01343 890258 **E-mail:** monks@pluscardenabbey.org

Contact: Brother Michael

Valliscaulian, founded 1230.

Location: MAP 17:A8, OS Ref. NJ142 576. On minor road 6m SW of Elgin. Follow B9010 for first mile.

Open: All year: 4.45am–8.30pm. Shop: 8.30am–5pm.

Admission: Free.

Pitmedden Garden

Leith Hall

PROVOST SKENE'S HOUSE

Guestrow, off Broad Street, Aberdeen AB10 1AS

Tel: 01224 641086 **Fax:** 01224 632133

Owner: Aberdeen City Council **Contact:** Shonagh Bain

Built in the 16th century, Provost Skene's House is one of Aberdeen's few remaining examples of early burgh architecture. Splendid room settings include a suite of Georgian rooms, an Edwardian nursery, magnificent 17th century plaster ceilings and wood panelling. The house also features an intriguing series of religious paintings in the Painted Gallery and changing fashions in the Costume Gallery.

Location: MAP 17:E11, OS Ref. NJ943 064. Aberdeen city centre, off Broad Street.

Open: Mon–Sat, 10am–5pm, Closed Suns.

Admission: Free.

ST MACHAR'S CATHEDRAL TRANSEPTS

Old Aberdeen

Tel: 01667 460232 **www.historic-scotland.gov.uk**

Owner: In the care of Historic Scotland

The nave and towers of the Cathedral remain in use as a church, and the ruined transepts are in care. In the south transept is the fine altar tomb of Bishop Dunbar (1514–32).

Location: MAP 17:E11, OS Ref. NJ939 088. In old Aberdeen. ½m N of King's College.

Open: Open all year.

Admission: Free.

SPYNIE PALACE

Elgin, IV30 5QG

Tel: 01343 546358 **www.historic-scotland.gov.uk**

Owner: Historic Scotland **Contact:** The Monument Manager

Spynie Palace was the residence of the Bishops of Moray from the 14th century to 1686. The site is dominated by the massive tower built by Bishop David Stewart (1461–77) and affords spectacular views across Spynie Loch.

Location: MAP 17:A8, OS Ref. NJ231 659. 2m N of Elgin off the A941.

Open: 1 Apr–30 Sept: daily, 9.30am–5.30pm, 1 Oct–31 Mar 9.30am–4.30pm weekends only. Last ticket 30 mins before closing.

Admission: Adult £3.70, Child £2.20, Conc. £3.00 (2010 prices). Joint entry ticket with Elgin Cathedral available.

Picnic area. Closes for lunch. Partial. WCs. €

TOLQUHON CASTLE

Aberdeenshire, AB41 7LP

Tel: 01651 851286 **www.historic-scotland.gov.uk**

Owner: In the care of Historic Scotland **Contact:** The Monument Manager

Tolquhon was built for the Forbes family. The early 15th century tower was enlarged between 1584 and 1589 with a large mansion around the courtyard. Noted for its highly ornamented gatehouse and pleasance.

Location: MAP 17:E10, OS Ref. NJ874 286. 15m N of Aberdeen on the A920.

Open: 1 Apr–30 Sept: daily, 9.30am–5.30pm, 1 Oct –31 Mar 9.30am–4.30pm, weekends only. Last ticket 30 mins before closing.

Admission: Adult £3.70, Child £2.20, Conc. £3.00 (2010 prices).

Picnic area. Closes for lunch. By arrangement. On leads. €

■ Owner

The Dowager Countess Cawdor

■ Contact

The Administrator
David Broadfoot MBE
Cawdor Castle
Nairn
Scotland IV12 5RD
Tel: 01667 404401
Fax: 01667 404674
E-mail: info@cawdorcastle.com

■ Location

MAP 16:O9
OS Ref. NH850 500

From Edinburgh A9, 3½ hrs, Inverness 20 mins, Nairn 10 mins. Main road: A9, 14m.

Rail: Nairn Station 5m.

Bus: Inverness to Nairn bus route 200 yds.

Taxi: Cawdor Taxis 01667 404315.

Air: Inverness Airport 5m.

■ Opening Times

Summer
1 May–2 October
Daily: 10am–5.30pm.
Last admission 5pm.

Winter
October–April
Groups by appointment, admission prices on application.

Auchindoune Garden
May–July: Tue & Thurs, 10am–4.30pm.

Otherwise by appointment.

■ Admission

Summer
House & Garden

Adult	£9.00
Child (5–15yrs)	£5.50
OAP	£8.00
Student	£8.00
Family (2+5)	£27.00
Groups (20+)	
Adult	£7.50
OAP/Student	£6.95
Garden only	
Per person	£5.00

RHS Access
Free admission to gardens May, June, September & October.

■ Special Events

16th July
Twelfth Night - Illyria

24th September
Living Food Festival

For concerts, garden tours and other events see website www.cawdorcastle.com

CAWDOR CASTLE

www.cawdorcastle.com

This splendid romantic castle, dating from the late 14th century, was built as a private fortress by the Thanes of Cawdor, and remains the home of the Cawdor family to this day. The ancient medieval tower was built around the legendary holly tree.

Although the house has evolved over 600 years, later additions, mainly of the 17th century, were all built in the Scottish vernacular style with slated roofs over walls and crow-stepped gables of mellow local stone. This style gives Cawdor a strong sense of unity, and the massive, severe exterior belies an intimate interior that gives the place a surprisingly personal, friendly atmosphere.

Good furniture, fine portraits and pictures, interesting objects and outstanding tapestries are arranged to please the family rather than to echo fashion or impress. Memories of Shakespeare's *Macbeth* give Cawdor an elusive, evocative quality that delights visitors.

Gardens

The flower garden also has a family feel to it, where plants are chosen out of affection rather than affectation. This is a lovely spot between spring and late summer. The walled garden has been restored with a holly maze, paradise garden, knot garden and thistle garden. The wild garden beside its stream leads into beautiful trails through spectacular mature mixed woodland, in which paths are helpfully marked and colour-coded. The Tibetan garden and traditional Scottish vegetable garden are at the Dower House at Auchindoune.

- 9 hole golf course, putting green, golf clubs for hire, Conferences, whisky tasting, musical entertainments, specialised garden visits. No photography, video taping or tripods inside. No large day sacks inside castle.
- Gift, book and wool shops.
- Lunches, sherry or champagne receptions.
- Visitors may alight at the entrance. WC. Only ground floor accessible.
- Licensed Courtyard Restaurant, May–Oct, groups should book.
- By arrangement.
- 250 cars and 25 coaches.
- £5.50 per child. Room notes, quiz and answer sheet can be provided.
- Guide dogs only in castle and grounds. Dog walking trail available.

€

DUNVEGAN CASTLE & GARDENS

www.dunvegancastle.com

Any visit to the Isle of Skye is incomplete without savouring the wealth of history offered by Dunvegan Castle & Gardens. Built on a rock in an idyllic loch side setting, Dunvegan is the oldest continuously inhabited castle in Scotland and has been the ancestral home of the Chiefs of MacLeod for 800 years.

Today visitors can enjoy tours of an extraordinary castle and Highland estate steeped in history and clan legend, delight in the beauty of its formal gardens, take a boat trip onto Loch Dunvegan to see the seal colony (voted '1 of the Best UK Days Out' by The Sunday Times Travel Magazine), stay in one of its charming estate cottages, enjoy an appetising meal at the MacLeods Table Cafe or browse in one of its four shops offering a wide choice to suit everyone. There is a wealth of activities in the area ranging from walking, fishing and sightseeing to fine local cuisine, arts and craft and camping at the estate's Glenbrittle Campsite at the foot of the majestic Cuillin mountain range.

Over time, we have given a warm Highland welcome to visitors including Sir Walter Scott, Dr Johnson and Queen Elizabeth II and we look forward to welcoming you.

Gardens

Dunvegan Castle's five acres of formal gardens began life in the 18th century. In stark contrast to the barren moorland and mountains that dominate Skye's landscape, the gardens are a hidden oasis featuring an eclectic mix of plants as you make your way through woodland glades, past shimmering pools fed by waterfalls and streams flowing down to the sea. Having experienced the Water Garden with its ornate bridges and islands replete with a rich and colourful plant variety, you can take a stroll through the elegant surroundings of the formal Round Garden featuring a Box-wood Parterre as its centrepiece. In what was formerly the castle's vegetable garden, the Walled Garden now features a diverse range of plants and flowers that compliment the attractive features including the stone worked MacLeod Clan Parliament Seating, a water lily pond and a Larch Pergola. A considerable amount of replanting and landscaping has taken place over the last thirty years to restore the gardens to their former glory and provide a legacy which future generations can enjoy.

The Gardens

- Boat trips to seal colony. Fishing trips and loch cruises. No photography in Castle.
- Gift and craft shops.
- Partial. WCs.
- Licensed.
- By appointment in English or Gaelic at no extra charge. Self guided.
- 120 cars and 10 coaches. If possible please book. Seal boat trip dependent upon weather.
- Welcome by arrangement. Guide available on request.
- On leads.
- 3 self-catering holiday cottages each sleeping 6.

Owner

Hugh Macleod of Macleod

Contact

Estate Manager
Dunvegan Castle
Isle of Skye
Scotland IV55 8WF

Tel: 01470 521206
Fax: 01470 521205
E-mail: info@dunvegancastle.com

Location

MAP 15:F9
OS Ref. NG250 480

1m N of village. NW corner of Skye.

From Inverness A82 to Invermoriston, A887 to Kyle of Lochalsh. From Fort William A82 to Invergarry, A87 to Kyle of Lochalsh.

Kyle of Lochalsh to Dunvegan via Skye Bridge.

Ferry: Maillaig to Armadale.

Rail: Inverness to Kyle of Lochalsh.

Opening Times

1 April–15 October
Daily: 10am–5.30pm.
Last admission 5pm.

16 October–31 March
Open by appointment weekdays only.

Castle & Gardens closed Christmas and New Year.

Admission

Summer
Castle & Gardens

Adult	£9.00
Child (5–15yrs)	£4.50
Senior/Student/Group (minimum 10 adults)	£7.00
Family Ticket (2 Adults, 3 Children)	£24.00

Gardens only

Adult	£7.00
Child (5–15yrs)	£3.50
Senior/Student/Group	£6.00

Seal Boats

Adult	£6.00
Child (5–15yrs)	£4.00
Senior/Student/Group	£5.00
Infant (under 5yrs)	Free

Loch Cruises & Fishing Trips

Adult	£37.00
Child (5–15yrs)	£26.00

Events & Weddings
Catering for up to 60 guests.

Film & TV
Unique location for film, TV or advertising.

BALLINDALLOCH CASTLE

Ballindalloch, Banffshire AB37 9AX

Tel: 01807 500205 **Fax:** 01807 500210 **E-mail:** enquiries@ballindallochcastle.co.uk

www.ballindallochcastle.co.uk

Owner: Mr & Mrs Oliver Russell **Contact:** Mrs Clare Russell

Ballindalloch Castle is, first and foremost, a much-loved home, lived in by its original family, the Macpherson-Grants, since 1546. Filled with family memorabilia, including an important collection of 17th century Spanish paintings. Beautiful rock and rose gardens and river walks. The estate is home to the famous Aberdeen-Angus breed of cattle.

Location: MAP 17:A9, OS Ref. NJ178 366. 14 m NE of Grantown-on-Spey on A95. 22 m S of Elgin on A95.

Open: Good Fri–30 Sept: 10.30am–5pm. Closed Saturdays. Coaches outwith season by arrangement.

Admission: House & Grounds: Adult £8, Child (6–16) £4, Conc £6, Family (2+3) £20, Groups (20+) Adult £5, Child £2.50, Season Ticket £20. Grounds only: Adult £4, Child (6–16) £2, Conc £3, Family (2+3) £10, Season Ticket £12. (*2010 prices & opening times).

Ground floor and grounds only. WCs. In dog walking area.

Cawdor Castle

CASTLE OF OLD WICK

Wick, IV

Tel: 01667 460232 **www.historic-scotland.gov.uk**

Owner: Historic Scotland **Contact:** Monument Manager

This dramatically located castle is one of the best preserved Norse castles in Scotland. The castle is a simple square keep of at least three storeys. In addition to the tower the site contains the low-lying ruins of other buildings.

Location: MAP 17:B3, OS Ref. ND368 487. 1m S of Wick on Shore Road, signposted from Wick town centre.

Open: Open all year.

Admission: Free.

CAWDOR CASTLE

See page 440 for full page entry.

THE DOUNE OF ROTHIEMURCHUS

By Aviemore PH22 1QH

Tel: 01479 812345 **E-mail:** info@rothie.net **www.rothiemurchus.net**

Owner: John Grant of Rothiemurchus, Lord Huntingtower

Contact: Rothiemurchus Centre

The family home of the Grants of Rothiemurchus since 1560, was nearly lost as a ruin and has been under an ambitious repair programme since 1975. The exterior and work on this exciting project in its unexpected setting may be visited on Mondays throughout the summer and the first Monday of every month. Book at the Rothiemurchus Centre or online for visits to restored rooms which can be enjoyed on the 1.5 hours 'Highland Lady Tour' which explores the haunts of Elizabeth Grant of Rothiemurchus, born 1797, author of 'Memoirs of a Highland Lady'. Her charming bestseller vividly describes the Doune of Rothiemurchus and its surroundings from the memories of her childhood.

Location: MAP 16:P11, OS Ref. NH900 100. 2m S of Aviemore on E bank of Spey river.

Open: Restoration and grounds open Apr–Aug: Mon 10am–12.30pm & 2–4.30pm (or dusk) also 1st Mon in the month during winter excl. Xmas & New Year. House open every Wednesday as part of a Highland Lady Tour or by special arrangement excl. Xmas and New Year. Groups by special arrangement.

Admission: Restoration and grounds donation to charity; Tours: £20pp (min 2 people) 2 hours; Groups: On application.

Rothiemurchus Centre. Obligatory. Limited. In grounds, on leads.

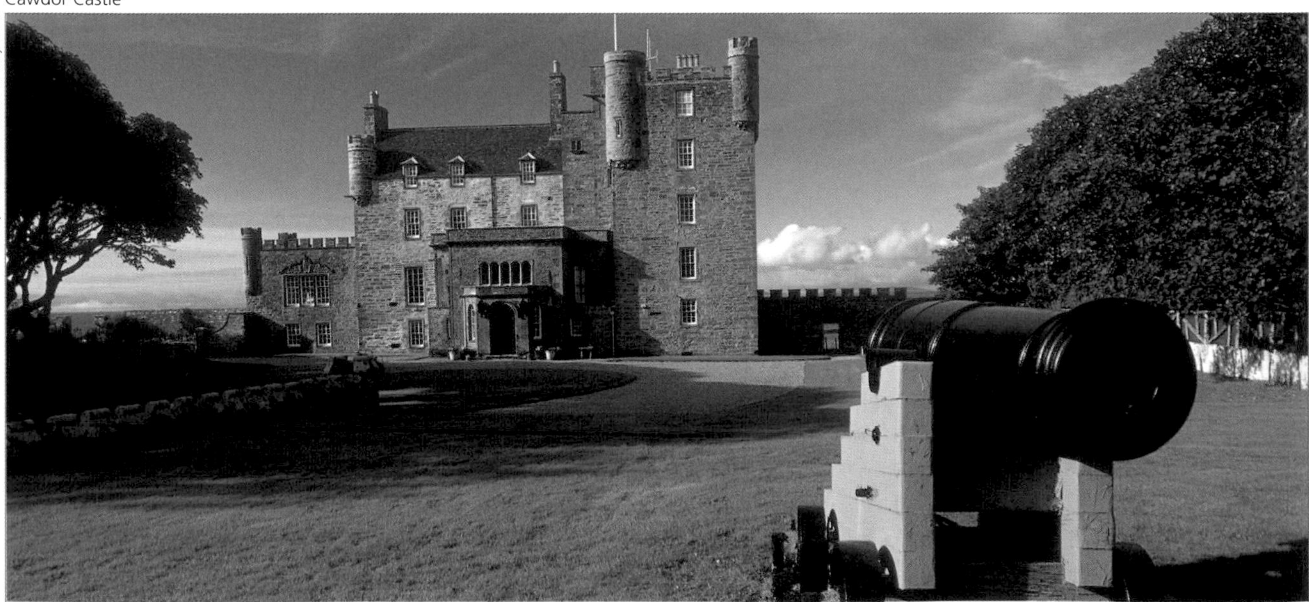

The Queen Elizabeth Castle of Mey Trust

CASTLE OF MEY

THURSO, CAITHNESS KW14 8XH

www.castleofmey.org.uk

Tel: 01847 851473 **Fax:** 01847 851475 **E-mail:** enquiries@castleofmey.org.uk

Owner: The Queen Elizabeth Castle of Mey Trust **Contact:** James Murray

The holiday home of The Queen Mother in Caithness and the only property in Britain that she owned. She bought the Castle in 1952, saved it from becoming a ruin and developed the gardens. It became her ideal holiday home because of the beautiful surroundings and the privacy she was always given. There is a purpose-built Visitor Centre with shop and tearoom and also an animal centre for children.

Location: MAP 17:B2, OS Ref. ND290 739. On A836 between Thurso and John O'Groats, just outside the village of Mey. 12m Thurso station, 18m Wick airport.

Open: 1 May–30 Sept: daily, 10.30am–last entries 4pm. Closed 28 Jul–8 Aug 2011 inclusive.

Admission: Adult £10.00, Child (16yrs and under) £4.50, Conc £9.00. Family £24.00. Booked groups (15+): £9.00. Gardens & grounds only: Adult £4.50.

No photography in the Castle. Partial. WCs. Licensed. By arrangement. Guide dogs only.

DUNROBIN CASTLE

GOLSPIE, SUTHERLAND KW10 6SF

www.dunrobincastle.co.uk

Tel: 01408 633177 **Fax:** 01408 634081 **E-mail:** info@dunrobincastle.co.uk

Owner: The Sutherland Dunrobin Trust **Contact:** Scott Morrison

Dates from the 13th century with additions in the 17th, 18th and 19th centuries. Wonderful furniture, paintings, library, ceremonial robes and memorabilia. Victorian museum in grounds with a fascinating collection including Pictish stones. Set in fine woodlands overlooking the sea. Magnificent formal gardens, one of few remaining French/Scottish formal parterres. Falconry display, telephone to confirm times.

Location: MAP 16:O6, OS Ref. NC850 010. 50m N of Inverness on A9. 1m NE of Golspie.

Open: 1 Apr–15 Oct: Apr, May, Sept & October, Mon–Sat, 10.30am–4.30pm, Sun, 12 noon–4.30pm. No Falconry display on Sundays. Last entry half an hour before closing. Jun, Jul & Aug, daily, 10.30am–5.30pm. Falconry displays every day. Last entry half an hour before closing. Falconry displays at 11.30am & 2pm.

Admission: Adult £9, Child £5, OAP/Student. £7.50, Family (2+2) £24. Groups (minimum 10): Adult £7.50, Child £4.70, OAP. £6.50. Please note these rates also include entry to the falconry display, museum and gardens.

Unsuitable for wheelchairs. By arrangement.

DUNVEGAN CASTLE & GARDENS

See page 441 for full page entry.

EILEAN DONAN CASTLE

Dornie, Kyle of Lochalsh, Wester Ross IV40 8DX

Tel: 01599 555202 **Fax:** 01599 555262 **E-mail:** eileandonan@btconnect.com

www.eileandonancastle.com **Contact:** David Win – Castle Keeper

A fortified site for eight hundred years, Eilean Donan now represents one of Scotland's most iconic images. Located at the point where three great sea lochs meet amidst stunning highland scenery on the main road to Skye. Spiritual home of Clan Macrae with century old links to Clan Mackenzie.

Location: MAP 16:J10, OS Ref. NG880 260. On A87 8m E of Skye Bridge.

Open: Mar–Oct: 10am–5pm.

Admission: Adult £5.50, Conc £4.50.

Dunrobin Castle

FORT GEORGE

ARDERSIER BY INVERNESS IV2 7TD

www.historic-scotland.gov.uk

Tel/Fax: 01667 460232

Owner: In the care of Historic Scotland **Contact:** The Monument Manager

Built following the Battle of Culloden to subdue the Highlands, Fort George never saw a shot fired in anger. One of the most outstanding artillery fortifications in Europe with reconstructed barrack room displays. The Queen's Own Highlanders' Museum.

Location: MAP 16:O6, OS Ref. NH762 567. 11m NE of Inverness off the A96 by Ardersier.

Open: Apr–Sep 9.30am–5.30pm daily, Oct–Mar 9.30am–4.30pm daily. Last ticket sold 45 mins before closing.

Admission: Adult £6.70, Child £4.00, Conc. £5.40. (2010 prices). 10% discount for groups (11+).

WCs. Free if pre-booked. On leads. €

URQUHART CASTLE

DRUMNADROCHIT, LOCH NESS, IV63 6XJ

www.historic-scotland.gov.uk

Tel: 01456 450551

Owner: In the care of Historic Scotland **Contact:** The Monument Manager

One of the largest castles in Scotland, it dominates a rocky promontory on Loch Ness. Most of the existing buildings date from the 16th century. Explore the visitor centre with original artefacts, audio-visual presentation, shop and café.

Location: MAP 16:M10, OS Ref. NH531 286. On Loch Ness near Drumnadrochit on the A82.

Open: 1 Apr–30 Sept: daily, 9.30am–6pm. 1–31 Oct 9.30–5pm, 1 Nov–31 Mar 9.30am–4.30pm. Last entry 45 mins before closing.

Admission: Adult £7.00, Child £4.20, Conc £5.60 (2010 prices).

WCs. Limited for coaches. Free if pre-booked. €

BALFOUR CASTLE

Shapinsay, Orkney Islands KW17 2DY

Tel: 01856 711282 **Fax:** 01856 711283

Owner/Contact: Mrs Lidderdale

Built in 1848. Now a small private hotel specialising in house parties, weddings etc. A beautiful island escape.

Location: MAP 14, OS Ref. HY475 164 on Shapinsay Island, 3½m NNE of Kirkwall.

Open: By appointment only.

Admission: Bookings essential. Contact property for details.

BISHOP'S & EARL'S PALACES

Kirkwall, Orkney, KW15 1PD

Tel: 01856 871918 **www.historic-scotland.gov.uk**

Owner: Historic Scotland **Contact:** The Monument Manager

The Bishop's Palace is a 12th century hall-house with a round tower built by Bishop Reid in 1541–48. The adjacent Earl's Palace built in 1607 has been described as the most mature and accomplished piece of Renaissance architecture left in Scotland.

Location: MAP 14, Bishop's Palace: OS Ref. HY447 108. Earl's Palace: OS Ref. HY448 108. In Kirkwall on A960.

Open: 1 Apr–31 Oct: daily, 9.30am–5.30pm. Last ticket 30 mins before closing.

Admission: Adult £3.70, Child £2.20, Conc. £3.00 (2010 prices). Explorer Pass available for entry to all Historic Scotland's Orkney attractions.

Closes for lunch. On leads. €

THE BLACKHOUSE, ARNOL

Arnol, Isle of Lewis, HS2 9DB

Tel: 01851 710395 **www.historic-scotland.gov.uk**

Owner: Historic Scotland **Contact:** The Monument Manager

A traditional Lewis thatched house, fully furnished, complete with attached barn, byre and stockyard. A peat fire burns in the open hearth. Includes a fascinating visitor centre.

Location: MAP 15, OS Ref. NB311 492. In Arnol village, Isle of Lewis, 14m NW of Stornoway on A858.

Open: 1 Apr–30 Sept 9.30am–5.30pm. 1 Oct–31 Mar. 9.30am–4.30pm. Closed on Sunday all year round. Last ticket 30 mins before closing.

Admission: Adult £2.50, Child £1.50, Conc. £2.00 (2010 prices).

WCs. Limited for coaches. On leads. €.

BROCH OF GURNESS

Aikerness, Orkney, KW17 2NH

Tel: 01856 751414 **www.historic-scotland.gov.uk**

Owner: Historic Scotland **Contact:** The Monument Manager

A noted icon of Orkney's rich archaeological heritage, the broch is one of the most outstanding surviving examples of a later prehistoric (Iron Age) settlement that is unique to northern Scotland.

Location: MAP 14, OS Ref. HY383 268. At Aikerness, about 14m NW of Kirkwall on A966.

Open: 1 Apr–31 Oct: daily, 9.30am–5.30pm. Last ticket 30 mins before closing.

Admission: Adult £4.70, Child £2.80, Conc. £3.80 (2010 prices). Explorer Pass available for entry to all Historic Scotland's Orkney attractions.

Closes for lunch. By arrangement. Limited for coaches. On leads. €

JARLSHOF PREHISTORIC & NORSE SETTLEMENT

Shetland, Sumburgh Head, ZE3 9JN

Tel: 01950 460112 **www.historic-scotland.gov.uk**

Owner: Historic Scotland **Contact:** The Monument Manager

Over 3 acres of remains spanning 3,000 years from the Stone Age. Oval-shaped Bronze Age houses, Iron Age broch and wheel houses. Viking long houses, medieval farmstead and 16th century laird's house.

Location: MAP 17, OS Ref. HU399 095. At Sumburgh Head, 22m S of Lerwick on the A970.

Open: 1 Apr–30 Sept: daily, 9.30am–5.30pm. Last ticket 30 mins before closing.

Admission: Adult £4.70, Child £2.80, Conc. £3.80 (2010 prices).

Visitor Centre. Closes for lunch. Limited for coaches. On leads. €

KISIMUL CASTLE

Castlebay, Isle of Barra HS9 5UZ

Tel: 01871 810313 **www.historic-scotland.gov.uk**

Owner: Historic Scotland **Contact:** The Monument Manager

The traditional seat of the chiefs of Clan Macneil, the castle stands on a rocky islet just off the island of Barra. It is the only significant surviving medieval castle in the Western Isles. It makes a delightful place to visit, offering excellent views of the sea & the island.

Location: MAP 15 C:12. OS Ref. NL665 979. In Castlebay, Isle of Barra, five minute boat trip (weather permitting).

Open: 1 Apr–30 Sept: daily, 9.30am–5.30pm.

Admission: Adult £4.70, Child £2.80, Conc. £3.80 (2010 prices). Includes boat trip. Last ticket 30 mins before closing.

Closes for lunch. Sturdy footwear recommended. €

Earl's Palace

Skara Brae

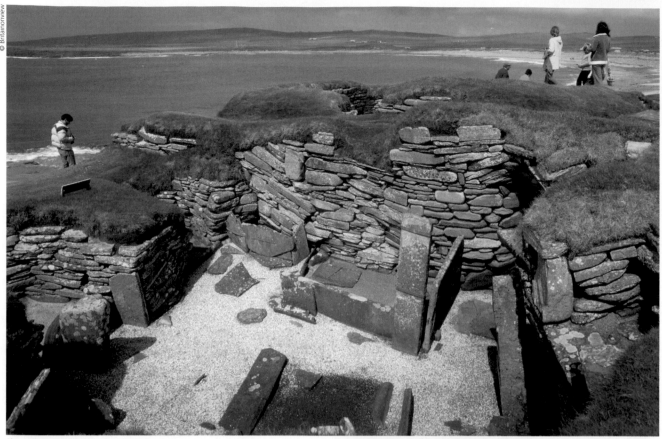

MAESHOWE CHAMBERED CAIRN

Orkney, KW16 3HA

Tel: 01856 761606 **www.historic-scotland.gov.uk**

Owner: Historic Scotland **Contact:** The Monument Manager

This world-famous tomb was built in Neolithic times, before 2700 BC. The large mound covers a stone-built passage and a burial chamber with cells in the walls. Runic inscriptions tell of how it was plundered of its treasures by Vikings.

Location: MAP 14, OS Ref. HY318 128. 9m W of Kirkwall on the A965.

Open: 1 Apr–30 Sept: daily, 9.30am–5pm. 1 Oct–31 Mar: daily, 9.30am–4.30pm.

Admission: Adult £5.20, Child £3.10, Conc. £4.20 (2010 prices) Timed ticketing in place – please telephone for details, and to book. Admission and shop at nearby Tormiston Mill. Ask about Explorer Passes, available for entry to all Historic Scotland's Orkney attractions.

Timed Tours, booking in advance advisable. Obligatory.

Limited for cars. No coaches. €

RING OF BRODGAR STONE CIRCLE AND HENGE

Stromness, Orkney

Tel: 01856 841815 **www.historic-scotland.gov.uk**

Owner: Historic Scotland **Contact:** The Monument Manager

A magnificent circle of upright stones with an enclosing ditch spanned by causeways, dating to the late Neolithic period. Part of the Heart of Neolithic Orkney World Heritage Site.

Location: MAP 14, OS Ref. HY294 134. 5m NE of Stromness on the B9055.

Open: All year.

Admission: Free.

Ranger Service on site to give guided walks. Contact 01856 841 732 for details. Limited for coaches. On leads.

TANKERNESS HOUSE

Broad Street, Kirkwall, Orkney

Tel: 01856 873535 **Fax:** 01856 871560

Owner: Orkney Islands Council **Contact:** Steve Callaghan

A fine vernacular 16th century town house contains The Orkney Museum.

Location: MAP 14, OS Ref. HY446 109. In Kirkwall opposite W end of cathedral.

Open: Oct–Apr: Mon–Sat, 10.30am–12.30pm & 1.30–5pm. May–Sept: Mon–Sat, 10.30am–5pm. Gardens always open. Please telephone in advance to confirm up to date opening times.

Admission: Free.

SKARA BRAE & SKAILL HOUSE

SANDWICK, ORKNEY, KW16 3LR

www.historic-scotland.gov.uk

Tel: 01856 841815

Owner: Historic Scotland / Major M R S Macrae **Contact:** Monument Manager

Skara Brae is one of the best preserved groups of Stone Age houses in Western Europe. Built before the Pyramids, the houses contain stone furniture, hearths and drains. Visitor centre and replica house with joint admission with Skaill House – 17th century home of the laird who excavated Skara Brae.

Location: MAP 14, OS6 HY231 188. 19m NW of Kirkwall on the B9056.

Open: Apr–Sept: daily, 9.30am–5.30pm. Oct–Mar: daily, 9.30am–4.30pm. Last ticket 45 mins before closing.

Admission: Apr–Sept: Adult £6.70, Child £4.00, Conc. £5.40. Oct–Mar: Adult £5.70, Child £3.40, Conc. £4.70 (2010 prices). 10% discount for groups (11+) Explorer Pass available for entry to all Historic Scotland's Orkney attractions.

WCs. Limited for coaches. Free school visits when booked. On leads.

€

Interior Castell Coch

Wales

The traditional border between Wales and England is Offa's Dyke, built by King Offa between 757 and 796AD. North Wales is a holiday area attracting lovers of coast and countryside alike. To the west lies Snowdon, a popular destination for climbers and walkers. To the east is a gentler landscape of moorlands, valleys and the hills of the Welsh Borders. Further south, the Gower Peninsula was the first place in Britain to be designated an Area of Outstanding Natural Beauty.

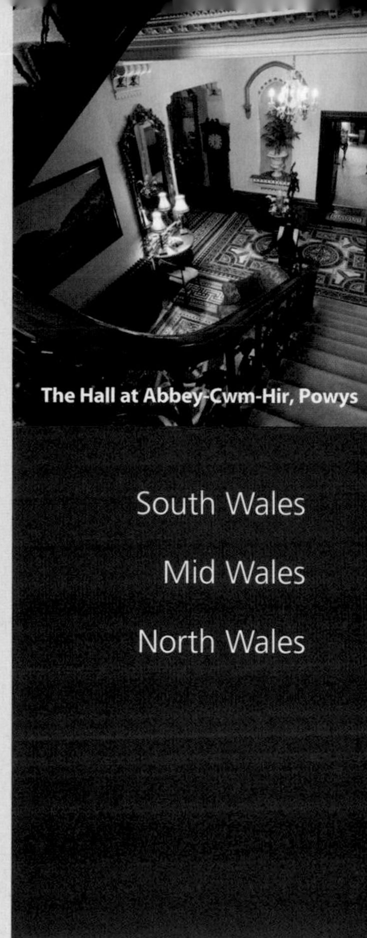

The Hall at Abbey-Cwm-Hir, Powys

South Wales

Mid Wales

North Wales

NORTH WALES

MID WALES

SOUTH WALES

Gwydir Castle, Gwynedd

Tintern Abbey, Monmouthshire

Pembroke Castle, Pembroke

■ **Owner**

Newport City Council

■ **Contact**

The Manager
Newport
South Wales
NP10 8YW

Tel: 01633 815880
Fax: 01633 815895
E-mail: tredegar.house@newport.gov.uk

■ **Location**

MAP 2:M1
OS Ref. ST290 852

M4 J28 signposted from London 2½hrs, from Cardiff 20 mins. 2m SW of Newport town centre.

■ **Opening Times**

Easter–Sept:
Wed–Sun & BHs,
Guided tours only
11am–4pm.

Evening tours & groups by appointment all year round.

Events throughout the year including Christmas & Halloween.

■ **Admission**

Adult	£6.50
Conc.	£4.90
Children 15 & under	Free

(when accompanied by a paying adult)

(2010 prices)

TREDEGAR HOUSE & PARK

Tredegar House is one of the architectural wonders of Wales and one of the most significant late seventeenth century houses in the whole of the British Isles. For over five hundred years it was the home to one of the greatest Welsh families, the Morgan's, later Lords Tredegar.

Visitors are taken on a lively and entertaining guided tour which includes the magnificent State Rooms, the elegant family apartments, and the intriguing warren of rooms 'below stairs'.

The House is set in 90 acres of parkland with nineteenth century planting of sequoia, rhododendron and other shrubs, formal gardens, lake and children's playground. The basic medieval garden plan survives on two sides of the House in a series of walled gardens, which have been rescued from the brink of decay. An outstanding early eighteenth century Orangery Garden has been recreated from surviving documentary and archaeological evidence. Late eighteenth century landscaping by Mickle swept away all but one of the avenues of oaks and chestnuts radiating from the House. His plan to demolish the magnificent late seventeenth century stable block was, thankfully never carried out.

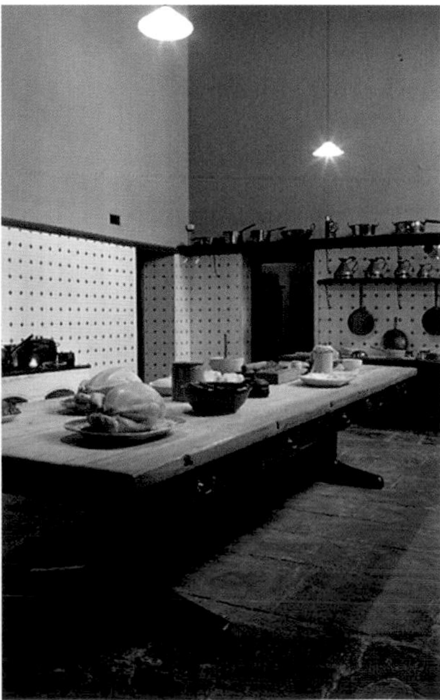

Photography by prior arrangement.

Partial. WCs.

Obligatory.

In grounds, on leads.

Oct–Mar booked tours only.

ABERCAMLAIS

Brecon, Powys LD3 8EY

Tel: 01874 636206 **Fax:** 01874 636964 **E-mail:** info@abercamlais.co.uk

www.abercamlais.co.uk

Owner/Contact: Mrs S Ballance

Splendid Grade I mansion dating from middle ages, altered extensively in early 18th century with 19th century additions, in extensive grounds beside the river Usk. Still in same family ownership and occupation since medieval times. Exceptional octagonal pigeon house, formerly a privy.

Location: MAP 6:I10, OS Ref. SN965 290. 5m W of Brecon on A40.

Open: Apr–Oct: by appointment.

Admission: Adult £5, Child Free.

No photography in house. Obligatory.

ABERDULAIS FALLS

Aberdulais, Vale of Neath SA10 8EU

Tel: 01639 636674 **Fax:** 01639 645069

Owner: National Trust **Contact:** The Property Warden

For over 300 years this famous waterfall has provided the energy to drive the wheels of industry, from the first manufacture of copper in 1584 to present day remains of the tinplate works. It has also been visited by famous artists such as J M W Turner in 1796. The site today houses a unique hydro-electrical scheme which has been developed to harness the waters of the Dulais river.

Location: MAP 5:G12, OS Ref. SS772 995. On A4109, 3m NE of Neath. 4m from M4/J43, then A465.

Open: 9 Jan–7 Mar: Sat & Sun 11am–4pm; 15 Feb–19 Feb: Mon–Thu 11am–4pm; 13 Mar–31 Oct: Daily 10am–5pm; 5 Nov–19 Dec: Fri, Sat & Sun 11am–4pm.

***Admission:** Adult £4.40, Child £2.20, Family £11. Children must be accompanied by an adult. Includes a voluntary donation but visitors can choose to pay the standard prices displayed at the property and on the website.

Light refreshments (Summer only). Limited.

ABERGLASNEY GARDENS

Llangathen, Carmarthenshire SA32 8QH

www.aberglasney.org

Tel/Fax: 01558 668998 **E-mail:** info@aberglasney.org

Owner: Aberglasney Restoration Trust **Contact:** Booking Department

Aberglasney is undoubtedly one of the finest gardens in Wales and dates back to the Elizabethan period. The gardens cover 10 acres and contain an amazing and diverse plant collection. It includes three walled gardens, areas of formal and informal garden and an amazing award-winning indoor garden.

Location: MAP 5:F11, OS Ref. SN581 221. 4m W of Llandeilo. Follow signs from A40.

Open: All year: daily (except Christmas Day). Apr–Sept: 10am–6pm, last entry 5pm. Oct–Mar: 10.30am–4pm.

Admission: Adult £7, Child £4, Conc. £7, Booked groups (10+) Adult £6, Child £3.

Licensed. Licensed. Limited for coaches. Guide dogs only.

BLAENAVON IRONWORKS

North Street, Blaenavon, Blaenau, Gwent NP4 9RN

Tel: 01495 792615 **www.cadw.wales.gov.uk**

Owner: In the care of Cadw **Contact:** The Custodian

The famous ironworks at Blaenavon were a milestone in the history of the Industrial Revolution. Visitors can view cottages furnished in three time periods. Recently used for BBC Coalhouse as 'Stack Square'. Part of a World Heritage site.

Location: MAP 6:J11, OS Ref. SO248 092. Via A4043 follow signs to Big Pit Mining Museum and Blaenavon Ironworks. Abergavenny 8m. Pontypool 8m. From car park, cross road, then path to entrance gate.

Open: 1 Apr–31 Oct: 10am–5pm Daily. 1 Nov–31 Mar: closed Mon–Thurs, 9.30am–4pm, Fri–Sat, 11am–4pm, Sun. Closed 24, 25, 26 Dec, 1 Jan.

Admission: Free. Under 16s must be accompanied by an adult. All opening times and prices are correct at time of going to press (Autumn 2010) but may be subject to change from March 2011 – Please see site for details.

Disabled parking, Toilets, Cycle stands. WCs. Limited for coaches. On leads. €

CAE HIR GARDENS

Cae Hir, Cribyn, Lampeter, Cardiganshire SA48 7NG

Tel: 01570 470839

Owner/Contact: Mr W Akkermans

This transformed 19th century smallholding offers a succession of pleasant surprises and shows a quite different approach to gardening.

Location: MAP 5:F9, OS Ref. SN521 520. NW on A482 from Lampeter, after 5m turn S on B4337. Cae Hir is 2m on left.

Open: Easter Sunday-October 31st, 10am–5pm.

Admission: Adults & OAPs £5, Child (6-16) £1, Child (under6) Free. Free to RHS members.

CAERLEON ROMAN BATHS & AMPHITHEATRE

High Street, Caerleon NP18 1AE

Tel: 01633 422518 **www.cadw.wales.gov.uk**

Owner: In the care of Cadw **Contact:** The Custodian

Caerleon is the most varied and fascinating Roman site in Britain – incorporating fortress and baths, well-preserved amphitheatre and a row of barrack blocks, the only examples currently visible in Europe.

Location: MAP 2:N1, OS Ref. ST340 905. 4m ENE of Newport by B4596 to Caerleon, M4/J25 (westbound), M4/J26 (eastbound).

Open: Apr–Oct: daily, 9.30am–5pm. Nov–Mar: Mon–Sat, 9.30am–5pm. Sun 11am–4pm. Closed 24, 25, 26 Dec, 1 Jan. Last admission 30 minutes before closing. All opening times are correct at time of going to press (Autumn 2010) but may be subject to change from April 2011 – Please contact site for details.

Admission: Free. Under 16s must be accompanied by an adult.

Video presentation. Ample for cars. Guide dogs only €

CAERPHILLY CASTLE

Caerphilly CF83 1JD

Tel: 029 2088 3143 **www.cadw.wales.gov.uk**

Owner: In the care of Cadw **Contact:** The Custodian

Often threatened, never taken, this vastly impressive castle is much the biggest in Wales. 'Red Gilbert' de Clare, Anglo-Norman Lord of Glamorgan, flooded a valley to create the 30 acre lake, setting his fortress on 3 artificial islands. Famous for its leaning tower and replica siege engines.

Location: MAP 2:L1, OS Ref. ST156 871. Centre of Caerphilly, A468 from Newport, A470, A469 from Cardiff.

Open: Last admission 30 minutes before closing. Mar–June: 9.30am–5pm daily. July–Aug: 9.30am–6pm daily. Sept–Oct: 9.30am–5pm daily. Nov-Feb: 10am–4pm. Sun, 11am–4pm. Closed 24, 25, 26 Dec, 1 Jan.

Admission: Adults £3.60, Concessions £3.20, Family Ticket £10.40 (2 adults and all children under 16yrs). Children under 5 free. Under 16s must be accompanied by an adult. All opening times and prices are correct at time of going to press (Autumn 2010) but may be subject to change from April 2011 – Please phone site for details.

Baby changing, Induction loop, Cycle stands, Disabled visitors can be dropped off by car at the main entrance. WCs. €

Caerphilly Castle

CALDICOT CASTLE & COUNTRY PARK

CHURCH ROAD, CALDICOT, MONMOUTHSHIRE NP26 4HU

www.caldicotcastle.co.uk

Tel: 01291 420241 **Fax:** 01291 435094
E-mail: caldicotcastle@monmouthshire.gov.uk
Owner: Monmouthshire County Council **Contact:** Castle Development Officer

Caldicot's magnificent castle is set in fifty acres of beautiful parkland. Founded by the Normans, developed in royal hands in the Middle Ages and restored as a Victorian home. Discover the Castle's past with an audio tour. Visitors can relax in tranquil gardens, explore medieval towers, discover children's activities and play giant chess. Medieval Banquet evenings and unique wedding location.

Location: MAP 2:N1, OS Ref. ST487 887. From M4 take J23a and B4245 to Caldicot. From M48 take J2 and follow A48 & B4245. Castle signposted from B4245.

Open: Castle: 1 Apr–31 Oct: daily, 11am–5pm. Active winter events programme, please telephone for winter opening times. Country Park: All year daily.

Admission: Adult £3.75, Child/Conc £2.50. Groups (10–100): Adult £3, Child/Conc £2.

Partial. WCs. By arrangement. Free for formal educational visits. In Castle, on leads.

CARDIFF CASTLE

Castle Street, Cardiff CF10 3RB
Tel: 029 2087 8100 **Fax:** 029 2023 1417
Owner: City and County of Cardiff **Contact:** Booking Office

2000 years of history, including Roman Walls, Norman Keep and Victorian interiors.

Location: MAP 2:M1, OS Ref. ST181 765. Cardiff city centre, signposted from M4.

Open: Open every day except 25 Dec, 26 Dec and 1 Jan. Mar–Oct: 9am–6pm (last tour 5pm / last entry 5pm). Nov–Feb: 9am–5pm (last tour 4pm / last entry 4pm).

Admission: Full Tour: Adult £10.50, Child (5-16) £7.95, Senior/Student £9. Curator Tours: Adult £13.50, Child (5-16 years) £10, Senior / Student £11.50.

CARMARTHEN CASTLE

Carmarthen, South Wales
Tel: 0126 7224923 **E-mail:** clgriffiths@carmarthenshire.gov.uk
Owner/Contact: The Conservation Department, Carmarthenshire County Council

The fortress, originally founded by Henry I in 1109, witnessed several fierce battles, notably in the 15th century when the Welsh hero Owain Glyndwr burnt the town and took the castle from the English.

Location: MAP 5:E11, OS Ref. SN413 200. In the town centre.

Open: Throughout the year.

Admission: Free.

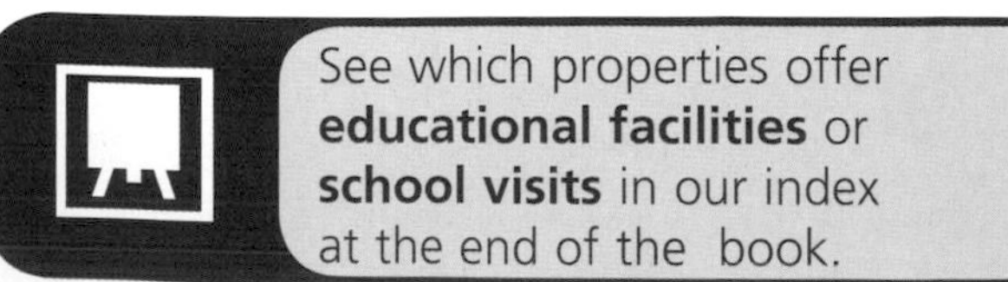
See which properties offer **educational facilities** or **school visits** in our index at the end of the book.

CARREG CENNEN CASTLE

Tir y Castell Farm, Llandeilo, Carmarthenshire SA19 6TS
Tel: 01558 822291 **www.cadw.wales.gov.uk**
Owner: In the care of Cadw **Contact:** The Manager

Spectacularly crowning a remote crag 300 feet above the River Cennen, the castle is unmatched as a wildly romantic fortress sought out by artists and visitors alike. The climb from Rare Breeds Farm is rewarded by breathtaking views and the chance to explore intriguing caves beneath.

Location: MAP 5:G11, OS Ref. SN668 190. Minor roads from A483(T) to Trapp village. 5m SE of A40 at Llandeilo.

Open: 1 Apr–31 Oct: daily, 9.30am–6.30pm. 1 Nov–31 Mar, daily, 9.30am–4pm. Closed 25 Dec.

Admission: Adult £3.60, Concessions £3.25, Family (2 adults and all children under 16yrs) £10.50. Child under 5 yrs free. Under 16s must be accompanied by an adult. All opening times and prices are correct at time of going to press (Autumn 2010) but may be subject to change from April 2011. Please phone site for details.

Induction loop. Toilets. Partial. Guide dogs only.

CADW: Crown Copyright

CASTELL COCH

TONGWYNLAIS, CARDIFF CF15 7JS

www.cadw.wales.gov.uk

Tel: 029 2081 0101
Owner: In the care of Cadw **Contact:** The Custodian

A fairytale castle in the woods, Castell Coch embodies a glorious Victorian dream of the Middle Ages. Designed by William Burges as a country retreat for the 3rd Lord Bute, every room and furnishing is brilliantly eccentric, including paintings of Aesop's fables on the drawing room walls.

Location: MAP 2:L1, OS Ref. ST131 826. M4/J32, A470 then signposted. 5m NW of Cardiff city centre.

Open: Mar–June: 9.30am–5pm daily. July–Aug: 9.30am–6pm daily, Sept–Oct 9.30am–5pm daily, Nov–Feb 10am–4pm, Sun 11am–4pm. Closed 24, 25, 26 Dec, 1–28 Jan 2011 inclusive.

Admission: Adult £3.60, Concessions £3.20, Family (2 adults and all children under 16 yrs) £10.40. Child under 5yrs free. Under 16s must be accompanied by an adult. All opening times and prices are correct at time of going to press (Autumn 2010) but may be subject to change from March 2011. Please phone site for details.

Toilets. Cycle stands. Baby changing. Induction loop. Partial. Limited for coaches. Guide dogs only. €

CHEPSTOW CASTLE

Chepstow, Monmouthshire NP16 5EY
Tel: 01291 624065 **www.cadw.wales.gov.uk**
Owner: In the care of Cadw **Contact:** The Custodian

The oldest stone fortification in Britain. So powerful was this castle that it continued in use until 1690, being finally adapted for cannon and musket after an epic Civil War siege. This huge, complex, grand castle deserves to be explored.

Location: MAP 2:O1, OS Ref. ST533 941. Chepstow via A466, B4235 or A48. 1½m N of M48/J22.

Open: Last admission 30 minutes before closing. Mar–June: 9.30am–5pm daily; July–Aug: 9.30am–6pm daily; Sept–Oct: 9.30am–5pm daily; Nov–Feb: Mon–Sat 10am–4pm, Sun 11am–4pm. Closed 24, 25, 26 Dec, 1 Jan.

Admission: Adult £3.60, Concessions £3.20, Family (2 adults and all children under 16yrs) £10.40. Child under 5yrs free. Under 16s must be accompanied by an adult. All opening times and prices are correct at time of going to press (Autumn 2010) but may be subject to change from March 2011. Please phone site for details.

Induction loop; mobility scooter. Pay and display. On leads. €

Cornwall House

CILGERRAN CASTLE

Cardigan, Pembrokeshire SA43 2SF

Tel: 01239 621339 **www.cadw.wales.gov.uk**

Owner: In the care of Cadw **Contact:** The Custodian

Perched high up on a rugged spur above the River Teifi, Cilgerran Castle is one of the most spectacularly sited fortresses in Wales. It dates from the 11th–13th centuries.

Location: MAP 5:D10, OS Ref. SN195 431. Main roads to Cilgerran from A478 and A484. 3½m SSE of Cardigan.

Open: Last admission 30 minutes before closing. Apr–Oct: daily, 10am–5pm. Nov–Mar 10am–4pm.

Admission: Adult £3, Concessions £2.60, Family (2 adults and all children under 16yrs) £8.60. child under 5yrs free. Under 16s must be accompanied by an adult. All opening times and prices are correct at time of going to press (Autumn 2010) but may be subject to change from April 2011. Please see site for details.

Toilets. Induction loop. Partial. WCs. On leads. €

CLYNE GARDENS

Mill Lane, Blackpill, Swansea SA3 5BD

Tel: 01792 401737 **E-mail:** botanics@swansea.gov.uk

Owner: City and County of Swansea **Contact:** Steve Hopkins

50 acre spring garden, large rhododendron collection, 4 national collections, extensive bog garden, native woodland.

Location: MAP 2:I1, OS Ref. SS614 906. S side of Mill Lane, 500yds W of A4067 Mumbles Road, 3m SW of Swansea.

Open: All year.

Admission: Free.

COLBY WOODLAND GARDEN

Amroth, Narbeth, Pembrokeshire SA67 8PP

Tel: 01834 811885 **Fax:** 01834 831766

Owner: National Trust

This 3½ ha (8 acre) garden has a fine display of colour in spring, with rhododendrons, magnolias, azaleas and camellias, underplanted with bluebells. Later highlights are the summer hydrangeas and autumn foliage. Open and wooded pathways through the valley offer lovely walks.

Location: MAP 5:D12, OS Ref. SN155 080. ½m inland from Amroth beside Carmarthen Bay. Signs from A477.

Open: Woodland Garden & Shop: 13 Feb–31 Oct: Daily 10am–5pm. Tea-room: 27 Mar–31 Oct: Daily 10am–5pm. Walled Garden & Gallery: 27 Mar–31 Oct: Daily 11am–5pm. Last admission 30 minutes before closing.

***Admission:** Adult £4.40, Child £2.20, Family £11. *Includes a voluntary donation but visitors can choose to pay the standard prices displayed at the property and on the website.

Gallery events.

CORNWALL HOUSE

58 Monnow Street, Monmouth NP25 3EN

Tel/Fax: 01600 712031

Owner/Contact: Ms Jane Harvey

Town house, dating back to at least the 17th century. Red brick garden façade in Queen Anne style, dating from 1752. Street façade remodelled in Georgian style (date unknown). Many original features, including fine staircase. Delightful town garden with original walled kitchen garden.

Location: MAP 6:L11, OS Ref. SO506 127. Half way down main shopping street in Monmouth.

Open: 9–25 Apr, 30 Apr–2 May, 28–30 Aug, 10–11 Sept, 2–5pm.

Admission: Adult £4, Conc. £2.

Obligatory. Public car park nearby. €

CRESSELLY

Kilgetty, Pembrokeshire SA68 0SP

E-mail: hha@cresselly.com **www.cresselly.com**

Owner/Contact: H D R Harrison-Allen Esq MFH

Home of the Allen family for 250 years. The house is of 1770 with matching wings of 1869 and contains good plasterwork and fittings of both periods. The Allens are of particular interest for their close association with the Wedgwood family of Etruria and a long tradition of foxhunting.

Location: MAP 5:C11, OS Ref. SN065 065. W of the A4075.

Open: 4–31 Jul Inclusive, 10am–1pm. Guided tours only, on the hour. Coaches and at other times by arrangement.

Admission: Adult £4, no children under 12.

Ground floor only. Obligatory. Coaches by arrangement.

DINEFWR PARK AND CASTLE

Llandeilo SA19 6RT

Tel: 01558 823902 **Fax:** 01558 825925 **E-mail:** dinefwr@nationaltrust.org.uk

Owner: National Trust **Contact:** Janet Philpin, Property Administrator

Historic site including 12th century Welsh castle, magnificent parkland with historic deer park and Newton House.

Location: MAP 5:G11, OS Ref. SN625 225. On outskirts of Llandeilo.

Open: Park & Castle: 14 Feb–30 Jun: Daily 11am–5pm; 1 Jul–31 Aug: Daily 11am–6pm; 1 Sept–31 Oct: Daily 11am–5pm; 5 Nov–19 Dec: Fri–Sun 11am–4pm.

***Admission:** Park & Castle: Adult £6.70, Child £3.35, Family £16.75. *Includes a voluntary donation but visitors can choose to pay the standard prices displayed at the property and on the website.

By arrangement. Limited for coaches. In grounds on leads.

DYFFRYN GARDENS AND ARBORETUM

ST NICHOLAS, Nr CARDIFF CF5 6SU

www.dyffryngardens.com

Tel: 029 2059 3328 **Fax:** 029 2059 1966

Owner: Vale of Glamorgan Council **Contact:** Ms G Donovan

Dyffryn Gardens is a beautiful Grade I registered Edwardian garden, set in the heart of the Vale of Glamorgan countryside. The 55-acre gardens are the result of a unique collaboration between the eminent landscape architect, Thomas Mawson, and the passionate plant collector, Reginald Cory. The garden includes great lawns, herbaceous borders, many individual themed garden 'rooms' and a well established Arboretum including 17 champion trees. The magnificent gardens have been undergoing extensive restoration work with assistance from the Heritage Lottery Fund, including a striking Visitor Centre and tearooms. Ongoing work includes the Walled Garden and new glasshouses, which are due for completion later this year.

Location: MAP 2:L2, OS Ref. ST095 723. 3m NW of Barry, J33/M4. 1½m S of St Nicholas on A48.

Open: All year. For details please telephone 029 2059 3328.

Admission: Summer: Adult £6.50, Child £2.50. Conc. £4.50. Winter: Adult £3.50, Child £1.50. Conc. £2.50. Discount for groups (15+).

© Skyscan

FONMON CASTLE

FONMON, BARRY, VALE OF GLAMORGAN CF62 3ZN

Tel: 01446 710206 **Fax:** 01446 711687 **E-mail:** Fonmon_Castle@msn.com

Owner: Sir Brooke Boothby Bt **Contact:** Anne Broadway

Occupied as a home since the 13th century, this medieval castle has the most stunning Georgian interiors and is surrounded by extensive gardens. Available for weddings, dinners, corporate entertainment and multi-activity days.

Location: MAP 2:L2, OS Ref. ST047 681. 15m W of Cardiff, 1m W of Cardiff airport.

***Open:** 1 Apr–30 Sept: Tue & Wed, 2–5pm (last tour 4pm). Other times by appointment. Groups: by appointment.

***Admission:** Adult £5, Child Free.

*2010 prices/opening.

Conferences. By arrangement (up to 120). WC. Guide dogs only.

KIDWELLY CASTLE

Kidwelly, Carmarthenshire SA17 5BQ

Tel: 01554 890104 **www.cadw.wales.gov.uk**

Owner: In the care of Cadw **Contact:** The Custodian

A chronicle in stone of medieval fortress technology this strong and splendid castle developed during more than three centuries of Anglo-Welsh warfare. The half-moon shape stems from the original 12th century stockaded fortress, defended by the River Gwendraeth on one side and a deep crescent-shaped ditch on the other.

Location: MAP 5:E12, OS Ref. SN409 070. Kidwelly via A484. Kidwelly Rail Station 1m.

Open: Last admission 30 minutes before closing. Mar–June: 9.30am–5pm. July-Aug: 9.30am-6pm. Sept-Oct: 9.30am-5pm. Nov–Feb: Mon–Sat, 10.00am–4pm, Sun 11am–4pm. Closed 24, 25, 26 Dec, 1 Jan.

Admission: Adult £3, Concessions £2.60, Family (2 adults and all children under 16yrs) £8.60. Child under 5yrs free. Under 16s must be accompanied by an adult. All opening times and prices are correct at time of going to press (Autumn 2010) but may be subject to change from April 2011. Please phone site for details.

Baby changing. Induction loop. Toilets. Partial. WCs.
Limited for cars. No coaches. On leads. €

LAMPHEY BISHOP'S PALACE

Lamphey, Pembroke SA71 5NT

Tel: 01646 672224 **www.cadw.wales.gov.uk**

Owner: In the care of Cadw **Contact:** The Custodian

Lamphey marks the place of the spectacular Bishop's Palace but it reached its height of greatness under Bishop Henry de Gower who raised the new Great Hall. Today the ruins of this comfortable retreat reflect the power enjoyed by the medieval bishops.

Location: MAP 5:C12, OS Ref. SN018 009. A4139 from Pembroke or Tenby. N of village (A4139).

Open: Last admission 30 minutes before closing. Apr–Oct: daily, 10am–5pm. The visitor centre will be closed during the winter but the grounds accessible between 10am and 4pm. Closed 24, 25, 26 December, 1 Jan.

Admission: Adult £3, Concessions £2.60, Family (2 adults and all children under 16yrs) £8.60. Child under 5yrs free. Under 16s must be accompanied by an adult. All opening times and prices are correct at time of going to press (Autumn 2010) but may be subject to change from April 2011. Please phone site for details.

Limited for cars, no coaches. On leads. €

LAUGHARNE CASTLE ✚

King Street, Laugharne, Carmarthenshire SA33 4SA

Tel: 01994 427906 **www.cadw.wales.gov.uk**

Owner: In the care of Cadw **Contact:** The Custodian

Picturesque Laugharne Castle stands on a low ridge overlooking the wide Taf estuary, one of a string of fortresses controlling the ancient route along the South Wales coast. Inspired Richard Huges and near to Dylan Thomas's Boathouse.

Location: MAP 5:E11, OS Ref. SN303 107. 4m S of A48 at St Clears via A4066.

Open: Last admission 30 minutes before closing. April–Oct: daily, 10am–5pm. The Monument is closed at all other times.

Admission: Adult £3, Concessions £2.60, Family (2 adults and all children under 16yrs) £8.60. Child under 5 yrs free. Under 16s must be accompanied by an adult. All opening times and prices are correct at time of going to press (Autumn 2010) but may be subject to change from April 2011. Please phone site for details.

Induction loop. Partial. Guide dogs only. €

LLANVIHANGEL COURT

Nr Abergavenny, Monmouthshire NP7 8DH

Tel: 01873 890217 **E-mail:** jclarejohnson@googlemail.com

www.llanvihangel-court.co.uk

Owner/Contact: Julia Johnson

Grade I Tudor Manor. The home in the 17th century of the Arnolds who built the imposing terraces and stone steps leading to the house. The interior has a fine hall, unusual yew staircase and many 17th century moulded plaster ceilings. Delightful grounds. 17th century features, notably Grade I stables.

Location: MAP 6:K11, OS Ref. SO433 139. 4m N of Abergavenny on A465.

Open: 28 Apr–12 May & 10–19 Aug, inclusive, daily 2.30–5.30pm. Last tour 5pm.

Admission: Entry and guide, Adult £5.00, Child/Conc. £2.50.

No inside photography. Partial. Limited. On leads.

NATIONAL BOTANIC GARDEN OF WALES

Llanarthne, Carmarthenshire SA32 8HG

Tel: 01558 668768 **Fax:** 01558 668933 **E-mail:** info@gardenofwales.org.uk

www.gardenofwales.org.uk

Owner: National Botanic Garden of Wales **Contact:** David Hardy or Max Sewter

Opened in 2000, the first botanic garden of the 21st century is already becoming an enduring icon for Wales. Extraordinarily beautiful in parts, it has as its centrepiece Lord Foster's stunning Great Glasshouse which shelters a fantastic Mediterranean plant collection. From national nature reserve to Japanese Garden, there are nearly 600 acres of rolling Welsh countryside to explore.

Location: MAP 5:F11, OS Ref. SN159 175. ¼m from the A48 midway between Crosshands & Carmarthen. Clearly signposted from A48 & Carmarthen. Train & Bus in Carmarthen (7m).

Open: BST 10am–6pm. BWT 10am–4.30pm. Closed Christmas Day.

Admission: Adult £8.50, Under 16s £4.50, Under 5s Free, Concessions £7, Family (2+4) £21. Groups (10+): Adult £7.50, Children £3.50, Concessions £6.

Tearoom, licensed. Licensed. By arrangement. Ample for cars & coaches. Guide dogs only. Excluding Christmas Day. Details available on request or website.

OXWICH CASTLE ✚

Oxwich, Swansea SA3 1NG

Tel: 01792 390359 **www.cadw.wales.gov.uk**

Owner: In the care of Cadw **Contact:** The Custodian

Beautifully sited in the lovely Gower peninsula, Oxwich Castle is a striking testament to the pride and ambitions of the Mansel dynasty of Welsh gentry.

Location: MAP 2:I1, OS159 Ref. SS497 864. A4118, 11m SW of Swansea, in Oxwich village.

Open: Last admission 30 minutes before closing. Apr–Sept: daily, 10am–5pm. The Monument is closed at all other times.

Admission: Adult £2.60, Concessions £2.25, Family (2 adults and all children under 16yrs) £7.45. Child under 5yrs free. Under 16s must be accompanied by an adult. All opening times and prices are correct at time of going to press (Autumn 2010) but may be subject to change from April 2011. Please phone see site for details.

Baby changing. Toilets. Induction loop. Cycle stands. Partial. No coaches. On leads. €

PEMBROKE CASTLE

PEMBROKE SA71 4LA

www.pembrokecastle.co.uk

Tel: 01646 681510 **Fax:** 01646 622260 **E-mail:** info@pembrokecastle.co.uk

Owner: Trustees of Pembroke Castle **Contact:** Mr D Ramsden

Pembroke Castle is situated within minutes of beaches and the breathtaking scenery of the Pembrokeshire Coastal National Park. This early Norman fortress, birthplace of the first Tudor King, houses many fascinating displays and exhibitions. Enjoy a picnic in the beautifully kept grounds, or on the roof of St. Anne's Bastion and take in the views along the estuary. Events every weekend in July and August.

Location: MAP 5:C12, OS Ref. SM983 016. W end of the main street in Pembroke.

Open: All year. 1 Apr–Sept: daily, 9.30am–6pm. Mar & Oct: daily, 10am–5pm. Nov–Feb: daily, 10am–4pm. Closed 24–26 Dec & 1 Jan. Cafe closed Dec–Jan. Brass rubbing centre open Summer months and all year by arrangement.

Admission: Adult £4.50, Child/Conc. £3.50, Family (2+2) £12. Groups (20+): Adult £4, OAP/Student £3.

Closed Jan. End of May–Sept by arrangement. In grounds, on leads.

Laugharne Castle

PICTON CASTLE & WOODLAND GARDENS

THE RHOS, NEAR HAVERFORDWEST, PEMBROKESHIRE SA62 4AS

www.pictoncastle.co.uk

Tel/Fax: 01437 751326 **E-mail:** info@pictoncastle.co.uk
Owner: The Picton Castle Trust **Contact:** Mr Dai W Evans

A beautiful 13th century castle with wonderful Georgian interiors, Picton Castle is set in 44 acres of magnificent woodland and walled garden. The friendly guides bring the history alive and in 2011 new areas of the castle will be open to view tours. The nationally important woodland gardens contain unique rhododendrons and roses, rare conifers, tree ferns and bamboos and are of the RHS access scheme. The Gallery features a programme of exhibitions ranging from fine art to fine quality arts & crafts. Events include plant fairs, outdoor theatre, music evenings, family fun days.

Location: MAP 5:C11, OS Ref. SN011 135. 4m E of Haverfordwest, just off A40.

Open: 29 Mar–31 Sept, daily, 10.30am–5pm. Check website for dates and times of February and October half term opening and occasional winter weekend openings. Entrance to castle by guided tours only - please phone for details.

Admission: Gardens and Gallery ticket: Adult £5.00, Seniors £4.75, Child £2.50. With Castle Tour: Adult £7.50, Child £4. Groups (20+): reduced prices by prior arrangement.

Special Events: Christmas at the Castle - The unique atmosphere with mulled wine, log fires and Christmas trees. A quality indoor festive gift market with the castle traditionally decorated for Christmas end November. In December Christmas Classics Concert in the Great Hall. Phone for details or see website.

WCs Licensed. Licensed. Obligatory. On leads.

Chepstow Castle

Treowen

RAGLAN CASTLE ✠

RAGLAN, MONMOUTHSHIRE NP15 2BT

www.cadw.wales.gov.uk

Tel: 01291 690228

Owner: In the care of Cadw **Contact:** The Custodian

Undoubtedly the finest late medieval fortress-palace in Britain, it was begun in the 1430s by Sir William ap Thomas who built the mighty 'Yellow Tower'. His son William Lord Herbert added a palatial mansion defended by a gatehouse and many towered walls.

Location: MAP 6:K12, OS Ref. SO415 084. Raglan, NE of Raglan village off A40 (eastbound) and signposted.

Open: Last admission 30 minutes before closing. Mar–Jun: 9.30am–5pm, daily ; Jul–Aug: 9.30am–6pm daily, Sept–Oct: 9.30am–5pm daily; Nov–Feb: Mon–Sat 10am–4pm, Sun 11am–4pm. Closed 24, 25, 26 Dec, 1 Jan.

Admission: Adult £3, Concessions £2.60, Family (2 adults and all children under 16yrs) £8.60. Child under 5yrs free. Under 16s must be accompanied by an adult. All opening times and prices are correct at time of going to press (Autumn 2010) but may be subject to change from April 2011. Please phone site for details.

[i] Toilets. Baby changing. Induction loop. Bluetooth. Partial. WCs. On leads. €

ST DAVIDS BISHOP'S PALACE ✠

St Davids, Pembrokeshire SA62 6PE

Tel: 01437 720517 **www.cadw.wales.gov.uk**

Owner: In the care of Cadw **Contact:** The Custodian

The city of St Davids boasts the most impressive medieval Bishops Palace in Wales. Built in the elaborate 'decorated' style of gothic architecture, the palace is lavishly encrusted with fine carving. Be sure to explore the undercrofts and see the extensive conservation works already complete.

Location: MAP 5:B11, OS Ref. SM750 254. A487 to St Davids, minor road past the Cathedral.

Open: Last admission 30 minutes before closing. Mar–June: 9.30am–5pm daily; July-Aug: 9.30am-6pm daily; Sept-Oct: 9.30am-5pm daily; Nov–Feb: Mon-Sat, 10am–4pm, Sun 11am–4pm. Closed 24, 25, 26 Dec, 1 Jan.

Admission: Adult £3, Concessions £2.60, Family (2 adults and all children under 16yrs) £8.60. Child under 5yrs free. Under 16s must be accompanied by an adult. All opening times and prices are correct at time of going to press (Autumn 2010) but may be subject to change from April 2011. Please phone site for details.

[i] Induction loop. Cycle stands. Partial. On leads. €

ST DAVIDS CATHEDRAL

St Davids, Pembrokeshire SA62 6QW

Tel: 01437 720691 **Fax:** 01437 721885

Contact: Mr R G Tarr

Over eight centuries old. Many unique and 'odd' features.

Location: MAP 5:B11, OS Ref. SM751 254. 5–10 mins walk from car/coach parks: signs for pedestrians.

Open: Daily, may be closed for services in progress. Sun services: 8am, 9.30am, 11.15am & 6pm. Weekday services: 8am & 6pm. Weds extra service: 10am.

Admission: Donations. Guided tours Adult £4, must be booked.

ST FAGANS: NATIONAL HISTORY MUSEUM

St Fagans, Cardiff CF5 6XB

Tel: 029 2057 3500 **Fax:** 029 2057 3490

One of the world's best-loved open-air museums. Original buildings have been moved from all over Wales and re-erected at the Museum – these include a Victorian school, industrial ironworkers' cottages and a rural chapel. St Fagans Castle, an Elizabethan Manor House, also stands within the grounds.

Location: MAP 2:L2, OS Ref. ST118 772. 4m W of city centre, 1½ m N of A48, 2m S of M4/J33. Follow the brown signs (Museum of Welsh Life). Entrance drive is off A4232 (southbound only).

Open: All year: daily, 10am–5pm. Closed 24–26 Dec & 1 Jan.

Admission: Free.

TINTERN ABBEY

TINTERN, MONMOUTHSHIRE NP16 6SE

www.cadw.wales.gov.uk

Tel: 01291 689251

Owner: In the care of Cadw **Contact:** The Custodian

Tintern is the best preserved abbey in Wales and ranks among Britain's most beautiful historic sites. Elaborately decorated in 'gothic' architecture style this church stands almost complete to roof level. Turner sketched and painted here, while Wordsworth drew inspiration from the surroundings.

Location: MAP 6:L12, OS Ref. SO533 000. Tintern via A466, from M4/J23. Chepstow 6m.

Open: Last admission 30 minutes before closing. Mar–June: 9.30am–5pm, daily, July–Aug: 9.30am–6pm daily, Sept–Oct: 9.30am–5pm daily, Nov–Feb: Mon–Sat 10am–4pm, Sun 11am–4pm. Closed 24, 25, 26 Dec, 1 Jan.

Admission: Adult £3.60, Concessions £3.20, Family (2 adults and all children under 16yrs) £10.40. Child under 5yrs free. Under 16s must be accompanied by an adult. All opening times and prices are correct at time of going to press (Autumn 2010) but may be subject to change from April 2011. Please phone site for details.

Induction loop. Toilets. Baby changing. WCs. On leads. €

Kidwelly Castle

TREBERFYDD

Bwlch, Powys LD3 7PX

Tel: 01874 730205 **E-mail:** david.raikes@btinternet.com **www.treberfydd.com**

Owner: David Raikes

Treberfydd is a Grade I listed Victorian country house, built in the Gothic style in 1847–50. The house was designed by J L Pearson, and the garden and grounds by W A Nesfield.

Location: MAP 6:I10, From A40 in Bwlch take road to Llangors, after ¼m turn left, follow lane for 2m until white gates and Treberfydd sign.

Open: 1–29 Aug. Guided tours of the House: 2 & 4pm, telephone or e-mail to secure a place on a tour. Grounds: 2–6pm.

Admission: House & grounds: Adult £4, Child (under 12yrs) Free. Grounds only: £2.50.

Obligatory. Limited. None for coaches. On leads, in grounds.

TREBINSHWN

Nr Brecon, Powys LD3 7PX

Tel: 01874 730653 **Fax:** 01874 730843

Owner/Contact: R Watson

16th century mid-sized manor house. Extensively rebuilt 1780. Fine courtyard and walled garden.

Location: MAP 6:I10, OS Ref. SO136 242. 1½m NW of Bwlch.

Open: Easter–31 Aug: Mon–Tue, 10am–4.30pm.

Admission: Free.

TREDEGAR HOUSE & PARK

See page 448 for full page entry.

TREOWEN

Wonastow, Nr Monmouth NP25 4DL

Tel: 01600 712031 **E-mail:** john.wheelock@treowen.co.uk **www.treowen.co.uk**

Owner: R A & J P Wheelock **Contact:** John Wheelock

Early 17th century mansion built to double pile plan with magnificent well-stair to four storeys.

Location: MAP 6:L11, OS Ref. SO461 111. 3m WSW of Monmouth.

Open: May, Jun, Aug & Sept: Fri, 10am–4pm. Also 26/27 Mar; 14/15 & 21/22 May; 17/18 & 24/25 Sept: 2–5pm. HHA Friends Free on Fri only.

Admission: £5 (£3 if appointment made). Groups by appointment only.

By arrangement. Entire house let, self-catering. Sleeps 25+.

TRETOWER COURT & CASTLE

Tretower, Crickhowell NP8 1RD

Tel: 01874 730279 **www.cadw.wales.gov.uk**

Owner: In the care of Cadw **Contact:** The Custodian

A fine fortress and an outstanding medieval manor house, Tretower Court and Castle range around a galleried courtyard, further enhanced by a beautiful recreated medieval garden.

Location: MAP 6:J11, OS Ref. SO187 212. Signposted in Tretower Village, off A479, 3m NW of Crickhowell.

Open: Last admission 30 minutes before closing. April-Oct: 10am-5pm daily; Nov-Mar: Mon-Thurs closed; Fri-Sat: 10am-4pm; Sun 11am-4pm.

Admission: Adult: £3, Concessions: £2.60, Family: £8.60 (2 adults and all children uner 16 yrs) Under 5yrs free. Under 16s must be accompanied by an adult. All opening times and prices are correct at time of going to press (Autumn 2010) but may be subject to change from April 2011. please phone site for details.

Toilets. Induction loop. Cycle stands. Picnic tables. No coaches. Guide dogs only. €

TUDOR MERCHANT'S HOUSE

Quay Hill, Tenby SA70 7BX

Tel/Fax: 01834 842279

Owner: National Trust **Contact:** The Custodian

A late 15th century town house, characteristic of the area at the time when Tenby was a thriving trading port. The house is furnished to recreate family life from the Tudor period onwards. There is access to the small herb garden, weather permitting.

Location: MAP 5:D12, OS Ref. SN135 004. Tenby. W of alley from NE corner of town centre square.

Open: 22 Mar–31 Oct: Sun–Thu 11am–5pm. Open Saturdays on Bank Holiday weekends, 11–5. Last admission 30 minutes before closing.

Admission: Adult £3, Child £1.50, Family £7.50. Groups: Adult £2.30, Child £1.15.

No indoor photography. No parking. Guide dogs only.

St Davids Cathedral

USK CASTLE

Usk, Monmouthshire NP5 1SD

Tel: 01291 672563 **E-mail:** info@uskcastle.com **www.uskcastle.com**

Owner/Contact: J H L Humphreys

Romantic, ruined castle overlooking the picturesque town of Usk. Inner and outer baileys, towers and earthwork defences. Surrounded by enchanting gardens (open under NGS) incorporating The Castle House, the former medieval gatehouse.

Location: MAP 6:K12, OS Ref. SO376 011. Up narrow lane off Monmouth road in Usk, opposite fire station.

Open: Castle ruins: daily, 11am–5pm. Groups by appointment. Gardens: private visits welcome & groups by arrangement. House: May & BHs: 2–5pm, small groups & guided tours only.

Admission: Castle ruins: Adult £2, Child Free. Gardens: Adult £4 to NGS, private visits welcome. House: Adult £6, Child £3.

Partial. By arrangement. No coaches. In grounds, on leads.

© Cadw, Welsh Assembly Government (Crown Copyright)

Tretower Court

WEOBLEY CASTLE ✠

Weobley Castle Farm, Llanrhidian SA3 1HB

Tel: 01792 390012 **www.cadw.wales.gov.uk**

Owner: In the care of Cadw **Contact:** The Custodian

Perched above the wild northern coast of the beautiful Gower peninsula, Weobley Castle was the home of the Knightly de Bere family. Its rooms include a fine hall and private chamber as well as numerous 'garderobes' or toilets and an early Tudor porch block.

Location: MAP 2:I1, OS Ref. SN477 928. B4271 or B4295 to Llanrhidian Village, then minor road for 1½m.

Open: Last admission 30 minutes before closing. Apr–Oct: daily, 9.30am–6pm; Nov–Mar 9.30am-5pm. Closed 24, 25, 26 Dec, 1 Jan.

Admission: Adult £2.60, Concessions £2.25, Family (2 adults and all children under 16yrs) £7.50. Child under 5yrs free. Under 16s must be accompanied by an adult. All opening times and prices are correct at time of going to press (Autumn 2010) but may be subject to change from April 2011. Please phone site for details.

Toilets. Limited for cars. No coaches. Guide dogs only.

WHITE CASTLE ✠

Llantillio Crossenny, Monmouthshire NP7 8UD

Tel: 01600 780380 **www.cadw.wales.gov.uk**

Owner: In the care of Cadw **Contact:** The Custodian

With its high walls and round towers reflected in the still waters of its moat, White Castle is the ideal medieval fortress. Rebuilt in the mid-13th century to counter a threat from Prince Llywelyn the Last. Plenty of wildlife to discover.

Location: MAP 6:K11, OS Ref. SO380 167. By minor road 2m NW from B4233 at A7 Llantilio Crossenny. 8m ENE of Abergavenny.

Open: Open 1 Apr–31 Oct daily, 10am–5pm. Open at all other times generally between 10am–4pm, but unstaffed. Closed 24, 25, 26 December, 1 January.

Admission: Adult £2.60, Concessions £2.25, Child under 5yrs Free, Family (2 adults and all children under 16yrs) £7.45. Child under 5yrs free. Under 16s must be accompanied by an adult. All opening times and prices are correct at time of going to press (Autumn 2010) but may be subject to change from March 2011 – Please phone site for details.

Induction loop. Cycle stands. Partial. Limited for cars. No coaches. On leads. €

■ **Owner**

Paul and Victoria Humpherston

■ **Contact**

Paul Humpherston
The Hall at Abbey-Cwm-Hir
Nr Llandrindod Wells
Powys LD1 6PH

Tel: 01597 851727
E-mail: info@abbeycwmhir.com

■ **Location**

MAP 6:I8
OS Ref. SO054 711

7m NW of Llandrindod Wells, 6m E of Rhayader, turn for Abbey-Cwm-Hir 1 mile north of Crossgates on the A483.

■ **Opening Times**

All year daily for pre-booked tours only, at 10.30am, 2pm and 7pm for couples, small parties or groups.

■ **Admission**

House Tour & Gardens

Adult	£14.00
Child (under 12)	£5.00
Groups (10+) or repeat visitors	£12.00

Gardens only

Adult	£5.00

■ **Gift Vouchers**

Gift vouchers for tours may be purchased as a heartfelt gift. They are redeemable at any time within 12 months of purchase.

■ **Special Events**

1 November–6 January
Each of the 52 rooms is decorated for Christmas, for an entirely unique experience. Morning, afternoon and evening tours for individuals, small parties or groups.

St. Valentines Day & Easter
Contact us for more details.

THE HALL AT ABBEY-CWM-HIR

www.abbeycwmhir.com

In a mid Wales setting of breathtaking beauty, history and romance, The Hall and its 12 landscaped acres overlook the ruins of the 12th century Cisterian 'Abbey of the Long Valley', in which Llewellyn the Last is buried, and the church. It is Grade II* listed as one of Wales' finest examples of Victorian Gothic Revival architecture. Having spent nine years restoring the house and the gardens, the owners now personally conduct unique tours of all 52 rooms in a true family atmosphere. The tours are not just about the architecture of an historic house. Visitors also experience stunning interior designs in all rooms, and items from a lifetime of collecting used as furnishings. Each of the 52 rooms contain their original features. In the formal reception rooms and bedrooms these include 14 marble fireplaces; rococco and stained glass ceilings; gothic windows and shutters; and a Maw tiled floor. In the former domestic rooms, features include 10 further iron fireplaces; original slate slab surfaces; and vaulted cellar ceilings. The house bursts with interior design ideas. These include images hand-painted on to existing wallpapers; bathrooms themed to trains, castles and the 1930s; bedrooms themed to schooldays, the seaside and transport; the Arthurian room; and the eclectic Garden Room.

Overall collections include clocks and phonographs; signs and packaging; kitchen memorabilia and children's books in original bindings; china and vehicles; and The Abbey-Cwm-Hir Art and Photographic Collections. The gardens (also listed) include a romantic walled garden; a lake and a waterfall; sweeping lawns and terraces; 4 courtyards; and some particularly fine mixed woodland.

Visitors are asked to remove outside shoes for the tour of the house, slippers can be provided.

Partial.

Licensed.

Licensed.

Obligatory.

Ample for cars, limited for coaches.

In grounds on leads.

HAFOD

Hafod Estate, Pontrhydygroes, Ystrad-Meurig, Ceredigion SY25 6DX

Tel: 01974 282568 **Fax:** 01974 282579 **E-mail:** hafod.estate@forestry.gsi.gov.uk

www.hafod.org

Owner: Forestry Commission Wales **Contact:** The Hafod Trust

Picturesque landscape, one of the most significant in Britain located in a remote valley and improved by Col Thomas Johnes 1780–1816. Ten miles of restored walks featuring cascades, bridges and wonderful views in 500 acres of wood and parkland. The epitome of the Picturesque and Sublime. Georgian Group Award winner.

Location: MAP 5:G8, OS Ref. SN768 736. 15 miles E of Aberystwyth near Devils Bridge, car park, off B4574.

Open: All year, daylight hours.

Admission: Free – guide book available at local shops or website.

WC. By arrangement. In grounds on leads.

THE HALL AT ABBEY-CWM-HIR

See page 458 for full page entry.

THE JUDGE'S LODGING

Broad Street, Presteigne, Powys LD8 2AD

Tel: 01544 260650 **E-mail:** info@judgeslodging.org.uk

www.judgeslodging.org.uk

Owner: Powys County Council **Contact:** Gabrielle Rivers

Explore the fascinating world of the Victorian judges, their servants and felonious guests at this award-winning, totally hands-on historic house. From sumptuous judge's apartments to the gas-lit servants' quarters below, follow an 'eavesdropping' audio tour featuring actor Robert Hardy. Damp cells, vast courtroom and local history rooms included.

Location: MAP 6:K8, OS Ref. SO314 644. In town centre, off A44 and A4113. Easy reach from Herefordshire and mid-Wales.

Open: 1 Mar–31 Oct: Tues–Sun, 10am–5pm. 1 Nov–31 Nov: Wed–Sun, 10am–4pm, 1 Dec–22 Dec: Sat–Sun 10am–4pm. Open BH Mon's. Bookings by arrangement accepted all year.

Admission: Adult £5.95, Child £3.95, Conc. £4.95, Family £16. Groups (10–80): Adult £5.25, Child/Conc. £4.50, Family £16, Schools £4.25.

Partial (access via a lift). By arrangement. In town. Guide dogs only.

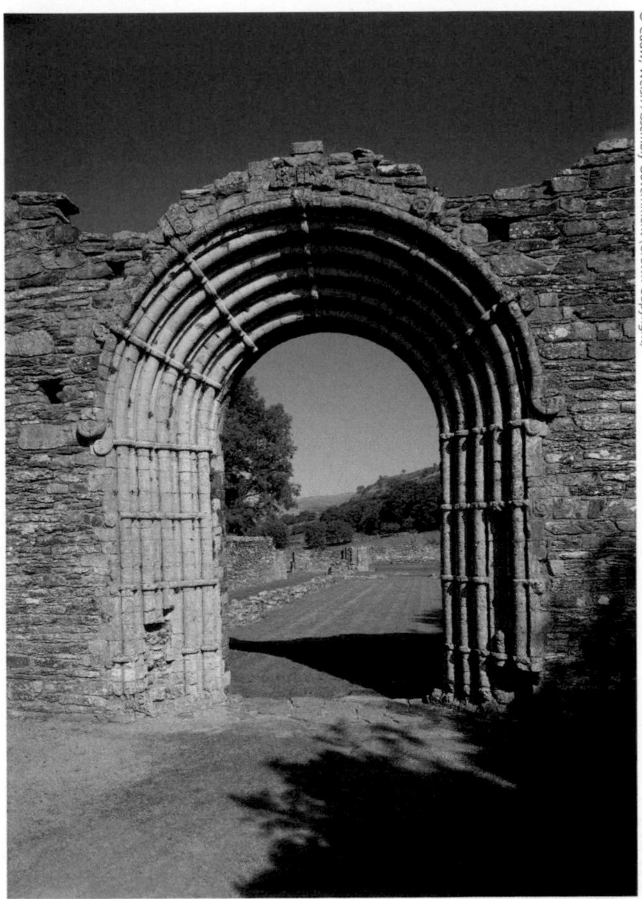

Strata Florida Abbey

LLANERCHAERON

Ciliau Aeron, Nr Aberaeron, Ceredigion SA48 8DG

Tel: 01545 570200

Owner: National Trust

This rare example of a self-sufficient 18th century Welsh minor gentry estate has survived virtually unaltered. The Villa, designed in the 1790s, is the most complete example of the early work of John Nash. It has its own service courtyard with dairy, laundry, brewery and salting house, and walled kitchen gardens produce fruit, vegetables, herbs and plants, all on sale in season. The Home Farm complex has an impressive range of traditional and atmospheric outbuildings and is now a working organic farm with Welsh Black Cattle, Llanwenog Sheep and rare Welsh Pigs. Visitors can see farming activities in progress, such as lambing, shearing and hay-making.

Location: MAP 5:F8, OS Ref. SN480 602. 2½ miles East of Aberaeron off A482 / 2½ mile foot/cycle track from Aberaeron to property along old railway track.

Open: House: 15–19 Feb, Mon-Fri; 24 Feb–18 Mar, Wed & Thu; 24 Mar–11 Apr, Mon–Sun; 14 Apr–18 Jul, Wed–Sun; 20 Jul–5 Sep, Tue–Sun. 8 Sep–31 Oct, Wed–Sun. Farm/Garden as House but 11am–5pm.

***Admission:** Adult £6.90, Child £3.50, Family £17.30. Reduced rate when arriving by cycle, on foot or by public transport. Adult £5.90, child £2.95. *Prices include a voluntary donation but visitors can choose to pay the standard prices displayed at the property and on the website.

POWIS CASTLE & GARDEN

Nr Welshpool SY21 8RF

Tel: 01938 551929 **Infoline:** 01938 551944 **Fax:** 01938 554336

E-mail: powiscastle@nationaltrust.org.uk

Owner: National Trust **Contact:** Visitor Services Manager

The world-famous garden, overhung with enormous clipped yew trees, shelters rare and tender plants in colourful herbaceous borders. Laid out under the influence of Italian and French styles, the garden retains its original lead statues and, an orangery on the terraces. Perched on a rock above the garden terraces, the medieval castle contains one of the finest collections of paintings and furniture in Wales.

Location: MAP 6:J6, OS Ref. SJ216 064. 1m W of Welshpool, car access on A483.

Open: Castle & Museum: 1–29 Mar: Mon, Thu, Fri, Sat, Sun, 1–4pm; 1 Apr–31 Oct: Mon, Thu, Fri, Sat, Sun, 1–5pm. Garden, Restaurant & Shop: 1–29 Mar: Mon, Thu, Fri, Sat, Sun, 11am–4.30pm; 1 Apr–31 Oct: Mon, Thu, Fri, Sat, Sun, 11am–5.30pm; 6 Nov–28 Nov: Sat, Sun, 11am–3.30pm. Restaurant & Shop: 4–19 Dec: Sat, Sun, 11am–3.30pm. Last entry 45 mins before closing.

***Admission:** Castle & Garden: Adult £11.50, Child £5.75, Family (2+3) £28.75, Family (Single adult family) £17.25. Garden only: Adult £8.50, Child £4.25, Family (2+3) £21.25, Family (Single adult family) £12.75. *Prices include a voluntary donation but visitors can choose to pay the standard prices displayed at the property and on the website.

No indoor photography. Partial. Licensed. By arrangement. Limited for coaches. Guide dogs only.

STRATA FLORIDA ABBEY

Ystrad Meurig, Pontrhydfendigaid SY25 6ES

Tel: 01974 831261 **www.cadw.wales.gov.uk**

Owner: In the care of Cadw **Contact:** The Custodian

Remotely set in the green, kite-haunted Teifi Valley with the lonely Cambrian mountains as a backdrop, the ruined Cistercian abbey has a wonderful doorway with Celtic spiral motifs and preserves a wealth of beautiful medieval tiles. Explore the poetic connections with Dafydd ap Gwilym.

Location: MAP 5:H8, OS Ref. SN746 658. Minor road from Pontrhydfendigaid 14m SE of Aberystwyth by the B4340.

Open: Last admission 30 minutes before closing. Apr–Sept: daily, 10am–5pm. Open at all other times generally between 10am–4pm, but unstaffed. Closed 24, 25, 26 Dec, 1 Jan.

Admission: Adult £3, Concessions £2.60, Family (2 adults and all children under 16yrs) £8.60. Child under 5yrs free. Under 16s must be accompanied by an adult. All opening times and prices are correct at time of going to press (Autumn 2010) but may be subject to change from March 2011. Please phone site for details.

Induction loop. Partial. Limited for cars. No coaches. On leads. €

TREWERN HALL

Trewern, Welshpool, Powys SY21 8DT

Tel: 01938 570243

Owner: Chapman Family **Contact:** M Chapman

Trewern Hall is a Grade II* listed building standing in the Severn Valley. It has been described as *'one of the most handsome timber-framed houses surviving in the area'*. The porch contains a beam inscribed RF1610, though it seems likely that parts of the house are earlier. The property has been in the ownership of the Chapman family since 1918.

Location: MAP 6:J6 , OS Ref. SJ269 113. Off A458 Welshpool–Shrewsbury Road, 4m from Welshpool.

Opening: Last week in Apr, 1–31 May: Mon–Fri, 2–5pm.

Admission: Adult £2, Child/Conc. £1.

Unsuitable. Limited. None for coaches.

ABERCONWY HOUSE

Castle Street, Conwy LL32 8AY

Tel: 01492 592246 **Fax:** 01492 564818

Owner: National Trust

Dating from the 14th century, this is the only medieval merchant's house in Conwy to have survived the turbulent history of this walled town for nearly six centuries. Furnished rooms and an audio-visual presentation show daily life from different periods in its history.

Location: MAP 5:H2, OS Ref. SH781 777. At junction of Castle Street and High Street.

Open: House: 13 Feb–31 Oct: Mon, Wed–Sun 11am–5pm. Shop: 2 Jan–12 Mar: Wed–Sun 11am–5pm. 13 Mar–31 Oct: Daily 10am–5.30pm. 3 Nov–31 Dec: Daily 11am–5pm. (House: open Tuesdays July and August. Shop: opens 11 on Sundays; closed 25 and 26 December. Last admission 30 minutes before closing).

Admission: Adult £3, Child £1.50, Family (2+2) £7.50.

No indoor photography. All year. By arrangement. In town car parks only. Guide dogs only.

BEAUMARIS CASTLE

BEAUMARIS, ANGLESEY LL58 8AP

www.cadw.wales.gov.uk

Tel: 01248 810361

Owner: In the care of Cadw **Contact:** The Custodian

The most technically perfect medieval castle in Britain, standing midway between Caernarfon and Conwy, commanding the old ferry crossing to Anglesey. Part of a World Heritage Inscribed Site.

Location: MAP 5:G2, OS Ref. SH608 762. 5m NE of Menai Bridge (A5) by A545. 7m from Bangor.

Open: Mar–June: daily, 9.30am–5pm; July–Aug: 9.30am–6pm; Sept–Oct: 9.30am–5pm; Nov–Feb: Mon–Sat, 10.00am–4pm, Sun 11am–4pm. Closed 24, 25, 26 Dec, 1 Jan. Last admission 30 minutes before closing.

Admission: Adult £3.60, Child (under 16 yrs)/Conc. £3.20, Child under 5yrs Free, Family (2 adults and all children under 16yrs) £10.40. Under 16s must be accompanied by an adult. All opening times and prices are correct at time of going to press (Autumn 2010) but may be subject to change from April 2011 – Please phone site for details.

Guide dogs only. €

BODELWYDDAN CASTLE

Bodelwyddan, Denbighshire LL18 5YA

Tel: 01745 584060 **Fax:** 01745 584563 **E-mail:** enquiries@bodelwyddan-castle.co.uk

www.bodelwyddan-castle.co.uk

Owner: Bodelwyddan Castle Trust **Contact:** Bookings and Information Team

Journey back in time as you tour this magnificently restored Victorian country house and view exquisite pieces from the National Portrait Gallery, Royal Academy and Victoria & Albert Museum. Explore 260 acres of parkland including formal gardens, woodland walks and WW1 practice trenches. Hands on Victorian Toys and Games Room. Exciting events and exhibition schedule. Café specialising in traditional, freshly prepared products.

Location: MAP 6:I2, OS Ref. SH999 749. Follow signs Junction 25 off A55 expressway. 2m W of St Asaph, opposite Marble Church.

Open: Various dates throughout the year. Please telephone or visit our website to check opening dates and times.

Admission: Adult £6, Child (5–16yrs) £2.50 (under 4yrs free), Conc. £5, Disabled £3.50. Family (1+3) £12, (2+2) £15. Discounts for schools & groups. Season ticket available.

BODNANT GARDEN

Tal-y-Cafn, Colwyn Bay LL28 5RE

Tel: 01492 650460 **Fax:** 01492 650448 **E-mail:** office@bodnantgarden.co.uk

www.bodnantgarden.co.uk

Owner: National Trust

Bodnant Garden is one of the finest gardens in the country not only for its magnificent collections of rhododendrons, camellias and magnolias but also for its idyllic setting above the River Conwy with extensive views of the Snowdonia range.

Location: MAP 5:H2, OS Ref. SH801 723. 8 miles S of Llandudno and Colwyn Bay, off A470. Signposted from A55, exit at Junction 19.

Open: 20 Feb–31 Oct, daily, 10am–5pm, and 1–21 Nov, daily, 10am–4pm. Last entry is 30 minutes prior to closing.

Admission: Adult £7.90, Child £3.95. Groups (20+): Adult £5.50, Child £3.25. National Trust members and RHS members free with valid membership card. Prices include a voluntary donation which will be put towards the upkeep of this property; visitors can, however, choose to pay standard admission prices displayed at the property.

Partial. WCs. Guide dogs only.

BRYN BRAS CASTLE

Llanrug, Caernarfon, Gwynedd LL55 4RE

www.brynbrascastle.co.uk

Tel/Fax: 01286 870210 **E-mail:** holidays@brynbrascastle.co.uk

Owner: Mr & Mrs N E Gray-Parry **Contact:** Marita Gray-Parry

Built in the Neo-Romanesque style in c1830, on an earlier structure, and probably designed by Thomas Hopper, it stands in the Snowdonian Range. The tranquil garden includes a hill-walk with fine views of Mt Snowdon, Anglesey and the sea. Bryn Bras, a much loved home, offers a delightful selection of apartments for holidays for twos within the Grade II* listed castle. Many local restaurants, inns.

Location: MAP 5:F3, OS Ref. SH543 625. ½m off A4086 at Llanrug, 4½m E of Caernarfon.

Open: Only by appointment.

Admission: By arrangement. No children please.

Self-catering apartments for two within castle.

Denbigh Castle

CAERNARFON CASTLE ✠

CASTLE DITCH, CAERNARFON LL55 2AY

www.cadw.wales.gov.uk

Tel: 01286 677617

Owner: In the care of Cadw **Contact:** The Custodian

The most famous, and perhaps the most impressive castle in Wales. Taking nearly 50 years to build, it proved the costliest of Edward I's castles. Part of a World Heritage Inscribed site.

Location: MAP 5:F3, OS Ref. SH477 626. In Caernarfon, just W of town centre.

Open: Last admission 30 minutes before closing. March–June: daily 9.30am–5pm. July–Aug: daily 9.30am–6pm. Sept–Oct: daily 9.30am–5pm. Nov–Feb: Mon–Sat 10am–4pm, Sun 11am–4pm. Closed 24, 25, 26 Dec, 1 Jan.

Admission: Adult £4.95, Concessions £4.60, Family (2 adults and all children under 16yrs) £14.50. Child under 5 yrs free. Under 16s must be accompanied by an adult. All opening times and prices are correct at time of going to press (Autumn 2010) but may be subject to change from April 2011 – Please phone site for details.

Induction loop. Toilets. Partial. Guide dogs only. €

CHIRK CASTLE

Chirk LL14 5AF

Tel: 01691 777701 **Fax:** 01691 774706 **E-mail:** chirkcastle@nationaltrust.org.uk

Owner: National Trust

700 year old Chirk Castle, a magnificent marcher fortress, commands fine views over the surrounding countryside. Rectangular with a massive drum tower at each corner, the castle has beautiful formal gardens with clipped yews, roses and a variety of flowering shrubs. The dramatic dungeon is a reminder of the castle's turbulent history, whilst later occupants have left elegant state rooms, furniture, tapestries and portraits. The castle was sold for five thousand pounds to Sir Thomas Myddelton in 1595, and his descendants continue to live in part of the castle today.

Location: MAP 6:J4, OS Ref. SJ275 388. 8m S of Wrexham off A483, 2m from Chirk village.

Open: Garden, tower, shops and tea-rooms: 6–14 Feb & 27–28 Feb: Sat & Sun, 10am–4pm; 17–21 Feb: Wed–Sun, 10am–4pm; 3 Mar–27 Jun & 1 Sept–31 Oct: Wed–Sun, 10am–5pm; 1 Jul–29 Aug: Tue–Sun, 10am–5pm; 6 Nov–19 Dec: Sat & Sun, 10am–4pm. State rooms:* 3 Mar–27 Jun & 1 Sep–31 Oct: Wed–Sun, 11am–5pm; 1 Jul–29 Aug: Tue–Sun, 11am–5pm. February, March and October closes 4. Open Bank Holiday Mondays. Last admission to garden and tower one hour before closing. *State rooms by guided tour only 11 to 12, free-flow 12 to closing.

***Admission:** Full Castle: Adult £9.60, Child £4.80, Family £24. Pre-booked groups (15+): Adult £7.50, Child £3.75. Garden & Tower: Adults £6.80, Child £3.40, Family £17. Includes a voluntary donation but visitors can choose to pay the standard prices displayed at the property and on the website.

No indoor photography. Licensed. By arrangement. Guide dogs only.

Dolwyddelan Castle

COCHWILLAN OLD HALL

Talybont, Bangor, Gwynedd LL57 3AZ

Tel: 01248 355853

Owner: R C H Douglas Pennant **Contact:** Miss M D Monteith

A fine example of medieval architecture with the present house dating from about 1450. It was probably built by William Gryffydd who fought for Henry VII at Bosworth. Once owned in the 17th century by John Williams who became Archbishop of York. The house was restored from a barn in 1971.

Location: MAP 5:G2, OS Ref. SH606 695. 3½m SE of Bangor. 1m SE of Talybont off A55.

Open: By appointment.

Admission: Please telephone for details.

CONWY CASTLE ✠

CONWY LL32 8AY

www.cadw.wales.gov.uk

Tel: 01492 592358

Owner: In the care of Cadw **Contact:** The Custodian

The castle and town walls are the most impressive of the fortresses built by Edward I. Explore the almost complete medieval town walls and enjoy the spectacular views. Part of a World Heritage Inscribed site.

Location: MAP 5:H2, OS Ref. SH783 774. Conwy by A55 or B5106.

Open: Last admission 30 minutes before closing. Apr–June: 9.30am–5pm daily; July–Aug: 9.30am–6pm daily; Sept–Oct: 9.30am–5pm daily; Nov–Feb: Mon–Sat, 10am–4pm, Sun 11am–4pm. Closed 24, 25, 26 Dec, 1 Jan.

Admission: Adult £4.60, Concessions £4.10, Family (2 adults and all children under 16yrs) £13.30. Joint ticket for Conwy Castle and Plas Mawr Town House: Adult £6.85, Conc. £5.85, Family (2 adults and all children under 16yrs) £19.55. Child under 5yrs free. Under 16s must be accompanied by an adult. All opening times and prices are correct at time of going to press (Autumn 2010) but may be subject to change from April 2011. Please phone site for details.

Induction loop. Toilets. Partial. WCs. By arrangement. Guide dogs only. €

© Cadw, Welsh Assembly Government (Crown Copyright)

Beaumaris Castle

CRICCIETH CASTLE ✠

Castle Street, Criccieth, Gwynedd LL52 0DP

Tel: 01766 522227 **www.cadw.wales.gov.uk**

Owner: In the care of Cadw **Contact:** The Custodian

Overlooking Cardigan Bay, Criccieth Castle is the most striking of the fortresses built by the Welsh Princes. Its inner defences are dominated by a powerful twin-towered gatehouse.

Location: MAP 5:F4, OS Ref. SH500 378. A497 to Criccieth from Porthmadog or Pwllheli.

Open: Last admission 30 minutes before closing. April–Oct: 10am-5pm daily: Nov–Mar: Fri & Sat, 9.30am–4pm, Sun, 11am–4pm. Closed 24, 25, 26 Dec, 1 Jan.

Admission: Adult £3, Concessions £2.60, Family (2 adults and all children under 16yrs) £8.60. Child under 5yrs free. Under 16s must be accompanied by an adult. All opening times and prices are correct at time of going to press (Autumn 2010) but may be subject to change from April 2011. Please phone site for details.

Induction loop. Toilets. Partial. Limited for cars, no coaches. On leads. €

DENBIGH CASTLE ✠

Denbigh, Denbighshire LL16 3NB

Tel: 01745 813385 **www.cadw.wales.gov.uk**

Owner: In the care of Cadw **Contact:** The Custodian

Crowning the summit of a prominent outcrop overlooking the Vale of Clwyd, the principal feature of this spectacular site is the great gatehouse dating back to the 11th century. Sections of the Town Walls are open to visitors. Don't miss Leicester's Church, Denbigh Friary and the Burgess Gate.

Location: MAP 6:I2, OS Ref. SJ052 658. Denbigh via A525, A543 or B5382.

Open: Last admission 30 minutes before closing. Apr–31 Oct: daily, 10am–5pm. At all other times this monument will be open but unstaffed between 10am and 4pm. Closed 24, 25, 26 December and 1 January.

Admission: Adult £3, Concessions. £2.60, Family (2 adults and all children under 16yrs) £8.60. Child under 5 yrs free. Under 16s must be accompanied by an adult. All opening times and prices are correct at time of going to press (Autumn 2010) but may be subject to change from April 2011. Please see site for details.

Cycle stands. Induction loop. Toilets. Partial. On leads. €

DOLBELYDR

Trefnant, Denbighshire LL16 5AG

Tel: 01628 825925 **E-mail:** bookings@landmarktrust.org.uk **www.landmarktrust.org.uk**

Owner/Contact: The Landmark Trust

A 16th century, Grade II* listed building, a fine example of a 16th century gentry house and has good claim to be the birthplace of the modern Welsh language. It was at Dolbelydr that Henry Salesbury wrote his Grammatica Britannica. Dolbelydr is cared for by The Landmark Trust, a building preservation charity who let it for holidays. Full details of Dolbelydr and 189 other historic and architecturally important buildings are featured in the Landmark Trust Handbook (£10 plus p&p refundable against a booking) and on the website.

Location: MAP 6:I2, OS Ref. SJ031 709.

Open: Available for holidays for up to 6 people throughout the year. Open Days on 8 days throughout the year. Other visits by appointment. Contact the Landmark Trust for details.

Admission: Free on Open Days and visits by appointment.

DOLWYDDELAN CASTLE ✠

Dolwyddelan, Gwynedd LL25 0JD

Tel: 01690 750366 **www.cadw.wales.gov.uk**

Owner: In the care of Cadw **Contact:** The Custodian

Standing proudly on a ridge, this stone keep tower remains remarkably intact and visitors cannot fail to be impressed with the great solitary square tower, built by Llewelyn the Great in the early 13th century.

Location: MAP 5:G3, OS Ref. SH722 522. A470(T) Blaenau Ffestiniog to Betws-y-Coed, 1m W of Dolwyddelan.

Open: Last admission 30 minutes before closing. Apr–Sept: Mon–Sat, 10am–5pm. Sun 11.30am–4pm. Oct–Mar: Mon–Sat, 10am–4pm. Sun, 11.30am–4pm. Closed 24, 25, 26 Dec, 1 Jan.

Admission: Adult £2.60, Concessions £2.25, Family (2 adults and all children under 16yrs) £7.50. child under 5yrs free. Under 16s must be accompanied by an adult. All opening times and prices are correct at time of going to press (Autumn 2010) but may be subject to change from April 2011. Please phone site for details.

Guide dogs only.

ERDDIG

Nr Wrexham LL13 0YT

Tel: 01978 355314 **Fax:** 01978 313333 **Info Line:** 01978 315151

Owner: National Trust

One of the most fascinating houses in Britain, not least because of the unusually close relationship that existed between the family of the house and their servants. The beautiful and evocative range of outbuildings includes kitchen, laundry, bakehouse, stables, sawmill, smithy and joiner's shop, while the stunning state rooms display most of their original 18th & 19th century furniture and furnishings, including some exquisite Chinese wallpaper.

Location: MAP 6:K3, OS Ref. SJ326 482. 2m S of Wrexham.

Open: House: 13 Mar–31 Oct: Mon, Tue, Wed, Sat & Sun, 12–5pm; 3 Jul–31 Aug: Mon, Tue, Wed, Thu Sat & Sun, 12–5pm; 6 Nov–19 Dec: Sat & Sun, 12–4pm. Garden, restaurant and shop: 13 Feb–7 Mar: Daily 11am–4pm; 13 Mar–31 Oct: Mon, Tue, Wed, Sat & Sun, 11am–6pm; 3 Jul–31 Aug: Mon, Tue, Wed, Thu, Sat & Sun, 11am–6pm; 6 Nov–19 Dec: Sat & Sun, 11–4pm; 26 Dec–31 Dec: Daily 11–4pm. Last admission one hour before closing. July and August: access to house by guided tour only on Thursday.

***Admission:** Adult £10.30, Child £5.15, Family (2+3) £25.75. Groups, Adult £7.20, Child £3.60. Garden & Outbuildings only: Adult £6.72, Child £3.36, Family £16.80. NT members Free. Includes a voluntary donation but visitors can choose to pay the standard prices displayed at the property and on the website.

Partial. WCs. Licensed. AV presentation. Guide dogs only.

FFERM

Pontblyddyn, Mold, Flintshire

Tel: 01352 770204

Owner: The Executors of the late Dr M Jones Mortimer

Contact: Miss Miranda Kaufmann

17th century farmhouse. Viewing is limited to 7 persons at any one time. Prior booking is recommended. No toilets or refreshments.

Location: MAP 6:J3, OS Ref. SJ279 603. Access from A541 in Pontblyddyn, 3½m SE of Mold.

Open: 2nd Wed in every month, 2–5pm. Pre-booking is recommended.

Admission: £4.

GWYDIR CASTLE

LLANRWST, GWYNEDD LL26 0PN

www.gwydircastle.co.uk

Tel: 01492 641687 **E-mail:** info@gwydircastle.co.uk

Owner/Contact: Mr & Mrs Welford

Gwydir Castle is situated in the beautiful Conwy Valley and is set within a Grade I listed, 10 acre garden. Built by the illustrious Wynn family c1500, Gwydir is a fine example of a Tudor courtyard house, incorporating re-used medieval material from the dissolved Abbey of Maenan. Further additions date from c1600 and c1828. The important 1640s panelled Dining Room has now been reinstated, following its repatriation from the New York Metropolitan Museum.

Location: MAP 5:H3, OS Ref. SH795 610. ½m W of Llanrwst on B5106.

Open: 1 Mar–31 Oct: daily, 10am–4pm. Closed Mons & Sats (except BH weekends). Limited openings at other times. Please telephone for details.

Admission: Adult £4, Child £2, OAP £3.50. Group discount 10%.

Partial. By arrangement. By arrangement. 2 doubles.

HARLECH CASTLE

Castle Square, Harlech LL46 2YH

Tel: 01766 780552 **www.cadw.wales.gov.uk**

Owner: In the care of Cadw **Contact:** The Custodian

Set on a towering rock above Tremadog Bay, this seemingly impregnable fortress is the most dramatic of all the castles of Edward I. Discover the Castle's connections with Owain Glyn Dŵr and its importance in Welsh history. Part of a World Heritage Inscribed site.

Location: MAP 5:F4, OS Ref. SH581 312. Harlech, Gwynedd on A496 coast road.

Open: Last admission 30 minutes before closing. Mar-June: daily, 9.30am–5pm; July-Aug daily, 9.30am-6pm; Sept-Oct daily 9.30am-5pm; Nov–Feb: Mon–Sat, 10.00am–4pm. 11am–4pm Sun. Closed 24, 25, 26 Dec, 1 Jan.

Admission: Adult £3.60, Concessions £3.20, Family (2 adults and all children under 16yrs) £10.40. Child under 5yrs free. Under 16s must be accompanied by an adult. All opening times and prices are correct at time of going to press (Autumn 2010) but may be subject to change from April 2011. Please phone site for details.

Induction loop. Toilets. Pay and Display. Cycle stands. Guide dogs only. €

HARTSHEATH

Pontblyddyn, Mold, Flintshire

Tel/Fax: 01352 770204

Owner: The Executors of the late Dr M Jones Mortimer

Contact: Miss Miranda Kaufmann

18th and 19th century house set in parkland. Viewing is limited to 7 persons at any one time. Prior booking is recommended. No toilets or refreshments.

Location: MAP 6:J3, OS Ref. SJ287 602. Access from A5104, 3½m SE of Mold between Pontblyddyn and Penyffordd.

Open: 1st, 3rd & 5th Wed in every month, 2–5pm.

Admission: £4.

ISCOYD PARK

Nr WHITCHURCH, SHROPSHIRE SY13 3AT

www.iscoydpark.com

Tel: 01948 780785 **E-mail:** info@iscoydpark.com

Owner/Contact: Mr & Mrs P L Godsal

A Grade II* red brick Georgian house in an idyllic 18th century parkland setting, very much a family home. After extensive refurbishment of the house and gardens we are now open for Weddings, parties, corporate events and conferences of all kinds. We can offer a wide range of B&B accommodation. All events considered!

Location: MAP 6:L4, OS Ref. SJ504 421. Car: 2m W of Whitchurch off A525.

Rail: Whitchurch station via Crewe. Air: Manchester/Liverpool.

Open: House visits by written appointment.

Private dinners a speciality. WCs. Licensed. Licensed. Obligatory.

Ample for cars. Limited for coaches.

PENRHYN CASTLE

Bangor LL57 4HN

Tel: 01248 353084 **Infoline:** 01248 371337 **Fax:** 01248 371281

Owner: National Trust

This dramatic neo-Norman fantasy castle sits between Snowdonia and the Menai Strait. Built by Thomas Hopper between 1820 and 1845 for the wealthy Pennant family, who made their fortune from Jamaican sugar and Welsh slate. The castle is crammed with fascinating things such as a 1-ton slate bed made for Queen Victoria.

Location: MAP 5:G2, OS Ref. SH602 720. 1m E of Bangor, at Llandygai (J11, A55).

Open: Stable Block: 13–21 Feb: Mon, Wed–Sun 11am-4pm. Castle: 24 Mar–30 Jun: Mon, Wed–Sun 12–5pm; 1 Jul–30 Aug: Mon, Wed–Sun 11am–5pm; 1 Sept–31 Oct: Mon, Wed–Sun 12–5pm. Stable block, shop and museums: 24 Mar–31 Oct: Mon, Wed–Sun 11am–5pm. Grounds and tea-room: as castle but open one hour earlier. Victorian kitchen: as castle but last admission 4.45pm. Last audio tour 4pm. *Half-term opening, stable block only, adult £2.

Admission: Castle: Adult £10, Child £5, Family (2+2) £25. Grounds and and stable block exhibitions only: adult £6.60, child £3.50.

Licensed. Guide dogs only.

PLAS BRONDANW GARDENS

Plas Brondanw, Llanfrothen, Gwynedd LL48 6SW

Tel: 01743 241181/07788 425713 **Email:** davinagriffiths@balfours.co.uk

Owner: Trustees of the Clough Williams-Ellis Foundation.

Italianate gardens with topiary.

Location: MAP 5:G4, OS Ref. SH618 423. 3m N of Penrhyndeudraeth off A4085, on Croesor Road.

Open: All year: daily, 9.30am–5.30pm. Coaches accepted, please book.

Admission: £3 first adult, £2 subsequent adults. Accompanied children free.

For **special events** in North Wales see our special index at the end of the book.

Cadw: Crown Copyright

PLAS MAWR

HIGH STREET, CONWY LL32 8DE

www.cadw.wales.gov.uk

Tel: 01492 580167

Owner: In the care of Cadw **Contact:** The Custodian

The best preserved Elizabethan town house in Britain, the house reflects the status of its builder Robert Wynn. A fascinating and unique place allowing visitors to sample the lives of the Tudor gentry and their servants, Plas Mawr is famous for the quality and quantity of its furnishings.

Location: MAP 5:I2, OS Ref. SH781 776. Conwy by A55 or B5106 or A547

Open: Last admission 45 minutes before closing. Apr–Sept: Tues–Sun, 9am–5pm. Oct: Tues–Sun, 9.30am–4pm. Closed on Mons (except BH weekends) between 1 Apr–31 Oct. Closed at all other times.

Admission: Adult £4.95, Concessions £4.60, Family (2 adults and all children under 16yrs) £14.50. Child under 5yrs free. Children under 16 must be accompanied by an adult. Joint ticket for Plas Mawr and Conwy Castle: Adult £6.85, Conc. £5.85, Family (2 adults and all children under 16yrs) £19.55. Under 16s must be accompanied by an adult. All opening times and prices are correct at time of going to press (Autumn 2010) but may be subject to change from April 2011. Please phone site for details.

Toilets. Induction loop. Partial. Guide dogs only. €

© Cadw, Welsh Assembly Government (Crown Copyright)

Rug Chapel

PLAS NEWYDD

Llanfairpwll, Anglesey LL61 6DQ

Tel: 01248 714795 **Infoline:** 01248 715272 **Fax:** 01248 713673

www.nationaltrust.org.uk/plasnewydd **Email:** plasnewydd@nationaltrust.org.uk

Owner: National Trust

Set amidst breathtaking beautiful scenery with spectacular Snowdonia views. Fine spring garden and Australasian arboretum, summer terrace, massed hydrangeas and Autumn colour. Rhododendron garden April–early June. Elegant 18th century house housing Rex Whistler's largest mural. Waterloo museum contains relics of 1st Marquess of Anglesey. Second-hand bookshop, children's adventure playground.

Location: MAP 5:F2, OS Ref. SH521 696. 2m SW of Llanfairpwll. A55 Junctions 7 and 8a, A4080 to Brynsiencyn. Bus: Arriva 42 Bangor-Llangefni. Rail: Llanfairpwll 1.75 miles.

Open: House, Coffee Shop & Garden: 19 Mar–2 Nov, Sat–Wed, 11am–5pm. Tours from 11.15, house open for free flow from 1pm, last entry 4.30. Shop, Tea Room & Adventure Playground: 3 Jan–19 Mar, Sat & Sun, 11am–4pm. 19 Mar–2 Nov, daily, 10am–5.30pm. 2 Nov–31 Dec, daily, 11am–4pm. Rhododendron Garden: 2 Apr–8 Jun, 11am–5.30pm (subject to flowering). The property is closed on Christmas Day.

Admission: Gift aid on Entry: House & Garden: Adult £9.30, Child £4.65, Family £23.25. Garden only: Adult £7.30, Child £3.65. NT Members Free.

No indoor photography. WCs. Licensed. Licensed. By arrangement. Guide dogs only. Special events throughout the year, see our website for details.

PLAS YN RHIW

Rhiw, Pwllheli LL53 8AB

Tel/Fax: 01758 780219

Owner: National Trust

A small manor house, with garden and woodlands, overlooking the west shore of Porth Neigwl (Hell's Mouth Bay) on the Llyn Peninsula. The house is part medieval, with Tudor and Georgian additions, and the ornamental gardens have flowering trees and shrubs, divided by box hedges and grass paths, rising behind to the snowdrop wood.

Location: MAP 5:D5, OS Ref. SH237 282. 16m SW of Pwllheli, 3m S of the B4413 to Aberdaron. No access for coaches.

Open: 25 Mar–2 May: Thur–Sun 12–5pm; 5 May–30 Aug: Mon, Wed–Sun 12–5pm; 2 Sept–30 Sep: Mon, Thur–Sun 12–5pm; 1 Oct–31 Oct: Thur–Sun 12–4pm. Open Bank Holidays. Garden and snowdrop wood open occasionally at weekends in January and February. Last admission 30 minutes before closing.

Admission: Adult £5, Child £2.50, Family (2+3) £12.50.

Partial. WCs. By arrangement. Limited. Guide dogs only.

PORTMEIRION

Portmeirion, Gwynedd LL48 6ET

Tel: 01766 770000 **Fax:** 01766 771331 **E-mail:** enquiries@portmeirion-village.com

Owner: The Portmeirion Foundation **Contact:** Mr R Llywelyn

Built by Clough Williams-Ellis as an 'unashamedly romantic' village resort.

Location: MAP 5:F4, OS Ref. SH590 371. Off A487 at Minffordd between Penrhyndeudraeth and Porthmadog.

Open: All year: daily, 9.30am–5.30pm. Closed 25 Dec.

Admission: Adults £8, Concessions £6.50, Children 4-16 years £4 (under 4 free). Half Price Entry 3.30–7.30pm. Family tickets available.

RHUDDLAN CASTLE ✠

Castle Street, Rhuddlan, Rhyl LL18 5AD

Tel: 01745 590777 **www.cadw.wales.gov.uk**

Owner: In the care of Cadw **Contact:** The Custodian

Guarding the ancient ford of the River Clwyd, Rhuddlan was the strongest of Edward I's castles in North-East Wales. Linked to the sea by an astonishing deep water channel nearly 3 miles long, it still proclaims the innovative genius of its architect.

Location: MAP 6:I2, OS Ref. SJ025 779. SW end of Rhuddlan via A525 or A547.

Open: 1 Apr–31 Oct: daily, 10am–5pm. The monument is closed at all other times.

Admission: Adult £3, Concessions £2.60, Family (2 adults and all children under 16yrs) £8.60. Under 16s must be accompanied by an adult. Child under 5 yrs go free. All opening times and prices are correct at time of going to press (Autumn 2010) but may be subject to change from April 2011. Please phone site for details.

Cycle stands. Toilets. Induction loop. Baby changing. Free childrens' quiz. WCs Limited for coaches. On leads. €

RUG CHAPEL & LLANGAR OLD PARISH CHURCH ✠

Rug, Corwen, Nr Llangollen LL21 9BT

Tel: 01490 412025 **www.cadw.wales.gov.uk**

Owner: In the care of Cadw **Contact:** The Custodian

Prettily set in a wooded landscape, Rug Chapel's exterior gives little hint of the highly decorative and colourful wonders within. Nearby the attractive medieval Llangar Church still retains its charming early Georgian furnishings.

Location: Rug Chapel: MAP 6:I4, OS Ref. SJ065 439. Off A494, 1m N of Corwen. Llangar Church: MAP 6:I4, OS Ref. SJ064 423. Off B4401, 1m S of Corwen.

Open: Last admission 30 minutes before closing. **Rug** Apr–Oct: Wed–Sun (open BH Mons), 10am–5pm. **Llangar** (By appointment) Apr–Oct: Wed–Sun (open BH Mons) Prior arrangement to access Llangar must be made through Custodian at Rug Chapel. Telephone 01490 412025 for details.

Admission: Adult £3.60, Concessions £3.20, Family (2 adults and all children under 16yrs) £10.40. Child under 5 yrs free. Under 16s must be accompanied by an adult. All opening times and prices are correct at time of going to press (Autumn 2010) but may be subject to change from April 2011. Please phone site for details.

Facilities at Rug Chapel only. Toilets. Cycle stands. Induction loops. WCs. Limited for coaches. Guide dogs only. €

TOWER

Nercwys Road, Mold, Flintshire CH7 4EW

Tel: 01352 700220 **E-mail:** enquiries@towerwales.co.uk **www.towerwales.co.uk**

Owner/Contact: Charles Wynne-Eyton

This Grade I listed building is steeped in Welsh history and bears witness to the continuous warfare of the time. A fascinating place to visit or for overnight stays.

Location: MAP 6:J3, OS Ref. SJ240 620. 1m S of Mold. SAT NAV – use CH7 4EF.

Open: 2–30 May incl. 29 Aug: 2–4.30pm. Groups also welcome at other times by appointment. It is strongly recommended that visitors travelling significant distances should phone in advance to check opening days.

Admission: Adult £3, Child £2.

TŶ MAWR WYBRNANT

Penmachno, Betws-y-Coed, Conwy LL25 0HJ

Tel: 01690 760213

Owner: The National Trust

Situated in the beautiful and secluded Wybrnant Valley, Tŷ Mawr was the birthplace of Bishop William Morgan, first translator of the entire Bible into Welsh. The house has been restored to its probable 16th-17th century appearance and houses a display of Welsh Bibles. A footpath leads from the house through woodland and the surrounding fields, which are traditionally managed.

Location: MAP 5:H3, OS Ref. SH770 524. From A5 3m S of Betws-y-Coed, take B4406 to Penmachno. House is 2½m NW of Penmachno by forest road.

Open: 25 Mar–31 Oct: Thur–Sun 12–5pm. Open Bank Holiday Mondays. Last admission 30 minutes before closing.

Admission: Adult £3, Child £1.50, Child under 5 yrs Free, Family £7.50. Children under 16 must be accompanied by an adult. Groups: Adult £2.50, Child £1.

Ground floor. Guide dogs only.

VALLE CRUCIS ABBEY ✠

Llangollen, Denbighshire LL20 8DD

Tel: 01978 860326 **www.cadw.wales.gov.uk**

Owner: In the care of Cadw **Contact:** The Custodian

Set in a beautiful valley location, Valle Crucis Abbey is the best preserved medieval monastery in North Wales, enhanced by the only surviving monastic fish pond in Wales.

Location: MAP 6:J4, OS Ref. SJ205 442. B5103 from A5, 2m NW of Llangollen, or A542 from Ruthin.

Open: Apr–Oct: daily, 10am–5pm. Unstaffed with no admission charge during winter, generally between 10am–4pm. Last admission 30 minutes before closing. Closed 23, 24, 25 December and 1 January.

Admission: Adult £2.60, Concessions £2.25, Family (2 adults and all children under 16yrs) £7.45. Child under 5yrs free. Under 16s must be accompanied by an adult. All opening times and prices are correct at time of going to press (Autumn 2010) but may be subject to change from March 2010. Please phone site for details.

Induction loop. Limited for cars. On leads. €

WERN ISAF

Penmaen Park, Llanfairfechan LL33 0RN

Tel: 01248 680437

Owner/Contact: Mrs P J Phillips

This Arts and Crafts house was built in 1900 by the architect H L North as his family home and it contains much of the original furniture and William Morris fabrics. It is situated in a woodland garden and is at its best in the Spring. It has extensive views over the Menai Straits and Conwy Bay. One of the most exceptional houses of its date and style in Wales.

Location: MAP 5:G2, OS Ref. SH685 75. Off A55 midway between Bangor and Conwy.

Open: 2–30 Mar: daily 1–3pm, except Tues.

Admission: Free.

Rhuddlan Castle

City Hall, Belfast, Northern Ireland

Ireland

Visitors come largely to enjoy the countryside and what it has to offer. Fishing (both river and sea) and golf are two of the most popular attractions. There are many heritage properties both in private ownership and owned by the National Trust for Ireland that have fascinating histories, among them Mount Stewart, once the home of Lord Castlereagh.

The East Hall at The Argory, County Armagh, Northern Ireland ©NTPL/Andreas von Einsiedel

Ballywater Park, Co Down

ARDRESS HOUSE

64 Ardress Road, Portadown, Co Armagh BT62 1SQ

Tel 028 8778 4753 **Fax:** 028 3885 1236 **E-mail:** ardress@nationaltrust.org.uk

www.ntni.org.uk

Owner: National Trust **Contact:** The Custodian

Nestled in the apple orchards of Armagh, Ardress is a 17th century house with elegant 18th century decoration. On display is the 1799 table made for the Speaker of the Irish Parliament upon which King George V signed the Constitution of Northern Ireland on 22 June 1921.

Location: MAP 18:N4, OS Ref. H912 561. On B28, 5m from Moy, 5m from Portadown, 3m from M1/J13.

Open: 20–21 Feb: Sat, Sun 12–4pm, 13 Mar–27 Jun: Sat, Sun 1–5pm, 2–11 Apr: Daily 1–5pm, 3 Jul–29 Aug: Thur–Sun 1–5pm, 4–26 Sep: Sat, Sun 1–5pm, 28–31 Oct: Thur–Sun 12–5pm. Admission by guided tour (last admission one hour before closing). Open Bank Holiday Mondays and all other public holidays in Northern Ireland including 17 March. Grounds ('The Lady's Mile') open daily all year, dawn to dusk.

***Admission:** Farmyard only: Adult £3, Child £1.50, Family £7.50. Farmyard and house: Adult £5, Child £2.50, Family £12.50. *Includes a voluntary donation but visitors can choose to pay the standard prices displayed at the property and on the website.

Ground floor. WC. Obligatory. On leads.

THE ARGORY

Moy, Dungannon, Co Tyrone BT71 6NA

Tel: 028 8778 4753 **Fax:** 028 8778 9598

E-mail: argory@nationaltrust.org.uk **www.ntni.org.uk**

Owner: National Trust **Contact:** The Property Manager

The Argory was built in the 1820s on a hill and has wonderful views over the gardens and 320 acre wooded riverside estate. This former home of the McGeough-Bond family has a splendid stable yard with horse carriages, harness room, acetylene gas plant and laundry.

Location: MAP 18:N4, OS Ref. H871 577. On Derrycaw road, 4m from Moy, 3m from M1/J13 or J14 (coaches J13).

Open: House: 13 Mar–28 Jun: Thur–Mon 11am–5pm. 2–11 Apr: Daily 11am–5pm. 1 Jul–31 Aug: Daily 11am–5pm. 2–30 Sep: Thur–Mon 11am–5pm. 1–31 Oct: Thur–Mon 11am–4pm. Grounds: 1 Jan–30 Apr: Daily 10am–5pm. 1 May–30 Sep: 10am–6pm. 1 Oct–31 Dec: Daily 10am–5pm. Admission to house by guided tour (last admission one hour before closing). Open Bank Holiday Mondays and all other public holidays in Northern Ireland, including 17 March. Tea-room, shop and second-hand bookshop open as house, but weekends only 1 September to 31 October.

Admission: *House tour: Adult £6, Child £3, Family £15. Grounds (Standard Admission): Adult £2.75, Child £1.25, Family £6.75. *includes a voluntary donation but visitors can choose to pay the standard prices displayed at the property and on the website.

Ground floor. WC. Obligatory. On leads.

BALLYWALTER PARK

BALLYWALTER, NEWTOWNARDS, CO DOWN BT22 2PP

www.ballywalterpark.com

Tel: 028 4275 8264 **Fax:** 028 4275 8818 **E-mail:** enq@dunleath-estates.co.uk

Owner: The Lord and Lady Dunleath

Contact: Mrs Sharon Graham, The Estate Office

Ballywalter Park was built, in the Italianate Palazzo style, between 1846 and 1852 by Sir Charles Lanyon for the present owner's great, great, great, grandfather Andrew Mulholland. A single-storey Gentlemen's wing, comprising Billiard Room, Smoking Room and Conservatory, was added in 1870 for Andrew's son, John Mulholland, later 1st Baron Dunleath. Further Edwardian additions were made by W J Fennell. The house has a fine collection of original furniture and paintings, complemented by contemporary pieces added by the present owner. The house has undergone major conservation works over the past 20 years, with the magnificent domed conservatory being restored in 2008/9.

Location: MAP 18:P3, OS Ref. J610 723. Off A2 on unclassified road, 1 km S of Ballywalter village.

Open: By prior appointment only; please contact The Estate Office.

Admission: House or Gardens: £7. House & Gardens: £10. Groups (max 50): £7.

No photography indoors. By prior arrangement. Obligatory.

Tel for details. €

The Argory

BARONS COURT

Newtownstewart, Omagh, Co Tyrone BT78 4EZ

Tel: 028 8166 1683 **Fax:** 028 8166 2059 **E-mail:** info@barons-court.com

www.barons-court.com

Contact: The Agent

The home of the Duke and Duchess of Abercorn, Barons Court was built between 1779 and 1782, and subsequently extensively remodelled by John Soane (1791), William and Richard Morrison (1819–1841), Sir Albert Richardson (1947–49) and David Hicks (1975–76).

Location: MAP 18:M3, OS Ref. H236 382. 5km SW of Newtownstewart.

Open: By appointment only.

Admission: Adult £9. Groups max. 50.

No photography. Partial. By arrangement. €

CASTLE COOLE

Enniskillen, Co Fermanagh BT74 6JY

Tel: 028 6632 2690 **Fax:** 028 6632 5665 **E-mail:** castlecoole@nationaltrust.org.uk

www.ntni.org.uk

Owner: National Trust **Contact:** The Property Manager

Surrounded by its stunning landscape park on the edge of Enniskillen, this majestic 18th century home of the Earls of Belmore, designed by James Wyatt, was created to impress. The surrounding wooded landscape park sloping down to Lough Coole is ideal for long walks.

Location: MAP 18:L4, OS Ref. H245 436. On A4, 1.5m from Enniskillen on A4, Belfast–Enniskillen road.

Open: Grounds: 1 Jan–28 Feb: Daily 10am–4pm. 1 Mar–31 Oct: Daily 10am–7pm. 1 Nov–31 Dec: Daily 10am–4pm. House, tea-room and shop: 13 Mar–30 May: Sat & Sun 11am–5pm. 2–11 Apr: Daily 11am–5pm. 1–30 Jun: Fri–Wed 11am–5pm. 1 Jul–31 Aug: Daily 11am–5pm. 4–30 Sept: Sat & Sun 11am–5pm. House: admission by guided tour (last tour one hour before closing). Open Bank Holiday Mondays and all other public holidays in Northern Ireland including 17 March. Last admission 30 minutes before closing.

***Admission:** House tour: Adult £5.50, child £2.50, Family £13.50. Grounds: car (£3.50). *Includes a voluntary donation but visitors can choose to pay the standard prices displayed at the property and on the website.

Partial. WC. In grounds, on leads.

CASTLE WARD HOUSE & DEMESNE

Strangford, Downpatrick, Co Down BT30 7LS

Tel: 028 4488 1204 **Fax:** 028 4488 1729 **E-mail:** castleward@nationaltrust.org.uk

www.nationaltrust.org.uk/castleward

Owner: National Trust **Contact:** Jacqueline Baird, Visitor Services Manager

Situated in a stunning location within an 820 acre walled demesne overlooking Strangford Lough, the lawns rise up to the unique 18th century house and its Gothic façade. This fascinating house features both Gothic and Classical styles of architectural treatment, internally and externally.

Location: MAP 18:P4, OS Ref. J573 498. On A25, 7m from Downpatrick and 1½m from Strangford.

Open: House: Mid Feb–End Oct. Grounds: All year: daily, 10am–4pm (8pm Apr–Sept).

***Admission:** Grounds & House Tour: Adult £6, Child £2.70, Family £14.70. Groups: £4.00. Grounds: Adult £6, Child £3, Family £14.70, Groups £4.00 *includes a voluntary donation but visitors can choose to pay the standard prices displayed at the property and on the website.

WCs. By arrangement. On leads. Caravan park, holiday cottages, basecamp. Summer Jazz Series, Cream Teas in Lord Bangor's Sitting Room €

CROM

Newtownbutler, Co Fermanagh BT92 8AP

Tel/Fax: 028 6773 8118 (Visitor Centre) 028 6773 8174 (Estate)

E-mail: crom@nationaltrust.org.uk **www.ntni.org.uk**

Owner: National Trust **Contact:** The Visitor Facilities Manager

Crom is one of Ireland's most important nature conservation areas. It is set in 770 hectares of romantic and tranquil islands, woodland and ruins on the shores of Upper Lough Erne.

Location: MAP 18:M4, OS Ref. H359 246. 3m from A34, well signposted from Newtownbutler. Jetty at Visitor Centre.

Open: Grounds: 13 Mar–31 May: Daily 10am–6pm. 1 Jun–31 Aug: Daily 10am–7pm. 1 Sep–31 Oct: Daily 10am–6pm. Visitor Centre: 13 Mar–26 Sept: Daily 11am–5pm. Open Bank Holiday Mondays and all other public holidays in Northern Ireland including 17 March. Last admission one hour before closing. Telephone for tea-room opening arrangements.

***Admission:** Grounds and Visitor Centre: Adult £3.25, Child £1, Family £7.50. *Includes a voluntary donation but visitors can choose to pay the standard prices displayed at the property and on the website.

7 x 4-star holiday cottages & play-area.

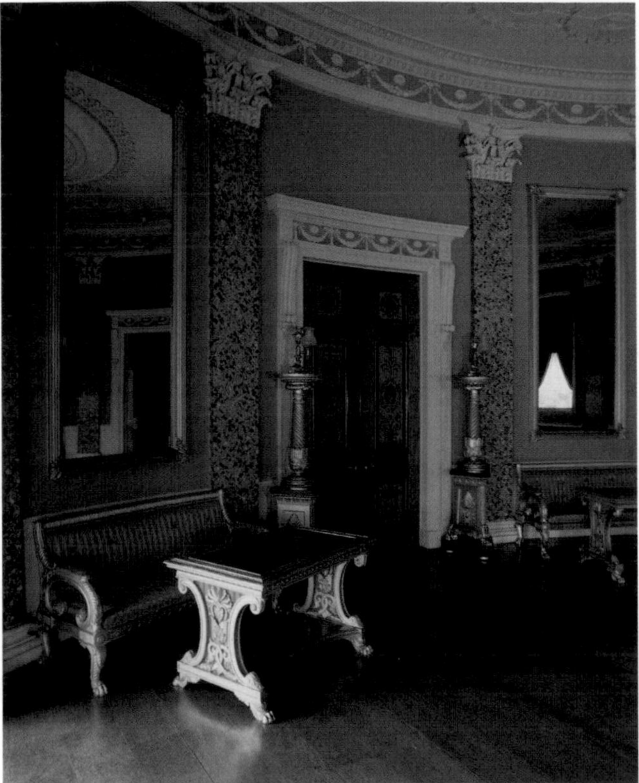

Castle Coole – The Saloon

THE CROWN BAR

46 Great Victoria Street, Belfast BT2 7BA

Tel: 028 9027 9901

Belfast has many watering holes but none quite like The Crown! Rich in colour and design, it is famous for its special atmosphere, gas lamps, cosy snugs, fine ales and wines, and delicious lunch-time cuisine. The most famous pub in Belfast and one of the finest high-Victorian gin palaces in the UK, with an ornate interior of brightly-coloured tiles, carvings and glass. Wonderfully atmospheric setting in which to down a pint.

Location: MAP 18:O3, OS Ref. J336 736. Central Belfast.

Open: Mon–Sat: 11.30am–11pm, Sun: 12.30–10pm.

Admission: Free.

DERRYMORE

Bessbrook, Newry, Co Armagh BT35 7EF

Tel: 028 8778 4753 **Fax:** 028 8778 9598 **E-mail:** derrymore@nationaltrust.org.uk

www.ntni.org.uk

Owner: National Trust

An elegant late 18th century thatched cottage, built by Isaac Corry, who represented Newry in the Irish House of Commons. Park laid out in the style of 'Capability' Brown.

Location: MAP 18:O5, OS Ref. J059 276. On A25, 2m from Newry on road to Camlough.

Open: 1 Jan–30 Apr: Daily 10am–4pm. 1 May–30 Sept: Daily 10am–6pm. 1 Oct–31 Dec: Daily 10am–4pm. Treaty Room only open 3 & 31 May, 12 & 13 July, 30 Aug, 2–5:30pm. Last admission 30 minutes before closing.

***Admission:** Treaty Room Tour: Adult £3.70, Child £1.80, Family £9.20. *includes a voluntary donation but visitors can choose to pay the standard prices displayed at the property and on the website.

On leads.

DIVIS & THE BLACK MOUNTAIN

12 Divis Road, Hannahstown, Belfast BT17 0NG

Tel: 028 9082 5434 **Fax:** 028 9082 5065 **E-mail:** divis@nationaltrust.org.uk

With spectacular panoramic views over Belfast, Divis and the Black Mountain is a haven for those seeking the wild countryside experience. On a clear day there are views of Strangford Lough, the Mournes and the Sperrins, as well as Scotland and Donegal.

Location: MAP 18:O3, OS Ref. J265 740. Access from Divis Road, off Upper Springfield Road. Signed from M1 Kennedy Way roundabout.

Open: All year.

Admission: Free

Mount Stewart – The Hall

FLORENCE COURT

Enniskillen, Co Fermanagh BT92 1DB
Tel: 028 6634 8249 **Fax:** 028 6634 8873 **E-mail:** florencecourt@nationaltrust.org.uk
www.ntni.org.uk
Owner: National Trust **Contact:** The Property Manager

Florence Court is a fine mid-18th century house and estate set against the stunning backdrop of the Cuilcagh Mountains. House tour includes service quarters popular with all ages. Beautiful walled garden and lots of walks in grounds.

Location: MAP 18:L4, OS Ref. H178 347. 8m SW of Enniskillen via A4 and then A32 to Swanlinbar.

Open: Gardens & Park: 1 Jan–28 Feb: Daily 10am–4pm. 1 Mar–31 Oct: Daily 10am–7pm. 1 Nov–31 Dec: Daily 10am–4pm. House, tea-room and shop: 13 Mar–25 Apr: Sat & Sun 11am–5pm. 2 Apr–11 Apr: Daily 11am–5pm. 1 May–30 Jun: Wed–Mon 11am–5pm. 1 Jul–31 Aug: Daily 11am–5pm. 1–30 Sept: Wed–Mon 11am–5pm. 2–31 Oct: Sat & Sun 11am–5pm. House: admission by guided tour (last admission one hour before closing). Open Bank Holiday Mondays and all other public holidays in Northern Ireland, including 17 March.

Admission: *House tour: Adult £5 (£4.54), Child £2 (£1.81), Family £12 (£10.90). Grounds (Standard Admission). Adult £3.25, Child £1.75, Family £7.75. *includes a voluntary donation but visitors can choose to pay the standard prices displayed at the property and on the website.

Ground floor. WC. Obligatory. In grounds, on leads.
Holiday cottage.

GIANT'S CAUSEWAY

North Coast Office, 60 Causeway Road, Bushmills BT57 8SU
Tel: 028 2073 1582 / 2972 **Fax:** 028 2073 2963
E-mail: giantscauseway@nationaltrust.org.uk

The Giant's Causeway, renowned for its polygonal columns of layered basalt, is the only World Heritage Site in Northern Ireland. Resulting from a volcanic eruption 60 million years ago, this is the focal point of a designated Area of Outstanding Natural Beauty and has attracted visitors for centuries. It harbours a wealth of local and natural history. Geology, flora and fauna of international importance. Beautiful coastal path extends 11 miles to the Carrick-a-Rede rope bridge with wonderful views and coastal scenery.

Location: MAP 18:O1, OS Ref. C952 452. Off A2 Bushmills to Ballintoy road.

Open: Open all year: Daily Dawn till dusk. Telephone for shop and tea-room opening arrangements. Last admission 30 minutes before closing.

Admission: Contact us for guided tour prices.

Suitable for picnics. For groups (15+), must be booked.
Charge (including NT). On leads

GRAY'S PRINTING PRESS

49 Main Street, Strabane, Co Tyrone BT82 8AU
Tel: 028 8674 8210 **E-mail:** grays@nationaltrust.org.uk **www.ntni.org.uk**
Owner: National Trust **Contact:** Property Manager

Nestled in Strabane, Gray's Printing Press is an icon of Strabane's 18th century reputation as Ireland's capital of publishing and the home of John Dunlop, the printer of the American Declaration of Independence. Fascinating guided tours and demonstrations.

Location: MAP 18:J3, OS Ref. H345 976. in the centre of Strabane.

Open: By appointment and 4 Jul, 2–5pm; 8 Aug, 2–5pm; 10 Sept, 2–5pm.

Admission: Tour: Adult £3.50, Child £2.10, Family £9.10. Group £2.60 (outside normal hours £4). *includes a voluntary donation but visitors can choose to pay the standard prices displayed at the property and on the website.

HEZLETT HOUSE

107 Sea Road, Castlerock, Coleraine, Co Londonderry BT51 4TW
Tel/Fax: 028 8778 4753 **E-mail:** downhillcastle@nationaltrust.org.uk
www.ntni.org.uk
Owner: National Trust **Contact:** The Custodian

Charming 17th century thatched house with 19th century furnishings. One of only a few pre-18th century Irish buildings still surviving.

Location: MAP 18:N1, OS Ref. C773 356. 5m W of Coleraine on Coleraine–Downhill coast road, A2.

Open: Contact the property for visiting times.

***Admission:** Adult £4.50, Child £2.25, family £11.25. *includes a voluntary donation but visitors can choose to pay the standard prices displayed at the property and on the website.

Ground floor. Obligatory. In grounds, on leads.

KILLYLEAGH CASTLE

Killyleagh, Downpatrick, Co Down BT30 9QA
Tel/Fax: 028 4482 8261 **E-mail:** gatehouses@killyleagh.plus.com
www.killyleaghcastle.com
Owner/Contact: Mrs G Rowan-Hamilton

Oldest occupied castle in Ireland. Self-catering towers available to sleep 4–15. Swimming pool and tennis court available by arrangement. Access to garden.

Location: MAP 18:P4, OS Ref. J523 529. At the end of the High Street.

Open: By arrangement. Groups (30–50): by appointment.

Admission: Adult £3.50, Child £2. Groups: Adult £2.50, Child £1.50.

No photography in house. Wedding receptions. Unsuitable. Obligatory.

LARCHFIELD ESTATE BARN & GARDENS

Bailliesmills Road, Lisburn, Co Antrim BT27 6XL
Tel: 02892 638 025 **E-mail:** enquiries@larchfieldestate.co.uk
www.larchfieldestate.co.uk
Owner: Mr & Mrs G Mackie **Contact:** Gavin Mackie

Just 20 minutes from Belfast City are the converted barn and spectacular walled gardens at Larchfield Estate. A stunning location year round, this venue offers exclusive use for private parties, weddings and corporate events. A private estate, viewings are strictly by appointment only.

Location: MAP 18:O4, OSNI J301 592. 4 Miles S of Lisburn, on the Bailliesmills Road, 10m SW of Belfast, BT27 6XJ.

Open: Not open to general public. Weddings, events and conferences only.

MOUNT STEWART

Newtonards, Co Down BT22 2AD
Tel: 028 4278 8387 **Fax:** 028 4278 8569 **E-mail:** mountstewart@nationaltrust.org.uk
Owner: National Trust **Contact:** The Property Manager

Home of the Londonderry family since the early 18th century, Mount Stewart was Lord Castlereagh's house and played host to many prominent political figures. The magnificent gardens planted in the 1920s have made Mount Stewart famous and earned it a World Heritage Site nomination.

Location: MAP 18:P3, OS Ref. J556 703. On A20, 5m from Newtownards on the Portaferry road.

Open: Lakeside gardens: Open all year: Daily 10am–6pm. Formal gardens: 13 Mar–31 Oct: Daily 10am–6pm. House: 13 Mar–31 Oct: Thur–Tue 11am–6pm. 2–11 Apr: Daily 11am–6pm. Temple of the Winds: 14 Mar–31 Oct: Sun 2–5pm. Open Bank Holiday Mondays and all other public holidays in Northern Ireland, including 17 March. House: admission by guided tour (timed tickets only); last admission one hour before closing. Lakeside gardens closed 25 and 26 December. Telephone for shop and restaurant opening times.

***Admission:** House tour and gardens: Adult £7.80, Child £3.90, Family £19.30. Gardens only: Adult £5.90, Child £2.90, Family £14.70. *includes a voluntary donation but visitors can choose to pay the standard prices displayed at the property and on the website.

Obligatory. In grounds, on leads. Lakeside area. €

Properties that **open all year** appear in the special index at the end of the book.

MUSSENDEN TEMPLE & DOWNHILL DEMESNE

North Coast Office, 60 Causeway Road, Bushmills BT57 8SU

Tel/Fax: 028 2073 1582 **E-mail:** downhilldemesne@nationaltrust.org.uk

www.ntni.org.uk

Owner: National Trust

Set on a stunning and wild headland with fabulous views over Ireland's north coast is the landscaped demesne of Downhill.

Location: MAP 18:N1, OS Ref. C757 357. 1m W of Castlerock.

Open: Grounds: Dawn to dusk all year.

Admission: Contact property for admission rates.

On leads.

PATTERSON'S SPADE MILL

751 Antrim Road, Templepatrick BT39 0AP

Tel: 028 9443 3619 **Fax:** 028 9443 9713 **E-mail:** pattersons@nationaltrust.org.uk

Owner: National Trust

Listen to the hammers, smell the grit, feel the heat and witness the thrill of the only surviving water-driven spade mill in Ireland. Visitors can watch as red-hot billets of steel are removed from the forge and fashioned into spades using the mill's massive trip hammer.

Location: MAP 18:O3, OS Ref. J263 852. 2m NE of Templepatrick on A6. M2/J4.

Open: 13 Mar–30 May: Sat & Sun 2–6pm. 2–11 Apr: Daily 2–6pm. 2 Jun–30 Aug: Wed–Mon 2–6pm. 4–26 Sep: Sat & Sun 2–6pm. Admission by guided tour. Open Bank Holiday Mondays and all other public holidays in Northern Ireland including 17 March. Last admission one hour before closing.

***Admission:** Adult £5, Child £2.80, Family £12.80. *Includes a voluntary donation but visitors can choose to pay the standard prices displayed at the property and on the website.

Suitable for picnics. In grounds, on leads.

ROWALLANE GARDEN

Saintfield, Ballynahinch, Co Down BT24 7LH

Tel: 028 9751 0721 **Fax:** 028 9751 1242 **E-mail:** rowallane@nationaltrust.org.uk

www.ntni.org.uk

Owner: National Trust **Contact:** Head Gardener

Rowallane is an enchanting garden enclosed within a demesne landscape of some 21 hectares, planted with an outstanding collection of trees, shrubs and other plants from many parts of the world, creating a beautiful display of form and colour throughout the year.

Location: MAP 18:P4, OS Ref. J405 585. On A7, 1m from Saintfield on road to Downpatrick.

Open: 2 Jan–28 Feb: Daily 10am–4pm. 1 Mar–30 Apr: Daily 10am–6pm. 1 May–31 Aug: Daily 10am–8pm. 1 Sept–31 Oct: Daily 10am–6pm. 1 Nov–31 Dec: Daily 10am–4pm. Closed 1 Jan, 25 & 26 Dec. Telephone for tea-room opening times. Last admission 30 minutes before closing.

***Admission:** Adult £5.50, Child £2.70, Family £13.70. *Includes a voluntary donation but visitors can choose to pay the standard prices displayed at the property and on the website.

Grounds. WC. Apr–Aug. In grounds, on leads.

SPRINGHILL HOUSE & COSTUME COLLECTION

20 Springhill Road, Moneymore, Co Londonderry BT45 7NQ

Tel/Fax: 028 8674 8210 **E-mail:** springhill@nationaltrust.org.uk **www.ntni.org.uk**

Owner: National Trust **Contact:** The Property Manager

Described as 'one of the prettiest houses in Ulster'. A charming plantation house with a significant book collection, portraits and decorative arts that bring to life the many generations of Lenox- Conynghams who lived here from 1680. The old laundry houses one of Springhill's most popular attractions, the Costume Collection with some exceptionally fine 18th to 20th century pieces.

Location: MAP 18:N3, OS Ref. H845 819. 1m from Moneymore on B18 to Coagh, 5m from Cookstown.

Open: 17 Mar–30 Jun: Sats, Suns & BH/PHs (6–15 Apr, daily); 1 Jul–31 Aug: daily; Sept: Sats & Suns, 12–5pm.

***Admission:** House & Costume Museum: Adult £6.60, Child £3.40, Family £16.60. Grounds & Costume Museum: Adult £3.40, Child £1.70, Family £8.50. Groups outside of normal hours £5.25. *includes a voluntary donation but visitors can choose to pay the standard prices displayed at the property and on the website. (2010).

In grounds, on leads.

TEMPLETOWN MAUSOLEUM

Templepatrick, Antrim BT39

Tel: 028 9082 5870

The mausoleum or monumental tomb was erected in 1789 by the Hon Sarah Upton to the Rt Hon Arthur Upton and displays some of Robert Adam's best classical work which is chaste, crisp and elegant. Given to the National Trust in 1965 by William Henderson Smith and Sir Robin Kinahan, it stands in the graveyard of Castle Upton. Castle Upton is privately owned and not open to the public.

Location: MAP 18:P4, OS Ref. J225 855. At Templepatrick on the Belfast-Antrim Road.

Open: All year.

Admission: Free access. Please contact Belfast Properties Office for further information.

WELLBROOK BEETLING MILL

20 Wellbrook Road, Corkhill, Co. Tyrone BT80 9RY

Tel: 028 8674 8210/8675 1735 **E-mail:** wellbrook@nationaltrust.org.uk

www.ntni.org.uk

Owner: National Trust **Contact:** The Custodian

If you come to the mill when there is a flax pulling you will find a hive of industry and when the beetling engines are running their thunder fills the valley. There are hands-on demonstrations of the linen process, led by costumed guides, original hammer machinery, used to beat a sheen into the cloth, lovely walks and picnic opportunities by the Ballinderry River. A truly unique experience.

Location: MAP 18:N3, OS Ref. H750 792. 4m from Cookstown, following signs from A505 Cookstown–Omagh road.

Open: 13 Mar–27 Jun: Sat & Sun 2–6pm. 2–6 Apr: Fri–Tue 1–6pm. 1 Jul–31 Aug: Sat–Thur 2–6pm. 4–26 Sep: Sat & Sun 2–6pm. Admission by guided tour. Open Bank Holiday Mondays and all other public holidays in Northern Ireland including 17 March. Last admission one hour before closing. Telephone for shop opening arrangements.

***Admission:** Mill Tour: Adult £4.20, Child £2.40, Family £10.60. *includes a voluntary donation but visitors can choose to pay the standard prices displayed at the property and on the website.

Mussenden Temple

JOHN O' GROATS
WESTERN ISLES
HIGHLANDS & SKYE
GRAMPIAN HIGHLANDS
PERTHSHIRE/FIFE
WEST HIGHLANDS & ISLANDS
GREATER GLASGOW
EDINBURGH
27
BORDERS
17
26
SOUTH WEST SCOTLAND
NORTHERN IRELAND
TYNE & WEAR
5
DURHAM
4
CUMBRIA
6
YORKSHIRE
25
24
ISLE OF MAN
LANCS
ISLE OF ANGLESEY
MERSEYSIDE
29
30
7
NOTTS
LINCS
CHESHIRE
16
NORFOLK
STAFFS
15
LEICS & RUTLAND
NORTH WALES
SALOP
WEST MIDS
NORTHANTS
CAMBS
WORCS
22
HEREFORDSHIRE
BEDS
SUFFOLK
SOUTH WALES
28
BUCKS
11
19
18
HERTS
ESSEX
10
1
OXON
23
LONDON
BERKS
20
WILTS
SURREY
KENT
14
HANTS
SOMERSET
21
W. SUSSEX
E. SUSSEX
DEVON
9
13
8
12
ISLE OF WIGHT
CORNWALL
2
3

Historic Places to Stay

Alpha by area/hotel name

Hudsons Heritage
http://www.hudsonsheritage.com
HUDSONS HERITAGE
OPEN NOW
Home
Accommodation
Weddings
Open All Year
National Trust
English Heritage
HHA
I'm planning a trip to...
Find Attractions
Over 2,000 Heritage Attractions
for trips, functions, weddings and special events.
Use the search box above or Click on a map region to begin..
Beaulieu
Heritage Property in Hampshire
Latest news
More
Campaign launched to save DH Lawrence visitor centre
Work begins on £36m home for Tudor flagship Mary Rose
Featured Attractions
HUDSONSHERITAGE.COM
HUDSONS HERITAGE
OUR BRAND NEW SITE
A brand new digital guide to the very best of Britain's fabulous historic properties and gardens.
Planning a weekend away or short break? Take a look at the super choice of Places to Stay available at many heritage properties.

Gravetye Manor

Elizabethan Splendour and Unique Gardens

Gravetye Manor is a truly enchanting place. Close to the pleasures of London, yet far from its hustle and bustle. This beautiful Elizabethan manor sits proudly amongst the winding pathways and abundant flower beds of William Robinson's own garden, the grandfather of the English natural garden.

From the hushed quiet of the wood panelled restaurant to the crackle of log fires, guests cannot fail to be charmed by this most quintessential English country house. Summer or winter, the sweeping countryside views, first class cuisine and attentive yet unobtrusive service will ensure an unforgettable experience.

Location: 30 miles from Central London - 12 miles from Gatwick Airport station - 5 miles from East Grinstead station.

Gravetye Manor, near West Hoathly, Susssex RH19 4LJ - www.gravetyemanor.co.uk - 01342 810 567

Now part of the National Trust
All profits donated to the charity

National Trust

THE THREE HISTORIC HOUSE HOTELS

Past, Present and Future Perfect

Since 1980, Historic House Hotels has acquired three rundown country houses, beautifully and accurately restoring them back to what they once were, and reinstating many lost features. More than just hotels, the beauty of the exterior of the buildings is matched by the meticulous attention to the detail of their contents.

The grounds surrounding each house are worthy of a visit in their own right, with walled gardens, follies, greenhouses, statues, woodland gardens and parterres of great beauty. The award-winning food, cooked to perfection in the hotel kitchens, also pursues the theme of tradition coupled with excellence. Each house has its own Spa, with a superb indoor pool, exercise facilities and a selection of therapeutic and invigorating treatments for the mind, body and soul. First class business facilities featuring the latest technologies satisfy the need of the discerning business traveller.

These beautifully restored houses provide the very best of British hospitality, retaining the atmosphere of a well-kept, well furnished private country house.

BODYSGALLEN HALL & SPA

Standing in over 200 acres of its own parkland to the south of Llandudno in North Wales, with spectacular views of Snowdonia and Conwy Castle and providing the best in country house hospitality. With a choice of 15 bedrooms in the main house and 16 adjacent cottage suites, it is ideally situated as a base for exploring and discovering some of the most attractive scenery in Europe.

Bodysgallen Hall & Spa
Llandudno, North Wales LL30 1RS
T 01492 584466 F 01492 582519
info@bodysgallen.com www.bodysgallen.com

HARTWELL HOUSE & SPA

One of Buckinghamshire's finest houses, in the tranquil Vale of Aylesbury, just one hour by car or rail from central London. Formally the home in exile of King Louis XVIII of France, the house now stands in 90 acres of parkland and provides 46 individual bedrooms, magnificent drawing rooms and superb dining rooms. It is easily reached from both LHR, Luton and Gatwick airports.

Hartwell House & Spa
Oxford Road nr Aylesbury, Buckinghamshire HP17 8NR

T 01296 747444 F 01296 747450
info@hartwell-house.com www.hartwell-house.com

MIDDLETHORPE HALL & SPA

A distinguished 30 bedroom William III house standing in its own grounds, and very close to York Racecourse. An obvious choice for the racegoer, it is also only a mile and a half from York railway station and the historic city centre. The beauty of the Yorkshire Dales, the open splendour of the North York Moors, the Howardian Hills and the wonderful coastal scenery are all within easy reach.

Middlethorpe Hall & Spa
Bishopthorpe Road, York YO23 2GB
T 01904 641241 F 01904 620176
info@middlethorpe.com www.middlethorpe.com

Award winning holiday and short break destination

Operated by the charity Leonard Cheshire Disability, located on the Royal Sandringham estate near King's Lynn in West Norfolk, Park House Hotel offers a holiday experience for people with mobility difficulties or disabilities, with or without their carer or companion.

Park House is an impressive Victorian country house set in its own grounds amidst the soaring trees and rolling parklands of the Estate. The main house was the birthplace of Princess Diana.

Fully accessible, the hotels is equipped to the very highest standards:

- 16 ensuite bedrooms (8 single/8 twin)
- Digital T.V., radio, direct dial telephone
- Tea/Coffee making facilities
- Well stocked library. Broadband enabled computer
- Relaxing lounge with 42" television
- Movie/games room, piano and art equipment
- Optional Entertainment most evenings

The picturesque grounds are fully accessible; both garden and woodland areas. A heated outdoor swimming pool with Arjo hoist is available May-September.

Only the finest, locally sourced ingredients are used by our team of chefs in preparing international menus complemented by a comprehensive wine list.

Optional, escorted excursions ensure that all guests have a chance to visit their choice of local attractions. The Royal residence at Sandringham House is adjacent to the hotel and is a popular destination, along with the myriad other stately homes within the local area.

Park House Hotel is the ideal country house destination for people with mobility difficulties or disabilities providing peace of mind and a holiday for everyone.

Park House Hotel, Sandringham,
King's Lynn, Norfolk PE35 6EH
t 01485 543000 e parkinfo@LCDisability.org
w www.parkhousehotel.org.uk
enjoyEngland.com
★★
HOTEL
Leonard
Cheshire
Disability
OPEN
BRITAIN

CASTLE AND ESTATE

www.pentillie.co.uk

Experience the magic of Pentillie Castle and Estate ...

Standing in its own magnificent riverside gardens, Pentillie Castle, had been closed to visitors for 40 years. Now, following its inheritance by the latest generation of the Coryton family, the 17th Century castle has been extensively refurbished, under the watchful eye of Channel 4's Country House Rescue, and is now open as an exclusive wedding venue, luxury B&B and events venue.

Its location is stunning but highly accessible: the Castle is just a few miles from the historic harbour town of Plymouth on the banks of the River Tamar, in an area of outstanding natural beauty. St Mellion International Golf resort is minutes away, and it is surprisingly close to the A38, and major rail and air links.

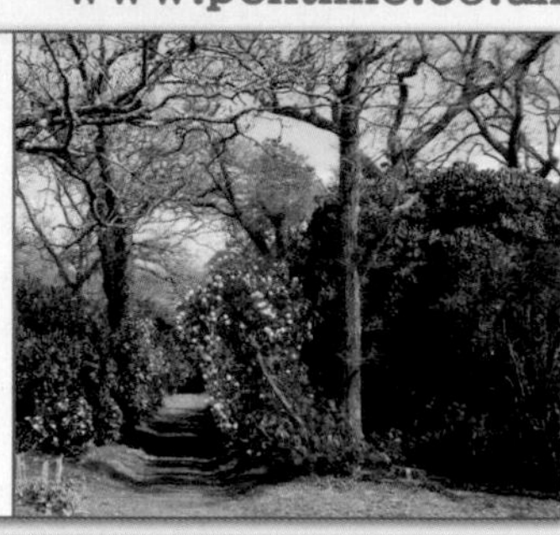

Luxury B&B ...

A stay at Pentillie is relaxing and memorable. The Castle boasts 5 star accommodation for 18, and all the beautifully decorated spacious bedrooms have elegant en-suites and views overlooking the river or gardens. Guests can enjoy dinner in the beautiful Georgian dining room and breakfast on the terrace. Then explore the gardens, which are studded with delightful secrets: the bathing house, the lime tree avenue, the American Gardens, and a walk across the estate will reveal Jimmy Tillie's intriguing mausoleum.

Weddings ...

Weddings at Pentillie are beautifully romantic and luxurious. The bride and groom can enjoy private and exclusive use of the house and its magical grounds. And the friendly and experienced staff will tailor the event to ensure it's the wedding of your dreams. Civil marriages can take place in 4 licensed areas around the house, including outside under the Southern Loggia. Weddings for 60 can be accommodated in the main house, or with marquees on the lawns, up to 250.

Guests can also be treated to a candlelit dinner in the bathing house by the river. The grounds can accommodate helicopters or hot air balloons, or, if the bride and groom wish to leave in style, a boat can pick them up from the jetty to take them on honeymoon. Pentillie is full of beautiful photo opportunities.

Events ...

Whether it's the launch of an exciting new project, a party that no-one will forget, or a business strategy day which delivers results, Pentillie has the flexibility, privacy and magic to ensure your event is special. With catering facilities, break out areas, conference rooms and beautiful open spaces.

Pentillie will be memorable and a pleasure to visit. The staff are friendly, efficient and will tailor things to suit your requirements.

Warner Leisure Hotels
EXCLUSIVELY FOR ADULTS
UK SHORT BREAKS
Thoresby Hall Hotel
Nottingham
Holme Lacy House Hotel
The Wye Valley
Nidd Hall Hotel
Harrogate
Historic Room
Four-star hotels steeped in Luxury and History
AA
★★★★
FEATURING FOUR STAR COUNTRY HOUSE HOTELS AND COASTAL PROPERTIES
13 STUNNING LOCATIONS
Warner Leisure Hotels' portfolio features three grand buildings that boast opulent accommodation, fine dining, beautiful surroundings and a wide choice of things to see and do.
Thoresby Hall, Holme Lacy House and Nidd Hall are the jewels in the Warner crown. These four-star hotels offer sumptuous food in their main restaurants and Thoresby Hall's Blue Room and Holme Lacy's Orchard restaurant offer you AA Rosette standard cuisine. All of these hotels offer you the chance to enjoy a UK short break in a luxurious setting.
The choice is yours
As well as our four-star hotels, Warner also offers a choice of hotels nestled in the countryside and some superb, inviting coastal spots.
Breaks by the sea
If the tang of a fresh sea breeze is more your thing, you're sure to love our Coastal Hotels and Villages. Snuggled in popular areas including East Anglia, the south coast and the Isle of Wight, our coastal spots provide classic UK holidays.
Whatever you want from your break, whether it's celebrating a special occasion in luxury or enjoying a laid-back break in a relaxed atmosphere, we have something for you.
Nidd Hall
Bodelwyddan Castle
Alvaston Hall
Thoresby Hall
Corton
Gunton Hall
Holme Lacy House
Littlecote House
Cricket St. Thomas
Bembridge Coast
Norton Grange
Sinah Warren
Lakeside
Bembridge Coast Hotel
Isle of Wight
Try something different
We are sure you'll remember your break with us for a very long time - but why not guarantee lasting memories by trying one of our Experiences? We have over 1,000 to choose from, ranging from hot air ballooning to zookeeping, and your chosen Experience may even change your life!
For more information call on 0800 1 388 399.
Request your FREE copy of our new 2011 brochure
NOW!
BREAKS AT ALL OUR 13 LOCATIONS INCLUDE:
Stylish en suite accommodation
Full English or continental breakfasts
Fantastic entertainment
Three-course evening meals
A child-free environment
TO BOOK OR FOR MORE INFORMATION
FREEPHONE 0800 1 388 399
www.warnerleisurehotels.co.uk
Travel Agent

BIBURY COURT

REFUGE ■ RETREAT

BIBURY, CIRENCESTER,
GLOUCESTERSHIRE, GL7 5NT
TEL: 01285 740337, FAX: 01285 740660
EMAIL: INFO@BIBURYCOURT.COM
WWW.BIBURYCOURT.COM

BIBURY COURT, PRIVATELY OWNED SINCE 1968, IS AN EIGHTEEN BEDROOMED MANOR HOUSE HOTEL. A REFUGE AND RETREAT FROM THE PRESSURES OF MODERN LIFE.

THE HOTEL IS OPEN TO NON RESIDENTS FOR MORNING COFFEE, LUNCH AND AFTERNOON TEA AND DINNER. LUNCH AND DINNER BOOKINGS ARE ADVISABLE.

THE CONSERVATORY, CATERING FOR TO 32 PEOPLE , AND THE STUDY CATERING FOR UP TO 12 PEOPLE ARE BOTH AVAILABLE FOR PRIVATE FUNCTIONS INCLUDING WEDDINGS AND CORPORATE EVENTS.

PLEASE CONTACT THE HOTEL FOR FURTHER INFORMATION AND TO RECEIVE A COPY OF OUR BROCHURE.

BOVEY CASTLE.

YOU'VE ARRIVED.

Luxurious yet relaxed, Bovey Castle is nestled in the heart of the Dartmoor National Park.

A round of golf, a spa treatment, afternoon tea in front of a roaring log fire, fine dining and even finer views.

For more information please call 01647 445 000 or visit
www.boveycastle.com

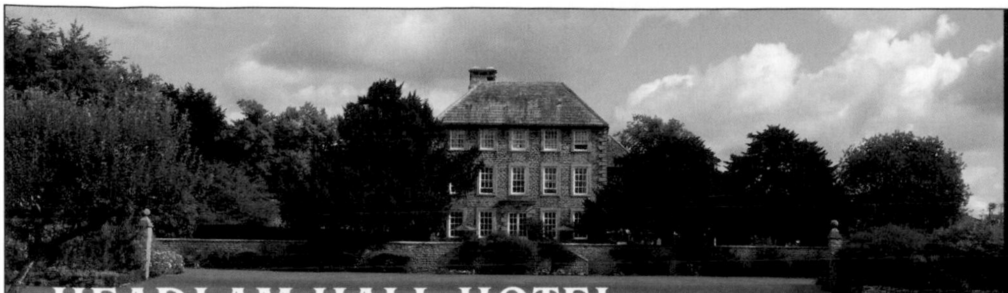

HEADLAM HALL
HOTEL • SPA • GOLF

HEADLAM HALL HOTEL

THE PERFECT BASE FOR BREAKS TO YORKSHIRE & NORTHUMBRIA

This superb seventeenth century Jacobean mansion stands in beautiful walled gardens surrounded by its own spa, golf course and rolling farmland. The picturesque hamlet of Headlam is located in a quiet corner of Teesdale in County Durham and offers rural peace and seclusion as well as good accessibility to the region's main attractions, including the incomparable Bowes Museum, Raby Castle and numerous fine other castles, houses and gardens in County Durham and Northumberland.

Headlam Hall is a family owned and run hotel. Guests have the choice of 40 beautiful, individually appointed bedrooms combining traditional and contemporary design.

The hotel's "Taste-Durham" award-winning restaurant serves the highest standards of freshly prepared modern British cuisine in relaxed and charming surroundings.

Residents can enjoy the stunning new Headlam Spa which includes a swimming pool, outdoor hydrotherapy pool, thermal zone and fully equipped gym. Nearby, our 9-hole USGA golf course is both picturesque and challenging and includes a PGA Pro shop and ten bay driving range.

Short Breaks at Headlam Hall are offered year-round and are great value - the latest special offers from the hotel can always be found at **www.headlamhall.co.uk**

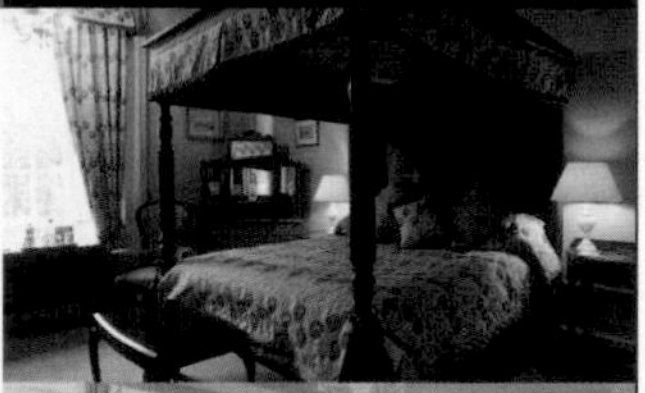

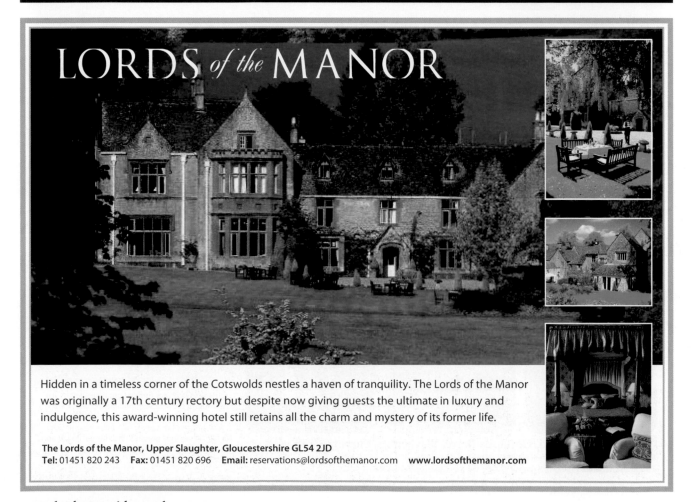

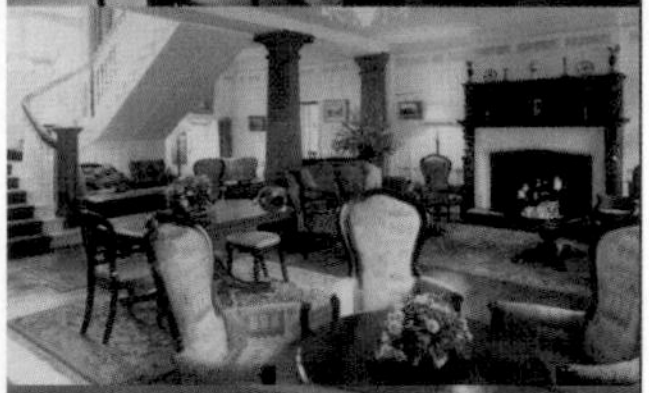

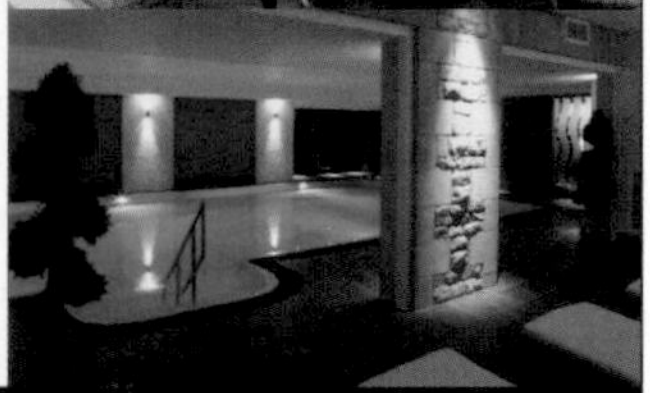

Headlam, Nr Gainford, Darlington, Co Durham DL2 3HA Tel: (01325) 730238 Fax: (01325) 730790 Email: admin@headlamhall.co.uk www.headlamhall.co.uk

LORDS *of the* MANOR

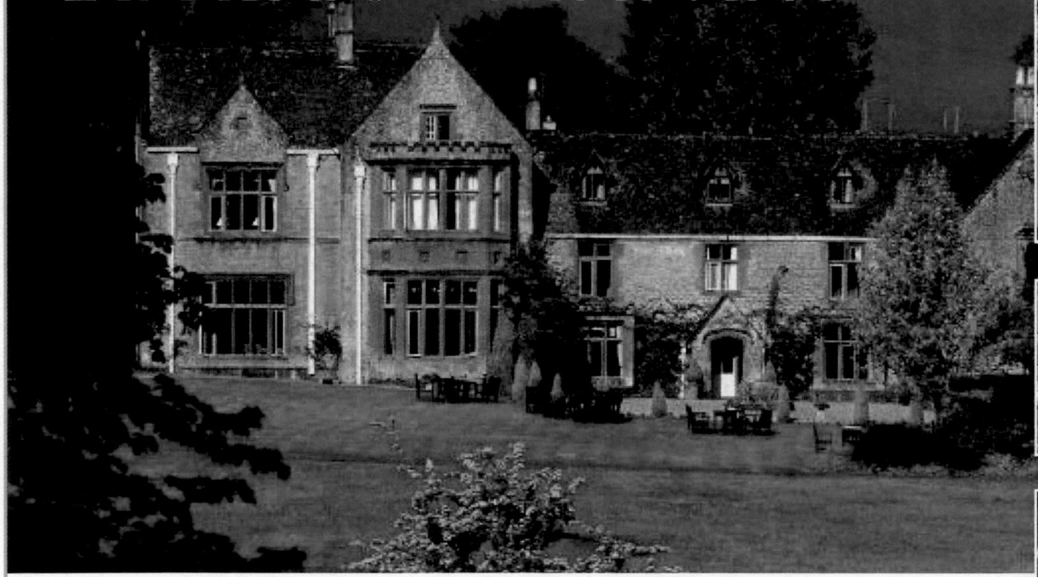

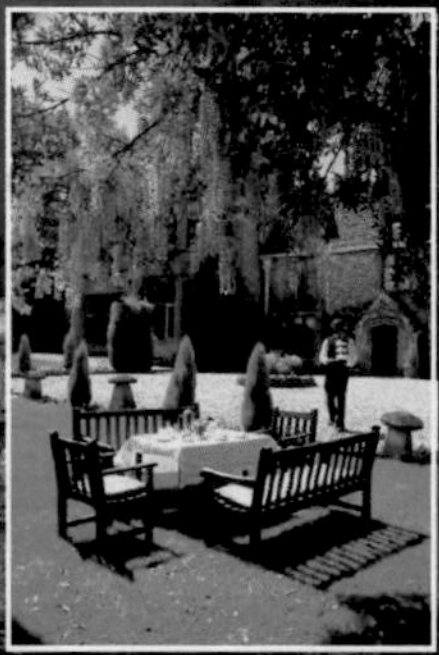

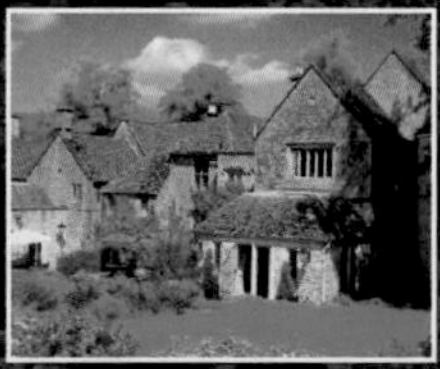

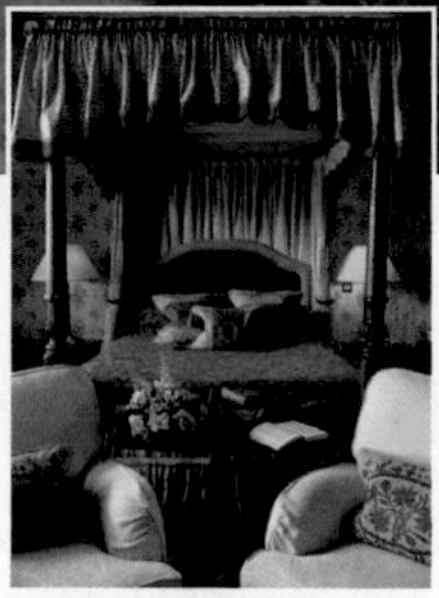

Hidden in a timeless corner of the Cotswolds nestles a haven of tranquility. The Lords of the Manor was originally a 17th century rectory but despite now giving guests the ultimate in luxury and indulgence, this award-winning hotel still retains all the charm and mystery of its former life.

The Lords of the Manor, Upper Slaughter, Gloucestershire GL54 2JD
Tel: 01451 820 243 **Fax:** 01451 820 696 **Email:** reservations@lordsofthemanor.com **www.lordsofthemanor.com**

Fully upgraded 4 ** Town House boutique hotel in the middle of medieval World Heritage walled town.**

28 bedrooms & suites offering luxury contemporary accommodation offering free broadband WiFi throughout.

Open 7 days a week serving 'gastro pub' and brasserie style meals in Dawson's Bar & Restaurant

See 'Special Offer's' and Christmas & New Year programme on **www.castlewales.co.uk**

Castle Hotel, High Street, Conwy. LL32 8DB
Call 01492 582800
Visit us at www.castlewales.co.uk

Langtry Manor

Built by a King for the woman he loved

"Best Hotel in Bournemouth"
- The Guardian

Built by King Edward VII as a love-nest for his mistress, Lillie Langtry, this unique hotel still casts its spell today. From four-poster beds to flat-screen TVs, it combines the very best of contemporary comfort and service with classic Edwardian elegance and stunning modern cuisine.

0844 372 5435 (Local Rate)
www.langtrymanor.co.uk

Derby Road, East Cliff, Bournemouth BH1 3QB

The stunning North Cornish coast is the perfect backdrop for this intimate family run Georgian manor house hotel.

Our hotel has a wonderful relaxed atmosphere and all our guests are assured of a warm welcome. We have a choice of 19 bedrooms and suites, all tastefully appointed with high levels of comfort.

Choose from our delicious 3 course Table d'hote menu in our Valley Restaurant, or try our fabulous traditional Sunday Lunches.

Perfectly located in 11 acres of gardens, woodland and pasture, just 2 1/2 miles from Perranporth beach and 5 minutes from the A30. A perfect base for exploring the gardens of Cornwall.

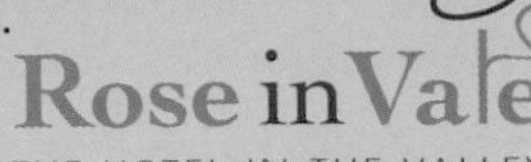

Awarded a Rosette by the AA for culinary excellence

AA

Mithian St Agnes Cornwall

T: 01872 552202 www.rose-in-vale-hotel.co.uk

A unique piece of living history

Over 900 years old Traquair has played host to 27 Scottish monarchs including Mary Queen of Scots. Today it remains a unique family home open to the public and offers accommodation with three spacious double bedrooms furnished with antique furniture.

Various offers available throughout the year please contact us or visit www.traquair.co.uk for more information.

TRAQUAIR HOUSE, INNERLEITHEN, PEEBLESSHIRE, EH44 6PW

TEL: 01896 830 323 FAX: 01896 830 639

Email: enquiries@traquair.co.uk

COUNTRY HOUSE HOTEL, RESTAURANT & SPA

An historic 4 star country house hotel with an award winning restaurant and luxury health spa nestling in the heart of White Cliffs Country. With stunning four-poster bedrooms in the old manor and contemporary rooms in converted Kentish barns. A perfect base from which to explore the history, heritage & culture of Kent.

WALLETT'S COURT COUNTRY HOUSE HOTEL

Westcliffe, St. Margaret's-at-Cliffe, Dover, Kent CT15 6EW

T: 01304 852424 E: MAIL@WALLETTSCOURT.COM

WWW.WALLETTSCOURT.COM

A beautiful country manor house, set in 12 acres of Oxfordshire countryside on the edge of the Cotswolds.

The perfect environment for a variety of events: leisure breaks, celebrations, weddings, meetings or team building

Weston Manor Hotel is located 2 miles from Junction 9 of the M40, just minutes from the spires of Oxford.

Weston-on-the-Green Oxfordshire OX25 3QL

www.westonmanor.co.uk

events@westonmanor.co.uk

Tel: 01869 350621

Quote Hudson's

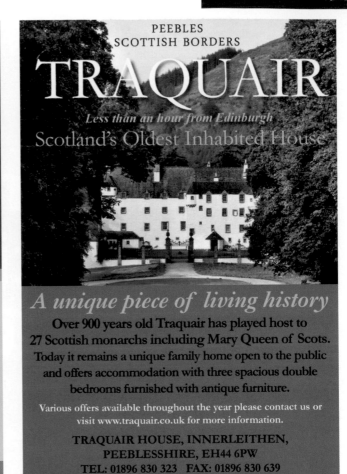

Indexes

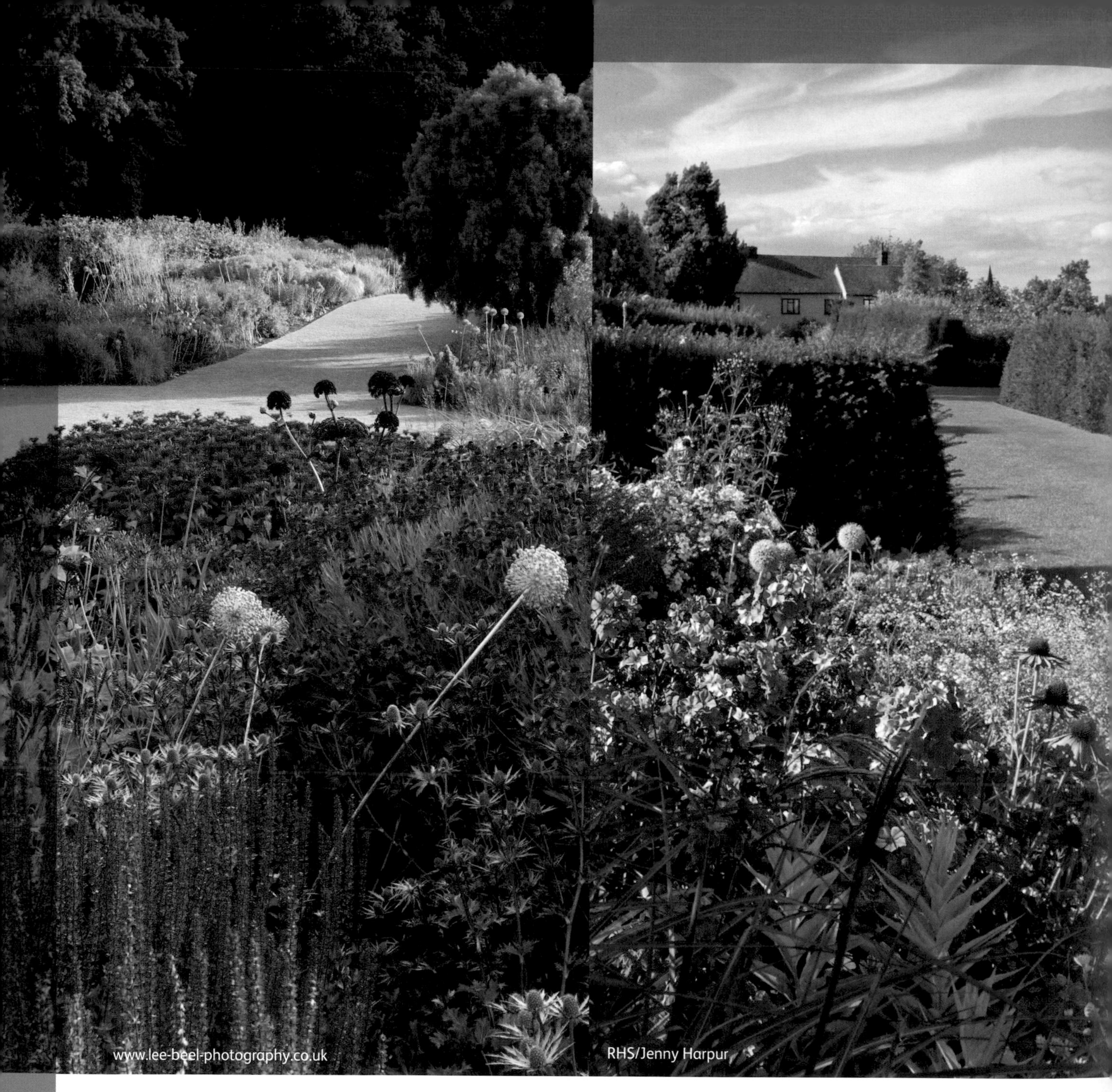

Britain's most beautiful days out

RHS GARDEN HARLOW CARR
North Yorkshire

RHS GARDEN HYDE HALL
Essex

RHS GARDEN ROSEMOOR
Devon

RHS GARDEN WISLEY
Surrey

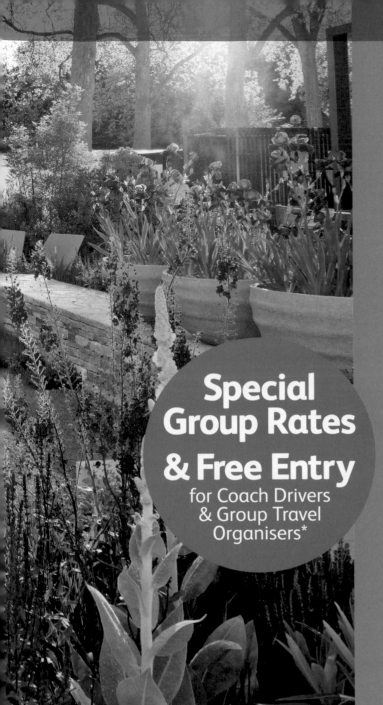

Plant Sales

Properties where plants are offered for sale.

ENGLAND

LONDON

SOUTH EAST

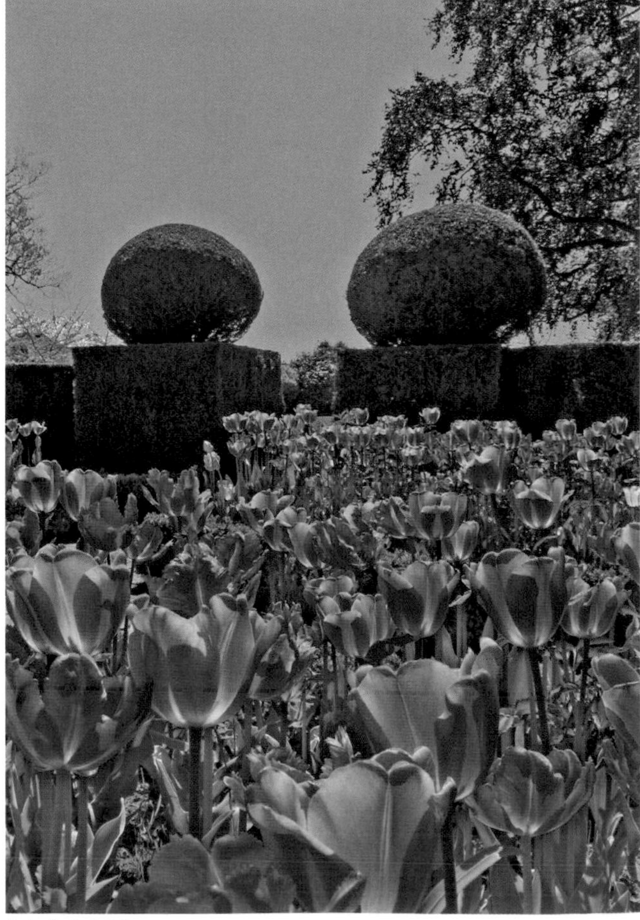

Hole Park Gardens

Hartland Abbey

SOUTH WEST

EASTERN REGION

EAST MIDLANDS

Burton Agnes Hall

HEART OF ENGLAND

YORKSHIRE & THE HUMBER

Rode Hall

NORTH WEST

NORTH EAST

SCOTLAND

WALES

SOUTH WALES

MID WALES

NORTH WALES

NORTHERN IRELAND

Muncaster Castle Gardens & Owl Centre

From left to right
Temple Pond Autumn, Portmeirion ©
Portmeirion, Penshurst Place peony border © Joe
Dale, Painswick Rococo Garden, Syon Park © Tony Marshall
Daylilies at Sandringham - By Gracious Permission of H.M. The Queen

Abbotsbury Sub-Tropical Gardens
Jan – Feb & Oct-Dec

Aberglasney Gardens
Jan Mar & Dec (except for 4-5 Dec)

Alnwick Garden
When open (gardens only)

Anglesey Abbey Gardens
When open (gardens only, except special event days)

Arley Hall & Gardens
When open (gardens only, except special event days)

Belvoir Castle
Apr & Jul, Mon-Sat

Benington Lordship Gardens
5-11 Feb, 12-4pm & May Bank Holiday, Sun 2-5pm, Mon 12-5pm

Blenheim Palace Park & Gardens
12 Feb - 29 May (except Easter) & 19 Sept – 16 Dec (park & gardens only)

Borde Hill
Jun-Jul

Bodnant Garden
When open

Branklyn Gardens
When open

Burton Agnes Gardens
When open

Cae Hir Gardens
When open (except special event days)

Caerhays Castle Garden
14 Feb - 13 Mar

Cawdor Castle & Gardens
May - Jun & Sept - Oct (Gardens only)

Cholmondeley Castle Garden
May

Cottesbrooke Hall & Gardens
When open (gardens only, except special event days)

Coughton Court
When open (gardens only, except special event days)

Dalemain
3-30 Apr, 1-30 Sept and 1-27 Oct (gardens only, except special event days)

Docton Mill Gardens
Saturdays 1 Mar - 31 Oct inclusive

Doddington Hall
When open

The Dorothy Clive Garden
Jul - Sept (except special event days and group visits)

Drummond Castle
May, Sept and Oct

Duncombe Park Gardens
When open (except special event days)

Dunrobin Castle Gardens
When open

Dyffryn Gardens & Arboretum
When open (except special event days)

Elton Hall
When open (gardens only)

Exbury Gardens
Mar and Sept

Floors Castle Gardens
When open (gardens only, except special event days)

Forde Abbey & Gardens
Jan-Feb & Oct - Dec (gardens only)

Furzey Gardens
When open

Glenwhan Garden
1 Aug -30 Sept and 1-31 Oct by appointment

Grimsthorpe Castle
Apr, May & Sept

Harewood House
13 Feb – 20 Jun & 6 Sept – 12 Dec (except special event days and bank holidays)

Harmony Garden
When open, except special event days

Hergest Croft
Jan- Apr, Jul-Sept & Nov-Dec

Hestercombe Gardens
Jan – Mar & Oct – Dec (gardens only)

Hever Castle
When open (gardens only)

Hill of Tarvit Mansionhouse & Garden
When open (gardens only, except special event days)

Holker Hall & Gardens
When open (gardens only, except special event days)

Houghton Hall
June (gardens only)

Kellie Castle & Garden
When open (except special event days)

Kelmarsh Hall
When open (except special event days)

Leith Hall and Garden
When open (except special event days)

Loseley Park
May & Sept (garden only, except NGS day on 9th May)

RHS Partner Gardens

Properties in Hudson's that offer free garden access at specified times to RHS Members.

Royal
Horticultural
Society

Iannington Gardens
Vhen open (garden only, xcept special event days)

Iapperton Gardens
Vhen open (except pecial event days)

Iational Botanic Garden of Vales, The
an - Mar & Oct - Dec

Iewby Hall & Gardens
pr, May & Sept (gardens only, xcept special event days)

Iymans
Vhen open

ainswick Rococo Garden
Vhen open (except Feb nd group visits)

arcevall Hall Gardens
pr, May & Oct.

arham Park
Vhen open (except group visits)

enshurst Place & Gardens
Vhen open (except group visits)

icton Castle
Vhen open (gardens nd gallery only)

las Brondanw Gardens
Vhen open (except NGS day the first week of May)

ortmeirion
Vhen open

aby Castle
Vhen open (except pecial event days)

agley Hall
Vhen open (Gardens only, ot special event days)

Renishaw Hall
When open (gardens only, except special event days and bank holidays)

Ripley Castle Gardens
When open (except special event days)

Rode Hall
When open

Ryton Gardens
When open (except special event days)

Sandringham
When open (gardens only)

Sausmarez Manor
First week of every month when open

Scone Palace & Grounds
When open

Sheffield Park Garden
When open (except special event days)

Syon Park
When open (gardens only, except special event days)

Tapeley Park
8 Jun - 8 Jul

Tatton Park
When open (gardens only)

Thorp Perrow Arboretum
Jan, Feb, Jul, Sept and Dec (except special event days)

Threave Garden & Estate
Apr-May and Sept-Oct (except special event days)

Trentham Estate
Jan-Mar and Oct-Dec (except special event days)

Trebah Garden
1 Jan- 31 Mar '11 and 1 Nov '11- 31 Mar '12

Trewithen Gardens
Jul - Sept

Waddesdon Manor
Mar & Sept – Oct (gardens only)

Wentworth Castle Gardens
When open

West Dean
Feb-Mar and Nov-Dec (except special event days)

Wilton House
When open (except regular access to adventure playground and special event days)

Wyken Hall Gardens
When open

York Gate Garden
Apr-May & Sept (except 24-25 Apr, 1-2 May and 29-30 May)

N.B. Free access applies to one member per policy. Information correct at time of going to print. Please check before travelling. For more information log on to www.rhs.org.uk/Gardens/RHS-Recommended-Gardens

Join the RHS today **£10 off**

RHS Members enjoy:

- free access to more than 140 independently owned gardens*, (including all the gardens listed here)
- unlimited free access to the 4 RHS Gardens with a family guest
- The Garden monthly magazine, worth £51 a year
- Privileged entry and discounted tickets to the RHS Flower Shows
- RHS expert gardening advice
- And much more...

Join by Direct Debit and receive £10 off (normal price £49) Call **0845 130 4646** (lines open 9am-5pm, Monday to Friday) or visit **www.rhs.org.uk/join** quoting code 3171 for your discount.

* Card holder 1 only

 Corporate Hospitality

Properties which are able to accommodate corporate functions, wedding receptions and events. Some properties specialise in corporate hospitality and are open, only rarely, if ever, to day visitors. Others do both. See entry for details.

ENGLAND

LONDON

SOUTH EAST

SOUTH WEST

EASTERN REGION

EAST MIDLANDS

HEART OF ENGLAND

YORKSHIRE & THE HUMBER

NORTH WEST

NORTH EAST

SCOTLAND

WALES

SOUTH WALES

MID WALES

NORTH WALES

NORTHERN IRELAND

Beaulieu

Education

The properties listed below provide special facilities for schools' groups. The range of these services varies, so it is vital that you contact the property directly when preparing to arrange a school trip. English Heritage offers free admission for pre-booked educational groups. For a free teacher's information pack: e-mail: education@english-heritage.org.uk or visit the website www.english-heritage.org.uk/education

ENGLAND

LONDON

SOUTH EAST

SOUTH WEST

EASTERN REGION

EAST MIDLANDS

HEART OF ENGLAND

YORKSHIRE & THE HUMBER

NORTH WEST

NORTH EAST

SCOTLAND

WALES

SOUTH WALES

MID WALES

NORTH WALES

NORTHERN IRELAND

Accommodation

Accommodation for individuals in historic hotels is listed on page 525. The historic properties listed below are not hotels. Their inclusion indicates that accommodation can be arranged, often for groups only. The type and standard of rooms offered vary widely – from the luxurious to the utilitarian. Full details can be obtained from each individual property.

ENGLAND

SOUTH EAST

SOUTH WEST

West Dean College

EASTERN REGION

EAST MIDLANDS

HEART OF ENGLAND

YORKSHIRE & THE HUMBER

NORTH WEST

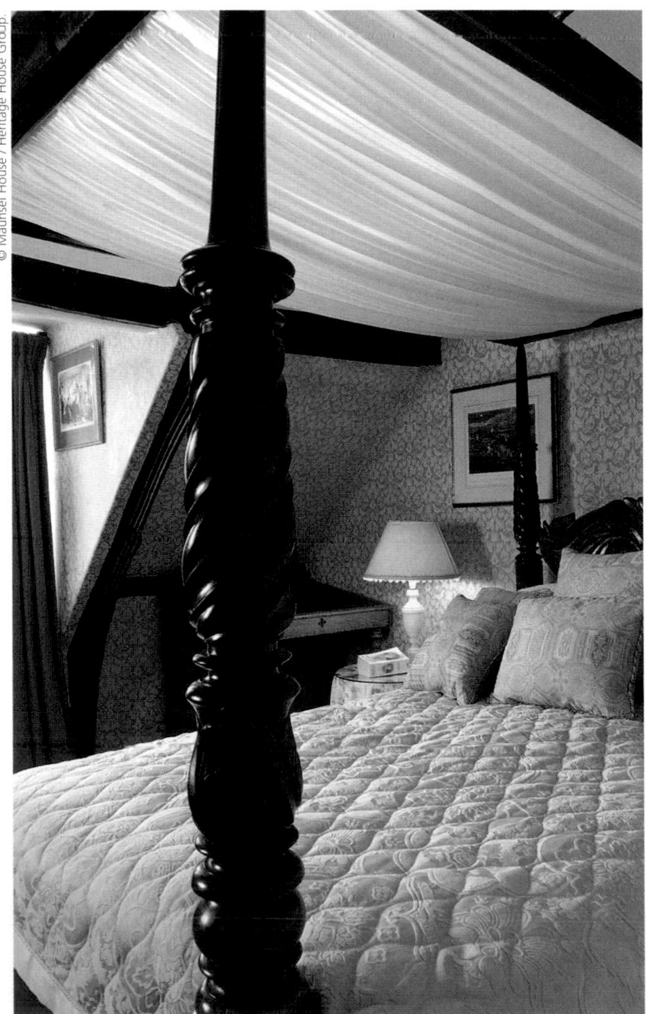

Maunsel House

West Dean College

NORTH EAST

SCOTLAND

WALES

SOUTH WALES

NORTH WALES

NORTHERN IRELAND

Civil Wedding Venues

Places at which the marriage or Civil partnership ceremonies can take place – many will also be able to provide facilities for wedding receptions.

Full details about each property are available in the regional listings. There are numerous other properties included within *Hudson's* which do not have a Civil Wedding Licence but which can accommodate wedding receptions. In Scotland religious wedding ceremonies can take place anywhere, subject to the Minister being prepared to perform them.

ENGLAND

LONDON

SOUTH EAST

© Peggy Porschen

Forde Abbey & Gardens

SOUTH WEST

EASTERN REGION

EAST MIDLANDS

HEART OF ENGLAND

Capesthorne Hall

YORKSHIRE & THE HUMBER

NORTH WEST

NORTH EAST

SCOTLAND

Claydon

Glenham Hall

WALES

SOUTH WALES

MID WALES

NORTH WALES

NORTHERN IRELAND

Open All Year

Properties included in this list are open to some extent for all or most of the year. See individual entries for details.

ENGLAND

LONDON

SOUTH EAST

SOUTH WEST

EASTERN REGION

EAST MIDLANDS

HEART OF ENGLAND

YORKSHIRE & THE HUMBER

NORTH WEST

NORTH EAST

SCOTLAND

WALES

SOUTH WALES

MID WALES

NORTH WALES

NORTHERN IRELAND

Special Events

This is merely a selection of special events being staged in 2011 – more information can be obtained from individual property websites – for quick access to these sites visit: www.hudsonsguide.co.uk

FEBRUARY

Blair Castle, Perthshire
Snowdrop Festival

Arley Hall & Gardens, Cheshire
Wedding Fair

Feb–Mar

The Savill Garden (Windsor Great Park, Berkshire)
Camellias and daffodils

6 & 13

Hartland Abbey, Devon
Snowdrop Sundays (11–4pm)

13 & 20

Deene Park, Northamptonshire
Snowdrop Sundays (Gardens Only), 11am–4pm

MARCH

Arley Hall & Gardens, Cheshire
Mother's Day Celebrations

Arundel Castle

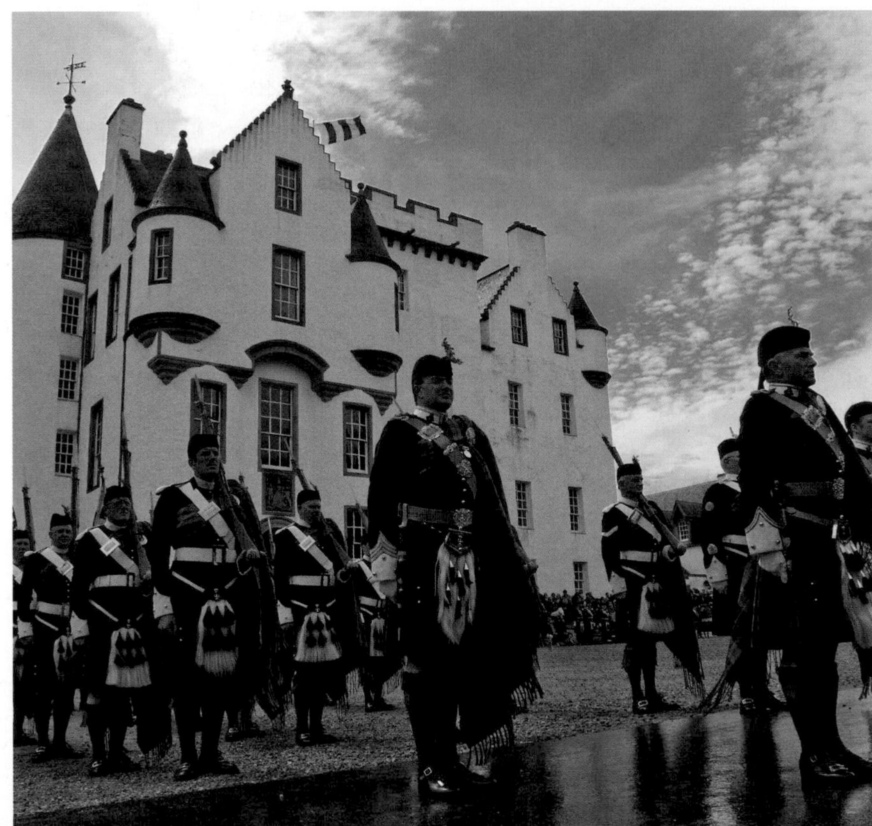

Blair Castle

2–3

Boconnoc, Cornwall
Cornwall Garden Society Spring Flower Show

4–6

Wilton House, Wiltshire
Antiques Fair

6

Boconnoc, Cornwall
Wedding Fair, 10am–4pm

12–27

Blenheim Palace, Oxfordshire
Exhibition: Gladys Deacon – The Life and Loves of an Edwardian Duchess 1921–1934

15

Boconnoc, Cornwall
Red Cross Concert

20

Hartland Abbey, Devon
Daffodil Day (11–4pm)

27

Deene Park, Northamptonshire
Daffodil Day (Gardens Only), 11am–4pm

31

Boconnoc, Cornwall
Floral Art Exhibition, 6–8pm

APRIL

Glamis Castle, Perthshire
Easter at Glamis

Arley Hall & Gardens, Cheshire
Spring Plant Fair
Bluebell Walks

Apr–May

The Savill Garden (Windsor Great Park, Berkshire)
Azalea and rhododendrons. Easter events and Spring Gardens Week

3

Hartland Abbey, Devon
Regis Car Tour

10

Blenheim Palace, Oxfordshire
The Orvis Fly Fishing Fair

17

Beaulieu, Hampshire
Boatjumble

22–25

Blenheim Palace, Oxfordshire
Great Blenheim Palace Easter Egg Challenge Easter Weekend

22 & 25

Hartland Abbey, Devon
Good Friday & Easter Monday – Bluebell Days

Easter

Clovelly, Devon
Red Letter Days

24–25

Lamport Hall & Gardens, Northamptonshire
Antiques and Collectors Fair (Easter Sunday and Monday)

Rockingham Castle, Northamptonshire
Easter Sunday & Monday

24

Traquair, Borders
Easter Egg Extravaganza

25

Chenies Manor House, Buckinghamshire
BH Mon 2–5pm – Fun for Children, a special Easter Event

27 April–8 May (inc.)

Pashley Manor Gardens, Sussex
Tulip Festival

30 Apr – 2 May

Blenheim Palace, Oxfordshire
Jousting Tournament featuring "The Knights of Royal England" May Bank Holiday

Chavenage

Skipton Castle

MAY

Clovelly, Devon
Celebration of Ales & Ciders

1–2

Hartland Abbey, Devon
Bluebell Days

2

Chenies Manor House, Buckinghamshire
BH Monday Tulip Festival, 2–5pm

First May BH
Penshurst Place & Gardens, Kent
Weald of Kent Craft Show

5–9

Hatfield House, Hertfordshire
Living Crafts

8

Boconnoc, Cornwall
History Lecture in Church, 11.30am

11–12

Boconnoc, Cornwall
Spring Fair

Hartland Abbey

14–15

Beaulieu, Hampshire
Spring Motormart & Autojumble

15

Boconnoc, Cornwall
St. John Ambulance Run
History Lecture in Church, 3pm

21–30

Pashley Manor Gardens, Sussex
Sculpture in Particular

22

Boconnoc, Cornwall
Precious Lives Dog Show

28–30

Blenheim Palace, Oxfordshire
"Art, Design and a Taste of Summer"
Whitsun Holiday

28

Blair Castle, Perthshire
Atholl Highlanders' Parade

28–30

Lamport Hall & Gardens, Northamptonshire
May BH Weekend – Festival of Country Life

28–29

Traquair, Borders
Medieval Fayre

29

Blair Castle, Perthshire
Highland Games

30

Chenies Manor House, Buckinghamshire
BH Mon – House & Garden open

JUNE

Arley Hall & Gardens, Cheshire
Arley Garden Festival

First week in June

Penshurst Place & Gardens, Kent
Glorious Gardens Week

June–July

The Savill Garden (Windsor Great Park, Berkshire)
Rose Garden, Hidden Gardens and the Dry Garden. Celebration of the Rose and Art Week

28

Tissington Hall, Derbyshire
Well Dressing: Annual week–long event with six village wells decorated in a fabulous montage of flowers, moss and twigs, depicting scenes from the Bible

3–5

Holker Hall & Gardens, Cumbria
Holker Garden Festival

4–5

Blenheim Palace, Oxfordshire
Blenheim Triathlon

Beaulieu, Hampshire
Steam Revival

5

Stonor, Oxfordshire
VW Owners' Rally

8–11 & 13–18

Blenheim Palace, Oxfordshire
Outdoor Summer Theatre by The Oxford School of Drama

Capesthorne Hall

12

Rockingham Castle, Northamptonshire
Jousting & Medieval Living History Village

Bowood House & Gardens, Wiltshire
Bowood Dog Show

15

Deene Park, Northamptonshire
Head Gardener's Tour with Supper

17

Hartland Abbey, Devon
Flower Festival

17–19

Pashley Manor Gardens, Sussex
Special Rose Weekend

19

Beaulieu, Hampshire
Hot Rod & Custom Car Show

Hartland Abbey, Devon
Atlantic Coast Express MG Car Rally (arrival pm)

24–26

Pashley Manor Gardens, Sussex
Kitchen Garden Weekend

24

Boconnoc, Cornwall
Music in the Park

25–26

Hartland Abbey, Devon
Country Fair Weekend

26

Beaulieu, Hampshire
Motorcycle Muster

JULY

Glamis Castle, Perthshire
Scottish Transport Extravaganza

Clovelly, Devon
Clovelly Maritime Festival
Woolsery Agricultural Show
Lundy Row

Goodwood House, Sussex
Festival of Speed
Glorious Goodwood Race–week

July – August

Blenheim Palace, Oxfordshire
Living History Interpretation – Summer Holiday Entertainment
Wings, Wheels & Steam

1–3

Scone Palace & Grounds, Perthshire
The Scottish Game Fair

2–3

Boconnoc, Cornwall
Endurance Horse Ride

10

Rockingham Castle, Northamptonshire
Falconry & Owl Day

Mid July–Mid August

Pashley Manor Gardens, Sussex
Lily Time

16

Blenheim Palace, Oxfordshire
Battle Proms Concert

Cawdor Castle, Highlands & Skye
Twelfth Night – Illyria

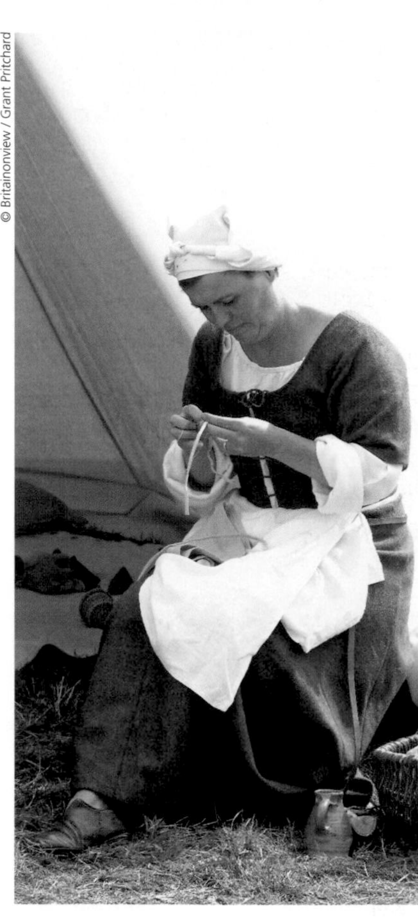
© Britainonview / Grant Pritchard

5–7

Blenheim Palace, Oxfordshire
Jousting Tournament featuring "The Knights of Royal England"

Hatfield House, Hertfordshire
Art in Clay

6–7

Traquair, Borders
Traquair Fair

18–21

Blair Castle, Perthshire
Blair Castle International Horse Trials and Country Fair

19–21

Hatfield House, Hertfordshire
Hatfield House Country Show

26–29

Stonor, Oxfordshire
Chilterns Craft Fair

27–29

Pashley Manor Gardens, Sussex
Sussex Guild Craft Show

28–29

Blenheim Palace, Oxfordshire
Classic Car Show August BH

Lamport Hall & Gardens, Northamptonshire
BH Sunday and Monday Antiques and Collectors Fair

Rockingham Castle, Northamptonshire
Vikings! Of Middle England

29

Chenies Manor House, Buckinghamshire
BH Monday 2–5pm Dahlia Festival

SEPTEMBER

Glamis Castle, Perthshire
Scotland's Countryside Festival

Clovelly, Devon
Lobster & Crab Feast

Goodwood House, Sussex
Goodwood Revival

17

Chenies Manor House, Buckinghamshire
10am–5pm – Famous Plant & Garden Fair (Manor opens from 2pm)

22–24

Blenheim Palace, Oxfordshire
CLA Game Fair

Boconnoc, Cornwall
Steam Fair

AUGUST

Glamis Castle, Perthshire
A Grand Scottish Prom

Clovelly, Devon
Lifeboat Day
Clovelly Gig Regatta

Goodwood House, Sussex
Vintage Goodwood

August–September

The Savill Garden (Windsor Great Park) Berkshire
Herbaceous borders and Golden Jubilee Garden Open Air Theatre

Glamis Castle

8–11

Blenheim Palace, Oxfordshire
Blenheim Palace International Horse Trials

9-11

Penshurst Place & Gardens, Kent
Weald of Kent Craft Show

10–11

Beaulieu, Hampshire
International Autojumble

10

Boconnoc, Cornwall
Sheepdog trials

15–18

Blenheim Palace, Oxfordshire
The Independent Woodstock Literary Festival

24

Cawdor Castle, Highlands & Skye
Living Food Festival

© Britainonview

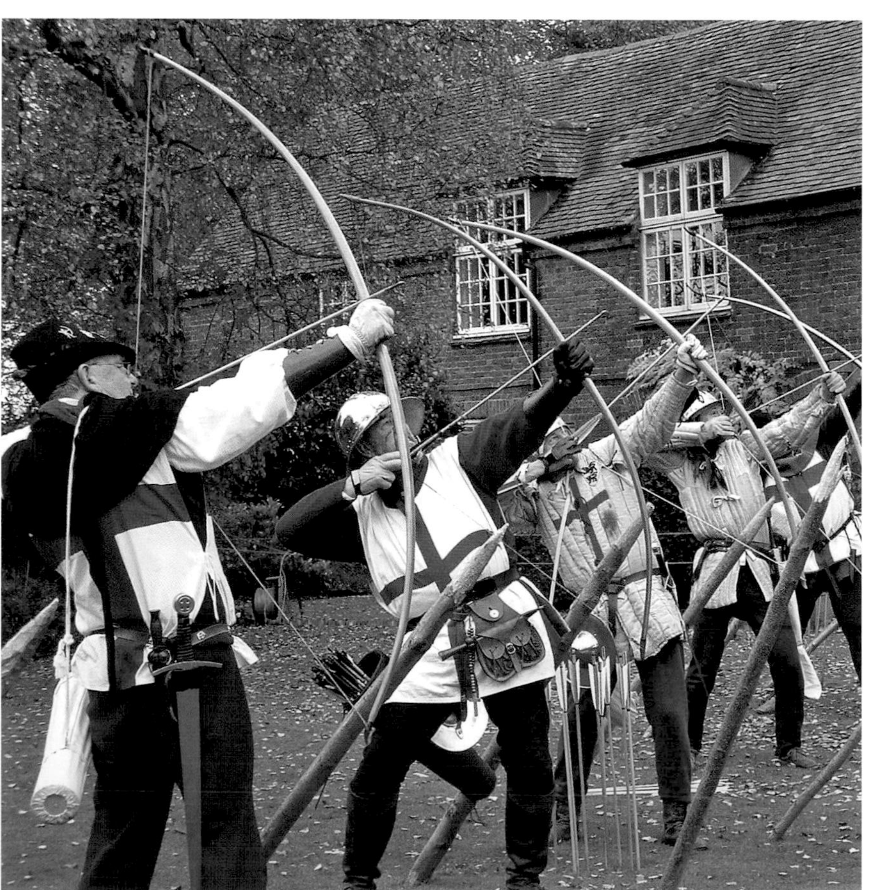

Harvington Hall

OCTOBER

Glamis Castle, Perthshire
Halloween at Glamis

Arley Hall & Gardens, Cheshire
Halloween Murder Mystery Evening

October–November

The Savill Garden (Windsor Great Park) Berkshire
Autumn Wood and The New Zealand Garden

2

Blenheim Palace, Oxfordshire
Breast Cancer Care's Bike Blenheim Palace

3–4

Boconnoc, Cornwall
Michaelmas Fair

8–9

Lamport Hall & Gardens, Northamptonshire
Autumn Gift and Craft Fair

22–30

Blenheim Palace, Oxfordshire
Half Term – Halloween Entertainment

26–27

Chenies Manor House, Buckinghamshire
Special opening for children Wednesday & Thursday 2–5pm 'Spooks and Surprises' fun for Children

28–29

Traquair, Borders
Halloween Experience

29

Beaulieu, Hampshire
Fireworks Spectacular

NOVEMBER

Glamis Castle, Perthshire
Winter programme of events

Clovelly, Devon
Clovelly Herring Festival

November – December

Blair Castle, Perthshire
Christmas Castle

Rockingham Castle

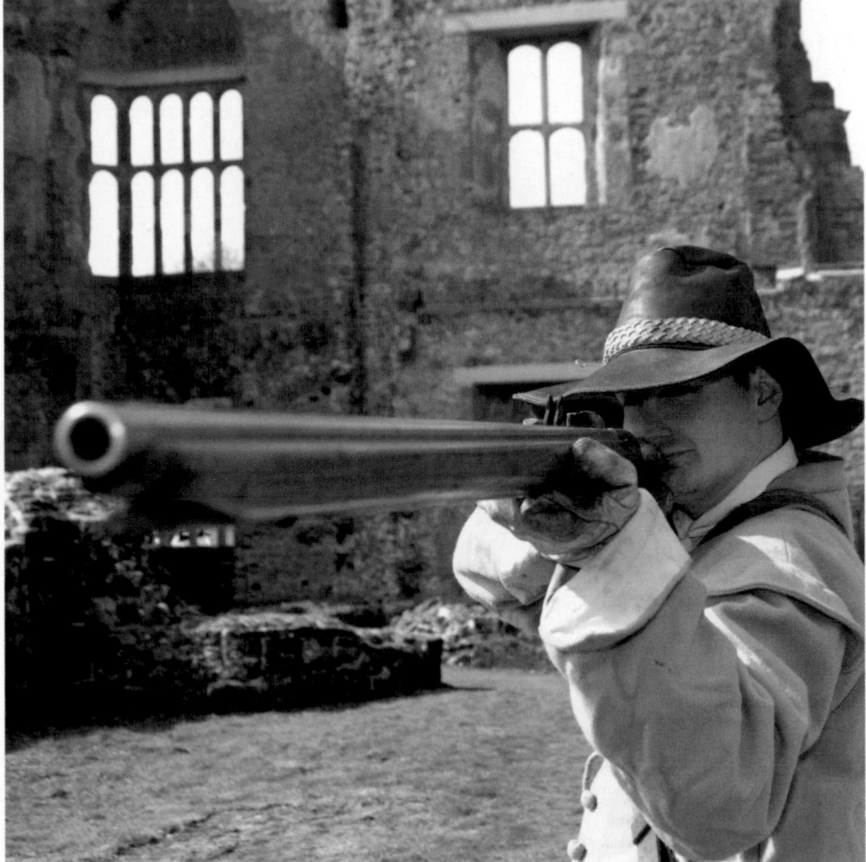

Cowdray Park

November – January

The Hall at Abbey-Cwm-Hir, Mid Wales
52 rooms decorated for Christmas

12–16

Blenheim Palace, Oxfordshire
Christmas at Blenheim Palace

18–20

Blenheim Palace, Oxfordshire
Living Crafts for Christmas

21–25

Rockingham Castle, Northamptonshire
Christmas at Rockingham Castle

25–27

Hopetoun House, Edinburgh
Christmas Shopping Fair

26–27

Traquair, Borders
Christmas Opening

DECEMBER

Glamis Castle, Perthshire
Winter programme of events

Arley Hall & Gardens, Cheshire
Christmas Floral Extravaganza

Clovelly, Devon
Christmas Lights

December–January

The Savill Garden (Windsor Great Park) Berkshire
Mahonia National Collection and a packed programme of Christmas festivities in the Savill Building. The Winter Garden

3–21

Holker Hall & Gardens, Cumbria
Christmas at Holker

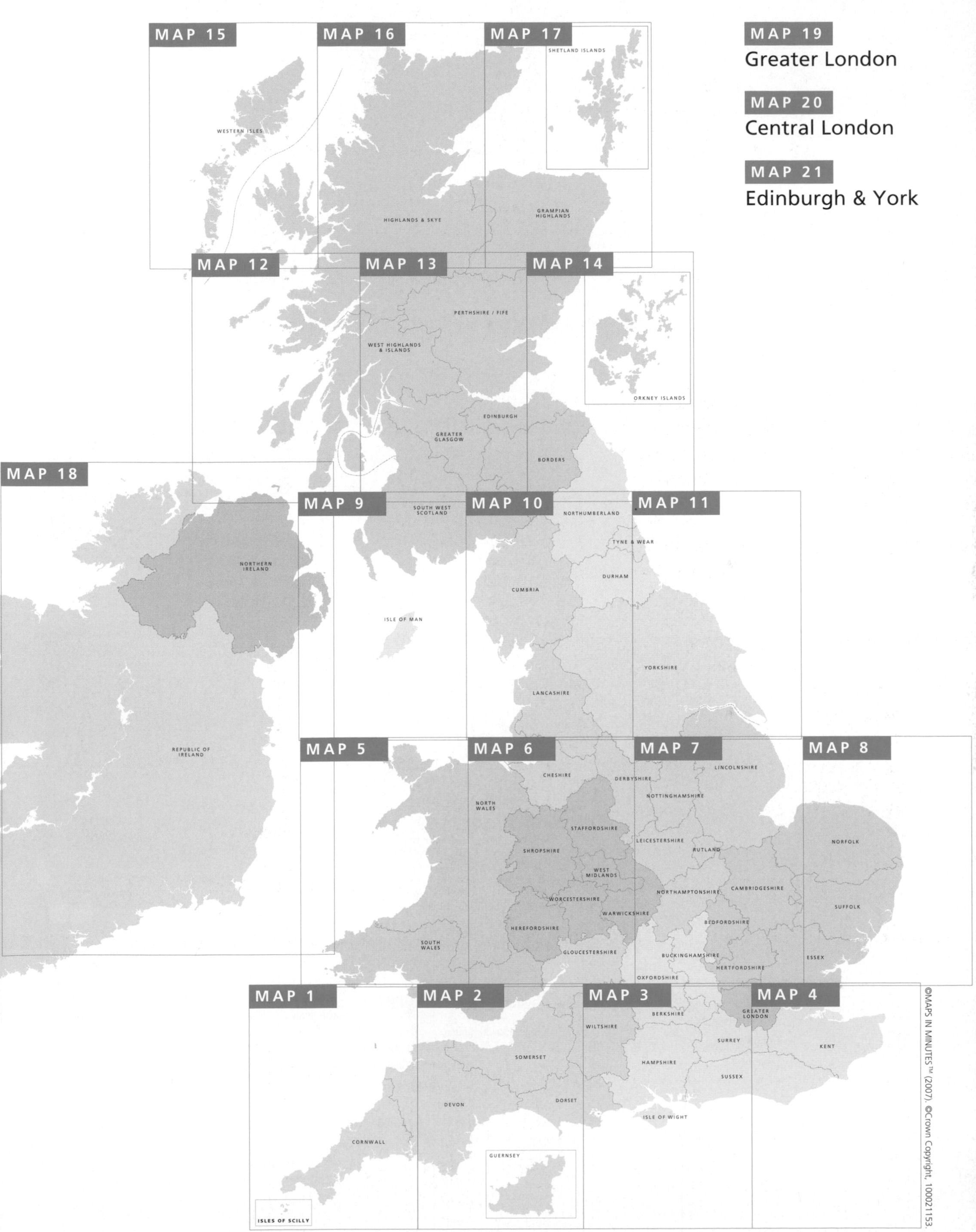
MAP 15
MAP 16
MAP 17
SHETLAND ISLANDS
MAP 19
Greater London
MAP 20
Central London
MAP 21
Edinburgh & York
WESTERN ISLES
HIGHLANDS & SKYE
GRAMPIAN HIGHLANDS
MAP 12
MAP 13
MAP 14
PERTHSHIRE / FIFE
WEST HIGHLANDS & ISLANDS
ORKNEY ISLANDS
EDINBURGH
GREATER GLASGOW
BORDERS
MAP 18
MAP 9
SOUTH WEST SCOTLAND
MAP 10
NORTHUMBERLAND
MAP 11
TYNE & WEAR
NORTHERN IRELAND
DURHAM
CUMBRIA
ISLE OF MAN
YORKSHIRE
LANCASHIRE
REPUBLIC OF IRELAND
MAP 5
MAP 6
MAP 7
MAP 8
CHESHIRE
DERBYSHIRE
LINCOLNSHIRE
NORTH WALES
NOTTINGHAMSHIRE
STAFFORDSHIRE
LEICESTERSHIRE
NORFOLK
SHROPSHIRE
RUTLAND
WEST MIDLANDS
NORTHAMPTONSHIRE
CAMBRIDGESHIRE
WORCESTERSHIRE
SUFFOLK
WARWICKSHIRE
BEDFORDSHIRE
HEREFORDSHIRE
SOUTH WALES
GLOUCESTERSHIRE
BUCKINGHAMSHIRE
ESSEX
HERTFORDSHIRE
OXFORDSHIRE
MAP 1
MAP 2
MAP 3
MAP 4
BERKSHIRE
GREATER LONDON
WILTSHIRE
SURREY
KENT
SOMERSET
HAMPSHIRE
SUSSEX
DORSET
DEVON
ISLE OF WIGHT
CORNWALL
GUERNSEY
ISLES OF SCILLY

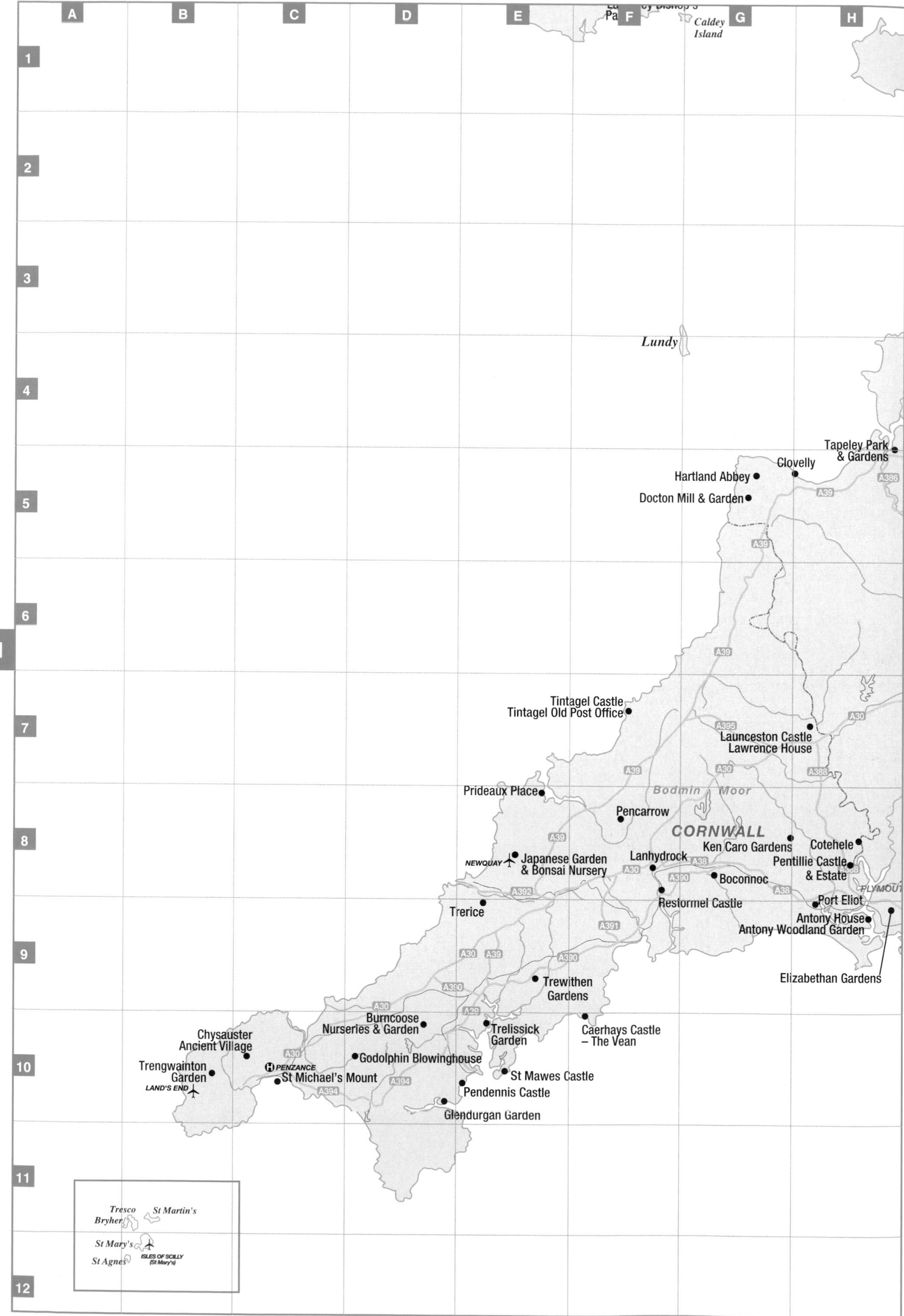

MAP 1
A
B
C
D
E
F
G
H
1
2
3
4
5
6
7
8
9
10
11
12
Caldey Island
Lundy
Tapeley Park & Gardens
Clovelly
Hartland Abbey
Docton Mill & Garden
Tintagel Castle
Tintagel Old Post Office
Launceston Castle
Lawrence House
Bodmin Moor
Prideaux Place
Pencarrow
CORNWALL
Ken Caro Gardens
Cotehele
NEWQUAY
Japanese Garden & Bonsai Nursery
Lanhydrock
Pentillie Castle & Estate
Boconnoc
PLYMOUTH
Restormel Castle
Port Eliot
Trerice
Antony House
Antony Woodland Garden
Elizabethan Gardens
Trewithen Gardens
Burncoose Nurseries & Garden
Trelissick Garden
Caerhays Castle – The Vean
Chysauster Ancient Village
PENZANCE
Trengwainton Garden
St Michael's Mount
Godolphin Blowinghouse
St Mawes Castle
LAND'S END
Pendennis Castle
Glendurgan Garden
Tresco
St Martin's
Bryher
St Mary's
St Agnes
ISLES OF SCILLY (St Mary's)
A39
A386
A395
A30
A388
A38
A390
A392
A391
A394

MAP 2
DEVON
SOMERSET
DORSET
Exmoor
Dartmoor
GUERNSEY
Weobley Castle
Oxwich Castle
Clyne Gardens
Tythegston Court
St Fagans: National History Museum
Castell Coch
Caerphilly Castle
Cardiff Castle
National Museum of Wales
Dyffryn Gardens & Arboretum
Fonmon Castle
Caerleon Roman Baths
Chepstow Castle
Caldicot Castle
Tredegar House & Park
Westbury Court Garden
Clevedon Court
Tyntesfield
Gatcombe Court
Beckford Tower
Bradford on-Avon Tithe Barn
Englishcombe Tithe Barn
No 1 Royal Crescent
Building of Bath Museum
Crowe Hall
Holburne Museum of Art
The Georgian House
Brean Down
Peto Gardens at Iford Manor
King John's Hunting Lodge
Farleigh Hungerford Castle
Chambercombe Manor
Holnicote Estate
Dunster Working Watermill
Dunster Castle
Fairfield
Kentsford
Orchard Wyndham
Cleeve Abbey
Dodington Hall
Coleridge Cottage
Hall Farm High Barn
Great House Farm
Milton Lodge Gardens
Wells Cathedral
Nunney Castle
Longleat
Stourton House Flower Garden
Stourhead
Arlington Court
Marwood Hill Garden
Anderton House
Glastonbury Tribunal, Abbey & Tor
Maunsel House
Robin Hood's Hut
Stembridge Tower Mill
Hestercombe Gardens
Priest's House
Muchelney Abbey
Lytes Cary Manor
Cothay Manor
Woodlands Castle
Treasurer's House
Tintinhull Garden
Sandford Orcas Manor House
Barrington Court
Rowlands Mill
Sherborne Old Castle
Sherborne Castle
Stoke sub-Hamdon Priory
Montacute House
Knightshayes Court
Stock Gayland House
Tiverton Castle
Lower Severalls
Merchant's House
Hemyock Castle
Killerton House
Lancin Farmhouse
Higher Melcombe
Fursdon House
Forde Abbey & Gardens
Minterne Gardens
Milton Abbey Church
Downes
Loughwood Meeting House
Mapperton
Markers Cottage
Athelhampton House & Gardens
Clouds Hill
Okehampton Castle
Finch Foundry
Exeter Cathedral
Custom House Exeter
Shute Barton
Church of Our Lady & St Ignatius
Wolfeton House
Hardy's Birthplace
Castle Drogo
Great Fulford
Culver House
Cadhay
Sand
Branscombe Mill
Max Gate
Abbotsbury Subtropical Gardens
Powderham Castle
A La Ronde
Lulworth Castle & Park
Portland Castle
Buckfast Abbey
Bradley Manor
Buckland Abbey
Dartington Hall
Compton Castle
Totnes Castle
Greenway
Berry Pomeroy Castle
Saltram House
Coleton Fishacre House & Garden
Dartmouth Castle
Overbeck's
Sausmarez Manor

MAP 3

A B C D E F G H

1 2 3 4 5 6 7 8 9 10 11 12

Chavenage
Parsonage
Coxwell Barn
Culham Manor Dovecote
Milton Manor House
Priory Cottages
West Wycombe
Wycombe Museum
Chiltern Open Air Museum
John Milton's Cottage
Wildmere Farm Chapel
Stonor
Hall Barn
Freeman Mausoleum
Gothic Temple
Cliveden
Greys Court
Boston Manor House
SWINDON
Richard Jeffries Farmhouse & Museum
Ardington House
Ashdown House
Lambourn
LYNEHAM
Mapledurham & Watermill
Dorney Court
Eton College
Basildon Park
WEST BERKSHIRE
St George's Chapel
Windsor Castle
Frogmore House
Osterley Park
Kew Gdns
Kew Palace
The Octagon
Corsham Court
Lacock Abbey
Bowood House
READING
WINDSOR & MAIDENHEAD
Runnymede
Savill Garden
Ham House
Strawberry Hill
Donnington Castle
Shaw House
WOKINGHAM
BRACKNELL FOREST
HEATHROW
Great Fosters
Garricks Temple
Hampton Court
WILTSHIRE
Stratfield Saye House
Claremont Landscape Garden
Whitehall
Great Chalfield Manor
Avebury Manor
Avebury Stone Circle
Alexander Keiller Museum
Sandham Memorial Chapel
Highclere Castle, Gardens & Egyptian Exhibition
Painshill Park Landscape Garden
Clandon Park & Hatchlands Park
The Vyne
Basing House
SURREY
Polesden Lacey
Box Hill
Salisbury Plain
Loseley Park
Shalford Mill
Farnham Castle Keep
Farnham Castle
Goddards
Leith Hill
GATWICK
Stonehenge
HAMPSHIRE

Great Hall & Queen Eleanor's Garden
Winchester Cathedral
Winchester City Mill
Wolvesey Castle

Northington Grange
Oakhurst Cottage
Jane Austen's House
Old Sarum

Mompesson House
Salisbury Cathedral

Houghton Lodge
Avington Park
Ramster Garden
Gilbert White's House
Wilton House
Mottisfont Abbey & Garden
Petworth Cottage Museum
Petworth House & Park
Hinton Ampner Garden
Nymans
Old Wardour Castle
Newhouse
Medieval Merchant's House
King John's House
Norrington Manor
Hamptworth Lodge
Whitsbury Down
Abbey Church of SS Mary and Ethelflaeda
Cowdray Ruins
Shipley Windmill
W. SUSSEX
Broadlands
SOUTHAMPTON
Uppark
Parham House & Gardens
Bishop's Waltham Palace
West Dean Gardens
Furzey Gardens
Bignor Roman Villa
Bramber Castle
St Mary's
Edmondsham House
Stansted Park
Boxgrove Priory
Netley Abbey
Goodwood House
New Forest
Titchfield Abbey
SHOREHAM
Kingston Lacy
Eling Tide Mill
Portchester Castle
Fishbourne Roman Palace
Denmans
Calshot Castle
St Agatha's Church
PORTSMOUTH
White Mill
BOURNEMOUTH
Beaulieu
Fort Brockhurst
Chichester Cathedral
Pallant House
Highdown Gardens
POOLE
Knoll Gardens
Exbury Gardens
Portsmouth Cathedral
BOURNEMOUTH
Highcliffe Castle
Osborne House
Charles Dickens' Birthplace Museum
Arundel Castle
Arundel Cathedral
Hurst Castle
Newtown Old Town Hall
Nunwell House & Gardens
Yarmouth Castle
Bembridge Windmill
Brownsea Island
Carisbrooke Castle
Morton Manor
The Needles
Needles Old Battery
Brighstone Shop & Museum
Mottistone Manor Garden
ISLE OF WIGHT
Corfe Castle
Clavell Tower
Appuldurcombe House
Isle of Wight

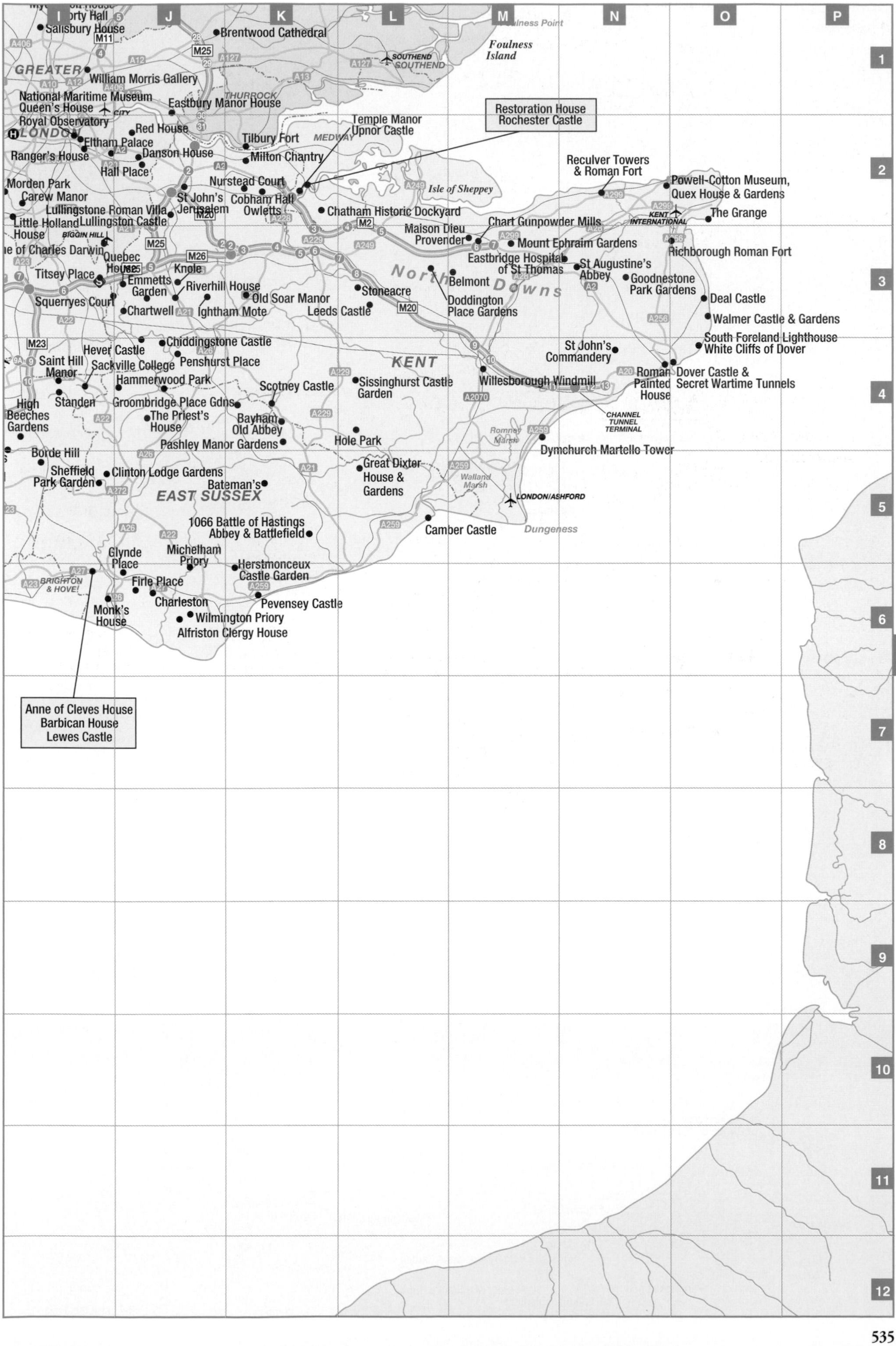

MAP 4

Restoration House
Rochester Castle

Anne of Cleves House
Barbican House
Lewes Castle

Salisbury House
Brentwood Cathedral
William Morris Gallery
National Maritime Museum
Queen's House
Royal Observatory
Eastbury Manor House
Red House
Eltham Palace
Danson House
Ranger's House
Hall Place
Tilbury Fort
Milton Chantry
Temple Manor
Upnor Castle
Morden Park
Carew Manor
Little Holland House
Lullingstone Roman Villa
Lullingstone Castle
Nurstead Court
St John's Jerusalem
Cobham Hall
Owletts
Chatham Historic Dockyard
Home of Charles Darwin
Quebec House
Titsey Place
Emmetts Garden
Knole
Riverhill House
Squerryes Court
Chartwell
Ightham Mote
Old Soar Manor
Stoneacre
Leeds Castle
Maison Dieu
Provender
Chart Gunpowder Mills
Mount Ephraim Gardens
Eastbridge Hospital of St Thomas
Belmont
Doddington Place Gardens
Reculver Towers & Roman Fort
Powell-Cotton Museum, Quex House & Gardens
The Grange
Richborough Roman Fort
St Augustine's Abbey
Goodnestone Park Gardens
Deal Castle
Walmer Castle & Gardens
South Foreland Lighthouse
White Cliffs of Dover
Dover Castle & Secret Wartime Tunnels
Roman Painted House
St John's Commandery
Willesborough Windmill
Hever Castle
Chiddingstone Castle
Penshurst Place
Saint Hill Manor
Sackville College
Hammerwood Park
Standen
High Beeches Gardens
Groombridge Place Gdns
The Priest's House
Scotney Castle
Bayham Old Abbey
Sissinghurst Castle Garden
Pashley Manor Gardens
Hole Park
Dymchurch Martello Tower
Borde Hill
Sheffield Park Garden
Clinton Lodge Gardens
Bateman's
Great Dixter House & Gardens
Camber Castle
1066 Battle of Hastings Abbey & Battlefield
Glynde Place
Michelham Priory
Herstmonceux Castle Garden
Firle Place
Charleston
Monk's House
Pevensey Castle
Wilmington Priory
Alfriston Clergy House

MAP 5

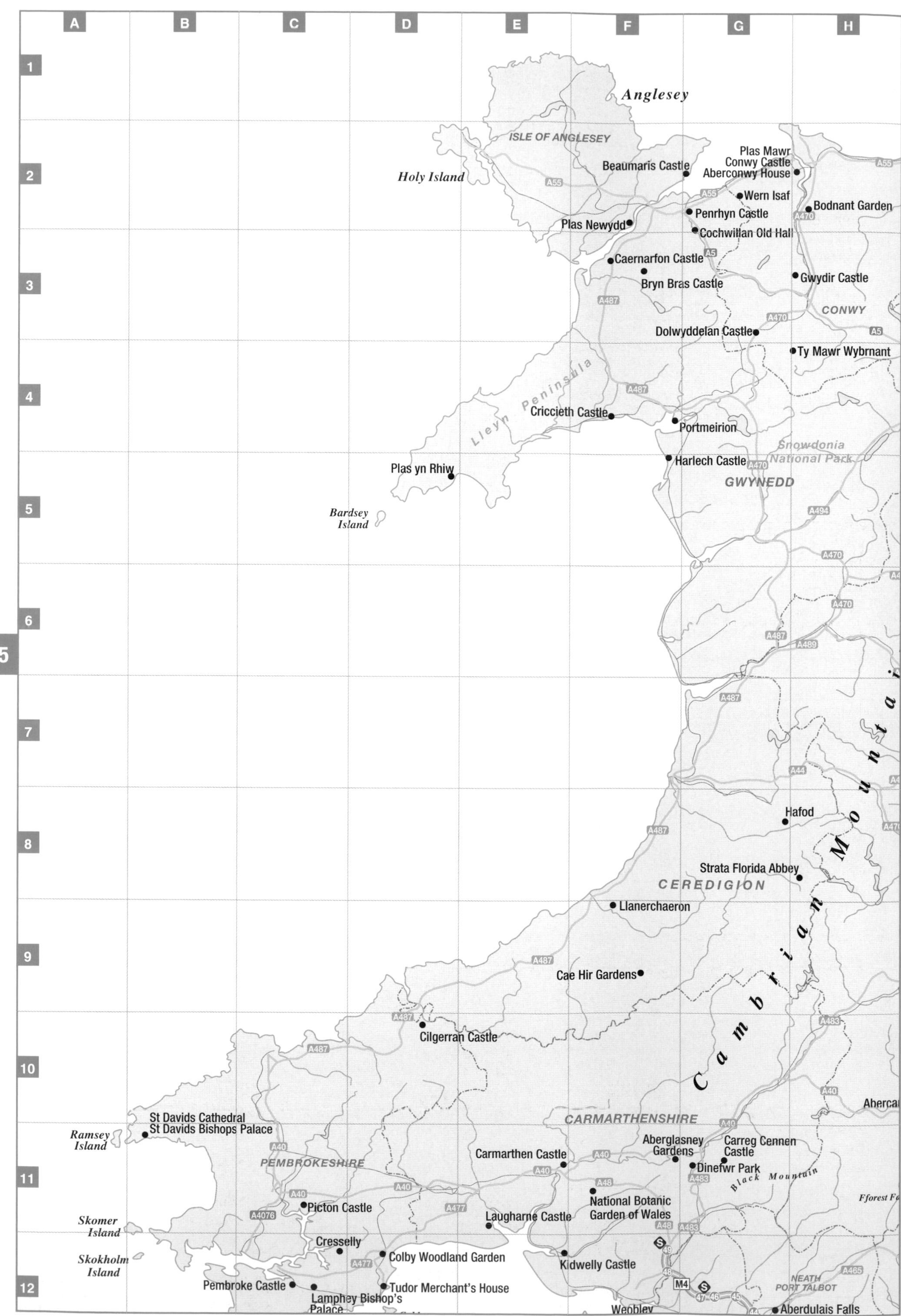

A
B
C
D
E
F
G
H
1
2
3
4
5
6
7
8
9
10
11
12
Anglesey
ISLE OF ANGLESEY
Holy Island
Beaumaris Castle
Plas Mawr
Conwy Castle
Aberconwy House
Wern Isaf
Penrhyn Castle
Bodnant Garden
Plas Newydd
Cochwillan Old Hall
Caernarfon Castle
Bryn Bras Castle
Gwydir Castle
CONWY
Dolwyddelan Castle
Ty Mawr Wybrnant
Lleyn Peninsula
Criccieth Castle
Portmeirion
Snowdonia National Park
Harlech Castle
GWYNEDD
Plas yn Rhiw
Bardsey Island
Cambrian Mountains
Hafod
Strata Florida Abbey
CEREDIGION
Llanerchaeron
Cae Hir Gardens
Cilgerran Castle
CARMARTHENSHIRE
Abercar
Ramsey Island
St Davids Cathedral
St Davids Bishops Palace
PEMBROKESHIRE
Carmarthen Castle
Aberglasney Gardens
Carreg Cennen Castle
Dinefwr Park
Black Mountain
Fforest Fa
National Botanic Garden of Wales
Picton Castle
Skomer Island
Laugharne Castle
Cresselly
Colby Woodland Garden
Kidwelly Castle
Skokholm Island
Pembroke Castle
Lamphey Bishop's Palace
Tudor Merchant's House
NEATH PORT TALBOT
Aberdulais Falls
Weobley
A55
A5
A470
A487
A494
A489
A44
A483
A40
A48
A477
A4076
A465
M4

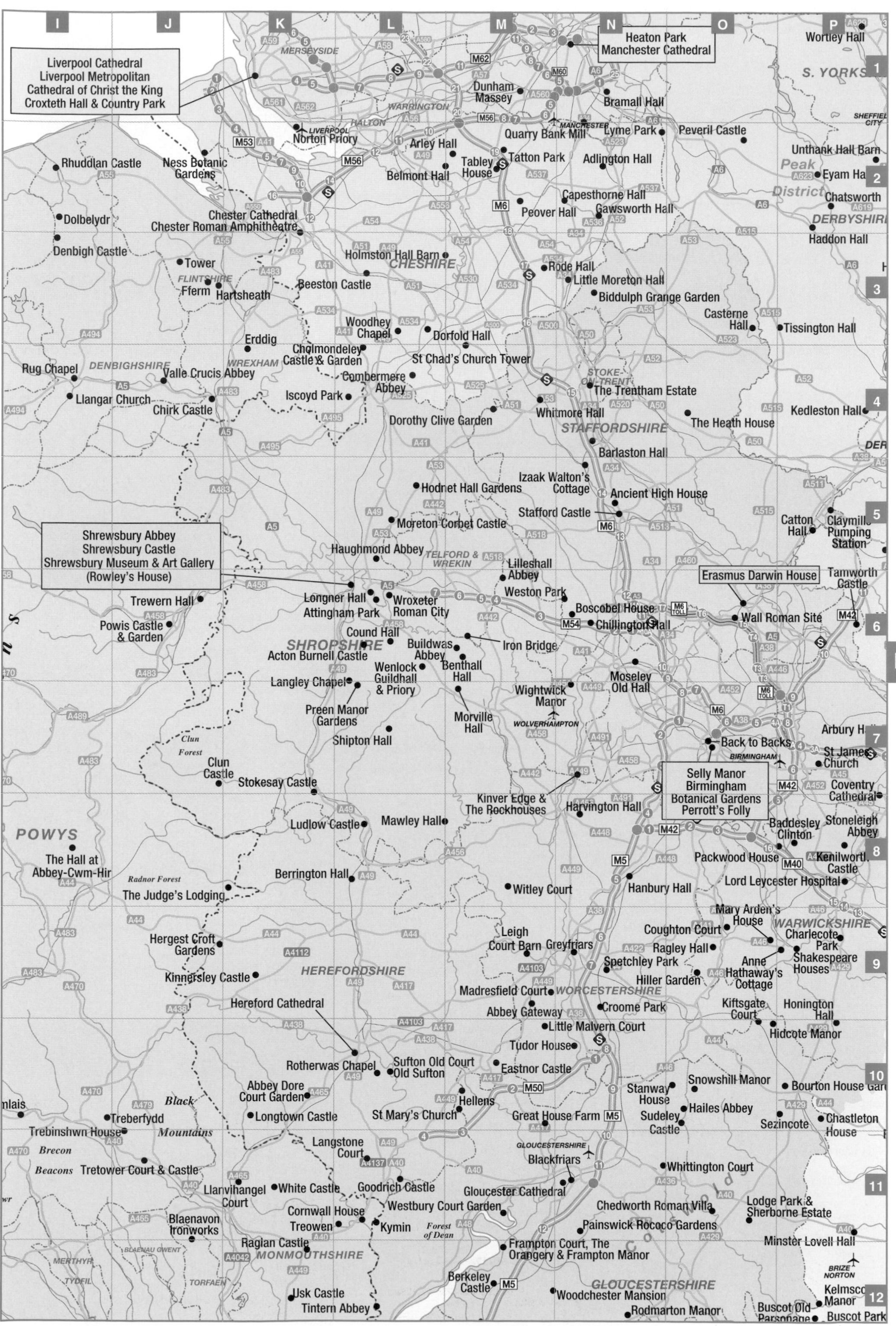
MAP 6
Liverpool Cathedral
Liverpool Metropolitan Cathedral of Christ the King
Croxteth Hall & Country Park
Heaton Park
Manchester Cathedral
Wortley Hall
Dunham Massey
Bramall Hall
Norton Priory
Arley Hall
Quarry Bank Mill
Lyme Park
Peveril Castle
Rhuddlan Castle
Ness Botanic Gardens
Tabley House
Tatton Park
Adlington Hall
Unthank Hall Barn
Belmont Hall
Eyam Hall
Capesthorne Hall
Chatsworth
Peover Hall
Gawsworth Hall
Dolbelydr
Chester Cathedral
Chester Roman Amphitheatre
Haddon Hall
Denbigh Castle
Holmston Hall Barn
Tower
Rode Hall
Little Moreton Hall
Fferm
Hartsheath
Beeston Castle
Biddulph Grange Garden
Casterne Hall
Tissington Hall
Woodhey Chapel
Dorfold Hall
Erddig
Cholmondeley Castle & Garden
St Chad's Church Tower
Rug Chapel
Valle Crucis Abbey
Combermere Abbey
The Trentham Estate
Llangar Church
Iscoyd Park
Chirk Castle
Whitmore Hall
Kedleston Hall
Dorothy Clive Garden
The Heath House
Barlaston Hall
Izaak Walton's Cottage
Hodnet Hall Gardens
Ancient High House
Stafford Castle
Moreton Corbet Castle
Catton Hall
Claymills Pumping Station
Shrewsbury Abbey
Shrewsbury Castle
Shrewsbury Museum & Art Gallery (Rowley's House)
Haughmond Abbey
Lilleshall Abbey
Erasmus Darwin House
Tamworth Castle
Weston Park
Trewern Hall
Longner Hall
Attingham Park
Wroxeter Roman City
Boscobel House
Chillington Hall
Wall Roman Site
Powis Castle & Garden
Cound Hall
Buildwas Abbey
Iron Bridge
Acton Burnell Castle
Benthall Hall
Wenlock Guildhall & Priory
Moseley Old Hall
Langley Chapel
Wightwick Manor
Preen Manor Gardens
Morville Hall
Shipton Hall
Arbury Hall
Back to Backs
St James Church
Clun Castle
Stokesay Castle
Selly Manor
Birmingham Botanical Gardens
Perrott's Folly
Coventry Cathedral
Kinver Edge & The Rockhouses
Harvington Hall
Ludlow Castle
Mawley Hall
Baddesley Clinton
Stoneleigh Abbey
The Hall at Abbey-Cwm-Hir
Packwood House
Kenilworth Castle
Berrington Hall
Lord Leycester Hospital
Witley Court
Hanbury Hall
The Judge's Lodging
Mary Arden's House
Coughton Court
Charlecote Park
Hergest Croft Gardens
Leigh Court Barn
Greyfriars
Ragley Hall
Anne Hathaway's Cottage
Shakespeare Houses
Spetchley Park
Kinnersley Castle
Hiller Garden
Madresfield Court
Hereford Cathedral
Croome Park
Kiftsgate Court
Honington Hall
Abbey Gateway
Little Malvern Court
Hidcote Manor
Tudor House
Rotherwas Chapel
Sufton Old Court
Old Sufton
Eastnor Castle
Snowshill Manor
Abbey Dore Court Garden
Stanway House
Bourton House Garden
Hellens
Hailes Abbey
Treberfydd
St Mary's Church
Great House Farm
Longtown Castle
Sudeley Castle
Chastleton House
Trebinshwn House
Sezincote
Langstone Court
Blackfriars
Whittington Court
Tretower Court & Castle
Llanvihangel Court
White Castle
Goodrich Castle
Gloucester Cathedral
Lodge Park & Sherborne Estate
Chedworth Roman Villa
Cornwall House
Westbury Court Garden
Blaenavon Ironworks
Treowen
Kymin
Painswick Rococo Gardens
Minster Lovell Hall
Raglan Castle
Frampton Court, The Orangery & Frampton Manor
Berkeley Castle
Usk Castle
Kelmscott Manor
Woodchester Mansion
Tintern Abbey
Rodmarton Manor
Buscot Old Parsonage
Buscot Park
MERSEYSIDE
WARRINGTON
HALTON
LIVERPOOL
MANCHESTER
S. YORKS
SHEFFIELD CITY
Peak District
DERBYSHIRE
CHESHIRE
FLINTSHIRE
DENBIGHSHIRE
WREXHAM
STOKE-ON-TRENT
STAFFORDSHIRE
TELFORD & WREKIN
SHROPSHIRE
WOLVERHAMPTON
BIRMINGHAM
Clun Forest
POWYS
Radnor Forest
WARWICKSHIRE
HEREFORDSHIRE
WORCESTERSHIRE
GLOUCESTERSHIRE
Black Mountains
Brecon Beacons
Forest of Dean
MONMOUTHSHIRE
BLAENAU GWENT
MERTHYR TYDFIL
TORFAEN
BRIZE NORTON
I
J
K
L
M
N
O
P
1
2
3
4
5
6
7
8
9
10
11
12

MAP 7

Clumber Park
Gainsborough Old Hall
Roche Abbey
Hodsock Priory
Renishaw Hall Gardens
Lincoln Medieval Bishop's Palace
Sutton Scarsdale Hall
Bolsover Castle
Doddington Hall & Gardens
Rufford Abbey
LINCOLNSHIRE
Lincolnshire Wolds
Hardstoft Herb Garden
Hardwick Hall
Stainsby Mill
Hardwick Old Hall
NOTTINGHAMSHIRE
Aubourn Hall
Winkburn Hall
Tattershall Castle
Newstead Abbey
D H Lawrence Heritage
Papplewick Hall
Leadenham House
Fulbeck Manor
Sibsey Trader Windmill
NOTTINGHAM
Nottingham Castle
Holme Pierrepont Hall
Wollaton Hall & Park
Marston Hall
Belton House
Belvoir Castle
Easton Walled Gardens
NOTTINGHAM EAST MIDLANDS
Thrumpton Hall
Sandringham
Woolsthorpe Manor
Castle Rising Castle
Melbourne Hall
Staunton Harold Church
Calke Abbey
Ashby de La Zouch Castle
Grimsthorpe Castle Park & Gardens
Ayscoughfee Hall Museum & Gardens
St George's Guildhall
Clifton House
The Fens
LEICESTERSHIRE
Donington le Heath Manor House
Bradgate Park
Quenby Hall
RUTLAND
Burghley House
Peckover House & Garden
Octavia Hill's Birthplace House
LEICESTER
Kirby Muxloe Castle
PETERBOROUGH
Lyddington Bede House
Longthorpe Tower
Peterborough Cathedral
Rockingham Castle
Kirby Hall
Deene Park
Elton Hall
Southwick Hall
Ely Cathedral
Old Palace
Oliver Cromwell's House
Rushton Triangular Lodge
Lyveden New Bield
Eleanor Cross
CAMBRIDGESHIRE
Stanford Hall
Kelmarsh Hall
Boughton House
COVENTRY
Ryton Gardens
Cottesbrooke
Lamport Hall
Coton Manor Garden
NORTHAMPTONSHIRE
The Manor, Hemingford Grey
Island Hall
Kimbolton Castle
Denny Abbey & Farmland Museum
Holdenby House
Althorp
78 Derngate
Bushmead Priory
Anglesey Abbey
Compton Verney
Castle Ashby Gardens
BEDFORDSHIRE
University Botanic Garden
CAMBRIDGE
Ickworth Park &
Canons Ashby
Cowper & Newton Museum
Turvey House
MILTON KEYNES
Wimpole Hall
Farnborough Hall
Stoke Park Pavilions
Moggerhanger Park
Bromham Mill & Gallery
Upton House
Brook Cottage
Wakefield Lodge
Weston Hall
Swiss Garden
Queen Anne's Summerhouse
Docwra's Manor Garden
Houghton House
Broughton Castle
Stowe House
Stowe Landscape Gardens
De Grey Mausoleum
Wrest Park
Old Palace
Audley End House & Gardens
Garden
Deddington Castle
Buckingham Chantry Chapel
Woburn Abbey
Cromer Windmill
Prior's Hall Barn
Rousham House
Claydon House
Ascott
Ford End Windmill
LUTON
Benington Lordship
Old Friends Meeting House
STANSTED
BUCKINGHAMSHIRE
HERTFORDSHIRE
Ditchley Park
Boarstall Duck Decoy
Waddesdon Manor
Pitstone Windmill
Knebworth
Shaw's Corner
Woodhall Park
Blenheim Palace
Wotton House
Boarstall Tower
Ashridge
Bridgewater Monument
Hertford Museum
Scott's Grotto
OXFORDSHIRE
Gorhambury House
Nether Winchendon House
Hatfield House
Chelmsford Cathedral
Waterperry Gardens
Berkhamstead Castle
Town Hall
Redbournbury Mill
Cathedral & Abbey Church of St Albans
Copped Hall
Rycote Chapel
Chenies Manor House
Kingston Bagpuize
26A East St Helen Street
Capel Manor
Waltham Abbey Gatehouse & Bridge

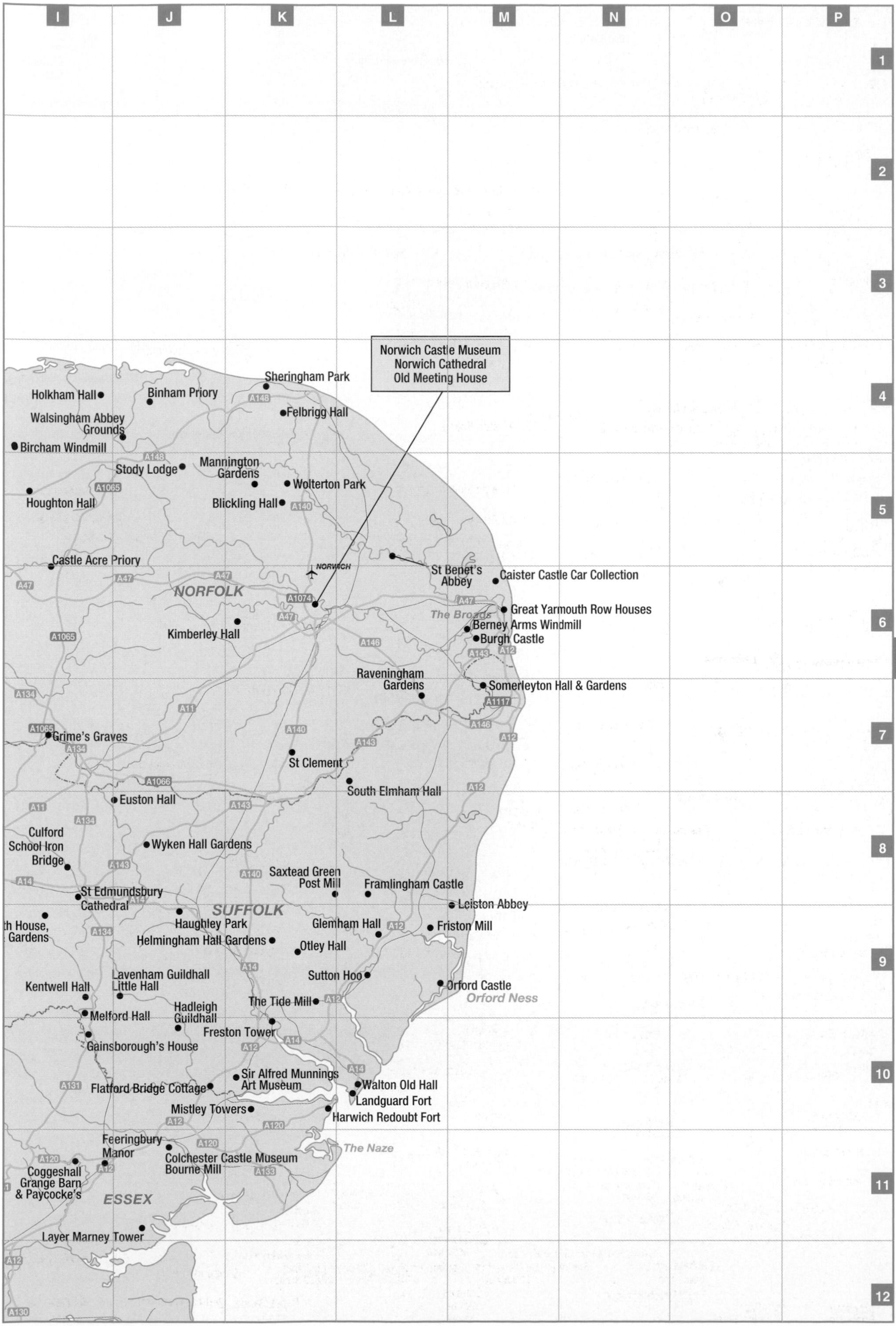

I J K L M N O P

1 2 3 4 5 6 7 8 9 10 11 12

MAP 8

Norwich Castle Museum
Norwich Cathedral
Old Meeting House

NORFOLK

Holkham Hall
Binham Priory
Sheringham Park
Felbrigg Hall
Walsingham Abbey Grounds
Bircham Windmill
Stody Lodge
Mannington Gardens
Wolterton Park
Houghton Hall
Blickling Hall
Castle Acre Priory
NORWICH
St Benet's Abbey
Caister Castle Car Collection
Great Yarmouth Row Houses
The Broads
Berney Arms Windmill
Burgh Castle
Kimberley Hall
Raveningham Gardens
Somerleyton Hall & Gardens
Grime's Graves
St Clement
South Elmham Hall
Euston Hall

SUFFOLK

Culford School Iron Bridge
Wyken Hall Gardens
Saxtead Green Post Mill
Framlingham Castle
St Edmundsbury Cathedral
Leiston Abbey
th House, Gardens
Haughley Park
Glemham Hall
Friston Mill
Helmingham Hall Gardens
Otley Hall
Lavenham Guildhall
Sutton Hoo
Kentwell Hall
Little Hall
Orford Castle
Orford Ness
The Tide Mill
Melford Hall
Hadleigh Guildhall
Freston Tower
Gainsborough's House
Sir Alfred Munnings Art Museum
Walton Old Hall
Flatford Bridge Cottage
Landguard Fort
Mistley Towers
Harwich Redoubt Fort
The Naze

ESSEX

Feeringbury Manor
Colchester Castle Museum
Bourne Mill
Coggeshall Grange Barn & Paycocke's
Layer Marney Tower

A148 A1065 A140 A47 A1074 A146 A143 A12 A1117 A134 A11 A1066 A14 A131 A120 A133 A130

MAP 9

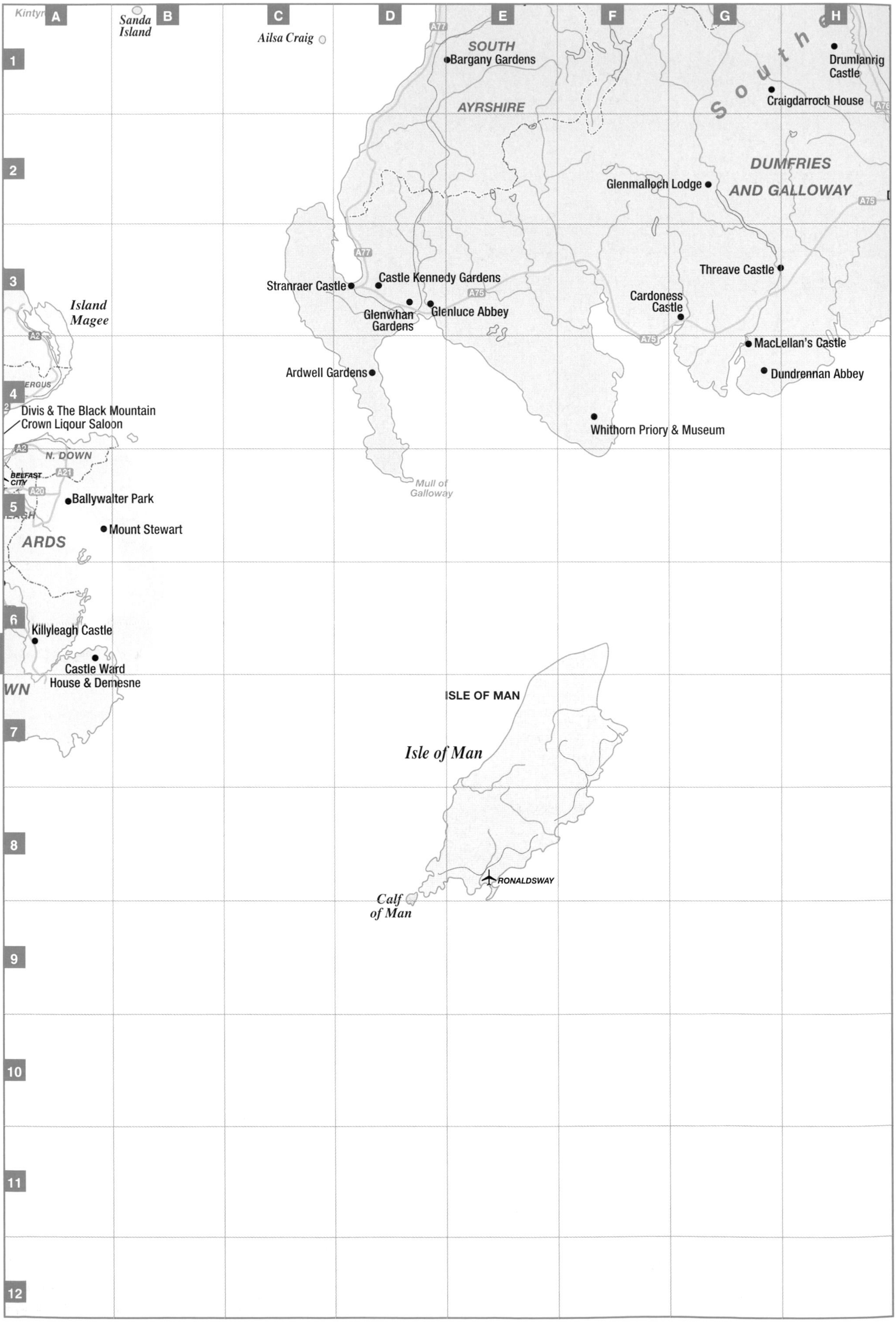

A
B
C
D
E
F
G
H
1
2
3
4
5
6
7
8
9
10
11
12
Kintyre
Sanda Island
Ailsa Craig
SOUTH AYRSHIRE
Bargany Gardens
Drumlanrig Castle
Craigdarroch House
DUMFRIES AND GALLOWAY
Glenmalloch Lodge
Threave Castle
Stranraer Castle
Castle Kennedy Gardens
Glenwhan Gardens
Glenluce Abbey
Cardoness Castle
MacLellan's Castle
Dundrennan Abbey
Ardwell Gardens
Whithorn Priory & Museum
Mull of Galloway
Island Magee
Divis & The Black Mountain
Crown Liqour Saloon
N. DOWN
BELFAST CITY
Ballywalter Park
Mount Stewart
ARDS
Killyleagh Castle
Castle Ward House & Demesne
ISLE OF MAN
Isle of Man
RONALDSWAY
Calf of Man
A77
A75
A76
A2
A21
A20

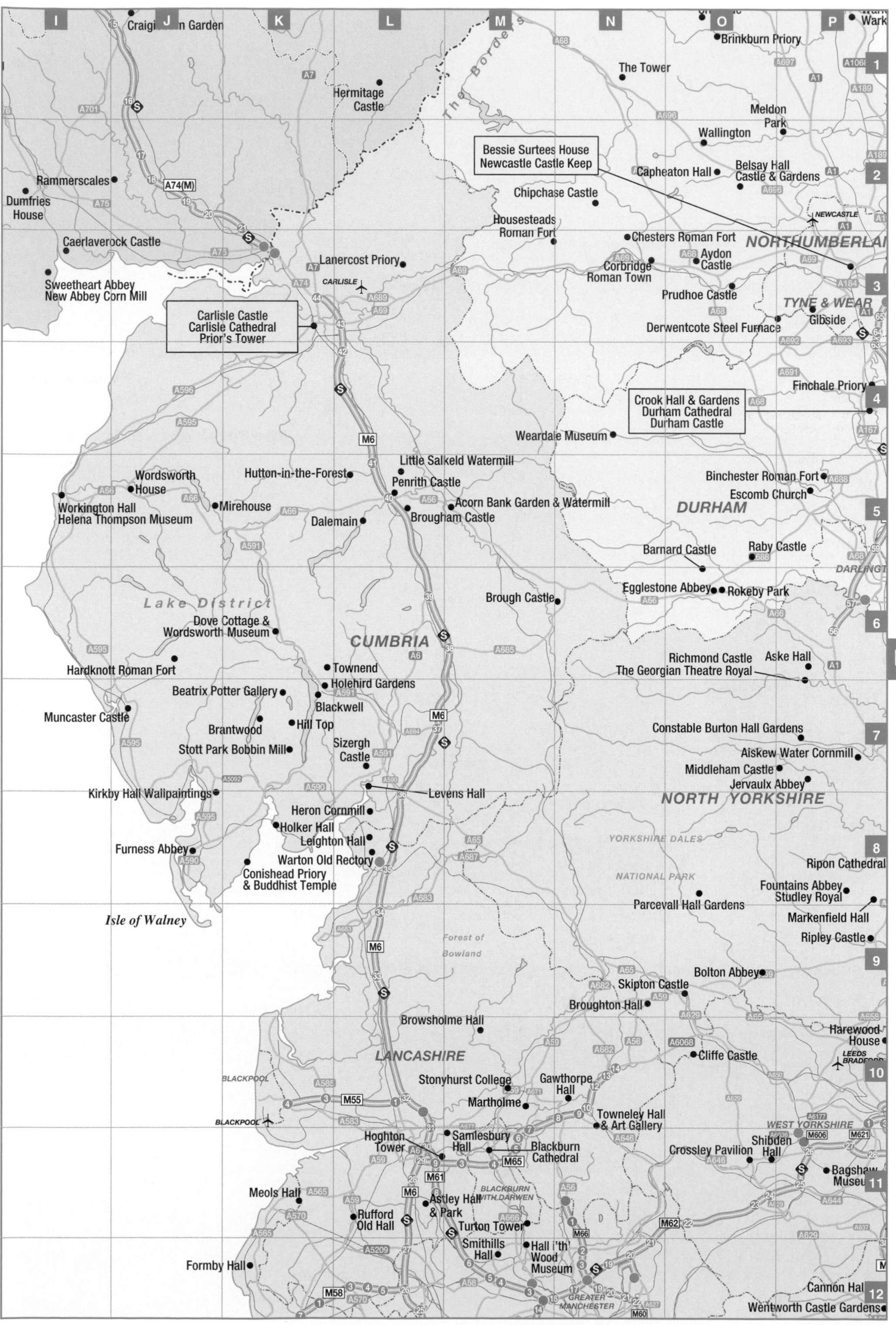

MAP 10
Craigieburn Garden
Hermitage Castle
The Tower
Brinkburn Priory
Meldon Park
Wallington
Bessie Surtees House
Newcastle Castle Keep
Capheaton Hall
Belsay Hall Castle & Gardens
Rammerscales
Dumfries House
Chipchase Castle
Housesteads Roman Fort
Chesters Roman Fort
NORTHUMBERLAND
Caerlaverock Castle
Lanercost Priory
Corbridge Roman Town
Aydon Castle
Sweetheart Abbey
New Abbey Corn Mill
CARLISLE
Prudhoe Castle
TYNE & WEAR
Gibside
Carlisle Castle
Carlisle Cathedral
Prior's Tower
Derwentcote Steel Furnace
Finchale Priory
Crook Hall & Gardens
Durham Cathedral
Durham Castle
Weardale Museum
Little Salkeld Watermill
Hutton-in-the-Forest
Wordsworth House
Penrith Castle
Binchester Roman Fort
Escomb Church
Workington Hall
Helena Thompson Museum
Mirehouse
Acorn Bank Garden & Watermill
Brougham Castle
Dalemain
DURHAM
Barnard Castle
Raby Castle
Egglestone Abbey
Rokeby Park
Lake District
Brough Castle
Dove Cottage & Wordsworth Museum
CUMBRIA
Hardknott Roman Fort
Townend
Richmond Castle
Aske Hall
The Georgian Theatre Royal
Beatrix Potter Gallery
Holehird Gardens
Blackwell
Muncaster Castle
Brantwood
Hill Top
Constable Burton Hall Gardens
Stott Park Bobbin Mill
Sizergh Castle
Aiskew Water Cornmill
Middleham Castle
Jervaulx Abbey
Kirkby Hall Wallpaintings
Levens Hall
NORTH YORKSHIRE
Heron Cornmill
Holker Hall
YORKSHIRE DALES
Leighton Hall
Furness Abbey
Warton Old Rectory
Ripon Cathedral
Conishead Priory & Buddhist Temple
NATIONAL PARK
Fountains Abbey
Studley Royal
Parcevall Hall Gardens
Markenfield Hall
Isle of Walney
Ripley Castle
Forest of Bowland
Bolton Abbey
Skipton Castle
Broughton Hall
Browsholme Hall
Harewood House
Cliffe Castle
LANCASHIRE
LEEDS BRADFORD
BLACKPOOL
Stonyhurst College
Gawthorpe Hall
Martholme
Towneley Hall & Art Gallery
WEST YORKSHIRE
Hoghton Tower
Samlesbury Hall
Blackburn Cathedral
Crossley Pavilion
Shibden Hall
Bagshaw Museum
BLACKBURN WITH DARWEN
Meols Hall
Astley Hall & Park
Rufford Old Hall
Turton Tower
Smithills Hall
Hall i' th' Wood Museum
Formby Hall
GREATER MANCHESTER
Cannon Hall
Wentworth Castle Gardens

MAP 11

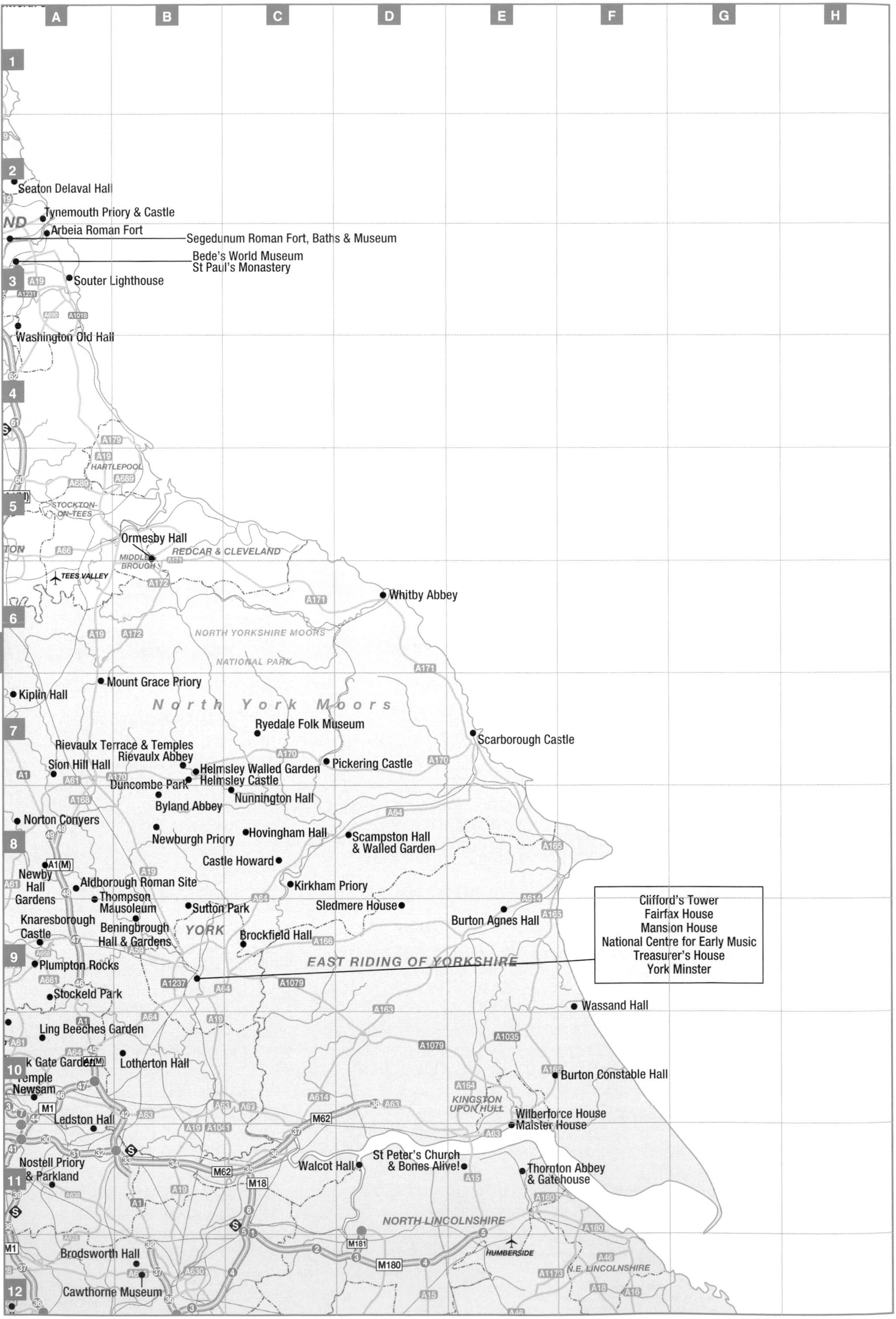

A B C D E F G H

1 2 3 4 5 6 7 8 9 10 11 12

Seaton Delaval Hall
Tynemouth Priory & Castle
Arbeia Roman Fort
Segedunum Roman Fort, Baths & Museum
Bede's World Museum
St Paul's Monastery
Souter Lighthouse
Washington Old Hall
HARTLEPOOL
STOCKTON-ON-TEES
Ormesby Hall
MIDDLESBROUGH
REDCAR & CLEVELAND
TEES VALLEY
Whitby Abbey
NORTH YORKSHIRE MOORS NATIONAL PARK
Mount Grace Priory
Kiplin Hall
North York Moors
Ryedale Folk Museum
Scarborough Castle
Rievaulx Terrace & Temples
Rievaulx Abbey
Sion Hill Hall
Helmsley Walled Garden
Helmsley Castle
Pickering Castle
Duncombe Park
Nunnington Hall
Byland Abbey
Norton Conyers
Newburgh Priory
Hovingham Hall
Scampston Hall & Walled Garden
Castle Howard
Newby Hall Gardens
Aldborough Roman Site
Thompson Mausoleum
Kirkham Priory
Sutton Park
Sledmere House
Knaresborough Castle
Beningbrough Hall & Gardens
YORK
Brockfield Hall
Burton Agnes Hall
Clifford's Tower
Fairfax House
Mansion House
National Centre for Early Music
Treasurer's House
York Minster
Plumpton Rocks
EAST RIDING OF YORKSHIRE
Stockeld Park
Wassand Hall
Ling Beeches Garden
Lotherton Hall
Burton Constable Hall
Temple Newsam
KINGSTON UPON HULL
Ledston Hall
Wilberforce House
Maister House
Nostell Priory & Parkland
St Peter's Church & Bones Alive!
Walcot Hall
Thornton Abbey & Gatehouse
NORTH LINCOLNSHIRE
HUMBERSIDE
N.E. LINCOLNSHIRE
Brodsworth Hall
Cawthorne Museum

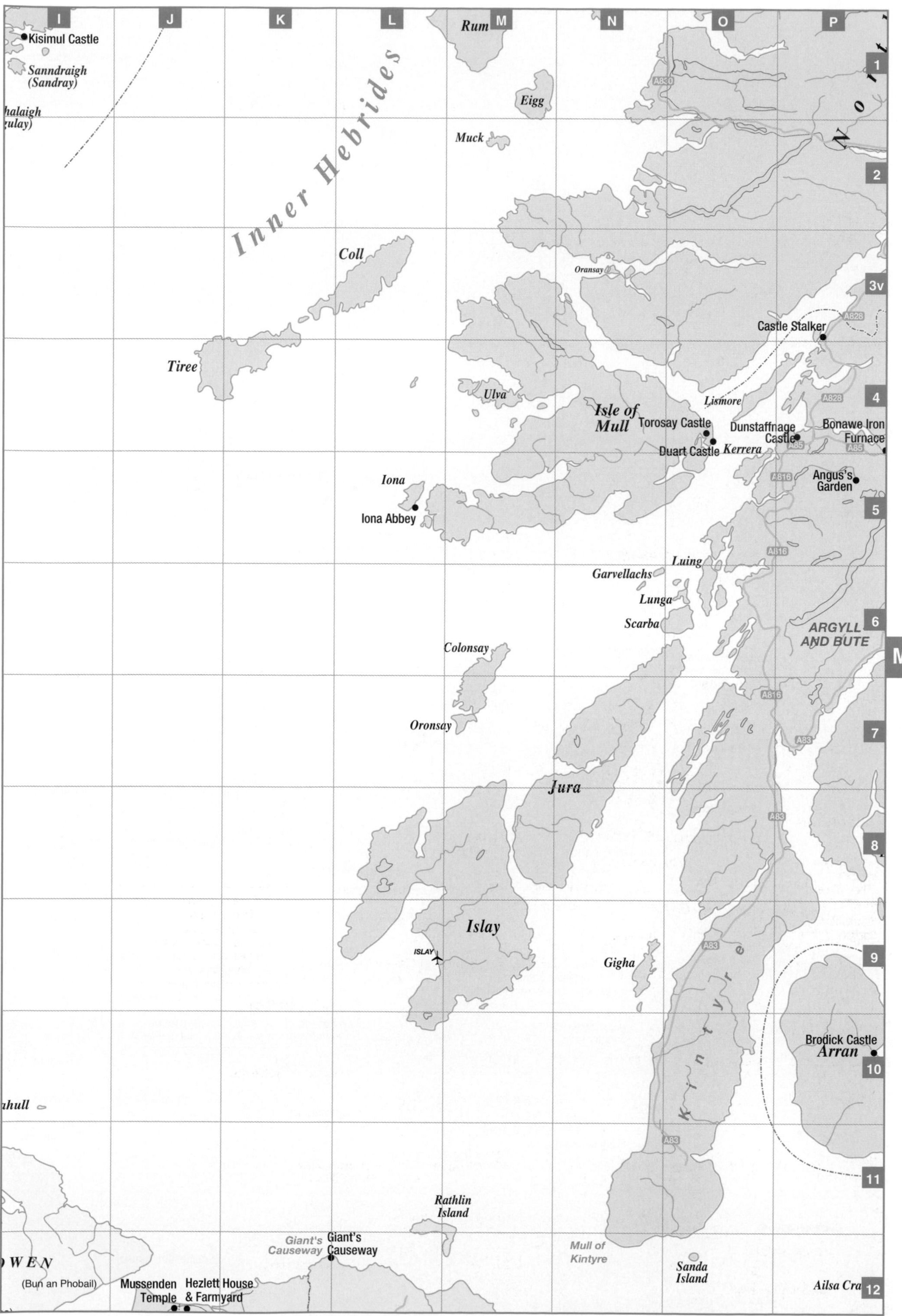

I
J
K
L
M
N
O
P
1
2
3v
4
5
6
7
8
9
10
11
12
Kisimul Castle
Sanndraigh (Sandray)
Rum
Eigg
Muck
Inner Hebrides
Coll
Tiree
Oransay
Castle Stalker
Ulva
Isle of Mull
Lismore
Torosay Castle
Duart Castle
Kerrera
Dunstaffnage Castle
Bonawe Iron Furnace
Angus's Garden
Iona
Iona Abbey
Luing
Garvellachs
Lunga
Scarba
ARGYLL AND BUTE
Colonsay
Oronsay
Jura
Islay
ISLAY
Gigha
Kintyre
Brodick Castle
Arran
Rathlin Island
Giant's Causeway
Giant's Causeway
Mull of Kintyre
Sanda Island
(Bun an Phobail)
Mussenden Temple
Hezlett House & Farmyard
A830
A828
A85
A816
A83

MAP 12

MAP 13

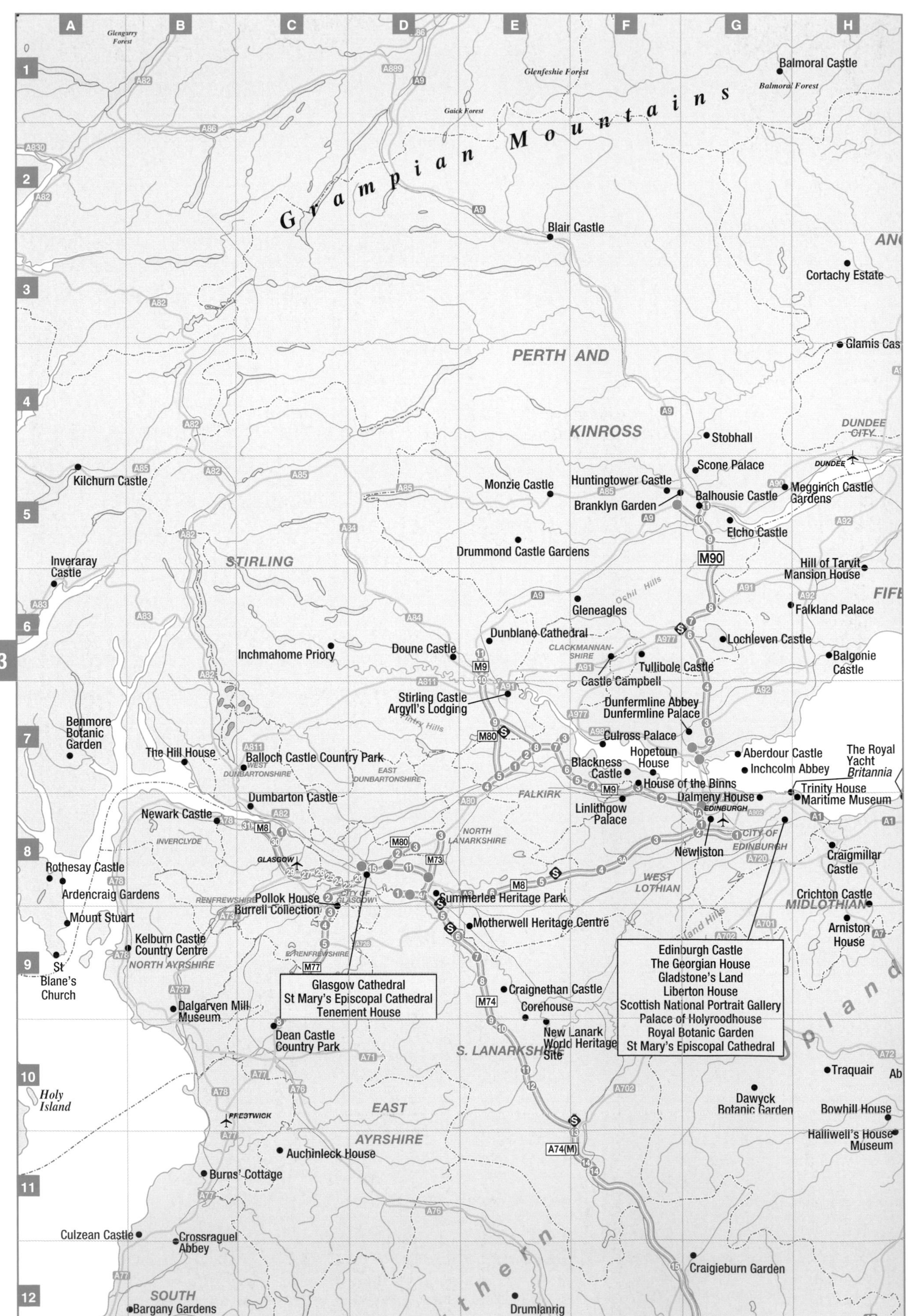
Grampian Mountains
Balmoral Castle
Blair Castle
Cortachy Estate
Glamis Castle
PERTH AND KINROSS
Stobhall
Scone Palace
Kilchurn Castle
Monzie Castle
Huntingtower Castle
Balhousie Castle
Branklyn Garden
Megginch Castle Gardens
Elcho Castle
Drummond Castle Gardens
Inveraray Castle
STIRLING
Hill of Tarvit Mansion House
Gleneagles
Falkland Palace
Dunblane Cathedral
Lochleven Castle
Inchmahome Priory
Doune Castle
Tullibole Castle
Castle Campbell
Balgonie Castle
Stirling Castle Argyll's Lodging
Dunfermline Abbey Dunfermline Palace
Benmore Botanic Garden
Culross Palace
The Hill House
Balloch Castle Country Park
Hopetoun House
Aberdour Castle
Inchcolm Abbey
The Royal Yacht Britannia
Blackness Castle
House of the Binns
Trinity House Maritime Museum
Dumbarton Castle
Dalmeny House
Linlithgow Palace
Newark Castle
Newliston
Craigmillar Castle
Rothesay Castle
Ardencraig Gardens
Pollok House
Burrell Collection
Summerlee Heritage Park
Crichton Castle
Mount Stuart
Motherwell Heritage Centre
Arniston House
Kelburn Castle Country Centre
St Blane's Church
Glasgow Cathedral
St Mary's Episcopal Cathedral
Tenement House
Edinburgh Castle
The Georgian House
Gladstone's Land
Liberton House
Scottish National Portrait Gallery
Palace of Holyroodhouse
Royal Botanic Garden
St Mary's Episcopal Cathedral
Craignethan Castle
Corehouse
Dalgarven Mill Museum
Dean Castle Country Park
New Lanark World Heritage Site
Traquair
Holy Island
Dawyck Botanic Garden
Bowhill House
Halliwell's House Museum
Auchinleck House
Burns' Cottage
Culzean Castle
Crossraguel Abbey
Craigieburn Garden
Bargany Gardens
Drumlanrig

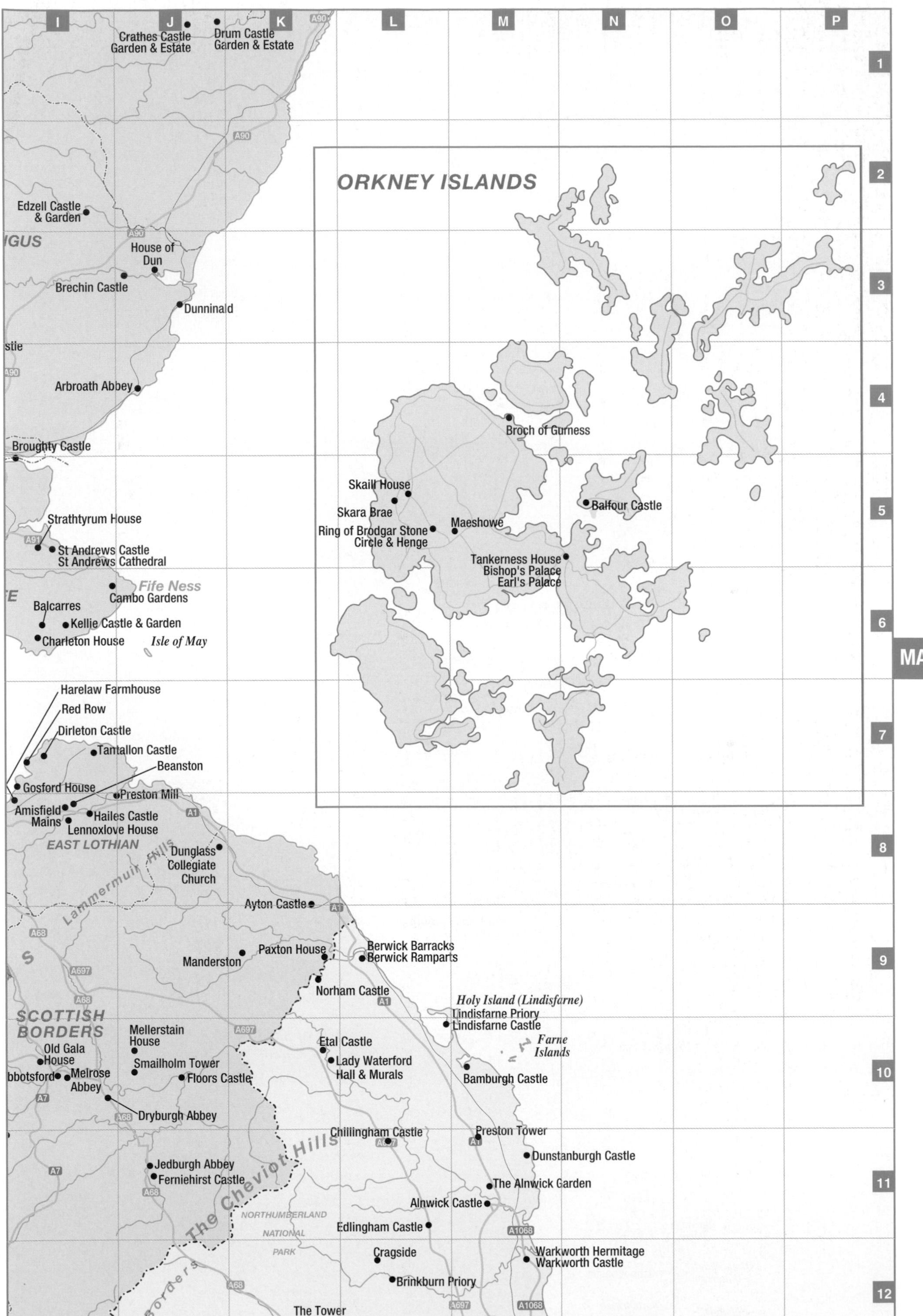
I
J
K
L
M
N
O
P
1
2
3
4
5
6
7
8
9
10
11
12
MAP 14
Crathes Castle Garden & Estate
Drum Castle Garden & Estate
Edzell Castle & Garden
House of Dun
Brechin Castle
Dunninald
Arbroath Abbey
Broughty Castle
Strathtyrum House
St Andrews Castle
St Andrews Cathedral
Fife Ness
Cambo Gardens
Balcarres
Kellie Castle & Garden
Charleton House
Isle of May
Harelaw Farmhouse
Red Row
Dirleton Castle
Tantallon Castle
Beanston
Gosford House
Preston Mill
Amisfield Mains
Hailes Castle
Lennoxlove House
EAST LOTHIAN
Lammermuir Hills
Dunglass Collegiate Church
Ayton Castle
Paxton House
Manderston
Berwick Barracks
Berwick Ramparts
Norham Castle
Holy Island (Lindisfarne)
Lindisfarne Priory
Lindisfarne Castle
Farne Islands
SCOTTISH BORDERS
Mellerstain House
Old Gala House
Smailholm Tower
Etal Castle
Lady Waterford Hall & Murals
Bamburgh Castle
bbotsford
Melrose Abbey
Floors Castle
Dryburgh Abbey
Chillingham Castle
Preston Tower
Dunstanburgh Castle
Jedburgh Abbey
Ferniehirst Castle
The Cheviot Hills
The Alnwick Garden
Alnwick Castle
NORTHUMBERLAND NATIONAL PARK
Edlingham Castle
Cragside
Warkworth Hermitage
Warkworth Castle
Brinkburn Priory
The Tower
Borders
ORKNEY ISLANDS
Broch of Gurness
Skaill House
Skara Brae
Balfour Castle
Maeshowe
Ring of Brodgar Stone Circle & Henge
Tankerness House
Bishop's Palace
Earl's Palace
A90
A91
A1
A68
A697
A7
A1068

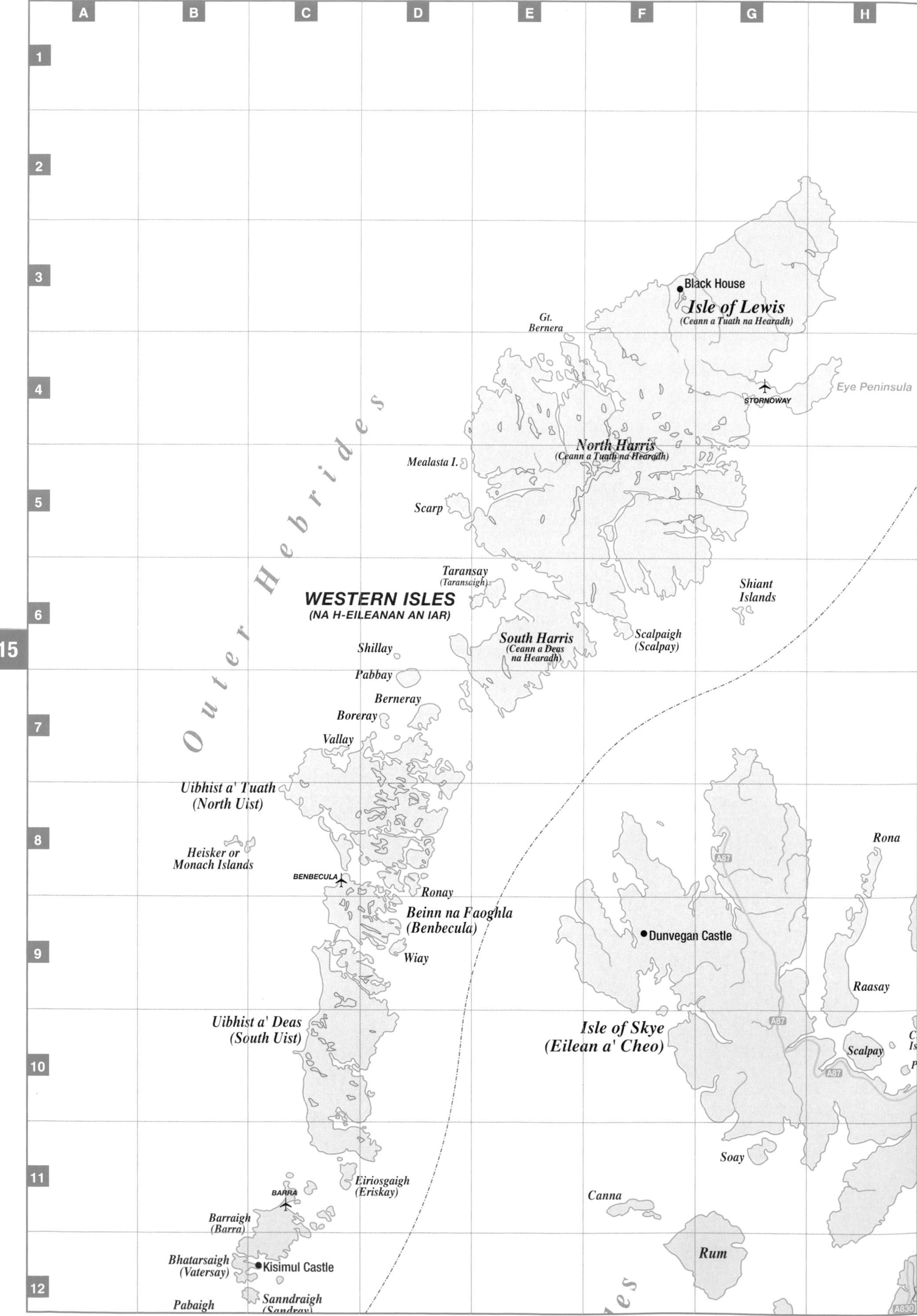
A
B
C
D
E
F
G
H
1
2
3
4
5
6
7
8
9
10
11
12
Black House
Isle of Lewis
(Ceann a Tuath na Hearadh)
Gt.
Bernera
Eye Peninsula
STORNOWAY
Outer Hebrides
North Harris
(Ceann a Tuath na Hearadh)
Mealasta I.
Scarp
Taransay
(Taransaigh)
WESTERN ISLES
(NA H-EILEANAN AN IAR)
Shiant
Islands
South Harris
(Ceann a Deas
na Hearadh)
Scalpaigh
(Scalpay)
Shillay
Pabbay
Berneray
Boreray
Vallay
Uibhist a' Tuath
(North Uist)
Heisker or
Monach Islands
BENBECULA
Ronay
Beinn na Faoghla
(Benbecula)
Wiay
Rona
A87
Dunvegan Castle
Raasay
Uibhist a' Deas
(South Uist)
Isle of Skye
(Eilean a' Cheo)
A87
Scalpay
A87
Soay
Eiriosgaigh
(Eriskay)
BARRA
Canna
Barraigh
(Barra)
Rum
Bhatarsaigh
(Vatersay)
Kisimul Castle
Pabaigh
Sanndraigh
A830

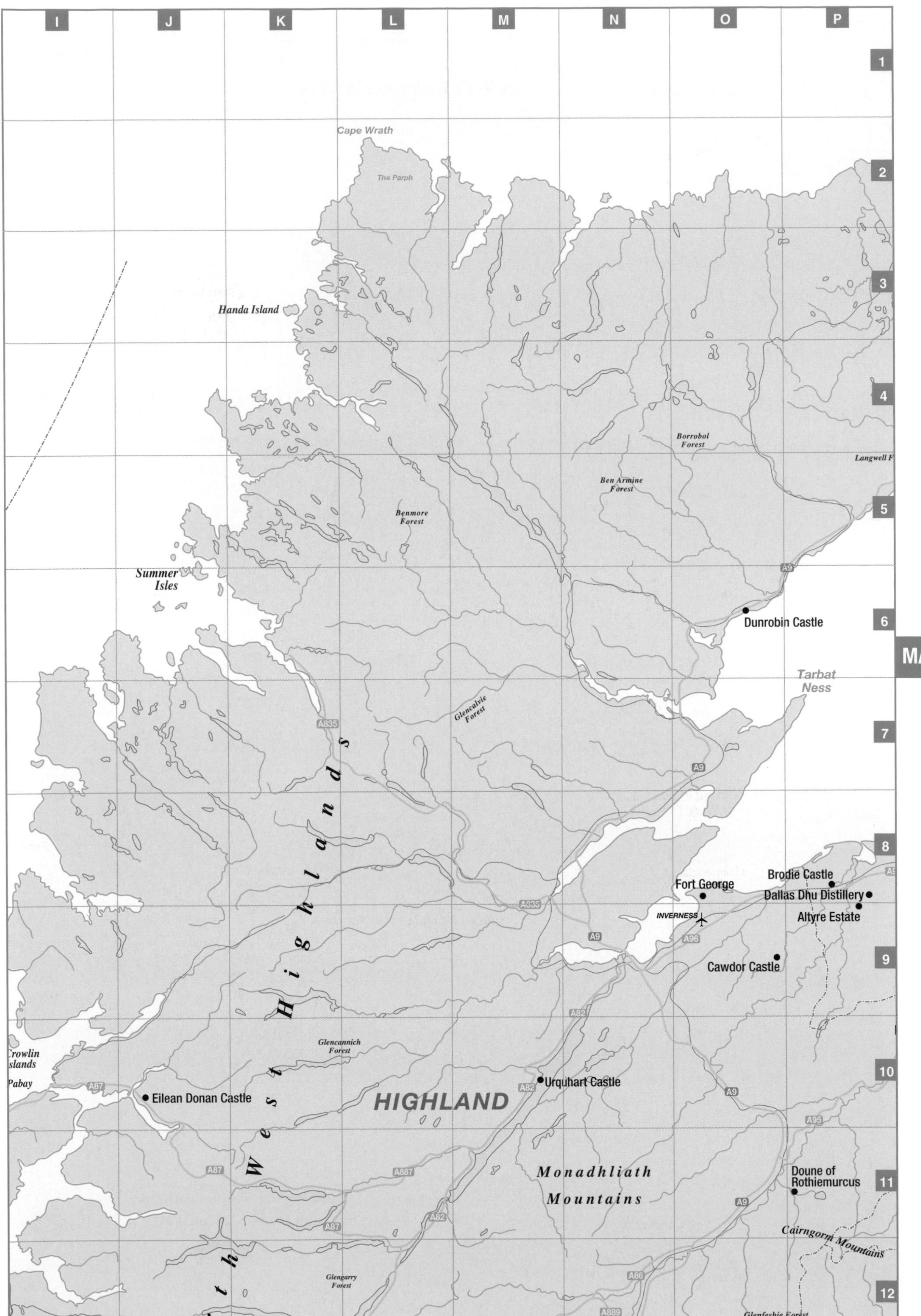
I
J
K
L
M
N
O
P
1
2
3
4
5
6
7
8
9
10
11
12
Cape Wrath
The Parph
Handa Island
Borrobol Forest
Langwell F
Ben Armine Forest
Benmore Forest
Summer Isles
Dunrobin Castle
MAP 16
Tarbat Ness
Glencalvie Forest
A835
A9
West Highlands
Brodie Castle
Fort George
Dallas Dhu Distillery
INVERNESS
Altyre Estate
A96
Cawdor Castle
A82
Glencannich Forest
Crowlin Islands
Pabay
A87
Eilean Donan Castle
Urquhart Castle
HIGHLAND
A95
Monadhliath Mountains
Doune of Rothiemurcus
A887
Cairngorm Mountains
A86
Glengarry Forest
A889
Glenfeshie Forest

MAP 17
Island of Stroma
Castle of Mey
WICK
Castle of Old Wick
SHETLAND ISLANDS
Jarlshof Prehistoric & Norse Settlement
Spynie Palace
Elgin Cathedral
Pluscarden Abbey
Duff House
Cairness House
Craigston Castle
Delgatie Castle
Drummuir Castle
Balvenie Castle
Huntly Castle
Fyvie Castle
Ballindalloch Castle
MORAY
Haddo House
Leith Hall & Garden
Tolquhon Castle
Pitmedden Garden
Craig Castle
Lickleyhead Castle
ABERDEENSHIRE
Kildrummy Castle
Kildrummy Castle Gardens
ABERDEEN
Castle Fraser & Garden
Corgarff Castle
Cruickshank Botanic Garden
David Welch Winter Gardens - Duthie Park
Provost Skene's House
St Machar's Cathedral Transepts
Crathes Castle Garden & Estate
Drum Castle Garden & Estate
Balmoral Castle

MAP 18
INISHOWEN
Giant's Causeway
Mussenden Temple
Hezlett House & Farmyard
Sanda Island
Mull of Kintyre
MOYLE
Inch I.
COLERAINE
LONDONDERRY
(Derry)
LIMAVADY
DERRY
BALLYMONEY
ANTRIM HILLS
BALLYMENA
(Leitir Ceanainn)
EGAL
Gray's Printing Press
(Leifear)
(Bealach Feich)
(Srath an Urláir)
STRABANE
SPERRIN MTS
MAGHERAFELT
LARNE
Island Magee
ANTRIM
Barons Court
Springhill House & Costume Collection
NEWTOWNABBEY
CARRICKFERGUS
Patterson's Spade Mill
Divis & The Black Mountain
Crown Liqour Saloon
BELFAST INTERNATIONAL
Wellbrook Beetling Mill
OMAGH
COOKSTOWN
N. DOWN
BELFAST
BELFAST CITY
LISBURN
CASTLEREAGH
Ballywalter Park
Mount Stewart
CRAIGAVON
ARDS
DUNGANNON
The Argory
Ardress House
Templetown Mausoleum
Rowallane Garden
FERMANAGH
Castle Coole
Killyleagh Castle
Castle Ward House & Demesne
Florence Court
ARMAGH
BANBRIDGE
DOWN
(Muineachán)
MONAGHAN
Crom
(Cluain Eois)
NEWRY & MOURNE
MOURNE MTS
Derrymore
(Baile na Lorgan)
(An Cabhán)
(Dun Dealgan)
CAVAN
(Carrig Mhachaire)
LOUTH
LONGFORD
(An Longfort)
(Ceanannus Mór)
(Droichead Átha)
M1 Toll
WESTMEATH
MEATH
(Baile Brigin)
(An Muileann gCearr)
(Baile Átha Troim)
(Na Sceirí)
DUBLIN
(An Ros)
Lambay Island
(Sord)
M4 Toll
DUBLIN
(Mullach Íde)
(Má Nuad)
DUBLIN
(BAILE ÁTHA CLIATH)
(Tulach Mhór)
OFFALY
(An Nás)
(Mainistir Eimhin)
KILDARE
(Móinteach Milic)
(Bré)
(Na Clocha Liathe)
©MAPS IN MINUTES™ (2007). ©Crown Copyright, 100021153 & Ordnance Survey Northern Ireland 2007 Permit No. NI 1675.

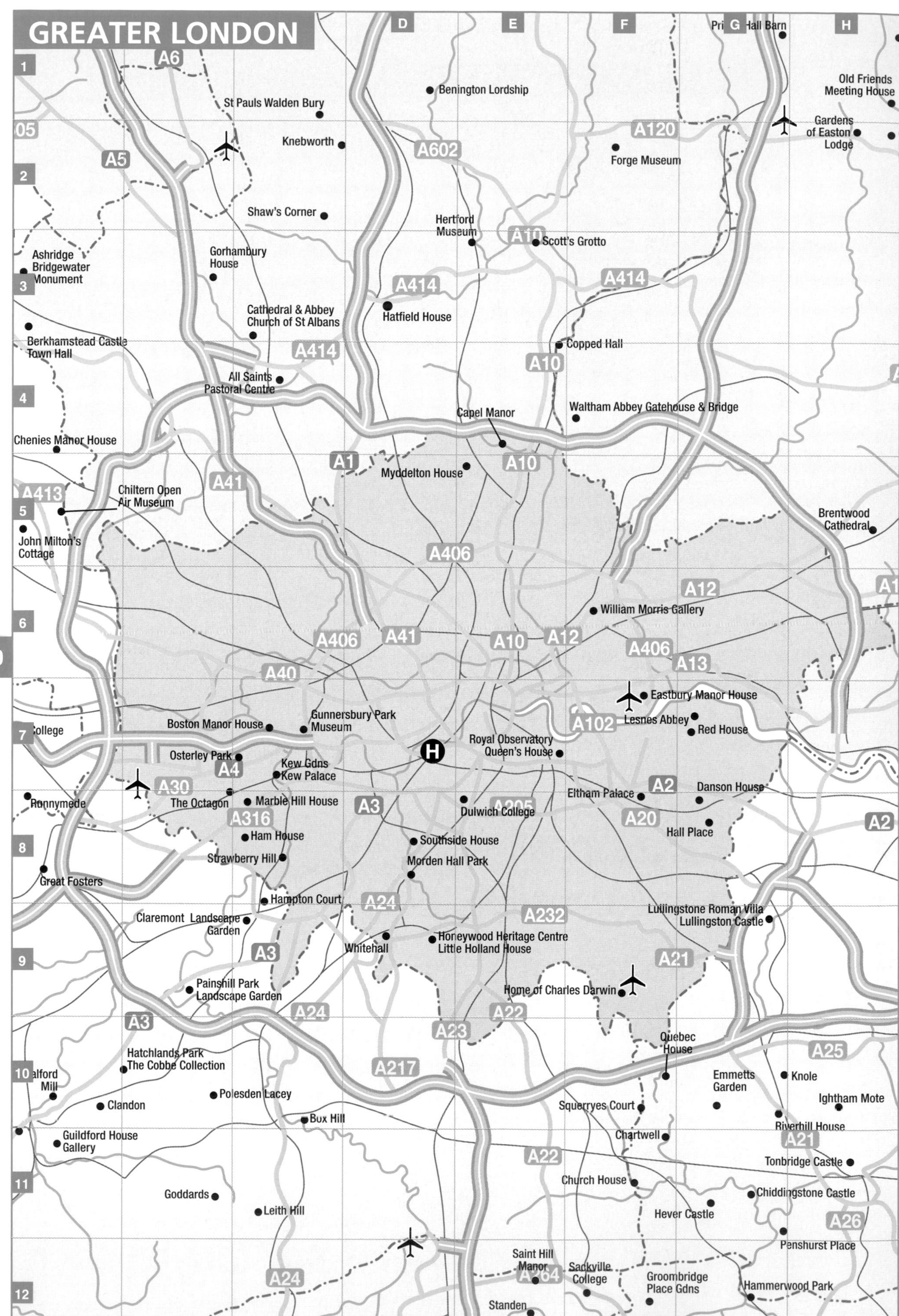
GREATER LONDON
MAP 19
D
E
F
G
H
1
2
3
4
5
6
7
8
9
10
11
12
A6
A5
A1
A10
A41
A413
A602
A120
A414
A406
A12
A13
A102
A40
A4
A30
A316
A3
A205
A2
A20
A24
A232
A21
A22
A23
A217
A25
A26
A264
St Pauls Walden Bury
Knebworth
Benington Lordship
Old Friends Meeting House
Gardens of Easton Lodge
Forge Museum
Shaw's Corner
Hertford Museum
Scott's Grotto
Ashridge Bridgewater Monument
Gorhambury House
Hatfield House
Cathedral & Abbey Church of St Albans
Berkhamstead Castle Town Hall
Copped Hall
All Saints Pastoral Centre
Waltham Abbey Gatehouse & Bridge
Capel Manor
Chenies Manor House
Myddelton House
Chiltern Open Air Museum
John Milton's Cottage
Brentwood Cathedral
William Morris Gallery
Eastbury Manor House
Lesnes Abbey
Red House
Boston Manor House
Gunnersbury Park Museum
Royal Observatory Queen's House
Osterley Park
Kew Gdns Kew Palace
Runnymede
The Octagon
Marble Hill House
Dulwich College
Eltham Palace
Danson House
Hall Place
Ham House
Southside House
Strawberry Hill
Morden Hall Park
Great Fosters
Hampton Court
Claremont Landscape Garden
Lullingstone Roman Villa Lullingston Castle
Whitehall
Honeywood Heritage Centre Little Holland House
Painshill Park Landscape Garden
Home of Charles Darwin
Quebec House
Hatchlands Park The Cobbe Collection
Emmetts Garden
Knole
Ightham Mote
Polesden Lacey
Clandon
Squerryes Court
Box Hill
Riverhill House
Guildford House Gallery
Chartwell
Tonbridge Castle
Church House
Chiddingstone Castle
Goddards
Hever Castle
Leith Hill
Penshurst Place
Saint Hill Manor
Sackville College
Groombridge Place Gdns
Hammerwood Park
Standen

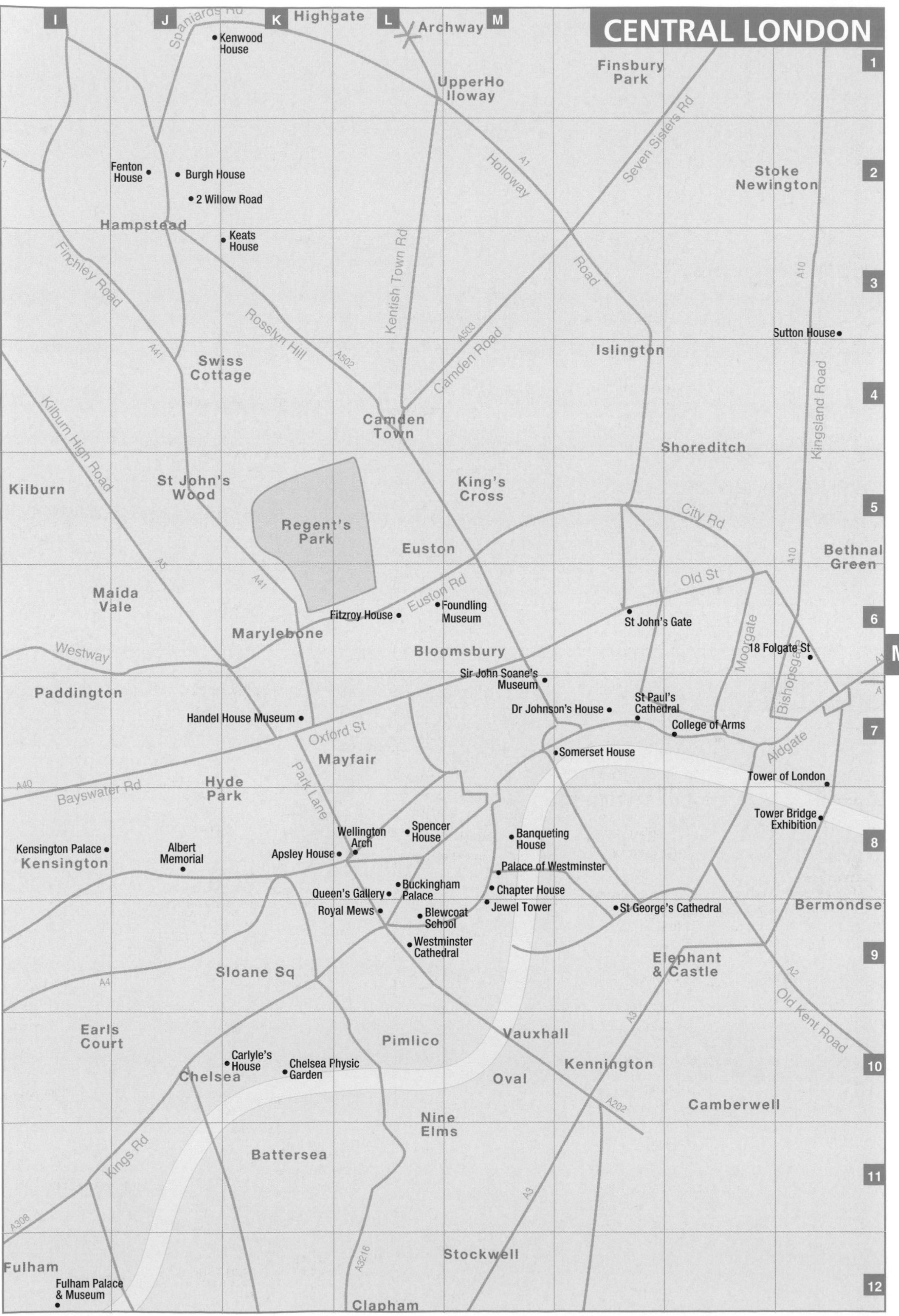

CENTRAL LONDON
MAP 20
I
J
K
L
M
1
2
3
4
5
6
7
8
9
10
11
12
Highgate
Archway
Spaniards Rd
Kenwood House
Finsbury Park
UpperHo lloway
Seven Sisters Rd
Holloway Road
A1
Stoke Newington
Fenton House
Burgh House
2 Willow Road
Hampstead
Keats House
Finchley Road
Kentish Town Rd
A10
Rosslyn Hill
A503
Camden Road
A502
A41
Sutton House
Swiss Cottage
Islington
Kingsland Road
Kilburn High Road
Camden Town
Shoreditch
Kilburn
St John's Wood
King's Cross
Regent's Park
City Rd
Euston
Bethnal Green
A5
Maida Vale
Euston Rd
Old St
Fitzroy House
Foundling Museum
St John's Gate
Marylebone
Moorgate
18 Folgate St
Westway
Bloomsbury
Bishopsgate
Paddington
Sir John Soane's Museum
Dr Johnson's House
St Paul's Cathedral
Handel House Museum
College of Arms
Oxford St
Mayfair
Somerset House
Aldgate
A40
Bayswater Rd
Hyde Park
Park Lane
Tower of London
Tower Bridge Exhibition
Wellington Arch
Spencer House
Banqueting House
Kensington Palace
Kensington
Albert Memorial
Apsley House
Palace of Westminster
Buckingham Palace
Queen's Gallery
Chapter House
Jewel Tower
St George's Cathedral
Royal Mews
Blewcoat School
Bermondse
Westminster Cathedral
Elephant & Castle
Sloane Sq
A4
A2
Old Kent Road
Earls Court
Vauxhall
A3
Pimlico
Carlyle's House
Chelsea Physic Garden
Kennington
Chelsea
Oval
A202
Camberwell
Nine Elms
Battersea
Kings Rd
A308
A3216
Stockwell
Fulham
Fulham Palace & Museum
Clapham

EDINBURGH

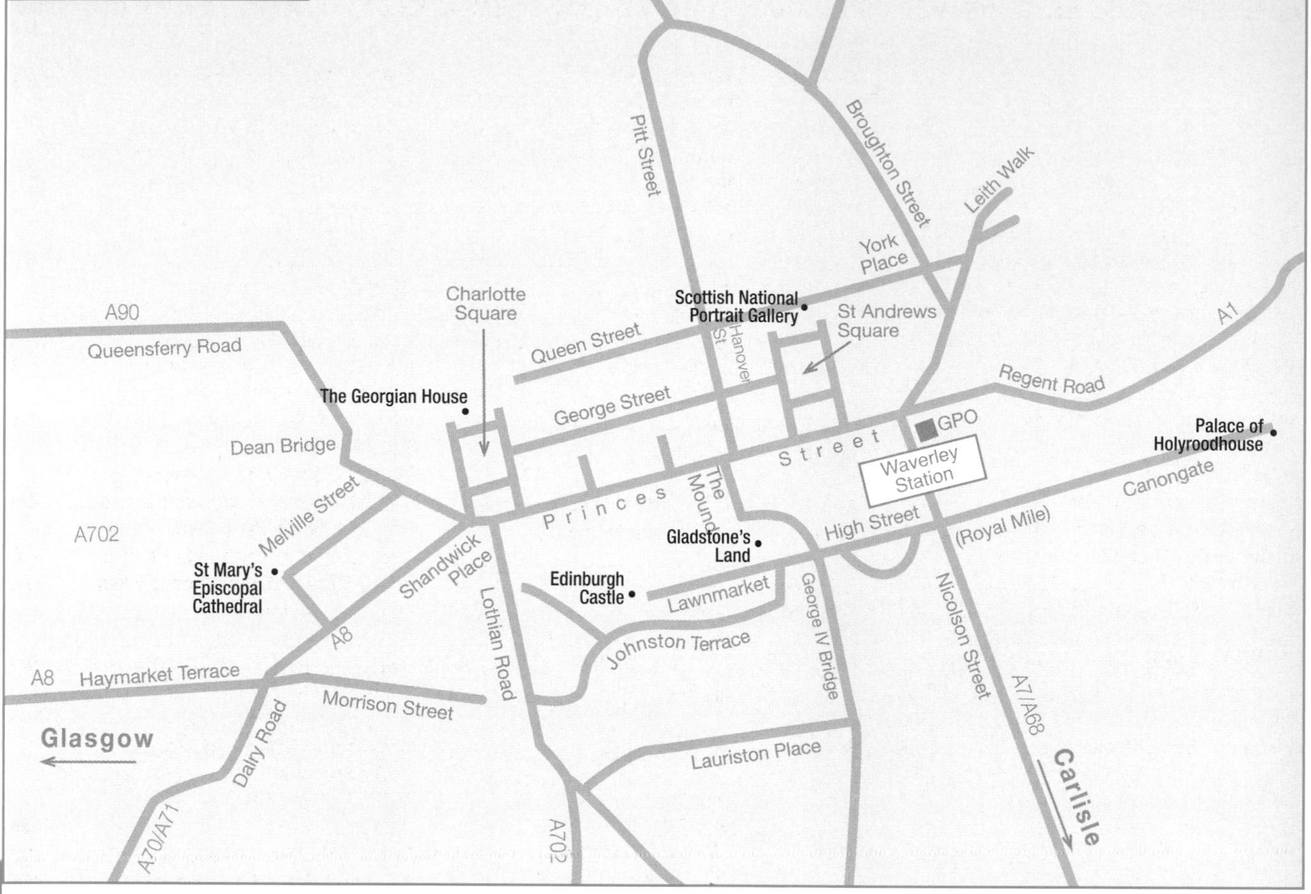

Royal Botanic Garden
Pitt Street
Broughton Street
Leith Walk
York Place
Scottish National Portrait Gallery
Hanover St
St Andrews Square
Charlotte Square
Queen Street
A90
Queensferry Road
The Georgian House
George Street
Regent Road
A1
GPO
Palace of Holyroodhouse
Dean Bridge
Princes Street
The Mound
Waverley Station
Canongate
Melville Street
A702
High Street
(Royal Mile)
Gladstone's Land
St Mary's Episcopal Cathedral
Shandwick Place
Edinburgh Castle
Lawnmarket
George IV Bridge
Nicolson Street
A8
Johnston Terrace
Lothian Road
A7/A68
A8
Haymarket Terrace
Morrison Street
Glasgow
Dalry Road
Lauriston Place
Carlisle
A70/A71
A702

MAP 21

YORK

A19 Thirsk
Bootham
Gillygate
Lord Mayors Walk
A1036 (A64) Scarborough
Monkgate
Bootham Bar
Treasurer's House
St Leonards Place
York Minster
St Maurice's Rd
Deangate
Aldwark
Museum Street
Duncombe Place
Foss Islands Road
CITY CENTRE
River Ouse
Stonebow
Station Road
Railway Station
Ousegate
Piccadilly
Fossgate
Fairfax House
National Centre for Early Music
Tower Street
Micklegate
Micklegate Bar
Walmgate
City Wall
Clifford's Tower
City Wall
A59
Nunnery Lane
A166 & A1079
Fishergate
The Mount
A1036 (A64) Blossom St
Leeds
Bishopgate Street
Paragon Street

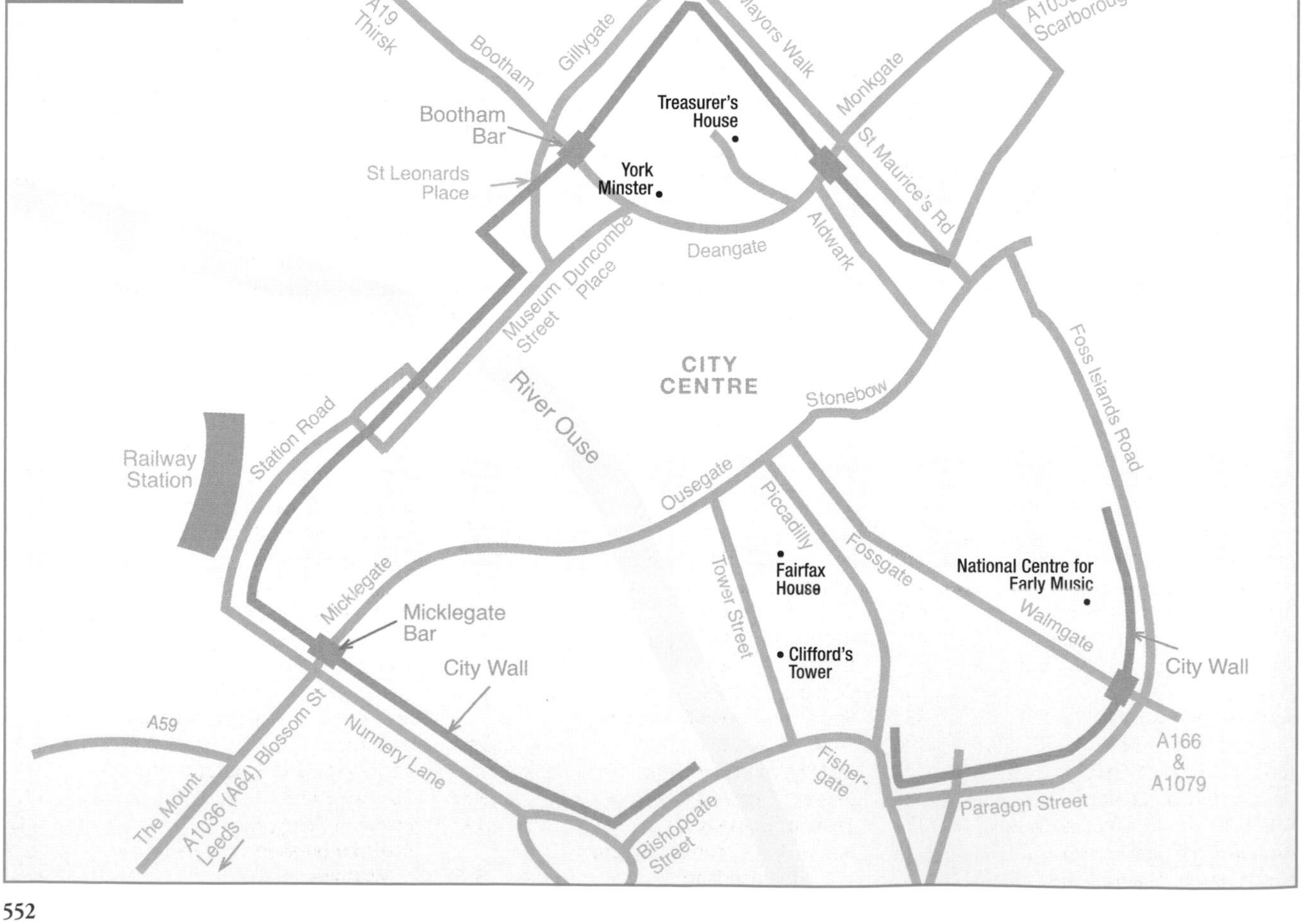

A

B

C

G

H

I

J

K

L

M

N

O

P

Q

T

U

V

W

Y